Rick Steves'

FRANCE

Rick Steves & Steve Smith

2013

CONTENTS

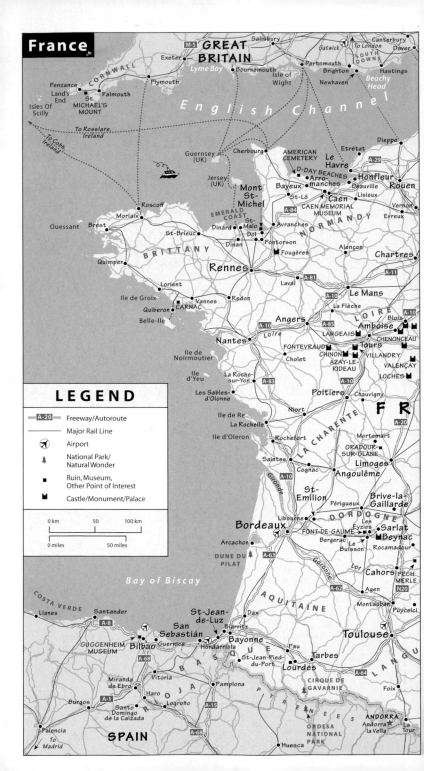

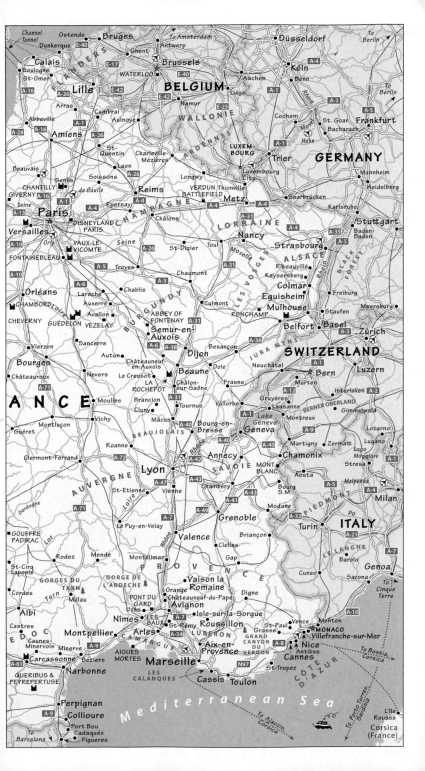

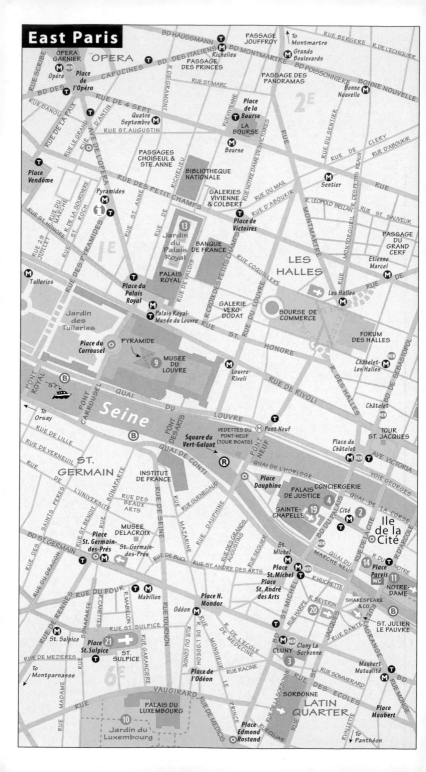

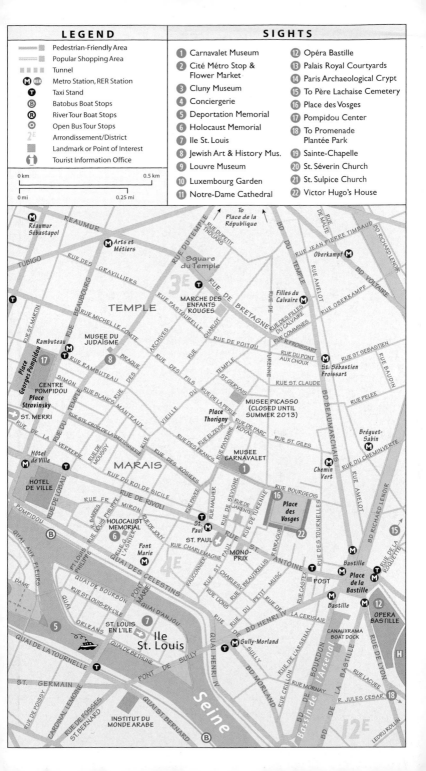

LEGEND

- ▬▬▬ ▪ Pedestrian-Friendly Area
- ┄┄┄ ▪ Popular Shopping Area
- ▪ ▪ ▪ ▪ Tunnel
- Ⓜ RER Metro Station, RER Station
- Ⓣ Taxi Stand
- Ⓑ Batobus Boat Stops
- Ⓡ River Tour Boat Stops
- Ⓞ Open Bus Tour Stops
- 2ᴱ Arrondissement/District
- ▪ Landmark or Point of Interest
- Tourist Information Office

0 km   0.5 km
0 mi   0.25 mi

SIGHTS

1. Carnavalet Museum
2. Cité Métro Stop & Flower Market
3. Cluny Museum
4. Conciergerie
5. Deportation Memorial
6. Holocaust Memorial
7. Ile St. Louis
8. Jewish Art & History Mus.
9. Louvre Museum
10. Luxembourg Garden
11. Notre-Dame Cathedral
12. Opéra Bastille
13. Palais Royal Courtyards
14. Paris Archaeological Crypt
15. To Père Lachaise Cemetery
16. Place des Vosges
17. Pompidou Center
18. To Promenade Plantée Park
19. Sainte-Chapelle
20. St. Séverin Church
21. St. Sulpice Church
22. Victor Hugo's House

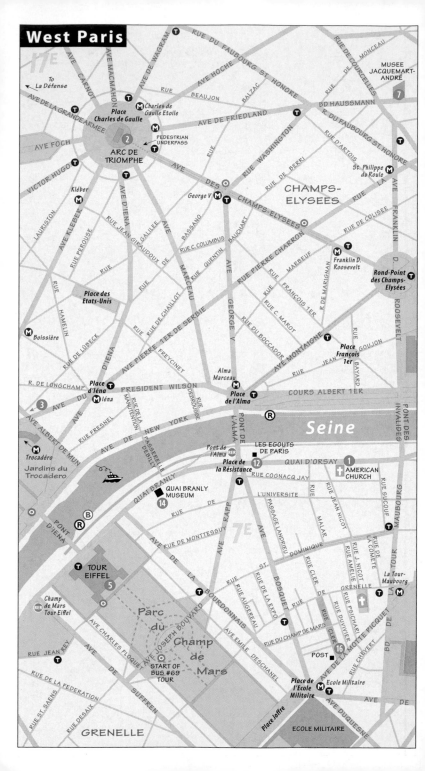

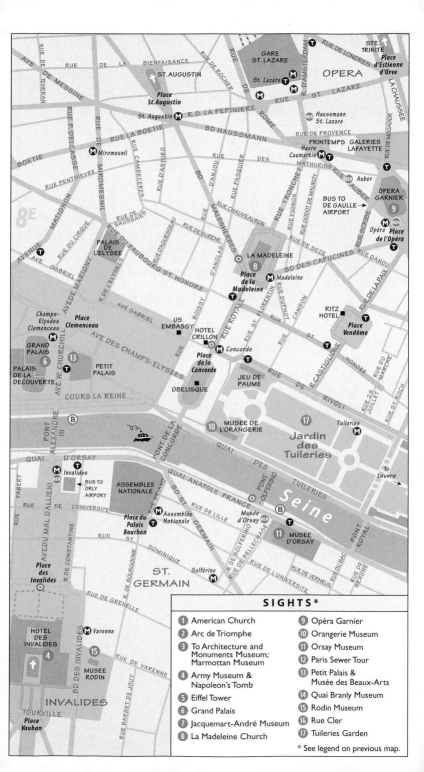

SIGHTS*

1. American Church
2. Arc de Triomphe
3. To Architecture and Monuments Museum; Marmottan Museum
4. Army Museum & Napoleon's Tomb
5. Eiffel Tower
6. Grand Palais
7. Jacquemart-André Museum
8. La Madeleine Church
9. Opéra Garnier
10. Orangerie Museum
11. Orsay Museum
12. Paris Sewer Tour
13. Petit Palais & Musée des Beaux-Arts
14. Quai Branly Museum
15. Rodin Museum
16. Rue Cler
17. Tuileries Garden

* See legend on previous map.

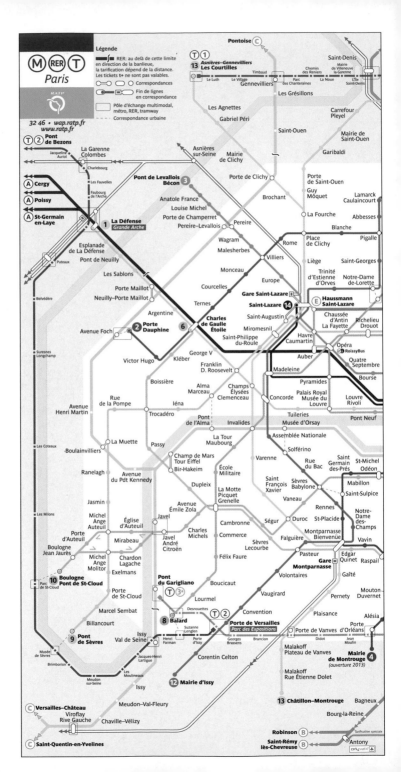

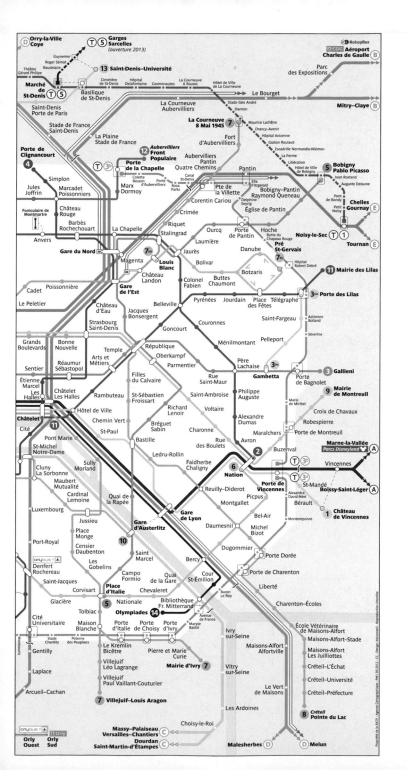

France

Bienvenue! You've chosen well. France is Europe's most diverse, tasty, and, in many ways, most exciting country to explore. It's a complex cultural bouillabaisse.

France is a place of gentle beauty, where the play of light transforms the routine into the exceptional. Here, travelers are treated to a blend of man-made and natural beauty like nowhere else in Europe. With luxuriant forests, forever coastlines, truly grand canyons, and Europe's highest mountain ranges, France has a cover-girl beauty from top to bottom. You'll also discover a dizzying array of artistic and architectural wonders—soaring cathedrals, chandeliered châteaux, and museums filled with the cultural icons of the Western world.

In many ways, France is a yardstick of human achievement. Travelers can trace the whole of European history, from the earliest prehistoric cave paintings to Roman ruins that rival Italy's. In medieval times, France cultivated Romanesque and Gothic architecture, erecting the great cathedrals and basilicas of Notre-Dame, Chartres, Vézelay, and a dozen others. With their innovative designs, French architects set the trends for cities throughout Europe—and with their revolutionary thinking, French philosophers refined modern thought and politics. The châteaux of the Loire Valley and the grand palace of Versailles announced France's emergence as the first European superpower and first modern government. It was France that gave birth to Impressionism and the foundations

of modern art. Today's travelers can gaze dreamy-eyed at water lilies in Claude Monet's Giverny, rejoice amid the sunflowers of Provence that so moved a troubled Vincent van Gogh, and roam the sunny coastlines that inspired Picasso and Matisse. And after all these centuries, France still remains at the forefront of technology, fashion, and—of course—cuisine.

There are two Frances: Paris...and the rest of the country. France's top-down government and cultural energy have always been centered in Paris, resulting in an overwhelming concentration of world-class museums, cutting-edge architecture, and historic monuments. Travelers can spend weeks in France and never leave Paris. Many do.

The other France venerates land, tradition, and a slower pace of life. After Paris, most travelers will be drawn to romantic hill towns and castles, meandering rivers and canals, and seas of vineyards that carpet this country's landscape. Village life has survived in France better than in most other European countries because France was slow to urbanize. It was an agricultural country right up until World War II (when a smaller proportion of French citizens lived in cities than Italians did 500 years earlier). And today, even as young people are chasing jobs in the cities, France remains farm country.

Everyone values the soil *(le terroir)* that brings the flavor to their foods and wines and nourishes a rural life that French people dream about. So although the country's brain resides in Paris, its soul lives in its villages—and that's where you'll feel the real pulse of France.

France offers more diversity than any other nation in Europe; moving from region to region, you feel as if you're crossing into a different country. Paris and the region around it (called Ile de France) is the "island" in the middle that anchors France. To the west are the dramatic D-Day beaches and English-style, thatched-roofed homes of Normandy; to the south lie the river valleys of the Loire and Dordogne, featuring luxurious châteaux, medieval castles, and hillside villages. Explore under-the-radar France to the far south and west, in the Spanish-tinged  Languedoc and Basque regions. Closer to Italy, sun-baked and windswept Provence offers Roman ruins and rustic charm, while the Riviera has sunny beaches and yacht-filled harbors. And in the north and east, travelers encounter snow-capped Alps, the venerable vineyards of Burgundy, and the Germanic villages and cuisine of Alsace.

The forte of French cuisine is its regional diversity. You'll enjoy Swiss-like fondue in the Alps, Italian-style pasta and pesto on the Riviera, Spanish paella in Languedoc, and German sauerkraut mixed with fine wine sauces in the Alsace. *C'est magnifique*—you can taste a good slice of Europe without stepping outside of France.

Each region also produces a wine that complements its cuisine—such as rich Burgundy wines that go perfectly with *coq*

au vin, meaty wines from Languedoc to counter heavy cuisine (such as cassoulet), fruity Côtes du Rhône wines that work well with herb-infused Provençal dishes, and dry whites in Alsace that meld perfectly with the Germanic cuisine. And in Normandy and Brittany, you'll enjoy apple ciders with crêpes and fresh seafood.

As if that weren't enough, France is also famous for its many pâtés, foie gras, hundreds of different cheeses, sizzling

escargots, fresh oysters, *herbes de Provence,* raw meats, fine wine sauces, French fries, duck and lamb dishes, pastries, bonbons, crème brûlée, and sorbets.

L'art de vivre—the art of living—is not just a pleasing French expression; it's a building block for a sound life. With five weeks of paid vacation, plus every Catholic holiday ever invented, the French are forced to enjoy life. It's no accident that France is home to café lounging, fine cuisine, Club Med vacations, barge cruising, and ballooning. You'll run headlong into that mindful approach to life at mealtime. The French insist on the best-quality croissants, mustard, and sparkling water;

they linger over lunches; and an evening's entertainment is often no more than a lovingly prepared meal with friends. France demands that the traveler slow down and savor the finer things; a hurried visitor will miss the *"this is what matters"* barge and blame the French for being lazy. One of your

co-authors learned this lesson the hard way while restoring a farm house in Burgundy—and found that it's counterproductive to hurry a project past its "normal pace."

In spite of lavish attention to relaxation, the French are a productive people. French inventors gave us the metric system, pasteurization, high-speed trains, and Concorde airplanes. More importantly, this country rose from the ashes of two

France Almanac

Official Name: It's officially the République Française, but locals, and everyone else, just call it France.

Population: France has 65 million people (more than the combined population of California and Texas). They're a mix of Celtic, Latin, and Teutonic DNA, plus many recent immigrants from around the globe—especially North Africa. Four out of five French are (at least nominally) Roman Catholic. Every French citizen is expected to speak French.

Area: At 215,000 square miles, it's Western Europe's largest nation. (But Texas is still 20 percent bigger.)

Latitude and Longitude: 46°N and 2°E (similar latitude to the states of Washington, North Dakota, and Maine).

Geography: The terrain consists of rolling plains in the north and mountains in the southwest (Pyrenees), southeast (Alps), and south-central (Massif Central). Capping the country on both ends are 1,400 miles of coastline (Mediterranean and Atlantic). The Seine River flows east-west through Paris, the Rhône rumbles north-south 500 miles from the Alps to the Mediterranean, and the Loire travels east-west, roughly dividing the country into north and south. Mont Blanc (15,771 feet) is Western Europe's highest point.

Major Cities: Nearly one in five lives in greater Paris (12 million in the metropolitan area, 2.2 million in the city). Marseille, on the Mediterranean coast, and Lyon, in the southeast, both have about 1.4 million people.

Economy: France's gross domestic product is $2.2 trillion (bigger than California's $1.85 trillion); the GDP per capita is $35,000

(America's is $48,100). Though the French produce nearly a quarter of the world's wine, they drink much of it themselves. France's free-market economy is tempered by the government: high taxes (one of Europe's highest rates at nearly 50 percent of GDP—compared to 22 percent in the US), government investment in industry, and social spending (to narrow the income gap between rich and poor). Despite the three-hour lunch stereotypes, the French work as much as their EU neighbors— that is, 20 percent less than Americans (but with greater per-hour productivity).

Government: President Francois Hollande, elected by popular vote in 2012, heads a socialist government along with president-appointed Prime Minister Jean-Marc Ayrault. The upper-house Senate (348 seats) is chosen by an electoral college; the National Assembly (577 seats) by popular vote. Though France is a cornerstone of the European Union, many French are Euro-skeptics.

Flag: The Revolution produced the well-known tricolore, whose three colors are vertical bands of blue, white, and red.

The Average Jean: The average French person is 39 years old and will live 81 years. This person eats lunch in 22 minutes (four times as fast as 20 years ago) and consumes a glass and a half of wine and a pound of fat a day. The average French citizen pops a bottle of Champagne about every four months. The average worker enjoys five weeks of holiday and vacation a year. A dog is a part of one in three French households; cats are animals non grata.

debilitating world wars to generate the world's seventh-largest economy. This is thanks in part to determined government intervention that continues today (government spending is 56 percent of GDP). Wine, tourism, telecommunications, pharmaceuticals, cars, and Airbus planes are big moneymakers. France is also the European Union's leading agricultural producer and a chief competitor of the US. You'll pass endless wheat farms in the north, dairy farms in the west, vegetable farms and fruit orchards in the south...and vineyards everywhere.

With no domestic oil production, France has focused on nuclear power generation, which now accounts for more than 75 percent of the country's electricity production. Electricity is expensive, so the French are careful to turn out lights and conserve—something to remember when you leave your hotel room for the day or evening. Although France's economy may be one of the world's largest, the French remain skeptical about the virtues of capitalism and the work ethic. Business conversation is generally avoided, as it implies a fascination with money that the French find vulgar. (It's considered gauche even to ask what someone does for a living.) In France, CEOs are not glorified as celebrities—chefs are.

The French believe that the economy should support social

good, not vice versa. This has produced a cradle-to-grave social security system of which the French are proud. France's poverty rate is half of that in the US, proof to the French that they are on the right track. On the other hand, if you're considering starting a business in France, think again—taxes are formidable (figure a total small-business tax rate of around 66 percent). France is routinely plagued with strikes, demonstrations, and slow-downs as workers try to preserve their hard-earned rights in the face of a competitive global economy.

As you travel, you'll find that the most "French" thing about France is the French themselves. Be prepared to embrace (or at least understand) the cultural differences between

yourself and your French hosts. You'll find the French to be reserved in the north and comparatively carefree in the sunny south. Throughout the country, they're more formal than you are. When you enter a store, you'll be greeted not simply with a *"Bonjour,"* but with *"Bonjour, Monsieur (or Madame)."* The proper response to the shopkeeper is *"Bonjour, Monsieur (or Madame)."* If there are others present, you'd say, *"Bonjour, Messieurs (or Mesdames)"*—just to make sure you don't leave anyone out. (For more on the French attitude toward language, see page 1104.)

The French are overwhelmingly Catholic but not very devout, and are quick to separate church from state. They are less active churchgoers than Americans, whom they find *très* evangelical. And in France you don't go to church to socialize or to help in charitable deeds (that's what taxes are for). France is also Europe's largest Muslim nation, with well over five million followers (there are twice as many Muslims in France as Protestants). The influx of Muslim immigrants has led to considerable problems of assimilation and remains one of France's thorniest issues to resolve.

The French don't seem particularly athletic—unless you  consider tossing little silver balls in the dirt *(pétanque, a.k.a. boules)* a sport. A few jog and exercise regularly, and fewer play on recreational teams—though you will find country lanes busy with bike riders hunched over handlebars on weekends. The French are avid sports-watchers. Soccer is king (even though the national team disgraced itself at the 2010 World Cup), bike racing is big, and rugby is surprisingly popular for such a refined place. *Le basket* (basketball) is making a move, with a French league and several French NBA stars, including Tony (formerly "Mr. Eva Longoria") Parker.

Another passion the French share with Americans is their love of movies. They admire Hollywood blockbusters, but they've also carved out their own niche of small-budget romantic comedies and thought-provoking thrillers.

Today's France will challenge many of your preconceptions. The French have a Michelin Guide-certainty in their

judgments and are often frank in how they convey their opinions. (Just ask about the best wine to serve with any given course.)

Simply put, the French see the world differently than we do. The right to bear arms, the death penalty, minuscule paid vacations, and health care as a privilege rather than a basic human right—these American concepts confound the average Jean. And they don't understand the American need for everyone to be in agreement all the time. Whether it's Iraq, Vietnam, or globalization, the French think it's important to question authority and not blindly submit to it. Blame this aversion to authority on their Revolution hangover.

The French can be a complicated people to understand for hurried travelers. But remember where they've come from: In just a few generations, they've seen two world wars destroy entire cities, villages, landscapes, and their self-respect. They've watched as America replaced them as the world's political and cultural superpower. On the bright side, they've seen their country re-emerge as a global force, with nuclear weapons, a space program, an international spy network, and their own ideas about geopolitics. Like Americans, they're trying to find their place in an increasingly global, multicultural world. Today, they just don't want to be taken for granted. And while the French may—or may not—love your country's politics, this has no bearing on how they will treat you as an individual.

As you travel through this splendid country, come with an appetite to understand and a willingness to experience. Welcome new ideas and give the locals the benefit of your doubt. Accept France on its own terms and don't judge. Above all, slo-o-o-ow down. Spend hours in cafés lingering over un café, make a habit of making unplanned stops, hop on the l'art de vivre barge, and surrender to the play of light as the Impressionists did.

INTRODUCTION

France is a big country by European standards—and would be one of the biggest states if it ever joined the US (unlikely). Geographically, it's a bit smaller than Texas, but has 65 million people (Texas has 25 million) and some 400 different cheeses (Texas has... not that many). *Diversité* is a French forte. This country features three impressive mountain ranges (the Alps, the Pyrenees, and the Massif Central), two coastlines as different as night and day (Atlantic and Mediterranean), cosmopolitan cities (such as Paris, Lyon, Strasbourg, and Nice), and countless sleepy villages. From the Swiss-like Alps to the *molto* Italian Riviera, and from the Spanish Pyrenees to *das* German Alsace, you can stay in France and feel like you've sampled much of Europe—and never be more than a short stroll from a *bon vin rouge*.

We've covered the predictable must-sees while mixing in a healthy dose of Back Door intimacy. Along with seeing the Eiffel Tower, Mont St-Michel, and the French Riviera, you'll take a minivan tour of the D-Day beaches, pedal your way from village to vineyard in the Alsace, marvel at 15,000-year-old cave paintings, and paddle a canoe down the lazy Dordogne River. You'll find a *magnifique* hill-town perch to catch a Provençal sunset, ride Europe's highest mountain lift over the Alps, and touch the quiet Romanesque soul of Burgundian abbeys and villages. You'll learn about each region's key monuments and cities with our thoughtfully presented walking tours and background information. Just as important, you'll meet the intriguing people who run your hotel, bed-and-breakfast, or restaurant. We've also listed our favorite local guides, all well worth the time and money, to help you gain a better understanding of this marvelous country's past and present.

The destinations covered in this book are balanced to include the most interesting cities and intimate villages, from jet-setting

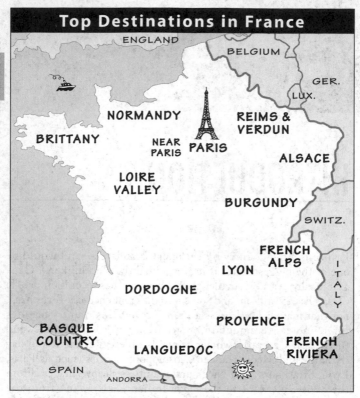

Top Destinations in France

ENGLAND

BELGIUM

GER.

LUX.

NORMANDY

NEAR PARIS

PARIS

REIMS & VERDUN

ALSACE

BRITTANY

LOIRE VALLEY

BURGUNDY

SWITZ.

FRENCH ALPS

LYON

ITALY

DORDOGNE

PROVENCE

BASQUE COUNTRY

LANGUEDOC

FRENCH RIVIERA

SPAIN

ANDORRA

beach resorts to the traditional heartland. This book is selective, including only the most exciting sights and romantic villages—for example, there are hundreds of beautiful châteaux in the Loire region, but we cover only the top 12. And though there are dozens of Loire towns you could use for a home base, we recommend just the best two: Amboise and Chinon.

The best is, of course, only our opinion. But after spending half of our adult lives writing and lecturing about travel, guiding tours, and gaining an appreciation for all things French, we've developed a sixth sense for what touches the traveler's imagination.

About This Book

Rick Steves' France 2013 is a personal tour guide in your pocket. Better yet, it's actually two tour guides in your pocket: The co-author of this book is Steve Smith. Steve lived in France as a child and as an adult and has been traveling to France—as a guide, researcher, homeowner, and devout Francophile—every year since 1985. He restored a 300-year-old farmhouse in Burgundy and today keeps one foot on each side of the Atlantic. Together, Steve and I

Key to This Book

Updates

This book is updated every year, but things change. For the latest, visit www.ricksteves.com/update. For a valuable list of reports and experiences—good and bad—from fellow travelers, check www.ricksteves.com/feedback.

Abbreviations and Times

I use the following symbols and abbreviations in this book:

Sights are rated:

▲▲▲	Don't miss
▲▲	Try hard to see
▲	Worthwhile if you can make it
No rating	Worth knowing about

Tourist information offices are abbreviated as **TI,** and bathrooms are **WCs.** To categorize accommodations, I use a **Sleep Code** (described on page 24).

Like Europe, this book uses the **24-hour clock.** It's the same through 12:00 noon, then keep going: 13:00, 14:00, and so on. For anything over 12, subtract 12 and add p.m. (14:00 is 2:00 p.m.).

When giving **opening times,** I include both peak season and off-season hours if they differ. So if a museum is listed as "May-Oct daily 9:00-16:00," it should be open from 9 a.m. until 4 p.m. from the first day of May until the last day of October (but expect exceptions).

For **transit** or **tour departures,** I first list the frequency, then the duration. So, a train connection listed as "2/hour, 1.5 hours" departs twice each hour, and the journey lasts an hour and a half.

keep this book current (though, for simplicity, from this point "we" will shed our respective egos and become "I").

This book is organized by destinations. Each destination is a mini-vacation on its own, filled with exciting sights, strollable neighborhoods, affordable places to stay, and memorable places to eat. In the following chapters, you'll find these sections:

Planning Your Time suggests a schedule for how to best use your limited time.

Orientation includes specifics on public transportation, helpful hints, local tour options, easy-to-read maps, and tourist information.

Sights describes the top attractions and includes their cost and hours.

Self-Guided Walks take you through interesting neighborhoods, with a personal tour guide in hand.

Sleeping describes my favorite hotels, from good-value deals

Map Legend

⅃ Viewpoint	✈ Airport	)▬(Tunnel
✚ Entrance	Ⓣ Taxi Stand	▬▬ Pedestrian Zone
❶ Tourist Info	▣ Tram Stop	------ Railway
WC Restroom	Ⓑ Bus Stop	·········· Ferry/Boat Route
▟ Castle	Ⓟ Parking	⊢⊣ Tram
♱ Church	Ⓡ RER Train	▥▥▥ Stairs
▪ Statue/Point of Interest	Ⓑ Batobus Stop	·----- Walk/Tour Route
▥ Park	Ⓜ Métro Stop	
◎ Fountain	)(Mtn. Pass	------ Trail

Use this legend to help you navigate the maps in this book.

to cushy splurges.

Eating serves up a range of options, from inexpensive cafés to fancy restaurants.

Connections outlines your options for traveling to destinations by train, bus, and plane. In car-friendly regions, I've included route tips for drivers.

France: Past and Present gives you a quick overview of French history, notable citizens, and current political issues.

The **appendix** is a traveler's tool kit, with telephone tips, transportation basics (on trains, buses, car rentals, driving, and flights), recommended books and films, useful phone numbers and websites, a festival list, a climate chart, a handy packing checklist, a hotel reservation form, a pronunciation guide for place names, and French survival phrases.

Browse through this book, choose your favorite destinations, and link them up. Then have a *fantastique* trip! Traveling like a temporary local, you'll get the absolute most out of every mile, minute, and dollar. As you visit places I know and love, I'm happy that you'll be meeting some of my favorite French people.

Planning

This section will help you get started planning your trip—with advice on trip costs, when to go, and what you should know before you take off.

Travel Smart

Your trip to France is like a complex play—easier to follow and to really appreciate on a second viewing. While no one does the same trip twice to gain that advantage, reading this book in its entirety before your trip accomplishes much the same thing.

Design an itinerary that enables you to visit sights at the best possible times. Note festivals, holidays, street-market days, and days when sights are closed or most crowded (all covered in this book). To get between destinations smoothly, read the tips in this book's appendix on taking trains and buses, and renting a car and driving. A smart trip is a puzzle—a fun, doable, and worthwhile challenge.

Be sure to mix intense and relaxed periods in your itinerary. To maximize rootedness, minimize one-night stands. It's worth taking a long drive after dinner (or a train ride with a dinner picnic) to get settled in a town for two nights. Hotels are more likely to give a better price to someone staying more than one night. Every trip—and every traveler—needs slack time (laundry, picnics, people-watching, and so on). Pace yourself. Assume you will return.

Reread this book as you travel, and visit local TIs. Upon arrival in a new town, lay the groundwork for a smooth departure; get the schedule for the train or bus you'll take when you depart. Drivers can study the best route to their next destination.

Get online at Internet cafés or your hotel, though I encourage you to disconnect from life back home and immerse yourself in the French experience. Carry a mobile phone (or use a phone card) to make travel plans: You can find tourist information, learn the latest on sights (special events, tour schedule, etc.), book tickets and tours, make reservations, reconfirm hotels, research transportation connections, and keep in touch with your loved ones.

Enjoy the friendliness of the French people. Connect with the culture. Learn a new French expression each day and practice it. Cheer for your favorite bowler at a *boules* match, leave no chair unturned in your quest for the best café, find that perfect hill-town view, and make friends with a waiter. Slow down to appreciate the sincerity of your French hosts, and be open to unexpected experiences. Ask questions—most locals are eager to point you in their idea of the right direction. Keep a notepad in your pocket for confirming prices, noting directions, and organizing your thoughts. Wear your money belt, learn the currency, and figure out how to estimate prices in dollars. Those who expect to travel smart, do.

Trip Costs

Five components make up your trip costs: airfare, surface transportation, room and board, sightseeing and entertainment, and shopping and miscellany.

Airfare: Paris and Nice have the most convenient flights from the US. A basic round-trip flight from the US to Paris or Nice can cost, on average, about $900 to $2,000 total, depending on where

INTRODUCTION

France at a Glance

These attractions are listed (as in this book) looping counter-clockwise around France, starting in Paris and ending in Champagne.

Paris World capital of art, fashion, food, literature, and ideas, offering historic monuments, grand boulevards, corner cafés, chic boutiques, cutting-edge architecture, and world-class art galleries, including the Louvre and Orsay.

Near Paris Europe's best palace at Versailles, the awesome cathedral of Chartres, Monet's flowery gardens at Giverny, and a mouse-run amusement park.

Normandy Pastoral mix of sweeping coastlines, half-timbered towns, and exciting cities, including bustling Rouen (Gothic architecture, Joan of Arc sites), the little romantic port town of Honfleur, historic Bayeux (remarkable tapestry on the Battle of Hastings), stirring D-Day sites and museums, and the almost surreal island abbey of Mont St-Michel.

Brittany Windswept and rugged, with a forgotten interior, well-discovered coast, Celtic ties, and two notable towns: Dinan (Brittany's best medieval center) and the beach resort of St-Malo.

The Loire Picturesque towns (such as Amboise and Chinon) and more than a thousand castles and palaces, including Chenonceaux (arcing across its river), the huge Château de Chambord, Villandry (wonderful gardens), lavishly furnished Cheverny, and many more.

Dordogne Prehistoric caves, rock-sculpted villages, lazy canoe rides past medieval castles, market towns such as pedestrian-friendly Sarlat, and nearby, for wine lovers, St-Emilion.

Basque Country Isolated yet beautiful region anchored by the mellow resort village of St-Jean-de-Luz, with other attractions scattered through the countryside and across the border into Spain.

Languedoc Sunny region with a Spanish flair, featuring Albi (fortress-like cathedral and a beautiful Toulouse-Lautrec museum), medieval Carcassonne (walled town with towers, turrets, and cobblestones), remote Cathar castles, and the lovely coastal village of Collioure.

Provence Attracts writers and artists, boasts Arles (Van Gogh sights, evocative Roman arena), Avignon (famous bridge and brooding Palace of the Popes), the ancient Roman aqueduct of Pont du Gard, Orange (Roman theater), the beautiful Côtes du Rhone wine road, and rock-top villages such as Les Baux, Roussillon, and Vaison la Romaine.

The French Riviera A string of coastal resorts, including Nice (big city with seafront promenade and art museums), easygoing Villefranche-sur-Mer, glitzy Monaco (casino), romantic Antibes (silky-sandy beaches), and little hilltop Eze-le-Village, with magnificent Mediterranean views.

The French Alps Spectacular scenery featuring the drop-dead gorgeous town of Annecy, Mont Blanc (Europe's highest peak), and the world-famous ski resort of Chamonix, with hikes galore and lifts to stunning alpine views.

Burgundy Aged blend of vineyards and spirituality, with the compact town of Beaune (world-famous vineyards), Fontenay (France's best-preserved medieval abbey), Vézelay (magnificent Romanesque church), the one-of-a-kind medieval castle under construction at Guédelon, Cluny's grand medieval abbey, and the modern-day religious community of Taizé.

Lyon Metropolitan city, located between Burgundy and Provence, with two Roman theaters, a terrific Gallo-Roman museum, the stirring French Resistance Center, and France's best cuisine at affordable prices.

Alsace Franco-Germanic region dotted with wine-road villages, starring half-timbered Colmar and its world-class art, and high-powered Strasbourg and its sensational cathedral.

Reims and Verdun Champagne-soaked Reims with caves serving the sparkling brew, and nearby Verdun, site of brutal WWI battles, with a compelling, unforgettable memorial.

you fly from and when (cheaper in winter). Smaller budget airlines may provide bargain service from several European capitals to many cities in France. Within France, these inexpensive flights can get you between Paris and other major cities (such as Nice, Marseille, Strasbourg, Toulouse, Lyon, and Bordeaux).

Consider saving time and money in Europe by flying into one city and out of another; for instance, into Nice and out of Paris. Most find the easygoing Mediterranean city of Nice far easier than Paris as a starting point for their trip.

Surface Transportation: For a three-week whirlwind trip of my recommended destinations, allow $750 per person for public transportation (trains and buses). For a three-week car rental, tolls, gas, and insurance, allow $1,000 per person (based on two people sharing). Figure about $250 total per week for just gas and tolls. Leasing is worth considering for three weeks or more. Car rentals and leases are cheapest if arranged from the US. Rentals are usually less expensive if you pick up and drop off outside a train station or airport (where surcharges are often applied). Learn your options.

Train passes are normally available only outside of Europe, but aren't necessarily your best option—you may save money by simply buying tickets as you go. For more on public transportation and car rental, see "Transportation" in the appendix.

Room and Board: Outside Paris you can thrive in France in 2013 on $145 a day per person for room and board. This allows $13 for breakfast, $18 for lunch, $44 for dinner with drinks, and $70 for lodging (based on two people splitting the cost of a $140 double room). That's definitely doable. Allow 20 percent more for your days in Paris. Students and tightwads can enjoy France for as little as $60 a day ($30 per bed, $30 for meals and snacks).

Sightseeing and Entertainment: Figure about $10-20 per major sight (Louvre-$14, Abbey of Mont St-Michel-$12), $7 for minor ones (climbing church towers), $30 for guided walks, and $25-60 for bus tours and splurge experiences (concerts in Paris' Sainte-Chapelle or a ride on the Chamonix gondola).

An overall average of $30 a day works for most people. Don't skimp here. After all, this category is the driving force behind your trip—you came to sightsee, enjoy, and experience France.

Shopping and Miscellany: Figure $5 per ice-cream cone, coffee, or soft drink. Shopping can vary in cost from nearly nothing to a small fortune. Good budget travelers find that this category has little to do with assembling a trip full of lifelong and wonderful memories.

Sightseeing Priorities

Depending on the length of your trip, and taking geographic proximity into account, here are my recommended priorities:

3 days:	Paris and maybe Versailles
5 days, add:	Normandy
7 days, add:	Loire
10 days, add:	Dordogne, Carcassonne
15 days, add:	Provence, the Riviera
18 days, add:	Burgundy, Chamonix
21 days, add:	Alsace, northern France
23 days, add:	Basque Country

For a day-by-day itinerary of a three-week trip, see the sidebars (one for drivers and one for people using trains and buses) later in this chapter.

If all you have is a week and it's your first trip to France, do Paris, Normandy, and the Loire.

For a more focused 10- to 14-day trip that highlights Paris, Provence, and the Riviera, fly into Paris and out of Nice. After touring Paris, take the TGV train from Paris to Avignon, rent a car there, and drop it in Nice (or use trains, buses, and minivan tours to get around). This trip also works in reverse.

Travelers with a little more time could add Burgundy and/or the Alps, which are about halfway between Paris and Provence and easy to explore by car or train.

When to Go

Late spring and fall are best, with generally good weather and lighter crowds, though summer brings festivals, reliable weather, and long opening hours at sights.

Europeans vacation in July and August, jamming the Riviera, the Dordogne, and the Alps (worst from mid-July to mid-August), but leaving the rest of the country just lively enough for tourists. And though many French businesses close in August, the traveler hardly notices. May weekends can be busy—many French holidays fall in this month—but June is generally quiet (outside of Paris).

Winter travel is fine for Paris, Nice, and Lyon, but you'll find smaller cities and villages buttoned up tight. Winter weather is gray, noticeably milder in the south (unless the wind is blowing), and colder and wetter in the north. Sights and tourist information offices keep shorter hours, and some tourist activities (such as English-language castle tours) vanish altogether. On the other hand, winter travel allows you to see cities through the lens of a local, as hotels, restaurants, and sights are wonderfully tourist-free. See the climate chart in the appendix for an idea of what to expect from the weather.

What's Blooming When

Thanks to France's relatively mild climate, fields of flowers greet the traveler much of the year:

Whirlwind (Kamikaze) Three-Week Trip Through France for Drivers

Day	Plan
1	Fly into Paris, pick up your car, visit Giverny, and overnight in Honfleur (1 night). Save Paris sightseeing for the end of your trip.
2	Spend today at D-Day sights: Arromanches, American Cemetery, and Pointe du Hoc (and Utah Beach Landing Museum, if you're moving fast). Dinner and overnight in Bayeux (1 night).
3	Bayeux Tapestry and church, Mont St-Michel, sleep on Mont St-Michel (1 night).
4	Spend your morning on Mont St-Michel, then head for châteaux country in the Loire Valley. Tour Chambord, then stay in Amboise (2 nights).
5	Do a day trip, touring Chenonceaux and Cheverny or Chaumont. Save time at the end of the day for Amboise and its sights.
6	Head south to the Dordogne region, stopping en route at Oradour-sur-Glane. End in a Dordogne village—your choice of the handful of lodgings I recommend (2 nights).
7	Browse the town and market of Sarlat, take a canoe trip, and tour a prehistoric cave.
8	Head to the Languedoc region, lunch in Puycelci or Albi, and spend the evening in Carcassonne (1 night).
9	Morning in Carcassonne, then on to Provence with a stop at the Pont du Gard aqueduct. Stay in or near Arles (2 nights).
10	All day for Arles and Les Baux.
11	Visit a Provençal hill town such as Roussillon, then depart for the Riviera, staying in Nice, Antibes, or Villefranche-sur-Mer (2 nights).
12	Sightsee in Nice and Monaco.
13	Make the long drive north to the Alps, and sleep in Chamonix (2 nights).
14	If the weather is clear, take the mountain lifts up to Aiguille du Midi and beyond.
15	Allow a half-day for the Alps (in Chamonix or Annecy). Then head for Burgundy, ending in Beaune for wine-tasting. Sleep in Beaune (1 night).

16   Spend the morning in Beaune, then move on to Colmar (2 nights).

17   Enjoy Colmar and the Route du Vin villages.

18   Return to Paris, visiting Verdun or Reims en route. Collapse in Paris hotel (4 nights).

19   Sightsee Paris.

20   More time in Paris.

21   Finish your sightseeing in Paris, and consider side-tripping to Versailles.

Mid-April-May: Crops of brilliant yellow colza bloom, mostly in the north (best in Burgundy). Wild red poppies *(coquelicots)* begin sprouting in the south.

June: Red poppies pop up throughout the country. Late in June, lavender blooms begin covering the hills of Provence.

July: Lavender is in full swing in Provence, and sunflowers are awakening. Cities, towns, and villages everywhere overflow with carefully tended flowers.

August-September: Sunflowers flourish north and south.

October: In the latter half of the month, the countryside glistens with fall colors, as most trees are deciduous. Vineyards go for the gold.

Know Before You Go

Your trip is more likely to go smoothly if you plan ahead. Check this list of things to arrange while you're still at home.

You need a **passport**—but no visa or shots—to travel in France. You may be denied entry into certain European countries if your passport is due to expire within three to six months of your ticketed date of return. Get it renewed if you'll be cutting it close. It can take up to six weeks to get or renew a passport (for more on passports, see www.travel.state.gov). Pack a photocopy of your passport in your luggage in case the original is lost or stolen.

Book rooms well in advance if you'll be traveling during peak season (spring through fall) or any major holidays (see page 1144). Some famous Parisian restaurants (but not ones I recommend) require reservations several weeks in advance.

Call your **debit- and credit-card companies** to let them know the countries you'll be visiting, to ask about fees, request your PIN (it will be mailed to you), and more. See page 18 for details.

Do your homework if you want to buy **travel insurance.** Compare the cost of the insurance to the likelihood of your using it and your potential loss if something goes wrong. Also, check whether your existing insurance (health, homeowners, or renters) covers you and your possessions overseas. For more tips, see www.ricksteves.com/insurance.

Consider buying a **railpass** after researching your options (see page 1115 and www.ricksteves.com/rail for all the specifics).

All **high-speed TGV trains** in France require a seat reservation—book as early as possible, as these trains fill fast, and some routes use TGV trains almost exclusively. This is especially true if you're traveling with a railpass, as TGV passholder reservations are limited, and usually sell out well before other seat reservations do. If you're taking an overnight train (especially between a French destination and Barcelona or Madrid), and you need a *couchette* (overnight bunk)—and you *must* leave on a certain day—consider booking it in advance through a US agent (such as www.rail europe.com). For more on train travel, see the appendix.

If you're planning on **renting a car** in France, bring your driver's license.

To avoid long ticket-buying lines at the **Eiffel Tower,** book an entry time in advance using its online reservation system (see page 111).

If you plan to hire a **local guide,** reserve ahead by email. Popular guides can get booked up.

If you're bringing a **mobile device,** download any apps you might want to use on the road, such as translators, maps, and transit schedules. Check out **Rick Steves Audio Europe,** featuring audio tours of major sights in Paris, hours of travel interviews on France, and more (via www.ricksteves.com/audioeurope, iTunes, Google Play, or the Rick Steves Audio Europe smartphone app; for details see page 1138).

If you'll be **traveling with children,** read my pre-trip suggestions on page 34.

Check the **Rick Steves guidebook updates** page for any recent changes to this book (www.ricksteves.com/update).

Because **airline carry-on restrictions** are always changing, visit the Transportation Security Administration's website (www.tsa.gov/travelers) for an up-to-date list of what you can bring on the plane with you...and what you have to check.

Practicalities

Emergency and Medical Help: In France, dial 17 for English-speaking police. To summon an ambulance, call 15. If you get sick, do as the French do and go to a pharmacist for advice. Or ask at your hotel for help—they'll know the nearest medical and emergency services.

Theft or Loss: To replace a passport, you'll need to go in person to an embassy or consulate. You'll find the US embassy in Paris and consulates in Lyon, Marseille, Nice, and Strasbourg (see page 1114; full list at www.usembassy.gov). If your credit and debit cards disappear, cancel and replace them (see "Damage Control for Lost Cards" on page 18). File a police report either on the spot or within a day or two; it's required if you submit an insurance claim for lost or stolen railpasses or travel gear, and can help with replacing your passport or credit and debit cards. For more information, see www.ricksteves.com/help. Precautionary measures can minimize the effects of loss—back up your photos and other files frequently.

Time Zones: France, like most of continental Europe, is

Whirlwind Three-Week Tour of France by Train and Bus

This itinerary is designed for train travelers. To do this trip by train and bus, make liberal use of minivan tours and taxis. You'll need 12 days of train travel to complete this trip. Buy a France Flexipass with nine train days and buy point-to-point tickets for days 5, 7, and 14 (short and cheap trips). Book any TGV trips as far ahead as possible—I have identified those trips with an * below (TGV trains fill fast; slower trains not requiring reservations are usually possible, but can be very inconvenient). A car is especially handy for exploring Normandy, the Dordogne, and Provence. If you only have two weeks, end your tour in Nice and skip Honfleur. Bonne route and bon courage!

Day	Plan
1	Fly into Paris.
2	Sightsee Paris.
3	More time in Paris.
4	*Train and bus to Mont St-Michel via Rennes (4 hours, arrive in Mont St-Michel about 13:00). Afternoon and night on Mont St-Michel.
5	Train to Bayeux (2 hours, arrive by noon). Afternoon for visiting Bayeux. Sleep in Bayeux.
6	All day for D-Day beaches by minivan, taxi, bike, bus, or a combination of these. Sleep in Bayeux.
7	*Train to Amboise via Caen and St-Pierre des Corps (5-6 hours). Sleep in Amboise.
8	All day for touring Loire châteaux (good options by bus, bike, or minivan tour). Sleep in Amboise.
9	Early train to Sarlat (6 hours, arrive about 13:30). Afternoon and evening in Sarlat. Sleep in Sarlat.
10	All day for caves and canoes by train and bike or minivan/taxi tour. Sleep in Sarlat.

generally six/nine hours ahead of the East/West Coasts of the US. The exceptions are the beginning and end of Daylight Saving Time: Europe "springs forward" the last Sunday in March (two weeks after most of North America), and "falls back" the last Sunday in October (one week before North America). For a handy online time converter, see www.timeanddate.com/worldclock.

Business Hours: You'll find much of rural France closed weekdays from noon to 14:00 (lunch is sacred). On Sunday, most businesses are closed (family is sacred), though some small shops, *boulangeries* (bakeries), and street markets are open until noon, special events and weekly markets pop up, and museums are open all day (but public transportation options are fewer). On Mondays,

11   Train or bus to Carcassonne (5.5 hours). Dinner and eve-
     ning wall walk. Sleep in Carcassonne.

12   Morning wall walk, then train to Arles (3 hours). Afternoon
     in Arles.

13   Train to Nîmes, then bus to Pont du Gard. Tour the Pont
     du Gard, then bus to Avignon and spend your afternoon/
     evening there (consider dinner). Train back to Arles (while
     not TGV, some of these trains may require reservations).
     Sleep in Arles.

14   Morning in Arles or Les Baux (by taxi or tour), afternoon
     train to Nice via Marseille (4 hours—many *trains from
     Marseille to Nice are TGV and require a reservation), set
     up in Nice. Sleep in Nice (3 nights).

15   All day for Nice (and maybe Antibes). Sleep in Nice (3
     nights).

16   All day for Villefranche-sur-Mer and Monaco. Sleep in
     Nice.

17   *Morning train to Annecy (7 hours). Afternoon and night
     in Annecy.

18   Morning in Annecy, midday train to Chamonix (2 hours),
     afternoon and evening in Chamonix. Sleep in Chamonix.

19   If the weather is clear, take the mountain lifts up to
     Aiguille du Midi and beyond. Sleep in Chamonix.

20   *Linger in Chamonix or take an early train to Paris (7
     hours) or, closer, Lyon (4 hours). Last afternoon and night
     in Paris or Lyon. (Or make it a 22-day tour with a night
     in Burgundy—stay in Beaune, a 6.5-hour train ride from
     Chamonix—or a 23-day tour with a scenic 6.5-hour train
     through Switzerland to Colmar, spend two nights there,
     then take the TGV back to Paris.)

21   Fly home.

* Indicates TGV option—book well in advance.

some businesses are closed until 14:00 and possibly all day. Smaller
towns are often quiet and downright boring on Sundays and
Mondays, unless it's market day. Saturdays are virtually weekdays
(without the rush hour).

Watt's Up? Europe's electrical system is 220 volts, instead of
North America's 110 volts. Most newer electronics (such as lap-
tops, battery chargers, and hair dryers) convert automatically, so
you won't need a converter plug, but you will need an adapter plug
with two round prongs, sold inexpensively at travel stores in the
US. Avoid bringing older appliances that don't automatically convert voltage; instead, buy a cheap replacement in Europe. You can
buy low-cost hair dryers and other small appliances at Darty and

Monoprix stores, which you'll find in major cities (ask your hotelier for the closest branch).

Discounts: Discounts aren't always listed in this book. However, many sights offer discounts for youths (up to age 18), students (with proper identification cards, www.isic.org), families, and groups of 10 or more. Always ask. Seniors (age 60 and over) may get the odd discount, though most require European citizenship. To inquire about a senior discount, ask, *"Réduction troisième âge?"* (ray-dook-see-ohn twah-zee-ehm ahzh).

Money

This section offers advice on how to pay for purchases on your trip (including getting cash from ATMs and paying with plastic), dealing with lost or stolen cards, VAT (sales tax) refunds, and tipping.

What to Bring

Bring both a credit card and a debit card. You'll use the debit card at cash machines (ATMs) to withdraw local cash for most purchases, and the credit card to pay for larger items. Some travelers carry a third card, in case one gets demagnetized or eaten by a temperamental machine.

For an emergency reserve, bring several hundred dollars in hard cash in $20 bills. Keep in mind, though, that French banks won't exchange dollars; should you need to exchange your US bills, go to a currency-exchange booth (and be prepared for lousy rates and/or outrageous fees).

Cash

Cash is just as desirable in Europe as it is at home. Small businesses (hotels, restaurants, and shops) prefer that you pay your bills with cash. Some vendors will charge you extra for using a credit card, and some won't take credit cards at all. Cash is the best—and sometimes only—way to pay for bus fare, taxis, and local guides.

Throughout Europe, ATMs are the standard way for travelers to get cash. Stay away from "independent" ATMs such as Travelex, Euronet, and Forex, which charge huge commissions and have terrible exchange rates.

To withdraw money from an ATM (known as a *distributeur;* dee-stree-bew-tur), you'll need a debit card (ideally with a Visa or MasterCard logo for maximum usability), plus a PIN code. Know your PIN code in numbers; there are only numbers—no letters—on European keypads. For security, it's best to shield the keypad when entering your PIN at an ATM. Although you can use a credit card for ATM transactions, it's generally more expensive (and only makes sense in an emergency) because it's considered a

Exchange Rate

1 euro (€) = about $1.30

To convert prices in euros to dollars, add about 30 percent: €20 = about $26, €50 = about $65. (Check www.oanda.com for the latest exchange rates.) Just like the dollar, one euro (€1) is broken down into 100 cents. You'll find coins ranging from €0.01 to €2, and bills from €5 to €500.

"cash advance" rather than a withdrawal. Try to withdraw large sums of money to reduce the number of per-transaction bank fees you'll pay.

Pickpockets target tourists. To safeguard your cash, wear a money belt—a pouch with a strap that you buckle around your waist like a belt and tuck under your clothes. Keep your cash, credit cards, and passport secure in your money belt, and carry only a day's spending money in your front pocket.

Credit and Debit Cards

For purchases, Visa and MasterCard are more commonly accepted than American Express. Just like at home, credit or debit cards work easily at larger hotels, restaurants, and shops. I typically use my debit card to withdraw cash to pay for most purchases. I use my credit card only in a few specific situations: to book hotel reservations by phone, to cover major expenses (such as car rentals, plane tickets, and hotel stays), and to pay for things near the end of my trip (to avoid another visit to the ATM). While you could use a debit card to make most large purchases, using a credit card offers a greater degree of fraud protection (because debit cards draw funds directly from your account).

Ask Your Credit- or Debit-Card Company: Before your trip, contact the company that issued your debit or credit cards.

• Confirm your **card will work overseas,** and alert them that you'll be using it in Europe; otherwise, they may deny transactions if they perceive unusual spending patterns.

• Ask for the specifics on transaction **fees.** When you use your credit or debit card—either for purchases or ATM withdrawals— you'll often be charged additional "international transaction" fees of up to 3 percent (1 percent is normal) plus $5 per transaction. Some banks have agreements with European partners that reduce or eliminate the transaction fee. For example, Bank of America debit-card holders can use French BNP Paribas ATMs without being charged the transaction fee (but they still pay a 1 percent international fee). If your card's fees seem high, consider getting a different card just for your trip: Capital One (credit cards only, www.capitalone.com) and most credit unions have low to no international fees.

• If you plan to withdraw cash from ATMs, confirm your daily **withdrawal limit,** and if necessary, ask your bank to adjust it. Some travelers prefer a high limit that allows them to take out more cash at each ATM stop (saving on bank fees), whereas others prefer to set a lower limit in case their card is stolen. Note that foreign banks also set maximum withdrawal amounts for their ATMs.

• Get your bank's emergency **phone number** in the US (but not its 800 number, which isn't accessible from overseas) to call collect if you have a problem.

• Ask for your credit card's **PIN** in case you need to make an emergency cash withdrawal or if you encounter Europe's "chip-and-PIN" system; the bank won't tell you your PIN over the phone, so allow time for it to be mailed to you.

Chip and PIN: If your card is declined for a purchase in Europe, it may be because Europeans are increasingly using chip-and-PIN cards, which are embedded with an electronic chip (rather than the magnetic stripe used on our American-style cards). Much of Europe is adopting this system, and some merchants rely on it exclusively. You're most likely to encounter chip-and-PIN problems at automated payment machines, such as those at train and subway stations, toll roads, parking garages, luggage lockers, and self-serve gas pumps.

But don't panic. To prevent problems, carry plenty of euros (you can always use an ATM with your magnetic-stripe debit card). Memorizing the PIN lets you use it at some chip-and-PIN machines—just enter it when prompted. If a machine won't take your card, find a cashier who can make your card work (they can print a receipt for you to sign), or find a machine that takes cash.

If you're still concerned, you can apply for a chip card in the US (though I think it's overkill). While big US banks offer these cards with high annual fees, a better option is the no-annual-fee GlobeTrek Visa, offered by Andrews Federal Credit Union in Maryland (open to all US residents; see www.andrews fcu.org).

Dynamic Currency Conversion: If merchants offer to convert your purchase price into dollars (called dynamic currency conversion, or DCC), refuse this "service." You'll pay even more in fees for the expensive convenience of seeing your charge in dollars.

Damage Control for Lost Cards

If you lose your credit, debit, or ATM card, you can stop people from using your card by reporting the loss immediately to the respective global customer-assistance centers. Call these 24-hour US numbers collect: Visa (tel. 303/967-1096), MasterCard (tel. 636/722-7111), and American Express (tel. 336/393-1111). In France, to make a collect call to the US, dial 00 00 11. For another option (with the same results), you can call these toll-free numbers in France: Visa (tel. 08 00 90 11 79) and MasterCard (tel. 08 00 90 13 87). American Express has a Paris office, but the call isn't free (tel. 01 47 77 70 00, greeting is in French only, dial 1 to speak with someone in English). Diners Club has offices in the US (tel. 303/799-1504, call collect) and Paris (tel. 08 10 31 41 59).

At a minimum, you'll need to know the name of the financial institution that issued you the card, along with the type of card (classic, platinum, or whatever). Providing the following information will allow for a quicker cancellation of your missing card: full card number, whether you are the primary or secondary cardholder, the cardholder's name exactly as printed on the card, billing address, home phone number, circumstances of the loss or theft, and identification verification (your birthdate, your mother's maiden name, or your Social Security number—memorize this, don't carry a copy). If you are the secondary cardholder, you'll also need to provide the primary cardholder's identification-verification details. You can generally receive a temporary card within two or three business days in Europe (see www.ricksteves.com/help for more).

If you report your loss within two days, you typically won't be responsible for any unauthorized transactions on your account, although many banks charge a liability fee of $50.

Tipping

Tipping *(donner un pourboire)* in France isn't as automatic and generous as it is in the US, but for special service, tips are appreciated, if not expected. As in the US, the proper amount depends on your resources, tipping philosophy, and the circumstances, but some general guidelines apply.

Restaurants: Prices at cafés and restaurants include a 12-15 percent service charge (referred to as *service compris* or *prix net* but generally not broken out on your bill). Most French never tip (credit-card receipts don't even have space to add a tip). But if you feel the service was *exceptional*, it's kind to tip up to 5 percent extra. If you want the waiter to keep the change when you pay, say, "*C'est bon*" (say bohn), meaning, "It's good." Never feel guilty if you don't leave a tip.

Taxis: To tip the cabbie, round up. For a typical ride, round up your fare a bit (for instance, if the fare is €13, pay €14). If the cabbie hauls your bags and zips you to the airport to help you catch your flight, you might want to toss in a little more. But if you feel like you're being driven in circles or otherwise ripped off, skip the tip.

Services: In general, if someone in the service industry does a super job for you, a small tip of a euro or two is appropriate...but not required. If you're not sure whether (or how much) to tip for a service, ask your hotelier or the TI.

Getting a VAT Refund

Wrapped into the purchase price of your French souvenirs is a Value-Added Tax (VAT) of about 19.6 percent. You're entitled to get most of that tax back if you purchase more than €175 (about $230) worth of goods at a store that participates in the VAT-refund scheme. Typically, you must ring up the minimum at a single retailer—you can't add up your purchases from various shops to reach the required amount.

Getting your refund is usually straightforward and, if you buy a substantial amount of souvenirs, well worth the hassle. If you're lucky, the merchant will subtract the tax when you make your purchase. (This is more likely to occur if the store ships the goods to your home.) Otherwise, you'll need to:

Get the paperwork. Have the merchant completely fill out the necessary refund document, *Bordereau de Vente à l'Exportation*, also called a "cheque." You'll have to present your passport. Get the paperwork done before you leave the store to ensure you'll have everything you need (including your original sales receipt).

Get your stamp at the border or airport. Process your VAT document at your last stop in the EU (e.g., at the airport) with the customs agent who deals with VAT refunds. Before checking in for your flight, find the local customs office, and be prepared to stand in line. It's best to keep your purchases in your carry-on for viewing, but if they're too large or dangerous to carry on (such as knives), have your purchases easily accessible in the bag you're about to check, ready to show the customs agent. You're not supposed to use your purchased goods before you leave. If you show up at customs wearing your chic new shoes, officials might look the other way—or deny you a refund.

Collect your refund. You'll need to return your stamped document to the retailer or its representative. Many merchants work with a service, such as Global Blue or Premier Tax Free, that has offices at major airports, ports, or border crossings (either before or after security, probably strategically located near a duty-free shop). These services, which extract a 4 percent fee, can refund your money immediately in cash or credit your card (within two billing cycles). If the retailer handles VAT refunds directly, it's up to you to contact the merchant for your refund. You can mail the documents from your home, or more quickly, from your point of departure (using a stamped, addressed envelope you've prepared or one that's been provided by the merchant). You'll then have to wait—it can take months.

Customs for American Shoppers

You are allowed to take home $800 worth of items per person duty-free, once every 30 days. You can also bring in duty-free a liter of alcohol. As for food, you can take home many processed and packaged foods: vacuum-packed cheeses, dried herbs, jams, baked goods, candy, chocolate, oil, vinegar, mustard, and honey. Fresh fruits and vegetables and most meats are not allowed. However, canned goose, duck, and pork pâté can be imported to the US, but not beef. Any liquid-containing foods (and often canned pâté) must be packed in checked luggage, a potential recipe for disaster. To check customs rules and duty rates, visit www.cbp.gov.

Sightseeing

Sightseeing can be hard work. Use these tips to make your visits to France's finest sights meaningful, fun, efficient, and painless.

Plan Ahead

Set up an itinerary that allows you to fit in all your must-see sights. For a one-stop look at opening hours, see the "At a Glance" side-bars for Paris, Nice, Lyon, and the Loire Valley châteaux. Most sights keep stable hours, but you can easily confirm the latest by checking with the TI or visiting museums' websites.

Don't put off visiting a must-see sight—you never know when a place will close unexpectedly for a holiday, strike, or restoration. On holidays (see list on page 1144), expect reduced hours or closures. In summer, some sights may stay open late. Off-season, many museums have shorter hours.

Going at the right time helps avoid crowds. This book offers tips on specific sights. Try visiting popular sights very early (arrive at least 15 minutes before opening time) or very late. Evening visits are usually peaceful, with fewer crowds. For example, Paris' Louvre and Orsay museums are open selected evenings, and the Pompidou Center is open late every night except Tuesday (when it's closed all day).

Many French monuments and cities (and some villages) are beautifully lit at night, making evening walks a joy. At Mont St-Michel and Carcassonne, it's best to arrive at about 17:00, spend the night, and explore in the morning before the crowds descend. Visit these sights first thing or late in the day: Château de Chenonceau, Les Baux, and Pont du Gard.

Several cities offer sightseeing passes that are worthwhile

values for busy sightseers; do the math to see if they'll save you money.

Study up. To get the most out of the sight descriptions in this book, read them before you visit.

At Sights

Here's what you can typically expect:

Some important sights require you to check daypacks and coats. To avoid checking a small backpack, carry it under your arm like a purse as you enter. From a guard's point of view, a backpack is generally a problem while a purse is not. If you check a bag, the attendant may ask you (in French) if it contains anything of value—such as a camera, phone, money, or passport—because these cannot be checked.

At churches—which often offer interesting art (usually free) and a cool, welcome seat—a modest dress code (no bare shoulders or shorts) is encouraged.

Flash photography is often banned, but taking photos without flash is usually allowed. Flashes damage oil paintings and distract others in the room. Even without a flash, a handheld camera will take a decent picture (or buy postcards or posters at the museum bookstore).

Museums may have special exhibits in addition to their permanent collection. Some exhibits are included in the entry price; others come at an extra cost (which you may have to pay even if you don't want to see the exhibit).

Expect changes—artwork can be on tour, on loan, out sick, or shifted at the whim of the curator. To adapt, pick up any available free floor plans as you enter, and ask the museum staff if you can't find a particular item. Say the title or artist's name, or point to the photograph in this book, and ask for its location by saying, *"Où est?"* (oo ay).

Many sights offer audioguides, which generally offer useful recorded descriptions in English (about €6, sometimes included with admission). If you bring along your earbuds, you can enjoy better sound and avoid holding the device to your ear. To save money, bring a Y-jack and share one audioguide with your travel partner. I've produced free downloadable audio tours of some of the major sights in Paris; see page 1138.

Important sights may have an on-site café or cafeteria (usually a handy place to rejuvenate during a long visit). The WCs at sights are free and generally clean.

Many sights sell postcards that highlight their attractions. Before you leave a sight, scan the postcards and thumb through the biggest guidebook (or skim its index) to be sure that you haven't overlooked something that you'd like to see.

Most sights stop admitting people 30-60 minutes before closing time, and some rooms may close early (often about 45 minutes before the actual closing time). Guards usher people out, so don't save the best for last.

Every sight or museum offers more than what is covered in this book. Use the information in this book as an introduction—not the final word.

Sleeping

Good-value accommodations in France generally are easy to find. Choose from one- to five-star hotels (two stars is my mainstay), bed-and-breakfasts (*chambres d'hôtes*, usually cheaper than hotels),

hostels, campgrounds, and even homes (*gîtes,* rented by the week).

I favor hotels and restaurants that are handy to your sightseeing activities. Rather than list hotels scattered throughout a city, I describe two or three favorite neighborhoods and recommend the best accommodations values in each, from dorm beds to fancy doubles with all of the comforts.

A major feature of this book is its extensive listing of good-value rooms. I like places that are clean, central, relatively quiet at night, reasonably priced, friendly, small enough to have a hands-on owner and stable staff, run with a respect for French traditions, and not listed in other guidebooks. (In France, for me, six out of these eight criteria means it's a keeper.) I'm more impressed by a handy location and a fun-loving philosophy than flat-screen TVs and shoeshine machines.

Book your accommodations well in advance if you'll be traveling during busy times. Reserving ahead is especially important for Paris—the sooner, the better. Wherever you're staying, be ready for crowds during these holiday periods: Easter weekend; Labor Day; Ascension weekend; Pentecost weekend; Bastille Day and the week during which it falls; and the winter holidays (mid-Dec-early Jan). See page 1144 for a list of major holidays and festivals in France; for tips on making reservations, see page 28.

Rates and Deals

I've described my recommended accommodations using a Sleep Code (see sidebar). Prices listed are for one-night stays in peak season, do not include breakfast, and assume you're booking directly (not through a TI or online hotel-booking engine). Using an

Sleep Code

(€1 = about $1.30, country code: 33)

Price Rankings

To help you sort easily through my listings, I've divided the accommodations into three categories based on the price for a double room with bath during high season:

> **$$$ Higher Priced**
> **$$ Moderately Priced**
> **$ Lower Priced**

I always rate hostels as $, whether or not they have double rooms, because they have the cheapest beds in town.

Prices can change without notice; verify the hotel's current rates online or by email.

Abbreviations

To pack maximum information into minimum space, I use the following code to describe the accommodations in this book. Prices listed are per room, not per person. When a price range is given for a type of room (such as double rooms listing for €100-130), it means the price fluctuates with the season, size of room, or length of stay; expect to pay the upper end for peak-season stays.

S = Single room (or price for one person in a double).

D = Double or twin room.

T = Triple (generally a double bed with a single).

Q = Quad (usually two double beds; adding an extra child's bed to a T is usually cheaper).

b = Private bathroom with toilet and shower or tub.

s = Private shower or tub only (the toilet is down the hall).

* = French hotel rating system, ranging from zero to five stars.

According to this code, a couple staying at a "Db-€100" hotel would pay a total of €100 (about $130) for a double room with a private bathroom. Unless otherwise noted, breakfast is not included (but is usually optional), hotel staff speak basic English, and credit cards are accepted.

There's almost always Wi-Fi and/or Internet access available, either free or for a fee.

online booking service costs the hotel about 20 percent and logically closes the door on special deals. Book direct.

These days, many hotels change prices from day to day, according to demand. Given the economic downturn, hoteliers may be willing to make a deal (rare in Paris). You could email several hotels to ask for their best price, though you'll almost always find the best offers on their websites. Comparison-shop and make your choice. Drivers can save big by sleeping in characterless—but clean and cheap—chain hotels outside of cities (some are located in town centers in which case I have usually listed them; see "Modern Hotel Chains," later).

As you look over the listings, you'll notice that some accommodations promise special prices to my readers who book direct (without using a room-finding service or hotel-booking website, which take a commission). To get these rates, you must mention this book when you reserve, and then show the book upon arrival. Rick Steves discounts apply to readers with ebooks as well as printed books. Discounts may not apply to promotional rates.

In general, prices can soften if you stay at least three nights or mention this book. You can also try asking for a cheaper room or a discount. To save money off-season, consider arriving without a reservation and dropping in at the last minute.

Types of Accommodations
Hotels
In this book, the price for a double room ranges from €40 (very simple, toilet and shower down the hall) to €400-plus (grand lobbies, maximum plumbing, and the works), with most clustering around €80-110 (with private bathrooms).

The French have a simple hotel-rating system based on amenities and rated by stars (indicated in this book by asterisks, from * through *****). One star is modest, two has most of the comforts, and three is generally a two-star with a fancier lobby and more elaborately designed rooms. Four stars offer more luxury than you usually have time to appreciate, and five stars is a new classification that I can't fathom (the addition of this category enabled many hotels to add a star with no change in comfort or services provided). Two- and three-star hotels are required to have an English-speaking staff, though nearly all hotels I recommend have someone who speaks English (unless I note otherwise in the listing).

Types of Rooms and Beds

Study the price list on the hotel's website or posted at the desk, so you know your options. Receptionists often don't mention the cheaper rooms (they assume you want a private bathroom or a bigger room). Here are the types of rooms and beds:

une chambre sans douche et WC	room without a private shower or toilet (uncommon these days)
une chambre avec cabinet de toilette	room with a toilet but no shower (some hotels charge for down-the-hall showers)
une chambre avec bain et WC	room with private bathtub and toilet
une chambre avec douche et WC	room with private shower and toilet
chambres communiquantes	connecting rooms (ideal for families)
un grand lit	double bed (55 inches wide)
deux petits lits	twin beds (30-36 inches wide)
un lit single	true single room bed
un lit de cent-soixante	queen-size bed (literally, 160 centimeters, or 63 inches, wide)
le king size	king-size bed (usually two twins pushed together)
un lit pliant	folding bed
un berceau	baby crib
un lit d'enfant	child's bed

The number of stars doesn't generally reflect room size or guarantee quality. Some two-star hotels are better than many three-star hotels. One- and two-star hotels are inexpensive, but some three-star (and even a few four-star) hotels offer good value, justifying the extra cost. Unclassified hotels (no stars) can be bargains or depressing dumps.

Most hotels have lots of doubles and a few singles, triples, and quads. Traveling alone can be expensive in France, as singles (except for the rare closet-type rooms that fit only one twin bed) are simply doubles used by one person—so they cost about the same as a double. Room prices vary within each hotel depending on size and whether the room has a bath or shower, twin beds or a double bed (tubs and twins cost more than showers and double beds). A triple is often just a double room with a double (or queen-size) bed plus a sliver-size single. Quad rooms usually have two double beds.

Keep Cool

If you're visiting France in the summer, the extra expense of an air-conditioned room can be money well spent, particularly in the south. Most hotel rooms with air-conditioners come with a control stick (like a TV remote) that generally has the similar symbols and features: fan icon (click to toggle through wind power, from light to gale); louver icon (choose steady airflow or waves); snowflake and sunshine icons (cold air or heat, depending on season); clock ("O" setting: run *X* hours before turning off; "I" setting: wait *X* hours to start); and the temperature control (21 or 22 degrees Celsius is comfortable; also see the thermometer diagram on page 1148).

Hotels cannot legally allow more in the room than what's shown on their price list. Modern hotels generally have a few family-friendly rooms that open to each other *(chambres communiquantes)*.

Hotels in France must charge a daily tax *(taxe du séjour)* of about €1-2 per person per day. Some hotels include it in the listed prices, but most add it to your bill.

You can save as much as €25 by finding the rare room without a private shower or toilet. A room with a bathtub usually costs more than a room with a shower and is generally larger. Hotels often have more rooms with tubs than showers and are inclined to give you a room with a tub (which the French prefer).

A double bed is usually cheaper than twins, though rooms with twin beds tend to be larger, and French double beds are smaller than American double beds. Many hotels have queen-size beds (a bed that's 63 inches wide—standard doubles are 55). To find out whether a hotel has queen-size beds, ask, *"Avez-vous des lits de cent-soixante?"* (ah-vay-voo day lee duh sahn-swah-sahnt). Some hotels push two twins together under king-size-sheets and blankets to make *le king size*.

If you prefer a double bed (instead of twins) and a shower (instead of a tub), you need to ask for it—and you can save up to €20. If you'll take either twins or a double, ask for a generic *une chambre pour deux* (room for two) to avoid being needlessly turned away.

Hotel lobbies, halls, and breakfast rooms are off-limits to smokers, though they can light up in their rooms. Still, I seldom smell any smoke in the hundreds of rooms I check each year. Some hotels have non-smoking rooms or floors—ask about them if this is important to you. If your room smells of smoke, ask for a different one.

Most hotels offer some kind of breakfast, but it's rarely included in the room rates—pay attention when comparing rates

Making Hotel Reservations

Given the good value of the accommodations I've found for this book, I'd recommend that you reserve your rooms several weeks in advance, particularly if you'll be traveling during peak times (for Paris, reserve several months ahead—for any time of year). Note that some national holidays jam things up and merit your making reservations far in advance (see "Holidays and Festivals" on page 1144).

Requesting a Reservation: It's usually easiest to book your room through the hotel's website; many have a reservation-request form built right in. (For the best rates, be sure to use the hotel's official site and not a booking agency's site.) Just type in your preferred dates and the website will automatically display a list of available rooms and prices. Simpler websites will generate an email to the hotelier with your request. If there's no reservation form, or for complicated requests, send an email from your personal address. Other options include calling (see "Phoning" below, but be mindful of time zones) or faxing. Most of my recommended hotels are accustomed to guests who speak only English.

The hotelier wants to know these key pieces of information (also included in the sample request form in the appendix):
- number and type of rooms
- number of nights
- date of arrival
- date of departure
- any special needs (e.g., bathroom in the room or down the hall, twin beds vs. double bed, air-conditioning, quiet, view, ground floor, etc.)

When you request a room, use the European style for writing dates: day/month/year. For example, for a two-night stay in July 2013, I would request: "1 double room for 2 nights, arrive 16/07/13, depart 18/07/13." Consider carefully how long you'll stay; don't just assume you can tack on extra days once you arrive. Make sure you mention any discounts—for Rick Steves readers or otherwise—when you make the reservation.

If you don't get a response to your email, it usually means the hotel is already fully booked—but try sending the message again or call to follow up.

Confirming a Reservation: Most hoteliers will request your credit-card number to hold the room. To confirm a room using a hotel's secure online reservation form, enter your contact information and credit-card number; the hotel will email a confirmation.

If you sent an email to request a reservation, the hotel will reply with its room availability and rates. This is not a confirmation. You must email back to say that you want the room at the given rate. While you can email your credit-card information (I do), it's safer to share that confidential info via phone call, two emails (splitting your number between them), or the hotel's secure online reservation form.

Canceling a Reservation: If you must cancel your reservation, it's courteous to do so with as much advance notice as possible. Simply make a quick phone call or send an email. Family-run places lose money if they turn away customers while holding a room for someone who doesn't show up. Understandably, many hoteliers bill no-shows for one night.

Cancellation policies can be strict: For example, you might lose a deposit if you cancel within two weeks of your reserved stay, or you might be billed for the entire visit if you leave early. Internet deals may require prepayment, with no refunds for cancellations. Ask about cancellation policies before you book.

If canceling via email, request confirmation that your cancellation was received to avoid being accidentally billed.

Reconfirming Your Reservation: Always call to reconfirm your room reservation a few days in advance. Smaller hotels and *chambres d'hôtes* appreciate your estimated time of arrival. If you'll be arriving late (after 17:00), let them know. On the small chance that a hotel loses track of your reservation, bring along a hard copy of their confirmation.

Reserving Rooms as You Travel: You can make reservations as you travel, calling hotels or *chambres d'hôtes* a few days to a week before your arrival. If everything's full, don't despair. Call a day or two in advance and fill in a cancellation. If you'd rather travel without any reservations at all, you'll have greater success snaring rooms if you arrive at your destination early in the day. When you anticipate crowds (weekends are worst), call hotels at about 9:00 or 10:00 on the day you plan to arrive, when the receptionist knows who'll be checking out and just which rooms will be available. If you encounter a language barrier, ask the fluent receptionist at your current hotel to call for you. If all else fails, local TIs can help you find a room.

Phoning: To call France from the US or Canada, dial 011-33 and then the local number (drop the local number's initial 0). The 011 is our international access code, and 33 is France's country code. If you're calling France from another European country, dial 00-33-local number (drop the local number's initial 0). The 00 is Europe's international access code. To make calls within France, simply dial the local number. For more tips on calling, see page 1105.

between hotels. The price of breakfast correlates with the price of the room: The more expensive the room, the more expensive the breakfast. This per-person charge can add up, particularly for families. Hotels hope you'll buy their breakfast, but it's optional unless otherwise noted (for more on breakfast, see page 36).

Some hotels, especially in coastal resort towns, strongly encourage their peak-season guests to take *demi-pension* (half-pension)—that is, breakfast and either lunch or dinner. By law, they can't require you to take half-pension unless you are staying three or more nights, but, in practice, many do during summer. And though the food is usually good, it limits your ability to shop around. I've indicated where I think *demi-pension* is a good value.

Most hotel rooms have a TV, phone, and Wi-Fi *(le wee-fee)*. Budget rooms are short on outlets (buying a cheap French extension cord helps). To turn on your TV, press the channel-up or channel-down button on the remote. If it still doesn't work, see if there's a power button on the TV itself, then press the up or down button again. Hotel elevators, while becoming more common, are often very small, forcing you to send your bags up separately—pack light.

Towels aren't routinely replaced every day. Hang up your towel to dry. Extra pillows and blankets are sometimes in the closet or available on request. To get a pillow, ask for *"Un oreiller, s'il vous plaît"* (un oh-ray-yay, see voo play).

If you're arriving early in the morning, your room probably won't be ready. You can drop your bag safely at the hotel and dive right into sightseeing.

Hoteliers can be a great help and source of advice. Most know their city well, and can assist you with everything from public transit and airport connections to calling an English-speaking doctor, or finding a good restaurant, the nearest Internet café *(café internet,* kah-fay an-ter-net), or self-service launderette *(laverie automatique,* lah-vay-ree oh-to-mah-teek).

Even at the best places, mechanical breakdowns occur: Air-conditioning malfunctions, sinks leak, hot water turns cold, and toilets gurgle and smell. Report your concerns clearly and calmly at the front desk. For more complicated problems, don't expect instant results.

If you suspect night noise will be a problem (if, for instance, your room is over a café), ask for a quieter room in the back or on an upper floor. To guard against theft in your room, keep valuables out of sight. Some rooms come with a safe, and other hotels have safes at the front desk. I've never bothered using one.

Checkout can pose problems if surprise charges pop up on your bill. If you settle your bill the afternoon before you leave, you'll have time to discuss and address any points of contention (before 19:00, when the night shift usually arrives).

Some hoteliers will ask you to sign their *Livre d'Or* ("Golden Book," for client comments). They take this seriously and enjoy reading your remarks.

Above all, keep a positive attitude. Remember, you're on vacation. If your hotel is a disappointment, spend more time out enjoying the city you came to see.

Modern Hotel Chains: France is littered with ultramodern hotels, often located on cheap land just outside of town, providing drivers with low-stress accommodations (though you'll find some in city centers as well). The antiseptically clean and cheap Formule 1 and ETAP chains (about €40-50/room for up to three people), the more attractive and spacious Ibis hotels (€80-110 for a double), and the cushier Mercure and Novotel hotels (€110-200 for a double) are all run by the same company, Accor (US tel. 800-515-5679, www.accorhotels.com). Though hardly quaint, these can be a good value (particularly if you find deals on their website), and some are centrally located (I find Ibis hotels to be a solid middle-of-the-road value when they are centrally located—you'll see many listed in this book). Another chain, Kyriad, offers midrange prices often in central locations (tel. 01 64 62 59 70, www.kyriad.com). Best Western Hotels are generally reliable and often centrally located (US tel. 800-780-7234, www.bestwestern.com). Château Hotels have more cushy digs (www.chateaucountry.com). For a long listing of various hotels throughout France, see www.france.com.

Bed-and-Breakfasts

B&Bs (*chambres d'hôtes*, abbreviated CH) are generally found in smaller towns and rural areas. They're a great deal, offering double the cultural intimacy yet costing much less than most hotel rooms. And though you may lose some hotel conveniences—such as lounges, in-room phones, frequent bed-sheet changes, and the ability to pay with a credit card—I happily make the trade-off for the personal touches and lower rates. Your hosts may not speak English, but they will almost always be enthusiastic and pleasant.

You'll find CHs in this book and through local TIs, often listed by the owner's family name. To find small-town TIs online, do a web search for *"office du tourisme"* with the name of town you want (if that doesn't work start with the nearest large city TI and go from there). Though some CHs post small *Chambres* or *Chambres d'hôte* signs in their front windows, many are found only through the local TI. It's always OK to ask to see the room before you commit.

I recommend reliable CHs that offer a good value and/or unique experience (such as CHs in renovated mills, châteaux, and wine *domaines*). Although *chambres d'hôtes* have their own star-rating system, it doesn't correspond to the hotels' rating system. So, to avoid confusion, I haven't listed these stars for CHs. Most of my recommended CHs have private in-room bathrooms, and some have common rooms with refrigerators. Doubles with breakfast generally cost €60-80 (€100-120 for the fancy ones).

Tables d'hôte are CHs that offer an optional, reasonably priced home-cooked dinner; the meals are almost always worth springing for, and they must be requested in advance.

Hostels

You'll pay about €22 per bed to stay at a hostel *(auberge de jeunesse)*. Travelers of any age are welcome if they don't mind dorm-style accommodations (usually in rooms of four to eight beds) and meeting other travelers. Cheap meals are sometimes offered, and most hostels offer kitchen facilities, Internet access, Wi-Fi, and self-service laundry. Nowadays, concerned about bedbugs, hostels are likely to provide all bedding, including sheets. Expect youth groups in spring, crowds in the summer, snoring, and variability in quality from one hostel to the next. Family and private rooms may be available on request.

Independent hostels tend to be easygoing, colorful, and informal (no membership required); see www.hostelz.com, www.hosteleurope.com; www.hostels.com; and www.hostelbookers.com. **Official hostels** are part of Hostelling International (HI) and share an online booking site (www.hihostels.com). HI hostels typically require that you either have a membership card or pay extra per night.

Camping

In Europe, camping is more of a social than an environmental experience. It's a great way for American travelers to make European friends. Camping averages about €18 per campsite per night (though most municipal sites cost less), and almost every destination recommended in this book has a campground within a reasonable walk or bus ride from the town center and train station. A tent, pillow, and sleeping bag are all you need. Many campgrounds have small grocery stores and washing machines, and some even come with cafés and miniature golf. French TIs have camping information. You'll find more detailed information in the annually updated *Michelin Camping France,* available in the US and at most French bookstores.

Gîtes, Apartments, and Hotel Barges

Throughout France, you can find reasonably priced rental homes that are ideal for families and small groups wanting to explore a region more closely.

Gites (pronounced "zheet") are homes in the countryside (usually urbanites' second homes) rentable by the week, from Saturday to Saturday. The objective of the *gite* program was to save characteristic rural homes from abandonment and to make it easy and affordable for families to enjoy the French countryside. The government offers subsidies to renovate such homes, then coordinates rentals to make it financially feasible for the owner. Today, France has thousands of *gites*. One of your co-authors restored a farmhouse a few hours north of Provence, and even though he and his wife are American, they received the same assistance that French owners get.

Gites are best for drivers (they're usually rural, with little public-transport access) and ideal for families and small groups (because they can sleep many for a reasonable price). Homes range in comfort from simple cottages and farmhouses to restored châteaux. Most have at least two bedrooms, a kitchen, a living room, and a bathroom or two—but no sheets or linens (though you can usually rent them for extra). Like hotels, all *gites* are rated for comfort from one to four (using ears of corn—*épis*—rather than stars). Two or three *épis* are generally sufficient quality, but I'd lean toward three for more comfort. Prices generally range from €400 to €1,300 per week, depending on house size and amenities such as pools (if it's less than €400 per week, I'd think twice). If your owner does not speak English, be prepared for doing business in French—all the contracts are in French. For more information on *gites*, visit www.gites-de-france.com or www.gite.com.

Apartments, less common than *gites*, are available in cities and in towns. You'll find long lists of homes and apartments for rent through TIs and on the Internet, though these are usually more expensive than staying in a *gite*. Here are three good independent sources to consider: **VRBO** is an international network of apartment rentals (houses, apartments, *gites*, etc.), that cuts out the middleman by putting you directly in touch with the owners (www.vrbo.com). **France Homestyle** is run by Claudette, a service-oriented French woman from Seattle who handpicks every home and apartment she lists (US tel. 206/325-0132, www.francehomestyle.com, info@francehomestyle.com). Or try **Ville et Village,** which has a bigger selection of high-end places (US tel. 510/559-8080, www.villeetvillage.com, rentals@villeetvillage.com).

Hotel barges are a fun option in canalside towns; I've listed a few in this book. If you're interested in renting one for more than a night or two, try **Papillon Barge** (mobile 06 86 28 11 55, www.hotelbarge.com) or **Barge Nilaya** (May-Sept mobile 06 89 18 80 67, Oct-April UK mobile—from the US dial 00-11-44-7909-151-611, www.bargenilaya.com).

Traveling with Kids

France is kid-friendly for young children, partly because so much of it is rural. (Teenagers, on the other hand, tend to prefer cit-ies.) Both of this book's authors have kids (from 11 to 25 years old), and we've used our substantial experience traveling with children to improve this book. Our kids have greatly enriched our travels, and we hope the same will be true for you.

My kids' favorite places have been Mont St-Michel, the Alps, the Loire châteaux, Carcassonne, and Paris (especially the Eiffel Tower and Seine River boat ride)—and any hotel with a pool. To make your trip fun for everyone in the family, mix heavy-duty sights with kids' activities (playing miniature golf, renting bikes, and riding the little tourist trains popular in many towns). And though Disneyland Paris is the predictable draw, my kids had more fun for half the expense simply by enjoying the rides in the Tuileries Garden in downtown Paris.

Minimize hotel changes by planning three-day stops. Aim for hotels with restaurants, so the older kids can go back to the room while you finish a quiet dinner.

I've listed public pools in many places (especially the south), but be warned: Public pools in France commonly require a small, Speedo-like bathing suit for boys and men (American-style swim trunks won't do)—though they usually have these little suits to loan. At hotel pools, either kind of suit will do.

For breakfast, croissants are a hit, though a good *pain au chocolat* (croissant with chocolate bits) will be appreciated even more. Hot chocolate, fruit, and yogurt are usually available. For lunch and dinner, it's easy to find fast-food places and restaurants with kids' menus, or *crêperies,* which have a wide variety of kid-friendly stuffings for both savory crêpes and sweet dessert crêpes. In the south of France, pizza is omnipresent. Many restaurants have a kid's menu. For food emergencies, I travel with a plastic container of peanut butter brought from home and smuggle small jars of jam from breakfast.

Kids homesick for friends can keep in touch with cheap international phone cards and by email. Cybercafés and hotels with Internet access are a godsend for parents with teenagers. Readily available Wi-Fi makes bringing a laptop, smartphone, or tablet computer worthwhile. Some parents find buying a French mobile phone—or roaming with an American mobile phone—a helpful investment; adults can stay connected to teenagers while allowing them maximum independence (see page 1108). Some American mobile-phone plans have automatic call forwarding and text settings that can save you money—and satisfy your teen.

Swap babysitting duties with your partner if one of you wants to take in an extra sight, or ask at hotels for babysitting services. And for memories that will last long after the trip, keep a family journal. Pack a small diary and a glue stick. While relaxing at a café over a *citron-pressé* (lemonade), take turns writing down the day's events, and include mementos such as ticket stubs from museums, postcards, or stalks of lavender.

What to Bring: Children's books in English are scarce and pricey in France. My children read more when traveling in Europe than while at home in the US, so don't skimp here. If your kids love peanut butter, bring it from home (hard to find in France)... or help them acquire a taste for Nutella, the tasty hazelnut-chocolate spread available everywhere.

Choose items that are small and convenient for use on planes, trains, and in your hotel room: compact travel games, a deck of cards, a handheld video game, an MP3 player, and a tablet or lightweight laptop. Bring your own drawing paper, pens, and crayons (expensive in France). A small travel journal and a glue stick make saving museum ticket stubs a fun activity.

For younger kids, Legos are easily packed and practical (it's also fun to purchase kits overseas, as Legos are sometimes different in Europe from those in the US). Budding fashionistas might enjoy traveling with—and buying new outfits for—a Corelle doll or another 16-inch doll. The French have wonderful doll clothes, with a better selection than what you'll typically find in the US.

For those traveling with younger kids, car-rental agencies usually rent car seats, though you must reserve one in advance (verify the price ahead of time—you may want to bring your own). According to French law, kids under 10 must be in a car seat in the back seat (unless all other seats are also taken by kids in car seats; if in front, car seats must face backward). And though most hotels have some sort of crib, I brought a portable crib and did not regret it.

Cameras are a great investment to get your kids involved. Give younger kids an old digital camera that you don't use anymore. For longer drives, audio books can be fun for the whole family. I recommend Peter Mayle's *A Year in Provence,* available on CD (or put it on your MP3 player/iPod).

Eating

The French eat long and well. Relaxed lunches, three-hour dinners, and endless hours sitting in outdoor cafés are the norm. Here, chefs are as famous as great athletes, and mamas hope their babies grow up to be great cooks. Cafés, cuisine, and wines should become a highlight of any French adventure: It's sightseeing for your palate.

Even if the rest of you is sleeping in cheap hotels, let your taste buds travel first class in France. (They can go coach in England.) You can eat well without going broke—but choose carefully: You're just as likely to blow a small fortune on a mediocre meal as you are to dine wonderfully for €20. Carefully read the information that follows, consider my restaurant suggestions in this book, and you'll do fine.

When restaurant-hunting, choose a spot filled with locals, not the place with the big neon signs boasting, "We Speak English and Accept Credit Cards." Venturing even a block or two off the main drag leads to higher-quality food for less than half the price of the tourist-oriented places. Locals eat better at lower-rent locales.

The no-smoking revolution hit France in 2008, when a law mandated that all café and restaurant interiors be smoke-free. Today the only smokers you'll find are at outside tables, which—unfortunately—may be exactly where you want to sit.

Waiters probably won't overwhelm you with friendliness. As their tip is already included in the bill (see "Tipping," page 19), there's less schmoozing than we're used to at home. Notice how hard they work. They almost never stop. Cozying up to clients (French or foreign) is probably the last thing on their minds. They're often stuck with client overload, too, because the French rarely hire part-time employees, even to help with peak times. To get a waiter's attention, try to make meaningful eye contact, which is a signal that you need something. If this doesn't work, raise your hand and simply say, "*S'il vous plaît*" (see voo play)—"please."

To get the most out of dining—slow down. Allow enough time, engage the waiter, show you care about food, and enjoy the experience as much as the food itself.

Breakfast

You'll almost always have the option of breakfast at your hotel, which is usually pleasant and convenient. A few hotels serve a classic continental breakfast, called *petit déjeuner* (puh-tee day-zhuh-nay). Traditionally, this consisted of a café au lait, hot chocolate, or tea; a roll with butter and marmalade; and a croissant. But these days most hotels put out a buffet breakfast (cereal, yogurt, fruit, cheese, croissants, juice, and the occasional hard-boiled egg).

Market Day (*Jour du Marché*)

Market days are a big deal throughout France. They have been a central feature of life in rural areas since the Middle Ages.

No single event better symbolizes the French preoccupation with fresh products, and their strong ties to the soil, than the weekly market. Many locals mark their calendars with the arrival of fresh produce.

Notice the signs as you enter towns indicating the *jours du marché*—essential information to any civilized soul, and a reminder not to park on the streets the night before (*stationnement interdit* means "no parking").

Most *marchés* take place once a week in the town's main square and, if large enough, spill onto nearby streets. Markets combine fresh produce; samples of wine and other locally produced beverages (such as brandies and ciders); and a smattering of nonperishable items, such as knives, berets, kitchen goods, and cheap clothing. The bigger the market, the greater the overall selection—particularly for nonperishable goods. Bigger towns (such as Beaune and Arles) may have two weekly markets. The biggest market days are usually on weekends, so that everyone can go.

Market day is as important socially as it is commercially—it's a weekly chance to resume friendships and get the current gossip. Neighbors catch up on Henri's barn renovation, see photos of Jacqueline's new grandchild, and relax over *un café*. Dogs are tethered to café tables while friends exchange kisses. Tether yourself to a café table and observe: three cheek-kisses for good friends (left-right-left, a fourth for friends you haven't seen in a while); the appropriate number of kisses varies by region—Paris, Lyon, and Provence all have different standards. It's bad form to be in a hurry on market day. Allow the crowd to set your pace.

Buy some of your picnics at an open-air market. Most perishable items are sold directly from the producers—no middlemen, no Visa cards, just really fresh produce (*du pays* means "grown locally"). Space rental is cheap (about €5-10, depending on the size). Most vendors follow a weekly circuit of markets they feel work best for them, showing up in the same spot every week, year in and year out. Notice how much fun they have chatting up their customers and one another. Many vendors speak enough English to assist you in your selection. Markets end by 13:00—in time for lunch, allowing the town to reclaim its streets and squares.

If all you want is coffee or tea and a croissant, the corner café offers more atmosphere and is less expensive (though you get more coffee at your hotel). Go local at the café and ask for *une tartine* (oon tart-een; baguette slathered with butter or jam) with your café au lait. To keep it cheap, pick up some fruit at a grocery store and pastries at your favorite *boulangerie* (bakery), and have a picnic breakfast, then savor your coffee at the bar *(comptoir)* while standing, like the French do. Some cafés and bakeries offer worthwhile breakfast deals with juice, croissant, and coffee or tea for about €5. If you crave eggs for breakfast, drop into a café and order *une omelette* or *œufs sur le plat* (fried eggs). As a less atmospheric alternative, some fast-food places offer cheap breakfasts.

Picnics and Snacks

Great for lunch or dinner, French picnics can be first-class affairs and adventures in high cuisine. Be daring. Try the smelly cheeses, ugly pâtés, sissy quiches, and minuscule yogurts. Shopkeepers are accustomed to selling small quantities of produce. Get a tasty salad-to-go and ask for a plastic fork *(une fourchette en plastique)*. A small container is *une barquette*. A slice is *une tranche*. If you need a knife *(couteau)* or corkscrew *(tire-bouchon)*, borrow one from your hotelier. And though wine is taboo in public places in the US, it's *pas de problème* in France.

Assembling a Picnic: Visit several small stores to put together a complete meal. Shop early, as many shops close from 12:00 to 15:00 for their lunch break. Say *"Bonjour"* as you enter, then point to what you want and say, *"S'il vous plaît."* Or visit open-air markets *(marchés)*, which are fun and photogenic but shut down around 13:00 (many are listed in this book; French TIs have complete lists).

At the *boulangerie* (bakery), buy some bread. A baguette usually does the trick, or choose from the many square loaves of bread on display: *pain aux céréales* (whole grain with seeds), *pain de campagne* (country bread, made with unbleached bread flour), *pain complet* (wheat bread), or *pain de seigle* (rye bread). To ask to have it sliced, say, *"Tranché s'il vous plaît."* The sales clerk will invariably ask if you would like anything else. If you've ordered all the treats you want, you can reply, *"C'est tout, merci"* (say too, mehr-see), meaning, "That'll be all, thanks."

At the *pâtisserie* (pastry shop, which is often the same place you bought the bread), choose a dessert that's easy to eat with your hands. My favorites are *éclairs* (*chocolat* or *café* flavored), individual fruit *tartes* (*framboise* is raspberry, *fraise* is strawberry, *citron* is lemon), and *macarons* (made of flavored cream sandwiched between two meringues, not coconut cookies like in the US).

At the *crémerie* or *fromagerie* (cheese shop), choose a sampling

Picnic Vocabulary

English	French	Pronounced
please	s'il vous plaît	see voo play
a plastic fork	une fourchette en plastique	oon foor-sheht ahn plah-steek
a small box	une barquette	oon bar-keht
a knife	un couteau	uhn koo-toh
corkscrew	tire-bouchon	teer-boo-shohn
sliced	tranché	trahn-shay
a slice	une tranche	oon trahnsh
a small slice	une petite tranche	oon puh-teet trahnsh
more	plus	ploo
less	moins	mwan (rhymes with fan)
It's just right.	C'est bon.	say bohn
That'll be all.	C'est tout.	say too
Thank you.	Merci.	mehr-see

of cheeses. I usually get one hard cheese (such as Comté, Cantal, or Beaufort), one soft cow's milk (such as Brie or Camembert), one goat's milk cheese (anything that says *chèvre*), and one blue cheese (Roquefort or Bleu d'Auvergne). Goat cheese usually comes in individual portions. For all other large cheeses, point to the cheese you want and ask for *une petite tranche* (a small slice). The shopkeeper will place a knife on the cheese indicating the size of the slice they are about to cut, then look at you for approval. If you'd like more, say, "*Plus.*" If you'd like less, say, "*Moins.*" If it's just right, say, "*C'est bon!*"

At the ***charcuterie*** or ***traiteur*** (for deli items, prepared salads, meats, and pâtés), I like a slice of *pâté de campagne* (country pâté made of pork) and *saucissons sec* (dried sausages, some with pepper crust or garlic—you can ask to have it sliced thin like salami). I get a fresh salad, too. Typical options are *carottes râpées* (shredded carrots in a tangy vinaigrette), *salade de betteraves* (beets in vinaigrette), and *céleri rémoulade* (celery root with a mayonnaise sauce). The food comes in easy-to-carry takeout boxes, and they may supply a plastic fork *(fourchette)*.

At a ***cave à vin***, you can buy chilled wines that the merchant is usually happy to open and re-cork for you. Note: Bottles of Champagne don't require a corkscrew to open!

At a ***supermarché, épicerie***, or ***magasin d'alimentation*** (small grocery store or minimart), you'll find plastic cutlery and glasses, paper plates, napkins, drinks, chips, and sometimes a meek display of produce. *Supermarchés* are less colorful than smaller stores, but cheaper, more efficient, and offer adequate quality. Department stores often have supermarkets in the basement. On the outskirts of cities, you'll find the monster *hypermarchés*. Drop in for a glimpse of hyper-France in action.

In stores, unrefrigerated soft drinks, bottled water, and beer are one-third the price of cold drinks. Bottled water and boxed fruit juice are the cheapest drinks. Avoid buying drinks to-go at streetside stands; they cost far less in a shop. Hang on to the half-liter mineral-water bottles (sold everywhere for about €1). Buy juice in cheap liter boxes, then drink some and store the extra in your water bottle. Of course, water quenches your thirst better and cheaper than anything you'll find in a store or café. I drink tap water throughout France, filling my bottle in hotel rooms as I go.

Sandwiches and Other Quick Bites

Throughout France you'll find bakeries and small stands selling baguette sandwiches, quiche, and pizza-like items to go for about €4. Usually filling and tasty, they also streamline the picnic process. Here are some sandwiches you'll see:

Fromage (froh-mahzh): Cheese (white on beige).

Jambon beurre (zhahn-bohn bur): Ham and butter (boring for most).

Jambon crudités (zhahn-bohn krew-dee-tay): Ham with tomatoes, lettuce, cucumbers, and mayonnaise.

Pain salé (pan sah-lay) or *fougasse* (foo-gahs): Bread rolled up with salty bits of bacon, cheese, or olives.

Poulet crudités (poo-lay krew-dee-tay): Chicken with tomatoes, lettuce, maybe cucumbers, and always mayonnaise.

Saucisson beurre (saw-see-sohn bur): Thinly sliced sausage and butter.

Thon crudités (tohn krew-dee-tay): Tuna with tomatoes, lettuce, and maybe cucumbers, but definitely mayonnaise.

Anything served *à la provençale* (ah lah proh-vehn-sahl) has marinated peppers, tomatoes, and eggplant. A sandwich *à la italienne* is a grilled *panini*.

Typical **quiches** you'll see at shops and bakeries are *lorraine* (ham and cheese), *fromage* (cheese only), *aux oignons* (with onions), *aux poirreaux* (with leeks—my favorite), *aux champignons* (with mushrooms), *au saumon* (salmon), or *au thon* (tuna).

Café Culture

French cafés and brasseries provide user-friendly meals and a refuge from sightseeing overload. They're not necessarily cheaper than restaurants. Their key advantage is flexibility: they offer long serving hours, and you're welcome to order just a salad, a sandwich, or

Coffee and Tea Lingo

By law, the waiter must give you a glass of tap water with your coffee or tea if you request it; ask for *"un verre d'eau, s'il vous plaît"* (uhn vayr doh, see voo play).

Coffee

French	Pronounced	English
un café	uhn kah-fay	shot of espresso
un café allongé (also called *café longue*)	uhn kah-fay ah-lohn-zhay (kah-fay lohn)	closest to an American cup of coffee
une noisette	oon nwah-zeht	espresso with a shot of milk
café au lait	kah-fay oh lay	coffee with lots of steamed milk (closest to an American latte)
un grand crème	uhn grahn krehm	big café au lait
un petit crème	uhn puh-tee krehm	small café au lait
un décaffiné	uhn day-kah-fee-nay	decaf—available for any of the above drinks

Tea

French	Pronounced	English
un thé nature	uhn tay nah-tour	plain tea
un thé au lait	uhn tay oh lay	tea with milk
un thé citron	uhn tay see-trohn	tea with lemon
une infusion	oon an-few-see-yohn	herbal tea

a bowl of soup, even for dinner. It's also OK to split starters and desserts, though not main courses.

Cafés and brasseries usually open by 7:00, but closing hours vary. Unlike restaurants, which open only for dinner and sometimes for lunch, some cafés and all brasseries serve food throughout the day (though with a more limited menu than at restaurants), making them the best option for a late lunch or an early dinner. (Note that many cafés in smaller towns close their kitchens from about 14:00 until 18:00.)

If you're a novice, it's easier to sit and feel comfortable when you know the system. Check the price list first, which by law must be posted prominently (if you don't see one, go elsewhere). There are two sets of prices: You'll pay more for the same drink if you're seated at a table *(salle)* than if you're seated at the bar or counter *(comptoir)*. For tips on coffee and tea, see the sidebar.

Standard Menu Items: *Croque monsieur* (grilled ham-and-cheese sandwich) and *croque madame* (*monsieur* with a fried egg on top) are generally served day and night. Sandwiches are least expensive, but very plain (*boulangeries* serve better ones). To get more than a piece of ham *(jambon)* on a baguette, order a sandwich *jambon crudités*, which means garnished with veggies. Omelets come lonely on a plate with a basket of bread. The daily special—*plat du jour* (plah dew zhoor), or just *plat*—is your fast, hearty, and garnished hot plate for €10-18. At most cafés, feel free to order only *entrées* (which in French means the starter course); many find these lighter and more interesting than a main course. A vegetarian can enjoy a tasty, filling meal by ordering two *entrées*. Regardless of what you order, bread is free, but almost never comes with butter; to get more, just hold up your bread basket and ask, "*Encore, s'il vous plaît?*"

Salads: They're typically large and often can be ordered with warm ingredients mixed in, such as melted goat cheese, fried gizzards, or roasted potatoes. One salad is perfect for lunch or a light dinner. To get salad dressing on the side, order "*la sauce à côté*" (lah sohs ah koh-tay). Classic salads include:

Salade niçoise (sah-lahd nee-swahz), a specialty from Nice, usually includes green salad topped with green beans, boiled potatoes, tomatoes, anchovies, olives, hard-boiled eggs, and lots of tuna. It's filling and easy on the budget.

Salade au chèvre chaud is a mixed green salad topped with warm goat cheese on small pieces of toast.

Salade composée is "composed" of any number of ingredients, such as *lardons* (bacon), Comté (a Swiss-style cheese), Roquefort (blue cheese), *œuf* (egg), *noix* (walnuts), and *jambon* (ham, generally thinly sliced).

Salade paysanne usually comes with potatoes *(pommes de terre)*, walnuts *(noix)*, tomatoes, ham, and egg.

Salade aux gésiers is a salad with chicken gizzards (and often slices of duck).

Restaurants

Choose restaurants filled with locals. Consider my suggestions and your hotelier's opinion, but trust your instincts. If a restaurant doesn't post its prices outside, move along. Refer to my restaurant recommendations to get a sense of what a reasonable meal should cost.

Restaurants usually open for dinner at 19:00 and are typically most crowded at about 20:30 (the early bird gets the table). Last seating is about 21:00 or 22:00 in cities (even later in Paris and on the Riviera), and earlier in small villages during the off-season.

If a restaurant serves lunch, it generally begins at 12:00 and goes until 14:30, with last orders taken at about 14:00. In contrast, some cafés and all brasseries offer a minimal menu (or more) all day (described earlier under "Café Culture").

If you ask for the *menu* (muh-noo) at a restaurant, you won't get a list of dishes; you'll get a fixed-price meal. *Menus*, which usually include two or three courses, are a good value if you're hungry. With a three-course *menu*, you'll select a starter (entrée), a main course with vegetables *(plat principal)*, plus a cheese course or a choice of desserts. Two-course *menus* (often referred to as *formules*) always include the *plat principal* and usually a choice between a starter or a dessert *(entrée et plat* or *plat et dessert)*. These fixed-price *menus* are a great way to pace your meal: Make your selection, then sit back and enjoy as the waves of food land on your table.

Restaurants and cafés usually offer great-value lunch *menus*, and many offer a reasonable *menu-enfant* (kid's meal). If all you want is a salad or soup, go to a café or brasserie instead.

Ask for *la carte* (lah kart) if you want to see an actual menu and order à la carte rather than get a fixed-price meal. Consider the waiter's recommendations and anything *de la maison* (of the house), as long as it's not an organ meat (tripes, *rognons*, and andouillette).

Galloping gourmets should bring a menu translator; the *Rick Steves' French Phrase Book & Dictionary*, with a menu decoder, works well for most travelers (see page 1140 for other menu translators).

Customers ordering à la carte typically get *une entrée* and *un plat,* or *un plat* and *un dessert,* or just *un plat.* Two people can split an entrée or a big salad (as small-size dinner salads are usually not offered á la carte) and then each get a *plat principal.* At better restaurants, it's considered inappropriate for two diners to share courses.

Tune into the relaxed pace of French dining. The French don't do dinner and a movie on date nights; they just do dinner. Evening meals last a long time in restaurants, and once you've been seated, that table is yours for the night. At the end of your meal, your server is likely to ask if you're finished—*"Vous-avez terminé?"* (voo-zah-vay tehr-mee-nay), or if you enjoyed it—*"Ça vous a plû?"* (sah voo zah ploo), then ask if you'd like anything else—*"Desirez-vous autre chose?"* (day-zee-ray-voo oh-truh shohz).

In restaurants, a waiter will never bring you the check unless you request it. For a French person, having the bill dropped off before asking for it is akin to being kicked out—*très* rude. But busy travelers are often ready for the check sooner rather than later. Here's a tip: When your server comes to clear your plates, he or she will often ask if you would like a post-meal coffee. It's the waiter's way of asking, "Are you done, or can I get you anything else?" Here's your chance. First, say *"oui"* or *"non"* to the coffee, and then ask for the bill, by saying, *"L'addition* (lah-dee-see-yohn), *s'il vous*

INTRODUCTION

plait." If you don't ask now, the wait staff may become scarce as they leave you to digest in peace.

Restaurants are almost always a better value in the countryside than in Paris. If you're driving, look for red-and-blue *Relais Routier* decals on main roads outside cities, indicating that the place is recommended by the truckers' union. These truck-stop cafés offer inexpensive and hearty fare.

Beverages

Water: The French are willing to pay for bottled water with their meal (*eau minérale;* oh mee-nay-rahl) because they prefer the taste over tap water. Badoit is my favorite carbonated water (*l'eau gazeuse;* loh gah-zuhz). To get a free pitcher of tap water, ask for *une carafe d'eau* (oon kah-rahf doh). Otherwise, you may unwittingly buy bottled water.

Coffee and Tea: See the "Coffee and Tea Lingo" sidebar, earlier.

Wine and Beer: Wines are often listed in a separate *carte des vins.* House wine at the bar is generally cheap and good (about €3-5/glass). At a restaurant, a bottle or carafe of house wine costs €8-18. To order inexpensive wine at a restaurant, ask for table wine (*un vin du pays;* uhn van duh pay) in a pitcher (*un pichet;* uhn pee-shay—only available when seated and when ordering food), rather than a bottle. Note, though, that finer restaurants usually offer only bottles of wine.

If all you want is a glass of wine, ask for *un verre de vin rouge* for red wine or *blanc* for white wine (uhn vehr duh van roozh/blahn). A half-carafe of wine is *un demi-pichet* (uhn duh-mee pee-shay); a quarter-carafe (ideal for one) is *un quart* (uhn kar).

The local beer, which costs about €4 at a restaurant, is cheaper on tap (*une pression;* oon pres-yohn) than in the bottle (*bouteille;* boo-teh-ee). France's best beer is Alsatian; try Kronenbourg or the heavier Pelfort. *Une panaché* (oon pah-nah-shay) is a tasty French shandy (beer and lemon soda).

Regional Specialty Drinks: For a refreshing before-dinner drink, order a *kir* (pronounced keer)—a thumb's level of *crème de cassis* (black currant liqueur) topped with white wine. If you like brandy, try a *marc* (regional brandy, e.g., *marc de Bourgogne*) or an Armagnac, cognac's cheaper twin brother. *Pastis,* the standard southern France aperitif, is a sweet anise (licorice) drink that comes on the rocks with a glass of water. Cut it to taste with lots of water.

Soft Drinks: For a fun, bright, nonalcoholic drink of 7-Up with mint syrup, order *un diabolo menthe* (uhn dee-ah-boh-loh mahnt). For 7-Up with fruit syrup, order *un diabolo grenadine* (think

Shirley Temple). Kids love the local orange drink, *Orangina,* a car-bonated orange juice with pulp and without caffeine. They also like the flavored syrups mixed with bottled water (*sirops à l'eau;* see-roh ah loh). In France *limonade* (lee-moh-nahd) is Sprite or 7-Up.

Ordering Beverages: Be clear when ordering drinks—you can easily pay €8 for an oversized Coke and €12 for a big beer. When you order a drink, state the size in centiliters (don't say "small," "medium," or "large," because the waiter might bring a bigger drink than you want). For something small, ask for 25 *cen-tilitres* (vant-sank sahn-tee-lee-truh; about 8 ounces); for a medium drink, order 33 cl (trahnte-twah; about 12 ounces—a normal can of soda); a large is 50 cl (san-kahnt; about 16 ounces); and a super-size is one liter (lee-truh; about a quart—which is more than I would ever order in France). The ice cubes melted after the last Yankee tour group left.

French Cuisine

The following listing of items found commonly throughout France should help you navigate a typical French menu. For dishes specific to each region, see the "Cuisine Scene" section in every chapter but Paris (which borrows cuisines from all regions).

First Course (Entrée)

Crudités: A mix of raw and lightly cooked fresh vegetables, usu-ally including grated carrots, celery root, tomatoes, and beets, often with a hefty dose of vinaigrette dressing.

Escargots: Snails cooked in parsley-garlic butter. You don't even have to like the snail itself. Just dipping your bread in garlic butter is more than satisfying. Prepared a variety of ways, the clas-sic is *à la bourguignonne* (served in their shells).

Foie gras: Rich and buttery in consistency—and hefty in price—this pâté is made from the swollen livers of force-fed geese (or ducks, in *foie gras de canard*). Spread it on bread with your knife, and never add mustard. For a real French experience, try this dish with some sweet white wine (often offered by the glass for an addi-tional cost). For more on foie gras, see the sidebar on page 494.

Huîtres: Oysters, served raw any month, are particularly pop-ular at Christmas and on New Year's Eve, when every café seems to have overflowing baskets in their window.

Œuf mayo: A simple hard-boiled egg topped with a dollop of flavorful mayonnaise.

Pâtés and *terrines:* Slowly cooked ground meat (usually pork, though game, poultry liver, and rabbit are also common) that is highly seasoned and served in slices with mustard and *cornichons* (little pickles). Pâtés are smoother than the similarly prepared but

French Wine-Tasting 101

France is peppered with wineries and wine-tasting opportunities. The American wine-tasting experience (I'm thinking Napa Valley) is generally informal, chatty, and entrepreneurial (logo-adorned baseball caps and golf shirts). In France, your hosts are not there to make small talk; you're likely to find them "all business." For some people, it can be overwhelming to try to make sense of the vast range of French wines, particularly when faced with a no-nonsense winemaker or sommelier. Take a deep breath, do your best to follow the instructions in this sidebar, and don't linger where you don't feel welcome. (I've tried to identify which vineyards are most accepting of wine novices.) Visit several private wineries, or stop by a *cave coopérative*—an excellent opportunity to taste wines from a number of vintners in a single, less intimidating setting. You'll have a better experience if you call ahead to let them know you're coming—even if the winery is open all day, it's good form to announce your visit (ask your hotelier for help). Avoid visiting places between noon and 14:00, when many are closed—and those that are open are staffed by people who would rather be at lunch.

Winemakers are happy to work with you...*if* they can figure out what you want (which they expect you to already know). When you enter a winery, it helps to know what you like (drier or sweeter, lighter or full-bodied, fruity or more tannic, and so on). The people serving you may know those words in English, but you're wise to know and use the key words in French (see "French Wine Lingo" on the facing page).

French wines usually have a lower alcohol level than American or Australian wines. Whereas many Americans like a big, full-bodied wine, most French tend to prefer more subtle flavors. They judge a wine by virtue of how well it pairs with a meal—and a big, oaky wine would overwhelm most French cuisine. The French also enjoy sampling younger wines to determine how they will taste in a few years, allowing them to buy at cheaper prices and stash the bottles in their cellars. Americans want it now—for today's picnic.

Remember that the vintner is hoping that you'll buy at least a bottle or two. If you don't buy, you may be asked to pay a minimal fee for the tasting. They understand that Americans can't take much wine with them, and they don't expect to make a big

chunkier *terrines*.

Salades: With the exception of a *salade mixte* (simple green salad, often difficult to find), the French get creative with their *salades*. (See page 42 for good salad suggestions.)

Soupe à l'oignon: Hot, salty, filling, and hard to find in some parts, French onion soup is a beef broth served with a baked cheese-and-bread crust over the top.

sale, but they do hope you'll look for their wines in the US. Some of the places I list will ship your purchase home—ask.

French Wine Lingo

Here are the steps you should follow when entering any wine-tasting:

1. Greetings, Sir/Madam: *Bonjour, Monsieur/Madame.*
2. We would like to taste a few wines.
   Nous voudrions déguster quelques vins.
   (noo voo-dree-ohn day-goo-stay kehl-kuh van)
3. We want a wine that is _____ and _____.
   Nous voudrions un vin _____ et _____.
   (noo voo-dree-ohn uhn van _____ ay _____)

Fill in the blanks with your favorites from this list:

English	French	Pronounced
wine	*vin*	van
red	*rouge*	roozh
white	*blanc*	blahn
rosé	*rosé*	roh-zay
light	*léger*	lay-zhay
full-bodied, heavy	*robuste*	roh-boost
fruity	*fruité*	frwee-tay
sweet	*doux*	doo
tannic	*tannique*	tah-neek
jammy	*confituré*	koh-fee-tuh-ray
fine	*fin, avec finesse*	fahn, ah-vehk fee-nehs
ready to drink (mature)	*prêt à boire*	preh ah bwar
not ready to drink	*fermé*	fair-may
oaky	*goût de la chêne*	goo duh lah sheh-nuh
from old vines	*de vieille vignes*	duh vee-yay-ee veen-yah
sparkling	*pétillant*	pay-tee-yahn

Main Course *(Plat Principal)*

Duck, lamb, and rabbit are popular in France, and each is prepared in a variety of ways. You'll also encounter various stew-like dishes that vary by region. The most common regional specialties are available almost everywhere and are described here.

   Bœuf bourguignon: A Burgundian specialty, this classy beef stew is cooked slowly in red wine, then served with onions, potatoes, and mushrooms.

Confit de canard: A Southwest favorite from the Dordogne region is duck that has been preserved in its own fat, then cooked in its own fat, and often served with potatoes (cooked in the same fat). Not for dieters. (*Magret de canard,* sliced duck breast, is very different in taste.)

Coq au vin: This Burgundian dish is rooster marinated ever so slowly in red wine, then cooked until it melts in your mouth. It's served (often family-style) with vegetables.

Daube: Generally made with beef, but sometimes lamb, this is a long and slowly simmered dish, typically paired with noodles or other pasta.

Escalope normande: A favorite from Normandy, this is turkey or veal in a cream sauce.

Gigot d'agneau: A specialty of Provence, this is a leg of lamb often grilled and served with white beans. The best lamb is *pré salé,* which means the lamb has been raised in salt-marsh lands (like at Mont St-Michel).

Poulet roti: Found everywhere, it's roasted chicken on the bone—French comfort food.

Saumon and *truite:* You'll see salmon dishes served in various styles. The salmon usually comes from the North Sea and is always served with sauce, most commonly a sorrel *(oseille)* sauce. (*Saumon tartare* is raw salmon; some love it, while others are careful to avoid it.) Trout *(truite)* is also fairly routine on menus.

Steak: Referred to as *pavé* (thick hunk of prime steak), *bavette* (skirt steak), *faux fillet* (sirloin), and *entrecôte* (rib steak). French steak is usually thinner and tougher than American steak and is always served with sauces (*au poivre* is a pepper sauce; *une sauce roquefort* is a blue-cheese sauce). French cows get more exercise, so their beef is somewhat stringy and chewy. Because steak is usually better (fattier) in North America, I usually avoid it in France (unless the sauce sounds good). You will also see *steak haché,* which is a lean, gourmet hamburger patty served *sans* bun. When it's served as *steak haché à cheval,* it comes with a fried egg on top.

By American standards, the French undercook meats (to allow you to actually get your teeth through the leaner, tougher meat). Their version of rare, *saignant* (seh-nyahn), means "bloody" and is close to raw. What they consider medium, *à point* (ah pwan), is what an American would call rare. Their term for well-done, *bien cuit* (bee-yehn kwee), would translate as medium for Americans.

Steak tartare: This wonderfully French dish is for adventurous types only. It's very lean, raw hamburger served with savory seasonings (usually Tabasco, capers, raw onions, salt, and pepper on the side) and topped with a raw egg yolk. This is not hamburger as we know it, but freshly ground beef. While it can be extremely tasty, it's very rich, and the portions are large.

Cheese Course *(Le Fromage)*

In France, the cheese course is served just before (or instead of) dessert. It not only helps with digestion, it gives you a great opportunity to sample the tasty regional cheeses—and time to finish up your wine. There are more than 400 different French cheeses to try. Some restaurants will offer a cheese platter, from which you select a few different kinds. A good platter has at least four cheeses: a hard cheese (such as Emmentaler—a.k.a. "Swiss cheese"), a flowery cheese (Brie or Camembert), a blue or Roquefort cheese, and a goat cheese.

Those most commonly served are Brie de Meaux (mild and creamy, from just outside Paris), Camembert (semi-creamy and pungent, from Normandy), chèvre (goat cheese with a sharp taste, usually from the Loire), and Roquefort (strong and blue-veined, from south-central France).

If you'd like to sample several types of cheese from the cheese plate, say: *"Un assortiment, s'il vous plaît"* (uhn ah-sor-tee-mahn, see voo play). If you serve yourself from the cheese plate, observe French etiquette and keep the shape of the cheese. It's best to politely shave off a slice from the side or cut small wedges.

If you've run out of wine, consider ordering more. A glass of good red wine complements your cheese course in a heavenly way.

Dessert *(Le Dessert)*

If you order espresso, it will always come after dessert. To have coffee with dessert, ask for *"café avec le dessert"* (kah-fay ah-vehk luh day-sayr). See the list of coffee terms earlier in this chapter.

Here are the types of treats you'll see:

Baba au rhum (bah-bah oh room): Brioche-like cake, drenched in rum and served with whipped cream.

Café gourmand (kah-feh goor-mahn): An assortment of small desserts selected by the restaurant—a great way to sample several desserts and learn your favorite.

Crème brûlée (krehm broo-lay): A rich, creamy, dense, caramelized custard.

Crème caramel (krehm kah-rah-mehl): Flan in a caramel sauce.

Fondant au chocolat (fohn-dahnt oh shoh-koh-lah): A molten chocolate cake with a runny (not totally cooked) center. Also known as *moelleux* (meh-leh) *au chocolat*.

Fromage blanc (froh-mahzh blahn): A light dessert similar to plain yogurt (yet different), served with sugar or herbs.

Glace (glahs): Ice cream—typically vanilla, chocolate, or

> ## How Was Your Trip?
>
> Were your travels fun, smooth, and meaningful? If you'd like to share your tips, concerns, and discoveries, please fill out the survey at www.ricksteves.com/feedback. I value your feedback. Thanks in advance—it helps a lot.

strawberry *(fraise)*.

Ile flottante (eel floh-tahnt): A light dessert consisting of islands of meringue floating on a pond of custard sauce.

Mousse au chocolat (moos oh shoh-koh-lah): Chocolate mousse.

Profiteroles (proh-fee-tuh-rohl): Cream puffs filled with vanilla ice cream, smothered in warm chocolate sauce.

Riz au lait (ree zoh lay): Rice pudding.

Sorbets: Light, flavorful, and fruity ices (known to us as sherbets), sometimes laced with brandy.

Tartes (tart): Narrow strips of fresh fruit, baked in a crust and served in thin slices (without ice cream).

Tarte tatin (tart tah-tan): Apple pie like grandma never made, with caramelized apples, cooked upside down, but served upright.

Traveling as a Temporary Local

We travel all the way to France to enjoy differences—to become temporary locals. You'll experience frustrations. Certain truths that we find "God-given" or "self-evident," such as cold beer, ice in drinks, bottomless cups of coffee, hot showers, and bigger being better, are suddenly not so true. One of the benefits of travel is the eye-opening realization that there are logical, civil, and even better alternatives.

With a history rich in human achievement, France is an understandably proud country. To enjoy its people, you need to celebrate the differences. A willingness to go local ensures that you'll enjoy a full dose of French hospitality.

Europeans generally like Americans. But if there is a negative aspect to the French image of Americans, it's that we are loud, wasteful, ethnocentric, too informal (which can seem disrespectful), and a bit naive.

The French (and Europeans in general) place a high value on speaking quietly in restaurants and on trains. Listen while on the bus or in a restaurant—the place can be packed, but the decibel level is low. Try to adjust your volume accordingly to show respect for the culture.

While the French look bemusedly at some of our Yankee excesses—and worriedly at others—they nearly always afford us

individual travelers all the warmth we deserve.

Judging from all the happy feedback I receive from travelers who have used this book, it's safe to assume you'll enjoy a great, affordable vacation—with the finesse of an independent, experienced traveler.

Thanks, and *bon voyage!*

Back Door Travel Philosophy

From *Rick Steves' Europe Through the Back Door*

Travel is intensified living—maximum thrills per minute and one of the last great sources of legal adventure. Travel is freedom. It's recess, and we need it.

Experiencing the real Europe requires catching it by surprise, going casual..."Through the Back Door."

Affording travel is a matter of priorities. (Make do with the old car.) You can eat and sleep—simply, safely, and enjoyably— anywhere in Europe for $120 a day plus transportation costs. In many ways, spending more money only builds a thicker wall between you and what you traveled so far to see. Europe is a cultural carnival, and time after time, you'll find that its best acts are free and the best seats are the cheap ones.

A tight budget forces you to travel close to the ground, meeting and communicating with the people. Never sacrifice sleep, nutrition, safety, or cleanliness to save money. Simply enjoy the local-style alternatives to expensive hotels and restaurants.

Connecting with people carbonates your experience. Extroverts have more fun. If your trip is low on magic moments, kick yourself and make things happen. If you don't enjoy a place, maybe you don't know enough about it. Seek the truth. Recognize tourist traps. Give a culture the benefit of your open mind. See things as different, but not better or worse. Any culture has plenty to share.

Of course, travel, like the world, is a series of hills and valleys. Be fanatically positive and militantly optimistic. If something's not to your liking, change your liking.

Travel can make you a happier American, as well as a citizen of the world. Our Earth is home to seven billion equally precious people. It's humbling to travel and find that other people don't have the "American Dream"—they have their own dreams. Europeans like us, but with all due respect, they wouldn't trade passports.

Thoughtful travel engages us with the world. In tough economic times, it reminds us what is truly important. By broadening perspectives, travel teaches new ways to measure quality of life.

Globetrotting destroys ethnocentricity, helping us understand and appreciate other cultures. Rather than fear the diversity on this planet, celebrate it. Among your most prized souvenirs will be the strands of different cultures you choose to knit into your own character. The world is a cultural yarn shop, and Back Door travelers are weaving the ultimate tapestry. Join in!

PARIS

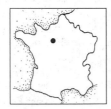

Paris—the City of Light—has been a beacon of culture for centuries. As a world capital of art, fashion, food, literature, and ideas, it stands as a symbol of all the fine things human civilization can offer. Come prepared to celebrate this, rather than judge our cultural differences, and you'll capture the romance and *joie de vivre* this city exudes.

Paris offers sweeping boulevards, chatty crêpe stands, chic boutiques, and world-class art galleries. Sip decaf with deconstructionists at a sidewalk café, then step into an Impressionist painting in a tree-lined park. Climb Notre-Dame and rub shoulders with the gargoyles. Cruise the Seine, zip to the top of the Eiffel Tower, and saunter down Avenue des Champs-Elysées. Master the Louvre and Orsay museums. Save some after-dark energy for one of the world's most romantic cities.

Planning Your Time

I've listed sights in descending order of importance, filling up to five very busy but doable days in Paris. Therefore, if you have only one day, just do Day 1; for two days, add Day 2; and so on. When planning where to plug in Versailles (see next chapter), keep in mind that the Château is closed on Mondays and especially crowded on Sundays and Tuesdays—try to avoid these days. For other itinerary considerations on a day-by-day basis, check the "Daily Reminder" on page 62.

Day 1
Morning: Follow my Historic Paris Walk, featuring Ile de la Cité, Notre-Dame, the Latin Quarter, and Sainte-Chapelle.

Afternoon: Tour the Louvre.

Evening: Enjoy the Trocadéro scene and a twilight ride up the Eiffel Tower.

Day 2

Morning: Wander the Champs-Elysées from the Arc de Triomphe down the grand Avenue des Champs-Elysées to the Tuileries Garden.

Afternoon: Cross the pedestrian bridge from the Tuileries Garden, then tour the Orsay Museum.

Evening: Take one of the tours by bus, taxi, or retro-chic Deux Chevaux car (see page 152). (If you're staying more than two days, save this for your last-night finale.)

Day 3

Morning: Catch the RER suburban train by 8:00 to arrive early at Versailles (before it opens at 9:00) and tour the palace's interior. (If you get a later start, reverse today's plan by doing the gardens first and the château's interior later in the afternoon.)

Midday: Have lunch in the gardens at Versailles.

Afternoon: Spend the afternoon touring the gardens, the Trianon Palaces, and Domaine de Marie-Antoinette.

Evening: Have dinner in Versailles town or return to Paris. For dessert, cruise the Seine River.

Day 4

Morning: Visit Montmartre (one-time stomping ground of Impressionist painters) and the Sacré-Cœur Basilica. Have lunch on Montmartre.

Afternoon: Continue your Impressionist theme by touring the Orangerie and the Rodin Museum, or switch gears and tour the Army Museum and Napoleon's Tomb.

Evening: Enjoy dinner on Ile St. Louis, then a floodlit walk by Notre-Dame.

Day 5

Morning: Ride scenic bus #69 to the Marais and tour this neighborhood, including the Pompidou Center.

Afternoon: Tour the Opéra Garnier, and end your day enjoying the glorious rooftop views at the Galeries Lafayette and Printemps department stores.

Evening: Stroll the Champs-Elysées at night.

PARIS

Orientation to Paris

Paris (population of city center: 2,234,000) is split in half by the Seine River, divided into 20 arrondissements (proud and independent governmental jurisdictions), circled by a ring-road freeway (the *périphérique*), and speckled with Métro stations. You'll find Paris easier to navigate if you know which side of the river you're on, which arrondissement you're in, and which Métro stop you're closest to. If you're north of the river (the top half of any city map), you're on the Right Bank (Rive Droite). If you're south of it, you're on the Left Bank (Rive Gauche). The bull's-eye of your Paris map is Notre-Dame, which sits on an island in the middle of the Seine. Most of your sightseeing will take place within five blocks of the river.

Arrondissements are numbered, starting at the Louvre and moving in a clockwise spiral out to the ring road. The last two digits in a Parisian zip code indicate the arrondissement number. The abbreviation for "Métro stop" is "Mo." In Parisian jargon, the Eiffel Tower is on *la Rive Gauche* (the Left Bank) in the *7ème* (7th arrondissement), zip code 75007, Mo: Trocadéro.

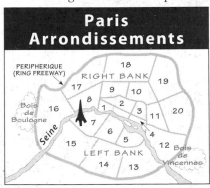

Paris Métro stops are used as a standard aid in giving directions, even for those not taking the Métro. As you're tracking down addresses, these words and pronunciations will help: Métro (may-troh), *place* (plahs; square), *rue* (roo; road), *avenue* (ah-vuh-noo), *boulevard* (boo-luh-var), and *pont* (pohn; bridge).

Tourist Information

Paris TIs can provide useful information but may have long lines. Pick up the free *Paris for You!* booklet. If you're looking for a map, they may charge you for it (all you really need are the freebie maps available at any hotel or in the front of this book). TIs also sell individual tickets to sights (see "Avoiding Lines with Advance Tickets" on page 61), as well as Paris Museum Passes (see page 58). If you plan to get a Museum Pass, it's quicker to buy these at participating sights (except major museums, where lines can be long).

Paris has several TI locations, including **Pyramides** (daily May-Oct 9:00-19:00, Nov-April 10:00-19:00, at Pyramides Métro stop between the Louvre and Opéra), **Gare du Nord** (daily 8:00-18:00), and two in **Montmartre,** both with a focus on their neighborhood (one on Place du Tertre, daily 10:00-18:00, tel. 01 42 62 21 21, and the other above the Anvers Métro stop, daily 10:00-18:00). In summer, TI kiosks may pop up in the squares in front of Notre-Dame and Hôtel de Ville. The official website for Paris' TIs is www.parisinfo.com.

Both **airports** have handy information offices with long hours and short lines (see page 210).

Pariscope: The weekly €0.40 *Pariscope* magazine (or one of its clones, available at any newsstand) lists museum hours, art exhibits, concerts, festivals, plays, movies, and nightclubs. Smart sightseers rely on this for the latest listings.

Other Publications: *L'Officiel des Spectacles* (€0.35), which is similar to *Pariscope,* also lists goings-on around town (in French). The *Paris Voice*, with snappy reviews of concerts, plays, and current events, is available only online at www.parisvoice.com. For a schedule of museum hours and English museum tours, get the free *Musées, Monuments Historiques, et Expositions* booklet at any museum.

Helpful Websites: These websites come highly recommended for local information and events: www.gogoparis.com, www.secretsofparis.com, and www.bonjourparis.com.

American Church and Franco-American Center: This interdenominational church—in the Rue Cler neighborhood, facing the river between the Eiffel Tower and Orsay Museum—is a nerve center for the American expat community. Worship services are held every Sunday (traditional services at 9:00 and 11:00, contemporary service at 13:30). The coffee hour after the 11:00 service and the free Sunday concerts (generally Sept-June at 17:00—but not every week and not in Dec) are a good way to get a taste of émigré life in Paris (reception open Mon-Sat 9:00-12:00 & 13:00-22:00, Sun 14:30-19:00, 65 Quai d'Orsay, Mo: Invalides, tel. 01 40 62 05 00, www.acparis.org). It's also a handy place to pick up free

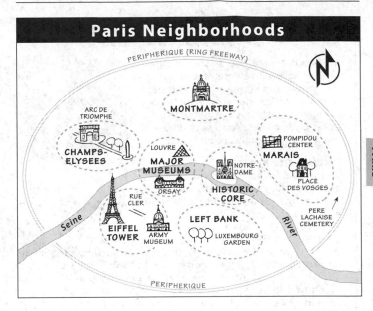

Paris Neighborhoods

PARIS

copies of *France-USA Contacts*, an advertisement paper with info on housing and employment for the 50,000 Americans living in Paris (www.fusac.fr).

Arrival in Paris

For a comprehensive rundown of the city's train stations and airports, see "Paris Connections," at the end of this chapter. For information on parking a car, see "Helpful Hints," next.

Helpful Hints

Theft Alert: Thieves thrive near famous monuments and on Métro and RER lines that serve high-profile tourist sights. Beware of pickpockets working busy lines (e.g., at ticket windows at train stations). Pay attention when it's your turn and your back is to the crowd—keep your bag firmly gripped in front of you.

In general, it's smart to wear a money belt, put your wallet in your front pocket, loop your day bag over your shoulders, and keep a tight grip on your purse or shopping bag. Muggings are rare, but they do occur. If you're out late, avoid the dark riverfront embankments and any place where the lighting is dim and pedestrian activity is minimal.

Paris is taking action to combat crime by stationing police at monuments, on streets, and on the Métro, as well as security cameras at key sights. You'll go through quick and reassuring airport-like security checks at many major attractions.

Paris Museum Pass

In Paris there are two classes of sight-seers—those with a Paris Museum Pass, and those who stand in line. The pass admits you to many of Paris' most popular sights, allowing you to skip ticket-buying lines. You'll save time and money by getting this pass.

Buying the Pass

The pass pays for itself with four key admissions in two days (for example, the Louvre, Orsay, Sainte-Chapelle, and Versailles), and it lets you skip the ticket line at most sights (2 days/€39, 4 days/€54, 6 days/€69, no youth or senior discount). It's sold at participating museums, monuments, FNAC department stores, and TIs (even at airports). Try to avoid buying the pass at a major museum (such as the Louvre), where the supply can be spotty and lines long. For more info, visit www.parismuseumpass.com or call 01 44 61 96 60.

To see if the pass is a good value for your trip, tally up what you want to see from the list on the facing page. And remember, an advantage of the pass is that you skip to the front of most (but not all) lines, which can save hours of waiting, especially in summer. Another benefit of the pass is that you can pop into lesser sights that otherwise might not be worth the expense.

Families: The pass isn't worth buying for children and teens, as most museums are free or discounted for those under 18 (teenagers may need to show ID as proof of age). If parents have a Museum Pass, kids can usually skip the ticket lines as well. A few places, such as the Arc de Triomphe and Army Museum, require everyone—even passholders—to stand in line to collect your child's free ticket.

What the Paris Museum Pass Covers

Most of the sights listed in this chapter are covered by the pass. It even covers Versailles' two major sights—worth €25 alone. Notable exceptions that are *not* covered by the pass include: the Eiffel Tower, Montparnasse Tower, Marmottan Museum, Opéra Garnier, Notre-Dame Treasury, Jacquemart-André Museum, Grand Palais, Catacombs, Montmartre Museum, Sacré-Cœur's dome, Dalí Museum, Museum of Erotic Art, and the ladies of Pigalle.

Here's a list of key included sights and their admission prices without the pass:

Louvre (€11)	Notre-Dame Tower (€8.50)
Orsay Museum (€9)	Paris Archaeological Crypt (€4)
Orangerie Museum (€7.50)	Paris Sewer Tour (€4.30)
Sainte-Chapelle (€8.50)	Cluny Museum (€8)
Arc de Triomphe (€9.50)	Pompidou Center (€11-13)
Rodin Museum (€6)	Jewish Art and History Museum (€7)
Army Museum (€9)	National Maritime Museum (€7)
Conciergerie (€8.50)	Delacroix Museum (€5)
Panthéon (€8.50)	Quai Branly Museum (€8.50)

Architecture and Monuments Museum (€8)

Versailles (€25 total—€15 for Château, €10 for Trianon Palaces and Domaine de Marie-Antoinette)

Activating and Using the Pass

The pass is activated the first time you use it—you must write the starting date on the pass. Validate it only when you're ready to tackle the covered sights on consecutive days. Plan carefully to make the most of your pass. First, make sure the sights you want to visit will be open (many museums are closed Mondays or Tuesdays). The pass provides the best value on days when sights close later, letting you extend your sightseeing day. Take advantage of these late hours. For instance, the Arc de Triomphe and Pompidou Center are always open later, while the Notre-Dame Tower, Sainte-Chapelle, Louvre, Orsay, and Army Museum and Napoleon's Tomb have late hours on selected evenings (or at certain times of year). On days that you don't have pass coverage, plan to visit free sights and those not covered by the pass (see page 84 for a list of free sights).

To use your pass at sights, boldly walk to the front of the ticket line (after going through security if necessary), hold up your pass, and ask the ticket-taker: *"Entrez, pass?"* (ahn-tray pahs). You'll either be allowed to enter at that point, or you'll be directed to a special entrance. For major sights, such as the Louvre and Orsay museums, I've identified passholder entrances on the maps in this book. Don't be shy—some places (Sainte-Chapelle and the Arc de Triomphe, in particular) have long lines where passholders wait needlessly. At a few sights (including the Louvre, Sainte-Chapelle, Notre-Dame Tower, and Château de Versailles), everyone has to shuffle through the slow-moving baggage-check lines for security—but you still save time by avoiding the ticket line.

ATM Alert: When withdrawing money from a cash machine, use your hand to shield your PIN number from prying eyes. Don't engage with anyone who offers to "help" you use an ATM (which works just like ours do) or warns you that it isn't working properly. If that happens, cancel your operation and find a different machine.

Tourist Scams: Be aware of the latest scams, including these current favorites. The "found ring" scam involves an innocent-looking person who picks up a ring off the ground and asks if you dropped it. When you say no, the person examines the ring more closely, then shows you a mark "proving" that it's pure gold. He offers to sell it to you for a good price—several times more than he paid for it before dropping it on the sidewalk.

In the "friendship bracelet" scam, a vendor approaches you and asks if you'll help him with a demonstration. He proceeds to make a friendship bracelet right on your arm. When finished, he asks you to pay for the bracelet he created just for you. And since you can't easily take it off on the spot, he counts on your feeling obliged to pay up.

Distractions by a stranger—often a "salesman," someone asking you to sign a petition, or someone posing as a deaf person to show you a small note to read—can all be tricks that function as a smokescreen for theft. As you try to wriggle away from the pushy stranger, an accomplice picks your pocket.

In popular tourist spots (such as in front of Notre-Dame) young ladies ask if you speak English, then pretend to beg for money while actually angling to get your wallet.

To all these scammers, simply say "no" firmly, don't apologize, don't smile, and step away purposefully.

Pedestrian Safety: Parisian drivers are notorious for ignoring pedestrians. Look both ways (many streets are one-way) and be careful of seemingly quiet bus/taxi lanes. Don't assume you have the right of way, even in a crosswalk. When crossing a street, keep your pace constant and don't stop suddenly. By law, drivers are allowed to miss pedestrians by up to just one meter—a little more than three feet (1.5 meters in the countryside). Drivers calculate your speed so they won't hit you, provided you don't alter your route or pace.

Watch out for bicyclists. This popular and silent transportation may come at you from unexpected places and directions—cyclists ride in specially marked bike lanes on wide sidewalks and also have a right to use lanes reserved for buses and taxis. Bikes commonly go against traffic, as many bike paths are on one-way streets. Always look both ways.

Busy Parisian sidewalks are much like freeways, so conduct yourself as if you were a foot-fueled-car: Stick to your lane, look to the left before passing a slow-moving pedestrian, and if you need to stop, look for a safe place to pull over.

Medical Help: The American Hospital, established by a group of expat doctors, provides medical attention from English-speaking staff (63 Boulevard Victor Hugo, in Neuilly suburb, Mo: Porte Maillot, then bus #82, tel. 01 46 41 25 25, www.american-hospital.org).

Museum Strategies: The worthwhile Paris Museum Pass, covering most sights in the city, is sold at museums and monuments, as well as TIs and FNAC stores (no surcharge). For detailed information, see the sidebar on page 58. For other museum strategies, see "Sightseeing" on page 21.

Avoiding Lines with Advance Tickets: If a Museum Pass does not fit your needs, you do have other line-skipping options. TIs and FNAC stores sell individual fast-track *"coupe-file"* tickets, letting you use the Museum Pass entrance at sights. TIs sell these tickets for no extra fee, but FNACs add a surcharge of 10-20 percent—often worth it, as these stores are everywhere, even on the Champs-Elysées (ask your hotelier for the nearest one). For sights that can otherwise have long waits (such as the Arc de Triomphe, Opéra Garnier, Versailles, and Monet's gardens in Giverny), these tickets are a good idea. (Note that Versailles and the Arc de Triomphe are covered by the Paris Museum Pass).

For some sights, you can book tickets online and print a receipt (either from home or at your hotel) that serves as your entry pass. This works great at the Eiffel Tower (though you must choose an entry time), Monet's gardens at Giverny, and the Jacquemart-André Museum, as well as for activities like the Bateaux-Mouches cruises and Sainte-Chapelle concerts. Increasingly, other sights are adding this helpful service. However, buying Paris Museum Passes and certain tickets online is not worth the cost or hassle because you have to either pay dearly to have them shipped to you or print vouchers and redeem them in person at a Paris TI.

Bookstores: Paris has many English-language bookstores, where you can pick up guidebooks (at nearly double their American prices). Most carry this book. My favorites include:

• **Red Wheelbarrow Bookstore** (in the Marais neighborhood, for sale and may be gone in 2013; if open, generally Mon 10:00-18:00, Tue-Sat 10:00-19:00, Sun 14:00-18:00; 22 Rue St. Paul, Mo: St. Paul, tel. 01 48 04 75 08).

• **Shakespeare and Company** (some used travel books, Mon-Fri 10:00-23:00, Sat-Sun 11:00-23:00, 37 Rue de la

PARIS

Daily Reminder

Sunday: Many sights are free on the first Sunday of the month, including the Louvre, Orsay, Rodin, Cluny, Pompidou, Quai Branly, and Delacroix museums. During the winter, the Arc de Triomphe (Oct-March) and all the sights at Versailles (Nov-March) are also free. These free days at popular sights attract hordes of visitors.

Versailles is more crowded than usual on Sunday—but on the upside, the garden's fountains are running (April-Oct).

Look for organ concerts at St. Sulpice and possibly other churches. The American Church often hosts a free concert (usually classical piano and vocals, generally Sept-June at 17:00—but not every week and not in Dec). Summer brings puppet shows to Luxembourg Garden and the Champ de Mars park.

Most of Paris' stores are closed on Sunday, but shoppers will find relief along the Champs-Elysées and in the Marais neighborhood's lively Jewish Quarter, where many stores are open. Many recommended restaurants in the Rue Cler neighborhood are closed for dinner.

Monday: These sights are closed today: Orsay, Rodin, Marmottan, Carnavalet, Catacombs, Petit Palais, Victor Hugo's House, Quai Branly, Paris Archaeological Crypt, Deportation Memorial, and Versailles. The Louvre is more crowded because of these closings. The Army Museum and Napoleon's Tomb is closed the first Monday of every month (though the tomb is open every Mon in June-Aug). Market streets such as Rue Cler and Rue Mouffetard are dead today. Some banks are closed. It's discount night at many cinemas.

Bûcherie, across the river from Notre-Dame, Mo: St. Michel, tel. 01 43 25 40 93).

• **W. H. Smith** (Mon-Sat 9:00-19:00, Sun 12:30-19:00, 248 Rue de Rivoli, Mo: Concorde, tel. 01 44 77 88 99).

• **San Francisco Book Company** (Mon-Sat 11:00-21:00, Sun 14:00-19:30, 17 Rue Monsieur le Prince, Mo: Odéon, tel. 01 43 29 15 70).

Public WCs: Most public toilets are free. If it's a pay toilet, the price will be clearly indicated. If the toilet is free but there's an attendant, it's polite (but not necessary) to leave a tip of €0.20-0.50. Booth-like pay toilets on the sidewalks provide both relief and a memory (don't leave small children inside unattended). The restrooms in museums are free and the best you'll find. Or walk into any sidewalk café like you own the place, and find the toilet in the back. If you have to buy something, your cheapest option is to order a shot of espresso (*un*

Tuesday: Many sights are closed today, including the Louvre, Orangerie, Cluny, Pompidou, National Maritime, Delacroix, and Architecture and Monuments museums. The Orsay and Versailles are particularly busy today; the fountains at Versailles run today from late May until late June. The Army Museum may be open until 21:00 (April-Sept).

Wednesday: All sights are open, and some have late hours, including the Louvre (until 21:45, last entry 21:00) and the Rodin Museum (until 20:45). The weekly *Pariscope* magazine comes out today. Most schools are closed, so many kids' sights are busy, and in summer the puppet shows play in Luxembourg Garden and the Champ de Mars park. Some cinemas offer discounts.

Thursday: All sights are open except the Sewer Tour. Some sights are open late, including the Orsay (until 21:45, last entry 21:00), Marmottan (20:00), and the Holocaust Memorial (22:00). Some department stores are open late.

Friday: All sights are open (Louvre until 21:45, last entry 21:00) except the Sewer Tour. Afternoon trains and roads leaving Paris are crowded. Restaurants are busy—it's smart to book ahead at popular places.

Saturday: All sights are open except the Jewish Art and History Museum and the Holocaust Memorial. The fountains run at Versailles (April-Oct). Department stores are jammed today. The Jewish Quarter is quiet. Restaurants throughout Paris get packed; reserve in advance if you have a particular place in mind. Luxembourg Garden and the Champ de Mars park host puppet shows in summer.

café) standing at the bar. Keep toilet paper or tissues with you, as some WCs are poorly stocked.

Parking: Street parking is generally free at night (19:00 to 9:00), all day Sunday, and anytime in August, when many Parisians are on vacation. To pay for streetside parking, you must go to a tabac and buy a parking card *(une carte de stationnement)*, sold in €10, €20, and €30 denominations. Insert the card into the meter (chip-side in) and punch the desired amount of time (generally €1-2/hour), then take the receipt and display it in your windshield. Meters limit street parking to a maximum of two hours. For a longer stay, park for less at an airport (about €10/day) and take public transport or a taxi into the city. Underground lots are numerous in Paris—you'll find them under Ecole Militaire, St. Sulpice Church, Les Invalides, the Bastille, and the Panthéon; all charge about €30-40/day (€60/3 days, €10/day more after that, for locations see

PARIS

www.vincipark.com). Some hotels offer parking for less—ask your hotelier.

Tobacco Stands *(Tabacs):* These little kiosks—usually just a counter inside a café—are handy and very local. They sell public-transit tickets, cards for parking meters, postage stamps (though not all sell international postage—to mail something home, use two domestic stamps, or go to a post office), prepaid phone cards, and...oh yeah, cigarettes. To find one of these kiosks, just look for a *Tabac* sign and the red cylinder-shaped symbol above certain cafés. A *tabac* can be a godsend for avoiding long ticket lines at the Métro, especially at the end of the month when ticket booths get crowded with locals buying next month's pass.

Winter Activities: The City of Light sparkles year-round. For background on what to do and see here in winter months, see www.ricksteves.com/pariswinter.

Updates to this Book: For news about changes to this book's coverage since it was published, see www.ricksteves.com/update.

Getting Around Paris

Paris is easy to navigate. Your basic choices are Métro (in-city subway), RER (suburban rail tied into the Métro system), public bus, and taxi. (Also consider the hop-on, hop-off bus and boat tours, described under "Tours in Paris," later.)

You can buy tickets and passes at Métro stations and at many *tabacs.* Staffed ticket windows in stations are gradually being phased out in favor of ticket machines, so expect some stations to have machines only—be sure to carry coins or small bills of €20 or less (not all machines take bills and none takes American credit cards). If a ticket machine is out of order or if you're out of change, buy tickets at a *tabac.*

Public-Transit Tickets: The Métro, RER, and buses all work on the same tickets. You can make as many transfers as you need on a single ticket, except when transferring between the Métro/RER system and the bus system, which requires using an additional ticket. A **single ticket** costs €1.70. To save money, buy a *carnet* (kar-nay) of 10 tickets for €12.70 (cheaper for ages 4-10). *Carnets* can be shared among travelers.

Passe Navigo: You can buy a chip-embedded card, called the Passe Navigo (though for most tourists, *carnets* are a better deal). You pay a one-time €5 fee for the Navigo card itself (which also requires a postage-stamp-size photo of yourself—bring your own, print a color photo, or use the €4 photo booths in major Métro stations). For a weekly *(hebdomadaire)* version good for travel in central Paris (zones 1-2), you'll pay €19.15, which gives you free run of the bus, Métro, and non-suburban RER system from Monday to

Sunday (expiring on Sunday, even if you buy it on, say, a Thursday). A monthly version is also available.

To use the Navigo, whether at a Métro turnstile or on the bus, touch the card to the purple pad, wait for the green validation light and the "ding," and you're on your way. The basic pass covers only central Paris, not regional destinations such as Versailles.

Navigo or *Carnet*? It's hard to beat the *carnet*. Two 10-packs of *carnets*—enough for most travelers staying a week—cost €25.40, are shareable, and don't expire. Though similar in price, the Passe Navigo is more of a hassle to buy, cannot be shared, and only becomes worthwhile for visitors who stay a full week (or more), start their trip early in the week (on a Monday or Tuesday), and use the system a lot.

Other Passes: A handy one-day bus/Métro pass (called **Mobilis**) is available for €6.40. The overpriced **Paris Visite** passes are poorly designed for tourists and offer minor reductions at minor sights (1 day/€9.75, 2 days/€15.85, 3 days/€21.60, 5 days/€31.15).

By Métro

In Paris, you're never more than a 10-minute walk from a Métro station. Europe's best subway system allows you to hop from sight to sight quickly and cheaply (runs daily 5:30-24:30, Fri-Sat until 2:00 in the morning, www.ratp.fr). Learn to use it. Begin by studying the color Métro map at the beginning of this book (also free at Métro stations and included on freebie Paris maps at your hotel).

Using the Métro System: To get to your destination, determine the closest "Mo" stop and which line or lines will get you there. The lines are color-coded and numbered, and you can tell their direction by their end-of-the-line stops. For example, the La Défense/Château de Vincennes line, also known as line 1 (yellow), runs between La Défense, on its west end, and Vincennes on its east end. Once in the Métro station, you'll see the color-coded line numbers and/or blue-and-white signs directing you to the train going in your direction (e.g., *direction: La Défense*). Insert your ticket in the automatic turnstile, reclaim your ticket, pass through, and keep it until you exit the system (some stations require you to pass your ticket through a turnstile to exit). The smallest stations are unstaffed and have ticket machines (coins are essential). Be warned that fare inspectors regularly check for cheaters and accept absolutely no excuses—keep that ticket or pay a minimum fine of €25.

Be prepared to walk significant distances within Métro stations (especially when you transfer). Transfers are free and can be made wherever lines cross, provided you do so within 1.5 hours. When you transfer, follow the appropriately colored line number for your next train, or find orange *correspondance* (connection) signs

PARIS

Métro Basics

- The same tickets are good on the Métro, RER (within the city), and city buses (but not to transfer between Métro/RER and bus).
- Save money by buying a *carnet* of tickets or a Passe Navigo.
- Beware of pickpockets, and don't buy tickets from men roaming the stations.
- Find your train by its end-of-the-line stops.
- Insert your ticket into the turnstile, retrieve it, and keep it until the end of your journey.
- Transfers (*correspondances*) within the Métro and RER system are free.

Key Words for the Métro and RER

French	Pronounced	English
direction	dee-rek-see-ohn	direction
ligne	leen-yuh	line
correspondance	kor-res-pohn-dahns	connection/transfer
sortie	sor-tee	exit
carnet	kar-nay	discounted set of 10 tickets
Pardon, madame/ monsieur.	par-dohn, mah-dahm/ mes-yur	Excuse me, ma'am/ sir.
Je descends.	juh day-sahn	I'm getting off.
Donnez-moi mon porte-monnaie!	duh-nay-mwah mohn port-moh-nay	Give me back my wallet!

that lead to your next line.

When you reach your destination, look for the blue-and-white

sortie signs pointing you to the exit. Before leaving the station, check the helpful *plan du quartier* (map of the neighborhood) to get your bearings. At stops with several *sorties,* you can save time by choosing the best exit.

After you exit the system, toss or tear your used ticket so you don't confuse it with unused tickets—they look almost identical.

Beware of Pickpockets: Thieves dig the Métro and RER. Be on guard. If your pocket is picked as you pass through a turnstile, you end up stuck on the wrong side (after the turnstile bar

Etiquette

- When your train arrives, board only after everyone leaving the car has made it out the door.
- Avoid using the hinged seats near the doors of some trains when the car is crowded; they take up valuable standing space.
- Always offer your seat to the elderly, those with disabilities, and pregnant women.
- Talk softly in cars. Listen to how quietly Parisians communicate (if at all) and follow their lead.

- If you find yourself blocking the door at a stop, step out of the car to let others off, then get back on.
- When you're getting off at a stop, the door may open automatically. If it doesn't, open the door by either pushing a square button (green or black) or lifting a metal latch.
- Métro doors close automatically. Don't try to hold open the door for late-boarding passengers.
- Dispose of used tickets after you complete your ride and leave the station (not before) to avoid confusing them with fresh ones.
- On escalators, stand on the right and pass on the left.
- When leaving a station, hold the door for the person behind you.

has closed behind you) while the thief gets away. Stand away from Métro doors to avoid being a target for a theft-and-run just before the doors close. Any jostling or commotion—especially when boarding or leaving trains—is likely the sign of a thief or a team of thieves in action. See page 57 for tips on keeping your bag close. Make any fare inspector show proof of identity (ask locals for help if you're not certain). Never show anyone your wallet.

By RER

The RER (Réseau Express Régionale; air-ay-air) is the suburban arm of the Métro, serving outlying destinations such as Versailles, Disneyland Paris, and the airports. These routes are indicated by thick lines on your subway map and identified by the letters A, B, C, and so on.

Within the city center, the RER works like the Métro and can be speedier if it serves your destination directly, because it makes fewer stops. Métro tickets and the Passe Navigo card are good on the RER when traveling in the city center. You can transfer between the Métro and RER systems with the same ticket. But to travel outside the city (to Versailles or the airport, for example), you'll need a separate, more expensive ticket. Unlike the Métro, not every train stops at every station along the way; check the sign or screen over the platform to see if your destination is listed as a stop (*"toutes les gares"* means it makes all stops along the way), or confirm with a local before you board. For RER trains, you may need to insert your ticket in a turnstile to exit the system.

By City Bus

Paris' excellent bus system is worth figuring out. Buses don't seem as romantic as the famous Métro and are subject to traffic jams, but savvy travelers know that buses can have you swinging through the city like Tarzan in an urban jungle.

Buses require less walking and fewer stairways than the Métro, and you can see Paris unfold as you travel. Bus stops are everywhere, and every stop comes with all the information you need: a good city bus map, route maps showing exactly where each bus that uses this stop goes, a frequency chart and schedule, a *plan du quartier* map of the immediate neighborhood, and a *soirées* map explaining night service, if available (www.ratp.fr). Bus-system maps are also available in any Métro station (and in the €6.50 *Paris Pratique* map book sold at newsstands). For longer stays, consider buying the €6 *Le Bus* book of bus routes.

Using the Bus System: Buses use the same tickets and passes as the Métro and RER. One Zone 1 ticket buys you a bus ride any-

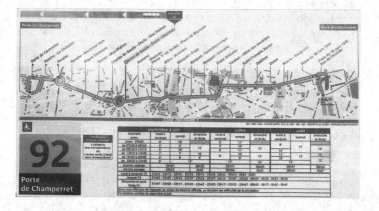

PARIS

Hop on the Bus, Gus

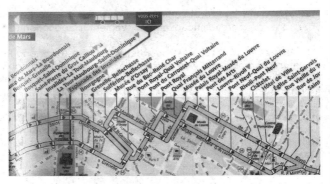

Just like the Métro, every bus stop has a name, and every bus is headed to one end-of-the-line stop or the other. The photo shows the route for bus #69. First, find your stop on the chart. It says *"vous êtes ICI"* ("you are HERE") at Esplanade des Invalides. Next, find your destination stop—let's say Bosquet-Grenelle, located a few stops to the west. Now, find out exactly where to catch the bus going in that direction. On the map showing the bus route, notice the triangle-shaped arrows pointing in the direction the bus is headed. You'll see that Esplanade des Invalides has two different bus stops—one for buses headed east, one for those going west. If you want to go west to Bosquet-Grenelle, head for that street corner to catch the bus. (With so many one-way streets in Paris, it's easy to get on the bus in the wrong direction.) When the bus pulls up, double-check that the sign on the front of the bus has the end-of-the-line stop going in your direction—to "Champ de Mars," in this case.

where in central Paris within the freeway ring road *(le périphérique)*. Use your Métro ticket or buy one on board for €0.20 more. (The ticket system has a few quirks—see "More Bus Tips," later.)

Board your bus through the front door. (Families with stroll-

ers can use any doors—the ones in the center are wider. To open the middle or back doors on long buses, push the green button located by those doors.) Validate your ticket in the machine and reclaim it. With a Passe Navigo, scan it on the purple touchpad. Keep track of what stop is coming up next by following the on-board

Scenic Buses for Tourists

Of Paris' many bus routes, these are some of the most scenic. They provide a great, cheap, and convenient introduction to the city.

Bus #69 runs east-west between the Eiffel Tower and Père Lachaise Cemetery by way of Rue Cler (recommended hotels), Quai d'Orsay, the Louvre, and the Marais (recommended hotels). For more on this route, see the sidebar on page 72.

Bus #87 also links the Marais and Rue Cler areas, but stays mostly on the Left Bank, connecting the Eiffel Tower, St. Sulpice Church, Luxembourg Garden (recommended hotels and restaurants), St. Germain-des-Prés, the Latin Quarter, the Bastille, and Gare de Lyon.

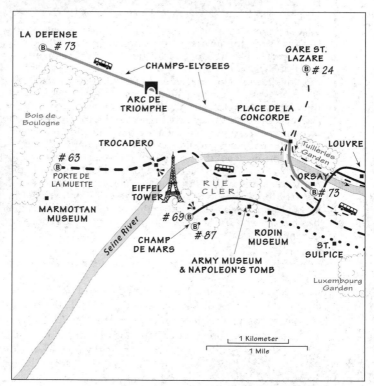

Bus #24 runs east-west along the Seine riverbank from Gare St. Lazare to Madeleine, Place de la Concorde, Orsay Museum, the Louvre, St. Michel, Notre-Dame, and Jardin des Plantes, all the way to Bercy Village (cafés and shops).

Bus #63 is another good east-west route, connecting the Marmottan Museum, Trocadéro (Eiffel Tower), Pont de l'Alma, Orsay Museum, St. Sulpice Church, Luxembourg Garden, Latin Quarter/Panthéon, and Gare de Lyon.

Bus #73 is one of Paris' most scenic lines, starting at the Orsay Museum and running westbound around Place de la Concorde, then up the Champs-Elysées, around the Arc de Triomphe, and down Avenue Charles de Gaulle to La Défense.

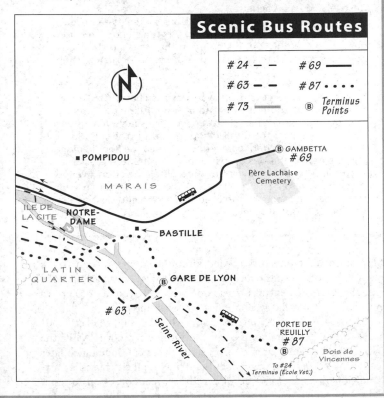

Scenic Bus Routes

# 24 – –	# 69 ———
# 63 – –	# 87 • • • •
# 73 ———	Ⓑ Terminus Points

Ⓑ GAMBETTA # 69

Père Lachaise Cemetery

■ POMPIDOU

M A R A I S

ILE DE LA CITE

NOTRE-DAME

BASTILLE

LATIN QUARTER

Ⓑ GARE DE LYON

63

Seine River

PORTE DE REUILLY Ⓑ # 87

Bois de Vincennes

To #24 Terminus (Ecole Vet.)

Scenic Bus Route #69

Why pay €25 for a tour company to give you an overview of Paris, when city bus #69 can do it for the cost of a Métro ticket? Get on the bus and settle in for a ride through some of the city's most interesting neighborhoods. Or use this line as a handy way to lace together many of Paris' most important sightseeing districts (you'll need a new ticket each time you board the bus). This scenic route crosses the city east-west, running between the Eiffel Tower and Père Lachaise Cemetery, and passing these great monuments and neighborhoods: Eiffel Tower, Ecole Militaire, Rue Cler, Les Invalides (Army Museum and Napoleon's Tomb), Louvre Museum, Ile de la Cité, Ile St. Louis, Hôtel de Ville, Pompidou Center, Marais, Bastille, and Père Lachaise.

You'll learn how great the city's bus system is—and you'll wonder why you've been tunneling by Métro under this gorgeous city. And if you're staying in the Marais or Rue Cler neighborhoods, line #69 is a useful route for just getting around town.

You can board daily until 22:30 (last departure from Eiffel Tower stop). It's best to avoid weekday rush hours (8:00-9:30 & 17:30-19:30) and hot days (no air-conditioning). Sundays are quietest, and it's easy to get a window seat. Evening bus rides are magical from fall through spring (roughly Sept-April), when it gets dark early enough to see the floodlit monuments before the bus stops running. In the Rue Cler area, eastbound line #69 leaves from the Eiffel Tower on Avenue Joseph Bouvard. The first stop is at the southwestern end of the avenue; the second stop is at the eastern end (just before Avenue de la Bourdonnais).

diagram or listening to recorded announcements. When you're ready to get off, push the red button to signal you want a stop, then exit through the central or rear door. Even if you're not certain you've figured out the system, do some joyriding.

More Bus Tips: Avoid rush hour (Mon-Fri 8:00-9:30 & 17:30-19:30), when buses are jammed and traffic doesn't move. While the Métro shuts down at about 24:30, some buses continue much later (called *Noctilien* lines, www.noctilien.fr). Not all city buses are air-conditioned, so they can become rolling greenhouses on summer days. You can transfer from one bus to another on the same ticket (within 1.5 hours, revalidate your ticket on the next bus), but you can't do a round-trip or hop on and off on the same line. You also can't transfer between the bus and the Métro/RER systems using the same ticket, or between buses with a ticket bought on board (go figure).

For a list of Paris' most scenic and convenient routes, see the sidebar on page 70. I've also listed the handiest bus routes for each recommended hotel neighborhood under "Sleeping in Paris," later.

By Taxi

Parisian taxis are reasonable, especially for couples and families. The meters are tamper-proof. Fares and supplements (described in English on the rear windows) are straightforward and tightly regulated.

A taxi can fit three people comfortably. Cabbies are legally required to accept four passengers, though they don't always like it. If you have five in your group, you can book a larger taxi in advance (your hotelier can call), or try your luck at a taxi stand. Beyond three passengers, expect to pay €3 extra per person. For a sample taxi tour of the city at night, see page 153.

Rates: All Parisian taxis start with €2.40 on the meter and have a minimum charge of €6.40. A 20-minute ride (e.g., Bastille to the Eiffel Tower) costs about €20 (versus €1.27/person to get anywhere in town using a *carnet* ticket on the Métro or bus). Drivers charge higher rates at rush hour, at night, all day Sunday, for extra passengers (see above), and to any of the airports. Each piece of luggage you put in the trunk is €1 extra (though it won't appear on the meter, it is a legitimate charge). To tip, round up to the next euro (at least €0.50).

How to Catch *un Taxi:* You can try waving down a taxi, but it's often easier to ask someone for the nearest taxi stand (*"Où est une station de taxi?"*; oo ay ewn stah-see-ohn duh "taxi"). Taxi stands are indicated by a circled "T" on good city maps, and on many maps in this book. To order a taxi in English, call 01 41 27 66 99, or ask your hotelier for help. When you summon a taxi by phone, the meter starts running as soon as the call is received, often adding €6 or more to the bill.

Taxis are tough to find during rush hour, when it's raining, on weekend nights, or on any night after the Métro closes (Sun-Thu at 24:30, Fri-Sat at 2:00 in the morning). If you need to catch a train or flight early in the morning, book a taxi the day before (especially for weekday departures). Some taxi companies require a €5 reservation fee by credit card for weekday morning rush-hour departures (7:00-10:00) and only have a limited number of reservation spots.

By Bike

Paris is surprisingly easy by bicycle. The city is flat, and riders have access to more than 370 miles of bike lanes and the many priority lanes for buses and taxis (though be careful on these). I biked along the river from Notre-Dame to the Eiffel Tower in 15 wonderfully scenic minutes.

PARIS

Urban bikers will find Paris a breeze. First-timers will get the hang of it quickly enough by following some simple rules. Always stay to the right in your lane, bike single-file, stay off sidewalks, watch out for opening doors on parked cars, signal with your arm before making turns, and use bike paths when available. Obey the traffic laws as if you were driving a car. Parisians use the same road rules as Americans, with two exceptions: When passing vehicles or other bikes, always pass on the left (it's illegal to pass on the right); and where there is no stop-

light, always yield to traffic merging from the right, even if you're on a major road and the merging driver is on a side street. You'll find a bell on your bike; use it like a horn to warn pedestrians who don't see you.

The TIs have a helpful "Paris à Vélo" map, which shows all the dedicated bike paths. Many other versions are available for sale at newsstand kiosks, some bookstores, and department stores.

Renting a Bike: The following two rental companies offer organized bike tours as well (see "Tours in Paris—Tour by Bike," later). **Bike About Tours** is your best bet for bike rental. Some of their units are foldable, which allows you to collapse your bike and jump on the Métro if the weather turns bad or if you get tired (€15/day during office hours, €20/24 hours; includes locks, helmets, and comfy gel seats; daily mid-Feb-Dec 9:00-18:00, closed Dec-mid-Feb; shop located near Hôtel de Ville in Vinci parking garage—see map on page 164, Mo: Hôtel de Ville, www.bikeabouttours.com, info@bikeabouttours.com). **Fat Tire Bike Tours** has a limited supply of bikes for rent, so call ahead to check availability (€4/hour, €25/24 hours, includes helmets and locks, credit-card imprint required for deposit, €2 daily rental discount with this book; office open daily 9:00-18:30, May-Aug bike rental only after 11:30 as priority is given to those taking a tour, 24 Rue Edgar Faure—see map on page 111, Mo: Dupleix, tel. 01 56 58 10 54, www.fattirebike toursparis.com).

You'll see many bike-rack stations throughout Paris. The city's **Vélib'** program (from *vélo* + *liberté* or *libre* = "bike freedom" or "free bike") gives residents access to more than 20,000 bikes, which they can unlock from the nearly 1,500 stations scattered around the city. You can use the Vélib' system, too, but only if you have a certain kind of credit card (American Express or a chip-and-PIN card—see page 18) or if you buy a subscription online (€1.70/1 day, €8/7 days, http://en.velib.paris.fr—click on "Subscriptions and Fees," tel. 01 30 79 79 30). The first 30 minutes of any trip are included with your subscription; after that there's a fee for each additional 30 minutes.

By Rollerblade

Inline skaters take to the streets Sunday afternoons and Friday evenings. It's serious skaters only on Fridays (they meet at 21:30 and are ready to roll at 22:00), but anyone can join in on Sundays (at 14:30). Police close off different routes each week to keep locals engaged, but the starting points are always the same. On Sunday, skaters leave from the south side of Place de la Bastille (for the route, see www.rollers-coquillages.org); on Fridays it's from Place Raoul Dautry (Mo: Montparnasse; see route at www.pari-roller .com). You can rent skates near Sunday's starting point at Nomades (€5/half-day, €9/day, Tue-Fri 11:00-13:30 & 14:30-19:30, Sat 10:00-19:00, Sun 12:00-18:00, closed Mon, 37 Boulevard Bourdon, near Place de la Bastille, Mo: Bastille, tel. 01 44 54 07 44, www .nomadeshop.com).

By Scooter

Left Bank Scooters will deliver and pick-up rental scooters to daring travelers over 20 years old with a valid driver's license (€80-100/day, price depends on size of the scooter and how long you keep it, mobile 06 78 12 04 24, www.leftbankscooters.com).

Tours in Paris

To sightsee on your own, download my series of free audio tours that illuminate some of Paris' top sights and neighborhoods, including the Historic Paris Walk, Louvre, Orsay, and Versailles Palace (see page 1138 for details).

Tours by Bus

Bus Tours—Paris Vision (also called Cityrama) offers bus tours of Paris, day and night (advertised in hotel lobbies). I'd consider a Paris Vision tour only for their nighttime tour (see page 152). During the day, you'll get a better value and more versatility by taking a hop-on, hop-off tour by bus (described next) or Batobus boat (see "By Boat," later), which provide transportation between sights.

Hop-on, Hop-off Bus Tours—Double-decker buses connect Paris' main sights, allowing you to hop on and off along the way. You get a disposable set of earbuds to listen to a basic running commentary (dial English for the so-so narration). You can get off at any stop, tour a sight, then catch a later bus. These are best in good weather, when you can sit up top. There are two compa-nies: L'Open Tours and Les Cars Rouges (pick up their brochures showing routes and stops from any TI or on their buses). You can start either tour at just about any of the major sights, such as the Eiffel Tower.

L'Open Tours uses bright yellow buses and provides more extensive coverage (and slightly better commentary) on four different routes, rolling by most of the important sights in Paris. Their Paris Grand Tour (the green route) offers the best introduction. The same ticket gets you on any of their routes within the validity period. Buy your tickets from the driver (1 day-€31, 2 days-€34, kids 4-11 pay €15 for 1 or 2 days, allow 2 hours per tour). Two to four buses depart hourly from about 10:00 to 18:00; expect to wait 10-15 minutes at each stop (stops can be tricky to find—look for yellow signs; tel. 01 42 66 56 56, www.parislopentour.com). A combo-ticket includes the Batobus boats, too (2 days-€43, 3 days-€46, kids 4-11 pay €20 for 2 or 3 days; described later).

Les Cars Rouges' bright red buses offer one route with just nine stops and recorded narration, but for a little less (adult-€29, kids 4-12 pay €15, good for 2 days, 10 percent cheaper if you book online, tel. 01 53 95 39 53, www.carsrouges.com).

Tours by Boat

Seine Cruises—Several companies run one-hour boat cruises on the Seine. For the best experience, cruise at twilight or after dark. (To dine while you cruise, see "Dinner Cruises" on page 209.) Two of the companies—Bateaux-Mouches and Bateaux Parisiens—are convenient to the Rue Cler hotels, and both run daily year-round (April-Oct 10:00-22:30, 2-3/hour; Nov-March shorter hours, runs hourly). Some offer discounts for early online bookings.

Bateaux-Mouches, the oldest boat company in Paris, departs from Pont de l'Alma's right bank and has the biggest open-top, double-decker boats (higher up means better views). But this company caters to tour groups, making their boats jammed and noisy (€11.50, kids 4-12 pay €5.50, tel. 01 42 25 96 10, www.bateaux -mouches.fr).

Bateaux Parisiens has smaller covered boats with handheld audioguides, fewer crowds, and only one deck. It leaves from right in front of the Eiffel Tower. From April to October, they usually have a second departure point on the Quai de Montebello near Notre-Dame (€12, kids 3-12 pay €5, half-price if you have a valid France or France-Switzerland railpass—does not use up a day of a flexipass, tel. 01 76 64 14 45, www.bateauxparisiens.com).

Vedettes du Pont Neuf offers essentially the same one-hour tour as the other companies, but starts and ends at Pont Neuf, closer to recommended hotels in the Marais and Luxembourg Garden neighborhoods. The boats feature a live guide whose delivery (in English and French) is as stiff as a recorded narration—and as hard to understand, given the quality of their sound system (€13, €11 if you book direct with this book in 2013, online booking costs just €9, kids 4-12 pay €7, tip requested, nearly 2/hour, daily 10:30-22:30, tel. 01 46 33 98 38, www.vedettesdupontneuf.com).

Hop-on, Hop-off Boat Tour—**Batobus** allows you to get on and off as often as you like at any of eight popular stops along the Seine. The boats, which make a continuous circuit, stop in this order: Eiffel Tower, Orsay Museum, St. Germain-des-Prés, Notre-Dame, Jardin des Plantes, Hôtel de Ville, the Louvre, and Pont Alexandre III, near the Champs-Elysées (1 day-€15, 2 days-€18, 5 days-€21, April-Aug boats run every 20 minutes 10:00-21:30, Sept-March every 25 minutes 10:00-19:00, 45 minutes one-way, 1.5-hour round-trip, worthless narration, www.batobus.com). If you use this for getting around—sort of a scenic, floating alternative to the Métro—it can be worthwhile, especially with a five-day pass. But if you just want a guided boat tour, the Seine cruises are a better choice (described above).

Low-Key Cruise on a Tranquil Canal—**Canauxrama** runs a lazy 2.5-hour cruise on a peaceful canal out of sight of the Seine. Tours start from Place de la Bastille and end at Bassin de la Villette (near Mo: Stalingrad). During the first segment of your trip, you'll pass through a long tunnel (built by order of Napoleon in the early 19th century, when canal boats were vital for industrial transport). Once outside, you glide—not much faster than you can walk—through sleepy Parisian neighborhoods and slowly climb through four double locks as a guide narrates the trip in French and English (adults-€16, kids 12 and under-€8.50, check online for discounts for advance booking, departs at 9:45 and 14:30 across from Opéra Bastille, just below Boulevard de la Bastille, opposite #50—where the canal meets Place de la Bastille, tel. 01 42 39 15 00, www.canauxrama.com). The same tour also goes in the opposite direction, from Bassin de la Villette to Place de la Bastille (departs at 9:45 and 14:45). It's OK to bring a picnic on board.

Tours on Foot

Paris Walks—This company offers a variety of two-hour walks, led by British and American guides. Tours are thoughtfully prepared and entertaining. Don't hesitate to stand close to the guide to hear (€12-15, generally 2/day—morning and afternoon, private tours available, family guides and Louvre tours a specialty, call 01 48 09 21 40 for schedule in English or check printable online

PARIS

Connecting with the Culture

Paris hosts more visitors than any other city in the world, and with such a robust tourism industry, many travelers feel cut off from the "real life" in the City of Light. Fortunately, Paris offers *beaucoup* ways for you to connect with locals—and thereby make your trip more personal...and more memorable. These get good reviews:

Meeting the French puts travelers in touch with Parisians by organizing dinners in private homes, workplace tours to match your interests/career, and more (tel. 01 42 51 19 80, www.meetingthefrench.com).

Paris Greeter is an all-volunteer organization that connects travelers with English-speaking Parisians who want to share their knowledge of Paris. These volunteer "guides" are not licensed to give historical tours; rather they act as informal companions who can show you "their Paris"—it's like seeing Paris through the eyes of a friend. The tours are free (though donations are welcome), and you must sign up five weeks before your visit (www.parisiendunjour.fr).

Cooking Schools: It's easy to hook up with small cooking schools that provide an unthreatening and personal experience, such as trips to markets (see page 1142 for a list of several schools).

Wine Tasting: Young, enthusiastic Olivier Magny and his team of sommeliers teach fun wine-tasting classes at **Ô Château** wine school/bar near the Louvre, in the 17th-century residence of Madame de Pompadour, King Louis XV's favorite mistress. Olivier's goal is to "take the snob out of wine." At these informal classes, you'll learn the basics of French wine regions, the techniques of tasting, and how to read a French wine label. Classes include Introductory Tasting (€30, 1 hour), Tour de France of Wine (€50, 2 hours), Wine and Cheese lunches (€75, 1.5 hours), Grands Crus tasting (€120, 2 hours), and a wine-tasting dinner (€100, about 2 hours). Register online using code "RS2013" for a 10 percent discount (68 Rue Jean-Jacques Rousseau, Mo: Louvre-Rivoli or Etienne Marcel, tel. 01 44 73 97 80, www.o-chateau.com).

Conversation Swap: Parler Paris is a free-form conversation group organized for native French and English speakers who want to practice in a relaxed environment. In a small group, you'll discuss interesting topics—for the first 45 minutes in French, then for 45 minutes in English. Your first visit is free; after that it's €12 a session (several meetings per week possible, tel. 01 48 42 26 10 or 01 40 27 97 59, www.parler parlor.com, info@parlerparlor.com).

schedule at www.paris-walks.com). Tours focus on the Marais (4/week), Montmartre (3/week), medieval Latin Quarter (Mon), Ile de la Cité/Notre-Dame (Mon), the "Two Islands" (Ile de la Cité and Ile St. Louis, Wed), the Revolution (Tue), and Hemingway's Paris (Fri). They also run less-regular tours of Paris' **Puces St. Ouen** flea market and of the Catacombs, plus a themed walk on the Occupation and Resistance in Paris during the 1940s. Call a day or two ahead to hear the current schedule and starting point. Most tours don't require reservations, but specialty tours—such as the Louvre, fashion, or chocolate tours—require advance reservations and prepayment with credit card (deposits aren't refundable).

Context Paris—These "intellectual by design" walking tours, geared for serious learners, are led by docents (historians, architects, and academics). They cover both museums and specific neighborhoods, and range from traditional topics such as French art history in the Louvre and the Gothic architecture of Notre-Dame to more thematic explorations like immigration and the changing face of Paris, jazz in the Latin Quarter, and the history of the baguette. It's best to book in advance—groups are limited to six participants and can fill up fast (€40-90/person, admission to sights extra, generally 3 hours, tel. 01 72 81 36 35, US tel. 800-691-6036, www.contextparis.com). They also offer private tours and excursions outside Paris.

Classic Walks—The antithesis of Context Paris' walks, these lowbrow, lighter-on-information but high-fun walking tours are run by Fat Tire Bike Tours. Their 3.5-hour Classic Walk covers most major sights (€20, departs May-Sept daily at 10:00; Mon, Wed, Fri and Sun only March-April and Oct; meet at their office at 24 Rue Edgar Faure, Mo: Dupleix, tel. 01 56 58 10 54, www .classicwalksparis.com). They also offer neighborhood walks of Montmartre, the Marais, and Latin Quarter, as well as themed walks on the French Revolution and World War II (€20, tours leave several times a week—see website for details). Their Easy Pass tours are designed to allow you to skip the lines at major sights. They run tours of the Louvre, Catacombs, Eiffel Tower, Pompidou, Orsay, and Versailles (€45-85/person, includes entry and guided tour, www.easypasstours.com). Also ask about their skip-the-line tickets to key sights. The company promises a €2 discount on all walks with this book.

Local Guides—For many, Paris merits hiring a Parisian as a personal guide. **Arnaud Servignat** is an excellent licensed guide (€190/half-day, also does car tours of the countryside around Paris for a little more, mobile 06 68 80 29 05, www.french-guide.com, arnotour@me.com). **Thierry Gauduchon** is a terrific guide well worth his fee (€200/half-day, €400/day, tel. 01 56 98 10 82, mobile 06 19 07 30 77, tgauduchon@aol.com). **Elisabeth Van Hest** is another likable and capable guide (€190/half-day, tel. 01 43 41 47 31, elisa.guide@gmail.com).

Food Tours—Friendly Canadian **Rosa Jackson** designs personalized "Edible Paris" itineraries based on your interests and three-hour "food-guru" tours of Paris led by her or one of her two colleagues (unguided itineraries from €125, €300 guided tours for up to 3, mobile 06 81 67 41 22, www.edible-paris.com, rosa@rosa jackson.com).

Tours by Bike, Segway, or Pedicab

A bike tour is a fun way to see Paris. Two companies—Bike About Tours and Fat Tire Bike Tours—offer tours, sell bottled water and bike maps of Paris, and give advice on cycling routes in the city. Their tour routes cover different areas of the city, so avid cyclists could do both without much repetition.

Bike About Tours—Run by Christian (American) and Paul (New Zealander), this company offers easygoing tours with a focus on the eastern half of the city. Their four-hour tours run daily year-round at 10:00 (also at 15:00 June-Sept). You'll meet at the statue of Charlemagne in front of Notre-Dame, then walk to the nearby rental office to get bikes. The tour includes a good back-street visit of the Marais, Rive Gauche outdoor sculpture park, Ile de la Cité, heart of the Latin Quarter (with a lunch break), Louvre, Les Halles, and Pompidou Center. Group tours have a 12-person maximum—reserve online to guarantee a spot, or show up and take your chances (€30, €5 discount with this book, maximum 2 discounts per book, 15 percent discount for families, includes helmets upon request, private tours available, see listing on page 74 for contact info).

Fat Tire Bike Tours—A hardworking gang of young anglophone expats runs an extensive program of bike, Segway, and walking tours (see Classic Walks listing, earlier). Their high-energy guides run four-hour bike tours of Paris, by day and by night (adults-€30, kids-€28, show this book to get a €4 discount per person, maximum 2 discounts per book, reservations not necessary—just show up). Kid-sized bikes are available, as are nifty tandem attachments that hook on to a parent's bike.

On the day tour, you'll pedal with a pack of 10-20 riders, mostly in parks and along bike lanes, with a lunch stop in the Tuileries Garden (tours leave daily rain or shine at 11:00, April-Oct at 15:00 as well, no minimum number of participants required). Livelier night tours follow a route past floodlit monuments and include a boat cruise on the Seine (April-Oct daily at 19:00, March daily at 18:00, end of Feb and all of Nov Tue, Thu, and Sat-Sun at 18:00, no night tours Dec-mid-Feb). Both tours meet at the south pillar of the Eiffel Tower, where you'll get a short history lesson, then walk six minutes to the Fat Tire office to pick up bikes (helmets available upon request at no extra charge, for contact info see listing on page 74). They also run bike tours to Versailles and Giverny (reservations required, see website for details). Their office has Internet access with English keyboards.

Fat Tire's pricey four-hour **City Segway Tours**—on stand-up motorized scooters—are novel in that you learn to ride a Segway

while exploring Paris (you'll get the hang of it after about half an hour). These tours take no more than eight people at a time, so reservations are required (€85, daily at 9:30, April-Oct also at 14:00 and 18:30, March and Nov also at 14:00, tel. 01 56 58 10 54, www.citysegwaytours.com).

TripUp Pedicab Tours—You'll see these space-age pedicabs *(cyclopolitains)* everywhere in central Paris. The hard-pedaling, free-spirited drivers (who get some electrical assistance) are happy to either transport you from point A to B or give you a tour at a snail's pace—which is a lovely way to experience Paris (€40-50/hour, www.tripup.fr).

Weekend Tour Packages for Students in Paris

Andy Steves (Rick's son) runs **Weekend Student Adventures,** offering experiential three-day weekend tours for €250 designed for American students studying abroad (see www.wsaeurope.com for details on tours of Paris and other great European cities).

Excursions from Paris

Most of the local guides listed earlier will do excursion tours from Paris using your rental car. Or consider these companies, which provide transportation:

Paris Webservices, a reliable outfit, offers many services, including day trips with English-speaking chauffeur-guides in cushy minivans for private groups to several of the destinations covered in this book, including Versailles, Giverny, Burgundy, Normandy, and the Loire (price depends on tour, use promo code "RSteves 77" and show current edition of this book for a 10 percent discount on tours and airport transfers—discount not valid on services they book for you through other companies; see contact info in listing on page 214).

Many companies offer bus tours to regional sights, including all of the day trips described in the next chapter. **Paris Vision** runs uninspired minivan and bus tours to several popular regional destinations, including the Loire Valley, Champagne region, D-Day beaches, and Mont St-Michel (tel. 01 42 60 30 01, www.parisvision.com). Their minivan tours are pricier, but more personal and given in English, and most offer convenient pickup at your hotel (half-day tour about €80/person, day tour about €190/person). Their full-size bus tours (operated by their Cityrama subsidiary, www.pariscityrama.fr) are multilingual, mass-marketed, and mediocre at best, but cheaper than the minivan tours—worthwhile for some travelers simply for the ease of transportation to the sights (about €70-150, destinations include Versailles, Giverny, and more).

Self-Guided Walk

Historic Paris

(This information is distilled from the Historic Paris Walk chapter in *Rick Steves' Paris*, by Rick Steves, Steve Smith, and Gene Openshaw. You can download a free audio version of this walk to your mobile device; see page 1138.)

Allow four hours to do justice to this three-mile walk; just follow the dotted line on the "Historic Paris Walk" map. Start where the city did—on the Ile de la Cité, the island in the Seine River and the physical and historic bull's-eye of your Paris map. The closest Métro stops are Cité, Hôtel de Ville, and St. Michel, each a short walk away.

• *On the square in front of Notre-Dame Cathedral, view the facade from the bronze plaque on the ground marked "Point Zero" (30 yards from the central doorway). You're standing at the center of the country, the point from which all distances in France are measured. Find the circular window in the center of the cathedral's facade.*

▲▲▲Notre-Dame Cathedral

This 700-year-old cathedral is packed with history and tourists. Study its sculpture and windows, take in a Mass, eavesdrop on guides, and walk all around the outside.

Cost and Hours: Cathedral—free, Mon-Fri 8:00-18:45, Sat-Sun 8:00-19:15; Treasury—€4, not covered by Museum Pass, Mon-Fri 9:30-17:40, Sat-Sun 9:30-18:10; audioguide-€5, free English tours—normally Wed-Thu at 14:15, Sat-Sun at 14:30. The cathedral hosts several Masses every morning, plus Vespers at 17:45. The international Mass is held Sun at 11:30, with an organ concert at 16:30. Call or check the website for a full schedule. On Good Friday and the first Friday of the month at 15:00, the (visu-

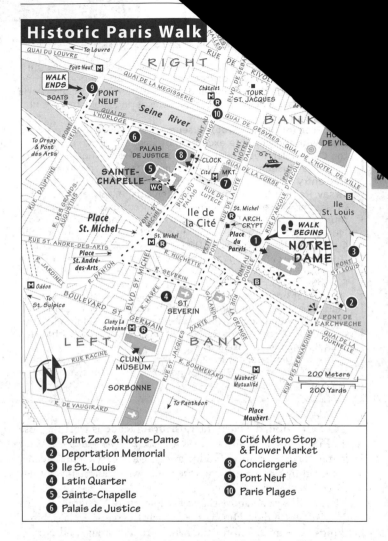

Historic Paris Walk

1. Point Zero & Notre-Dame
2. Deportation Memorial
3. Ile St. Louis
4. Latin Quarter
5. Sainte-Chapelle
6. Palais de Justice
7. Cité Métro Stop & Flower Market
8. Conciergerie
9. Pont Neuf
10. Paris Plages

ally underwhelming) relic known as Jesus' Crown of Thorns goes on display (Mo: Cité, Hôtel de Ville, or St. Michel; tel. 01 42 34 56 10, www.notredamedeparis.fr).

Tower Climb: The entrance for Notre-Dame's towers is outside the cathedral, along the left side. It's 400 steps up, but it's worth it for the gargoyle's-eye view of the cathedral, Seine, and city (€8.50, covered by Museum Pass but no bypass line for passholders; daily April-Sept 10:00-18:30, Sat-Sun until 23:00 in July-Aug, Oct-March 10:00-17:30, last entry 45 minutes before closing; to avoid long lines arrive before 10:00 or after 17:00—after 16:00 in winter; tel. 01 53 10 07 00, www.notre-dame-de-paris.monuments-nationaux.fr).

Sights

... with lots of pricey sights, ... Smart, budget-minded ... g the most out of a **Paris** ... sidering these frugal sight-

... : Some museums are always ... special exhibits), including ... lugo's House, and Fragonard ... nost famous museums offer ... month, including the Louvre, Orsay, ... ter, Quai Branly, and Delacroix museums. These sig... the first Sunday of off-season months: the Arc de Triomphe (Oct-March) and Versailles (Nov-March). Expect big crowds on free days. You can also visit the Orsay Museum for free at 17:00 (or Thu at 21:00), an hour before the museum closes. One of the best everyday values is the Rodin Museum's garden, where it costs just €1 to experience many of Rodin's finest works in a lovely outdoor setting.

Other Freebies: Many worthwhile sights don't charge entry, including the Notre-Dame Cathedral, Père Lachaise Cemetery, Deportation Memorial, Holocaust Memorial, Paris Plages (summers only), Sacré-Cœur Basilica, St. Sulpice Church (with organ recital), and La Défense mall.

Paris' glorious, entertaining parks are free, of course. These include Luxembourg Garden, Champ de Mars (under the Eiffel

● **Self-Guided Tour:** The **cathedral facade** is worth a close look. The church is dedicated to "Our Lady" *(Notre Dame)*. Mary is center stage—cradling God, right in the heart of the facade, surrounded by the halo of the rose window. Adam is on the left and Eve is on the right.

Below Mary and above the arches is a row of 28 statues known as the Kings of Judah. During the French Revolution, these biblical kings were mistaken for the hated French kings, and Notre-Dame represented the oppressive Catholic hierarchy. The citizens stormed the church, crying, "Off with their heads!" All were decapitated, but have since been recapitated.

Speaking of decapitation, look at the carving to the left of the doorway on the left. The man with his head in his hands is St. Denis. Back when there was a Roman temple on this spot, Christianity began making converts. The fourth-century bishop of Roman Paris, Denis was beheaded as a warning to those forsaking the Roman gods. But those early Christians were hard to keep down. The man who would become St. Denis got up, tucked his head under his arm, headed north, paused at a fountain to wash it

Tower), Tuileries Garden (between the Louvre and Place de la Concorde), Palais Royal Courtyards, Jardin des Plantes, Parc Monceau, the Promenade Plantée walk, and Versailles' gardens (except when the fountains perform on Tue late May-late June and weekends April-Oct).

Reduced Prices: Several sights offer a discount if you enter later in the day, including the Orsay (Fri-Wed after 16:15 and Thu after 18:00), the Orangerie (after 17:00), and the Army Museum and Napoleon's Tomb (after 17:00). The Eiffel Tower costs less if you're willing to restrict your visit to the two lower levels—and even less if you're willing to use the stairs.

Free Concerts: Venues offering free or cheap (€6-8) concerts include the American Church, Hôtel des Invalides, St. Sulpice Church, La Madeleine Church, and Notre-Dame Cathedral. For a listing of free concerts, check *Pariscope* magazine (under the "Musique" section) and look for events marked *entrée libre*.

Good-Value Tours: At €12-15, Paris Walks' tours are a good value. The €11-13 Seine River cruises, best after dark, are also worthwhile. The scenic bus route #69, which costs only the price of a transit ticket, could be the best deal of all.

Pricey...but worth it? Certain big-ticket items—primarily the top of the Eiffel Tower, the Louvre, and Versailles—are expensive and crowded, but offer once-in-a-lifetime experiences. All together they amount to less than a ticket to Disneyland—only these are real.

off, and continued until he found just the right place to meet his maker: Montmartre. (Although the name "Montmartre" comes from the Roman "Mount of Mars," later generations—thinking of their beheaded patron, St. Denis—preferred a less pagan version, "Mount of Martyrs.") The Parisians were convinced by this miracle, Christianity gained ground, and a church soon replaced the pagan temple.

Medieval art was OK if it embellished the house of God and told biblical stories. For a fine example, move to the base of the central column (at the foot of Mary, about where the head of St. Denis could spit if he were really good). Working around from the left, find God telling a barely created Eve, "Have fun, but no apples." Next, the sexiest serpent I've ever seen makes apples à la mode. Finally, Adam and Eve, now ashamed of their nakedness, are expelled by an angel. This is a tiny example in a church covered with meaning.

Enter the church at the right doorway (the line moves quickly). You'll be routed around the ambulatory, in much the same way medieval pilgrims were. Notre-Dame has the typical basilica floor plan shared by so many Catholic churches: a long central nave lined with columns and flanked by side aisles. It's designed in the shape of a cross, with the altar placed where the crossbeam intersects. The church can hold up to 10,000 faithful, and it's probably buzzing with visitors now, just as it was 600 years ago. The quiet, deserted churches we see elsewhere are in stark contrast to the busy, center-of-life places they were in the Middle Ages.

Don't miss the **rose windows** that fill each of the transepts. Just past the altar is the **choir,** enclosed with carved-wood walls, where more intimate services can be held in this spacious building. Circle the choir—the back side of the choir walls features **scenes of the resurrected Jesus** (c. 1350). Just ahead on the right is the **Treasury.** It contains lavish robes, golden reliquaries, and the humble tunic of King (and St.) Louis IX, but it probably isn't worth the entry fee.

Back outside, walk around the church through the park on the riverside for a close look at the **flying buttresses.** The Neo-Gothic 300-foot **spire** is a product of the 1860 reconstruction of the dilapidated old church. Around its base (visible as you approach the back end of the church) are apostles and evangelists (the green men) as well as Eugène-Emmanuel Viollet-le-Duc, the architect in charge of the work. The apostles look outward, blessing the city, while the architect (at top) looks up the spire, marveling at his fine work.

Nearby: The **archaeological crypt** is a worthwhile 15-minute stop if you have a Paris Museum Pass (€4 without Museum Pass, Tue-Sun 10:00-18:00, closed Mon, last entry 30 minutes before closing, enter 100 yards in front of the cathedral, tel. 01 55 42 50 10). You'll see remains of the many structures that have stood on this spot in the center of Paris: Roman buildings that surrounded a temple of Jupiter; a wall that didn't keep the Franks out; the main medieval road that once led grandly up the square to Notre-Dame; and even (wow) a 19th-century sewer.

• *Behind Notre-Dame, cross the street and enter through the iron gate into the park at the tip of the island. Look for the stairs and head down to reach the...*

▲Deportation Memorial
(Mémorial de la Déportation)

This memorial to the 200,000 French victims of the Nazi concentration camps (1940-1945) draws you into their experience. France was quickly overrun by Nazi Germany, and Paris spent the war years under Nazi occupation. Jews and dissidents were rounded up and deported—many never returned.

As you descend the steps, the city around you disappears. Surrounded by walls, you have become a prisoner. Your only freedom is your view of the sky and the tiny glimpse of the river below.

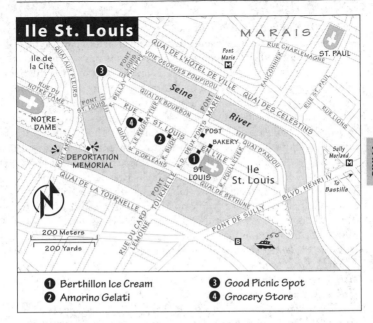

Ile St. Louis

❶ Berthillon Ice Cream
❷ Amorino Gelati
❸ Good Picnic Spot
❹ Grocery Store

Enter the dark, single-file chamber up ahead. Inside, the circular plaque in the floor reads, "They went to the end of the earth and did not return."

The hallway stretching in front of you is lined with 200,000 lighted crystals, one for each French citizen who died. Flickering at the far end is the eternal flame of hope. The tomb of the unknown deportee lies at your feet. Above, the inscription reads, "Dedicated to the living memory of the 200,000 French deportees shrouded by the night and the fog, exterminated in the Nazi concentration camps." The side rooms are filled with triangles—reminiscent of the identification patches inmates were forced to wear—each bearing the name of a concentration camp. Above the exit as you leave is the message you'll find at many other Holocaust sites: "Forgive, but never forget."

Cost and Hours: Free, April-Sept Tue-Sun 10:00-19:00, Oct-March Tue-Sun 10:00-18:00, closed Mon year-round, may randomly close at other times; at the east tip of the island named Ile de la Cité, behind Notre-Dame and near Ile St. Louis (Mo: Cité); tel. 06 14 67 54 98.

• *Back on street level, look across the river (north) to the island called...*

Ile St. Louis

If Ile de la Cité is a tugboat laden with the history of Paris, it's towing this classy little residential dinghy, laden only with high-rent apartments, boutiques, characteristic restaurants (see page 200), and famous ice cream shops.

Ile St. Louis wasn't developed until much later than Ile de la Cité (17th century). What was a swampy mess is now harmonious Parisian architecture and one of Paris' most exclusive neighborhoods. If you won't have time to return here for an evening stroll (see page 151), consider taking a brief detour across the pedestrian bridge, Pont St. Louis. It connects the two islands, leading right to Rue St. Louis-en-l'Ile. This spine of the island is lined with appealing shops and reasonably priced restaurants. A short stroll takes you to the famous Berthillon ice cream parlor at #31. Gelato-lovers head instead to Amorino Gelati at 47 Rue St. Louis-en-l'Ile. When you're finished exploring, loop back to the pedestrian bridge along the parklike quays (walk north to the river and turn left). This walk is about as peaceful and romantic as Paris gets.

• *From the Deportation Memorial, cross the bridge to the Left Bank. All those* **padlocks** *adorning the railing are akin to lighting candles in a church. Locals and tourists alike honor loved ones by writing a brief message on the lock and attaching it to the railing. You can buy a lock (called* cadenas, *€5) at a nearby bookseller's stall along the river.*

Turn right after crossing the bridge and walk along the river, toward the front end of Notre-Dame. Stairs detour down to the riverbank if you need a place to picnic. This side view of the church from across the river is one of Europe's great sights and is best from river level. For the best view and the sweetest crêpes you've ever had, look for the old river barge Daphné *and see if* Valeria *is open (€2.50-3.50). If the sun is out, he should be there.*

After passing the Pont au Double (the bridge leading to the facade of Notre-Dame), watch on your left for **Shakespeare and Company**, *an atmospheric reincarnation of the original 1920s bookshop and a good spot to page through books (37 Rue de la Bûcherie; see page 61). Before returning to the island, walk a block behind Shakespeare and Company, and take a spin through the...*

▲Latin Quarter

This area's touristy fame relates to its intriguing, artsy, bohemian character. This was perhaps Europe's leading university district in the Middle Ages, when Latin was the language of higher education.

The neighborhood's main boulevards (St. Michel and St. Germain) are lined with cafés—once the haunts of great poets and philosophers, now the hangouts of tired tourists. Though still youthful and artsy, much of this area has become a tourist ghetto filled with cheap North African eateries. Exploring a few blocks up- or downriver from here gives you a better chance of feeling the pulse of what survives of Paris' classic Left Bank. For colorful wandering and café-sitting, afternoons and evenings are best.

Walking along Rue St. Séverin, you can still see the shadow of the medieval sewer system. The street slopes into a central channel of bricks. In the days before plumbing and toilets, when people still went to the river or neighborhood wells for their water, flushing meant throwing it out the window. At certain times of day, maids on the fourth floor would holler, *"Garde de l'eau!"* ("Watch out for the water!") and heave it into the streets, where it would eventually wash down into the Seine.

Consider a visit to the **Cluny Museum** for its medieval art and unicorn tapestries (see page 118). The **Sorbonne**—the University of Paris' humanities department—is also nearby; visitors can ogle at the famous dome, but they are not allowed to enter the building (two blocks south of the river on Boulevard St. Michel).

Be sure to see **Place St. Michel.** This square (facing the Pont St. Michel) is the traditional core of the Left Bank's artsy, liberal, hippie, bohemian district of poets, philosophers, and winos. In less commercial times, Place St. Michel was a gathering point for the city's malcontents and misfits. In 1830, 1848, and again in 1871, the citizens took the streets from the government troops, set up barricades *Les Miz*-style, and fought against royalist oppression. During World War II, the locals rose up against their Nazi oppressors (read the plaques under the dragons at the foot of the St. Michel fountain). Even today, whenever there's a student demonstration, it starts here.

• *From Place St. Michel, look across the river and find the prickly steeple of the Sainte-Chapelle church. Head toward it. Cross the river on Pont St. Michel and continue north along the Boulevard du Palais. On your left, you'll see the doorway to Sainte-Chapelle (usually with a line of people).*

You'll need to pass through a strict security checkpoint to get into the Sainte-Chapelle complex (this is more than a tourist attraction: France's Supreme Court meets to the right of Sainte-Chapelle in the Palais de Justice). Expect a long wait unless you arrive before it opens. (The Annexe Café across the street sells €1 coffee to-go—perfect for sipping while you wait in line.) First comes the security line (all sharp objects are confiscated). No one can skip this line. Security lines are shortest on weekday mornings and on weekends (when the courts are closed). Once past security, you'll enter the courtyard outside Sainte-Chapelle, where you'll find WCs and information about upcoming church concerts (for concert details, see page 149). You'll also encounter another line to buy tickets to go into the church. Those with combo-tickets or Museum Passes can skip the ticket-buying line.

▲▲▲Sainte-Chapelle

This triumph of Gothic church architecture is a cathedral of glass like no other. It was speedily built between 1242 and 1248 for King

Louis IX—the only French king who is now a saint—to house the supposed Crown of Thorns. Its architectural harmony is due to the fact that it was completed under the direction of one architect and in only six years—unheard of in Gothic times. In contrast, Notre-Dame took over 200 years.

Cost and Hours: €8.50, €12.50 combo-ticket with Conciergerie, under 18 free, covered by Museum Pass, audioguide-€4.50; daily March-Oct 9:30-18:00, Wed until 21:30 mid-May-mid-Sept, Nov-Feb 9:00-17:00; last entry 30 minutes before closing, be prepared for long lines, evening concerts—see page 149, 4 Boulevard du Palais, Mo: Cité, tel. 01 53 40 60 80, www.sainte-chapelle.monuments-nationaux.fr.

Visiting the Church: Though the inside is beautiful, the exterior is basically functional. The muscular buttresses hold up the stone roof, so the walls are essentially there to display stained glass. The lacy spire is Neo-Gothic—added in the 19th century.

Inside, the layout clearly shows an *ancien régime* approach to worship. The low-ceilinged basement was for staff and other common folks—worshipping under a sky filled with painted fleurs-de-lis, a symbol of the king. Royal Christians worshipped upstairs. The paint job, a 19th-century restoration, helps you imagine how grand this small, painted, jeweled chapel was. (Imagine Notre-Dame painted like this...) Each capital is playfully carved with a different plant's leaves.

Climb the spiral staircase to the **Chapelle Haute.** Fill the place with choral music, crank up the sunshine, face the top of the altar, and really believe that the Crown of Thorns is there, and this becomes one awesome space.

Fiat lux. "Let there be light." From the first page of the Bible, it's clear: Light is divine. Light shines through stained glass like God's grace shining down to earth. Gothic architects used their new technology to turn dark stone buildings into lanterns of light. The glory of Gothic shines brighter here than in any other church.

There are 15 separate panels of **stained glass** (6,500 square feet—two thirds of it 13th-century original), with more than 1,100 different scenes, mostly from the Bible. These cover the

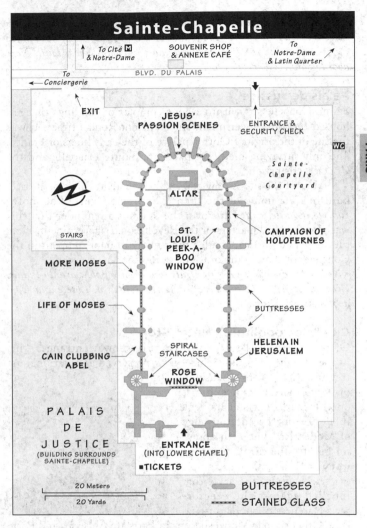

Sainte-Chapelle

↑ To Cité Ⓜ & Notre-Dame

SOUVENIR SHOP & ANNEXE CAFÉ

To Notre-Dame & Latin Quarter ↗

To Conciergerie ←

BLVD. DU PALAIS

EXIT

JESUS' PASSION SCENES

ENTRANCE & SECURITY CHECK

WC

PARIS

Sainte-Chapelle Courtyard

ALTAR

ST. LOUIS' PEEK-A-BOO WINDOW

CAMPAIGN OF HOLOFERNES

STAIRS

MORE MOSES

LIFE OF MOSES

BUTTRESSES

CAIN CLUBBING ABEL

SPIRAL STAIRCASES

HELENA IN JERUSALEM

ROSE WINDOW

P A L A I S

D E

J U S T I C E
(BUILDING SURROUNDS SAINTE-CHAPELLE)

ENTRANCE
(INTO LOWER CHAPEL)

■TICKETS

20 Meters

20 Yards

▬▬ **BUTTRESSES**

┄┄┄ **STAINED GLASS**

entire Christian history of the world, from the Creation in Genesis (first window on the left, as you face the altar), to the coming of Christ (over the altar), to the end of the world (the round "rose"-shaped window at the rear of the church). Each individual scene is interesting, and the whole effect is overwhelming.

The **altar** was raised up high to better display the Crown of Thorns, the relic around which this chapel was built. The supposed crown cost King Louis more than three times as much as this church. Today it is kept by the Notre-Dame Treasury (though it's occasionally brought out for display).

• *Exit Sainte-Chapelle. Back outside, as you walk around the church exterior, look down to see the foundation and take note of how much Paris has risen in the 750 years since Sainte-Chapelle was built. Next door to Sainte-Chapelle is the...*

Palais de Justice

Sainte-Chapelle sits within a huge complex of buildings that has housed the local government since ancient Roman times. It was the site of the original Gothic palace of the early kings of France. The only surviving medieval parts are Sainte-Chapelle and the Conciergerie prison.

Most of the site is now covered by the giant Palais de Justice, built in 1776, home of the French Supreme Court. The motto *Liberté, Egalité, Fraternité* over the doors is a reminder that this was also the headquarters of the Revolutionary government. Here they doled out justice, condemning many to imprisonment in the Conciergerie downstairs or to the guillotine.

• *Now pass through the big iron gate to the noisy Boulevard du Palais. Cross the street to the wide, pedestrian-only Rue de Lutèce and walk about halfway down.*

Cité "Metropolitain" Métro Stop

Of the 141 original early-20th-century subway entrances, this is one of only a few survivors—now preserved as a national art treasure. (New York's Museum of Modern Art even exhibits one.) It marks Paris at its peak in 1900—on the cutting edge of Modernism, but with an eye for beauty. The curvy, plantlike ironwork is a textbook example of Art Nouveau, the style that rebelled against the erector-set squareness of the Industrial  Age. Other similar Métro stations in Paris are Abbesses and Porte Dauphine.

The flower and plant market on Place Louis Lépine is a pleasant detour. On Sundays this square flutters with a busy bird market. And across the way is the Préfecture de Police, where Inspector Clouseau of *Pink Panther* fame used to work, and where the local resistance fighters took the first building from the Nazis in August of 1944, leading to the Allied liberation of Paris a week later.

• *Pause here to admire the view. Sainte-Chapelle is a pearl in an ugly architectural oyster. Double back to the Palais de Justice, turn right onto Boulevard du Palais, and enter the...*

PARIS

▲Conciergerie

Though pretty barren inside, this former prison echoes with history (and is free with the Museum Pass—remember that passholders can skip the ticket-buying line). Positioned next to the courthouse, the Conciergerie was the gloomy prison famous as the last stop for 2,780 victims of the guillotine, including France's last *ancien régime* queen, Marie-Antoinette. Before then, kings had used the building to torture and execute failed assassins. (One of its towers along the river was called "The Babbler," named for the pain-induced sounds that leaked from it.) When the Revolution (1789) toppled the king, the building kept its same function, but without torture. The progressive Revolutionaries proudly unveiled a modern and more humane way to execute people—the guillotine.

Inside, pick up a free map and breeze through the one-way circuit. It's well-described in English. See the spacious, low-ceilinged Hall of Men-at-Arms (Room 1), used as the guards' dining room, with four large fireplaces (look up the chimneys). This big room gives a feel for the grandeur of the Great Hall (upstairs, not open to visitors), where the Revolutionary tribunals grilled scared prisoners on their political correctness.

You'll also see a re-creation of Marie-Antoinette's cell, which houses a collection of her mementos. In another room, a list of those made "a foot shorter at the top" by the "national razor" includes ex-King Louis XVI, Charlotte Corday (who murdered the Revolutionary writer Jean-Paul Marat in his bathtub), and—oh, the irony—Maximilien de Robespierre, the head of the Revolution, the man who sent so many to the guillotine.

Cost and Hours: €8.50, €12.50 combo-ticket with Sainte-Chapelle, covered by Museum Pass, daily March-Oct 9:30-18:00, Nov-Feb 9:00-17:00, last entry 30 minutes before closing, 2 Boulevard du Palais, Mo: Cité, tel. 01 53 40 60 80, www.conciergerie.monuments-nationaux.fr.

• *Back outside, turn left on Boulevard du Palais and head north. On the corner is the city's oldest public clock. The mechanism of the present clock is from 1334, and even though the case is Baroque, it keeps on ticking.*

Turn left onto Quai de l'Horloge and walk west along the river, past "The Babbler" tower. The bridge up ahead is the Pont Neuf, where we'll end this walk. At the first corner, veer left into a sleepy triangular square called Place Dauphine. Marvel at how such coziness could be lodged in the midst of such greatness. At the equestrian statue of Henry

PARIS

IV (at the other end of Place Dauphine), turn right onto the old bridge and take refuge in one of the nooks halfway across, on the Eiffel Tower side.

Pont Neuf

This "new bridge" is now Paris' oldest. Built during Henry IV's reign (about 1600), its arches span the widest part of the river. Unlike other bridges, this one never had houses or buildings growing on it. The turrets were originally for vendors and street entertainers. In the days of Henry IV, who promised his peasants "a chicken in every pot every Sunday," this would have been a lively scene. From the bridge, look downstream (west) to see the next bridge, the pedestrian-only Pont des Arts. Ahead on the Right

Bank is the long Louvre Museum. Beyond that, on the Left Bank, is the Orsay. And what's that tall black tower in the distance?

• *Our walk is finished. From here, you can tour the Seine by boat (the departure point for Seine river cruises offered by Vedettes du Pont Neuf is through the park at the end of the island—see page 77), continue to the Louvre, or (if it's summer) head to the...*

▲Paris Plages (Paris Beaches)

The Riviera it's not, but this string of fanciful faux beaches— assembled in summer along a one-mile stretch of the Right Bank of the Seine—is a fun place to stroll, play, and people-watch on a sunny day. Each summer, the Paris city government closes the embankment's highway and trucks in potted palm trees, hammocks, lounge chairs, and 2,000 tons of sand to create colorful urban beaches. You'll also find "beach cafés," climbing walls, prefab pools, trampolines, *boules*, a library, beach volleyball, badminton, and Frisbee areas.

Cost and Hours: Free, mid-July-mid-Aug daily 8:00-24:00, no beach off-season; on Right Bank of Seine, just north of Ile de la Cité, between Pont des Arts and Pont de Sully; for information, go to www.paris.fr, click on "English," then "Visit," then "Highlights."

Sights in Paris

Major Museums Neighborhood

Paris' grandest park, the Tuileries Garden, was once the private property of kings and queens. Today it links the Louvre, Orangerie,

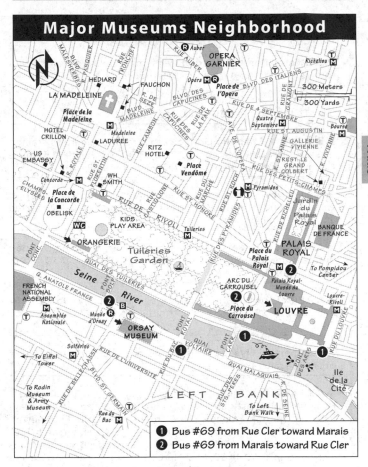

Major Museums Neighborhood

300 Meters

300 Yards

❶ Bus #69 from Rue Cler toward Marais
❷ Bus #69 from Marais toward Rue Cler

Jeu de Paume, and Orsay museums. And across from the Louvre are the tranquil, historic courtyards of the Palais Royal.

▲▲▲Louvre (Musée du Louvre)

This is Europe's oldest, biggest, greatest, and second-most-crowded museum (after the Vatican). Housed in a U-shaped, 16th-century palace (accentuated by a 20th-century glass pyramid), the Louvre is Paris' top museum and one of its key landmarks. It's home to *Mona Lisa*, *Venus de Milo*, and hall after hall of Greek and Roman masterpieces, medieval jewels, Michelangelo statues, and paintings by the greatest artists from the

Paris at a Glance

▲▲▲**Notre-Dame Cathedral** Paris' most beloved church, with towers and gargoyles. **Hours:** Cathedral Mon-Fri 8:00-18:45, Sat-Sun 8:00-19:15; tower daily April-Sept 10:00-18:30, Sat-Sun until 23:00 in July-Aug, Oct-March 10:00-17:30; Treasury Mon-Fri 9:30-17:40, Sat-Sun 9:30-18:10. See page 82.

▲▲▲**Sainte-Chapelle** Gothic cathedral with peerless stained glass. **Hours:** Daily March-Oct 9:30-18:00, Wed until 21:30 mid-May-mid-Sept, Nov-Feb 9:00-17:00. See page 89.

▲▲▲**Louvre** Europe's oldest and greatest museum, starring *Mona Lisa* and *Venus de Milo*. **Hours:** Wed-Mon 9:00-18:00, Wed and Fri until 21:45, closed Tue. See page 95.

▲▲▲**Orsay Museum** Nineteenth-century art, including Europe's greatest Impressionist collection. **Hours:** Tue-Sun 9:30-18:00, Thu until 21:45, closed Mon. See page 105.

▲▲▲**Eiffel Tower** Paris' soaring exclamation point. **Hours:** Daily mid-June-Aug 9:00-24:00, Sept-mid-June 9:30-23:00. See page 110.

▲▲▲**Champs-Elysées** Paris' grand boulevard. **Hours:** Always open. See page 124.

▲▲▲**Versailles** The ultimate royal palace (Château), with a Hall of Mirrors, vast gardens, a grand canal, plus a queen's playground (Trianon Palaces and Domaine de Marie-Antoinette). **Hours:** Château April-Oct Tue-Sun 9:00-18:30, Nov-March Tue-Sun 9:00-17:30, closed Mon year-round. Trianon/Domaine April-Oct Tue-Sun 12:00-18:30, Nov-March Tue-Sun 12:00-17:30, closed Mon year-round; in winter only the two Trianon Palaces are open. Gardens generally open April-Oct daily 9:00-20:30, Nov-March Tue-Sun 8:00-18:00, closed Mon. See the Versailles chapter.

▲▲**Orangerie Museum** Monet's water lilies, plus works by Utrillo, Cézanne, Renoir, Matisse, and Picasso, in a lovely setting. **Hours:** Wed-Mon 9:00-18:00, closed Tue. See page 104.

▲▲**Army Museum and Napoleon's Tomb** The emperor's imposing tomb, flanked by museums of France's wars. **Hours:** Museum—daily April-Sept 10:00-18:00, may be open Tue until 21:00, Oct-March 10:00-17:00, closed first Mon of month year-round. Tomb—daily April-June and Sept 10:00-18:00, may be open Tue until 21:00; July-Aug 10:00-19:00, may be open Tue until 21:00; Oct-March 10:00-17:00, closed first Mon of month Sept-May. See page 115.

▲▲**Rodin Museum** Works by the greatest sculptor since Michelangelo, with many statues in a peaceful garden. **Hours:** Tue-Sun 10:00-17:45, Wed until 20:45, closed Mon. See page 116.

▲▲**Marmottan Museum** Untouristy art museum focusing on Monet. **Hours:** Tue-Sun 10:00-18:00, Thu until 20:00, closed Mon. See page 117.

▲▲**Cluny Museum** Medieval art with unicorn tapestries. **Hours:** Wed-Mon 9:15-17:45, closed Tue. See page 118.

▲▲**Arc de Triomphe** Triumphal arch with viewpoint, marking start of Champs-Elysées. **Hours:** Interior—daily April-Sept 10:00-23:00, Oct-March 10:00-22:30. See page 128.

▲▲**Jacquemart-André Museum** Art-strewn mansion. **Hours:** Daily 10:00-18:00, Mon and Sat until 21:00 during special exhibits. See page 130.

▲▲**Pompidou Center** Modern art in colorful building with city views. **Hours:** Wed-Mon 11:00-21:00, closed Tue. See page 136.

▲▲**Sacré-Cœur and Montmartre** White basilica atop Montmartre with super views. **Hours:** Daily 6:00-22:30; dome climb daily May-Sept 9:00-19:00, Oct-April 9:00-17:00. See page 139.

▲**Panthéon** Neoclassical monument celebrating the struggles of the French. **Hours:** Daily 10:00-18:30 in summer, until 18:00 in winter. See page 122.

▲**Opéra Garnier** Grand belle époque theater with a modern ceiling by Chagall. **Hours:** Generally daily 10:00-17:00, mid-July-Aug until 18:00. See page 129.

▲**La Défense and La Grande Arche** The city's own "little Manhattan" business district and its colossal modern arch. **Hours:** Always open. See page 131.

▲**Jewish Art and History Museum** Displays history of Judaism in Europe. **Hours:** Sun-Fri 11:00-18:00, closed Sat. See page 135.

▲**Carnavalet Museum** Paris' history wrapped up in a 16th-century mansion. **Hours:** Tue-Sun 10:00-18:00, closed Mon. See page 134.

▲**Père Lachaise Cemetery** Final home of Paris' illustrious dead. **Hours:** Mon-Fri 8:00-18:00, Sat 8:30-18:00, Sun 9:00-18:00, closes at 17:30 in winter. See page 138.

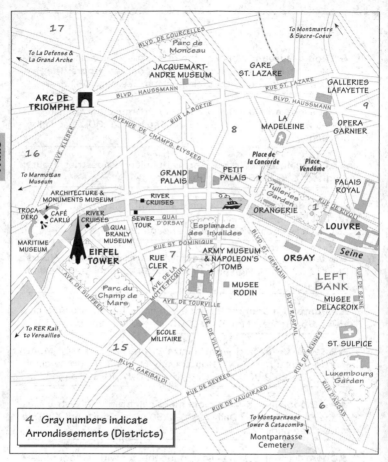

To La Defense &
La Grand Arche

17

BLVD. DE COURCELLES

Parc de
Monceau

To Montmartre
& Sacre-Coeur

JACQUEMART-
ANDRE MUSEUM

GARE
ST. LAZARE

RUE ST. LAZARE

GALLERIES
LAFAYETTE

ARC DE
TRIOMPHE

BLVD. HAUSSMANN

RUE LA BOETIE

BLVD. HAUSSMANN

9

AVENUE DE CHAMPS ELYSEES

8

LA
MADELEINE

OPERA
GARNIER

16

AVE. KLEBER

Place de
la Concorde

Place
Vendôme

PALAIS
ROYAL

To Marmottan
Museum

GRAND
PALAIS

PETIT
PALAIS

Tuileries
Garden

RUE DE RIVOLI

ARCHITECTURE &
MONUMENTS MUSEUM

RIVER
CRUISES

ORANGERIE

LOUVRE

TROCA-
DERO

CAFÉ
CARLÚ

RIVER
CRUISES

SEWER
TOUR

QUAI
D'ORSAY

ORSAY

Seine

MARITIME
MUSEUM

QUAI
BRANLY
MUSEUM

Esplanade
des Invalides

RUE DE SEINE

EIFFEL
TOWER

RUE ST. DOMINIQUE

RUE
CLER

7

ARMY MUSEUM
& NAPOLEON'S
TOMB

BLVD. ST. GERMAIN

LEFT
BANK

AVE. DE LA MOTTE-PICQUET

MUSEE
RODIN

MUSEE
DELACROIX

AVE. DE SUFFREN

Parc du
Champ de
Mars

AVE. DE TOURVILLE

BLVD. RASPAIL

To RER Rail
to Versailles

ECOLE
MILITAIRE

AVE. DE VILLARS

ST. SULPICE

15

BLVD. GARIBALDI

RUE DE SEVRES

RUE DE RENNES

Luxembourg
Garden

RUE D'ASSAS

RUE DE VAUGIRARD

6

4   Gray numbers indicate
Arrondissements (Districts)

To Montparnasse
Tower & Catacombs

Montparnasse
Cemetery

Renaissance to the Romantics (mid-1800s).

Touring the Louvre can be overwhelming, so be selective.
Focus on the Denon wing (south, along the river), with Greek
sculptures, Italian paintings (by Raphael and da Vinci), and—of
course—French paintings (Neoclassical and Romantic), and the
adjoining Sully wing, with Egyptian artifacts and more French
paintings. For extra credit, tackle the Richelieu wing (north,
away from the river), displaying works from ancient Mesopotamia
(today's Iraq), as well as French, Dutch, and Northern art.

Expect changes—the sprawling Louvre is constantly shuf-
fling its collection. Rooms are periodically closed for renovation,
and pieces are removed from display if they're being restored or
loaned to other museums. The new Islamic art space—with its
glass roof modeled on a head scarf (visible in the Cour de Visconti
courtyard of the Denon wing) may be open by the time you visit.

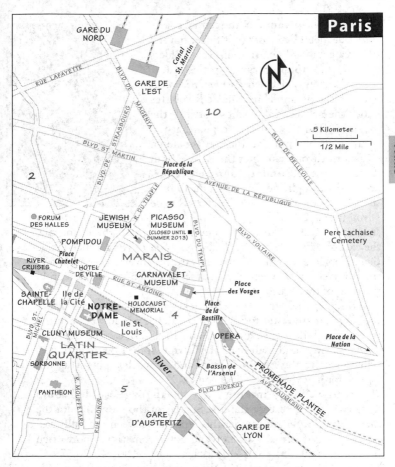

Various galleries devoted to decorative arts are in flux until at least the spring of 2013. If you don't find the artwork you're looking for, ask the nearest guard for its new location.

Cost and Hours: €11, free on first Sun of month, covered by Museum Pass, tickets good all day, reentry allowed; Wed-Mon 9:00-18:00, Wed and Fri until 21:45 (except on holidays), closed Tue, galleries start shutting 30 minutes before closing, last entry 45 minutes before closing; crowds worst in the morning (arrive 30 minutes before opening) and all day Sun, Mon, and Wed; several cafés, tel. 01 40 20 53 17, recorded info tel. 01 40 20 51 51, www.louvre.fr.

Getting There: It's at the Palais Royal-Musée du Louvre Métro stop. (The old Louvre Métro stop, called Louvre-Rivoli, is farther from the entrance.) Bus #69 also runs past the Louvre.

Getting In: There is no grander entry than through the main

entrance at the **pyramid** in the central courtyard, but metal detectors (not ticket-buyers)
can create a long line. Museum Pass holders
can use the **group entrance** in the pedestrian passageway (labeled *Pavilion Richelieu*)
between the pyramid and Rue de Rivoli. It's
under the arches, a few steps north of the
pyramid; find the uniformed guard at the
security checkpoint entrance, at the down
escalator. Anyone can enter the Louvre from
its less crowded **underground entrance,**
accessed through the Carrousel du Louvre
shopping mall. Enter the mall at 99 Rue de

Rivoli (the door with the red awning) or directly from the Métro
stop Palais Royal-Musée du Louvre (stepping off the train, take
the exit to *Musée du Louvre-Le Carrousel du Louvre*). Once inside
the underground mall, continue toward the inverted pyramid and
the Louvre's security entrance. Museum Pass holders can skip to
the head of the security line.

Buying Tickets: Self-serve ticket machines located under
the pyramid are faster to use than the ticket windows (machines
accept euro bills, coins, and chip-and-PIN Visa cards). The *tabac*
in the underground mall (near the Carrousel du Louvre entrance)
sells tickets to the Louvre, Orsay, and Versailles, plus Museum
Passes, for no extra charge (cash only).

Tours: Ninety-minute English-language **guided tours**
leave twice daily (except the first Sunday of the month) from the
Accueil des Groupes area, under the pyramid between the Sully and
Denon wings (normally at 11:00 and 14:00, sometimes more often
in summer; €9 plus your entry ticket, tour tel. 01 40 20 52 63).
Videoguides on Nintendo 3DS portable game consoles provide
tech-savvy visitors with commentary on about 700 masterpieces
(€5, available at entries to the three wings, at the top of the escalators). A free Louvre **smartphone app** is available at iTunes, where
you can also download my free self-guided Louvre **audio tour** (see
page 1138). You'll also find English explanations throughout the
museum.

Baggage Check: The free *bagagerie* is under the pyramid, to
the right of the Denon wing entrance (it is signed *visiteurs indivi-
duels*). Large bags must be checked, and you can also check small
bags to lighten your load. The baggage-claim clerk might ask you
in French, "Does your bag contain anything of value?" You can't
check cameras, money, passports, or other valuables.

Services: WCs are located under the pyramid, behind the
escalators to the Denon and Richelieu wings. Once you're in the
galleries, WCs are scarce.

⊘ **Self-Guided Tour:** Start in the Denon Wing and visit the highlights, in the following order (thanks to Gene Openshaw for his help writing this tour).

Look for the famous *Venus de Milo (Aphrodite)* statue (pic-

tured here). You'll find her not far from another famous statue, the *Winged Victory of Samothrace.* This goddess of love (c. 100 B.C., from the Greek island of Melos) created a sensation when she was discovered in 1820. Most "Greek" statues are actu- ally later Roman copies, but *Venus* is a rare Greek original. She, like Golden Age Greeks, epitomizes stability, beauty, and balance.

After viewing *Venus*, wander through the **ancient Greek and Roman works** to room 6 to see the Parthenon frieze (stone fragments that once decorated the exterior of the greatest Athenian temple), mosaics from the ancient city of Antioch, Etruscan sarcophagi, and Roman portrait busts.

Later Greek art was Hellenistic, adding motion and drama. For a good example, see the exciting *Winged Victory of Samothrace* (*Victoire de Samothrace,* on the landing). This statue of a woman with wings, poised on the prow of a ship, once stood on a hilltop to commemorate a naval victory. This is the *Venus de Milo* gone Hellenistic.

The **Italian collection**—including the *Mona Lisa*—is scat- tered throughout the rooms of the long Grand Gallery, to the right (as you face her) of *Winged Victory* (look for **two Botticelli frescoes** as you enter). In painting, the Renaissance meant realism, and for the Italians, realism was spelled "3-D." Painters were inspired by the realism and balanced beauty of Greek sculpture. Painting a 3-D world on a 2-D surface is tough, and after a millennium of Dark Ages, artists were rusty. Living in a religious age, they painted mostly altarpieces full of saints, angels, Madonnas-and- bambinos, and crucifixes floating in an ethereal gold-leaf heaven. Gradually, though, they brought these otherworldly scenes down to earth.

Two masters of the Italian High Renaissance (1500-1600) were Raphael (see his *La Belle Jardinière,* showing the Madonna, Child, and John the Baptist) and Leonardo da Vinci. The Louvre has the greatest collection of Leonardos in the world—five of them, including the exquisite *Virgin and Child with St. Anne;* the neigh- boring *Virgin of the Rocks;* and the androgynous *John the Baptist.*

But his most famous, of course, is the *Mona Lisa* (*La Joconde* in French), located in the Salle des Etats, midway down the Grand Gallery, on the right. After several years and a €5 million renova- tion, Mona is alone behind glass on her own false wall. Leonardo

PARIS

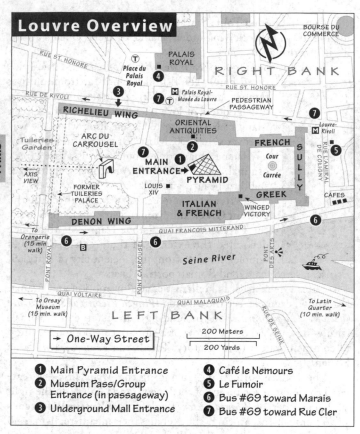

Louvre Overview

BOURSE DU
COMMERCE

RUE ST. HONORE

Place du
Palais
Royal ④

PALAIS
ROYAL

RIGHT BANK

RUE ST. HONORE

RUE DE RIVOLI ③

Palais Royal-
Musée du Louvre ⑦

PEDESTRIAN
PASSAGEWAY

RICHELIEU WING

Louvre-
Rivoli ⑦

Tuileries
Garden

ARC DU
CARROUSEL

ORIENTAL
ANTIQUITIES

FRENCH

Cour
Carrée

S
U
L
L
Y

⑤

RUE L'AMIRAL DE COLIGNY

⑦

AXIS
VIEW

MAIN
ENTRANCE ① ②

PYRAMID

CAFÉS

LOUIS
XIV

GREEK

FORMER
TUILERIES
PALACE

ITALIAN
& FRENCH

WINGED
VICTORY

To
Orangerie
(15 min
walk)

DENON WING

QUAI FRANÇOIS MITTERAND

⑥

⑥ B

⑥

PONT ROYAL

PONT CARROUSEL

Seine River

PONT
DES
ARTS

QUAI VOLTAIRE

QUAI MALAQUAIS

To Orsay
Museum
(15 min. walk)

LEFT BANK

RUE DE SEINE

To Latin
Quarter
(10 min.)

→ One-Way Street

200 Meters

200 Yards

① Main Pyramid Entrance
② Museum Pass/Group
   Entrance (in passageway)
③ Underground Mall Entrance

④ Café le Nemours
⑤ Le Fumoir
⑥ Bus #69 toward Marais
⑦ Bus #69 toward Rue Cler

was already an old man when François I invited him to France. Determined to pack light, he took only a few paintings with him. One was a portrait of Lisa del Giocondo, the wife of a wealthy Florentine merchant. When Leonardo arrived, François immediately fell in love with the painting, making it the centerpiece of the small collection of Italian masterpieces that would, in three centuries, become the Louvre museum. He called it *La Gioconda* (*La Joconde* in French)—a play on both her last name and the Italian word for "happiness." We know it as the *Mona Lisa*—a contraction of the Italian for "my lady Lisa." Warning: François was impressed, but *Mona* may disappoint you. She's smaller than you'd expect, darker, engulfed in a huge room, and hidden behind a glaring pane of glass.

The huge canvas opposite *Mona* is Paolo

Veronese's *The Marriage at Cana*, showing the Renaissance love of beautiful things gone hog-wild. Venetian artists like Veronese painted the good life of rich, happy-go-lucky Venetian merchants.

Now for something **Neoclassical**. Exit behind *Mona Lisa* and turn right into the Salle Daru to find *The Coronation of Emperor Napoleon* by Jacques-Louis David. Neoclassicism, once the rage in France (1780-1850), usually features Greek subjects, patriotic sentiment, and a clean, simple style. After Napoleon quickly conquered most of Europe, he insisted on being made emperor (not merely king) of this "New Rome." He staged an elaborate coronation ceremony in Paris, and rather than let the pope crown him, he crowned himself. The setting was Notre-Dame Cathedral, with Greek columns and Roman arches thrown in for effect. Napoleon's mom was also added, since she couldn't make it to the ceremony. A key on the frame describes who's who in the picture.

The **Romantic** collection, in an adjacent room (Salle Mollien), has works by Théodore Géricault (*The Raft of the Medusa*—one

of my favorites) and Eugène Delacroix *(Liberty Leading the People)*. Romanticism, with an emphasis on motion and emotion, is the flip side of cool, balanced Neoclassicism, though they both flourished in the early 1800s. Delacroix's *Liberty*, commemorating the stirrings of democracy in France, is also an appropriate tribute to the Louvre, the first museum ever opened to the common rabble of humanity. The good things in life don't belong only to a small, wealthy part of society, but to everyone. The motto of France is *Liberté, Egalité, Fraternité*—liberty, equality, and the brotherhood of all.

Exit the room at the far end (past Café Mollien) and go downstairs, where you'll bump into the bum of a large, twisting male nude looking like he's just waking up after a thousand-year nap. The two *Slaves* (1513-1515) by Michelangelo are a fitting end to this museum—works that bridge the ancient and modern worlds. Michelangelo, like his fellow Renaissance artists, learned from the Greeks. The perfect anatomy, twisting poses, and idealized faces appear as if they could have been created 2,000 years earlier. Michelangelo said that his purpose was to carve away the marble to reveal the figures God put inside. The *Rebellious Slave*, fighting against his bondage, shows the agony of that process and the ecstasy of the result.

Although this makes for a good first tour, there's so much more. After a break (or on a second visit), consider a stroll through a few rooms of the Richelieu wing, which contain some of the

Louvre's most ancient pieces. Bible students, amateur archaeologists, and Iraq War vets may find the collection especially
interesting.

Nearby: Across from the Louvre are the lovely **Palais Royal
courtyards.** Although the palace is closed to the public, the
courtyards are always open and free (directly north of the Louvre
on Rue de Rivoli, Mo: Palais Royal-Musée du Louvre). Enter
through a whimsical (locals say tacky) courtyard filled with stubby,
striped columns and playful fountains (with fun, reflective metal
balls). Next, you'll pass into another, perfectly Parisian garden.
This is where in-the-know Parisians come to take a quiet break,
walk their poodles and kids, or enjoy a rendezvous—amid flowers
and surrounded by a serene arcade. Bring a picnic and create your
own quiet break, or have a drink at one of the outdoor cafés at the
courtyard's northern end. This is Paris.

Exiting the courtyard at the side facing away from the Seine
brings you to the Galeries Colbert and Vivienne, attractive examples of shopping arcades from the early 1900s.

▲▲Orangerie Museum (Musée de l'Orangerie)

Step out of the tree-lined, sun-dappled Impressionist painting that
is the Tuileries Garden, and into the Orangerie (oh-rahn-zheh-
ree), a little bijou of
select works by Claude
Monet and his contem-
poraries. Start with the
museum's claim to fame:
Monet's water lilies.
These eight mammoth-
scale paintings are dis-
played exactly as Monet
intended them—surrounding you in oval-shaped rooms—so you
feel as though you're immersed in his garden at Giverny.

Working from his home there, Monet built a special studio with skylights and wheeled easels to accommodate the canvases—1,950 square feet in all. Each canvas features a different
part of the pond, painted from varying angles at distinct times of
day—but the true subject of these works is the play of reflected
light off the surface of the pond. The Monet rooms are considered the first art installation, and the blurry canvases signaled the
abstract art to come.

Downstairs you'll see artists that bridge the Impressionist
and Modernist worlds—Renoir, Cézanne, Utrillo, Matisse, and
Picasso. Together they provide a snapshot of what was hot in the
world of art collecting, circa 1920.

Cost and Hours: €7.50, €5 after 17:00, under 18 free, €14 combo-ticket with Orsay Museum (valid for four days, one visit per sight), covered by Museum Pass; Wed-Mon 9:00-18:00, closed Tue, galleries shut down 15 minutes before closing time; audio-guide-€5, €6 English tours usually offered Mon and Thu at 14:30; located in Tuileries Garden near Place de la Concorde (Mo: Concorde), 15-minute stroll from the Orsay, tel. 01 44 77 80 07, www.musee-orangerie.fr.

▲▲▲Orsay Museum (Musée d'Orsay)

The Musée d'Orsay (mew-zay dor-say) houses French art of the 1800s and early 1900s (specifically, 1848-1914), picking up where the Louvre's art collection leaves off.

For us, that means Impressionism, the art of sun-dappled fields, bright colors, and crowded Parisian cafés. The Orsay houses the best general collection anywhere of Manet, Monet, Renoir, Degas, Van Gogh, Cézanne, and Gauguin.

Cost and Hours: €9, €6.50 Fri-Wed after 16:15 and Thu after 18:00, free on first Sun of month and right when the ticket booth stops selling tickets (Tue-Wed and Fri-Sun at 17:00, Thu at 21:00; they won't let you in much after that), covered by Museum Pass, €14 combo-ticket with Orangerie Museum (valid for four days, one visit per sight); Tue-Sun 9:30-18:00, Thu until 21:45, closed Mon, Impressionist galleries start shutting 45 minutes before closing, last entry one hour before closing (45 minutes before on Thu); crowded on Tue, when Louvre is closed; cafés and restaurant, tel. 01 40 49 48 14, www.musee-orsay.fr.

Getting There: The museum, at 1 Rue de la Légion d'Honneur, sits above the RER-C stop called Musée d'Orsay; the nearest Métro stop is Solférino, three blocks southeast of the Orsay. Bus #69 also stops at the Orsay. From the Louvre, it's a lovely 15-minute walk through the Tuileries Garden and across the pedestrian bridge to the Orsay.

Getting In: As you face the museum from Rue de la Légion d'Honneur (with the river on your left), passholders and ticket-holders enter on the right (Entrance C). Ticket purchasers enter closer to the river (Entrance A).

Tours: Audioguides cost €5. English guided tours usually run daily at 11:30 (€7.50/1.5 hours, none on Sun, may run at other times—inquire when you arrive). Or you can download my free self-guided Orsay **audio tour** (see page 1138).

Background: The Impressionist painters rejected camera-like

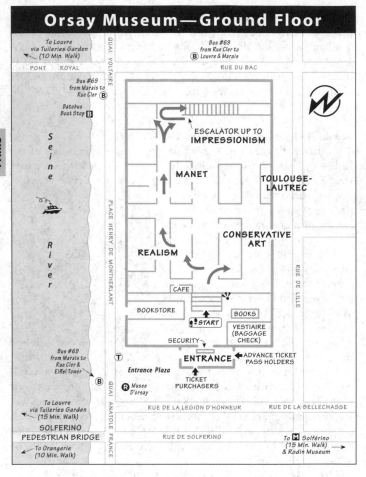

Orsay Museum—Ground Floor

detail for a quick style more suited to capturing the passing moment. Feeling stifled by the rigid rules and stuffy atmosphere of the Academy (the state-funded art school), the Impressionists took as their motto, "Out of the studio, into the open air." They grabbed their berets and scarves and went on excursions to the country, where they set up their easels (and newly invented tubes of premixed paint) on riverbanks and hillsides, or they sketched in cafés and dance halls. Gods, goddesses, nymphs, and fantasy scenes were out; common people and rural landscapes were in.

The quick style and everyday subjects were ridiculed and called childish by the "experts." Rejected by the Salon (where works were exhibited to the buying public), the Impressionists staged their own exhibition in 1874. They brashly took their name from an insult thrown at them by a critic who laughed at one of Monet's "impressions" of a sunrise. During the next decade, they exhibited their own work independently. The public, opposed at first, was slowly won over by the simplicity, the color, and the vibrancy of Impressionist art.

Ə Self-Guided Tour: This former train station, or *gare*, barely escaped the wrecking ball in the 1970s, when the French realized it'd be a great place to exhibit the enormous collections of 19th-century art scattered throughout the city. The ground floor (level 0) houses early 19th-century art, mainly conservative art of the Academy and Salon, plus Realism. On the top floor is the core of the collection—the Impressionist rooms. If you're pressed for time, go directly there. Keep in mind that the collection is always on the move—paintings on loan, in restoration, or displayed in different rooms. The museum updates its website daily with the latest layout (www.musee-orsay.fr).

PARIS

Conservative Art to Realism: In the Orsay's first few rooms, you're surrounded by visions of idealized beauty—nude women in languid poses, Greek mythological figures, and anatomically perfect statues. This was the art adored by French academics and the middle-class *(bourgeois)* public.

Farther along on the ground floor, you'll witness the shift to Realism. **Jean-François Millet's** *The Gleaners* (*Les Glaneuses,* 1867) depicts the poor women who pick up the meager leftovers after a field has already been harvested by the wealthy. This is "Realism" in two senses. It's painted "realistically," not prettified. And it's the "real" world—not the fantasy world of Greek myth, but the harsh life of the working poor.

Alexandre Cabanel's *The Birth of Venus* (*La Naissance de Vénus,* 1863) and **Edouard Manet's** *Olympia* (1863) offer two opposing visions of Venus. Cabanel's Venus is a perfect fantasy, an orgasm of beauty. Manet's nude is a Realist's take on the traditional Venus. Manet doesn't gloss over anything. The pose is classic, but the sharp outlines and harsh, contrasting colors are new and shocking. Manet replaced soft-core porn with hard-core art.

Impressionism: The Impressionist collection is scattered somewhat randomly through rooms 29-36 of the top floor. You'll see Monet hanging next to Renoir, Manet sprinkled among Pissarro, and a few Degas here and a few Cézannes there. Shadows dance and the displays mingle. Where they're hung is a lot like their brushwork...delightfully sloppy.

In **Manet's** *Luncheon on the Grass* (*Le Déjeuner sur l'Herbe,* 1863), a new revolutionary movement is starting to bud—Impressionism. Notice the background: the messy brushwork of trees and leaves, the play of light on the pond, and the light that filters through the trees onto the woman who stoops in the haze. Also note the strong contrast of colors (white skin, black clothes, green grass). This is a true out-of-doors painting, not a studio production.

Edgar Degas blended classical lines with Impressionist color, spontaneity, and everyday subjects from urban Paris. He loved the unposed "snapshot" effect, catching his models off guard. In *The Dance Class* (*La Classe de Danse*, c. 1873-1875), bored, tired dancers scratch their backs restlessly at the end of a long rehearsal. *In a Café*, or *Absinthe* (*Au Café, dit L'Absinthe*, 1876) captures a weary lady of the evening meeting morning with a last, lonely, nail-in-the-coffin drink in the glaring light of a four-in-the-morning café. Degas approaches his dance students, women at work, and café scenes from odd angles that aren't always ideal, but that make the scenes seem more real.

To paint common Parisians living and loving in the afternoon sun, **Pierre-Auguste Renoir** headed for the fields on Butte Montmartre (near the Sacré-Cœur basilica) on Sunday afternoons, when working-class folk would dress up and dance, drink, and eat little crêpes (galettes) till dark. In *Dance at the Moulin de la Galette* (*Bal du Moulin de la Galette*, 1876), the sunlight filtering through the trees creates a kaleidoscope of colors—the 19th-century equivalent of a mirror ball throwing darts of light onto the dancers. Like a photographer who uses a slow shutter speed to show motion, Renoir paints a waltzing blur.

Next, it's the father of Impressionism, **Claude Monet.** Look for paintings from his garden at Giverny and *The Cathedral of Rouen* (*La Cathédrale de Rouen*, 1893), "a series of differing impressions" of the cathedral facade at various times of day and year. In all, he did 30 paintings of the cathedral, and each is unique. The time-lapse series shows the sun passing slowly across the sky, creating different-colored light and shadows.

Post-Impressionism: It was **Paul Cézanne** who brought Impressionism into the 20th century. Compared with the color of Monet, the warmth of Renoir, and Van Gogh's passion, Cézanne's rather impersonal canvases can be difficult to appreciate. Bowls of fruit, landscapes, and a few portraits were Cézanne's passion. Because of his style (not his content), he is often called the first modern painter.

Find his paintings in room 36. In *Landscape* (*Rochers près des Grottes au-dessus de Château-Noir*, 1904), Cézanne uses chunks of green, tan, and blue paint as building blocks to construct this rocky brown cliff. These chunks are like little "cubes" (a style that later influenced the...Cubists). The subjects of Cézanne's *The Card Players* (*Les Joueurs de Cartes*, c. 1890-1895) aren't people—they're studies in color and pattern. The subject matter—two guys playing cards—is less important than the pleasingly balanced pattern they make on the canvas, two sloping forms framing a cylinder (a bottle) in the center. Later, abstract artists would focus solely on shapes and colors.

Like Michelangelo, Beethoven, Rembrandt, Wayne Newton, and a select handful of others, **Vincent van Gogh** put so much of himself into his work that art and life became one. In the Orsay's collection of Van Goghs (level 2), you'll see both the artist's painting style and his life unfold.

Encouraged by his art-dealer brother, Van Gogh moved to Paris, and *voilà!* The color! He met Monet, drank with Paul Gauguin and Henri de Toulouse-Lautrec, and soaked up the Impressionist style. In his *Self-Portrait, Paris* (*Portrait de l'Artiste*, 1887), you can see how he built a bristling brown beard with thick, side-by-side strokes of red, yellow, and green.

The social life of Paris became too much for the solitary Van Gogh, and he moved to southern France. At first, in the glow of the bright spring sunshine, he had a period of incredible creativity and happiness, as he was overwhelmed by the bright colors, landscape vistas, and common people—an Impressionist's dream. But being alone in a strange country began to wear on him. An ugly man, he found it hard to get a date. The close-up perspective of *Van Gogh's Room at Arles* (*La Chambre de van Gogh à Arles*, 1889) makes his tiny rented room look even more cramped.

Van Gogh wavered between happiness and madness, even mutilating his own ear at one point. He despaired of ever being sane enough to continue painting. His *Self-Portrait, St. Rémy* (1889) shows a man engulfed in a confused background of brushstrokes that swirl and rave, setting in motion the waves of the jacket. But in the midst of this rippling sea of mystery floats a still, detached island of a face with probing, questioning, yet wise eyes. Do his troubled eyes know that only a few months on, he will take a pistol and put a bullet through his chest? Vincent van Gone.

Nearby are the paintings of **Paul Gauguin,** who got the travel bug early in childhood and grew up wanting to be a sailor. He traveled to the South Seas in search of the exotic, finally settling on Tahiti. There he found his Garden of Eden. *Arearea,* or *Joyousness* (*Joyeusetés,* 1892) shows native women and a dog. In the "distance" (there's no attempt at traditional 3-D here), a procession goes by with a large pagan idol.

Pointillism, as illustrated by many paintings in the next rooms, brings Impressionism to its logical conclusion. Little dabs of pure colors are placed side by side to blend in the viewer's eye. In works such as *The Circus* (*Le Cirque,* 1891), **Georges Seurat** (1859-1891) used only red, yellow, blue, and green points of paint to create a mosaic of colors that shimmers at a distance, capturing the wonder of the dawn of electric light.

The Rest of the Orsay: The open-air mezzanine of level 2 is lined with statues. Stroll the mezzanine, enjoying the works of great French sculptors, including **Auguste Rodin,** who combined classical solidity with Impressionist surfaces. Look for *The Walking Man* (*L'Homme Qui Marche,* c. 1900) by room 71. Like this statue, Rodin had one foot in the past, while the other was stepping into the future. With no mouth or hands, the subject speaks with his body. The rough, "unfinished" surface reflects light in the same way the rough Impressionist brushwork does, making the statue come alive, never quite at rest in the viewer's eye. Rodin's powerful, haunting works are a good place to end this tour. With a stable base of 19th-century stone, he launched art into the 20th century.

Eiffel Tower Area
▲▲▲Eiffel Tower (La Tour Eiffel)
It's crowded, expensive, and there are probably better views in Paris, but visiting this 1,000-foot-tall ornament is worth the trouble. Visitors to Paris may find *Mona Lisa* to be less than expected, but the Eiffel Tower rarely disappoints, even in an era of skyscrapers.

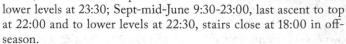

Cost: €14 for an elevator ride all the way to the top, €8.50 if you're only going up to the two lower levels, not covered by Museum Pass; save some time in line by climbing the stairs to the first and second levels for €5 (€3.50 if you're under 25); once inside the tower, you can buy your way to the top with no penalty—ticket booths and machines on the first and second levels sell supplements for €5.50.

Hours: Daily mid-June-Aug 9:00-24:00, last ascent to top at 23:00 and to lower levels at 23:30; Sept-mid-June 9:30-23:00, last ascent to top at 22:00 and to lower levels at 22:30, stairs close at 18:00 in off-season.

Reservations: Frankly, you'd be crazy to show up without a reservation. At www.tour-eiffel.fr, you can book an entry time and skip the initial line (the longest)—at no extra cost. Book well in advance, as soon as you know when you'll be in Paris. Just pay online with a credit card and print your own ticket. When buying tickets online, make sure you select "Lift entrance ticket with access to the summit" in order to go all the way to the top. For "Type of ticket," it doesn't really matter whether you pick "Group" or "Individual"; a "Group" ticket just gives you one piece of paper covering everyone in your party. You must enter a mobile phone number for identification purposes, so if you don't have one, make one up—and jot it down so you won't forget it (French mobile

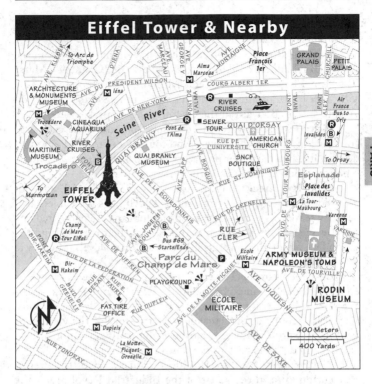

Eiffel Tower & Nearby

phone numbers begin with 06 or 07 and have 10 digits). Arrive at the tower 10 minutes before your entry time and look for either of the two entrances marked *Visiteurs avec Reservation (Visitors with Reservation)*, where attendants scan your ticket and put you on the first available elevator. Alternatively, Classic Walks may have tickets with reservations (see page 79).

When to Go: For the best of all worlds, arrive with enough light to see the views, then stay as it gets dark to see the lights. The views are grand whether you ascend or not. At the top of the hour, a five-minute display features thousands of sparkling lights (best viewed from Place du Trocadéro or the grassy park below).

Avoiding Lines: Crowds overwhelm this place much of the year, with one- to two-hour waits to get in (unless it's rainy, when lines can evaporate). Weekends and holidays are worst, but prepare for ridiculous crowds almost any time. The best solution is to make an online reservation (see above) and to take the stairs down (from first or second levels). If you don't have a reservation, go early; get in line 30 minutes before the tower opens. Going later is the next-best bet (after 19:00 May-Aug, after 17:00 off-season, a bit earlier in winter as it gets dark by 17:00). When you buy tickets, all members of your party must be with you. You can bypass some (but not all) lines if you have a reservation at either of the tower's view restaurants or hike the stairs.

Getting There: The tower is about a 10-minute walk from the Métro (Bir-Hakeim or Trocadéro stops) or train (Champ de Mars-Tour Eiffel RER stop). The Ecole Militaire Métro stop in the Rue Cler area is 20 minutes away. Buses #69 and #87 stop nearby on Avenue Joseph Bouvard in the Champ de Mars park.

Pickpockets: Beware. Street thieves plunder awestruck visitors gawking below the tower. And tourists in crowded elevators are like fish in a barrel for predatory pickpockets. *En garde.* There's a police station at the Jules Verne pillar.

Security Check: Bags larger than 19" × 8" × 12" are not allowed, but there is no baggage check. All bags are subject to a security search. No knives, glass bottles, or cans are permitted.

Services: Free WCs are at the base of the tower, behind the east pillar. Inside the tower itself, WCs are on all levels, but they're small, with long lines.

Best Views of the Tower: The best place to view the tower is from Place du Trocadéro to the north. It's a 10-minute walk across the river, a happening scene at night, and especially fun for kids. Consider arriving at the Trocadéro Métro stop for the view, then walking toward the tower. Another delightful viewpoint is from the Champ de Mars park to the south.

Background: Built on the 100th anniversary of the French Revolution (and in the spirit of the Industrial Revolution), the tower was the centerpiece of a World Expo designed simply to show off what people could build in 1889. Bridge-builder Gustave Eiffel (1832-1923) won the contest to construct the fair's centerpiece by beating out rival proposals such as a giant guillotine. To a generation hooked on technology, the tower was the marvel of the age, a symbol of progress and human ingenuity. Not all were so impressed, however; many found it a monstrosity. The writer Guy de Maupassant (1850-1893) routinely ate lunch in the tower just so he wouldn't have to look at it.

Visiting the Tower: Delicate and graceful when seen from afar, the Eiffel Tower is massive—even a bit scary—close up. You don't appreciate its size until you walk toward it; like a mountain, it seems so close but takes forever to reach. Despite the tower's 7,300 tons of metal and 60 tons of paint, it is so well-engineered that it weighs no more per square inch at its base than a linebacker on tiptoes.

There are three observation platforms, at roughly 200, 400, and 900 feet. To get to the top, you'll wait in line to ride an elevator to the second level. A separate elevator—with another line—shuttles between the second level and the top. (Note: Whether you have a ticket for the top or just for the second level, elevators going up do not stop at the first level. You can see the first level on the way back down, but not all elevators descending from the second level stop at the first level—ask before boarding.) Although being on the windy top of the Eiffel Tower is a thrill you'll never forget, the view is better from the second level, where you can actually see Paris' monuments.

The stairs—yes, you can walk up to the first and second levels—are next to the entrance to the pricey Jules Verne restaurant. As you ascend through the metal beams, imagine being a worker, perched high above nothing, riveting this thing together.

The **top level,** called *le sommet,* is tiny. (It can close temporarily without warning when it reaches capacity or in windy conditions.) All you'll find here are wind and grand, sweeping views. The city lies before you (pick out sights with the help of the panoramic maps). On a good day, you can see for 40 miles.

The **second level** has the best views because you're closer to the sights, and the monuments are more recognizable. (While the best views are up the short stairway, on the platform without the wire-cage barriers, at busy times much of that zone is taken up by people waiting for the elevator to the top.) This level has souvenir shops, public telephones to call home, and a small stand-up café. While you'll save no money, consider taking the elevator up and the stairs down (5 minutes from second level to first, 5 minutes more to ground) for good exercise and views.

The **first level** has more great views, all well-described by the tower's panoramic displays. There are a number of photo exhibits on the tower's history, WCs, a conference hall (closed to tourists), an ATM, and souvenirs. A small café sells pizza and sandwiches (outdoor tables in summer). This level also has two fine restaurants run by famous French chef Alain Ducasse: 58 Tour Eiffel (listed on page 190) has more accessible prices than the Jules Verne Restaurant (€90 weekday lunch *menu,* €170-220 weekend lunch *menus,* €220 dinner *menu,* reserve 2-3 months in advance, tel. 01 45 55 61 44, www.lejulesverne-paris.com). In winter, part of the first level is set up for winter activities (most recently as an ice-skating rink). Climb the stairs to Cineiffel for a small gallery and theater. A tired eight-minute video that shows continuously features clips of the tower's construction, its paint job, its place in pop culture, and the millennium fireworks.

After Your Visit: Descend back to earth. From here, consider catching the Bateaux Parisiens boat for a Seine cruise (see page 76) or visiting one of the following nearby sights: the Quai Branly Museum (page 114), Rue Cler market street, Army Museum and Napoleon's Tomb (page 115), or Rodin Museum (page 116).

For a final peek at the tower, stroll across the river to Place du Trocadéro or to the end of the Champ de Mars and look back for great views. However impressive it may be by day, the tower is an awesome thing to see at twilight, when it becomes engorged with light, and virile Paris lies back and lets night be on top. When darkness fully envelops the city, the tower seems to climax with a spectacular light show at the top of each hour...for five minutes.

Near the Eiffel Tower

▲**Architecture and Monuments Museum (Cité de l'Architecture et du Patrimoine)**—This museum, on the east side of Place du Trocadéro, takes you through 1,000 years of French architecture, brilliantly displaying casts and models of some of France's most cherished monuments from the 11th to 21st centuries. Gaze into the eyes of medieval statues and wander under doorways, tympanums, and arches from the abbey of Cluny, Chartres Cathedral, Château de Chambord, and much more. You'll see how colorfully painted the chapels were in Romanesque churches and discover a vast array of models from modern projects, along with thought-provoking designs for low-income housing. The views from the upper rooms to the Eiffel Tower are sensational, as are those from the terrace of the on-site café, Café Carlu.

Cost and Hours: €8, covered by Museum Pass, audio-guide-€3; Wed-Mon 11:00-19:00, Thu until 21:00, closed Tue; excellent English explanations, great view café (reasonable prices, open same hours as museum and does not require entry into the museum), 1 Place du Trocadéro, Mo: Trocadéro, RER: Champ de Mars-Tour Eiffel, tel. 01 58 51 52 00, www.citechaillot.fr.

Quai Branly Museum (Museé du Quai Branly)—This is the best collection I've seen anywhere of so-called Primitive Art from Africa, Polynesia, Asia, and America. It's presented in a wild, organic, and strikingly modern building that caused a stir in Paris when it opened in 2006. Masks, statuettes, musical instruments, clothes, voodoo dolls, and a variety of temporary exhibitions and activities are artfully presented and exquisitely lit. It's not, however, accompanied by much printed English information—to really appreciate the exhibit, you need to rent the audioguide. Even if you skip the museum, drop by its peaceful garden café for fine Eiffel Tower views (closes 30 minutes before museum) and enjoy the intriguing gardens. The pedestrian bridge that crosses the river and runs up to the museum has terrific views of the Eiffel Tower.

Cost and Hours: €8.50, free on first Sun of the month, covered by Museum Pass, audioguide-€5; museum—Tue-Sun 11:00-19:00, Thu-Sat until 21:00, closed Mon, ticket office closes one hour before closing; gardens—Tue-Sun 9:15-19:30, Thu-Sat until 21:15, closed Mon; 37 Quai Branly, 10-minute walk east (upriver) of Eiffel Tower, along the river (RER: Champ de Mars-Tour Eiffel or Pont de l'Alma), tel. 01 56 61 70 00, www.quaibranly.fr.

National Maritime Museum (Musée National de la Marine)—This extensive museum houses an amazing collection of ship models, submarines, torpedoes, cannonballs, *beaucoup* bowsprits, and naval you-name-it, including a small boat made for Napoleon. Don't miss the model and story of how the obelisk on Place de la Concorde was delivered from Egypt to Paris entirely by waterways (behind stairs leading down to special exhibits space). Take advantage of the audioguide that explains key exhibits and adds important context to your visit. Kids love it, too.

Cost and Hours: €7, 26 and under free, includes audioguide, covered by Museum Pass; Mon and Wed-Fri 11:00-18:00, Sat-Sun 11:00-19:00, closed Tue; on left side of Place du Trocadéro with your back to Eiffel Tower, tel. 01 53 65 69 69, www.musee-marine.fr.

▲**Paris Sewer Tour (Les Egouts de Paris)**—Discover what happens after you flush. This quick, interesting, and slightly stinky visit (a perfumed hanky helps) takes you along a few hundred yards of water tunnels in the world's first underground sewer system. Pick up the helpful English self-guided tour, then drop down into Jean Valjean's world of tunnels, rats, and manhole covers. (Victor Hugo was friends with the sewer inspector when he wrote *Les Misérables.*) You'll pass well-organized displays with helpful English information explaining the history of water distribution in Paris, from Roman times to the present. The evolution of this amazing network of sewers is surprisingly fascinating. More than 1,500 miles of tunnels carry 317 million gallons of water daily through this underworld. It's the world's longest sewer system—so long, they say, that if it was laid out straight, it would stretch from Paris all the way to Istanbul.

In the gift shop, you can ask about the slideshow and occasional tours in English. The WCs are just beyond the gift shop.

Cost and Hours: €4.30, covered by Museum Pass, May-Sept Sat-Wed 11:00-17:00, Oct-April Sat-Wed 11:00-16:00, closed Thu-Fri, located where Pont de l'Alma greets the Left Bank—on the right side of the bridge as you face the river, Mo: Alma-Marceau, RER: Pont de l'Alma, tel. 01 53 68 27 81.

▲▲**Army Museum and Napoleon's Tomb (Musée de l'Armée)**—The Hôtel des Invalides, a former veterans' hospital topped by a golden dome, houses Napoleon's over-the-top-ornate tomb, as well as Europe's greatest military museum. Visiting the Army Museum's different sections, you can watch the art of war unfold from stone axes to Axis powers.

At the center of the complex, Napoleon Bonaparte lies majestically dead inside several coffins under a grand dome—a goosebumping pilgrimage for historians. Your visit continues through an impressive range of museums filled with medieval armor, cannons and muskets, Louis XIV-era uniforms and weapons, and Napoleon's horse—stuffed and mounted.

The best section is dedicated to the two World Wars. Walk chronologically through displays on the trench warfare of World War I, the victory parades, France's horrendous loss of life, and the humiliating Treaty of Versailles that led to World War II. The WWII rooms use black-and-white photos, maps, videos, and a few artifacts to trace Hitler's rise, the Blitzkrieg that overran France, America's entry into the war, D-Day, concentration camps, the atomic bomb, and the eventual Allied victory. There's special insight into France's role (the French Resistance) and how it was Charles de Gaulle who actually won the war.

Cost and Hours: €9, €7 after 17:00, free for military personnel in uniform, free for kids but they must wait in line for ticket, covered by Museum Pass, audioguide-€6; museum—daily April-Sept 10:00-18:00, may be open Tue until 21:00, Oct-March 10:00-17:00, closed first Mon of month year-round; tomb—daily April-June and Sept 10:00-18:00, may be open Tue until 21:00; July-Aug 10:00-19:00, may be open Tue until 21:00; Oct-March 10:00-17:00, closed first Mon of month Sept-May, last tickets sold 30 minutes before closing, cafeteria, tel. 01 44 42 38 77 or 08 10 11 33 99, www.invalides.org.

Getting There: The Hôtel des Invalides is at 129 Rue de Grenelle; Mo: La Tour Maubourg, Varenne, or Invalides. Bus #69 from the Marais and Rue Cler area also takes you there, or it's a 10-minute walk from Rue Cler.

▲▲Rodin Museum (Musée Rodin)—This user-friendly museum is filled with passionate works by the greatest sculptor since Michelangelo. Note that the museum  is undergoing a major renovation until 2014. Expect some statues to be moved around and some rooms to be closed altogether. The gardens remain open. To compensate for the closures, the museum has added a few rarely displayed pieces to its exhibits.

Auguste Rodin (1840-1917) sculpted human figures on an epic scale, revealing through their bodies his deepest thoughts and feelings. Like many of Michelangelo's unfinished works, Rodin's statues rise from the raw stone around them, driven by the life force. With missing limbs and scarred skin, these are prefab classics, making ugliness noble. Rodin's people are always moving restlessly. Even the famous *Thinker* is moving. While he's plopped down solidly, his mind is a million miles away.

Rodin worked with many materials—he chiseled marble (though not often), modeled clay, cast bronze, worked plaster, painted on canvas, and sketched on paper. He often created different versions of the same subject in different media.

Rodin lived and worked in this mansion, renting rooms alongside Henri Matisse, the poet Rainer Maria Rilke (Rodin's secretary), and the dancer Isadora Duncan. The well-displayed exhibits trace Rodin's artistic development, explain how his bronze statues were cast, and show some of the studies he created to work up to his masterpiece (the unfinished *Gates of Hell*). Learn about Rodin's tumultuous relationship with his apprentice and lover, Camille Claudel. Mull over what makes his sculptures some of the most evocative since the Renaissance. And stroll the gardens, packed with many of his greatest works (including *The Thinker, Balzac,* the *Burghers of Calais,* and the *Gates of Hell*). The beautiful gardens are ideal for artistic reflection.

Cost and Hours: €6, under 18 free, free on first Sun of the month, €1 for garden only (possibly Paris' best deal, as many works are on display there), both museum and garden covered by Museum Pass, audioguide-€4; Tue-Sun 10:00-17:45, Wed until 20:45, closed Mon; gardens close at 18:00, Oct-March at 17:00; last entry 30 minutes before closing, mandatory baggage check, self-service café in garden, near the Army Museum and Napoleon's Tomb at 79 Rue de Varenne, Mo: Varenne, tel. 01 44 18 61 10, www.musee-rodin.fr.

▲▲Marmottan Museum (Musée Marmottan Monet)— This intimate, less-touristed mansion on the southwest fringe of urban Paris has the best collection of works by the father of Impressionism, Claude Monet (1840-1926). Fiercely independent and dedicated to his craft, Monet gave courage to the other Impressionists in the face of harsh criticism.

Though the museum is not arranged chronologically, you can trace his life. You'll see black-and-white sketches from his youth, his discovery of open-air painting, and the canvas—*Impression: Sunrise*—that gave Impressionism its name. There are portraits of his wives and kids, and his well-known "series" paintings (done at different times of day) of London, Gare St. Lazare, and the Cathedral of Rouen. The museum's highlight is scenes from his garden at Giverny—the rose trellis, the Japanese bridge, and the larger-than-life water lilies.

In addition, the Marmottan features a world-class collection of works by Berthe Morisot and other Impressionists; an eclectic collection of non-Monet objects (furniture, illuminated manuscript drawings); and temporary exhibits.

Cost and Hours: €10, not covered by Museum Pass, audioguide-€3, Tue–Sun 10:00-18:00, Thu until 20:00, closed Mon, last entry 30 minutes before closing, 2 Rue Louis-Boilly, Mo: La Muette, tel. 01 44 96 50 33, www.marmottan.com.

Left Bank

Opposite Notre-Dame, on the left bank of the Seine, is the Latin Quarter. (For more information on this neighborhood, see my self-guided walk of historic Paris, earlier.)

▲▲Cluny Museum (Musée National du Moyen Age)—This treasure trove of Middle Ages (Moyen Age) art fills old Roman baths, offering close-up looks at stained glass, Notre-Dame carvings, fine goldsmithing and jewelry, and rooms of tapestries. The highlights are several original stained-glass windows from Sainte-Chapelle and the exquisite Lady and the Unicorn series of six tapestries: A delicate, as-medieval-as-can-be noble lady introduces a delighted unicorn to the senses of taste, hearing, sight, smell, and touch. This museum helps put the Middle Ages in perspective, reflecting a time when Europe was awakening from a thousand-year slumber and Paris was emerging on the world stage. Trade  was booming, people actually owned chairs, and the Renaissance was moving in like a warm front from Italy.

Cost and Hours: €8, free on first Sun of month, covered by Museum Pass, ticket includes audioguide though passholders must pay €1; Wed–Mon 9:15-17:45, closed Tue, ticket office closes at 17:15; near corner of Boulevards St. Michel and St. Germain at 6 Place Paul Painlevé; Mo: Cluny-La Sorbonne, St. Michel, or Odéon; tel. 01 53 73 78 16, www.musee-moyenage.fr.

St. Germain-des-Prés—A church was first built on this site in A.D. 558. The church you see today was constructed in 1163 and is all that's left of a once sprawling and influential monastery. The colorful interior reminds us that medieval churches were originally painted in bright colors. The surrounding area hops at night with venerable cafés, fire-eaters, mimes, and scads of artists.

Cost and Hours: Free, daily 8:00-20:00, Mo: St. Germain-des-Prés.

▲St. Sulpice Church—Since it was featured in *The Da Vinci Code,* this grand church has become a trendy stop for the book's many fans. But the real reason to visit is to see and hear its intimately accessible organ. For pipe-organ enthusiasts, this is one

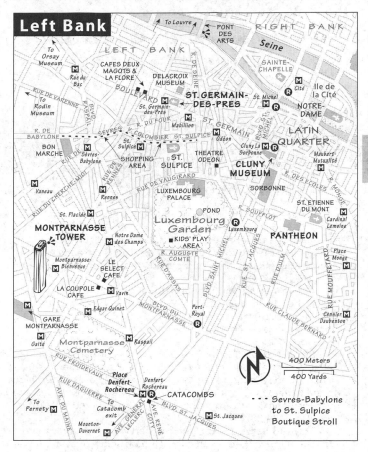

Left Bank

To Louvre · PONT DES ARTS · RIGHT BANK · Seine · LEFT BANK · To Orsay Museum · SAINTE-CHAPELLE · Rue du Bac · CAFES DEUX MAGOTS & LA FLORE · BOULEVARD · DELACROIX MUSEUM · R. DE SEINE · St. Michel · M Cité · Ile de la Cité · RUE DE VARENNE · To Rodin Museum · BLVD RASPAIL · ST. GERMAIN-DES-PRES · St. Germain-des-Prés · M · NOTRE-DAME · R. DE BABYLONE · R. DU FOUR · Mabillon · ST. GERMAIN · BLVD. ST. · LATIN QUARTER · SEVRES · COLOMBIER · ST. SULPICE · Odéon · Cluny La Sorbonne · M · BON MARCHE · St. Sulpice · Sèvres-Babylone · SHOPPING AREA · ST. SULPICE · THEATRE ODEON · CLUNY MUSEUM · Maubert-Mutualité · RUE DE RENNES · RUE DE VAUGIRARD · SORBONNE · R. DES ECOLES · RUE MONGE · Vaneau · M · Rennes · LUXEMBOURG PALACE · POND · R. SOUFFLOT · ST. ETIENNE DU MONT · RUE DU CHERCHE-MIDI · St. Placide · M · Luxembourg Garden · M Luxembourg · PANTHEON · Cardinal Lemoine · MONTPARNASSE TOWER · Notre Dame des Champs · KIDS' PLAY AREA · BLVD. SAINT MICHEL · RUE ST. JACQUES · Place Monge · Montparnasse-Bienvenue · M · R. AUGUSTE COMTE · RUE D'ASSAS · RUE D'ULM · RUE MOUFFETARD · M · LE SELECT CAFE · Vavin · LA COUPOLE CAFE · M · BLVD. DU MONTPARNASSE · Port-Royal · RUE CLAUDE BERNARD · GARE MONTPARNASSE · Edgar Quinet · M · Censier Daubenton · M · Gaîté · Montparnasse Cemetery · Raspail · M · 400 Meters · 400 Yards · RUE FROIDEVAUX · Place Denfert-Rochereau · Denfert-Rochereau · CATACOMBS · RUE DAGUERRE · AVE. DU MAINE · To Catacomb exit · BLVD. ST. JACQUES · St. Jacques · M · Sevres-Babylone to St. Sulpice Boutique Stroll · To Pernety · M · AVE. GENERAL LECLERC · AVE. RENE COTY · Mounton-Duvernet

N

of Europe's great musical treats. The Grand Orgue at St. Sulpice Church has a rich history, with a succession of 12 world-class organists—including Charles-Marie Widor and Marcel Dupré—

that goes back 300 years. Widor started the tradition of opening the loft to visitors after the Sunday morning service. Daniel Roth (or his understudy) continues to welcome guests in three languages while playing five keyboards.

Cost and Hours: Free, church open daily 7:30-19:30, Mo: St. Sulpice or Mabillon. See www.stsulpice.com for special concerts.

Sunday Organ Visits: The 10:30-11:30 Sunday Mass (come appropriately dressed) is followed by a high-powered 25-minute

PARIS

Best Views over the City of Light

Your trip to Paris is played out in the streets, but the brilliance of the City of Light can only be fully appreciated by rising above it all. Invest time to marvel at all the man-made beauty, seen best in the early morning or around sunset. Many of the viewpoints I've listed are free or covered by the Museum Pass; otherwise, expect to pay €8-14. Here are some prime locations for soaking in the views:

Eiffel Tower: It's hard to find a grander view of Paris than from the tower's second level. Go around sunset and stay after dark to see the tower illuminated; or go in the early morning to avoid the midday haze and crowds (not covered by Museum Pass, see page 110).

Arc de Triomphe: Without a doubt, this is the perfect place to see the glamorous Champs-Elysées (if you can manage the 284 steps). It's great during the day, but even greater at night, when the boulevard positively glitters (covered by Museum Pass, see page 128).

Notre-Dame's Tower: This viewpoint is brilliant—it couldn't be more central—but it requires climbing 400 steps and is usually crowded with long lines (try to arrive early or late). Up high on the tower, you'll get an unobstructed view of gargoyles, the river, the Latin Quarter, and the Ile de la Cité (covered by Museum Pass, see page 82).

Steps of Sacré-Cœur: Join the party on Paris' only hilltop. Walk uphill or take the funicular (if it's running), then hunker down on Sacré-Cœur's steps to enjoy the sunset and territorial views over Paris. Stay in Montmartre for dinner, then see the view

recital. Then, at noon, the small, unmarked door is opened (left of entry as you face the rear). Visitors scamper like 16th notes up spiral stairs, past the 19th-century StairMasters that five men once pumped to fill the bellows, into a world of 7,000 pipes. You can see the organ and visit with Daniel (or his substitute, who might not speak English). Space is tight—only 15 people are allowed in at a time, and only a few can gather around the organist at once—you need to be quick to allow others a chance to meet him. You'll likely have about 20 minutes to kill before watching the master play during the next Mass (church views are great, and there's a small lounge to wait in); you can leave at any time. If you're late or rushed, show up around 12:30 and wait at the little door (last entry again after dark (free, see page 139).

Galeries Lafayette or Printemps: Take the elevator or escalator to the top floor of either department store (they sit side by side) for a stunning overlook of the old Opéra district (free, see page 143).

Montparnasse Tower: The top of this solitary skyscraper has some of the best views in Paris, though they're disappointing after dark. Zip up 56 floors on the elevator, then walk to the rooftop (not covered by Museum Pass, see page 123).

Pompidou Center: Take the escalator up and admire the beautiful cityscape along with the exciting modern art. There may be better views over Paris, but this is the best one from a museum (covered by Museum Pass, see page 136).

Place du Trocadéro and Café Carlu: This is *the* place to see the Eiffel Tower. Come for a look at Monsieur Eiffel's festive creation day or night (when the tower is lit up). Consider starting or ending your Eiffel Tower visit here (free, see page 114) and having a drink or snack at Café Carlu. With its privileged spot on Place du Trocadéro, this café offers dramatic views of the Eiffel Tower from its terrace (Wed-Mon 11:00-19:00, closed Tue, in Architecture and Monuments Museum but open to public).

Arab World Institute (Institut du Monde Arabe): This building near Ile St. Louis has free views from its terrific roof terrace (Tue-Sun 10:00-18:00, closed Mon, 1 Rue des Fossés Saint-Bernard, Place Mohammed V, Mo: Jussieu, www.imarabe.org).

Panthéon: Climb to the top for great Paris views (must be escorted by guide, covered by Museum Pass, may be closed for renovation in 2013, see page 122).

Bar at Hôtel Concorde-Lafayette: This otherwise unappealing hotel is noteworthy for its 33rd-floor bar, where you can sip wine and enjoy a stunning Parisian panorama (free elevator but pricey drinks, bar open daily 17:00-1:30 in the morning, tel. 01 40 68 50 68, www.concorde-lafayette.com).

is at 13:00). As someone leaves, you can slip in, climb up, and catch the rest of the performance.

Nearby: Tempting boutiques surround the church, and Luxembourg Garden is nearby.

Delacroix Museum (Musée National Eugène Delacroix)— This museum for Eugène Delacroix (1798-1863) was once his home and studio. A friend of bohemian artistic greats—including George Sand and Frédéric Chopin—Delacroix is most famous for the flag-waving painting *Liberty Leading the People*, which is displayed at the Louvre, not here.

Cost and Hours: €5, free on first Sun of the month, covered by Museum Pass, Wed-Mon 9:30-17:00, Sat-Sun until 17:30 in summer, closed Tue, last entry 30 minutes before closing, 6 Rue de Furstenberg, Mo: St. Germain-des-Prés, tel. 01 44 41 86 50, www .musee-delacroix.fr.

▲Luxembourg Garden (Jardin du Luxembourg)—Paris' most beautiful, interesting, and enjoyable garden/park/recreational area, le Jardin du Luxembourg, is a great place to watch Parisians at rest and play. This 60-acre garden, dotted with fountains and statues, is the property of the French Senate, which meets here in the Luxembourg Palace.

Luxembourg Garden has special rules governing its use (for example, where cards can be played, where dogs can be walked, where joggers can run, and when and where music can be played). The brilliant flower beds are changed three times a year, and the boxed trees are brought out of the *orangerie* in May. Children enjoy the rentable toy sailboats. The park hosts marionette shows several times weekly (Les Guignols, Wed 15:30, Sat-Sun 11:00 and 15:30). Pony rides are available from April through October. (Meanwhile, the French CIA plots espionage in their underground offices beneath the park.)

Challenge the card and chess players to a game (near the tennis courts), or find a free chair near the main pond and take a well-deserved break.

Cost and Hours: Free, daily dawn until dusk, Mo: Odéon, RER: Luxembourg.

Nearby: The grand Neoclassical-domed Panthéon, now a mausoleum housing the tombs of great French notables, is three blocks away (see below).

Other Parks: If you enjoy Luxembourg Garden and want to see more green spaces, you could visit the more elegant **Parc Monceau** (Mo: Monceau), the colorful **Jardin des Plantes** (Mo: Jussieu or Gare d'Austerlitz, RER: Gare d'Austerlitz), or the hilly and bigger **Parc des Buttes-Chaumont** (Mo: Buttes-Chaumont).

▲Panthéon—This state-capitol-style Neoclassical monument celebrates France's illustrious history and people, balances Foucault's pendulum, and is the final home of many French VIPs.

Cost and Hours: €8.50, under 18 free, covered by Museum Pass, daily 10:00-18:30 in summer, until 18:00 in winter, last entry 45 minutes before closing, Mo: Cardinal Lemoine. Ask about occasional English tours or call ahead for schedule; tel. 01 44 32 18 00, www.pantheon.monuments-nationaux.fr.

Visiting the Panthéon: Inside the vast building (360' by 280' by 270') are monuments tracing the celebrated struggles of

the French people: a beheaded St. Denis (painting on left wall of nave), St. Geneviève saving the fledgling city from Attila the Hun, and scenes of Joan of Arc (left transept).

Foucault's pendulum swings gracefully at the end of a 220-foot cable suspended from the towering dome. It was here in 1851 that the scientist Léon Foucault first demonstrated the rotation of the earth. Stand a few minutes and watch the pendulum's arc (appear to) shift as you and the earth rotate beneath it.

Stairs in the back lead down to the crypt, where a pantheon of greats is buried. Rousseau is along the right wall as you enter, Voltaire faces him across the hall. Also buried here are scientist Marie Curie, Victor Hugo *(Les Misérables, The Hunchback of Notre-Dame)*, Alexandre Dumas *(The Three Musketeers, The Count of Monte Cristo)*, and Louis Braille, who invented the script for the blind.

Dome Climb: For fine views, climb 206 steps to the dome gallery. Visits are by escort only and leave every hour until 17:30 from the bookshop near the entry—see schedule as you go in. Note that in 2013, dome access may be closed for renovation.

Montparnasse Tower (La Tour Montparnasse)—This sadly out-of-place 59-story superscraper has one virtue: Its sensational

views are cheaper and far easier to access than the Eiffel Tower's. Come early in the day for clearest skies and be treated to views from a comfortable interior and from up on the rooftop. (Some say it's the very best view in Paris, as you can see the Eiffel Tower clearly... and you can't see the Montparnasse Tower at all.)

Exit the elevator at the 56th floor, passing the eager photographer (they'll superimpose your group's image with the view) to views of *tout Paris*. Here you can have a drink or a light lunch (OK prices), peruse the gift shop, or use the good WCs. Take time to explore every corner of the floor. Dioramas identify highlights of the star-studded vista. From here it's easy to admire Georges-Eugène Haussmann's grand-boulevard scheme. Notice the lush courtyards hiding behind grand street fronts. The exhibits change often, but you'll likely see historic photos and enjoy a plush little theater playing a continuous video.

For more views, climb to the open terrace on the 59th floor to enjoy the surreal scene of a lonely man in a box and a helipad surrounded by the window-cleaner track. Here, 690 feet above Paris, you can scan the city with the wind in your hair.

Cost and Hours: €13, not covered by Museum Pass; April-Sept daily 9:30-23:30; Oct-March Sun-Thu 9:30-22:30, Fri-Sat 9:30-23:00; last entry 30 minutes before closing, sunset is great, but views are disappointing after dark, entrance on Rue de l'Arrivée, Mo: Montparnasse-Bienvenüe—from the Métro stay inside the station and follow the signs for *La Tour*; tel. 01 45 38 52 56, www.tourmontparnasse56.com.

Sightseeing Tip: The tower is an efficient stop when combined with a day trip to Chartres, which begins at the Montparnasse train station (see the next chapter for details).

▲**Catacombs**—Descend 60 feet below the street and walk a one-mile (one-hour) route through tunnels containing the anonymous bones of six million permanent Parisians.

In 1786, health-conscious Parisians looking to relieve congestion and improve the city's sanitary conditions emptied the church cemeteries and moved the bones here, to former limestone quarries. For decades, priests led ceremonial processions of black-veiled, bone-laden carts into the quarries, where the bones were stacked in piles five feet high and as much as 80 feet deep. Ignore the sign announcing, "Halt, this is the empire of the dead," and walk through passageways of skull-studded tibiae, past more cheery signs: "Happy is he who is forever faced with the hour of his death and prepares himself for the end every day." You emerge far from where you entered, with white-limestone-covered toes, telling everyone you've been underground gawking at bones. Note to wannabe Hamlets: An attendant checks your bag at the exit for stolen souvenirs.

Cost and Hours: €8, not covered by Museum Pass, Tue-Sun 10:00-17:00, closed Mon, ticket booth closes at 16:00; tel. 01 43 22 47 63, www.catacombes-de-paris.fr.

Warning: Lines are long (figure an hour wait) and hard to avoid. Arrive no later than 14:30 or risk not getting in.

Getting There: 1 Place Denfert-Rochereau. Take the Métro to Denfert-Rochereau, then find the lion in the big traffic circle; if he looked left rather than right, he'd stare right at the green entrance to the Catacombs.

After Your Visit: You'll exit at 36 Rue Rémy Dumoncel, far from where you started. Turn right out of the exit and walk to Avenue du Général Leclerc, where you'll be equidistant from Métro stops Alésia (walk left) and Mouton Duvernet (walk right).

Champs-Elysées and Nearby

▲▲▲**Champs-Elysées**—This famous boulevard is Paris' backbone, with its greatest concentration of traffic. From the Arc de

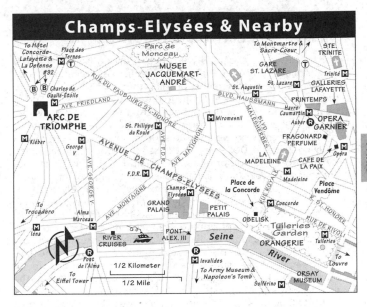

Champs-Elysées & Nearby

To Hôtel
Concorde-
Lafayette &
La Defense
#92

Place des
Ternes

Parc de
Monceau

MUSÉE
JACQUEMART-
ANDRÉ

To Montmartre &
Sacre-Coeur

STE.
TRINITE

GARE
ST. LAZARE

Trinité

Charles de
Gaulle-Étoile

St. Augustin

St. Lazare

GALLERIES
LAFAYETTE

AVE. FRIEDLAND

RUE DU FAUBOURG ST-HONORE

BLVD. HAUSSMANN

Havre-
Caumartin

PRINTEMPS

ARC DE
TRIOMPHE

Miromesnil

BLVD
MALESHERBES

Auber

OPERA
GARNIER

Kléber

St. Philippe
du Roule

FRAGONARD
PERFUME

Opéra

George
V

AVENUE DE CHAMPS-ELYSÉES

AVE. MATIGNON

LA
MADELEINE

CAFÉ DE
LA PAIX

AVE. F.D.R.

Madeleine

Place
Vendôme

F.D.R.

Trocadero

Alma
Marceau

AVE. MONTAIGNE

AVE. GEORGE V

Champs-
Elysées

GRAND
PALAIS

Place de
la Concorde

RUE ROYALE

R. ST. HONORE

PETIT
PALAIS

Concorde

RUE DE RIVOLI

Iéna

RIVER
CRUISES

PONT
ALEX. III

OBELISK

Seine

Tuileries
Garden

To
Louvre

ORANGERIE

Tuileries

Pont
de l'Alma

1/2 Kilometer

River

To
Eiffel Tower

1/2 Mile

Invalides

To Army Museum &
Napoleon's Tomb

ORSAY
MUSEUM

Solférino

PARIS

Triomphe down Avenue des Champs-Elysées, all of France seems to converge on Place de la Concorde, the city's largest square. And though the Champs-Elysées has become as international as it is Parisian, a walk here is still a must.

Background: In 1667, Louis XIV opened the first section of the street as a short extension of the Tuileries Garden. This year is considered the birth of Paris as a grand city. The Champs-Elysées soon became *the* place to cruise in your carriage. (It still is today; traffic can be gridlocked even at midnight.) One hundred years later, the café scene arrived. From the 1920s until the 1960s, this boulevard was pure elegance; Parisians actually dressed up to come here. It was mainly residences, rich hotels, and cafés. Then, in 1963, the government pumped up the neighborhood's commercial metabolism by bringing in the RER (commuter train). Suburbanites had easy access, and *pfft*—there went the neighborhood.

The *nouveau* Champs-Elysées, revitalized in 1994, has newer benches and lamps, broader sidewalks, all-underground parking, and a fleet of green-suited workers who drive motorized street cleaners. Blink away the modern elements, and it's not hard to imagine the boulevard pre-1963, with only the finest structures lining both sides all the way to the palace gardens.

Le Tour de France

For three weeks every July, French sporting life comes to a standstill as the Tour de France whizzes across the nation's landscape and television screens, pushing the world's top cyclists to their physical extremes and fans to the edges of their seats. What began in 1903 as a six-day publicity stunt for a cycling newspaper—in the era of wood-framed bikes and wine-and-cigarette breaks—has since grown into the sport's most prestigious race: a grueling 21-day, 2,000-mile test of strength and stamina, fueled by cutting-edge equipment and training regimens. The route changes each year (and usually spills into a neighboring country or two), but always finishes in Paris, on the Champs-Elysées.

Professional cycling is hugely popular in France, and while the Tour's on, media coverage is inescapable (despite—or perhaps thanks to—recent doping scandals). If you're here in July, it's easy to get caught up in the excitement. Casual spectators can appreciate the Tour's athletic demands and visual appeal, as cyclists travel in high-speed, multicolored packs through some of Europe's most scenic landscapes. But serious fans also love the complex, overlapping tests of speed, endurance, and strategy.

The long race is divided into daily stages, during which riders compete both as individuals and as members of their nine-man team. While the Tour produces only one overall winner, cycling is very much a team sport, and each member is critical (the loss of any rider along the way generally dooms a team's chances).

Minimizing air resistance is key to strategy, and riders spend most of each stage "drafting" behind *domestiques* ("servants," usually young riders still paying their dues), who take turns pedaling in front. The team's constant internal maneuvering is a matter of choreographed precision, aimed at minimizing fatigue... and the chance of a collision. At the end of each stage, fans breathlessly watch for that critical moment when the lead riders break away for the final sprint. Meanwhile, the team must jockey its way as a whole to the best position within the peloton (cluster

● **Self-Guided Walk:** To reach the top of the Champs-Elysées, take the Métro to the Arc de Triomphe (Mo: Charles de Gaulle-Etoile), then saunter down the grand boulevard (Métro stops every few blocks, including George V and Franklin D. Roosevelt). If you plan to tour the Arc de Triomphe (see next listing), do it before starting this walk.

Fancy car dealerships include **Peugeot,** at #136 (showing off its futuristic concept cars, often alongside the classic models), and **Mercedes-Benz,** a block down at #118, where you can pick up a Mercedes watch and cufflinks to go with your new car. In the 19th century this was an area for horse stables; today, it's the district of garages, limo companies, and car dealerships. If you're serious of riders), all while plotting how best to tap its members' varied talents over the course of the race.

Specialists ride not just to bolster their team, but also compete for their own distinctions: Climbers, usually smaller racers, battle to wear the *maillot à pois rouges* (red-polka-dot jersey), awarded to the "King of the Mountains." Bigger riders are usually sprinters, who save their energy for short bursts of speed, while vying for the *maillot vert* (green jersey). Time trialists help lower the team's aggregate time by excelling at individual races, where they must maintain high speeds over a long distance. The team's star is its captain, usually a solid "all-rounder." He's going for the famous *maillot jaune* (yellow jersey), worn by whoever holds the overall lead in the "general classification" standings at the end of each stage. (It may be called "the" yellow jersey, but each day's jersey is a new, unsweaty one.) A complex points system helps determine who has the lowest cumulative time—and, ultimately, who gets the €1.5 million (about $2 million) prize, and recognition as the world's greatest cyclist.

Unlike most spectator sports, cycling is perhaps best enjoyed on TV, where the intricate maneuvering is easier to follow, and the action stays in the camera's frame. Each day's race climax occurs around 17:00. If you're in France, just turn on your set at that time, flip among the first few channels, and you'll find coverage.

If you do catch the Tour in person, you'll experience the excitement firsthand and hear the loud whoosh of passing cyclists—but they're gone in a blink (viewing is best—and most crowded—on uphill slopes; for dates and details, see www.letour.fr).

Any time of year, you can at least picture the Tour's final stretch here on the nation's grandest avenue, where cheering crowds cram the sidewalks, necks craned for a glimpse of the yellow jersey.

about selling cars in France, you must have a showroom on the Champs-Elysées.

Next to Mercedes is the famous **Lido,** Paris' largest cabaret (and a multiplex cinema). You can walk all the way into the lobby. Paris still offers the kind of burlesque-type spectacles that have been performed here since the 19th century, combining music, comedy, and scantily clad women. Movie-going on the Champs-Elysées provides another kind of fun, with theaters showing the very latest releases. Check to see if there are films you recognize, then look for the showings *(séances)*. A "v.o." *(version originale)* next to the time indicates the film will be shown in its original language; a "v.f." stands for *version française*.

The flagship store of leather-bag maker **Louis Vuitton** may be the largest single-brand luxury store in the world. Step inside. The store insists on providing enough salespeople to treat each customer royally—if there's a line, it means shoppers have overwhelmed the place.

Fouquet's café-restaurant (#99), under the red awning, is a popular spot among French celebrities, serving the most expensive shot of espresso I've found in downtown Paris (€8). Opened in 1899 as a coachman's bistro, Fouquet's gained fame as the hangout of France's WWI biplane fighter pilots—those who weren't shot down by Germany's infamous "Red Baron." It also served as James Joyce's dining room.

Since the early 1900s, Fouquet's has been a favorite of French actors and actresses. The golden plaques at the entrance honor winners of France's Oscar-like film awards, the Césars (one is cut into the ground at the end of the carpet). There are plaques for Gérard Depardieu, Catherine Deneuve, Roman Polanski, Juliette Binoche, and several famous Americans (but not Jerry Lewis). More recent winners are shown on the floor just inside.

Ladurée (two blocks downhill at #75) is a classic 19th-century tea salon/restaurant/*pâtisserie*. Non-patrons can discreetly wander around the place, though photos are not allowed. A coffee here is *très élégant* (only €3.50).

From posh cafés to stylish shops, monumental sidewalks to glimmering showrooms, the Champs-Elysées is Paris at its most Parisian.

▲▲Arc de Triomphe—Napoleon had the magnificent Arc de Triomphe commissioned to commemorate his victory at the battle of Austerlitz. There's no triumphal arch bigger (165 feet high, 130 feet wide). And, with 12 converging boulevards, there's no traffic circle more thrilling to experience—either from behind the wheel or on foot (take the underpass).

The foot of the arch is a stage on which the last two centuries of Parisian history have played out—from the funeral of Napoleon to the goose-stepping arrival of the Nazis to the triumphant return of Charles de Gaulle after the Allied liberation. Examine the carvings on the pillars, featuring a mighty Napoleon and excitable Lady Liberty. Pay your respects at the Tomb of the Unknown Soldier. Then climb the 284 steps to the observation deck up top, with sweeping skyline panoramas and a mesmerizing view down onto the traffic that swirls around the arch.

Cost and Hours: Outside and at the base—free, always viewable; steps to rooftop—€9.50, under 18 free, free on first Sun of month Oct-March, covered by Museum Pass; daily April-Sept 10:00-23:00, Oct-March 10:00-22:30, last entry 30 minutes before closing; Place Charles de Gaulle, use underpass to reach arch, Mo: Charles de Gaulle-Etoile, tel. 01 55 37 73 77, www.arc-de -triomphe.monuments-nationaux.fr.

Avoiding Lines: Bypass the slooow ticket line with your Museum Pass (though if you have kids, you'll need to line up to get the free tickets for children). There may be another line (that you can't skip) at the entrance to the stairway up the arch. Lines disappear after 17:00—come for sunset.

▲**Opéra Garnier**—This gleaming grand theater of the belle époque was built for Napoleon III and finished in 1875. (For the best view, stand in front of the Opéra Métro stop.) From Avenue de l'Opéra, once lined with Paris' most fashionable haunts, the facade suggests "all power to the wealthy." And a shimmering Apollo, holding his lyre high above the building, seems to declare, "This is a temple of the highest arts."

Cost and Hours: €9, not covered by Museum Pass, erratic hours due to performances and rehearsals, but generally daily 10:00-17:00, mid-July-Aug until 18:00, last entry 30 minutes before closing, 8 Rue Scribe, Mo: Opéra, RER: Auber.

Tours: English tours of the building run during summer and off-season on weekends and Wed, usually at 11:30 and 14:30—call to confirm schedule (€13.50, includes entry, 1.5 hours, tel. 01 40 01 17 89 or 08 25 05 44 05, press 2 for tours).

Visiting the Theater: You'll enter around the left side of the building—as you face the front, find the red carpet across from American Express on Rue Scribe. As you pass the bust of the architect, Monsieur Garnier, pay your respects and check out the bronze floor plan of the complex etched below. Notice how little space is given to seating.

The building is huge—though the auditorium itself seats only 2,000. The real show was before and after the performance, when the elite of Paris—out to see and be seen—strutted their elegant stuff in the extravagant lobbies. Think of the grand marble stairway as a theater. As you wander the halls and gawk at the decor, imagine this place in its heyday, filled with beautiful people. The massive foundations straddle an underground lake (inspiring the mysterious world of the *Phantom of the Opera*). Visitors can peek from two boxes into the actual red-velvet performance hall to view Marc Chagall's colorful ceiling (1964) playfully dancing around the eight-ton chandelier (guided tours take you into the performance hall; you can't enter when they're changing out the stage). Note the box seats next to the stage—the most expensive in the house, with an obstructed view of the stage...but just right if you're here only to be seen.

The elitism of this place prompted former President François Mitterrand to have an opera house built for the people in the 1980s, situated symbolically on Place de la Bastille, where the French Revolution started in 1789. This left the Opéra Garnier home only to ballet and occasional concerts. The library/museum will interest opera buffs, but anyone will enjoy the second-floor grand foyer and Salon du Glacier, iced with decor typical of 1900.

Nearby: The Fragonard Perfume Museum (described next) is on the left side of the Opéra, and the venerable Galeries Lafayette department store (marvelous views from roof terrace) is just behind. Across the street, the illustrious Café de la Paix has been a meeting spot for the local glitterati for generations. If you can afford the coffee, this spot offers a delightful break.

Fragonard Perfume Museum—Near Opéra Garnier, this perfume shop masquerades as a museum. Housed in a beautiful 19th-century mansion, it's the best-smelling museum in Paris—and you'll learn a little about how perfume is made, too (ask for the English handout).

Cost and Hours: Free, Mon-Sat 9:00-18:00, Sun 9:00-17:00, 9 Rue Scribe, Mo: Opéra, RER: Auber, tel. 01 47 42 04 56, www.fragonard.com.

▲▲Jacquemart-André Museum (Musée Jacquemart-André)—This thoroughly enjoyable museum (with an elegant café) showcases the lavish home of a wealthy, art-loving, 19th-century Parisian couple. After wandering the grand boulevards, get inside for an intimate look at the lifestyles of the Parisian rich and fabulous. Edouard André and his wife Nélie Jacquemart—who had no children—spent their lives and fortunes designing, building, and then decorating this sumptuous mansion. What makes the visit so rewarding is the excellent audioguide tour (in English, included with admission—plan on spending an hour with the audioguide). The place is strewn with paintings by Rembrandt, Botticelli, Uccello, Mantegna, Bellini, Boucher, and Fragonard—enough to make a painting gallery famous.

Cost and Hours: €11, includes audioguide, not covered by Museum Pass; daily 10:00-18:00, Mon and Sat until 21:00 during special exhibits; can avoid lines by purchasing tickets online (€2 fee) and printing receipt, 158 Boulevard Haussmann, Mo: Miromesnil or St. Philippe-du-Roule, bus #80 makes a convenient connection to Ecole Militaire; tel. 01 45 62 11 59, www.musee-jacquemart-andre.com.

After Your Visit: Consider a break in the sumptuous museum tearoom, with delicious cakes and tea (daily 11:45-17:30). From here walk north on Rue de Courcelles to see Paris' most beautiful park, Parc Monceau.

▲**Petit Palais (and its Musée des Beaux-Arts)**—This free museum displays a broad collection of paintings and sculpture from the 1600s to the 1900s. It's a museum of second-choice art, but the building itself is impressive, and there are a few 19th-century diamonds in the rough, including pieces by Courbet, Monet, the American painter Mary Cassatt, and other Impressionists. The Palais also has a pleasant garden courtyard and café.

Cost and Hours: Free, Tue-Sun 10:00-18:00, Thu until 20:00 for temporary exhibitions, closed Mon; across from Grand Palais on Avenue Winston Churchill, a looooong block west of Place de la Concorde; tel. 01 53 43 40 00, www.petitpalais.paris.fr.

Grand Palais—This grand exhibition hall, built for the 1900 World's Fair, is used for temporary exhibits. The building's Industrial Age, erector-set, iron-and-glass exterior is striking, but the steep entry price is only worthwhile if you're interested in any of the several different exhibitions (each with different hours and costs, located in various parts of the building). Many areas are undergoing renovations, which may still be under way during your visit. Get details on the current schedule from a TI, in *Pariscope*, or from the website.

Cost and Hours: Admission prices and hours vary with each exhibition; major exhibitions usually €11, not covered by Museum Pass; generally open daily 10:00-20:00, Wed until 22:00, some parts of building closed Mon, other parts closed Tue, closed between exhibitions; Avenue Winston Churchill, Mo: Rond Point or Champs-Elysées, tel. 01 44 13 17 17, www.grandpalais.fr.

▲**La Défense and La Grande Arche**—Though Paris keeps its historic center classic and skyscraper-free, this district, nicknamed "le petit Manhattan," offers an impressive excursion into a side of Paris few tourists see: that of a modern-day economic superpower. La Défense was first conceived more than 60 years ago as a US-style forest of skyscrapers that would accommodate the business needs of the modern world. Today La Défense is a thriving commercial and shopping center, home to 150,000 employees and 55,000 residents.

For an interesting visit, take the Métro to the La Défense Grande Arche stop, follow *Sortie Grande Arche* signs, and climb the steps of La Grande Arche for distant city views. Then stroll gradually downhill among the glass buildings to the Esplanade de la Défense Métro station, and return home from there.

La Grande Arche de la Fraternité: This is the centerpiece of this ambitious complex. Inaugurated in 1989 on the 200th anniversary of the French Revolution, it was, like the Revolution, dedicated to human rights and brotherhood. The place is big—Notre-Dame Cathedral could fit under its arch. The "cloud"—a huge canvas canopy under the arch—is an attempt to cut down on the wind-tunnel effect this gigantic building creates.

Lunch on the Steps: Join the locals and picnic on the arch steps; good to-go places are plentiful (and cafés are nearby).

The Esplanade: La Défense is much more than its eye-catching arch. Survey the skyscraping scene from the top of the steps. Wander from the arch back toward the city center (and to the next Métro stop) along the Esplanade (a.k.a. "le Parvis"). The Esplanade is a virtual open-air modern art gallery, sporting pieces by Joan Miró (blue, red, and yellow), Alexander Calder (red), and Yaacov Agam (the fountain with colorful stripes and rhythmically dancing spouts), among others. *La Défense de Paris,* the statue that gave the area its name, recalls the 1871 Franco-Prussian war—it's a rare bit of old Paris out here in the 'burbs.

As you descend the Esplanade, notice how the small gardens and *boules* courts (reddish dirt areas) are designed to integrate tradition into this celebration of modern commerce. Note also how the buildings decrease in height and increase in age—the Nexity Tower (closest to central Paris) looks old compared to the other skyscrapers. Dating from the 1960s, it was one of the first buildings at La Défense. Your walk ends at the amusing fountain of Bassin Takis, where you'll find the Esplanade de la Défense Métro station that zips you out of all this modernity and directly back into town.

Marais Neighborhood and Nearby

The Marais neighborhood extends along the Right Bank of the Seine, from the Pompidou Center to the Bastille, the prison of Revolution fame. But don't waste time looking for the Bastille; the building is long gone, and just the square remains.

With more pre-Revolutionary lanes and buildings than anywhere else in town, the Marais is more atmospheric than touristy. It's medieval Paris, and the haunt of the old nobility. During the reign of Henry IV, this area—originally a swamp *(marais)*—became the hometown of the French aristocracy. In the 17th century, big shots built their private mansions *(hôtels)* close to Henry's stylish Place des Vosges.

With the Revolution, the aristocratic splendor of this quarter passed, and the Marais became a dumpy bohemian quarter so sordid it was nearly slated for destruction. In the mid-1800s, the wrecking ball was poised over the Marais: Napoleon III had

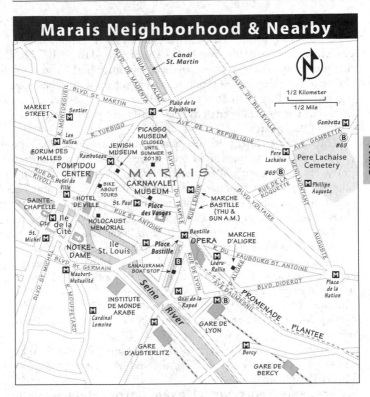

Marais Neighborhood & Nearby

ordered Baron Georges-Eugène Haussmann to modernize Paris by blasting out narrow streets to construct broad boulevards (wide enough for the big guns of the army, too wide for revolutionary barricades). By 1910, the renovation was almost complete, and a big boulevard was planned to slice right through the Marais. But then the march of "progress" was halted by one tiny little event—World War I.

Today the Marais is a thriving, trendy, real community—home to fashion boutiques, quiet cafés, Jewish bakeries, nightlife, and actual Parisians. When strolling the Marais, stick to the west-east axis formed by Rue Ste. Croix de la Bretonnerie, Rue des Rosiers (heart of Paris' Jewish community), and Rue St. Antoine. On Sunday afternoons, this trendy area pulses with shoppers and café crowds.

Place des Vosges and West

The following sights are listed roughly in geographical order from east to west, starting at the heart of the Marais.

▲**Place des Vosges**—Henry IV (r. 1589-1610) built this centerpiece of the Marais in 1605 and called it "Place Royal." As he'd hoped, it turned the Marais into Paris' most exclusive neighborhood. Walk to the center, where Louis XIII, on horseback, gestures, "Look at this wonderful square my dad built." He's surrounded by locals enjoying their community park. You'll see children frolicking in the sandbox, lovers warming benches, and pigeons guarding their fountains while trees shade this escape from the glare of the big city (you can refill your water bottle in the center of the square).

Study the architecture: nine pavilions (houses) per side. The two highest—at the front and back—were for the king and queen (but were never used). Warm red brickwork—some real, some fake—is topped with sloped slate roofs, chimneys, and another quaint relic of a bygone era: TV antennas. The insightful writer **Victor Hugo** lived at #6—at the southeast corner of the square, marked by the French flag—from 1832 to 1848. This was when he wrote much of his most important work, including his biggest hit, *Les Misérables*. Inside you'll wander through eight plush rooms and enjoy a fine view of the square (free, fee for optional exhibits—usually about €7, and usually not worth paying for, audioguide-€5, Tue-Sun 10:00-18:00, closed Mon, last entry at 17:40, 6 Place des Vosges; Mo: Bastille, St. Paul, or Chemin Vert; tel. 01 42 72 10 16, www.musee-hugo.paris.fr).

Sample the upscale art galleries ringing the square, then exit the square at its northwest corner, and head west on Rue des Francs-Bourgeois.

▲**Carnavalet Museum (Musée Carnavalet)**—At the Carnavalet Museum, French history unfolds in a series of stills—like a Ken Burns documentary, except you have to walk. The Revolution is the highlight, but you get a good overview of everything—from Louis XIV-period rooms to Napoleon to the belle époque. Though explanations are in French only, many displays are fairly self-explanatory.

The Revolution section is the best. No period of history is as charged with the full range of human drama: bloodshed, martyrdom, daring speeches, murdered priests, emancipated women, backstabbing former friends—all in the name of government "by, for, and of the people."

You'll see paintings of the Estates-General assembly that planted the seeds of democracy and a model of the Bastille, the hated prison that was the symbol of oppression. Read the "Declaration of the Rights of Man." See pictures of the ill-fated King Louis XVI and Queen Marie-Antoinette, and the fate that awaited them—the guillotine. You'll see portraits of all the major players in the Revolutionary spectacle—Maximilien de Robespierre, Georges Danton, Charlotte Corday—as well as the dashing general who would inherit democracy and turn it into dictatorship...Napoleon Bonaparte.

Cost and Hours: Free, fee for some temporary (but optional) exhibits, audioguide-€5, Tue-Sun 10:00-18:00, closed Mon; avoid lunchtime (12:30-14:30), when many rooms may be closed; 23 Rue de Sévigné, Mo: St. Paul, tel. 01 44 59 58 58, www.carnavalet .paris.fr.

▲▲**Picasso Museum (Musée Picasso)**—This museum, closed for a major renovation until summer 2013, contains the world's largest collection of Picasso's paintings, sculptures, sketches, and ceramics, along with his small collection of Impressionist art.

Rue des Rosiers: Paris' Jewish Quarter—This tiny yet colorful Jewish district of the Marais was once considered the largest in Western Europe. Today, Rue des Rosiers is lined with Jewish shops and kosher eateries, and the district is being squeezed by the trendy boutiques of modern Paris. Visit any day but Saturday, when most businesses are closed—it's best on Sunday. The intersection of Rue des Rosiers and Rue des Ecouffes marks the heart of the small neighborhood that Jews call the Pletzl ("little square"). Lively Rue des Ecouffes, named for a bird of prey, is a derogatory nod to the moneychangers' shops that once lined this lane.

Eating: If you're visiting at lunchtime, you'll be tempted by kosher pizza and plenty of cheap fast-food joints selling falafel "to go" *(emporter)*. **L'As du Falafel,** with its bustling New York deli atmosphere, is terrific (at #34, sit-down or to go). The **Sacha Finkelsztajn** Yiddish bakery at #27 is also good (Polish and Russian cuisine, pop in for a tempting treat, sit for the same price as take-away). Nearby, the recommended **Chez Marianne** cooks up traditional Jewish meals and serves excellent falafel to go (at corner of Rue des Rosiers and Rue des Hospitalières-St-Gervais).

▲**Jewish Art and History Museum (Musée d'Art et Histoire du Judaïsme)**—This fine museum, located in a beautifully restored Marais mansion, tells the story of Judaism in France and throughout Europe, from the Roman destruction of Jerusalem to the theft of famous artworks during World War II. Displays illustrate the cultural unity maintained by this continually dispersed population. You'll learn about the history of Jewish traditions, from bar mitzvahs to menorahs, and see the exquisite traditional costumes and objects central to daily life. The museum also displays paintings by famous Jewish artists, including Marc Chagall, Amedeo Modigliani, and Chaim Soutine. The English explanations posted in many rooms provide sufficient explanation for most; the included audioguide provides greater detail.

Cost and Hours: €7, includes audioguide, covered by Museum Pass, Sun-Fri 11:00-18:00, closed Sat, last entry 45 minutes before closing, 71 Rue du Temple; Mo: Rambuteau or Hôtel de Ville a few blocks farther away, RER: Châtelet-Les Halles; tel. 01 53 01 86 60, www.mahj.org.

Holocaust Memorial (Mémorial de la Shoah)—This sight commemorates the lives of the more than 76,000 Jews deported from France in World War II. It has several facets: a WWII deportation memorial, a museum on the Holocaust, and a Jewish resource center. Displaying original deportation records, the museum takes you through the history of Jews in Europe and France, from medieval pogroms to the Nazi era. But its focal point is underground, where victims' ashes are buried.

Cost and Hours: Free, Sun-Fri 10:00-18:00, Thu until 22:00, closed Sat and certain Jewish holidays, south of Rue de Rivoli at 17 Rue Geoffroy l'Asnier, tel. 01 42 77 44 72, www.memorialdela shoah.org.

▲▲Pompidou Center (Centre Pompidou)—One of Europe's greatest collections of far-out modern art is housed in the Musée National d'Art Moderne, on the fourth and fifth floors of this colorful exhibition hall. The building itself is "exoskeletal" (like Notre-Dame or a crab), with its functional parts—the pipes, heating ducts, and escalator—on the outside and the meaty art inside. It's the epitome of Modern architecture, where "form follows function." Created ahead of its time, the 20th-century art in this collection is still waiting for the world to catch up.

Cost and Hours: €11-13 depending on current exhibits, free on first Sun of month, Museum Pass covers permanent collection and view escalators, €3 Panorama Ticket lets you ride to the top for the view (doesn't include museum entry); Wed-Mon 11:00-21:00, closed Tue, ticket counters close at 20:00, arrive after 17:00 to avoid crowds (mainly for special exhibits); café on mezzanine, pricey view restaurant on Level 6, Mo: Rambuteau or farther-away Hôtel de Ville, tel. 01 44 78 12 33, www.centrepompidou.fr.

Visiting the Museum: Buy your ticket on the ground floor, then ride up the escalator (or run up the down escalator to get in the proper mood). When you see the view, your opinion of the Pompidou's exterior should improve a good 15 percent. Find the permanent collection—the entrance is either on the fourth or fifth floor (it varies). Enter, show your ticket, and get the current floor plan *(plan du musée)*.

The 20th century—accelerated by technology and fragmented by war—was exciting and chaotic, and the art reflects the turbulence of that century of change. In this free-flowing and airy museum, you'll come face-to-face with works from the first half of the 20th century, including pieces by Pablo Picasso, Marc Chagall, Henri Matisse, Wassily Kandinsky, Piet Mondrian, Paul Klee, Salvador Dalí, Max Ernst, Jackson Pollock, and many more.

The contemporary collection highlights post-1960 works, including Andy Warhol's pop art. You'll also see fewer traditional canvases or sculptures and lots of mixed-media work, combining painting, sculpture, welding, photography, video, computer programming, new resins, plastics, industrial techniques, and lighting and sound systems. Even skeptics of modern art will find that after so many Madonnas-and-children, a piano smashed to bits and glued to the wall is refreshing.

View from the Pompidou: Ride the escalator for a great city view from the top (ticket or Museum Pass required).

Nearby: The Pompidou Center and the square that fronts it are lively, with lots of people, street theater, and activity inside and out—a perpetual street fair. Kids of any age enjoy the fun, colorful fountain (called *Homage to Stravinsky*) next to the Pompidou Center.

Hôtel de Ville—Looking more like a grand château than a public building, Paris' city hall stands proudly on the river (a few blocks south of the Pompidou Center). The Renaissance-style building (built 1533-1628, and reconstructed after a 19th-century fire) displays hundreds of statues of famous Parisians on its facade. Peek through the doors to see elaborate spiral stairways reminiscent of Château de Chambord in the Loire. Playful fountains energize the big, lively square in front.

This spacious stage has seen much of Paris' history. On July 14, 1789, Revolutionaries rallied here on their way to the Bastille. In 1870, it was home to the radical Paris Commune. During World War II, General Charles de Gaulle appeared at the windows to proclaim Paris' liberation from the Nazis. And in 1950, Robert Doisneau snapped a famous black-and-white photo of a kissing couple, with Hôtel de Ville as a romantic backdrop.

Today, this is the symbolic heart of the city of Paris. Demonstrators gather here to speak their minds. Crowds cheer during big soccer games shown on huge TV screens. In summer, the square hosts sand volleyball courts; in winter, a big ice-skating rink. And year-round, the place is always beautifully lit after dark.

East of Place des Vosges

Promenade Plantée Park (Viaduc des Arts)—This two-mile-long, narrow garden walk on an elevated viaduct was once used for train tracks and is now a fine place for a refreshing stroll or run. Botanists appreciate the well-maintained and varying vegetation. From west (near Opéra) to east, the first half of the path is elevated until the midway point, the pleasant Jardin de Reuilly (a good stopping point for most, near Mo: Dugommier), then it continues on street level—with separate paths for pedestrians and cyclists—out to Paris' ring road, the *périphérique*.

Cost and Hours: Free, opens Mon-Fri at 8:00, Sat-Sun at 9:00, closes at sunset (17:30 in winter, 20:30 in summer). It runs from Place de la Bastille (Mo: Bastille) along Avenue Daumesnil to St. Mandé (Mo: Michel Bizot) or Porte Dorée, passing within a block of Gare de Lyon.

Getting There: To get to the park from Place de la Bastille (exit the Métro following *Sortie Rue de Lyon* signs), walk a looooong block down Rue de Lyon hugging the Opéra on your left. Find the low-key entry and steps up the red-brick wall a block after the Opéra.

▲Père Lachaise Cemetery (Cimetière du Père Lachaise)—Littered with the tombstones of many of the city's most illustrious dead, this is your best one-stop look at Paris' fascinating, romantic past residents. Enclosed by a massive wall and lined with 5,000 trees, the peaceful, car-free lanes and dirt paths of Père Lachaise cemetery encourage park-like meandering. Named for Father *(Père)* La Chaise, whose job was listening to Louis XIV's sins, the cemetery is relatively new, having opened in 1804 to accommodate Paris' expansion. Today, this city of the dead (pop. 70,000) still accepts new residents, but real estate prices are sky high (a 21-square-foot plot costs more than €11,000).

The 100-acre cemetery is big and confusing, with thousands of graves and tombs crammed every which way, and only a few pedestrian pathways to help you navigate. The maps available from any of the nearby florists help direct you to the graves of Frédéric Chopin, Molière, Edith Piaf, Oscar Wilde, Gertrude Stein, Jim Morrison, Héloïse and Abélard, and many more.

Cost and Hours: Free, Mon-Fri 8:00-18:00, Sat 8:30-18:00, Sun 9:00-18:00, closes at 17:30 in winter, last entry 15 minutes before closing; two blocks from Mo: Gambetta (not Mo: Père Lachaise) and two blocks from bus #69's last stop; tel. 01 55 25 82 10, searchable map available at non-official website: www.pere-lachaise.com.

Montmartre

Stroll along Paris' highest hilltop (420 feet) for a different perspective on the City of Light. Walk in the footsteps of the people who've lived here—monks stomping grapes (1200s), farmers grinding grain in windmills (1600s), dust-coated gypsum miners (1700s), Parisian liberals (1800s), Modernist painters (1900s), and all the struggling artists, poets, dreamers, and drunkards who came here for cheap rent, untaxed booze, rustic landscapes, and cabaret nightlife. With vineyards, wheat fields, windmills, animals, and a village tempo of life, it was the perfect escape from grimy Paris.

For restaurant recommendations in this area, see page 208.

▲▲**Sacré-Cœur**—The Sacré-Cœur (Sacred Heart) Basilica's exterior, with its onion domes and bleached-bone pallor, looks

ancient, but was finished only a century ago by Parisians humiliated by German invaders. Otto von Bismarck's Prussian army laid siege to Paris for more than four months in 1870. Things got so bad for residents that urban hunting for dinner (to cook up dogs, cats, and finally rats) became accepted behavior. Convinced they were being punished for the country's liberal sins, France's Catholics raised money to build the church as a "praise the Lord anyway" gesture.

The five-domed, Roman-Byzantine-looking basilica took 44 years to build (1875-1919). It stands on a foundation of 83 pillars sunk 130 feet deep, necessary because the ground beneath was honeycombed with gypsum mines. The exterior is laced with gypsum, which whitens with age.

Take a clockwise spin around the crowded interior to see impressive mosaics, and to give St. Peter's bronze foot a rub. For an unobstructed panoramic view of Paris, climb 260 feet (300 steps) up the tight and claustrophobic spiral stairs to the top of the dome (especially worthwhile if you have kids with excess energy).

Cost and Hours: Church—free, daily 6:00-22:30, last entry at 22:15; dome—€6, not covered by Museum Pass, daily May-Sept 9:00-19:00, Oct-April 9:00-17:00; tel. 01 53 41 89 00, www.sacre-coeur-montmartre.com.

Getting There: You have several options. You can take the Métro to the Anvers stop (to avoid the stairs up to Sacré-Cœur, buy one more Métro ticket and ride the funicular, though it's sometimes closed for maintenance). The Abbesses stop is closer but less scenic. Or you can go to Place Pigalle, then take the tiny electric Montmartrobus, which drops you right by Place du Tertre, near Sacré-Cœur (costs one Métro ticket, 4/hour). A taxi to the top of the hill saves time and avoids sweat (about €13, €20 at night).

The Heart of Montmartre—Montmartre's main square (**Place du Tertre**), one block from the church, was once the haunt of

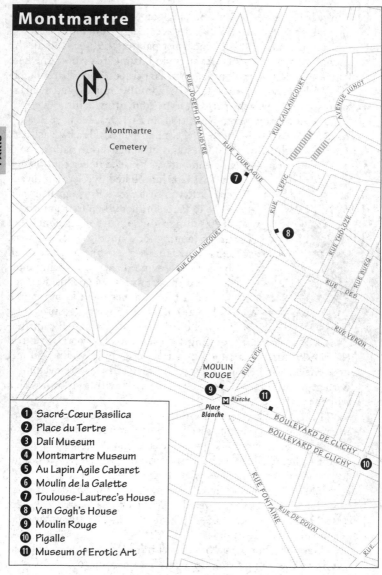

Montmartre

Montmartre
Cemetery

MOULIN
ROUGE

*Place
Blanche*

Ⓜ *Blanche*

BOULEVARD DE CLICHY

BOULEVARD DE CLICHY

❶ Sacré-Cœur Basilica
❷ Place du Tertre
❸ Dalí Museum
❹ Montmartre Museum
❺ Au Lapin Agile Cabaret
❻ Moulin de la Galette
❼ Toulouse-Lautrec's House
❽ Van Gogh's House
❾ Moulin Rouge
❿ Pigalle
⓫ Museum of Erotic Art

Henri de Toulouse-Lautrec and the original bohemians. Today, it's mobbed with tourists and unoriginal bohemians, but it's still fun (to beat the crowds, go on a weekday or early on weekend mornings). From here, head up Rue des Saules to find Paris' lone vineyard and the **Montmartre Museum** (described later). Return uphill, then follow Rue Lepic down to the old windmill, **Moulin de la Galette,** which once pressed monks' grapes and farmers'

PARIS

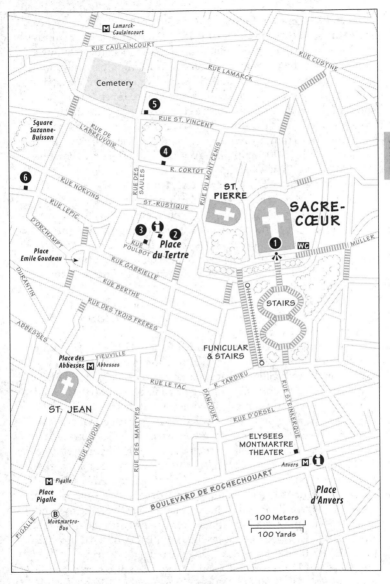

grain, and crushed gypsum rocks into powdery plaster of Paris (there were once 30 windmills on Montmartre). When the gypsum mines closed (c. 1850) and the vineyards sprouted apartments, this windmill turned into the ceremonial centerpiece of a popular outdoor dance hall. Farther down Rue Lepic, you'll pass near the former homes of **Toulouse-Lautrec** (at Rue Tourlaque—look for the brick-framed art-studio windows under the heavy mansard roof) and **Vincent van Gogh** (54 Rue Lepic).

Dalí Museum (L'Espace Dalí)—This beautifully lit black gallery (well-described in English) offers a walk through statues, etchings, and paintings by the master of Surrealism. The Spaniard found fame in Paris in the 1920s and '30s. He lived in Montmartre for a while, hung with the Surrealist crowd in Montparnasse, and shocked the world with his dreamscape paintings and experimental films. Don't miss the printed interview on the exit stairs.

PARIS

Cost and Hours: €11, not covered by Museum Pass, audioguide-€3, daily 10:00-18:00, July-Aug until 20:00, 11 Rue Poulbot, tel. 01 42 64 40 10, www.daliparis.com.

Montmartre Museum (Musée de Montmartre)—This 17th-century home re-creates the traditional cancan-and-cabaret Montmartre scene, with paintings, posters, photos, music, and memorabilia. Once the residence of Pierre-Auguste Renoir and Maurice Utrillo, the museum now houses the original *Lapin Agile* sign, the famous Chat Noir poster, and Toulouse-Lautrec's dashing portrait of red-scarved Aristide Bruant, the earthy cabaret singer and club owner.

Cost and Hours: €8, includes good audioguide, not covered by Museum Pass, daily 10:00-18:00, 12 Rue Cortot, tel. 01 49 25 89 39, www.museedemontmartre.fr.

Pigalle—Paris' red light district, the infamous "Pig Alley," is at the foot of Butte Montmartre. *Ooh la la.* It's more racy than dangerous. Walk from Place Pigalle to Place Blanche, teasing desperate barkers and fast-talking temptresses. In bars, a €150 bottle of (what would otherwise be) cheap champagne comes with a friend. Stick to the bigger streets, hang on to your wallet, and exercise good judgment. Cancan can cost a fortune, as can con artists in topless bars. After dark, countless tour buses line the streets, reminding us that tour guides make big bucks by bringing their groups to touristy nightclubs like the famous Moulin Rouge (Mo: Pigalle or Abbesses).

Museum of Erotic Art (Musée de l'Erotisme)—Paris' sexy museum has five floors of risqué displays—mostly paintings and drawings—ranging from artistic to erotic to disgusting, with a few circa-1920 porn videos and a fascinating history of local brothels tossed in. It's in the center of the Pigalle red light district.

Cost and Hours: €10, €7 online, no...it's not covered by the Museum Pass, daily 10:00-2:00 in the morning, 72 Boulevard de Clichy, Mo: Blanche, tel. 01 42 58 28 73, www.musee-erotisme.com.

Shopping in Paris

Even staunch anti-shoppers may be tempted to indulge in chic Paris. Wandering among elegant and outrageous boutiques provides a break from the heavy halls of the Louvre and, if you

French Shopping Etiquette

Before you enter a Parisian store, remember the following points:

- In small stores, always say, *"Bonjour, Madame* or *Mademoiselle* or *Monsieur"* when entering. And remember to say *"Au revoir, Madame* or *Mademoiselle* or *Monsieur"* when leaving.
- The customer is not always right. In fact, figure the clerk is doing you a favor by waiting on you.
- Except in department stores, it's not normal for the customer to handle clothing. Ask first before you pick up an item: *"Je peux?"* (zhuh puh), meaning, "Can I?"
- For clothing size comparisons between the US and France, see page 1147 of the appendix.
- Forget returns (and don't count on exchanges).
- Saturday afternoons are *très* busy and not for the faint of heart.
- Observe French shoppers. Then imitate.
- Stores are generally closed on Sunday, except at the Carrousel du Louvre (underground shopping mall at the Louvre) and some shops near Sèvres-Babylone, along the Champs-Elysées, and in the Marais.
- Some small stores don't open until 14:00 on Mondays.
- Don't feel obliged to buy. If a shopkeeper offers assistance, just say, *"Je regarde, merci."*

approach it right, a little cultural enlightenment. Even if you don't intend to buy anything, budget some time for window-shopping. The expression for "window-shopping" in French is *faire du lèche-vitrines*—"window-licking." Here are a few of your options for picking up gifts, souvenirs, and something special for yourself.

Souvenir Shops

Avoid souvenir carts in front of famous monuments. You can find cheaper gifts around the Pompidou Center, on the streets of Montmartre, and in some department stores. The riverfront stalls near Notre-Dame sell a variety of used books, old posters and postcards, magazines, refrigerator magnets, and other tourist paraphernalia in the most romantic setting. You'll find better deals at the souvenir shops that line Rue d'Arcole between Notre-Dame and Hôtel de Ville and on Rue de Rivoli, alongside the Louvre.

Department Stores *(Les Grands Magasins)*

Like cafés, department stores were invented here (surprisingly, not in America). Parisian department stores begin with their showy perfume sections, almost always central on the ground floor and worth a visit to see how much space is devoted to pricey, smelly water. Helpful information desks are usually located at the main entrances near the perfume section (with floor plans in English). Stores generally have affordable restaurants (some with view terraces) and a good selection of fairly priced souvenirs and toys. Shop at these great Parisian department stores: Galeries Lafayette (Mo: Chaussée d'Antin-La Fayette, Havre-Caumartin, or Opéra), Printemps (next door to Galeries Lafayette), and Bon Marché (Mo: Sèvres-Babylone). Opening hours are customarily Monday through Saturday from 10:00 to 19:00. Some are open later on Thursdays, and all are jammed on Saturdays and closed on Sundays (except in December).

Boutique Strolls

Give yourself a vacation from your sightseeing-focused vacation by sifting through window displays, pausing at corner cafés, and feeling the rhythm of neighborhood life. (Or have you been playing hooky and doing this already?) Though smaller shops are more intimate, sales clerks are more formal—so mind your manners. Here are three very different areas to lick some windows.

Sèvres-Babylone to St. Sulpice

This Left Bank shopping stroll lets you sample smart clothing boutiques and clever window displays while enjoying one of Paris' more attractive neighborhoods.

Start at the **Bon Marché** (Mo: Sèvres-Babylone), Paris' oldest department store. From the Bon Marché, follow Rue de Sèvres, where you'll find **La Maison du Chocolat** at #19, selling handmade chocolates in exquisitely wrapped boxes. Be sure to lick the chocolate off your fingers before entering **Hermès** (next door, at #17), famous for pricey silk scarves—and for the former designer of its fashion house, Jean-Paul Gaultier. Don't let the doorman intimidate you: Everyone's welcome here. This store, opened in 2011, is housed in the original Art Deco swimming pool of Hôtel Lutetia, built in 1935. Take a spin through this ultra-trendy space, which covers more than 20,000 square feet. Across the street sits the marvelously old-school **Au Sauvignon Café** (10 Rue de Sèvres, open daily).

Continue a block farther down Rue de Sèvres to Place Michel Debré, where a *Centaur* statue stands guard. From Place Michel Debré, boutique-lined streets fan out like spokes on a wheel. Definitely make a short detour up Rue du Cherche-Midi (follow the horse's fanny). This street offers an ever-changing but always chic selection of shoe, purse, and clothing stores. Find Paris' most celebrated bread—beautiful round loaves with designer crust—at the low-key **Poilâne** at #8 (Mon-Sat 7:15-20:15, closed Sun).

Return to the *Centaur* in Place Michel Debré. Check out the **Comtesse du Berry** pâté store, which sells small gift packs. Then turn right and head down Rue du Vieux Colombier, where you'll pass the **Théâtre du Vieux-Colombier** (1913), **Longchamps** (#21), selling stylish French handbags, **Aubade** for lingerie, **Lola** for ladies' clothes, and **Victoire** for the gentlemen. If the man or *petit-garçon* in your life needs a swimsuit, check out **Vilebrequin** (#5). Spill into Place St. Sulpice, with its big, twin-tower church. **Café de la Mairie** is a great spot to sip a *café crème* and admire the lovely square.

Place de la Madeleine to Place Vendôme

The ritzy streets connecting these high-priced squares form a miracle mile of gourmet food shops, glittering jewelry stores, four-star hotels, exclusive clothing boutiques, and people who spend more on clothes in one day than I do all year (note that these shops are closed on Sundays).

Start at Place de la Madeleine (Mo: Madeleine). **Fauchon,** at #30 Place de la Madeleine, is a bastion of over-the-top food products that has faded from its glory days. Today it caters to a largely tourist clientele—though it can still make your mouth water and your pocketbook ache. **Hédiard,** across the square at #21, is an older, more appealing, and more accessible gourmet food shop. Two doors down, at #19, **La Maison de la Truffe** sells black mushrooms for up to €1,000 a pound and white truffles from Italy for €2,500 a pound. Small jars of black truffles cost €45-70. Next door, at **Caviar Kaspia** (#17), you can add Iranian caviar, eel, and vodka to your truffle collection. Find the price list on the counter. The stronger caviars are cheaper (€110 for a small tin). The "finer" caviars sell for up to €12,000 a kilo. (I have a hard time visualizing 2.2 pounds of caviar, and a harder time visualizing paying for it.)

From Place de la Madeleine, you can head south down Rue Royale, passing the classy Village Royale shopping courtyard. At #16 Rue Royale, an out-of-this-world pastry break awaits at **Ladurée,** with its 19th-century setting. Turning left on Rue du Faubourg St. Honoré takes you past numerous clothing boutiques, and another left on Rue de Castiglione leads to Place Vendôme, a *très* elegant square that's home to the original Hôtel Ritz and upper-crust **jewelry stores,** including Van Cleef & Arpels, Dior, Chanel, Cartier, and others (if you have to ask how much...).

The Marais

For more eclectic, avant-garde boutiques, peruse the artsy shops between Place des Vosges and the Pompidou Center. Starting at Place des Vosges, stick to the west-east axis formed by Rue des Francs-Bourgeois, Rue des Rosiers, and Rue Ste. Croix de la Bretonnerie. This area is rich with jewelry, shoes, and trendy clothing boutiques. On Sunday afternoons, when the rest of Paris naps, the neighborhood comes alive with shoppers and café crowds, and enjoys little car traffic. But it's quiet on Saturdays, when the Jewish community rests.

Flea Markets

Paris' sprawling flea markets (*marché aux puces;* mar-shay oh-poos; *puce* is French for "flea") are oversized garage sales. They started in the Middle Ages, when middlemen sold old, flea-infested clothes and discarded possessions of the wealthy at bargain prices to eager peasants. Buyers were allowed to rummage through piles of aristocratic garbage.

Puces St. Ouen—Located at Porte de Clignancourt, Puces St. Ouen (poos san-wahn) is the mother of all flea markets, with more than 2,000 vendors selling everything from flamingos to faucets, but mostly antiques (Sat 9:00-18:00, Sun 10:00-18:00, Mon 11:00-17:00, closed Tue-Fri, pretty dead the first 2 weeks of Aug, tel. 01 58 61 22 90, www.st-ouen-tourisme.com and www.les-puces.com).

This market shows off Paris' gritty, suburban underbelly and can be intimidating (in Paris, the have-nots live in the burbs, while the haves want to be as central as they can get). No event brings together the melting-pot population of Paris better than this carnival-like market. Some find it claustrophobic, overcrowded, and threatening; others find French *diamants*-in-the-rough and return happy. (Wear your money belt; pickpockets and scam artists thrive in these wall-to-wall-shopper events—and don't use ATM machines here.) The markets actually get more peaceful the farther in you go. You can bargain a bit (best deals are made with cash at the end of the day), though don't expect swinging deals here.

Getting There: Take Métro line 4 to the end of the line at Porte de Clignancourt, then carefully follow *Sortie, Marché aux Puces* signs. Walk straight out of the Métro down Avenue de la Porte de Clignancourt, passing by leather stores and through blocks of stalls hawking trinkets and cheap clothing. Your destination is just beyond the elevated freeway (white bridge).

Other Flea Markets—**Puces de Vanves** is comparatively tiny and civilized, and preferred by many flea-market connoisseurs (Sat-Sun 7:00-17:00, best to arrive before 13:00—when the best stalls close, closed Mon-Fri, Mo: Porte de Vanves). The mega-**Puces de Montreuil** is the least organized and most traditional of them all, with chatty sellers and competitive buyers (Sat-Mon 8:00-18:00, closed Tue-Fri, Mo: Porte de Montreuil).

Market Streets

Several traffic-free street markets overflow with flowers, produce, fish vendors, and butchers, illustrating how most Parisians shopped before there were supermarkets and department stores. **Rue Cler** is like a refined street market, serving an upscale neighborhood near the Eiffel Tower (Mo: Ecole Militaire). **Rue Montorgueil** (Mo: Etienne Marcel), a thriving and less touristy market street, is famous as the last vestige of the once-massive Les Halles market; gather a picnic here and take it to the park at Les Halles. **Rue Mouffetard,** hiding several blocks behind the Panthéon (Mo: Censier Daubenton), has an upper stretch that is pedestrian and touristic and a bottom stretch that is purely Parisian. Shops are open daily except Sunday afternoons, Monday, and lunchtime throughout the week (13:00-15:00).

Entertainment in Paris

Paris is brilliant after dark. Save energy from your day's sightseeing and experience the City of Light lit. Whether it's a concert at Sainte-Chapelle, a boat ride on the Seine, a walk in Montmartre, a hike up the Arc de Triomphe, or a late-night café, you'll see Paris at its best. Night walks in Paris are wonderful.

Adjust your expectations to the changing times. Paris will always be the City of Light, but it shines a little dimmer these days. In an effort to go green and save money, Paris has toned down the lighting on several monuments, including the Arc de Triomphe and the Louvre's glass pyramid.

Music

Jazz and Blues Clubs—With a lively mix of American, French, and international musicians, Paris has been an internationally acclaimed jazz capital since World War II. You'll pay €12-25 to enter a jazz club (may include one drink; if not, expect to pay €5-10 per drink; beer is cheapest). See *Pariscope* magazine under "Musique" for listings, or, even better, the *Paris Voice* website for a good monthly review (www.parisvoice.com). You can also check Time Out's website (www.timeout.fr/paris) or each club's website (all have English versions), or drop by the clubs to check out the calendars posted on their front doors. Music starts after 21:00 in most clubs. Some offer dinner concerts from about 20:30 on. Here are several good bets:

Caveau de la Huchette, a characteristic old jazz/dance club, fills an ancient Latin Quarter cellar with live jazz and frenzied dancing every night (admission about €12 on weekdays, €14 on weekends, €6-8 drinks, daily 21:30-2:30 in the morning or later, 5 Rue de la Huchette, Mo: St. Michel, recorded info tel. 01 43 26 65 05, www.caveaudelahuchette.fr).

Autour de Midi et Minuit is a an Old World bistro at the foot of Montmartre, sitting above a *cave à jazz*. Eat upstairs if you like (see page 209 for details), then make your way down to the basement to find bubbling jam sessions on Tuesday and Wednesday and concerts on Thursday, Friday, and Saturday (no cover, €5 minimum Tue-Wed; €16 cover Thu-Sat includes one drink; jam sessions at 21:30, concerts usually at 22:00; no music Sun-Mon; 11 Rue Lepic, Mo: Blanche or Abbesses, tel. 01 55 79 16 48, www.autourdemidi.fr).

For a spot teeming with late-night activity and jazz, go to the two-block-long Rue des Lombards, at Boulevard Sébastopol, midway between the river and the Pompidou Center (Mo: Châtelet). **Au Duc des Lombards** is one of the most popular and respected jazz clubs in Paris, with concerts nightly in a great, plush, 110-seat theater-like setting (admission €20-30, buy online and arrive early for best seats, cheap drinks, shows at 20:00 and 22:00, 42 Rue des Lombards, tel. 01 42 33 22 88, www.ducdeslombards.fr). **Le Sunside,** run for 18 years by Stephane Portet, is just a block away. The club offers two little stages (ground floor and downstairs): "le Sunset" stage tends toward contemporary world jazz; "le Sunside" stage features more traditional and acoustic jazz (concerts range from free to €25, check their website; generally at 20:00, 21:00, and 22:00; 60 Rue des Lombards, tel. 01 40 26 46 60, www.sunset-sunside.com).

For a less pricey—and less central—concert club, try **Utopia.** From the outside it's a hole in the wall, but inside it's filled with devoted fans of rock and folk blues. Though Utopia is officially a private club (and one that permits smoking), you can pay €3 to join for an evening, then pay a reasonable charge for the concert (usually €10 or under, concerts start about 22:00). It's located in the Montparnasse area (79 Rue de l'Ouest, Mo: Pernety, tel. 01 43 22 79 66, www.utopia-cafeconcert.fr).

Old-Time Parisian Cabaret on Montmartre: Au Lapin Agile—This historic little cabaret tries its best to maintain the atmosphere of the heady days when bohemians would gather here to enjoy wine, song, and sexy jokes. Today, you'll mix in with a few locals and many tourists (the Japanese love the place) for a drink and as many as 10 different performers—mostly singers with a piano. Performers range from sweet and innocent Amélie types to naughty Maurice Chevalier types. And though tourists are welcome, there's no accommodation for English speakers (except on their website), so non-French-speakers will be lost. You sit at carved wooden tables in a dimly lit room, taste the traditional drink (a small brandy with cherries), and are immersed in an old-time Parisian ambience. The soirée covers traditional French standards, love ballads, sea chanteys, and more (€24, €7 drinks, Tue-Sun 21:00-2:00 in the morning, closed Mon, best to reserve ahead, 22 Rue des Saules, tel. 01 46 06 85 87, www.au-lapin-agile.com).

Classical Concerts—For classical music on any night, consult *Pariscope* magazine (check "Concerts Classiques" under "Musique" for listings), and look for posters at tourist-oriented churches.

From March through November, these churches regularly host concerts: St. Sulpice, St. Germain-des-Prés, La Madeleine, St. Eustache, St. Julien-le-Pauvre, and Sainte-Chapelle.

Sainte-Chapelle: Enjoy the pleasure of hearing Mozart, Bach, or Vivaldi, surrounded by 800 years of stained glass (unheated—bring a sweater). The acoustical quality is surprisingly good. There are usually two concerts per evening, at 19:00 and 20:30; specify which one you want when you buy or reserve your ticket. VIP tickets get you a seat in the first eight rows (€40), Prestige tickets cover the next 15 rows (€30) and Normal tickets are the last five rows (€16). Seats are unassigned within each section, so arrive at least 30 minutes early to get through the security line and snare a good view.

You can book at the box office, by phone, or online. Two different companies present concerts, but the schedule will tell you who to contact for tickets to a particular performance. The small box office (with schedules and tickets) is to the left of the chapel entrance gate (4 Boulevard du Palais, Mo: Cité), or call 01 42 77 65 65 or 06 67 30 65 65 for schedules and reservations. You can leave your message in English—just speak clearly and spell your name. You can check schedules at www.archetspf.asso.fr, but if you want to book online, visit www.classictic.com, which lets you conveniently print out your email confirmation as your ticket.

Flavien from Euromusic offers last-minute discounts with this book when seats are available (limit 2 tickets per book). VIP tickets are discounted to €30 and Prestige tickets to €25. The offer applies only to Euromusic concerts and must be purchased with cash only at the Sainte-Chapelle ticket booth close to concert time.

The evening entrance is at 4 Boulevard du Palais, between the gilded gate of the Palais de Justice and the Conciergerie. You'll enter through the law courts hall, directly into the royal upper chapel, just as St. Louis once did.

Salle Pleyel: This concert hall on the Right Bank hosts world-class artists, from string quartets and visiting orchestras to international opera stars. Tickets range from €10 to €150, depending on the artist and seats you choose, and are usually hard to come by, so it's best to order online in advance (252 Rue du Faubourg St. Honoré, Mo: Ternes, tel. 01 42 56 13 13, www.sallepleyel.fr).

Other Venues: Look also for daytime concerts in parks, such as the Luxembourg Garden. Even the Galeries Lafayette department store offers concerts. Many of these concerts are free *(entrée libre)*, such as the Sunday atelier concert sponsored by the American Church (generally Sept-June at 17:00 but not every week and not in Dec, 65 Quai d'Orsay, Mo: Invalides, RER: Pont de l'Alma, tel. 01 40 62 05 00, www.acparis.org).

Opera—Paris is home to two well-respected opera venues. The **Opéra Bastille** is the massive modern opera house that dominates Place de la Bastille. Come here for state-of-the-art special effects and modern interpretations of classic ballets and operas. In the spirit of this everyman's opera, unsold seats are available at a big discount to seniors and students 15 minutes before the show. Standing-room-only tickets for €15 are also sold for some performances (Mo: Bastille). The **Opéra Garnier,** Paris' first opera house, hosts opera and ballet performances. Come here for less expensive tickets and grand belle époque decor (Mo: Opéra). To get tickets for either opera house, it's easiest to reserve online at www.operadeparis.fr, or call 01 71 25 24 23 outside France or toll tel. 08 92 89 90 90 inside France. You can also go directly to the Opéra Bastille's ticket office (open daily 11:00-18:00).

Evening Museum Visits

Various **museums** are open late on different evenings—called *visites nocturnes*—offering the opportunity for more relaxed, less crowded visits: the Louvre (Wed and Fri until 21:45), Orsay (Thu until 21:45), Pompidou Center (Wed-Mon until 21:00), Grand Palais (Wed until 22:00), Holocaust Memorial (Thu until 22:00), Quai Branly (Thu-Sat until 21:00), Rodin Museum (Wed until 20:45), and Marmottan Museum (Thu until 20:00). The Army Museum may be open Tuesdays until 21:00 (April-Sept).

   Summer Night Spectacle: An elaborate sound-and-light show (Grandes Eaux Nocturnes) takes place at the Château in Versailles on Saturdays (€23, mid-June-Aug at 21:00, www .chateauversailles.fr).

Night Walks

Go for an evening walk to best appreciate the City of Light. Break for ice cream, pause at a café, and enjoy the sidewalk entertainers as you join the post-dinner Parisian parade. Remember to avoid poorly lit areas and stick to main thoroughfares. Consider the following suggestions.

   ▲▲▲Trocadéro and Eiffel Tower—This is one of Paris' most spectacular views at night. Take the Métro to the Trocadéro stop and join the party on Place du Trocadéro for a magnificent view of the glowing Eiffel Tower (see the "Best Views over the City of Light" sidebar on page 120). It's a festival of hawkers, gawkers, drummers, and entertainers.

   Walk down the stairs, passing the fountains and rollerbladers, then cross the river to the base of the tower, well worth the effort even if you don't go up (tower open daily mid-June-Aug until 24:00, Sept-mid-June until 23:00).

From the Eiffel Tower you can stroll through the Champ de Mars park past tourists and romantic couples, and take the Métro home (Ecole Militaire stop, across Avenue de la Motte-Picquet from far southeast corner of park). Or there's a handy RER stop (Champ de Mars-Tour Eiffel) two blocks west of the Eiffel Tower on the river.

▲▲**Champs-Elysées and the Arc de Triomphe**—The Avenue des Champs-Elysées glows after dark. Start at the Arc de Triomphe (observation deck open daily, April-Sept until 23:00, Oct-March until 22:30), then stroll down Paris' lively grand promenade. A right turn on Avenue George V leads to the Bateaux-Mouches river cruises. A movie on the Champs-Elysées is a fun experience (weekly listings in *Pariscope* under "Cinéma"), and a drink or snack at Renault's futuristic car café is a kick (at #53, toll tel. 08 11 88 28 11).

▲**Ile St. Louis and Notre-Dame**—This stroll features floodlit views of Notre-Dame and a taste of the Latin Quarter. Take the Métro (line 7) to the Pont Marie stop, then cross Pont Marie to Ile St. Louis. Turn right up Rue St. Louis-en-l'Ile, stopping for dinner—or at least a Berthillon ice cream (at #31) or Amorino Gelati (at #47). At the end of Ile St. Louis, cross Pont St. Louis to Ile de la Cité, with a great view of Notre-Dame. Wander to the Left Bank on Quai de l'Archevêché, and drop down to the river for the best floodlit views. From May through September you'll find several permanently moored barges *(péniches)* that operate as bars. Although I wouldn't eat dinner on one of these barges, the atmosphere is great for a drink, often including live music on weekends (daily until 2:00 in the morning, closed Oct-April, live music often Thu-Sun from 21:00). End your walk on Place du Parvis Notre-Dame in front of Notre-Dame (tower open Sat-Sun until 23:00 in July-Aug), or go back across the river to the Latin Quarter.

Open-Air Sculpture Garden—Day or night, this skinny riverfront park dotted with modern art makes for a pleasant walk, but it's especially fun on balmy evenings in the summer, when you may encounter rock and salsa dancing. It's on the Left Bank across from Ile St. Louis, running between the Arab World Institute and Jardin des Plantes (free, music around 20:00, very weather-dependent, Quai St. Bernard, Mo: Cardinal Lemoine plus an eight-minute walk up Rue Cardinal Lemoine toward the river).

After-Dark Tours

Several companies offer evening tours of Paris. You can take a traditional, mass-produced bus tour for €25 per person, or for a little more (around €100 per couple), take an hour-long, vintage-car tour with a student guide. A pedicab will take you around for €40-50 per hour. Do-it-yourself-ers can save money by hiring a cab for a private tour (€50 for one hour). All options are described below.

▲▲▲Deux Chevaux Car Tours—If rumbling around Paris and sticking your head out of the rolled-back top of a funky old 2CV car *à la* Inspector Clouseau sounds like your kind of fun, do this. Two enterprising companies have assembled a veritable fleet of these "tin-can" cars (France's version of the VW "bug," which hasn't been made since 1985) for giving tourists tours of Paris day and night (Paris Authentic and 4 Roues Sous 1 Parapluie). Night is best. The student-guides are informal, speak English, and are passionate about showing you their city. Appreciate the simplicity of the vehicle you're in. Notice the bare-bones dashboard. Ask your guide to honk the horn, to run the silly little wipers, and to open and close the air vent—*c'est magnifique!* They'll pick you up and drop you at your hotel or wherever you choose. Paris Authentic offers many options (€45/person for 2 people for a 1-hour tour, €33/person for 3 people; €160/couple for a 2-hour tour that includes Montmartre and a bottle of champagne, 10 percent tip is appropriate, 23 Rue Jean-Jacques Rousseau, mobile 06 64 50 44 19, www.parisauthentic.com, infos@parisauthentic.com). 4 Roues Sous 1 Parapluie, which translates to "4 wheels under 1 umbrella," offers comparable tours with candy-colored cars and drivers dressed in striped shirts and berets. Evening tours last 1.5 hours and cost €90 per person for two, €60 per person if you fit three passengers, and €180 if you want the whole backseat to yourself (tel. 08 00 80 06 31, mobile 06 67 32 26 68, www.4roues-sous-1parapluie.com, info@4roues-sous-1parapluie.com)

Pedicab Tours—Experience the City of Light at an escargot's pace with your private chauffeur pedaling a sleek, human-powered tricycle from TripUp Pedicab Tours. Call ahead, book online, or flag one down; they usually work until about 22:00 (€40-50/hour, mobile 06 98 80 69 33, www.tripup.fr, contact@tripup.fr).

▲Nighttime Bus Tours—Below I've listed two different night tours run by the same parent company (Paris Vision). Tickets are sold through your hotel (no booking fee, brochures in lobby) or directly at the Paris Vision office at 214 Rue de Rivoli, across the street from the Tuileries Métro stop.

The nightly **Paris Illuminations** tour is run by Cityrama and connects all the great illuminated sights of Paris with a 100-minute bus tour in 12 languages. The double-decker buses have huge windows, but the most desirable front seats are sometimes reserved for customers who've bought tickets for the overrated Moulin Rouge. Left-side seats are better. Visibility is fine in the rain.

These tours are not for everyone. You'll stampede on with a United Nations of tourists, get a set of headphones, dial up your language, and listen to a tape-recorded spiel (which is interesting, but includes an annoyingly bright TV screen and a pitch for the other, more expensive excursions). Uninspired as it is, the ride provides an entertaining overview of the city at its floodlit and scenic best. Bring your city map to stay oriented as you go. You're always on the bus, but the driver slows for photos at viewpoints (€25, kids-€12.50, 1.75 hours, departs from 2 Rue des Pyramides at 20:00 Nov-March, at 22:00 April-Oct, reserve one day in advance, arrive 30 minutes early to wait in line for best seats, Mo: Pyramides, tel. 01 42 60 30 01, www.pariscityvision.com/en/cityrama/paris -illuminations).

Paris Vision also offers **Paris Illuminations-By Minibus,** which are minivan night tours following a similar route to the bus tours. They will pick you up and drop you off at your hotel (€55, kids-€40, 2 hours, tel. 01 42 60 30 01, www.parisvision.com).

▲▲▲**Do-It-Yourself Floodlit Paris Taxi Tour**—I recommend a loop trip that takes about an hour and connects these sights: Notre-Dame, Hôtel de Ville, Ile St. Louis, the Orsay Museum, Esplanade des Invalides, Champ de Mars park at Place Jacques Rueff (five-minute stop), Eiffel Tower from Place du Trocadéro (five-minute stop), Arc de Triomphe, Champs-Elysées, Place de la Concorde, and the Louvre. The trip should cost about €45 (taxis have a strict meter of €33/hour plus about €1/kilometer).

Sleeping in Paris

I've focused most of my recommendations in four safe, handy, and colorful neighborhoods: the village-like Rue Cler (near the Eiffel Tower), the artsy and trendy Marais (near Place de la Bastille), the historic island of Ile St. Louis (next door to Notre-Dame), and the lively and Latin yet classy Luxembourg Garden neighborhood (on the Left Bank). Before choosing a hotel, read the descriptions of the neighborhoods closely. Each offers different pros and cons: Your neighborhood is as important as your hotel for the success of your trip.

You'll also find recommendations for good budget accommodations in two more neighborhoods—Montmartre and along lively Rue Mouffetard—plus a few bed-and-breakfast and apartment-rental agencies, and suggestions for sleeping near Paris' airports.

Reserve ahead for Paris—the sooner, the better. In August and at other times when business is slower, some hotels offer lower rates to fill their rooms. Check hotel websites for the best deals. See page 1144 for a list of major holidays and festivals in Paris; for tips on making reservations, see page 28.

Old, characteristic, budget Parisian hotels have always been cramped. Retrofitted with toilets, private showers, and elevators (as most are today), they are even more cramped.

Get suggestions from your hotelier for safe parking (for parking basics, see page 63).

Sleep Code

(€1 = about $1.30, country code: 33)
S = Single, **D** = Double/Twin, **T** = Triple, **Q** = Quad, **b** = bathroom,
s = shower only, * = French hotel rating system (0-5 stars).

Unless otherwise noted, hotel staff speak basic English, credit cards are accepted, and breakfast is not included (but is usually optional). All hotels in these listings have elevators, air-conditioning, Internet access (a public terminal in the lobby for guests to use), and Wi-Fi, unless otherwise noted. "Wi-Fi only" means there's no public computer available.

To help you easily sort through my listings, I've divided the accommodations into three categories based on the price for a standard double room with bath during high season:

$$$ Higher Priced—Most rooms €200 or more.
$$ Moderately Priced—Most rooms between €150-200.
$ Lower Priced—Most rooms €150 or less.

Prices can change without notice; verify the hotel's current rates online or by email.

In the Rue Cler Neighborhood
(7th arrondissement, Mo: Ecole Militaire, La Tour Maubourg, or Invalides)

Rue Cler, lined with open-air produce stands six days a week, is a safe, tidy, village-like pedestrian street. It's so French that when I step out of my hotel in the morning, I feel like I must have been a poodle in a previous life. How such coziness lodged itself between the high-powered government district, the Eiffel Tower, and Les Invalides, I'll never know. This is a neighborhood of wide, tree-lined boulevards, stately apartment buildings, and lots of Americans. The American Church (see page 56), American Library, American University, and many of my readers call this area home. Hotels here are a relatively good value, considering the elegance of the neighborhood and the higher prices of the more cramped hotels in other central areas. And for sightseeing, you're within walking distance of the Eiffel Tower, Army Museum, Quai Branly Museum, Seine River, Champs-Elysées, and Orsay and Rodin museums.

Become a local at a Rue Cler café for breakfast, or join the afternoon crowd for *une bière pression* (a draft beer). On Rue Cler you can eat and browse your way through a street full of cafés, pastry shops, delis, cheese shops, and colorful outdoor produce stalls. Afternoon *boules* (outdoor bowling) on the Esplanade des Invalides is a relaxing spectator sport (look for the dirt area to the upper right as you face the front of Les Invalides; see the sidebar on page 1141). The manicured gardens behind the golden dome of the Army Museum are free, peaceful, and filled with flowers (at southwest corner of grounds, closes at about 19:00).

Though hardly a happening nightlife spot, Rue Cler offers many low-impact after-dark activities. Take an evening stroll above the river through the parkway between Pont de l'Alma and Pont des Invalides. For an after-dinner cruise on the Seine, it's a 15-minute walk to the river and the Bateaux-Mouches (see page 76). For a post-dinner cruise on foot, saunter into the Champ de Mars park to admire the glowing Eiffel Tower. For more ideas on Paris after hours, see "Entertainment in Paris," earlier.

Services: There's a large **post office** at the end of Rue Cler on Avenue de la Motte-Picquet and a handy **SNCF Boutique** at 80 Rue St. Dominique (Mon-Sat 8:30-19:30, closed Sun, get there when it opens to avoid a long wait). At both of these offices, take a number and wait your turn. A smaller post office is closer to the Eiffel Tower on Avenue Rapp, one block past Rue St. Dominique toward the river. You can buy your Paris Museum Pass at **Tabac La Cave à Cigares** on Avenue de la Motte-Picquet, across from where the Rue Cler ends.

Markets: Cross the Champ de Mars park to mix it up with bargain-hunters at the twice-weekly open-air market, **Marché Boulevard de Grenelle,** under the Métro, a few blocks southwest of the Champ de Mars park (Wed and Sun 7:00-12:30, between Mo: Dupleix and Mo: La Motte-Picquet-Grenelle). Two minuscule grocery stores, both on Rue de Grenelle, are open until midnight: **Epicerie de la Tour** (at #197) and **Alimentation** (at corner with Rue Cler). **Rue St. Dominique** is the area's boutique-browsing street and well worth a visit if shopping for clothes.

Internet Access: Com Avenue is good (about €5/hour, shareable and multi-use accounts, Mon-Sat 10:00-20:00, closed Sun, 24 Rue du Champ de Mars, tel. 01 45 55 00 07).

Laundry: Launderettes are omnipresent; ask your hotel for the nearest. Here are three handy locations: on Rue Augereau, on Rue Amélie (both between Rue St. Dominique and Rue de Grenelle), and at the southeast corner of Rue Valadon and Rue de Grenelle.

Booking Agency: To book tickets for key sights, or for assistance with hotels, transportation, or excursions, contact the helpful staff at **Paris Webservices** (Mon-Fri 9:00-21:00, Sat-Sun 9:00-18:00, 12 Rue de l'Exposition, Mo: Ecole Militaire, RER: Pont de l'Alma, tel. 09 52 06 02 59, www.pariswebservices.com, contactpws@pariswebservices.com).

Métro Connections: Key Métro stops are Ecole Militaire, La Tour Maubourg, and Invalides. The useful RER-C line runs from the Pont de l'Alma and Invalides stations, serving Versailles to

PARIS

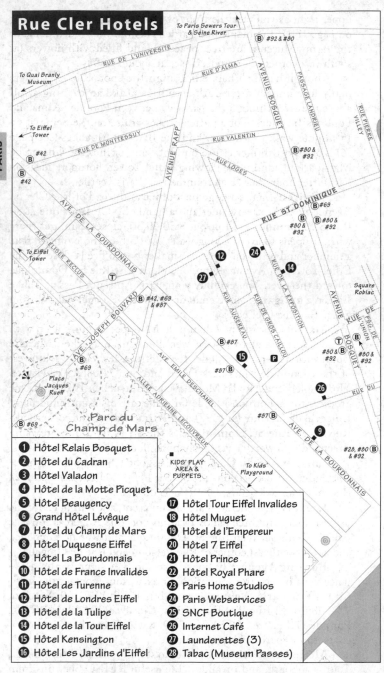

Rue Cler Hotels

To Paris Sewers Tour & Seine River

To Quai Branly Museum

To Eiffel Tower

RUE DE L'UNIVERSITE

RUE D'ALMA

AVENUE BOSQUET

PASSAGE LANDRIEU

RUE PIERRE VILLEY

RUE DE MONTESSUY

AVENUE RAPP

RUE VALENTIN

RUE LOGES

B #42

B #42

AVE. DE LA BOURDONNAIS

AVE. ELISEE RECLUS

To Eiffel Tower

T

AVE. JOSEPH BOUVARD

B #42, #69 & #87

AVE. EMILE DESCHANEL

ALLEE ADRIENNE LECOUVREUR

B #69

Place Jacques Rueff

B #69

Parc du Champ de Mars

RUE ST. DOMINIQUE

B #69

B #80 & #92

B #80 & #92

RUE AUGEREAU

RUE DE GROS CAILLOU

RUE DE LA EXPOSITION

12

27

24

14

AVENUE DE

RUE DE PSG. DE L'UNION

Square Roblac

B #80 & #92

T

B #80 & #92

B #87

B #87

15

P

#87 B

26

RUE DU

9

#28, #80 B & #92

AVE. DE LA BOURDONNAIS

KIDS' PLAY AREA & PUPPETS

To Kids' Playground

1 Hôtel Relais Bosquet
2 Hôtel du Cadran
3 Hôtel Valadon
4 Hôtel de la Motte Picquet
5 Hôtel Beaugency
6 Grand Hôtel Lévêque
7 Hôtel du Champ de Mars
8 Hôtel Duquesne Eiffel
9 Hôtel La Bourdonnais
10 Hôtel de France Invalides
11 Hôtel de Turenne
12 Hôtel de Londres Eiffel
13 Hôtel de la Tulipe
14 Hôtel de la Tour Eiffel
15 Hôtel Kensington
16 Hôtel Les Jardins d'Eiffel

17 Hôtel Tour Eiffel Invalides
18 Hôtel Muguet
19 Hôtel de l'Empereur
20 Hôtel 7 Eiffel
21 Hôtel Prince
22 Hôtel Royal Phare
23 Paris Home Studios
24 Paris Webservices
25 SNCF Boutique
26 Internet Café
27 Launderettes (3)
28 Tabac (Museum Passes)

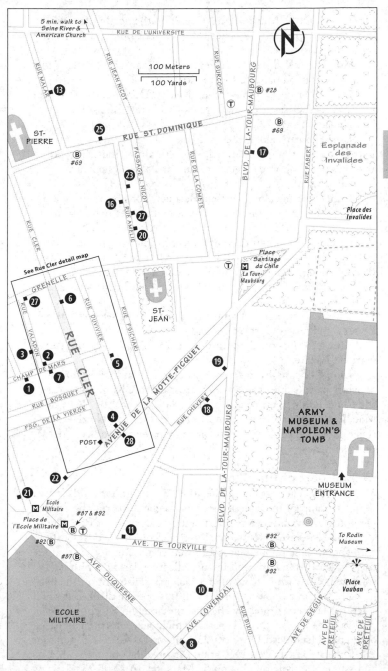

the southwest; the Marmottan Museum to the northwest; and the Orsay Museum, Latin Quarter (St. Michel stop), and Austerlitz train station to the east.

Bus Routes: Smart travelers take advantage of these bus routes (see map on page 70 for stop locations):

Line #69 runs east-west along Rue St. Dominique and serves Les Invalides, Orsay, Louvre, Marais, and Père Lachaise Cemetery (see sidebar on page 72).

Line #63 runs along the river (the Quai d'Orsay), serving the Latin Quarter along Boulevard St. Germain to the east (ending at Gare de Lyon), and Trocadéro and areas near the Marmottan Museum to the west.

Line #92 runs along Avenue Bosquet, north to the Champs-Elysées and Arc de Triomphe (faster than the Métro) and south to the Montparnasse Tower and Gare Montparnasse.

Line #87 runs from Avenue Joseph Bouvard in the Champ de Mars park up Avenue de la Bourdonnais and serves the Sèvres-Babylone shopping area, St. Sulpice Church, Luxembourg Garden, the Bastille, and Gare de Lyon (also more convenient than Métro for these destinations).

Line #80 runs on Avenue Bosquet, crosses the Champs-Elysées, and serves Gare St. Lazare.

Line #28 runs on Boulevard de la Tour Maubourg and serves Gare St. Lazare.

Line #42 runs from Avenue Joseph Bouvard in the Champs de Mars park (same stop as #87), crosses the Champs-Elysées at the Rond-Point, then heads to Place de la Concorde, Place de la Madeleine, Opéra Garnier, and finally to Gare du Nord—a long ride to the train station but less tiring than the Métro if you're carrying suitcases.

In the Heart of Rue Cler

Many of my readers stay in the Rue Cler neighborhood. If you want to disappear into Paris, choose a hotel elsewhere. The following hotels are within Camembert-smelling distance of Rue Cler.

$$$ Hôtel Relais Bosquet*** is a fine hotel in an ideal location, with comfortable public spaces and well-configured rooms that are large by local standards and feature effective darkness blinds. The staff are politely formal and offer a 15 percent discount off the public rate to anyone booking direct with this book in 2013. But you'll often get far better rates by "liking" the hotel on Facebook. Book well in advance for the best rates, which vary enormously based on demand (standard Db-€150-235, bigger Db-€175-275, superior Db-€190-305, extra bed-€29, good €15 breakfast buffet with eggs and sausage, 19 Rue du Champ de Mars, tel. 01 47 05 25 45, www.hotel-paris-bosquet.com, hotel@relaisbosquet.com).

$$$ Hôtel du Cadran*, perfectly located a *boule* toss from Rue Cler, is daringly modern—with a *chocolat-et-macaron* shop/bar in the lobby, efficient staff, and über-stylish yet tight rooms featuring cool colors, mood lighting, and every comfort (Db-€250-290; 5 percent discount off lowest rates—including Internet deals—and free, big breakfast when you use the code "RickSteves rate" and book by email or through their website; 10 Rue du Champ de Mars, tel. 01 40 62 67 00, fax 01 40 62 67 13, www.cadranhotel .com, resa@cadranhotel.com).

$$$ Hôtel Valadon*, almost across the street, is really an annex of Hôtel du Cadran (listed above), where you'll check in and have breakfast. The Valadron's 12 cute-and-quiet rooms are larger than those at the Cadran, with the same comfort, prices, and discounts (Tb available, one good family suite, 16 Rue Valadon, tel. 01 47 53 89 85, www.hotelvaladon.com, info@hotelvaladon.com).

$$ Hôtel de la Motte Picquet*, at the corner of Rue Cler and Avenue de la Motte-Picquet, is an intimate, modest little place with narrow halls, comfortable but compact rooms, and a terrific staff (Moe and Tina). Get a room off the street to avoid street noise (standard Db-€150, bigger Db-€230, Tb/Qb-€270-350, 30 Avenue de la Motte-Picquet, tel. 01 47 05 09 57, fax 01 47 05 74 36, www.hotelmottepicquetparis.com, book@hotelmottepicquetparis .com).

$$ Hôtel Beaugency*, a good value on a quieter street a short block off Rue Cler, has 30 smallish rooms with standard furnishings and a lobby that you can stretch out in (Sb-€120, Db-€155, twin Db-€165, occasional discounts for Rick Steves readers—ask when you book, 21 Rue Duvivier, tel. 01 47 05 01 63, fax 01 45 51 04 96, www.hotel-beaugency.com, infos@hotel-beaugency.com).

Warning: The next two hotels are very busy with my readers (reserve long in advance).

$$ Grand Hôtel Lévêque, ideally located on Rue Cler, is all about location. It's a busy place with a sliver-size elevator, a sleek breakfast room that doubles as a lounge, impersonal service, and so-so accommodations (some rooms are fine, while others feel neglected). Rooms on Rue Cler come with fun views but morning noise as the market sets up (S-€75-120, Db-€140-170, Tb-€200, don't let them talk you into a pricier room than the one you booked, 29 Rue Cler, tel. 01 47 05 49 15, fax 01 45 50 49 36, www.hotel-leveque.com, info@hotel-leveque.com).

$ Hôtel du Champ de Mars, with adorable rooms and serious owners Françoise and Stephane, is a cozy Rue Cler option. This plush little hotel has a small-town feel from top to bottom. The rooms are snug but lovingly kept, and single rooms can work as tiny doubles. It's an excellent value despite the lack of air-conditioning (Sb-€100, Db-€120, 30 yards off Rue Cler at 7 Rue du Champ de Mars, tel. 01 45 51 52 30, fax 01 45 51 64 36, www.hotelduchampdemars.com, reservation@hotelduchampde mars.com).

Near Rue Cler, Close to Ecole Militaire Métro Stop

The following listings are a five-minute walk from Rue Cler, near Métro stop Ecole Militaire or RER: Pont de l'Alma.

$$$ **Hôtel Duquesne Eiffel*****, a few blocks farther from the action, is calm, hospitable, and very comfortable. It features handsome rooms (some with terrific Eiffel Tower views for only €20 more), a welcoming lobby, and a big, hot breakfast for €13 (Db-€190-250, price grows with room size, Tb-€270, 10 percent less with this book in 2013, 23 Avenue Duquesne, tel. 01 44 42 09 09, fax 01 44 42 09 08, www.hotel-duquesne-eiffel-paris.com, contact@hde.fr).

$$$ **Hôtel La Bourdonnais***** is *très* Parisian, mixing an Old World feel with creaky, comfortable rooms and generous public spaces. Its mostly spacious rooms are traditionally decorated, and its bathrooms are due for an upgrade (Db-€200-300, Tb-€240-320, Qb-€280-350, Sophie promises free breakfast with this book through 2013, 111-113 Avenue de la Bourdonnais, tel. 01 47 05 45 42, fax 01 45 55 75 54, www.hotellabourdonnais.fr, hlb@hotella bourdonnais.fr).

$$ **Hôtel de France Invalides**** is an OK mid-range option away from most other hotels I list. It's run by a brother-sister team (Alain and Marie-Hélène) with a small bar/lounge and 60 well-maintained rooms, some with knockout views of Invalides' golden dome. Rooms on the courtyard are very quiet, while those facing Les Invalides face a large street (Sb-€115, standard Db-€140-250, 5 percent discount with this book in 2013, connecting rooms possible for families, no air-con, 102 Boulevard de la Tour Maubourg, tel. 01 47 05 40 49, fax 01 45 56 96 78, www.hoteldefrance.com, contact@hoteldefrance.com).

$ **Hôtel de Turenne**** is modest, with the cheapest air-conditioned rooms I've found and a lobby with windows on the world. Rooms are simple but comfortable, and the price is right. There are five true singles and several connecting rooms good for families (Sb-€70, Db-€85-107, Tb-€150, Wi-Fi only, 20 Avenue de Tourville, tel. 01 47 05 99 92, fax 01 45 56 06 04, www.hotel -turenne-paris.com, info@hotel-turenne-paris.com).

Near Rue Cler, Closer to Rue St. Dominique (and the Seine)

$$$ **Hôtel de Londres Eiffel***** is my closest listing to the Eiffel Tower and the Champ de Mars park. Here you get immaculate,

warmly decorated rooms (several are connecting for families), snazzy public spaces, and a service-oriented staff. Some rooms are pretty small—request a bigger room. It's less convenient to the Métro (10-minute walk), but very handy to buses #69, #80, #87, and #92, and to RER-C: Pont de l'Alma (Sb-€175, small Db-€190, bigger Db-€205, Db with Eiffel Tower view-€230, Tb-€270, 1 Rue Augereau, tel. 01 45 51 63 02, fax 01 47 05 28 96, www.hotel -paris-londres-eiffel.com, info@londres-eiffel.com, helpful Cédric and Arnaud). The owners also run a good two-star hotel with similar comfort in the cheaper Montparnasse area, **$$ Hôtel Apollon Montparnasse** (Db-€140-170, look for Web deals, 91 Rue de l'Ouest, Mo: Pernety, tel. 01 43 95 62 00, fax 01 43 95 62 10, www .apollon-montparnasse.com, info@apollon-montparnasse.com).

$$ Hôtel de la Tulipe*,** three blocks from Rue Cler toward the river, feels pricey but unique. The 20 small and simple rooms surround a seductive, wood-beamed lounge and a peaceful, leafy courtyard. The owners promise a 10 percent discount when you book direct with this book in 2013 (Sb-€160, Db-€182, Tb-€224, 4-person apartment-€335, 2-room suite for up to 5 people-€365, no air-con, no elevator, 33 Rue Malar, tel. 01 45 51 67 21, fax 01 47 53 96 37, www.paris-hotel-tulipe.com, hoteldelatulipe@wanadoo.fr).

$ Hôtel de la Tour Eiffel** is a good two-star value on a quiet street near several of my favorite restaurants. The rooms are well-designed and comfortable, but some have thin walls and none have air-conditioning (snug Db-€110, bigger Db-€120-140, no breakfast offered, Wi-Fi only, 17 Rue de l'Exposition, tel. 01 47 05 14 75, fax 01 47 53 99 46, www.hotel-toureiffel.com, hte7@wanadoo.fr).

$ Hôtel Kensington** is a good budget value close to the Eiffel Tower and run by elegant, though formal, Daniele. It's an unpretentious place with mostly small, basic, but well-kept rooms (Sb-€65-74, Db-€80-97, big Db on back side-€98-117, Eiffel Tower views for those who ask, no air-con, pay Internet access, 79 Avenue de la Bourdonnais, tel. 01 47 05 74 00, fax 01 47 05 25 81, www .hotel-kensington.com, hk@hotel-kensington.com).

Near La Tour Maubourg Métro Stop

The next four listings are within three blocks of the intersection of Avenue de la Motte-Picquet and Boulevard de la Tour Maubourg.

$$$ Hôtel Les Jardins d'Eiffel*,** on a quiet street, feels like the modern motel it is, with professional service, its own parking garage (€24/day), and a spacious lobby. Most rooms are big and quiet by Parisian standards (standard Db-€180-210, renovated Db-€215-240, 15 percent Rick Steves discount when you book direct in 2013, check website for special discounts, 8 Rue Amélie, tel. 01 47 05 46 21, fax 01 45 55 28 08, www.hoteljardinseiffel.com, reservations@hoteljardinseiffel.com).

$$$ Hôtel Tour Eiffel Invalides*** advertises its Best Western status proudly and offers a generous-size lobby with a small courtyard and good, traditionally decorated rooms with big beds but no firm prices (the Internet decides). Allow about €220-280 for a double but look for better rates on their website. Ask for a non-smoking room (35 Boulevard de la Tour Maubourg, tel. 01 45 56 10 78, fax 01 47 05 65 08, www.timhotel.fr, invalides@tim hotel.fr).

$$$ Hôtel Muguet*,** a peaceful, stylish, immaculate refuge, gives you three-star comfort for a two-star price. This delightful spot offers 43 tasteful rooms, a greenhouse lounge, and a small garden courtyard. The hands-on owner, Catherine, gives her guests a restful and secure home in Paris (Sb-€140-175, Db-€195-245—more with view, Tb-€195-245, strict cancellation policy: cancel 7 days before arrival or lose deposit, 11 Rue Chevert, tel. 01 47 05 05 93, fax 01 45 50 25 37, www.hotelparismuguet.com, muguet @wanadoo.fr).

$$$ Hôtel de l'Empereur** is well-run and offers good service. It delivers smashing views of Invalides from most of its very comfortable and tastefully designed rooms. Fifth-floor rooms have small balconies, and all rooms have queen-size beds (Sb-€140-175, Db-€195-245—more with view, Tb-€195-245, two-room Qb-€370, strict cancellation policy: cancel 7 days before arrival or lose deposit, 2 Rue Chevert, tel. 01 45 55 88 02, fax 01 45 51 88 54, www.hotelempereurparis.com, contact@hotelempereur.com).

Lesser Values in the Rue Cler Area

Given how fine this area is, these are acceptable last choices.

$$$ Hôtel 7 Eiffel** is an ultra-modern, high-design, four-star splurge, complete with bar and fireplace lounge in lobby, colorful rooftop terrace, room service, and all the usual comforts of a business hotel (Db-€270-370, check Web for deals, 17 bis Rue Amélie, tel. 01 45 55 10 01, fax 01 47 05 28 68, www.7eiffel.com, reservation@7eiffel.com).

$ Hôtel Prince,** across from the Ecole Militaire Métro stop, has a spartan lobby, drab halls, and plain-but-acceptable rooms for the price (Sb-€109, Db-€130, Tb-€150, free breakfast with this book in 2013, Wi-Fi only, 66 Avenue Bosquet, tel. 01 47 05 40 90, fax 01 47 53 06 62, www.hotel-paris-prince.com, paris@hotel -prince.com).

$ Hôtel Royal Phare,** facing the busy Ecole Militaire Métro stop, is a humble place. The 34 basic, pastel rooms are unimaginative but sleepable. Rooms on the courtyard are quietest, with peek-a-boo views of the Eiffel Tower from the fifth floor up (Sb-€84, Db with shower-€98, Db with tub-€108, Tb-€120, fridges in rooms, no air-con but fans, no Wi-Fi, 40 Avenue de la Motte-Picquet, tel. 01 47 05 57 30, fax 01 45 51 64 41, www.hotel-royalphare-paris .com, hotel-royalphare@wanadoo.fr, friendly manager Hocin).

In the Marais Neighborhood
(4th arrondissement, Mo: Bastille, St. Paul, and Hôtel de Ville)
Those interested in a more SoHo/Greenwich Village-type locale should make the Marais their Parisian home. Once a forgotten Parisian backwater, the Marais—which runs from the Pompidou Center east to the Bastille (a 15-minute walk)—is now one of Paris' most popular residential, tourist, and shopping areas. This is jumbled, medieval Paris at its finest, where classy stone mansions sit alongside trendy bars, antiques shops, and fashion-conscious boutiques. The streets are a fascinating parade of artists, students, tourists, immigrants, and baguette-munching babies in strollers. The Marais is also known as a hub of the Parisian gay and lesbian scene. This area is *sans doute* livelier (and louder) than the Rue Cler area.

In the Marais you have these major sights close at hand: the Carnavalet Museum, Victor Hugo's House, the Jewish Art and History Museum, the Pompidou Center, and the Picasso Museum (closed until summer 2013). You're also a manageable walk from Paris' two islands (Ile St. Louis and Ile de la Cité), home to Notre-Dame and Sainte-Chapelle. The Opéra Bastille, Promenade Plantée park, Place des Vosges (Paris' oldest square), Jewish Quarter (Rue des Rosiers), the Latin Quarter, and night-life-packed Rue de Lappe are also walkable. Strolling home (day or night) from Notre-Dame along Ile St. Louis is marvelous.

Most of my recommended hotels are located a few blocks north of the Marais' main east-west drag, Rue St. Antoine/Rue de Rivoli.

Tourist Information: The nearest TI is at the Pyramides Métro stop (daily May-Oct 9:00-19:00, Nov-April 10:00-19:00).

Services: Most banks and other services are on the main street, Rue de Rivoli, which becomes Rue St. Antoine. Marais **post offices** are on Rue Castex and at the corner of Rue Pavée and Rue des Francs Bourgeois. There's a busy **SNCF Boutique** where you can take care of all train needs on Rue St. Antoine at Rue de Turenne (Mon-Fri 8:00-20:30, Sat 10:00-20:30, closed Sun). A quieter SNCF Boutique is nearer Gare de Lyon at 5 Rue de Lyon (Mon-Sat 8:30-18:00, closed Sun).

Markets: The Marais has two good open-air markets: the sprawling **Marché de la Bastille,** along Boulevard Richard Lenoir, on the north side of Place de la Bastille (Thu and Sun until 14:30); and the more intimate, untouristy **Marché d'Aligre** (Tue-Sat 9:00-14, closed Mon, cross Place de la Bastille and walk about 10 blocks down Rue du Faubourg St. Antoine, turn right at Rue de Cotte to

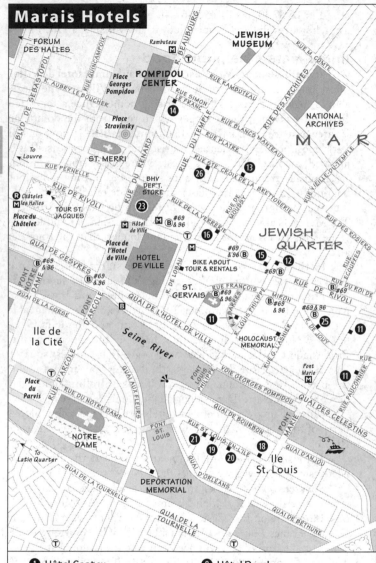

Marais Hotels

- ① Hôtel Castex
- ② Hôtel Bastille Spéria
- ③ Hôtel St. Louis Marais
- ④ Hôtel du 7ème Art
- ⑤ Hôtel de la Place des Vosges
- ⑥ Hôtel Original Paris
- ⑦ Hôtel Jeanne d'Arc
- ⑧ Hôtel Daval
- ⑨ Sully Hôtel
- ⑩ Hôtel Pratic
- ⑪ MIJE Hostels (3)
- ⑫ Hôtel Caron de Beaumarchais
- ⑬ Hôtel de la Bretonnerie
- ⑭ Hôtel Beaubourg

PARIS

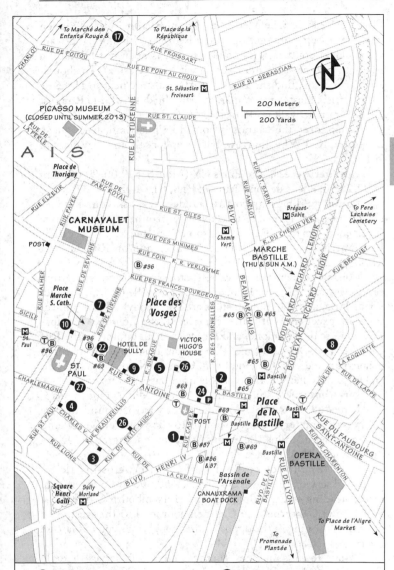

⑮	Hôtel de Nice	㉒	SNCF Boutique
⑯	Hôtel du Loiret	㉓	BHV Department Store
⑰	To Hôtel du Vieux Saule	㉔	Late-Night Grocery
⑱	Hôtel du Jeu de Paume	㉕	Internet Café
⑲	Hôtel de Lutèce	㉖	Launderettes (3)
⑳	Hôtel des Deux-Iles	㉗	Red Wheelbarrow Books
㉑	Hôtel Saint-Louis		

Place d'Aligre; or, take Métro line 8 from Bastille in the direction of Créteil-Préfecture, get off at the Ledru-Rollin stop, and walk a few blocks southeast). A small **grocery** is open until 23:00 on Rue St. Antoine (near intersection with Rue Castex). To shop at a Parisian Sears, find the **BHV** department store next to Hôtel de Ville. Paris' oldest covered market, **Marché des Enfants Rouges,** lies a 10-minute walk north of Rue de Rivoli.

Bookstore: The Marais is home to a fine English-language bookstore, **Red Wheelbarrow,** but it's up for sale and may close in 2013.

Internet Access: Try **Paris CY** (Mon-Sat 10:00-20:00, Sun 13:00-20:00, 8 Rue de Jouy, Mo: St. Paul, tel. 01 42 71 37 37).

Laundry: There are many launderettes; ask your hotelier for the nearest. Here are three you can count on: on Impasse Guémenée (north of Rue St. Antoine), on Rue Ste. Croix de la Bretonnerie (just east of Rue du Temple), and on Rue du Petit Musc (south of Rue St. Antoine).

Métro Connections: Key Métro stops in the Marais are, from east to west: Bastille, St. Paul, and Hôtel de Ville (Sully-Morland, Pont Marie, and Rambuteau stops are also handy). Métro connections are excellent, with direct service to the Louvre, Champs-Elysées, Arc de Triomphe, and La Défense (all on line 1); the Rue Cler area and Opéra Garnier (line 8 from Bastille stop); and four major train stations: Gare de Lyon, Gare du Nord, Gare de l'Est, and Gare d'Austerlitz (all accessible from Bastille stop).

Bus Routes: For stop locations, see the "Marais Hotels" map.

Line #69 on Rue St. Antoine takes you eastbound to Père Lachaise Cemetery and westbound to the Louvre, Orsay, and Rodin museums, plus the Army Museum, ending at the Eiffel Tower (see sidebar on page 72).

Line #87 runs down Boulevard Henri IV, crossing Ile St. Louis and serving the Latin Quarter along Boulevard St. Germain, before heading to St. Sulpice Church/Luxembourg Garden, the Eiffel Tower, and the Rue Cler neighborhood to the west. The same line, running in the opposite direction, brings you to Gare de Lyon.

Line #96 runs on Rues Turenne and Rivoli, serves Ile de la Cité and St. Sulpice Church (near Luxembourg Garden), and ends at Gare Montparnasse.

Line #65 runs from Gare de Lyon up Rue de Lyon, around Place de la Bastille, and then up Boulevard Beaumarchais to Gare de l'Est and Gare du Nord.

Line #67 runs from Place d'Italie to the Jardin des Plantes (just south of the Seine), across Ile St. Louis (on Boulevard Henri IV), along Rue de Rivoli past the Louvre, then up to Montmartre.

Taxis: You'll find taxi stands on Place de la Bastille (where

PARIS

Boulevard Richard Lenoir meets the square), on the south side of Rue St. Antoine (in front of St. Paul Church), behind the Hôtel de Ville on Rue du Lobau (where it meets Rue de Rivoli), and a quieter one on the north side of Rue St. Antoine (where it meets Rue Castex).

Near Place des Vosges

$$ Hôtel Castex*,** on a quiet street near Place de la Bastille, is a well-located place with tile-floored rooms (that amplify noise). Their clever system of connecting rooms allows families total privacy between two rooms, each with its own bathroom. The 30 rooms are narrow (Sb-€145, Db-€175, Tb-€220, free buffet breakfast with this book through 2013, just off Place de la Bastille and Rue St. Antoine at 5 Rue Castex, Mo: Bastille, tel. 01 42 72 31 52, fax 01 42 72 57 91, www.castexhotel.com, info@castexhotel.com).

$$ Hôtel Bastille Spéria*,** a short block off Place de la Bastille, offers business-type service in a great location. The 42 well-configured rooms are modern and comfortable, with big beds (Sb-€135-150, Db-€165-185, good buffet breakfast-€13, 1 Rue de la Bastille, Mo: Bastille, tel. 01 42 72 04 01, fax 01 42 72 56 38, www .hotelsperia.com, info@hotelsperia.com).

$$ Hôtel St. Louis Marais*,** an intimate little hotel, lies on a quiet street closer to the river. The well-maintained rooms come with character and reasonable rates (Db-€175-195, 1 Rue Charles V, tel. 01 48 87 87 04, www.saintlouismarais.com).

$$ Hôtel Original Paris*,** on a busy street barely off Place de la Bastille, has artsy rooms and a good location (Db-€155-190, 8 Boulevard Beaumarchais, Mo: Bastille, tel. 01 47 00 91 50, fax 01 47 00 06 31, www.hoteloriginalparis.com, info@hoteloriginalparis .com).

$ Hôtel du 7ème Art,** two blocks south of Rue St. Antoine toward the river, is a young, carefree, Hollywood-nostalgia place with a full-service café-bar and Charlie Chaplin murals. Its 23 good-value rooms have brown 1970s decor, but are comfortable enough. Sadly, smoking is allowed in all rooms, so you might detect an odor. The large rooms are American-spacious (small Db-€100, standard Db-€115, large Db-€130-160, Tb-€150-180, extra bed-€20, no elevator, 20 Rue St. Paul, Mo: St. Paul, tel. 01 44 54 85 00, fax 01 42 77 69 10, www.paris-hotel-7art.com, hotel 7art@wanadoo.fr).

$ Hôtel de la Place des Vosges** has simple, chic rooms and is brilliantly located between Rue St. Antoine and Place des Vosges. Amenities are sparse, there's no air-conditioning, and the elevator skips floors five and six, but the price is right (Db-€95-140, 12 Rue de Biraque, Mo: St. Paul, tel. 01 42 72 60 46, fax 01 42 72 02 64, www.hotelplacedesvosges.com, contact@hpdv.net).

$ Hôtel Jeanne d'Arc**, a lovely little hotel with a stylish lobby and thoughtfully appointed rooms, is ideally located for (and very popular with) connoisseurs of the Marais. It's a fine value and worth booking way ahead (three months in advance, if possible). Sixth-floor rooms have views, and corner rooms are wonderfully bright in the City of Light. Rooms on the street can be noisy until the bars close (Sb-€65-96, Db-€96, larger twin Db-€119, Tb-€149, good Qb-€164, no air-con, Wi-Fi only—in lobby, 3 Rue de Jarente, Mo: St. Paul, tel. 01 48 87 62 11, fax 01 70 24 83 38, www.hoteljeannedarc.com, information@hoteljeannedarc.com).

$ Hôtel Daval**, an unassuming place on the wild side of Place de la Bastille, is ideal for night owls. The rooms are tiny and the halls are narrow, but the rates are good for an air-conditioned place. Ask for a quieter room on the courtyard side if sleep matters (Sb-€86, Db-€92-101, Tb-€112, Qb-€131, Wi-Fi only, 21 Rue Daval, Mo: Bastille, tel. 01 47 00 51 23, fax 01 40 21 80 26, www.hoteldaval.com, info@hoteldaval.com).

$ Sully Hôtel, sitting right on Rue St. Antoine, is a basic, cheap dive run by no-nonsense Monsieur Zeroual. The rooms are frumpy, dimly lit, and can smell of smoke, and the entry is narrow, but the price fits (Db-€80, Tb-€90, Qb-€110, no elevator, no air-con, Wi-Fi only, 48 Rue St. Antoine, Mo: St. Paul, tel. 01 42 78 49 32, fax 01 44 61 76 50, www.sullyhotelparis.com, sullyhotel @orange.fr).

$ Hôtel Pratic, just off the quiet and charming Place du Sainte Catherine, works for travelers who don't mind squeezing sideways to make it past the bed into the bathroom. The half-timbered interior gives this hotel a modest level of charm, but also makes for dark rooms and hallways (Sb-€69, Db-€69-119, Tb-€119-159, more for rooms with view of square, no elevator, no air-con, 9 Rue d'Ormesson, tel. 01 48 87 80 47, fax 01 48 87 40 04, www.pratichotelparis.com, pratic.hotel@wanadoo.fr).

$ *MIJE Youth Hostels:* The Maison Internationale de la Jeunesse et des Etudiants (MIJE) runs three classy old residences, ideal for budget travelers. Each is well-maintained, with simple, clean, single-sex (unless your group takes a whole room), one- to four-bed rooms for travelers of any age. The hostels are **MIJE Fourcy** (biggest and loudest, €11 dinners available with a membership card, 6 Rue de Fourcy, just south of Rue de Rivoli), **MIJE Fauconnier** (no elevator, 11 Rue du Fauconnier), and **MIJE Maubisson** (smallest and quietest, no outdoor terrace, 12 Rue des Barres). None have double beds or air-conditioning; all have private showers in every room (all prices per person: Sb-€51, Db-€38, Tb-€33, Qb-€31, credit cards accepted, includes breakfast but not towels, required membership card-€2.50 extra/person, 7-day maximum stay, rooms locked 12:00-15:00, curfew at 1:00 in the morning). They all share the same contact information (tel. 01 42 74 23 45, fax 01 40 27 81 64, www.mije.com, info@mije.com) and Métro stop (St. Paul). Reservations are accepted (six weeks ahead online, 10 days ahead by phone)—though you must show up by noon, or call the morning of arrival to confirm a later arrival time.

Near the Pompidou Center

These hotels are farther west, closer to the Pompidou Center than to Place de la Bastille. The Hôtel de Ville Métro stop works well for all of these hotels, unless a closer stop is noted.

PARIS

$$ Hôtel Caron de Beaumarchais***, on a busy corner, feels like a fluffy folk museum, with 20 pricey but cared-for and char-acter-filled rooms. Its small lobby is cluttered with bits from an elegant 18th-century Marais house (small Db in back-€165, larger Db facing the front-€195, Wi-Fi only, 12 Rue Vieille du Temple, tel. 01 42 72 34 12, fax 01 42 72 34 63, www.carondebeaumarchais .com).

$$ Hôtel de la Bretonnerie***, three blocks from the Hôtel de Ville, makes a fine Marais home. It has a warm, welcoming lobby and 29 well-appointed, good-value rooms with an antique, open-beam warmth but no air-conditioning (standard "clas-sic" Db-€145, bigger "charming" Db-€175, Db suite-€200, Tb/ Qb-€225, between Rue Vieille du Temple and Rue des Archives at 22 Rue Ste. Croix de la Bretonnerie, tel. 01 48 87 77 63, fax 01 42 77 26 78, www.bretonnerie.com, hotel@bretonnerie.com).

$$ Hôtel Beaubourg*** is a solid three-star value on a small street in the shadow of the Pompidou Center. The lounge is invit-ing, and the 28 rooms are comfy, well-appointed, and quiet (stan-dard Db-€140, bigger twin or king-size Db-€160 and worth the extra cost, rates vary wildly with availability, 11 Rue Simon Le Franc, Mo: Rambuteau, tel. 01 42 74 34 24, fax 01 42 78 68 11, www .beaubourg-paris-hotel.com, reservation@hotelbeaubourg.com).

$ Hôtel de Nice**, on the Marais' busy main drag, features a turquoise-and-fuchsia "Marie-Antoinette-does-tie-dye" decor. Its narrow halls are littered with paintings and layered with carpets, and its 23 Old World rooms have thoughtful touches and tight bathrooms. Twin rooms, which cost the same as doubles, are larger and on the street side—but have effective double-paned windows (Sb-€80-130, Db-€110-160, Tb-€135-170, reception on second floor, 42 bis Rue de Rivoli, tel. 01 42 78 55 29, fax 01 42 78 36 07, www.hoteldenice.com, contact@hoteldenice.com, laissez-faire management).

$ Hôtel du Loiret* is a centrally located and rare Marais bud-get hotel. It's basic, but the rooms are surprisingly sharp, consid-ering the price and location (Db-€80-100, Tb-€130, no air-con, expect some noise, 8 Rue des Mauvais Garçons, tel. 01 48 87 77 00, fax 01 48 04 96 56, www.hotel-du-loiret.fr, hotelduloiret@hotmail .com).

Near the Marché des Enfants Rouges

$$ Hôtel du Vieux Saule* has 27 simple rooms with little character in a great location. Rooms are tight and modern. Avoid the smoking rooms on the first floor (Sb-€95-140, Db-€110-160, *supérieure* Db-€145-190, deluxe Db-€180-250, rates vary greatly with season, check online for best deals, small sauna free for guests, 6 Rue de Picardie, Mo: Filles du Calvaire or Temple, tel. 01 42 72 01 14, fax 01 40 27 88 21, www.hotelvieuxsaule.com, reserv @hotelvieuxsaule.com).

On Ile St. Louis
(4th arrondissement; Mo: Pont Marie and Sully-Morland)
The peaceful, residential character of this river-wrapped island, with its brilliant location and homemade ice cream, has drawn Americans for decades. There are no budget values here—all of the hotels are three-star or more—though prices are reasonable for the level of comfort. The island's village ambience and proximity to the Marais, Notre-Dame, and the Latin Quarter make this area well worth considering. All of the following hotels are on the island's main drag, Rue St. Louis-en-l'Ile, where I list several restaurants (see page 200). For nearby services, see the Marais neighborhood section; for locations, see the Marais Hotels map, earlier.

$$$ Hôtel du Jeu de Paume**,** occupying a 17th-century tennis center, is the most expensive hotel I list in Paris. When you enter its magnificent lobby, you'll understand why. Greet Scoop, *le chien*, then take a spin in the glass elevator for a half-timbered-tree-house experience. The 30 rooms are carefully designed and tasteful, though not particularly spacious (you're paying for the location and public areas). Most rooms face a small garden; all are pin-drop peaceful (standard Db-€290-330, deluxe Db-€400-560, €18 breakfast, 54 Rue St. Louis-en-l'Ile, tel. 01 43 26 14 18, fax 01 40 46 02 76, www.jeudepaumehotel.com, info@jeudepaumehotel .com).

$$$ Hôtel de Lutèce* comes with a sit-awhile wood-paneled lobby and a real fireplace. Rooms at this appealing hotel are handsome, and those on lower floors have high ceilings. Twin rooms are larger and the same price as double rooms. Rooms with bathtubs are on the louder street-side, while those with showers are on the courtyard (Db-€220, Tb-€255, 65 Rue St. Louis-en-l'Ile, tel. 01 43 26 23 52, fax 01 43 29 60 25, www.hoteldelutece .com, info@hoteldelutece.com).

$$$ Hôtel des Deux-Iles* has the same owners and same prices as the Lutèce (listed above), with a tad less personality (59

Rue St. Louis-en-l'Ile, tel. 01 43 26 13 35, fax 01 43 29 60 25, www .hoteldesdeuxiles.com, info@hoteldesdeuxiles.com).

$$ Hôtel Saint-Louis* blends character with modern comforts. The well-maintained rooms come with cool stone floors and exposed beams. Rates are reasonable...for the location (Db-€175-195, top-floor Db with micro-balcony-€245, Tb-€289, iPads available for guest in-room use, 75 Rue St. Louis-en-l'Ile, tel. 01 46 34 04 80, fax 01 46 34 02 13, www.hotelsaintlouis.com, slouis@noos.fr).

PARIS

In the Luxembourg Garden Area (St. Sulpice to Panthéon)

(5th and 6th arrondissements, Mo: St. Sulpice, Mabillon, Odéon, and Cluny-La Sorbonne; RER: Luxembourg)

This neighborhood revolves around Paris' loveliest park and offers quick access to the city's best shopping streets and grandest café-hopping. Hotels in this central area are more expensive than those in the Rue Cler area or Marais neighborhood, but a better value than accommodations on Ile St. Louis. Sleeping in the Luxembourg area offers a true Left Bank experience without a hint of the low-end commotion of the nearby Latin Quarter tourist ghetto. The Luxembourg Garden, Boulevard St. Germain, Cluny Museum, and Latin Quarter are all at your doorstep. Here you get the best of both worlds: youthful Left Bank energy and the classic trappings that surround the monumental Panthéon and St. Sulpice Church.

Having the Luxembourg Garden as your backyard allows strolls through meticulously cared-for flowers, a great kids' play area, and a purifying escape from city traffic. Place St. Sulpice presents an elegant, pedestrian-friendly square and quick access to some of Paris' best boutiques. Sleeping in the Luxembourg area also puts several movie theaters at your fingertips (at Métro stop: Odéon), as well as lively cafés on Boulevard St. Germain, Rue de Buci, Rue des Canettes, Place de la Sorbonne, and Place de la Contrescarpe, all of which buzz with action until late.

While it takes only 15 minutes to walk from one end of this neighborhood to the other, I've located the hotels by the key monument they are close to (St. Sulpice Church, the Odéon Theater, and the Panthéon). Most hotels are within a five-minute walk of the Luxembourg Garden (and none is more than 15 minutes away).

Services: The nearest **TI** is across the river at the Pyramides Métro stop (daily May-Oct 9:00-19:00, Nov-April 10:00-19:00). There are two useful **SNCF Boutiques** for easy train reservations and ticket purchase: at 79 Rue de Rennes (Mon-Sat 10:00-19:00, closed Sun) and at 54 Boulevard St. Michel (Tue-Sat 8:15-19:45, Mon 13:00-19:45, closed Sun).

PARIS

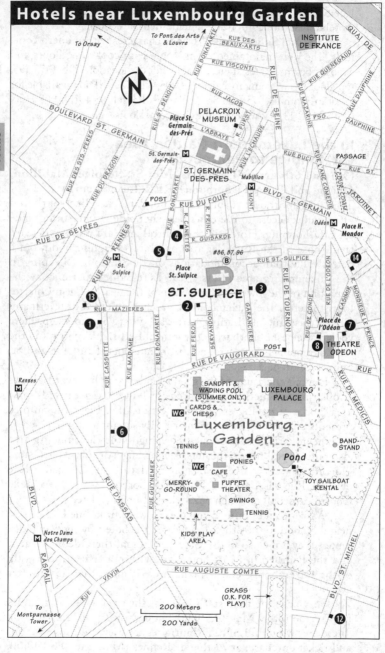

Hotels near Luxembourg Garden

To Orsay

To Pont des Arts & Louvre

INSTITUTE DE FRANCE

QUAI DE

RUE DES BEAUX-ARTS

RUE VISCONTI

RUE BONAPARTE

RUE DE SEINE

RUE MAZARINE

RUE QUEREGAUD

RUE DAUPHINE

DAUPHINE

PSG

RUE JACOB

RUE ST. BENOIT

BOULEVARD ST. GERMAIN

Place St. Germain-des-Prés

DELACROIX MUSEUM

L'ABBAYE

R. FURST.

St. Germain-des-Prés Ⓜ

ST. GERMAIN-DES-PRÉS

RUE DE L'ÉCHAUDE

RUE BUCI

PASSAGE

RUE ST.

RUE DES SIS.-PERES

RUE DU DRAGON

Mabillion

Ⓜ

R. MONT.

BLVD. ST. GERMAIN

RUE ST. ANC. COMEDIE

COUR. COMM.

ST. JARDINET

BOULEVARD ST. GERMAIN

POST

RUE DU FOUR

RUE BONAPARTE

R. CANETTES

R. PRINC

RUE DE SEVRES

RUE DE RENNES

4

5

Odéon Ⓜ Place H. Mondor

R. GUISARDE

#86, 87, 96

Ⓑ

RUE ST. SULPICE

14

St. Sulpice Ⓜ

Place St. Sulpice

ST. SULPICE

3

Place de l'Odéon

RUE DE L'ODEON

RUE DE TOURNON

RUE DE CONDE

R. CASIMIR

MONSIEUR LE PRINCE

13

RUE MAZIERES

2

GARANCIERE

7

RUE CASSETTE

RUE MADAME

RUE BONAPARTE

RUE FEROU

SERVANDONI

POST

8 THEATRE ODEON

1

Rennes Ⓜ

RUE DE VAUGIRARD

RUE

RUE DE MEDICIS

BLVD.

RUE GUYNEMER

SANDPIT & WADING POOL (SUMMER ONLY)

CARDS & CHESS

WC

LUXEMBOURG PALACE

TENNIS

Luxembourg Garden

BAND-STAND

6

WC

PONIES

CAFE

Pond

MERRY-GO-ROUND

PUPPET THEATER

TOY SAILBOAT RENTAL

RUE D'ASSAS

SWINGS

TENNIS

RASPAIL

Notre Dame des Champs Ⓜ

KIDS' PLAY AREA

RUE VAVIN.

RUE

RUE AUGUSTE COMTE

GRASS (O.K. FOR PLAY)

BLVD. ST. MICHEL

To Montparnasse Tower

200 Meters

200 Yards

12

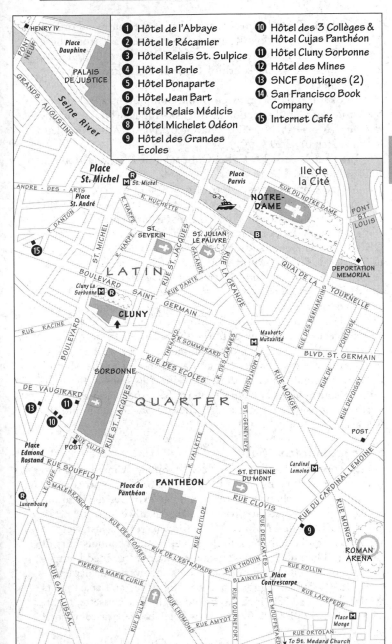

1 Hôtel de l'Abbaye
2 Hôtel le Récamier
3 Hôtel Relais St. Sulpice
4 Hôtel la Perle
5 Hôtel Bonaparte
6 Hôtel Jean Bart
7 Hôtel Relais Médicis
8 Hôtel Michelet Odéon
9 Hôtel des Grandes Ecoles
10 Hôtel des 3 Collèges & Hôtel Cujas Panthéon
11 Hôtel Cluny Sorbonne
12 Hôtel des Mines
13 SNCF Boutiques (2)
14 San Francisco Book Company
15 Internet Café

Markets: The colorful street market at the south end of Rue Mouffetard is a worthwhile 10- to 15-minute walk from these hotels (Tue-Sat 10:00-13:00 & 16:00-19:00, Sun 10:00-13:00, closed Mon, five blocks south of Place de la Contrescarpe, Mo: Place Monge).

Bookstore: San Francisco Book Company is a welcoming bookstore with a full selection of English-language books, including mine (Mon-Sat 11:00-21:00, Sun 14:00-19:30, 17 Rue Monsieur le Prince, tel. 01 43 29 15 70).

Internet Access: Try **Cyber Cube** at 5 Rue Mignon (Mon-Sat 10:00-10:00, closed Sun).

Métro Connections: Métro lines 10 and 4 serve this area (10 connects to the Austerlitz train station, and 4 runs to the Montparnasse, Est, and Nord train stations). Neighborhood stops are Cluny-La Sorbonne, Mabillon, Odéon, and St. Sulpice. RER-B (Luxembourg station is handiest) provides direct service to Charles de Gaulle airport and Gare du Nord trains, and access to Orly airport via the Orlybus (transfer at Denfert-Rochereau).

Bus Routes: Buses #86 and #87 run eastbound through this area on or near Boulevard St. Germain, and westbound along Rue des Ecoles, stopping on Place St. Sulpice. Lines #63 and #87 provide a direct connection west to the Rue Cler area. Line #63 also serves the Orsay and Marmottan museums to the west and Gare de Lyon to the east. Lines #86 and #87 run east to the Marais, and #87 continues to Gare de Lyon. Line #96 stops at Place St. Sulpice southbound en route to Gare Montparnasse and runs north along Rue de Rennes and Boulevard St. Germain into the Marais.

Near St. Sulpice Church

These hotels are all within a block of St. Sulpice Church and two blocks from famous Boulevard St. Germain. This is nirvana for boutique-minded shoppers—and you'll pay extra for the location. Métro stops St. Sulpice and Mabillon are equally close.

$$$ Hôtel de l'Abbaye**** is a lovely refuge just west of Luxembourg Garden; it's a find for well-heeled connoisseurs of this area. The hotel's four-star luxury includes refined lounges inside and out, with 44 sumptuous rooms and every amenity (standard Db-€265-285, bigger Db-€385-415, suites and apartments available for €480-580, includes breakfast, 10 Rue Cassette, tel. 01 45 44 38 11, fax 01 45 48 07 86, www.hotelabbayeparis.com, hotel.abbaye@wanadoo.fr).

$$$ Hôtel le Récamier**, romantically tucked in the corner of Place St. Sulpice, is high-end defined, with designer public spaces, elaborately appointed rooms, a courtyard tea salon, and professional service (classic Db-€260, deluxe Db-€300, traditional Db-€330, deluxe rooms offer best value, 3 bis Place St. Sulpice, tel. 01 43 26 04 89, fax 01 43 26 35 76, www.hotelrecamier.com, contact@hotelrecamier.com).

$$$ Hôtel Relais St. Sulpice*, burrowed on the small street just behind St. Sulpice Church, is a high-priced boutique hotel with a cozy lounge and 26 dark, stylish rooms, most surrounding a leafy glass atrium. Top-floor rooms get more light and are worth requesting (Db-€222-270 depending on size, much less off-season, sauna free for guests, 3 Rue Garancière, tel. 01 46 33 99 00, fax 01 46 33 00 10, www.relais-saint-sulpice.com, relaisstsulpice@wanadoo.fr).

$$$ Hôtel la Perle*** is a spendy pearl in the thick of the lively Rue des Canettes, a block off Place St. Sulpice. This modern, business-class hotel is built around a central bar and atrium (standard Db-€210, bigger Db-€225, luxury Db-€250, check website or call for last-minute deals within 5 days of your stay, 14 Rue des Canettes, tel. 01 43 29 10 10, fax 01 46 34 51 04, www.hotellaperle.com, frontdesk@hotellaperle.com).

$ Hôtel Bonaparte,** an unpretentious and welcoming place wedged between boutiques, is a few steps from Place St. Sulpice. Although the 29 Old World rooms don't live up to the handsome entry, they're plenty comfortable and spacious by Paris standards, with big bathrooms, traditional decor, and molded ceilings (Sb-€104-128, Db-€130-169, Tb-€171, 61 Rue Bonaparte, tel. 01 43 26 97 37, fax 01 46 33 57 67, www.hotelbonaparte.fr, reservation@hotelbonaparte.fr; helpful Fréderic and owner Eric at reception).

West of Luxembourg Garden

$ Hôtel Jean Bart** feels like it's from another era—prices included. Run by smiling Madame Lechopier, it's a rare budget hotel find in this neighborhood, one block from Luxembourg Garden. Beyond the dark, retirement home-like lobby, you'll find 33 spotless rooms with creaking floors and tight bathrooms. The cheapest rooms share one shower on the first floor (S-€57, Sb-€70, D-€57, Db-€78-82, cash only, no air-con, 9 Rue Jean-Bart, tel. 01 45 48 29 13, fax 01 45 48 10 79, hotel.jean.bart@gmail.com).

Near the Odéon Theater

These two hotels are between the Odéon Métro stop and Luxembourg Garden (five blocks east of St. Sulpice) and may have rooms when others don't. In addition to the Odéon Métro stop, the RER-B Luxembourg stop is a short walk away.

$$$ Hôtel Relais Médicis*** is ideal if you've always wanted to live in a Monet painting and can afford it. A glassy entry hides 17 rooms surrounding a fragrant little garden courtyard and fountain, giving you a countryside break fit for a Medici in the heart of Paris. This delightful refuge is tastefully decorated with floral Old World charm and permeated with thoughtfulness (Sb-€172, Db-€208-228, deluxe Db-€258, Tb-€298, Qb-€348, €30 cheaper mid-July-Aug and Nov-March, includes extravagant continental breakfast, faces the Odéon Theater at 5 Place de l'Odéon, tel. 01 43 26 00 60, fax 01 40 46 83 39, www.relaismedicis.com, reservation@relais medicis.com, kind Marie at reception).

$ Hôtel Michelet Odéon** sits in a corner of Place de l'Odéon with big windows on the square. Though it lacks personality, it's a fair value in this pricey area, with 24 simple rooms with modern decor and views of the square (Db-€120-140, Tb-€170, Qb-€190, no air-con, 6 Place de l'Odéon, tel. 01 53 10 05 60, fax 01 46 34 55 35, www.hotelmicheletodeon.com, hotel@micheletodeon.com).

Near the Panthéon and Rue Mouffetard

$ Hôtel des Grandes Ecoles** is idyllic. A private cobbled lane leads to three buildings that protect a flower-filled garden courtyard, preserving a sense of tranquility rare in this city. Its 51 rooms are French-countryside-pretty and reasonably spacious, but have no air-conditioning. This romantic spot is deservedly popular, so book ahead. Reservations are not accepted more than four months in advance; new openings become available on the 15th of each month (Db-€120-150 depending on size, extra bed-€20, no TVs in rooms, parking garage-€30/day, 75 Rue du Cardinal Lemoine, Mo: Cardinal Lemoine, tel. 01 43 26 79 23, fax 01 43 25 28 15, www .hotel-grandes-ecoles.com, hotel.grandes.ecoles@free.fr; mellow Marie speaks English, Mama does not).

$ Hôtel des 3 Collèges** greets clients with a bright lobby, narrow hallways, and unimaginative rooms. Rates are fair and the smiling staff is eager to please (Sb-€89-114, Db-€111-160, Tb-€160-180, 16 Rue Cujas, tel. 01 43 54 67 30, fax 01 46 34 02 99, www.3colleges.com, hotel@3colleges.com).

$ Hôtel Cujas Panthéon** gives boring, standard two-star comfort with air-conditioning at fair prices (Db-€130-145, Tb-€170-180, free Wi-Fi, 18 Rue Cujas, tel. 01 43 54 58 10, fax 01 43 25 88 02, www.cujas-pantheon-paris-hotel.com, hotel-cujas -pantheon@wanadoo.fr).

$ Hôtel Cluny Sorbonne** is a modest place located in the thick of things across from the famous university and below the Panthéon. Rooms are well-worn with thin walls (small Db-€105-110, really big Db/Tb/Qb-€160, check website for deals, no air-con, Wi-Fi only, 8 Rue Victor Cousin, tel. 01 43 54 66 66, fax 01 43 29 68 07, www.hotel-cluny.fr, cluny@club-internet.fr).

South of Luxembourg Garden

$$ Hôtel des Mines** is less central, but its 50 well-maintained rooms are a fair value and come with updated bathrooms and an inviting lobby (Sb-€125, Db-€160, Tb-€190, Qb-€220, less for last-minute bookings and stays of 3 nights or more, frequent Web deals, between Luxembourg and Port-Royal stations on the RER-B line, a 10-minute walk from Panthéon, one block past Luxembourg Garden at 125 Boulevard St. Michel, tel. 01 43 54 32 78, fax 01 46 33 72 52, www.hoteldesminesparis.com, hotel @hoteldesminesparis.com).

PARIS

Budget Accommodations Away from the Center

Acceptable budget accommodations in central neighborhoods are few and far between in Paris. I've listed the best I could find in the neighborhoods described previously, most at about €100 for a double room. These are great (moderate) budget options, but if you want even lower rates or greater selection, you need to look farther away from the river (prices drop proportionately with distance from the Seine). Below you'll find more budget listings in less-central, but still-appealing neighborhoods. You'll spend more time on the Métro or bus getting to sights but save money by sleeping in these areas.

At the Bottom of Rue Mouffetard

These accommodations, away from the Seine and other tourists in an appealing workaday area, offer more room for your euro. Rue Mouffetard is the bohemian soul of this area. Two thousand years ago, it was the principal Roman road south to Italy. Today, this small, meandering street has a split personality. The lower half thrives in the daytime as a pedestrian shopping street. The upper half sleeps during the day, but comes alive after dark. Use Métro stop Censier Daubenton or Les Gobelins. A terrific Saturday market sprawls along Boulevard Port Royal, just east of the Port Royal Métro stop.

$ Port-Royal-Hôtel* has only one star, but don't let that fool you. Its 46 rooms are polished top to bottom and have been well-run by the same proud family for 81 years. You could eat off the floors of its spotless, comfy rooms...but you won't find air-conditioning, Internet access, or Wi-Fi. Ask for a room away from the street (S-€49-60, D-€60, Db-€86-96 depending on size, big shower down the hall-€3, cash only, nonrefundable cash deposit required, on busy Boulevard de Port-Royal at #8, Mo: Les Gobelins, tel. 01 43 31 70 06, fax 01 43 31 33 67, www.hotelportroyal.fr, portroyal hotel@wanadoo.fr).

PARIS

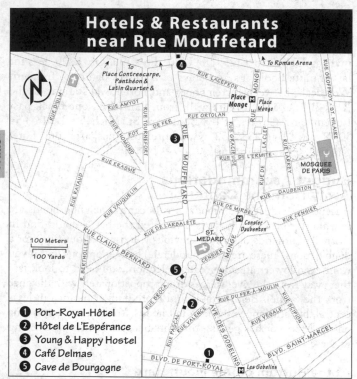

Hotels & Restaurants near Rue Mouffetard

① Port-Royal-Hôtel
② Hôtel de L'Espérance
③ Young & Happy Hostel
④ Café Delmas
⑤ Cave de Bourgogne

$ Hôtel de L'Espérance** is simply a terrific two-star value. It's quiet and cushy, with soft rooms, canopy beds, and nice public spaces (Sb-€85, Db-€85-100, Tb-€120, 15 Rue Pascal, Mo: Censier Daubenton, tel. 01 47 07 10 99, fax 01 43 37 56 19, www.hotelde lesperance.fr, hotel.esperance@wanadoo.fr).

$ Young & Happy Hostel is easygoing, well-run, and English-speaking, with Internet access, kitchen facilities, and acceptable hostel conditions. It sits dead-center in the Rue Mouffetard action...which can be good or bad (all rates per person: bunk in 4- to 10-bed co-ed dorm-€24-32, in 3- to 5-bed female-only dorm-€28, in double room-€35, includes breakfast, sheet deposit-€5, towel-€1, credit cards accepted, no air-con, no lockers but safety box at reception, pay Wi-Fi, 11:00-16:00 lockout but reception stays open, no curfew, 80 Rue Mouffetard, Mo: Place Monge, tel. 01 47 07 47 07, fax 01 47 07 22 24, www.youngand happy.fr, smile@youngandhappy.fr, friendly Alex at the helm).

Montmartre

Montmartre is surprisingly quiet once you get away from the touristy top of the hill. Ditch the flow of visitors streaming from

Place d'Anvers to Sacré-Cœur Basilica, and you'll find a charming neighborhood happily living in the shadow of the hulking monument. Montmartre is a mix of young families, artists, and sprightly senior citizens, and is becoming increasingly popular with the *bobo* crowd (*bourgeois bohemian*, French for "hipster"). Travelers will find good deals on hotel rooms and a lively atmosphere, especially in the evenings when the terraces are full and tiny bars spill crowds onto the narrow streets. There's a TI at the Anvers Métro stop (daily 10:00-18:00, 72 Boulevard Rochechouart).

Most of the action is centered around Rue des Abbesses, starting at Place des Abbesses, and stretching several blocks to Rue Lepic. Rue Lepic is also lively, but the lower you go the seedier it gets: Scammers and shady characters swarm the base of the hill after hours (along Boulevard Clichy and Boulevard Rochechouart, where you'll find what's left of Paris' red light district). For fun nightlife, explore the narrow streets uphill from Rue des Abbesses around Rue Durantin and Rue des Trois Frères. For restaurant suggestions, see page 208.

Métro and Bus Connections: Métro line 12 is the handiest (use the Abbesses stop). Line 2 is also close, using the Blanche, Pigalle, or Anvers stops, but requires a four-block uphill walk to reach my recommended hotels. There's only one bus line on the hill—the Montmartrobus electric bus—which connects Pigalle, Abbesses, and Place du Tertre in 10 minutes (4/hour). At the base of the hill you can catch bus #67 (next to the Pigalle Métro station) and ride straight to the Louvre, along the Seine, across Ile St. Louis, and eventually to the Jardin des Plantes.

$$$ Le Relais Montmartre is a spotless hotel with cushy public spaces, pastel paint, and 26 cozy rooms sporting floral curtains. There are lots of guest-centered amenities, including a shared iPad, fireplace, and quiet central courtyard (Db-€185-240 depending on room size, 6 Rue Constance, tel. 01 70 64 25 25, fax 01 70 64 25 00, www.relaismontmartre.fr, contact@relaismontmartre.fr).

$ Hôtel Regyn's Montmartre** is located directly on the lively Abbesses square, with 22 small but adequate rooms, no air-conditioning, and mediocre bathrooms. Rooms in the front come with pleasant views and noise from the square. Guests in fourth- and fifth-floor rooms can see all the way to the Eiffel Tower (Sb-€91-110, Db-€122-142, check website for specials, 18 Place des Abbesses, tel. 01 42 54 45 21, fax 01 42 59 08 85, www.hotel-regyns-paris.com, info@hotel-regyns-montmartre.net).

$ Hôtel André Gill ** makes me smile. It's a family affair: The front desk is run by two lovely sisters, two lap dogs, and two fat cats. Breakfast is included and served in a living room filled with plastic flowers and photos of the sisters' grandchildren. The hallways and elevator are alarmingly dark and narrow, but the rooms

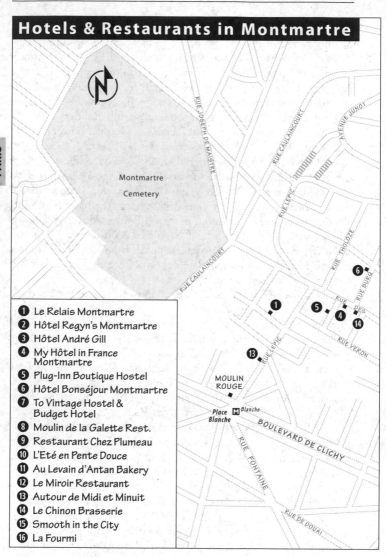

Hotels & Restaurants in Montmartre

Montmartre Cemetery

MOULIN ROUGE

Place Blanche

BOULEVARD DE CLICHY

1 Le Relais Montmartre
2 Hôtel Regyn's Montmartre
3 Hôtel André Gill
4 My Hôtel in France Montmartre
5 Plug-Inn Boutique Hostel
6 Hôtel Bonséjour Montmartre
7 To Vintage Hostel & Budget Hotel
8 Moulin de la Galette Rest.
9 Restaurant Chez Plumeau
10 L'Eté en Pente Douce
11 Au Levain d'Antan Bakery
12 Le Miroir Restaurant
13 Autour de Midi et Minuit
14 Le Chinon Brasserie
15 Smooth in the City
16 La Fourmi

themselves are bright and clean (Sb-€45, Db-€63-89, Tb-€105, large double with Eiffel Tower view-€120-150, 4 Rue André Gill, tel. 01 42 62 48 48, fax 01 42 62 77 92, andregill@hotmail.com).

$ **My Hôtel in France Montmartre,** a chain hotel, has 41 small, basic-but-good-value rooms on six floors, with no elevator or air-conditioning. Twin rooms are larger than doubles for the same price. Continental breakfast and a sandwich lunch-box are included (Sb-€80-89, Db-€90-99, prices vary greatly depending on occupancy, 57 Rue des Abbesses, tel. 01 42 51 50 00, fax 01

42 51 08 68, www.myhotelinfrance-montmartre.com, montmartre @my-hotel-in-france.com).

$ Plug-Inn Boutique Hostel is part hotel and part hostel, but with a hotel vibe. Half a block off Rue des Abbesses, it has a young clientele, bathrooms in all 30 rooms, free Wi-Fi, and several public computer terminals. Early arrivals can leave their luggage and take a shower. Not all rooms are available online, so book by phone or email (all prices per person: bunk in dorm-€29-36, private Db room-€49-52, female-only rooms available, includes breakfast, kitchen facilities, elevator, 24-hour front desk staff, no curfew, 7 Rue Aristide Bruant, tel. 01 42 58 42 58, fax 01 42 23 93 88, www.plug-inn.fr, bonjour@plug-inn.fr).

$ Hôtel Bonséjour Montmartre, run by eager Michel and his family, is an old, worn, hostelesque place with dirt-cheap prices. All rooms have sinks, but share a hallway toilet. Some rooms share one public shower on main floor, and others have small, oddly placed shower cabins right next to the bed (S-€35-50, D-€56-69, Tb-€80, higher price for private shower, no elevator, no air-con, 11 Rue Burq, tel. 01 42 54 22 53, fax 01 42 54 25 92, www.hotel-bonse jour-montmartre.fr, hotel-bonsejour-montmartre@wanadoo.fr).

$ The Vintage Hostel & Budget Hotel sits halfway between the hill of Montmartre and Gare du Nord (both destinations are a 10-minute walk away). This hostel/hotel hybrid appeals to young-sters and oldsters alike. Private double rooms—an especially good value—are on the top two floors, and most come with romantic balconies just big enough for a table and two chairs (bunk in dorm room with private toilet and shower-€35-45, Sb-€75-85, Db-€90-120, includes breakfast, towel-€1, Wi-Fi only—in lobby, 73 Rue de Dunkerque, tel. 01 40 16 16 40, www.vintage-hostel.com, contact @vintage-hostel.com).

At or near Paris' Airports
At Charles de Gaulle Airport
Both of these places are located outside the T-3 RER stop, and both have restaurants. For locations, see the map on page 211.

$$ Novotel* is a step up from cookie-cutter airport hotels (Db-€145-200, can rise to €290 for last-minute rooms, tel. 01 49 19 27 27, fax 01 49 19 27 99, www.novotel.com, h1014@accor.com).

$ Hôtel Ibis CDG Airport** is huge and offers standard air-port accommodations (Db-€115-155, tel. 01 49 19 19 19, fax 01 49 19 19 21, www.ibishotel.com, h1404@accor.com).

Near Charles de Gaulle Airport, in Roissy
The small village of **Roissy-en-France** (you'll see signs just before the airport as you come from Paris), which gave its name to the airport (Roissy Charles de Gaulle), has better-value chain hotels with free shuttle service to and from the airport (4/hour, 15 min-utes, look for *navettes hôtels* signs to reach these hotels). Hotels have reasonably priced restaurants with long hours, though it's more pleasant to walk into the town, where you'll find a bakery, pizzeria, cafés, and a few restaurants. Most Roissy hotels list spe-cials on their websites. These hotels are within walking distance of the town: **$ Hôtel Ibis CDG Paris Nord 2**** (Db-€90-110, usu-ally cheaper than the Ibis right at the airport, 335 Rue de la Belle Etoile, tel. 01 48 17 56 56, fax 01 48 17 56 51, www.ibishotel.com,

h0815@accor.com), **$ Hôtel Campanile Roissy***** (Db-€90-120, allée des Vergers, tel. 01 34 29 80 40, fax 01 34 29 80 39, www .campanile-roissy.fr, roissy@campanile.fr), and **$$ Hôtel Golden Tulip Paris CDG***** (Db-€130-200, 11 Allée des Vergers, tel. 01 34 29 00 00, fax 01 34 29 00 11, www.goldentulipcdgvillepinte .com, info@goldentulipcdgvillepinte.com). The cheapest option is **$ B&B Hôtel Roissy CDG***, where many flight attendants stay (Db-€55, 17 Allée des Vergers, tel. 01 34 38 55 55, fax 01 34 38 55 00, www.hotelbb.com).

To avoid rush-hour traffic, drivers can consider sleeping north of Paris in either **Auvers-sur-Oise** (30 minutes west of airport) or in the pleasant medieval town of **Senlis** (15 minutes north of airport). In Auvers, **$$ Hostellerie du Nord***** is small, friendly, and polished—a treat for those who want to sleep in luxury. It has modern, spacious rooms and a seriously good restaurant that requires reservations (Db-€100-130, suites-€190, *menus* from €60, a block from train station at 6 Rue du Général de Gaulle, tel. 01 30 36 70 74, fax 01 30 36 72 75, www.hostelleriedunord.fr). In Senlis, **$ Hôtel Ibis Senlis**** is a few minutes from town (Db-€80-110, Route Nationale A1, tel. 03 44 53 70 50, fax 03 44 53 51 93, www.ibishotel .com, h0709@accor.com). If you don't have a car, sleep elsewhere.

Near Orly Airport

Two chain hotels, owned by the same company and very close to the Sud terminal, are your best options near Orly. Both have free shuttles *(navettes)* to the terminal.

$$$ Hôtel Mercure Paris Orly*** provides high comfort for a high price; check their website for discounts (Db-€140-220, book early for better rate, tel. 01 49 75 15 51, fax 01 49 75 15 51, www .accorhotel.com, h1246@accor.com).

$ Hôtel Ibis Orly Aéroport** is reasonable and basic (Db-€85-110, tel. 01 56 70 50 60, fax 01 56 70 50 70, www.ibishotel.com, h1413@accor.com).

Apartment Rentals

Among the many English-speaking organizations renting apartments in Paris, the following have proven most reliable (for a list of agencies renting apartments countrywide, see page 32). Their websites are good and essential to understanding your options. Read the rental conditions very carefully.

Paris Perfect has offices in Paris with English-speaking staff who seek the "perfect apartment" for their clients and are selective about what they offer. Their service gets rave reviews. Many units have Eiffel Tower views, and most include free Internet, free local and international phone calls, satellite TV, air-conditioning, and washers and dryers (studio-€125/night, one-bedroom apartment-€199/night, two-bedroom apartment-€285/night, 5 percent discount off regular rates for Rick Steves readers, US toll-free tel. 888-520-2087, www.parisperfect.com).

Cobblestone Paris Rentals is a small, American-run outfit offering furnished rentals with a focus on the Marais and central Paris. All apartments offer free Wi-Fi, free international phone calls, and free cable TV. Apartments come stocked with English-language DVDs, coffee, tea, cooking spices, and basic bathroom amenities (two free river cruises for Rick Steves readers who book a stay of five nights or more, www.cobblestoneparis.com, reservations@cobblestoneparis.com).

Paris Appartements Services rents studios (€100-170/night) and one-bedroom apartments (€150-230/night) in central neighborhoods (20 Rue Bachaumont, tel. 01 40 28 01 28, fax 01 40 28 92 01, www.paris-appartements-services.com, info@paris-apts.com).

Home Rental Service has been in business for 18 years and offers a big selection of apartments throughout Paris with no agency fees (120 Champs-Elysées, tel. 01 42 25 65 40, fax 01 42 25 65 45, www.homerental.fr, info@homerental.fr).

Locaflat offers accommodations ranging from studios to five-room apartments, with occasional specials online (63 Avenue de la Motte-Picquet, tel. 01 43 06 78 79, fax 01 40 56 99 69, www.locaflat.com, locaflat@gmail.com).

Immo Marais has over 100 apartments in all sizes in the Marais (60 Rue Roi de Sicile, tel. 01 42 74 06 17, fax 01 42 74 68 82, www.parislocationsmeublees.com, contact@palocme.com).

Paris Home is a small outfit with only two small studios, but both are located on Rue Amélie in the heart of the Rue Cler area (see map on page 156). Each has modern furnishings and laundry facilities. Friendly Slim, the owner, is the best part (€590/week, no minimum stay, special rates for longer stays, credit cards accepted, free Internet access and US or France telephone calls, free maid service, airport/train station transfers possible, mobile 06 19 03 17 55, www.parishome2000.com, parishome2000@yahoo.fr).

Paris for Rent, a San Francisco-based group, has been renting top-end apartments in Paris for more than a decade (US tel. 866-4-FRANCE, www.parisforrent.com).

Tournights, run by Frederick and Mayra, rents several apartments around Paris (www.tournights.com).

Cross-Pollinate is a reputable online booking agency representing B&Bs and apartments in a handful of European cities. Paris listings range from a Bastille B&B room for two for €90 per night to a two-bedroom Montmartre apartment sleeping six for €160 per night. Minimum stays vary from one to five nights (US tel. 800-270-1190, France tel. 09-75-18-11-10, www.cross-pollinate.com, info@cross-pollinate.com).

Eating in Paris

The Parisian eating scene is kept at a rolling boil. Entire books (and lives) are dedicated to the subject. Paris is France's wine-and-

cuisine melting pot. Though it lacks a style of its own (only French onion soup is truly Parisian; otherwise, there is no "Parisian cuisine" to speak of), it draws from the best of France. Paris could hold a gourmet Olympics and import nothing.

My recommendations are centered on the same great neighborhoods listed earlier, under "Sleeping in Paris"; you can come home exhausted after a busy day of sightseeing and find a good selection of restaurants right around the corner. And evening is a fine time to explore any of these delightful neighborhoods, even if you're sleeping elsewhere.

To save piles of euros, go to a bakery for takeout, or stop at a café for lunch. Cafés and brasseries are happy to serve a *plat du jour* (garnished plate of the day, about €12-18) or a chef-like salad (about €10-13) day or night. To save even more, consider picnics (tasty take-out dishes are available at charcuteries).

Linger longer over dinner—restaurants expect you to enjoy a full meal. Most restaurants I've listed have set-price *menus* between €20 and €35. In most cases, the few extra euros you pay are well-spent, and open up a variety of better choices. Remember that a service charge is included in the prices (so little or no tipping is expected). Eat early with tourists or late with locals. Before choosing a seat outside, remember that smokers love outdoor tables.

In the Rue Cler Neighborhood

The Rue Cler neighborhood caters to its residents. Its eateries, while not destination places, have an intimate charm. I've provided a full range of choices—from cozy ma-and-pa diners to small and trendy boutique restaurants to classic, big, boisterous bistros. For all restaurants listed in this area, use the Ecole Militaire Métro stop (unless another station is listed).

On Rue Cler

$ Café du Marché boasts the best seats, coffee, and prices on Rue Cler. The owner's philosophy: Brasserie on speed—crank out good food at great prices to chic locals and savvy tourists. It's high-energy, with young waiters who barely have time to smile... *très* Parisian. This place is ideal if you don't mind a limited selection and want to eat an inexpensive one-course meal among a

PARIS

Good Picnic Spots

Paris is picnic-friendly. Almost any park will do. Many have benches or grassy areas, though some lawns are off-limits—obey the signs. Parks generally close at dusk, so plan your sunset picnics carefully. Hoteliers frown on in-room picnics. Here are some especially scenic areas located near major sights:

Palais Royal: Escape to a peaceful courtyard full of relaxing locals across from the Louvre (Mo: Palais Royale). The nearby Louvre courtyard surrounding the pyramid is less tranquil, but very handy.

Place des Vosges: Relax in an exquisite grassy courtyard in the Marais, surrounded by royal buildings (Mo: Bastille).

Square du Vert-Galant: For great river views, try this little triangular park on the west tip of Ile de la Cité. It's next to the statue of King Henry IV (Mo: Pont Neuf).

Pont des Arts: Munch from a perch on this pedestrian bridge over the Seine (near the Louvre)—it's equipped with benches (Mo: Pont Neuf).

Along the Seine: A grassy parkway runs along the left bank of the Seine between Les Invalides and Pont de l'Alma (Mo: Invalides, near Rue Cler).

Tuileries Garden: Have an Impressionist "Luncheon on the Grass" nestled between the Orsay and Orangerie museums (Mo: Tuileries).

Luxembourg Garden: The classic Paris picnic spot is this expansive Left Bank park (Mo: Odéon).

Les Invalides: Take a break from the Army Museum and Napoleon's Tomb in the gardens behind the complex (Mo: Varenne).

Champ de Mars: The long grassy strip below the Eiffel Tower has breathtaking views of this Paris icon. However, you must eat along the sides of the park, as the central lawn is off-limits (Mo: Ecole Militaire).

Pompidou Center: There's no grass, but the people-watching is unbeatable; try the area by the *Homage to Stravinsky* fountains (Mo: Rambuteau or Hôtel de Ville).

commotion of people. The chalkboard lists your choices: good, hearty €10 salads or more filling €10-12 *plats du jour*. If coming for dinner, arrive before 19:30; it's packed at 21:00, and service can be slow (Mon-Sat 11:00-23:00, Sun 11:00-17:00, at the corner of Rue Cler and Rue du Champ de Mars, 38 Rue Cler, tel. 01 47 05 51 27).

$ Tribeca Italian Restaurant, next door to Café du Marché, is run by the same people with essentially the same formula *à la italienne*. They offer similar value and more space with a calmer ambience. Choose from family-pleasing €13 pizzas and Italian *plats* (open daily, tel. 01 45 55 12 01).

Restaurant Price Code

To help you choose among these listings, I've divided the restaurants into three categories, based on the price for a typical main course.

$$$ Higher Priced—Most main courses €25 or more
 $$ Moderately Priced—Most main courses between €15-25.
  $ Lower Priced—Most main courses €15 or less.

$ Le Petit Cler is a small, authentic, and adorable café with long leather booths, a vintage interior, a handful of outdoor tables, and simple, delicious, inexpensive dishes (€9 omelets, €7 soup of the moment, €12 salads, €13 *plats*, mouthwatering *petit pots* of chocolate or vanilla pudding, closed Mon, next to Grand Hôtel Lévêque at 29 Rue Cler, tel. 01 45 50 17 50).

$ Café le Roussillon offers good-value café food at fair prices (daily, indoor seating only, at the corner of Rue de Grenelle and Rue Cler, tel. 01 45 51 47 53).

$ Crêperie Ulysée en Gaule offers cheap seats on Rue Cler with crêpes to go. Readers of this book don't have to pay an extra charge to sit if they buy a drink. The family adores its Greek dishes, but their crêpes are your least expensive hot meal on this street (28 Rue Cler, tel. 01 47 05 61 82).

$ Brasserie Aux PTT, a simple traditional café delivering fair-value fare, reminds Parisians of the old days on Rue Cler. Rick Steves diners are promised a free *kir* with their dinner (closed Sun, 2-minute walk from most area hotels, opposite 53 Rue Cler, tel. 01 45 51 94 96).

Close to Ecole Militaire

$$ Le Florimond is fun for a special occasion. The setting is intimate and welcoming. Locals come for classic French cuisine at fair prices. Friendly English-speaking Laurent, whose playful ties change daily, gracefully serves one small room of tables and loves to give suggestions. The stuffed cabbage and the *confit de canard* are particularly tasty, and the house wine is wonderful (€36 *menu*, affordable wine selection, closed Sun, reservations smart, 19 Avenue de la Motte-Picquet, tel. 01 45 55 40 38).

$$ Café le Bosquet is a modern Parisian brasserie with dressy waiters. Dine in their snappy interior or at tables on a broad sidewalk. Come here for standard café fare—salad, French onion soup, steak, or a *plat du jour* for about €14-19. The escargots are tasty, and the house red wine is plenty good (continental breakfast for €6, free Wi-Fi, closed Sun, reservations smart Fri-Sat, corner of Rue

Rue Cler Restaurants

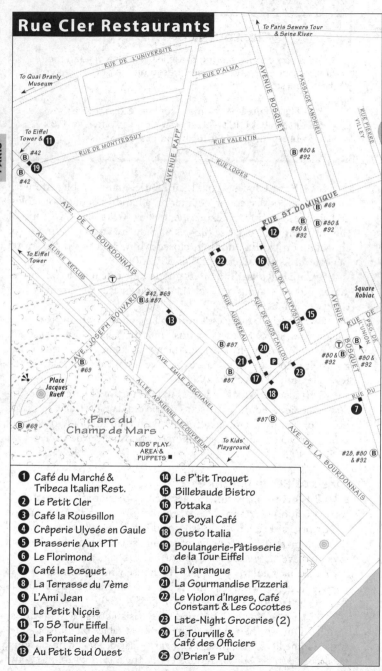

To Paris Sewers Tour & Seine River

To Quai Branly Museum

RUE DE L'UNIVERSITÉ

RUE D'ALMA

AVENUE BOSQUET

PASSAGE LANDRIEU

RUE PIERRE VILLEY

To Eiffel Tower & ⑪ Ⓑ #42

RUE DE MONTTESSUY

RUE VALENTIN

RUE LOGES

Ⓑ #80 & #92

⑲ Ⓑ #42

AVENUE RAPP

RUE ST. DOMINIQUE

Ⓑ #69

AVE. DE LA BOURDONNAIS

⑫ Ⓑ #80 & #92

Ⓑ #80 & #92

To Eiffel Tower

AVE. ELISÉE RECLUS

Ⓣ

㉒ ⑯

RUE DE L'EXPOSITION

RUE AUGEREAU

RUE DE GROS CAILLOU

Square Robiac

#42, #69 Ⓑ & #87

AVE. JOSEPH BOUVARD

⑬

⑭ ⑮

AVENUE DE

RUE DE PSG. DE L'UNION

Ⓣ Ⓑ #80 & #92 Ⓑ #80 & #92

Ⓑ #87

⑳

Ⓑ #69

AVE. EMILE DESCHANEL

Place Jacques Rueff

㉑ ㉓

Ⓑ #87

⑰

P

RUE DU

Parc du Champ de Mars

ALLÉE ADRIENNE LECOUVREUR

⑱

⑦

Ⓑ #69

KIDS' PLAY AREA & PUPPETS ■

To Kids' Playground

#87 Ⓑ

AVE. DE LA BOURDONNAIS

#28, #80 Ⓑ & #92

❶ Café du Marché & Tribeca Italian Rest.
❷ Le Petit Cler
❸ Café la Roussillon
❹ Crêperie Ulysée en Gaule
❺ Brasserie Aux PTT
❻ Le Florimond
❼ Café le Bosquet
❽ La Terrasse du 7ème
❾ L'Ami Jean
❿ Le Petit Niçois
⓫ To 58 Tour Eiffel
⓬ La Fontaine de Mars
⓭ Au Petit Sud Ouest

⓮ Le P'tit Troquet
⓯ Billebaude Bistro
⓰ Pottaka
⓱ Le Royal Café
⓲ Gusto Italia
⓳ Boulangerie-Pâtisserie de la Tour Eiffel
⓴ La Varangue
㉑ La Gourmandise Pizzeria
㉒ Le Violon d'Ingres, Café Constant & Les Cocottes
㉓ Late-Night Groceries (2)
㉔ Le Tourville & Café des Officiers
㉕ O'Brien's Pub

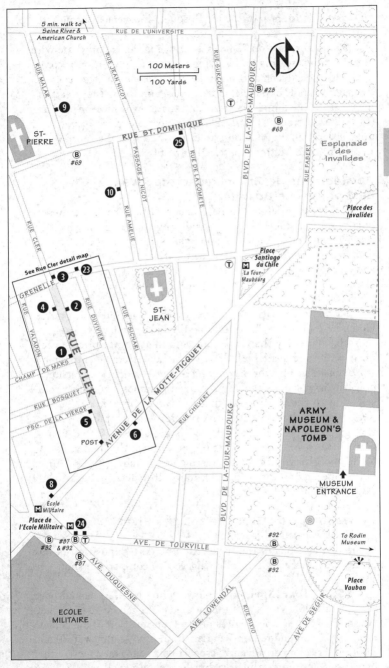

See Rue Cler detail map

PARIS

du Champ de Mars and Avenue Bosquet, 46 Avenue Bosquet, tel. 01 45 51 38 13).

$$ La Terrasse du 7ème is a sprawling, happening café with grand outdoor seating and a living room-like interior with comfy love seats. Located on a corner, it overlooks a busy intersection with a constant parade of people. Chairs are set up facing the street, as a meal here is like dinner theater—and the show is slice-of-life Paris (€16-22 *plats*, good €13 *salade niçoise*, no fixed-price *menu*, daily until at least 24:00 and sometimes until 2:00 in the morning, at Ecole Militaire Métro stop, tel. 01 45 55 00 02).

Between Rue de Grenelle and the River, East of Avenue Bosquet

$$$ L'Ami Jean offers top Basque specialties. You'll get hearty portions at palatable prices (considering the quality), while sitting in snug-but-fun, get-to-know-your-neighbor spaces. Parisians detour long distances to savor the gregarious chef's special cuisine and convivial atmosphere. Arrive by 19:30 or call ahead (€43 *menu*, closed Sun-Mon, 27 Rue Malar, Mo: La Tour-Maubourg, tel. 01 47 05 86 89).

$$ Le Petit Niçois celebrates fish from southern France. Come here for everything from bouillabaisse to bass to paella to mussels, and enjoy the area's top seafood at decent prices (a few meat dishes are available). Start with the delectable *escargot à la provençale*, dive into the *marmite du pêcheur*—a delicious version of bouillabaisse, sample the sinful puréed potatoes, and finish yourself off with the lemon twist finale *(citron confit givré aux frais)* or *café gourmand* desserts. The atmosphere is contemporary—warm though formal—and the welcome is genuine (€22 two-course *menu*, €32 three-course *menu*; better yet, ask the owner, caring Carlos, to give you the royal treatment—matching three courses with wine and apéritifs for €50; daily, 10 Rue Amélie, Mo: La Tour Maubourg, tel. 01 45 51 83 65).

Between Rue de Grenelle and the River, West of Avenue Bosquet

Some of these places line peaceful Rue de l'Exposition (a few blocks west of Rue Cler), allowing you to comparison shop *sans* stress.

$$$ 58 Tour Eiffel, on the tower's first level, is popular both for its incredible views and the cuisine of its famed French chef, Alain Ducasse. Dinner here is pricey (you must order a complete *menu*—€70-85) and requires a reservation (two seatings: 18:30 and 21:00; reserve long in advance, especially if you want a view, either by calling or going online; within France, dial toll tel. 08 25 56

66 62; from outside France, dial 01 76 64 14 64; www.restaurants -toureiffel.com). Lunch is easier (€20 *menu*, daily 11:30-16:00, no reservations possible, Mo: Bir-Hakeim or Trocadéro, RER: Champ de Mars-Tour Eiffel).

$$$ La Fontaine de Mars, a longtime favorite and neighborhood institution, draws Parisians who want to be seen. It's charmingly situated on a tiny, jumbled square with tables jammed together for the serious business of eating. Reserve in advance for a table on the ground floor or on the square, and enjoy the same meal Barack Obama did. Street-level seats come with the best ambience (€20-30 *plats du jour,* superb foie gras, superb-er desserts, 129 Rue St. Dominique, tel. 01 47 05 46 44).

$$ Au Petit Sud Ouest has stone walls and wood beams, making it a cozy place to sample fine cuisine from southwestern France. Duck, goose, foie gras, *cassoulet,* and truffles are among its specialties. Tables come with toasters to heat your bread—it enhances the flavors of the foie gras (closed Sun-Mon, 46 Avenue de la Bourdonnais, tel. 01 45 55 59 59).

$$ Le P'tit Troquet is a petite eatery taking you back to the Paris of the 1920s. Marie welcomes you warmly, and chef José cooks a delicious three-course €33 *menu* with a range of traditional choices prepared creatively. The homey charm and gourmet quality make this restaurant a favorite of connoisseurs (opens at 18:30, closed Sun, reservations smart, 28 Rue de l'Exposition, tel. 01 47 05 80 39).

$$ Billebaude, run by patient Pascal, is a small, authentic Parisian bistro popular with locals. The focus is on what's fresh, including catch-of-the-day fish and meats from the hunt (available in the fall and winter). Chef Sylvain, an avid hunter (as the decor will remind you), is determined to deliver quality at a fair price— and he succeeds. Try *filet de bar* (sea bass) for your main course and *œufs à la neige* for dessert (€33 *menu,* closed Sun-Mon, 29 Rue de l'Exposition, tel. 01 45 55 20 96).

$$ Pottaka is a snug eatery where in-the-know locals go for delicious Basque cuisine at reasonable prices (€34 *menu,* €19 *plats,* reservations smart for Wed-Sat nights, 4 Rue de l'Exposition, tel. 01 45 51 88 38).

$ Le Royal is a tiny neighborhood fixture. This humble time-warp place, with prices and decor from another era, comes from an age when cafés sold firewood and served food as an afterthought. Parisians dine here because "it's like eating at home." Gentle Michele runs the counter while hustling Giles tends to the tables (€5 omelets, €9 *plats,* filling three-course *menu*-€13, closed Sat-Sun, 212 Rue de Grenelle, tel. 01 47 53 92 90).

$ Gusto Italia serves up tasty, good-value Italian cuisine in a shoebox-size place with a few tables outside. Arrive early or plan to wait (€12 salads, €14 pasta, daily, 199 Rue de Grenelle, tel. 01 45 55 00 43).

$ Boulangerie-Pâtisserie de la Tour Eiffel delivers inexpensive salads, quiches, and sandwiches. Enjoy the views of the Eiffel Tower (daily, outdoor and indoor seating, one block southeast of the tower at 21 Avenue de la Bourdonnais, tel. 01 47 05 59 81).

$ La Varangue is an entertaining one-man show featuring English-speaking Philippe, who once ran a catering business in Pennsylvania. He now lives upstairs and has found his niche serving a mostly American clientele. The food is cheap and basic, the tables are few, and he opens at 17:30. Norman Rockwell would dig his minuscule dining room—with the traditional kitchen sizzling just over the counter. Try his snails and chocolate cake—but not together (€12 *plats*, €18 *menu*, always a vegetarian option, closed Sun, 27 Rue Augereau, tel. 01 47 05 51 22).

$ La Gourmandise is a kid-friendly, cheap pizzeria across from La Varangue (closed Sun, eat in or take out, 28 Rue Augereau, tel. 01 45 55 45 16).

The Constant Lineup: Ever since leaving the venerable Hôtel Crillon, famed chef Christian Constant has made a career of taking the "snoot" out of French cuisine—and making it accessible to people like us. Today you'll find three of his restaurants strung along one block of Rue St. Dominique between Rue Augereau and Rue de l'Exposition. Each is distinct, and each offers a different experience and price range. None of these places is cheap, but they all deliver top-quality cuisine.

$$$ Le Violon d'Ingres, where Christian won his first Michelin star, makes for a good excuse to dress up and really dine finely in Paris. Glass doors open onto a lively and chic eating scene, service is formal yet helpful, and the cuisine is what made this restaurateur's reputation (€60-80 *menus*, daily, reservations essential, 135 Rue St. Dominique, tel. 01 45 55 15 05).

$$ Les Cocottes is a trendy, bar-stool-only place serving simple dishes in small iron pots to yuppie Parisians (daily, no reservations taken, 135 Rue St. Dominique).

$$ Café Constant is a cool, two-level place that feels more like a small bistro-wine bar than a café. Delicious and fairly priced dishes are served in a fun setting to a dedicated clientele. Arrive early to get a table (downstairs seating is better); the friendly staff speak English (€11 *entrées*, €16 *plats*, €7 desserts, closed Sun-Mon, no reservations taken, corner of Rue Augereau and Rue St. Dominique, next to recommended Hôtel Londres Eiffel, tel. 01 47 53 73 34).

Picnicking near Rue Cler

Rue Cler is a festival of food. The street is lined with businesses run by people whose lives seem to be devoted to their specialty: polished produce, rotisserie chicken, freshly made crêpes, or deliciously stinky cheese.

For a magical picnic dinner at the Eiffel Tower, assemble it in no fewer than five shops on Rue Cler. Then lounge on the best grass in Paris, with the dogs, Frisbees, a floodlit tower, and a cool breeze in the Champ de Mars park (picnics are allowed off to the sides, but not in the central area, which is off-limits).

Asian delis (generically called *traiteurs asiatique*) provide low-stress, low-price take-out treats (€8 dinner plates; the one on Rue Cler near Rue du Champ de Mars has tables). **Crêperie Ulysée en Gaule,** the Greek restaurant on Rue Cler across from Grand Hôtel Lévêque, sells take-away crêpes (see page 187). For the cheapest, easiest meals, consider getting sandwiches or kebabs, just beyond the cute zone a few steps past the Ecole Militaire Métro stop on Avenue de Tourville.

Small, **late-night groceries** are at 197 Rue de Grenelle (open daily until midnight), as well as where Rues Cler and Grenelle cross.

Breakfast on Rue Cler

Hotel breakfasts, though convenient, are generally not a good value. For a great Rue Cler start to your day, drop by **Brasserie Aux PTT,** where Rick Steves readers are promised a *deux pour douze* breakfast special (two "American" breakfasts—juice, a big coffee, croissant, bread, ham, and eggs—for €12; closed Sun, 53 Rue Cler). For a continental breakfast for about €6, try nearby **Café le Bosquet** (closed Sun, 46 Avenue Bosquet).

Nightlife in Rue Cler

This sleepy neighborhood was not made for night owls, but there are a few notable exceptions. The focal point of before- and after-dinner posing occurs along the broad sidewalk at the intersection of Avenues de la Motte-Picquet and Tourville (Mo: Ecole Militaire). **Le Tourville** and **Café des Officiers** gather a sea of outward-facing seats for the important business of people-watching—and fashion-model recruiting.

La Terrasse du 7ème, across the avenue, has a less-pretentious clientele (see listing, earlier). Nearby, **Café du Marché** (listed earlier) attracts a Franco-American crowd until at least midnight, as does the younger **Café Roussillon** (good French pub atmosphere, corner of Rue de Grenelle and Rue Cler). **O'Brien's Pub** is a relaxed Parisian rendition of an Irish pub, full of Anglophones (77 Rue St. Dominique, Mo: La Tour Maubourg).

In the Marais Neighborhood

The trendy Marais is filled with diners enjoying good food in colorful and atmospheric eateries. The scene is competitive and changes all the time. I've listed an assortment of eateries—all handy to recommended hotels—that offer good food at decent prices, plus a memorable experience.

On Romantic Place des Vosges

This square offers Old World Marais elegance, a handful of eateries, and an ideal picnic site until dusk, when the park closes (use Bastille or St. Paul Métro stops). Strolling around the arcade after dark is more important than dining here—fanciful art galleries alternate with restaurants and cafés. Choose a restaurant that best fits your mood and budget; most have arcade seating and provide big space heaters to make outdoor dining during colder months an option. Also consider a drink or dessert on the square at Café Hugo or Carette after eating elsewhere.

$$$ **Ma Bourgogne** is a vintage eatery where you'll sit under warm arcades in a whirlpool of Frenchness, as bow-tied and black-aproned waiters serve you traditional French specialties: blood-red steak (try the *brochette de bœuf*), piles of fries, escargot, and good red wine. Monsieur Cougoureux (koo-goo-ruh) has commanded this ship since de Gaulle was sniveling at Americans. He offers anyone with this book a free *amuse-bouche* ("amusement for your mouth") of his homemade *steak tartare*—but you may need to remind him (show him my picture in this book). This is your chance to try this "raw spiced hamburger" delicacy without dedicating an entire meal to it (€40 *menu*, daily, cash only, at northwest corner at #19, tel. 01 42 78 44 64).

$$ **La Place Royale** offers a fine location on the square; there's comfortable seating inside or you can sit outside under the arches. The cuisine is traditional, well-priced, and served nonstop all day (€23-39 *menus*, daily, 2 bis Place des Vosges, tel. 01 42 78 58 16).

$$ **Café Hugo,** named for the square's most famous resident, is best for drinks only, as the cuisine does not live up to its setting (daily, 22 Place des Vosges, tel. 01 42 72 64 04).

Near Place des Vosges

$$ **Les Bonnes Soeurs,** a block from the square, blends modern and traditional fare with simple, contemporary ambience. Portions are big and inventive. The delicious and filling *pressé de chèvre* starter (a hunk of goat cheese topped with tapenade and tomatoes) begs to be shared. Their hearty French hamburger comes with a salad and the best fries I've tasted in Paris (*plats* from €16, no *menu*, daily, 8 Rue du Pas de la Mule, tel. 01 42 74 55 80).

$$ **Chez Janou,** a Provençal bistro, tumbles out of its corner

building and fills its broad sidewalk with happy eaters. At first glance, you know this place has a following. Don't let the trendy and youthful crowd intimidate you: It's relaxed and charming, with helpful and patient service. The curbside tables are inviting, but I'd sit inside (with very tight seating) to immerse myself in the happy commotion. The style is French Mediterranean, with an emphasis on vegetables (€16-20 *plats du jour* that change with the season, daily from 19:45—book ahead or arrive when it opens, 2 blocks beyond Place des Vosges at 2 Rue Roger Verlomme, tel. 01 42 72 28 41). They're proud of their 81 varieties of *pastis* (licorice-flavored liqueur, €3.50 each, browse the list above the bar).

$ Café des Musées is an unspoiled, zinc-countered bistro serving traditional dishes with little fanfare and a €22 daily *menu* special that's hard to beat. The place is just far enough away to be overlooked by tourists but packed with locals, so arrive early or book ahead (daily, 49 Rue de Turenne, tel. 01 42 72 96 17).

Near the Bastille
To reach these restaurants, use the Bastille Métro stop.

$$$ Brasserie Bofinger, an institution for over a century, is famous for fish and traditional cuisine with Alsatian flair. You'll eat in a sprawling interior, surrounded by brisk, black-and-white-attired waiters. It's a high-energy feast for all the senses. Downstairs rooms are elaborately decorated and reminiscent of the Roaring Twenties, while upstairs rooms have traditional Alsatian decor. Eating under the grand 1919 *coupole* is a memorable treat (as is using the "historic" 1919 WC downstairs). Check out the boys shucking and stacking seafood platters out front before you enter. Their €29 two-course and €34 three-course *menus,* while not top cuisine, are a good value. If you've always wanted one of those picturesque seafood platters, this is a good place—you can take the standard platter or create one à la carte (open daily for lunch and for dinner, fun kids' menu, reasonably priced wines, 5 Rue de la Bastille, don't be confused by the lesser "Petite" Bofinger across the street, tel. 01 42 72 87 82).

$$ Au Temps des Cerises is a cozy place serving wines by the glass and simple meals with a smile. The woody 1950s atmosphere has tight seating and wads of character. Come for a glass of wine and move on, or better yet, stay for a tasty dinner (€9 starters, €18 *plats*, cheap wine, daily, at Rue du Petit Musc and Rue de la Cerisaie, tel. 01 42 72 08 63).

In the Heart of the Marais
These are closest to the St. Paul Métro stop.

$$ Robert et Louise (now run by Pascal *et* François) crams tables into a tiny, rustic-as-it-gets interior, warmed by a fireplace

PARIS

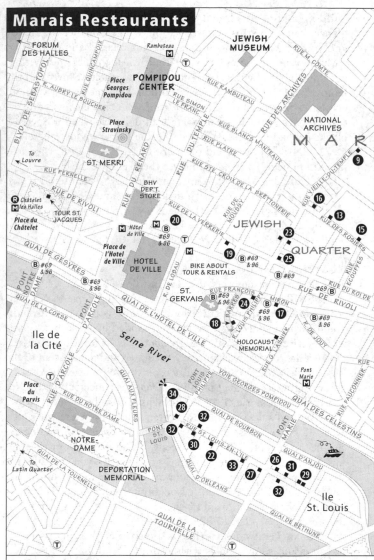

Marais Restaurants

1. Ma Bourgogne
2. La Place Royale
3. Café Hugo
4. Les Bonnes Soeurs
5. Chez Janou
6. Café des Musées
7. Brasserie Bofinger
8. Au Temps des Cerises
9. Robert et Louise Restaurant
10. Breizh Café
11. Le Bistrot des Compères
12. Place du Marché Ste. Catherine Eateries
13. Chez Marianne
14. Le Loir dans la Théière
15. L'As du Falafel
16. La Droguerie Crêperie
17. Au Bourguignon du Marais

PARIS

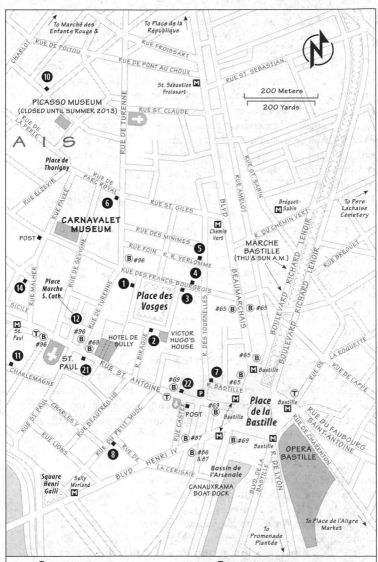

18 L'Ebouillanté

19 Pizza Sant'Antonio

20 BHV Cafeteria

21 Monoprix (Grocery)

22 Late-Night Groceries (2)

23 Au Petit Fer à Cheval &
La Belle Hortense

24 La Perla Bar

25 Le Pick-Clops Bar Rest.

26 Le Tastevin

27 Nos Ancêtres les Gaulois

28 La Brasserie de l'île St. Louis

29 L'Orangerie & Auberge de
la Reine Blanche

30 Café Med

31 Bakery

32 Berthillon Ice Cream (3)

33 Amorino Gelati

34 Good Picnic Spot

grill. The food is red-meat good, well-priced, and popular with tourists (€7 starters, €18 *plats*, €6 desserts, closed Mon, 64 Rue du Vieille du Temple, tel. 01 42 78 55 89).

$ Breizh (Brittany) Café is worth the walk. It's a simple Breton joint serving organic crêpes and small rolls made for dipping in rich sauces and salted butter. The crêpes are the best in Paris and run the gamut from traditional andouille (pork sausage) to Asian fusion (buckwheat crêpe topped with seaweed butter). They also serve oysters, have a fantastic list of sweet crêpes, and talk about cider like a sommelier would talk about wine. Try a sparkling cider, a Breton cola, or my favorite—*lait ribot*, a buttermilk-like drink (€7-12 dinner crêpes and *plats*, serves nonstop from 12:00 to late, closed Mon-Tue, 109 Rue du Vieille du Temple, tel. 01 42 72 13 77).

$ Le Bistrot des Compères has a privileged location on a quiet corner in the thick of the Marais; there's a warm and welcoming feel whether you sit inside or out. The cuisine is traditional with creative twists, the staff is relaxed, and the prices are very fair (€7 starters, €15 *plats*, €7 desserts, closed Sun-Mon, 16 Rue Charlemagne, tel. 01 42 72 14 16).

$ *On Place du Marché Ste. Catherine:* This small, romantic square, just off Rue St. Antoine, is an international food festival cloaked in extremely Parisian, leafy-square ambience. On a balmy evening, this is clearly a neighborhood favorite, with a handful of restaurants offering €20-30 three-course meals. Study the square, and you'll find three popular French bistros with similar features: **La Terrasse Ste. Catherine**, **Le Marché,** and **Au Bistrot de la Place** (all open daily with €24 three-course *menus* on weekdays, must order à la carte on weekends, tight seating on flimsy chairs indoors and out). Other inviting eateries nearby serve a variety of international food. You'll eat under the trees, surrounded by a futuristic-in-1800 planned residential quarter.

$ Several hardworking **Asian fast-food eateries,** great for an €8 meal, line Rue St. Antoine.

On Rue des Rosiers in the Jewish Quarter: These places line up along the same street in the heart of the Jewish Quarter.

$ Chez Marianne is a neighborhood fixture that blends delicious Jewish cuisine with Parisian *élan* and wonderful atmosphere. Choose from several indoor zones with a cluttered wine shop/deli feeling, or sit outside. You'll select from two dozen *Zakouski* elements to assemble your €12-16 *plat*. Vegetarians will find great options (€8 falafel sandwich—only €6 if you order it to go, long hours daily, corner of Rue des Rosiers and Rue des Hospitalières-St.-Gervais, tel. 01 42 72 18 86). For takeout, pay inside first and get a ticket before you order outside.

$ Le Loir dans la Théière ("The Dormouse in the Teapot") is a cozy, mellow teahouse offering a welcoming ambience for tired travelers. It's ideal for lunch and popular for weekend brunch. They offer a daily assortment of creatively filled quiches, and bake up an impressive array of homemade desserts that are proudly displayed in the dining room. Try the mile-high lemon meringue "pie" or the oversized *mille-feuille* (Mon-Fri 12:00-19:00, Sat-Sun 10:00-19:00, 3 Rue des Rosiers, tel. 01 42 72 90 61).

$ L'As du Falafel rules the falafel scene in the Jewish quarter. Monsieur Isaac, the "Ace of Falafel" here since 1979, brags, "I've got the biggest pita on the street...and I fill it up." (Apparently it's Lenny Kravitz's favorite, too.) Your inexpensive meal comes on plastic plates, in a bustling setting that seems to prove he's earned his success. The €7 "special falafel" is the big hit (€6 to go), but many Americans enjoy his lighter chicken version *(poulet grillé)* or the tasty and massive *assiette de falafel* (€9). Wash it down it a cold Maccabee beer. Their take-out service draws a constant crowd (long hours daily except closed Fri evening and all day Sat, air-con, 34 Rue des Rosiers, tel. 01 48 87 63 60).

$ La Droguerie, an outdoor crêpe stand a few blocks farther down Rue des Rosiers, is an option if falafels don't work for you, but cheap does (€5 dinner crêpes, closed Mon, 56 Rue des Rosiers).

Near Hôtel de Ville

To reach these eateries, use the Hôtel de Ville Métro stop.

$$ Au Bourguignon du Marais is a handsome wine bar/bistro for Burgundy lovers, where excellent wines (Burgundian only, available by the glass) blend with a good selection of well-designed dishes and efficient service. The *œufs en meurette* are mouthwatering, and the *bœuf bourguignon* could feed two (€10-14 starters, €20-26 *plats*, closed Sun-Mon, pleasing indoor and outdoor seating, 52 Rue François Miron, tel. 01 48 87 15 40).

$ L'Ebouillanté is a breezy crêperie-café, romantically situated near the river on a broad, cobbled pedestrian lane behind a church. With great outdoor seating and an artsy, cozy interior, it's perfect for an inexpensive and relaxing tea, snack, or lunch—or for dinner on a warm evening. Their *Brick*, a Tunisian-inspired dish that looks like a stuffed omelet, has several filling options and comes with a small salad (€15); it left me stuffed (*plats* and big salads-€13, daily 12:00-21:30 except closed Mon Nov-March, a block off the river at 6 Rue des Barres, tel. 01 42 71 09 69).

$ Pizza Sant'Antonio is bustling and cheap, serving up €11 pizzas and salads on a fun Marais square (daily, barely off Rue de Rivoli at 1 Rue de la Verrerie, tel. 01 42 77 78 47).

$ BHV Department Store's fifth-floor cafeteria provides nice views, good prices, and no-brainer, point-and-shoot cafeteria cuisine (Mon-Sat 11:30-18:00, closed Sun, at intersection of Rue du Temple and Rue de la Verrerie, one block from Hôtel de Ville).

Picnicking in the Marais

Picnic at peaceful Place des Vosges (closes at dusk) or on the Ile St. Louis *quais* (described later). Stretch your euros at the basement supermarket of the **Monoprix** department store (closed Sun, near Place des Vosges on Rue St. Antoine). You'll find small **groceries** open until 23:00 at 48 Rue St. Antoine and on Ile St. Louis.

Nightlife in the Marais

Trendy cafés and bars—popular with gay men—cluster on Rue des Archives and Rue Ste. Croix de la Bretonnerie (closing at about 2:00 in the morning). There's also a line of bars and cafés providing front-row seats for the buff parade on Rue Vieille du Temple, a block north of Rue de Rivoli (the horseshoe-shaped **Au Petit Fer à Cheval** bar-restaurant and the atmospheric **La Belle Hortense** bookstore/wine bar are the focal points of the action). Nearby, Rue des Rosiers bustles with youthful energy, but there are no cafés to observe from. **La Perla** dishes up inexpensive Tex-Mex and is stuffed with Parisian yuppies in search of the perfect margarita (26 Rue François Miron, tel. 01 42 77 59 40).

$ Le Pick-Clops bar-restaurant is a happy peanuts-and-lots-of-cocktails diner with bright neon, loud colors, and a garish local crowd. It's perfect for immersing yourself in today's Marais world—a little boisterous, a little edgy, a little gay, fun-loving, easygoing... and no tourists. Sit inside on old-fashioned diner stools, or streetside to watch the constant Marais parade. The name means "Steal the Cigarettes"—but you'll pay €11 for your big salad (daily 7:00-24:00, 16 Rue Vieille du Temple, tel. 01 40 29 02 18).

More Options: The best scene for hard-core clubbers is the dizzying array of wacky eateries, bars, and dance halls on **Rue de Lappe.** Just east of the stately Place de la Bastille, it's one of the wildest nightspots in Paris and not for everyone.

The most enjoyable peaceful evening may be simply mentally donning your floppy "three musketeers" hat and slowly strolling Place des Vosges, window-shopping the art galleries.

On Ile St. Louis

This romantic and peaceful neighborhood is filled with promising and surprisingly inexpensive possibilities; it merits a trip for dinner even if your hotel is elsewhere. Cruise the island's main street for a variety of options, from cozy *crêperies* to Italian eateries to Alsatian brasseries and romantic bistros. After dinner, sample Paris' best ice cream and stroll across to Ile de la Cité to see a floodlit Notre-Dame. These recommended spots line the island's main drag, Rue St. Louis-en-l'Ile (see map on page 196; to get here use the Pont Marie Métro stop).

$$$ Le Tastevin is an intimate mother-and-son-run restaurant serving top-notch traditional French cuisine with white-table-cloth, candlelit, gourmet elegance under heavy wooden beams. The romantic setting (and the elegantly romantic Parisian couples enjoying the place) naturally makes you whisper. The *menus*, which start at €31 (two courses) and rise to €40-54 (three courses), offer a handful of classic choices that change with the season (daily, reserve for late-evening dining, fine wine list, 46 Rue St. Louis-en-l'Ile, tel. 01 43 54 17 31, owner Madame Puisieux and her gentle son speak just enough English).

$$$ Nos Ancêtres les Gaulois ("Our Ancestors the Gauls"), famous for its rowdy, medieval-cellar atmosphere, is made for hungry warriors and wenches who like to swill hearty wine. They serve up a rustic all-you-can-eat buffet with straw baskets of raw veggies and bundles of sausage (cut whatever you like with your dagger), massive plates of pâté, a meat course, and all the wine you can stomach for €41. The food is just food; burping is encouraged. If you want to overeat, drink too much wine, be surrounded with tourists (mostly French), and holler at your friends while receiving smart-aleck buccaneer service, you're home (daily, 39 Rue St. Louis-en-l'Ile, tel. 01 46 33 66 07).

$$ La Brasserie de l'Ile St. Louis is situated at the prow of the island's ship as it faces Ile de la Cité, offering purely Alsatian cuisine (try the *choucroute garnie* or *coq au riesling* for €19), served in a vigorous, Teutonic setting with no-nonsense, slap-it-down service on wine-stained paper tablecloths. This is a good, balmy-evening perch for watching the Ile St. Louis promenade. If it's chilly, the interior is fun for a memorable night out (closed Wed, no reservations, 55 Quai de Bourbon, tel. 01 43 54 02 59).

$$ L'Orangerie is an inviting place with soft lighting and comfortable seating where diners speak in hushed voices so that everyone can appreciate the delicious cuisine and tasteful setting (€35 three-course *menu*, €27 two-course *menu*, Tue-Sun from 19:00, closed Mon, 28 Rue St. Louis-en-l'Ile, tel. 01 46 33 93 98).

$ Auberge de la Reine Blanche welcomes diners willing to rub elbows with their neighbors under heaving beams. Earnest owner Michel serves traditional cuisine at reasonable prices. The giant goat-cheese salad is a beefy meal in itself (€20 two-course *menu*, €25 three-course *menu*, daily from 18:00, 30 Rue St. Louis-en-l'Ile, tel. 01 46 33 07 87).

$ Café Med, near the pedestrian bridge to Notre-Dame, is a tiny, cheery *crêperie* with good-value salads, crêpes, and €11 *plats*

(€14 and €20 *menus*, daily, limited wine list, 77 Rue St. Louis-en-l'Ile, tel. 01 43 29 73 17). Two similar *crêperies* are just across the street.

Riverside Picnic for Impoverished Romantics

On sunny lunchtimes and balmy evenings, the *quai* on the Left Bank side of Ile St. Louis is lined with locals who have more class than money, spreading out tablecloths and even lighting candles for elegant picnics. And tourists can enjoy the same budget meal. A handy grocery store at #67 on the main drag (open until 22:00, closed Tue) has tabouli and other simple, cheap take-away dishes for your picnicking pleasure. The bakery a few blocks down at #40 serves quiche and pizza (open until 20:00, closed Sun-Mon).

Ice-Cream Dessert

Half the people strolling Ile St. Louis are licking an ice-cream cone, because this is the home of *les glaces Berthillon* (now sold throughout Paris). The original **Berthillon** shop, at 31 Rue St. Louis-en-l'Ile, is marked by the line of salivating customers (closed Mon-Tue). For a less famous but at least as satisfying treat, the homemade Italian gelato a block away at **Amorino Gelati** is giving Berthillon competition (no line, bigger portions, easier to see what you want, and they offer little tastes—Berthillon doesn't need to, 47 Rue St. Louis-en-l'Ile, tel. 01 44 07 48 08). Having some of each is not a bad thing.

In the Luxembourg Garden Area

Sleeping in the Luxembourg neighborhood puts you near many appealing dining and after-hours options. Because my hotels in this area cluster near St. Sulpice Church and the Panthéon, I've organized restaurant listings the same way. Restaurants around St. Sulpice tend to be boisterous; those near the Panthéon are calmer; it's a short walk from one area to the other. Anyone sleeping in this area is close to the inexpensive eateries that line the always-bustling Rue Mouffetard. You're also within a 15-minute walk of the *grands cafés* of St. Germain and Montparnasse (with Paris' first café and famous artist haunts).

Near St. Sulpice Church

The eateries in this section are served by the St. Sulpice, Mabillon, and St. Germain-des-Prés Métro stops. The streets between St. Sulpice Church and Boulevard St. Germain abound with restaurants, *crêperies*, wine bars, and jazz haunts (for this area, use Mo: St. Sulpice). Find Rue des Canettes and Rue Guisarde, and window-shop the many French and Italian eateries—most with similar prices, but each with a slightly different feel.

$$ Lou Pescadou-Chez Julien offers a comfortable atmosphere and above-average bistro fare in a zone where every restaurant looks the same (€9 starters, €18 *plats*, daily, some outdoor seating, 16 Rue Mabillon, tel. 01 43 54 56 08).

$$ Boucherie Roulière has a dark interior crammed with locals in search of a thick steak or other meat dish (€9 *entrées*, €19 *plats*, closed Mon, 24 Rue des Canettes, tel. 01 43 26 25 70).

$$ Santa Lucia draws positive reviews with wood-fired pizza, good pasta, and killer tiramisu (€12-14 pizza and pastas, €22 *plats*, closed Mon, 22 Rue des Canettes, tel. 01 43 26 42 68).

$ La Crêpe Rit du Clown cooks up yummy crêpes (Mon-Sat 12:00-23:00, closed Sun, 6 Rue des Canettes, tel. 01 46 34 01 02).

Chez Georges is a bohemian pub lined with black-and-white photos of the artsy and revolutionary French '60s. Have a drink as you sit in a cool little streetside table nook, or venture downstairs to find a hazy, drippy-candle, traditionally French world in the Edith Piaf-style dance cellar (cheap drinks from old-fashioned menu, Tue-Sat 14:00-2:00 in the morning, closed Sun-Mon and in Aug, 11 Rue des Canettes, tel. 01 43 26 79 15).

Near Boulevard St. Germain: A five-minute walk from St. Sulpice Church, this venerable boulevard is home to some of Paris' most famous cafés and best pre- or post-dinner strolling. Consider a light dinner with a table facing the action at Hemingway's **Les Deux Magots** or at Sartre's **Le Café de Flore** (figure about €12 for an omelet and €18-28 for a salad or *plat*). A block north (toward the river), **Rue de Buci** offers a lineup of bars, cafés, and bistros targeted to a young clientele who are more interested in how they look than how the food tastes. It's terrific theater for passersby from 18:00 until late.

$$ La Cigale Récamier, near the Sèvres-Babylone shopping area, is a classy place for a quiet meal at reasonable prices with appealing indoor and outdoor seating. It's about 10 minutes west of Place St. Sulpice, on a short pedestrian square a block off Rue de Sèvres (€20 *plats*, à la carte only, closed Sun, 4 Rue Récamier, Mo: Sèvres-Babylone, tel. 01 46 48 86 58).

Near the Odéon Theater

To reach these, use the Odéon or Cluny-la Sorbonne Métro stops. In this same neighborhood, you'll find the historic Café le Procope, Paris' more-than-300-year-old café.

$ L'Avant Comptoir is a little stand-up-only hors d'oeuvres bar serving up a delightful array of French-Basque tapas for €3-6 on a sleek zinc counter. The menu is fun and accessible; it has a good list of wines by the glass; and crêpes are made fresh to go (daily 12:00-23:00, 9 Carrefour de l'Odéon, tel. 01 44 27 07 97).

$$ Brasserie Bouillon Racine takes you back to 1906 with an

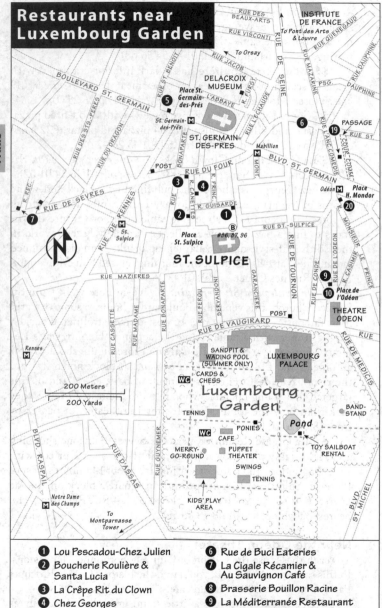

Restaurants near Luxembourg Garden

1. Lou Pescadou-Chez Julien
2. Boucherie Roulière & Santa Lucia
3. La Crêpe Rit du Clown
4. Chez Georges
5. Les Deux Magots & Le Café de Flore
6. Rue de Buci Eateries
7. La Cigale Récamier & Au Sauvignon Café
8. Brasserie Bouillon Racine
9. La Méditerranée Restaurant
10. Café de l'Odéon
11. Restaurant Polidor

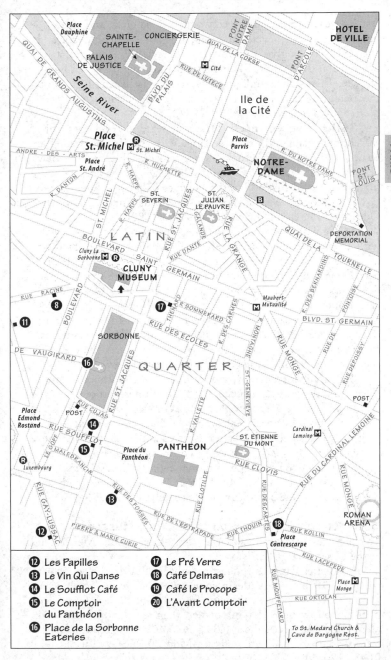

⑫ Les Papilles

⑬ Le Vin Qui Danse

⑭ Le Soufflot Café

⑮ Le Comptoir
  du Panthéon

⑯ Place de la Sorbonne
  Eateries

⑰ Le Pré Verre

⑱ Café Delmas

⑲ Café le Procope

⑳ L'Avant Comptoir

Art Nouveau carnival of carved wood, stained glass, and old-time lights reflected in beveled mirrors. The over-the-top decor and energetic waiters give it an inviting conviviality. Check upstairs before choosing a table. Their roast suckling pig (€19) is a house favorite. There's Belgian beer on tap and a fascinating history on the menu (€18-23 *plats*, €31 *menu*, a few fish options and lots of meat, daily, 3 Rue Racine, tel. 01 44 32 15 60).

$$ La Méditerranée is all about seafood from the south served in a pastel and dressy setting...with similar clientele. The scene and the cuisine are sophisticated yet accessible, and the view of the Odéon is *formidable*. The sky-blue tablecloths and the lovingly presented dishes add to the romance (€28 two-course *menus*, €33 three-course *menus*, daily, reservations smart, facing the Odéon at 2 Place de l'Odéon, tel. 01 43 26 02 30).

$$ Café de l'Odéon offers a great chance to savor light meals with a classy crowd on a peaceful and elegant square in front of a venerable theater. Though limited, the menu is accessible and decently priced, and you'll feel like a winner eating so well and so reasonably in such a Parisian setting. From May to October, the café is outdoors-only and serves lunch and dinner—or just go for drinks (good €14 salads, €17 *plats* such as salmon and *steak tartare*; May-Oct daily 12:00-23:00—weather permitting, no reservations, Place de l'Odéon, tel. 01 44 85 41 30). In the winter (Nov-April) they serve lunch only inside the palatial theater lobby.

$ Restaurant Polidor, a bare-bones neighborhood fixture since the 19th century, is much loved for its unpretentious quality cooking, fun old-Paris atmosphere, and fair value. Stepping inside, you know this is a winner—noisy, happy diners sit tightly at shared tables as waiters chop and serve fresh bread. The selection features classic bourgeois *plats* from every corner of France; their *menu fraicheur* is designed for lighter summer eating (€12-17 *plats*, €25-35 three-course *menus*, daily 12:00-14:30 & 19:00-23:00, cash only, no reservations, 41 Rue Monsieur-le-Prince, tel. 01 43 26 95 34).

Between the Panthéon and the Cluny Museum
To reach these restaurants, use the Cluny-La Sorbonne Métro stop or the Luxembourg RER stop.

$$ At Les Papilles you just eat what's offered...and you won't complain. It's a foodie's dream come true—one *menu*, no choices, and no regrets. Choose your wine from the shelf or ask for advice from the burly rugby-playing owner, then relax and let the food arrive. Book this place ahead (€34 *menu*, €16 daily *marmite du marché*—a.k.a. market stew, closed Sun-Mon, 30 Rue Gay Lussac, tel. 01 43 25 20 79).

$$ Le Vin Qui Danse is a warm little place serving a good selection of tasty dishes and well-matched wines to appreciative clients (€27 two-course *menu*, add €15 for three wines selected to complement your meal, daily, 4 Rue des Fossés St. Jacques, tel. 01 43 54 80 81).

$ On Rue Soufflot with Panthéon Views: Facing each other are two cafés—**Le Soufflot** and **Le Comptoir du Panthéon**—that are well-positioned for afternoon sun and soft evening light. A block in front of the Panthéon, they deliver dynamite views of the inspiring dome. Both serve classic café food all day until late and are great for a pensive drink or a light meal—simply choose the one that appeals.

$ Place de la Sorbonne: This appealing little square surrounds a gurgling fountain and faces Sorbonne University, just a block from the Cluny Museum. It offers several opportunities for a good outdoor lunch or a pleasant dining experience. At amiable Carole's tiny **Baker's Dozen,** you'll pay take-away prices for light fare you can sit down to eat (€5 salads and sandwiches, Mon-Sat until 15:30, closed Sun, tel. 01 44 07 08 09). **Café de l'Ecritoire** is a typical brasserie with salads, *plats du jour,* and good seating inside and out (daily, tel. 01 43 54 60 02). **Patios** serves basic Italian cuisine, including pizza, at decent prices (daily until late, tel. 01 45 38 71 19). **Le Bac de la Sorbonne** is a tad cheaper, but you get what you pay for.

$$ Le Pré Verre, a block from the Cluny Museum, is a chic wine bistro—a refreshing alternative in a part of the Latin Quarter mostly known for low-quality, tourist-trapping eateries. Offering imaginative, modern cuisine at fair prices, the place is packed. The bargain lunch *menu* includes a starter, main course, glass of wine, and coffee for €14. The three-course dinner *menu* at €30 is worth every *centime*. They pride themselves equally on their small-producers' wine list, so follow your server's advice (closed Sun-Mon, 8 Rue Thénard, reservations necessary, tel. 01 43 54 59 47).

On Rue Mouffetard

Several blocks behind the Panthéon, Rue Mouffetard is a conveyor belt of comparison-shopping eaters with wall-to-wall budget options (fondue, crêpes, Italian, falafel, and Greek). Come here to sift through the crowds and eat cheaply. This street stays up late and likes to party (particularly around Place de la Contrescarpe). The gauntlet begins on top, at thriving Place de la Contrescarpe, and ends below where Rue Mouffetard stops at St. Médard Church. Both ends offer fun cafés where you can watch the action. The upper stretch is pedestrian and touristy; the bottom stretch is purely Parisian. Anywhere between is no-man's land for consistent quality. Still, strolling with so many fun-seekers is enjoyable, whether you eat or not. To get here, use the Censier Daubenton or Place Monge Métro stop.

$$ Café Delmas, at the top of Rue Mouffetard on picturesque Place de la Contrescarpe, is *the* place to see and be seen. Come here for a before- or after-dinner drink on the terrace, typical but pricey café cuisine, or great chocolate ice cream (open daily).

$ Cave de Bourgogne, a young and local hangout, has reasonably priced café fare at the bottom of Rue Mouffetard. The outside has picture-perfect tables on a raised terrace; the interior is warm and lively (€13-16 *plats*, specials listed on chalkboards, daily, 144 Rue Mouffetard—see map on page 178).

In Montmartre

Much of Montmartre is extremely touristy, with mindless mobs following guides to cancan shows. But the ambience is undeniably fun, so either join in the touristic fray or walk a few blocks away and find a quieter, more authentic meal at one of the places I've listed below. For locations, see map on page 180.

Near Sacré-Cœur

The steps in front of Sacré-Cœur are perfect for a picnic with a view, though the spot comes with lots of company. For a quieter setting, consider the park directly behind the church. Along the touristy main drag (near Place du Tertre and just off it), several fun piano bars serve mediocre crêpes but offer great people-watching. The options become less touristy and far more tasty as you get away from the top of the hill (skip any place on Place du Tertre). The Anvers Métro stop works well if you're visiting Sacré-Cœur. The Abbesses Métro stop will land you in the heart of the residential Montmartre neighborhood.

$$$ Moulin de la Galette lets you dine with Renoir under the historic windmill in a comfortable setting with good prices. Find the old photos scattered about the place (€23 two-course and €29 three-course *menus* at lunch only; €15 starters and €28 *plats* for dinner, daily, 83 Rue Lepic, Mo: Abbesses, tel. 01 46 06 84 77).

$$ Restaurant Chez Plumeau, just off jam-packed Place du Tertre, is touristy yet moderately priced, with formal service but great seating on a tiny, characteristic square (elaborate €17 salads, €18-22 *plats,* closed Tue Oct-April and Wed year-round, 4 Place du Calvaire, Mo: Abbesses, tel. 01 46 06 26 29).

$ L'Eté en Pente Douce is a good Montmartre choice, hiding under the generous branches of street trees. Just downhill from the crowds on a classic neighborhood corner, it features cheery indoor and outdoor seating, €10 *plats du jour* and salads, vegetarian options, and good wines (daily, many steps below Sacré-Cœur to the left as you leave, down the stairs below the WC, 23 Rue Muller, Mo: Anvers, tel. 01 42 64 02 67).

Near Place des Abbesses

At the bottom of Montmartre, residents pile into a long lineup of brasseries and cafés near Place des Abbesses, especially along Rue des Abbesses and Rue des Martyrs. The food is average; the atmosphere is anything but. Come here for a lively, tourist-free scene. Rue des Abbesses is perfect for a picnic-gathering stroll with cheese shops, delis, wine stores, and bakeries. In fact, the baker at **Au Levain d'Antan** won the award for the best baguette in Paris in 2011 (Mon-Fri 7:30-20:00, closed Sat-Sun, 6 Rue des Abbesses). Unless another Métro stop is listed, use the Abbesses stop.

$$ Le Miroir's kitchen is run by a young and enthusiastic chef cooking up seasonal French fare. Go for high-quality ingredients served to a locals-only crowd. If you enjoyed the wine you had with your meal, cross the street to their wine shop and pick up a bottle to go (€26-33 two or three-course *menus*, Tue-Sat lunch and dinner, Sun lunch only, closed Mon, 94 Rue des Martyrs, tel. 01 46 06 50 73).

$$ Autour de Midi et Minuit is a classic French bistro sitting on top of a jazz cellar (see the Entertainment in Paris chapter for concert details). Hot food served upstairs; cool jazz served downstairs (lunch €15, dinner €26-33, closed Mon, 11 Rue Lepic, Mo: Blanche or Abbesses, tel. 01 55 79 16 48).

$ Le Chinon Brasserie offers good seating inside and out and is the best bet for café/wine bar ambience and food (daily, 49 Rue des Abbesses, tel. 01 42 62 07 17).

$ Smooth in the City provides a much-needed break from rich French fare. For €8.50 you get a fresh fruit smoothie, a healthy salad or veggie-packed sandwich, and a homemade dessert. Order it to go for your walk up the hill, or sit at one of their three outdoor tables (daily 10:00-19:00, 11 Rue des Abbesses, tel. 01 83 56 56 55).

$ La Fourmi sits at the bottom of the hill. Open all day, they offer the cheapest coffee and croissants in Montmartre, and simple, affordable lunches (€8-12). In the evening, the place is taken over by hilltop hipsters who come for the inexpensive beer and generous cheese plates (daily, 74 Rue des Martyrs, Mo: Anvers or Pigalle, tel. 01 42 64 70 35).

Dinner Cruises

The following companies all offer dinner cruises (reservations required). Bateaux-Mouches and Bateaux Parisiens have the best reputations and the highest prices. They offer multicourse meals and music in aircraft-carrier-size dining rooms with glass tops and good views. For both, proper dress is required—no denim, shorts, or sport shoes; Bateaux-Mouches requires a jacket and tie for men. The main difference between these companies is the music:

Bateaux-Mouches offers violin and piano to entertain your romantic evening, whereas Bateaux Parisiens boasts a lively atmosphere with a singer, band, and dance floor.

Bateaux-Mouches, started in 1949, is hands-down the most famous. You can't miss its sparkling port on the north side of the river at Pont de l'Alma. The boats usually board 19:30-20:15, depart at 20:30, and return at 22:45 (€100-155/person, RER: Pont de l'Alma, tel. 01 42 25 96 10, www.bateaux-mouches.fr).

Bateaux Parisiens leaves from Port de la Bourdonnais, just east of the bridge under the Eiffel Tower. Begin boarding at 19:45, leave at 20:30, and return at 23:00 (€66-165/person, price depends on departure time, view seating, and *menu* option; tel. 01 76 64 14 45, www.bateauxparisiens.com). The middle level is best. Pay the few extra euros to get seats next to the windows—it's more romantic and private, with sensational views.

Le Capitaine Fracasse offers the budget option (€50/person, €80 with wine or champagne; reserve ahead—easy online—or get there early to secure a table; boarding times vary by season and day of week, walk down stairs in the middle of Bir-Hakeim bridge near the Eiffel Tower to Iles aux Cygne, Mo: Bir-Hakeim or RER: Champ de Mars-Tour Eiffel, tel. 01 46 21 48 15, www.croisiere-paris.com).

Paris Connections

Whether you're aiming to catch a train or plane, budget plenty of time to reach your departure point. Paris is a big, crowded city, and getting across town on time is a goal you'll share with millions of other harried people. Factor in traffic delays and walking time through huge stations and vast terminals. At the airport, expect lines at ticketing, check-in, baggage check, and security points. Always keep your luggage safely near you. Pickpockets prey on jet-lagged and confused tourists on public transportation.

By Plane
Charles de Gaulle Airport

Paris' main airport has three terminals: T-1, T-2, and T-3. Most flights from the US use T-1 or T-2 (check your ticket, or contact your airline). All three terminals have ATMs *(distributeurs)*, shops, bars, and access to ground transportation into Paris. You can travel between terminals on the free CDGVAL automated shuttle train (departs every 5 minutes, 24/7). Allow 30 minutes to travel between terminals and an hour for total travel time between your gates at T-1 and T-2.

When leaving Paris, plan to arrive at the airport two to three hours early for an overseas flight, or one to two hours for flights

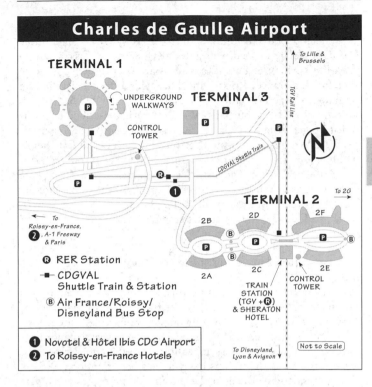

Charles de Gaulle Airport

TERMINAL 1

UNDERGROUND WALKWAYS

TERMINAL 3

CONTROL TOWER

CDGVAL Shuttle Train

TGV Rail Line

To Lille & Brussels

N

To 2G

TERMINAL 2

To Roissy-en-France, A-1 Freeway & Paris

2B   2D   2F

2A   2C   2E

TRAIN STATION (TGV + Ⓡ) & SHERATON HOTEL

CONTROL TOWER

Ⓡ RER Station

▬■ CDGVAL Shuttle Train & Station

Ⓑ Air France/Roissy/ Disneyland Bus Stop

❶ Novotel & Hôtel Ibis CDG Airport

❷ To Roissy-en-France Hotels

To Disneyland, Lyon & Avignon ▼

Not to Scale

PARIS

within Europe (particularly on budget airlines, which can have especially long check-in lines). For flight info, dial either 3950 from French landlines (€0.35/minute) or, from the US, dial 011 33 1 70 36 39 50, or visit www.adp.fr (airport code: CDG).

Terminal 1 (T-1): This circular terminal has three key floors—arrival *(arrivées)* on the top floor, and two floors for departures *(départs)* below. After passing through customs on the **arrival level** *(niveau arrivée)* you'll exit between doors *(porte)* 34 and 36. Nearby are orange information counters with English-speaking staff, a TI (where you can buy a Paris Museum Pass), a café, a newsstand, and an ATM. Walk clockwise around the terminal to find ground transportation: Air France and Roissy buses (door 32), Disneyland shuttles (door 30), and taxis (door 10). Car rentals are at doors 24-30. On the **departure levels** *(niveaux départ)*, departure screens help you find out which hall you should use to check in. Halls 1-4 are on floor 2, and 5-6 are downstairs on floor 1. Also on floor 1 are the CDGVAL shuttle train, cafés, a post office (PTT), pharmacy, boutiques, and a handy grocery. Boarding gates and duty-free shopping are located on floor 3, which is only accessible with a boarding pass.

Terminal 2 (T-2): This long, horseshoe-shaped terminal is divided into six halls, labeled A through F. It's a busy place, so take a deep breath and follow signage carefully. The orange information desks are located near gate 6/8 in each hall (ask where to buy a Paris Museum Pass). Taxi stops are well signed. To locate stops for Air France, Roissy, and Disneyland buses—marked on the map on page 211—follow *Paris by Bus* signs. T-2 has a train station, with RER suburban trains into Paris (described later), as well as longer-distance trains to the rest of France (including high-speed TGV trains). It's located between halls C/D and E/F, below the Sheraton Hotel (prepare for a long walk to reach your train).

Car-rental offices, post offices, pharmacies, and ATMs are all well-signed. You can stash your bags at Baggage du Monde, located above the train station in T-2, but it's pricey (€15 for 24 hours), so I'd use a train station's storage instead (tel. 01 34 38 58 97, www.bagagesdumonde.com).

Transportation Between Charles de Gaulle Airport and Paris

Buses, airport vans, commuter trains, and taxis link the airport's terminals with central Paris. If you're traveling with two or more companions, carrying lots of baggage, or are just plain tired, taxis are worth the extra cost. If you're arriving on a weekday morning, however, taxis are much less appealing, as traffic into Paris can be bad—in that case, the train is likely to be a better option.

By Bus: **Roissy-Buses** make the 50-minute trip to the Opéra Métro stop in central Paris, arriving on Rue Scribe. From there, it's an easy Métro ride to anywhere in the city. To get to the Métro entrance or nearest taxi stand, turn left as you exit the bus and walk counterclockwise around the lavish Opéra building to its front (€10, runs 6:00-23:00, 4/hour until 20:45, 3/hour after that, 50 minutes, buy ticket on bus).

"Les Cars" Air France buses run at least twice hourly from 5:45 until 23:00 (tel. 08 92 35 08 20). **Bus #2** goes to the Etoile stop on Rue Carnot, near the Arc de Triomphe (€16.50, 45 minutes) and Porte Maillot (with connections to Beauvais Airport, described later). Once at the Arc de Triomphe, catch city bus #92 (one block away; see map on page 125) to the Rue Cler area. **Bus #4** runs to Gare de Lyon (45 minutes) and the Montparnasse Tower/train station (€16.50, 1 hour). **Bus #3** goes to Orly airport (€19, 1 hour). Buy tickets from the driver (round-trip tickets or 2 persons traveling together save 20 percent) or online, which saves you an additional 10 percent (www.lescarsairfrance.com).

From Paris to the airport, catch Air France buses at Etoile/Arc de Triomphe (on Avenue Carnot—the non-Champs-Elysées side), Porte Maillot (on Boulevard Gouvion-St-Cyr—right side of the Palais des Congres), Gare Montparnasse (on Rue du

Public Transportation to Recommended Hotels

You have many options for traveling between Charles de Gaulle Airport and Paris; which alternative makes the most sense depends not only on your budget, but where you're staying in the city. Here are my tips for getting to recommended hotels, according to the neighborhood they're in. Keep in mind that, at the airport, using buses (and taxis) require shorter walks than taking RER trains.

Rue Cler Area: The Roissy-Bus, RER, and "Les Cars" Air France bus all work well for Rue Cler hotels. If taking the Roissy-Bus, ride it all the way to the Opéra stop, then take Métro line 8 (direction: Balard) and get off at the La Tour Maubourg or Ecole Militaire stop. Or hop the RER-B from the airport, change at the St. Michel stop for the RER-C (direction: Versailles Rive Gauche or Pontoise), and, depending on where exactly your hotel is, either change again at the Invalides stop to Métro line 8 (direction: Balard; get off either at La Tour Mauberg or Ecole Militaire), or stay on the RER for one more stop, and get off at Pont de l'Alma. If riding the Air France bus, take it to the Arc de Triomphe, then grab the #92 city bus and hop off at one of the stops along Avenue Bosquet, shortly after crossing the river (for stop locations near the Arc, see the map on page 125; for stop locations on Avenue Bosquet, see page 156).

Marais and Ile St. Louis: Take "Les Cars" Air France bus (#4) to Gare de Lyon, find the Métro entry near the bus stop, then take a quick trip on Métro line 1 (direction: La Défense). Get off at the Bastille or St. Paul stops for the Marais, or the Hôtel de Ville stop for Ile St. Louis. Or, take RER-B from the airport to the Châtelet-Les Halles stop and transfer to Métro line 1 (direction: Château de Vincennes; long walk in a huge station), and get off at Hôtel de Ville, St. Paul, or Bastille.

Luxembourg Garden: RER-B to the Luxembourg stop.

Commandant Mouchotte—facing the station with the tower behind you, it's around the left side), or Gare de Lyon (in front of #20 Boulevard Diderot—the main street in front of the station).

By Airport Van: The shuttle vans from Charles de Gaulle work like those at home, carrying passengers directly to and from their hotels, with stops along the way to pick up other passengers. Shuttles work best for trips from your hotel to the airport, since they require you to book a precise pickup time in advance—even though you can't ever know exactly when your flight will actually arrive. Airport vans cost about €32 for one person, €46 for two, and €58 for three. While these vans take longer to reach the airport than a taxi does, compared to taxis they're a good value for single travelers and big families. Have your hotelier book at least a day in advance.

Several companies offer shuttle service; I usually just go with the one my hotel normally uses. Otherwise, try **Paris Shuttles Network** (tel. 01 45 26 01 58, www.shuttlesnetwork.com) or **Airport Connection** (tel. 01 43 65 55 55, www.supershuttle.fr).

Paris Webservices actually works well from the airport to Paris, because they meet you inside the terminal and will wait for you if you're late (tel. 01 53 62 02 29, fax 01 53 01 35 84, www .pariswebservices.com, contactpws@pariswebservices.com). For a one-way trip they charge about €30 for one person, or €44 for 2 people. Booking a round trip costs about €160-180 for up to 4 people. Claim a 10 percent discount by mentioning promo code "RSteves77" when you book, then showing your driver a current edition of this book. They also sell Museum Passes with no extra fee (order ahead) and offer excursions (see page 81).

By Commuter Train: The RER, Paris's suburban commuter train, is your cheapest (though not most convenient) option for getting between the airport and the city center (€9.30, runs 5:00-24:00, 4/hour, 30 minutes to Gare du Nord). It runs directly to well-located RER/Métro stations (including Gare du Nord, Châtelet-Les Halles, St. Michel, and Luxembourg); from there, you can hop the Métro to get exactly where you need to go. It's handy and cheap, but it can require walking with your luggage through big, crowded stations.

From the airport terminal, follow *Paris by Train* signs, then *RER* signs. (If you're landing at Terminals 1 or 3, you'll need to take the CDGVAL shuttle to reach the RER station.) The RER station at T-2 is also a crowded train station, with long ticket-window lines. It's faster to buy tickets from the machines (use the green-colored machines that read *Paris/Ile de France,* coins required, break your bills at an airport shop). Beware of pickpockets; wear your money belt, and keep your bags close. For step-by-step instructions on taking the RER into Paris, see http://parisbytrain.com (see the options under "CDG Airport to Paris").

If you're taking the RER from central Paris out to the airport, allow plenty of time to get to your departure gate (plan for a 10-minute Métro or bus ride to the closest RER station, a 15-minute wait for your RER, plus a 30-minute ride, plus walking time through the stations and airport). At the RER station, make sure the sign over the platform shows *Aéroport Roissy-Charles de Gaulle* as a stop served. (The line splits, so not every line B train serves the airport.) If you're not clear, ask another rider, *"Air-o-por sharl duh gaul?"* Once at the airport, hop out either at T-2 or T-1/3 (where you can connect to T-1 or T-3 on the CDGVAL shuttle).

By Taxi: The 50-minute trip costs about €65 (more if traffic is bad). Taxis can carry three people with bags comfortably, and are legally required to accept a fourth passenger for €3 extra (though they may not like it). Larger parties can wait for a larger vehicle. Expect to pay €1/bag handling fee. Don't take an unauthorized taxi from cabbies greeting you on arrival. Official taxi stands are well-signed.

For trips from Paris to the airport, have your hotel arrange it. Specify that you want a real taxi *(un taxi normal)*, not a limo service that costs €20 more (and gives your hotel a kickback). For weekday morning departures (7:00-10:00), reserve at least a day ahead (€5 reservation fee payable by credit card). For more on taxis in Paris, see page 73.

By Car: Car-rental desks are well-signed from the arrival halls. When returning your car, allow ample time to reach the check-in desks, especially if flying out of Terminal 2—its imperfect signage can make it especially confusing to navigate.

From Charles de Gaulle Airport to Disneyland Paris

The Val d'Europe (VEA) **Disneyland shuttle bus** leaves from each terminal (€19, runs every 20 minutes 8:30-20:00ish, 30 minutes, www.vea-shuttle.co.uk). TGV trains also run to Disneyland from the airport in 10 minutes, but leave less frequently (hourly) and require shuttle buses at each end—take the shuttle van instead.

Orly Airport

This easy-to-navigate airport feels small, but has all the services you'd expect at a major airport: ATMs and currency exchange, car-rental desks, cafés, shops, a post office, a TI, and more (for flight info from French landlines dial 3950, from the US dial 011 33 1 70 36 39 50, www.adp.fr, airport code: ORY). Orly is good for rental-car pickup and drop-off, as it's closer to Paris and far easier to navigate than Charles de Gaulle Airport.

Orly has two terminals: Ouest (west) and Sud (south). Air France and a few other carriers arrive at Ouest; most others use Sud. At both terminals, arrivals are on the ground level (level 0) and departures are on level 1. You can connect the terminals with the free Orlyval shuttle train (departs from Ouest departures level 1 at exit A; from Sud at exit K) or with any of the shuttle buses *(navettes)* that also travel into downtown Paris.

Transportation Between Orly Airport and Paris

Shuttle buses *(navettes)*, the RER, taxis, and airport vans connect Paris with either terminal.

By Bus: **"Les Cars" Air France bus #1** runs to Gare Montparnasse, Invalides, and Etoile Métro stops, all of which have connections to several Métro lines. Upon request, drivers will also stop at the Porte d'Orléans Métro stop. For the Rue Cler neighborhood, take the bus to Invalides, then the Métro to La Tour Maubourg or Ecole Militaire. Buses depart from Ouest arrival level exit B-C or Sud exit L: Look for signs to *navettes* (€12 one-way, 4/hour, 40 minutes to Invalides, buy ticket from driver or save 10 percent by booking online, round-trip tickets or 2 persons traveling together save 20 percent, www.lescarsairfrance.com).

The **Orlybus** goes directly to the Denfert-Rochereau Métro stop. From there, you can catch the Métro or RER-B to central Paris, including the Luxembourg Garden area, Notre-Dame Cathedral, and Gare du Nord. The Orlybus departs from Ouest arrival level exit D and Sud exit H (€7, 3/hour, 30 minutes).

A different bus called **"Paris par le train"** takes you to the Pont d'Orly RER station, where you can catch the RER-C to Gare d'Austerlitz, St. Michel/Notre-Dame, Musée d'Orsay, Invalides (change here for Rue Cler hotels), and Pont de l'Alma. Catch this bus at Ouest arrival level exit G or Sud exit F (€7 total, 4/hour, 40 minutes).

The **Orlyval shuttle train** takes you to the Antony RER station, where you can catch RER-B (direction: Mitry-Claye or Aéroport Charles de Gaulle) to Luxembourg and many recommended hotels, Châtelet-Les Halles, St. Michel, and Gare du Nord. Catch the Orlyval at Ouest arrival level exit A or Sud exit K (€11 total, 6/hour, 40 minutes).

By Taxi: Taxis are outside Ouest arrival level exit B, and to the far right as you leave terminal Sud, at exit M. Allow €40-50 with bags for a taxi into central Paris.

By Airport Van: Airport vans are a good means of getting from Paris to the airport, especially for single travelers or families of four or more (too many for most taxis; see page 214). From Orly, figure about €23 for one person or €30 for two people (less per person for larger groups and kids).

From Orly Airport to Disneyland Paris
The Val d'Europe (VEA) **shuttle bus to Disneyland** departs from Ouest arrival level platform A, exit I; and from the Sud bus station platform 2, exit G (€18, hourly 9:00-19:30, 45 minutes).

Beauvais Airport (airport code: BVA)
Budget airlines such as Ryanair use this small airport, offering dirt-cheap airfares but leaving you 50 miles north of Paris. Still, this airport has direct buses to Paris (see below) and is handy for travelers heading to Normandy or Belgium (car rental available). The airport is basic, waiting areas are crowded, and services are sparse, but improvements are gradually on the way (airport tel. 08 92 68 20 66—lines open daily 8:00-20:00, www.aeroportbeauvais

.com; Ryanair tel. 08 92 78 02 10—lines open Mon-Fri 9:00-19:00, Sat 10:00-17:00, Sun 11:00-17:00; www.ryanair.com).

Transportation Between Beauvais Airport and Paris

By Bus: Buses depart from the airport when they're full (about 20 minutes after flights arrive) and take 1.5 hours to reach Paris. Buy your ticket (€15 one-way) at the little kiosk to the right as you exit the airport. Buses arrive at Porte Maillot on the west edge of Paris (on Métro line 1 and RER-C). The closest taxi stand is at Hôtel Concorde-Lafayette.

Buses heading to Beauvais Airport leave from Porte Maillot about 3.25 hours before scheduled flight departures. Catch the bus in the parking lot on Boulevard Pershing next to Hôtel Concorde-Lafayette. Arrive with enough time to purchase your bus ticket before boarding (*parking* Pershing ticket booth tel. 01 58 05 08 45, airport ticket booth tel. 03 44 11 46 86).

By Train: Trains connect Beauvais' city center and Paris' Gare du Nord (20/day, 1.25 hours). To reach Beauvais' train station, take the Beauvais *navette* (€4, 6/day, 30 minutes) or local bus #12 (€1, 12/day, 30 minutes).

By Taxi: You can take a taxi from Beauvais Airport to Beauvais' train station or city center (€14) or to central Paris (allow €130 and 1.25 hours).

From Beauvais Airport to Disneyland

The Val d'Europe (VEA) **shuttle bus to Disneyland** runs three times a day from Beauvais via Charles de Gaulle Airport (€30, 2.5 hours).

Connecting Paris' Airports

"Les Cars" Air France bus #3 directly and conveniently links Charles de Gaulle and Orly airports (€19.50, stops at Charles de Gaulle Terminals 1 and 2 and Orly Ouest exit B-C or Sud exit L, roughly 2/hour, 5:45-23:00, 1 hour).

RER line B connects Charles de Gaulle and Orly but requires a transfer to the Orlyval train. It isn't as easy as the Air France bus mentioned above, though it's faster when there's traffic (€18, 5/hour, 1.5 hours). This line splits at both ends: Heading to Orly, take trains that serve the Antony stop (direction: St-Rémy-les-Chevreuse), then transfer to Orlyval train; heading to Charles de Gaulle, take trains that end at the airport ("Aéroport Charles de Gaulle-Roissy"), not Mitry-Claye. You can also connect Charles de Gaulle or Orly airports to Beauvais via train. Take the RER-B to Gare du Nord, catch a train to Beauvais, and then a shuttle or local bus to Beauvais Airport (see "Beauvais Airport," earlier).

Three Val d'Europe (VEA) **buses** a day run between Beauvais and Charles de Gaulle, en route to Disneyland (€15, www.vea -shuttle.co.uk).

Taxis are easiest, but pricey (about €80 between Charles de Gaulle and Orly, €115 between Charles de Gaulle and Beauvais, €135 between Orly and Beauvais).

By Train

Paris is Europe's rail hub, with six major stations and one minor one, with trains heading in different directions:

- Gare du Nord (northbound trains)
- Gare Montparnasse (west- and southwest-bound trains)
- Gare de Lyon (southeast-bound trains)
- Gare de l'Est (eastbound trains)
- Gare St. Lazare (northwest-bound trains)
- Gare d'Austerlitz (southwest-bound trains)
- Gare de Bercy (smaller station with non-TGV southbound trains)

All six main train stations have banks or currency exchanges, ATMs, train information desks, telephones, cafés, newsstands, and clever pickpockets (pay attention in ticket lines—keep your bag firmly gripped in front of you). Because of security concerns, not all have baggage checks.

Any train station has schedule information, can make reservations, and can sell tickets for any destination. Or you can save time and stress by buying train tickets or making train reservations at an SNCF Boutique. These small branch offices of the French national rail company are conveniently located throughout Paris, with offices near most of my recommended hotels and museums and at Charles de Gaulle and Orly Airports. Arrive when they open to avoid lines (generally open Mon-Sat 8:30-19:00 or 20:00, closed Sun). For a complete list of SNCF Boutiques, see www .megacomik.info/boutiquesncf.htm.

Each station offers two types of rail service: long distance to other cities, called Grandes Lignes (major lines); and suburban service to nearby areas, called Banlieue, Transilien, or RER. You also may see ticket windows identified as *Ile de France*. These are for Transilien trains serving destinations outside Paris in the Ile de France region (usually no more than an hour from Paris). When arriving by Métro, follow signs for *Grandes Lignes–SNCF* to find the main tracks. Métro and RER trains, as well as buses and taxis, are well-marked at every station.

Budget plenty of time before your departure to factor in ticket lines and making your way through large, crowded stations. Paris train stations can be intimidating, but if you slow down, take a deep breath, and ask for help, you'll find them manageable and efficient. Bring a pad of paper for clear communication at ticket/

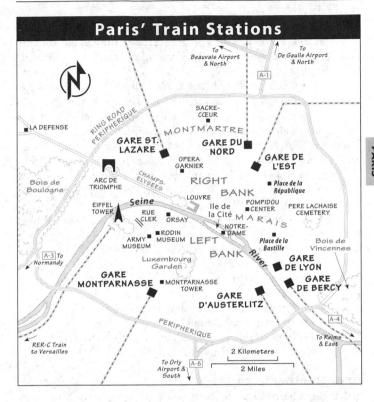

Paris' Train Stations

PARIS

info windows. All stations have helpful information booths *(accueil)*; the bigger stations have roving helpers, usually wearing red or blue vests. They're capable of answering rail questions more quickly than the staff at the information desks or ticket windows. I make a habit of confirming my track number and departure time with these helpers.

To make your trip go more smoothly, be sure to review the many train tips starting on page 1115.

Gare du Nord

The granddaddy of Paris' train stations serves cities in northern France and international destinations north of Paris, including Copenhagen, Amsterdam (see "To Brussels and Amsterdam by Thalys Train," later), and the Eurostar to London (see "To London by Eurostar Train," also later).

Arrive early to allow time to navigate this station. From the Métro, follow *Grandes Lignes* signs (main lines) to reach the tracks at street level. Grandes Lignes trains depart from tracks 2-21 (tracks 20 and 21 are around the corner), suburban Banlieue/Transilien lines from tracks 30-36 (signed *Réseau Ile-de-France*), and RER trains from tracks 37-44 (tracks 41-44 are one floor below). Glass train information booths *(accueil)* are scattered throughout the station, and information-helpers circulate (all rail staff are required to speak English).

There's a helpful TI (labeled *Paris Tourisme*) kiosk near track 19 that provides free maps and sells Paris Museum Passes and fast-pass (a.k.a. *"coupe-file"*) tickets. Monet-esque views over the trains and peaceful, air-conditioned cafés hide on the upper level by the Eurostar check-in (find the cool view WCs down the steps in the café). Other WCs are down the stairs across from track 10 (€0.50). Baggage check and rental cars are near track 3 and down the steps. Taxis are out the door past track 3. Steps down to the Métro are opposite tracks 10 and 19.

Key Destinations Served by Gare du Nord Grandes Lignes: **Brussels** (about 2/hour, 1.5 hours), **Bruges** (at least hourly, 2.5-3 hours, change in Brussels), **Amsterdam** (8-10/day, 3.5 hours direct), **Berlin** (4/day, 8.25 hours, 1-2 changes, via Belgium, non-Belgium-traversing trains leave from Gare de l'Est), **Koblenz** (8/day, 5 hours, change in Köln, more from Gare de l'Est that don't cross Belgium), **Copenhagen** (7/day, 14-18 hours, 1 night train), and **London** via Eurostar Chunnel train (12-15/day, 2.5-3 hours).

By Banlieue/RER Lines: Charles de Gaulle Airport (4/hour, 45 minutes, runs 5:00-24:00, track 4).

Gare Montparnasse

This big, modern station covers three floors, serves lower Normandy and Brittany, and has TGV service to the Loire Valley and southwestern France, as well as suburban service to Chartres.

Baggage check *(consigne)* and WCs are on the mezzanine level. Most services are provided on the second (top) level, where the Grandes Lignes and some Banlieue trains arrive and depart. Trains to Chartres usually depart from tracks 10-19, and the main rail information office *(accueil)* is opposite track 15. With your back to the tracks, taxis are to the far left, car rental is to the far right, and Air France buses to Orly and Charles de Gaulle Airports stop outside the exit to the far right. City buses are out the front of the station (down the escalator through the glassy facade). Bus #96 is good for connecting to Marais and Luxembourg area hotels, while #92 is best for Rue Cler hotels (easier than the Métro).

Key Destinations Served by Gare Montparnasse: Chartres (10/day, 65 minutes), **Amboise** (12/day in 1.5 hours with change in St-Pierre-des-Corps, requires TGV reservation; non-TGV trains leave from Gare d'Austerlitz), **Pontorson/Mont St-Michel** (3/day, 3.5-4.5 hours, via Rennes or Dol), **Dinan** (6/day, 4 hours, change in Rennes and Dol), **Bordeaux** (20/day, 3.5 hours), **Sarlat** (3/day, 5.5-6.5 hours, change in Libourne or Bordeaux), **Toulouse** (13/day, 5-7 hours, most require change, usually in Bordeaux or Montpellier), **Albi** (6/day, 6.5-9 hours, change in Toulouse, also night train), **Tours** (10/day, 1.25 hours), **Madrid** (3/day, 12-14 hours, expensive overnight trains from Gare d'Austerlitz), and **Lisbon** (2/day, 21-24 hours via Irun).

Gare de Lyon

This huge, bewildering station offers TGV and regular service to southeastern France, Italy, Switzerland, and other international destinations.

From the RER or Métro, follow signs for *Grandes Lignes Arrivées* and take the escalator up to reach the street-level platforms (Grandes Lignes and Banlieue lines share the same tracks). Grande Ligne trains are divided into two areas: Hall 1 (tracks A-N in the blue area) and Hall 2 (tracks 5-23 in the yellow area). Monitors show either yellow or blue even before the track is posted, so you know which general area your train leaves from. The two areas are connected by the hallway adjacent to track A and opposite track 9. This hallway has all the services. Transilien ticket windows are just inside the hall adjacent to track A *(billets Ile de France)*. Train information booths are opposite tracks A, M, and 11 (others are downstairs).

Don't leave this station without visiting the recommended Le Train Bleu Restaurant, up the stairs opposite track G. Its pricey but way-cool bar-lounge works well as a quiet waiting area; otherwise find a seat near the baggage check—from opposite track 13 follow *consigne* signs down one floor (baggage check available daily 6:15-22:00, €4-10).

Taxi stands are well-signed in front of, and underneath, the station. "Les Cars" Air France buses to Gare Montparnasse (easy transfer to Orly Airport) and direct to Charles de Gaulle Airport stop outside the station's main entrance (opposite tracks A-L, walk across the parking lot—the stop is a block down from the Café Européen on the right across from Café Les Deux Savoies; normally at :15 and :45 after the hour; see "By Bus" on page 212).

Key Destinations Served by Gare de Lyon: Vaux-le-Vicomte (train to Melun, 2/hour by train, 30 minutes; 3/hour by RER, 45 minutes), **Fontainebleau** (2/hour, 40 minutes; some depart from the Grandes Lignes level, more frequent departures are from one level down—follow *RER-D* signs, and ask at any information booth or ticket window where the next departure leaves from), **Disneyland** (RER line A-4 to Marne-la-Vallée-Chessy, at least 3/hour, 45 minutes), **Beaune** (roughly hourly at rush hour but few mid-day, 2.5 hours, most require change in Dijon; direct trains from Paris' Bercy station take an hour longer), **Dijon** (roughly hourly at rush hour but few mid-day, 1.5 hours), **Chamonix**

(7/day, 5.5-7 hours, some change in Switzerland), **Annecy** (hourly, 4 hours, many with change in Lyon), **Lyon** (at least hourly, 2 hours), **Avignon** (9/day in 2.5 hours to Avignon TGV Station, 5/day in 3.5 hours to Avignon Centre-Ville station, more connections with change—3-4 hours), **Arles** (11/day, 2 direct TGVs—4 hours, 9 with change in Avignon—5 hours), **Nice** (hourly, 5.75 hours, may require change, 11.5-hour night train possible out of Gare d'Austerlitz), **Carcassonne** (8/day, 7-8 hours, 1 change, night trains leave from Gare d'Austerlitz), **Zürich** (6/day direct, 4 hours), **Venice** (5/day, 10-12 hours with 1-3 changes; 1 direct overnight, 14 hours, operated by private company Thello—which doesn't accept railpasses, important to reserve ahead at www.thello.com; 4 more night trains with changes), **Rome** (3/day, 11-16 hours; 1 night train, 14 hours, may transfer in Milan, operated by private company Thello—which doesn't accept railpasses, important to reserve ahead at www.thello.com), **Bern** (9/day, otherwise 4-5.5 hours), **Interlaken** (7/day, 5-6.5 hours, 1-3 changes, 2 more from Gare de l'Est), and **Barcelona** (2/day, 7.5 hours, change in Figueres; night train possible from Gare d'Austerlitz).

Gare de l'Est

This two-floor station (with underground Métro) serves northeastern France and international destinations east of Paris. It's easy to navigate: All trains depart at street level from tracks 1-30. Check the departure monitors to see which section your train leaves from: Departures marked with a yellow square leave from tracks 2-12, while those marked with a blue square depart from tracks 22-30 (suburban Banlieue trains depart from tracks 13-21). A train information office is opposite track 17, and ticket sales are at each end of the station through the halls opposite tracks 8 and 25. Most other services are down the escalator through the hall opposite tracks 12-20 (baggage lockers, car rental, WC, small grocery store, more shops, and Métro access). There's a post office at track level, near the top of the escalators. Access to taxis and buses is out the front of the station (exit with your back to the tracks).

Key Destinations Served by Gare de l'Est: Colmar (12/day with TGV, 3.5 hours, change in Strasbourg), **Strasbourg** (hourly with TGV, 2.5 hours), **Reims** (9/day with TGV, 45 minutes), **Verdun** (4/day with TGV, 1.5 hours; 3 hours by regional train with transfer in Chalôns-en-Champagne), **Interlaken** (2/day, 6.5 hours, 2-3 changes, 7 more from Gare de Lyon), **Zürich** (7/day, 5-6 hours, 1-2 changes, faster direct trains from Gare de Lyon), **Frankfurt** (5 direct/day, 4 hours; 4 more/day with change in Karlsruhe, 4.5 hours), **Vienna** (7/day, 12-17 hours, 1-3 changes, night train via Munich or Frankfurt), **Prague** (5/day, 12-18 hours, night train via Mannheim or Berlin), **Munich** (6/day, 6 hours, most with 1 change, 1 direct night train), and **Berlin** (5/day, 8.5 hours, 1-2 changes; 1 direct night train, 12.5 hours).

Gare St. Lazare

This compact station serves upper Normandy, including Rouen and Giverny. All trains arrive and depart one floor above street level.

From the Métro, follow signs to *Grandes Lignes* to reach the tracks (long walk). Grandes Lignes to all destinations listed below depart from tracks 23-27; Banlieue trains depart from 1-16. The ticket office and car rental are near track 27. Train information offices *(accueil)* are scattered about the station. This station has no baggage check, but it does have a three-floor shopping mall with food, clothing, and more (with your back to the tracks, head a few steps through the halls). Taxis, the Métro, and buses are well-signed.

Key Destinations Served by Gare St. Lazare: Giverny (train to Vernon, 8/day Mon-Sat, 6/day Sun, 45 minutes), **Rouen** (nearly hourly, 1.5 hours), **Honfleur** (13/day, 2-3.5 hours, via Lisieux, then bus), **Bayeux** (9/day, 2.5 hours, some change in Caen), **Caen** (14/day, 2 hours), and **Pontorson/Mont St-Michel** (2/day, 4-5.5 hours, via Caen; more trains from Gare Montparnasse).

Gare d'Austerlitz

This small station provides non-TGV service to the Loire Valley, southwestern France, and Spain. All tracks are at street level. The information booth is opposite track 17, and all ticket sales are in the hall opposite track 10. Baggage check, WCs (with €6 showers that include towel, soap, and the works), and car rental are along the side of the station, opposite track 21. To get to the Métro and RER, you must walk outside and along either side of the station.

Key Destinations Served by Gare d'Austerlitz: Versailles (via RER line C, 4/hour, 35 minutes), **Amboise** (6/day direct in 2 hours, 5/day with transfer in Blois or Les Aubrais-Orléans; faster TGV connection from Gare Montparnasse), **Sarlat** (1/day, 6.25 hours, requires change to bus in Souillac, 3 more/day via Gare Montparnasse), **Carcassonne** (1 direct night train, 7.5 hours, plus a decent night train via Toulouse; better day trains from Gare de Lyon), **Cahors** (5/day, 5 hours, at least 1 direct night train; slower trains from Gare Montparnasse), **Barcelona** (1/night, 12.5 hours, make mandatory reservation at least 2 weeks ahead; day trains from Gare de Lyon), and **Madrid** (1 direct night train, 13-14 hours, make mandatory reservation at least 2 weeks ahead, 16 hours via Irun; day trains from Gare Montparnasse).

Gare de Bercy

This smaller station handles southbound non-TGV trains (Mo: Bercy, one stop east of Gare de Lyon on line 14, exit the Métro station and it's across the street). Facilities are limited—just a WC and a sandwich-fare take-out café.

To Brussels and Amsterdam by Thalys Train

The pricey Thalys train has the monopoly on the rail route between Paris and Brussels (for a cheaper option, try the Eurolines bus, tel. 08 36 69 52 52, www.eurolines.com). Without a railpass you'll pay about €65-120 second class for the Paris-Amsterdam train (compared to €50 by bus) or about €40-70 second class for the Paris-Brussels train (compared to €30 by bus). Even with a railpass, you need to pay for train reservations (second class-€27-39; first class-€42-62, includes a meal). Book at least a day ahead, as seats are limited (www.thalys.com). Or hop on the bus, Gus.

To London by Eurostar Train

The fastest and most convenient way to get from the Eiffel Tower to Big Ben is by rail. Eurostar, a joint service of the Belgian, British, and French railways, is the speedy passenger train that zips you (and up to 800 others in 18 sleek cars) from downtown Paris to downtown London (1-2/hour, 2.5 hours) faster and more easily than flying. The train goes 190 mph both before and after the English Channel crossing. The actual tunnel crossing is a 20-minute, silent, 100-mile-per-hour nonevent. Your ears won't even pop. Get ready for more high-speed connections: Eurostar's monopoly

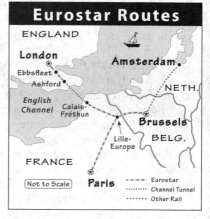

expired at the beginning of 2010, and Germany's national railroad is negotiating to run its bullet trains to London by 2013.

Eurostar Fares: Unlike most trains in Western Europe, Eurostar is not covered by railpasses and always requires a separate, reserved train ticket. Eurostar fares vary depending on how far ahead you reserve, whether you can live with restrictions, and whether you're eligible for any discounts (such as those for early purchase or round-trip travel).

A **one-way, full-fare ticket** (with no restrictions on refundability) runs about $400 for first class and $300 for second class. **Discounts** can lower fares substantially (figure $60-160 for second class, one way) for children under 12, youths under 26, seniors 60 or older, and railpass holders. The early bird gets the best price. If you're ready to commit, you can book tickets as early as 6-9 months in advance at www.eurostar.com.

Buying Eurostar Tickets: Because only the most expensive (full-fare) ticket is fully refundable, don't reserve until you're sure of your plans. But if you wait too long, the cheapest tickets will get bought up.

Once you're confident about the time and date of your crossing, you can check and book fares by phone or online. Ordering online through Eurostar or major agents offers a print-at-home e-ticket option. You can also order by phone through Rail Europe at US tel. 800-387-6782 for home delivery before you go, or through Eurostar (French tel. 08 92 35 35 39, priced in euros) and pick up your ticket at the train station. In Europe you can buy your Eurostar ticket at any major train station in any country, at neighborhood SNCF offices (see page 218), or at any travel agency that handles train tickets (expect a booking fee). You can purchase passholder discount tickets at Eurostar departure stations, through US agents, or by phone with Eurostar, but they may be harder to get at other train stations and travel agencies, and are a discount category that can sell out.

Remember France's time zone is one hour later than Britain's. Times printed on tickets are local times (departure from Paris is French time, arrival in London is British time).

Taking the Eurostar: Eurostar trains depart from and arrive at Paris' Gare du Nord. Check in at least 30 minutes in advance for your Eurostar trip. It's very similar to an airport check-in: You pass through airport-like security, fill out a customs form, show your passport to customs officials, and find a TV monitor to locate your departure gate. The currency-exchange booth here has rates about the same as you'll find on the other end.

By Bus

The main bus station is Gare Routière du Paris-Gallieni (28 Avenue du Général de Gaulle, in suburb of Bagnolet, Mo: Gallieni, tel. 01 49 72 51 51). Buses provide cheaper—if less comfortable and more time-consuming—transportation to major European cities. The bus is also the cheapest way to cross the English Channel; book at least two days in advance for the best fares. Eurolines' buses depart from here (tel. 08 36 69 52 52, www.eurolines.com). Look on their website for offices in central Paris.

NEAR PARIS

Versailles • Chartres • Giverny • Disneyland Paris

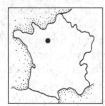

Efficient trains bring dozens of day trips within the grasp of temporary Parisians. Europe's best palace at Versailles, the awesome cathedral of Chartres, the flowery gardens at Giverny that inspired Monet, and a mouse-run amusement park await the traveler looking for a refreshing change from urban Paris.

Versailles

Every king's dream, Versailles (vehr-"sigh") was the residence of French monarchs and the cultural heartbeat of Europe for about 100 years—until the Revolution of 1789 changed all that. The Sun King (Louis XIV) created Versailles, spending freely from the public treasury to turn his dad's hunting lodge into a palace fit for the gods (among whom he counted himself). Louis XV and Louis XVI spent much of the 18th century gilding Louis XIV's lily. In 1837, about 50 years after the royal family was evicted by citizen-protesters, King Louis-Philippe opened the palace as a museum. Today you can visit parts of the huge palace and wander through acres of manicured gardens sprinkled with fountains and studded with statues. Europe's next-best palaces are just Versailles wannabes.

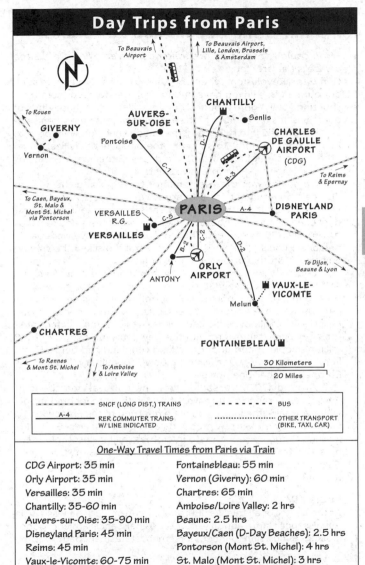

Day Trips from Paris

To Beauvais Airport

To Beauvais Airport,
Lille, London, Brussels
& Amsterdam

N

To Rouen

GIVERNY

Vernon

**AUVERS-
SUR-OISE**

Pontoise

CHANTILLY

Senlis

**CHARLES
DE GAULLE
AIRPORT**
(CDG)

To Reims
& Epernay

D-1

C-1

B-3

To Caen, Bayeux,
St. Malo &
Mont St. Michel
via Pontorson

VERSAILLES
R.G.

VERSAILLES

C-5

PARIS

A-4

**DISNEYLAND
PARIS**

C-2

B-2

D-2

**ORLY
AIRPORT**

ANTONY

To Dijon,
Beaune & Lyon

**VAUX-LE-
VICOMTE**

Melun

CHARTRES

FONTAINEBLEAU

To Rennes
& Mont St. Michel

To Amboise
& Loire Valley

30 Kilometers

20 Miles

‑‑‑‑‑‑ SNCF (LONG DIST.) TRAINS	‑ ‑ ‑ ‑ BUS
A-4 RER COMMUTER TRAINS W/ LINE INDICATED	·········· OTHER TRANSPORT (BIKE, TAXI, CAR)

NEAR PARIS

One-Way Travel Times from Paris via Train

CDG Airport: 35 min	Fontainebleau: 55 min
Orly Airport: 35 min	Vernon (Giverny): 60 min
Versailles: 35 min	Chartres: 65 min
Chantilly: 35-60 min	Amboise/Loire Valley: 2 hrs
Auvers-sur-Oise: 35-90 min	Beaune: 2.5 hrs
Disneyland Paris: 45 min	Bayeux/Caen (D-Day Beaches): 2.5 hrs
Reims: 45 min	Pontorson (Mont St. Michel): 4 hrs
Vaux-le-Vicomte: 60-75 min	St. Malo (Mont St. Michel): 3 hrs

Worth ▲▲▲, Versailles offers three blockbuster sights. The main attraction is the palace itself, called the **Château.** Here you walk through dozens of lavish, chandeliered rooms once inhabited by Louis XIV and his successors. Next come the expansive **Gardens** behind the palace, a landscaped wonderland dotted with statues and fountains. Finally, at the far end of the Gardens, is the pastoral area called the **Trianon Palaces and Domaine de**

Kings and Queens and Guillotines

• *You could read this on the train ride to Versailles. Relax...the palace is the last stop.*

Come the Revolution, when they line us up and make us stick out our hands, will you have enough calluses to keep them from shooting you? A grim thought, but Versailles raises these kinds of questions. It's the symbol of the *ancien régime*, a time when society was divided into rulers and the ruled, when you were born to be rich or to be poor. To some it's the pinnacle of civilization; to others, the sign of a civilization in decay. Either way, it remains one of Europe's most impressive sights.

Versailles was the residence of the king and the seat of France's government for a hundred years. Louis XIV (r. 1643-1715) moved out of the Louvre in Paris, the previous royal residence, and built an elaborate palace in the forests and swamps of Versailles, 10 miles west. The reasons for the move were partly personal—Louis XIV loved the outdoors and disliked the sniping environs of stuffy Paris—and partly political.

Louis XIV was creating the first modern, centralized state. At Versailles he consolidated his government's scattered ministries so that he could personally control policy. More importantly, he invited France's nobles to Versailles in order to control them. Living a life of almost enforced idleness, the "domesticated" aristocracy couldn't interfere with the way Louis ran things. With 18 million people united under one king (England had only 5.5 million), a booming economy, and a powerful military, France was Europe's number-one power.

Around 1700, Versailles was the cultural heartbeat of Europe, and French culture was at its zenith. Throughout Europe, when you said "the king," you were referring to the French king—Louis XIV. Every king wanted a palace like Versailles. Everyone learned French. French taste in clothes, hairstyles, table manners, theater, music, art, and kissing spread across the Continent. That cultural dominance continued, to some extent, right up to the 20th century.

Louis XIV

At the center of all this was Europe's greatest king. He was a true Renaissance Man, a century after the Renaissance: athletic, good-looking, a musician, dancer, horseman, statesman, patron of the

Marie-Antoinette (a.k.a. Trianon/Domaine), designed for frolicking blue bloods and featuring several small palaces and Marie's Hamlet—perfect for getting away from the mobs at the Château.

Visiting Versailles can seem daunting because of its size and hordes of visitors. But if you follow my tips, a trip here during even the busiest times is manageable.

arts, and lover. For all his grandeur, he was one of history's most polite and approachable kings, a good listener who could put even commoners at ease in his presence.

Louis XIV called himself the Sun King because he gave life and warmth to all he touched. He was also thought of as Apollo, the Greek god of the sun. Versailles became the personal temple of this god on earth, decorated with statues and symbols of Apollo, the sun, and Louis XIV himself. The classical themes throughout underlined the divine right of France's kings and queens to rule without limit.

Louis XIV was a hands-on king who personally ran affairs of state. All decisions were made by him. Nobles, who in other countries were the center of power, became virtual slaves dependent on Louis XIV's generosity. For 70 years he was the perfect embodiment of the absolute monarch. He summed it up best himself with his famous rhyme—*"L'état, c'est moi!"* (lay-tah say-mwah): "The state, that's me!"

Another Louis or Two to Remember

Three kings lived in Versailles during its century of glory. Louis XIV built it and established French dominance. Louis XV, his great-grandson (Louis XIV reigned for 72 years), carried on the tradition and policies, but without the Sun King's flair. During Louis XV's reign (1715-1774), France's power abroad was weakening, and there were rumblings of rebellion from within.

France's monarchy was crumbling, and the time was ripe for a strong leader to re-establish the old feudal order. They didn't get one. Instead, they got Louis XVI (r. 1774-1792), a shy, meek bookworm, the kind of guy who lost sleep over revolutionary graffiti...because it was misspelled. Louis XVI married a sweet girl from the Austrian royal family, Marie-Antoinette, and together they retreated into the idyllic gardens of Versailles while revolutionary fires smoldered.

Getting There

By Train: The town of Versailles is 35 minutes southwest of Paris. Take the **RER-C train** (4/hour, 35 minutes one-way, €6.50 round-trip) from any of these Paris RER stops: Gare d'Austerlitz, St. Michel, Musée d'Orsay, Invalides, Pont de l'Alma, or Champ de Mars. You can buy your train tickets at any Métro ticket window in Paris—for no extra cost it will include the connection from that

Métro stop to the RER. At the RER station, catch any train listed as "Versailles R.G." or "Versailles Rive Gauche" (Rive Gauche is the Versailles station closest to the Château—there are two others). Ride to the last stop.

At the Versailles R.G. train station, exit through the turnstiles by inserting your ticket. Ignore the hawkers peddling guided Versailles tours and tickets. To reach the **palace,** just follow the crowds: Turn right out of the station, then left at the first boulevard, and walk 10 minutes. To return to Paris, all trains serve all downtown Paris RER stops on the C line.

A Phébus shuttle bus links the Versailles R.G. train station to the **Trianon/Domaine,** but doesn't go to the palace. It's ideal if you are visiting the Trianon/Domaine first, before the Château—or if you want to return to the train station from the Trianon/Domaine (1-2/hour, runs mid-April-Oct only, €1.70 or one Métro ticket, check current schedule for "Ligne TRI" at www.phebus.tm.fr).

By Taxi: The 30-minute ride (without traffic) between Versailles and Paris costs about €60.

By Car: Get on the *périphérique* freeway that circles Paris, and take the toll-free A-13 autoroute toward Rouen. Exit at Versailles, follow signs to *Versailles Château*, and park in the huge pay lot at Place d'Armes (€5.50/2 hours, €10/4 hours, €15/8 hours).

Planning Your Time

Versailles merits a full sightseeing day and is much more enjoyable with a relaxed, unhurried approach. Here's what I'd do on a first visit:

• Get a pass in advance (explained on page 231, under "Passes").

• Avoid Sundays and Tuesdays, when crowds smother the palace interior.

• Leave Paris by 8:00 and arrive at the palace just before it opens at 9:00. Or consider leaving Paris a bit earlier to take advantage of the impressive €9 buffet breakfast at the recommended

Hôtel Ibis Versailles (across from the train station). In the morning, tour the Château following my self-guided tour, which hits the highlights.

• Have a canalside lunch at one of the sandwich kiosks or cafés in the Gardens. Spend the afternoon touring the Gardens, Trianon Palaces, and Domaine de Marie-Antoinette. On spring or summer weekends (also on Tue late May-late June), catch the Fountain Spectacles in the Gardens. Stay for dinner in Versailles town (see recommended restaurants on page 242), or head back to Paris.

• If you need to shorten your visit, skip the Trianon/Domaine, which takes an additional 1.5 hours, plus a 30-minute walk each way.

• An alternate plan (for late risers) is to visit the uncrowded Trianon Palaces and Domaine de Marie-Antoinette first (opens at noon), then work your way back through the Gardens to the Château, arriving after the crowds have died down. To do this, take advantage of the direct shuttle bus from the Versailles R.G. train station to the Grand Trianon (described earlier).

• In general, allow 1.5 hours each for the Château, the Gardens, and the Trianon/Domaine. Add another two hours for round-trip transit, plus another hour for lunch, and you're looking at an eight-hour day—at the very least.

Orientation

Cost: Buy either a Paris Museum Pass or a Versailles Le Passeport Pass, both of which give you access to the most important parts of the complex (see "Passes" below).

If you don't get a pass, buy individual tickets for each of the three different sections.

The Château: €15, includes audioguide, under 18 free. Covers the famous Hall of Mirrors, the king and queen's living quarters, many lesser rooms, and any temporary exhibitions. For €1 more, you can get a guided tour of the Château—a great deal (see "Guided Tours," later). Free on the first Sunday of off-season months (Nov-March).

The Trianon Palaces and Domaine de Marie-Antoinette: €10, no audioguide available, under 18 free. Covers the Grand Trianon and its gardens, the Petit Trianon, the queen's Hamlet, and a smattering of nearby buildings. Free on the first Sunday of off-season months (Nov-March).

The Gardens: Free, except on Fountain Spectacle days, when admission is €8.50 (weekends April-Oct plus Tue late May-late June; see "Fountain Spectacles in the Gardens," later).

Passes: The following passes can save money and allow you to skip the long ticket-buying lines (but not security checks before entering the palaces). Both passes include the Château audioguide.

The **Paris Museum Pass** (see page 58) covers the Château and the Trianon/Domaine area (a €25 value) and is the best solution for most. It doesn't include the Gardens on Fountain Spectacle days.

The **Le Passeport** one-day pass costs €18 and covers the Château and the Trianon/Domaine area. The price bumps up to €25 on Fountain Spectacle days.

Buying Passes and Tickets: It's best to buy tickets or passes in advance. They're available at any Paris TI or FNAC department store (small fee), or online at www.chateauversailles.fr (print out your pass/ticket or pick it up near the entrance).

In Versailles, passes are sold at the city TI (€2 fee; for TI details, see "Information," later).

Your last option is to buy your pass or ticket at the Château ticket-sales office (to the left as you face the palace). Ticket windows accept American credit cards but have long lines in the morning—avoid the wait by using the ticket machines at the back of the room (you'll need a chip-and-PIN card or bills—which half the machines accept).

Hours: The **Château** is open April-Oct Tue-Sun 9:00-18:30, Nov-March Tue-Sun 9:00-17:30; closed Mon year-round.

The **Trianon Palaces and Domaine de Marie-Antoinette** are open April-Oct Tue-Sun 12:00-18:30, Nov-March Tue-Sun 12:00-17:30; closed Mon year-round (off-season only the two Trianon Palaces are open, not the Hamlet or other outlying buildings).

The **Gardens** are open April-Oct daily 9:00-20:30, but may close earlier for special events; Nov-March Tue-Sun 8:00-18:00, closed Mon.

Last entry to all areas is 30 minutes before closing.

Crowd-Beating Strategies: Versailles can be packed May-Sept 10:00-13:00. Avoid Tuesdays and Sundays, when the place is jammed with a slow shuffle of tourists from open to close. Ticket and security lines can be long: To skip the ticket-buying line, use a Paris Museum Pass or Le Passeport, buy tickets in advance, or book a guided tour (below). Everyone—including holders of advance tickets and passes—must go through security (longest lines 10:00-12:00). Before queuing up at the security entrance, check for signs that they might have opened up a special, shorter line for passholders (but don't count on it). For strategies once you get into the palace and its grounds, see "Planning Your Time," earlier.

Pickpockets: Assume pickpockets are working the tourist crowds.

Information: Before you go, check the excellent website for updates and special events—www.chateauversailles.fr. The palace's general contact number is tel. 01 30 83 78 00. Versailles has two information offices. You'll pass the city TI on your walk from the RER station to the palace—it's just past the Pullman Hôtel (daily 9:00-19:00, tel. 01 39 24 88 88). The information office at the Château is on the left side of the courtyard as you face the Château (WCs, toll tel. 08 10 81 16 14). Pick up the free, useful map just inside the Château.

Guided Tours: The 1.5-hour English guided tour gives you access to a few extra rooms (the lineup varies) and lets you skip ticket-buying lines if you came *sans* pass. Ignore the tours hawked as you leave the train station. Book at the guided-tours office in the Château courtyard—it's to your right as you approach the palace (look for *Visites Conférences* signs). You can book a tour online on the palace's website or reserve immediately upon arrival—tours can sell out by 13:00 (€16 includes palace entry—just €1 more than entry alone, €7 if you have pass, tours run about hourly from 9:00-15:00).

Audioguide Tours: A free audioguide to the Château is included in your admission (pick up just inside the palace, return as you leave).

You can download a free Rick Steves audio tour of Versailles; see page 1138. Other podcasts and digital tours are available in the "multimedia" section at www.chateau versailles.fr.

The palace audioguide and my audio tour complement one another: Eager students can easily transfer earbuds between devices and listen to both tours as you shuffle through the lavish rooms.

Baggage Check: Large bags and baby strollers are not allowed in the Château and the two Trianons (use a baby backpack or hire a babysitter for the day); you must use the free baggage check and retrieve your items one hour before closing.

Services: There are WCs on either side of the Château courtyard (in the ticket-sales office and in the guided-tours office), immediately upon entering the Château (Entrance H), and near the exit from the Dauphin's Apartments. You'll also find WCs near the Grand Café d'Orléans, in the Gardens near the Latona Basin, at the Grand Canal, in the Grand Trianon and Petit Trianon, and at several other places scattered around the grounds. Any café generally has a WC.

Photography: Allowed, but no flash indoors.

Eating: To the left of the Château's golden Royal Gate entrance, the Grand Café d'Orléans offers good value self-service meals (€5 sandwiches and small salads, great for picnicking in the Gardens). In the Gardens, you'll find several restaurants, cafés, and snack stands. Most are located near the Latona Fountain (less crowded) and in a delightful cluster at the Grand Canal (more crowds and more choices, including two restaurants).

In **town,** restaurants are on the street to the right of the parking lot (as you face the Château). Handy McDonald's and

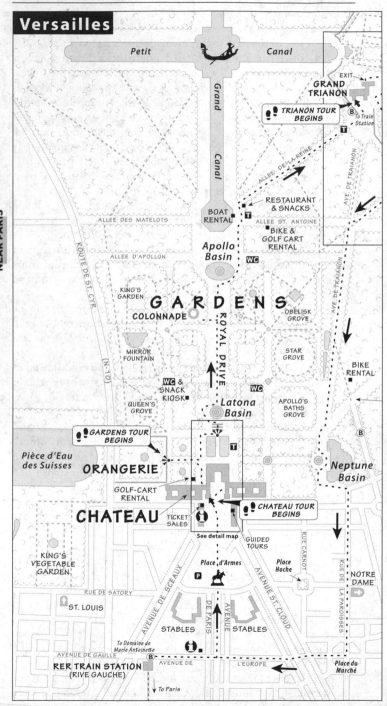

Versailles

NEAR PARIS

Petit Canal

Grand Canal

GRAND TRIANON

EXIT

TRIANON TOUR BEGINS

To Train Station

ALLEE DE LA REINE

AVE. DE TRIANON

RESTAURANT & SNACKS

BOAT RENTAL

ALLEE DES MATELOTS

ALLEE ST. ANTOINE

BIKE & GOLF CART RENTAL

Apollo Basin

WC

ALLEE D'APOLLON

ROUTE DE ST. CYR

KING'S GARDEN

COLONNADE

GARDENS

OBELISK GROVE

AVE. DE TRIANON

MIRROR FOUNTAIN

ROYAL DRIVE

STAR GROVE

BIKE RENTAL

WC & SNACK KIOSK

QUEEN'S GROVE

Latona Basin

APOLLO'S BATHS GROVE

WC

GARDENS TOUR BEGINS

Pièce d'Eau des Suisses

ORANGERIE

Neptune Basin

GOLF-CART RENTAL

CHATEAU

TICKET SALES

See detail map

CHATEAU TOUR BEGINS

GUIDED TOURS

KING'S VEGETABLE GARDEN

Place d'Armes

Place Hoche

RUE CARNOT

RUE DE LA PAROISSES

NOTRE DAME

RUE DE SATORY

ST. LOUIS

AVENUE DE SCEAUX

DE PARIS

AVENUE

AVENUE ST. CLOUD

STABLES

STABLES

To Domaine de Marie Antoinette

AVENUE DE GAULLE

RER TRAIN STATION (RIVE GAUCHE)

AVENUE DE

L'EUROPE

Place du Marché

To Paris

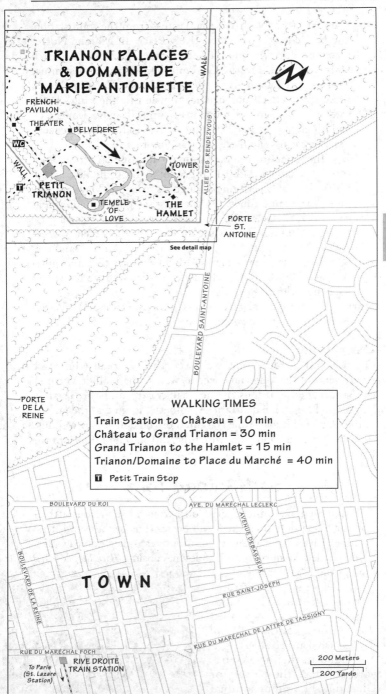

TRIANON PALACES & DOMAINE DE MARIE-ANTOINETTE

WALL

FRENCH PAVILION

THEATER

BELVEDERE

WC

WALL

PETIT TRIANON

TEMPLE OF LOVE

TOWER

THE HAMLET

ALLÉE DES RENDEZVOUS

PORTE ST. ANTOINE

See detail map

NEAR PARIS

BOULEVARD SAINT-ANTOINE

PORTE DE LA REINE

WALKING TIMES

Train Station to Château = 10 min
Château to Grand Trianon = 30 min
Grand Trianon to the Hamlet = 15 min
Trianon/Domaine to Place du Marché = 40 min

🚋 Petit Train Stop

BOULEVARD DU ROI

AVE. DU MARÉCHAL LECLERC

AVENUE DE BASSEUX

T O W N

RUE SAINT-JOSEPH

RUE DU MARÉCHAL DE LATTRE DE TASSIGNY

BOULEVARD DE LA REINE

RUE DU MARÉCHAL FOCH

To Paris (St. Lazare Station)

RIVE DROITE TRAIN STATION

200 Meters

200 Yards

Starbucks (both with WCs) are across from the train station. The best choices are on the lively Place du Marché Notre-Dame in the town center (listed on page 242).

Fountain Spectacles in the Gardens: On spring and summer weekends, the Gardens charge a mandatory admission fee for these spectacles. Loud classical music fills the king's backyard, and the Gardens' fountains are in full squirt. Louis XIV had his engineers literally reroute a river to fuel these gushers. Even by today's standards, they are impressive.

The fountains run on Saturdays and Sundays from April through October (11:00-12:00 & 15:30-17:30; finale starts at 17:20). They also perform on Tuesdays from late May until late June at the same times. On these "spray days," the Gardens cost €8.50. (Pay at the Gardens entrance; covered by Le Passeport but not Paris Museum Pass.) The calendar of spectacles also includes a few music-only days (on the rare Tue, €8.50) and elaborate sound-and-light displays (Sat mid-June-Aug at 21:00, €23). Check the Versailles website for what's happening during your visit.

Starring: Luxurious palaces, endless gardens, Louis XIV, Marie-Antoinette, and the *ancien régime*.

Overview

On this self-guided tour, we'll see the Château (the State Apartments of the king and queen as well as the Hall of Mirrors), the landscaped Gardens in the "backyard," and the Trianon Palaces and Domaine de Marie-Antoinette, located at the far end of the Gardens. If your time is limited or you don't enjoy walking, skip the Trianon/Domaine, which is a 30-minute hike from the Château.

Self-Guided Tour

This commentary, which leads you through the various attractions at Versailles, covers just the basics. For background, first read the "Kings and Queens and Guillotines" sidebar on page 228. For a detailed room-by-room rundown, consider *Rick Steves' Paris* (buy in the US or at any of the English-language bookstores in Paris listed in the previous chapter) or the guidebook called *The Châteaux, the Gardens, and Trianon* (sold at Versailles).

Stand in the huge courtyard and face the palace, or Château. The golden Royal

Gate in the center of the courtyard, nearly 260 feet long and decorated with 100,000 gold leaves, is a recent replica of the original. The ticket-buying office is to the left; guided-tour sales are to the right. The entrance to the Château (once you have your ticket or pass) is through the modern concrete-and-glass security checkpoint, marked *Entrance A*. After passing through security, you spill out into the open-air courtyard on the other side of the golden Royal Gate.

Enter the Château from the courtyard at Entrance H—the State Apartments. Inside are an info desk (get a free map), WCs, and free audioguides.

The Château: The one-way walk through the palace leads you past the dazzling 700-seat **Royal Opera House;** by the intimate, two-tiered **Royal Chapel;** and through the glamorous **State Apartments.** In the **King's Wing** you'll see a billiard room, a royal make-out room, the Swiss bodyguard room, Louis' official bedroom, his grand throne room (the **Apollo Room**—with a 10-foot-tall canopied throne), and his war rooms.

Next you'll visit the magnificent **Hall of Mirrors**—250 feet long, with 17 arched mirrors matching 17 windows looking out upon royal garden views. The mirrors—a luxury at the time—reflect an age when beautiful people loved to look at themselves. In another age altogether, this was the room in which the Treaty of Versailles was signed, ending World War I.

You'll finish in the **Queen's Wing,** where you'll visit the Queen's bedchamber, the guard room where Louis XVI and Marie-Antoinette surrendered to the Revolution, and Napoleon's coronation room.

Getting Around the Gardens: It's a 30- to 45-minute **walk** from the palace, down to the Grand Canal, past the two Trianon palaces, to the Hamlet at the far end of Domaine de Marie-Antoinette. Allow more time if you stop along the way. After enduring the slow Château shuffle, stretching your legs out here feels pretty good.

There's a **bike rental** station by the Grand Canal. A bike won't save you that much time (you can't take it inside the grounds of the Trianon/Domaine; park it near an entrance while you tour

NEAR PARIS

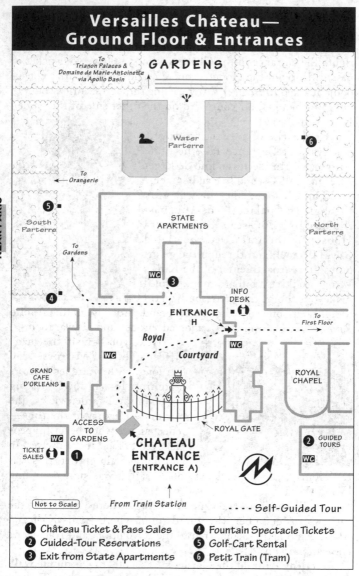

Versailles Château— Ground Floor & Entrances

GARDENS

To Trianon Palaces & Domaine de Marie-Antoinette via Apollo Basin

Water Parterre

← To Orangerie

STATE APARTMENTS

South Parterre

North Parterre

To Gardens

WC **3**

INFO DESK ℹ

4

ENTRANCE H →

To First Floor

Royal

WC

WC

Courtyard

GRAND CAFE D'ORLEANS

ROYAL CHAPEL

ACCESS TO GARDENS

ROYAL GATE

WC

TICKET SALES ℹ **1**

CHATEAU ENTRANCE (ENTRANCE A)

2 GUIDED TOURS

WC

Not to Scale

From Train Station

- - - - Self-Guided Tour

1 Château Ticket & Pass Sales
2 Guided-Tour Reservations
3 Exit from State Apartments
4 Fountain Spectacle Tickets
5 Golf-Cart Rental
6 Petit Train (Tram)

inside). Instead, simply enjoy pedaling around the greatest royal park in all of Europe (€6.50/hour or €15/half-day, kid-size bikes and tandems available).

The fast-looking, slow-moving **tram** *(petit train)* leaves from behind the Château (north side). It stops at the Grand Canal and at the Grand and Petit Trianons (two of the entrance points to the Trianon/Domaine). You can hop on and off as you like (€7, pay driver, free for kids under 11, 4/hour, runs 11:00-18:00).

Another option is to rent a **golf cart** for a fun drive through the Gardens. You can't drive it in the Trianon/Domaine, but you can park it outside the entrance while you sightsee inside (€30/hour, 4-person limit per cart, rent down by the canal or at Orangerie side of palace).

The Phébus **shuttle bus** can save you 30 minutes of walking time, if you want to return directly to the train station from the Trianon/Domaine (see page 230).

Palace Gardens: The Gardens offer a world of royal amuse-

ments. The warmth from the Sun King was so great that he could even grow orange trees in chilly France. Louis XIV had a thousand of these to amaze his visitors. In winter they were kept in the greenhouses (beneath your feet) that surround the courtyard. On sunny days, they were wheeled out in their silver planters and scattered around the grounds.

With the palace behind you, it seems as if the grounds stretch out forever. Versailles was laid out along an eight-mile axis that included the grounds, the palace, and the town of Versailles itself, one of the first instances of urban planning since Roman times and a model for future capitals, such as Washington, D.C., and Brasilia. A promenade leads from the palace to the Grand Canal, where France's royalty floated up and down in imported Venetian gondolas.

Trianon Palaces and Domaine de Marie-Antoinette: Versailles began as an escape from the pressures of kingship. But in a short time, the Château had become as busy as Paris ever was. Louis XIV needed an escape from his escape and built a smaller palace out in the boonies. Later, his successors retreated still farther from the Château and French political life, ignoring the real world that

was crumbling all around them. They expanded the Trianon area, building a fantasy world of palaces and pleasure gardens—the enclosure called Marie-Antoinette's Domaine.

The beautifully restored **Grand Trianon Palace** is as sumptuous as the main palace, but much smaller. With its pastel-pink

NEAR PARIS

colonnade and more human scale, this is a place you'd like to call home. Nearby are the **French Pavilion,** Marie-Antoinette's **Theater,** and the octagonal **Belvedere** palace.

You can almost see princesses bobbing gaily in the branches as you walk through the enchanting forest, past the white marble **Temple of Love** to the queen's fake-peasant **Hamlet** *(le Hameau).*

Marie-Antoinette's happiest days were spent at the Hamlet, under a bonnet, tending her perfumed sheep and manicured gardens in a thatch-happy wonderland.

Despite her bad reputation with the public, Marie-Antoinette was a sweet girl from Vienna who never quite fit in with the fast, sophisticated crowd at Versailles. She made the **Petit Trianon,** a masterpiece of Neoclassical architecture, a place to get away and re-create the simple home life she remembered from her childhood. Here she played, while in the cafés of faraway Paris, revolutionaries plotted the end of the *ancien régime.*

Lesser Sights near the Palace

Equestrian Performance Academy (Académie du Spectacle Equestre)—The art of horseback riding has returned to Versailles. On most weekends from May through mid-December, you can either watch a basic training session or enjoy a choreographed performance—including "equestrian fencing"—performed to classical music (training session-€12, includes a visit through the stables, Sat-Sun and some Thu at 11:15; musical shows-€25, Sun and some Thu at 15:00 plus Sat at 20:00 May-July and at 18:00 Sept-Dec, but sporadic schedule—confirm online). The stables (Grandes Ecuries) are across the parking square from the Château, next to the post office (information tel. 01 39 02 07 14, reservations tel. 08 92 68 18 91, www.acadequestre.fr).

The King's Vegetable Garden (Le Potager du Roi)—When Louis XIV demanded fresh asparagus in the middle of winter, he got it, thanks to his vegetable garden. The 22-acre garden—still productive—is open to visitors. Stroll through symmetrically laid-out plots planted with vegetables both ordinary and exotic, among thousands of fruit trees. Even today, the garden sprouts 20 tons of vegetables and 50 tons of fruit a year, which you can buy in season.

Cost and Hours: €4.50 weekdays, €6.50 weekends, April-Oct Tue-Sun 10:00-18:00, closed Mon, limited winter hours, 10 Rue du Maréchal Joffre, tel. 01 39 24 62 62, www.potager-du-roi.fr.

Sleeping in Versailles

For a less expensive and laid-back alternative to Paris, the town of Versailles can be a good overnight stop, especially for drivers. Park in the palace's main lot while looking for a hotel, or leave your car there overnight (€5.50/2 hours, €14.80/8 hours). Get a map of Versailles at your hotel or at the TI.

$$ Hôtel de France*,** in an 18th-century townhouse, offers Old World class, with mostly air-conditioned, appropriately royal rooms, a pleasant courtyard, a bar, and a restaurant (Db-€143, Tb-€180, Qb-€244, Wi-Fi, just off parking lot across from Château at 5 Rue Colbert, tel. 01 30 83 92 23, fax 01 30 83 92 24, www.hotelfrance-versailles.com, hotel-de-france-versailles @orange.fr).

$ Hôtel le Cheval Rouge,** built in 1676 as Louis XIV's stables, now boards tourists. Tucked into a corner of Place du Marché, this modest hotel has a big, scruffy courtyard with free parking and sufficiently comfortable rooms connected by long, narrow halls (Db-€82-98, Tb-€120, Qb-€130, Wi-Fi, 18 Rue André Chénier, tel. 01 39 50 03 03, fax 01 39 50 61 27, www.chevalrougeversailles .fr, chevalrouge@sfr.fr).

$ Hôtel Ibis Versailles** offers a good weekend value and modern comfort, with 85 air-conditioned rooms (Mon-Thu Db-€135, Fri-Sun Db-€90, extra bed-€10, good-value breakfast-€9, Internet access and Wi-Fi, parking-€12, across from RER station

NEAR PARIS

Sleep Code

(€1 = about $1.30, country code: 33)
S = Single, **D** = Double/Twin, **T** = Triple, **Q** = Quad, **b** = bathroom, **s** = shower only, * = French hotel rating system (0-5 stars). Everyone speaks English and accepts credit cards.

To help you easily sort through these listings, I've divided the accommodations into two categories, based on the price for a standard double room with bath,

$$ Higher Priced—Most rooms more than €100.
$ Lower Priced—Most rooms €100 or less.

Prices can change without notice; verify the hotel's current rates online or by email.

Versailles Town Hotels & Restaurants

❶ Hôtel de France
❷ Hôtel le Cheval Rouge
❸ Hôtel Ibis Versailles
❹ Au Chien qui Fume Restaurant
❺ A la Côte Bretonne Restaurant
❻ La Boulangerie
❼ Equestrian Performances

at 4 Avenue du Général de Gaulle, tel. 01 39 53 03 30, fax 01 39 50 06 31, www.ibishotel.com, h1409@accor.com).

Eating in Versailles

In the pleasant town center, around Place du Marché Notre-Dame, you'll find a thriving open market (food market Sun, Tue, and Fri mornings until 13:00; clothing market all day Wed-Thu and Sat) and a variety of reasonably priced restaurants, cafés, and a few cobbled lanes. The square—a 15-minute walk from the Château (veer left as you leave the Château)—is lined with colorful and inexpensive eateries. Troll the intriguing options or try one of these:

Au Chien qui Fume is a good choice, with cozy seating inside and out, a playful staff, and reliable, traditional cuisine (€30 *menu*, €16 *plats*, closed Sun, 72 Rue de la Paroisse, tel. 01 39 53 14 56).

A la Côte Bretonne is your best bet for crêpes in a friendly, cozy setting. Fluent in English Yann-Alan and his family have served up the cuisine of their native Brittany region since 1951 (€4-10 crêpes from a fun and creative menu, Tue-Sun 12:00-14:00 & 19:00-22:30, closed Mon, fine indoor and outdoor seating, a few steps off the square on traffic-free Rue des Deux Portes at #12, tel. 01 39 51 18 24).

La Boulangerie has mouthwatering sandwiches, salads, quiches, and more (Tue-Sun until 20:00, closed Mon, 60 Rue de la Paroisse).

Chartres

Chartres, about 50 miles southwest of Paris, gives travelers a pleasant break in a lively, midsize town with a thriving, pedestrian-friendly old center. But the big reason to come to Chartres (shar-truh) is to see its famous cathedral—arguably Europe's best example of pure Gothic.

Planning Your Time

Chartres is an easy day trip from Paris. But with its statues glowing in the setting sun—and with hotels and restaurants much less expensive than those in the capital—Chartres also makes a worthwhile overnight stop. Dozens of Chartres' most historic buildings are colorfully illuminated at night (May-Sept), adding to the town's after-hours appeal.

If coming just for the day, leave Paris in the morning by train. Chartres is a one-hour ride from Paris' Gare Montparnasse (10/day, about €13 one-way; see page 220 for Gare Montparnasse details). Jot down return times to Paris before you exit the Chartres train station (last train generally departs Chartres around 21:00).

Upon arrival in Chartres, head for the cathedral. Allow an hour to savor the church on your own as you follow my self-guided tour. Then join the excellent cathedral tour led by Malcolm Miller (1.25 hours; tours usually Mon-Sat at 12:00 and 14:45). Take another hour to wander the appealing old city. On Wednesday and Saturday mornings, an outdoor market sets up a few short blocks from the cathedral on Place Billard.

Orientation to Chartres

Tourist Information

At the **TI,** pick up the English brochure with a good map and basic information on the town and cathedral (Mon-Sat 9:30-18:30, Sun 10:00-17:30, in the historic Maison du Saumon building, 10 Rue de la Poissonnerie, tel. 02 37 18 26 26, www.chartres-tourisme.com). The TI has specifics on cathedral tours with Malcolm Miller. They

1 Hôtel Châtelet

2 Hôtel le Bœuf Couronné

3 Hôtellerie Saint Yves

4 To Auberge de Jeunesse

5 Le Bistrot de la Cathédrale, Le Serpente & Café des Arts

6 Le Cloître Gourmand

7 Le Pichet Restaurant

8 Crypt Tours (via "La Crypte" Bookstore)

9 Launderette

also rent audioguides for the old town; the narration, while thin, is relaxing and easy to follow (€5.50, €8.50/double set, about 2 hours). Skip the Chartres Pass, which is sold here.

Arrival in Chartres

Exiting Chartres' train station, you'll see the spires of the cathedral dominating the town. It's a five-minute walk up Avenue Jehan de Beauce to the cathedral (or you can take a taxi for about €6.50).

Helpful Hints

Internet Access: For a computer and free Wi-Fi, head to the TI (described earlier), or try the Wi-Fi signal at McDonald's (Place des Epars).

Laundry: The town has several launderettes. The most central is a few blocks from the cathedral (by the TI) at 16a Place de la Poissonnerie (daily 10:00-13:00 & 14:00-18:00).

Taxi: To call a taxi, try tel. 02 37 36 00 00.

Sights in Chartres

▲▲▲Chartres Cathedral

Chartres' old church burned to the ground on June 10, 1194. So the small town built a big-city church, one of the most impres-

sive structures in all of Europe—fit to contain a prize relic, what was supposedly the veil of Mary, mother of Jesus. Some of the children who watched the original church's destruction were actually around to help rebuild the cathedral and attend its dedication Mass in 1260. That's astonishing, considering that other Gothic cathedrals, such as Paris' Notre-Dame, took literally centuries to build. Having been built so quickly, the cathedral has a unity of architecture, statuary, and stained glass that captures the spirit of the Age of Faith like no other church.

NEAR PARIS

Cost: Free, €7.50 to climb the 300-step north tower (free on first Sun of the month and for those under 18).

Hours: Church—daily 8:30-19:30; tower—May-Aug Mon-Sat 9:30-12:30 & 14:00-17:30, Sun 14:00-17:30, Sept-April closes daily at 16:30 (entrance inside church after bookstore on left). Mass times vary by season: usually Mon-Fri at 9:00 and/or 11:45; Sat at 11:45 and 18:00; Sun at 9:15 (Gregorian), 11:00, and 18:00 (some services held in the crypt). Call or go online to confirm times given here—tel. 02 37 21 59 08, or go to www.diocese-chartres.com, and click on the *La Cathédrale* (then *Infos Pratiques*, then *Horaires des Messes*).

Restoration: The interior is undergoing a multiyear restoration. While you'll encounter some scaffolding inside and out, it affects only about 10 percent of the church.

Tours: Malcolm Miller, a fascinating English scholar who moved here 50+ years ago when he was 24, has dedicated his life to studying this cathedral and sharing its wonder through his guided lecture tours. He's still going strong, and his 1.25-hour tours are riveting even if you've taken my self-guided tour. No reservation is needed; just show up (€10, €5 for students, includes headphones that allow him to speak softly, offered Mon-Sat at 12:00 and 14:45; no tours last half of Aug, Jan-Feb, or if fewer than 12 people show up). Some visitors take two tours on the same day, as every tour is different. Tours begin just inside the church at the *Visites de la Cathédrale* sign. Consult this sign for changes or cancellations. He also offers private tours (tel. 02 37 28 15 58, millerchartres@aol .com). Miller's guidebook provides a detailed look at Chartres'

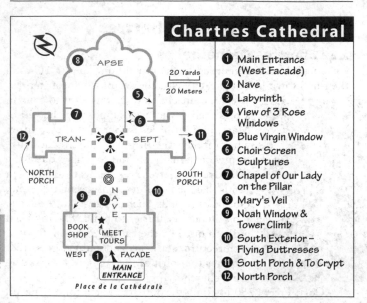

Chartres Cathedral

1. Main Entrance (West Facade)
2. Nave
3. Labyrinth
4. View of 3 Rose Windows
5. Blue Virgin Window
6. Choir Screen Sculptures
7. Chapel of Our Lady on the Pillar
8. Mary's Veil
9. Noah Window & Tower Climb
10. South Exterior – Flying Buttresses
11. South Porch & To Crypt
12. North Porch

windows, sculpture, and history (sold at cathedral).

You can rent **audioguides** from the bookstore inside the cathedral (near the entrance). Routes include the cathedral (€4.30, 45 minutes), the choir only (€3.30, 25 minutes), or both (€6.40, 70 minutes).

Boring **crypt tours** take you into the foundations of the previous ninth-century church. The only way to see the crypt, this guided tour in French (with English handout) lets you view remnants of the earlier churches, a modern copy of the old wooden Mary-and-baby statue, and hints of the old well and Roman wall (€2.80; April-Oct daily at 11:00, 14:15, 15:30, and 16:30 except no 11:00 tour on Sun; late June-mid-Sept also at 17:15; 2/day Nov-March, 30-minute tours start in the cathedral's other bookstore—La Crypte, located outside church near south porch, tel. 02 37 21 75 02).

Bring: Binoculars are a big help for studying the cathedral art. You can rent binoculars cheaply at souvenir shops around the cathedral.

Background: The church is (at least) the fourth one on this spot dedicated to Mary, who has been venerated here for some 1,700 years. There's even speculation that the pagan Romans dedicated a temple here to a mother-goddess. In earliest times Mary was honored next to a natural spring of healing waters (not visible today).

In 876, the church acquired the torn veil (or birthing gown) supposedly worn by Mary when she gave birth to Jesus. The 2,000-year-old veil (now on display) became the focus of worship at the church. By the 11th century the cult of saints was strong. And Mary, considered the "Queen of All Saints," was hugely popular. God was enigmatic and scary, but Mary was maternal and accessible, providing a handy go-between for Christians and their Creator. Chartres, a small town of 10,000 with a prized relic, found itself in the big time on the pilgrim circuit.

When the fire of 1194 incinerated the old church, the veil was feared lost. Lo and behold, several days later, townspeople found it miraculously unharmed in the crypt (beneath today's choir). Whether the veil's survival was a miracle or a marketing ploy, the people of Chartres were so stoked, they worked like madmen to erect this grand cathedral in which to display it. Thinkers and scholars gathered here, making Chartres a leading center of learning in the Middle Ages (until the focus shifted to Paris' university).

By the way, the church is officially called the Cathédrale Notre-Dame de Chartres. Many travelers think that "Notre-Dame" is in Paris. That's true. But more than a hundred churches dedicated to Mary—"Notre-Dames"—are scattered around France. Chartres Cathedral is one of them.

❍ Self-Guided Tour: Start in front of the main entrance (west facade, c. 1150). Chartres' soaring (if mismatched) steeples announce to pilgrims that they've arrived. The right (south) tower, with a Romanesque stone steeple, survived the fire. The left (north) tower lost its wooden steeple in the fire. In the 1500s, it was topped with the flamboyant Gothic steeple we see today.

Enter the church (from a side entrance, if the main one is closed) and wait for your pupils to enlarge. The place is huge—the **nave** is 427 feet long, 20 feet wide, and 120 feet high.

Try to picture the church in the Middle Ages—painted in greens, browns, and golds (like colorful St. Aignan Church in the old town, described later). It was full of pilgrims, and was a rough cross between a hostel, a soup kitchen, and a flea market. The broad, round **labyrinth** inlaid in black marble on the floor is a spiritual journey. Mazes like this were common in medieval churches. Pilgrims enter from the west rim, by foot or on their knees, and wind inward, meditating, on a metaphorical journey to Jerusalem. About 900 feet later, they hope to meet God in the middle.

Walk up the nave to where the transept crosses. As you face the altar, north is to the left. The three big, round "rose" (flower-shaped) **windows** over the entrances receive sunlight at different times of day. All three are predominantly blue and red, but each has different "petals," and each tells a different part of the Christian story in a kaleidoscope of fragmented images.

Now walk around the altar to the right (south) side and find the **Blue Virgin** window with a big, blue Mary (second one from the right). Mary, dressed in blue on a rich red background, cradles Jesus, while the dove of the Holy Spirit descends on her. This very old window (mid-12th century) was the central window behind the altar of the church that burned in 1194. It survived and was reinserted into this frame in the new church around 1230. Mary's glowing dress is an example of the famed "Chartres blue," a sumptuous color made by mixing cobalt oxide into the glass (before cheaper materials were introduced).

The **choir** (enclosed area around the altar where church officials sat) is the heart *(coeur)* of the church. A stone screen rings it with **41 statue groups** illustrating Mary's life. The plain windows surrounding the choir date from the 1770s, when the dark mystery of medieval stained glass was replaced by the open light of the French Enlightenment.

Do an about-face and find the **Chapel of Our Lady on the Pillar.** A 16th-century statue of Mary and baby—draped in cloth, crowned and sceptered—sits on a 13th-century column in a wonderful carved-wood alcove. This is today's pilgrimage center, built to keep visitors from clogging up the altar area.

Double back a bit around the ambulatory, heading toward the back of the church. In the next chapel you encounter (Chapel of the Sacred Heart of Mary), you'll find a gold frame holding a venerated fragment of Mary's veil (described under "Background," earlier). These days it's kept—for its safety and preservation—out of the light and behind bulletproof glass.

Return to the west end and find the last window on the right (near the tower entrance), the **Noah Window.** In the bottom diamond, God tells Noah he'll destroy the earth. Up near the top (diamond #7), a rainbow (symbolizing God's promise never to bring another flood) arches overhead, God drapes himself over it, and Noah and his family give thanks.

To climb the **north tower,** find the entrance nearby. Then exit the church (through the main entrance or the door in the south transept) to view its south side. Six flying buttresses (the arches that stick out from the upper walls) push against six pillars lining the nave inside, helping to hold up the heavy stone ceiling and sloped, lead-over-wood roof. The three doorways of the **south porch** show the world from Christ's time to the present, as Christianity triumphs over persecution.

Reach the north side by circling around the back end of the church (great views). The **north porch** tells the earliest part of the Christian story, from Creation up to the coming of Christ.

Imagine all this painted and covered with gold leaf in preparation for the dedication ceremonies in 1260, when the Chartres generation could finally stand back and watch as their great-grandchildren, carrying candles, entered the cathedral.

More Sights in Chartres

International Stained Glass Center (Centre International du Vitrail)—The low-key glass center (on the north side of cathe-

dral) is worth a visit to learn about the techniques behind the mystery of this fragile but enduring art. Borrow the helpful English booklet (€8 deposit) and take the self-guided tour. A 20-minute video in English describes how glass is made, and a 10-minute French-only video (follow along with the English booklet) explains how it is turned into stained glass.

Cost and Hours: €4, Mon-Fri 9:30-12:30 & 13:30-18:00, Sat 10:00-12:30 & 14:30-18:00, Sun 14:30-18:00, 5 Rue du Cardinal Pie, just 50 yards from cathedral, tel. 02 37 21 65 72, www.centre-vitrail.org, secretariat@centre-vitrail.org. The center offers a worthwhile tour and glass-making demonstrations (€6.50-9.50, 1.5 hours) as well as classes lasting from one to seven days; call ahead or email for topics and dates.

Chartres Town—While overshadowed by its cathedral, Chartres' old town thrives (except on Monday) and is worth some explo-

ration. You can rent an audio-guide from the TI, or better, just wander. In medieval times Chartres was actually two towns—the pilgrims' town around the cathedral, and the industrial town along the river, which was powered by water-mills. A 45-minute loop takes

you around the cathedral, through the old pilgrims' town, down along the once-industrial riverbank, and back to the cathedral. Along the way you'll discover a picnic-perfect park behind the cathedral, see the colorful pedestrian zone, and wander quiet alleys and peaceful lanes.

Sleeping in Chartres

(€1 = about $1.30, country code: 33)

$$ Hôtel Châtelet*,** a block up from the train station, is friendly and comfortable. Don't let the facade fool you—inside is a comfy place with a huge fireplace in the lobby and 40 spotless, spacious, and well-furnished rooms. Several have connecting rooms for families and many have partial cathedral views (streetside Db-€115, quiet side Db-€123, Db with cathedral view-€143, add €25/person

NEAR PARIS

for Tb and Qb, minibars, air-con, handy and safe parking-€8, 6 Avenue Jehan de Beauce, tel. 02 37 21 78 00, fax 02 37 36 23 01, www.hotelchatelet.com, reservation@hotelchatelet.com).

$ Hôtel le Bœuf Couronné** is a vintage two-star hotel, warmly run by Madame Vinsot, with 18 freshly renovated, good-value rooms and a handy location halfway between the station and cathedral (standard Db-€80, big Db-€115, a few good family rooms, no air-con, elevator, Internet access and Wi-Fi, restaurant, 15 Place Châtelet, tel. 02 37 18 06 06, fax 02 37 21 72 13, www.le boeufcouronne.com, resa@leboeufcouronne.fr).

$ Hôtellerie Saint Yves, which hangs on the hillside just behind the cathedral, delivers well-priced simplicity with 50 spic-and-span rooms in a renovated monastery with meditative garden areas (Sb-€45, Db-€65, Tb-€75, small but workable bathrooms, breakfast-€7.50, Wi-Fi, TV in the lounge only, 1 Rue Saint Eman, tel. 02 37 88 37 40, fax 02 37 88 37 49, www.hotellerie-st-yves.com, contact@hotellerie-st-yves.com).

$ Auberge de Jeunesse (youth hostel), a 20-minute walk from the historic center, is located in a modern building with good views of the cathedral from its terrace (€14/bunk in 4- to 6-bed dorms, sheet rental-€2.30, cheap meals, Wi-Fi, kitchen access, 23 Avenue Neigre, tel. 02 37 27 64, fax 02 37 36 75 85, www.auberge-de -jeunesse-chartres.com, auberge-jeunesse-chartres@wanadoo.fr).

Eating in Chartres

Dining out in Chartres is a good deal—particularly if you've come from Paris. Troll the places basking in cathedral views, and if it's warm, find a terrace table (several possibilities). Then finish your evening cathedral-side, sipping a hot or cold drink at the recommended Le Serpente.

Le Bistrot de la Cathédrale has the best view terrace—particularly enjoyable on a balmy summer evening—and serves reliable, classic French fare. The owner has a thing for wine, so the list is good. He also insists on fresh products (*menus* from €22, *plats* from €14, closed Wed, 1 Cloître Notre-Dame, tel. 02 37 36 59 60).

Le Serpente saddles up next door to the cathedral, with view tables on both sides of Rue des Changes, a teapot collector's interior, and cool sling chairs ideal for appreciating the Gothic grandeur. Food is basic bistro, and the prices are fair (daily, 2 Cloître Notre-Dame, tel. 02 37 21 68 81).

Café des Arts is one of several places that strings out along pedestrian-friendly Rue des Changes with comfortable indoor and outdoor seating. They are best at good-value €8-12 dinner-size tartines, salads, crêpes, and *plats du jour*; the house wine is a fine value (closed Mon, 45 Rue des Changes, tel. 02 37 21 07 05).

Le Cloître Gourmand, facing the cathedral's left transept, boasts a small terrace and an intimate, traditional interior. The young chef loves his meat and prides himself on using only the freshest ingredients (€25 *menu*, closed Mon, 21 Cloître Notre-Dame, tel. 02 37 21 49 13).

Le Pichet, just below the TI, is run by endearing Marie-Sylvie and Xavier. This local-products shop and cozy bistro makes a fun lunch stop, with cheap homemade soups and a good selection of *plats*—split the pot-au-feu three ways or try the rabbit with plums (€15 *plats*, Thu-Tue 11:00-18:00, closed Wed, 19 Rue du Cheval Blanc, tel. 02 37 21 08 35).

Giverny

Claude Monet's gardens at Giverny are like his paintings—brightly colored patches that are messy but balanced. Flowers

were his brushstrokes, a bit untamed and slapdash, but part of a carefully composed design. Monet spent his last (and most creative) years cultivating his garden and his art at Giverny (zhee-vayr-nee), the spiritual home of Impressionism. Visiting the Marmottan and/or the Orangerie museums in Paris before your visit here will heighten your appreciation of these gardens.

In 1883, middle-aged Claude Monet, his wife Alice, and their eight children from two families settled into a farmhouse here, 50 miles west of Paris. Monet, already a famous artist and happiest at home, would spend 40 years in Giverny, traveling less with each passing year. He built a pastoral paradise complete with a Japanese garden and a pond full of floating lilies.

Getting to Giverny

Drivers can get in and out of Giverny in a half-day with ease. The trip is also doable in a half-day by public transportation with a train/bus connection, but because trains are not frequent (and less so on the weekend), be prepared for a full six-hour excursion.

By Tour: Big tour companies do a Giverny day trip from Paris for around €70. If you're interested, ask at your hotel—but you can easily do the trip yourself by train and bus for about €30.

By Car: From Paris' Périphérique ring road, follow A-13 toward Rouen, exit at *Sortie 14* to Vernon, and follow *Centre Ville* signs, then signs to *Giverny*. You can park right at Monet's house or at one of several nearby lots.

By Train to Vernon: Take the Rouen-bound train from the Paris Gare St. Lazare station to Vernon, about four miles from Giverny (normally leaves from tracks 20-25, 45 minutes one-way, about €25 round-trip). The train that leaves Paris at around 8:15 is ideal for this trip, with departures about every two hours after that (8/day Mon-Sat, 6/day Sun). Before boarding, use an information desk in Gare St. Lazare to get return times from Vernon to Paris.

Getting from Vernon's Train Station to Giverny: From the Vernon station to Monet's garden (4 miles one-way), you have four good options: bus, taxi, bike, or on foot. If you have bags, you can check them at the Café-Tabac de la Gare (a block past the train station bus stop—described below—at 138 Rue d'Albuféra, tel. 02 32 51 01 00).

The Vernon-Giverny **bus** meets every train from Paris for the 15-minute run to Giverny and connects to every return train to Paris (€6.50 round-trip). A bus-and-train timetable is available at the station bus stop, the Giverny stop, and on the bus—note return times. To reach the bus stop to Giverny, walk through the station, then follow the tracks—the stop is across from the L'Arrivée de Giverny café. Don't dally in the station—the bus leaves soon after your train arrives. During busy times, a line can form while the driver sells tickets and loads the bus. The bus leaves Giverny from the same stop where it drops you off (see map). Be there at least 15 minutes early to ensure a space (if the bus fills, you may have to wait up to two hours for the next one).

Taxis wait in front of the station in Vernon. If you miss the return bus from Giverny, ask any shop, restaurant, or hotel to call a taxi for you (mobile 06 77 49 32 90).

You can rent a **bike** at L'Arrivée de Giverny, the café opposite the train station (€14, tel. 02 32 21 16 01), and follow a paved bike path *(piste cyclable)* that runs from near Vernon along an abandoned railroad right-of-way (figure about 30 minutes to Giverny). Get the easy-to-follow map to Giverny when you rent your bike, and you're in business.

Hikers can go on **foot** to Giverny (about 1.5 hours one way), following the bike instructions above, and take a bus or taxi back.

Extension to Rouen: Consider combining your morning Giverny visit with an afternoon excursion to nearby Rouen—together they make an efficient, workable, and memorable day trip from Paris. From Vernon (the halfway point between Rouen and Paris), it's about 40 minutes by train to Rouen; the return trip from Rouen back to Paris takes 70-90 minutes. Plan to arrive at Monet's garden when it opens (at 9:30), so you can be back to the Vernon train station by about noon. You'll land in Rouen by 13:30 (you'll

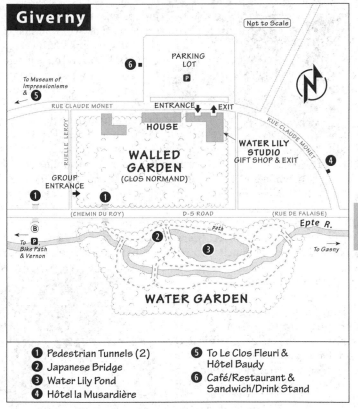

Giverny

Not to Scale

PARKING LOT

To Museum of Impressionisms &

RUE CLAUDE MONET

ENTRANCE   EXIT

HOUSE

WATER LILY STUDIO
GIFT SHOP & EXIT

WALLED GARDEN
(CLOS NORMAND)

RUELLE LEROY

GROUP ENTRANCE

(CHEMIN DU ROY)   D-5 ROAD   (RUE DE FALAISE)

Epte R.

Path

To Bike Path & Vernon

To Gasny

WATER GARDEN

NEAR PARIS

1 Pedestrian Tunnels (2)
2 Japanese Bridge
3 Water Lily Pond
4 Hôtel la Musardière

5 To Le Clos Fleuri & Hôtel Baudy
6 Café/Restaurant & Sandwich/Drink Stand

find a lunchtime train from Vernon to Rouen), and have plenty of time to see Rouen's cathedral and surrounding medieval quarter (Rouen's museums are closed Tue). If you leave Rouen around 17:30, you'll pull into Paris shortly before 19:00, having spent a wonderful day sampling rural and urban Normandy.

Sights in Giverny

▲Monet's Garden and House

There are two gardens, split by a busy road, plus the house, which displays Monet's prized collection of Japanese prints. The gardens are always flowering with something; they're at their most colorful April through July.

Cost and Hours: €9, not covered by Paris Museum Pass, daily April-Oct 9:30-18:00, closed Nov-March, last entry at 17:30, tel. 02 32 51 90 31, www.fondation-monet.com. An audioguide is being developed and may be available when you visit—ask.

Crowd-Beating Tips: Though lines may be long and tour

groups may trample the flowers, true fans still find magic in the gardens. Minimize crowds by arriving a little before 9:30, when it opens, or come after 16:00 and stay until it closes. Crowds recede briefly during lunch (12:00-13:30), but descend en masse after lunch. The busiest months here are May and June.

If you can't arrive early or late, buy your tickets online (www.fondation-monet.com) or, for a bit more, at any FNAC store in Paris. Both allow you to skip the ticket-buying line here and use the group entrance.

Visiting the Garden and House: After you get in, go directly into the **Walled Garden** (Clos Normand) and work your way around clockwise. Smell the pretty scene. Monet cleared this land of pine trees and laid out symmetrical beds, split down the middle by a "grand alley" covered with iron trellises of climbing roses. In his carefree manner, Monet throws together hollyhocks, daisies, and poppies. The color scheme of each flowerbed contributes to the look of the whole garden.

In the far corner of the Walled Garden, you'll find a pedestrian tunnel that leads under the road to the **Water Garden.** Follow the meandering path to the Japanese bridge, under weeping willows, over the pond filled with water lilies, and past countless scenes that leave artists aching for an easel. Find a bench. Monet landscaped like he painted—he built an Impressionist pattern of blocks of color. After he planted the gardens, he painted them, from every angle, at every time of day, in all kinds of weather.

Back on the main side, continue your visit with a wander through Monet's mildly interesting **home** (pretty furnishings, Japanese prints, old photos, and a room filled with copies of his paintings). The gift shop at the exit is the actual sky-lighted studio where Monet painted his water-lily masterpieces (displayed at the Orangerie Museum in Paris). Many visitors spend more time in this tempting gift shop than in the gardens themselves.

Nearby Sights

All of Giverny's sights and shops string along Rue Claude Monet, which runs in front of Monet's house.

Museum of Impressionisms (Musée des Impression-nismes)—This bright, modern museum, dedicated to the history of Impressionism and its legacy, houses temporary exhibits of Impressionist art. Check its website for current shows or just drop in. It also has picnic-pleasant gardens in front.

Cost and Hours: €6.50, April-Oct daily 10:00-18:00, closed Nov-March; to reach it, turn left after leaving Monet's place and walk 200 yards; tel. 02 32 51 94 00, www.mdig.fr.

Vernon Town—If you have time to kill at Vernon's train station, take a five-minute walk into town and sample the peaceful village. Walk between the tracks and the café across the street from the station, and follow the street as it curves left and becomes Rue d'Albuféra. You'll find a smattering of half-timbered Norman homes near Hôtel de Ville (remember, you're in Normandy) and several good cafés and shops.

Sleeping and Eating in Giverny

(€1 = about $1.30, country code: 33)

$ Hôtel la Musardière** is nestled in the village of Giverny two blocks from Monet's home (exit right when you leave Monet's). Carole welcomes you with 10 sweet rooms that Claude himself would have felt at home in, a reasonable and homey *crêperie*-restaurant (€9 crêpes, €26 non-crêpe *menu*), and a lovely yard with outdoor tables (Db-€83-95, Tb-€120-130, Qb-€140, Wi-Fi, 123 Rue Claude Monet, tel. 02 32 21 03 18, fax 02 32 61 60 00, www.lamusardiere.fr, resa@lamusardiere.fr).

$ Le Clos Fleuri is a family-friendly B&B in a modern house with three fine rooms, handy cooking facilities, and a lovely garden. It's a 15-minute walk from Monet's place and is run by charming, English-speaking Danielle, who serves up a generous breakfast (Db-€80 for two or more nights, €95 for one night, cash only, Wi-Fi, 5 Rue de la Dîme, tel. 02 32 21 36 51, www.giverny-leclos fleuri.fr).

Eating: A flowery **café/restaurant** and a **sandwich/drink stand** sit right next to the parking lot across from Monet's home. Enjoy your lunch in the nearby gardens of the Museum of the Impressionisms.

Rose-colored **Hôtel Baudy,** once a hangout for American Impressionists, offers an appropriately pretty setting for lunch or dinner (outdoor tables in front, *menus* from €24, popular with tour groups, daily, 5-minute walk past Museum of Impressionisms at 81 Rue Claude Monet, tel. 02 32 21 10 03). Don't miss a stroll through the artsy gardens behind the restaurant.

Disneyland Paris

Europe's Disneyland is a remake of California's, with most of the same rides and smiles. The main difference is that Mickey Mouse speaks French, and you can buy wine with your lunch. My kids went ducky for it.

Disneyland is easy to get to, and may be worth a day—if Paris is handier for you than Florida or California.

Getting to Disneyland Paris

By Train: The slick 45-minute RER trip is the best way to get to Disneyland from downtown Paris. Take RER line A-4 to Marne-la-Vallée-Chessy (check the signs over the platform to be sure Marne-la-Vallée-Chessy is served, because the line splits near the end). Catch it from Paris' Charles de Gaulle-Etoile, Auber, Châtelet-Les Halles, or Gare de Lyon stations (at least 3/hour, drops you 45 minutes later right in the park, about €8 each way). The last train back to Paris leaves shortly after midnight. When returning, remember to use the same RER ticket for your Métro connection in Paris.

By Bus and Train from the Airport: Both of Paris' major airports have direct shuttle buses to Disneyland Paris (every 20 minutes, daily 8:30-20:00ish, €19). Fast TGV trains run from Charles de Gaulle to Disneyland in 10 minutes, but they're less frequent and pricier—the shuttle bus makes more sense.

By Car: Disneyland is about 40 minutes (20 miles) east of Paris on the A-4 autoroute (direction Nancy/Metz, exit #14). Parking is about €15/day at the park.

Dis-Orientation

The Disneyland Paris Resort is a sprawling complex housing two theme parks (Disneyland Paris and Walt Disney Studios), a few entertainment venues, and several hotels. Opened in 1992, it was the second Disney resort built outside the US (Tokyo was first). With upward of 15 million visitors a year, it quickly became Europe's single leading tourist destination. Mickey has arrived.

Disneyland Paris: This park has a corner on the fun market, with the classic rides and Disney characters you expect to see. You'll find familiar favorites wrapped in French packaging, like Space Mountain (a.k.a. *De la Terre à la Lune*) and Pirates of the Caribbean *(Pirates des Caraïbes).*

Walt Disney Studios: This zone has a Hollywood focus geared for an older crowd, with animation, special effects, and movie magic "rides." The cinema-themed rides include CinéMagique (a slow-motion cruise through film history on a people-mover, mixing film clips, audio-animatronic figures, and live actors); Studio Tram Tour: Behind the Magic (another slow-mo ride, this time mostly outdoors, through a "movie backlot"); and Moteurs... Action! Stunt Show Spectacular (an actual movie sequence is filmed with stunt drivers, audience bit players, and brash MTV-style hosts). The top thrill rides include the Rock 'n' Roller Coaster (which starts out by accelerating from a standstill to 57 miles per hour in less than three seconds, all while Aerosmith tunes blast in your ears) and the Twilight Zone Tower of Terror (which drops passengers from a precarious 200-foot-high perch).

Skipping Lines: The free FASTPASS system is a worthwhile timesaver for the nine most popular rides. At the ride, insert your park admission ticket into the FASTPASS machine, which spits out a ticket printed with your return time—often within 45 minutes (you may only have one FASTPASS ticket at a time). You'll also save time by buying your park tickets ahead (at airport TIs, some Métro stations, or along the Champs-Elysées at the Disney Store or Virgin Megastore).

Cost: Disneyland Paris and Walt Disney Studios charge the same. You can pay separately for each or buy a combined "Hopper" ticket for both. A one-day pass to either park is about €50 for adults and €45 for kids aged 3-11 (check their website for special offers). Kids under 3 are free.

A two-day Hopper ticket for entry to both parks is about €120 for adults (less for kids); a three-day Hopper ticket is about €150. Regular prices are discounted about 25 percent Nov-March, and promotions are offered occasionally (check www.disneylandparis .com).

Hours: Disneyland—daily 10:00-19:00, later on weekends, until 23:00 mid-May-Aug, hours fluctuate with the seasons— check website for precise times. Walt Disney Studios—summer daily 10:00-19:00; winter Mon-Fri 10:00-18:00, Sat-Sun until 19:00.

Information: Disney brochures are in every Paris hotel. For more info and to make reservations, call 01 60 30 60 53, or try www.disneylandparis.com.

Avoiding Crowds: Saturday, Sunday, Wednesday, public holidays, and any day in July and August are the most crowded. After

NEAR PARIS

dinner, crowds are gone.

Eating with Mickey: Food is fun and not outrageously priced. (Still, many smuggle in a picnic.)

Sleeping at Disneyland

Most are better off sleeping in the real world (i.e., Paris), though with direct buses and freeways to both airports, Disneyland makes a convenient first- or last-night stop. Seven different Disney-owned hotels offer accommodations at or near the park in all price ranges. Prices are impossible to pin down, as they vary by season and by the package deal you choose (deals that include park entry are usually a better value). To reserve any Disneyland hotel, call 01 60 30 60 53, or check www.disneylandparis.com. The prices you'll be quoted include entry to the park. **Hôtel Santa Fe**** offers a fair mid-range value, with frequent shuttle service to the park. Another cheap option is **Davy Crockett's Ranch,** but you'll need a car to stay there. The most expensive is the **Disneyland Hotel******, right at the park entry, about three times the price of the Santa Fe. The **Dream Castle Hotel****** is another higher-end choice, with nearly 400 rooms done up to look like a lavish 17th-century palace (40 Avenue de la Fosse des Pressoirs, tel. 01 64 17 90 00, www.dreamcastle-hotel.com, info@dreamcastle-hotel.com).

NORMANDY

Rouen • Honfleur • Bayeux • D-Day Beaches
• Mont St-Michel

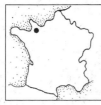

Sweeping coastlines, half-timbered towns, and thatched roofs decorate the rolling green hills of Normandy. Parisians call Normandy "the 21st arrondissement." It's their escape—the nearest beach. The Brits also consider this area close enough for a weekend away (you'll notice that the BBC comes through loud and clear on your car radio).

Despite the peacefulness you feel today, the region's history is filled with war. Normandy was founded by Viking Norsemen who invaded from the north, settled here in the ninth century, and gave the region its name. A couple hundred years later, William the Conqueror invaded England from Normandy. His victory is commemorated in a remarkable tapestry at Bayeux. A few hundred years after that, France's greatest cheerleader, Joan of Arc (Jeanne d'Arc), was convicted of heresy in Rouen and burned at the stake by the English, against whom she rallied France during the Hundred Years' War. And in 1944, Normandy hosted a World War II battle that changed the course of history.

The rugged, rainy coast of Normandy harbors wartime bunkers and enchanting fishing villages like Honfleur. And, on the border it shares with Brittany, the almost surreal island abbey of Mont St-Michel rises serene and majestic, oblivious to the tides of tourists.

Planning Your Time

Honfleur, the D-Day beaches, and Mont St-Michel each merit overnight visits. At a minimum, you'll want a full day for the D-Day beaches and a half-day each in Honfleur and on Mont St-Michel.

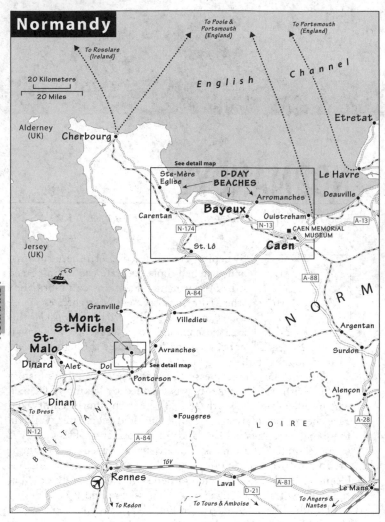

Normandy

If you're driving between Paris and Honfleur, Giverny (see previous chapter) or Rouen (covered in this chapter) are worthwhile stops. By train, they're best as day trips from Paris. The WWII memorial museum in Caen works well as a stop between Honfleur and Bayeux (and the D-Day beaches). Mont St-Michel must be seen early or late to avoid the masses of midday tourists. Dinan, just 45 minutes by car from Mont St-Michel, offers a fine introduction to Brittany (see next chapter). Drivers can enjoy Mont St-Michel as a day trip from Dinan.

For practical information in English about Normandy, see http://normandy.angloinfo.com or www.normandie-tourisme.fr.

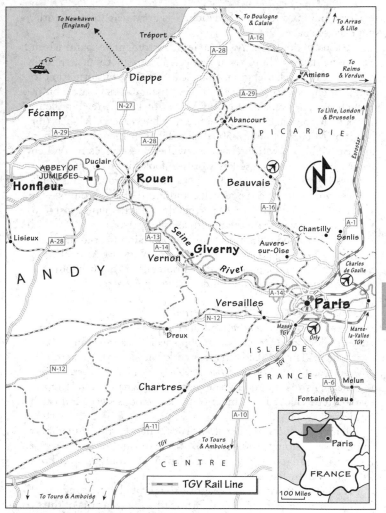

To Newhaven
(England)

To Boulogne
& Calais

To Arras
& Lille

Tréport

A-28

A-16

To Reims
& Verdun

Dieppe

Amiens

Fécamp

N-27

A-29

Abancourt

To Lille, London
& Brussels

A-28

Duclair

ABBEY OF
JUMIÈGES

Rouen

P I C A R D I E

Honfleur

Beauvais

Lisieux

A-28

Seine

Giverny

A-13

A-14

Vernon

River

A-16

Chantilly

Auvers-
sur-Oise

A-1

Senlis

Charles
de Gaulle

A N D Y

A-14

Versailles

Paris

N-12

Massy
TGV

Orly

Marne-
la-Vallée
TGV

Dreux

I S L E   D E

N-12

F R A N C E

A-6

Melun

Chartres

Fontainebleau

A-10

A-11

TGV

To Tours
& Amboise

C E N T R E

Paris

FRANCE

TGV Rail Line

To Tours & Amboise

100 Miles

Getting Around Normandy

This region is ideal with a **car.** If you're driving into Honfleur from the north, take the impressive but pricey Normandy Bridge (Pont de Normandie, about €5 toll). If you're driving from Mont St-Michel into Brittany, follow my recommended scenic route to the town of St-Malo (see page 371).

Trains from Paris serve Rouen, Caen, Bayeux, Mont St-Michel (via Pontorson or Rennes), and Dinan, though service between these sights can be frustrating (try linking by bus—see below). Mont St-Michel is a headache by train, except from Paris. Enterprising hotel owners in Bayeux operate a minivan service between Bayeux and Mont St-Michel—a great help to those without cars (see page 307).

Buses make Giverny, Honfleur, Arromanches, and Mont St-Michel accessible to train stations in nearby towns, though Sundays can be challenging. Plan ahead: For bus information in English, check with the local TI. Or, if you can navigate a bit in French, try the websites for Bus Verts (for Le Havre, Honfleur, Bayeux, Arromanches, and Caen, www.busverts.fr), Manéo (for Mont St-Michel, www.vtni50.fr), and Tibus or Illenoo (for Dinan and St-Malo, www.tibus.fr or www.illenoo-services.fr). When navigating these sites, the key words to look for are "Horaires" or "Fiches Horaires" (schedules) and "Lignes" (bus route). Bus companies commonly offer good value and multi-ride discounts—for example, Bus Verts offers a 20 percent discount if you buy just four tickets (even if you share them with another person).

Another good option is to use an **excursion tour** to link destinations. **Westcapades** provides trips to Mont St-Michel from Dinan and St-Malo, and **Afoot in France** leads quality tours for small groups or individuals (for details, see page 356).

Normandy's Cuisine Scene

Normandy is known as the land of the four C's: Calvados, Camembert, cider, and *crème*. The region specializes in cream sauces, organ meats (sweetbreads, tripe, and kidneys—the "gizzard salads" are great), and seafood *(fruits de mer)*. You'll see *crêperies* offering inexpensive and good value meals everywhere. A galette is a savory crêpe enjoyed as a main course; a crêpe is sweet and eaten for dessert.

Dairy products are big, too. Local cheeses are Camembert (mild to very strong; see sidebar), Brillat-Savarin (buttery), Livarot (spicy and pungent), Pavé d'Auge (spicy and tangy), and Pont l'Evêque (earthy flavor).

What, no wine? That's right. You're in the rare region of France where wine is not a local forte. Still, you won't die of thirst. Normandy is famous for its many apple-based beverages. You can't miss the powerful Calvados apple brandy or the Bénédictine brandy (made by local monks). The local dessert, *trou Normand*, is apple sorbet swimming in Calvados. The region also produces three kinds of alcoholic apple ciders: *cidre* can be *doux* (sweet), *brut* (dry), or *bouché* (sparkling—and the strongest). You'll also find bottles of Pommeau, a tasty blend of apple juice and Calvados (sold in many shops), as well as *poiré*, a tasty pear cider. And don't leave Normandy without sampling a *kir Normand*, a mix of crème de cassis and cider. Drivers in Normandy should be on the lookout for *Route de Cidre* signs (with a bright red apple); this tourist trail leads

Camembert Cheese

This cheap, soft, white, Brie-like cheese is sold all over France (and America) in distinctive, round wooden containers. Camembert has been known for its cheese for 500 years, but local legend has it that today's cheese got its start in the French Revolution, when a priest on the run was taken in by Marie Harel, a Camembert farmer. He repaid the favor by giving her the secret formula from his own hometown—Brie.

From cow to customer, Camembert takes about three weeks to make. High-fat milk from Norman cows is curdled with rennet, ladled into round, five-inch molds, sprinkled with *Penicillium camemberti* bacteria, and left to dry. In the first three days, the cheese goes from the cow's body temperature to room temperature to refrigerator cool (50 degrees).

Two weeks later, the ripened and aged cheese is wrapped in wooden bands and labeled for market. Like wines, Camembert cheese is controlled by government regulations and must bear the "A.O.C." *(Appellation d'Origine Contrôlée)* stamp of approval.

you to small producers of handcrafted cider and brandy.

Remember, restaurants serve only during lunch (11:30-14:00) and dinner (19:00-21:00, later in bigger cities); cafés serve food throughout the day.

Rouen

This 2,000-year-old city mixes Gothic architecture, half-timbered houses, and contemporary bustle like no other place in France.

Busy Rouen (roo-ahn) is France's fifth-largest port and Europe's biggest food exporter (mostly wheat and grain). Although its cobbled old town is a delight to wander, the city feels less welcoming at night (you'll notice a surprising number of panhandlers). Rouen works best for me as a day trip from Paris, or as a stop between Paris and Honfleur.

Rouen is nothing new. It was a regional capital during Roman times, and France's second-largest city in medieval times (with 40,000 residents—only Paris had more). In the ninth century, the

Normans made the town their capital. William the Conqueror called it home before moving to England. Rouen walked a political tightrope between England and France for centuries, and was an English base during the Hundred Years' War. Joan of Arc was burned here (in 1431).

Rouen's historic wealth was based on its wool industry and trade—for centuries, it was the last bridge across the Seine River before the Atlantic. In April of 1944, as America and Britain weakened German control of Normandy prior to the D-Day landings, Allied bombers destroyed 50 percent of Rouen. And though the industrial suburbs were devastated, most of the historic core survived, keeping Rouen a pedestrian haven.

Planning Your Time

If you want a dose of a smaller—yet lively—French city, Rouen is an easy day trip from Paris, with convenient train connections to Gare St. Lazare (nearly hourly, 70-90 minutes). Considering the convenient Paris connection and Rouen's handy location in Normandy, drivers can save money and headaches by taking the train to Rouen and picking up a rental car there. Leave the car (with your bags in it) in the secure rental lot, and visit Rouen before heading out (for car-rental companies, see "Helpful Hints," later). Even if you don't have a car, you can visit Rouen on your way from Paris to other Normandy destinations, thanks to the good bus and train service (free daytime bag check available Wed-Mon at the Museum of Fine Arts, closed Tue).

Orientation to Rouen

Although Paris embraces the Seine, Rouen ignores it. The area we're most interested in is bounded by the river to the south, the Museum of Fine Arts (Esplanade Marcel Duchamp) to the north, Rue de la République to the east, and Place du Vieux Marché to the west. It's a 20-minute walk from the train station to the Notre-Dame Cathedral or TI. Everything else of interest is within a 10-minute walk of the cathedral or TI.

Tourist Information

Pick up the map with information on Rouen's museums at the TI, which faces the cathedral. The TI also has €5 audioguide tours covering the cathedral and Rouen's historic center, though this book's self-guided walk is enough for most (May-Sept Mon-Sat 9:00-19:00, Sun 9:30-12:30 & 14:00-18:00; Oct-April Mon-Sat 9:30-12:30 & 13:30-18:00, closed Sun; 25 Place de la Cathédrale, tel. 02 32 08 32 40, www.rouentourisme.com). A small office in the TI changes money (closed during lunch year-round).

Arrival in Rouen

By Train: Rue Jeanne d'Arc cuts down from Rouen's train station through the town center to the Seine River. Day-trippers should **walk** from the station down Rue Jeanne d'Arc toward Rue du Gros Horloge—a busy pedestrian mall in the medieval center. This cobblestone street connects Place du Vieux Marché and Joan of Arc Church (to your right, the starting point of my self-guided walk) with Notre-Dame Cathedral (to your left). Note that the station has no baggage storage. If you have luggage, walk or taxi a few blocks downhill from the station to the Museum of Fine Arts, where you can check your bags for free (for museum hours, see page 276). You can enjoy this lovely museum at the end of your walking tour.

Rouen's **subway** (Métrobus) whisks travelers from under the train station to the Palais de Justice in one stop (€1.80; descend and buy tickets from machines one level underground, then validate ticket on subway two levels down; subway direction: Technopôle or Georges Braque). Returning to the station, take a subway in direction: Boulingrin and get off at Gare-Rue Verte.

Taxis (to the right as you exit station) will take you to any of my recommended hotels for about €8.

By Bus: Rouen's bus station is a half-block off Rue Jeanne d'Arc, near the river (CNA bus information office open Mon-Sat 9:00-19:00, closed Sun, Compagnie Normande d'Autobus, tel. 08 25 07 60 27). To reach the center, exit the station to the right, turn left up Rue Jeanne d'Arc, then turn right on pedestrian-friendly Rue du Gros Horloge to reach most hotels and the cathedral. (To find the start of my self-guided walk, turn left on Rue du Gros Horloge.)

By Car: Assume you'll get lost for a while. Follow signs for *Centre-Ville* and *Rive Droite* (right bank). For day-trippers taking my self-guided walk of Rouen, the parking lot near Place du Vieux Marché is best. Other lots are scattered about the city center (see map on next page). You can park for free overnight along the river (metered until 19:00), or pay for more secure parking in one of many well-signed underground lots. La Haute Vieille Tour parking garage, between the cathedral and the river, is handy (about €12/day). When you get turned around (likely, because of the narrow, one-way streets), aim for the highest cathedral spires you spot.

If leaving Rouen for Honfleur, follow blue autoroute signs to *Le Havre,* then *Caen* (toll freeway). You'll spot exit signs for Honfleur before reaching Caen.

Helpful Hints

Closed Days: Most of Rouen's museums are closed on Tuesday, and many sights also close midday (12:00-14:00). The cathedral is

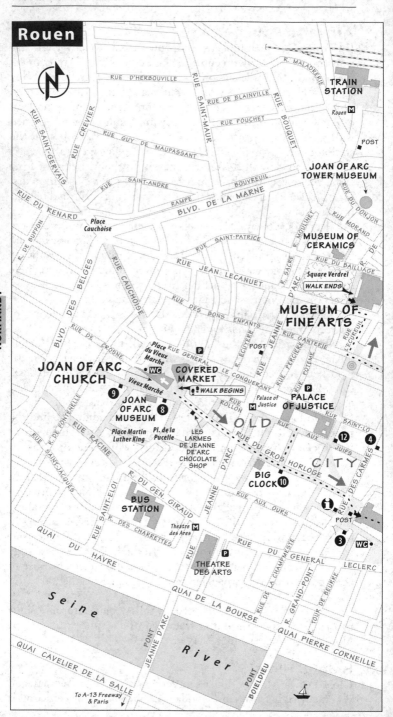

Rouen

NORMANDY

RUE D'HERBOUVILLE
RUE SAINT-MAUR
RUE DE BLAINVILLE
RUE FOUCHET
RUE CREVIER
RUE GUY DE MAUPASSANT
RUE SAINT-GERVAIS
RUE SAINT-ANDRE
RUE DU RENARD
RAMPE
BLVD. DE LA MARNE
Place Cauchoise
R. DE BUFFON
RUE SAINT-PATRICE
RUE JEAN LECANUET
RUE CAUCHOISE
RUE DES BONS ENFANTS
BLVD. DES BELGES
RUE DE CROSNE
Place du Vieux Marche
RUE GENERAL
WC
COVERED MARKET
JOAN OF ARC CHURCH
Vieux Marché
WALK BEGINS
JOAN OF ARC MUSEUM
Place Martin Luther King
Pl. de la Pucelle
LES LARMES DE JEANNE DE' ARC CHOCOLATE SHOP
RUE DE FONTENELLE
RUE RACINE
RUE SAINT-JACQUES
R. DU GEN GIRAUD
BUS STATION
RUE SAINT-ELOI
R. DES CHARRETTES
Théâtre des Arts
THEATRE DES ARTS
QUAI DU HAVRE
QUAI DE LA BOURSE
Seine
River
QUAI CAVELIER DE LA SALLE
To A-13 Freeway & Paris
PONT JEANNE D'ARC
PONT BOIELDIEU
QUAI DE LA BOURSE

TRAIN STATION
Rouen M
R. MALADRERIE
RUE SAINT-MAUR
RUE BOUQUET
POST
JOAN OF ARC TOWER MUSEUM
RUE DU DONJON
RUE MORAND
MUSEUM OF CERAMICS
R. MOULINET
RUE DU BAILLAGE
R. SACRE
Square Verdrel
WALK ENDS
MUSEUM OF FINE ARTS
RUE JEANNE D'ARC
RUE GANTERIE
POST
RUE ECUYERE
LE CONQUERANT
RUE PERCIERE
RUE POTEME
RUE ROLLON
Palace of Justice
M
PALACE OF JUSTICE
P
RUE SAINT-LO
OLD
RUE AUX JUIFS
12
4
CITY
RUE DU GROS HORLOGE
BIG CLOCK 10
RUE DES CARMES
RUE AUX OURS
i
POST
3
WC
RUE DU GENERAL LECLERC
RUE DE LA CHAMPMESLE
RUE GRAND-PONT
RUE TOUR DE BEURRE
QUAI PIERRE CORNEILLE

9
8

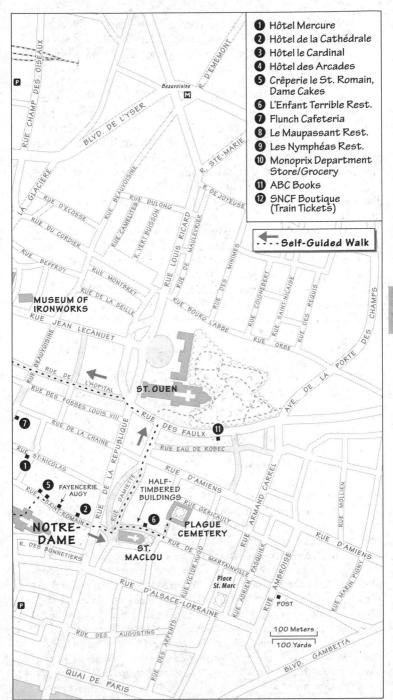

1 Hôtel Mercure
2 Hôtel de la Cathédrale
3 Hôtel le Cardinal
4 Hôtel des Arcades
5 Crêperie le St. Romain, Dame Cakes
6 L'Enfant Terrible Rest.
7 Flunch Cafeteria
8 Le Maupassant Rest.
9 Les Nymphéas Rest.
10 Monoprix Department Store/Grocery
11 ABC Books
12 SNCF Boutique (Train Tickets)

◄ - - - - Self-Guided Walk

NORMANDY

closed Monday morning and during Mass (usually Tue-Sat at 10:00, July-Aug at 18:00; Sun and holidays at 8:30, 10:00, and 12:00). The Joan of Arc Church is closed Friday and Sunday mornings, and during Mass.

Market Days: The best open-air market is on Place St. Marc, a few blocks east of St. Maclou Church. It's filled with antiques and other good stuff (all day Tue, Fri, and Sat; on Sun until about 12:30). A smaller market is on Place du Vieux Marché, near the Joan of Arc Church (Tue-Sun until 13:30, closed Mon). The TI has a list of all weekly markets.

Supermarket: It's inside the **Monoprix,** at the back of the store (Mon-Sat 8:30-21:00, closed Sun, on Rue du Gros Horloge).

Internet Access: Ask at the TI about where you can get connected.

English Bookstore: ABC Books has nothing but English-language books—some American, but mostly British (Tue-Sat 10:00-18:00, closed Sun-Mon, south of St. Ouen Church at 11 Rue des Faulx, tel. 02 35 71 08 67).

Taxi: Call **Les Taxi Blancs** at 02 35 61 20 50 or 02 35 88 50 50.

Car Rental: Agencies with an office in the train station include **Europcar** (tel. 02 35 88 21 20), **Avis** (tel. 02 35 88 60 94), and **Hertz** (tel. 02 35 70 70 71). They have similar hours (normally Mon-Fri 8:00-12:00 & 14:00-19:00, Sat 8:30-12:00 & 14:00-17:00, closed Sun).

SNCF Boutique: For train tickets, visit the SNCF office in town at the corner of Rue aux Juifs and Rue Eugène Boudin (Mon-Sat 10:00-19:00, closed Sun).

Self-Guided Walk

Welcome to Rouen

On this 1.5-hour walk, you'll see the essential Rouen sights. Remember that many sights are closed midday (12:00-14:00). This walk is designed for day-trippers coming by train (who will start with a 10-minute downhill walk from the station). Drivers should park at or near Place du Vieux Marché (parking garage available).

From Place du Vieux Marché, you'll walk the length of Rue du Gros Horloge to Notre-Dame Cathedral. From there, walk four blocks west to the plague cemetery (Aître St. Maclou), loop up to the church of St. Ouen, and return along Rues de l'Hôpital and Ganterie, ending at the Museum of Fine Arts (a 5-minute walk to the train station). The map on page 266 highlights our route.

• *If arriving by train, walk down Rue Jeanne d'Arc and turn right on Rue du Guillaume le Conquérant (notice the Gothic Palais de Justice building across Rue Jeanne d'Arc—we'll get to that later). This takes you to our starting point...*

The Hundred Years' War
(1336-1453)

It would take a hundred years to explain all the causes, battles, and political maneuverings of this century-plus of warfare between France and England, but here goes:

In 1300, before the era of the modern nation-state, the borders between France and England were fuzzy. French-speaking kings had ruled England, English kings owned the south of France, and English merchants dominated trade in the north. Dukes and lords in both countries were aligned more along family lines than by national identity. When the French king died without a male heir (1328), both France and England claimed the crown, and the battle was on.

England invaded the more populous country (1345) and—thanks to skilled archers using armor-penetrating longbows—won big battles at Crécy (1346) and Poitiers (1356). Despite a truce, roving bands of English mercenaries stayed behind and supported themselves by looting French villages. The French responded with guerrilla tactics.

In 1415, the English took still more territory, with Henry V's big victory at Agincourt. But rallied by the heavenly visions of young Joan of Arc, the French slowly drove the invaders out. Paris was liberated in 1436, and when Bordeaux fell to French forces (1453), the fighting ended without a treaty.

Place du Vieux Marché
• *Stand near the entrance of the striking Joan of Arc Church.*
Surrounded by half-timbered buildings, this old market square has a covered produce market, a park commemorating Joan of Arc's burning, and a modern church named after her. A tall aluminum cross, planted in a flowery garden near the church entry, marks the spot where Rouen publicly punished and executed people. The pillories stood here, and during the Revolution, the town's guillotine made 800 people "a foot shorter at the top." In 1431, Joan of Arc—only 19 years old—was burned at this site. Find her flaming statue facing the cross. As the flames engulfed her, an English soldier said, "Oh my God, we've killed a saint." (Nearly 500 years later, Joan was canonized, and the soldier was proved right.)

▲▲Joan of Arc Church (Eglise Jeanne d'Arc)
This modern church is a tribute to the young woman who was canonized in 1920 and later became the patron saint of France. The church, completed in 1979, feels Scandinavian inside and out—another reminder of Normandy's Nordic roots. Sumptuous 16th-century windows, salvaged from a church lost during World War II, were worked into the soft architectural lines (the €0.50 English

Joan of Arc
(1412-1431)

The cross-dressing teenager who rallied French soldiers to drive out English invaders was the illiterate daughter of a humble farmer. One summer day, in her dad's garden, 13-year-old Joan heard a heavenly voice accompanied by bright light. It was the first of several saints (including Michael, Margaret, and Catherine) to talk to her during her short life.

In 1429, the young girl was instructed by the voices to save France from the English. Dressed in men's clothing, she traveled to see the king and predicted that the French armies would be defeated near Orléans—as they were. King Charles VII equipped her with an ancient sword and a banner that read "Jesus, Maria," and sent her to rally the troops.

Soon "the Maid" (la Pucelle) was bivouacking amid rough soldiers, riding with them into battle, and suffering an arrow wound to the chest—all while liberating the town of Orléans. On July 17, 1429, she held her banner high in the cathedral of Reims as Charles was officially proclaimed king of a resurgent France.

Joan and company next tried to retake Paris (1429), but the English held out. She suffered a crossbow wound through the thigh, and her reputation of invincibility was tarnished. During a battle at Compiègne (1430), she was captured and turned over to the English for £10,000. The English took her to Rouen where she was chained by the neck inside an iron cage, while the local French authorities (allied with the English) plotted against her. The Inquisition—insisting that Joan's voices were "false and diabolical"—tried and sentenced her to death for being a witch and heretic.

On May 30, 1431, Joan of Arc was tied to a stake on Rouen's old market square (Place du Vieux Marché). She yelled, "Rouen! Rouen! Must I die here?" Then they lit the fire; she fixed her eyes on a crucifix and died chanting, "Jesus, Jesus, Jesus."

After her death, Joan's place in history was slowly rehabilitated. French authorities proclaimed her trial illegal (1455), prominent writers and artists were inspired by her, and the Catholic Church finally beatified (1909) and canonized her (1920) as St. Joan of Arc.

pamphlet provides some background and describes the stained-glass scenes). Similar to modern churches designed by the 20th-century architect Le Corbusier, this is an uplifting place to be, with a ship's-hull vaulting and sweeping wood ceiling that sail over curved pews and a wall of glass below. Make time to savor this unusual place.

Cost and Hours: Free; April-Oct Mon-Thu and Sat 10:00-

12:00 & 14:00-18:00, Fri and Sun 14:00-17:30; Nov-March daily 14:00-18:00; closed during Mass. A public WC is 30 yards straight ahead from the church doors.

• *Turn left out of the church and step over ruins of a 15th-century church that once stood on this spot (destroyed during the French Revolution). Straight ahead is the waxy...*

Joan of Arc Museum

Enter through a souvenir shop sandwiched between big restaurants. This museum tells the story of this inspirational teenager of supreme faith who, after hearing voices for several years, won the confidence of her countrymen, was given an army, and rallied the French against their English invaders. Those touched by her story will enjoy this little museum, with excellent English information and nifty models throughout.

Cost and Hours: €5, daily mid-April-Sept 9:30-18:00, Oct-mid-April 10:00-12:00 & 14:00-17:30, tel. 02 35 88 02 70, www.jeanne-darc.com.

• *Leave the square and join the busy pedestrian street, Rue du Gros Horloge—the town's main shopping street since Roman times. A block up on your right (at #163) is Rouen's most famous chocolate shop...*

Les Larmes de Jeanne d'Arc

The chocolate-makers of Les Larmes de Jeanne d'Arc would love to tempt you with their chocolate-covered almond "tears *(larmes)* of Joan of Arc." Although you must resist touching the chocolate fountain, you are welcome to taste a tear. The first one is free; a small bag costs about €8 (Mon-Sat 9:00-19:00, closed Sun).

• *Your route continues past a medieval McDonald's and across busy Rue Jeanne d'Arc to the...*

▲Big Clock (Gros Horloge)

This impressive, circa-1528 Renaissance clock, le Gros Horloge (groh oar-lohzh), decorates the former city hall. Is something missing? Not really. In the 16th century, an hour hand offered sufficient precision; minute hands became necessary only in a later, faster-paced age. The lamb at the end of the hour hand is a reminder that wool rules—it was the source of Rouen's wealth. The town medallion features a sacrificial lamb, which has both religious and commercial significance (center, below the clock). The black-and-silver orb above the clock makes one revolution in 29 days. The clock's artistic highlight fills the underside of the arch (walk underneath and stretch your back), with the "Good Shepherd" and lots of sheep.

To see the inner workings and an extraordinary panorama over Rouen (including a memorable view of the cathedral), climb

NORMANDY

the clock tower's 100 steps. You'll tour several rooms with the help of an audioguide that suffers from a Goldilocks-and-the-Three-Bears narration. The big bells ring on the hour—a deafening experience if you're in the tower.

Cost and Hours: €6, includes audioguide; April-Oct Tue-Sun 10:00-12:00 & 13:00-18:00; Nov-March Tue-Sun 14:00-18:00; closed Mon year-round.

• *Walk under le Gros Horloge, then take a one-block detour left on Rue Thouret to see the...*

Palace of Justice (Palais de Justice)

Years of cleaning have removed the grime that once covered this fabulously flamboyantly Gothic building, the former home of Normandy's *parlement*. The result is striking; think of this as you visit Rouen's other Gothic structures; many are awaiting baths of their own. Pockmarks on the side of the building that faces Rue Jeanne d'Arc are leftovers from bombings during the Normandy invasion. Look for the English-language plaques on the iron fence—they provide some history, and describe the damage and tedious repair process.

• *Double back and continue up Rue du Gros Horloge. In a block you'll see a plaque dedicated to Cavelier de la Salle (high on the left), who explored the mouth of the Mississippi River, claimed the state of Louisiana for France, and was assassinated in Texas in 1687. Soon you'll reach...*

▲▲Notre-Dame Cathedral (Cathédrale Notre-Dame)

This cathedral is a landmark of art history. You're seeing essen-

tially what Claude Monet saw as he painted 30 different studies of this frilly Gothic facade at various times of the day. Using the physical building only as a rack upon which to hang light, mist, dusk, and shadows, Monet was capturing "impressions." One of the results is in Rouen's Museum of Fine Arts; four others are at the Orsay Museum in Paris. Find the plaque showing two of these paintings (in the corner of the square, about 30 paces to your right if you were exiting the TI).

Look up at the soaring facade and find the cleaned sections, with bright statues on either side of the central portal—later, we'll meet some of their friends face to face inside the cathedral.

Cost and Hours: Tue-Sun 8:00-19:00, Mon 14:00-19:00; closed during Mass Tue-Sat at 10:00, July-Aug also at 18:00, Sun at 8:30, 10:30, and 12:00; also closed Nov-March daily 12:00-14:00.

Visiting the Cathedral: Stand at the back and look down the **nave.** This is a classic Gothic nave—four stories of pointed-arch arcades, the top filled with windows to help light the interior. Today, the interior is lighter than intended, because the original colored glass (destroyed mostly in World War II) was replaced by clear glass. Why such a big cathedral here? Until the 1700s, Rouen was the second largest city in France—rich from its wool trade and its booming port.

Circle counterclockwise around the church along the side aisle. The side chapels and windows have descriptions in English. Each is dedicated to a different saint. These chapels display the changing assortment of styles through the centuries. Look for photos halfway down on the right that show devastating WWII bomb damage to the cathedral.

Passing through an iron gate after the high altar (closed during Mass; may be open on the opposite side even during Mass), you come to several **stone statues.** These figures were lifted from the facade during a cleaning and will eventually be installed in a museum. For us, it's a rare chance to stand toe-to-toe with a saint (weird feeling).

There are several **stone tombs** on your left, dating from when Rouen was the Norman capital. The first tomb is for Rollo, the first duke of Normandy in 933 (and great-great-great-great grandfather of William the Conqueror, seventh duke of Normandy, c. 1028). As the first duke, Rollo was chief of the first gang of Vikings (the original "Normans") who decided to settle here. Called the "Father of Normandy," Rollo died at the age of 80, but he is portrayed on his tomb as if he were 33 (as was the fashion, because Jesus died at that age). Because of later pillage and plunder, only Rollo's femur is inside the tomb.

And speaking of body parts, the next tomb contains the heart of Richard the Lionhearted. (The rest of his body lies in the Abbey of Fontevraud, described on page 456 in the Loire chapter.) A descendant of William the Conqueror, Richard was both a king of England and the 12th duke of Normandy. A photo mounted on the wall opposite Richard shows damage from a violent 1999 storm that blew the spire off the roof and sent it crashing to the cathedral floor.

Circle behind the altar. The beautiful **windows** with bold blues and reds are generally from the 13th century. Look back above the entry to see a rare black-and-white rose window (its medieval colored glass is long gone). You'll come to a display for the window dedicated to St. Julien with pane-by-pane descriptions in English. The panels showing damage from the WWII bombing are captivating.

Continue a few paces, then look up to the **ceiling** over the

NORMANDY

nave. Looking directly above Rollo's femur on the opposite side of the apse, you can see the patchwork in the ceiling where the spire crashed through the roof. Perhaps this might be a good time to exit? Pass through the small iron gate, turn right, and leave through the side door (north transept).

Stepping outside, look back at the **facade.** The fine carved tympanum (the area over the door) shows a graphic Last Judgment. Jesus stands between the saved (on the left) and the damned (on the right). Notice the devil grasping a miser, who clutches a bag of coins. Look for the hellish hot tub, where even a bishop (pointy hat) is eternally in hot water.

Most of the facade has been cleaned—blasted with jets of water—but the limestone carving is still black. It's too delicate to survive the hosing, and instead awaits a more expensive laser cleaning (as do many other monuments in Rouen).

• *From this courtyard, a gate deposits you on a traffic-free street. Turn right and walk along...*

Rue St. Romain

This street has half-timbered buildings and lanes worth a look. In a short distance, you can look through an arch, back at the cathedral's spire. Made of cast iron in the late 1800s—about the same time Gustave Eiffel was building his tower in Paris—the spire is, at 490 feet, the tallest in France. You can also see the former location of the missing smaller (green) spire—downed in that 1999 storm.

• *Farther down the street, find a shop that shows off a traditional art form in action.*

At **Fayencerie Augy** (at #26), Monsieur Augy welcomes shoppers to browse his studio/gallery/shop and see Rouen's clay "china" being made the traditional way. First, the clay is molded and fired. Then it's dipped in white enamel, dried, lovingly hand-painted, and fired a second time. Rouen was the first city in France to make faience, earthenware with colored glazes. In the 1700s, the town had 18 factories churning out the popular product (Tue-Sat 9:00-19:00, closed Sun, 26 Rue St. Romain, VAT tax refunds nearly pay for the shipping, www.fayencerie-augy.com). For more faience, visit the local Museum of Ceramics (described later, under "Sights in Rouen").

• *Continue along Rue St. Romain, which (after crossing Rue de la République) leads to the fancy...*

St. Maclou Church

This church's unique, bowed facade is textbook Flamboyant Gothic (sadly, its doorways are blackened by pollution—visualize the brilliant exterior of the Palais de Justice, and what a world without pollution would be like). Notice the flame-like tracery decorating its gable. Because this was built at the very end of the Gothic age—and construction took many years—the doors are from the next age: the Renaissance (c. 1550). The bright and airy interior is worth a quick peek.

Cost and Hours: Free, Fri-Mon 10:00-12:00 & 14:00-17:30, closed Tue-Thu.

• *Leaving the church, turn right, and then take another right (giving the little boys on the corner wall a wide berth). Wander past a fine wall of half-timbered buildings fronting Rue Martainville, to the end of St. Maclou Church.*

Half-Timbered Buildings

Because the local stone—a chalky limestone from the cliffs of the Seine River—was of poor quality (your thumbnail is stronger), and because local oak was plentiful, half-timbered buildings became a Rouen specialty from the 14th through 19th centuries. Cantilevered floors were standard until the early 1500s. These top-heavy designs made sense: City land was limited, property taxes were based on ground-floor square footage, and the cantilevering minimized unsupported spans on upper floors. The oak beams provided the structural skeleton of the building, which was then filled in with a mix of clay, straw, pebbles...or whatever was available.

• *A block farther down on the left, at 186 Rue Martainville, a covered lane leads to the...*

Plague Cemetery (Aître St. Maclou)

During the great plagues of the Middle Ages, as many as two-thirds of the people in this parish died. For the decimated community, dealing with the corpses was an overwhelming task. This half-timbered courtyard (c. 1520) was a mass grave, an ossuary where the bodies were "processed." Bodies would be dumped into the grave (where the well is now) and drenched in liquid lime to help speed decomposition. Later, the bones would be stacked in alcoves above the colonnades that line this courtyard. Notice the ghoulish carvings (c. 1560s) of gravediggers' tools, skulls, crossbones, and characters doing the "dance of death." In this *danse macabre,* Death, the great equalizer, grabs people of all social classes. The place is now an art school. Peek in on the young artists. As you leave, spy the dried black cat (died c. 1520, in tiny glass case to the left of the door). To overcome evil, it was buried during the building's construction.

Cost and Hours: Free, daily mid-March-Oct 8:00-20:00, Nov-mid-March 8:00-19:00.

Nearby: Farther down Rue Martainville, at Place St. Marc, a colorful market blooms Sunday until about 12:30 and all day

NORMANDY

Tuesday, Friday, and Saturday. If it's not market day, you can double back to the cathedral and Rue du Gros Horloge, or continue with me to explore more of Rouen and find the Museum of Fine Arts (back toward the train station).

• *To reach the museum, turn right upon leaving the boneyard, then right again at the little boys (onto Rue Damiette), and hike up antique row to the vertical St. Ouen Church (a seventh-century abbey turned church in the 15th century, fine park behind). Turn left at the church on Rue des Faulx (an English-language bookstore, ABC Books, is a block to the right—see "Helpful Hints," page 268), and cross the busy street. (The horseman you see to the right is a short yet majestic Napoleon Bonaparte, who welcomes visitors to Rouen's city hall.) Continue down Rue de l'Hôpital's traffic-free lane, which becomes Rue Ganterie. A right at the modern square on Rue l'Ecrueil leads you to the Museum of Fine Arts and the Museum of Ironworks (both described next, under "Sights in Rouen"). This is the end of our tour. The tower where Joan of Arc was imprisoned (also explained later) is a few blocks uphill, on the way back to the train station.*

Sights in Rouen

The first three museums are within a block of one another, closed on Tuesdays, never crowded, and can all be visited with the same €8 combo-ticket (www.rouen-musees.com).

▲**Museum of Fine Arts (Musée des Beaux-Arts)**—Paintings from many periods are beautifully displayed in this overlooked two-floor museum, including works by Caravaggio, Peter Paul Rubens, Paolo Veronese, Jan Steen, Théodore Géricault, Jean-Auguste-Dominique Ingres, Eugène Delacroix, and several Impressionists. With its reasonable entry fee and calm interior, this museum is worth a short visit for the Impressionists and a surgical hit of a few other key artists. The museum café is good for a peaceful break from the action outside.

Cost and Hours: €5, occasional temporary exhibitions cost extra, €8 combo-ticket includes ironworks and ceramics museums; open Wed-Mon 10:00-18:00, 15th-17th-century rooms closed 13:00-14:00, closed Tue; a few blocks below train station at 26 bis Rue Jean Lecanuet, tel. 02 35 71 28 40.

Visiting the Museum: Pick up the essential museum map at the ticket desk. Climb the stairs to the upper floor, where you'll focus your time and savor the complete lack of crowds. Find the excellent handheld English descriptions in key rooms. There's a gallery dedicated to Géricault and a good collection of Ingres' work (smaller paintings than at the Louvre, but worth a look). In the next rooms you'll find scenes inspired by Normandy's landscape—painted by Impressionists Monet, Sisley, and Pissarro—

and a handful of paintings from Renoir, Degas, and Corot. Room 2.25 showcases a must-see scene of Rouen's busy port in 1855.

Other rooms on the upper floor are devoted to French painters from the 17th and 18th centuries (Boucher, Fragonard, and Poussin) and Italian works, including several by Veronese. A gripping Caravaggio canvas, depicting the flagellation of Christ, demands attention with its dramatic lighting and realistic faces.

Back on the ground floor, pass through the bookstore to find an intriguing collection of backlit panels created in homage to hometown boy Marcel Duchamp. Several colorful Modiglianis and one grand-scale Delacroix are nearby.

Museum of Ironworks (Musée le Secq des Tournelles, a.k.a. Musée de la Ferronnerie)—This deconsecrated church houses iron objects, many of them more than 1,500 years old. Locks, chests, keys, tools, thimbles, coffee grinders, corkscrews, and flatware from centuries ago—virtually anything made of iron is on display. You can duck into the entry area for a glimpse of a medieval iron scene without passing through the turnstile.

Cost and Hours: €3, €8 combo-ticket includes fine arts and ceramics museums, no English explanations—bring a French/English dictionary, Wed-Mon 10:00-13:00 & 14:00-18:00, closed Tue, behind Museum of Fine Arts, 2 Rue Jacques Villon, tel. 02 35 88 42 92.

Museum of Ceramics (Musée de la Céramique)—Rouen's famous faience (earthenware), which dates from the 16th to 18th centuries, fills this fine old mansion. Unfortunately, there's not a word of English.

Cost and Hours: €3, €8 combo-ticket includes fine arts and ironworks museums, Wed-Mon 10:00-13:00 & 14:00-18:00, closed Tue, 1 Rue Faucon, tel. 02 35 07 31 74.

Joan of Arc Tower (Le Tour Jeanne d'Arc)—This tower (1204), part of Rouen's brooding castle, was Joan's prison before her untimely death. Cross the deep moat and find three small floors (and 122 spiral steps) covering tidbits of Rouen's and Joan's history, well-described in English. The top floor gives a good peek at an impressive wood substructure but no views.

Cost and Hours: €1.50, Wed-Sat and Mon 10:00-12:30 & 14:00-18:00, Sun 14:00-18:30, closed Tue, one block uphill from the Museum of Fine Arts on Rue du Bouvreuil, tel. 02 35 98 16 21.

Near Rouen

The Route of the Ancient Abbeys (La Route des Anciennes Abbayes)—This route—punctuated with abbeys, apples, and Seine River views—provides a pleasing detour for drivers connecting Rouen and destinations farther west (if you're traveling *sans* car, skip it). Follow D-982 west of Rouen to Jumièges (visit its abbey), then cross the Seine on the car ferry at Duclair (about €2).

Drivers can stop to admire the gleaming Romanesque church at the **Abbey of St. Georges de Boscherville** (but skip the abbey grounds). The romantically ruined twin-towered **Abbey of Jumièges** is the top sight to visit on this route. Founded in A.D. 654, it was destroyed by Vikings and rebuilt by William the Conqueror, only to be torn down again by French Revolutionaries. Today, nature is gradually reclaiming its stone, as there is no roof to protect the abbey (€5, helpful English handout, more detailed booklet for sale, daily mid-June-mid-Sept 9:30-18:30, mid-Sept-mid-June 9:30-13:00 & 14:30-17:30, last entry 30 minutes before closing, tel. 02 35 37 24 02). Several decent lunch options lie across the street from the abbey.

Sleeping in Rouen

Although I prefer Rouen by day, sleeping here presents you with a mostly tourist-free city (most hotels cater to business travelers). These hotels are perfectly central, within two blocks of Notre-Dame Cathedral.

$$$ Hôtel Mercure*,** ideally situated a block north of the cathedral, is a concrete business hotel with a professional staff, a sprawling lobby and bar, and 125 rooms loaded with modern comforts. Suites come with views of the cathedral, but are overpriced and not much bigger than a double. Look for promotional rates with big discounts (Db-€180-200, suite-€290, breakfast-€16, air-con, elevator, free Internet access and Wi-Fi, parking garage-€12/day, 7 Rue Croix de Fer, tel. 02 35 52 69 52, fax 02 35 89 41 46, www.mercure.com, h1301@accor.com).

$$ Hôtel de la Cathédrale** welcomes you with a lovely courtyard and a cozy, wood-beamed breakfast room. Guest rooms are mostly country-French with basic bathrooms, imperfect sound insulation, and mushy beds (Sb-€60-80, Db with shower-€78, Db with tub-€108, Tb-€130, Qb-€145, elevator, free Internet access and Wi-Fi, nearby parking-€5 overnight or €11/24 hours, 12 Rue St. Romain, a block from St. Maclou Church, tel. 02 35 71 57 95, fax 02 35 70 15 54, www.hotel-de-la-cathedrale.fr, contact@hotel -de-la-cathedrale.fr).

$$ Hôtel le Cardinal** offers good rooms facing the cathedral, without the street appeal of the Hôtel de la Cathédrale. Nearly all of its 14 rooms look right onto the cathedral (Sb-€75, Db-€85; Db-€130-160 for fourth-floor rooms—the hotel's largest and most cushy, with balconies and great cathedral views; non-smoking rooms available, breakfast-€9, elevator, free Wi-Fi, 1 Place de la Cathédrale, tel. 02 35 70 24 42, fax 02 35 89 75 14, www.cardinal-hotel.fr, hotelcardinal.rouen@wanadoo.fr).

Sleep Code

(€1 = $1.30, country code: 33)
S = Single, **D** = Double/Twin, **T** = Triple, **Q** = Quad, **b** = bathroom, **s** = shower only, ***** = French hotel rating system (0-5 stars). Unless otherwise noted, credit cards are accepted and English is spoken.

To help you easily sort through these listings, I've divided the accommodations into three categories based on the price for a standard double room with bath:

$$$ **Higher Priced**—Most rooms €90 or more.
$$ **Moderately Priced**—Most rooms between €60-90.
$ **Lower Priced**—Most rooms €60 or less.

Prices can change without notice; verify the hotel's current rates online or by email.

$ Hôtel des Arcades is bare-bones basic, but as cheap and central as it gets (S-€39, D-€43 plus €5 to shower down the hall, Db-€56-62, 52 Rue des Carmes, tel. 02 35 70 10 30, www.hotel-des-arcades.com, hotel_des_arcades@yahoo.fr).

Eating in Rouen

You can eat well in Rouen at fair prices. Because you're in Normandy, *crêperies* abound. For a simple meal inside or out, prowl the places between the St. Maclou and St. Ouen churches (along Rues Martainville and Damiette), or the ever-so-hip Rue de l'Eau de Robec. Otherwise, try the recommendations below.

Near the Cathedral

Crêperie le St. Romain, between the cathedral and St. Maclou Church, is an excellent budget option. It's run by gentle Mr. Pegis, who serves filling €9 crêpes with small salads in a warm setting (lunch Tue-Sat, dinner Thu-Sat, closed Sun-Mon, 52 Rue St. Romain, tel. 02 35 88 90 36).

Dame Cakes is ideal if it's lunchtime or teatime and you need a Jane Austen fix. The decor is from another, more precious era, and the baked goods are out of this world (€12-15 salads and *plats*, garden terrace in back, Mon-Sat 11:00-18:00, closed Sun, 70 Rue St. Romain, tel. 02 35 07 49 31).

L'Enfant Terrible is a sharp, wine-loving place serving well-prepared dishes at reasonable prices. There's plenty of contemporary music and lots of yellow (€18 two-course *menu*, €23 three-course *menu*, closed Sun-Mon, 234 Rue Martainville, tel. 02 35 89 50 02).

At **Flunch** you'll find family-friendly, cheap, point-and-shoot, cafeteria-style meals in a fast-food setting (*menus* under €10 include salad bar, main course, and drink; good kids' *menu*, open daily until 22:00, a block from cathedral at 66 Rue des Carmes, tel. 02 35 71 81 81).

On Place du Vieux Marché

A fun lineup of restaurants—where locals wouldn't be caught dead—faces Place du Vieux Marché, across from the Joan of Arc Church. **Le Maupassant** stands out as more welcoming, with an outdoor terrace and three lively floors filled with orange leather booths (regional *menus*, lunch from €16, dinner from €30, daily, 39 Place du Vieux Marché, tel. 02 35 07 56 90).

Les Nymphéas is *le place* to do it up well in Rouen. Indoor and garden tables are carefully set for lovers of fine cuisine (€44 and €54 *menus*, closed Sun-Mon, just off Place du Vieux Marché at 7 Rue de la Pie, tel. 02 35 89 26 69).

Rouen Connections

Rouen is well served by trains from Paris, via Amiens to other points north, and via Caen to other destinations west and south.

From Rouen by Train to: Paris' Gare St. Lazare (nearly hourly, 1.5 hours), **Bayeux** (6/day, 2 hours, change in Caen; more trips possible via Paris' Gare St. Lazare, 4-5 hours), **Pontorson/ Mont St-Michel** (2/day, 4 hours, change in Caen; more with change in Paris, 7 hours).

By Train and Bus to: Honfleur (6/day Mon-Sat, 3/day Sun, 1-hour train to Le Havre, then easy transfer to 30-minute bus over Normandy Bridge to Honfleur—Le Havre's bus and train stations are adjacent).

Honfleur

Gazing at its cozy harbor lined with skinny, soaring houses, it's easy to overlook the historic importance of this port. For more

than a thousand years, sailors have enjoyed Honfleur's (ohn-flur) ideal location, where the Seine River greets the English Channel. William the Conqueror received supplies shipped from Honfleur. Samuel de Champlain sailed from here in 1608 to North America, where he discovered the St. Lawrence River and

founded Quebec City. The town was also a favorite of 19th-century Impressionists who were captivated by Honfleur's unusual light—the result of its river-meets-sea setting. Eugène Boudin (boo-dahn) lived and painted in Honfleur, drawing Monet and other creative types from Paris. In some ways, modern art was born in the fine light of idyllic little Honfleur.

Honfleur escaped the bombs of World War II, and today offers a romantic port enclosed on three sides by sprawling outdoor cafés. Long eclipsed by the gargantuan port of Le Havre just across the Seine, Honfleur happily uses its past as a bar stool...and sits on it.

Orientation to Honfleur

Honfleur is popular—be ready for crowds on weekends and during summer. All of Honfleur's engaging streets and activities are within a short stroll of its old port (Vieux Bassin). The Seine River flows just east of the center, the hills of the Côte de Grâce form its western limit, and Rue de la République slices north-south through the center to the port. Honfleur has two can't-miss sights—the harbor and Ste. Catherine Church—and a handful of other intriguing monuments. But really, the town itself is its best sight.

Tourist Information

The TI is in the flashy glass public library *(Mediathéque)* on Quai le Paulmier, two blocks from Vieux Bassin toward Le Havre (July-Aug Mon-Sat 9:30-19:00, Sun 10:00-17:00; Sept-June Mon-Sat 9:30-12:30 & 14:00-18:00, Sun 10:00-12:30 & 14:00-17:00 except closed Sun afternoon Oct-Easter; free WCs inside, pay Internet access, tel. 02 31 89 23 30, www.ot-honfleur.fr). Here you can rent a €3.50 audioguide for a self-guided town walk, or pick up a town

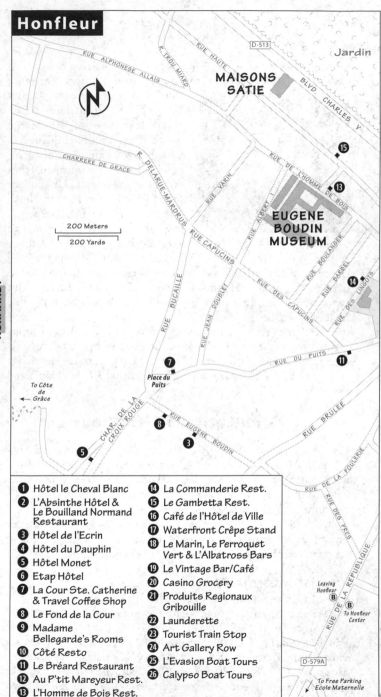

Honfleur

Jardin

D-513

RUE ALPHONESE ALLAIS
R. TROU MIARD
RUE HAUTE

MAISONS SATIE

BLVD. CHARLES V.

CHARRERE DE GRACE
R. DELARUE-MARDRUS

RUE DE L'HOMME DE BOIS

RUE VARIN

RUE CAPUCINS

RUE ALBERT I

EUGENE BOUDIN MUSEUM

200 Meters
200 Yards

RUE BUCAILLE
RUE JEAN DOUBLET
RUE DES CAPUCINS

RUE BOULANGER
RUE BARBEL
RUE DES LINGOTS

⑮
⑬

⑭

RUE DU PUITS

⑪

⑦

Place du Puits

To Côte de Grâce

CHAR. DE LA CROIX ROUGE

⑧   RUE EUGENE BOUDIN

③

⑤

RUE BRULEE

RUE DE LA FOULERIE

RUE DES PRES

Leaving Honfleur

Ⓑ

Ⓑ To Honfleur Center

RUE DE LA REPUBLIQUE

D-579A

To Free Parking
Ecole Maternelle

NORMANDY

① Hôtel le Cheval Blanc
② L'Absinthe Hôtel & Le Bouilland Normand Restaurant
③ Hôtel de l'Ecrin
④ Hôtel du Dauphin
⑤ Hôtel Monet
⑥ Etap Hôtel
⑦ La Cour Ste. Catherine & Travel Coffee Shop
⑧ Le Fond de la Cour
⑨ Madame Bellegarde's Rooms
⑩ Côté Resto
⑪ Le Bréard Restaurant
⑫ Au P'tit Mareyeur Rest.
⑬ L'Homme de Bois Rest.

⑭ La Commanderie Rest.
⑮ Le Gambetta Rest.
⑯ Café de l'Hôtel de Ville
⑰ Waterfront Crêpe Stand
⑱ Le Marin, Le Perroquet Vert & L'Albatross Bars
⑲ Le Vintage Bar/Café
⑳ Casino Grocery
㉑ Produits Regionaux Gribouille
㉒ Launderette
㉓ Tourist Train Stop
㉔ Art Gallery Row
㉕ L'Evasion Boat Tours
㉖ Calypso Boat Tours

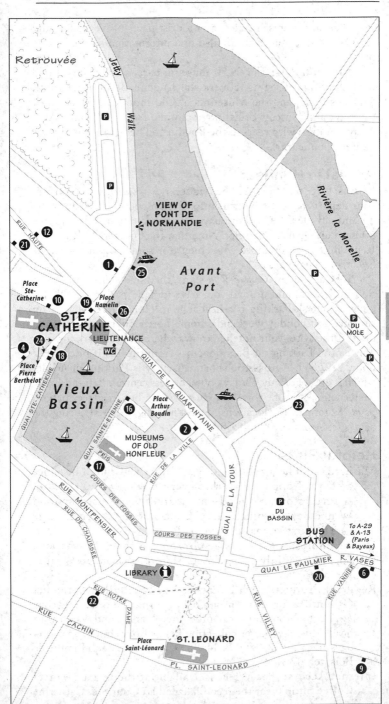

NORMANDY

map, bus and train schedules, and tourist maps of Normandy and the Calvados region. You can also find information on the D-Day beaches.

Museum Pass: The €9.50 museum pass, sold at the TI and participating museums, covers the Eugène Boudin Museum, Maisons Satie, and the Museums of Old Honfleur (Museum of the Navy and Museum of Ethnography and Norman Popular Art); it pays for itself with visits to the Boudin and Satie museums (www.musees-honfleur.fr).

Arrival in Honfleur

By Bus: Get off at the small bus station *(gare routière)*, and confirm your departure at the helpful information counter. To reach the TI and old town, turn right as you exit the station and walk five minutes up Quai le Paulmier. Note that the bus stop on Rue de la République may be more convenient for some accommodations (see map on page 282).

By Car: Follow *Centre-Ville* signs, then find your hotel (easier said than done) and unload your bags (double-parking is OK for a few minutes). Parking is a headache in Honfleur, especially on summer and holiday weekends. Some hotels offer parking...for a price. Otherwise, your hotelier knows where you can park for free. The central Parking du Bassin (across from the TI) is pricey (€2/hour, €12/day). Across the short causeway is Parking du Môle, which is cheaper (only €3/day), but a bit less central. Parking Ecole Maternelle is still farther (out Rue Brûlée), but free (see map on page 282 for parking locations). Street parking, metered during the day, is free from 20:00 to 8:00.

Helpful Hints

Market Day: The area around Ste. Catherine Church becomes a colorful open-air market every Saturday (9:00-13:00). A smaller organic-food-only market takes place here on Wednesday mornings, and a flea market takes center stage here the first Sunday of the month.

Grocery Stores: A good **Casino Grocery** is near the TI with long hours (daily July-Aug, closed Mon off-season, 16 Quai le Paulmier).

Regional Products with Panache: Visit **Produits Regionaux Gribouille** for any Norman delicacy you can dream up. Say *bonjour* to Monsieur Gribouille (gree-boo-ee) and watch your head—his egg-beater collection hangs from above (open 364 days a year, 9:30-13:00 & 14:00-19:00, 16 Rue de l'Homme de Bois, tel. 02 31 89 29 54).

Internet Access: Free Wi-Fi is available at the relaxed **Travel Coffee Shop** (near the recommended La Cour Ste. Catherine

B&B). The TI has a list of cybercafés with computer terminals and Wi-Fi.

Laundry: Lavomatique is a block behind the TI, toward the port (daily 7:00-20:00, 4 Rue Notre-Dame).

Taxi: Call 02 31 89 81 22 or mobile 06 18 18 38 38.

Tourist Train: Honfleur's *petit train* toots you up the Côte de Grâce—the hill overlooking the town—and back in about 50 minutes (€6.50, daily, departs from across gray swivel bridge that leads to Parking du Môle).

Sights in Honfleur

Vieux Bassin—Stand near the water facing Honfleur's square harbor, with the merry-go-round across the lock to your left,

and survey the town. The word "Honfleur" is Scandinavian, meaning the shelter *(fleur)* of Hon (a Norse settler). This town has been sheltering residents for about a thousand years. During the Hundred Years' War (14th century), the harbor was fortified by a big wall with twin gatehouses (the one surviving gatehouse, *La Lieutenance,* is on your right) and a narrow boat passage protected by a chain.

Those skinny houses on the right side were designed at a time when buildings were taxed based on their width, not height (and when knee replacements were unheard of). How about a room on the top floor, with no elevator? Imagine moving a piano into one of these units today. The spire halfway up the left side of the port belongs to Honfleur's oldest church and is now home to the Marine Museum. The port, once crammed with fishing boats, now harbors sleek sailboats. Walk toward the *La Lieutenance* gatehouse. In front of the barrel-vaulted arch (once the entry to the town), you can see a bronze bust of Samuel de Champlain—the explorer who sailed with an Honfleur crew 400 years ago to make his discoveries in Canada.

Turn around to see various tour and fishing boats and the high-flying Normandy Bridge (described later, under "Near Honfleur") in the distance. Fisherfolk catch flatfish, scallops, and tiny shrimp daily and bring them here. On the left you may see fishermen's wives selling *crevettes* (shrimp). You can buy them *cuites* (cooked) or *vivantes* (alive and wiggly). They are happy to let you sample one (rip off the cute little head and tail, and pop the middle into your mouth—*délicieuse!*), or buy a cupful to go for a few euros (daily in season).

NORMANDY

You'll probably see artists sitting at easels around the harbor, as Boudin and Monet did. Many consider Honfleur the birthplace of 19th-century Impressionism. This was a time when people began to revere, not fear, the out-of-doors, and started to climb mountains "because they were there." Pretty towns like Honfleur and the nearby coast were ideal subjects to paint—and still are—thanks to what locals called the "unusual luminosity" of the region. And with the advent of trains in the late 1800s, artists could travel to the best light like never before. Artists would set up easels along the harbor to catch the light playing on the line of buildings, slates, timbers, geraniums, clouds, and reflections in the water. Monet came here to visit the artist Boudin, a hometown boy, and the battle cry of the Impressionists—"Out of the studio and into the light!"—was born.

If you're an early riser, you can watch what's left of Honfleur's fishing fleet prepare for the day, and you just might experience that famous luminosity.

▲▲Ste. Catherine Church (Eglise Ste. Catherine)—The unusual wood-shingled exterior suggests that this church has a different story to tell than most. Walk inside. You'd swear that if it were turned over, it would float—the legacy of a community of sailors and fishermen, with plenty of boat-builders and no cathedral architects. When workers put up the first nave in 1466, it soon became apparent that more space was needed—so the second was built in 1497. Because it felt too much like a market hall, they added side aisles. Notice the oak pillars, some full length and others supported by stone bases. Trees come in different sizes, yet each pillar had to be the same thickness. In the last months of World War II, a bomb fell through the roof—but didn't explode. The pipe organ behind you is popular for concerts, and half of the modern pews are designed to flip so that you can face the music. Take a close look at the many medieval instruments carved into the railing below the organ—a 16th-century combo band in wood.

The church's bell tower is equally unusual, as it was built not adjacent to the church but across the square. That's so it wouldn't overburden the wooden church's roof, and to help minimize fire hazards. Historians consider the structure ugly—I kind of like it. Notice the funky shingled beams that run from its squat base to support the skinny tower, and find the small, faded wooden sculpture of St. Catherine over the door. Peek inside to appreciate the ancient wood framing. In the tiny museum, with a few church artifacts, a useful 15-minute video (in English) describes the tower's history.

Cost and Hours: Church—free, daily July-Aug 9:00-18:30, Sept-June 9:00-17:15; museum—not worth the entry fee but free with ticket to the Eugène Boudin Museum; April-Sept Wed-Mon

10:00-12:00 & 14:00-18:00; Oct-March Wed-Mon 14:00-18:00 only, closed Tue.

Honfleur's Museums and Galleries

Remember, the €9.50 museum pass covers all four museums described below and pays for itself with visits to just the Boudin and Satie museums (pass sold at TI and participating museums).

▲**Eugène Boudin Museum**—This pleasing little museum has three interesting floors with many paintings of Honfleur and the surrounding countryside. The first floor displays Norman folk costumes, the second floor has the Boudin collection, and the third floor houses the Hambourg/Rachet collection and the Katia Granoff room.

Cost and Hours: €5.80, €2 extra during special exhibits, covered by museum pass, €2 English audioguide covers selected works (no English explanations on display—but none needed); mid-March-Sept Wed-Mon 10:00-12:00 & 14:00-18:00, closed Tue; Oct-mid-March Wed-Fri and Mon 14:30-17:30, Sat-Sun 10:00-12:00 & 14:30-17:30, closed Tue; elevator, no photos, Rue de l'Homme de Bois, tel. 02 31 89 54 00.

➔ Self-Guided Tour: Pick up a map at the ticket counter, tip your beret to Eugène Boudin, and climb the stairs (or take the elevator).

First Floor (Costumes): Monsieur and Madame Louveau (see their photo as you enter) gave Honfleur this quality collection of local traditional costumes. The hats, blouses, and shoes are supported by paintings that place them in an understandable historical and cultural context. Of special interest are the lace bonnets, typical of 19th-century Normandy. You could name a woman's village by her style of bonnet. The dolls are not toys for tots, but marketing tools for traveling clothing merchants—designed to show off the latest fashions. The men's department is in the back of the room.

Second Floor (Boudin Collection and More): Making a right off the stairs leads you into a large room of appealing 20th-century paintings and sculpture, created by artists who produced most of their works while living in Honfleur (special exhibits sometimes occupy this space). A left off the stairs leads you through a temporary exhibition hall into the Salle Eugène Boudin, a small gallery of 19th-century paintings. In this room, Boudin's artwork is mixed with that of his colleagues and contemporaries; paintings by Claude Monet and Gustave Courbet are usually displayed. Find the glass display case in the rear titled *Précurseur de l'Impressionisme*, with little pastel drawings, and follow Boudin's art as it evolves chronologically, from Romanticism through Realism to Impressionism (the heart of this museum).

Eugène Boudin
(1824-1898)

Born in Honfleur, Boudin was the son of a harbor pilot. As an amateur teenage artist, he found work in an art-supply store that catered to famous artists from Paris (such as Jean-Baptiste-Camille Corot and Jean-François Millet) who came to paint the seaside. Boudin studied art in Paris but kept his hometown roots. Thanks to his Paris connections, Boudin's work was exhibited at the Paris salons.

At age 30 Boudin met the teenaged Claude Monet. Monet had grown up in nearby Le Havre, and, like Boudin, sketched the world around him—beaches, boats, and small-town life. Boudin encouraged him to don a scarf, set up his easel outdoors, and paint the scene exactly as he saw it. Today, we say: "Well, duh!" But "open-air" painting was unorthodox for artists trained to thoroughly study their subjects in the perfect lighting of a controlled studio setting. Boudin didn't teach Monet as much as give him the courage to follow his artistic instincts.

In the 1860s and 1870s, Boudin spent summers at his farm (St. Siméon) on the outskirts of Honfleur, hosting Monet, Edouard Manet, and others. They taught Boudin the Impressionist techniques of using bright colors and building a subject with many individual brushstrokes. Boudin adapted those "strokes" to build subjects with "patches" of color. In 1874, Boudin joined the renegade Impressionists at their "revolutionary" exhibition in Paris.

Upon showing their work in Paris, local artists—such as Eugène Boudin—created enough of a stir that Normandy came into vogue; many Parisian artists (including Monet and other early Impressionists) traveled to Honfleur to tune in to the action. Boudin himself made a big impression on the father of Impressionism by introducing Monet to the practice of painting outside. This collection of Boudin's paintings—which the artist gave to his hometown—shows how his technique developed, from realistic portrayals of subjects (outlines colored in, like a coloring book) to masses of colors catching light (Impressionism). Boudin's beach scenes, showing aristocrats taking a healthy saltwater dip, helped fuel that trend. His skies were good enough to earn him the nickname "King of Skies."

Third Floor (Hambourg/Rachet Collection): Follow the steps that lead from the Boudin room to the small Hambourg/Rachet collection (and a smashing painting of Honfleur at twilight). In 1988, André Hambourg and his wife, Nicole Rachet, donated their art to this museum. The collection is enjoyably

Impressionistic, but largely from the mid-20th century.

Third Floor (Salle Katia Granoff): Retrace your steps back to the main stairway to reach the other third-floor room, where you'll find a worthwhile collection of 20th-century pieces by artists who lived and learned in Honfleur. Find the few paintings by Raoul Dufy (a French Fauvist painter) and compare his imaginative scenes of Normandy with others you've seen. Don't miss the brilliant view of the Normandy Bridge through the windows.

Art Galleries—Eugène Boudin ignited Honfleur's artistic tradition that still burns today. The town is a popular haunt of artists, many of whom display their works in Honfleur's terrific selection of art galleries (the best ones are along the streets between Ste. Catherine Church and the port). As you walk around the town, take the time to enjoy today's art.

▲Maisons Satie—This peaceful museum, housed in composer Erik Satie's birthplace, presents his music in a creative and enjoyable way. As you wander from room to room with your included audioguide, infrared signals transmit bits of Satie's music, along with a first-person story (in English). As if you're living as an artist in 1920s Paris, you'll drift past winged pears, strangers in the window, and small girls with green eyes. (If you like what you hear...don't move; the infrared transmission is hypersensitive, and the soundtrack switches every few feet.) The finale—performed by you—is the *Laboratory of Emotions* pedal-go-round. For a relaxing sit, enjoy the 12-minute movie (4/hour, French only) featuring modern dance springing from Satie's collaboration with Picasso types.

Cost and Hours: €5.80, includes audioguide, covered by museum pass; May-Sept Wed-Mon 10:00-19:00, closed Tue; Oct-Dec and mid-Feb-April Wed-Mon 11:00-18:00, closed Tue; closed Jan-mid-Feb; last entry one hour before closing, 5-minute walk from harbor at 67 Boulevard Charles V, tel. 02 31 89 11 11.

Museums of Old Honfleur—Two side-by-side folk museums combine to paint a picture of daily life in Honfleur during the time when its ships were king and the city had global significance. The curator creatively supports the artifacts with paintings, making the cultural context clearer. Both museums have booklets with English explanations.

The **Museum of the Navy** (Musée de la Marine) faces the port and fills Honfleur's oldest church (15th century) with a cool collection of ship models, marine paraphernalia, and paintings. The **Museum of Ethnography and Norman Popular Art** (Musée d'Ethnographie et d'Art Populaire), located in the old prison and courthouse, re-creates typical rooms from various eras and crams them with objects of daily life (€3.70 each or €5 for both, covered by museum pass; both museums open April-Sept Tue-Sun

NORMANDY

10:00-12:00 & 14:00-18:30, closed Mon; March and Oct-mid-Nov Tue-Fri 10:00-12:00 & 14:30-17:30, Sat-Sun 10:00-12:00 & 14:00-17:30, closed Mon; closed mid-Nov-Feb).

Walks

▲**Côte de Grâce Walk**—For good exercise and a bird's-eye view of Honfleur and the Normandy Bridge, take the steep 20-minute walk (or quick drive) up to the Côte de Grâce viewpoint—best in the early morning or at sunset. From Ste. Catherine Church, walk or drive up Rue du Puits, then follow the blue-on-white signs to reach the splendid view. *Piétons* (walkers) should veer right up La Rampe du Mont Joli; *conducteurs* (drivers) should keep straight. Two hundred yards past the top, the **Chapel of Notre-Dame de Grâce** merits a visit. Built in the early 1600s by the mariners and people of Honfleur, the church oozes seafaring mementos. Model boats hang from the ceiling, pictures of boats balance high on the walls, and what's left is decorated by stained-glass images of sailors praying to the Virgin Mary while at sea. Even the holy water basins to the left and right of the entrance are in the shape of seashells.

Just below the chapel, a second lookout offers a sweeping view of super-industrial Le Havre, with the Manche (English Channel) to your left and the Normandy Bridge to your right.

Jetty/Park Walk—Take a level stroll in Honfleur along the water past the Hôtel le Cheval Blanc to see the mouth of the Seine River and big ships at sea. You'll pass kid-friendly parks carpeted with flowers and grass, and continue past the lock connecting Honfleur to the Seine and the sea. Grand and breezy vistas of the sea reward the diligent walker (allow one hour out and back for best views).

Near Honfleur

Boat Excursions—Boat trips in and around Honfleur depart near Hôtel le Cheval Blanc (Easter-Nov usually about 11:00-17:00). The tour boat *Calypso* takes good 45-minute spins around Honfleur's harbor (€6, tel. 02 31 89 07 77). *L'Evasion* boats cruise to the Normandy Bridge (see below), which, unfortunately, means two boring trips through the locks (€10/1.5 hours, €7/50 minutes, mobile 06 85 36 78 12).

▲**Normandy Bridge (Pont de Normandie)**—The 1.25-mile-long Normandie Bridge is the longest cable-stayed bridge in the Western world (about €5 toll each way). This is a key piece of a super-expressway that links the Atlantic ports from Belgium to Spain. View the bridge from Honfleur (better from an excursion boat or the Côte de Grâce viewpoint, and best at night, when bridge is floodlit). Also consider visiting the bridge's free Exhibition Hall (under tollbooth on Le Havre side, daily 8:00-

19:00). The Seine finishes its winding 500-mile journey here, dropping only 1,500 feet from its source. The river flows so slowly that, in certain places, a stiff breeze can send it flowing upstream.

▲**Etrétat**—France's answer to the White Cliffs of Dover, these chalky cliffs soar high above a calm, crescent beach (from Honfleur, it's about 50 minutes by car or 2 hours by bus via Le Havre). Walking trails lead hikers from the small seaside resort of Etrétat along a vertiginous route with sensational views (and crowds of hikers in summers and on weekends). You'll recognize these cliffs—and the arches and stone spire that decorate them—from countless Impressionist paintings, including several at the Eugène Boudin Museum in Honfleur. The small, Coney Island-like town holds plenty of cafés and a **TI** (Place Maurice Guillard, tel. 02 35 27 05 21, www.etretat.net).

Getting There: Etrétat is north of Le Havre. To get here by car, cross the Normandy Bridge and follow A-29, then exit at *sortie Etrétat*. Buses serve Etrétat from Le Havre's *gare routière,* adjacent to the train station (5/day, 1 hour, www.cars-perier.com).

Sleeping in Etrétat: **$$$ Hôtel Dormy** makes a nice splurge if the scenery moves you (Route du Havre at the edge of Etrétat, tel. 02 35 27 07 88, www.dormy-house.com, info@etretat-hotel .com).

Sleeping in Honfleur

(€1 = about $1.30, country code: 33)
Though Honfleur is popular in summer, it's busiest on weekends and holidays when prices can rise (blame Paris). English is widely spoken (Honfleur is a popular weekend getaway for Brits). A few moderate accommodations remain, but most hotels are pretty pricey. Budget travelers should consider the *chambres d'hôtes* listed.

Hotels
$$$ Hôtel le Cheval Blanc*, a Best Western, is a waterfront splurge with port views from all of its 32 plush and pricey rooms (many with queen-size beds), plus a rare-in-this-town elevator, but no air-conditioning—noise can be a problem with windows open (small Db with lesser view-€145, Db with full port view-€160-210, family rooms/suites-€280-425, must cancel by 16:00 the day before or forfeit deposit, free Wi-Fi, 2 Quai des Passagers, tel. 02 31 81 65 00, fax 02 31 89 52 80, www.hotel-honfleur.com, info@hotel -honfleur.com).

$$$ L'Absinthe Hôtel* offers 12 tastefully restored rooms, all with king-size beds. Rooms in the "old" section come with wood-beamed decor and Jacuzzi tubs, and share a cozy public lounge with a fireplace (Db-€155-185). Five rooms have port views

NORMANDY

and four-star, state-of-the-art comfort, including air-conditioning and saunas (Db-€175-250, Db suite-€265; breakfast-€13, private parking-€12, 1 Rue de la Ville, check in at L'Absinthe restaurant across alley, tel. 02 31 89 23 23, fax 02 31 89 53 60, www.absinthe .fr, reservation@absinthe.fr).

$$$ Hôtel de l'Ecrin*** is a true Old World refuge. Enter the private courtyard to find a vintage mansion with lovely gardens and ample grass, a big pool, a sauna, public spaces Eugène Boudin would appreciate, free on-site parking, and *très* traditional rooms (Db-€125, bigger Db-€145-160, big suites-€200-280, Wi-Fi, 10 minutes by foot from the harbor at 19 Rue Eugène Boudin, tel. 02 31 14 43 45, fax 02 31 89 24 41, www.honfleur.com, hotel.ecrin @honfleur.com).

$$ Hôtel du Dauphin** is centrally located and a good mid-range value, with a colorful lounge/breakfast room, many narrow stairs (normal in Honfleur), and an Escher-esque floor plan. The 30 mostly smallish rooms—some with open-beam ceilings, some with queen- or king-size beds—provide reasonable comfort. If you need a lower floor or bigger bed, request it when you book (Db-€80-100, Tb-€120-140, lovely Qb-€155-175, Wi-Fi in lobby,

a stone's throw from Ste. Catherine Church at 10 Place Pierre Berthelot, tel. 02 31 89 15 53, fax 02 31 89 92 06, www.hoteldu dauphin.com, info@hoteldudauphin.com). The same owners also run the **$$$ Hôtel des Loges***,** a few doors up, which offers larger rooms with less personality (Db-€110-135).

$$ Hôtel Monet,** on the road to the Côte de Grâce and a 10-minute walk down to the port (longer back up), is an overlooked find. This tranquil spot is an ivy-covered brick home with 16 mostly tight but good-value rooms facing a courtyard, many with a patio made for picnics. You'll meet welcoming owners Christoph and Sylvie (Db-€64-104, Tb-€80-115, Qb-€92-150, highest rates are for July-Sept, free and easy parking, Wi-Fi, Chartière du Puits, tel. 02 31 89 00 90, fax 02 31 89 97 16, www.hotel-monet.fr, contact@hotel-monet-honfleur.com).

$ Etap Hôtel is modern, efficient, trim, and cheap, with antiseptically clean rooms (Sb-€42, Db/Tb-€49, €6 for each extra person, reception is closed 21:00-6:00 but automatic check-in with credit card available 24 hours, elevator, pay Wi-Fi, across from bus station and main parking lot on Rue des Vases, tel. 08 92 68 07 81, fax 02 31 89 77 88, www.etaphotel.com).

Chambres d'Hôtes

The TI has a long list of Honfleur's many *chambres d'hôtes* (rooms in private homes), but most are too far from the town center. The three listed here are good values.

$$$ Le Fond de la Cour is where British expats Amanda, Chris, and big dog Pataud offer a good mix of accommodations, including a large cottage that can sleep six, three apartments with small kitchens (Db-€100-120, extra person-€30, short stays possible), and two sharp B&B rooms (Db-€95-105, Tb-€100, includes breakfast, Wi-Fi, free street parking, private parking-€9/day, 29 Rue Eugène Boudin, tel. 09 62 31 24 30, mobile 06 72 20 72 98, www.lefonddelacour.com, amanda.ferguson@orange.fr).

$$ La Cour Ste. Catherine, kitty-corner to Le Fond de la Cour, is an enchanting bed-and-breakfast run by the open-hearted Madame Giaglis ("call me Liliane") and her big-hearted husband, Monsieur Liliane. Her six big, modern rooms—each with firm beds and a separate sitting area—surround a perfectly Norman courtyard with a small terrace, fine plantings, a cozy lounge area ideal for cool evenings, and a happening coffee shop. The rooms are as cheery as the owner (Db-€90, Db suite-€110, Tb/Qb-€150, extra bed-€30, includes breakfast, small apartments that sleep up to 6 and cottage with kitchen also available, cash only, free Internet access and Wi-Fi, free parking in 2013 with this book, 200 yards up Rue du Puits from Ste. Catherine Church at #74, tel. 02 31 89 42 40, www.coursaintecatherine.com, coursaintecatherine @orange.fr). If you can't find a room in Honfleur, talk to Liliane— she wants to help, even when her place is full.

$ Sweet **Madame Bellegarde** offers two simple rooms in her traditional home (Db-€49-57, family-friendly Tb with great view from bathroom-€64, includes breakfast, cash only, 10-minute uphill walk from TI, 3 blocks up from St. Léonard Church in untouristy part of Honfleur, 54 Rue St. Léonard, look for small *chambres* sign in window, she'll try to hold a parking spot if you ask, tel. 02 31 89 06 52).

Eating in Honfleur

Eat seafood or cream sauces here. It's a tough choice between the irresistible waterfront tables of the many look-alike places lining the harbor and the eateries with more solid reputations elsewhere in town. Trust my dinner suggestions below and consider your hotelier's opinion. It's best to call ahead to reserve at most restaurants in Honfleur (particularly on weekends).

Le Bouilland Normand hides a block off the port on a pleasing square and offers a true Norman experience at reasonable prices. Annette and daughter Claire provide quality *Normand* cuisine and enjoy helping travelers (€18-26 *menus,* closed Wed-Thu, dine inside or out, on Rue de la Ville, tel. 02 31 89 02 41).

Côté Resto saddles up on the left side of Ste. Catherine Church and serves a top selection of seafood (including seafood *choucroute* and real cheesecake—not served together) in a classy setting. The value is excellent for those in search of a special meal (€22 two-course *menu*, €28 three-course *menu*, great selection, closed Thu, 8 Place Ste. Catherine, tel. 02 31 89 31 33).

Le Bréard serves exquisite modern French cuisine presented with care, style, and ingenuity. The chef has returned after several years in Paris' finer restaurants, bringing his considerable talent back to Honfleur. Book ahead, then savor a delicious, slow meal in a formal yet appealing setting—all for a fraction of the price you'd pay in Paris (€29-55 *menus,* closed Mon-Tue, 7 Rue du Puits, tel. 02 31 89 53 40).

Au P'tit Mareyeur is whisper-formal, intimate, all about seafood, and a good value. Reservations are particularly smart here (€30 four-course *menu,* closed Tue-Wed and Jan, 4 Rue Haute, tel. 02 31 98 84 23, friendly owner Julie speaks some English).

L'Homme de Bois combines great ambience with authentic Norman cuisine and decent prices (€19 three-course *menu* with few choices, €23 *menu* gives more choices, daily, a few outside tables, 30 Rue de l'Homme de Bois, tel. 02 31 89 75 27).

La Commanderie, specializing in pizza and crêpes (€10-12), is cozy and welcoming (daily July-Aug, closed Mon-Tue off-season, across from Le Corsaire restaurant on Place Ste. Catherine, tel. 02 31 89 14 92).

Le Gambetta is a good place whose sincere owners limit the selection in order to preserve the freshness of their products (€23 *menus,* closed Thu, 58 Rue Haute, tel. 02 31 87 05 01).

Travel Coffee Shop is an ideal breakfast or lunch option for travelers wanting conversation (in either English or French) and good food at very fair prices (Thu-Tue 8:00-19:00, closed Wed, 74 Rue du Puits).

Dining along the Harbor: If the weather cooperates, slide down to the harbor and table-shop the joints that line the high side. (The harbor's lower side offers views of the picturesque high side, but high-side restaurants allow you to dine right on the water. Skip either side if you don't land a table right on the harbor.) Several places have effective propane heaters that keep outdoor diners happy when it's cool. Although the cuisine is mostly mediocre, the setting is uniquely Honfleur—and, on a languid evening, hard to pass up. Take a stroll along the port and compare restaurant views, chair comfort, and menu selection (all of these places look the same to me). Then dive in and remember that you're paying for the setting, not the cuisine: Stick with basic dishes such as crêpes, omelets, pizza, or pasta. If you decide to eat elsewhere, at least come here for a before- or after-dinner drink—see "Nightlife," below.

Of the harbor-front options, **Café de l'Hôtel de Ville** owns the best afternoon sun exposure (and charges for it) and looks across to Honfleur's soaring homes (open daily July-Aug, closed Tue off-season, Place de l'Hôtel de Ville, tel. 02 31 89 07 29).

Breakfast: If it's even close to sunny, skip your hotel breakfast and enjoy ambience for a cheaper price by eating on the port, where several cafés offer *petit déjeuner* (€3-7 for continental fare, €7-13 for more elaborate choices). Morning sun and views are best from the high side of the harbor. If price or companionship matter, head to the Travel Coffee Shop for the best breakfast deal in town (described earlier).

Dessert: Honfleur is ice-cream crazy, with gelato and traditional ice cream shops on every corner. If you need a Ben & Jerry's ice cream fix or a scrumptious dessert crêpe, find the **waterfront stand** at the southeast corner of Vieux Bassin.

Nighttime Food to Go: Order a tasty pizza to go until late from **Il Parasole** (described earlier), and enjoy a picnic dinner with port views a few steps away in front of the *La Lieutenance* gatehouse.

Nightlife: Nightlife in Honfleur centers on the old port. Three bar/cafés sit almost side by side, halfway up the high-building side of the port. All offer waterfront tables if all you want is a drink: **Le Marin** (average), **L'Albatross** (pub-like with flags, banners, and a loyal following), and **Le Perroquet Vert** (existential—"those lights are so...").

Le Vintage, just off the port, is a happening bar/café with live piano and jazz on weekend nights. Casual outdoor seating and a vigorous interior make this a fun choice (closed Tue, 8 Quai des Passagers, tel. 02 31 89 05 28).

Honfleur Connections

Two bus routes, run by Bus Verts, conveniently connect Honfleur with Le Havre, Caen, Deauville, and Lisieux (all with direct rail service to Paris), where you'll catch a train to other points. Bus #50 runs between Le Havre, Honfleur and Lisieux; bus #20 connects Le Havre, Honfleur, Deauville, and Caen. Coming from Paris, the best train-to-bus transfers are usually in Lisieux or Deauville (Deauville train requires a quick transfer in Lisieux), but if you want to visit Rouen on the way, the bus via Le Havre works fine. At Lisieux's train station, bus #50 stops on your right as you walk out; bus #20 from Deauville's station is on the left (follow *Gare Routière* signs). Although train and bus service usually are coordinated, confirm your connection with the helpful staff at Honfleur's bus station (English information desk open Mon-Fri 9:30-12:00 & 13:00-18:00, in summer also Sat-Sun, tel. 02 31 89 28 41, www.busverts.fr). If the station is closed, you can get schedules at the TI. Railpass-holders will save money by connecting through Deauville, as bus fares increase with distance (Deauville to Honfleur-€2.30, Lisieux to Honfleur-€4.30).

From Honfleur by Bus and/or Train to: Caen (express buses 2/day, 1 hour; more scenic *par la côte* 9/day, 2 hours; or 1-hour bus to Lisieux, then 30-minute train to Caen); **Bayeux** (8/day, 1.5-3 hours by bus and train; 1-hour express bus or 2-hour bus via the coast to Caen, then 20-minute train to Bayeux; or 1-hour bus to Lisieux, then 1-hour train to Bayeux via Caen); **Rouen** (6/day Mon-Sat, 3/day Sun, bus-and-train combo involves 30-minute bus ride over Normandy Bridge to Le Havre, then easy transfer to 1-hour train to Rouen or by less frequent bus to Lisieux and train to Rouen); **Paris'** Gare St. Lazare (13/day, 2-3.5 hours, by bus to Lisieux, Deauville, or Le Havre, then train to Paris; buses from Honfleur meet most Paris trains).

Bayeux

Only six miles from the D-Day beaches, Bayeux was the first city liberated after the landing. Incredibly, the town was spared the bombs of World War II. After a local chaplain made sure London knew that his city was not a German headquarters and was of no strategic importance, a scheduled bombing raid was canceled—making Bayeux the closest city to the D-Day landing site not destroyed. Even without its famous medieval tapestry and proximity to the D-Day beaches, Bayeux would be worth a visit for its enjoyable town center and awe-inspiring cathedral, beautifully illuminated at night. Bayeux makes an ideal home base for visiting the area's sights, particularly if you lack a car.

Orientation to Bayeux

Tourist Information
The TI is on a small bridge two blocks north of the cathedral—conveniently located on the pedestrian street that connects Place St. Patrice (with its recommended hotels and a Saturday market) and the tapestry museum. Ask for the free *Exploration and Emotion: D-Day Landings* booklet, bus schedules to the beaches, and regional information, and inquire about special events and concerts (TI open July-Aug Mon-Sat 9:00-19:00, Sun 9:00-13:00

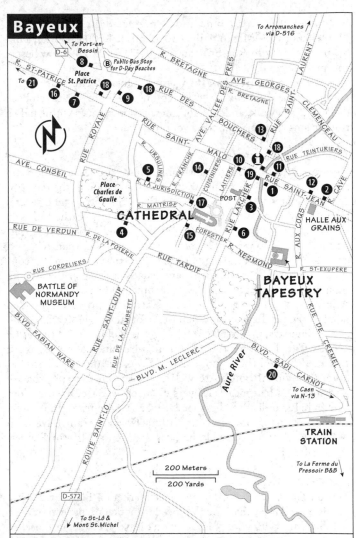

NORMANDY

1. Villa Lara, Hôtel Churchill & Carrefour City Grocery
2. Hôtel le Lion d'Or
3. Hôtel Reine Mathilde & Brasserie
4. Logis les Remparts B&B
5. Manoir Sainte Victoire
6. Le Bistro Bayeusain Chambres
7. Hôtel d'Argouges
8. Hôtel de Sainte Croix
9. Hôtel Mogador
10. Hôtel le Maupassant & Café

11. La Chaumière Deli
12. La Rapière Restaurant
13. L'Angle Saint Laurent
14. Le Pommier Restaurant
15. Pomme Cannelle Restaurant
16. Taverne des Ducs
17. Lace Conservatory
18. Launderettes (3)
19. Bike Rental & Internet Café
20. Scauto Car Rental
21. To Hertz Car Rental

& 14:00-18:00; April-June and Sept-Oct daily 9:30-12:30 & 14:00-18:00; Nov-March daily 9:30-12:30 & 14:00-17:30; on Pont St. Jean leading to Rue St. Jean, tel. 02 31 51 28 28, www.bessin -normandie.com).

For a **self-guided walking tour,** pick up the map called *Découvrez Vieux Bayeux* at the TI. Follow the bronze plates embedded in the sidewalk, and look for information plaques with English translations that correspond to your map.

Arrival in Bayeux

By Train and Bus: Trains and buses share the same station (no bag storage). It's a 15-minute walk from the station to the tapestry, and 15 minutes from the tapestry to Place St. Patrice (and several recommended hotels). To reach the tapestry, the cathedral, and the hotels, cross the major street in front of the station at the traffic light and follow Rue Cremel toward *l'Hôpital*, then turn left on Rue Nesmond. Find signs to the *Tapisserie* (tapestry) or continue on to the cathedral. Taxis are usually waiting at the station, though you may have to call (or ask someone to call one for you). Allow €7 for a taxi from the train station to any recommended hotel or sight in Bayeux, and €20 to Arromanches (€30 after 19:00 and on Sundays, taxi tel. 02 31 92 92 40 or mobile 06 70 40 07 96).

By Car: Look for the cathedral spires and follow signs for *Centre-Ville,* and then signs for the *Tapisserie* (tapestry) or your hotel (individual hotels are well-signed from the ring road—wait for yours to appear). Drivers connecting Bayeux with Mont St-Michel should use the speedy, free A-84 autoroute (closest entrance/exit for Bayeux is at Villers-Bocage; from Bayeux to A-84, take the underpass by the train station to Tilly-sur-Seulles, then Villers-Bocage).

Helpful Hints

Market Days: The Saturday open-air market on Place St. Patrice is much larger than the Wednesday market on pedestrian Rue St. Jean. Both end by 13:00. Don't leave your car on Place St. Patrice on a Friday night, as it will be towed early Saturday.

Grocery Store: Carrefour City, at Rue St. Jean 14, is next to the recommended Hôtel Churchill (Mon-Sat 7:00-22:00, Sun 8:30-12:00).

Internet Access: Right across from the TI, the souvenir shop **Aure Commun** has computer terminals and is open long hours (daily 9:00-20:00, tel. 02 31 22 27 86). The recommended **La Reine Mathilde Brasserie** has free Wi-Fi for customers.

Laundry: A launderette with big machines is a block behind the TI, on Rue Maréchal Foch. Two more launderettes are near Place St. Patrice: One is at 4 Rue St. Patrice and the other is at 69 Rue des Bouchers (both open daily 7:00-21:00).

Bike Rental: Vélos Location has what you need and will deliver to outlying hotels (daily April-Oct 8:00-20:30, closes earlier off-season, across from the TI at Impasse de Islet, tel. 02 31 92 89 16).

Taxi: Call 02 31 92 92 40 or mobile 06 70 40 07 96.

Car Rental: Bayeux offers few choices. **Scauto** (at the Renault dealership) is handiest, just below the train station at the BP gas station. A rental at about €74/day with a 200-kilometer limit is sufficient to see the key sights from Arromanches to Utah Beach—you'll drive about 180 kilometers (16 Boulevard Sadi-Carnot, tel. 02 31 51 18 51, fax 02 31 51 18 30). **Hertz** is the only agency in town that allows you to drop off in a different city (located west of the city center on Route de Cherbourg, off D-613, tel. 02 31 92 03 26).

Day Trip to Caen Memorial Museum: France's most complete D-Day museum (described on page 334) is a manageable day trip from Bayeux, thanks to frequent and quick (20-minute) rail service between Bayeux and Caen, and easy access to the museum from Caen's train station. It's a 30-minute drive from Bayeux to the museum.

Sights in Bayeux

▲▲▲**Bayeux Tapestry (Tapisserie de Bayeux)**—Made of wool embroidered onto linen cloth, this historically precious docu-

ment is a mesmerizing 70-yard-long cartoon. The tapestry tells the story of William the Conqueror's rise from duke of Normandy to king of England, and shows his victory over England's King Harold at the Battle of Hastings in 1066. Long and skinny, the tapestry was designed to hang in the nave of Bayeux's cathedral as a reminder for locals of their ancestor's courage. The terrific museum that houses the tapestry is an unusually good chance to teach your kids about the Middle Ages: Models, mannequins, a movie, and more make it an engaging, fun place to visit.

Cost and Hours: €8, includes an excellent audioguide for adults and a special kids' version, daily May-Aug 9:00-18:15, March-April and Sept-Oct 9:00-17:45, Nov-Feb 9:30-11:45 & 14:00-17:15—these are first and last entry times, tel. 02 31 51 25 50, www.tapisserie-bayeux.fr. To avoid crowds, arrive by 9:00 or late in the day.

Bayeux History—The Battle of Hastings

Because of this pivotal battle, the most memorable date of the Middle Ages is 1066. England's king, Edward the Confessor, was about to die without an heir. The big question: Who would succeed him—Harold, an English nobleman and the king's brother-in-law, or William, duke of Normandy and the king's cousin? Edward chose William, and sent Harold to Normandy to give William the news. On the journey, Harold was captured. To win his release, he promised he would be loyal to William and not contest the decision. To test his loyalty, William sent Harold to battle for him in Brittany. Harold was successful, and William knighted him. To further test his loyalty, William had Harold swear on the relics of the Bayeux cathedral that when Edward died, he would allow William to ascend the throne. Harold returned to England, Edward died... and Harold grabbed the throne.

William, known as William the Bastard, invaded England to claim the throne. Harold met him in southern England at the town of Hastings, where their forces fought a fierce 14-hour battle. Harold was killed, and his Saxon forces were routed. William—now "the Conqueror"—marched to London, claimed his throne, and became king of England (though he spoke no English) as well as duke of Normandy.

The advent of a Norman king of England muddied the political waters and set in motion 400 years of conflict between England and France—not to be resolved until the end of the Hundred Years' War (1453). The Norman conquest of England brought that country into the European mainstream (but still no euros). The Normans established a strong central English government. Historians speculate that had William not succeeded, England would have remained on the fringe of Europe (like Scandinavia), and French culture (and language) would have prevailed in the New World. Hmmm.

Film: When buying your ticket, ask when they'll show the English version of the 15-minute battle film (runs every 40 minutes, English times also posted at the base of the steps to the theater).

Visiting the Museum: Your visit has three separate parts that tell the basic story of the Battle of Hastings, provide historical context for the event, and explain how the tapestry was made. At a minimum, allow a full hour to appreciate this important artifact.

Your visit starts with the actual **tapestry,** accompanied by an included audioguide that gives a top-notch, fast-moving, 20-minute scene-by-scene narration complete with period music (if you lose your place, find subtitles in Latin). Learn to pause your audioguide so you can stop and focus when and where you want.

Pay attention to scene 23, where Harold reneges on his oath to William and takes the crown of England. Get close and (almost) feel the tapestry's texture.

Next you'll climb upstairs into a room filled with engaging exhibits, including a full-size replica of the boats William used to cross the Channel, mannequins (find William looking unmoved with his new crown), terrific models of castles (who knew that the Tower of London was a Norman project?), and medieval villages. Good explanations outline the events surrounding the invasion and the subsequent creation of the tapestry. Your visit finishes with a worthwhile 15-minute **film** that ties it all together one last time (in the cinema). You'll exit below, through a *formidable* boutique.

Remember, this is Norman propaganda—the English (the bad guys, referred to as *les goddamns,* after a phrase the French kept hearing them say) are shown with mustaches and long hair; the French (*les* good guys) are clean-cut and clean-shaven—with even the backs of their heads shaved for a better helmet fit.

▲▲**Bayeux Cathedral**—This massive building, as big as Paris' Notre-Dame, dominates the small town of Bayeux. (Make it a point to see the cathedral after dark, when it's beautifully illuminated.)

Cost and Hours: Free, daily July-Aug 8:30-19:00, Sept-June 8:30-18:00.

Visiting the Cathedral: To start your visit, find the small **square** opposite the front entry (information board about the cathedral in rear corner). Notice the two dark towers—originally Romanesque, they were capped later with tall Gothic spires. The cathedral's west facade is structurally Romanesque, but with a decorative Gothic "curtain" added.

Before entering, head just to the left of the cathedral and find the stairs at the top of a walking lane (another information panel is close by). The little rectangular stone house atop the near tower was the **watchman's home,** from which he'd keep an eye out for incoming English troops during the Hundred Years' War...and for Germans five centuries later (it didn't work—the Germans took the town in 1940). Bayeux was liberated on D-Day plus one: June 7. About the only casualty was the German lookout—shot while doing just that from the window of this stone house.

Now step inside the cathedral. The view of the **nave** from the top of the steps shows a mix of Romanesque and Gothic. Historians believe the Bayeux tapestry originally hung here. Imagine it proudly circling the Norman congregation, draped around the nave above the big arches. This section is brightly lit by the huge windows above, in the Gothic half of the nave. The glass was originally richly colored (see the rare surviving 13th-century bits in the high central window above the altar).

Walk down the nave and notice the areas between the big, round **arches.** That busy zigzag patterning characterizes Norman art in France as well as in England. These 11th-century Romanesque arches are decorated with a manic mix of repeated geometric shapes: half-circles, interlocking hatch marks, full circles, and diagonal lines. Notice also the creepy faces eyeing you, especially the ring of devil heads three arches up on the right. Yikes.

Information panels in the side aisles give the facts about the cathedral (in English). More 13th-century Norman Gothic is in the choir (the fancy area behind the central altar). Here, simple Romanesque carvings lie under Gothic arches with characteristic tall, thin lines adding a graceful verticality to the overall feel of the interior).

For maximum 1066 atmosphere, step into the spooky **crypt** (beneath the central altar), which was used originally as a safe spot for the cathedral's relics. The crypt displays two freestanding columns and bulky capitals with fine Romanesque carving. During a reinforcement of the nave, these two columns were replaced. Workers removed the Gothic veneer and discovered their true inner Romanesque beauty. Orange angel-musicians add color to this somber room.

River Walk—Join the locals and promenade along the meandering walking path that follows the little Aure River for about 2.5 miles through Bayeux. The path runs both ways from the TI (find the waterwheel behind the TI and keep walking; path marked on city maps).

Lace Conservatory (Conservatoire de la Dentelle)—Notable for its carved 15th-century facade, the Adam and Eve house (find Adam, Eve, and the snake) offers a chance to watch workers design and weave intricate lace, just as artisans did in the 1600s. Enter to the clicking sound of the small wooden bobbins used by the lacemakers, and appreciate the concentration that their work requires. You can also see examples of lace from the past.

Cost and Hours: Free, Mon-Sat 10:00-12:30 & 14:30-17:00, until 18:00 in summer, closed Sun, across from cathedral entrance, tel. 02 31 92 73 80, http://dentclledebayeux.free.fr.

Baron Gérard Museum—This museum, home to a modest painting gallery and a collection of porcelain and lace, should reopen in mid-2013, possibly under a different name and with an expanded collection. Ask at the TI for details.

▲Battle of Normandy Memorial Museum (Musée Memorial de la Bataille de Normandie)—This museum provides an excellent and manageable overview of WWII's Battle of Normandy. It's like a compact version of the Caen Memorial Museum—and worthwhile if you won't be visiting there. You'll get a good briefing on the Atlantic Wall (the German fortifications stretching along the coast—useful before visiting Longues-sur-Mer), learn why Normandy was selected as the landing site, understand General Charles de Gaulle's contributions to the invasion, and realize the key role played by aviation. You'll also appreciate the challenges faced by doctors, war correspondents, and civil engineers (who had to clean up after the battles—the gargantuan bulldozer on display looks useful).

Cost and Hours: €7, daily May-Sept 9:30-18:30, Oct-April 10:00-12:30 & 14:00-18:00, may close Jan-Feb, on Bayeux's ring road, 20 minutes on foot from center on Boulevard Fabian Ware, tel. 02 31 51 46 90, www.normandiememoire.com.

Film: A 25-minute film gives a good summary of the Normandy invasion from start to finish (shown in English May-Sept at 10:30, 12:00, 14:00, 15:30, and 17:00; Oct-April at 10:30, 14:45, and 16:15).

Nearby: A right out of the museum leads along a footpath to the **Monument to Reporters,** a grassy walkway lined with white roses and stone monuments listing, by year, the names of reporters who have died in the line of duty from 1944 to today. Some years have been kinder to journalists than others. The path continues to the **British Military Cemetery,** decorated with 4,144 simple gravestones marking the final resting places of these fallen soldiers. The memorial's Latin inscription reads, "In 1944, the British came to free the homeland of William the Conqueror." Interestingly, this cemetery has soldiers' graves from all countries involved in the battle of Normandy (even Germany) except the United States, which requires its soldiers to be buried on US property—such as the American Cemetery at Omaha Beach.

Sleeping in Bayeux

(€1 = about $1.30, country code: 33)
Hotels are a good value here, and it's just a short hop from Bayeux to the D-Day beaches. Drivers should see "Sleeping near Omaha Beach" (page 328) and "Sleeping in Arromanches" (page 319) for more options.

Near the Tapestry

The first two listings sit kitty-corner and share the same owners, who operate a shuttle van to Mont St-Michel (see "Bayeux Connections," later).

$$$ Villa Lara**** offers the town's most luxurious accommodations smack in the center of Bayeux. The 28 spacious and well-configured rooms all have brilliant views of the cathedral, and a few have small terraces. The professional owners—the Héberts—

NORMANDY

and their well-trained staff take excellent care of their guests (Db-€220-280, Db suite-€350-450, elevator, Wi-Fi, exercise room, ice machines, comfortable lounges, free and secure parking, between the tapestry museum and TI at 6 Place de Québec, tel. 02 31 21 31 80, fax 02 31 21 41 66, www.hotel-villalara.com, info@hotel-villalara.com).

$$$ Hôtel Churchill*,** on a traffic-free street across from the TI, could not be more central or more service-oriented, and is owned by the same people as the Villa Lara, above. It has 32 plush rooms with wood furnishings, big beds, and convivial public spaces (standard Db-€120, superior Db-€145, deluxe Db or Tb-€175, Qb-€195, Internet access and Wi-Fi in the comfortable bar/lounge, easy and free parking, 14 Rue St. Jean, tel. 02 31 21 31 80, fax 02 31 21 41 66, www.hotel-churchill.fr, info@hotel-churchill.fr).

$$$ Hôtel le Lion d'Or*,** General Eisenhower's favorite hotel in Bayeux, draws an older clientele willing to pay top euro for its Old World character, professional service, and elegant restaurant. The place lives on its reputation, but could use a little work (standard Db-€125, bigger Db-€150, still bigger Db-€175, extra bed-€30, breakfast-€13, no elevator, Wi-Fi, easy parking-€9/day, 71 Rue St. Jean, tel. 02 31 92 06 90, fax 02 31 22 15 64, www.liondor-bayeux.fr, info@liondor-bayeux.fr).

$$ Hôtel Reine Mathilde** is a solid, centrally located value with painless parking and good service. There are 16 tight but sharp rooms above an easygoing brasserie (Db-€60-85, Tb-€70-95, Qb-€85-100), and six larger rooms with three-star comfort next door (Db-€80-105, Tb-€90-125, breakfast-€7.50, Wi-Fi, one block from the TI at 23 Rue Larcher, tel. 02 31 92 08 13, www.hotel-bayeux-reinemathilde.fr, hotel.reinemathilde@orange.fr).

Chambres d'Hôtes near the Cathedral

$$ Logis les Remparts is a delightful, three-room bed-and-breakfast run by charming Christèle and situated above an atmospheric Calvados cider-tasting shop. Rooms are big, comfortable, and homey—one is a huge, two-room suite (Db-€55-90, Tb-€80-100, Qb-€130, cash only for payments under €100, breakfast-€6, Wi-Fi downstairs in shop, a few blocks above the cathedral on the park-like Place Charles de Gaulle at 4 Rue Bourbesneur, tel. 02 31 92 50 40, www.lecornu.fr, info@lecornu.fr).

$$ Manoir Sainte Victoire is a classy, 17th-century building with three comfortable rooms, each dedicated to a different modern artist, and each with views of the cathedral (Db-€90, includes breakfast; rooms have small kitchenettes, Internet access, and Wi-Fi; 32 Rue de la Jurisdiction, tel. 02 31 22 74 69, mobile 06 37 36 90 95, www.manoirsaintevictoire.com, contact@manoirsaintevictoire.com).

$ Le Bistro Bayeusain offers four vinyl-floor-simple, cheap rooms with shared bathrooms over a small restaurant. It's situated below the cathedral and run by the pleasant Alexandra (D-€35, 31 Rue Larcher, tel. 02 31 92 30 08, bistrobayeusain@orange.fr).

Near Place St. Patrice

These hotels just off the big Place St. Patrice (easy parking) are a 10-minute walk up Rue St. Martin from the TI (a 15-minute walk to the tapestry).

$$$ Hôtel d'Argouges*** (dar-goo-zhah) makes an impression as you enter. Named for its builder, Lord d'Argouges, this tranquil retreat has a mini-château feel, with classy public spaces, lovely private gardens, and standard-comfort rooms. The hotel is run by formal Madame Ropartz, who has had every aspect of the hotel renovated (Db-€134-149, Tb-€186, fine family suites-€238, deluxe mega-suite for up to 6 and good for two couples-€335, includes good breakfast, extra bed-€15, secure parking-€5/day, just off Place St. Patrice at 21 Rue St. Patrice, tel. 02 31 92 88 86, fax 02 31 92 69 16, www.hotel-dargouges.com, info@hotel-dargouges.com).

$$ Hôtel de Sainte Croix offers three big rooms with cavernous bathrooms in a traditional manor home (Db-€90, Tb-€130, Qb-€155, cash only, includes good breakfast, 12 Rue du Marché at Place St. Patrice, mobile 06 08 09 62 69, www.hotel-de-sainte-croix.com, contact@hotel-de-sainte-croix.com, friendly Florence).

$$ Hôtel Mogador** is a good two-star value. Choose between simple, wood-beamed rooms on the busy square, or quiet, more colorful, modern rooms off the street. There are no public areas beyond the small breakfast room and tiny courtyard (Sb-€45-55, Db-€55-65, Tb-€68-78, Qb-€81-91, breakfast-€6, Wi-Fi, 20 Rue Alain Chartier at Place St. Patrice, tel. 02 31 92 24 58, fax 02 31 92 24 85, www.hotelmo.fr, lemogador@gmail.com).

$ Hôtel le Maupassant offers 10 no-star, no-frills rooms with just enough comfort. The rooms are above a central café, and the bartender doubles as the receptionist (S-€39, D-€46, Db-€53, Ts-€78, Wi-Fi, 19 Rue St. Martin, tel. 02 31 92 28 53, h.lemaupassant@orange.fr).

In the Countryside near Bayeux

$$$ La Ferme du Pressoir is a lovely, traditional B&B on a big working farm that is immersed in Norman landscapes about 20 minutes south of Bayeux. The five rooms filled with wood furnishings are vintage French—and so are the kind owners, Jacques and Odile (Db-€95, Tb-€110, Qb-€130, 5 people-€140, includes good breakfast, tel. 02 41 40 71 07, Le Haut St-Louet, just off A-84, exit at Villers-Bocage, www.bandbnormandie.com, lafermedupressoir@bandbnormandie.com).

Eating in Bayeux

Drivers can also consider the short drive to Arromanches for seaside options (see page 320).

On or near Traffic-Free Rue St. Jean

This street is lined with cafés, *crêperies*, and inexpensive dining options.

La Chaumière is the best charcuterie (deli) in town; you'll find salads, quiches, and prepared dishes to go (Tue-Sun open until 19:30, closed Sun 13:00-15:00 and all day Mon; on Rue St. Jean across from Hôtel Churchill). The grocery store across the street has what you need to complete your picnic.

La Rapière is a lovely, traditional wood-beamed eatery filled with locals enjoying a refined meal and a rare-these-days cheese platter for your finale. The veal with Camembert sauce is memorable (€29-36 *menus*, closed Wed-Thu, 53 Rue St. Jean, tel. 03 31 21 05 45).

L'Angle Saint Laurent is a popular bistro, run by a husband-and-wife team (lovely Caroline manages the restaurant, Sébastien cooks). You'll dine well on *Normand* specialties in a smart setting (€25-36 *menus*, closed Sun-Mon, 2 Rue des Bouchers, tel. 02 31 92 03 01).

La Reine Mathilde Brasserie, a service-oriented spot, offers bistro fare all day (omelets, big salads, pizza). It also has a marvelous outside terrace with cathedral views (daily with nonstop service 12:00-21:00, a block from Rue St. Jean at 23 Rue Larcher).

Near the Cathedral

Le Pommier, with street appeal both inside and out, is a good place to sample regional products with clever twists in a relaxed yet refined atmosphere. Owner Thierry mixes old and new in his cuisine and decor. His fish and meat dishes are satisfying no matter how he prepares them (good three-course *menu* from €20, open daily, 38 Rue des Cuisiniers, tel. 02 31 21 52 10).

Pomme Cannelle is cheap and easy, featuring crêpes, salads, and more for €9, inexpensive *menus*, and best—a killer view of the cathedral from the front terrace (open daily, 2 Impasse Prud'Homme, tel. 02 31 92 95 09).

On Place St. Patrice

Taverne des Ducs provides big brasserie ambience, efficient and friendly service with English-speaking staff, comfortable seating inside and out, a full range of choices from *la carte* (including French onion soup, *choucroute*, and all the classics), and set *menus*. Try the cooked oysters with garlic sauce, or the *dos de cabillaud au*

NORMANDY

beurre (cod in butter sauce). They serve until 23:00 (*menus* from €18, open daily, 41 Rue St. Patrice, tel. 02 31 92 09 88).

Bayeux Connections

From Bayeux by Train to: Paris' Gare St. Lazare (9/day, 2.5 hours, some change in Caen), **Amboise** (12/day, 4-6 hours, 4 hours via Caen and Tours' St-Pierre des Corps, or 6 hours via Paris-Montparnasse and Tours' St-Pierre des Corps), **Rouen** (6/day, 2 hours, change in Caen; more trips possible via Paris' Gare St. Lazare, 4-5 hours), **Caen** (18/day, 20 minutes), **Honfleur** (8/day, 1.5-3 hours by train and bus; 20-minute train to Caen, then 1-hour express bus to Honfleur or more scenic 2-hour bus via the coast; or 1-hour train to Lisieux then 1-hour bus to Honfleur; for bus information, call 02 31 89 28 41, www.busverts.fr), **Pontorson/Mont St-Michel** (2-3/day, 2 hours to Pontorson, then bus to Mont St-Michel; also consider Hôtel Churchill's faster shuttle van—described later).

By Bus to the D-Day Beaches: Bus Verts du Calvados offers minimal service to D-Day beaches with stops in Bayeux at Place St. Patrice and at the train station (schedules at TI, tel. 08 10 21 42 14, www.busverts.fr). Lines #74/#75 run east to Arromanches and Juno Beach (3-5/day, none on Sun Sept-June; 30 minutes to Arromanches, 50 minutes to Juno Beach), and line #70 runs west to the American Cemetery and Vierville-sur-Mer (4/day in summer, 1-2/day off-season, 35 minutes to American Cemetery, 45 minutes to Vierville-sur-Mer). Because of the schedules, you're usually stuck with either too much or too little time at either sight if you try to take the bus round-trip; consider a taxi one way and a bus the other (for taxi information, see page 299).

By Shuttle Van to Mont St-Michel: The recommended **Hôtel Churchill** runs a shuttle van to Mont St-Michel for €58 per person round-trip (€50 one-way, 1.5 hours each way; available to the general public, though hotel clients get a small discount). The van leaves Bayeux at 8:30 and returns by 15:00, allowing travelers three hours at Mont St-Michel. The trip is a terrific deal as you'll get a free tour of Normandy along the way from your knowledgeable driver. For details, see www.hotel-churchill.fr.

D-Day Beaches

The 75 miles of Atlantic coast north of Bayeux, stretching from Ste-Marie-du-Mont to Ouistreham, are littered with WWII museums, monuments, cemeteries, and battle remains left in tribute to the courage of the British, Canadian, and American armies that successfully carried out the largest military operation in history: D-Day. (It's called *Jour J* in French—the letters "D" and "J" come from the first letter for the word "day" in either English or French.) It was on these serene beaches, at the crack of dawn on June 6, 1944, that the Allies finally gained a foothold in France, and Nazi Europe was doomed to crumble.

"The first 24 hours of the invasion will be decisive....The fate of Germany depends on the outcome....For the Allies, as well as Germany, it will be the longest day."
    —Field Marshal Erwin Rommel to his aide, April 22, 1944 (from *The Longest Day*, by Cornelius Ryan)

NORMANDY

June 2009 marked the 65th anniversary of the landings. It was hailed as the last of the great D-Day commemorations, as there likely won't be many veterans alive for the 70th. But that doesn't mean these events will end. All along this rambling coast, locals will never forget what the troops and their families sacrificed all those years ago. A warm regard for Americans has survived political disputes, from de Gaulle to "Freedom Fries." This remains particularly friendly soil for Americans—a place where their soldiers are still honored and the image of the US as a force for good has remained largely untarnished.

Planning Your Time

I've generally listed the D-Day sites in order of importance, with the most visit-worthy first (note that several are closed in January). Most Americans prefer to focus on the American sector (west of Arromanches), rather than the British and Canadian sectors (east of Arromanches), which have been overbuilt with resorts, making it harder to envision the events of June 1944. For more information on visiting the D-Day beaches, www.normandiememoire.com is a useful resource.

D-Day Sites in One Day

If you only have one day, I'd spend it entirely on the beaches and miss the Caen Memorial Museum. (If you want to squeeze in the museum, visit it on your way to or from the beaches—but remember that the American Cemetery closes at 18:00 May-Sept and at

17:00 Oct-April—and you need at least 1.5 hours there.) With the exciting sites and upgraded museums along the beaches, the Caen Memorial Museum is less important for most.

If you're traveling **by car,** begin on the cliffs above Arromanches and see the movie at the Arromanches 360° Theater to set your mood. Walk or drive a quarter-mile downhill to the town and visit Port Winston and the D-Day Landing Museum, then continue west to Longues-sur-Mer. Spend your afternoon visiting the American Cemetery, walking on the beach at Vierville-sur-Mer, and exploring the Pointe du Hoc Ranger Monument. Try to find time for the terrific Utah Beach Landing Museum, and consider visiting the strategic town of Ste-Mère Eglise to learn about the paratroopers' role in the invasion. Make a quick stop at the German Military Cemetery on your way back. Canadians will want to start at the Juno Beach Centre and Canadian Cemetery (in Courseulles-sur-Mer, 10 minutes east of Arromanches), then pick up the itinerary described above.

For those **sans car,** it's easiest to take a minivan tour or taxi from Bayeux, or—for a really full day—combine a visit to the Caen Memorial Museum with their guided minivan tour of the beaches. Public transport is available, though very limited. Many find that a one-day car rental works best.

With More Time
Ideally, spend one day at Arromanches and the Omaha Beach sites, and another half-day at the Utah Beach sites (then head off to Mont St-Michel or Honfleur).

Getting Around the D-Day Beaches

On Your Own
Though the minivan excursions listed below teach important history lessons—drawing Americans and Canadians out of their cars—**renting a car** is a good and less expensive way to visit the beaches, particularly for three or more people (for rental suggestions, see Bayeux's "Helpful Hints" on page 298). Park in monitored locations at the sites, since break-ins are a problem—particularly at the American Cemetery—and consider hiring a guide to join you (see "Private Tours," later).

Hardy souls can **bike** between some sites (though distances are long enough to discourage most). Very limited **bus service** links Bayeux, the coastal town of Arromanches, and the most impressive sites of D-Day (see Bus Verts du Calvados information on page 307). Consider a bus one way and taxi the other. For small groups, hiring a **taxi for the day** is far cheaper than taking a minivan tour, but you don't get the history.

By Taxi

Taxi minivans shuttle up to seven people between the key sites at reasonable rates (which vary depending on how far you choose to go). Allow €240 for an eight-hour taxi day (€300 on Sun) to visit the top Utah and Omaha beach sites. Figure about €20 each way between Bayeux and Arromanches, €34 between Bayeux and the American Cemetery, and €95 for a 2.5-hour visit to Omaha Beach sites from Bayeux or Arromanches (50 percent surcharge after 19:00 and on Sun, taxi tel. 02 31 92 92 40 or mobile 06 70 40 07 96, www.taxisbayeux.com, taxisbayeux@orange.fr). Abbeilles Taxis offer D-Day excursions from Caen (€130 for 3.5-hour visit to Omaha Beach sites, €280 for full-day visit, tel. 02 31 52 17 89, www.taxis-abbeilles-caen.com).

By Fully-Guided Minivan Tour

An army of small companies offers all-day excursions to the D-Day beaches from Bayeux or nearby. The tour companies and guides listed in this section are all quality operators that I trust. Most deliver riveting commentary about these moving sites. Because they pick up and drop off at select train stations, they are popular with day-trippers from Paris. To land one of these top-notch guides, book your tour as far in advance as possible  (three months is best), or pray for a last-minute cancellation. The best way to save on the cost is to hire a guide who offers half-day tours or one who is willing to join you in your rental car (noted in listings below).

Cost: These tours are pricey, because you're hiring a professional guide and driver/vehicle for the day. All guides seem to charge about the same. A few have regularly scheduled departures available for individual sign-up (expect to pay about €50-60/person for a half-day and €90/person for a full day), but many take only private groups (figure €475-500 for up to eight people). Most tours don't go inside museums (which are self-explanatory), but those that do usually include entry fees—ask. Although many operators offer all-day tours only, these guides may do half-day trips: Paul de Winter, Edward Robinson, Normandy Sightseeing Tours, Vanessa Letourneur, Eva Ruttger, Mathias Leclere, and Victory Tours.

Working with Your Guide: Request extra time at the American Cemetery to see the excellent visitor center. Don't be afraid to take charge of your tour if you have other specific interests (some guides can get lost in the minutiae of battles that you don't have time for). Many tours prefer to pick up in or near Bayeux, and a few levy a small surcharge for a Caen pickup. While some companies discourage children, others embrace them.

Scheduled Tours

The following guides accept individual sign-ups for their scheduled departures.

D-Day Historian Tours are run by Paul Woodadge, a passionate historian and teacher who takes your learning seriously. He offers regularly scheduled tours in his minivan several days a week (€85/day) and also gives private tours. His "Band of Brothers Tour" is excellent (tel. 02 31 22 28 82, www.ddayhistorian.com, paul @ddayhistorian.com).

Paul de Winter is clean-cut, serious about teaching, has a PhD in military history, and has written a book titled *Defeating Hitler*. History buffs will be happy, but so will others as Paul's delightful wife and driver, Fiona, helps balance out the conversation (€70/half-day, €95/day, 6-person maximum, private tours available, www.dewintertours.com, info@dewintertours.com).

Normandy Sightseeing Tours delivers a French perspective through the voices of its small fleet of licensed guides. They take individual sign-ups (€50/half-day, €90/day), and will pick you up anywhere you like (for a price). Because there are many guides, the quality of their teaching is less consistent—guides David, Olivier, and Karinne get the best reviews (tel. 02 31 51 70 52, fax 02 31 51 74 74, www.normandy-sightseeing-tours.com, fredericguerin @wanadoo.fr).

Vanessa Letourneur is another capable French native who can guide anywhere in Normandy. She offers half-day tours from Caen for €60/person (mobile 06 98 95 89 45, www.normandy panorama.com).

The **Caen Memorial Museum** runs a busy program of half-day tours covering the American and Canadian sectors in combination with a visit to the museum. This option works well for those who have limited time (see museum listing on page 334). The museum has many guides (some good, some mediocre) and is more likely to have availability when others don't.

Private Tours

The following guides offer tours only for private parties.

Dale Booth is a fine historian and a riveting storyteller. He leads tours for up to eight people to the American, Canadian, and British sectors using your vehicle or his (tel. 02 33 71 53 76, www .dboothnormandytours.com, dboothholidays@sfr.fr).

D-Day Battle Tours are run by WWII enthusiast Ellwood von Seibold. He drives a WWII Dodge Command Car, lives in a

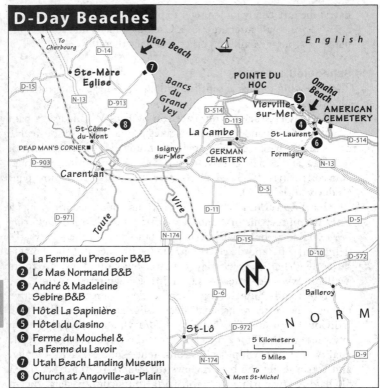

D-Day Beaches

1. La Ferme du Pressoir B&B
2. Le Mas Normand B&B
3. André & Madeleine Sebire B&B
4. Hôtel La Sapinière
5. Hôtel du Casino
6. Ferme du Mouchel & La Ferme du Lavoir
7. Utah Beach Landing Museum
8. Church at Angoville-au-Plain

home where an American paratrooper landed in the garden, and owns a café in Ste-Mère Eglise (C-47 Café) that has the rudder of a WWII-era C-47 transport plane as its centerpiece. He lives this stuff and can explain the events as if you were there (tel. 02 33 94 44 13, mobile 06 32 67 49 15, www.ddaybattletours.com, ellwood @ddaybattletours.com).

Nigel Stewart is a low-key yet capable British guide licensed to lead tours throughout Normandy. He will meet you anywhere in Normandy in his vehicle (4-person maximum), or join you in yours (mobile 06 71 55 51 30, www.dday-guide.com, nigel.normandy @gmail.com).

Normandy Battle Tours are led by likeable, easygoing Stuart Robertson, who loves teaching visitors about the landings. He also owns a bed-and-breakfast near Ste-Mère Eglise and offers combo accommodation/tour packages (tel. 02 33 41

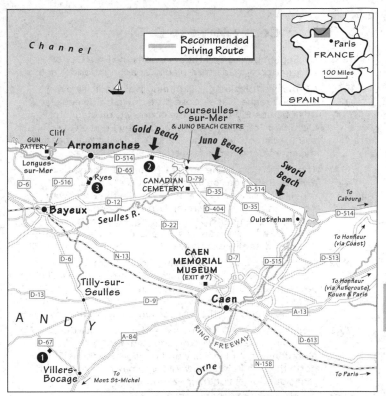

28 34, www.normandybattletours.com, stuart@normandybattle tours.com).

Michael Phillips has been guiding for 16 years and brings a gentle, personal perspective to his tours. He is easy to be with and specializes in private tours (British mobile 0780-246-8599, from France dial 00-44/780-246-8599, www.d-daytours.com, info@d-daytours.com).

Edward Robinson, Irish, informal, and chatty (a national trait?), has previously guided for the Caen Memorial Museum and knows his way around the beaches. He does a terrific tour of the Omaha Beach sector (particularly Pointe du Hoc) and fires important information at you like a machine gun. Taking up to eight passengers in his minivan, he tailors each tour to his clients' needs and tries to get off the beaten track (mobile 06 88 14 19 15, www.battleofnormandytours.com, edrobinson@battleofnormandy tours.com).

Eva Ruttger is young, smart, and energetic. She was raised in Germany and can speak to that perspective when touring the beaches. She offers full- and half-day tours in an eight-person

Countdown to D-Day

1939   On September 1, Adolf Hitler invades the Free City of Danzig (today's Gdańsk, Poland), sparking World War II.

1940   Germany's "Blitzkrieg" ("lightning war") quickly overwhelms France, Nazis goose-step down the Avenue des Champs-Elysées, and the country is divided into Occupied France (the north) and Vichy France (the south, ruled by right-wing French). Just like that, nearly the entire Continent is fascist.

1941   The Allies (Britain, the Soviet Union, and others) peck away at the fringes of "fortress Europe." The Soviets repel Hitler's invasion at Moscow, while the Brits (with American aid) battle German U-boats for control of the seas. On December 7, Japan bombs the US naval base at Pearl Harbor, Hawaii. The US enters the war against Japan and its ally, Germany.

1942   Three crucial battles—at Stalingrad, El-Alamein, and Guadalcanal—weaken the German forces and their ally Japan. The victorious tank battle at El-Alamein in the deserts of North Africa soon gives the Allies a jumping-off point (Tunis) for the first assault on the Continent.

1943   More than 150,000 Americans and Brits, under the command of George Patton and Bernard "Monty" Montgomery, land in Sicily and begin working their way north through Italy. Meanwhile, Germany has to fend off tenacious Soviets on their eastern front.

1944   On June 6, 1944, the Allies launch "Operation Overlord," better known as D-Day. The Allies amass three million soldiers and six million tons of *matériel* in England in preparation for the biggest fleet-led invasion in history—across the English Channel to France, then eastward to Berlin. The Germans, hunkered down in

minivan, or will join your car for less. For a multi-day tour, she can pick you up in Paris and guide in Giverny, Honfleur, or other towns on the way to the D-Day beaches (mobile 06 50 48 68 19, www.visitnormandybeaches.com, info@visitnormandybeaches .com).

Victory Tours is run by friendly Dutchman Roel (pronounced "rule"), who gives half-day, all-day, and two-day tours. His tours are informal and entertaining, but sufficiently informative for most (departs from Bayeux only, tel. 02 31 51 98 14, fax 02 72 68 61 66, www.victorytours.com, victorytours@orange.fr).

Lucie Hoffmann, hip, relaxed, and French, has been guiding for nine years throughout Normandy. Having worked for northern France, know an invasion is imminent, but the Allies keep the details top secret. On the night of June 5, 150,000 soldiers board ships and planes, not knowing where they are headed until they're under way. Each one carries a note from General Dwight D. Eisenhower: "The tide has turned. The free men of the world are marching together to victory."

At 6:30 on June 6, 1944, Americans spill out of troop transports into the cold waters off a beach in Normandy, code-named Omaha. The weather is bad, seas are rough, and the prep bombing has failed. The soldiers, many seeing their first action, are dazed, confused, and weighed down by heavy packs. Nazi machine guns pin them against the sea. Slowly, they crawl up the beach on their stomachs. More than a thousand die. They hold on until the next wave of transports arrives.

All day long, Allied confusion does battle with German indecision—the Nazis never really counterattack, thinking D-Day is just a ruse, not the main invasion. By day's end, the Allies take several beaches along the Normandy coast and begin building artificial harbors, providing a tiny port-of-entry for the reconquest of Europe. The stage is set for a quick and easy end to the war. Right.

1945 Having liberated Paris (August 26, 1944), the Allied march on Berlin from the west bogs down, hit by poor supply lines, bad weather, and the surprising German counterpunch at the Battle of the Bulge. Finally, in the spring, the Americans and Brits cross the Rhine, Soviet soldiers close in on Berlin, Hitler shoots himself, and— after nearly six long years of war—Europe is free.

NORMANDY

four years at the Caen Memorial Museum, she knows her WWII history. She also loves guiding kids (mobile 06 03 09 10 21, lucie hoffmann@msn.com).

Mathias Leclere brings a thoughtful, French perspective to his tour. Born four miles from Juno Beach to a family with three centuries of roots in Normandy, he is part of its soil. Mathias is a self-taught historian who leads half- and full-day tours in his minivan (www.ddayguidedtours.com).

Helpful Hints

Normandy Pass: If you plan to visit several D-Day sites, you can save a few euros by buying the Normandy Pass (€1 added to the full-price admission at your first site). You'll save €1 at most subsequent sites and €4 at the Caen Memorial Museum—but for the best value, don't visit the museum first since you have to pay full price at your first site. The pass is valid for one month and is transferrable to anyone.

Good Map: The free and well-done *Exploration and Emotion: D-Day Landings* booklet gives succinct reviews of 29 D-Day museums and sites with current opening times. It also suggests several driving itineraries that are linked to roadside signposts, helping you understand the significance of the area you are passing through. The map is available at TIs, but you usually need to ask for it.

Food Strategies: The D-Day landing sites are rural, and you won't find a restaurant or grocery on every corner. This is the time to pack that perfect French picnic. Especially if you are traveling with kids, load up on snacks and beverages before heading out. Otherwise, consider timing your lunch to coincide with your visit to Omaha Beach, where you'll find two recommended restaurants nearby (see page 321).

Arromanches

This small town was ground zero for the D-Day invasion. Almost overnight, it sprouted the immense Port Winston, which gave the Allies a foothold in Normandy, allowing them to begin their victorious push to Berlin and end World War II. The postwar period brought a decline. Only recently has the population of tiny Arromanches finally returned to its June 5, 1944, numbers. You'll find a good museum, an evocative beach and bluff (with an interesting film), and a touristy-but-fun little town that offers a pleasant cocktail of war memories, cotton candy, and beachfront trinket shops. Arromanches makes a great base for sightseeing (I've listed accommodations under "Sleeping in Arromanches," later). Sit on the seawall after dark and listen to the waves lick the sand while you contemplate the events that took place here nearly 70 years ago.

Orientation to Arromanches

Tourist Information

The TI has the *Exploration and Emotion: D-Day Landings* booklet, bus schedules, a photo booklet of area hotels, and a list of *chambres d'hôtes* (daily June-Aug 9:30-18:00, Sept-May 10:00-12:00 & 14:00-17:00, opposite the recommended Hôtel d'Arromanches at 2 Avenue Maréchal Joffre, tel. 02 31 22 36 45, www.ot -arromanches.fr).

Arrival in Arromanches

The main parking lot by the museum costs €1 per hour. For free parking and less traffic, look for the lot between the small grocery store and Ideale Hôtel Mountbatten as you enter Arromanches.

Helpful Hints

Post Office: The main **post office** (PTT)—which has an **ATM**—is opposite the museum.

Groceries: A little **supermarket** is a few blocks above the beach, across from the Ideale Hôtel Mountbatten.

Taxi: To get an Arromanches-based **taxi,** call mobile 06 66 62 00 99.

D-Day Sites in Arromanches

In this section, I've linked Arromanches' D-Day sites with some self-guided commentary.

▲▲▲**Port Winston Artificial Harbor**—Start on the cliffs above the town, overlooking the site of the impressive WWII harbor.

Getting There: Drive two minutes toward Courseulles-sur-Mer and pay €2 to park, or park in Arromanches and walk up. Non-drivers can hike 10 minutes uphill from Arromanches, or take the free white train from the museum to the top of the bluff (runs daily June-Sept, Sat-Sun only Oct-May).

◉ Self-Guided Tour: This commentary will lead you around the site.

• *Find the concrete viewpoint overlooking the town and the beaches and prepare for your briefing. Beyond Arromanches to the left is the American sector, with Omaha Beach and then Utah Beach (notice the sheer cliffs); below and to the right lie the British and Canadian sectors (more level terrain).*

Now get this: At a makeshift harbor below, the Allies arrived in the largest amphibious attack ever, launching the liberation of Western Europe. On June 7, 1944—after some pretty serious aerial and seaborne bombing—17 old ships sailed 90 miles across the English Channel under their own steam to Arromanches. Their crews sank them so that each bow faced the next ship's stern, forming a sea barrier. Then 500 tugboats towed 115 football-field-size cement blocks (called "Mulberries") across the channel. These were also sunk, creating a four-mile-long breakwater 1.5 miles offshore. Finally, engineers set up seven floating steel "pierheads" with extendable legs; they then linked these to shore with four mile-long floating roads made of concrete pontoons. Soldiers placed anti-aircraft guns on the Mulberries and pontoons, protecting a port the size of Dover, England. Within just six days of operation, 54,000 vehicles, 326,000 troops, and 110,000 tons of goods had crossed the English Channel. An Allied toehold on Normandy was secure. Eleven months later, Hitler was dead and the war was over.

The **Arromanches 360° Theater** behind you shows a moving film, *The Price of Freedom,* with D-Day footage that flashes back from quiet farmlands and beaches to June of 1944. It's a noisy montage of videos on a 360° screen—stand as near to the center as you can (€4.40, daily Feb-Dec 10:00-18:00, closed Jan, 2 shows/hour at :10 and :40 past the hour, 20 minutes, tel. 02 31 22 30 30, www.arromanches360.com).

• *Head down to the town's main parking lot and find the round bulkhead on the seawall, near the D-Day Landing Museum entry. Stand facing the sea.*

The world's first prefab harbor was created out there by the British. Since it was Churchill's brainchild, it was named Port Winston. Designed to be a temporary harbor (it was used for six months), it was supposed to wash out to sea over time—which is exactly what happened with its twin harbor at Omaha Beach (that one lasted only 12 days, thanks to a terrible storm). If the tide is out, you'll see several rusted floats mired on the sand close in—these supported the pontoon roads. If you stare hard enough at the concrete blocks in the sea to the right, you'll see that one still has what's left of an anti-aircraft gun on it. On the hill beyond the museum, you'll spot a Sherman tank, one of 50,000 deployed during the landings. Behind the museum (not viewable from here) you'll find a section of a pontoon road, an anti-aircraft gun, and a Higgins boat, which was used to ferry 36 soldiers at a time from naval ships to the beaches. If you can, walk down to the beach and wander among the concrete and rusted litter of the battle—and be thankful that all you hear are birds and surf.

▲**D-Day Landing Museum (Musée du Débarquement)**—The D-Day Landing Museum, facing the harbor, makes a worthwhile 45-minute visit and is the only way to get a full appreciation of how the artificial harbor was built. While gazing through windows at the site of this amazing endeavor, you can study helpful models, videos, and photographs illustrating the construction and use of the prefabricated harbor. Those blimp-like objects tethered to the port prevented German planes from getting too close (though the German air force had been made largely irrelevant by this time). Ponder the remarkable undertaking that resulted in this harbor being built in just 12 days, while battles raged. One video (8 minutes, ground floor) recalls D-Day; the other (15 minutes, upstairs) features the construction of the temporary port—ask for times when it is shown in English.

Cost and Hours: €7, daily May-Aug 9:00-19:00, Sept 9:00-

18:00, Oct-Dec and Feb-April 9:30-12:30 & 13:30-17:00, closed Jan, pick up English flier at door, tel. 02 31 22 34 31, www.arromanches-museum.com.

Sleeping in Arromanches

(€1 = about $1.30, country code: 33)
Arromanches, with its pinwheels and seagulls, has a salty beach-town ambience that makes it a good overnight stop. Park in the town's main lot at the museum (€1/hour, free 19:00-9:00). For evening fun, do what most do and head for the small bar at **Restaurant "Le Pappagall"** (see "Eating in Arromanches"), or, for more of a nightclub scene, have a drink at **Pub Marie Celeste,** around the corner on Rue de la Poste. Drivers should also consider my sleeping recommendations near Omaha Beach (see page 328).

$$$ Hôtel de la Marine*** has one of the best locations for D-Day enthusiasts, with point-blank views to the artificial harbor site from most of its 28 comfortable and non-smoking rooms (Db-€116, Tb-€150, Qb-€175, bigger family rooms, includes breakfast, elevator, Wi-Fi, view restaurant, half-board strongly encouraged—figure €85/person, Quai du Canada, tel. 02 31 22 34 19, fax 02 31 22 98 80, www.hotel-de-la-marine.fr, hotel.de.la.marine@wanadoo.fr).

$$ Hôtel d'Arromanches** sits behind Hôtel de la Marine and is a fine value, with nine mostly small but smartly appointed rooms (some with water views), all up a tight stairway. Here you'll find the cheery, recommended Restaurant "Le Pappagall" and English-speaking Louis at the helm (Db-€66, Tb-€72, breakfast-€9, Wi-Fi, 2 Rue Colonel René Michel, tel. 02 31 22 36 26, fax 02 31 22 23 29, www.hoteldarromanches.fr, reservation@hoteldarromanches.fr).

$$ Le Mulberry** is an intimate place with eight handsome rooms and a small restaurant, just a five-minute walk up from the touristy beach (Db-€83-105, Tb-€105-150, includes breakfast, reception closed 13:00-17:00 and after 19:00, a block below the church at 6 Rue Maurice Lihare, tel. 02 31 22 36 05, www.lemulberry.fr, mail@lemulberry.fr).

$$ Ideale Mountbatten Hôtel**, located a long block up from the water, is an eight-room, two-story, motel-esque place with generously sized, clean, and good-value lodgings. Upstairs rooms have a little view over the sea (Db-€80-90, Tb-€100, includes breakfast, Wi-Fi, easy and free parking, short block below the main post office—PTT—at 20 Boulevard Gilbert Longuet, tel. 02 31 22 59 70, fax 02 31 22 50 30, www.hotelmountbatten.com, mountbattenhotel@wanadoo.fr).

NORMANDY

In the Countryside near Arromanches

$$ Le Mas Normand, 10 minutes east of Arromanches in Ver-sur-Mer, is the child of *Provençale* Mylène and *Normand* Christian. Here you get a warm welcome and the best of both worlds: four lovingly decorated, Provence-style rooms wrapped in 18th-century Norman stone (a fifth room is in a renovated, four-person gypsy caravan). There's a lovely yard with ample grass, two dogs, some geese, and no smoking (Db-€70-90, Tb-€120, Qb-€140, discounts for longer stays Nov-March, includes breakfast, Wi-Fi; drive to the east end of little Ver-sur-Mer, turn right at Hôtel P'tit Bouchon, take another right where the road makes a "T," and find the sign at 8 Impasse de la Rivière; tel. & fax 02 31 21 97 75, www.lemasnormand.com, lemasnormand@wanadoo.fr). Book ahead for Christian's home-cooked gourmet dinner, including wine, cider, and coffee (€35/person, requires 4 people, kids' menus available).

$ At **André and Madeleine Sebire**'s B&B, you'll experience a real Norman farm. The hardworking owners offer four modest, homey, and dirt-cheap rooms in the middle of nowhere (Sb-€34, Db-€39, Tb-€44, includes breakfast, 2 miles from Arromanches in the tiny village of Ryes at Ferme du Clos Neuf, tel. 02 31 22 32 34, emmanuelle.sebire@wanadoo.fr, little English spoken). Try these directions: Follow signs into Ryes, then locate the faded green *Chambres d'Hôte* sign opposite the village's lone restaurant. Follow that sign onto Rue de la Forge, cross a tiny bridge, turn right onto Rue de la Tringale, and follow it for a half-mile until you see a small sign on the right to *Le Clos Neuf.* Park near the tractors.

Eating in Arromanches

You'll find cafés, *crêperies,* and shops selling sandwiches to go (ideal for beachfront picnics). The following restaurants offer reliable dining.

The lively **Le Bistro d'Arromanches,** on a short traffic-free street, has good prices and reliable, basic bistro fare (€8-12 pizza and pasta, €7-13 salads, daily, 19 Rue du Maréchal Joffre, tel. 02 31 22 31 32).

Restaurant "Le Pappagall" (French slang for "parakeet") has tasty mussels, filling fish *choucroute,* "*les* feesh and cheeps," salads, and a full menu with fair prices (€19-29 *menus,* see Hôtel d'Arromanches listing, earlier).

Lose the crowds at *crêperie* **La Ripaille,** a short block inland from the busy main drag. Sweet Sylvie will serve you a filling deep-dish crêpe with a green salad for €10 (closed Sun, 14 Rue du Colonel René Michel, tel. 02 31 51 02 31).

Hôtel de la Marine allows you to dine or drink in style on the water. The cuisine gets mixed reviews, but the view doesn't (*menus* from €24, cool bar with same views, daily, see hotel listing earlier).

Arromanches Connections

From Arromanches by Bus to: Bayeux (bus #74/#75, 3-5/day, Sept-June no bus Sun, 30 minutes); **Juno Beach** (bus #74/#75, 20 minutes). The bus stop is near the main post office, four long blocks above the sea (the stop for Bayeux is on the sea side of the street; the stop for Juno Beach is on the post office side).

American D-Day Sites West of Arromanches

The American sector is divided between Omaha and Utah beaches. Omaha Beach starts a few miles west of Arromanches and has the most important sites for visitors, including the American Cemetery and Pointe du Hoc (four miles west of Omaha). Utah Beach sites are farther away (on the road to Cherbourg), and though they may be less visited, they were also critical to the ultimate success of the Normandy invasion. The American Airborne sector covers a broad area behind Utah Beach and centers on Ste-Mère Eglise. You'll see memorials sprouting up all around the countryside.

Omaha Beach D-Day Sites

▲Longues-sur-Mer Gun Battery

Four German casemates (three with guns intact)—built to guard against seaborne attacks—hunker down at the end of a country road. The guns, 300 yards inland, were arranged in a semicircle to maximize the firing range east and west, and are the only original coastal artillery guns remaining in place in the D-Day region. (Much was scrapped after the war, long before people thought of tourism.) This battery was a critical link in Hitler's Atlantic Wall defense, which consisted of more than 15,000 structures stretching from Norway to the Pyrenees. The guns could hit targets up to 12 miles away with relatively fine accuracy if linked to good target information. The Allies had to take them out.

Enter the third bunker you pass. It took seven soldiers to manage each gun, which could be loaded and fired six times per minute (the shells weighed 40 pounds). Judging from the echoes you hear inside the bunker, you can imagine the terrible noise that was made each time the gun fired. Outside, climb above the bunker and find the hooks that were used to secure camouflage netting, making it impossible for bombers to locate them.

A lone observation bunker (look for the low-lying concrete bunker roof on the cliffs) was designed to direct the firing; field telephones connected the bunker to the gun batteries by underground wires. Walk to the observation bunker to appreciate the strategic view over the channel. From here you can walk along the glorious *Sentier du Littoral* (coastal path) above the cliffs and see Arromanches in the distance. Or enjoy more views by driving five minutes down to the water (continue on the small road past the parking lot).

Cost and Hours: Free and always open. The €5 booklet is helpful, but skip the €4 tour.

Getting There: You'll find the guns 10 minutes west of Arromanches on D-514. Follow *Port en Bessin* signs; once in Longues-sur-Mer, follow *Batterie* signs.

▲▲▲WWII Normandy American Cemetery and Memorial

"Soldiers' graves are the greatest preachers of peace."
—Albert Schweitzer

Crowning a bluff just above Omaha Beach and the eye of the D-Day storm, 9,387 brilliant white-marble crosses and Stars of David glow in memory of Americans who gave their lives to free Europe on the beaches below. You'll want to spend at least 1.5 hours at this stirring site.

Cost and Hours: Free, daily May-Sept 9:00-18:00, Oct-April 9:00-17:00, tel. 02 31 51 62 00, www.abmc.gov. Park carefully, as break-ins have been a problem. You'll find good WCs and water fountains at the parking lot. Guided tours are offered a few times a day in high season—call ahead for times.

Getting There: The cemetery is just east of St-Laurent-sur-Mer and northwest of Bayeux in Colleville-sur-Mer. From route D-514, directional signs will point the way.

➲ Self-Guided Tour: Your visit begins at the impressive **Visitor Center.** Pass security, pick up the handout, sign the register, and allow time to appreciate the superb exhibit. On the arrival floor, computer terminals provide access to a database containing the story of each US serviceman who died in Normandy.

Descend one level, where you'll learn about the invasion

preparations and the immense logistical challenges they presented. The heart of the center tells the stories of the individuals who gave their lives to liberate people they could not know, and shows the few possessions they died with. This adds a personal touch to the D-Day landings and prepares visitors for the fields of white crosses and Stars of David outside. The pressure on these men to succeed in this battle is palpable. There are a manageable number of display cases, a few moving videos (including an interview with Dwight Eisenhower), and a must-see 16-minute film (cushy theater chairs, on the half-hour, you can enter late).

A lineup of informational plaques provides a worthwhile and succinct overview of key events from September 1939 to June 5, 1944. Starting with June 6, 1944, the plaques present the progress of the landings in three-hour increments. Amazingly, Omaha Beach was secured within six hours of the landings.

A path from the visitor center leads to a bluff overlooking the piece of Normandy **beach** called "that embattled shore—portal of freedom." It's quiet and peaceful today, but the horrific carnage of June 6, 1944, is hard to forget. A good orientation table looks over the sea. Nearby, steps climb down to the beautiful beach below. A walk on the beach is a powerful experience and a must if you are *sans* both car and tour. Visitors with cars can drive to the beach at Vierville-sur-Mer (see next listing).

In the **cemetery,** you'll find a striking memorial with a soaring statue representing the spirit of American youth. Around the statue, giant reliefs of the Battle of Normandy and the Battle of Europe are etched on the walls. Behind is the semicircular Garden of the Missing, with the names of 1,557 soldiers who were never found. A small metal knob next to the name indicates one whose body was eventually found—there aren't many.

Finally, wander through the peaceful and poignant sea of headstones. Notice the names, home states, and dates of death (but no birth dates) inscribed on each. Dog-tag numbers are etched into the lower backs of the crosses. During the campaign, the dead were buried in temporary cemeteries throughout various parts of Normandy. After the war, the families of the soldiers could decide  whether their loved ones should remain with their comrades or be brought home (61 percent opted for repatriation).

A disproportionate number of officers are buried here, including General Theodore Roosevelt, Jr., who joined the invasion

NORMANDY

despite having a weak heart—he died from a heart attack one month after D-Day (you can find Ted's and his brother Quentin's graves along the sea, about 150 yards down, in the second grouping of graves just after the row 27 marker—look for the gold lettering). Families knew that these officers would want to be buried alongside the men with whom they fought. Also buried here are two of the Niland brothers, now famous from *Saving Private Ryan* (in the middle of the cemetery, just before the circular chapel, turn right just after the letter "F").

France has given the US permanent free use of this 172-acre site. It is immaculately maintained by the American Battle Monuments Commission.

▲Vierville-sur-Mer and Omaha Beach

This essential detour for drivers allows direct access onto Omaha Beach. From the American Cemetery, drive west along D-514 into St-Laurent, then take a one-way loop drive along the beach, following *Vierville par la Côte* signs on D-517. As you drop down toward the beach, stop at the **Omaha Beach Museum** (Musée Memorial d'Omaha Beach) parking lot. Outside the museum, you'll see a rusted metal object with several legs, called a "Czech hedgehog"—thousands of these were placed on the beaches by the Germans to foil the Allies' advance. Find the American 155 mm gun nearby, and keep this image in mind for your stop at Pointe du Hoc (this artillery piece is similar in size to the German guns that were targeted by US Army Rangers at that site). The Sherman tank is one of very few remaining along the D-Day beaches. The museum itself is worthwhile for those with time and curiosity to learn more about the Omaha Beach battles. Allow 45 minutes (€6, daily June-Sept 9:30-19:00, Oct-March 10:00-18:00, good 20-minute film).

A right turn along the water leads to **Le Ruquet** (where the road ends), a good place to appreciate the challenges that American soldiers faced on D-Day. The small German bunker and embedded gun protected this point, which offered the easiest access inland from Omaha Beach. It was here that the Americans would establish their first road inland.

Find your way out to the beach and stroll to the right, below the American Cemetery, to better understand the assignment that American forces were handed on June 6: You're wasted from a lack of sleep and nervous anticipation. Now you get seasick too, as you're about to land in a small, flat-bottomed boat, cheek-to-jowl with 35 other soldiers. Your water-soaked pack feels like a boulder, and your gun feels heavier. The boat's front ramp drops open, and you run for your life for 500 yards through water and sand onto this open beach, dodging bullets from above (the landings had to occur at low tide so that mines would be visible).

Omaha Beach witnessed by far the most intense battles of any along the D-Day beaches. The hills above were heavily fortified, and a single German machine gun could fire 1,200 rounds a minute. That's right—1,200. It's amazing that anyone survived. The highest casualty rates in Normandy occurred at Omaha Beach, nicknamed "Bloody Omaha." Though there are no accurate figures for D-Day, it is estimated that on the first day of the campaign, the Allies suffered 10,500 casualties (killed, wounded, and missing)—6,000 of whom were Americans. Estimates for Omaha Beach casualties range from 2,500 to 4,800 killed and wounded on that day, many of whom drowned after being wounded. But thanks to an overwhelming effort and huge support from the US and Royal navies, 34,000 Americans would land on the beach by day's end.

If the tide's out, you'll notice some remains of rusted metal objects. Omaha Beach was littered with obstacles to disrupt the landings. Thousands of metal poles and Czech hedgehogs, miles of barbed wire, and more than four million mines were scattered along these beaches. At least 150,000 tons of metal were taken from the beaches after World War II, and they still didn't get it all. They never will.

If your stomach is grumbling, **Hôtel La Sapinière's** airy and reasonable café is a short walk away (just west of the American Cemetery; see page 328).

Back in your car, retrace your route along the beach (look for worthwhile information boards along the sea) and hug the coast past the flags heading toward the Pointe de la Percée cliff, which, from here, looks very Pointe du Hoc-like (American Army

Rangers mistook this cliff for Pointe du Hoc, costing them time and lives). A local artist made that striking metal sculpture rising from the waves in honor of the liberating forces, and to symbolize the rise of freedom on the wings of hope. Keep hugging the coastline on D-517 and pull over about 100 yards before the Hôtel Casino to find the two German bunkers just below the hotel. Anti-tank guns housed in these bunkers were not aimed out to sea, but instead were positioned to fire directly up the beach.

Look out to the ocean. It was here that the Americans assembled their own floating bridge and artificial harbor (à la Arromanches). The harbor functioned for 12 days before being destroyed by an unusually vicious June storm (the artificial ports at

NORMANDY

Arromanches and Utah Beach were used until November of 1944). Have a seaside drink or lunch at the casino's café, and contemplate a stroll toward the jutting Pointe de la Percée.

Drive on past the Hôtel Casino on D-517. As you climb away from the beach, look to your left and try to find two small concrete window frames high in the cliff that served German machine gun nests, and notice the pontoon bridge on the right that had been installed at this beach. After the storm, it was moved to Arromanches and used as a second off-loading ramp. It was discovered only a few years ago...in a junkyard.

At the junction with D-514, turn right (west) toward Pointe du Hoc. Along the way, in the hamlet of Englesqueville la Percée, you'll see a 10th-century fortified farm on the left offering Calvados tastings. To try some, cross the drawbridge, ring the rope bell, and meet charming owners Souzic and Bernard Lebrec. Start with their cider, move on to Pommeau (a mix of apple juice and Calvados), and finish with Calvados. They also sell various other regional products, including D-Day Honey, which is made by one of the guides I recommend (tel. 09 60 38 60 17, mobile 06 76 37 46 41).

▲▲▲Pointe du Hoc

The intense bombing of the beaches by Allied forces is best experienced here, where US Army Rangers scaled impossibly steep cliffs to disable a German gun battery. Pointe du Hoc's bomb-cratered, lunar-like landscape and remaining bunkers make it one of the most evocative of the D-Day sites.

Cost and Hours: Pointe du Hoc is free and open daily May-Sept 9:00-18:00, Oct-April 9:00-17:00, tel. 02 31 51 62 00.

Getting There: It's off route D-514, 20 minutes west of the American Cemetery.

Visiting Pointe du Hoc: Park near the Information Center (WCs available), then follow the path toward the sea. Upon entering the site, you'll see an opening on your left that's as wide as a manhole cover and about six feet deep. This was a machine gun nest. Three soldiers would be holed up down there—a commander, a gun loader, and the gunner.

Climb to the viewing platform ahead and survey the scene. This point of land was the Germans' most heavily fortified position along the D-Day beaches and held six anti-ship guns capable of firing 12 miles east to west. Omaha Beach is 11 miles to the east; Utah Beach is seven miles to the west. For the American landings to succeed, the Allies had to run the Germans off this cliff. So they bombed it to smithereens, dropping over 1,500 tons of bombs on this one cliff top. That explains the craters. Heavy bombing started in April of 1944, continued into May, and hit its peak on June 6—making this the most intensely bombarded site of the D-Day targets. Even so, only about 5 percent of the bunkers were destroyed. The problem? Multiple direct hits were needed to destroy bunkers like these, which were well-camouflaged and whose thick, dense walls were heavily reinforced.

Walk around. The battle-scarred German bunkers and the cratered landscape remain much as the Rangers left them. You can crawl in and out of the bunkers at your own risk, but picnicking is forbidden—the bunkers are considered gravesites. Notice the six large, round open sites with short rusted poles stuck in a concrete center. Each held an anti-ship gun (picture the 155 mm gun you saw by the Omaha Beach Museum). Destroying these was the Rangers' goal.

Walk to the bunker hanging over the ocean with the stone column at its top. This memorial symbolizes the Ranger "Dagger," planted firmly in the ground. Read the inscription, then walk below the sculpture to peer into the narrow slit of the bunker. Look over the cliff, and think about the 225 handpicked Rangers who attempted a castle-style assault of its steep face. They landed to your right, used ladders borrowed from London fire departments to get a head start up the cliff, and fired rockets to position their grappling hooks and climbing ropes on the cliff face. Timing was critical, as they had just 30 minutes before the rising tide would overcome the men below. Only about a third of the Rangers survived the assault. After finally succeeding in their task, the Rangers found that the German guns had been moved (commander Erwin Rommel had directed that all coastal guns not under the cover of roofs be pulled back due to air strikes). They eventually found the guns stashed a kilometer inland and destroyed them.

Climb down into the bunker, which was the site's communication center, and find the room with the narrow opening. From here, men would direct the firing of the six anti-ship guns via telephone. Also in the bunker are rooms where soldiers ate and slept.

A museum dedicated to the Rangers is in nearby Grandcamp-Maisy.

▲German Military Cemetery

To ponder German losses, visit this somber, thought-provoking resting place of 21,000 German soldiers. This was the original site for the American Cemetery now on Omaha Beach. And compared to the American Cemetery, which symbolizes hope and victory, this one is a clear symbol of defeat and despair. The site seems appropriately bleak, with two graves per simple marker and dark, basalt crosses in groups of five scattered about. Birth and death dates (day/month/year) on the graves make clear the tragedy of the soldiers' short lives. The circular mound in the middle covers the remains of 207 unknown soldiers and 89 others. Notice the ages of the young soldiers who gave their lives for a cause they couldn't understand. A small visitor center gives more information on this and other German war cemeteries.

Cost and Hours: Free, daily April-Oct 8:00-19:00, Nov-March until 17:30, tel. 02 31 22 70 76.

Getting There: It's on N-13 in the village of La Cambe, 15 minutes south of Pointe du Hoc and 15 minutes west of Bayeux (follow signs reading *Cimetière Militaire Allemande*).

Sleeping near Omaha Beach

(€1 = about $1.30, country code: 33)
With a car, you can find better deals on accommodations and wake up a stone's throw from many landing sites. Besides these recommended spots, you'll pass scads of good-value *chambres d'hôtes* as you prowl the D-Day beaches.

$$ Hôtel la Sapinière** is a find just a few steps from the beach below the American Cemetery. A grassy, beach-bungalow kind of place, it has sharp, crisp rooms, all with private patios, and a lighthearted, good-value restaurant/bar (Db-€90, loft Db-€105, Tb/Qb-€130; in Le Ruquet in St-Laurent-sur-Mer—find it a little west of the American Cemetery by taking D-517 down to the beach and turning right; tel. 02 31 92 71 72, fax 02 31 92 92 12, www.la-sapiniere.fr, sci-thierry@wanadoo.fr).

$$ Hôtel du Casino** is a good place to experience Omaha Beach. This average-looking hotel has surprisingly comfortable rooms and sits alone, overlooking the beach in Vierville-sur-Mer, between the American Cemetery and Pointe du Hoc. The halls have pebble walls, and all rooms have views, but the best face the sea: Ask for *côté mer*. Don't expect an effusive greeting. Introverted owner Madame Clémenceau will leave you alone with the sand, waves, seagulls, and your thoughts (Db-€78, view Db-€84-87, extra bed-€16, view restaurant with *menus* from €27, café/bar on the beach below, tel. 02 31 22 41 02, fax 02 31 22 41 12, hotel-du-casino@orange.fr). Don't confuse this with the Hôtel du Casino in St-Valery en Caux.

$ At Ferme du Mouchel, animated Odile rents four colorful and good rooms with sweet gardens in a lovely farm setting (Db-€55, Tb-€72, Qb-€90, includes breakfast, a few minutes inland in the village of Formigny, well-signed from the beaches, tel. 02 31 22 53 79, mobile 06 15 37 50 20, www.ferme-du-mouchel.com, odile.lenourichel@orange.fr).

$ La Ferme du Lavoir has two good rooms at great prices (one is a huge quad) and cider/Calvados tastings (Db-€47, Tb-€60, Qb-€73, includes breakfast, about 2 miles south of American

Cemetery on Route de St-Laurent-sur-Mer in Formigny, tel. 02 31 22 56 89, www.fermedulavoir.fr, contact@fermedulavoir.fr).

Utah Beach D-Day Sites

▲▲▲Utah Beach Landing Museum (Musée du Débarquement)

This is the best museum on the D-Day beaches and worth the 45-minute drive from Bayeux. For the Allied landings to succeed, many coordinated tasks had to be accomplished: Paratroopers had to be dropped inland, the resistance had to disable bridges and cut communications, bombers had to deliver payloads on target and on time, the infantry had to land safely on the beaches, and supplies had to follow the infantry closely. This thorough yet manageable museum pieces those many parts together in a series of fascinating exhibits and displays.

Cost and Hours: €7.50, daily June-Sept 9:30-19:00, Oct-Nov and Feb-May 10:00-17:30, closed Dec-Jan, last entry one hour before closing, tel. 02 33 71 53 35, www.utah-beach.com. Guided museum tours are sometimes offered—call ahead or ask when you arrive (tours are free, tips appropriate).

Getting There: From Bayeux, travel west toward Cherbourg on N-13 and take the Utah Beach exit (two exits after passing Carentan). Turn right at the exit to reach the museum. An American flag leads to the entry as you approach. The road leaving the museum, the Route de la Liberté, runs all the way from Utah Beach to Cherbourg, and on to Paris and Berlin, with every kilometer identified with road markers.

Visiting the Museum: Built around the remains of a concrete German bunker, the museum nestles in the sand dunes on Utah Beach, with floors above and below sea level. Enter through the glass doors and learn about the American landings on Utah Beach, the German defenses there (Rommel was displeased at what he found two weeks before the invasion), and daily life before and after the occupation. Don't miss the display of objects American soldiers brought to the French (chewing gum, Coke, Nescafé, and good cigarettes).

The highlight of the museum are the exhibits of innovative invasion equipment and videos demonstrating how it worked: the remote-controlled Goliath mine, the LVT-2 Water Buffalo and Duck amphibious vehicles, the wooden Higgins landing craft (named for the New Orleans man who invented it), and a fully restored B-26 bomber with its zebra stripes and 11 menacing machine guns—without which the landings would not have been possible (the yellow bomb icons indicate the number of missions a pilot had flown). Take time to enter the simulated briefing

NORMANDY

room and sense the pilots' nervous energy—would your plane fly *LOW* or *HIGH*? The stunning grand finale is the large, glassed-in room overlooking the beach, with Pointe du Hoc looming to your right. From here, you'll peer over re-created German trenches and feel what it must have felt like to be behind enemy lines. Many German bunkers remain buried in the dunes.

Church at Angoville-au-Plain

At this simple Romanesque church, two American medics (Kenneth Moore and Robert Wright) treated German and American wounded while battles raged only steps away. On June 6, American paratroopers landed around Angoville-au-Plain a few miles inland of Utah Beach and met fierce resistance from German forces. The two medics set up shop in the small church, and treated American and German soldiers equally for 72 hours straight, saving many lives. German patrols entered the church on a few occasions. The medics insisted that the soldiers leave their guns outside or leave the church—incredibly, they did. In the ultimate coincidence, this 12th-century church is dedicated to two martyrs who were doctors as well.

Pass through the small cemetery and enter the church. Inside, several wooden pews toward the rear still have visible bloodstains. Find the new window that honors the American medics and another that honors the paratroopers. An informational display outside the church recounts the events here; an English handout is available inside.

Cost and Hours: Free, €3 requested donation for brochure, daily 9:00-18:00.

Getting There: Take the Utah Beach exit (D-913) from N-13 and turn right, then look for the turn-off to Angoville-au-Plain.

Dead Man's Corner Museum

In 1944, the Germans used this French home as a regional headquarters. Today, a tiny museum recounts the terrible battles that took place around the town of Carentan from June 6 to 11. A swampy inlet divided Omaha and Utah beaches, and it was critical for the Americans to take this land so that the armies on each beach could unite and move forward. But the Germans resisted, and a battle that was supposed to last one afternoon endured for  five days and left more than 2,000 Americans dead. American soldiers named the road below the museum "Purple Heart Lane."

NORMANDY

The museum is ideal for enthusiasts and best for collectors of WWII paraphernalia (but overkill for the average traveler). Every display case shows incredible attention to detail. Dutch owner/collector/perfectionist Michel Detrez displays only original material. He acquired much of his collection from American veterans who wanted their "souvenirs" to be preserved for others to see. The museum doubles as a sales outlet, with a remarkable collection of D-Day items for sale—both original items and replicas.

Cost and Hours: €6, daily 9:00-18:00 except closed Sun mid-Oct-April, tel. 02 33 42 00 42, www.paratrooper-museum.org/us /DMC.html.

Getting There: It's in St-Côme du Mont, 15 minutes south of Ste-Mère Eglise; from the N-13 highway, go two exits north of Carentan and turn left.

Ste-Mère Eglise

This celebrated village lies 15 minutes north of Utah Beach and was the first village to be liberated by the Americans, due largely to its strategic location on the Cotentin Peninsula. The area around Ste-Mère Eglise was the center of action for American paratroopers, whose objective was to land behind enemy lines in support of the American landing at Utah Beach.

For *The Longest Day* movie buffs, Ste-Mère Eglise is a necessary pilgrimage. It was around this village that many paratroopers, facing terrible weather and heavy anti-aircraft fire, landed off-target—and many landed in the town. One American paratrooper dangled from the town's church steeple for two hours (a parachute has been reinstalled on the steeple where Private John Steele's became snagged—though not in the correct corner). And though many paratroopers were killed in the first hours of the invasion, the Americans eventually overcame their poor start and managed to take the town. They played a critical role in the success of the Utah Beach landings by securing roads and bridges behind enemy lines. Today, the village greets travelers with flag-draped streets and a handful of worthwhile sights.

At the center of town, the 700-year-old **medieval church** on the town square was the focus of the action during the invasion. It now holds two contemporary stained-glass windows that acknowledge the heroism of the Allies. One features St. Michael, patron saint of paratroopers.

Also worth a visit is the **Airborne Museum** (€7, daily April-Sept 9:00-18:30, Oct-Dec and Feb-March 10:00-17:00, closed Jan, 14 Rue Eisenhower, tel. 02 33 41 41 35, www.airborne-museum .org). Housed in two parachute-shaped structures, its collection is dedicated to the daring aerial landings that were essential to the success of D-Day. During the invasion, in the Utah Beach sector

NORMANDY

alone, 23,000 men were dropped from planes (remarkably, only 197 died), along with 1,700 vehicles and 1,800 tons of supplies. In one building, you'll see a Waco glider (104 were flown into Normandy at first light on D-Day) used to land supplies in fields to support the paratroopers. Each glider could be used only once. Feel the canvas fuselage and check out the bare-bones interior. The second, larger building holds a Douglas C-47 plane that dropped parachutists, along with many other supplies essential to the successful landings.

Canadian D-Day Sites East of Arromanches

The Canadians' assignment for the Normandy invasions was to work with British forces to take the city of Caen. They hoped to make quick work of Caen, then move on. That didn't happen. The Germans poured most of their reserves, including tanks, into the city and fought ferociously for two months. The Allies didn't occupy Caen until August of 1944.

Juno Beach Centre

Located on the beachfront in the Canadian sector, this facility is dedicated to teaching travelers about the vital role Canadian forces played in the invasion, and about Canada in general. (Canada declared war on Germany two years before the United States, a fact little recognized by most Americans today.) After attending the 50th anniversary of the D-Day landings, Canadian veterans were  saddened by the absence of information on their contribution (after the US and Britain, Canada contributed the largest number of troops—14,000), so they generated funds to build this place (plaques in front honor key donors).

Cost and Hours: €7, €10.50 with guided tour of Juno Beach, daily April-Sept 9:30-19:00, Oct and March 10:00-18:00, Nov-Feb 10:00-13:00 & 14:00-17:00, tel. 02 31 37 32 17, www.junobeach.org.

Tours: The Centre's 45-minute, English-language guided tours of Juno Beach are definitely worthwhile (€4.50 for tour alone, €10.50 with Centre admission; April-Oct at 10:00, 12:00, and 15:00; July-Aug nearly hourly 10:00-16:00; verify times prior to your visit).

Getting There: It's in Courseulles-sur-Mer, about 15 minutes east of Arromanches off D-514.

Visiting Juno Beach: Your visit to the Centre includes a short film, then many thoughtful exhibits that bring to life Canada's unique ties with Britain, the US, and France, and explain how the war-front affected the home-front in Canada. The Centre also has rotating exhibits about Canada's geography, economy, and more.

To better understand the Canadians' role in the invasion, take advantage of the Centre's eager-to-help, red-shirted "exchange students" (young Canadians who work as guides at the Centre for a 4-month period). They are great resources for what to do and see in "their" area. Be sure to ask for the simple, hand-drawn map showing sights of interest.

The best way to appreciate this sector of the D-Day beaches is to take a tour with one of the Centre's Canadian guides, whose knowledge of the invasion is impressive. The tour covers important aspects of the battles and touches on the changes to the sand dunes and beaches since the war.

Nearby: When leaving the Juno Beach Centre, to the left about 400 yards away you'll spot a huge stainless steel cross. This is La Croix de Tourraine, which marks the site where General de Gaulle landed on June 14, 1944. Information plaques describe this important event, which cemented de Gaulle's role as the leader of free France.

Canadian Cemetery

This small, touching cemetery hides a few miles above the Juno Beach Centre and makes a modest statement when compared with  other, more grandiose cemeteries in this area. To me, it captures the understated nature of Canadians perfectly. Surrounded by beautiful farmland, with distant views to the beaches, you'll find graves marked with the soldiers' names and maple leaves, and decorated with live flowers or plants in their honor. From Courseulles-sur-Mer, follow signs to *Caen* on D-79. After about 2.5 miles (4 kilometers), take the Reviers turnoff at the roundabout.

Caen

Though it was mostly destroyed by WWII bombs, today's Caen (pronounced "kahn," population 115,000) is a thriving, workaday city packed with students and a few tourists. The WWII museum and the vibrant old city are the targets for travelers, though these sights come wrapped in a big city with rough edges. And though Bayeux or Arromanches—which are smaller—make the best base

NORMANDY

for most D-Day sites, train travelers with limited time might find urban Caen more practical because of its buses to Honfleur and easy access to the Caen Memorial Museum.

Orientation to Caen

The looming château, built by William the Conqueror in 1060, marks the city's center. West of here, modern Rue St. Pierre is a popular shopping area and pedestrian zone. To the east, the more historic Vagueux quarter has many restaurants and cafés in half-timbered buildings. A marathon race in honor of the Normandy invasion is held every June 8 and ends at the Memorial Museum.

Tourist Information

The TI is opposite the château on Place St. Pierre, 10 blocks from the train station (take the tram to the St. Pierre stop). Pick up a map and free visitor's guide filled with practical information (Mon-Sat 9:30-13:00 & 14:00-18:30, Sun 10:00-13:00 except closed Sun Oct-March, drivers follow *Parking Château* signs, tel. 02 31 27 14 14, www.tourisme.caen.fr).

Arrival in Caen

These directions assume you're headed for the town's main attraction, the Caen Memorial Museum.

By Car: Finding the memorial is quick and easy. It's a half-mile off the ring-road expressway (*périphérique nord,* take *sortie* #7, look for white *Le Mémorial* signs). When leaving the museum, follow *Toutes Directions* signs back to the ring road.

By Train: Caen is two hours from Paris (14/day) and 20 minutes from Bayeux (18/day). Caen's modern train station is next to the *gare routière,* where buses from Honfleur arrive. There is no baggage storage at the station, though free baggage storage is available at the Caen Memorial Museum. The efficient tramway runs right in front of both stations, and taxis usually wait in front. For detailed instructions on getting to the Caen Memorial Museum, see "Getting There" in the next section.

By Bus: Caen is one hour from Honfleur by express bus (2/day), or two hours by the scenic coastal bus (9/day). Buses stop near the train station.

Sights in Caen

▲▲▲Caen Memorial Museum (Le Mémorial de Caen)

Caen, the modern capital of lower Normandy, has the most thorough and by far priciest WWII museum in France. Located at

NORMANDY

the site of an important German headquarters during World War II, its official name is The Caen Memorial: Center for the History for Peace (Le Mémorial de Caen: La Cité de l'Histoire pour la Paix). With two video presentations and numerous exhibits on the lead-up to World War II, the actual Battle of Normandy, the Cold War, and more, it effectively puts the Battle of Normandy into a broader context. By June of 2013, General Wilhelm Richter's command bunker, which housed the aforementioned German headquarters, should be open in front of the museum.

Cost and Hours: €19, less with a Normandy Pass purchased elsewhere (see page 315), free for all veterans and kids under 10 (ask about family rates). An audioguide (€4) streamlines your visit by providing helpful background for each area of the museum. Open March-Oct daily 9:00-19:00; Nov-Dec and Feb Tue-Sun 9:30-18:00, closed Mon; closed most of Jan; last entry 75 minutes before closing, tel. 02 31 06 06 44—as in June 6, 1944, fax 02 31 06 06 70, www.memorial-caen.fr.

Getting There: Taxis normally wait in front of the train station and are the easiest solution (about €14 one-way, 15 minutes), particularly if you have bags. To reach the museum by public transport (allow 30 minutes for the one-way trip), take the tram from in front of the station. It's the first tram shelter after you leave the train station—do not cross the tram tracks (line A or B, buy €1.20 ticket from machine before boarding, ticket good on both tram and bus for one hour, validate it on tram, departs every few minutes). Get off at the third tram stop (Bernières), then transfer to frequent bus #2 (4-6/hour Mon-Sat, 2/hour Sun). To reach the bus stop (which is signed from the tram stop), exit the tram, cross the street to the left in front of the tram, and walk up Rue de Bernières until you see the bus shelter for #2. To experience the heart of Caen, get off the tram at the next stop, St. Pierre, and explore the pedestrian streets near the church and the château (and the TI), then head down Rue Saint-Jean to Rue de Bernières, turn right, and find bus #2 again.

Returning from the museum by bus and tram is a snap (taxi there and bus/tram back is a good compromise). Bus #2 waits across from the museum on the street's right side (the museum has the schedule), and whisks you to the Quatrans stop in downtown Caen (follow the stop diagram in the bus as you go), where you'll transfer to the tram and get off at the Gare SNCF stop.

Services: The museum provides free baggage storage and free supervised babysitting for children under 10 (for whom exhibits may be too graphic). There's a large gift shop with plenty of books in English, an excellent and reasonable all-day sandwich shop/café above the entry area, and a restaurant with a garden-side terrace (lunch only, located in the Cold War wing). Picnicking in the gardens is also an option.

Minivan Tours: The museum offers good-value minivan tours covering the key sites along the D-Day beaches. Two identical half-day tours leave the museum: one at 9:00 (€64/person) and one at 13:00 or 14:00—depending on the season (€80/person); both include entry to the museum. The all-day "D-Day Tour" package (€111, includes English information book) is designed for day-trippers and includes pick-up from the Caen train station (with frequent service from Paris), a tour of the Caen Memorial Museum followed by lunch, then a five-hour tour in English of the American sector. Your day ends with a drop-off at the Caen train station in time to catch a train back to Paris or elsewhere. Contact the museum for details, reservations, and advance payment.

Planning Your Museum Time: Allow a minimum of 2.5 hours for your visit, including 50 minutes for the movies. You could easily spend all day here; in fact, tickets purchased after 13:00 are valid for 24 hours, so you can return the next day. The museum is divided into two major wings: the "World Before 1945" (the lead-up to World War II and the battles and related events of the war), and the "World After 1945" (Cold War, nuclear threats, world peacemakers, and so on). Though each wing provides stellar exhibits and great learning, I'd spend most of my time on the "World Before 1945."

The museum is amazing, but it overwhelms some with its many interesting exhibits (all well-described in English). Limit your visit to the WWII sections and be sure to read the blue "Context" information boards that give a helpful overview of each subarea. Then feel free to pick and choose which displays to focus on. The audioguide provides similar context to the exhibits.

My recommended plan of attack: Start your visit with the *Jour J* movie that sets the stage, then tour the WWII sections and finish with the second movie *(Espérance)*.

❷ Self-Guided Tour: Begin by watching *Jour J (D-Day)*, a powerful 15-minute film that shows the build-up to D-Day itself (runs every 30 minutes from 10:00 to 18:00, pick up schedule as you enter, works in any language). Although snippets come from the movie *The Longest Day*, most of the film consists of footage from actual battle scenes.

On the opposite side of the entry hall from the theater, find *Début de la Visite* signs and begin your museum tour with a downward spiral stroll, tracing (almost psychoanalyzing) the path

Europe followed from the end of World War I to the rise of fascism to World War II.

The lower level gives a thorough look at how World War II was fought—from General Charles de Gaulle's London radio broadcasts to Hitler's early missiles to wartime fashion to the D-Day landings. Videos, maps, and countless displays relate the war's many side stories, including the Battle of Britain, the French Resistance, German death camps, and the Battle of Stalingrad. Remember to read the blue "Context" panels in each section, and then be selective about how much detail you want after that. Several powerful exhibits summarize the terrible human costs of World War II (Russia alone saw 21 million of its people die during the war; the US lost 300,000).

After exploring the WWII sections, try to see the second movie *(Espérance—"Hope"),* a thrilling sweep through the pains and triumphs of the 20th century (hourly, 20 minutes, good in all languages, shown in the main entry hall).

The Cold War wing sets the scene for this era with audio testimonies and photos of European cities destroyed during World War II. It continues with a helpful overview of the bipolar world that followed the war, with fascinating insights into the psychological battle waged by the Soviet Union and the US for the hearts and minds of their people until the fall of communism. The wing culminates with a major display recounting the fall of the Berlin Wall.

The museum also celebrates the irrepressible human spirit in the Gallery of Nobel Peace Prizewinners. It honors the courageous and too-often-inconspicuous work of people such as Andrei Sakharov, Elie Wiesel, and Desmond Tutu, who understood that peace is more than an absence of war.

An exhibit labeled *Taches d'Opinion* highlights the role of political cartoonists in expressing dissatisfaction with a range of government policies, from military to environmental to human rights issues.

The finale is a walk through the US Armed Forces Memorial Garden (Vallée du Mémorial). On a visit here, I was bothered at first by the seemingly mindless laughing of lighthearted children, unable to appreciate the gravity of their surroundings. Then I read this inscription on the pavement: "From the heart of our land flows the blood of our youth, given to you in the name of freedom." And their laughter made me happy.

Mont St-Michel

For more than a thousand years, the distant silhouette of this island abbey sent pilgrims' spirits soaring. Today, it does the same for tourists. Mont St-Michel, among the top four pilgrimage sites in Christendom through the ages, floats like a mirage on the horizon. Today, several million visitors—far more tourists than pilgrims—flood the single street of the tiny island each year.

The year 2012 was a momentous one for this timeless abbey. The causeway that for more than 100 years has brought tourists to Mont St-Michel's front door was closed to car traffic (it will eventually be demolished—see "The Causeway and Its Demise" sidebar). Instead of parking along the causeway, drivers now park on the mainland and either walk or ride a *navette* (shuttle) to the island.

Orientation to Mont St-Michel

Mont St-Michel is surrounded by a vast mudflat and connected to the mainland by a half-mile causeway (soon to be replaced by

a bridge). Think of the island as having three parts: the fortified abbey soaring above, the petite village squatting in the middle, and the lower-level medieval fortifications. The village has just one main street on which you'll find all the hotels, restaurants, and trinkets. Between 11:00 and 16:00, tourists trample the dreamscape (much like earnest pilgrims did 800 years ago). A ramble on the ramparts offers mudflat views and an escape from the tourist zone. Though several tacky history-in-wax museums tempt visitors, the only worthwhile sights are the abbey at the summit of the island, and views from the ramparts and quieter lanes as you descend.

Daytime Mont St-Michel is a touristy gauntlet—worth a stop, but a short one will do. Arrive late and depart early. To avoid the human traffic jam on the main drag, follow the detour path up or down the mount (described on page 345). The tourist tide recedes late each afternoon. On nights from autumn through spring, the island stands serene, its floodlit abbey towering above a sleepy village. The abbey interior should be open until 23:00 in July and August (Mon-Sat).

The "village" on the mainland side of the causeway (called La

NORMANDY

The Causeway and Its Demise

In 1878, a causeway was built that allowed Mont St-Michel's pilgrims to come and go regardless of the tide (and without hip boots). The causeway increased the flow of visitors, but stopped the flow of water around the island. The result: Much of the bay silted up, and Mont St-Michel is no longer an island.

An ambitious project is well under way to return the island to its original form (an information center located in the car parking lot does a good job of explaining the project). Plans involve replacing the causeway with a super-sleek bridge (allowing water to flow underneath) and moving all car and bus parking off-site. The first phase, completed in 2010, saw the construction of a dam *(barrage)* on the Couesnon River, which traps water at high tide and releases it at low tide, flushing the bay and forcing sediment out to the sea (the dam also provides great views of the abbey from its sleek wood benches). In 2011, public parking near the island was removed and the remote lot was built. In 2012, *navettes* (shuttles) began taking visitors from the parking lot to the island.

The entire project won't be completed until 2015. As you approach the island, expect to see cranes and busy workers. For the latest, visit www.projetmontsaintmichel.fr.

Caserne) consists of a line-up of modern hotels and a handful of shops.

Tourist Information

A good information center about the causeway project is in the car parking lot. It has an English-speaking staff and slick touch-screen monitors describing the various phases of construction (daily 9:00-18:00).

The full-service TI is on your left as you enter Mont St-Michel's gates. They have listings of *chambres d'hôtes* on the mainland, English tour times for the abbey, tour times for walks outside the island, bus schedules, and the tide table *(Horaires des Marées)*, which is essential if you plan to explore the mudflats outside Mont St-Michel (daily July-Aug 9:00-19:00, March-June and Sept-Oct 9:00-12:30 & 14:00-18:00, Nov-Feb 10:00-12:30 & 14:00-17:00; tel. 02 33 60 14 30, www.ot-montsaintmichel.com). A post office (PTT) and ATM are 50 yards beyond the TI.

Arrival in Mont St-Michel

Prepare for lots of walking, particularly if you arrive by car and are not sleeping on the island or in nearby la Caserne.

By Train: The nearest train station is in Pontorson (called

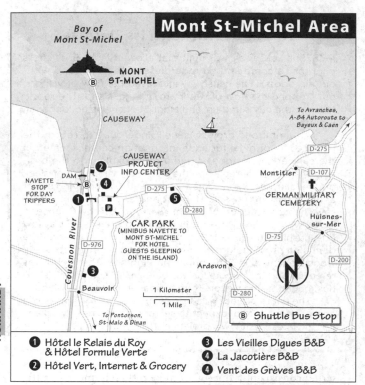

Mont St-Michel Area

Bay of Mont St-Michel

MONT ST-MICHEL

CAUSEWAY

To Avranches, A-84 Autoroute to Bayeux & Caen

D-275

CAUSEWAY PROJECT INFO CENTER

Montitier   D-107

NAVETTE STOP FOR DAY TRIPPERS

DAM

D-275

GERMAN MILITARY CEMETERY

D-280

Huisnes-sur-Mer

Couesnon River

D-976

CAR PARK (MINIBUS NAVETTE TO MONT ST-MICHEL FOR HOTEL GUESTS SLEEPING ON THE ISLAND)

D-75

D-200

Ardevon

N

Beauvoir

1 Kilometer

1 Mile

D-280

To Pontorson, St-Malo & Dinan

B Shuttle Bus Stop

❶ Hôtel le Relais du Roy & Hôtel Formule Verte

❷ Hôtel Vert, Internet & Grocery

❸ Les Vieilles Digues B&B

❹ La Jacotière B&B

❹ Vent des Grèves B&B

NORMANDY

Pontorson–Mont St-Michel). The few trains that stop here are met by a bus in front waiting to take passengers to Mont St-Michel (about €2.50, 12 buses/day July-Aug, 8/day Sept-June, fewer on Sun, 20 minutes; takes you to within 300 yards of the entry gate of Mont St-Michel). Taxis between Pontorson and Mont St-Michel get you to near the *navette* stop (350 yards from the entry gate) and cost about €18 (€26 after 19:00 and on weekends/holidays; tel. 02 33 60 33 23 or 02 33 60 82 70). If you plan to arrive on Saturday night, beware that Sunday train service from Pontorson is almost nonexistent.

By Bus: Buses from Rennes and St-Malo get you to within 300 yards of Mont St-Michel's entry gate (for details, see "Mont St-Michel Connections" at the end of this chapter). From Bayeux, it's faster to arrive on Hôtel Churchill's minivan shuttle (see page 307).

By Car: You'll be directed to a sea of parking as you approach Mont St-Michel (€8.50/24 hours, no re-entry privileges—if you leave and return on the same day, you'll pay another €8.50).

From the parking lot, it's a half-mile walk to the *navette* stop. From there you can either continue walking to the island, take the short ride on the free *navette* (departures every few minutes), or take the horse-drawn *maringote* (double-decker wagon, €4). Both the *navette* and *maringote* drop you off 350 yards from the island. There's talk of extending the *navette* service all the way to the car parking lot in 2013; check www.accueilmontsaintmichel.com for the latest.

Those staying at a hotel on the island have the option of riding a minibus *navette* (smaller than a regular *navette*) directly from the parking lot to the very foot of the island (avoiding the walk described above; must book in advance through your hotel). The minibus *navette* is also available to those with walking difficulties (best to call ahead to reserve a seat, tel. 02 14 13 20 00).

If you're staying overnight in La Caserne, your hotel will give you a code to pass through a barrier so you can park right at your hotel (€1.50 fee; get directions from your hotelier).

Helpful Hints

Tides: The tides here rise above 50 feet—the largest and most dangerous in Europe, and second in the world after the Bay of Fundy between New Brunswick and Nova Scotia, Canada. High tides *(grandes marées)* lap against the TI door (where you'll find tide hours posted).

Internet and Groceries: The industrious **Hôtel Vert,** located in La Caserne, has Internet access and Wi-Fi, a 24-hour grocery store and rooms for rent (hotel described under "Sleeping in Mont St-Michel," later).

Taxi: Call 02 33 60 33 23 or 02 33 60 26 39.

Guided Tours: Several top-notch guides can lead you through the abbey's complex history. The best are found in Bayeux, a good base for a daytrip to Mont St-Michel. **Nigel Stewart** and **Lucie Hoffmann** (see listings under "Getting Around the D-Day Beaches" on page 309) are good choices. **Westcapades** provides transportation from St-Malo with minimal commentary (tel. 02 96 39 79 52, www.westcapades.com, marc @westcapades.com; see page 356).

Guided Walks: The **TI** may offer guided walks of the village below the abbey (ask ahead). They also have information on inexpensive guided walks across the bay (with some English). **La Traversée Traditionelle** traces the footsteps of pilgrims, starting across the bay at Le Bec d'Andaine and walking over the mudflat to Mont St-Michel (verify that the guide speaks some English, weekends only, May-Oct; about €6, 4 miles— or 1.75 hours—each way, round-trip takes 4.5 hours, including one hour on Mont St-Michel; ask at TI or call 02 33 89 80 88, www.cheminsdelabaie.com). For a tour within the **abbey** itself, see my self-guided tour on page 345.

Crowd-Beating Tips: Arrive after 16:00 and leave by 11:00 to avoid the worst crowds. The island's main drag is wall-to-wall people from 11:00 to 16:00. Bypass this mess by following this book's suggested walking routes (under "Sights in Mont St-Michel").

Best Light: Because Mont St-Michel faces southwest, morning light from the causeway is eye-popping. Take a memorable walk before breakfast. And don't miss the illuminated island after dark (also best from the causeway).

Sights in Mont St-Michel

These sights are listed in the order by which you approach them from the mainland.

Surrounding the Island

The Bay of Mont St-Michel—The vast Bay of Mont St-Michel has long played a key role. Since the sixth century, hermit-monks in search of solitude lived here. The word "hermit" comes from an ancient Greek word meaning "desert." The next best thing to a desert in this part of Europe was the sea. Imagine the desert this bay provided as the first monk climbed the rock to get close to God. Add to that the mythic tide, which sends the surf speeding eight miles in and out with each tide cycle. Long before the causeway was built, when Mont St-Michel was an island, pilgrims would approach across the mudflat, aware that the tide swept in "at the speed of a galloping horse" (well, maybe a trotting horse—12 m.p.h., or about 18 feet per second at top speed).

Quicksand was another peril. A short stroll onto the sticky sand helps you imagine how easy it would be to get one or both feet stuck as the tide rolled in. The greater danger for adventurers today is the thoroughly disorienting fog and the fact that the sea can encircle unwary hikers. (Bring a mobile phone.) Braving these devilish risks for centuries, pilgrims kept their eyes on the spire crowned by their protector, St. Michael, and eventually reached their spiritual goal.

▲▲Stroll Around Mont St-Michel—To resurrect that Mont St-Michel dreamscape and evade all those tacky tourist stalls, you can walk out on the mudflats around the island (to reach the mudflats, pass through the *gendarmerie,* a former guard station), on the left side of the island as you face it). Take your shoes off and walk barefoot (handy faucets are available on your way back by the *gendarmerie*). At low tide, it's reasonably dry and a great memory-maker. But this can be hazardous, so don't go alone, don't stray far, and be sure to double-check the tides—or consider a guided walk (described under "Helpful Hints," earlier). Remember the scene

NORMANDY

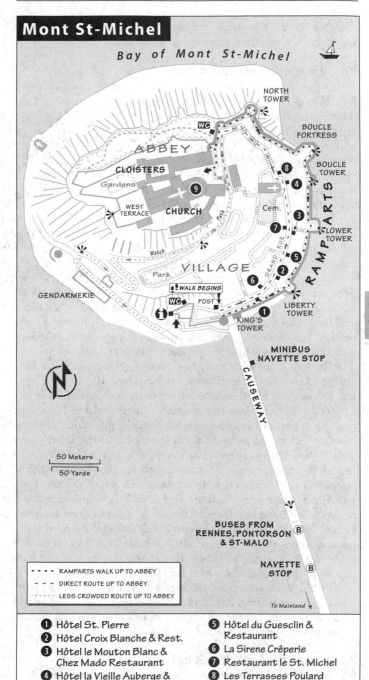

Mont St-Michel

Bay of Mont St-Michel

NORTH TOWER

BOUCLE FORTRESS

WC

ABBEY

CLOISTERS

Gardens

BOUCLE TOWER

8

4

9

WEST TERRACE

CHURCH

Cem.

3

7

LOWER TOWER

Path

Watch

VILLAGE

RAMPARTS

5

Park

6

2

GENDARMERIE

WALK BEGINS

WC

POST

1

LIBERTY TOWER

KING'S TOWER

NORMANDY

MINIBUS NAVETTE STOP

CAUSEWAY

50 Meters

50 Yards

BUSES FROM RENNES, PONTORSON & ST-MALO

B

NAVETTE STOP

B

To Mainland

- - - - RAMPARTS WALK UP TO ABBEY
- - - DIRECT ROUTE UP TO ABBEY
- - - - LESS CROWDED ROUTE UP TO ABBEY

1 Hôtel St. Pierre

2 Hôtel Croix Blanche & Rest.

3 Hôtel le Mouton Blanc & Chez Mado Restaurant

4 Hôtel la Vieille Auberge & Restaurant

5 Hôtel du Guesclin & Restaurant

6 La Sirene Crêperie

7 Restaurant le St. Michel

8 Les Terrasses Poulard

9 Entry to Abbey

from the Bayeux tapestry where Harold rescues Normans from the quicksand? It happened somewhere in this bay.

The Village Below the Abbey

Visitors usually enter the island through a stone arch at the lower left. However, during very high tides, you'll enter through the door in the central tower. The island's main 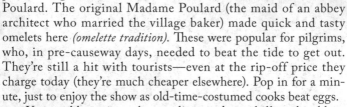 street (Rue Principale, or "Grande Rue"), lined with shops and hotels leading to the abbey, is grotesquely touristy. It is some consolation to remember that, even in the Middle Ages, this was a commercial gauntlet, with stalls selling souvenir medallions, candles, and fast food. With only 30 full-time residents, the village lives solely for tourists. After visiting the TI, check the tide warnings posted on the wall and pass through the imposing doors.

Before the drawbridge, on your left, peek through the door of Restaurant la Mère Poulard. The original Madame Poulard (the maid of an abbey architect who married the village baker) made quick and tasty omelets here *(omelette tradition)*. These were popular for pilgrims, who, in pre-causeway days, needed to beat the tide to get out. They're still a hit with tourists—even at the rip-off price they charge today (they're much cheaper elsewhere). Pop in for a minute, just to enjoy the show as old-time-costumed cooks beat eggs.

You could continue the grueling trudge uphill to the abbey, through the masses and past several gimmicky museums (all island hotel receptions are located on this street). But if the abbey's your goal, bypass the worst crowds and tourist kitsch by climbing the first steps on your right after the drawbridge and following the ramparts in either direction up and up to the abbey (quieter if you go right; ramparts described on page 349). I'd go up one way and return down the other. If crowds really get in your craw, leave the village from the island's main entry arch and make a hard right, passing under the stone arch of the *gendarmerie,* and follow the cobbled ramp up to the abbey (this is also the easiest route up thanks to the long ramps, which help you avoid most stairs).

Public WCs are next to the island TI at the town entry, partway up the main drag, and at the abbey entrance. You can attend Mass at the tiny St. Pierre Church (times posted on the door), opposite Les Terrasses Poulard gift shop.

▲▲Abbey of Mont St-Michel

Mont St-Michel has been an important pilgrimage center since A.D. 708, when the bishop of Avranches heard the voice of

Archangel Michael saying, "Build here and build high." With brilliant foresight, Michael reassured the bishop, "If you build it...they will come." Today's abbey is built on the remains of a Romanesque church, which stands on the remains of a Carolingian church. St. Michael, whose gilded statue decorates the top of the spire, was the patron saint of many French kings, making this a favored site for French royalty through the ages. St. Michael was particularly popular in Counter-Reformation times, as the Church employed his warlike image in the fight against Protestant heresy.

This abbey has 1,200 years of history, though much of its story was lost when its archives were taken to St-Lô for safety during World War II—only to be destroyed during the D-Day fighting. As you climb the stairs, imagine the centuries of pilgrims and monks who have worn down the edges of these same stone steps. Keep to the right, as tour groups can clog the left side of the steps.

Cost and Hours: €9; May-June daily 9:00-19:00; July-Aug Mon-Sat 9:00-23:00, Sun 9:00-19:00; Sept-April daily 9:30-18:00; closed Dec 25, Jan 1, and May 1; last entry one hour before closing (tel. 02 33 89 80 00). Buy your ticket to the abbey and keep climbing. Mass is held daily, except Monday, at 12:15 in the abbey church.

Visiting the Abbey: Allow 20 minutes to hike at a steady pace from the island TI. To avoid crowds, arrive by 10:00 or after 16:00 (the place gets really busy by 11:00). In summer evenings, when the abbey is open until 23:00 and crowds are gone, visits come with music and mood lighting (€9), called *Ballades Nocturnes*. It's worth paying a second admission to see the abbey so peaceful (nighttime program starts at 19:00; daytime tickets aren't valid for re-entry, but you can visit before 19:00 and stay on).

Tours: There are no English explanations in the abbey. Consider renting the excellent audioguide (€4.50, €6/2 people) or take a 1.25-hour English-language guided tour (free but tip requested, 2-4 tours/day, first and last tours usually around 10:00 and 15:00, confirm times at TI, meet at top terrace in front of church). The guided tours, which can be good, come with big crowds. You can start a tour, then decide if it works for you—but I'd skip it, instead following my directions below.

● **Self-Guided Tour:** Visit the abbey by following a one-way route. You'll climb to the ticket office, then climb some more. Stop after you pass a public WC, and look back to the church. That boxy Gothic structure across the steps is one of six cisterns that provided the abbey with water. Inside the room marked *Accueil* you'll find interesting models of the abbey through the ages.

• *Find your way to the big terrace, walk to the round lookout at the far end, and face the church.*

West Terrace: In 1776, a fire destroyed the west end of the church, leaving this grand view terrace. The original extent of the church is outlined with short walls (as well as the stonecutter numbers, generally not exposed like this—a reminder that they were paid by the piece). The buildings of Mont St-Michel are made of granite stones quarried from the Isles of Chausey (visible on a clear day, 20 miles away). Tidal power was ingeniously harnessed to load, unload, and even transport the stones, as barges hitched a ride with each incoming tide.

As you survey the Bay of Mont St-Michel, notice the polder land—farmland reclaimed by Normans in the 19th century with the help of Dutch engineers. The lines of trees mark strips of land used in the process. Today, this reclaimed land is covered by salt-loving plants and grazed by sheep whose salty meat is considered a local treat. You're standing 240 feet above sea level, at the summit of what was an island called "the big tomb." The small island just farther out is "the little tomb."

The bay stretches from Normandy (on the right as you look to the sea) to Brittany (on the left). The Couesnon River below marks the historic border between the two lands. Brittany and Normandy have long vied for Mont St-Michel. In fact, the river used to pass Mont St-Michel on the other side, making the abbey part of Brittany. Today, it's just barely—but definitively—on Norman soil. The new dam across this river (easy to see from here—it looks like a bridge when its gates are open) was built in 2010. Central to the dam is a system of locking gates that retain water upriver during high tide and release it six hours later, in effect flushing the bay and returning it to a mudflat at low tide (see "The Causeway and Its Demise" sidebar on page 339). Walk toward the sea side of the terrace, and look down at the gardens below (where this tour will end).

• Now enter the...

Abbey Church: Sit on a pew near the altar, under the little statue of the Archangel Michael (with the spear to defeat dragons and evil, and the scales to evaluate your soul). Monks built the church on the tip of this rock to be as close to heaven as possible. The downside: There wasn't enough level ground to support a sizable abbey and church. The solution: Four immense crypts were built under the church to create a platform to support each of its wings. While most of the church is Romanesque (round arches, 11th century), the light-filled apse behind the altar was built later, when Gothic arches were the rage. In 1421, the crypt that supported the apse collapsed, taking that end of the church with it. Few of the original windows survive (victims of fires, storms, lightning, and the Revolution).

In the chapel to the right of the altar stands a grim-looking statue of the man with the vision to build the abbey (St. Aubert).

Take a spin around the apse, and find the suspended pirate-looking ship and the glass-covered manhole (you'll see it again later from another angle).

• *After the church, enter the...*

Cloisters: A standard feature of an abbey, this was the peaceful zone that connected various rooms, where monks could meditate, read the Bible, and tend their gardens (growing food and herbs for medicine). The great view window is enjoyable today (what's the tide doing?), but it was of no use to the monks. The more secluded a monk could be, the closer he was to God. (A cloister, by definition, is an enclosed place.) Notice how the columns are staggered. This efficient design allowed the cloisters to be supported with less building material (a top priority, given the difficulty of transporting stone this high up). The carvings above the columns feature various plants and heighten the Garden-of-Eden ambience the cloister offered the monks. The statues of various saints, carved among some columns, were de-faced—literally—by French revolutionaries.

• *Continue on to the...*

Refectory: This was the dining hall where the monks consumed both food and the word of God in silence—one monk read in a monotone from the Bible during meals (pulpit on the right near the far end). The monks gathered as a family here in one undivided space under one big arch (an impressive engineering feat in its day). The abbot ate at the head table; guests sat at the table in the middle. The clever columns are thin but very deep, allowing maximum light while offering solid support. From 966 until 2001, this was a Benedictine abbey. In 2001, the last three Benedictine monks checked out, and a new order of monks from Paris took over.

• *Stairs lead down one flight to a...*

Round Stone Relief Sculpture of St. Michael: This scene depicts the legend of Mont St-Michel: The archangel Michael wanted to commemorate a hard-fought victory over the devil with the construction of a monumental abbey on a nearby island. He chose to send his message to the bishop of Avranches (St. Aubert), who saw Michael twice in his dreams. But the bishop did not trust his dreams until the third time, when Michael drove his thumb into the bishop's head, leaving a mark that he could not deny.

• *Continue down the stairs another flight to the...*

Guests' Hall: St. Benedict wrote that guests should be welcomed according to their status. That meant that when kings (or other VIPs) visited, they were wined and dined without a hint of monastic austerity. This room once exploded in color, with gold stars on a blue sky across the ceiling. (The painting of this room was said to be the model for Sainte-Chapelle in Paris.) The floor was composed of glazed red-and-green tiles. The entire space was bathed in glorious sunlight, made divine as it passed through a filter of stained glass. The big double fireplace, kept out of sight by hanging tapestries, served as a kitchen—walk under it and see the light.

• *Hike the stairs through a chapel to the...*

Hall of the Grand Pillars: Perched on a pointy rock, the huge abbey church had four sturdy crypts like this to prop it up. You're standing under the Gothic portion of the abbey church—this was the crypt that collapsed in 1421. Notice the immensity of the columns (15 feet around) in the new crypt, rebuilt with a determination not to let it fall again. Now look up at the round hole in the ceiling and recognize it as the glass manhole cover from the church altar above.

• *To see what kind of crypt collapsed, walk on to the...*

Crypt of St. Martin: This simple 11th-century Romanesque vault has minimal openings, since the walls needed to be solid and fat to support the buildings above. As you leave, notice the thickness of the walls.

• *Next, you'll find the...*

Ossuary (identifiable by its big treadwheel): The monks celebrated death as well as life. This part of the abbey housed the hospital, morgue, and ossuary. Because the abbey graveyard was small, it was routinely emptied, and the bones were stacked here.

During the Revolution, monasticism was abolished. Church property was taken by the atheistic government, and from 1793 to 1863, Mont St-Michel was used as an Alcatraz-type prison. Its first inmates were 300 priests who refused to renounce their vows. (Victor Hugo complained that using such a place as a prison was like keeping a toad in a reliquary.) The big treadwheel—the kind that did heavy lifting for big building projects throughout the Middle Ages—is from the decades when the abbey was a prison. Teams of six prisoners marched two abreast in the wheel—hamster-style—powering two-ton loads of stone and supplies up Mont St-Michel. Spin the rollers of the sled next to the wheel.

Finish your visit by walking through the Promenade of the Monks, under more Gothic vaults, and into the vast **Scriptorium Hall** (a.k.a. Knights Hall), where monks decorated illuminated manuscripts. You'll then spiral down to the gift shop, turn right, and follow signs to the *Jardin*. The room after the shop holds temporary exhibits related to Mont St-Michel.

• *Exit the room and walk out into the rear garden. From here, look up at the miracle of medieval engineering.*

The "Merveille": This was an immense building project—a marvel back in 1220. Three levels of buildings were created: the lower floor for the lower class, the middle floor for VIPs, and the top floor reserved for the clergy. It was a medieval skyscraper, built with the social strata in mind. The vision was even grander—the place where you're standing was to be built up in similar fashion, to support a further expansion of the church. But the money ran out, and the project was abandoned. As you leave the garden, notice the tall narrow windows of the refectory on the top floor.

• *Stairs lead from here back into the village. To avoid the crowds on your descent, turn right when you see the knee-high sign for* Musée Historique *and find your own route down or, at the same place, follow the Chemin des Ramparts to the left and hike down via the...*

Ramparts: Mont St-Michel is ringed by a fine example of 15th-century fortifications. They were built to defend against a new weapon: the cannon. They were low, rather than tall—to make a smaller target—and connected by protected passageways, which enabled soldiers to zip quickly to whichever zone was under attack. The five-sided Boucle Tower (1481, see map on page 343) was crafted with no blind angles, so defenders could protect it and the nearby walls in all directions. And though the English con-quered all of Normandy in the early 15th century, they never took this well-fortified island. Because of its stubborn success against the English in the Hundred Years' War, Mont St-Michel became a symbol of French national identity.

After dark, the island is magically floodlit. Views from the ramparts are sublime. For the best view, exit the island and walk out on the causeway a few hundred yards.

Near Mont St-Michel

German Military Cemetery (Cimetière Militaire Alle-mand)—Located three miles from Mont St-Michel, near tiny Huisnes-sur-Mer (well-signed east of Mont St-Michel, off D-275), this somber but thoughtfully presented cemetery-mortuary houses the remains of 12,000 German WWII soldiers brought to this location from all over France. (The stone blocks on the steps up indicate the regions in France from where they came.) A display of letters they sent home (with English translations) offers insights into the soldiers' lives. From the lookout, take in the sensational views over Mont St-Michel.

Sleeping in Mont St-Michel

(€1 = about $1.30, country code: 33)
Sleep on or near the island so that you can visit Mont St-Michel early and late. What matters is being here before or after the crush of tourists. Sleeping on the island—inside the walls—is a great experience for medieval romantics who don't mind the headaches associated with spending a night here, including average rooms

and baggage hassles. To reach a room on the island, you'll need to carry your bags 10 minutes uphill from the *navette* stop (you can take the hotel guest-only minibus *navette* directly from the parking area to the foot of the island, but you must book a seat in advance through your hotel). Take only what you need for one night in a smaller bag, but don't leave any luggage visible in your car.

Hotels near the island in la Caserne are a good deal cheaper and require less walking—you can park right at your hotel. All are a short walk from the free and frequent *navette* to the island, allowing easy access at any time.

On the Island

There are eight small hotels on the island, and because most visitors day-trip here, finding a room is generally no problem (but finding an elevator is). Though some pad their profits by requesting that guests buy dinner from their restaurant, *requiring* it is illegal. Higher-priced rooms generally have bay views. Several hotels are closed from November until Easter.

The following hotels are listed in order of altitude; the first hotels are lowest.

$$$ Hôtel St. Pierre*** and **Hôtel Croix Blanche*****, which share the same owners and reception desk, sit side by side (reception at St. Pierre). Each provides comfortable rooms at inflated prices, some with good views. Both have several family loft rooms (non-view Db-€150-190, view Db-€190-210, Tb or Qb-€220-260, €230 for luxury Db in wood-beamed annex—*Logis du Château;* lower rates are for Hôtel Croix Blanche, higher rates for Hôtel St. Pierre; breakfast-€15, Internet access and Wi-Fi, tel. 02 33 60 14 03, fax 02 33 48 59 82, www.auberge-saint-pierre.fr, contact @auberge-saint-pierre.fr).

$$$ Hôtel le Mouton Blanc** delivers a good midrange value, with 15 rooms split between two buildings. The main building *(bâtiment principal)* is best, with cozy rooms, wood beams, and decent bathrooms; the more modern "annex" has cramped bathrooms (Db-€110, loft Tb-€140, loft Qb-€150, tel. 02 33 60 14 08, fax 02 33 60 05 62, www.lemoutonblanc.fr, contact@lemouton blanc.fr).

$$$ Hôtel la Vieille Auberge** is a small place with sharp rooms at fair prices (Db-€120, Tb/Qb-€150-160; spring for one of the four great terrace rooms—Db-€150, Tb-€170; breakfast-€15, check in at their restaurant, but book through Hôtel St. Pierre, listed above).

$$ Hôtel du Guesclin** has the cheapest and best value rooms I list on the island and is the only family-run hotel left there. Rooms have traditional decor and are perfectly comfortable. Check in at the bar on the main street level (Db-€74-90, Tb-€90, breakfast-€9, tel. 02 33 60 14 10, fax 02 33 60 45 81, www.hoteldu guesclin.com, hotel.duguesclin@wanadoo.fr).

On the Mainland

Modern hotels gather in La Caserne on the mainland. These have soulless but cheaper rooms with easy parking and many tour groups. Remember to call at least a day ahead to get the code allowing you to skip the parking lot and drive to your hotel's front door (€1.50 fee).

$$$ Hôtel le Relais du Roy houses tight but well-configured and plush three-star rooms with small balconies allowing "lean-out" views to the abbey. Most rooms are on the river side and have nice countryside views (Db-€92-105, Wi-Fi, bar, restaurant, tel. 02 33 60 14 25, fax 02 33 60 37 69, www.le-relais-du-roy.com, reservation@le-relais-du-roy.com).

$$ Hôtel Vert** and **Hôtel Formule Verte****, located across the street from each other, are run by the same company. Both provide motel-esque rooms with Wi-Fi at good rates. **Hôtel Vert** is a step up in comfort (Db-€64-84, Tb-€75-95, Qb-€95-115, tel. 02 33 60 09 33, fax 02 33 60 20 02); **Hôtel Formule Verte** is modern and simple (Db-€48-68, Tb-€63-83, Qb-€80-103, tel. 02 33 60 14 13, fax 02 33 60 14 44). The hotels share the same website and email address (www.le-mont-saint-michel.com, stmichel@le-mont-saint-michel.com).

Chambres d'Hôtes

Simply great values, these converted farmhouses are near the village of Ardevon, a few minutes' drive from the island toward Avranches.

$$ Les Vieilles Digues, where charming, English-speaking Danielle pampers you, is two miles toward Pontorson on the main road (on the left if you're coming from Mont St-Michel). It has a lovely garden and seven nicely furnished and homey rooms with subtle Asian touches, all with showers (but no Mont St-Michel views). Ground-floor rooms have patios on the garden (D-€65, Db-€75, Tb-€95, includes good breakfast, easy parking, Internet access and Wi-Fi, 68 Route du Mont St-Michel, tel. 02 33 58 55 30, fax 02 33 58 83 09, www.bnb-normandy.com, danielle.tchen @wanadoo.fr).

$$ La Jacotière is closest to Mont St-Michel and within walking distance of the *navette* (allowing you to avoid the €8.50 fee to park). This place will likely be sold by 2013, so expect some changes to the information I've given here. There are six immaculate rooms and views of the island from the backyard (Db-€68, studio with great view from private patio-€70, extra bed-€12, includes breakfast, Wi-Fi, tel. 02 33 60 22 94, fax 02 33 60 20 48, www.lajacotiere.fr, la.jacotiere@wanadoo.fr).

$ Vent des Grèves is about a mile down D-275 from Mont St-Michel (green sign; if arriving from the north, it's just after Auberge de la Baie). Sweet Estelle (who speaks English) offers five bright, big, and modern rooms with good views of Mont St-Michel and a common deck with tables to let you soak it all in (Sb-€40, Db-€50, Tb-€60, Qb-€70, includes breakfast, credit cards OK, Wi-Fi, tel. 02 33 48 28 89, www.ventdesgreves.com, ventdesgreves@orange.fr).

Eating in Mont St-Michel

Puffy omelets (*omelette montoise*, or *omelette tradition*) are Mont St-Michel's specialty. Also look for mussels (best with crème fraîche), seafood platters, and locally raised lamb (a saltwater-grass diet gives the meat a unique taste, but beware of impostor lamb from New Zealand—ask where your dinner was raised). Muscadet wine (dry, white, and cheap) is the local wine and goes well with most regional dishes.

The menus at most of the island's restaurants look like carbon copies of one another (with *menus* from €18 to €28, cheap crêpes, and full à la carte choices). Some places have better views or more appealing decor, and a few have outdoor seating with views along the ramparts walk—ideal when it's sunny. If it's too cool to sit outside, window-shop the places that face the bay from the ramparts walk and arrive early to land a bay-view table. Unless noted otherwise, the listed restaurants are open daily for lunch and dinner.

La Sirene Crêperie offers a good island value and a cozy interior (€9 main-course crêpes, open daily for lunch, open for dinner only in summer, enter through gift shop across from Hôtel St. Pierre, tel. 02 33 60 08 60).

Hôtel du Guesclin is the top place for a traditional meal, with white tablecloths and beautiful views of the bay from its inside-only tables (book a window table in advance; see details under "Sleeping in Mont St-Michel—On the Island," earlier).

Restaurant le St. Michel is lighthearted, reasonable, family-friendly, and run by helpful Patricia (decent omelets, mussels, salads, and pasta; open daily for lunch only, may be open for dinner in summer, test its stone toilet, across from Hôtel le Mouton Blanc, tel. 02 33 60 14 37).

Chez Mado is a stylish three-story café-*crêperie*-restaurant one door up from Hôtel le Mouton Blanc. It's worth considering for its upstairs terrace, which offers the best outside table views up to the abbey (when their umbrellas don't block it). **La Vieille Auberge** has a broad terrace with the next-best views to the abbey and, so far, no big umbrellas. **La Croix Blanche** owns a small deck with abbey views and window-front tables with bay views, and **Les Terrasses Poulard** has indoor views to the bay.

Picnics: This is the romantic's choice. The small lanes above the main street hide scenic picnic spots, such as the small park at the base of the ancient treadwheel ramp to the upper abbey. You'll catch late sun by following the ramp that leads you through the *gendarmerie* and down behind the island (on the left as you face the main entry to the island). Sandwiches, pizza by the slice, salads, and drinks are all available to go at shops along the main drag. But you'll find a better selection at the modest **supermarket** located on the mainland (see "Helpful Hints" on page 341).

Mont St-Michel Connections

By Train, Bus, or Taxi

Bus and train service to Mont St-Michel is a challenge. Depending on where you're coming from, you may find that you're forced to arrive and depart early or late—leaving you with too much or too little time on the island.

From Mont St-Michel to Paris: There are several ways to get to Paris. Most travelers take the regional bus from Mont St-Michel to Rennes or Dol de Bretagne and connect directly to the TGV (4/day via Rennes, 1/day via Dol de Bretagne, 4 hours total via either route from Mont St-Michel to Paris' Gare Montparnasse; €12 for bus to Rennes, €6.50 for bus to Dol de Bretagne; not covered by railpass, all explained in English at www.keolis-emeraude.com/en). You can also take the 20-minute bus ride to Pontorson (see next) and catch one of a very few trains from there (3/day, 5.5 hours, transfer in Caen, St-Malo, or Rennes). In July and August (and on April-June and Sept weekends), you can take the SNCF bus to Villedieu les Poêles, and transfer there to the train to Paris' Gare Montparnasse (1/day, 4 hours total, bus and train covered by railpass).

From Mont St-Michel to Pontorson: The nearest train station to Mont St-Michel is five miles away, in Pontorson (called Pontorson/Mont St-Michel). It's connected to Mont St-Michel by a 20-minute bus ride (12/day July-Aug, 6/day Sept-June, www.vtni50.fr—under "Horaires," click on "Fiches horaires," choose "Horaires Manéo-Service Express," then "Ligne 6" for the Pontorson/Mont St-Michel schedule) or by taxi (€18, €26 at night and on weekends, tel. 02 33 60 33 23 or 02 33 60 82 70).

From Pontorson by Train to: Bayeux (2-3/day, 2 hours; also see Hôtel Churchill's shuttle van service—page 307); **Rouen** (2/day via Caen, 4 hours; 4/day via Paris, 7 hours); **Dinan** (3/day, 2 hours, transfer in Dol); **St-Malo** (2/day, 1-2 hours, transfer in Dol); **Amboise** (2-3/day; 5.5-7.5 hours via transfers in Caen and Tours, or

NORMANDY

via Rennes, Le Mans, and Tours).

From Mont St-Michel by Bus to: St-Malo (2/day, usually at about 9:20 and 15:45, 1-2 hours with change at the Pontorson train station; the 9:20 bus from Mont St-Michel with Pontorson transfer arrives in St-Malo at 11:00, where you can catch buses to Dinan—TI has schedules); **Rennes** (4/day direct, 1.75 hours). Keolis buses provide service to St-Malo and Rennes (tel. 02 99 19 70 80, www.keolis-emeraude.com/en).

Taxis are more expensive, but are helpful when trains and buses don't cooperate. Figure €80 from Mont St-Michel to St-Malo, and €100 to Dinan (50 percent more on Sun and at night).

By Car

From Mont St-Michel to St-Malo, Brittany: The direct (and free) freeway route takes 40 minutes. For a scenic drive into Brittany,

take the following route: Head to Pontorson, follow *D-19* signs to St-Malo, then look for *St. Malo par la Côte* and join D-797, which leads along *La Route de la Baie* to D-155 and on to the oyster capital of Cancale. In Cancale, keep tracking *St. Malo par la Côte* and *Route de la Baie* signs. You'll be routed through the town's port (good lunch stop), then emerge on D-201. Take time to savor Pointe du Grouin, then continue west on D-201 as it hugs the coast to St-Malo (see page 371 in Brittany chapter). If continuing on to Dinan: From St-Malo, signs direct you to Rennes, then Dinan. This drive adds about 2.5 hours (with stops; takes longer on weekends and in summer) to the fastest path between Mont St-Michel and Dinan, but is well worth it when skies are clear. For more details on this drive, see "Scenic Drive Between St-Malo and Mont St-Michel" on page 380 of the Brittany chapter.

From Mont St-Michel to Bayeux: Take the free and zippy A-84 toward Caen, exit at Villers-Bocage, then follow signs to Bayeux.

BRITTANY

Dinan • St-Malo

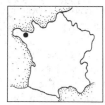

The bulky peninsula of Brittany is windswept and rugged, with a well-discovered coast, a forgotten interior, strong Celtic ties, and a craving for crêpes. This region of independent-minded locals is linguistically and culturally different from Normandy—and, for that matter, the rest of France. The Couesnon River skirts the western edge of Mont St-Michel, marking the border between Normandy and Brittany. Tradition is everything here, where farmers and fishermen still play a big part in the region's economy.

In 1491, the French King Charles VIII forced Brittany's 14-year-old Duchess Anne to marry him (at Château de Langeais in the Loire Valley). Their union made feisty, independent Brittany an unhappy small cog in a big country (the Kingdom of France). Brittany lost its freedom, but with Anne as queen gained certain rights, such as free roads. (Even today, more than 500 years later, Brittany's highways come with no tolls, which is unique in France.)

Locals take great pride in their distinct Breton culture. In Brittany, music stores sell more Celtic albums than anything else. It's hard to imagine that this music was forbidden as recently as the 1980s. During that repressive time, many of today's Breton pop stars were underground artists. And not long ago, a child would lose French citizenship if christened with a Celtic name.

But the freckled locals are now free to wave their black-and-white-striped flag, sing their songs, and *parler* their language (there's a Breton TV station and radio station). Look for bumper stickers and flags touting the region's Breton name, Breizh. Like their Irish counterparts, Bretons—many with red hair—are chatty, their music is alive with stories of struggles against an oppressor, and their identities are intrinsically tied to the sea.

Planning Your Time

With one full day, spend the morning in Dinan and the afternoon either along the Rance River (walking or biking are best, but driving works) or along Brittany's wild coast, where you can tour Fort la Latte and enjoy the massive views between Les Sable d'Or-les-Pins and Cap Fréhel. Try to find a few hours for St-Malo—ideally when connecting Mont St-Michel with Brittany. The coastal route between Mont St-Michel and St-Malo—via the town of Cancale (famous for oysters and a good place for lunch), with a stop at Pointe du Grouin (fabulous ocean views)—gives travelers with limited time a worthwhile glimpse at this photogenic province.

Getting Around Brittany

By Car: This is the ideal way to scour the ragged coast and watery towns. Autoroutes are free, and the traffic is generally negligible (except in summer along the coast).

By Train and Bus: Trains provide barely enough service to Dinan and St-Malo (on Sun, service all but disappears). Key transfer points by train include the big city of Rennes and the small town of Dol-de-Bretagne. Some trips are more convenient by bus (including Rennes to Dinan and Dinan to St-Malo).

By Minivan Tour: Westcapades runs daylong minivan tours covering Dinan, St-Malo, and Mont St-Michel (designed for daytrippers from Paris, trips officially begin at the train station in St-Malo and end at the train station in Rennes). These tours are flexible, but light on information. Because the guides are based in Dinan, you can do the entire round-trip from Dinan (about 9:45-19:30). Alternatively, you can start in St-Malo (at 10:30) and finish either in Dinan (about 19:30) or in Rennes (about 19:00), where you can catch the TGV train to Paris. You can also get off at Mont St-Michel (described in the Normandy chapter)—making this tour a convenient way to reach that remote island abbey (€85/day, tel. 02 96 39 79 52, www.westcapades.com, marc@westcapades.com). Another tour option starts at Rennes' TGV Station and includes Mont St-Michel and key parts of the D-Day beaches, ending at either the train station in Bayeux or in Caen.

Another small tour company, **Afoot in France,** provides tours in Brittany and Normandy for small groups or individuals. This service is ideal for people who'd like to have a local tour guide as their personal driver (tel. 02 97 66 17 19, http://escorted-tours .afootinfrance.com, afootinfrance@gmail.com). Both of its guides also lead tours for my company.

BRITTANY

Brittany's Cuisine Scene

Though the endless coastline suggests otherwise, there is more than seafood in this rugged Celtic land. Crêpes are to Bretons

what pasta is to Italians: a basic, reasonably priced, daily necessity. Galettes are savory buckwheat crêpes, commonly filled with ham, cheese, eggs, mushrooms, spinach, seafood, or a combination. Purists insist that a galette should not have more than three or four fillings—overfilling it masks the flavor (which is the point in certain places). Here, the word "crêpe" is used generically to mean a dessert.

Oysters *(huîtres)* are the second food of Brittany, and are available all year. Mussels, clams, and scallops are often served as main courses, and you can also find galettes with scallops and *moules marinières* (mussels steamed in white wine, parsley, and shallots). Farmers compete with fishermen for the hearts of locals by growing fresh vegetables, such as peas, beans, and cauliflower.

For dessert, look for *far breton,* a traditional custard often served with prunes. Dessert crêpes, made with white flour, come with a variety of toppings. Or try *kouign amann,* a puffy, caramelized Breton cake made with buckwheat dough (in Breton, *kouign* means "cake" and *amann* means "butter"). At bakeries, look for *ker-y-pom,* traditional Breton shortbread biscuits with butter, honey, and apple-pie fillings.

Cider is the locally produced drink. Order *une bolée de cidre* (a traditional bowl of hard apple cider) with your crêpes. Breton beer is strong and delicious; try anything local (Sant Erwann is my favorite).

Remember, restaurants serve food only during lunch (11:30-14:00) and dinner (19:00-21:00, later in bigger cities); cafés offer food throughout the day.

Dinan

If you have time for only one stop in Brittany, do Dinan. Hefty ramparts corral its half-timbered and cobbled quaintness into

Brittany's best medieval town center. And though it has a touristy icing—plenty of *crêperies,* shops selling Brittany kitsch, and colorful flags—it's a workaday Breton town filled with about 10,000 people who appreciate the beautiful place they call home. This impeccably preserved ancient city, which escaped the bombs of World War II, is peaceful and conveniently located (about a 45-minute drive from Mont St-Michel). For a memorable day, spend your morning exploring Dinan and your afternoon walking, biking, or boating the Rance River.

Orientation to Dinan

Dinan's old city, wrapped in its medieval ramparts, gathers on a hill well above the Rance River. Cobbled lanes climb steeply from Dinan's small river port to the vast Place du Guesclin (gek-lahn). There you'll find lots of parking, Château de Dinan, and the TI. Place des Merciers, just north of Place du Guesclin, is the center of most shopping activities.

Tourist Information

At the TI, pick up a free map and bus and train schedules, ask about boat trips on the Rance River, and check your email at the Internet terminal (July-Aug Mon-Sat 9:30-19:00, Sun 10:00-12:30 & 14:30-18:00; Sept-June Mon-Sat 9:30-12:30 & 14:00-18:00, closed Sun; just off Place du Guesclin near Château de Dinan at 9 Rue du Château, tel. 02 96 87 69 76, www.dinan-tourisme.com).

Arrival in Dinan

By Train: To get to the town center from Dinan's Old World train station (no lockers or baggage storage), find a taxi (see "Helpful Hints," below) or walk 20 steady minutes (see map on next page). If walking, head left out of the train station, make a right at Hôtel de la Gare up Rue Carnot, turn right on Rue Thiers following *Centre-Ville* signs, and go left across big Place Duclos-Pinot, passing just left of Café de la Mairie. To reach the TI and Place du Guesclin, go to the right of the café (on Rue du Marchix).

By Bus: Dinan's key intercity bus stop is in front of the post office on Place Duclos-Pinot, 10 minutes above the train station and five minutes below Place du Guesclin. To reach the historic core, cross the square, passing to the left of Café de la Mairie (for more bus information, see "Dinan Connections," later).

By Car: Dinan confuses drivers—take your time navigating here and keep in mind that you'll pay for most street parking. Follow *Centre-Ville* signs and park on Place du Guesclin (free parking 19:00-9:00 except July-Sept and on market days on Thu). If you enter Dinan near the train station, drive the route described above (see "By Train"), and keep to the right of Café de la Mairie to reach Place du Guesclin. Check with your hotelier before leaving your car overnight on Place du Guesclin; it will be towed before 8:00 on market or festival days.

Helpful Hints

Market Days: On Thursday, a big open-air market is held on Place du Guesclin (8:00-13:00). In July and August, Wednesday is flea-market day on Place St. Sauveur.

Internet Access: The **TI** has computers (small fee) but no Wi-Fi. Ask at your hotel or the TI for Wi-Fi availability.

Laundry: Pressing-Laverie's Madame Heurlin can usually do your laundry in a few hours (Tue-Fri 8:30-12:00 & 14:00-19:00, Sat 8:30-18:00, closed Sun-Mon, a few blocks from Place Duclos-Pinot at 19 Rue de Brest, tel. 02 96 39 71 35).

Supermarkets: Groceries are upstairs in the **Monoprix** (Mon-Sat 9:00-20:00, in summer also open Sun 9:00-13:00, 7 Rue du Marchix). Or try **Marché Plus,** on Place Duclos-Pinot (Mon-Sat 7:00-21:00, Sun 9:00-13:00).

Dinan

TRAIN STATION

RUE DEROYER
RUE CARNOT
RUE LECONTE DE LISLE
RUE DU COMTE DE GARAYE
❼
RUE PREJENTAIS
RUE LORD KITCHENER
RUE EVEN
RUE DES GRANDS JARDINS
RUE DES PIVENTS
RUE THIERS
RUE DE LA CROIX
RUE DE ST-CHARLES
R. SAGESSE
BOULANGERIE
ST. MALO
RUE CHALOTAIS
RUE PASTEUR
RUE LA TOUR
RUE SAINT-MARC
RUE DES ROUAIRIES
❶❾
Pl. Duclose Pinot
❷❶
GRAND RUE
❻
RUE MARCHIX FERRONNERIE
R. CHATEAUBRIAND
B
RAMPARTS
RUE DE BREST
❶❼
POST
PROMENADE DES
❶❽
PETITS FOSSES
CHATEAU

❶ Hôtel Le d'Avaugour	❶❺ Le Cottage Restaurant & Bakery
❷ Hôtel Arvor	❶❻ Rue de la Cordonnerie Bars
❸ Chambres d'Hôte le Logis du Jerzual	❶❼ Launderette
❹ Hôtel de la Tour de l'Horloge	❶❽ Monoprix (Groceries)
❺ Hôtel du Théâtre	❶❾ Marché Plus (Groceries)
❻ Hôtel Ibis Dinan	❷⓿ River Cruises
❼ Hôtel de la Gare	❷❶ Café de la Mairie
❽ Crêperie des Artisans	❷❷ Théâtre des Jacobins
❾ Le Cantorbery Restaurant	❷❸ Clock Tower
❶⓿ Fleur de Sel Restaurant	❷❹ La Craquanterie Shop
❶❶ Crêperie Ahna	❷❺ Rampart Walk Gates (2)
❶❷ La Lycorne Restaurant	❷❻ To Hôtel Manoir de Rigourdaine, Vue de la Rance Chambres & Bike Route to Port de Lyvet & St-Suliac
❶❸ La Tomate Restaurant	
❶❹ Café St. Sauveur	

Bike Rental: The TI has up-to-date information on bike-rental places. Try to rent your bike at the port, to avoid riding down and back up a big hill.

Taxi: Call 06 08 00 80 90 (www.taxi-dinan.com). Figure about €50 to St-Malo and €85 to Mont St-Michel.

Minivan Excursions: Helpful Marc Le Meur runs **Westcapades,** with guaranteed minivan departures at least three times a week from Dinan to St-Malo and Mont St-Michel (see "Getting Around Brittany," earlier).

Tourist Train: This *petit train* runs a circuit connecting the port and upper old town (€6, runs every 40 minutes, leaves in the old town from in front of the Théâtre des Jacobins, a block off Place du Guesclin).

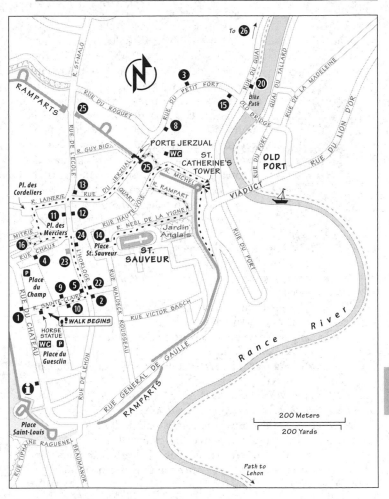

Picnic Park: The small but flowery Jardin Anglais hides behind the Church of St. Sauveur.

Self-Guided Walk

Welcome to Dinan

Frankly, I wouldn't go through a turnstile in Dinan. The attraction is the town itself. Enjoy the old town center, ramble around the ramparts, and explore the old riverfront harbor. Here are some ideas, laced together as a relaxed one-hour walk (not including exploring the port). Start near the TI, and as you wander, notice the pride locals take in their Breton culture.

• *Start in the center of Place du Guesclin, and find the statue of the horseback rider.*

Place du Guesclin: This sprawling town square/parking lot is named after Bertrand du Guesclin, a native 14th-century knight and hero (described as small in stature but big-hearted) who became a great French military leader, famous for his daring victories over England during the Hundred Years' War (like Joan of Arc, he was a key player in defeating the English). On this very square, he beat Sir Thomas of Canterbury in a nail-biter of a joust that locals still talk about to this day. The victory freed his brother, whom Thomas had taken prisoner in violation of a truce. For 700 years, merchants have filled this square to sell their produce and crafts (in modern times, it's Thu 8:00-13:00).

• *With the statue of Guesclin behind you, follow Rue Ste. Claire to the right, into the old town and to the...*

Théâtre des Jacobins: Fronting a pleasant little square, the theater was once one of the many convents that dominated the town. In fact, in medieval times, a third of Dinan consisted of convents. They're still common in Brittany, which remains the most Catholic part of France. The theater today offers a full schedule of events.

• *Turn left and walk down Rue de l'Horloge ("Clock Street") toward the clock tower. On the way, on your left, you'll see...*

Anybody's Tombstone: The tombstone without a head is a town mascot. It's actually a prefab tombstone, made during the Hundred Years' War, when there was more death than money in France. A portrait bust would be attached to this generic body for a proper, yet economical, burial.

• *Continue to the...*

Clock Tower: The old town spins around this clock tower, which has long symbolized the power of the town's merchants. The tower's 160 steps (the last few on a ladder) lead to a sweeping city view. Warning: Plug your ears at the quarter-hour, when the bells ring (€3, daily June-Sept 10:00-18:30, April-May 14:00-18:00, closed Oct-March).

• *Across the street from the clock tower find...*

La Craquanterie: This shop specializes in Breton cookies and treats. Look for *beurre salé* (salted butter—think salted caramel), *kouign amann* (a rich, caramelized cake), *gâteau breton* (butter cakes), and *craquantes* (crisp cookies with salted butter). They offer tastes of their goodies (daily 10:00-13:00 & 14:00-18:00, 12 Rue de l'Horloge, tel. 02 96 85 10 05).

• *Continue along Rue de l'Horloge, taking the first left into Dinan's historic commercial center, Place des Merciers. Stop under a porch.*

Old Town Center: The arcaded, half-timbered buildings around you are Dinan's oldest. They date from the time when property taxes were based on the square footage of the ground floor. To provide shelter from both the rain and taxes, buildings started with small ground floors, then expanded outward as they got taller. Notice the stone bases supporting the wood columns. Because trees did not come in standard lengths, it was easier to adjust the size of the pedestals.

Medieval shopkeepers sold goods in front of their homes under the shelter of leaning walls. Most streets are named for the key commerce that took place there. Wander further toward the square and locate picturesque Rue de la Cordonnerie ("Shoe Street," to the left of the pretty restaurant La Mère Pourcel), a good example of a medieval lane, with overhanging buildings whose roofs nearly touch. After a disastrous 18th-century fire, a law required that the traditional thatch be replaced by safer slate. From La Mère Pourcel, go up Rue de la Cordonnerie into the small maze of streets. Find "pub row" and the modern market stalls of La Cohue, then return to Place des Merciers.

• *Continue working your way through the square. (The building with the arched stone facade at the end of the square—Les Cordeliers—used to be a Franciscan monastery during the Middle Ages; today, it's a middle school...wrap your brain around that change.) Turn right on Rue de la Lainerie ("Street of Wool Shops"), which becomes...*

Rue du Jerzual: This spiraling road was the primary medieval link to the port and the focus of commercial activity in old Dinan.

The steep cobbled street (slippery when wet) was chock-a-block with potential customers making their way between the port and the upper city. Notice the waist-high stone and wooden shelves that front many of the buildings. Here, medieval merchants could display their products and tempt passersby. You can continue all the way down to the port (described later, under "Sights in Dinan"); it's a 10-minute walk down (remember, what goes down must come back up). If your knees balk, follow the path to the ramparts, described next.

• *For the best look at Dinan's impressive fortified wall, turn right after passing under the massive medieval gate (Porte du Jerzual) and work your way up the curving road. Turn right on Rue Michel, then turn right again through the green iron gate to walk along the...*

Ramparts: In the Middle Ages, this elevated walkway was

connected with Château de Dinan
(it's about a mile in either direction to the château from here).
Although the old port town was
repeatedly destroyed, these ramparts were never taken by force. If
an attacker got by the *contrescarpe*
(second outer wall, now covered
in vegetation) and through the
(dry) moat, he'd be pummeled by

ghastly stuff dropped through the holes lining the ramparts. Today,
the ramparts protect the town's residential charm and private gardens. Venture out on the (second) huge Governor's Tower to see
how the cannon slots enabled defenders to shoot in all directions.
The St-Malo tower is the last one you can see as you look uphill.
Our next destination is the farthest visible tower built into the wall
to the right (with your back to the upper old town). The tall church
further to the right is where our walk ends—the Church of St.
Sauveur.

• *Double back to Rue Michel and turn right. Take the first left, onto
Rue du Rempart. Walk to the round tower (in the corner of the park),
called...*

St. Catherine's Tower: This part of Dinan's medieval defense
system allows strategic views of the river valley and over the old
port (for more on the port, see below). Find the medieval bridge
below and the path that leads along the river to the right to Léhon
(described later, under "Sights in Dinan"). To the left you can follow the Rance River downstream as it meanders toward the sea.
The English gardens behind you are picnic-pleasant.

• *Walk through the gardens to the church behind you, and dip into the...*

Church of St. Sauveur: Enter this asymmetrical church (typical in Brittany) to see striking, modern stained-glass windows and
a beautifully lit nave. Pick up the English explanation (€.20) and
learn the church's raison d'être. The church is a thousand years
old—the wood balcony in the entry confirms that, as it heaves
under the weight of the organ. When built, the church sat lonely
on this hill, as all other activity was focused around the port.

• *Your tour is over. Good lunch cafés are across the square (see "Eating in
Dinan," later), and you are a block below the main Rue de l'Horloge.*

Sights in Dinan

Dinan's Old Port

Following the self-guided walk, you can reach Dinan's modest
little port by continuing down Rue du Jerzual (which becomes
Rue du Petit Fort). Notice the unusual wood-topped building

just before the port (across from Le Cottage restaurant). This was a leather tannery. Those wooden shutters could open to dry the freshly tanned hides while the nearby river flushed the toxic waste products (happily, swimming was not in vogue then). The last business before the port is a killer bakery with delicious local specialties, including *far breton* and *kouign amann* (you'll also find good picnic fixings and drinks to go). Try the *pomme* crumble. You deserve a baked break.

The port was the birthplace of Dinan a thousand years ago. For centuries, this is where people lived and worked, and today it's

a great place for a riverside drink or snack. This once-thriving port is connected to the sea—15 miles away—by the Rance River. By taxing river traffic, the town grew prosperous. The tiny Vieux Pont (Old Bridge) dates to the 15th century. Because the port area was so exposed, the townsfolk retreated to the bluff behind its current for-

tifications. Notice the viaduct high above, built in 1850 to alleviate congestion and to send traffic around the town. Until then, the main road crossed the tiny Old Bridge, heading up Rue du Jerzual to Dinan.

▲Rance River Valley

The best thing about Dinan's port is the access it provides to lush riverside paths that amble along the gentle Rance River Valley. You can walk, bike, drive, or boat in either interesting direction (perfect for families).

On Foot: For a breath of fresh Brittany air and an easy walk, visit the flower-festooned village of **Léhon.** Cross the Old Bridge in Dinan's port, turn right, and follow the level river trail for 30 minutes. You'll come to pristine little Léhon (a town of character, as the sign reminds you). Visitors are greeted by a beautiful ninth-century abbey that rules the roost (find the cloisters; interior closed to visitors). Explore the village's flowery cobbled lanes, but skip the town-topping castle ruin (free, 9:00-19:00). Enjoy a drink—or, even better, a meal at the adorable **La Marmite de l'Abbaye** café/restaurant, with seating inside or out. Your hostess, sweet Breton Madame Borgnic, serves wood-fire-grilled meats for lunch and dinner (closed Tue off-season, tel. 02 96 87 39 39). The trail continues on well past Léhon, but you'll need a bike to make a dent in it. The villages of Evran and Treverien are both reachable by bike (allow 45 minutes from Dinan to Evran, and an additional 25 minutes to Treverien).

By Bike: The Rance River Valley could not be more bike-friendly, as there's nary a foot of elevation gain (for bike rentals, ask at the TI). Here's what I'd do with three hours and a bike: Pedal to Léhon (following the "On Foot" route, above), then double back to Dinan and follow the bike path along the river downstream to the Port de Lyvet.

To reach the Port de Lyvet, ride through Dinan's port, staying on the old city side of the river. You'll join a parade of ocean-bound boats as the river opens up, becoming more like an inlet of the sea. It's a breezy, level 30-minute ride past rock faces, cornfields, and slate-roofed farms to the tiny **Port de Lyvet** (cross small dam to reach village, trail ends a short distance beyond). **L'Effet Mer** café/restaurant is well-positioned in the village (open daily for lunch, dinner, or a refreshing drink on its wooden deck, closed Wed off-season, tel. 02 96 83 21 10). Serious cyclists should continue on to St-Suliac via La Vicomte (described later, under "By Car").

By Boat: Boats depart from Dinan's port, at the bottom of Rue du Jerzual, 50 feet to the left of the Old Bridge on the Dinan side (schedules depend on tides, get details at TI). The snail-paced, one-hour cruise on the *Jaman IV* runs upriver to Léhon (the trip is better on foot or bike), taking you through a lock and past pretty scenery (€13, April-Oct 2-4/day, fewer off-season, mobile 06 07 87 64 90). A longer cruise with **Compagnie Corsaire** goes

to St-Malo (€31 round-trip, €25 one-way, runs April-Sept, 1/day, slow and scenic 2.5 hours one-way, schedule changes with the tide, tel. 08 25 16 81 20, www.compagniecorsaire.com, or ask at TI). Enjoy St-Malo (described later in this chapter), then take the bus or train back (or do the reverse—bus/train to St-Malo, then boat back). Get the bus schedule before leaving Dinan (4-6/day, 1 hour, no buses on Sun except in summer).

By Car: Meandering the Rance River Valley by car requires a good map (orange Michelin #309 worked for me). Drivers connecting Dinan and St-Malo can include this short Rance joyride detour: From Dinan, go down to the port, then follow D-12 with the river to your right toward Taden, then toward Plouër-sur-Rance (Dinan's port-front road is occasionally blocked, in which case you'll join this route beyond the port). Stay straight through La Hisse, then drop down and turn right, following signs to *Le Vicomte*. Cross the Rance on the small dam and find the cute **Port de Lyvet** (lunch café described earlier), then continue to La Vicomte and find D-29 north. Track your way to **St-Suliac**, a

BRITTANY

Sleep Code

(€1 = $1.30, country code: 33)
S = Single, **D** = Double/Twin, **T** = Triple, **Q** = Quad, **b** = bathroom,
s = shower only, ***** = French hotel rating system (0-5 stars).
Unless otherwise noted, credit cards are accepted and English
is spoken.

To help you sort easily through these listings, I've divided
the accommodations into three categories based on the price
for a standard double room with bath:

$$$ Higher Priced—Most rooms €95 or more.
$$ Moderately Priced—Most rooms between €60-95.
$ Lower Priced—Most rooms €60 or less.

Prices can change without notice; verify the hotel's
current rates online or by email.

---

pretty little port town with a handful of restaurants, a small grocery store, and a photogenic *boulangerie*. Stroll the ancient alleys,
find a bench on the grassy waterfront, and contemplate lunch. **La
Ferme du Boucanier Bistrot** is a good bet (*menus* from €30, closed
Tue-Wed, open for lunch weekends only, 2 Rue de l'Hôpital, tel.
02 23 15 06 35). From here, continue on to St-Malo or return to
Dinan.

Sleeping in Dinan

Dinan is popular. Weekends and summers are tight; book ahead
if you can. Dinan likes its nightlife, so be wary of rooms over loud
bars, particularly on lively weekends.

In the Old Center
$$$ Hôtel Le d'Avaugour**** is Dinan's most central four-star
hotel, with an efficient staff, stay-awhile lounge areas, full bar, and
backyard garden oasis. It faces busy Place du Guesclin, near the
town's medieval wall. The wood-furnished rooms have comfortable
queen- or king-sized beds and modern hotel amenities. Likeable
owner Nicolas strongly encourages two-night stays (streetside
Db-€120-150, garden-side Db-€120-190, third person-€16, suites
available, prices vary greatly by season, rooms over garden are best,
good breakfast-€14, elevator, bikes available, 1 Place du Champ,
tel. 02 96 39 07 49, fax 02 96 85 43 04, www.avaugourhotel.com,
contact@avaugourhotel.com).

$$ Hôtel Arvor** is a top-notch place with a fine stone
facade, ideally located in the old city a block off Place du Guesclin.

It's well-run, with 24 tastefully appointed and comfortable rooms (standard Db-€72-95, Tb-€88-125, €15/person extra for larger rooms accommodating up to 6 people, elevator, Wi-Fi, 15 free parking spaces, 5 Rue Pavie, tel. 02 96 39 21 22, fax 02 96 39 83 09, www.hotelarvordinan.com, hotel-arvor@wanadoo.fr).

$$ Chambres d'Hôte le Logis du Jerzual is just about as cozy as it gets, with five warmly decorated rooms and period furnishings and thoughtful touches throughout. Ideal hostess Sylvie Ronserray welcomes guests. Enjoy the terraced yard in this haven of calm close to the action: It's just up from the port but a long, steep walk below the main town (Db-€85-95, Db suite-€120, extra bed-€25, includes breakfast, 25 Rue du Petit Fort, tel. 02 96 85 46 54, fax 09 81 38 16 89, www.logis-du-jerzual.com, sylvie.logis @laposte.net). Drive up Rue du Petit Fort from the port (it's well-signed) and drop off your bags. Parking is nearby.

$$ Hôtel de la Tour de l'Horloge** is a good two-star bet burrowed deep in the town's center, with 12 imaginatively decorated and impeccably maintained rooms fronting the bar-lined Rue de la Chaux (some rooms can be noisy on weekends). Gentle Catherine speaks English and gives a warm welcome (Db-€68-77, Tb-€80-87, Qb-€90-105, Wi-Fi, 5 Rue de la Chaux, tel. 02 96 39 96 92, fax 02 96 85 06 99, www.hotel-dinan.com, hotel.pbdela tour@orange.fr).

$ Hôtel du Théâtre is good for serious budget travelers, with seven simple and slightly smelly (but clean) rooms above a scrappy café/bar, across from Hôtel Arvor (S/D-€24, Db-€29, Tb-€39, €4 more July-Aug, 2 Rue Ste. Claire, tel. 02 96 39 06 91, owner Patrick speaks some English).

Closer to the Train Station

$$ Hôtel Ibis Dinan**, with its shiny, predictable comfort, stands tall between Place du Guesclin and the train station. It works especially well for bus and train travelers, as it's central, reasonably priced, and next to the bus stop—convenient for hitting regional destinations such as St-Malo. They may have rooms when others don't (Db-€93, Tb-€124, Qb-€144, cheaper on weekends, 1 Place Duclos-Pinot, tel. 02 96 39 46 15, fax 02 96 85 44 03, www.ibis hotel.com, h5977@accor.com).

$ Hôtel de la Gare* faces the station and offers the full Breton Monty, with *charmant* Laurence and Claude (who both love Americans), a local-as-it-gets café hangout, and surprisingly quiet, clean, and comfy rooms for a bargain. The hotel has no email of its own, but offers free Wi-Fi thanks to the owners' teenage son (Ds-€36, Db-€50, Tb/Qb-€50-65, breakfast-€6, Place de la Gare, tel. 02 96 39 04 57, fax 02 96 39 02 29).

Near Dinan

To locate these places, see the map on page 360.

$$$ Hôtel Manoir de Rigourdaine** is *the* place to stay if you have a car and two nights to savor Brittany. Overlooking a

splendid scene of green meadows and turquoise water, this well-renovated farmhouse comes with wood beams, comfy public spaces, immaculate grounds, and three-star rooms (many with views) for two-star prices (Db-€89-97, extra person-€20, Internet access and Wi-Fi, 15-minute drive north of Dinan, tel. 02 96 86 89 96, fax 02 96 86 92 46, www.hotel-rigourdaine .fr, hotel.rigourdaine@wanadoo.fr). From Dinan, drop down to the port and follow D-12 toward Taden, then follow signs to *Plouër-sur-Rance*, then *Langrolay*, and look for signs to the hotel. If coming from the St-Malo area, take N-137 toward Rennes, then N-176 toward Dinan, take the Rance Plouër exit, and follow signs to *Langrolay* until you see hotel signs. From Rennes, take N-137 toward St-Malo, then N-176 toward Saint-Brieuc, take the Plouër-sur-Rance exit, and look for signs to *Langrolay* and then the hotel.

$$ Vue de la Rance Chambres is a three-room manor home about five minutes from Dinan (works well for drivers). You'll get terrific views over the Rance River Valley and sleep in clean and spacious rooms, but you'll need to stay for five nights, (Db-€60-80, Tb-€80-90, Qb-€90-110, includes good breakfast, Wi-Fi, 5 Rue des Grippas, La Hisse, Samson-sur-Rance, tel. 02 96 87 49 70, www.vuedelarance.com, reservations@vuedelarance.com).

Eating in Dinan

Dinan has good restaurants for every budget. Since galettes (savory crêpes) are the specialty, *crêperies* are a nice, inexpensive choice—and available on every corner. Be daring and try the crêpes with scallops and cream, or go for the egg-and-cheese crêpes. Ham-filled crêpes can be salty. For a good dinner, book Le Cantorbery or Le Cottage a day ahead if you can, and think hard about walking, riding, or driving to nearby Léhon for a charming village experience (see "Rance River Valley—On Foot," earlier).

Crêperie des Artisans is worth the walk for its delicious crêpes and warm ambience. Sincere owners Michel and Christelle are adamant about using only traditional fresh ingredients, and make the most authentic (and best) crêpes in town (both the mushroom-and-cheese galettes and the caramel-and-salted-butter crêpes are terrific). Try the *lait ribot* (a frothy, slightly sour milk drink) or the delicious handmade cider (€9-14 *menus,* closed Mon except July-Aug, 6 Rue du Petit Fort, halfway down to the port, tel. 02 96 39 44 10).

Le Cantorbery is a warm place (literally), where meats are grilled in the cozy dining-room fireplace *à la tradition.* The seafood is *très* tasty (*menus* from €28, closed Wed except July-Aug, just off Place du Guesclin at 6 Rue Ste. Claire, indoor dining only, two floors, tel. 02 96 39 02 52, well-run by sincere Madame Touchais).

Fleur de Sel, run by welcoming Monsieur Guilli, is where locals go for fish (meat dishes also served). The decor is appealing, and the choices are varied and reasonably priced (*menus* from €27-40, closed Sun-Mon, 7 Rue Ste. Claire, tel. 02 96 85 15 14).

Crêperie Ahna rocks Dinan. Locals jam the place: The price is right, the dishes are excellent, and young owner Gregory sets the tone for a fun experience. The cuisine goes well beyond crêpes; the do-it-yourself *pierrades*—where you cook your meat or fish on a hot stone at your table—are a treat (inside seating only, closed Sun, 7 Rue de la Poissonnerie, tel. 02 96 39 09 13).

La Lycorne is Dinan's place to go for a healthy serving of mussels prepared 20 different ways (€13, served with fries of course, many other dishes available as well). The ambience is fine inside or out, as it's situated on a traffic-free street (closed Mon, 6 Rue de la Poissonnerie, tel. 02 96 39 08 13).

La Tomate dishes up pizza and pasta for €10-12 with appealing indoor or outdoor seating (April-Sept open daily, Oct-March closed Sun-Mon, 4 Rue de l'Ecole, tel. 02 96 39 96 12).

Café St. Sauveur is a local watering hole/café with good prices and a hard-to-beat setting...when it's sunny (€7 for lunch salads and *plats,* open daily, across from the church at 19 Place St. Sauveur, tel. 02 96 85 30 20). The café next door offers a similar menu and prices.

At the Old Port: You'll find several restaurants at the old port. Have a pre-dinner drink—or a meal if the waterfront setting matters more than the cuisine—at one of the places on the river (La Terrasse is decent). Or you can hold out for dinner at **Le Cottage,** which merits the long, but picturesque, walk along a cobbled lane. The massive central fireplace here provides a warm ambience (it's no wonder that grilled dishes are a specialty). You'll find the portions are American-sized, and animated owner Claire wants to make you happy—trust her advice on what to order (€19-25 *menus*—I'd spring for the €25 *menu,* daily, 78 Rue du Petit Fort, tel. 02 96 87 96 70).

Nightlife: So many lively pub-like bars line the narrow, pedestrian-friendly **Rue de la Cordonnerie** that the street is nicknamed

"Rue de la Soif" ("Street of Thirst"). When the weather is good, you can sit outside at a picnic table and strike up a conversation with a friendly, tattooed Breton.

Dinan Connections

Locals take the bus to St-Malo or to Rennes, then catch trains from there (trains from Dinan require several changes, take longer than buses for regional destinations, and barely run on Sundays). Regional bus service is provided by Tibus (www.tibus.fr) or Illenoo (www.illenoo-services.fr).

From Dinan by Train to: Paris' Gare Montparnasse (6/day, 4 hours, change in Dol and Rennes), **Pontorson/Mont St-Michel** (3/day, 2 hours, change in Dol, then bus or taxi from Pontorson, see "Mont St-Michel Connections" on page 353), **St-Malo** (5/day, 1-2 hours, transfer in Dol, bus is better—see below), **Amboise** (6/day, 5-6 hours, via Rennes, then TGV to Paris with no station change needed in Paris; or better via Rennes, Le Mans, and Tours—2/day, 5-6 hours).

By Bus to: Rennes (with good train connections to many destinations, 7/day, 1 hour), **St-Malo** (5/day, none on Sun except in summer, 1 hour; faster and better than train, as bus stops in both cities are more central), **Mont St-Michel** (2/day, 3-4 hours, includes transfer with 1-hour wait in St-Malo or in Dol de Bretagne), **Dinard** (2/day, Mon-Sat only, 1 hour). Buses leave from the train station and from Place Duclos-Pinot, near the main post office.

BRITTANY

St-Malo

Come here to experience a true Breton beach resort. The old center (called Intra Muros) is your target, with pretty beaches, power-

ful ramparts that hug the entire town, and island fortifications that litter the bay. The inner city has an eerie, almost claus-trophobic feeling, thanks to the concentration of tall, dark stone buildings hemmed in by the towering ramparts (though a few pedestrian streets buck that sen-sation). The town feels better up

top on the walls, which are *the* sight here. St-Malo is packed in July and August, when the 8,000 people who call the old city home are

St-Malo's Seafaring Past

St-Malo has been a sailor's town since its origin as an ancient monastic settlement about 1,500 years ago. After the fall of the Roman Empire, monasteries provided security and stability for their regions, allowing communities like this one to grow and evolve into towns—and sometimes into important cities. By the 1100s, St-Malo was a powerful, fortified island guarding access to the Rance River Valley from one direction and the English Channel from the other. St-Malo later became notorious as the home of the corsairs—French mercenaries working for the King of France, and famous for daring raids on ships from other (unfriendly) countries. Unlike other pirates, these swashbuckling sailors were spared from the usual punishment for pillaging (death), as they were considered the king's combatants—a fine legal distinction. The corsairs of St-Malo were immensely profitable to the king (and themselves), and wreaked economic havoc on other countries (such as England) all the way up until the late 1700s.

joined by 12,000 additional daily "residents." But if you're willing to brave the crowds, it's an easy 45-minute drive—or a manageable bus or train ride—from Mont St-Michel or Dinan. (However, there's no baggage storage anywhere.) If you have a whole day here, circumnavigate St-Malo along its walls, take the walk to Alet, and visit Fort du Petit Bé.

BRITTANY

Orientation to St-Malo

Tourist Information

St-Malo's TI is across from the main city gate (Porte St. Vincent) on Esplanade St. Vincent (July-Aug Mon-Sat 9:00-19:30, Sun 10:00-18:00; Sept-June daily 9:00-13:00 & 14:00-18:30 except closed Sun Oct-March; tel. 08 25 13 52 00, www.saint-malo-tourisme.com). Pick up the helpful city map, along with schedules for the bus, train, or ferry (to Dinard). Downloadable walking tours of the city may be available in time for your visit—ask.

Arrival in St-Malo

By Train: The modern TGV Station is a five-minute bus ride on the #C-1 line to Porte St. Vincent (€1.20). If you'd rather walk, go for 15 minutes straight out of the station, then track the pointed spire in the distance for another five minutes.

By Bus: The main bus stops are near the Porte St. Vincent and TI (closer to town) and at the train station (confirm which stop your bus uses—some stop at both).

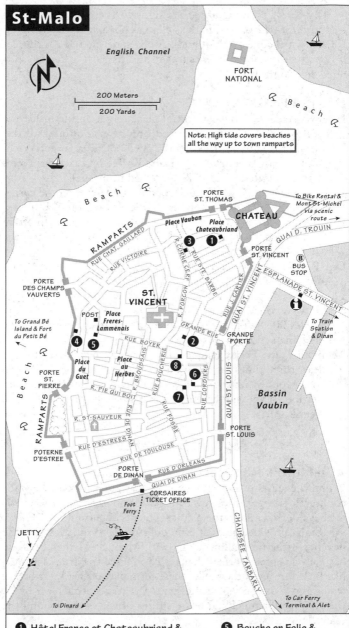

St-Malo

English Channel

FORT NATIONAL

Beach

200 Meters

200 Yards

Note: High tide covers beaches all the way up to town ramparts

Beach

PORTE ST. THOMAS

RAMPARTS

RUE CHAT. GAILLARD

RUE VICTOIRE

Place Vauban

Place Chateaubriand

❶

CHATEAU

To Bike Rental & Mont St-Michel via scenic route

QUAI D. TROUIN

PORTE ST. VINCENT

❸

R. CORNE CERF

RUE STE. BARBE

R. J. CARTIER

QUAI ST. VINCENT

ESPLANADE ST. VINCENT

B BUS STOP

PORTE DES CHAMPS VAUVERTS

ST. VINCENT

R. PORCON

GRANDE RUE

To Grand Bé Island & Fort du Petit Bé

POST

Place Freres-Lammenais

❹ ❺

RUE BOYER

Place du Guet

Place au Herbes

R. BROUSSAIS

RUE BOUCHERIE

❷

GRANDE PORTE

To Train Station & Dinan

ℹ

Beach

PORTE ST. PIERRE

R. PIE QUI BOIT

❽

❻

RUE CORDIERS

QUAI ST. LOUIS

Bassin Vaubin

RAMPARTS

R. ST-SAUVEUR

RUE DE DINAN

RUE FOSSE

❼

POTERNE D'ESTREE

RUE D'ESTREES

RUE DE TOULOUSE

PORTE ST. LOUIS

PORTE DE DINAN

RUE D'ORLEANS

QUAI DE DINAN

CORSAIRES TICKET OFFICE

CHAUSSEE TARBARLY

Foot Ferry

JETTY

To Dinard

To Car Ferry Terminal & Alet

BRITTANY

❶ Hôtel France et Chateaubriand & Le Chateaubriand Restaurant
❷ Hôtel du Louvre
❸ Hôtel le Nautilus
❹ Le Corps de Garde Crêperie

❺ Bouche en Folie & Tam's Kaffee
❻ Coté Sens
❼ Internet Café
❽ Launderette

By Car: Follow *Centre-Ville* signs to the old center (signs lead to *Intra-Muros*), and park as close as possible to the Porte St. Vincent (at the merry-go-round). A big underground parking lot is opposite the Porte St. Vincent, and smaller surface lots are scattered around the walls.

Helpful Hints

Internet Access: The most central place to get online inside the walls is at **Mokamalo** (closed Sun afternoon and all day Mon, 5 Rue de l'Orme, tel. 02 99 56 60 17). To get Wi-Fi for the price of a drink, try **Tam's Kaffee** on Place des Frères Lamennais (tel. 02 23 18 24 14, closed Mon-Tue).

Laundry: Inside the walls, you'll find a launderette on the corner of Rue de la Herse and Halle aux Blés (daily 7:00-21:00).

Bike Rental: There are several places to rent bikes near the train station and TI. Ask at the TI or find **Ty'Boost** bikes near the TI at 49 Quai Duguay-Trouin (tel. 02 99 56 47 18).

Car Rental: You'll find both **Avis** (tel. 02 99 40 18 54) and **Europcar** (tel. 02 99 56 75 17) inside the train station.

Foot Ferry: A nifty little ferry *(Bus de Mer)* shuttles passengers between St-Malo and Dinard in 10 minutes (€7 round-trip, runs 9:00-18:00, later in summer). Boats depart from the Cale de Dinan on the west side of the old city.

Minivan Tour: Westcapades guarantees minivan departures at least three times a week from St-Malo. Tours include Dinan and Mont St-Michel, and officially end at the Rennes train station so you can connect to Paris (see page 356 for more details).

Sights in St-Malo

▲St-Malo's Ramparts

Climb the stairs inside the Porte St. Vincent and tour the walls counterclockwise. It's a rewarding mile-long romp around the medieval fortifications (the oldest segments date from the 1100s).

Stairs provide access at each door *(porte)*. Walk down to the **beaches** if the tides allow (along with Mont St-Michel, St-Malo has Europe's greatest tidal changes). You'll see tree trunks planted like little forests on the sand—these form part of St-Malo's breakwater and must be replaced every 20 years. Storms blast in off the English Channel and bring surges of waves that pound the seawalls.

The **fortified islands** were built during the Hundred Years' War (late 1600s) by Louis XIV's military architect, Vauban, to defend the country against England. You can tour the closer forts when tides allow (each costs €5 to enter). **Fort National** is the first you'll come across (but can be visited only with a French-language tour, so I'd skip it unless you're a military architecture buff). Farther along, you'll see the more worthwhile **Fort du Petit Bé** (access is often submerged), which sits behind Ile du Grand Bé, where the famous poet Chateaubriand is buried. The island of Grand Bé is worth a romp if the tide agrees, and the views of Fort Petit du Bé will send your imagination soaring. The longer, low-slung island even farther out has no buildings and is off-limits until WWII mines are completely removed. Speaking of World War II, St-Malo was decimated by American bombs during the war as part of the campaign to liberate France. Eighty percent of St-Malo was leveled. Even though they look old, most of the town's buildings date from 1945 or later.

As you walk along the wall, soon after the recommended Le Corps de Garde Crêperie, you'll pass a *Chiens du Guet* restaurant sign. At one time, bulldogs were kept in the small, enclosed area behind the restaurant, then let loose late at night to patrol the beaches.

Nearby the **Québec flags** fly in honor of St-Malo's sister city, Québec City. (Explorer Jacques Cartier, who visited the future site of Québec City and is credited with discovering Canada, lived in and sailed from St-Malo.)

You'll eventually come to a long, concrete **jetty** that offers good views back to the ramparts. Across the bay is the belle époque resort city of Dinard (described later). Farther along, look for long, concrete-bordered *pétanque* (a.k.a. *boules*) courts below the walls (you may encounter games of *boule bretonne*—more like lawn bowling and with bigger balls). The **Corsaires ticket office,** located just before the commercial port, marks the departure point for the foot ferry to Dinard (you'll enjoy great views on your return ride to St-Malo).

From here, find your way inside the walls along Rue de Dinan, and return to the Porte St. Vincent on surface streets. The shopping streets Rue de la Vieille Boucherie and Rue Porcon de la Barbinais are among the most appealing.

Alet

The village of Alet is just a few minutes' drive past St-Malo's port (a 20-minute walk from the ramparts), but it feels a world apart. A splendid walking path leads around this small point with stunning views of crashing waves, the city of Dinard, the open sea, and, finally, St-Malo (allow 30 minutes at a relaxed pace, go in a clockwise direction). World War II bunkers cap the small hill, and there's a small museum you can visit. Several popular cafés face the bay back near the Tour de Solidor.

To get to Alet by car (see map page 373), follow signs to

Centre-Ville, then *Intra-Muros*. With the rampart walls on your right and the Bassin Vauban port on your left, follow *Toutes Directions* signs south until you spot *Alet* signs, and park near the Tour de Solidor or a block farther at Place St. Pierre. To reach the start of the walking path, walk several blocks (with the sea on your left).

On foot from St-Malo, walk from Porte St. Louis along the road and across the drawbridge (note the dry dock as you pass the second roundabout). Go past the Olympique Piscine (swimming pool), then cut right through the parking lot to the walking path that leads around the harbor. When you reach the seawall, look left for a set of steps that connects to a path around the point. At the top of the steps, you'll find more steps that lead to the small WWII museum and bunkers.

Sleeping in St-Malo

(€1 = $1.30, country code: 33)
Spending a night here gives you more time to enjoy the sunset and sea views from the town walls.

$$$ Hôtel France et Chateaubriand*** is a venerable establishment near the Porte St. Vincent, with 80 rooms at decent rates (Db-€100-170, most rooms around €110, breakfast-€11, secure parking-€15/day, Wi-Fi, 12 Place Chateaubriand, tel. 02 99 56 66 52, fax 02 99 40 10 04, www.hotel-chateaubriand-st-malo.com).

$$$ Hôtel du Louvre***, a modern three-star hotel within the city walls, is run by helpful Philippe and his wife Anne. The hotel has comfortable and chic—if small—rooms (Db-€85-142, breakfast-€12, elevator, Internet access and Wi-Fi, parking-€7.50-12/day, 2 Rue des Marins, tel. 02 99 40 86 62, www.hoteldulouvre-saintmalo.com, contact@hoteldulouvre-saintmalo.com).

$$ Hôtel le Nautilus** is a good place run by the affable team of Loïck and Jean-Michel. It's conveniently located inside the walls near the Porte St. Vincent (Db-€68, Tb-€82, elevator, Internet access and free Wi-Fi, parking-€5/day, 9 Rue de la Corne de Cerf, easiest to park outside walls and walk in through the Porte St. Vincent, tel. 02 99 40 42 27, www.lenautilus.com, info@lenautilus.com).

Eating in St-Malo

St-Malo is all about seafood and crêpes. There's no shortage of restaurants, many serving the local specialty of mussels *(moules)* and oysters *(huitres)*. Look also for bakeries selling *ker-y-pom*, traditional Breton apple-filled shortbread biscuits that are the best-tasting treat in town, especially when warmed.

BRITTANY

Le Corps de Garde Crêperie is my favorite lunch stop. It's up on the walls, with St-Malo's only view tables. They serve original crêpes at fair prices from noon to 22:00, with cool ambience indoors or out (daily, 3 Montée Notre Dame, tel. 02 99 40 91 46).

Bouche en Folie matches tasty specialties that change daily with a cozy setting; it's traditional without being kitsch (*menus* from €25, closed Mon, 14 Rue du Boyer, mobile 06 72 49 08 89).

Coté Sens is my St-Malo splurge. Enthusiastically run by the wife and husband team of Sandrine and Oliver, Coté Sens has a small but delightfully fresh selection that Sandrine happily translates for you (*menus* from €35, daily, 16 Rue de la Herse, tel. 02 99 20 08 12).

Le Chateaubriand, inside the Porte St. Vincent, delivers a grand, Old World aura and offers a full range of choices at decent prices (*menus* from €19, daily, inside and outdoor dining, Place Chateaubriand, tel. 02 99 56 66 52).

St-Malo Connections

From St-Malo by Train to: Dinan (5/day, 1-2 hours, transfer in Dol, bus is better—see below), **Pontorson** (with bus connections to **Mont St-Michel;** 3/day, 1-2 hours, transfer in Dol).

By Bus to: Dinan (5/day, none on Sun except in summer, 1 hour; faster and better than train, as bus stops in both cities are more central), **Mont St-Michel** (2/day, 2 hours, via Pontorson), **Rennes** (4/day). Regional bus service is provided by Tibus (www.tibus.fr) or Illenoo (www.illenoo-services.fr).

Best Way to Mont St-Michel: There are a precious few train-to-bus and bus-to-bus trips that work well (1-2 hours to Mont St-Michel), depending on the time of day. And schedules change like the wind, so let the TI explain your options.

Near St-Malo

Dinard

This upscale-traditional resort comes with a kid-friendly beach and an old-time, Coney Island-style, beach-promenade feel (2 buses/day from Dinan, Mon-Sat only, 1 hour). Its Saturday market is worth going out of your way to see. The small passenger-only ferry from St-Malo *(Bus de Mer)* provides the most scenic arrival (€7 round-trip, runs 9:00-18:00, later in summer, departs Dinard from below Promenade du Clair de Lune at Embarcadère). A visit to Dinard ties in well with a coastal drive to Fort la Latte and Cap Fréhel (described later).

The **TI,** between the casino and Place de la République parking lot, is at 2 Boulevard Féart (daily 10:00-12:30 & 14:00-18:00, tel. 02 99 46 94 12, www.ot-dinard.com). To get to the TI from Place de la République, walk toward the water, take the first right, and make another right onto Boulevard Féart.

Dinard is a 10- to 20-minute drive from St-Malo. Leaving St-Malo, follow *Barrage de la Rance* signs through the unappealing port; when you arrive in Dinard, follow *Centre-Ville* signs, and park on Place de la République.

▲▲Scenic Drive to Coastal Capes and Castles

For drivers, the coastline immediately west of St-Malo and Dinard offers sweeping views of sandy beaches with wind-sculpted rocks, immense cliffs overlooking crashing waves, and sleepy fishing hamlets. The star is Fort la Latte, a medieval castle built on a rocky spur over the ocean—so picturesque that it was featured in a Hollywood movie.

Allow a half day for the entire trip. You'll first drive to the farthest point of the journey—the resort town of Sables-d'Or-les-Pins—and then slowly work your way back toward St-Malo (this route also works well in the opposite direction). If you don't have much time and just want to see the fort, it's about an hour's drive from St-Malo or Dinan.

During summer or on a weekend, do this drive early to avoid crowds. If it's Saturday and off-season, consider starting at the market in Dinard (described earlier) and then follow my directions.

Getting to Sables-d'Or-les-Pins: Coming from St-Malo, take D-168 west, which becomes D-786 near Ploubalay. Continue on D-786 to Sables-d'Or-les-Pins. If you are coming from the south via Dinan, take D-794 to Plancoët, then follow D-19 through Saint-Lormel and join D-786.

Sables-d'Or-les-Pins: This is your first stop. Park near the grand casino and venture out on the sand. Take your shoes off. If the tide's out, you'll see beached fishing boats and miles of sand. Cap Fréhel, your next destination, is a lovely 15-minute drive away. Follow D-34 and drive slowly: View pullouts are there for a reason.

Cap Fréhel: This popular destination lies at the tip of a long peninsula and features walking paths over soaring cliffs with views in all directions. The place gets jammed in the afternoon—if time is tight, skip this stop and head directly to Fort la Latte. You'll pay €2 to park near the stone lighthouse. Views from the trails are sufficiently expansive, but it is possible to climb the lighthouse each afternoon (€2, daily 15:00-17:00). That's Fort la Latte to the east, your next destination. Step down into the cool **Café-Restaurant La Fauconnière** for tables with views and reasonable café fare (drinks, snacks, desserts) at any time and good meals from 12:00-14:00 (open daily until 18:00, tel. 02 96 41 54 20).

Fort la Latte: This mighty fortress, worth ▲▲, is a five-minute drive east of Cap Fréhel. From the parking lot, it's a

10-minute walk to stunning views of a medieval castle hugging onto a massive rock above the ocean (€5, daily 10:30-18:30, tel. 02 96 41 57 11, www.castlelalatte.com). Pick up the English flier and learn the historical background of the castle, then tour it at your own pace.

The first fort on this site, made out of wood, was built as a lookout for those nasty Normans. What you see today dates from the 14th and 15th centuries, when wars between England and France caught Brittany in the middle for well over a hundred years. While the castle was never successfully attacked from the sea, in 1597 its garrison of 25 men was overwhelmed by a force of 2,000 soldiers coming from land. Later, Louis XIV's military architect Vauban oversaw work shoring up the castle's outer defenses. The castle was used well into the 18th century.

Touring the site, you'll cross two impressive drawbridges (notice the spiked gates), peer into dungeons (one still houses a prisoner), and wander ramparts towering high above the ocean. The guardroom houses a small gift shop (there's a good book about the castle in English for €5). The small chapel was added in the 18th century, replacing the original chapel, and is dedicated to St. Michael, protector of warriors. The largest structure inside the fort is the governor's lodge (closed to the public).

The highlight of a visit to Fort la Latte is the climb to the top of the castle keep, with its 360-degree view. You'll pass several beautifully vaulted rooms on the way up.

Once on top, as you gaze out from this invincible castle, clinging for its life to a rock, think of Fort la Latte as a symbol of Brittany's determination to remain independent from France. It's no surprise that Hollywood used this castle in the 1958 film *The Vikings* with Kirk Douglas. The low-slung *four à boulets* in the western end served as a kiln to heat cannon balls. The defenders aimed hot shots at ships to set them afire. That's cool. One hundred cannon balls could be heated at a time.

If you want to stretch your legs, a trail leaves from behind the ticket kiosk links to Cap Fréhel. A 10-minute walk up this path rewards you with killer views back to the fort; it takes 75 minutes to walk all the way to the cape. There's also a short trail down to a rocky beach, giving you a sea-level perspective of the fortress.

Fort la Latte to St-Malo: Take D-16 back to D-786 and head east. A worthwhile detour on the way is **Pointe du Chevet.** Drive through the sweet little town of St-Jacut-de-la-Mer, then track signs to *Pointe Chevet*—and don't park until the road ends. Beautiful views (and far fewer people) surround you. If the tide is out, you can hike to an island and study the impressive rows of wooden piers sunk into the bay. These are used to grow mussels, which cling to the wooden poles; farmers eventually harvest them using a machine that pushes a ring around the poles. From here, return to D-786 heading toward Ploubalay and find signs to *St-Malo* or *Dinan*.

▲▲Scenic Drive Between St-Malo and Mont St-Michel

If you have less time, consider this lovely ride—worth ▲▲▲ if it's clear (see route on map on page 357). This quick taste-of-Brittany driving tour samples a bit of the rugged peninsula's coast, with lots of views but no dramatic forts. Allow two hours for the drive between Mont St-Michel and St-Malo, including stops (a more direct route takes 45 minutes). On a weekend or in summer, the drive will take longer—start early. These directions are from St-Malo to Mont St-Michel, but the drive works just as well in reverse order.

St-Malo to the Emerald Coast: From St-Malo, take the scenic road hugging the coast east on D-201 to Pointe du Grouin, where the appropriately named Emerald Coast (Côte d'Emeraude) begins. Leave St-Malo, following *Cancale* signs and passing countless roundabouts, then look for signs to *Rothéneuf,* where you'll access D-201, which skirts in and out of camera-worthy views. Brown signs lead to short worthwhile detours to the coast; these are my favorites:

Ile Besnard and Dunes de Chevets: A five-minute detour off D-201 leads to this pretty, sandy beach arcing alongside a crescent bay. There are rocks rising from the water to scramble on, a nature trail above the beach, and a view restaurant by the campground (Les Chevets Bar/Restaurant, closed Mon-Tue). From the hamlet of La Guimorais, a 10-minute drive from Rothéneuf, follow signs to *Ile Besnard* and *Dunes de Chevets* to the very end (past the campground), and park at the far end of the lot.

Pointe du Grouin: This striking rock outcrop yields views from easy trails in all directions. Park near Hôtel du Grouin (outdoor café with views), and continue on foot. Pass the *semaphore du grouin* (signal station), where paths lead everywhere. Breathe in the sea air. Can you spot Mont St-Michel in the distance? The big rock below is L'Ile des Landes, an island earmarked for a fort during the French Revolution. The fort was never built, and the island remains home to thousands of birds. What fool would build on an island in this bay?

Cancale: Return to your car and leave Pointe du Grouin, following signs to *Cancale*, Brittany's appealing oyster capital. Its harbor *(le port)* is lined with restaurants, all offering oysters and mussels. Upon arrival in Cancale, follow *par la côte* signs to arrive on the port side. Slurp oysters here.

Cancale to Mont St-Michel: Cancale is a 45-minute drive from Mont St-Michel. Head out of Cancale toward Mont St-Michel on D-155, then D-797, and drive along *la Route de la Baie,* which skirts the bay and passes big-time oyster farming, windmill towers (most lacking their sails), flocks of sheep, and, at low tide, grounded boats waiting for the sea to return. On a clear day, look for Mont St-Michel in the distance. On a foggy day, look harder.

Fougères

BRITTANY

The very Breton city of Fougères, worth ▲, is a handy stop for drivers traveling between the Loire châteaux and Mont St-Michel.

Fougères has one of Europe's largest medieval castles, a lovely old city center, and a panoramic park viewpoint. Drivers follow *Centre-Ville* signs, then *Château,* and park at the free lot just past the château.

For a memorable, leg-stretching stroll, start from the parking lot near the château. Walk into Fougères with the water-filled moat on your left, then follow *Jardin Public* signs. Stop for a peek in the handsome church of St. Sulpice (English handout inside); the woodwork is exceptional, from the paneled walls and ceiling to the choir stalls and the carved altar. Then let the *Jardin Public* signs lead you through back streets, passing gingerbread-like Breton homes, up into the lush park. Walk through manicured gardens to the base of St. Léonard Church and find the floral panorama. Double back most of the way you came, then veer right to the château and under the stone gate. There's no reason to enter the château unless you need more exercise or a town map (€8, includes audioguide, daily 10:00-12:30 & 14:00-18:00, July-Aug until 19:00, Oct-April until 17:30, tel. 02 99 99 79 59, www.chateau-fougeres.com). For a good view of the castle without the previous climb, walk a block above the castle (up Rue de la Pinterie) and find the short ramparts across from the *crêperie* recommended next.

Eating in Fougères: You'll find a gaggle of cafés and *crêperies* near the castle with good choices and prices. **Le Bonheur Est Dans le Blé** is a notch above the others, serving tasty crêpes on a lovely little terrace overlooking the valley (closed Tue evening except July-Aug, a block up from the château at 3 Rue Fourchette, tel. 02 99 94 99 72).

THE LOIRE

Amboise • Chinon • Beaucoup de Châteaux

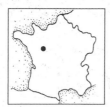

As it glides gently east to west, officially separating northern from southern France, the Loire River has come to define this popular tourist region. The importance of this river and the valley's prime location, in the center of the country just south of Paris, have made the Loire a strategic hot potato for more than a thousand years. The Loire was the high-water mark for the Moors as they pushed into Europe from Morocco. (Loire means "impassable" in Arabic.) Today, this region is still the dividing line for the country—for example, weather forecasters say, "north of the Loire…and south of the Loire…"

Because of its history, this region is home to more than a thousand castles and palaces of all shapes and sizes. When a "valley address" became a must-have among 16th-century hunting-crazy royalty, rich Renaissance palaces replaced outdated medieval castles.

Hundreds of these castles and palaces are open to visitors, and it's castles that you're here to see (you'll find better villages and cities elsewhere). Old-time aristocratic château-owners, struggling with the cost of upkeep, enjoy financial assistance from the government if they open their mansions to the public.

Today's Loire Valley is carpeted with fertile fields, crisscrossed by rivers, and laced with rolling hills. It's one of France's most important agricultural regions. It's also under some development pressure, thanks to TGV bullet trains that link it to Paris in an hour, and cheap flights to England that make it a prime second-home spot for many Brits, including Sir Mick Jagger.

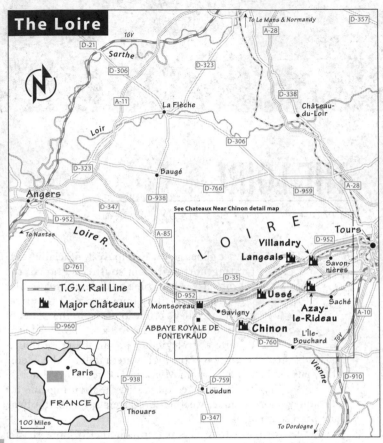

The Loire

T.G.V. Rail Line

Major Châteaux

100 Miles

Paris

FRANCE

To Nantes

Angers

Loire R.

Sarthe

La Flèche

Loir

Baugé

Montsoreau

ABBAYE ROYALE DE
FONTEVRAUD

Savigny

Chinon

See Chateaux Near Chinon detail map

L O I R E

Villandry

Langeais

Ussé

Azay-
le-Rideau

L'Île-
Bouchard

Saché

Savon-
nières

Tours

Château-
du-Loir

Thouars

Loudun

To Dordogne

To Le Mans & Normandy

Choosing a Home Base

This is a big, unwieldy region for travelers, so I've divided it into
two halves, each centered around a good, manageable town to use
as a base: Amboise and Chinon. Châteaux-holics and gardeners
can stay longer and sleep in both towns. Amboise is east of the
big city of Tours, and Chinon lies to Tours' west. The drive from
Amboise to Chinon takes over an hour; if you sleep on one side of
Tours and intend to visit castles on the other side, you're looking at
a long round-trip drive—certainly doable, but not my idea of good
travel. Instead, sleep in or near the town nearest the castles you
plan to visit, and avoid crossing the traffic-laden city of Tours. The
A-85 autoroute is the quickest way to link Amboise with châteaux
near Chinon. Thanks to this uncrowded freeway, sleepy Azay-le-
Rideau is another good base for destinations west of Tours, and
also works as a base for sights on both sides of Tours.

Amboise is the best home base for first-timers to this area, as

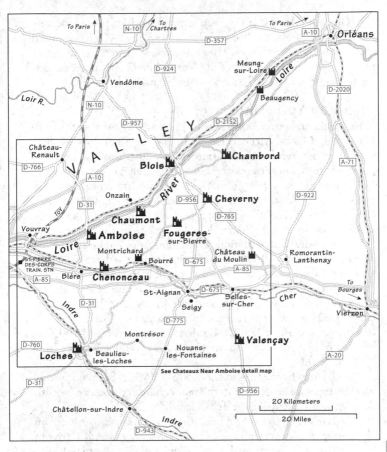

it offers handy access to these important châteaux: Chenonceau, Blois, Chambord, Cheverny, Fougères-sur-Bièvre, Chaumont-sur-Loire, Loches, and Valençay. Amboise also has better train connections from Paris and better public transportation options to nearby sights, making it the preferable choice if you don't want to rent a car or bike.

Chinon, Azay-le-Rideau, and their nearby châteaux don't feel as touristy, and appeal to gardeners and road-less-traveled types. The key sights in this area include the châteaux of Chinon, Azay-le-Rideau, Langeais, Villandry, Chatonnière, Rivau, Ussé, and the Abbaye Royale de Fontevraud. Chinon and Azay-le-Rideau are good for cyclists, with convenient rental shops, decent access to bike paths, and interesting destinations within pedaling distance.

Loches is a more remote home-base option for drivers wanting to sleep away from the tourist fray.

THE LOIRE

Château Hotels: If ever you wanted to sleep in a castle surrounded by a forest, the Loire Valley is the place—you have several choices in all price ranges. However, you'll need a car to get to most of these places. Most of my "castle hotel" recommendations are within 15 minutes of Amboise (see page 410).

Planning Your Time

With frequent, convenient trains to Paris and a few direct runs to Charles de Gaulle Airport, the Loire can be a good first or last stop on your French odyssey (more than 20 trains/day between Paris' Gare Montparnasse or Gare d'Austerlitz and Amboise, 1.5-2 hours; some trains from Gare d'Austerlitz require an easy transfer in Orléans, and all trains from Montparnasse require a change in St-Pierre-des-Corps; 5 trains/day between Charles de Gaulle Airport and St-Pierre-des-Corps, 2 hours; easy car rental at St-Pierre-des-Corps Station, 15 minutes from Amboise).

A day and a half is sufficient to sample the best châteaux. Don't go overboard. Two châteaux, possibly three (if you're a big person), make up the recommended daily dosage. Famous châteaux are least crowded early and late in the day. Most open at about 9:00 and close between 18:00 and 19:00. During the off-season, some close at 17:00 and midday from 12:00 to 14:00. The Festival of Gardens at Chaumont runs May to mid-October from 10:00 to 20:00.

A day trip from Paris to the Loire is doable. Several minivan and bus tours make getting to the main châteaux a breeze (see "By Bus, Minivan Excursion, or Taxi," later).

Drivers: For the single best day in the Loire, consider this plan: Sleep in or near Amboise and visit Chenonceau early (arrive by 9:00), when crowds are small; spend midday at Chambord (30-minute drive from Chenonceau); and enjoy Chaumont or Cheverny on the way back to your hotel (the hunting dogs are fed at 17:00 on most days at Cheverny). Remember to allow time to visit Amboise. With a second full day, move to Chinon, visiting Villandry and Langeais en route, then devote your afternoon to Chinon.

The best map of the area is Michelin #518, covering all the sights described in this chapter (the TI's free map of Touraine, the area surrounding Tours, is also good).

Try to see one château on your drive in (for example, if arriving from the north, visit Chambord, Cheverny, or Blois; if coming from the west or the south, see Azay-le-Rideau, Chinon, Langeais, or Villandry). If you're coming from Burgundy, don't miss the one-of-a-kind Château de Guédelon (see page 966 in the Burgundy chapter). If you're driving to the Dordogne from the Loire, the A-20 autoroute via Limoges (near Oradour-sur-Glane) is fastest and toll-free until Brive-la-Gaillarde.

Without a Car and on a Budget: Sleep in Amboise. The next morning, rent a bike or catch the public bus, shuttle van (high season only), or train from Amboise to the town of Chenonceaux, tour Chenonceau (the château), then return to Amboise in the afternoon to enjoy its château and Leonardo's last stand at Clos-Lucé. With a second day, take the short (and cheap) train ride to Blois, tour its castle and old town, and take the €6 excursion bus (runs April-Aug) to Chambord and Cheverny. (For more train and bus specifics, see "Amboise Connections" on page 413 and "Blois Connections" on page 427.) Those connecting Paris with Amboise or Chinon can layover in Blois en route (baggage check available at château).

Fit budget travelers based in Chinon can bike to Langeais, Ussé, and Villandry, and/or take the train to Azay-le-Rideau and Langeais (but keep in mind that the train trips are long and not a good option for most).

Without a Car but Not Broke (Yet): Take a minivan excursion directly from Amboise or Tours (described in the next section).

Getting Around the Loire Valley

If you're looking to hunt down remote châteaux, rent a car. Day rentals are reasonable and easy in Amboise and at the St-Pierre-des-Corps train station in Tours (but not in Chinon). Trains, buses, minivan tours, bikes, or taxis help non-drivers reach the well-known châteaux. To get to the less-famous châteaux without a car, you can take a taxi, arrange a custom minivan excursion (affordable for small groups), or ride a bike (great option for those with time and stamina). Parking is free at all châteaux except Chambord.

By Train

With easy access from Amboise and Chinon, the big city of Tours is the transport hub for travelers bent on using trains or buses to explore the Loire (but it has little else to offer visitors—I wouldn't sleep there). Tours has two important train stations and a major bus station (with service to several châteaux). The main train station is called Tours SNCF, and the smaller, suburban TGV Station (located between Tours and Amboise) is St-Pierre-des-Corps. Check the schedules carefully, as service is sparse on some lines. The châteaux of Amboise, Blois, Chenonceau, Chaumont (via the town of Onzain plus a long walk), Langeais, Chinon, and Azay-le-Rideau all have train and/or bus service from Tours' main SNCF Station; Amboise, Blois, Chaumont, and Chenonceau are also served from Tours' St-Pierre-des-Corps Station. Look under each sight for specifics, and seriously consider a minivan excursion (described next).

Loire Valley Châteaux at a Glance

Which châteaux should you visit—and why? Here's a quick summary. Remember, TIs sell bundled tickets for several châteaux that save you money and time in ticket lines (see page 395).

Châteaux East of Tours

▲▲▲**Chenonceau** For sheer elegance arching over the Cher River, and for its lovely gardens. **Hours:** Daily mid-March-mid-Sept 9:00-19:30, July-Aug until 20:00, closes earlier off-season. See page 417.

▲▲**Blois** For its urban setting, beautiful courtyard, and fun sound-and-light show. **Hours:** Daily July-Aug 9:00-19:00, April-June and Sept 9:00-18:30, Oct 9:00-17:30, Nov-March 9:00-12:30 & 14:00-17:30. See page 424.

▲▲**Chambord** For its grandeur (440 rooms), fun rooftop views, and evocative setting surrounded by a forest. **Hours:** Daily April-Sept 9:00-18:15, Oct-March 9:00-17:15. See page 428.

▲▲**Cheverny** For its intimate feel, lavishly furnished rooms, and daily feeding of the hunting dogs. **Hours:** Daily July-Aug 9:15-19:00, April-June and Sept 9:15-18:15, Oct 9:45-17:30, Nov-March 9:45-17:00. See page 432.

▲▲**Chaumont-sur-Loire** For its imposing setting over the Loire River, intriguing rooms, and impressive Festival of the Gardens. **Hours:** Daily July-Aug 10:00-19:00, May-June and early Sept 10:00-18:00, April and late Sept 10:30-17:30, Oct-March 10:00-17:00. See page 434.

Chenonceau

Chambord

THE LOIRE

▲**Amboise** For terrific views over Amboise and Leonardo da Vinci memories. **Hours:** Daily April-June 9:00-18:30, July-Aug 9:00-19:00, Sept-Oct and March 9:00-18:00, Nov-Jan 9:00-12:00 & 14:00-16:45, Feb 9:00-12:00 & 13:30-17:30. See page 400.

▲**Clos-Lucé (in Amboise)** For a chance to see Leonardo da Vinci's final home, and to stroll through gardens decorated with models of his creations. **Hours:** Daily April-Oct 9:00-19:00, Nov-Dec and Feb-March 9:00-18:00, Jan 9:00-17:00. See page 402.

Châteaux West of Tours

▲▲**Azay-le-Rideau** For its fairy-tale facade and setting on a romantic reflecting pond, and for its beautifully furnished rooms. **Hours:** Daily July-Aug 9:30-19:00, April-June and Sept-Oct 9:30-18:00, Nov-March 10:00-17:15. See page 449.

▲▲**Villandry** For the best gardens in the Loire Valley. **Hours:** Daily April-Sept 9:00-19:00, March and Oct 9:00-18:00, Nov-Feb 9:00-17:00. See page 453.

▲**Chinon** For its Joan of Arc history. **Hours:** Daily March-Oct 9:30-18:00, until 19:00 in May-Aug; Nov-Feb 9:30-17:00. See page 442.

▲**Langeais** For its fortress-like setting above an appealing little village, and its 16th-century furnished rooms. **Hours:** Daily July-Aug 9:00-19:00, April-June and Sept-mid-Nov 9:30-18:30, mid-Nov-March 10:00-17:00. See page 452.

Chaumont-sur-Loire

Azay-le-Rideau

THE LOIRE

By Bus, Minivan Excursion, or Taxi

A few bus and shuttle van routes and minivan excursions offer painless transportation to the valley's châteaux (but little information). These organized itineraries make life far easier for those without a car, and can save you time (in line) and money (on admissions) when you purchase your château ticket at a discounted group rate from the driver. TIs in the region have details on the options listed here, and on others offering similar services.

Although the minivan companies don't visit all the castles in this chapter, they organize custom excursions, and will pick up your small group in Amboise, Chinon, or Azay-le-Rideau (€20-35/person for scheduled half-day itineraries from Tours, €45-50 for all day; figure €220 for custom groups of up to 7 for 4 hours, €390 for all day).

From Amboise to East of Tours

This area's three big-name castles—Chenonceau, Chambord, and Cheverny—are reachable by bus or shuttle van; minivan tours offer visits to the same three, and quick glances at a few others.

By Bus: If you're on a budget and visiting in high season, the region's buses are workable. A handy excursion bus departs from the Blois train station—an easy train ride from Amboise—and runs a loop route connecting Blois, Chambord, Cheverny, and (skippable) Beauregard, allowing visits to the châteaux with your pick of return times. This service runs from April through August (see "Blois Connections," page 427). Buses also connect Amboise and Chenonceaux (1-2/day; see "Amboise Connections," page 413).

By Minivan Excursion: Quart de Tours runs a high-season-only shuttle service between Amboise and the Château de Chenonceau, and between Amboise, Chambord, and Cheverny. **Touraine Evasion** runs a similar shuttle combining Chambord and Chenonceau (see "Amboise Connections," page 413).

Based in Amboise, **Acco-Dispo** is a small, well-run minibus company with good all-day, English-language château tours from Amboise and Tours. Costs vary with the itinerary (from Amboise—half-day-€34/person, full-day-€52; from Tours—half-day-€21/person, full-day-€52; daily, free hotel pickups, small groups of 2-8 people, mobile 06 82 00 64 51, fax 02 47 57 67 13, www.accodispo-tours.com). While on the road, you'll usually get a fun and enthusiastic running commentary covering each château's background, as well as the region's contemporary scene—but you're on your own at the château itself. (You're responsible for entry fees but can buy discounted tickets from the driver.) All-day tours depart 8:30-10:30 (varies by itinerary); afternoon tours depart 13:00-13:30. Both return to Amboise or Tours at about 18:30. Most itineraries include Chenonceau, and some throw in a wine-tasting.

Reserve a week ahead by email, or two or three days ahead by phone. (Day-trippers from Paris find this service convenient; after a one-hour TGV ride to Tours, you're met near the Tours SNCF Station and returned there at day's end.) Acco-Dispo also runs multi-day tours of the Loire and Brittany.

Another minivan option, **Loire Valley Tours** offers all-day itineraries from Amboise to either châteaux near Amboise or châteaux near Chinon. The tours are fully guided and include admissions, lunch, and wine-tasting (about €135/person, tel. 02 54 33 99 80, www.loire-valley-tours.com, contact@loire-valley -tours.com).

By Taxi: Taxi excursions from the Blois train station to nearby châteaux can be affordable when split among several people. For details, see "Blois Connections," page 427, or call the Blois TI at tel. 02 54 90 41 41.

From Chinon to Châteaux West of Tours

Tours is a one-hour train ride from Chinon (11 trains or SNCF buses/day). Minivan excursions leave from Tours' TI to many châteaux, including Azay-le-Rideau and Villandry. Try **Acco-Dispo** or **Quart de Tours,** with daily three-hour tours to Azay-le-Rideau and Villandry for about €22 (both companies described earlier). **Touraine Evasion** offers similar services and prices with an audio-guide (mobile 06 07 39 13 31, www.tourevasion.com).

By Bike

Cycling options are endless in the Loire, where the elevation gain is generally manageable. (However, if you have only a day or two, rent a car or stick to the châteaux easily reached by buses and mini-vans.) Amboise, Chenonceaux, Blois, Azay-le-Rideau, and Chinon all make good biking bases and have rental options (ask at the TI in each city for bike rental shops). A network of nearly 200 miles of bike paths and well-signed country lanes connect many châteaux near Amboise. Pick up the free bike-path map at any TI, buy the more detailed map available at TIs, or study the route options at www.loireavelo.fr. (I also list several accommodations with easy access to these bike paths.)

Near Chinon, a 30-mile bike path runs along the Loire River, passing by Ussé and Langeais, then meeting the Cher River at Villandry and continuing along the Cher to Tours and beyond. To follow this route, pick up the *La Loire à Vélo* brochure at any area TI.

Détours de Loire can help you plan your bike route and will deliver rental bikes to most places in the Loire for reasonable rates. They have a full range of bikes from kid-size to tandems, and will shuttle luggage to your next stop. They have shops in Amboise,

THE LOIRE

Hot-Air Balloon Rides

In France's most popular regions, you'll find hot-air balloon companies eager to take you for a ride (Burgundy, the Loire, Dordogne, and Provence are best suited for ballooning). It's not cheap, but it's unforgettable—a once-in-a-lifetime chance to sail serenely over châteaux, canals, vineyards, Romanesque churches, and villages. Balloons don't go above 3,000 feet and usually fly much lower than that, so you get a bird's-eye view of France's sublime landscapes.

Most companies offer similar deals and work this way: Trips range from 45 to 90 minutes of air time, to which you should add two hours for preparation, champagne toast, and transport back to your starting point. Deluxe trips add a gourmet picnic, making it a four-hour event. Allow about €190 for a short tour, and about €270 for longer flights. Departures are, of course, weather-dependent, and are usually scheduled first thing in the morning or in early evening. If you've booked ahead and the weather turns bad, you can reschedule your flight, but you can't get your money back. Most balloon companies charge about €25 more for a bad-weather refund guarantee; unless your itinerary is very loose, it's a good idea.

Flight season is April through October. It's smart to bring a jacket for the breeze, though temperatures in the air won't differ too much from those on the ground. Air sickness is usually not a problem, as the ride is typically slow and even. Baskets have no seating, so count on standing the entire trip. Group (and basket) size can vary from 4 to 16 passengers. Area TIs have brochures. **France Montgolfières** gets good reviews and offers flights in the areas that I recommend (tel. 02 54 32 20 48, fax 02 54 32 20 07, www.france-mont golfiere.com). Others are **Aérocom Montgolfière** (tel. 02 54 33 55 00, www.aerocom.fr) and **Touraine Montgolfière** (tel. 02 47 56 42 05, www.touraine-montgolfiere.fr).

Blois, and Tours and allow one-way rentals between shops at no added charge (www.locationdevelos.com).

By Car

You can rent a car most easily at Tours' St-Pierre-des-Corps train station, or in Amboise (see page 398). I've listed specific driving instructions for each destination covered in this chapter.

The Loire Valley's Cuisine Scene

Here in "the garden of France," locally produced food is delicious. Loire Valley rivers yield fresh trout *(truite)*, salmon *(saumon)*, and smelt *(éperlau)*, which are often served fried *(friture)*. *Rillettes*, a stringy pile of cooked and whipped pork, makes for a cheap, mouthwatering sandwich spread (use lots of mustard and add a baby pickle, called a *cornichon*). The area's wonderful goat cheeses include Crottin de Chavignol (*crottin* means horse dung, which is what this cheese, when aged, resembles), Saint-Maure Fermier (soft and creamy), and Selles-sur-Cher (mild). For dessert, try a delicious *tarte tatin* (upside-down caramel-apple tart).

Remember, restaurants serve food only during lunch (11:30-14:00) and dinner (19:00-21:00, later in bigger cities); bigger cafés offer eats throughout the day.

Wines of the Loire

Loire wines are overlooked, and that's a shame—there is gold in them thar grapes. The Loire is France's third-largest producer of wine and grows the greatest variety of any region. Four main grapes are grown in the Loire: two reds, Gamay and Cabernet Franc, and two whites, Sauvignon Blanc and Chenin Blanc.

The Loire is divided into four subareas, and the name of a wine (its *appellation*) generally refers to where its grapes were grown. The Touraine subarea encompasses the wines of Chinon and Amboise. Using 100 percent Cabernet Franc grapes, growers in Chinon and Bourgeuil are the main (and best) producers of reds. Thanks to soil variation and climate differences year in and out, wines made from a single grape have a remarkable range in taste. The best and most expensive white wines are the Sancerres, made on the less-touristed eastern edge of the Loire. Less expensive, but still tasty, are Touraine Sauvignons and the sweeter Vouvray, whose grapes are grown near Amboise. Vouvray is also famous for its light and refreshing sparkling wines (called *vins pétillants*)—locals will tell you the only proper way to begin any meal in this region is with a glass of it, and I can't disagree (try the *rosé pétillant* for a fresh sensation). A dry rosé is popular in the Loire in the summer and can be made from a variety of grapes.

You'll pass vineyards as you travel between châteaux, though there's no scenic wine road to speak of (the closest thing is around Bourgeuil). Remember that it's best to call ahead before visiting a winery.

THE LOIRE

East of Tours

Amboise

Straddling the widest stretch of the Loire River, Amboise is an inviting town with a pleasing old quarter below its hilltop château.

A castle has overlooked the Loire from Amboise since Roman times. Leonardo da Vinci retired here... just one more of his many brilliant ideas.

As the royal residence of François I (r. 1515-1547), Amboise wielded far more importance than you'd imagine from a lazy walk through its pleasant, pedestrian-only commercial zone. In fact, its residents are quite conservative, giving the town an attitude—as if no one told them they're no longer the second capital of France. The locals keep their wealth to themselves; consequently, many grand mansions hide behind nondescript facades.

With or without a car, Amboise is an ideal small-town home base for exploring the best of château country.

Orientation to Amboise

Amboise (pop. 14,000) covers ground on both sides of the Loire, with the "Golden Island" (Ile d'Or) in the middle. The train station is on the north side of the Loire, but nearly everything else is on the south (château) side, including the TI and steady traffic. Pedestrian-friendly Rue Nationale parallels the river a few blocks inland and leads from the base of Château d'Amboise through the town center and past the clock tower—once part of the town wall—to the striking Romanesque Church of St. Denis.

Tourist Information

The information-packed TI is on Quai du Général de Gaulle (May-Sept Mon-Sat 9:30-18:30, Sun 10:00-13:00 & 14:00-17:00; Oct-April Mon-Sat 10:00-13:00 & 14:00-18:00, Sun 10:00-13:00; tel. 02 47 57 09 28, www.amboise-valdeloire.com). Pick up the brochures with self-guided walking tours in and around the city, and consider pre-purchasing tickets to key area châteaux (saving time in ticket lines—explained under "Helpful Hints," later). Ask about sound-and-light shows in the region (generally summers only). The TI stores bags (€2.50 each), books local guides, and can reserve a room for you in a hotel or *chambre d'hôte* (€2.50 fee). Their free English-speaking service, SOS Chambres d'Hôtes, can tell you which rooms are still available when the TI is closed (tel. 02 47 23 27 42).

Arrival in Amboise

By Train: Amboise's train station is birds-chirping peaceful. You can't store bags here, but you can leave them at the TI (see above). Turn left out of the main station (you may have to cross under the tracks first), make a quick right, and walk down Rue Jules Ferry five minutes to the end, then turn right and cross the long bridge leading over the Loire River to the city center. It's a €6 taxi ride from the station to central Amboise, but taxis seldom wait at the station (taxi tel. 02 47 57 13 53 or 02 47 57 30 39).

By Car: Drivers set their sights on the flag-festooned château that caps the hill. Most recommended accommodations and restaurants either have or can help you locate parking (it's free in the big lot along the river).

Helpful Hints

Save Time and Money: The TI sells tickets in bundles of two or more to sights and châteaux around Amboise and Chinon (called "le Pass," valid for a year). This will save you some on entry fees—and, more important, time spent in line at each sight (for example, the pass for Clos-Lucé and the châteaux of Amboise, Chambord, and Chaumont saves €3.50 over individual ticket prices). You can also get discounted tickets if you take a minivan tour (see "Getting Around the Loire Valley" on page 387).

Market Days: Open-air markets are held on Friday (smaller but more local; food only) and Sunday (the big one) in the parking lot behind the TI on the river (both 8:30-13:00).

Regional Products: Galland, at 29 Rue Nationale, sells fine food and wine products from the Loire (daily 9:30-19:00).

Supermarket: Carrefour City is near the TI (Mon-Sat 7:00-21:00, Sun 9:00-13:00), though the shops on pedestrian-only Rue Nationale are infinitely more pleasing.

Internet Access: The **TI** has a public computer terminal and can tell you where to find Wi-Fi.

Bookstore: Maison de la Presse is a good bookstore with a small selection of English novels and a big selection of maps and English guidebooks—such as Michelin's Green Guide *Châteaux of the Loire* (English version costs €16; they also sell English translations of bike-route books, open Mon 14:00-19:00, Tue-Sat 8:00-19:00, Sun 9:00-13:00, across from the TI at 5 Quai du Général de Gaulle).

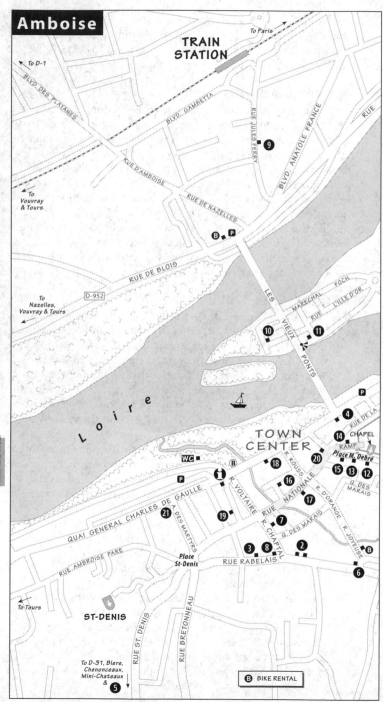

Amboise

TRAIN STATION

To Paris

To D-1

BLVD DES PLATANES

BLVD GAMBETTA

RUE JULES FERRY

RUE D'AMBOISE

BLVD ANATOLE FRANCE

RUE

To Vouvray & Tours

RUE DE NAZELLES

9

B **P**

RUE DE BLOIS

D-952

To Nazelles, Vouvray & Tours

LES VIEUX PONTS

RUE MARECHAL FOCH

RUE L'ILLE D'OR

10 **11**

Loire

P

RUE DE LA

4

CHAPEL

TOWN CENTER

14

RAMP

Place M. Debré

WC

B

18

R. ROUSS

20

15 **13** **12**

P

i

R. VOLTAIRE

16

RUE NATIONALE

R. D'ORANGE

17

Q. DES MARAIS

QUAI GENERAL CHARLES DE GAULLE

A DES MARTYRS

21

19

R. CHAPTAL

7

Q. DES MARAIS

R. JOYEUSE

B

RUE AMBROISE PARE

Place St-Denis

3 **8**

2

6

RUE RABELAIS

ST-DENIS

RUE ST-DENIS

RUE BRETONNEAU

To Tours

To D-31, Blere, Chenonceaux, Mini-Chateaux &

5

B BIKE RENTAL

THE LOIRE

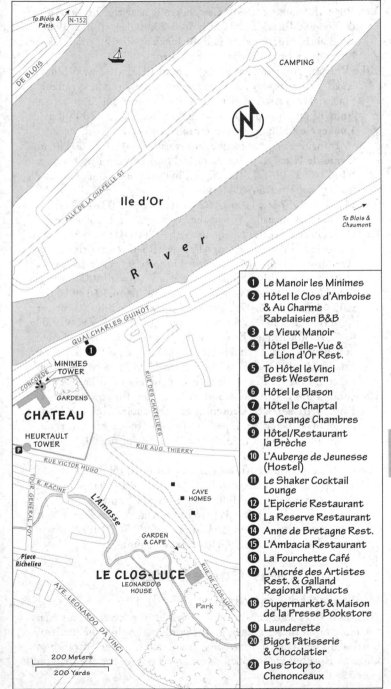

1. Le Manoir les Minimes
2. Hôtel le Clos d'Amboise & Au Charme Rabelaisien B&B
3. Le Vieux Manoir
4. Hôtel Belle-Vue & Le Lion d'Or Rest.
5. To Hôtel le Vinci Best Western
6. Hôtel le Blason
7. Hôtel le Chaptal
8. La Grange Chambres
9. Hôtel/Restaurant la Brèche
10. L'Auberge de Jeunesse (Hostel)
11. Le Shaker Cocktail Lounge
12. L'Epicerie Restaurant
13. La Reserve Restaurant
14. Anne de Bretagne Rest.
15. L'Ambacia Restaurant
16. La Fourchette Café
17. L'Ancrée des Artistes Rest. & Galland Regional Products
18. Supermarket & Maison de la Presse Bookstore
19. Launderette
20. Bigot Pâtisserie & Chocolatier
21. Bus Stop to Chenonceaux

THE LOIRE

Laundry: The handy coin-op **Lav'centre** is near the TI, up Allée du Sergent Turpin at #9 (daily 7:00-20:00, last wash at 19:00, English instructions). The door locks at closing time; leave beforehand, or you'll trigger the alarm.

Bike Rental: You can rent a bike (about €11/half-day, €15/day, leave your passport or a photocopy) at any of these reliable places: **Détours de Loire** (daily, in round building across from TI on Quai du Général de Gaulle, tel. 02 47 30 00 55), **Locacycle** (daily, full-day rentals can be returned the next morning, 2 Rue Jean-Jacques Rousseau, tel. 02 47 57 00 28), or **Cycles le Duc** (good bikes, closed Sun-Mon, 5 Rue Joyeuse, tel. 02 47 57 00 17). The signed bike route to Chenonceaux leads past Leonardo's Clos-Lucé.

Taxi: Call 02 47 57 13 53, 06 12 92 70 46, or 06 88 02 44 10 (allow €25 to Chenonceaux, €35 in the evening or on Sun).

Car Rental: You can rent cars at the St-Pierre-des-Corps train station (TGV service from Paris), a 15-minute drive from Amboise. On the outskirts of Amboise, **Garage Jourdain** rents cars (roughly €50/day for a small car with 100 kilometers/62 miles free, Mon-Fri 7:45-12:00 & 14:00-18:00, Sat 9:00-12:00 & 14:00-17:00, closed Sun, about a mile downriver from the TI at 105 Avenue de Tours, tel. 02 47 57 17 92, fax 02 47 57 77 50). Pricier **Europcar** is outside Amboise on Route de Chenonceaux at the Total gas station (about €68/day for a small car, tel. 02 47 57 07 64, fax 02 47 23 25 14, www.europ car.com). Figure €7 for a taxi from Amboise to either place.

Chocolate Fantasy: A tasty and historic stop for chocoholics is **Bigot Pâtisserie & Chocolatier.** Try their specialty, Puits d'Amour—"Well of Love" (daily, one block off the river, where Place Michel Debré meets Rue Nationale, tel. 02 47 57 04 46).

Private Guide: Fabrice Maret is an expert in all things Loire and a great teacher. He lives in Blois but can meet you in Amboise to give an excellent walking tour of the city and its sights, or join your car and guide you around the area's châteaux (€260/day plus transportation from Blois, tel. 02 54 70 19 59, www.chateauxloire.com, info@chateauxloire.com).

Self-Guided Walk

Welcome to Amboise

This short walk starts at the banks of the Loire River, winds past the old church of St. Denis, and meanders through the heart of town to a fine little city museum. You'll end near the entrance to Château Royal d'Amboise and Leonardo's house. See the map on page 396 to orient yourself.

• *Climb to the top of the embankment overlooking the river across from the TI.*

Amboise Riverbank: Survey the town, its island, bridge, and castle. If you have a passion for anything French—philosophy, history, food, wine—you'll feel it here, along the Loire. This river, the longest in France and the natural boundary between northern and southern France, is the last "untamed" river in the country (there are no dams or mechanisms to control periodic flooding). The region's châteaux line up along the Loire and its tributaries, because before trains and trucks, stones for big buildings were best shipped by boat. You may see a few of the traditional flat-bottomed Loire boats moored here. The bridge spanning the river isn't just any bridge. It marks a strategic river crossing and a longtime political border. That's why the first Amboise castle was built here. In the 15th century, this was one of the biggest forts in France.

The half-mile-long "Golden Island" is the only island in the Loire substantial enough to withstand flooding and to have permanent buildings (including a soccer stadium and a 13th-century church). It was important historically as the place where northern and southern France came together. Truces were made here.

• *Walk downstream and cross the busy Quai du Général de Gaulle when you see the post office (PTT) on the other side. Walk up Avenue des Martyrs de la Résistance and find the old church standing proudly on a bluff to the right (see map).*

Church of St. Denis (Eglise St. Denis): Ever since ancient Romans erected a Temple of Mars here, this has been a place of worship. According to legend, God sent a bolt of lightning that knocked down the statue of Mars, and Christians took over the spot. The current Romanesque church dates from the 12th century. A cute little statue of St. Denis (above the round arch) greets you as you step in. The delightful carvings capping the columns inside date from Romanesque times. The lovely pastel-painted *Deposition* to the right of the choir is restored to its 16th-century brilliance. The medieval stained glass in the windows, likely destroyed in the French Revolution, was replaced with 19th-century glass.

From the steps of the church, look out to the hill-capping Amboise château. For a thousand years, it's been God on this hill and the king on that one. It's interesting to ponder how, throughout French history, the king's power generally trumped the Church's, and how the Church and the king worked to keep people down—setting the stage for the French Revolution.

• *Retrace your steps down from the church and across Place St. Denis, go past Amboise's lone cinema, continue walking straight, and follow Rue Nationale through the heart of town toward the castle.*

Rue Nationale: In France, districts around any castle or church officially classified as historic are preserved. The broad, pedestrianized Rue Nationale, with its narrow intersecting lanes, survives from the 15th century. At that time, when the town spread at the foot of the king's castle, this was the "Champs-Elysées" of Amboise. Supporting the king and his huge entourage was a serious industry. The French king spilled money wherever he stayed.

As you walk along this spine of the town, spot surviving bits of rustic medieval oak in the half-timbered buildings. The homes of wealthy merchants rose from the chaos of this street. Side lanes can be more candid—they often show what's hidden behind modern facades.

Stop when you reach the impressive **clock tower** (Tour de l'Horloge), built into part of the town wall that dates back to the 15th century. This was once a fortified gate, opening onto the road to the city of Tours. Imagine the hefty wood-and-iron portcullis (fortified door) that dropped from above.

• *At the intersection with Rue François I (where you'll be tempted by the Bigot chocolate shop—see "Helpful Hints," earlier), turn left a couple of steps to the...*

City Hall Museum (Musée de l'Hôtel de Ville): This free museum is worth a quick peek for its romantic interior, town paintings, and historic etchings (mid-June-mid-Sept Wed-Mon 10:00-12:30 & 14:00-18:00, closed Tue and off-season). Upstairs, in the still-functioning city assembly hall, notice how the photo of the current president faces the lady of the Republic. (According to locals, her features change with the taste of the generation, and the bust of France's Lady Liberty is often modeled on famous supermodels of the day.)

• *Your walk ends here, but you can easily continue on to the nearby Château Royal d'Amboise (and beyond that, to Leonardo's last residence): Retrace your steps along Rue François I to Place Michel Debré, at the base of the château. Here, at one of the most touristy spots in the Loire, you can feel how important tourism is to the local economy. Notice the fat, round 15th-century fortified tower, whose interior ramp was built for galloping horses to spiral up to castle level. But to get to the castle without a horse, you'll have to walk up the long ramp.*

Sights in Amboise

▲Château Royal d'Amboise

This historic heap became the favored royal residence in the Loire under Charles VIII, who did most of the building in the late 15th century. Charles is famous for accidentally killing himself by walking into a door lintel on his way to a tennis match (seriously). Later occupants include Louis XII (who moved the royal court to Blois) and François I (who physically brought the Renaissance here in

1516, in the person of Leonardo da Vinci).

Cost and Hours: €10.30 plus €3.50 for audioguide (kid's version available), daily April-June 9:00-18:30, July-Aug 9:00-19:00, Sept-Oct and March 9:00-18:00, Nov-Jan 9:00-12:00 & 14:00-16:45, Feb 9:00-12:00 & 13:30-17:30, Place Michel Debré, tel. 02 47 57 00 98, www.chateau-amboise.com.

Visiting the Château: After climbing the long ramp to the ticket booth and picking up the good English handout, our first stop is the petite **chapel** where Leonardo da Vinci is supposedly buried. This flamboyant little Gothic chapel comes with two fireplaces "to comfort the king" and two plaques "evoking the final resting place" of Leonardo (one in French, the other in Italian). Where he's actually buried, no one seems to know. Look up at the ceiling to appreciate the lacy design.

The **gardens** come with grand river and château views. Each summer, bleachers are set up for sound-and-light spectacles—a

faint echo of the extravaganzas Leonardo orchestrated for the court. Modern art decorating the garden reminds visitors of the inquisitive and scientific Renaissance spirit that Leonardo brought to town. The flags are those of France and Brittany—a reminder that, in a sense, modern France was created at the nearby château of Langeais when Charles VIII (who was born here) married Anne of Brittany, adding her domain to the French kingdom.

Wandering through the **castle rooms,** the route takes you chronologically from Gothic-style rooms to those from the early Renaissance and on to the 19th century. In the Salle des Gardes, plans show the château's original, much larger size. Some wings added in the 15th and 16th centuries have disappeared. (The little chapel you just saw was once part of the bigger complex.) The rose-colored top-floor rooms are well-furnished from the post-Revolutionary 1800s and demonstrate the continued interest in this château among French nobility.

Climb to the top of the **Minimes Tower** for grand views. From here, the strategic value of this site is clear: The visibility is great, and the river below provided a natural defense. The bulky tower climbs 130 feet in five spirals—designed for a mounted soldier in a hurry.

There are two exits. While you can leave the way you came, it's more interesting to spiral down the **Heurtault Tower** (access through the gift shop near the top of the entry ramp). As with the castle's other tower, this was designed to accommodate a soldier on horseback. As you gallop down to the exit, notice the cute little characters and scenes left by 15th-century stone-carvers. While they needed to behave when decorating churches and palaces, here they could be a bit racier and more spirited.

Leaving the Château: The turnstile puts you on the road to Château du Clos-Lucé (described next; turn left and hike straight for 10 minutes). Along the way, you'll pass **troglodyte houses**—both new and old—carved into the hillside. Originally, poor people resided here—the dwellings didn't require expensive slate roofing, came with natural insulation, and could be dug essentially for free, as builders valued the stone quarried in the process. Today wealthy stone lovers are renovating them into stylish digs worthy of *Better Homes and Caves*. You can see chimneys high above. Unfortunately, none are open to the public.

▲Château du Clos-Lucé and Leonardo da Vinci Park

In 1516, Leonardo da Vinci packed his bags (and several of his favorite paintings, including the *Mona Lisa*) and left an imploding Rome for better wine and working conditions in the Loire Valley. He accepted the position of engineer, architect, and painter to France's Renaissance king, François I. This "House of Light" is the plush palace where Leonardo spent his last three years. (He died on May 2, 1519.) François, only 22 years old, installed the 65-year-old Leonardo here just so he could enjoy his intellectual company.

The house is a kind of fort-château of its own, with a fortified rampart walk and a 16th-century chapel. While the present owners keep the upstairs to themselves, an entire floor of finely decorated and furnished rooms is open to the public.

Leonardo came with disciples, who also stayed active here, using this house as a kind of workshop and laboratory. The place survived the Revolution because the quick-talking noble who owned it was sympathetic to the cause; he convinced the Revolutionaries that philosophically, Leonardo would have been on their side.

Cost and Hours: The €14 admission, while pricey, is worth it for Leonardo fans with two hours to spend taking full advantage of this sight. Daily April-Oct 9:00-19:00, Nov-Dec and Feb-March 9:00-18:00, Jan 9:00-17:00, follow the helpful free English handout, tel. 02 47 57 00 73, www.vinci-closluce.com. A free app in English includes background information and tours of the châ-

THE LOIRE

teau and grounds (download via iTunes).

Eating: The garden café is reasonably priced and appropriately meditative. For a view over Amboise, choose the terrace *crêperie*.

Getting There: It's a 10-minute walk uphill from Château Royal d'Amboise, past troglodyte homes (see end of previous listing). If you drive, note that the parking lot near Clos-Lucé is unsafe—don't leave valuables visible in your car.

Visiting the Château and Gardens: Your visit begins with a tour of Leonardo's elegant yet livable Renaissance **home.** This little residence was built in 1450—just within the protective walls of the town—as a guesthouse for the king's château nearby. Today it thoughtfully re-creates (with Renaissance music) the everyday atmosphere Leonardo enjoyed while he lived here, pursuing his passions to the very end. Find the touching sketch in Leonardo's bedroom of François I comforting his genius pal on his deathbed, and see copies of Leonardo's most famous paintings (including the *Mona Lisa*).

The basement level is filled with **sketches** recording the storm patterns of Leonardo's brain and **models** of his remarkable inventions (inspired by nature and built according to his notes). Leonardo was fascinated by water. All he lacked was steam power. It's hard to imagine that this Roman candle of creativity died nearly 500 years ago. Imagine Leonardo's résumé letter to kings of Europe: "I can help your armies by designing tanks, flying machines, wind-up cars, gear systems, extension ladders, and water pumps." The French considered him a futurist who never really implemented his visions.

Your visit finishes with a stroll through the whimsical and very kid-friendly **park grounds,** with life-size models of Leonardo's inventions (including some that function, such as a "revolving bridge"), "sound stations" (in English), and translucent replicas of some of his paintings. The models make clear that much of what Leonardo observed and created was based on his intense study of nature.

Other Sights

▲Château Royal d'Amboise Sound-and-Light Show—If you're into S&L, this is considered one of the best shows of its kind in the area. Although it's entirely in French, you can buy the English booklet for €5. Volunteer locals from toddlers to pensioners re-create the life of François I with costumes, juggling, impressive light displays, and fireworks. Dress warmly.

Cost and Hours: Bench-€14, chair-€17, family deals, only about 20 performances a year, 1.5-hour show, Wed and Sat late June-July 22:30-24:00, Aug 22:00-23:30, tel. 02 47 57 14 47, www.renaissance-amboise.com. The ticket window is on the ramp to

The Loire and Its Many Châteaux: A Historical Primer

It's hard to overstate the importance of the Loire River to France. Its place in French history goes back to the very foundation of the country. As if to proclaim its storied past, the Loire is the last major wild river in France, with no dams and no regulation of its flow.

Traditional flat-bottomed boats romantically moored along embankments are a reminder of the age before trains and trucks, when river traffic safely and efficiently transported heavy loads of stone and timber. With prevailing winds sweeping east from the Atlantic, barge tenders raised their sails and headed upriver; on the way back, boats flowed downstream with the current.

With this transportation infrastructure and the region's thick forests—providing plenty of timber, firewood, and hunting terrain—it's no wonder that castles were built here in the Middle Ages. The first stone fortresses went up here a thousand years ago, and many of the pleasure palaces you see today rose over the ruins of those original defensive keeps.

The Hundred Years' War—roughly 1336 to 1453—was a desperate time for France. Because of a dynastic dispute, the English had a serious claim to the French throne, and by 1415 they controlled much of the country, including Paris. France was at a low ebb, and its king and court retreated to the Loire Valley to rule what remained of their realm. Chinon was the refuge of the dispirited king, Charles VII. He was famously visited there in 1429 by the charismatic Joan of Arc, who inspired the king to get off his duff and send the English packing.

The French kings continued to live in the Loire region for the next two centuries, having grown comfortable with the château culture of the region. The climate was mild, hunting was good, dreamy rivers made nice reflections, wealthy friends lived in similar luxury nearby, and the location was close enough to Paris—but still far enough away. Charles VII ruled from Chinon, Charles VIII preferred Amboise, Louis XII reigned from Blois, and François I held court in Chambord and Blois.

This was a kind of cultural Golden Age. With peace and stability, there was no need for fortifications. The most famous luxury hunting lodges, masquerading as fortresses, were built during this period—including Chenonceau, Chambord, Chaumont, Amboise, and Azay-le-Rideau. Kings (François I), writers (Rabelais), poets (Ronsard), and artists (Leonardo da Vinci) made the Loire a cultural hub.

Because French kings ruled effectively only by being constantly on the move, many royal châteaux were used infrequently. The entire court—and its trappings—had to be portable. A castle kept empty and cold eleven months of the year would suddenly become the busy center of attention when the king came to town. As you visit the castles, imagine the royal roadies setting up a kingly room—hanging tapestries, unfolding chairs, wrestling big trunks with handles—in the hours just before the arrival of the royal entourage. The French word for furniture, *mobilier,* literally means "mobile."

When touring the châteaux, you'll notice the impact of Italian culture. From the Renaissance onward, Italian ways were fancy ways. French nobles and court ministers who traveled to Italy returned inspired by the art and architecture they saw. Kings imported Italian artists and architects. It's no wonder that the ultimate French Renaissance king, François I, invited the ultimate Italian artist, Leonardo da Vinci, to join his court in Amboise. Tastes in food, gardens, artists, and women were all influenced by Italian culture.

Women had a big impact on Loire château life. Big personalities like kings tickled more than one tiara. Louis XV famously decorated the palace of Chenonceau with a painting of the Three Graces—featuring his three favorite mistresses.

Châteaux were generally owned by kings, their ministers, or their mistresses. A high-maintenance and powerful mistress often managed to get her own place even when a king's romantic interest shifted elsewhere. In many cases, the king or minister would be away at work or at war for years at a time—leaving home-improvement decisions to the lady of the château, who had unlimited money. That helps explain the emphasis on comfort and the feminine touch you'll enjoy while touring many of the Loire châteaux.

In 1525, François I moved to his newly built super-palace at Fontainebleau, and political power left the Loire. From then on, châteaux were mostly used as vacation and hunting retreats. They become refuges for kings again during the French Wars of Religion (1562-1598)—a sticky set of squabbles over dynastic control that pitted Protestants (Huguenots) against Catholics. Its conclusion marked the end of an active royal presence on the Loire. With the French Revolution in 1789, symbols of the Old Regime, like the fabulous palaces along the Loire, were ransacked. Fast talking saved some châteaux, especially those whose owners had personal relationships with Revolutionary leaders.

Only in the 1840s did the châteaux of the Loire become appreciated for their historic value. The Loire was the first place where treasures of French heritage were officially recognized and protected by the national government. In the 19th century, Romantic Age writers—like Victor Hugo and Alexander Dumas— visited and celebrated the châteaux. Aristocrats on the Grand Tour stopped here. The Loire Valley and its historic châteaux found a place in our collective hearts and have been treasured to this day.

THE LOIRE

the château and opens at 20:30.

Mini-Châteaux—This five-acre park on the edge of Amboise (on the route to Chenonceaux) shows the major Loire châteaux in 1:25-scale models, forested with 2,000 bonsai trees and laced together by a model TGV train and river boats. For children, it's a fun introduction to the real châteaux they'll be visiting (and there's a cool toy store). Essential English information is posted throughout the sight.

You'll find other kid-oriented attractions at Mini-Châteaux; consider playing a round of mini-golf and feeding the fish in the moat (a great way to get rid of that old baguette).

Cost and Hours: Adults-€14, kids-€10, daily June-Aug 10:00-20:00, Sept-Oct 10:30-18:00, April-May 10:30-19:00, closed Nov-March, last entry one hour before closing, tel. 02 47 23 44 57, www.mini-chateaux.com.

Caveau des Vignerons—This small *cave* offers free tastings of cheeses, pâtés, and regional wines from 10 different vintners (daily mid-March-mid-Nov 10:00-19:00, under Château d'Amboise, across from recommended l'Epicerie restaurant, tel. 02 47 57 23 69).

Biking from Amboise—Allow an hour to Chenonceaux (about 8 miles one-way). The first two miles are uphill, and the entire ride is on a road with light traffic. White-and-green biking signs will guide you to Chenonceaux. Serious cyclists can continue to Chaumont in 1.5 hours, connecting Amboise, Chenonceaux, and Chaumont in an all-day, 37-mile pedal (see "Recommended Bike Route" on the map on page 414).

Canoe Trips from Amboise or Chenonceaux—Paddling under the Château de Chenonceau is a memorable experience. **Canoe Company** offers canoe rentals on the Loire and Cher rivers (€12-22/person depending on how far you go, tel. 06 70 13 30 61, www.canoe-company.fr).

Near Amboise

Wine-Tasting in Vouvray—In the nearby town of Vouvray, 10 miles toward Tours from Amboise, you'll find wall-to-wall opportunities for wine-tasting. From Amboise you can take the speedy D-952 there, or joyride on the more appealing D-1 (see map on page 414). Here are two top choices for testing the local sauce:

The big **Cave des Producteurs** is a smart place to start. It has an English-speaking staff, English-language tours of the winery, and a good selection from the 25 producers they represent, including wines from other Loire areas (free wine-tasting, cellar tour-€2, daily mid-May-mid-Sept 9:00-19:00, mid-Sept-mid-May 9:00-12:30 & 14:00-19:00, call ahead for times of cellar tour in English, tel. 02 47 52 75 03, www.cp-vouvray.com). It's just west of Vouvray in Rochecorbon. Go past the smaller Cave des Producteurs outlet you'll see along D-952 in Vouvray, turn when you see the blue signs to *Moncontour*, then follow the small brown signs to *Cave des Producteurs.*

For a more intimate experience, drop by **Marc Brédif,** where you'll find a top-quality selection of Vouvray wines, as well as red wines from Chinon and Bourgeuil. You can also tour their impressive 1.2 miles of cellars dug into the hillside (free wine-tasting, cellar tour-€5, Mon-Fri 9:00-13:00 & 14:00-18:00, Sat 10:30-13:00 & 14:00-18:00, Sun 10:30-13:00, tel. 02 47 52 50 07, www.deladoucette.net). Coming from Amboise, you'll pass it on D-952 after Vouvray; it's on the right, just after the Moncontour turnoff.

For tips on wine-tasting, see "French Wine-Tasting 101" on page 46.

ZooParc de Beauval—If you need a zoo fix, this is France's biggest and most impressive one, with thousands of animals from the land and sea. It's about 30 minutes southeast of Amboise toward Vierzon—pick up details at the TI (€22, kids 3-10-€16, daily from 9:00 to dusk, tel. 02 54 75 50 00, www.zoobeauval.com).

Sleeping in Amboise

Amboise is busy in the summer, but there are lots of reasonable hotels and *chambres d'hôtes* in and around the city; the TI can help with reservations (for a €2.50 fee).

In the Town Center

$$$ Le Manoir les Minimes**** is a good place to experience the refined air of château life in a 17th-century mansion, with antique furniture and precious art objects in the public spaces. Its 15 large, modern rooms work for those seeking luxury digs in Amboise (tall folks take note: top-floor attic rooms have low ceilings). Several rooms have views of Amboise's château (standard Db-€134-150, larger Db-€200, suite-€295, 3- to 4-person suites-€500, extra bed-€28, continental breakfast-€14, air-con, Wi-Fi, three blocks upriver from bridge at 34 Quai Charles Guinot, tel. 02 47 30 40 40, fax 02 47 30 40 77, www.manoirlesminimes.com, reservation @manoirlesminimes.com).

$$$ Hôtel le Clos d'Amboise*** This smart urban refuge opens onto beautiful gardens and a small, heated swimming pool. It offers stay-awhile lounges and well-designed rooms that mix a touch of modern with a classic, traditional look (standard Db-€110, bigger Db-€150-180, Db suites-€210-310, extra person-€20, check website for deals, good buffet breakfast-€12, mini-fridges, air-con, elevator, Wi-Fi, sauna, free parking, 27 Rue Rabelais, tel. 02 47 30 10 20, fax 02 47 57 33 43, www.leclosamboise.com,

Sleep Code

(€1 = about $1.30, country code: 33)
S = Single, **D** = Double/Twin, **T** = Triple, **Q** = Quad, **b** = bathroom, **s** = shower only, * = French hotel rating system (0-5 stars). Unless otherwise noted, credit cards are accepted and English is spoken.

To help you easily sort through these listings, I've divided the accommodations into three categories based on the price for a standard double room with bath:

$$$ Higher Priced—Most rooms €90 or more.
$$ Moderately Priced—Most rooms between €60-90.
$ Lower Priced—Most rooms €60 or less.

Prices can change without notice; verify the hotel's current rates online or by email.

info@leclosamboise.com, helpful Patricia or Olivier are ever-present).

$$$ Le Vieux Manoir* is an entirely different high-end splurge. American expats Gloria and Bob Belknap have restored this secluded but central onetime convent with an attention to detail that Martha Stewart would envy. The gardens are lovely—as is the atrium-like breakfast room—and its six bedrooms would make an antique collector drool. Eager-to-help Gloria is a one-person tourist office (Db-€160-185, cottages-€240-300 and require

3-night minimum stay, includes superb breakfast, air-con, Internet access and Wi-Fi in lobby, no room phones or TVs, free parking, 13 Rue Rabelais, tel. & fax 02 47 30 41 27, www.le-vieux-manoir.com, le_vieux_manoir@yahoo.com).

$$$ Hôtel le Vinci Best Western* is well-run and modern, providing pricey-but-reliable, mid-range comfort a mile from the town center. Meals are possible on the back terrace (standard Db-€90, superior Db-€110, extra person-€20, breakfast-€13, 12 Avenue Emile Gounin, tel. 02 47 57 10 90, fax 02 47 57 17 52, www.vinciloirevalley.com, reservation@vinciloirevalley.com).

$$ Hôtel Belle-Vue is a centrally located and traditional place overlooking the river where the bridge hits the town. Following a renovation project, the hotel is reopening in 2013, (Db-€70-105, Tb-€115, Qb-€135, elevator, Wi-Fi in lobby, 12 Quai

THE LOIRE

Charles Guinot, tel. 02 47 57 02 26, fax 02 47 30 51 23, www.hotel
-bellevue-amboise.com, contact@hotel-bellevue-amboise.com).

$$ Hôtel le Blason**, in a 15th-century, half-timbered
building on a busy street, is run by helpful Damien and Beranger,
who speak English. The rooms—some with ship's-cabin-like
bathrooms—are tight and bright, and have double-paned win-
dows. There's air-conditioning on the top floor (Sb-€53, Db-€63,
Tb-€73, Qb-€83, quieter rooms in back and on top floor, free
Internet access and Wi-Fi, secure parking-€3/day, 11 Place
Richelieu, tel. 02 47 23 22 41, fax 02 47 57 56 18, www.leblason.fr,
hotel@leblason.fr).

$ Hôtel le Chaptal** is a plain, modern hotel with small but
clean and cheap rooms (Db-€48-55, Tb-€68, Qb-€80, Wi-Fi, 11
Rue Chaptal, tel. 02 47 57 14 46, fax 02 47 57 67 83, www.hotel
-chaptal-amboise.fr, infos@hotel-chaptal-amboise.fr).

Chambres d'Hôtes

The heart of Amboise offers several solid bed-and-breakfast
options.

$$$ Au Charme Rabelaisien is a lovely place run by charm-
ing Madame Viard. Big doors from the street open onto a grand
courtyard with manicured gardens, a heated pool, and three sumptuous rooms surrounding it (small Db-€85-99, roomy Db-€155-
175, includes breakfast, air-con, Wi-Fi, private parking, 25 Rue
Rabelais, tel. 02 47 57 53 84, fax 02 22 44 19 24, www.au-charme
-rabelaisien.com, aucharmerabelaisien@wanadoo.fr).

$$ La Grange Chambres welcomes with an intimate, flow-
ery courtyard and four comfortable rooms, each tastefully restored
with modern conveniences and big beds. There's also a common
room with a fridge and tables for do-it-yourself dinners (Db-€78-
85, extra person-€20, includes breakfast, cash only, where Rues
Chậtal and Rabelais meet at 18 Rue Chậtal, tel. 02 47 57 57 22,
www.la-grange-amboise.com, info@la-grange-amboise.com).
Adorable Yveline Savin also rents a small two-room cottage (€440-
560/week, 2- to 3-day stays possible).

Near the Train Station

$$ Hôtel la Brèche*, a sleepy place near the station, has 14 top-
value rooms and a good restaurant. Many rooms overlook the
peaceful graveled garden, while those on the street are generally
larger and come with some traffic noise; all are tastefully decorated
(Sb-€55, Db-€59-67, Tb-€75, Qb-€90, room for up to six-€95,
breakfast-€7, Wi-Fi, 15-minute walk from city center and 2-min-
ute walk from station, 26 Rue Jules Ferry, tel. 02 47 57 00 79, fax 02
47 57 65 49, www.labreche-amboise.com, info@labreche-amboise
.com).

Hostel: **$** **L'Auberge de Jeunesse** (Centre Charles Péguy) is ideally located on the western tip of the "Golden Island," a 10-minute walk from the train station. Open to people of all ages, and popular with student groups, it's friendly and easy on the wallet. There are a handful of double rooms—some with partial views to the château—so book ahead (D-€26, bunk in 3- to 4-bed room-€14, sheets-€3, no surcharge for nonmembers, breakfast-€4.50, dinner-€10, reception open daily 15:00-20:00, no curfew, Ile d'Or, tel. 02 47 30 60 90, fax 02 47 30 60 91, www.mjcamboise.fr, cis @mjcamboise.fr).

Sleeping near Amboise

The area around Amboise is peppered with good-value accommodations of every shape, size, and price range. This region offers drivers the best chance to experience château life at affordable rates—and my recommendations justify the detour. For locations, see the map on page 414. Also consider the recommended accommodations in Chenonceaux and the Hôtel du Grand St. Michel at Chambord.

$$$ Château de Pray**** is a 750-year-old fortified castle with hints of its medieval origins. The 14 rooms in the main château come with character—and with tubs in most bathrooms. A newer annex offers four contemporary rooms (sleeping up to three each), with lofts, terraces, and views of the castle. A big pool and the restaurant's vegetable garden lie below the château (small Db in main build-

ing-€150, bigger Db-€200-260, Db in annex-€175, continental breakfast-€16, no air-con, 3-minute drive upriver from Amboise toward Chaumont on D-751, tel. 02 47 57 23 67, fax 02 47 57 32 50, http://praycastel.online.fr, praycastel@online.fr). The dining room is splendid and a relaxing place to splurge...and feel good about it (four-course *menus* from €57, reservations required).

$$$ At **Château de Nazelles Chambres,** gentle owners Veronique and Olivier Fructus offer five rooms in a 16th-century hillside manor house that comes with a cliff-sculpted pool, manicured gardens, a guest's kitchen (picnics are encouraged), views over Amboise, and a classy living room with billiards, computer access, and Wi-Fi. The two bedrooms in the main building are just grand, while the rooms cut into the rock come with private terraces and rock-walled bathrooms (Db-€120, bigger Db-€145, Qb-€280, includes breakfast, tel. & fax 02 47 30 53 79, www .chateau-nazelles.com, info@chateau-nazelles.com). From D-952, take D-5 into Nazelles-Négron, then turn left on D-1 and quickly veer right above the post office (PTT) to 16 Rue Tue-la-Soif.

$$$ Château des Arpentis***, a medieval château-hotel centrally located just minutes from Amboise, makes a fun and classy splurge. Flanked by woods and acres of grass, and fronted by a stream and a moat, you'll come as close as you can to château life during the Loire's Golden Age. Rooms are big, with tasteful decor—and the pool is even bigger (Db-€130-185, amazing family suites-€220-370, air-con, Wi-Fi, near St-Règle, tel. 02 47 23 00 00, fax 02 47 52 62 17, www.chateaudesarpentis.com, contact @chateaudesarpentis.com). It's on D-31 just southeast of Amboise; from the roundabout above the Leclerc Market, follow *Autrèche* signs, then look for small signs on the right next to a tall flagpole.

$$ L'Auberge de Launay, five miles upriver from Amboise, gets rave reviews for its easy driving access to many châteaux, its warm welcome, and its wonderful restaurant. Owners François and Hélène are natural hosts at this comfortable 15-room hotel and restaurant (roadside Db-€68, bigger garden-side Db-€78, Internet access and Wi-Fi; about 4 miles from Amboise, across the river toward Blois, at 9 Rue de la Rivière in Limeray; tel. 02 47 30 16 82, www.aubergedelaunay.com, info@aubergedelaunay.com). The star of this place is the country-classy restaurant, with *menus* from €27 (closed Sun except for hotel guests).

$$ Le Moulin du Fief Gentil is a lovely 16th-century mill house set on four acres with a backyard pond (fishing possible in summer, dinner picnics anytime, fridge and microwave at your disposal), and the possibility of home-cooked dinners by English-speaking owner Fleurance (twin Db-€87, bigger Db-€105-120, 2-room apartment-€140, extra person-€25, includes breakfast, four-course dinner *menu* with wine-€32, cash only, tel. 02 47 30 32 51, mobile 06 64 82 37 18, www.fiefgentil.com, contact@fief gentil.com). It's located on the edge of Bléré, a 15-minute drive from Amboise and Chenonceaux—from Bléré, follow signs toward *Luzillé*, and it's on the right.

$$ Hostellerie du Château de L'Isle is a rustic, lost-in-time place wrapped in a lush park with a pond and acres of grass on the Cher River. Located in Civray-de-Touraine, two minutes from Chenonceaux, it offers 12 sufficiently comfortable rooms with laissez-faire management. Rooms in the main building are better (small Db-€55, standard Db-€70, big Db-€85-105, tel. 02 47 23 63 60, www.chateau-de-lisle.com, chateaudelisle@wanadoo.fr). The gazebo-like restaurant, as lovely as a Monet painting, features the owner's cooking (€26-36 meals, limited choices). From the center of Civray-de-Touraine, follow D-81 toward Tours.

$ La Chevalerie owner Martine Aleksic rents four simple bargain *chambres* that are family-friendly in every way. You'll get a warm reception and total seclusion in a farm setting, with a swing set, tiny fishing pond, shared kitchens, and connecting rooms (Sb-€40, Db-€50, Tb-€60, Qb-€76, includes breakfast with fresh eggs, cash only, in La Croix-en-Touraine, tel. 02 47 57 83 64, lyoubisa .aleksic@orange.fr). From Amboise, take D-31 toward Bléré, look for the *Chambres d'Hôte* sign on your left at about three miles, and then turn left onto C-105.

Eating in Amboise

Amboise is filled with inexpensive and forgettable restaurants, but a handful of places are worth your attention. Some offer a good, end-of-meal cheese platter—a rarity in France these days. The epicenter of the city's dining action is on Place Michel Debré, along Rue Victor Hugo, and across from the château entrance. After dinner, make sure to cross the bridge for floodlit views of the castle, and consider a view drink at **Le Shaker Cocktail Lounge** (daily from 18:00 until later than you're awake, 3 Quai François Tissard).

Dining Below the Château

L'Epicerie, across from the château entry, serves delicious and well-presented traditional cuisine at fair prices. Choose a table outdoors facing the château or in the rustically elegant dining room. The snails are incredible, the sauces are delectable, and the service is attentive. The €26 and €34 *menus* come with an amazing cheese platter (July-Sept daily, Oct-June closed Mon-Tue, reserve ahead, 46 Place Michel Debré, tel. 02 47 57 08 94).

La Reserve feels like a wine bar-bistro with modern but tasteful decor, good *menu* choices at fair prices, and a loyal clientele (*menus* from €17-35, daily, 28 Place Michel Debré, tel. 02 47 57 97 96).

Anne de Bretagne offers typical, inexpensive café fare in a good location with charming ambience—come for the setting, not the cuisine. The outdoor tables are ideal for surveying the street scene (nonstop service daily 12:00-22:00, Place du Château, tel. 02 47 57 05 46).

L'Ambacia, with tables spilling out on the broad sidewalk, is a trendy, casual bistro serving everything from bagels to hamburgers to pasta (€9-14 *plats*, 12 Place Michel Debré, tel. 02 47 23 21 44).

Elsewhere in Amboise

La Fourchette is Amboise's family diner, with simple decor inside and out. Chef Christine makes everything fresh in her open kitchen, offering a limited selection at good prices (€15-24 *menus*, closed Sun-Mon, on a quiet corner near Rue Nationale at 9 Rue

Malebranche, mobile 06 11 78 16 98).

Le Lion d'Or has a chef who takes his job seriously and delivers quality regional cuisine at affordable prices. You'll dine in a contemporary setting (€22-28 *menus*, closed Sun-Mon, where the bridge meets the town at 7 Quai Charles Guinel, tel. 02 47 57 00 23).

L'Ancrée des Artistes is Amboise's reliable and central *crêperie*. It's a young-at-heart place with music to dine by and easygoing servers (€9 dinner crêpes, €14 three-course crêpe *menus*, 35 Rue Nationale, tel. 02 47 23 18 11).

Hôtel la Brèche serves a good-value €20 *menu* in their warm, traditional dining room and large garden. Stretch your legs and cross the river to the restaurant, then enjoy floodlit castle views on your walk home (daily; for details, see "Sleeping in Amboise," earlier).

Near Amboise

These places merit the short drive. It's best to call ahead to reserve. For a royal experience, consider making the quick drive to **Château de Pray** (see page 410). For a warm welcome and good cuisine, call to find out if Hélène can take you at **L'Auberge de Launay** (page 411). For vintage French cuisine, head for **Auberge du Cheval Rouge** (page 422) near Chenonceaux. To add a Michelin star to your portfolio, aim for Chenonceaux and the **Auberge du Bon Laboureur** (see page 421).

Amboise Connections

By Bus and Taxi

From Amboise to Nearby Châteaux: For easiest access to area châteaux, see "Getting Around the Loire Valley" on page 387.

By Bus to: Chenonceaux (1-2/day, Mon-Sat only, none on Sun, 20 minutes, one-way-€1.20; departs Amboise about 9:45, returns from Chenonceaux at about 12:15, allowing you about an hour and 20 minutes at the château; in summer, there's also an afternoon departure at about 15:00, with a return from Chenonceaux at about 17:20; confirm times with the TI; the Amboise stop—called Théâtre—is between Place St. Denis and the river on the west side of Avenue des Martyrs de la Résistance, across from the Théâtre de Beaumarchais; in Chenonceaux, the bus stops across the street from the TI and at the château; tel. 02 47 05 30 49, www.touraine filvert.com—click "Horaires," "Toutes les Lignes du Réseau," then "line C"); **Tours** (8/day Mon-Sat, none on Sun, buses are cheaper than trains—about €2.50).

By Shuttle Van to Chenonceaux, Chambord, and Cheverny: Quart de Tours runs two round-trips per day (high season only)

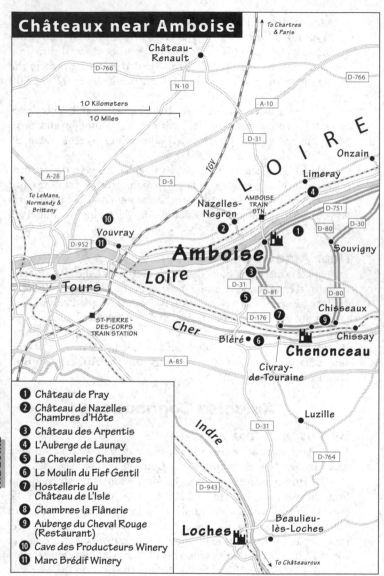

Châteaux near Amboise

To Chartres & Paris

Château-Renault

D-766

D-766

N-10

10 Kilometers

10 Miles

A-10

A-28

D-31

L O I R E

Onzain

D-5

TGV

Limeray

4

To LeMans, Normandy & Brittany

Nazelles-Negron

AMBOISE TRAIN STN.

D-751

D-30

10

2

1

D-80

Souvigny

Vouvray

Amboise

11

D-952

Loire

D-81

3

D-31

Chisseaux

Tours

5

9

Chissay

ST-PIERRE-DES-CORPS TRAIN STATION

Cher

D-176

7

Chenonceau

Bléré

6

A-85

Civray-de-Touraine

❶ Château de Pray

❷ Château de Nazelles
   Chambres d'Hôte

❸ Château des Arpentis

❹ L'Auberge de Launay

❺ La Chevalerie Chambres

❻ Le Moulin du Fief Gentil

❼ Hostellerie du
   Château de L'Isle

❽ Chambres la Flânerie

❾ Auberge du Cheval Rouge
   (Restaurant)

❿ Cave des Producteurs Winery

⓫ Marc Brédif Winery

Indre

D-31

Luzille

D-764

D-943

Beaulieu-lès-Loches

Loches

To Châteauroux

THE LOIRE

between Amboise and Chenonceaux (€15 round-trip, €10 one-way, includes €2.50 discount for château, 15-minute trip), and an afternoon excursion trip from Amboise to Chambord and Cheverny (€34, allow four hours). Book ahead, as seats are limited (mobile 06 30 65 52 01, www.quartdetours.com). **Touraine Evasion** runs a similar service combining Chambord and Chenonceaux (mobile

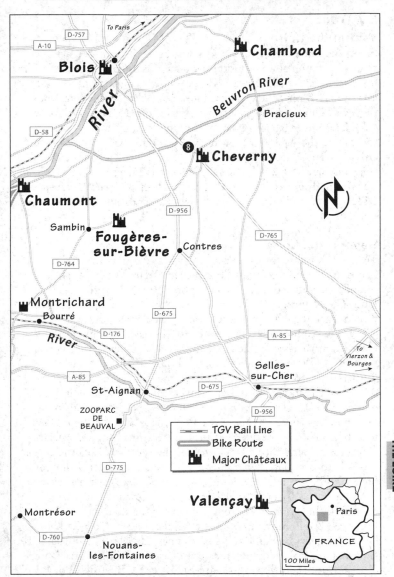

06 07 39 13 31, www.tourevasion.com). Check with the Amboise TI for details and pickup locations for both companies.

By Taxi: Most châteaux are too expensive by cab, but a taxi from Amboise to Chenonceaux costs about €26 (€36 on Sundays and after 19:00, tel. 02 47 57 13 53 or 02 47 57 30 39). The meter doesn't start until you do.

By Train
Within the Loire
From Amboise by Train to: Chenonceaux (trains are a more frequent, if a bit slower, option than the bus; 6/day, most about 1 hour, transfer at St-Pierre-des-Corps—check connections to avoid long waits), **Blois** (14/day, 20 minutes, bus or taxi excursions from there to Chambord and Cheverny—see "Blois Connections," page 427), **Chaumont** (about 14/day, 35 minutes, take 10-minute train to Onzain on the Amboise-Blois route 25-minute walk—you can see château from station), **Tours** (12/day, 25 minutes, allows connections to châteaux west of Tours), **Chinon** (12/day, 1.5-2.25 hours, transfer in Tours and possibly in St-Pierre-des-Corps), **Azay-le-Rideau** (6/day, 2 hours, transfer in Tours and possibly in St-Pierre-des-Corps).

Beyond the Loire
Twelve 15-minute trains link Amboise daily to the regional train hub of St-Pierre-des-Corps (in suburban Tours). There you'll find reasonable connections to distant points (including the TGV to Paris' Gare Montparnasse). Transferring in Paris can be the fastest way to reach many French destinations, even in the south.

From Amboise by Train to: Paris (12/day, 1.5 hours to Paris' Gare Montparnasse with change to TGV at St-Pierre-des-Corps, requires TGV reservation; 6/day, 2 hours direct to Paris' Gare d'Austerlitz, no reservation required; more to Gare d'Austerlitz or Paris RER stations with same travel time and transfers in Blois or Les Aubrais-Orléans), **Sarlat** (4/day, 5-6 hours, several routes possible, best is to change at St-Pierre-des-Corps, then TGV to Libourne or Bordeaux-St-Jean, then train through Bordeaux vineyards to Sarlat; it's a bit slower on the route via Les Aubrais-Orléans to Souillac then scenic SNCF bus to Sarlat), **Limoges** (near Oradour-sur-Glane, 11/day, 4.5 hours, change at St-Pierre-des-Corps and Vierzon or at Les Aubrais-Orléans and Vierzon, then tricky bus connection from Limoges to Oradour-sur-Glane—see page 513), **Pontorson/Mont St-Michel** (2-3/day, 5.5-7.5 hours by transfers at Caen and Tours or Rennes, Le Mans, and Tours), **Bayeux** (3/day, 5.5-6 hours, transfer in Paris—arrive at Paris' Gare d'Austerlitz, then Métro to Gare St. Lazare), **Beaune** (2/day, 5 hours, transfer in Dijon and Tours; plus 12/day, 6 hours, with changes in Paris and in Dijon—arrive at Paris' Gare d'Austerlitz or Gare Montparnasse, then Métro to Gare de Lyon), **Bourges** (roughly hourly—though fewer mid-day, 2-3 hours, change at St-Pierre-des-Corps).

Chenonceaux

This one-road, sleepy village—with a knockout château—makes a good home base for drivers and a workable base for train travelers who don't mind connections. The château itself, understandably the most popular in the region, is wonderfully organized for visitors. The gardens are open on summer evenings with mood lighting and music, making the perfect after-dinner activity for those sleeping here. Note that Chenonceaux is the name of the town, and Chenonceau (no "x") is the name of the château, but they're pronounced the same: shuh-nohn-soh.

Orientation to Chenonceaux

The small **TI** is on the main road from Amboise as you enter the village. It has Wi-Fi and Internet access (July-Aug daily 9:00-19:00; Sept-June Mon-Sat 10:00-12:30 & 14:00-18:30, closed Sun; tel. 02 47 23 94 45).

The **bus** stops at the TI (the Amboise-bound stop is unsigned and across the street from the TI) and at the château (1-2 buses/day to Amboise, Mon-Sat only, none on Sun, 15 minutes).

La Maison des Pages has some bakery items, sandwiches, cold drinks to go, and just enough groceries for a modest picnic (on the main drag between Hostel du Roy and Hôtel la Roseraie).

You can rent **bikes** at the recommended Relais Chenonceaux hotel (May-Sept daily 9:00-19:00; see "Sleeping in Chenonceaux," later).

Sights in Chenonceaux

▲▲▲Château de Chenonceau

Chenonceau is the toast of the Loire. This 16th-century Renaissance palace arches gracefully over the Cher River and is impeccably maintained, with fresh flower arrangements in the summer and roaring log fires in the winter. Chenonceau is one of the most-visited châteaux in France—so carefully follow my crowd-beating tips (next page). Plan on a 15-minute walk from the parking lot to the château. Warning: don't leave any valuables visible in your car.

Cost and Hours: Château-€11, wax museum-€2, daily mid-March-mid-Sept 9:00-19:30, July-Aug until 20:00, closes earlier off-season, tel. 02 47 23 90 07, www.chenonceau.com.

Chenonceau at Night *(Promenade Nocturne):* On summer nights, floodlights and period music create a romantic after-dinner cap to your Loire day. Just stroll over whenever and for as long as you like (€5, daily July-Aug 21:30-23:30, Fri-Sun in June).

Crowd-Beating Tips: Chenonceau's crowds are worth planning around. This place gets slammed in high season, when it's best to come early (by 9:00) or after 17:00. Avoid slow ticket lines by purchasing your ticket in advance (at area TIs) or from the ticket machines at the main entry (just follow the prompts, US credit cards work).

Tours: The interior is fascinating—but only if you take full advantage of the free, excellent 20-page **booklet** (included with entry), or rent the wonderful **iPod video/audioguide tour** (€4; two different versions available—45 or 60 minutes, each with the same stops; request the unhurried 60-minute version to enjoy full coverage). There's also an audioguide for kids. Pay for the audioguide when buying your ticket (before entering the château grounds), then pick up the iPod just inside the château's door. Or, before you visit, download the tour from www.chenonceau.com to your own mobile device for €3.

Services: WCs are available by the ticket office and behind the wax museum. There's a free bag check at the turnstile.

Wax Museum, Play Area, and Traditional Farm: The wax museum (La Galerie des Dames-Musée de Cires, located in the château stables), while tacky and designed for children, puts a waxy face on the juicy history of the château (tickets only available at the château ticket office). Reading the English displays requires a series of deep knee-bends. A kids' play area *(Kindergarten)* lies just past the wax museum, and a few steps beyond that you can stroll around a traditional farm and imagine the production needed to sustain the château (free, always open).

Eating: A reasonable cafeteria is next door to the wax museum. Fancy meals are served in the *orangerie* behind the stables. There's a cheap *crêperie*/sandwich shop at the entrance gate. While picnics are not allowed on the grounds, there are picnic tables in a park near the parking lot.

Boat Trips: In summer, the château has rental **rowboats**—an idyllic way to savor graceful château views (€6/30 minutes, July-Aug daily 10:00-19:00, 4 people/boat).

Background: Although earlier châteaux were built for defensive purposes, Chenonceau was the first great pleasure palace. Nicknamed "the château of the ladies," it housed many famous women over the centuries. The original builder's wife oversaw the construction of the main part of the château.

In 1547, King Henry II gave the château to his mistress, Diane de Poitiers, who added an arched bridge across the river to access the hunting grounds. She enjoyed her lovely retreat until Henry II died (pierced in a jousting tournament in Paris) and his vengeful wife, Catherine de Médicis, unceremoniously kicked her out (and into the château of Chaumont, described on page 434). Catherine added the three-story structure on Diane's bridge. She died before completing her vision of a matching château on the far side of the river, but not before turning Chenonceau into *the* place to see and be seen by local aristocracy. (Whenever you see a split coat of arms, it belongs to a woman—half her husband's and half her father's.)

❂ **Self-Guided Tour:** Strut like an aristocrat down the tree-canopied path to the château. (There's a fun plant maze partway up on the left.) You'll cross three moats and two bridges, and pass an old round tower, which predates the main building. Notice the tower's fine limestone veneer, added so the top would better fit the new château.

The main château's original **oak door** greets you with the coats of arms of the first owners. The knocker is high enough to be used by visitors on horseback. The smaller door within the large one could be for two purposes: to slip in after curfew, or to enter during winter without letting out all the heat.

Once inside, you'll tour the château in a clockwise direction (turn left upon entering). Take time to appreciate the beautiful brick floor tiles and lavishly decorated ceilings. As you continue, follow your pamphlet or audioguide, and pay attention to these details:

In the **guard room,** the best-surviving original floor tiles are near the walls—imagine the entire room covered with these tiles. And though the tapestries kept the room cozy, they also functioned to tell news or recent history (to the king's liking, of course). You'll see many more tapestries in this château.

The superbly detailed **chapel** survived the vandalism of the Revolution because the fast-thinking lady of the palace filled it with firewood. Angry masses were supplied with mallets and instructions to smash everything royal or religious. While this room was both, all they saw was stacked wood. The hatch door provided a quick path to the kitchen and an escape boat downstairs. The windows, blown out during World War II, are replacements from the 1950s.

The centerpiece of the **bedroom of Diane de Poitiers** is a severe portrait of her rival, Catherine de Médicis, at 40 years old. After the queen booted out the mistress, she placed her own portrait over the fireplace, but she never used this bedroom. The 16th-century tapestries are among the finest in France. Each one took an average of 60 worker-years to make. Study the complex compositions of the *Triumph of Charity* and the violent *Triumph of Force.*

At 200 feet long, the three-story **Grand Gallery** spans the river. (The upper stories house double-decker ballrooms and art exhibits.) Notice how differently the slate and limestone of the checkered floor wear after 500 years. Imagine grand banquets here. Catherine, a contemporary of Queen Elizabeth I of England, wanted to rule with style. She threw wild parties and employed her ladies to circulate and soak up all the political gossip possible from the well-lubricated Kennedys and Rockefellers of her realm. Parties included grand fireworks displays and mock naval battles on the river. The niches once held statues—Louis XIV took a liking to them, and consequently, they now decorate the palace at Versailles.

In summer and during holidays, you can take a quick walk outside for more good palace **views:** Cross the bridge, pick up a re-entry ticket, then stroll the other bank of the Cher (across the river from the château). During World War II, the river you crossed marked the border between the collaborationist Vichy government and Nazi-controlled France. Back then, Chenonceau witnessed many prisoner swaps. During World War I, the Grand Gallery served as a military hospital, where more than 2,200 soldiers were cared for—picture hundreds of beds lining the gallery.

Double back through the gallery to find the sensational state-of-the-art (in the 16th century) **kitchen** below. It was built near water (to fight the inevitable kitchen fires) and in the basement; because heat rises, the placement helped heat the palace. Cross the small bridge (watch your head) to find the stove and landing bay for goods to be ferried in and out.

The staircase leading **upstairs** wowed royal guests. It was the first non-spiral staircase they'd seen...quite a treat in the 16th century. The balcony provides lovely views of the gardens—which originally supplied vegetables and herbs. (Diane built the one to the right, Catherine the one to your left.) The estate is still full of wild boar and deer—the primary dishes of past centuries. You'll see more lavish bedrooms on this floor. Find the small side rooms that show fascinating old architectural sketches of the château. The walls, 20 feet thick, were honeycombed with the flues of 224 fireplaces and passages for servants to do their pleasure-providing work unseen. There was no need for plumbing. Servants fetched, carried, and dumped everything pipes do today. The long room stretching over the river usually contains a temporary modern-art exhibit.

Sleeping in Chenonceaux

(€1 = about $1.30, country code: 33)
Hotels are a good value in Chenonceaux, and there's one in each category, from one to four stars. You'll find them *tous ensemble* on

Rue du Dr. Bretonneau.

$$$ Auberge du Bon Laboureur**** turns heads with its ivied facade, lush terraces, and, inside, leathery lounges and bars. The staff acts a tad stiff, but if you get past the formal pleasantries, you have four-star rooms at three-star prices (Db-€125-175, suites-€210-300, pool, air-con, 6 Rue du Dr. Bretonneau, tel. 02 47 23 90 02, www.bonlaboureur.com, laboureur@wanadoo.fr).

$$ Hôtel la Roseraie* ** has a flowery terrace and 17 warmly decorated rooms. Sabine, Thierry, and Jerome run a good show (standard Db-€72-94, big Db-€135-155, Tb-€120-180, buffet breakfast-€11, queen- or king-size beds, air-con, Wi-Fi, free parking, heated pool, closed Jan-Feb, 7 Rue du Dr. Bretonneau, tel. 02 47 23 90 09, fax 02 47 23 91 59, www.hotel-chenonceau .com, laroseraie-chenonceaux @orange.fr). The traditional dining room and delightful terrace are ideal for a nice dinner available for guests  and non-guests alike who reserve ahead (€29 *menus*, closed Tue and mid-Nov-mid-March).

$$ Relais Chenonceaux,** above a restaurant, greets guests with a nice patio and unimaginative, wood-paneled rooms at fair rates. The coziest—and, in summer, hottest—rooms are on the top floor, but watch your head (Db-€72, Tb-€85, Qb-€105, Wi-Fi, tel. 02 47 23 98 11, fax 02 47 23 84 07, 10 Rue du Dr. Bretonneau, www .chenonceaux.com, info@chenonceaux.com).

$ Hostel du Roy* offers 30 basic budget rooms, some in a quiet garden courtyard, and a mediocre but inexpensive restaurant (Db-€44-53, Tb-€64, one-room Qb-€68, two-room Qb-€98, room for up to five-€110, Wi-Fi, 9 Rue du Dr. Bretonneau, tel. 02 47 23 90 17, fax 02 47 23 89 81, www.hostelduroy.com, hostel duroy@wanadoo.fr).

Eating in and near Chenonceaux

Reserve ahead to dine in formal style at the country-elegant **Auberge du Bon Laboureur** (*menus* at €50, €62, and €85). **Hôtel la Roseraie** serves good fixed-price meals in a stylish dining room or on a garden terrace (*menus* from €29, €5 more buys a cheese course, Mon and Wed-Sun 19:00-21:00, closed Tue and mid-Nov-mid-March). **Relais Chenonceaux** dishes up crêpes, salads, and *plats* at decent prices in a pleasant interior or on its terrace (daily). All of these are listed earlier, under "Sleeping in Chenonceaux."

THE LOIRE

For a French treat, book ahead and drive about a mile to Chisseaux and dine at the wonderfully traditional **Auberge du Cheval Rouge.** You'll enjoy some of the region's best cuisine at affordable prices, either inside or on a flower-filled patio (*menus* from €33, closed Tue-Wed, 30 Rue Nationale, Chisseaux, tel. 02 47 23 86 67).

Chenonceaux Connections

From Chenonceaux by Train to: Tours (8/day, 30 minutes), with connections to **Chinon, Azay-le-Rideau,** and **Langeais**; **Amboise** (6/day, 1 hour, transfer at St-Pierre-des-Corps).

By Bus to: Amboise (1-2/day, Mon-Sat only, none on Sun, 20 minutes, one-way-€1.20, departs Chenonceaux at about 12:15, and in summer also at about 17:20, catch bus at the château or across the street from the TI, tel. 02 47 05 30 49, www.tourainefilvert .com).

By Shuttle Van: Quart de Tours runs two round-trips per day (high season only) between Chenonceaux and Amboise (see "Amboise Connections" on page 413).

By Taxi to: Amboise (€26, €36 on Sun and after 19:00).

Blois

Bustling Blois (pronounced "blwah") feels like a megalopolis after all those rural villages. Blois owns a rich history, dolled-up pedestrian areas, an impressive château, and convenient access to Chambord and Cheverny by excursion bus, taxi, or car (see "Getting Around the Loire Valley" on page 387 and "Blois Connections," later). Good train service to Paris and Amboise enables easy stopovers in Blois (luggage lockers at château).

If Blois feels more important than other Loire towns, it was. From this once powerful city, the medieval counts of Blois governed their vast lands and vied with the king of France for dominance. The center of France moved from Amboise to Blois in 1498, when Louis XII inherited the throne (after Charles VIII had his unfortunate head-banging incident in Amboise). The château you see today is living proof of this town's 15 minutes of fame. But Blois is worth a visit for more than its château. Tour the flying-buttressed St. Nicholas Church, find the medieval warren of lanes below St. Louis Cathedral, and relax in a café on Place Louis XII.

Orientation to Blois

Unlike most other Loire châteaux, Blois' Château Royal sits right in the city center, with no forest, pond, moat, or river to call its own. It's an easy walk from the train station, near ample underground parking, and just above the TI. Below the château, Place Louis XII marks the hub of traffic-free Blois, with cafés and shops lining its perimeter. Rue du Commerce, leading up from the river, is Blois' primary shopping street. Atmospheric cafés and restaurants hide in the medieval tangle of lanes below St. Louis Cathedral and around St. Nicholas Church. Blois was heavily bombed in World War II, leaving much of the old town in ruins, but the château survived. Today, the city largely ignores its river.

Arrival in Blois

Train travelers can walk 10 minutes straight out of the station down Avenue Jean Laigret to the TI and château (follow small brown *Château* signs), or take a two-minute taxi from in front of the station. Although there's no bag check at the station, there are large, free **lockers** at the château—so you can drop off your luggage, visit the château and the town, and even take an excursion or taxi tour to Chambord and Cheverny (provided you're back in Blois to reclaim your bag before the château closes).

Drivers follow *Centre-Ville* and *Château* signs (metered parking along Avenue Jean Laigret or inside at Parking du Château—first 30 minutes free, then about €2/2.5 hours).

Tourist Information

The cramped TI is across from the château entrance (daily April-Sept 9:00-18:00, Oct-March 10:00-17:00, 23 Place du Château, tel. 02 54 90 41 41, www.bloispaysdechambord.com). Save time as you explore the center of Blois by using the TI's handy walking-tour brochure (brown and purple routes are best). The TI also has information on bike rentals.

Helpful Hints

Private Guide: Fabrice Maret lives in Blois and is a great teacher. He gives top-notch walking tours of his city or can join you in your car for a tour of area châteaux (€260/day plus transportation from Blois, tel. 02 54 70 19 59, www.chateauxloire.com, info@chateauxloire.com).

Bike Rental: Détours de Loire bike rental is at 3 Rue de la Garenne (tel. 02 54 56 07 73). Because they also have a shop in

Amboise, you can rent a bike for a one-way ride to Amboise, stopping at garden-rich Chaumont-sur-Loire on the way (40-mile trip).

Sights in Blois

▲▲Château Royal de Blois

Size up the château from the big square before entering. Unlike most other Loire châteaux, the Château Royal sits right in the city center. Even though parts of the building date from the Middle Ages, notice the complete absence of defensive towers, draw-bridges, and other fortifications. Gardens once extended behind the château and up the hill to a forest. A walk around the building's perimeter (to the right as you face it) reveals more of its beautiful Renaissance facade.

Kings Louis XII and François I built most of the château you see today, each calling it home during their reigns. That's Louis looking good on his horse in the niche. Catherine de Médicis (onetime owner of Chenonceau) spent her last night here, where she had been exiled by her son, Henry III.

Cost and Hours: €9.50, kids under 18-€7, €15 combo-ticket with House of Magic (described later, under "Other Sights") or Sound-and-Light Show (see next), €20 covers all three; daily July-Aug 9:00-19:00, April-June and Sept 9:00-18:30, Oct 9:00-17:30, Nov-March 9:00-12:30 & 14:00-17:30, free lockers available with entry, tel. 02 54 90 33 33, www.chateaudeblois.fr.

Sound-and-Light Show: This simple "show" takes place in the center courtyard and features projections on the château walls. An English version of the show runs on Wednesdays, though the French version is worthwhile any evening if you're sleeping in Blois (€7.50, €15 combo-ticket also covers daytime château entry, €20 gets you both plus the House of Magic; daily April-Sept at about 22:00).

Visiting the Château: At the ticket office, pick up the helpful English brochure, then read the well-presented English displays in each room.

Begin in the **courtyard,** where four different wings—ranging from Gothic to Neoclassical—underscore this château's importance over many centuries. Stand with your back to the entry to get oriented. The medieval parts of the château are the brick-patterned sections (to your left and behind you), both built by Louis XII. While work was under way on Chambord, François I added the elaborate Renaissance wing (to your right; early 16th century), centered on the protruding spiral staircase and festooned with his emblematic salamanders. Gaston d'Orléans inherited the place in the 1600s and wanted to do away with the mismatched styles. He demolished a large church that stood here (the chapel to your left is all that remains) and replaced it with the clean-lined, Neoclassical structure you see today.

Visit the interior counterclockwise, and focus on the Renaissance wing. Begin in the far-right corner (where you entered the courtyard) and walk under the stone porcupine relief, Louis' symbol, and up the steps into the dazzling **Hall of the Estates-General.** This is the oldest surviving part of the château (predating Louis and François), where the Estates-General met twice to help determine who would inherit the throne from Henry III, who had no male heir. (Keep reading to see how Henry resolved the problem.)

Continue into the small **lapidary museum** (down the steps by the wooden staircase), with an impressive display of statues and architectural fragments from the original château; here's your chance to look nasty salamanders and gargoyles in the eye.

Stone stairs lead up from the gargoyles to the **royal apartments of François I,** where you're greeted by a bust of the Renaissance king. The apartments cover two floors. Immerse yourself in richly tiled, ornately decorated rooms with some original furnishings, incredible ceilings, fireplaces (there's one in every room), and excellent English explanations. You'll see busts and portraits of some of the château's most famous residents, and near the end, learn about the dastardly 1588 murder of the duke of Guise, which took place in these apartments. In the late 1500s, the devastating Wars of Religion pitted Protestant against Catholic, and took a huge toll on this politically and religiously divided city—including the powerful Guise brothers. King Henry III (Catherine de Médicis' son) had the devoutly Catholic brothers assassinated to keep the duke off the throne.

Skip the Neoclassical wing (no English and little of interest), and end your visit with a walk through the small **fine-arts museum.** Located just over the château's entry, this 16th-century who's-who portrait gallery lets you put a face to the characters that made this château's history.

Other Sights

House of Magic (Maison de la Magie)—The home of Jean-Eugène Robert-Houdin, the illusionist whose name was adopted by Harry Houdini, offers an interesting but overpriced history of illusion and magic. Kids enjoy the gift shop. Several daily 30-minute shows have no words, so they work in any language.

THE LOIRE

Cost and Hours: Adults-€8, kids under 18-€5, €15 combo-ticket with château, €20 combo-ticket includes château and Sound-and-Light Show; daily 9:00-12:30 & 14:00-18:30, "séance" schedule posted at entry—usually at 11:15, 15:15, and 17:15, but hours may change in summer; at the opposite end of the square from the château, tel. 02 54 90 33 33, www.maisondelamagie.fr.

Wine Cooperative—Sample wines from a variety of local vintners on the château square, next to Le Marignan café (free, 8:30-12:30 & 14:00-17:30).

Historic Center—Take time to discover Blois' pedestrian-friendly center. Although much of the old town was destroyed by WWII bombs, the area has been tastefully rebuilt. Below the castle, you'll enter a network of lively walking streets with characteristic squares, cafés and restaurants, and a few noteworthy monuments. Use the TI's self-guided tours or poke about on your own. The towering **St. Nicholas Church,** with its flying buttresses, dates from the late 1100s and is worth a peek inside for its blend of Gothic and Romanesque styles. The maze of medieval lanes below Blois' other hill, crowned by **St. Louis Cathedral,** are also worth a wander. **Rue du Commerce** strings smart shops along its car-free path as it climbs from the river and turns into Rue de la Porte Chartraine. There's little to do along the river except to cross Pont Jacques Gabriel for views back to the city.

Biking from Blois—Blois is well-positioned as a starting point for biking forays into the countryside. Cycling from Blois to Chambord is a level, 70-minute, one-way ride along a well-marked route that gets more scenic the closer you get to Chambord. You can loop back to Blois without repeating the same route, and also connect to a good network of other bike paths (the TI's free *Le Pays des Châteaux á Vélo* map shows the bike routes in this area). Adding Cheverny makes a full-day, 30-mile round-trip. The TI has info on bike-rental shops in Blois.

Sleeping in Blois

(€1 = about $1.30, country code: 33)

Blois has a scarcity of worthwhile hotels. There's a **launderette** at 6 Rue St. Lubin.

$$$ **Hôtel Mercure Blois***** is modern and pricey but reliable, with a riverfront location 15 minutes from the château (Db-€140-180, air-con, 28 Quai Saint Jean, tel. 02 54 56 66 66, www.mercure.com).

$$$ **Best Western Blois Château***** has stylish decor, small-but-sharp rooms, and all the comforts you'd expect from this chain (Db-€125-150, air-con, Wi-Fi, loaner iPads, across from the train station and behind the château at 8 Avenue du Dr. Jean Laigret,

THE LOIRE

tel. 02 54 56 85 10, www.bestwesternblois.com, bwbloischateau @orange.fr).

$ Hôtel Anne de Bretagne** offers top value with 30 comfortable rooms at good prices, a central location near the château and train station, and a welcoming terrace (Sb-€46, Db-€58, Tb-€72, Qb-€85, Wi-Fi, 150 yards uphill from Parking du Château, 5-minute walk below the train station at 31 Avenue du Dr. Jean Laigret, tel. 02 54 78 05 38, fax 02 54 74 37 79, www.hotelannedebretagne .com, contact@hotelannedebretagne.com).

Eating in Blois

If you're stopping in Blois around lunchtime, plan on eating at **Le Marignan,** located on a breezy square in front of the château (daily, good salads and crêpes, €13-15 *menus,* fast service, 5 Place du Château, tel. 02 54 74 73 15). At the top of the hour, you can watch the stately mansion opposite the château become "the dragon house," as monsters crane their long necks out its many windows.

Between the Château and the River: The traffic-free streets between the château and the river are home to many cafés with standard, easy meals. **Le Clipper,** dishing up wood-fired pizza and basic café fare, has a favored location on Place Louis XII with great outdoor seating (daily, tel. 02 54 78 22 39). **La Banquette Rouge,** a block above St. Nicholas Church's left transept, delivers good regional cuisine with ambience to diners in long red booths—as the name suggests (€28 and €32 *menus,* closed Sun-Mon, 16 Rue des Trois Marchands, tel. 02 54 78 74 92). **Le Castelet,** also near St. Nicholas, is cozy, simple, cheap, and fun, with good vegetarian choices (*menus* from €19, closed Sun and Wed, 40 Rue St. Lubin, tel. 02 54 74 66 09).

Between the Cathedral and the River: Blois' most atmospheric square for an outdoor meal is Place de Grenier à Sel, between the river and St. Louis Cathedral, where you'll find a few simple options; **Le Murano** does a Franco-Italian mix (€22 *menus,* cheap pizza, daily, 11 Rue Vauvert, tel. 02 54 78 44 97). Nearby Rue Foulerie is ground zero for hip Blois. At **Vinomania,** wine lovers can combine relaxed wine-tastings with brasserie cuisine in a lively setting (daily, 12 Rue du Poids du Roi, tel. 02 54 90 17 66).

Blois Connections

From Blois by Train to: Amboise (14/day, 20 minutes), **Chinon** (6/day, 2-2.5 hours, transfer in Tours and possibly in St-Pierre-des-Corps), **Azay-le-Rideau** (6/day, 1.75-2.5 hours, transfer in Tours and possibly in St-Pierre-des-Corps), **Paris** (5/day direct, 1.5-2 hours, more with transfer in St-Pierre-des-Corps or Orléans).

By Bus to Chambord and Cheverny: From April through August, **Transports du Loir-et-Cher** (TLC) excursion buses to Chambord, Cheverny, and (less important) Beauregard leave from the Blois train station—look for them immediately to the left as you leave the station (TLC bus marked *Navette-Châteaux*). Morning departures from Blois station at 9:10 and 11:10 go to Chambord; from Chambord, departures link Cheverny and Beauregard with various return trips to Blois, allowing you from two to seven hours at a château. Verify these times at a TI or online (€6 bus fare, discounts offered on château entries including the Château Royal in Blois; buy tickets and get schedule from TI or bus driver, www.tlcinfo.net).

By Taxi: Blois taxis wait 30 steps in front of the station and offer excursion fares to **Chambord, Chaumont,** or **Cheverny** (€34 one-way from Blois to any of these three châteaux, €104 round-trip to Chambord and Cheverny, €48 more to add Chaumont, 8-person minivans available, tel. 02 54 78 07 65). These rates are per cab, making the per-person price downright reasonable for groups of three or four.

Château de Chambord

With its huge scale and prickly silhouette, Château de Chambord, worth ▲▲, is the granddaddy of the Loire châteaux. It's surrounded by Europe's largest enclosed forest park, a game preserve defined by a 20-mile-long wall and teeming with wild deer and boar. Chambord (shahn-bor) began as a simple hunting lodge for bored Blois counts and became a monument to the royal sport and duty of hunting. (Apparently, hunting was considered important to keep the animal population under control and the vital forests healthy.)

The château, six times the size of your average Loire castle, has 440 rooms and a fireplace for every day of the year. It consists of a keep in the shape of a Greek cross, with four towers and two wings surrounded by stables. Its four floors are each separated by 46 stairs, giving it very high ceilings. The ground floor has reception rooms, the first floor up houses the royal apartments, the second floor up houses a WWII exhibit and temporary art exhibits, and the rooftop offers a hunt-viewing terrace. Special exhibits describing Chambord at key moments in its history help animate the place. Because hunters could see best after autumn leaves fell,

Chambord was a winter palace (which helps explain the 365 fireplaces). Only 80 of Chambord's rooms are open to the public—and that's plenty.

Cost and Hours: €9.50, daily April-Sept 9:00-18:15, Oct-March 9:00-17:15, last entry 30 minutes before closing, parking-€3, tel. 02 54 50 40 00, www.chambord.org. There are two ticket offices: one in the village in front of the château, and another (less crowded) inside the actual château.

Getting There: The Blois excursion bus is best (€6, two daily departures from Blois station April-early Sept, taxis from Blois are reasonable as well; see "Blois Connections," earlier, for bus and taxi details).

Information and Tours: This château requires helpful information to make it come alive. Most rooms have adequate English explanations. You can rent an audioguide for a thorough history of the château and its rooms (€5, two can share one audioguide with volume turned to max).

Services: The bookshop in the château has a good selection of children's books. Among the collection of shops near the château, you'll find a TI (April-Oct daily 9:30-13:00 & 14:00-18:00, closed Nov-March, tel. 02 54 33 39 16), an ATM, WCs, local souvenirs, a wine-tasting room, and cafés. There's only one WC at the château itself (in a courtyard corner).

Biking Around the Park: You can rent bikes (€6/hour, €8/2 hours) to explore the park—a network of leafy lanes crisscrossing the vast expanse contained within its 20-mile-long wall.

Medieval Pageantry on Horseback Show: The 45-minute, family-friendly show (in the stables across the field from the château entry) is high-powered and full of clanging swords and pikes—performed on horseback and in medieval armor. Afterwards, the knights and horses come out to mingle and chat with children (€15; July-Aug daily at 11:45 and 16:30, May-June and Sept-early Oct Tue-Sun at 11:45, Sat-Sun also at 16:30, closed Mon; tel. 02 54 20 31 01, www.ecuries-chambord.com).

Views: For the best views, cross the small river in front of the château and turn right. The recommended Hôtel du Grand St. Michel has a broad view terrace, ideal for post-château refreshment.

Background: Starting in 1518, François I created this "weekend retreat," employing 1,800 workmen for 15 years. (You'll see his signature salamander symbol everywhere.) François I was an absolute monarch—with an emphasis on absolute. In 32 years of rule (1515-1547), he never once called the Estates-General to session (a rudimentary parliament in *ancien régime* France). This grand hunting palace was another way to show off his power. Countless guests, like Charles V—the Holy Roman Emperor and most

THE LOIRE

powerful man of the age—were invited to this pleasure palace of French kings...and were totally wowed.

The grand architectural plan of the château—modeled after an Italian church—feels designed as a place to worship royalty. Each floor of the main structure is essentially the same: four equal arms of a Greek cross branch off of a monumental staircase, which leads up to a cupola. From a practical point of view, the design pushed the usable areas to the four corners. This castle, built while the pope was erecting a new St. Peter's Basilica, is like a secular rival to the Vatican.

Construction started the year Leonardo died, 1519. The architect is unknown, but an eerie Leonardo-esque spirit resides here. The symmetry, balance, and classical proportions combine to reflect a harmonious Renaissance vision that could have been inspired by Leonardo's notebooks.

Typical of royal châteaux, this palace of François I was rarely used. Because any effective king had to be on the road to exercise his power, royal palaces sat empty most of the time. In the 1600s, Louis XIV renovated Chambord, but he visited it only six times (for about two weeks each visit).

⊘ Self-Guided Tour: This tour covers the highlights, floor by floor.

Ground Floor: This stark level shows off the general plan—four wings, small doors to help heated rooms stay warm, and a massive staircase. In a room just inside the front door, on the left, you can watch a worthwhile 18-minute video.

The attention-grabbing **double-helix staircase** dominates the open vestibules and invites visitors to climb up. Its two spirals are interwoven, so people can climb up and down and never meet. From the staircase, enjoy fine views of the vestibule action, or just marvel at the playful Renaissance capitals carved into its light tuff stone.

First Floor: Here you'll find the most interesting rooms. Starting opposite a big ceramic stove, tour this floor basically clockwise. You'll enter the lavish apartments in the **king's wing** and pass through the grand bedrooms of Louis XIV, his wife Maria Theresa, and, at the far end, François I (follow *Logis de François 1er* signs). Notice how the furniture in François' bedroom was designed to be easily disassembled and moved with him.

A highlight of the first floor is the fascinating seven-room **Museum of the Count of Chambord** (Musée du Comte de Chambord). The last of the French Bourbons, Henri d'Artois (a.k.a. the Count of Chambord) was next in line to be king when France decided it didn't need one. He was raring to rule—you'll see his coronation outfits and even souvenirs from the coronation that never happened. Check out his boyhood collection of little guns, including a working mini-cannon. The man who believed he should have become King Henry V lived in exile from the age of 10. Although he opened the palace to the public, he actually visited this château only once, in 1871.

The **chapel** tucked off in a side wing is interesting only for how unimpressive it is. It's dwarfed by the mass of this imposing château, clearly designed to trumpet the glories not of God, but of the king of France.

Second Floor: Beneath beautiful coffered ceilings (notice the "F" for François) is a series of ballrooms that once hosted post-hunt parties. From here, you'll climb up to the rooftop, but first lean to the center of the staircase and look down its spiral.

Rooftop: A pincushion of spires and chimneys decorates the rooftop viewing terrace. From a distance, the roof—with its frilly forest of stone towers—gives the massive château a deceptive lightness. From here, ladies could scan the estate grounds, enjoying the spectacle of their ego-pumping men out hunting. On hunt day, a line of beaters would fan out and work inward from the distant walls, flushing wild game to the center, where the king and his buddies waited. The showy lantern tower of the tallest spire glowed with a nighttime torch when the king was in.

Gaze up at the grandiose tip-top of the tallest tower, capped with the king's fleur-de-lis symbol. It's a royal lily—not a cross—that caps this monument to the power of the French king.

In the Courtyard: Leaving the main part of the château, turn left. In the corner (just past the summer café), a door leads to the classy **carriage rooms** and the fascinating **lapidary rooms.** Here you'll come face-to-face with original stonework from the roof, including the graceful lantern cupola, with the original palace-capping fleur-de-lis. Imagine having to hoist that load. The volcanic tuff stone used to build the spires was soft and easy to work, but not very durable—particularly when so exposed to the elements.

Sleeping near Chambord and Cheverny

(€1 = about $1.30, country code: 33)
$$ Hôtel du Grand St. Michel** lets you wake up with Chambord outside your window. It's an Old World, hunting-lodge kind of place with rooms in pretty good shape and a trophy-festooned dining room (*menus* from €20). Sleep here and you'll have a chance to roam the château grounds after the peasants have been run out (small Db-€62-72, bigger Db-€80, Db facing château-€85-100 and worth the extra euros, extra bed-€15, breakfast-€10, tel. 02 54 20 31 31, fax 02 54 20 36 40, on Place Saint Louis, www.saintmichel-chambord.com, hotelsaintmichel@wanadoo.fr).

$$ Chambres la Flânerie, on the bike route from Chambord to Cheverny, offers two family rooms in an adorable home. It's riddled with flowers, crawling with ivy, and surrounded by wheat fields and forests. The gentle Delabarres speak enough English and loan bikes to their fortunate guests (Db-€63, Tb-€78, Qb-€98, includes breakfast, 25 Rue de Gallerie, tel. 02 54 79 86 28, mobile 06 75 72 28 41, www.laflanerie.com, laflanerie@laflanerie.com). Coming from Blois on D-765, it's before Cheverny in the hamlet of Les Fées. Turn right where you see wooden bus shelters flanking the road, and follow signs to *Eric Auge Menuiserie* (see map on page 414).

Cheverny

This stately hunting palace, a ▲▲ sight, is one of the more lavishly furnished Loire châteaux. Because the immaculately preserved Cheverny (shuh-vehr-nee) was built and decorated in a relatively short 30 years, from 1604 to 1634, it offers a unique architectural harmony and unity of style. From the start, this château has been in the Hurault family, and Hurault pride shows in its flawless preservation and intimate feel. The viscount's family still lives on the  third floor (not open to the public, but you'll see some family photos). Cheverny was spared by the French Revolution; the owners were popular then, as today, even among the village farmers.

The château is flanked by a pleasant village, with a small grocery, cafés offering good lunch options, and a few hotels. You can get to Cheverny by bus from Blois (see "Blois Connections" on page 427) or by minivan tour from Amboise (see "Getting Around the Loire Valley" on page 387).

Cost and Hours: €9, €13.50 combo-ticket includes Tintin "adventure" rooms, family deals, daily July-Aug 9:15-19:00, April-June and Sept 9:15-18:15, Oct 9:45-17:30, Nov-March 9:45-17:00, tel. 02 54 79 96 29, www.chateau-cheverny.fr.

Visiting the Château: As you walk across the manicured grounds toward the gleaming château, the sound of hungry hounds will follow you. Medallions with portraits of Roman emperors, including Julius Caesar (above the others in the center), line up across the facade. As you enter the château, pick up the excellent English self-guided tour brochure, which describes the interior beautifully.

Your visit starts in the lavish **dining room,** decorated with leather walls and a sumptuous ceiling. As you climb the stairs to the private apartments, look out the window and spot the *orangerie* across the grass. It was here that the *Mona Lisa* was hidden (along

with other treasures from the Louvre) during World War II.

On the first floor up, you'll tour the I-could-live-here **family apartments** with silky bedrooms, kids' rooms, and an intimate dining room.

You'll pass though the **Arms Room** before landing in the **King's Bedchamber**—literally fit for a king. Study the fun ceiling art, especially the "boys will be boys" cupids. Following the tour booklet, in later rooms, find a grandfather clock with a second hand that's been ticking for 250 years, a family tree going back to 1490, and a letter of thanks from George Washington to this family for their help in booting out the English.

Nearby: Barking dogs remind visitors that the viscount still loves to hunt. The **kennel** (200 yards in front of the château, look for *Chenil* signs) is especially interesting at dinnertime, when the 70 hounds are fed (April-mid-Sept daily at 17:00, mid-Sept-March Mon and Wed-Fri at 15:00). The dogs—half English foxhound and half French Poitou—are bred to have big feet and bigger stamina. They're given food once a day, and the feeding *(la soupe des chiens)* is a fun spectacle that shows off their strict training. Before chow time, the hungry hounds fill the little kennel rooftop and watch the trainer bring in troughs stacked with delectable raw meat. He opens the gate, and the dogs gather enthusiastically around the food, yelping hysterically. Only when the trainer says to eat can they dig in. You can see the dogs at any time, but the feeding show is fun to plan for.

Also nearby, **Tintin** comic lovers can enter a series of fun rooms designed to take them into a Tintin adventure (called Les Secrets de Moulinsart, €13.50 combo-ticket with castle); hunters can inspect an antler-filled **trophy room;** and gardeners can prowl the château's fine **kitchen and flower gardens** (free, behind the dog kennel).

Wine-Tastings at the Château Gate: Opposite the entry to the château sits a slick wine-tasting room, **La Maison des Vins.** It's run by an association of 32 local vintners. Their mission: to boost the Cheverny reputation for wine (which is fruity, light, dry, and aromatic compared to the heavier, oaky wines made farther downstream). Tasters have two options. In the first, any visitor can have four free tastes from featured bottles of the day, offered with helpful guidance. Or, for a fee, you can sample more freely among the 32 labels, at your own pace, by using modern automated dispensers. Even if just enjoying the free samples, wander among the spouts. Each gives the specs of that wine in English (€6.50 for small tastes of 7 wines, €6-9 bottles, daily 11:00-13:15 & 14:15-19:00, tel. 02 54 79 25 16, www.maisondesvinsdecheverny.fr).

Fougères-sur-Bièvre

The feudal castle of Fougères-sur-Bièvre (foo-zher sewr bee-ehv) dominates its hamlet and is worth a stop, even if you don't go inside (but I would). Located 15 minutes from Cheverny on the way to Chenonceaux and Amboise, Fougères-sur-Bièvre was constructed for defense, not hunting. It was built over a small river to provide an unlimited water supply during sieges. Leveled in the Hundred Years' War, then rebuilt in the 1500s, it's completely restored. Although there are no furnishings (there weren't many in the Middle Ages in any case), it gives you a good look at how castles were built.

Follow the route with the helpful English handout (minimal English explanations are also provided in some rooms). You'll see models of castle-construction techniques, including interesting exhibits on the making of half-timbered walls (oak posts and cross-beams provided the structural skeleton, and the areas in between were filled in with a mix of clay, straw, and pebbles). Walk under medieval roof supports, gaze through loopholes, and stand over machicolations (holes for dropping rocks and scalding liquids on attackers) in the main tower. Seeing the main tower from within adds an entirely new appreciation of these structures' complexity, and the two medieval latrines demonstrate how little toilet technology has changed in 800 years. Before leaving, take a few minutes to visit the re-created medieval vegetable garden.

Cost and Hours: €5.50; May-mid-Sept daily 9:30-12:30 & 14:00-18:30; mid-Sept-April Wed-Mon 10:00-12:00 & 14:00-17:00, closed Tue; last entry 30 minutes before closing, tel. 02 54 20 27 18, http://fougeres-sur-bievre.monuments-nationaux.fr.

Getting There: Fougères-sur-Bièvre has no easy public-transport link from Amboise...or anywhere else. If you're *sans* rental car or bike, arrange for a custom minivan tour—or skip it.

Chaumont-sur-Loire

A castle has been located on this spot since the 11th century; the current version is a ▲▲ sight. The first priority at Chaumont (show-mon) was defense. You'll appreciate the strategic location on the long climb up from the village below. (Drivers can avoid the uphill hike except off-season—explained later.) Gardeners will

appreciate the elaborate Festival of Gardens that unfolds next to the château every year, and modern-art lovers will enjoy how works have been incorporated into the gardens, château, and stables.

Cost and Hours: Château and stables-€10; château open daily July-Aug 10:00-19:00, May-June and early Sept 10:00-18:00, April and late Sept 10:30-17:30, Oct-March 10:00-17:00, last entry 30 minutes before closing; stables close daily 12:00-14:00; English handout available, tel. 02 54 20 99 22, www.domaine-chaumont.fr.

Festival of Gardens: This annual exhibit, with 25 elaborate gardens arranged around a different theme each year, draws rave reviews from international gardeners (Garden Festival-€10; château, stables, and Garden Festival-€16; late April-mid-Oct daily 10:00-20:00, in 2013 may be open with special lighting until 24:00 July-Aug, tel. 02 54 20 99 22, www.domaine-chaumont.fr). When the festival is on, you'll find several little cafés and reasonable lunch options scattered about the hamlet (festival ticket not needed).

Getting There: There is no public transport to Chaumont, although the train between Blois and Amboise (8/day) can drop you in Onzain, a 25-minute roadside walk across the river to the château. Bikes (Chaumont is about 20 miles from Amboise or Blois), taxis (reasonable from Blois train station), and chartered minivans also work for non-drivers (see "Getting Around the Loire Valley" on page 387).

From May to mid-October, drivers can park up top, at an entrance open only during the Festival of Gardens (you don't need to buy tickets for the garden event). From the river, drive up behind the château (direction: Montrichard), take the first hard right turn (following *Stade du Tennis* signs), and drive to the lot beyond the soccer field.

Background: The Chaumont château you see today was built mostly in the 15th and 16th centuries. Catherine de Médicis forced Diane de Poitiers to swap Chenonceau for Chaumont; you'll see tidbits about both women inside. Louis XVI, Marie-Antoinette, Voltaire, and Benjamin Franklin all spent time here. Today's château offers a good look at the best defense design in 1500: on a cliff with a dry moat, big and small drawbridges with classic ramparts, loopholes for archers, and handy holes through which to dump hot oil on attackers.

❷ Self-Guided Tour: There's no audioguide or regular English tour. Your walk through the palace—restored mostly in the 19th century—is described by the English flier you'll pick up

THE LOIRE

when you enter. As the château has more rooms than period furniture, your tour will be peppered with modern-art exhibits that fill otherwise empty spaces. The rooms you'll visit first (in the east wing) show the château as it appeared in the 15th and 16th centuries. Your visit ends in the west wing, which features furnishings from the 19th-century owners.

The castle's medieval **entry** is littered with various coats of arms. As you walk in, take a close look at the two drawbridges (a new mechanism allows the main bridge to be opened with the touch of a button). Once inside, the heavy defensive feel is replaced with palatial luxury. Peek into the courtyard—during the more stable 1700s, the fourth wing, which had enclosed the courtyard, was taken down to give the terrace its river-valley view.

Entering the château rooms, signs direct you along a one-way loop path *(suite de la visite)* through the château's three wings. Catherine de Médicis, who missed her native Florence, brought a touch of Italy to all her châteaux, and her astrologer (Ruggieri) was so important that he had his own (plush) room—next to hers. **Catherine's bedroom** has a case with ceramic portrait busts dating from 1770, when the lord of the house had a tradition of welcoming guests by having their portrait sketched, then giving them a ceramic bust made from this sketch when they departed. Find Ben Franklin's medallion. The exquisitely tiled **Salle de Conseil** has a grand fireplace designed to keep this conference room warm. The treasury box in the **guard room** is a fine example of 1600s-era locksmithing. The lord's wealth could be locked up here as safely as possible in those days, with a false keyhole, no handles, and even an extra-secure box inside for diamonds.

A big spiral staircase leads up through a messy attic and then down to rooms decorated in 19th-century style. The **dining room**'s fanciful limestone fireplace is exquisitely carved. Find the food (frog legs, snails, goats for cheese), the maid with the bellows, and even the sculptor with a hammer and chisel at the top (on the left). Your visit ends with a stroll through the 19th-century library, the billiards room, and the living room.

In the **courtyard,** study the entertaining spouts and decor on the walls.

The **stables** *(ecuries)* were entirely rebuilt in the 1880s. The medallion above the gate reads *pour l'avenir* (for the future), which shows off an impressive commitment to horse technology. Inside, circle clockwise—you can almost hear the clip-clop of horses walking. Notice the deluxe horse stalls, padded with bins and bowls for hay, oats, and water, complete with a strategically placed drainage gutter. The horses were named for Greek gods and great châteaux. The Horse Kitchen (Cuisine des Chevaux) produced mash twice weekly for the animals. The "finest tack room in all of

France" shows off horse gear. Beyond the covered alcove where the horse and carriage were prepared for the prince, you'll see four carriages parked and ready to go. Finally, the round former kiln was redesigned to be a room for training the horses.

The estate is a **tree garden,** set off by a fine lawn. Trees were imported from throughout the Mediterranean world to be enjoyed—and to fend off any erosion on this strategic bluff.

Loches and Valençay

Loches

The overlooked town of Loches (lohsh), located about 30 minutes south of Amboise, makes a good base for drivers wanting to visit sights east and west of Tours (in effect triangulating between Amboise and Chinon), but has no easy train or bus connections. This pretty town sits on the region's loveliest river, the Indre, and holds an appealing mix of medieval monuments, stroll-worthy streets, and fewer tourists. Its château dominates the skyline and is worth a short visit. The Wednesday and Saturday street markets are lively; the Saturday market takes over many streets in the old city.

Sleeping in Loches: For an overnight stay, try **$$ Hôtel George Sand***,** located on the river, with a well-respected restaurant, an idyllic terrace, and rustic, comfortable rooms (Db-€60-72, luxury Db-€135, Tb-€95, Wi-Fi, no elevator, 300 yards south of TI at 39 Rue Quintefol, tel. 02 47 59 39 74, fax 02 47 91 55 75, www.hotelrestaurant-georgesand.com, contactGS@hotel restaurant-georgesand.com). **$$$ Le Logis du Bief,** a fine, welcoming *chambre d'hôte* in the center of town with four lovely, air-conditioned rooms, has a riverfront terrace and cozy living spaces (Db-€90-120, Tb-€145, 10 percent discount if staying 2 nights, includes breakfast, 21 Rue Quintefol, tel. 02 47 91 66 02, mobile 06 83 10 46 64, www.logisloches.com).

Valençay

The Renaissance château of Valençay (vah-lahn-say) is a massive, luxuriously furnished structure with echoes of its former owner Talleyrand (a famous French diplomat who helped broker the Louisiana Purchase) and lovely gardens. It has kid-friendly activities and elaborate big toys, and lots of summer events such as fencing demonstrations and candlelit visits.

Cost and Hours: €12, ask about family rates, free audioguide covers château and gardens, daily June 9:30-18:30, July-Aug 9:30-19:00, April-May and Sept 10:00-18:00, Oct 10:20-17:30, closed Nov-March, tel. 02 54 00 15 69, www.chateau-valencay.fr.

West of Tours

Chinon

This pleasing, sleepy town straddles the Vienne River and hides its ancient streets under a historic royal fortress. Today's Chinon (shee-nohn) is best known for its popular red wines. But for me it's also a top home base for seeing the sights west of Tours: Azay-le-Rideau (sound-and-light show), Langeais, Villandry, Chatonnière, Rivau, Ussé, and the Abbaye Royale de Fontevraud. Each of these worthwhile sights is no more than a 20-minute drive away. Trains provide access to many châteaux (via Tours) but are time-consuming, so you're better off with your own car or a minivan excursion (see "Getting Around the Loire Valley," on page 387, and "Chinon Connections," later).

Orientation to Chinon

Chinon stretches out along the Vienne River, and everything of interest to travelers lies between it and the hilltop fortress. Charming Place du Général de Gaulle—ideal for café-lingering—is in the center of town. Rue Rabelais is Chinon's traffic-free shopping street, with restaurants, bars, and cafés—as lively as they can be in peaceful Chinon.

Tourist Information

The TI is in the town center, near the base of the hill and a 15-minute walk from the train station. You'll find *chambre d'hôte* listings, wine-tasting details (wine-route maps available for the serious taster), bike-rental information, and an English-language self-guided tour of the town (May-Sept daily 10:00-19:00; Oct-April Mon-Sat 10:00-12:00 & 14:00-18:00, closed Sun; in village center on Place Hofheim, tel. 02 47 93 17 85, www.chinon-valdeloire .com). Free public WCs are around the back of the TI.

Helpful Hints

Market Days: A market takes place all day Thursday on Place Jeanne d'Arc (west end of town). There's a sweet little market on Sunday, around Place du Général de Gaulle.

Groceries: Carrefour City is across from the Hôtel de Ville, on Place du Général de Gaulle (Mon-Sat 7:00-20:00, Sun 9:00-13:00).

Laundry: Salon Lavoir is near the bridge at #7 Quai Charles VII (daily 7:00-21:00).

Bike and Canoe Rental: Canoe-Kayak & Vélo rents bikes and canoes on the river, next to the campground (bikes-€14/day; canoes-€10/2 hours or €19/half-day, shuttle included; €23 to combine bike and canoe in a full day; mobile 06 23 82 96 33, www.loisirs-nature.fr). For more on biking and canoeing, see page 444.

Taxi: Call 06 83 51 87 88 for an English-speaking taxi driver; tel. 02 47 95 85 48 for other taxi service.

Car Rental: It's best to book a car at the St-Pierre-des-Corps train station in Tours (see page 398).

Best Views: You'll find terrific rooftop views from the fortress and along Rue du Coteau St. Martin (between St. Mexme Church and the fortress—see map), and rewarding river views to Chinon by crossing the bridge in the center of town and turning right (small riverfront café May-Sept).

Self-Guided Walk

Welcome to Chinon

Chinon offers a peaceful world of quiet cobbled lanes, historic buildings, and few tourists. By following this walk (or the TI's self-guided tour brochure) and reading plaques at key buildings, you'll gain a good understanding of this city's historic importance.

• *Begin this short walk from the highest point of the bridge that crosses the Vienne River, and enjoy the great view.*

Chinon Riverbank: The linear city of Chinon is sandwiched between the Vienne River and an abrupt cliff. People have lived along the banks of this river since prehistoric times. The Gallo-Romans built the first defenses in Chinon 1,600 years ago. There's been a castle up on that hill for over a thousand years—which pretty much predates every other castle you'll visit in the Loire area. The strategic advantage of the castle's site is clear. You may see reproductions of traditional wooden boats moored below. These were once used to shuttle merchandise up and down the river; some boats ventured as far west as the Atlantic.

• *Walk toward the city, then make a right along the riverbank and find the big statue that honors a famous Renaissance writer and satirist.*

Rabelais Statue: The great French writer François Rabelais was born here in 1494. You'll see many references to him in his proud hometown. His best-known work, *Gargantua and Pantagruel,* describes the amusing adventures of father-and-son giants and was set in Chinon. Rabelais' vivid humor and savage wit are, for many, quintessentially French—there's even a French word for it: *rabelaisien*. In his bawdy tales, Rabelais critiqued society in ways that deflected outright censorship—though the Sorbonne called them obscene. A monk and a doctor, he's considered the first great

THE LOIRE

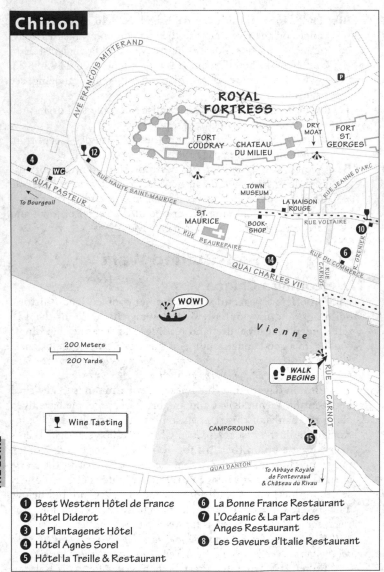

Chinon

ROYAL FORTRESS

FORT COUDRAY   CHATEAU DU MILIEU   DRY MOAT   FORT ST. GEORGES

P

AVE FRANÇOIS MITTERAND

4

12

WC

QUAI PASTEUR

To Bourgeuil

RUE HAUTE SAINT-MAURICE

RUE JEANNE D'ARC

TOWN MUSEUM

LA MAISON ROUGE

ST. MAURICE

BOOK-SHOP

RUE VOLTAIRE

RUE BEAUREPAIRE

RUE DU COMMERCE

R. GRENIER

10

6

14

QUAI CHARLES VII

RUE CARNOT

WOW!

Vienne

200 Meters
200 Yards

WALK BEGINS

RUE CARNOT

Wine Tasting

CAMPGROUND

15

QUAI DANTON

To Abbaye Royale de Fontevraud & Château du Rivau

THE LOIRE

1 Best Western Hôtel de France
2 Hôtel Diderot
3 Le Plantagenet Hôtel
4 Hôtel Agnès Sorel
5 Hôtel la Treille & Restaurant

6 La Bonne France Restaurant
7 L'Océanic & La Part des Anges Restaurant
8 Les Saveurs d'Italie Restaurant

French novelist, and his farces were a voice against the power of the Church and the king.

• *Turn your back on Rabelais and follow the brick sidewalk leading to the center of Chinon's main square.*

Place du Général de Gaulle: The town wall once sat on the wide swath of land running from this square down to the river, effectively walling the city off from the water. This explains why,

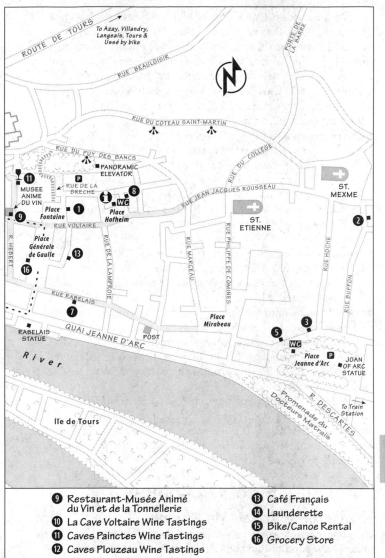

9 Restaurant-Musée Animé
   du Vin et de la Tonnellerie

10 La Cave Voltaire Wine Tastings

11 Caves Painctes Wine Tastings

12 Caves Plouzeau Wine Tastings

13 Café Français

14 Launderette

15 Bike/Canoe Rental

16 Grocery Store

even now, Chinon seems to turn its back on its river. In medieval times, as was typical of that age, the market was here, just outside the wall. The town hall building, originally an arcaded market, was renovated only in the 19th century. Today it flies three flags: Europe, France, and Chinon (with its three castles). From here, you can see the handy elevator that connects the town with its castle.

Turn left down **Rue Voltaire.** If the old wall still stood, you'd be entering town through the east gate. (Note the black info posts here and scattered throughout town.) Walk along a fine strip of 16th-, 17th-, and 18th-century houses. A few steps to the right on Rue du Dr. Gendron is the charming little **Musée Animé du Vin;** at the next corner is **Cave Voltaire,** and a right turn on the next small lane leads to **Caves Painctes** and the quarry where the stone for the castle originated (all covered later, under "Sights in Chinon.")

• *Continue walking a few blocks farther into the historic city center.*

Old Town: In the immediate post-WWII years, there was little money or energy to care for beautiful old towns. But in the 1960s, new laws and sensitivities kicked in, and old quarters like this were fixed up and preserved. Study the vernacular architecture. **La Maison Rouge** (at 38-42 Rue Voltaire) is a fine example of the town's medieval structures: a stone foundation and timber frame, filled in with whatever was handy. With dense populations crowding within the protective town walls, buildings swelled wider at the top to avoid blocking congested streets.

Pop into the ancient **bookshop** on the corner. I asked the owner where he got his old prints. He responded, "Did you ever enjoy a friend's mushrooms and ask him where he found them? Did he tell you?"

The **town museum** is across the street. Its plaque recalls that this building housed an Estates-General meeting, convened by Charles VII, in 1428. Just around the corner, find a good tower view (and a public WC).

• *From here the street changes names to Rue Haute St. Maurice. You can continue in the same direction and find the Caves Plouzeau wine cellars at #94 (described later). If you'd rather visit the castle, turn around, walk back and climb up Rue Jean d'Arc—or take the elevator near the TI—to the fortress.*

Sights in Chinon

▲Forteresse Royale de Chinon

Chinon's castle (or fortress) is more ruined and older than the more famous and visited châteaux of the Loire. It comes without a hint of pleasure palace. While there's not much left, its rich history makes the castle a popular destination for French tourists and school groups.

Cost and Hours: €7.50, daily March-Oct 9:30-18:00, until 19:00 May-Aug, Nov-Feb 9:30-17:00, tel. 02 47 93 13 45, www.forteressechinon.fr.

THE LOIRE

Castle Tours: Your admission includes a fun, self-guided tour booklet. Free English-language tours leave daily and can help bring the ruins to life. It's worth planning your visit around them (45 minutes, generally at 11:00, 14:00, and 17:00).

Getting There: It's a bracing walk up from town, or you can take the free "panoramic" elevator from behind the TI. You'll find a free parking lot 100 yards above the castle entry.

Background: Henry II and Eleanor of Aquitaine, who ruled a vast realm from Scotland to the Spanish border, reigned from here around 1150. They had eight children (among them two future kings, including Richard the Lionhearted). And it was in this castle that Joan of Arc pleaded with Charles VII to muster the courage to rally the French and take the throne back from the nasty English. Charles had taken refuge in this well-fortified castle during the Hundred Years' War, making Chinon France's capital city during that low ebb in Gallic history.

Visiting the Castle: The castle has three structures separated by moats. You'll enter via the oldest part, the 12th-century Fort Saint-Georges. Crossing a dry moat, you find yourself in the big courtyard of the Château du Milieu; at the far end is Fort Coudray.

Follow the arrows through eight stark and stony rooms, enjoying the clever teaching videos. There's a small museum devoted to the legendary Joan of Arc and her myth, developed through the centuries to inspire the French to pride and greatness. The fort comes with commanding views of town, the river, and the château-studded countryside. Chinon—both the city and the castle—developed as its political importance grew. It was the seat of French royalty in the 14th century. Most of the stones were quarried directly below the castle and hauled up through a well. The resulting caverns keep stores of local wine cool to this day.

Wine Sights and Tastings in and near Chinon

Chinon reds are among the most respected in the Loire, and there are a variety of ways to sample them.

La Cave Voltaire—At the most convenient of Chinon's wine-tasting options, pony-tailed, English-speaking sommelier Patrice would love to help you learn about his area's wines. He serves inexpensive appetizers and has wines from all regions of France—the best, of course, are from Chinon. It's a good place to come before dinner. The ambience inside is wine-shop cozy, but the tables outside are hard to resist (daily 10:00-22:00, near Place du Général de Gaulle at 13 Rue Voltaire, tel. 02 47 93 37 68, www.lacavevoltaire.fr).

Caves Plouzeau—This place offers another opportunity to walk through long, atmospheric *caves*—complete with mood lighting—

that extend under the château to a (literally) cool tasting room and reasonably priced wines (€6-11/bottle, April-Sept Tue-Sat 11:00-13:00 & 15:00-19:00, closed Sun-Mon and Oct-March, at the western end of town on 94 Rue Haute St-Maurice, tel. 02 47 93 16 34, http://plouzeau.com).

Caves Painctes—At this *cave*, summer travelers have a chance to sample Chinon wines, as well as to walk through the cool quarry from which stones for the castle and town's houses were cut. This rock (tuff) is soft and easily quarried, and when exposed to oxygen, it hardens. The *caves*, 300 feet directly below the castle, were dug as the castle was built. Its stones were hauled directly up to the building site with a treadmill-powered hoist (think Mont St-Michel, if you've visited there). Converted to wine cellars in the 15th century, the former quarry is a pilgrimage site of sorts for admirers of Rabelais, who featured it prominently in his writings. To visit, you must sign up for a tour, which takes about an hour and includes a 10-minute video and a tasting of three local wines. Designed to promote Chinon wines, it's run by a local winemakers' association (€3, July-Aug Tue-Sun at 11:00, 15:00, 16:30, and 18:00; closed Mon and Sept-June; off Rue Voltaire on Impasse des Caves Painctes, tel. 02 47 93 30 44).

Restaurant-Musée Animé du Vin et de la Tonnellerie ("Wine and Barrel Museum and Restaurant")—This combination museum/restaurant is the life's work of a passionate wine lover, the mustachioed Dédé la Boulange. You'll stroll through a few rooms animated by characters re-creating the production of local wines, and smile at the ingenuity of his handiwork (€4.50, €2.50 if you enjoy dinner at his recommended restaurant on the premises, daily mid-March-mid-Oct 10:00-22:00, closed off-season, 12 Rue Voltaire).

Domaine de la Chevalerie—For an authentic winery experience in the thick of the vineyards, drive about 25 minutes from Chinon to Domaine de la Chevalerie. This traditional winery has been run by the same family for 14 generations. Fun-loving and English-speaking daughter Stéphanie will take you through the cavernous hillside cellars crammed with 260,000 bottles, then treat you to a tasting of their 100 percent Cabernet Franc reds from seven different plots of land (daily 10:00-12:00 & 14:00-19:00, best to call ahead, off D-35 at 7 Rue du Peu Muleau, Restigné, tel. 02 47 97 46 32, www.domainedelachevalerie.fr).

Other Sights

▲**Biking from Chinon**—Many good options are available from Chinon (be sure to get maps from the TI or your bike rental shop). The easiest ride—thanks to the level terrain—is to the pretty village of Candes-St-Martin (cross the bridge and turn left, then bike along the river and follow signs). Most cyclists can manage the pleasant ride from Chinon to Ussé, and some will want to venture beyond. To avoid the monumental hill when leaving town, take your bike in the free elevator behind the TI up to the château level. At the top, turn right and then make quick left and you'll find the main road. Look for *Loire à Vélo* signs (route #4 on their map). You'll come to a quiet lane that crosses the Indre River, then, if you have the energy, follow the Loire River to Villandry (after Villandry, the path follows the Cher River into Tours). Connecting these châteaux towns is a full-day, 35-mile round-trip ride that only those in fit condition will enjoy. (See "Helpful Hints," earlier, for rental location and costs.)

Canoeing/Kayaking from Chinon—From May through September, you'll find plastic canoes and kayaks for rent next to the campground across the lone bridge in Chinon. The outfitters will shuttle you upriver to tiny Anché for a scenic and fun two-hour, four-mile float back to town—ending with great Chinon fortress views. They also offer a 10-mile, half-day float that starts in Chinon and ends downriver in the lovely village of Candes-St-Martin. Or do your own biathlon by canoeing one way and biking back (see "Helpful Hints," earlier, for rental location and costs).

Nighttime in Chinon—Café Français has live music several nights a week. Run by Jean François (a.k.a. "Jeff"), it's a characteristic local hangout and *the* place for any late-night fun in this sleepy town (open Tue-Sat from 18:00 and Sun from 19:00 until you shut it down, closed Mon, behind town hall at 37 Rue des Halles, tel. 02 47 93 32 78).

Sleeping in Chinon

(€1 = about $1.30, country code: 33)

Hotels are a good value in Chinon. If you stay overnight here, walk out to the river and cross the bridge for a floodlit view of the château walls.

$$$ Best Western Hôtel de France*** offers sufficient comfort without the personal touches of the other hotels I list. Still, I like the location—at Chinon's best square—as well as the open patios and half-timbered hallways inside the hotel (Db-€115-150, Tb/Qb-€160-200, includes breakfast, several rooms have balconies over the square, some have thin walls, some have air-con, Wi-Fi, 49 Place du Général de Gaulle, tel. 02 47 93 33 91, fax 02 47 98 37 03, www.bestwestern-hoteldefrance-chinon.com, elmachinon @aol.com).

$$ Hôtel Diderot** This handsome 18th-century manor house on the eastern edge of town is the closest hotel I list to the train station (drivers, look for signs from Place Jeanne d'Arc). It's a family affair, run by spirited Laurent and his equally spirited sisters, Françoise and Martine, who will adopt you into their clan if you're not careful. The hotel surrounds a carefully planted courtyard, and has a small bar with a good selection of area wines. Rooms in the main building vary in size and decor, but all are well-

maintained, with personal touches. Ground-floor rooms come with private patios. The four good family rooms have connecting rooms, each with a private bathroom. Breakfast (€9) includes a rainbow of Laurent's homemade jams (Sb-€58-75, Db-€68-92, extra bed-€12, Wi-Fi, limited parking-€7/day, 4 Rue de Buffon, tel. 02 47 93 18 87, fax 02 47 93 37 10, www.hoteldiderot.com, hoteldiderot @wanadoo.fr).

$$ Le Plantagenet has 30 comfortable rooms and may have space when others don't. There's a garden courtyard—picnics encouraged if you buy drinks from hotel, an onsite washer/dryer, and a great €10 breakfast (Db-€69 without air-con, Db-€83 with air-con, some rooms have balconies, 12 Place Jeanne d'Arc, tel. 02 47 93 36 92, www.hotel-plantagenet.com, resa@hotel-plantagenet .com).

$ Hôtel Agnès Sorel, at the western end of town, sits on the river and is handy for drivers, but it's a 30-minute walk from the train station and has some traffic noise. Of its ten sharp rooms, three have river views, two have balconies, and five surround a small courtyard. A few are air-conditioned (Db-€50-60, bigger Db-€85, big Db suite-€110, T/Qb suite-€135, Wi-Fi in lobby, 4 Quai Pasteur, tel. 02 47 93 04 37, fax 02 47 93 06 37, www.hotel -agnes-sorel.com, christine.tarre@hotel-agnes-sorel.com).

$ Hôtel la Treille has five rugged and rustic rooms for budget travelers (D-€32, Db-€42, Tb-€52, 4 Place Jeanne d'Arc, tel. 02 47 93 07 71, no fax, no email, no overhead).

Outside Chinon, near Ligré

$$$ Le Clos de Ligré lets you sleep in farmhouse silence, surrounded by vineyards and farmland. A 10-minute drive from Chinon, it has room to roam, a pool overlooking the vines, and a billiards room with a baby grand piano. English-speaking Martine Descamps spoils her guests with cavernous and creatively decorated rooms (Db-€110, good family rooms, includes breakfast, €35 dinner includes the works, cash only, 37500 Ligré, tel. 02 47 93 95 59, mobile 06 61 12 45 55, www.le-clos-de-ligre.com, martinedescamps@le-clos-de-ligre.com). From Chinon, cross the river and go toward Richelieu on D-760, turn right on D-115, and continue for about five kilometers (three miles). Turn left, following signs to *Ligré,* and look for signs to *Le Clos de Ligré* (see map on page 450).

Eating in Chinon

For a low-stress meal with ambience, choose one of the cafés on the photogenic Place du Général de Gaulle. Many places are closed Wednesday: Check before you go.

La Treille Hôtel-Restaurant is a good choice for dining on regional dishes at fair prices inside or out (under its namesake trellis). Stéphanie offers a limited selection, but the cuisine is fresh, inventive, and delicious (*menus* from €20, closed Wed-Thu, good wine list, 4 Place Jeanne d'Arc, tel. 02 47 93 07 71).

La Bonne France is sweet and simple, with homey and romantic seating indoors or in its quaint front yard. The chef, who excels at sauces, provides a good budget *menu* (€16 for two courses, €20 for three, €26 for four, closed Wed, 4 Place de la Victoire, tel. 02 47 98 01 34).

L'Océanic, in the thick of the pedestrian zone, is where locals go for fish and tasty desserts. It has the best wine list in town, formal indoor or relaxed outdoor seating, and chic Marie-Poule to take your order (*menus* from €26, closed Sun-Mon, 13 Rue Rabelais, tel. 02 47 93 44 55).

Les Saveurs d'Italie is a cheap and cheery deli/diner with a warm greeting and the town's best Italian cuisine (€10 pizzas and pasta, limited outside seating, closed Sun-Mon, next to TI at 3 Impasse J. Macé, tel. 02 47 58 80 62).

Restaurant-Musée Animé du Vin et de la Tonnellerie is a one-man show where jolly Dédé dishes up all the wine you can drink and *fouées* you can eat (little pastry shells filled with garlic paste, cheese, or *rillettes*—that's a meat spread), accompanied by *mâche*-and-walnut salad, green beans, dessert *fouées*, wine, and coffee—all for €19. Let your hair down in this get-to-know-your-neighbor kind of place as you watch Dédé slap the *fouées* in his rustic oven (daily for lunch and dinner, 12 Rue Voltaire, tel. 02 47 93 25 63).

La Part des Anges is an intimate little place on a traffic-free street. You'll appreciate its kind, young owners and good-value *menus* (€17 *menus*, €8.50 kid *menu*, good €9 salads, limited outdoor seating, daily, 5 Rue Rabelais, tel. 02 47 93 99 93).

Near Chinon

For a memorable countryside meal, drive 25 minutes to **Etape Gourmande at Domaine de la Giraudière,** in Villandry (see page

THE LOIRE

455). A trip here combines well with visits to Villandry and Azay-le-Rideau.

Chinon Connections

By Minivan
From Chinon to Loire Châteaux: Acco-Dispo and **Quart de Tours** offer fixed-itinerary minivan excursions from Tours. Take the train to Tours from Chinon, or get several travelers together to book your own van from Chinon (see "Getting Around the Loire Valley" on page 387).

By Train
Twelve trains and SNCF buses link Chinon daily with the city of Tours (1 hour, connections to other châteaux and minibus excursions from Tours—see "Getting Around the Loire Valley" on page 387) and to the regional rail hub of St-Pierre-des-Corps in suburban Tours (TGV trains to distant destinations, and the fastest way to Paris). Traveling by train to the nearby châteaux (except for Azay-le-Rideau) requires a transfer in Tours and healthy walks from the stations to the châteaux. Fewer trains run on weekends.

From Chinon to Loire Châteaux: Azay-le-Rideau (7/day, 20 minutes direct, plus long walk to château), **Langeais** (5/day, 2 hours, transfer in Tours), **Amboise** (12/day, 1.5-2.5 hours, transfer in Tours), **Chenonceaux** (8/day, 1.5 hours, transfer in Tours), **Blois** (6/day, 2-2.5 hours, transfer in Tours and possibly in St-Pierre-des-Corps).

To Destinations Beyond the Loire: Paris' Gare Montparnasse (9/day, 2-2.5 hours, transfer in Tours and sometimes also St-Pierre-des-Corps), **Sarlat** (5/day, 6 hours, change at St-Pierre-des-Corps, then TGV to Libourne or Bordeaux-St. Jean, then train through Bordeaux vineyards to Sarlat), **Pontorson/Mont St-Michel** (3/day, 6 hours with change at Tours main station and Caen, then bus from Pontorson; or 8 hours via Paris TGV with changes at St-Pierre-des-Corps and Paris' Gare Montparnasse, then bus from Rennes), **Bayeux** (9/day, 5-6 hours with change in Caen and Tours, or 7 hours via Tours, St-Pierre-des-Corps, and Paris' Gare Montparnasse).

Azay-le-Rideau

About 30 minutes west of Tours, Azay-le-Rideau (ah-zay luh ree-doh) is a pleasing little town with a small but lively pedestrian zone and a château that gets all the attention. Azay-le-Rideau works well as a base for visiting sights west of Tours by car or bike (but not by train—the train station is a half-mile walk from the town center). The town is close to the A-85 autoroute, offering drivers reasonable access to châteaux near Amboise. Travelers who bed down here will be tempted by the fun sound-and-light show at the château.

Orientation to Azay-le-Rideau

Tourist Information

Azay-le-Rideau's TI is just below Place de la République, a block to the right of the post office (July-Aug daily 10:00-19:00; Sept-Oct and April-June daily 9:00-13:00 & 14:00-18:00; Nov-March Mon-Sat 9:00-13:00 & 14:00-18:00, closed Sun; 4 Rue du Château, tel. 02 47 45 44 40). The TI has pay Internet access and Wi-Fi, and is a good place to pick up information on the sound-and-light show, bike rentals, and summer buses to Villandry and Langeais.

Arrival in Azay-le-Rideau

It's about a 25-minute walk from the station to the town center (taxi mobile 06 60 94 42 00). Walk down from the station, turn left, and follow *Centre-Ville* signs. Drivers can head for the château and park there.

Sights in Azay-le-Rideau

▲▲Château d'Azay-le-Rideau

This charming 16th-century château, the fairy-tale castle of the Loire, sparkles on an island in the Indre River, its image roman-

tically reflected in the slow-moving waters. The building is a prime example of an early-Renaissance château. With no defensive purpose, it was built simply for luxurious living in a luxurious setting. The ornamental facade is perfectly harmonious, and the interior—with its grand staircases and elegant loggias—is Italian-inspired.

The château was built from 1518 to 1527 by a filthy-rich banker—Gilles Berthelot, treasurer to the king of France. The

THE LOIRE

Near Chinon
1. Château de Chatonnière
2. Château du Rivau
3. Le Saut aux Loups Mushroom Caves & Restaurant
4. Domaine de la Chevalerie Wine-Tasting
5. Le Clos de Ligré B&B
6. Etape Gourmande Restaurant

structure has a delightfully feminine touch: Because Gilles was often away on work, his wife, Philippe, supervised the construction. The castle was so lavish that the king, François I, took note, giving it the ultimate compliment: He seized it, causing its owner to flee. Because this château survived the Revolution virtually unscathed, its interior capably demonstrates three centuries of royal styles. The French government purchased it in 1905.

Rooms are well-described in English, and a good audioguide gives even more information. Don't miss the newly opened attic *(combles)* showing off the roof's elaborate wooden supports. For many, the highlight of a visit is the romantic garden, designed in the 19th century to show off the already beautiful château. Stroll around the entire building to enjoy romantic views from all sides, especially of the fanciful turrets, gracefully framed by the trees reflected on the water.

Cost and Hours: €8.50; audioguide-€4.50, €6/2 people; daily July-Aug 9:30-19:00, April-June and Sept-Oct 9:30-18:00, Nov-March 10:00-17:15, last entry one hour before closing, tel. 02 47 45 42 04, http://azay-le-rideau.monuments-nationaux.fr/en.

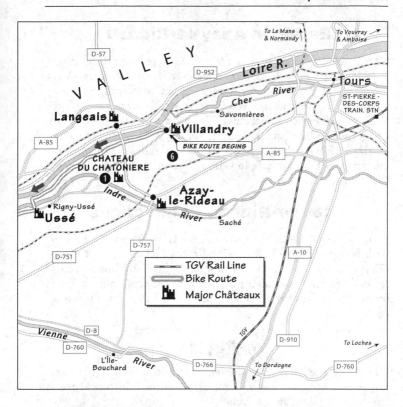

Sound-and-Light Show: The château hosts a sound-and-light show twice nightly in July and August (€11, gates open at 21:00, shows at 21:30 and 22:45). These shows allow you to meander through the grounds accompanied by flashy lighting and music.

Sleeping in Azay-le-Rideau

(€1 = about $1.30, country code: 33)

The town's appealing center may convince you to set up here (a good idea if you plan to see the sound-and-light show).

$$ Hôtel de Biencourt** is a find. Ideally located on a traffic-free street between Place de la République (easy parking) and the château, this sharp boutique hotel is a former convent whose gentle owners have completed a masterful renovation. Rooms offer three-star comfort at two-star prices. There's a pleasing garden terrace and a calming lounge area (Db-€62-70, Tb-€86, Qb-€100, Wi-Fi, shared fridge, open March-mid-Nov, 7 Rue de Balzac, tel. 02 47 45 20 75, fax 02 47 45 91 73, www.hotelbiencourt.com, biencourt @infonie.fr).

THE LOIRE

Eating in Azay-le-Rideau

Côte Cour is *the* place to dine for fresh and creative cuisine at reasonable prices. Friendly Sandra offers a few, select choices—local products and mostly organic foods—served in a warm interior or on a great outdoor terrace (€8.50 starters, €17 *plats*, closed Tue-Wed, faces the château gate at 19 Rue Balzac, tel. 02 47 45 30 36). **Crêperie du Roy** is small, central, and cheap (24 Rue Nationale, tel. 02 47 45 91 88). If you have a car, seriously consider the 15-minute drive to **Domaine de la Giraudière** in Villandry (see page 455).

Azay-le-Rideau Connections

From Azay-le-Rideau, the **train** runs to **Tours** (8/day, 30 minutes, with connections to Langeais and other châteaux), to **Chinon** (7/day, 20 minutes), and to **Blois** (6/day, 1.75-2.5 hours, transfer in Tours and possibly in St-Pierre-des-Corps). Summertime **buses** run to Villandry and Langeais twice a day (the TI has bus schedules).

Langeais

One of the most imposing-looking fortresses of the Middle Ages, Langeais—rated ▲—was built mostly for show. Towering above its

appealing little village, it comes with a moat, a drawbridge, lavish defenses, and turrets.

Cost and Hours: €8.50, daily July-Aug 9:00-19:00, April-June and Sept-mid-Nov 9:30-18:30, mid-Nov-March 10:00-17:00, last entry one hour before closing, tel. 02 47 96 72 60, www.chateau-de-langeais.com.

Getting There: Nine trains a day link Langeais and **Tours** (20 minutes), with about five connections a day from there to **Chinon** (2 hours total, faster by bike). Drivers should turn right at the foot of the castle and follow the road left (around the castle) to find the parking lot (on the right). You can also find free parking a block from the château at a lot adjacent to the town market square.

Background: Langeais is located at a strategic point on the Loire River and the road to Tours (15 miles upstream), which for a time was the French capital. The only remaining part of the original castle is the thousand-year-old tower standing across from the castle's garden. (That castle, an English stronghold, was destroyed by the French king in the Hundred Years' War.)

The new castle, built in the 15th century, dates from the age of cannons, which would have made quick work of its tough-looking facade. In fact, the imposing walls were mostly for show. This is a transitional piece of architecture: part medieval and part Renaissance. The mullioned windows overlooking the court-yard indicate this was a fancy residence more than a defensive fortress. While Langeais makes a show of its defenses, castles built just 50 years later (such as Azay-le-Rideau) give not a hint of fortification.

Visiting the Château: The interior is late-Middle Ages chic. It's the life's work of a 19th-century owner who was a lover of medieval art. He decorated and furnished the rooms with 15th- and 16th-century artifacts or good facsimiles. Most of what you see is modern-made in 16th-century style.

The palace is decked out as palaces were: designed to impress, and ready to pack and move. There were bedrooms for show and bedrooms for sleeping. The **banquet room** table would have groaned with food and luxury items—but just one long, communal napkin and no forks. Belgian tapestries on the walls still glimmer with 500-year-old silk thread. As you wander, notice how the rooms—with hanging tapestries, foldable chairs, and big chests with handles—could have been set up in a matter of hours. Big-time landowners circulated through their domains, moving every month or so.

In the so-called **Wedding Hall,** wax figures re-create the historic marriage that gave Langeais its 15 minutes of château fame. It was here that King Charles VIII secretly wed 14-year-old Anne (duchess of Brittany), a union that brought independent Brittany into France's fold. (An eight-minute sound-and-light show explains the event—usually in English at :15 past each hour.)

The top-floor museum has a rare series of 16th-century **tapestries** featuring nine heroes—biblical, Roman, and medieval. One of just three such sets in existence, seven of the original nine scenes survive.

Finish your visit by enjoying commanding **town views** from the ramparts.

Villandry

Villandry (vee-lahn-dree) is famous for its extensive gardens, considered to be the best in the Loire Valley. Its château is just another Loire palace, but the grounds—arranged in elaborate geometric patterns and immaculately maintained—make it a ▲▲ sight (worth ▲▲▲ for gardeners). Still, if you're visiting anyway, it's worth three extra euros to tour the château as well.

Cost and Hours: €9.50, €6.50 for gardens only, daily April-Sept 9:00-19:00, March and Oct 9:00-18:00, Nov-Feb 9:00-17:00, tel. 02 47 50 02 09, www .chateauvillandry.fr. Parking is free and easy between the trees across from the entry (hide valuables in your trunk).

Background: Finished in 1536, Villandry was the last great Renaissance château built on the Loire. It's yet another pet project of a fabulously wealthy finance minister of François I— Jean le Breton. While serving as ambassador to Italy, Jean picked up a love of Italian Renaissance gardens. When he took over this property, he razed the 12th-century castle (keeping only the old tower), put up his own château, and installed a huge Italian-style garden. The château was purchased in 1906 by the present owner's great-grandfather, and the garden—a careful reconstruction of what the original might have been—is the result of three generations of passionate dedication.

Visiting the Château and Gardens: The excellent English handout included with your admission leads you through the **château**'s elegant 19th-century rooms. They feel so lived-in that you'll wonder if the family just stepped out to get their poodle bathed. The 15-minute *Four Seasons of Villandry* slideshow (with period music and no narration) offers a look at the gardens throughout the year in a relaxing little theater. The literal high point of your château visit is the spiral climb to the top of the keep—the only surviving part of the medieval castle—where you'll find a grand view of the gardens and surrounding countryside.

The lovingly tended **gardens** are well-described by your handout. Follow its recommended route through the four garden types. The 10-acre Renaissance garden, inspired by the 1530s Italian-style original, is full of symbolism. Even the herb and vegetable sections are put together with artistic flair. The earliest Loire gardens were practical, grown by medieval abbey monks who needed vegetables to feed their community and medicinal herbs to cure their ailments. And those monks liked geometrical patterns. Later Italian influence brought decorative ponds, tunnels, and fountains. Harmonizing the flowers and vegetables was an innovation of 16th-century Loire châteaux. This example is the closest we have to that garden style. The 85,000 plants—half of which come from the family greenhouse—are replanted twice a year by 10 full-time gardeners. The place is as manicured as a putting green—just try to find a weed. Stroll under the grapevine trellis, through a good-looking salad zone, and among Anjou pears (from the nearby region of Angers). Charts posted throughout identify everything in English.

Bring bread for the piranha-like carp who prowl the fanciful moat. Like the carp swimming around other Loire châteaux, they're so voracious, they'll gather at your feet to frantically eat your spit.

You can stay as late as you like in the gardens, though you must enter before the ticket office closes.

Eating and Sleeping in Villandry

The pleasant little village of Villandry offers several cafés and restaurants, a small grocery store, a bakery, and good rates at the pleasant little **$$ Hôtel-Restaurant le Cheval Rouge**** right on the main drag (Db-€63-73, extra person-€9, dinner *menus* from €20, Wi-Fi, tel. 02 47 50 02 07, www.lecheval-rouge.com).

Eating near Villandry
Etape Gourmande at Domaine de la Giraudière offers a wonderfully rustic farmhouse dining experience. Gentle owner Beatrice takes time with every client, and the country-gourmet cuisine is simply delicious (ask her how she landed here). The *menu* is flexible: Choose just a starter and dessert, a starter and main course, or all three if you're starved. The dining room is *très* cozy, but the outside seating is pleasant, too (€17-33 *menus*, mid-March-mid-Nov daily 12:00-15:00 & 19:30-21:00, closed mid-Nov-mid-March, a half-mile from Villandry's château toward Druye, tel. 02 47 50 08 60, fax 02 47 50 06 60). This place works best for lunch, as it's between Villandry and Azay-le-Rideau on D-121. It also works for dinner when combined with a visit to Azay-le-Rideau's sound-and-light show.

More Château Gardens

Gardeners will be tempted by these untouristy "lesser châteaux" because of their pleasing plantings.

Château de Chatonnière—The grounds feature romantic paths through 12 exquisitely tended gardens of various themes. Surrounded by fields of wildflowers (my favorite part), it's a must-visit for gardeners and flower fanatics from May to early July, when the place positively explodes in fragrance and color. At other times,

THE LOIRE

when flowers are few, the entry fee is not worth it for most.

Cost and Hours: €7, daily mid-March–mid-Nov 10:00–20:00, closed mid-Nov–mid-March, château interior closed to visitors, between Langeais and Azay-le-Rideau just off D-57, tel. 02 47 45 40 29, www.lachatonniere.com.

Château du Rivau—Gleaming-white and medieval, this château lies wedged between wheat and sunflower fields, and makes for a memorable 15-minute drive from Chinon. Its owners have spared little expense in their 20-year renovation of the 15th-century castle and its extensive gardens. The 14 different flower and vegetable gardens and orchards are kid-friendly (with elf and fairy guides) and lovingly tended with art installations, topiaries, hammocks, birds, a maze, and much more. The stables—with projections about jousting and "Heroic Horses" from history—will delight most kids (English subtitles), but the medieval castle interior is skippable. A good little café serves reasonable meals in a lovely setting.

Cost and Hours: €10, daily April–Sept 10:00–18:00, Oct–mid-Nov 10:00–12:30 & 14:00–18:00, closed mid-Nov–March; in Lémeré on D-759—from Chinon follow *Richelieu* signs, then signs to the château; tel. 02 47 95 77 47, www.chateaudurivau.com.

Ussé

This château, famous as an inspiration for Charles Perrault's classic version of the Sleeping Beauty story, is worth a quick photo stop for its fairy-tale turrets and gardens, but don't bother touring the interior of this pricey pearl. The best view, with reflections and a golden-slipper picnic spot, is from just across the bridge.

Cost and Hours: €14, daily April–Aug 10:00–19:00, mid-Feb–March and Sept–mid-Nov 10:00–18:00, closed mid-Nov–mid-Feb, tel. 02 47 95 54 05, www.chateaudusse.fr.

Abbaye Royale de Fontevraud

The Royal Abbey of Fontevraud (fohn-tuh-vroh) is a 15-minute journey west from Chinon. This vast 12th-century abbey provides a fascinating look at medieval monastic life. The "abbey" was actually a 12th-century monastic city, the largest such compound in Europe—with four monastic complexes, all within a fortified wall.

Cost and Hours: €9, audio-guide–€4; April–Oct daily 9:30–18:30, until 19:30 July–Aug;

Nov-Dec and Feb-March Tue-Sun 9:30-18:30, closed Mon; closed Jan, tel. 02 41 51 73 52, www.abbayedefontevraud.com. Spring for the helpful audioguide (the free English leaflet gives light coverage). There's free parking 100 yards beyond the abbey entrance.

Background: The order of Fontevraud, founded in 1101, was an experiment of rare audacity. This was a double monastery, where both men and women lived under the authority of an abbess while observing the rules of St. Benedict (but influenced by the cult of the Virgin Mary). Men and women lived separately and chastely within the abbey walls. The order thrived, and in the 16th century, this was the administrative head of more than 150 monasteries. Four communities lived within these walls until the Revolution. In 1804, Napoleon made the abbey a prison, which actually helped preserve the building. It functioned as a prison for 150 years, until 1963, with five wooden floors filled with cells. Designed to house 800 inmates, the prison was notoriously harsh. Life expectancy here was eight months.

Visiting the Abbey: Thanks to the €4 audioguide, this abbey is well-presented for English speakers.

Your visit begins in the bright, 12th-century, Romanesque **abbey church.** Sit on the steps, savor the ethereal light and the cavernous setting, and gaze down the nave. At the end of it are four painted sarcophagi belonging to Eleanor of Aquitaine; her second husband, Henry II, the first of the Plantagenet kings; their son Richard the Lionhearted; and his sister-in-law. These are the tops of the sarcophagi only. Even though we know these Plantagenets were buried here (because they gave lots of money to the abbey), no one knows the fate of the actual bodies.

You'll leave the church through the right transept into the **cloister.** This was the center of the abbey, where the nuns read, exercised, checked their email, and washed their hands. While visiting the abbey, remember that monastic life was very simple: nothing but prayers, readings, and work. Daily rations were a loaf of bread and a half-liter of wine per person, plus soup and smoked fish.

Next you'll find the **chapter house,** where the nuns' meetings took place, as well as the **community room**—the only heated room in the abbey, where the nuns embroidered linen. In rooms leading off the cloister, Renaissance paintings feature portraits of the women in black habits who ran this abbey.

The nearby **refectory,** built to feed 400 silent monks at a time, was later the prison work yard, where inmates built wooden chairs.

Your abbey visit ends in the honeycombed 12th-century **kitchen,** with five bays covered by 18 chimneys to evacuate smoke. It likely served as a smokehouse for fish farmed in the abbey ponds.

Abbeys like this were industrious places, but focused on self-sufficiency rather than trade.

Finish your visit by wandering through the abbey's **medicinal gardens** out back.

Near Fontevraud: Mushroom Caves

For an unusual fungus find close to the abbey of Fontevraud, visit the mushroom caves at **Le Saut aux Loups**. France is the world's third-largest producer of mushrooms (after the US and China). Climb to a cliff ledge and visit 16 chilly rooms bored into limestone to discover everything about the care and nurturing of mushrooms. You'll see them raised in planters, plastic bags, logs, and straw bales, and you'll learn about their incubation, pasteurization, and fermentation. Abandoned limestone quarries like this are fertile homes for mushroom cultivation, and have made the Loire Valley the mushroom capital of France since the late 1800s. You'll ogle at the weird shapes and never take your 'shrooms for granted again. The growers harvest a ton of mushrooms a month in these caves; shitakes are their most important crop. Pick up the English booklet and follow the fungus. Many visitors come only for the on-site mushroom restaurant, whose wood-fired *galipettes* (stuffed mushrooms with crème fraîche and herbs) are the kitchen's forté.

Cost and Hours: €6, March-mid-Nov daily 10:00-18:00, closed mid-Nov-Feb; lunch served Wed-Mon in summer—otherwise weekends only; dress warmly, just north of Fontevraud at Montsoreau's west end along the river, tel. 02 41 51 70 30, www.troglo-sautauxloups.com.

Sleeping and Eating near Abbaye Royale de Fontevraud

(€1 = about $1.30, country code: 33)

$$$ Hôtel la Croix Blanche**, 10 steps from the abbey, welcomes travelers with open terraces and will have you sleeping and dining in comfort. This ambitious restaurant-hotel combines a hunting-lodge feel with polished service, comfortable open spaces, a pool, and 23 plush rooms (Db-€90-130, Db suites-€100-170, Wi-Fi, Place Plantagenets, tel. 02 41 51 71 11, fax 02 41 38 15 38, www.hotel-croixblanche.com, info@hotel-croixblanche.com).

The abbey faces the main square of a cute town with several handy eateries. The **boulangerie** opposite the entrance to the abbey serves mouthwatering quiche and sandwiches at impossibly good prices. You'll also find a few *créperies* and cafés near the abbey.

DORDOGNE

*Sarlat • Dordogne River Valley • Cro-Magnon Caves •
Oradour-sur-Glane • St-Emilion • Rocamadour •
Lot River Valley*

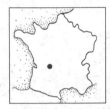

The Dordogne River Valley is a rich brew of natural and man-made beauty. Walnut orchards, tobacco plants, sunflowers, and cornfields carpet the valley, while stone fortresses patrol the cliffs above. During much of the on-again, off-again Hundred Years' War (when this region was called the Périgord), this strategic river—so peaceful today—separated warring Britain and France. Today's Dordogne River carries more travelers than goods, as the region's economy relies heavily on tourism.

The joys of the Dordogne include rock-sculpted villages, fertile farms surrounding I-should-retire-here cottages, memory-card-gobbling vistas, lazy canoe rides, and a local cuisine worth loosening your belt for. But its big draw is its concentration of prehistoric artifacts. Limestone caves decorated with prehistoric artwork litter the Dordogne region.

Planning Your Time

Although tourists inundate the region in the summer, the Dordogne's charm is protected by its relative inaccessibility. Given the time it takes to get here, I'd allow a minimum of two nights (ideally three) and most of two days...or I'd skip it. Your sightseeing obligations, in order of priority, are as follows: prehistoric cave art; the Dordogne River Valley, nearby villages, and castles; the town of Sarlat; and, if you have a bit more time, the less-traveled Lot River Valley (most efficiently viewed when heading to or from the south). Wine lovers work in a pilgrimage to St-Emilion, two hours west of Sarlat.

If you're connecting the Dordogne with the Loire region by car, the fastest path is on the A-20 autoroute (exit at Souillac for

Sarlat and nearby villages). Break up your trip from the north by stopping in Oradour-sur-Glane. If you need to spend the night in this area, consider tiny Mortemart. If you're connecting the Dordogne and Carcassonne, explore the Lot River Valley on your way south. If heading west, taste the Bordeaux wine region's prettiest town, St-Emilion.

Those serious about visiting the Dordogne's best caves (especially with a relatively rare English-speaking tour) need to book well in advance (explained on page 502).

The following three-day itinerary is designed for drivers, but it's doable—if you're determined—by taxi rides, a canoe trip (the best way to see the Dordogne regardless of whether you've got a car), and a minivan tour.

Day 1: Enjoy a morning in Sarlat (ideally on a market day— Sat or Wed), then spend the afternoon on a canoe trip, with time at the day's end to explore Beynac and Castelnaud. If it's not market day in Sarlat, do the canoe trip, Beynac, and Castelnaud first, and enjoy the late afternoon and evening in Sarlat. (Because the town's essential sights are outdoors, my Sarlat self-guided walk works great after dinner.) The sensational views from Castelnaud's castle and Domme are best in the morning; visit Beynac's castle or viewpoint late in the day for the best light. With a little lead time, canoe-rental companies can pick up non-drivers in

Sarlat. Taxis are reasonable between Sarlat and the river villages.

Day 2: Drivers can begin at Lascaux II (the best cave art intro in the area, even though it's a replica). Then follow the scenic Vézère River toward Les Eyzies-de-Tayac, stopping for lunch in idyllic little St-Léon before going on to the caves at La Roque St-Christophe (no reservations needed; doesn't close for lunch, unlike most other caves). In Les Eyzies-de-Tayac, visit the prehistory welcome center and museum, then see the real thing at the cave or caves of your choice (I prefer Grotte de Font-de-Gaume and Grotte de Rouffignac; be sure to book well ahead for Font-de-Gaume—for details, see page 506). Without a car, this day's full list of activities is only possible by taxi or excursion tour. By train, you can link Sarlat and Les Eyzies-de-Tayac.

Day 3: Head east and upriver to explore Rocamadour, Gouffre de Padirac, and storybook villages such as Carennac, Autoire, and Loubressac. And though Rocamadour is accessible by train and a short taxi ride, the rest of these places are feasible only with your own wheels, by taxi, or on an excursion tour.

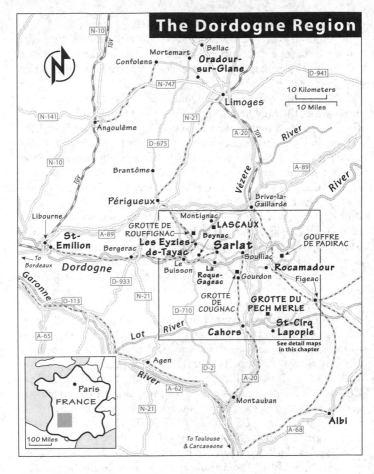

Choosing a Home Base

Sarlat is the only viable solution for train travelers, but those with a car should consider sleeping riverside in La Roque-Gageac (a beautiful village with good hotels) or Beynac (a *très* photogenic village with good *chambres d'hôtes* and hotels). For a grand château hotel experience that won't break the bank, sleep near the Lascaux caves at Château de la Fleunie (30 minutes north of Sarlat; see page 509). For the best view hotel I've found in the area, try Hôtel de l'Esplanade in Domme (see page 486). If you'd rather frolic on a real farm, sleep near Les Eyzies-de-Tayac at Auberge Veyret (see page 505). For a list of good *chambres d'hôtes* near Sarlat, try www .chambres-perigord.com (in French, but easy to navigate—click *Entrée,* then on the upper-left, click *Chambres/Auberges).*

DORDOGNE

Getting Around the Dordogne

This region is a joy with a car, and tough without one. Consider renting a car for a day, renting a canoe or bike, or taking a minivan excursion. If you're up for a splurge, consider a hot-air balloon ride (see page 392).

By Train: Connecting the Dordogne's sights by train is next to impossible. The only helpful train runs from Sarlat to Les Eyzies-de-Tayac, with a prehistory welcome center and museum and the Grotte de Font-de-Gaume (3/day, transfer in Le Buisson, 15-minute walk from station to museum, 30-minute walk from station to Font-de-Gaume cave).

By Car: Roads are small, slow, and scenic. There is no autoroute in the remote region near Sarlat, so you'll need more travel time than usual. Little Sarlat is routinely snarled with traffic on market days—particularly Saturdays. You can rent a car in Sarlat (see page 469), though bigger cities, such as Libourne, Périgueux, and Brive-la-Gaillarde, offer greater drop-off flexibility. In summer (mid-June-mid-Sept), you'll pay to park in most villages' riverfront lots between 10:00 and 19:00. Leave nothing in your car at night—thieves enjoy the Dordogne, too.

By Taxi: For taxi service from Sarlat to Beynac or La Roque-Gageac, allow €33 (€39 at night and on Sun); from Sarlat to Les Eyzies-de-Tayac, allow €46 one-way (€66 at night and on Sun) or €88 round-trip. Philippe (see next) can often pick you up within a few minutes if you call. Corinne, who runs Beynac-based **Taxi Corinne,** is helpful, speaks a little English, and is eager to provide good service to tourists (can provide regional as well as local transport, tel. 05 53 29 42 07, mobile 06 72 76 03 32, www.taxicorinne.com, corinne.brouqui@wanadoo.fr).

By Custom Taxi/Minivan Excursion: You have a few good options. **Allô-Philippe Taxi** is run by amiable Philippe, who speaks enough English and has a comfortable SUV with raised seats for better viewing. Philippe will custom-design your tour, help with cave reservations, and provide some commentary during your excursion. He can pick you up anywhere—including Bordeaux's airport (€320) or remote train stations. His taxi rates are the same as given above ("By Taxi"); for excursions, he charges €39/hour for up to six people (€57/hour on Sun). Book early (tel. 05 53 59 39 65, mobile 06 08 57 30 10, http://allophilippetaxi.monsite.orange.fr, allophilippetaxi@wanadoo.fr).

Gentle **Christoph Kusters** speaks flawless English and provides similar services in his Land Rover, which fits up to six people (€140/half-day, €280/day, mobile 06 08 70 61 67, www.taxialacarte.com, taxialacarte@gmail.com).

Ophorus Excursions offers a full range of scheduled half- and full-day trips to caves, castles, and villages as far as St-Emilion in a comfortable minivan with English-fluent guides (€65/half-day, €95-120/day, private tours also possible, mobile 06 33 05 10 09, www.ophorus.com info@ophorus.com).

Caves and Castles is run by a delightful British couple (Steve and Judie Burman) who offer tours to the area's main sights. Most excursions are several days in length, but it's worth asking about their day tours (tel. 05 53 50 31 21, www.cavesandcastles.com, enquiry@cavesandcastles.com).

Béatrice Mollart and Bruno Elure, a local guide team, are happy to drive and guide you throughout their region. They even offer a Deux Chevaux car option (mobile 06 79 63 28 47, loeildela gazelle@orange.fr).

By Boat: Non-drivers should rent a canoe, my favorite mode of transportation for exploring a slice of this region. A canoe offers easy access to the river's sights and villages, and canoe companies will pick you up in Sarlat for no extra charge. Since a canoe costs €12-18/person (for the trip I recommend, from Vitrac to Beynac), and you can spend all day on and off the river touring sights I cover, this is a swimmingly good deal. For the same scenery with less work, you can also take a boat cruise from Beynac or La Roque-Gageac. Details on all these options are covered later in this chapter.

By Bike or Moped: Cyclists find the Dordogne beautiful but hilly, with lots of traffic on key roads. Mopeds are an option. You can rent bikes in Sarlat (see page 469).

The Dordogne's Cuisine Scene

Gourmets flock to this area for its geese, ducks, and wild mush-

rooms. The geese produce (involuntarily) the region's famous foie gras. (They're force-fed, denied exercise during the last weeks of their lives, and slaughtered for their livers, meat, and fluffy down—see sidebar on page 494.) Foie gras tastes like butter and costs like gold. The duck specialty is *confit de canard* (duck meat preserved in its own fat—sounds terrible, but tastes great).

Pommes de terre sarladaises are mouthwatering, thinly sliced potatoes fried in duck fat and commonly served with *confit de canard*. Wild truffles are dirty black tubers that grow underground, generally on the roots of oak trees. Farmers traditionally locate them with sniffing pigs and then charge a fortune for their catch (roughly $250 per pound). Native cheeses are Cabécou (a silver-dollar-size, pungent, nutty-flavored goat cheese) and Echourgnac (made by local Trappist monks). You'll find walnuts *(noix)* in salads, cakes, liqueurs, salad dressings, and more.

Wines to sample are Bergerac (red, white, and rosé), Pecharmant (red, must be at least four years old), Cahors (a full-bodied red), and Monbazillac (sweet dessert wine). The *vin de noix* (sweet walnut liqueur) is delightful before dinner.

Remember, restaurants serve only during lunch (11:30-14:00) and dinner (19:00-21:00, later in bigger cities); bigger cafés serve food throughout the day.

Dordogne Markets

Markets are a big deal in rural France, and nowhere more so than in the Dordogne. I've listed good markets for every day of the week, so there's no excuse for drivers not to experience one. Here's what to look for:

Strawberries *(fraises):* For the French, the Dordogne is the region famous for the very tastiest strawberries. Available from April to November, they're gorgeous, and they smell even better than they look. Buy *une barquette* (small basket), and suddenly your two-star hotel room is a three-star. Look also for *fraises des bois,* the tiny, sweet, and less visually appealing strawberries found in nearby forests.

Fresh Veggies: Outdoor markets allow you to meet the farmer, and give you a chance to buy direct. (See what's fresh, and look for it on your menu this evening.) Subtly check out the hands of the person helping customers—if they're not gnarled and rough from working the fields, move on.

Cheeses *(fromages):* The region is famous for its Cabécou goat cheese (described earlier), though often you'll also find Auvergne cheeses (St. Nectaire and Cantal are the most common) from just east of the Dordogne (usually in big rounds), and Tomme and Brébis (sheep cheeses) from the Pyrenees to the south.

Truffles *(truffes):* Only the bigger markets will have these ugly, jet-black tubers on display. Truffle season is our off-season (Nov-Feb), when you'll find them at every market. During summer, the fresh truffles you might see are *truffes d'été,* a less desirable and cheaper, but still tasty species. If you see truffles displayed at other times, they've been sterilized (a preservative measure that can reduce flavor). On Sarlat market days, there's usually a guy in the center of Place de la Liberté with a photo of his grandfather and his truffle-hunting dog.

DORDOGNE

Anything with Walnuts *(aux noix):* *Pain aux noix* is a thick-as-a-brick bread loaf chock-full of walnuts. *Moutarde de noix* is walnut mustard. *Confiture de noix* is a walnut spread for hors d'oeuvres. *Gâteaux de noix* are tasty cakes studded with walnuts. *Liqueur de noix* is a marvelous creamy liqueur, great over ice or blended with a local white wine.

Goose or Duck Livers and Pâté (foie gras): This spread is made from geese (better) and ducks (still good), or from a mix of the two. You'll see two basic forms: *entier* and *bloc.* Both are 100 percent foie gras; *entier* is a piece cut right from the product, whereas *bloc* has been blended to make it easier to spread—*mousse* has been whipped for an even creamier consistency. Foie gras is best accompanied by a sweet white wine (such as the locally produced Monbazillac, or Sauterne from Bordeaux). You can bring the unopened tins back into the US, *pas de problème.* For more on foie gras, see the sidebar on page 494.

Confit de Canard: At butcher stands, look for hunks of duck smothered in white fat, just waiting for someone to take them home and cook them up.

Dried Sausages *(saucissons secs):* Long tables piled high with

dried sausages covered in herbs or stuffed with local goodies are a common sight in French markets. You'll always be offered a mouth-watering sample. Some of the variations you'll see include *porc, canard* (duck), *fumé* (smoked), *à l'ail* (garlic), *cendré* (rolled in ashes), *aux myrtilles* (with blueberries), *sanglier* (wild boar), and even *âne* (donkey)—and, but of course, *aux noix* (with walnuts).

Olive Oil *(huile d'olive):* You'll find stylish bottles of various olive oils, as well as vegetable oils flavored with truffles, walnuts, chestnuts *(châtaignes),* and hazelnuts *(noisettes)*—good for cooking, ideal on salads, and great as gifts. Pure walnut oil, pressed at local mills from nuts grown in the region, is a local specialty, best on salads. Don't cook with pure walnut oil, as it will burn quickly.

Olives and Nuts *(olives et noix):* These interlopers from Provence find their way to every market in France.

Brandies and Liqueurs: Although they're not made in this region, Armagnac, Cognac, and other southwestern fruit-flavored liquors are often available from a seller or two. Try the *liqueur de pomme verte,* and sample Armagnac in the tiny plastic cups.

Dordogne Market Days

The best markets are in Sarlat (Sat and Wed, in that order), followed

by the markets in Cahors on Saturday, St-Cyprien on Sunday, and Le Bugue on Tuesday. Markets usually shut down by 13:00.

Sunday: St-Cyprien (lively market, 10 minutes west of Beynac, difficult parking), Montignac (near Lascaux), and St-Geniès (a tiny, intimate market with few tourists; halfway between Sarlat and Montignac)

Monday: Les Eyzies-de-Tayac and a tiny one in Beynac

Tuesday: Cénac (you can canoe from here) and Le Bugue (great market 20 minutes west of Beynac)

Wednesday: Sarlat (big market)

Thursday: Domme

Friday: Souillac (transfer point to Cahors, Carcassonne)

Saturday: Sarlat and Cahors (both are excellent), and the little *bastide* village of Belvès (small market)

Sarlat

Sarlat (sar-lah) is a pedestrian-filled banquet of a town, serenely set amid forested hills. There are no blockbuster sights—the only

thing worth a visit is the cathedral (and that just barely). Still, Sarlat delivers a seductive tangle of traffic-free, golden cobblestone lanes peppered with beautiful buildings, lined with foie gras shops (geese hate Sarlat), and stuffed with tourists. The town is warmly lit at night and ideal for after-dinner strolls. It's just the right size—large enough to have a theater with four screens, but small enough so that everything is an easy meander from the town center. And though undeniably popular with tourists, it's the handiest home base for those without a car.

Orientation to Sarlat

Rue de la République slices like an arrow through the circular old town. Sarlat's smaller half has few shops and many quiet lanes. The action lies east of Rue de la République.

Tourist Information

The TI, with English-speaking staff, is 50 yards to the right of the Cathedral of St. Sacerdos as you face the front entrance (April-June and Sept-Oct Mon-Sat 9:00-12:00 & 14:00-18:00, Sun 10:00-13:00 & 14:00-17:00; July-Aug Mon-Sat 9:00-19:00, Sun 10:00-12:00 & 14:00-18:00; Nov-March closes at 18:00 and all day Sun; on Rue Tourny, tel. 05 53 31 45 45, www.sarlat-tourisme .com). Their €0.50 city map with English information is a good investment, and their free *Guide Pratique* booklet has rental information on cars, bikes, and canoes (this and other brochures can also be downloaded from the TI's website). Other booklets cover sights throughout the region. For €2, the TI will reserve you a hotel room or a time slot for a prehistoric cave visit (for more on cave reservations, see page 502).

The TI rents iPhone audioguides for self-guided tours of the city (€5 with two sets of earphones) and sells a laminated *City of Sarlat* walking-tour map (€6)—both are handy for exploring Sarlat. They also offer guided tours of Sarlat in English (€6, Wed at 11:00, mid-May-July and Sept-mid-Oct, no tours in Aug or off-season), and sell tickets for the panoramic elevator ride in the covered market hall (€5; described later, in my self-guided walk).

Arrival in Sarlat

By Train: The sleepy train station keeps a lonely vigil (without a shop, café, or hotel in sight). It's a mostly downhill, 20-minute walk to the town center (consider a taxi, about €7—see "Helpful Hints"). To walk into town, turn left out of the station and follow the *Centre-Ville* sign down Avenue de la Gare as it curves downhill, then turn right at the bottom, on Avenue Thiers, to reach the town center. Some trains (such as those from Limoges and Cahors) arrive at nearby Souillac, which is connected to Sarlat's train station by an SNCF bus.

By Car: Sarlat's streets are slammed on market days, when parking can be a headache. Try parking along Avenue Gambetta (at the north end of town), or in one of the signed lots on the ring road. The closest parking is metered (free Mon-Sat 12:00-14:00 & 19:00-9:00 and all day Sun).

Helpful Hints

Market Days: Sarlat has been an important market town since the Middle Ages. Outdoor markets thrive on Wednesday morning and all day Saturday. Saturday's market swallows the entire town and is best in the morning (produce and food vendors leave at noon). Come before 8:00 to watch them set up, and, once the market is under way, plant yourself at a well-positioned café to observe the civilized scene. Don't miss

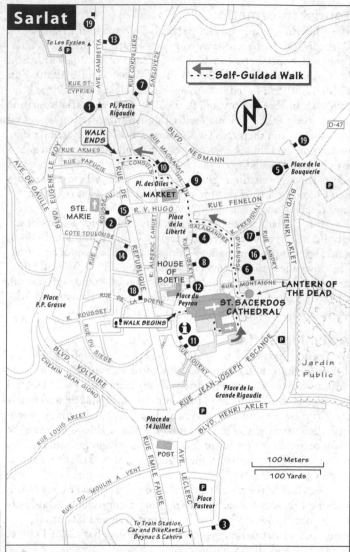

Sarlat

←---- Self-Guided Walk

- ❶ Hôtel Plaza Madeleine
- ❷ La Villa des Consuls
- ❸ Hôtel Montaigne
- ❹ Hôtel de la Mairie
- ❺ Hôtel la Couleuvrine
- ❻ La Lanterne Chambres
- ❼ Les Cordeliers Chambres
- ❽ Les Chambres du Glacier & Brasserie
- ❾ La Maison du Notaire Royal
- ❿ La Mirandol Restaurant
- ⓫ Chez le Gaulois Restaurant
- ⓬ Le Bistrot Restaurant
- ⓭ La Fourchette
- ⓮ Pizzeria Romane
- ⓯ Lemoine Café
- ⓰ Le Présidial Restaurant
- ⓱ L'Assiette de Foie Gras
- ⓲ Petit Casino Grocery
- ⓳ Launderette (2)

DORDOGNE

the market action inside the former Church of Ste. Marie. In summer months, a small organic market enlivens the town's lower (southern) side (Thu 18:00-22:00, Place du 14 Juillet). For tips on what to look for at the market, see "Dordogne Markets," earlier.

Supermarket: There's a **Petit Casino** grocery at 32 Rue de la République (Mon-Sat 8:00-12:30 & 15:00-19:30, Sun 9:00-12:00).

Internet Access: Ask the TI where you can get connected. The **Café de la Mairie** (at the recommended Hôtel de la Mairie) and the recommended **Brasserie le Glacier** have free Wi-Fi for customers.

Laundry: Madame Mazzocato runs a good launderette across from the recommended Hôtel la Couleuvrine (self-serve daily 24 hours, drop-off/pickup Mon-Fri 8:00-12:00 & 14:00-18:30, Sat 8:00-12:00, none Sun, 10 Place de la Bouquerie). And for my readers, she will drop off laundry at your (Sarlat) hotel. Another **self-serve laundry** is near the hotels north of the center (daily 7:00-21:00, 74 Avenue Gambetta).

Biking: Sarlat is surrounded by beautiful country lanes that would be ideal for biking were it not for all those hills. Villages along the Dordogne River make good biking destinations, though expect some traffic and hills between Sarlat and the river (the TI and bike-rental places can advise quieter routes).

You can rent bikes at **@toutLoc** (near the train station at 26 Route du Lot, tel. 05 53 28 18 33, atoutloc24@yahoo.fr). British-run **Aquitaine Bike** will deliver bikes to your hotel, and also organize two-day and longer independent bike tours (tel. 05 53 30 35 17, www.aquitainebike.com). The TI has information on bike rental outside Sarlat.

Taxi: Call Philippe of **Allô-Philippe Taxi** (tel. 05 53 59 39 65, mobile 06 08 57 30 10, also offers regional day trips—see page 462) or **Taxi Sarlat** (tel. 05 53 59 02 43, mobile 06 80 08 65 05).

Car Rental: Try **Europcar** (Le Pontet, at south end of Avenue Leclerc on roundabout, Place du Maréchal de Lattre de Tassigny, 15-minute walk from the center, tel. 05 53 30 30 40).

Self-Guided Walk

Welcome to Sarlat

This short walk starts facing the Cathedral of St. Sacerdos (a few steps from the TI). Although it's designed for daytime (when the cathedral is open), it also works beautifully after dinner, when the gas-lit lanes and candlelit restaurants twinkle. See the map on opposite page to help navigate this walk. For eager learners, the

TI's audioguide adds some additional stops to this tour.

• *Start in front of the Cathedral of St. Sacerdos, on the...*

Place du Peyrou: An eighth-century Benedictine abbey once stood where the Cathedral of St. Sacerdos is today. It provided the stability for Sarlat to develop into an important trading city during the Middle Ages. The old Bishop's Palace, built right into the cathedral (on the right, with its top-floor Florentine-style loggia), recalls Sarlat's Italian connection. The Italian bishop was the boyfriend of Catherine de Médicis (queen of France)—a connection that got him this fine residence. After a short stint here, he split to Paris with lots of local money. And though his departure scandalized the town, it left Sarlat with a heritage of Italian architecture. (Notice the fine Italianate house of Etienne de la Boëtie on the opposite side of the square, and the similar loggia to its right.)

Another reason for Sarlat's Italo-flavored urban design was its loyalty to the king during wartime. Sarlat's glory century was from about 1450 to 1550, after the Hundred Years' War (see sidebar on page 269). Loyal to the French cause—through thick and thin and a century of war—Sarlat was rewarded by the French king, who gave the town lots of money to rebuild itself in stone. Sarlat's new nobility needed fancy houses, complete with ego-boosting features. Many of Sarlat's most impressive buildings date from this prosperous era, when the Renaissance style was in vogue, and everyone wanted an architect with an Italian résumé.

• *Take a closer look (opposite the cathedral) at...*

The House of Etienne de la Boëtie: This house was a typical 16th-century merchant's home—family upstairs and open ground floor (its stone arch now filled in) with big, fat sills to display retail goods. Pan up, scanning the crude-but-still-Renaissance carved reliefs. It was a time when anything Italian was trendy (when yokels "stuck a feather in their cap and called it macaroni"). La Boëtie (lah bow-ess-ee), a 16th-century bleeding-heart liberal who spoke and wrote against the rule of tyrannical kings, remains a local favorite.

Notice how the house just to the left arches over the small street. This was a common practice to maximize buildable space in the Middle Ages. Sarlat enjoyed a population boom after the Hundred Years' War ended in 1468.

• *If you're doing this walk during the day, head into the cathedral now. If it's after hours, skip ahead to the Lantern of the Dead (below): Face the cathedral, walk around it to the left, up the lane, and through the little door in the wall to the rocket-shaped building on a bluff 30 yards behind the church.*

Cathedral of St. Sacerdos: Though the cathedral's facade has a few well-worn 12th-century carvings, most of it dates from the

18th and 19th centuries. Step inside this historic Sarlat interior. The faithful believed that Mary delivered them from the great plague of 1348, so you'll find a full complement of Virgin Marys here and throughout the town. The Gothic interiors in this part of France are simple, with clean lines and nothing extravagant. The first chapel on the left is the baptistery. Locals would come here to give thanks after they made the pilgrimage to Lourdes for healing and returned satisfied. A column on the right side of the nave shows a long list of hometown boys who gave their lives for France in World War I.

• *Exit the cathedral from the right transept (through a padded brown door) into what was once the abbey's cloisters. Snoop through two quiet courtyards, then turn left, making your way around to the back of the church, where you'll climb steps (above the monks' graveyard) to a bluff behind the church. You'll find a bullet-shaped building ready for some kind of medieval take-off, known as the...*

Lantern of the Dead (Lanterne des Morts): Dating from 1147, this is the oldest monument in town. In four horrible days, a quarter of Sarlat's population died in a plague (1,000 out of 4,000). People prayed to St. Bernard of Clairvaux for help. He blessed their bread—and instituted hygiene standards while he was at it, stopping the disease. This lantern was built in gratitude.

• *From the Lantern of the Dead, exit downhill and to the right, toward an adorable house. Cross one street and keep straight, turn left a block later on Impasse de la Vieille Poste, make a quick right on Rue d'Albusse, and then take a left onto...*

Rue de la Salamandre: The salamander—unfazed by fire or water—was Sarlat's mascot. Befitting its favorite animal, Sarlat was also unfazed by fire (from war) and water (from floods). Walk several steps down this "Street of the Salamander" and find the Gothic-framed doorway just below on your right. Step back and notice the tower that housed the staircase. Staircase towers like this (Sarlat has about 20) date from about 1600 (after the wars of religion between the Catholics and Protestants), when the new nobility needed to show off.

• *Continue downhill, passing under the salamander-capped arch, and pause near (or better, sit down at) the café on the...*

Place de la Liberté: This has been Sarlat's main market square since the Middle Ages, though it was significantly expanded in the 18th century. Sarlat's patriotic town hall stands behind you (with a café perfectly situated for people-watching). You can't miss the dark **stone roofs** topping the buildings across the square. They're typical of this region: Called *lauzes* in French, the flat limestone rocks were originally gathered by farmers clearing their fields, then made into cheap, durable roofing material (today few people can afford them). The unusually steep pitch of the *lauzes* roofs—which last up to 300 years—helps distribute the weight of the roof (about 160 pounds per square foot) over a greater area. Although most *lauze* roofs have been replaced by roofs made from more affordable materials, a great number remain. The small window is critical: It provides air circulation, allowing the lichen that coat the porous stone to grow—sealing gaps between the stones and effectively waterproofing the roof. Without that layer, the stone would crumble after repeated freeze-and-thaw cycles.

• *Walk right, to the "upper" end of the square. The bulky Church of Ste. Marie, right across from you, today serves as Sarlat's...*

Covered Market: Once a parish church dedicated to St. Marie, with a massive *lauzes* roof and a soaring bell tower, this building was converted into a gunpowder factory and then a post office before becoming today's indoor market (daily 8:30-13:00). Marvel at its tall, strangely modern, seven-ton doors. On the

opposite side of the building, a modern, glass-sided **panoramic elevator** whisks tourists up through the center of the ancient church's bell tower for bird's-eye views over the rooftops (€5, buy tickets at TI, 5/hour, visit lasts 12 minutes, June-Sept daily in good weather 9:00-19:00, shorter hours off-season—check with TI for times). Your elevator operator doubles as a guide, who gives a quick but effective history of Sarlat at the top (in English, if the group is mostly English-speaking; if your visit is in French, use the good English handout).

• *When you've returned to earth, head back into Place de la Liberté and turn left up the small lane past the big doors to meet the "Boy of Sarlat"—a statue marking the best view over Place de la Liberté. Notice the cathedral's tower, with a salamander swinging happily from its spire. Turn around and find...*

Foie Gras and Beyond: Tourist-pleasing stores like La Boutique du Badaud line the streets of Sarlat and are filled with the finest local products. This quiet shop sells it all, from truffles to foie gras to walnut wine to truffle liqueur. They also offer tastings (*dégustations*) of various products (see what's on the table to taste). To better understand what you're looking at, read the Foie Gras sidebar on pages 494-495.

• *Turn left (behind the boy statue) and trickle like medieval rainwater down the ramp into an inviting square. Here you'll find a little gaggle of geese.*

Place des Oies: Feathers fly when geese are traded on this "Square of the Geese" on market days (Nov-March). The birds are serious business here, and have been since the Middle Ages. Trophy homes surround this cute little square on all sides. Check out the wealthy merchant's home to the right as you enter the square—the **Manoir de Gisson**—with a tower built big enough to match his ego. The owner was the town counsel, a position that arose as cities like Sarlat exited the Middle Ages. Town counsels replaced priests in resolving civil conflicts and performing other civic duties. Touring the interior of the manor shows you how the wealthy lived in Sarlat. It's carefully decorated with authentic 16th- to 18th-century furniture, and offers a peek at the inside of its impressive *lauzes* roof (€7, daily April-Sept 10:00-19:00, closes earlier off-season, rotating exhibits in cellar, tel. 05 53 28 70 55, www.manoirdegisson.com).

• *Walk to the right along Rue des Consuls. Just before Le Mirandol restaurant, turn right toward a...*

Fourteenth-Century Vault and Fountain: For generations, this was the town's only source of water, protected by the Virgin Mary. Opposite the restaurant and fountain, find the wooden doorway (open only July-Aug) that houses a massive Renaissance stairway. These showy stairways, which replaced more space-efficient spiral ones, required a big house and a bigger income. Impressive.

• *Follow the curve along Rue des Consuls, and enter the straight-as-an-arrow...*

Rue de la République: This "modern" thoroughfare, known as *La Traverse* to locals, dates from the mid-1800s, when blasting big roads through medieval cities was standard operating procedure. It wasn't until 1963 that Sarlat's other streets would become off-limits to cars, thanks to France's forward-thinking minister of culture, André Malraux. The law that bears his name has served to preserve and restore important monuments and neighborhoods throughout France. Eager to protect the country's architectural heritage, private investors, cities, and regions worked together to create traffic-free zones, rebuild crumbling buildings, and make sure that no cables or ugly wiring marred the ambience of towns like this. Without the Malraux Law, Sarlat might well have more "efficient" roads like Rue de la République slicing through its once-charming old town center.

Your tour is over, but make sure you take time for a poetic ramble through the town's quiet side—or, better yet, stroll any of Sarlat's lanes after dark. This is the only town in France illuminated by gas lamps, which cause the warm limestone to glow, turning the romance of Sarlat up even higher. Now may also be a good time to find a café and raise a toast to Monsieur Malraux.

DORDOGNE

Sleeping in Sarlat

Even with summer crowds, Sarlat is the train traveler's best home base. Note that in July and August, some hotels require half-pension, and hotels in downtown Sarlat book up first. Parking can be a headache—drivers will find rooms and parking more easily just outside the town (see "Near Sarlat" on page 478) or in the nearby villages and destinations described later, under "The Best of the Dordogne River Valley" (most are a 15-minute drive away).

Hotels in the Town Center

$$$ **Hôtel Plaza Madeleine***** is a central and sharp three-star value with professional service, comfortable lounges, and 39 smart rooms with every comfort. You'll find a generously sized pool out back, exercise bikes, a sauna, and a Jacuzzi—all free for guests (standard Db-€120-155, most at €120; bigger Db-€155-175, extra person-€25, several connecting rooms for families, air-con, elevator, Internet access and Wi-Fi, garage-€10, at north end of ring road at 1 Place de la Petite Rigaudie, tel. 05 53 59 10 41, fax 05 53 31 03 62, www.hoteldelamadeleine-sarlat.com, hotel.madeleine @wanadoo.fr).

$$ **La Villa des Consuls*****, a cross between a B&B and a hotel, occupies a 17th-century home buried on Sarlat's quiet side with 12 lovely, spacious rooms with microwave ovens and refrigerators; most also have a kitchen and a living room. The rooms surround a small courtyard and come with wood floors, private decks, and high ceilings. English-fluent David helms the ship alone; as he's often out, arrange your arrival time in advance. He prices his rooms to encourage longer stays; these rates are for stays of two to

---

Sleep Code

(€1 = about $1.30, country code: 33)

S = Single, **D** = Double/Twin, **T** = Triple, **Q** = Quad, **b** = bathroom, **s** = shower only, ***** = French hotel rating system (0-5 stars). Unless otherwise noted, credit cards are accepted and English is spoken.

   To help you sort easily through these listings, I've divided the accommodations into three categories based on the price for a standard double room with bath:

  $$$ **Higher Priced**—Most rooms €95 or more.
  $$ **Moderately Priced**—Most rooms between €70-95.
   $ **Lower Priced**—Most rooms €70 or less.

   Prices can change without notice; verify the hotel's current rates online or by email.

six nights (Db-€92-110, big Db/Tb/Qb-€118-162, 10 percent more for 1-night stays, less for 7 or more days, air-con, Internet access and Wi-Fi, free washers and dryers, garage-€9/day, train station pickup-€7, 3 Rue Jean-Jacques Rousseau, tel. 05 53 31 90 05, fax 05 53 31 90 06, www.villaconsuls.fr, villadesconsuls@yahoo.fr).

$$ Hôtel Montaigne**, a rock-solid two-star value located a block south of the pedestrian zone, is well run by the smiling Martinats. The rooms are simple, spotless, comfortable, and air-conditioned. Of the hotels I recommend, this one is nearest the train station (Db-€59-79, extra person-€15, two-room family suites-€99-109, breakfast buffet-€9, air-con, elevator, Internet access and Wi-Fi, easy parking, Place Pasteur, tel. 05 53 31 93 88, fax 05 53 31 99 71, www.hotelmontaigne.fr, contact@hotel montaigne.fr).

$ Hôtel de la Mairie's** quirky but comfortable rooms are located above its namesake café, smack dab on the main square

(ideal for market days). The rooms, providing two-star comfort at fair prices, have effective double-paned windows, and most have beamed ceilings; rooms #3 and #6 have the best views (Db-€65, Tb-€70-85, Qb-€95, Wi-Fi, reception in café, Place de la Liberté, tel. 05 53 59 05 71, fax 05 53 59 59 95, www.hotel-mairie-sarlat .com, hoteldelamairie@orange.fr).

$ Hôtel la Couleuvrine** offers faded comfort at fair rates in a historic building with a handy location—across from the launderette and with easy parking (for Sarlat). Families enjoy *les chambres familles* (#19 and #20 are in the tower). Some rooms have tight bathrooms, a few have private terraces, and others could use new carpets (Db-€68, Db suite-€94, Tb-€94, Qb-€118, elevator, on ring road at 1 Place de la Bouquerie, tel. 05 53 59 27 80, fax 05 53 31 26 83, www.la-couleuvrine.com, lacouleuvrine@wanadoo.fr). Half-pension is encouraged during busy periods and in the summer—figure €70 per person for room, breakfast, and a good dinner in the classy restaurant.

Hotels North of Town

The following hotels are a 10-minute walk north of the old town on Avenue de Selves. All have easy parking.

$$$ Hôtel Clos la Boëtie***** is the place to stay if you need five-star comfort just a short walk from Sarlat. Located on a busy street next to the Hôtel de Selves (listed next), the hotel has spared no expense in decorating its 11 luxurious rooms (Db-€220-285, Db suite-€310-350, elaborate breakfast-€20, Wi-Fi, pool, sauna,

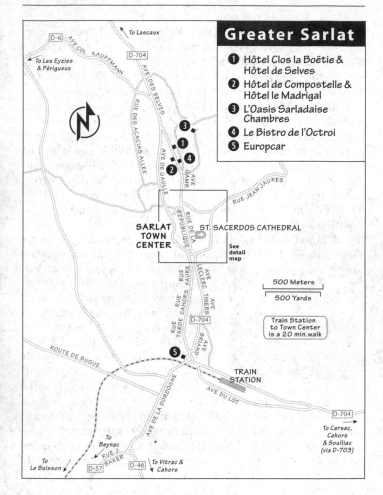

Greater Sarlat

1. Hôtel Clos la Boëtie & Hôtel de Selves
2. Hôtel de Compostelle & Hôtel le Madrigal
3. L'Oasis Sarladaise Chambres
4. Le Bistro de l'Octroi
5. Europcar

massages possible, parking-€12, 95 Avenue de Selves, tel. 05 53 29 44 18, fax 05 53 28 61 40, www.closlaboetie-sarlat.com, hotel @closlaboetie-sarlat.com).

$$$ Hôtel de Selves*** feels *très* American, with a spacious lobby, professional staff, and 40 well-equipped rooms in a modern shell with a year-round swimming pool (Db-€95-125, Db with balcony-€135-150, Tb-€152, two-room family suites-€214-234, all rooms non-smoking, air-con, elevator, Internet access, pay Wi-Fi, outside parking-€8, garage-€12/day, 93 Avenue de Selves, tel. 05 53 31 50 00, fax 05 53 31 23 52, www.selves-sarlat.com, hotel@selves -sarlat.com).

$$ Hôtel de Compostelle*** features a cheery, open lobby and well-maintained, mostly spacious rooms, including several big family rooms (Db-€83-95, Tb-€145, Qb-€165 for 4-6 people, air-con, elevator is one floor up, Wi-Fi, sweet backyard terrace, parking-€7, 64 Avenue de Selves, tel. 05 53 59 08 53, fax 05 53 30 31 65, www.hotel-compostelle-sarlat.com, info@hotel-compostelle -sarlat.com).

$$ Hôtel le Madrigal**, one block past Hôtel de Compostelle, is a charming nine-room hotel with good two-star rooms and rates, all with queen-size beds and smallish bathrooms. Check in at the Hôtel de Compostelle a few doors down (Db-€70, Tb-€90, Qb-€110, air-con, Wi-Fi, fitness room, parking-€7, 50 Avenue des Selves, tel. 05 53 59 21 98, fax 05 53 30 31 65, www.hotel-madrigal -sarlat.com, info@hotel-madrigal-sarlat.com).

Chambres d'Hôtes

These *chambres d'hôtes* are central and compare well with the hotels listed earlier.

$$ La Lanterne, named for the monument it faces, is home to welcoming Brits Terri and Roy Bowen (and dog Frodo), who have restored a 500-year-old building that could not be more central. Clients get cozy public spaces and thoughtfully appointed, quiet rooms that surround a sweet little courtyard (Db-€85-90, Tb studio-€95, breakfast-€8, cash or Paypal only, Wi-Fi, 9 bis Rue Montaigne, tel. 05 53 59 17 79, mobile 06 33 42 19 57, www.sarlat .biz, info@sarlat.biz).

$$ Les Cordeliers, owned by gentle Brits Chris and Amanda Johnson, offers four-star comfort at two-star prices. Most of the seven cushy rooms are huge; all are air-conditioned and well-furnished; and a small kitchen is at your disposal with serve-yourself snacks and drinks (Db-€95, extra bed-€20, 2-night minimum, big breakfast with fresh fruit and eggs-€7, closed Nov-Feb, 51 Rue des Cordeliers, tel. 05 53 31 94 66, www.hotelsarlat.com, info@hotel sarlat.com).

$ Les Chambres du Glacier, where kind Monsieur Da Costa offers four cavernous and surprisingly classy rooms above an outdoor café, is in the thick of Sarlat's pedestrian zone (perfect for market days). Rooms come with café noise, sky-high ceilings, big windows over Sarlat's world, polished wood floors, and bathrooms you can get lost in (Db-€70, Tb-€80, Qb-€90, Wi-Fi, Place de la Liberté, tel. 05 53 29 99 99, www.chambres-du-glacier-sarlat.com, carlos.da.costa.24@wanadoo.fr).

$ La Maison du Notaire Royal, run by friendly, English-speaking Pierre-Henri Toulemon and French-speaking Diane, has four large rooms with a private entry in a frumpy 17th-century home located a few steps above the main square. Guests have access to a fridge, microwave, and garden tables (Db-€63, €8/ extra person up to 5, includes breakfast, cash only, Internet access and Wi-Fi, parking-€1, no deposit required, call a day ahead to confirm approximate arrival time, look for big steps from northeast corner of Place de la Liberté, 4 Rue Magnanat, tel. 05 53 31 26 60, mobile 06 08 67 76 90, www.toulemon.com, contact@toulemon .com). They also rent two cottages with living rooms and kitchens a few blocks from the town center. One has two bedrooms and sleeps four; the other has three bedrooms and can sleep seven (3-day minimum, easy parking).

Near Sarlat

$ L'Oasis Sarladaise Chambres is a steal, giving travelers a true French experience two kilometers from the town center. Here, the eager-to-please Mazzocatos welcome you into a traditional neighborhood home where everything feels authentic, picnic dinners are encouraged (and well-provisioned), and the price can't be beat. All three rooms are bird-chirping-peaceful and overlook the garden (Db-€40, Tb/Qb with 2 bedrooms and big terrace-€70, rates go down if you stay more than one night, homemade breakfast-€5, cash only, Wi-Fi, no English spoken, 5-minute drive from the center at 9 Rue Jacques Monod, tel. 05 53 59 25 96, mobile 06 81 30 57 81, fred.mazzo@orange.fr).

Eating in Sarlat

Sarlat is stuffed with restaurants that cater to tourists, but you can still dine well and cheaply. The following places have been reliable; the last two are the most formal. If you have a car, consider driving to Beynac (see page 490) or La Roque-Gageac (page 487) for a riverfront dining experience. Wherever you dine, sample a glass of sweet Monbazillac wine with your foie gras.

La Mirandol is a popular place for budget cuisine, with reasonable salads, *plats du jour,* and €14-29 *menus* (daily, a block off Rue de la République at 7 Rue des Consuls, tel. 05 53 29 53 89).

Chez le Gaulois is a change from the traditional places that line Sarlat's lanes. Pyrenees-raised Olivier and Belgianborn Beatrice serve a hearty mountain cuisine featuring fondue, raclette, *tartiflette* (roasted potatoes mixed with ham and cheese—comes with a good salad for €14), and thinly sliced ham (Olivier spends all evening slicing away). Ask about the daily special and trust Beatrice's advice. They have a few sidewalk tables, but the fun is inside and the service is English-fluent. The ceiling is cluttered with ham hocks, and the soundtrack is jazz (good salads, try *la tarte au figues* for dessert, daily April-Oct, Nov-March closed Sun-Mon, near the TI at 1 Rue Tourny, tel. 05 53 59 50 64).

Le Bistrot, capably run by chef Nicolas, features fresh, local products at his perfect-for-people-watching location, opposite the cathedral. The ambience is delightful and the cuisine is reliably good, but service can be slow (daily, 14 Place du Peyrou, tel. 05 53 28 28 40).

Brasserie le Glacier offers great main-square views from its outdoor tables and good café fare at reasonable prices. Come here for good service; a big salad, pizza (€10), or *plat* (€12); and a view of the lights warming the town buildings (daily, Place de la Liberté, tel. 05 53 29 99 99, also rents rooms—see "Sleeping in Sarlat," earlier).

La Fourchette serves vegetarian meals only at reasonable prices in a pleasant indoor setting (lunch daily except Sun, dinner Fri-Sat only, 23 Avenue Gambetta, tel. 05 53 28 51 24).

Le Bistro de l'Octroi, a few blocks north of the old town, has to provide top cuisine and competitive prices to draw locals— and it does. Quality bistro fare (mostly meat dishes) is served on a generous garden terrace and within the warm interior (€20-30 three-course *menus*, daily, 111 Avenue des Selves—for location see map on page 476, tel. 05 53 30 83 40).

Pizzeria Romane is a cheap, spacious, and family-friendly eatery where you can watch your pizza cook (€9 pizza, lots of salads, closed Sun-Mon, on the quiet side of Sarlat at 3 Côte de Toulouse, tel. 05 53 59 23 88).

Lemoine is a classy café where you can enjoy rich chocolate cake (chocolate decadence) with a hot drink (daily, 13 Rue de la République, tel. 05 53 59 20 77).

Le Présidial is a lovely place for a refined meal in a historic mansion. The setting is exceptional—you're greeted with beautiful gardens (where you can dine in good weather), and the interior comes with high ceilings, stone walls, rich wood floors, and formal service (€28-42 *menus*, closed Sun, Rue Landry, tel. 05 53 28 92 47).

At **L'Assiette de Foie Gras,** a young chef and his wife are making their mark on Sarlat with creative cuisine that blends regional recipes with South American flavors (*le* chef is Argentinian, *le* wife is German, *le* result is *délicieux*). The interior seating feels good, and a handful of outdoor tables line the small lane in front (€22-30 *menus*, good wine list, daily, 4 Rue Landry, mobile 06 17 66 47 91).

Sarlat Connections

Sarlat's TI has train schedules. Souillac and Périgueux are the train hubs for points within the greater region. For all the following destinations, you can go west, on the Libourne/Bordeaux line (transferring in either city, depending on your connection), or east, by SNCF bus to Souillac (covered by railpass, bus leaves from Sarlat train station). I've listed the fastest path in each case. Sarlat train info: tel. 05 53 59 00 21.

From Sarlat by Train to: Les Eyzies-de-Tayac (3/day, 1-3 hours, transfer in Le Buisson), **Paris** (7/day, allow 6 hours: 3/day with change in Libourne or Bordeaux-St-Jean, then TGV; and 4/day by bus to Souillac, then train with possible change in Brive-la-Gaillarde), **Amboise** (4/day, 5-6 hours, via Libourne or Bordeaux-St-Jean, then TGV to Tours' St-Pierre-des-Corps, then local train to Amboise), **Bourges** (4/day, 6-7 hours, 2-4 changes), **Limoges/Oradour-sur-Glane** (slow and difficult trip with lots of changes, 5/day, 3-4 hours: 3/day by bus to Souillac and train to Limoges, then 15-minute walk to catch bus to Oradour-sur-Glane—and 2/day to Limoges with change in Le Buisson and Périgueux), **Cahors** (5/day, 3 hours, bus to Souillac or Siorac, then train to Cahors), **Albi** (6/day, 5-7 hours with 2-3 changes, some require bus from Sarlat to Souillac), **Carcassonne** (5/day, 5.5-7 hours, 1-3 changes, some require bus from Sarlat to Souillac), **St-Emilion** (3-4/day, 2 hours, no transfer, or 3/day to nearby Libourne, then bus or taxi to St-Emilion).

To Beynac, La Roque-Gageac, Castelnaud, and Domme: Remember, these are accessible only by taxi or bike (best rented in Sarlat). See Sarlat's "Helpful Hints" on page 467 for specifics.

The Best of the Dordogne River Valley

The most striking stretch of the Dordogne lies between Carsac and Beynac. Traveling by canoe is the best way to savor the highlights of the Dordogne River Valley, though several scenic sights lie off the river and require a car or bike. Following my "Dordogne Scenic Loop" directions (facing page), you can easily link Sarlat with La Roque-Gageac, Beynac and its château, and Castelnaud before returning to Sarlat.

Planning Your Time

Drivers should allow a minimum of a half-day to sample the river valley (a full day if they toss in a cave visit). Drive slowly to savor the scenery and to stay out of trouble (these are narrow, cliff-hanging roads). The area is picnic-perfect, but buy your supplies before leaving Sarlat; pickings are slim in the villages (though view cafés are in full supply). Vitrac (near Sarlat) is the best place to park for a canoe ride down the river. La Roque-Gageac, Beynac, and Domme have good restaurants. There are a few good places to witness the *gavage* (feeding of the geese and ducks to make foie gras) between Beynac and Sarlat—their dinnertime is generally about 18:00.

You'll pay €3 for all-day parking in most villages (display your parking chit on your dashboard; cars are checked).

I've given distances for drivers in kilometers to match up with your rental car's odometer.

Self-Guided Tours

▲▲Dordogne Scenic Loop

Following these directions, beginning and ending in Sarlat, you can see this area by car or bike (27 hilly miles). Cyclists can cut seven miles off this distance and still see most of the highlights by following D-704 from Sarlat toward Cahors, then taking the Montfort turn-off (well-signed at the roundabout by the big Leclerc grocery store) and tracking signs to Montfort—see the map on page 482. Once in Montfort, follow the river downstream to La Roque-Gageac.

Remember that most of the stops along this route are described in detail later in this chapter (see "Dordogne Towns and Sights").

The Tour Begins: From Sarlat, follow signs on D-704 toward *Cahors* and *Carsac*. Not long after leaving Sarlat, you'll pass the Rougie foie gras outlet store, then the limestone quarry that gives the houses in this area their lemony color. In about five minutes,

soon after passing through a short tunnel, be on the lookout for the little signposted turn-off on the right to the *Eglise de Carsac* (Church of Carsac). Set peacefully among cornfields, with its WWI monument, bonsai-like plane trees, and simple, bulky Romanesque exterior, the church is part of a vivid rural French scene. Take a break here and enter the church (usually open, find English handout). The small cornfields nearby are busy growing food for ducks and geese—locals are appalled that humans would eat the stuff.

From here, continue on, following signs to *Montfort*. About a kilometer west of Carsac, pull over to enjoy the scenic viewpoint (overlooking a bend in the river known as Cingle de Montfort). Across the Dordogne River, fields of walnut trees stretch to distant castles, and the nearby hills are covered in oak trees. This region of the Périgord is nicknamed "black Périgord" for its thick blanket of oaks, which stay leafy throughout the winter. The fairy-tale castle you see is **Montfort,** which was once the medieval home of Simon

DORDOGNE

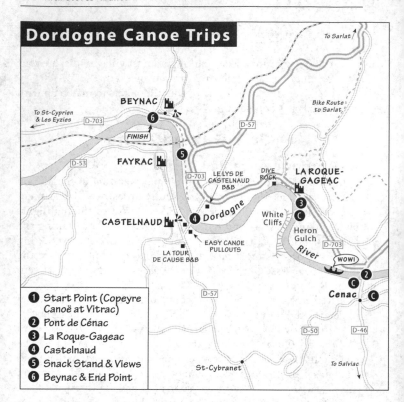

Dordogne Canoe Trips

To Sarlat

BEYNAC

To St-Cyprien
& Les Eyzies

D-703

Bike Route
to Sarlat

D-57

6

FINISH

FAYRAC

D-53

5

D-703

LE LYS DE
CASTELNAUD
B&B

DIVE
ROCK

LA ROQUE-
GAGEAC

Dordogne

3

C

CASTELNAUD

4

White
Cliffs

Heron
Gulch

D-703

LA TOUR
DE CAUSE B&B

EASY CANOE
PULLOUTS

River

WOWI

C

2

D-57

D-50

D-46

C

Cenac

C

St-Cybranet

To Salviac

1 Start Point (Copeyre
   Canoë at Vitrac)
2 Pont de Cénac
3 La Roque-Gageac
4 Castelnaud
5 Snack Stand & Views
6 Beynac & End Point

de Montfort, who led the Cathar Crusades in the early 13th century. Today it's considered mysterious by locals. (The hometown rumor is that the castle is now the home of a brother of the emir of Kuwait.) A plaque on the rock near where you parked honors those who fought the Nazi occupiers in this area in 1943.

Continue on, passing under Montfort's castle (not worth a stop). If you're combining a canoe trip with this drive, cross the river following signs to *Domme,* and find my recommended canoe rental on the right side (see "Dordogne Canoe Trip," next). The very touristy *bastide* (fortified village) of **Domme** is well worth a side-trip from Vitrac or La Roque-Gageac for its sensational views (best for lunch or dinner). Our driving route continues to the more important riverfront villages of **La Roque-Gageac,** then on to **Castelnaud,** and finally to **Beynac** (all described later in this chapter). From Beynac, it's a quick run back to Sarlat.

▲▲▲Dordogne Canoe Trip

For a refreshing break from the car or train, explore the riverside castles and villages of the Dordogne by canoe.

You can rent plastic boats—which are hard, light, and inde-

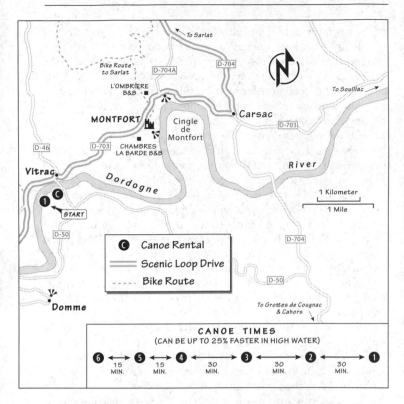

To Sarlat

D-704A   D-704

N

Bike Route
to Sarlat

L'OMBRIÈRE
B&B

To Souillac

MONTFORT

Cingle
de
Montfort

Carsac

D-703

CHAMBRES
LA BARDE B&B

D-46   D-703

Vitrac

Dordogne   *River*

1 Kilometer

1 Mile

C

1

START

D-50

D-704

C Canoe Rental

Scenic Loop Drive

Bike Route

D-50

Domme

To Grottes de Cougnac
& Cahors

CANOE TIMES
(CAN BE UP TO 25% FASTER IN HIGH WATER)

6 ←→ **5** ←→ **4** ←→ **3** ←→ **2** ←→ **1**
15   15   30   30   30
MIN.   MIN.   MIN.   MIN.   MIN.

structible—from many outfits in this area. Whether a one-person kayak or a two-person canoe, they're stable enough for beginners.

Many rental places will pick you up at an agreed-upon spot (even in Sarlat, provided that your group is big enough, and they aren't too busy). All companies let you put in anytime between 9:30 and 16:00 (if you start at 16:00, they'll pick you up at about 18:00). They all charge about the same (€12-18/person for two-person canoes, €17-23 for one-person kayaks). You'll get a life vest and, for a few extra euros, a watertight bucket in which to store your belongings. (The bucket is too big for just a camera, watch, wallet, and cell phone, so bring a resealable plastic baggie or something similar for dry storage in the canoe.)

The trip is fun even in light rain (if you don't mind getting wet)—but heavy rains can make the current too fast to handle, so be sure to check on river levels. If you don't see many other canoes in the river, the river is probably too high—ask before you rent.

Beach your boat wherever it works to take a break—it's light enough that you can drag it up high and dry to go explore. (The canoes aren't worth stealing, as they're cheap and clearly color-coded for their parent company.) It's OK if you're a complete novice—the only whitewater you'll encounter will be the rare wake of passing tour boats...and your travel partner frothing at the views.

Of the region's many canoe companies, only **Copeyre Canoë** has a pull-out arrangement in Beynac (to get to their Vitrac put-in base, from the main roundabout in the town of Vitrac, cross the Dordogne, and turn right). Readers of this book get a 10 percent discount in 2013, and they'll even pick you up in Sarlat for free (this allows non-drivers a chance to explore the riverfront villages for the price of a canoe trip—tip the driver a few euros for this helpful service; tel. 05 53 28 23 82, mobile 06 83 27 30 06, www .canoe-copeyre.com). Allow time to explore Beynac after your river paddle and before the return shuttle trip. Copeyre Canoë also arranges a 14-mile trip from Carsac to Beynac, adding the gorgeous Montfort loop, called *Cingle de Montfort* (longer two-day trip possible).

The Nine-Mile Paddle from Vitrac to Beynac: This is the most interesting, scenic, and handy trip if you're based in or near Sarlat. Vitrac, on the river close to Sarlat, is a good starting point. And, with its mighty castle and pleasant hotels and restaurants, Beynac delivers the perfect finale to your journey.

Here's a rundown of the two-hour Vitrac-Beynac adventure: Leave Vitrac, paddling at an easy pace through lush, forested land. The fortified hill town of Domme will be dead ahead. Pass through Heron Gulch, and after about an hour you'll come to La Roque-Gageac (one of two easy and worthwhile stops before Beynac).

Paddle past La Roque-Gageac's wooden docks (where the tour boats normally tie up) to the stone ramp at the town. Do a 180-degree turn and beach thyself, dragging the boat high and dry. From there you're in La Roque-Gageac's tiny town center, with a TI and plenty of restaurants nearby. Enjoy the town (described on page 487) before heading back to your canoe and into the water.

When leaving La Roque-Gageac, float backward to enjoy the village view. About 15 minutes farther downstream, you'll approach views of the feudal village and castle of Castelnaud. Look for the castle's huge model of a medieval catapult silhouetted menacingly against the sky (it's a steep but worthwhile climb to tour this castle—see page 489). About 15 minutes after you first spot the castle, you'll find two grassy pullouts flanking the bridge below the castle, and the bridge arches make terrific frames for castle views. Just past the grass there's a small market and charcuterie with all you need for a picnic, and a café/restaurant.

Another 15 minutes downstream brings views of Château de Fayrac on your left. The lords of Castelnaud built this to better spy on Beynac during the Hundred Years' War. It's another 15 minutes to your last stop: Beynac. The awesome Beynac castle—looming high above the town—gets better and better as you approach. Slow down and enjoy the ride (sometimes there's a snack stand with the same views at the bridge on the right). Keep to the right as you approach the Copeyre Canoë depot at the downstream end of town. You'll see the ramp just before the parking lot and wooden dock (where the tour boats generally tie up). Do another 180-degree turn, and beach yourself hard. The office is right there. Return your boat, and explore Beynac (described on page 490).

Other Canoe Options: All along the river you'll see canoe companies, each with stacks of plastic canoes. Depending on their location and relations with places to pull out, each one works best on a particular stretch of the river. All have essentially the same policies. Below Domme in Cénac, **Dordogne Randonnées** has canoes and kayaks for the scenic two-hour stretch to a pullout just past Beynac (to reach their office coming from Sarlat or Beynac, take the first left after crossing the bridge to Cénac, tel. 05 53 28 22 01, randodordogne@wanadoo.fr). In La Roque-Gageac, **Canoe-Dordogne** rents canoes for the worthwhile two-hour float to Château des Milandes, allowing canoers to stop in Beynac before the pullout (tel. 05 53 29 58 50). For a lazier no-paddle alternative, try a boat cruise on the river to Castelnaud and back, either from Beynac or La Roque-Gageac (€9, 50-60 minutes, both options are great for landlubbers and described in the next section).

Dordogne Towns and Sights

The towns and sights described below coincide with the Dordogne River Valley scenic loop outlined earlier (see page 481). In many villages, parking must be paid for during the day but is free overnight (19:00-10:00) and off-season. Be sure you pay; cars are checked. Parked cars are appealing to thieves—take everything out or stow belongings out of sight.

Those with a car can enjoy tranquil rural accommodations at great prices in these cozy villages. I like the comfort they provide and the views they offer. Read about the villages below, then make your choice—you can't go wrong.

Montfort

There's more to this castle-topped village than meets the eye—leave most tourists behind and find a few cafés, a pizzeria, and a handful of *chambres d'hôtes*, including these recommended listings (for locations, see map on page 482).

DORDOGNE

Sleeping and Eating in Montfort

$$ Chambres la Barde has five sumptuous rooms in a warm, modern stone home with a swimming pool, a cozy lounge, a big grass yard, a communal kitchen, a *pétanque* court, a game room, and views to Montfort castle from each room's terrace (Db-€63-85, extra person-€10, breakfast-€8, 2-room suite sleeps 5, cash only, Wi-Fi, below Montfort castle—green signs guide you there, tel. 05 53 28 24 34, mobile 06 86 88 60 93, www.perigord-dordogne -sarlat.com, labardemontfort@gmail.com).

$$ L'Ombriere, with four beautifully renovated rooms and caring Italian hosts Andrea and Barbara, is a calm B&B overlooking a walnut grove (Db-€80-90, some rooms have air-con, Wi-Fi, on east edge of Montfort village—watch for signs, tel. 05 53 28 11 38, www.lombriere.com, info@lombriere.com).

▲▲Domme

This busy little town merits a stop for its stunning view; it's ideal early or late, when crowds recede and the light is best. If you come for lunch or dinner, arrive early enough to savor the cliff-capping setting. Follow signs up to *La Bastide de Domme,* and drive right through the narrow gate of the fortified town walls. Park at a pay lot in town, then follow *Le Panorama* signs. You'll find picnic-perfect benches, cafés, and a view you won't soon forget.

Sleeping and Eating in Domme

The town has many forgettable restaurants, but a few places stand out.

$$$ Hôtel de l'Esplanade turns its back on the busy village and delivers the valley's most sensational views from many of its comfortable bedrooms and restaurant tables. If you come for the restaurant (€36-60 *menus*), book ahead for view seating (Db-€95-135, view Db-140-€160, air-con, Wi-Fi, tel. 05 53 28 31 41, fax 05 53 28 49 92, www .esplanade-perigord.com, esplanade.domme@wanadoo.fr).

Chabanoix et Châtaigne is a small bistro serving delicious Dordogne fare blended with international flavors. Enjoy the sunset from Domme's viewpoint, then come here for dinner, but book a table ahead—local foodies are all over this place (closed Wed and Sat, 3 Rue Geoffroy de Vivians, tel. 05 53 31 07 11).

Belvédère Café owns a privileged position at the viewpoint and serves café fare at good prices with million-dollar views from its outside tables (daily for lunch and dinner, at *Le Panorama,* tel. 05 53 31 12 01).

DORDOGNE

▲▲▲La Roque-Gageac

Whether you're joyriding or paddling the Dordogne, La Roque-Gageac (lah rohk-gah-zhahk) is an essential stop—and a strong contender on all the "cutest towns in France" lists. Called by most simply "La Roque" ("The Rock"), it looks sculpted out of the rock between the river and the cliffs.

Orientation: At the upstream end of town, you'll find plenty of parking; the **TI** (Easter-Sept daily 10:00-12:30 & 13:30-17:00, stays open later in summer, closed off-season, tel. 05 53 29 17 01); a WC; swings and slides for kids; canoe rental; and *pétanque (boules)* courts, which are lively on summer evenings (17:00-21:00). A small market brightens La Roque-Gageac on Friday mornings in summer. Though busy with day-trippers, the town is tranquil at night.

Town Overview—Stand along the river near the TI and survey La Roque-Gageac: it's a one-street town stretching along the river.

Cars and strollers compete for the same riverfront space. The highest stone work (on the far right) was home to the town's earliest inhabitants, in the 10th century. High above (about center), 12th-century cave dwellers built a settlement during the era of Norman (Viking) river raids. Long after the Vikings were tamed, French soldiers used this lofty perch as a barracks while fighting against England in the Hundred Years' War.

Now locate the exotic foliage by the church on the right. Tropical gardens (bamboo, bananas, lemons, and so on) are a village forte, because limestone absorbs heat.

La Roque-Gageac frequently endures winter floods that would leave you (standing where you are now) underwater. When there's a big rain in central France, La Roque-Gageac floods two days later. The first floors of all the riverfront buildings are vacated off-season. (A house about five buildings downriver from Hôtel Belle Etoile shows various high-water marks—*inondation* means "flood.") Looking farther downstream, notice the fanciful castle built in the 19th century by a British aristocrat (whose family still nurtures Joan of Arc dreams in its turrets). The old building just beyond that (downstream end of town) actually is historic—it's the quarantine house, where lepers and out-of-town visitors who dropped by in times of plague would be kept (after their boats were burned).

Those wooden boats on the river are modeled after boats called *gabarres*, originally built here to take prized oak barrels filled with local wine down to Bordeaux. Unable to return against the river current, those boats were routinely taken apart for their lumber. Today, tourists, rather than barrels, fill the boats on cruises down the river (described below). If you're experiencing a movie-based déjà vu, it's because these actual boats (dolled up, of course) were used by Johnny Depp, who delighted viewers and Juliette Binoche alike in the movie *Chocolat*.

Climb into the town by strolling up the cobbled lane to the right of the Hôtel Belle Etoile. Where the stepped path ends, go right to find the exotic garden and viewpoint (in front of the simple church). A left turn at the end of the stepped path takes you to the privately owned Fort Troglodytique (long closed to the public). For a terrific medieval fort experience, visit La Roque St-Christophe (described on page 511).

Boat Tours—Tour boats make one-hour cruises from La Roque-Gageac to Castelnaud and back (€9, 2/hour, April-Nov daily, tel. 05 53 29 40 44).

Sleeping and Eating in and near La Roque-Gageac

Along with Beynac, this is one of the region's most beautiful villages. Park in the lot at the eastern end of town if you're staying in La Roque-Gageac, and take everything of value out of your car.

$$ Hôtel la Belle Etoile**, a well-managed hotel-restaurant located on the river in the center of La Roque-Gageac, is a great deal. Hostess Danielle and chef Régis (ray-geez) make the ideal team. The comfy rooms are well-maintained, and most have river views (non-riverview Db-€56, riverview Db-€67 or €77, gorgeous suite-€120-150, air-con, Wi-Fi, reserve private parking ahead, closed Nov-March, tel. 05 53 29 51 44, fax 05 53 29 45 63, www .belleetoile.fr, hotel.belle-etoile@wanadoo.fr). I discovered this place through its **restaurant**—it's where locals go for a fine meal. They serve a memorable dinner of classic French cuisine in a romantic setting. The serving sizes are not great, but the quality is (*menus* from €27, closed for lunch Wed and all day Mon; book a few days ahead).

$$ Hôtel le Périgord**, a modern hotel across the river from the hill town of Domme, offers traditionally decorated rooms at fair rates with nice gardens, a view pool, tennis courts, a game room, and a restaurant (Db-€64-74, view Db-€84, extra person-€17, dinner *menus* from €25, Port de Domme, tel. 05 53 28 36 55, fax 05 53 28 38 73, www.hotelleperigord.eu, bienvenue@hotelleperigord.eu).

$ L'Auberge des Platanes**, across from La Roque-Gageac's TI and parking lot, rents 13 rooms above a sprawling café and a restaurant—guests take a back seat to café clients. Half the rooms are simple, traditional, and cheap; the other half are modern, with all the comforts, and pricier (Sb-€39, Db-€50-65, Tb-€58-110, tel. 05 53 29 51 58, fax 05 53 31 19 32, www.aubergedesplatanes.com, contact@aubergedesplatanes.com).

▲▲Château de Castelnaud

This crumbling castle looks less mighty than Château de Beynac (across the river), but it packs a powerful medieval punch. Now a

museum devoted to medieval warfare, every room in the château has a story to tell. Several rooms display weaponry and artifacts from the Hundred Years' War, and others have videos (with English subtitles), interactive computers (in English), and castle models. The whole experience is designed to teach you about daily castle life,
from the battlefield (armory) to the dinner table (kitchen). The upper courtyard has a 150-foot-deep well (drop a pebble). The rampart views are as unbeatable as the siege machines are formidable. Pick up the free, essential English explanations and follow *Suite de la Visite* signs to stay the course.

Cost and Hours: €8.20, daily July-Aug 9:00-20:00, April-June and Sept 10:00-19:00, Oct and Feb-March 10:00-18:00, Nov-Jan 14:00-17:00, last entry one hour before closing, daily demonstrations of medieval warfare mid-July-Aug, several restaurants near the castle's parking lot or down below at the river's edge, tel. 05 53 31 30 00, www.castelnaud.com.

Getting There: From the river, it's a steep 25-minute hike through the village to the castle. Drivers can park in the €3 lot near the castle gate (10-minute walk uphill from there). You can stop at Castelnaud on your canoe trip, or hike an hour from Beynac along a riverside path (though it's tricky to follow in parts—it hugs the river as it passes through campgrounds and farms—determined walkers do fine).

Sleeping near Castelnaud

This village, ideally situated between La Roque-Gageac and Beynac, has two excellent B&B choices nearby (see map on page 482).

$$ La Tour de Cause is where California refugees Albert and Caitlin have found their heaven, amid their renovated farmhouse with five top-quality rooms, a big pool, and, best of all, a *pétanque* court. Albert restores homes in California, and has brought his considerable talent to France (Sb-€75, Db-€92, includes breakfast, cash only, 2-night minimum, en-suite bathrooms—some with immense walk-in showers, closed Nov-April, Internet access and

DORDOGNE

Wi-Fi, tel. 05 53 30 30 51, US tel. Nov-March 707/527-5051, www.latourdecause.com, info@latourdecause.com). From the Dordogne River, cross the bridge to Castelnaud, follow signs toward *Daglan*, then make a hard right turn in the hamlet of Pont de Cause and park near their gate.

$ Le Lys de Castelnaud is run by French medieval enthusiasts Nathalie and Dominique. Nathalie is a Joan of Arc fanatic and speaks sufficient English to explain her passion. The decor is steeped in the Middle Ages, with knights in armor, tapestries, and old swords. The four rooms are well-priced (three have Castelnaud views) and have all the modern conveniences (Db-€68, Tb/Qb-€90-110, cash only, Internet access, tel. 05 53 28 20 27, mobile 06 09 57 21 97, www.chambres-dordogne.com, contact @chambres-dordogne.com). It's well-signed at the foot of the road that leads across the river to Castelnaud.

▲▲▲Beynac

Four miles downstream from La Roque-Gageac, Beynac (bay-nak) is the other must-see, picture-perfect Dordogne village. It comes with a big, foreboding bonus: one of the most imposing castles in France.

This feudal village tumbles down a steep hill from its majestic castle to the river far below. You'll have the Dordogne River at your doorstep and a perfectly preserved medieval village winding, like a sepia-tone film set, from the beach to the castle above. Except for the castle, there's nothing to "tour." The purely stone village—with steep streets that still have their Languedoc (old French) names—is just plain pretty. The floodlit village is always open for evening strollers.

Orientation: The **TI** is across from the recommended Hôtel du Château (daily 10:00-12:30 & 14:00-17:30, tel. 05 53 29 43 08). Pick up the *Plan de Beynac* in English for a simple self-guided walking tour, and get information on hiking and canoes. A few steps down from the TI is the post office (which has an ATM). If you need a lift, call Beynac-based **Taxi Corinne** (see page 462). From June to September, there's a sweet little market on Monday mornings in the river parking lot. Drivers can park at pay lots located on the river, way up at the castle (follow signs to *Château de Beynac*), or halfway between. The same parking ticket works up at the château if you decide against the climb.

Walks—A too-busy road separates Beynac from its river. The village climbs steeply uphill from river to château—the farther you get from the road, the more medieval the village feels. (You can drive up via a long lane looping around the back of town.) Another trail begins across from Hôtel Bonnet at the eastern end of town and follows the river toward Castelnaud, with great views back toward Beynac and—for able route-finders—a healthy one-hour hike to Castelnaud. Make time to walk at least a few hundred yards along this trail to enjoy the view to Beynac.

▲▲**Château de Beynac**—Beynac's brooding, cliff-clinging château soars 500 feet above the Dordogne River. During the

Hundred Years' War (see sidebar on page 269), the castle of Beynac housed the French, while the British set up camp across the river at Castelnaud. From the condition of the castles, I'd say France won. This sparsely furnished castle is best for its valley views, but it still manages to evoke a powerful medieval feel. (These castles never had much furniture in any case.) When buying your ticket, notice the list showing the barons of Beynac *(Beynac et Ses Barons)*—Richard the Lionhearted *(Coeur de Lion)* spent 10 years here. As you tour the castle, swords, spears, and crossbows keep you honest, and the two stone WCs keep kids entertained. I like the soldiers' party room best—park your sword at the door and hang your crossbow on the hooks above, *s'il vous plaît*. Authentic-looking wooden stockades were installed for the 1998 filming of the movie *The Messenger: The Story of Joan of Arc*.

Cost and Hours: €7.50, daily May-Oct 10:00-18:00, Nov-April closes at 16:00 or 17:00—depending on weather and whim, last entry 45 minutes before closing, tel. 05 53 29 50 40.

Information: You're free to wander on your own, though occasional tours are available in English; call ahead for times (tip expected). Pick up the English explanations (€0.15) or spring for the excellent €5 pamphlet.

Viewpoints—Even if you pass on the castle, hike or drive up to the town lookout for a commanding top-of-the-village view, which overlooks several castles and the river. Walk outside the village at the top (parking available), turn right in front of the little cemetery, and walk uphill until the view opens up. Castelnaud's castle hangs on the hill in the distance straight ahead; Château de Fayrac (owned by a Texan) is just right of the rail bridge in front of Castelnaud; it was originally constructed by the lords of Castelnaud to keep a closer eye on the castle of Beynac. The Château de Marqueyssac, on a hill to the left, was built by the barons of Beynac to keep a closer eye on the boys at Castelnaud. More

DORDOGNE

than a thousand such castles were erected in the Dordogne alone during the Hundred Years' War (1336-1453).

Three exceptional views of Beynac lie far below. The first is along the riverside path opposite Hôtel Bonnet (walk as far as you can for great views back to Beynac). A second viewpoint is about a half-mile drive toward La Roque-Gageac; turn right at the Ferme du Château restaurant, and follow the road to its end. For the best (and easiest) village view, climb the short wall between the parking lot and the river—just try fitting it all in your camera's viewfinder.

Boat Trips—Boats leave from Beynac's riverside parking lot for relaxing, 50-minute river cruises to Castelnaud and back (€9, nearly hourly, departures Easter-Oct daily 10:00-12:30 & 14:00-18:00, more frequent trips July-Aug, written English explanations, tel. 05 53 28 51 15).

Sleeping in Beynac

My favorite village on the river comes with some traffic noise.

$$ Hôtel du Château**, on the river at Beynac's only (but busy) intersection, provides adequate comfort with 16 rooms, most with queen-size beds. Some have street noise, though it's mitigated by air-conditioning (available in some rooms) and insulated windows. Other rooms have terraces facing the river; four rooms can sleep up to three people, and one has a full kitchen. Ask about their three-room house next door (Sb-€50-60, Db-€70-88, buffet breakfast-€8, Internet access and Wi-Fi, tel. 05 53 29 19 20, fax 05 53 28 55 56, www.hotel-beynac-dordogne.com, contact@hotel -beynac-dordogne.com).

$ Le Petit Versailles does its name justice, with five immacu- late rooms that Louis would have appreciated. The place has a quiet terrace and garden, and—best of all—the welcoming Fleurys, Jean-Claude and Françoise, who speak just enough English (Db- €70 for 1 night, less if you stay longer, 3 rooms have fine views, all have big beds, includes large English breakfast, cash only, no smoking anywhere, Internet access and Wi-Fi, laundry facilities, Route du Château, mobile 06 71 88 59 72, www.lepetitversailles .fr, info@lepetitversailles.fr). With the river on your right, take the small road—wedged between the hill and Hôtel Bonnet—for a half-mile, turn right when you see their sign and continue 100 yards, then take a right down a steep driveway.

Eating in Beynac

Beynac has a handful of worthwhile restaurants and a bakery with handy picnic-ready lunch items (across from the TI). Have a drink up high at the café opposite the castle entry, or down below at the café that hides right on the river (walk down the steps across from Hôtel du Château); stay for dinner if the spirit moves you.

DORDOGNE

Hôtel du Château features a relaxed dining room, air-conditioned comfort, and reasonable prices (€22-39 dinner *menus*, great €19 *omelet aux cèpes*, daily, see hotel listing earlier). From mid-June through mid-September, they offer a light, "between meals" mid-afternoon menu for those too late for lunch and too starving to wait until dinnertime—a typical dilemma for busy tourists on the river.

Taverne/Café des Remparts, Beynac's scenic eatery, faces the castle at the top of the town and serves copious salads, good omelets, and *plats*. I can't imagine leaving Beynac without relaxing at their view-perfect café for at least a drink; it's best at night. Sophie promises a free apéritif with this book. Call ahead to be sure they're open (July-Aug daily for lunch and dinner, otherwise open daily for lunch and weekends for dinner, closed in winter, across from castle, tel. 05 53 29 57 76).

La Petite Tonnelle, cut into the rock, has a romantic interior and a fine terrace out front. Locals love it for its tasty cuisine served at fair prices. It's a block up from Hôtel du Château (€16-33 *menus*, on the road to the castle, tel. 05 53 29 95 18).

Foie Gras Farms

During the evenings, many farms in this area let you witness the force-feeding of geese for the "ultimate pleasure" of foie gras.

Look for *Gavage* signs, but beware: It's hard for the squeamish to watch (read the sidebar for a description before you visit). Of the two places listed here, the first is by far the best, with the only real tour. The second is tiny, homey, and has more flexible hours. For locations, see the map on page 498.

Elevage du Bouyssou—This big, homey goose farm a short drive from Sarlat is run by a couple who enjoy their work. Denis Mazet (the latest in a long line of goose farmers here) spends five hours a day feeding his gaggle of geese. His wife, Nathalie—clearly in love with country life—speaks wonderful English and enthusiastically shows guests around their idyllic farm. Each evening, she leads a one-hour, kid-friendly tour. You'll meet the geese babies, do a little unforced feeding, and hear how every part of the goose (except heads and feet) is used—even feathers (for pillows). Nathalie explains why locals see force-feeding as humane (comparable to raising any other animal for human consumption) before you step into the dark barn where about a hundred geese await another

DORDOGNE

Foie Gras and Force-Feeding the Geese and Ducks

Force-feeding geese and ducks has the result of quickly fattening their livers, the principal ingredient of the Dordogne specialty foie gras. The practice is as controversial among animal-rights activists as bullfighting. And though some view these birds as tortured prisoners, here's the (politically incorrect) perspective of those who produce and consume such farm-raised animals.

French enthusiasts of *la gavage* (as the force-feeding process is called) say the animals are calm, in no pain, and are designed to take in food in this manner because of their massive gullets and expandable livers (used to store lots of fat for their long migrations). Geese and ducks do not have a gag reflex, and the linings of their throats are tough (they swallow rocks to store in their gizzards for grinding the food they eat). They can eat lots of food easily, without choking. They live lives at least as comfy as the chickens, cows, and pigs that many people have no problem eating, and are slaughtered as humanely as any nonhuman can expect in this food-chain existence.

The quality of foie gras depends on a stress-free environment; the birds do best with the same human feeder and a steady flow of good corn. These mostly free-range geese and ducks live six months (most of our factory-farmed chickens in the US live less than two months, and are plumped with hormones). Their "golden weeks" are the last three or four, when they go into the

dinner. The tour finishes in the little shop. They raise and slaughter a thousand geese annually, producing about 1,500 pounds of foie gras—most of which is sold directly to visitors at good prices.

Hours: Tours daily at 18:30 year-round, groups welcome, English tour on request at any time by reservation (tel. 05 53 31 12 31, elevage.bouyssou@wanadoo.fr). In July and August, Nathalie includes a tasting of her products paired with a sweet wine.

Getting There: Leave Sarlat on the Carsac-bound road (D-704), go about seven kilometers in the direction of Carsac, turn left at the cement plant, and follow *Bouyssou* signs until you reach the farm.

La Ferme de l'Angle—At this tiny goose farm in the scenic middle of nowhere, a short distance north of Sarlat, Christiane (who speaks English) and son Cyril (who speaks goose) enjoy playing host to the guests who drop by. While there's no formal tour here pen to have their livers fattened. With two or three feedings a day, their liver grows from about a quarter-pound to nearly two pounds. A goose with a fattened liver looks like he's waddling around with a full diaper under his feathers. (Signs and placards in the towns of the region show geese with this unique and, for foie-gras lovers, mouthwatering shape.) The same process is applied to ducks to get the marginally less exquisite and less expensive duck-liver foie gras.

The varieties of product you'll be tempted to buy (or order in restaurants) can be confusing. Here's a primer: first, *foie gras* means "fattened liver"; *foie gras d'oie* is from a goose, and *foie gras de canard* is from a duck (you'll also see a blend of the two). *Pâté de foie gras* is a "paste" of foie gras combined with other meats, fats, and seasonings (think of liverwurst). Most American consumers get the chance to eat foie gras only in the form of pâtés.

The *foie gras d'oie entier* (a solid chunk of pure goose liver) is the most expensive and prized version of canned foie gras, costing about €18 for 130 grams (about a tuna-can-size tin). The *bloc de foie gras d'oie* is made of chunks of pure goose liver that have been pressed together; it's more easily spreadable (figure €14 for 130 grams). The *medaillons de foie gras d'oie* must be at least 50 percent foie gras (the rest will be a pâté filler, about €8 for 130 grams). A small tin of blended duck-and-goose foie gras costs about €5. When choosing, look for a *"production locale"* label to be assured that your foie gras is indeed locally made. Note: Airport security may require you to carry these in your checked baggage, not your carry-on.

After a week in the Dordogne, I leave feeling a strong need for foie gras detox.

and only a handful of geese, this is an easy way to see the *gavage* in action—Cyril will demonstrate at just about any time.

Hours: Daily 10:30-12:00 & 16:30-18:00, tel. 05 53 31 16 63.

Getting There: To get to the farm, located five kilometers from Sarlat, take D-704 (direction: Brive/Montignac); at Restaurant la Vieille Grange, take a left and follow signs.

▲Château de Commarque

This mystical medieval castle ruin is ripe for hikers wanting to get away from it all. From the remote and secluded parking lot, it's a 20-minute walk down through a forest of chestnut trees to a clearing, where the mostly ruined castle appears...like a mirage. Pay the entry fee, pick up the English brochure, and you're free to scour the sight. The main event is the castle, but you'll also discover the remains of a chapel and several other buildings. Owner Hubert de

Commarque bought the castle in 1968 and has been digging it out of the forest ever since. During the summer, you may see archaeology students doing excavating work.

Cost and Hours: €6.50, daily May-Sept 10:00-19:00, until 20:00 in July-Aug, April 10:00-18:00, closed Oct-March, last entry one hour before closing, WCs back at the parking lot, off D-47 and D-6 between Sarlat and Les Eyzies-de-Tayac—see map on page 498, www.commarque.com.

Getting There: From Sarlat, follow signs to *Les Eyzies*, then follow the D-6 to Marquay. As you pass through Marquay, keep right, following *Commarque* signs, then go about two kilometers and turn right. Notice that this is very close to the Abri du Cap Blanc Cro-Magnon cave (see page 507).

Maison Forte de Reignac

For over 700 years, a powerful lord ruled from this unusual home carved from a rock face high above the Vézère River. After a short but steep hike to the entry, you'll climb through several floors of well-furnished rooms, some with fireplaces lit. Kids love this tree house of a place. Your tour concludes in a room that houses torture devices and highlights man's creative abilities to inflict unthinkable pain...and a slow death. You'll see full-size models of interrogation chairs, a spike-covered rack, a guillotine, and a warden's corset. The loaner English handout provides good context.

Cost and Hours: €7, daily July-Aug 10:00-20:00, May-June and Sept 10:00-19:00, April 10:00-18:00, closed most of Oct-March, just north of the village of Tursac, tel. 05 53 50 69 54, www.maison-forte-reignac.com.

Getting There: From Les Eyzies-de-Tayac, it's a twisty 10-minute drive up D-706 (direction: La Roque St-Christophe).

Cro-Magnon Caves

The towns and sights of the Dordogne region—including Les Eyzies-de-Tayac, Grotte de Font-de-Gaume, Abri du Cap Blanc, Grotte de Rouffignac, Lascaux II, and Grotte de Cougnac—have a rich history of prehistoric cave art. The paintings you'll see here are famous throughout the world for their remarkably modern-looking technique, beauty, and mystery. To fully appreciate them, take time to read the following information, written by Gene Openshaw, on the purpose of the art and the Cro-Magnon style of painting.

Cave Art 101

From 18,000 to 10,000 B.C., long before Stonehenge, before the pyramids, before metalworking, farming, and domesticated dogs,

back when mammoths and saber-toothed cats still roamed the earth, prehistoric people painted deep inside limestone caverns in southern France and northern Spain. These are not crude doodles with a charcoal-tipped stick. They're sophisticated, costly, and time-consuming engineering projects planned and executed by dedicated artists supported by a unified and stable culture—the Magdalenians.

The Magdalenians (c. 18,000-10,000 B.C.): These hunter-gatherers of the Upper Paleolithic period (40,000-10,000 B.C.) were driven south by the Second Ice Age. (Historians named them after the Madeleine archaeological site near Les Eyzies-de-Tayac.) The Magdalenians flourished in southern France and northern Spain for eight millennia—long enough to chronicle the evolution and extinction of several animal species. (Think: Egypt lasted a mere 3,000 years; Rome lasted 1,000; America fewer than 250 so far.)

Physically, the people were Cro-Magnons. Unlike hulking, beetle-browed Neanderthals, Cro-Magnons were fully developed *Homo sapiens* who could blend in to our modern population. We know these people by the possessions found in their settlements: stone axes, flint arrowheads, bone needles for making clothes, musical instruments, grease lamps (without their juniper wicks), and cave paintings and sculpture. Many objects are beautifully decorated.

The Magdalenians did not live in the deep limestone caverns they painted (which are cold and difficult to access). But many did live in the shallow cliffside caves that you'll see throughout your Dordogne travels, which were continuously inhabited from prehistoric times until the Middle Ages.

The Paintings: Though there are dozens of caves painted over a span of more than 8,000 years, they're all surprisingly similar. These Stone Age hunters painted the animals they hunted—bison or bulls (especially at Lascaux and Grotte de Font-de-Gaume), horses, deer, reindeer, ibex (mountain goats), wolves, bears, and cats, plus animals that are now extinct—mammoths (the engravings at Grotte de Rouffignac), woolly rhinoceros (at Grotte de Font-de-Gaume), and wild oxen.

Besides animals, you'll see geometric and abstract designs, such as circles, squiggles, and hash marks. There's scarcely a *Homo*

Cro-Magnon Caves near Sarlat

To Perigueux &
St-Emilion
via A-89

D-45

D-32

2 Kilometers

2 Miles

GROTTE DE ROUFFIGNAC

St-Léon

D-706

LA ROQUE ST-CHRISTOPHE

D-710

D-47

River

MAISON DE REIGNAC

D-65

AUBERGE VEYRET

ABRI DU CAP BLANC

D-48

Les Eyzies-de-Tayac

GROTTE DE FONT-DE-GAUME

CHATEAU DE COMMARQUE

D-47

Vézère

Le Bugue

D-703

(WELCOME CENTER & MUSEUM)

D-48

D-35

D-703

D O R D O G N E

St-Cyprien

Le Buisson

D-29

D-51

D-703

D-53

D-25

Dordogne

River

CHATEAU DES MILANDES

D-25

To Bergerac & St-Emilion

D-703

Siorac-en-Périgord

D-710

D-53

DORDOGNE

Belves

D-53

Paris

FRANCE

100 Miles

■ Prehistoric Sites

🦆 Foie Gras Farm

▨ Scenic Loop

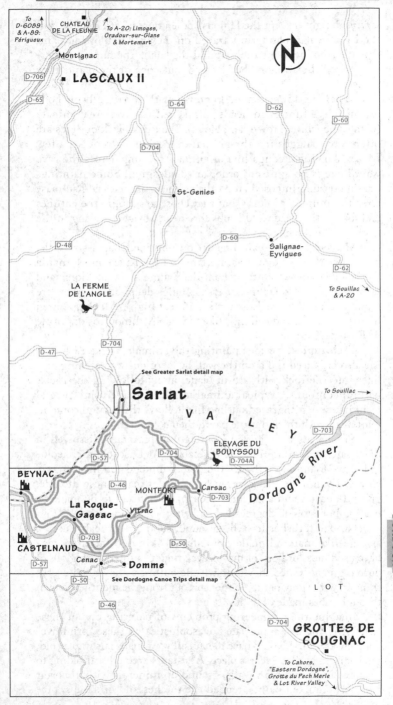

To
D-6089
& A-89:
Périgueux

CHATEAU
DE LA FLEUNIE

To A-20: Limoges,
Oradour-sur-Glane
& Mortemart

Montignac

D-706

■ **LASCAUX II**

D-65

D-64

D-62

D-60

D-704

St-Genies

D-48

D-60

Salignae-
Eyvigues

D-62

**LA FERME
DE L'ANGLE**

To Souillac
& A-20

D-704

D-47

See Greater Sarlat detail map

Sarlat

V A L L E Y

To Souillac

D-703

ELEVAGE DU
BOUYSSOU

D-704A

D-57

D-704

Dordogne River

BEYNAC

D-46

MONTFORT

Carsac

**La Roque-
Gageac**

Vitrac

D-703

D-703

D-50

CASTELNAUD

D-57

Cenac

Domme

D-50

See Dordogne Canoe Trips detail map

L O T

D-46

D-704

**GROTTES DE
COUGNAC**

To Cahors,
"Eastern Dordogne",
Grotte du Pech Merle
& Lot River Valley

DORDOGNE

sapiens in sight (except the famous "fallen hunter" at Lascaux), but there are human handprints traced on the wall by blowing paint through a hollow bone tube around the hand. The hunter-gatherers painted the animals they hunted, but none of the plants they gathered.

Style: The animals stand in profile, with unnaturally big bodies and small limbs and heads. Black, red, and yellow dominate (with some white, brown, and violet). The thick black outlines are often wavy, suggesting the animal in motion. Except for a few friezes showing a conga line of animals running across the cave wall, there is no apparent order or composition. Some paintings are simply superimposed atop others. The artists clearly had mastered the animals' anatomy, but they chose to simplify the outlines and distort the heads and limbs for effect, always painting in the distinct Magdalenian style.

Many of the cave paintings are on a Sistine Chapel-size scale. The "canvas" was huge: Lascaux's main caverns are more than a football field long; Grotte de Font-de-Gaume is 430 feet long; and Grotte de Rouffignac meanders six miles deep. The figures are monumental (bulls at Lascaux are 16 feet high). All are painted high up on walls and ceilings, like the woolly rhinoceros of Grotte de Font-de-Gaume.

Techniques: Besides painting the animals, these early artists also engraved them on the wall by laboriously scratching outlines into the rock with a flint blade, many following the rock's natural contour. A typical animal might be made using several techniques—an engraved outline that follows the natural contour, reinforced with thick outline paint, then colored in.

The paints were mixed from natural pigments dissolved in cave water and oil (animal or vegetable). At Lascaux, archaeologists have found more than 150 different minerals on hand to mix paints. Even basic black might be a mix of manganese dioxide, ground quartz, and a calcium phosphate that had to be made by heating bone to 700 degrees Fahrenheit, then grinding it.

No paintbrushes have been found, so artists probably used a sponge-like material made from animal skin and fat. They may have used moss or hair, or maybe even finger-painted with globs of pure pigment. Once they'd drawn the outlines, they filled everything in with spray paint—either spit out from the mouth or blown through tubes made of hollow bone.

Imagine the engineering problems of painting one of these caves, and you can appreciate how sophisticated these "primitive" people were. First, you'd have to haul all your materials into a cold, pitch-black, hard-to-access place. Assistants erected scaffolding to reach ceilings and high walls, ground up minerals with a mortar and pestle, mixed paints, tended the torches and oil lamps, prepared the "paintbrushes," laid out major outlines with a connect-the-dots series of points...then stepped aside for Magdalenian Michelangelos to ascend the scaffolding and create.

Dating: Determining exactly how old this art is—and whether it's authentic—is tricky. (Because much of the actual paint is mineral-based with no organic material, carbon-dating techniques are often ineffective.) As different caves feature different animals, prehistorians can derive which caves are relatively older and younger, since climate change caused various animal species to come and go within certain regions. In several cases, experts confirmed the authenticity of a painting because the portrayals of the animals showed anatomical details not previously known—until they were discovered by modern technology. (For instance, in Grotte de Rouffignac, the mammoths are shown with a strange skin flap over their anus, which was only discovered during the 20th century on a preserved mammoth found in Siberian permafrost.) They can also estimate dates by checking the amount of calcium glaze formed over the paint, which can sometimes only be seen by infrared photography.

Why?: No one knows the purpose of the cave paintings. Interestingly, the sites the artists chose were deliberately awe-

inspiring, out of the way, and special. They knew their work here would last for untold generations, as had the paintings that came before theirs. Here are some theories of what this first human art might mean:

It's no mystery that hunters would paint animals, the source of their existence. The first scholar to study the caves, Abbé Henri Breuil, thought the painted animals were magic symbols made by hunters to increase the supply of game. Or perhaps hunters thought that if you could "master" an animal by painting it, you could later master it in battle. Some scholars think the paintings teach the art of hunting, but there's very little apparent hunting technique shown. Did they worship animals? The paintings definitely depict an animal-centered (rather than a human-centered) universe.

The paintings may have a religious purpose, and some of the caverns are large and special enough that rituals and ceremonies could have been held there. But the paintings show no sacrifices, rituals, or ceremonies. Scholars writing on primitive art in other parts of the world speculate that art was made by shamans in a religious or drug-induced trance, but France's paintings are very methodical.

The order of paintings on the walls seems random. Could

DORDOGNE

it be that the caves are a painted collage of the history of the Magdalenians, with each successive generation adding its distinct animal or symbol to the collage, putting it in just the right spot that established their place in history?

The fact that styles and subject matter changed so little over the millennia might imply that the artists purposely chose timeless images to relate their generation with those before and after. Perhaps they simply lived in a stable culture that did not value innovation. Or were these people too primitive to invent new techniques and topics?

Maybe the paintings are simply the result of the universal human drive to create, and these caverns were Europe's first art galleries, bringing the first tourists.

Very likely there is no single meaning that applies to all the paintings in all the caves. Prehistoric art may be as varied in meaning as current art.

Picture yourself as a Magdalenian viewing these paintings: You'd be guided by someone into a cold, echoing, and otherworldly chamber. In the darkness, someone would light torches and lamps, and suddenly the animals would flicker to life, appearing to run around the cave, like a prehistoric movie. In front of you, a bull would appear, behind you a mammoth (which you'd never seen in the flesh), and overhead a symbol that might have tied the whole experience together. You'd be amazed that an artist could capture the real world and reproduce it on a wall. Whatever the purpose—religious, aesthetic, or just plain fun—there's no doubt the effect was (and is) thrilling.

Today, you can visit the caves and share a common experience with a caveman. Feel a bond with these long-gone people... or stand in awe at how different they were from us. Ultimately, the paintings are as mysterious as the human species.

Helpful Hints

Drivers Fare Best: All the prehistoric caves listed here are within a reasonable drive of Sarlat. Considering the scarcity of public transit, if you don't have a car, you'll be like a caveman without a spear (see page 462 for guided tours that connect some of these sights).

Book Ahead: July, August, and holiday weekends are busiest, so book as far ahead as you can during these times. Saturdays are generally quiet. Four caves take reservations (by phone, fax, or email): Lascaux II (July-Aug only), Grotte de Font-de-Gaume, Abri du Cap Blanc, and Grotte du Pech Merle. The rest are first-come, first-served. Remember that Sarlat's TI and some hotels can reserve cave visits for you (and are likely to be more effective in landing a reservation).

Cave Tips: Read "Cave Art 101" (previous section) to gain a better understanding of what you'll see. Dress warmly, even if it's hot outside. Tours can last up to an hour, and the caves are all a steady, chilly 55 degrees Fahrenheit, with 98 or 99 percent humidity. While on tour, lag behind the group to have the paintings to yourself for a few  moments. Photos, day packs, big purses, and strollers are not allowed. (You can take your camera—without using it—and check the rest at the site.)

Local Guide: Angelika Siméon is a qualified guide eager to teach you about the caves (book ahead; €125/half-day, €215/day, tel. 05 53 35 19 30, mobile 06 24 45 96 28, angelika.simeon @wanadoo.fr).

Les Eyzies-de-Tayac

This single-street town is the touristy hub of a cluster of Cro-Magnon caves, castles, and rivers. It merits a stop for its Prehistory Welcome Center, National Museum of Prehistory, and the Grotte de Font-de-Gaume cave (a 15-minute walk outside town; described later, under "Caves near Les Eyzies-de-Tayac"). Les Eyzies-de-Tayac is world-famous because it's where the original Cro-Magnon man was discovered in 1870. That breakthrough set of bones was found just behind the hotel of Monsieur Magnon—Hôtel le Cro-Magnon, which is in business to this day on the main street in Les Eyzies-de-Tayac. The name "Cro-Magnon" translates as "Mr. Magnon's Hole."

Orientation: Les Eyzies-de-Tayac's **TI** rents bikes and has free Wi-Fi (July-Aug Mon-Sat 9:00-19:00, Sept-June Mon-Sat 10:00-12:00 & 14:00-18:00, closed Sun except June-Sept 10:00-12:00 & 14:00-17:00, tel. 05 53 06 97 05, fax 05 53 06 90 79, www .tourisme-vezere.com). The train station is a level 500 yards from the town center (turn right from the station to get into town).

Sights in Les Eyzies-de-Tayac

Prehistory Welcome Center (Pôle International de la Préhistoire)

Start your prehistoric explorations at the Pôle International de la Préhistoire (PIP) at the Sarlat (east) end of town. This glass-and-concrete facility gives a helpful introduction to this region's important prehistoric sites. The low-slung building houses time-lines, slideshows, and exhibits (all in English) that work together to give visitors a primer on the origins of man. The English-speaking staff is happy to provide maps of the region, and give suggestions on places to visit—and (incredibly) it's all free. Park here (for free), then walk 200 yards into Les Eyzies for its National Museum of Prehistory.

Cost and Hours: Free; mid-May-Sept daily 10:00-18:00; Oct-mid-May Sun-Fri 10:00-17:00, closed Sat; free parking across the street, located east of downtown Les Eyzies-de-Tayac at 30 Rue du Moulin—watch for tall silver *PIP* sign, tel. 05 53 06 06 97, www.pole-prehistoire.com.

▲National Museum of Prehistory (Musée National de Préhistoire)

This modern museum houses more than 18,000 bones, stones, and crude little doodads that were uncovered locally. It takes you

through prehistory—starting 400,000 years ago— and is good preparation for your cave visits. The museum does a great job presenting its exhibits, although you have to work at following the serious teaching style.

Appropriately located on a cliff inhabited by humans for 35,000 years (above Les Eyzies-de-Tayac's TI), the museum's sleek design is intended to help it blend into the surrounding rock. Inside, you'll see many worthwhile exhibits, including videos demonstrating scratched designs, painting techniques, and how spearheads were made. You'll also see full-size models of Cro-Magnon people, and animals that stare at racks of arrowheads.

Cost and Hours: €5; July-Aug daily 9:30-18:30; June and Sept Wed-Mon 9:30-18:00, closed Tue; Oct-May Wed-Mon 9:30-12:00 & 14:00-17:30, closed Tue; tel. 05 53 06 45 45, www.musee-prehistoire-eyzies.fr.

Information: For context, read "Cave Art 101," on page 497, before you go.

Tours: To get the most out of your visit, consider a private or semi-private English-language guided tour of the museum; for details, call 05 53 06 45 65 or email reservation.prehistoire @culture.gouv.fr.

Visiting the Museum: Pick up the museum layout with your ticket. Enter by walking in the footsteps of your ancestors, then greet the 10-year-old *Turkana Boy*, whose bone fragments were found in Kenya in 1984 by Richard Leakey and date from 1.5 million years ago.

The **first floor** up sets the stage, describing human evolution and the fundamental importance of tools. Find the numbered English info sheets provided at regular intervals and match them to exhibit numbers to make sense of what you're seeing.

The **second floor** up is better, and highlights prehistoric artifacts found in France. Some of the most interesting objects you'll see are displayed in this order: a handheld arrow launcher, a 5,000-year-old flat-bottomed boat (pirogue) made from oak, prehistoric fire pits, amazing cavewoman jewelry (including a necklace made of 70 stag teeth—pretty impressive, given that stags only have two teeth each...do the math), engravings on stone (don't miss the unflattering yet impressively realistic female figure), a handheld lamp used to light cave interiors *(lampe à manche)*, and beautiful rock sculptures of horses (much like the paintings at the cave of Abri du Cap Blanc).

Your visit ends on the **cliff edge,** with a Fred Flintstone-style photo op on a stone ledge (through the short tunnel) that some of our ancient ancestors once called home.

Sleeping in and near Les Eyzies-de-Tayac

(€1 = about $1.30, country code: 33)
Train travelers wanting to see the museum and nearby caves will find Les Eyzies-de-Tayac a practical place to sleep, as will drivers interested in rural accommodations.

$$ Auberge Veyret, a 15-minute drive from Les Eyzies-de-Tayac, is a fun farm experience. Mama greets you with nary a word of English, her son cooks, and her daughter (Laurence) and husband (Patrick) do everything else. The rooms are spotless and furnished like Grandma's, but with modern conveniences. Several family-friendly wooden chalets have two rooms, private decks, and kitchenettes. You'll be expected to dine here—and you'd be a fool not to, since dinner includes everything from apéritif to *digestif*, with five courses in between and wine throughout (Db-€60, breakfast-€7.50, half-board-€60/person, lower rates for kids, 4-person chalet-€120 per night plus linen fee, cash only, large pool, en route to Abri du Cap Blanc—look for any sign that says *Veyret,* tel. 05 53 29 68 44, fax 05 53 31 58 28, www.auberge-veyret.com, contact @auberge-veyret.com).

$$ Le Chevrefeuille, halfway between Les Eyzies-de-Tayac and St-Cyprien, is a family-friendly place offering modern comfort in a farm setting. Warm and helpful Ian and Sara Fisk moved to France from England (via Brazil) to raise their children, and expert cook Ian prepares scrumptious dinners several nights a week in season. Five guest rooms and suites in various configurations

DORDOGNE

handle singles to family groups; common areas include a lounge and kitchen area (Db-€65-90, family rooms/suites-€90-120, includes breakfast, pay laundry facilities, cash only, swimming pool and play areas, closed Nov-Easter, tel. 05 53 59 47 97, www.lechevrefeuille.com, info@lechevrefeuille.com). From near Les Eyzies, head south on D-48 about six kilometers, turn right into the small hamlet of Pechboutier, and look for their sign.

$ Madame Bauchet (call her "Nanou") owns the closest rooms to the Les Eyzies-de-Tayac train station, and they're a good, clean value. Madame Bauchet does not speak English, but she's a creative communicator and will pick you up at the station if you ask ahead (Db-€40, Tb/Qb with air-con-€55, breakfast-€6, cash only, closed Nov-March, 200 yards from the station at 40 Avenue de la Préhistoire—look for the brown *Chambres* sign, tel. 05 53 06 97 71, http://chez.nanou.pagespro-orange.fr, bauchetgerard@orange.fr).

Caves near Les Eyzies-de-Tayac

▲▲▲Grotte de Font-de-Gaume

Even if you're not a connoisseur of Cro-Magnon art, you'll dig this cave—the last one in France with prehistoric multicolored (polychrome) paintings still open to the public. (Lascaux—45 minutes down the road—has replica caves for visitors instead.) Access to Font-de-Gaume is restricted, however, so plan ahead. This cave, made millions of years ago—not by a river, but by the geological activity that created the Pyrenees Mountains—is entirely natural.  It contains 15,000-year-old paintings of 230 animals, 82 of which are bison.

On a carefully guided and controlled 100-yard walk, you'll see about 20 red-and-black bison—often in elegant motion—painted with a moving sensitivity. When two animals face each other, one is black, and the other is red. Your guide, with a laser pointer and great reverence, will trace the faded outline of the bison and explain how, 15 millennia ago, cave dwellers used local minerals and the rock's natural contours to give the paintings dimension. Some locals knew about the cave long ago, when there was little interest in prehistory, but the paintings were officially discovered in 1901 by the village schoolteacher.

Cost and Hours: €7.50, free first Sun of the month Nov-May, open mid-May-mid-Sept Sun-Fri 9:30-17:30, mid-Sept-mid-May

Sun-Fri 9:30-12:30 & 14:00-17:30, closed Sat year-round, last tour departs 1.5 hours before closing, no photography or large bags, tel. 05 53 06 86 00, fax 05 53 35 26 18, www.eyzies.monuments-nationaux.fr, fontdegaume@monuments-nationaux.fr. Those planning to also visit the Abri du Cap Blanc cave (described next) can reserve and buy tickets here.

Getting a Ticket: To preserve the precious and fragile art, the number of daily visitors allowed is strictly regulated (96 people per day, in small groups). Of the 96 spots available, all are kept open for those wanting to enter badly enough to come early and wait for a ticket (reservations are no longer possible). Except during winter, you'll want to arrive by 7:30; in winter, you should be OK if you pop in by 9:00. It's worth trying to request an English-language tour (and cross your fingers that space is available for that time). You can drop by the sight at any time during opening hours and get the latest on how early you need to show up to get a ticket; you can also call the sight (10:30-12:00 or 14:30-16:00) to see if spots happen to be open before doing the early-morning bit. You must check in 15 minutes before your tour, or you'll lose your place to the sightseeing vultures waiting to snatch up the spots of late arrivals. You can always join this flock and try to snag a place (some ticket holders don't show).

Drivers who can't get a ticket here should try the caves at Grotte de Rouffignac (see page 509), or aim for the more remote Grotte du Pech Merle, about 30 minutes east of Cahors (see page 531).

Tours: Because English tours are limited (usually Sept-May at 11:00, July-Aug also at 13:00 and 15:00), you'll likely make the visit with a French guide. (In the off-season, the guide may simply poll tour members to arrive at a mutually agreeable language.) The English-info flier is useless, but depending on the guide, the actual tour can be either illuminating and enthusiastic, or little more than pointing out legs, eyes, heads, and bellies of the bison. Don't fret if you're not on an English tour—most important is experiencing the art itself.

Getting There: You'll find the cave at the corner of D-47 and D-48, about a two-minute drive (or a 15-minute walk) east of Les Eyzies-de-Tayac (toward Sarlat). There's easy on-site parking. After checking in at the ticket house, walk 400 yards on an uphill path to the cave entrance (where there's a free, safe bag check and a WC).

▲Abri du Cap Blanc

In this prehistoric cave (a 10-minute drive from Grotte de Font-de-Gaume), early artists used the rock's natural contours to add dimension to their sculpture. Your guide spends the tour in a single stone room explaining the 14,000-year-old carvings. The small museum (with English explanations) helps prepare you for your visit, and the useful English handout describes what the French-speaking guide is talking about. Look for places where the artists smoothed or roughened the surfaces to add depth. Impressive as these carvings are, their subtle majesty is lost on some.

Cost and Hours: €7.50, 17 and under free; includes required 45-minute tour, 7 tours/day, call to verify tour times, cave open mid-May-mid-Sept Sun-Fri 10:00-18:00, mid-Sept-mid-May Sun-Fri 10:00-12:30 & 14:00-17:30, closed Sat year-round, no photos, tel. 05 53 59 60 30. Tickets and reservations are also available at the Font-de-Gaume cave (fontdegaume@monuments-nationaux.fr).

Getting There: Abri du Cap Blanc is well-signed and is located about three kilometers after Grotte de Font-de-Gaume on the road to Sarlat. From the parking lot, walk 200 yards down to the entry. Views of the Château de Commarque (described on page 495) are terrific as you arrive.

More Cro-Magnon Caves

▲▲Lascaux II

The region's—and the world's—most famous cave paintings are at Lascaux, 14 miles north of Sarlat and Les Eyzies-de-Tayac. The Lascaux caves were discovered accidentally in 1940 by four kids and their dog. From 1948 to 1963, more than a million people climbed through this prehistoric wonderland—but these visitors tracked in fungus on their shoes and changed the temperature and humidity with their heavy breathing. In just 15 years, the precious art deteriorated more than during the previous 15,000 years, and the caves were closed. A copy cave—accurate to within one centimeter, reproducing the best 40-yard-long stretch, and showing 90 percent of the paintings found in Lascaux—was opened next to the original in 1983. Guides assure visitors that the original is every bit as crisp and has just as much contrast as the facsimile you'll see.

At impressive Lascaux II, the reindeer, horses, and bulls of Lascaux I are painstakingly reproduced by top artists using the same dyes, tools, and techniques their predecessors did 15,000 years ago. Of course, seeing the real thing at the other caves is important, but come here first (taking one of the scheduled English-language tours) for a great introduction to the region's cave art. Although it feels

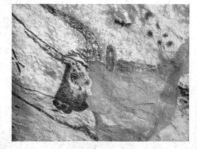

a bit rushed—40 people per tour are hustled through the two-room cave reproductions—the guides are committed to teaching, the paintings are astonishing, and the experience is mystifying. (Forget that they're copies, and enjoy being swept away by the prehistoric majesty of it all.) The cave is a constant 56 degrees year-round, so dress warmly. Pleasant Montignac is worth a wander if you have time to kill.

Cost and Hours: €9.20; July-Aug daily 9:00-20:00; April-June and Sept-Oct daily 9:00-18:00; Nov-Dec and Feb-March Tue-Sun 10:00-12:00 & 14:00-17:30, closed Mon; closed Jan.

Getting Tickets: You'll see Lascaux II with a 40-minute English tour (4/day May-Sept—usually 2 tours in the morning and 2 more in the afternoon, about 2/day off-season, call 05 53 51 96 23 for ticket availability and estimated English tour times, reservations possible July-Aug only). Unless you're visiting in winter (Oct-March), you must buy your ticket before coming to Lascaux; the ticket office is next to the TI in Montignac, five minutes away by car. Deep-blue signs direct drivers to *La Billetterie* in Montignac (follow signs for *Centre-Ville,* then look for *La Billetterie*—don't double-park); Lascaux is well-signed from there. In July and August, tours are usually sold out by 13:00, so book ahead.

Sleeping near Lascaux: **$$$ Château de la Fleunie*** offers regal 15th-century château accommodations surrounded by pastures and mountain goats, the biggest private pool I've seen in France, tennis courts, and a restaurant with *beaucoup d'ambiance* (€29-45 *menus*). Rooms are either in the château or in the modern annex—book ahead to snag a château room (Db-€80-120, bigger Db-€130-150, most around €125, tower room for two-€170-190, extra person-€20, half-pension required July-Aug, 10-minute drive north of Montignac on road to Brive-la-Gaillarde, in Condat-sur-Vézère, tel. 05 53 51 32 74, fax 05 53 50 58 98, www.lafleunie.com, lafleunie@free.fr).

▲▲Grotte de Rouffignac

Rouffignac provides a different experience from other prehistoric caves in this area. Here you'll ride a clunky little train down a giant subterranean riverbed, exploring about half a mile of this six-mile-long gallery. The cave itself was known to locals for decades—hence the graffiti (with dates going back to the 18th century) littering the ceiling—but the 13,000-year-old paintings were discovered only in 1956.

Cost and Hours: €6.50, daily July-Aug 9:00-11:30 & 14:00-18:00, April-June and Sept-Nov 10:00-11:30 & 14:00-17:00, closed Dec-March, one-hour guided tours run 2/hour, no reservations, tel. 05 53 05 41 71, www.grottederouffignac.fr. Dress warmly. It's

DORDOGNE

really crowded only mid-July-August—especially in the afternoons. Weekends tend to be quietest.

Getting There: Grotte de Rouffignac is well-signed from the route between Les Eyzies-de-Tayac and Périgueux; allow 25 minutes from Les Eyzies-de-Tayac.

Visiting the Cave: Your tour likely will be in French (guides may answer questions in English), but here's the gist of what they're saying on the stops of your train ride:

The cave was created by the underground river. It's entirely natural, but it was much shallower before the train-track bed was excavated. As you travel, imagine the motivation and determination of the painters who crawled so deep into this dark and mysterious cave. They left behind their art...and the wonder of people who crawled in centuries later to see it all.

All along the way, you'll see crater-like burrows made by hibernating bears long before the first humans painted here. There are hundreds of them—not because there were so many bears, but because year after year, a few of them would return, preferring to make their own private place to sleep (rather than using some other bear's den). After a long winter nap, bears would have one thing on their mind: Cut those toenails. The walls are scarred with the scratching of bears in need of clippers (look to the right as you ride).

Stop 1: The images of woolly mammoths etched into the walls can be seen only when lit from the side (as your guide will demonstrate). As the rock is very soft here, these were simply gouged out by the artists' fingers.

Stop 2: Look for images of finely detailed rhinoceroses in black paintings. The rock is harder here, so nothing is engraved.

Stop 3: On the left, you'll see woolly mammoths and horses engraved with tools in the harder rock. On the right is the biggest composition of the cave: a herd of peaceful mammoths. A mysterious calcite problem threatens to cover the paintings with ugly white splotches.

Off the Train: When you get off the train, notice how high the original floor was (the bear-crater level), and imagine both the prehistoric makers and viewers of this art crawling back here with pretty lousy flashlight-substitutes. Here, the ceiling is covered with a remarkable gathering of animals. You'll see a fine 16-foot-long horse, a group of mountain goats, and a grandpa mammoth. Art even decorates the walls far down the big, scary hole. When the group chuckles, it's because the guide is explaining how the mammoth with the fine detail (showing a flap of skin over its anus) helped authenticate the paintings: These paintings couldn't be fakes, because no one knew about this anatomical detail until the preserved remains of an actual mammoth were found in Siberian permafrost in modern times. (The discovery explained the painted skin flap, which had long puzzled French prehistorians.)

▲La Roque St-Christophe

Five fascinating terraces carved by the Vézère River have provided shelter to people here for 50,000 years. Although the terraces were inhabited in prehistoric times, there's no prehistoric art on display—the exhibit (except for one small cave) is entirely medieval. The official recorded history goes back to A.D. 976, when people settled here to steer clear of the Viking raiders who'd routinely sail up the river. (Back then, in this part of Europe, the standard closing of a prayer wasn't "amen," but "and deliver us from the Norseman, amen.")

A clever relay of river watchtowers kept an eye out for raiders. When they came, cave dwellers gathered their kids, hauled up their animals (see the big, re-created winch), and pulled up the ladders. Although there's absolutely nothing old here except for the carved-out rock (with holes for beams, carved out of the soft limestone), it's easy to imagine the entire village—complete with butcher, baker, and candlestick-maker—in this family-friendly exhibit. This place is a dream for kids of any age who hold fond tree-house memories.

It's simple to visit: There's a free parking lot across the stream, with picnic tables, a WC, and—adjacent to the babbling brook—a pondside café (providing good salads, omelets, and drinks—the nearby pretty village of St-Léon provides more lunch choices). Borrow the English booklet (or buy it for €2) at the turnstile; stop to take in the picture showing its medieval buildings; and climb through the one-way circuit, which is slippery when damp.

Cost and Hours: €8, daily July-Aug 10:00-20:00, Sept-Dec and Feb-June 10:00-18:00, Jan 14:00-17:00, last entry 45 minutes before closing, lots of steps, eight kilometers north of Les Eyzies-de-Tayac, follow signs to *Montignac,* tel. 05 53 50 70 45. Note that this sight is very near the Maison Forte de Reignac (described on page 496).

▲▲Grottes de Cougnac

Located 23 kilometers south of Sarlat (allow 30 minutes) and three well-signed kilometers north of Gourdon on D-704, this cave holds fascinating rock formations and the oldest (14,000-25,000-year-old) paintings open to the public. Less touristy than other sites, it provides a more intimate look at cave art, as guides take more time

DORDOGNE

to explain the caves and paintings (your guide should give some explanations in English—ask if he or she doesn't).

The 1.5-hour tour begins in a cave where the guide explains the geological formations (you'll learn that it takes 70 years for water to make it from the earth's surface into the cave). From this first cave, you'll return to the fresh air and walk 15 minutes to a second cave—and the paintings you came to see. They are worth the wait. Vivid depictions (about 10) of ibex, mammoths, and giant deer *(Megaloceros)*, as well as a few nifty representations of humans, are outlined in rust or black. The rendering of the giant deer's antlers is exquisite, and many paintings use the cave's form to add depth and movement.

Because access is first-come, first-served (and groups are limited to 25), try to arrive first thing (ideally 10 minutes before opening). In the off-season, be careful not to arrive too close to the last tour before lunch (11:30)—if that tour is full, you'll have to wait for the 14:30 departure. The caves are damp, so expect a few drops on your head (hats or hoods help). English-only tours happen on occasion (call ahead to check times); you can also buy a €5 English booklet about the site.

Cost and Hours: €7.50; these hours correspond to first/last tour times: July-Aug daily 10:00-18:00; April-June and Sept daily 10:00-11:30 & 14:30-17:00; Oct Mon-Sat 14:00-16:00, closed Sun; closed Nov-March; free WCs, beverages sold on-site, tel. 05 65 41 47 54, www.grottesdecougnac.com.

Oradour-sur-Glane

Located two hours north of Sarlat and 27 kilometers west of Limoges, Oradour-sur-Glane is one of the most powerful sights in France—worth ▲▲▲. French schoolchildren know this town well; most make a pilgrimage here. **Village des Martyrs,** as it is known, was machine-gunned and burned on June 10, 1944, by Nazi troops. The Nazis were either seeking revenge for the killing of one of their officers

(by French Resistance fighters in a neighboring village) or simply terrorizing the populace in preparation for the upcoming Allied invasion (this was four days after D-Day). With cool attention to detail, the Nazis methodically rounded up the entire population of 642 townspeople. The women and children were herded into the town church, where they were tear-gassed and machine-gunned. Plaques mark the place where the town's men were grouped and executed. The town was then set on fire, its victims left under a blanket of ashes. Today, the ghost town, left untouched for almost 70 years, greets every pilgrim who enters with only one English word: Remember.

Cost and Hours: Entering the village is free, but the museum costs €8 (audioguide-€2, ample English explanations posted). Both are open daily mid-May-mid-Sept 9:00-19:00, off-season until 17:00 or 18:00, last visit one hour before closing, tel. 05 55 43 04 30, www.oradour.org. Allow two hours for your visit.

Getting There: Oradour-sur-Glane is well-signed off A-20 for drivers coming from the Dordogne. Those driving from the Loire should take A-10 to Poitiers, then follow signs for *Limoges*.

Taking public transport here requires dedication. Bus #12 connects Limoges with Oradour in 30 minutes (4/day, 15-minute walk from Limoges train station to bus stop on Place Winston Churchill). Consider a taxi. Limoges is a stop on an alternative train route between Amboise and Sarlat (Limoges TI tel. 05 55 34 46 87).

Touring Oradour-sur-Glane: Follow *Village des Martyrs* signs to the parking lot and start at the rust-colored **underground museum** (Centre de la Mémoire), which provides a good social and political context for the event. Thorough English explanations are posted for every exhibit (though the audioguide makes it easier to take in). The exhibits convey a good sense of daily life in Oradour before June 10, 1944, and explain SS terror tactics. You'll see home movies of locals before the attack and disturbing footage of similar events elsewhere. English subtitles are scant in the 12-minute film shown in the theater, but (with the help of audioguide translations) its message is powerful.

From the museum, join other hushed visitors to walk the length of Oradour's **main street,** past gutted, charred buildings in the shade of lush trees. *Lieu de Supplice* signs show where locals were tormented. The plaques on the buildings provide the names and occupations of the people who lived there (*laine* means wool, *sabotier* is a maker of wooden shoes, *couturier* is a tailor, *quincaillerie* is a hardware store, *cordonnier* is shoe repair, *menuisier* is a carpenter, and *tissus* are fabrics). You'll pass streetcar tracks, several cafés, and a hôtel-restaurant. This village was not so different from those you have enjoyed on your trip. Visit the **church,** with its bullet-pocked altar, and walk into the **cemetery** where most lives ended on that June day. The names of all who died in the massacre are etched into the rear wall. Across from the cemetery, find the **underground memorial** and see cases with rusted toys, broken crucifixes, dishes, and town mementos.

St-Emilion and Bordeaux Wine Country

Two hours due west of Sarlat and just 40 minutes from Bordeaux, St-Emilion is another pretty face just waiting to flirt with you.

Unlike other French lookers, this one seduces in English—the historic presence of British interest in the wine industry has given the town an almost bilingual feel. It's an easy place for Anglophones.

Carved like an amphitheater into the bowl of a limestone hill, St-Emilion's tidy streets connect a few inviting squares with heavy cobbles and scads of well-stocked wine shops. There's little to do in this town of well-heeled and well-wined residents other than enjoy the setting, and, *bien sûr*, sample the local sauce. Wine has been good to St-Emilion, though it accounts for barely 5 percent of Bordeaux's famous red-wine production. Also try a tasty homemade *macaron*, sold at many shops. Sunday is market day in St-Emilion.

Orientation to St-Emilion

Tourist Information

The enterprising TI is a critical stop, at the top of the town on Place des Créneaux, across from the town's highest bell tower. It's located in a onetime abbey and connected to pretty cloisters (these go ignored by most tourists—find the door in the rear of the TI). The TI is well-armed with good information in English (daily mid-June-mid-Sept 9:30-19:00, mid-Sept-mid-June 9:30-12:30 & 13:30-18:30 except Nov-March closes at 18:00, Place Pioceau, tel. 05 57 55 28 28, fax 05 57 55 28 29, www.saint-emilion-tourisme.com, st-emilion.tourisme@wanadoo.fr).

The TI has information on St-Emilion's few sights and has a helpful booklet on *chambres d'hôtes*. Ask about English-language **tours** of the city, the underground church, and the vineyards (vineyard and underground tours described later, under "Sights in St-Emilion"). The TI also rents **bikes,** and has helpful English-language handouts outlining several self-guided cycling routes, as well as themed, well-marked **walking routes** through the vineyards.

Arrival in St-Emilion

By Train: It's a 20-minute walk through the vineyards from St-Emilion's train station into town; taxis don't wait at the station, but you can call one (see "Helpful Hints—Taxi and Local Guide," below; 6 trains/day Mon-Fri from Bordeaux, 4/day Sat-Sun). You can also get off in Libourne (five miles away, with better train service including TGV trains, and easy car rental). From Libourne you can catch a cab (€25) or take an infrequent bus to St-Emilion (3/day, June-Sept only) from the bus station *(gare routière)* next to the train station.

By Car: If you're coming from Sarlat, take the autoroute from Périgueux and save 40 minutes over the local roads. If coming from the Loire, take the autoroute to Poitiers, then follow N-10 south toward Angoulême, then Bordeaux. You'll find parking (€2/hour) in lots at the upper end of the town, or along the wall.

Helpful Hints

Taxi and Local Guide: Jolly **Robert Faustin,** who drives a comfortable station wagon and speaks enough English, can advise you and arrange visits to wineries (he knows them all), and is an enjoyable person to spend time with (tel. & fax 05 57 25 17 59, mobile 06 77 75 36 64, www.taxi-lussac-winetour-st emilion.com, robert.faustin@wanadoo.fr).

Tourist Train: A *petit train* toots you from St-Emilion through vineyards and back in 35 minutes (€6.50, 10/day, stop is behind TI by vineyards).

Sights in St-Emilion

Wine-Tasting—They've been making wine in St-Emilion for over 1,800 years—making it the oldest wine-producing area in the Bordeaux region. Blending Cabernet Franc and Merlot grapes, St-Emilion wines are also the most robust in Bordeaux. About 60 percent of the grapes you see are Merlot. To ensure a smooth visit, read "French Wine-Tasting 101" on page 46 before you go.

Maison du Vin: Located next to the TI, this is a fair starting point for oenophiles, where you get an introduction to wine, beginning with an hour-long video (played on the hour, English subtitles). In the next room, read the description of the wine-making process and sniff cool aluminum cylinders that let you guess at elements (musk, blackberry, currant) in the wines before you taste them (free, daily 9:30-12:30 & 14:00-18:30, tel. 05 57 55 50 55, www.maisonduvinsaintemilion.com, maisonduvin@vins -saint-emilion.com). They also offer 1.5-hour wine-tasting classes for €25 (mid-July-mid-Sept daily at 11:00, register in advance).

Château Visits and Minivan Excursions: The TI can send

you to a tasting at selected châteaux (no charge, but a tasting fee may apply) and offers a minivan tour through the vineyards—in English and French—that includes a tasting at one château (€14, 1.5-2 hours, English tour usually departs from the TI at 14:00, usually May-mid Sept only; verify times).

Wine Shops: St-Emilion's many wine shops offer a free and easy way to sample the array of local wines. Keepers of small shops greet visitors in flawless English, with a central tasting table, maps of the vineyards, and several open bottles (most shops open daily 10:00-19:00, until 20:00 in summer). And though it's hard to distinguish these classy wine stores from each other, you'll be pleasantly surprised at the passionate shopkeepers' welcoming attitude. Americans may represent only about 15 percent of the visitors, but we buy 40 percent of their wine. Although the owners hope that you'll buy a bottle (particularly if you taste many wines), and shipping is easy (except to California and Texas), there's no fee for the tastings.

Vignobles & Châteaux is a polished wine shop offering wine-tasting classes at their "Ecole de Vin" upstairs (about €30 for 1.5-hour class, offered 1/week, more extensive classes and visits to prestigious wineries available; 4 Rue du Clocher, tel. 05 57 24 61 01, www.vignobleschateaux.fr).

Cercle des Oenophiles is an easygoing place where you can taste wines and tour nearby cellars storing more than 400,000 bottles of wine (free, daily 10:00-19:00, at 12 Rue Guadat, tel. 05 57 74 45 55).

Views over St-Emilion—You can climb the **bell tower** in front of the TI for a good view (€1.25, give ID at TI in exchange for the key, open daily same hours as TI), but the view is best from the **Tour du Roy** several blocks below (€1.25, Mon-Fri 14:00-18:00, Sat-Sun 10:00-18:00).

Tours of St-Emilion—The TI offers two guided tours in St-Emilion: an underground tour and a city walk. The somewhat interesting 45-minute **underground tour** makes three stops: the catacombs (sorry, no bones); the monolithic church, which literally rocks below; and Trinity Chapel. Learn who St. Emilion was, and be impressed that it took dedicated Benedictine monks 300 years to dig this monolithic church out of one big rock (9th-12th centuries). You'll also learn that there are about 125 miles of underground tunnels in the St-Emilion area. Originally dug as quarries, they're ideal for wine storage today. The tour is mandatory if you want to see these sights. If time's limited and you can't get on an English tour, skip this (€7, English tour daily at 14:00, more in French, thorough English handout given on French tours). The **city walking tour** takes 1.5 hours and covers aboveground sights and the back streets of St-Emilion (€12, daily at 11:00).

Quickie Vineyard Loop by Car or Bike—This 10-kilometer loop can be done in 20 minutes if driving, and in two hours if pedaling. Leave the upper end of St-Emilion on D-243E-1 and head to St-Christophe des Bardes. Pass through the village (direction: St-Genès), then follow signs to the right to *St. Laurent des Combes*. Joyride your way down through hillsides of vines, then find signs looping back to St-Emilion's lower end via D-245 and D-122.

Sleeping in St-Emilion

(€1 = about $1.30, country code: 33)
There are no cheap hotels in St-Emilion. *Chambres d'hôtes* offer a better value. Hotel prices skyrocket during the VinExpo festival at the end of June, and during harvest time (late Sept).

Hotels
The first two places are a few doors apart, at the upper end of the city.

$$$ Au Logis des Remparts* offers top comfort in tasteful rooms, plus a pool and a tranquil garden with vineyards to touch (standard Db-€105, nicer Db with bathtubs-€150, Db with garden views-€170-190, suites-€250-400, air-con, pay Wi-Fi, book ahead for limited on-site parking, tel. 05 57 24 70 43, fax 05 57 74 47 44, www.logisdesremparts.com, contact@logisdesremparts.com).

$$ L'Auberge de la Commanderie welcomes visitors with a neon entry and Modernist decor in its two buildings—a main hotel and an annex. Run by an amiable owner, the hotel's 16 rooms are well-maintained. Rooms in the main building come with interesting murals; annex rooms have more subtle stone walls and more space (Db-€85-105, Tb-€120-150, 2-room apartment for up to 4 people-€170, closed Jan-Feb, air-con or ceiling fans, elevator, Internet access and Wi-Fi, free parking, tel. 05 57 24 70 19, fax 05 57 74 44 53, www.aubergedelacommanderie.com, contact @aubergedelacommanderie.com).

Chambres d'Hôtes
$$$ La Maison d'Aline is a peaceful and central place with three good rooms run by calming Marie-Christine. Each of the traditional rooms has a view over the village (Db-€110-150, includes breakfast, 2 blocks past L'Auberge de la Commanderie, across from Cordeliers winery at 7 Rue Port Brunet, tel. 05 57 24 65 47, mobile 06 23 77 38 90, www.alinebb.com, mcclemot@alinebb.com).

$$ Le Logis de la Tourelle rents five simple-but-spacious rooms at the lower end of town for fair rates (Db-€70-80, on Rue Guadet, tel. 05 57 24 79 65, mobile 06 80 25 14 51, restaurant.lacote braisee@wanadoo.fr). Check in at La Côte Braisée restaurant at

DORDOGNE

3 Rue du Tertre de la Tente, and they'll escort you to the rooms several blocks away.

Near St-Emilion

The vineyards that surround St-Emilion hide many good-value *chambres d'hôtes*. Places below the town are scattered among the villages and are hard to find: Get good directions before you go. You can meander the villages just outside St-Emilion's upper entry point, then pick the place you prefer (the village of Montagne has many good *chambres d'hôtes*). Or stop by the TI for a long list with small photos (no room-booking fee).

$$ Moulin la Grangère, dreamily wrapped in hills of vineyards, offers the perfect haven from which to appreciate the Bordeaux wine country.  Charming Marie-Annick and Alain Noel rent three modern rooms in a well-renovated, blue-shuttered 19th-century mill with manicured gardens, a big pool, a *pétanque* court, and sublime scenery in every direction (Db-€80, Tb/Qb-€100, €10 less for stays of 2 nights or more, includes breakfast, cash only, Internet access and Wi-Fi, tel. 05 57 24 72 51, www.moulin-la-grangere.com, alain.noel25@orange.fr). It's 10 minutes from St-Emilion, near St-Christophe des Bardes (head up D-243E-1 from its intersection with D-245, then look for the small *Moulin la Grangère* signs, on the left in about 200 yards).

Eating in St-Emilion

Skip the cafés lining the street by the TI and instead head to the melt-in-your-chair square, Place du Marché.

Amelia-Canta Café is *the* happening spot on Place du Marché for lunch or dinner on a warm evening. It has café fare, salads, and veggie options (€16-25 *menus*, daily March-Nov, 2 Place de l'Eglise Monolithe, tel. 05 57 74 48 03).

L'Envers du Décor wine bar-bistro is about fun, wine, and food—in that order. It's perfect for this wine-happy town: The restaurant's tabletops are wooden wine crates, and the floor is paved with cool blue-and-brown tiles. Meat dishes are their forte (lunch *menus* from €19, dinner *menus* from €30, daily, a few doors from the TI at 11 Rue du Clocher, tel. 05 57 74 48 31).

Logis de la Cadène has street appeal with a pleasing patio terrace, a warm interior, and fine, traditional cuisine (€25-32 *menus*, closed Sun-Mon, just above Amelia-Canta Café at 3 Place du Marché du Bois, tel. 05 57 24 71 40).

L'Huitrier Pie, a local favorite, serves up the town's best oysters, fish, and other seafood. Cool terraces flank the restaurant (€33 standard *menu*, €50 tasting *menu*, closed Tue-Wed, at the lower/south end of town on 11 Rue de la Porte Bouqueyre, tel. 05 57 24 69 71).

The Overlooked Eastern Dordogne

Many find this remote, less-visited section of the Dordogne (Quercy *région*) even more beautiful than the countryside around Sarlat. Its undisputed highlight is the pilgrimage town of Rocamadour, but there's so much more to see. For a good introduction to this area, follow this self-guided driving tour connecting Sarlat and Rocamadour.

Self-Guided Driving Tour

Welcome to the Eastern Dordogne

For the most scenic route from Sarlat to Rocamadour, follow the Dordogne River heading east, driving about an hour upriver from Souillac, to connect these worthwhile stops: Martel, Carennac, Château de Castelnau-Bretenoux, Loubressac, and Autoire. Rocamadour lies a short hop south of this area, as do the Tom Sawyer-like Gouffre de Padirac caves (both described later in this chapter). Allow 45 minutes from Sarlat to Souillac, then 15 minutes to Martel, and 20 minutes to Carennac (Château de Castelnau-Bretenoux and Loubressac are within 10 minutes of Carennac). From Carennac, it's 25 minutes south to Rocamadour. On Mondays, these towns are very quiet, and most shops are closed.

• *From Souillac's center, take D-803 east to...*

Martel: This well-preserved medieval town of 1,500 souls and seven towers offers a good chance to stretch your legs and stock up on picnic items (market days are Wed and Sat on the atmospheric Place des Consuls). Neither on a river nor crowning a hilltop, Martel is largely overlooked by tourists. Pick up a copy of the TI's well-done walking-tour pamphlet (in English, TI closed 12:00-13:00 and Sun), and enjoy the handsome pedestrian area lined with historic buildings. The walking tour starts at Martel's terrific main square (Place des Consuls)—with a medieval covered market and reasonable lunch cafés—and connects the town's seven

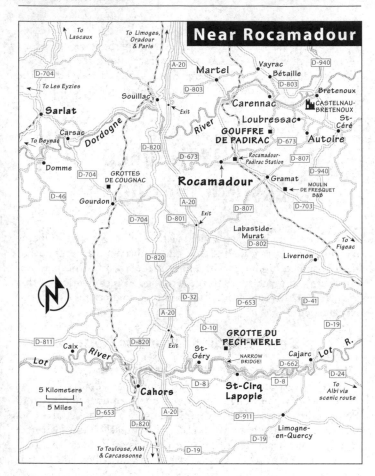

Near Rocamadour

DORDOGNE

towers and the fortress-like church of St. Maur. The town is said to be named for Charles Martel, Charlemagne's grandfather and role model, who stopped the Moors' advance into northern France in 732.

• *From Martel, continue east on D-803 toward Vayrac and Bétraille, then cross the Dordogne on D-20 to find...*

Carennac: This jumble of peaked roofs and half-timbered walls, lassoed between the river and D-20, demands to be photographed. Park along D-20 and wander through the village to the river on foot. Find the fortified Prieuré St.-Pierre. Explore this evocative church and examine its exquisitely carved tympanum. It was built as an outpost of the Cluny Abbey in the 10th century, and then fortified in the 1500s during the French Wars of Religion (a series of civil wars between Catholic and Protestant factions). For a good lunch or dinner inside or out, head to **Le Prieuré**

Restaurant (closed Mon except July-Aug, across from the church, tel. 05 65 39 76 74). Cross the small bridge behind the restaurant for more village views.

• *From here, head east on D-30, tracking the Dordogne River. On the left you'll pass the splendidly situated and once-powerful military castle called...*

Château de Castelnau-Bretenoux: This château has views in all directions and a few well-furnished rooms. The reddish-golden stone and massive 12th-century walls make an impression, as does its height—almost 800 feet. Consider detouring for a closer look, but skip the interior unless you're a castle-holic. You'll be required to take a 30-minute, French-only tour of the seven furnished rooms, but then you're free to wander (€7.50, €2 to park; July-Aug daily 10:00-19:00; Sept-June daily 10:00-12:30 & 14:00-18:30; Oct-March Wed-Mon 10:00-12:30 & 14:00-17:30, closed Tue; last entry one hour before closing, tel. 05 65 10 98 00).

• *From D-30, turn right on D-14 and then left on D-118. You'll come to...*

Loubressac: Mystical Loubressac hangs atop a beefy ridge, with outlandish views and a gaggle of adorable homes at its eastern end. If this is not the most beautiful village in France, I'd like to see the one that is. Park along the central green (with a small grocery store), take a loop stroll through the village, and consider a *café* or meal at the *très* traditional and reasonable **Hôtel Lou Cantou****. Or, if you're really on vacation, spend the night, have dinner (restaurant closed Fri and Sun nights), and let owner Marie-Claude take good care of you (Db-€56-70, half with valley views, Wi-Fi, tel. 05 65 38 20 58, fax 05 65 38 25 37, lou_cantou@orange.fr).

• *From here it's a short hop on D-118 to lovely little...*

Autoire: The *other* most beautiful village in France, this one lies a few minutes beyond Loubressac. Visit and decide which village is fairest of them all.

• *From here you can follow signs to Gramat, then on to Rocamadour.*

Rocamadour

An hour east of Sarlat, this historic town with its dramatic rock-face setting is a ▲▲ sight after dark. Once one of Europe's top pilgrimage sites, today it feels more tacky than spiritual. Still, if you can get into the medieval mindset, its peaceful and dramatic setting—combined with the memory of the countless thousands of faithful who trekked from all over Europe to worship here—overwhelms the kitschy tourism, and it becomes a nice (short) stop.

Those who visit only during the day might wonder why they bothered, as there's little to do here except climb the pilgrims' steps (with people who aren't pilgrims) to a few churches, and then stare at the view. Travelers who arrive late and spend the night enjoy fewer crowds—and a floodlit spectacle. To scenically connect Rocamadour and Sarlat, follow the driving tour outlined in the previous section.

Orientation to Rocamadour

Rocamadour has three basic levels, connected by steps or elevators. The bottom level (La Cité Médiévale, or simply La Cité) is a long, single pedestrian street lined with shops and restaurants. The sanctuary level (Cité Religieuse) is up 223 holy steps. Its centerpiece is a church with seven chapels gathered around a small square. A switchback trail, the Way of the Cross (Chemin de la Croix), leads to the top level (called L'Hospitalet) and château (public access to ramparts only) that crowns the cliff and offers a great view and free parking. For most, the goal is the sanctuary at midlevel.

Tourist Information

There are two TIs in Rocamadour (www.rocamadour.com): the glassy TI that most drivers come to first, in the village of **L'Hospitalet** above Rocamadour (daily July-Aug 9:30-19:00, April-June and Sept-Oct 10:00-12:00 & 14:00-18:00, Nov-March until 17:00); and another on the level pedestrian street in **La Cité Médiévale** (roughly the same hours, tel. 05 65 33 22 00). On the same pedestrian street, you'll find an ATM next to the post office (PTT).

Arrival in Rocamadour

By Train: Five daily trains (transfer in Brive-la-Gaillarde) leave you 2.5 miles from the village at an unstaffed station. It's a €10 taxi ride to Rocamadour (see "Helpful Hints—Taxi," next page).

By Car: Drivers can park above or below the town, but I prefer the upper lot, which is easier and cheaper. From the upper town, follow *P Château* signs and drive all the way to the western end of town until you see the *ascenseur incliné* (elevator), where the parking is free. Walk or take the elevator down (see below).

To park below the town, follow signs to *La Cité* and *Parking de la Vallée*. Walk 15 minutes into La Cité Médiévale, or take the little tourist train (4/hour, €3.50 round-trip); then either climb the stairs or take the elevator to the sanctuary level.

DORDOGNE

Helpful Hints

Elevators: For pilgrims preferring not to climb the stairs or hike the Way of the Cross, this vertical town has two handy elevators. The *ascenseur cité* (€2 one-way, €3 round-trip) links the lower town with the sanctuary, and the *ascenseur incliné* (€2.50 one-way, €4.10 round-trip) connects the church with the château and parking lot at the top. If you buy a round-trip, keep the receipt for your return ride. Each elevator is run like any other: on demand (push the button if no one is there). Managed by two different companies, they're within 50 yards of one another at the sanctuary level.

Views After Dark: If you're staying overnight, don't miss the views of a floodlit Rocamadour from the opposite side of the valley (doable by car, on foot, or by tourist train; see below). It's best as a half-hour (round-trip) stroll. From the town's southeast end (Porte du Figuier), follow the quiet road down, cross the bridge, and head up the far side of the gorge opposite the town. Leave before it gets dark, as the floodlighting is best at twilight. Wear light-colored or reflective clothing, or take a flashlight—it's a dark road with no shoulder. Within the town, climb the steps to just below the sanctuary, and consider a drink with a view at the Hôtel Sainte Marie.

Tourist Train: You can take the cheesy but convenient *petit train* to enjoy the view after dark (runs evenings only), complete with 50 other travelers, a bad sound system blaring worthless commentary in four languages, a flashing yellow light, and a rooftop crimping your view (€5, 30-minute round-trip, 2 trips/evening, departures starting at twilight—the first one is by far the best, check at the TI or call 05 65 33 67 84). Or you can walk the same route in 30 minutes (see above), and take much better photos.

Small Grocery Store: It's on Place de l'Europe next to the hotel Amadour, in the upper city (open daily 8:00-20:00).

Taxi: Call 06 73 44 79 98 or 06 86 18 71 55.

Sights in Rocamadour

In the Upper Town (L'Hospitalet)

If you're coming from Sarlat or from the north, your first view of Rocamadour is the same as the one seen by medieval pilgrims—at the top of the gorge from the hamlet of **L'Hospitalet,** named for the hospitality it gave pilgrims. Stop here for the sweeping views (a right turn takes you to the *Château* parking lot described above; a left leads to the glassy TI and the lower Cité). Imagine the impact of this sight in the 13th century, as awestruck pilgrims

Rocamadour's Religious History

Rocamadour was once one of Europe's top pilgrimage sights. Today tourists replace the pilgrims, enjoying a dramatically situated one-street town under a pretty forgettable church—all because of a crude little thousand-year-old black statue of the Virgin Mary.

Of France's roughly 200 "Black Virgins," this was perhaps the most venerated. Black Virgins date to the end of the pagan era—when Europe was forcefully being Christianized. In Europe's pagan religions, black typically symbolized fertility and motherhood. For newly converted (and still reluctant) pagans, it was easier to embrace the Virgin if she was black.

A thousand years ago, many Europeans expected the world to end, and pilgrimages became immensely popular. About that time, the first pilgrims came here—to a little cave in a cliff over a gorge created by the Alzou River—to pray to a crude statue of a Black Virgin. Then, in 1166, a remarkably intact body was found beneath the threshold of the troglodyte chapel. People assumed this could only be a hermit (certainly a saintly hermit) who had lived in this cave. He was given the name Amadour (servant of Mary), and the place was named Rocamadour (the rock of the servant of Mary).

Suddenly, this humble site was on the map. The Benedictines moved in to develop the spot, building a church over the cave. Like Mont St-Michel, a single-street town sprouted at its base to

first gazed on the sanctuary cut from the limestone cliffs. It was through L'Hospitalet's fortified gate that medieval pilgrims gained access to the "Holy Way," the path leading from L'Hospitalet to Rocamadour.

Château—Dating from the 14th century, the original château fortified a bluff that was an easy base for bandits to attack the wealthy church below. Today's structure is a 19th-century private house that was transformed into a reception spot for pilgrims. It's *privé* unless you are a pilgrim (in which case you can sleep here). All it offers tourists is a short rampart walk for a grand view (not worth the €2 fee; turnstile requires exact change).

The zigzag **Way of the Cross** (Chemin de la Croix—a path marked with 14 Stations of the Cross, with a chapel for each station) gives religious purpose to the 15-minute hike between the château and the sanctuary below.

Grotte Préhistorique des Merveilles—This cave, located next to the upper TI, has the usual geological formations and a handful of small, blurred cave paintings. It's of no interest if you have seen or will see other prehistoric caves—its sole advantages are that it requires little effort to visit (with only about 10 steps down), and handle the needs of its growing pilgrim hordes. During Europe's great age of pilgrimages (12th and 13th centuries), the greatest of pilgrims (St. Louis, St. Dominique, Richard the Lionhearted, and so on) all trekked to this spot to pray. Rocamadour became a powerful symbol of faith and hope.

During the 14th-century, up to 8,000 people lived in Rocamadour, earning their living off of the pilgrims—who arrived in numbers of up to 20,000 a day. But with the 16th-century Wars of Religion and the Age of Enlightenment (in the 18th century), pilgrimages declined...and so did Rocamadour.

During the Romantic Age of the 19th century, pilgrimages were again in vogue, and Rocamadour rebounded. Local bishops rebuilt the château above the sanctuary, making it a pilgrims' reception center, and connecting it to the church with the Way of the Cross. (Most of the current buildings in the Sanctuary of Our Lady of Rocamadour date from the 19th century.) But there hasn't been a bona fide miracle here for eight centuries...and that's not good for the pilgrimage business.

Since the mid-20th century, Rocamadour has become more of a tourist attraction, and today, its 650 inhabitants earn a living off its million visitors a year. The vast majority of those who climb the holy steps to the sanctuary are tourists—more interested in burning calories than incense.

the guide can answer questions in English on the 40-minute tour.

Cost and Hours: €6, daily July-Aug 9:30-19:00, April-June and Sept 10:00-12:00 & 14:00-18:00, Oct until 17:00, closed Nov-March, decent handout available, tel. 05 65 33 67 92, www.grotte-des-merveilles.com.

In the Lower Town (La Cité Médiévale)

Rocamadour's town is basically one long street traversing the cliff below the sanctuary. For eight centuries it has housed, fed, and sold souvenirs to the site's countless visitors. There's precious little here other than tacky trinket shops, but I enjoy popping into the **Galerie le Vieux Pressoir** (named for its 13th-century walnut millstone). It fills a medieval vaulted room with the fine art of a talented couple: Richard Begyn and Veronique Guinard.

Of Rocamadour's 11 original **gates,** seven survive (designed to control the pilgrim crowds). In the 14th century, as many as 20,000 people a day from all over Europe would converge on this spot. From the western end of town, 223 steps lead up to the church at the sanctuary level. Traditionally, pilgrims kneel on each and pray an "Ave Maria" to Our Lady.

DORDOGNE

Between the Upper and Lower Towns (La Cité Religieuse)

These sights form the heart of your vertical sightseeing. From the **upper town,** descend the Way of the Cross path, or take the elevator. From the **lower town,** ride the elevator up or climb the steps (as pilgrims once did), passing a plaque listing key medieval pilgrims, such as St. Bernard, St. Dominique, and St. Louis (the only French king to become a saint; he brought the Crown of Thorns to Paris and had Sainte-Chapelle constructed to house it). Either way, your destination will be signed *Sanctuaires* (free, open daily generally 8:00-19:00).

▲▲**Sanctuary of Our Lady of Rocamadour**—Stand in the small square with the cliff to your left, and look up to the open door of the Church of St. Saveur. Though the buildings originated much earlier, most of what you see was rebuilt in the 19th century. Crammed onto a ledge on a cliff, the church couldn't follow the standard floor plan, so its seven chapels surround the square (called the *parvis*) rather than the church. The bishop's palace is behind you and to your right, and houses a gift shop selling various pilgrimage mementos, including modern versions of the medallions that pilgrims prized centuries ago as proof of their visit (€11 for a tiny one). The two most historic chapels are to your left on either side of the steps.

Walk up the flight of steps to the cliff, where a tomb is cut into the rock. This is where the miraculously preserved body of St. Amadour was found in 1166. Places of pilgrimage do better with multiple miracles, so, along with its Black Virgin and the miracle of St. Amadour's body (see sidebar on page 524), Rocamadour has the **Sword of Roland.** The rusty sword of Charlemagne's nephew sticks in the cliffside, above Amadour's tomb (to the right, about where the church roof meets the cliff). According to medieval sources, Roland was about to die in battle, but the great warrior didn't want his sword to fall into enemy hands. He hurled it from the far south of France, and it landed here—stuck miraculously into the Rocamadour cliffs just above the Black Virgin. (The sword is clearly from the 18th century, but never mind.)

St. Michael's Chapel is built around the original cave to your left (open only to pilgrims, with little to see inside). To your right, the **Chapel of the Virgin** (Chapelle Notre-Dame) is the focal point for pilgrims. Step inside. Sitting above the altar is the much-venerated Black Virgin, a 12th-century statue (covered with a thin plating of blackened silver—see sidebar on page 524) that depicts Mary presenting Jesus to the world. The oldest thing in the sanctuary—from the ninth century—is a simple rusted bell hanging from the ceiling. The suspended sailboat models are a reminder that sailors relied on Mary for safe passage.

DORDOGNE

The adjacent **Church of St. Saveur** is the sanctuary's main place of worship. A copy of the Black Virgin is displayed on the rear wall to give visitors a closer look. The rebuilt wooden balcony overhead was for the monks. Imagine attending a Mass here in centuries past, when pilgrims filled the church and monks lined the balconies. While Rocamadour's church seems more like a tourist attraction, it remains a sacred place of worship. A sign reminds tourists "to admire, to contemplate, to pray. You're welcome to respectfully visit." A bulletin board on the wall usually displays fliers for pilgrimages to Lourdes or Santiago de Compostela. Rocamadour has been both a key destination and staging point for pilgrims for centuries.

From here you can walk under the Church of St. Saveur and find the Way of the Cross (Chemin de la Croix) and elevators up *(Château par ascenseur)* or down *(La Cité par ascenseur)*.

Near Rocamadour

▲**Gouffre de Padirac**—Twenty minutes from Rocamadour is the huge sinkhole of Padirac, with its underground river and miles of stalagmites and stalactites (but no cave art). Though it's an impressive cave, if you've seen caves already, it's slow in comparison, with an insufficient payoff (lots of climbing and not much English). But the mechanics of the visit are easy, and there's not much to communicate anyway. Here's the drill: After paying, hike the stairs (with big views of the sinkhole—a round shaft about 100 yards wide and deep), or ride the elevator to the river level. Line up and wait for your boat. Pack into the boat with about a dozen others for the slow row past a fantasy world of hanging cave formations. Get out and hike a big circle with your group and guide, enjoying lots of caverns, underground lakes, and mighty stalagmites and stalactites. Get back on the boat and retrace your course. Two elevators zip you back to the sunlight. The visit takes 1.5 hours (crowds make it take longer in summer, when I'd skip it). Dress warmly.

Cost and Hours: €10, reserve online at least 48 hours ahead and save lots of waiting, daily July-Aug 9:30-20:30, April-June and Sept-early Nov 9:30-18:00, closed early Nov-March, tel. 05 65 33 64 56, www.gouffre-de-padirac.com. For a knickknack Padirac, don't miss the shop.

Sleeping in Rocamadour

(€1 = about $1.30, country code: 33)

Hotels are a deal here. Those in the upper La Cité (near L'Hospitalet) have views down to Rocamadour and easier parking, but the spirit of St. Amadour is more present below, in the medieval city (which I prefer). Every hotel—including the ones I

DORDOGNE

recommend—has a restaurant where they'd like you to dine.

$ Hôtel Belvédère**, in La Cité Religieuse, has 17 well-maintained, modern, and appealing rooms, five of which have views over Rocamadour, and seven of which have valley views (rooms #14-18 have best views, Db with no view-€65, Db with view-€77, tel. 05 65 33 63 25, fax 05 65 33 69 25, www.hotel-le-belvedere.fr, lebelvedere-rocamadour@orange.fr).

$ Hôtel-Restaurant le Terminus des Pèlerins**, at the western end of the pedestrian street in La Cité Medievale, has immaculate, comfortable rooms with wood furnishings; the best have balconies and face the valley. Helpful owner Geneviève was born in this hotel (Db-€56, Db with view and balcony-€74, Tb/Qb-€82, tel. 05 65 33 62 14, fax 05 65 33 72 10, www.terminus-des-pelerins .com, contact@terminus-des-pelerins.com).

Near Rocamadour: **$$ Moulin de Fresquet** is simply idyllic. Here gracious Gérard and his wife, Claude, have lovingly restored an ancient mill in a lush, park-like setting. The five antique-furnished rooms come with wood beams, oodles of character, lovely terraces, chaise lounges, and a duck pond (with at least 50 ducks for pets, not for dinner). If you're really on vacation, stay here... and if Claude is cooking, eat here (dinner with wine-€28, daily except Thu). Book well ahead (Db-€69-99, Db suite-€118, Tb suite-€138, includes breakfast, cash only, closed Nov-March, in Gramat, tel. 05 65 38 70 60, mobile 06 08 85 09 21, fax 05 65 33 60 13, www.moulindefresquet.com, info@moulindefresquet.com). Go to Gramat, then follow signs toward *Figeac.* The *chambres d'hôte* is well-signed at the east end of Gramat, at a big roundabout.

Eating in Rocamadour

Hôtel Belvédère, in the upper town, has the best interior view from its modern dining room. Book ahead for a window-side table, ideally for a meal just before sunset (*menus* from €19, daily, tel. 05 65 33 63 25; also listed under "Sleeping in Rocamadour," earlier).

The **Bar l'Esplanade** hunkers cliffside below Hôtel Belvédère and owns unobstructed views from the tables in its garden café. It's open for lunch, dinner, drinks, and snacks (daily, tel. 05 65 33 18 45).

DORDOGNE

Lot River Valley

An hour and a half south of the Dordogne, the overlooked Lot River meanders through a strikingly beautiful valley under stubborn cliffs and past tempting villages.  The fortified bridge at Cahors, the prehistoric cave paintings at Grotte du Pech Merle, and the breathtaking town of St-Cirq Lapopie are worthwhile sights in this valley—each within a half-hour of the others. These sights can be combined to make a terrific day for travelers willing to invest the time (doable as a long day trip from the Sarlat area). They also work well as a day trip from Rocamadour, and are worthwhile for drivers connecting the Dordogne with Albi or Carcassonne. (If you're going to or coming from the south, you can scenically connect this area with Albi via Villefranche-de-Rouergue and Cordes-sur-Ciel.) With extra time, spend a night in St-Cirq Lapopie, which makes a good base for visiting the area.

St-Cirq Lapopie

This spectacularly situated village, clinging to a ledge sailing above the Lot River, knows only two directions—straight up and way  down. In St-Cirq Lapopie, there's little to do but wander the rambling footpaths, inspect the flowers and stones, and thrill over the vistas. You'll find picnic perches, a handful of galleries and restaurants, and views from the bottom and top of the village that justify the pain.

St-Cirq Lapopie is well-signed 30 minutes east of Cahors, an hour south of Rocamadour, and just 20 minutes from the cave paintings of Grotte du Pech Merle.

Orientation to St-Cirq Lapopie

St-Cirq Lapopie is busy on weekends and in high season (July-Aug), but is pin-drop peaceful after-hours in any season. Arrive later in the day and spend the night to best appreciate where you

DORDOGNE

are—your first views of St-Cirq Lapopie are eye-popping enough to convince you to stay.

Tourist Information: The TI is located across from the recommended Auberge du Sombral (May-Sept daily 10:00-13:00 & 14:00-18:00 except July-Aug 10:00-19:00, Oct-April until 17:00 and closed Sun, tel. 05 65 31 31 31). Pick up the visitor's guide in English, with brief descriptions of 22 historic buildings, and ask for information on hikes in the area.

Arrival in St-Cirq Lapopie: Arriving by car from the west, you'll pass the town across the Lot River, then cross a narrow bridge and climb. There are three well-signed parking options: a small, free, dirt parking lot partway up, leaving you with a hefty uphill walk; a much closer pay lot at village level (€3, exact change required); and a third lot that lies at the top (€3, great views from here). Pull over for photo stops as you climb.

Riverside Trail: Called Chemin de Halage, a beautiful trail below St-Cirq Lapopie was originally used for pulling flat-bottomed boats upriver. Long sections of the trail are cut into the limestone cliff. Once riverside, walking downriver toward Cahors, you'll reach the cut-out section in about 20 minutes. The best stretch lies between St-Cirq Lapopie and Bouziés, a six-mile-round-trip level walk—but it's a steep hike down to the river and a long climb back up. Get details at the TI.

Sleeping and Eating in St-Cirq Lapopie

(€1 = about $1.30, country code: 33)
The village has all of 18 rooms, none of which are open off-season (mid-Nov-March).

$$ Auberge du Sombral**, run with panache by Madame Hardeveld and daughter Marion (who speaks English), is a good value in the town center below the TI. They'll welcome you with an oh-so-cozy lobby area and eight comfortable rooms above in various sizes, most with double beds (small Sb-€52, Db-€73-80, tel. 05 65 31 26 08, fax 05 65 30 26 37, www.lesombral.com, aubergesombral@gmail.com). The good restaurant serves reliable lunches (every day but Thu) and dinners (Fri-Sat only) in its lovely dining room or out front on a photogenic terrace (€15 lunch *menus*, €28 dinner *menus*).

As restaurants go, **Lou Boulat Brasserie** works for me. It serves low-risk lighter meals (salads, crêpes, and *plats*) in a low-stress setting, with good views from the side terrace (daily for lunch, Thu-Sun for dinner, at the upper end of town, off the main road by the post office/PTT, tel. 05 65 30 29 04).

L'Oustal is the most traditional restaurant in town, with a handful of cozy tables inside and out on a little terrace (€16 and €22 *menus*, €15 *plats du jour*, closed Wed, beneath the towering church, tel. 05 65 31 20 17).

Picnicking: This town was made for picnics; consider picking up dinner fixings in the hamlet of La Tour de Faure. There's a small grocery store on the other side of the river just west of the bridge to St-Cirq Lapopie, and a bakery a short way east of the bridge.

More Sights in the Lot River Valley

▲**Cahors and the Pont Valentré**—One of Europe's best medieval monuments, this fortified bridge was built in 1308 to keep the English out of Cahors. It worked. Learn the story of the devil on the center tower. The steep trail on the non-city side leads to great views (views are actually better partway up; be careful if the trail is wet) and was once part of the pilgrimage route to Santiago de Compostela in northwest Spain. Imagine that cars were allowed to cross this bridge until recently.

If you need an urban fix, stroll the pedestrian-friendly alleys between Cahors' cathedral and the river, a thriving place filled with good lunch options. To find this area by car, follow *Centre-Ville* and *St. Urcisse Eglise* signs, and park where you can.

▲▲**Grotte du Pech Merle**—This cave, about 30 minutes east of Cahors, has prehistoric paintings of mammoths, bison, and horses—rivaling the better-known cave art at Grotte de Font-de-Gaume. Although this cave is easier to view, as more people per day are allowed in (700), that also makes the cave a bit less special. Still, it has brilliant cave art and interesting stalactite and stalagmite formations. I like the mud-preserved Cro-Magnon footprint. Allow a total of two hours for your visit, starting at the small museum, continuing with a 20-minute film subtitled in English, and finishing with the caves. If you can't join an English tour, ask for the English booklet.

Cost and Hours: €9, daily March-mid-Nov 9:30-12:00 & 13:30-17:00, closes earlier off-season, fewer visitors on weekends, tel. 05 65 31 27 05, fax 05 65 31 20 47, www.pechmerle.com. Before you visit, read "Cave Art 101" on page 497.

Getting Tickets: It's smart to reserve your spot in advance (by phone or online), as private groups can fill the cave's quota. Book a week ahead in summer; if you visit without a reservation, arrive by 9:30 and line up.

DORDOGNE

BASQUE COUNTRY

*Euskal Herria: St. Jean-de-Luz • Bayonne • Biarritz •
San Sebastián • Guernica • Bilbao*

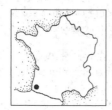

Straddling two nations on the Atlantic Coast—stretching about 100 miles from Bayonne, France south to Bilbao, Spain—lies the ancient, free-spirited land of the Basques. The Basque Country is famous for its sunny beaches and scintillating modern architecture...and for its feisty, industrious natives. It's also simply beautiful: Bright white chalet-style homes with deep-red and green shutters scatter across lush, rolling hills; the Pyrenees Mountains soar high above the Atlantic; and surfers and sardines share the waves.

Insulated from mainstream Europe for much of their history, the plucky Basques have wanted to be left alone for more than 7,000 years. An easily crossed border separates the French *Pays Basque* from the Spanish *País Vasco,* allowing you to sample both sides from a single base (in France, I hang my beret in cozy St-Jean-de-Luz; in Spain, I prefer fun-loving San Sebastián).

Much unites the French and Spanish Basque regions: They share a cuisine, Union Jack-style flag (green, red, and white), and common language (Euskara), spoken by about a half-million people. (Virtually everyone also speaks French and/or Spanish.) And both have been integrated by their respective nations, sometimes forcibly. The French Revolution quelled French Basque ideas of independence; 130 years later, Spain's fascist dictator, Generalísimo Francisco Franco, attempted to tame his own separatist-minded Basques.

But over the last generation, things have started looking up. The long-suppressed Euskara language is enjoying a resurgence. And, as the European Union celebrates ethnic regions rather than nations, the French and Spanish Basques are feeling more united. This heavily industrialized region is enjoying a striking 21st-century renaissance. In France, long-ignored cities such as Bayonne and the surfing mecca of Biarritz are being revitalized. And in Spain, the dazzling architecture of the Guggenheim Bilbao modern-art museum and the glittering resort of San Sebastián are drawing enthusiastic crowds. At the same time, traditional small towns—like France's St-Jean-de-Luz and nearby mountain villages, and Spain's Lekeitio and Hondarribia—are also thriving, making the entire region colorful, fun, welcoming...and unmistakably Basque.

Planning Your Time

One day is enough for a quick sample of the Basque Country, but two or three days lets you breathe deep and hold it in. Where you go depends on your interests: France or Spain? Cities (such as Bayonne and Bilbao) or resorts (such as St-Jean-de-Luz and San Sebastián)?

If you want to slow down and focus on Spain, spend one day relaxing in San Sebastián and the second side-tripping to Bilbao (and Guernica, if you have a car).

Better yet, Basque on both sides of the border. Sleep in one country, then side-trip into the other, devoting one day to France (St-Jean-de-Luz and Bayonne), and a second day to Spain (San Sebastián and maybe Bilbao).

Wherever you go, your Basque sightseeing should be a fun blend of urban, rural, cultural, and culinary activities.

Getting Around the Basque Country

The tourist's Basque Country—from Bayonne to Bilbao—stays close to the coastline. Fortunately, everything is connected by good roads and public transportation.

By Bus and Train: In France, the three main towns (St-Jean-de-Luz, Bayonne, and Biarritz) are connected by bus (trains also zip between St-Jean-de-Luz and Bayonne). Even if you rent a car, I'd do these three towns by public transit. To go between France and San Sebastián, a train—with a transfer in Hendaye—is your best bet (2/hour, about an hour between St-Jean-de-Luz and San Sebastián; less frequent by bus: Mon-Sat 2/day direct, 1 hour). From San Sebastián, the bus is the best way to reach Bilbao (and from there, Guernica). Specific connections are explained in each section.

Note that a few out-of-the-way areas—France's Basque villages of the interior, Spain's Lekeitio and Bay of Biscay—are impractical by public transportation...but worth the trouble by car.

By Car: Bayonne, St-Jean-de-Luz, San Sebastián, and Bilbao are connected by a convenient expressway, called A-63 in France

Who Are the Basques?

To call the Basques "mysterious" is an understatement. Before most European nations had ever set sail, Basque whalers competed with the Vikings for control of the sea. During the Industrial Revolution and lean Franco years, Basque steel kept the Spanish economy alive. In the last few decades, the separatist group ETA has given the Basque people an unwarranted reputation for violence. And through it all, the Basques have spoken a unique language that to outsiders sounds like gibberish or a secret code.

So just who are the Basques? Even for Basques, that's a difficult question. According to traditional stereotypes, Basques are thought of as having long noses, heavy eyebrows, floppy ears, stout bodies, and a penchant for wearing berets. But widespread Spanish and French immigration has made it difficult to know who actually has Basque ethnic roots. (In fact, some of the Basques' greatest patriots have had no Basque blood.) And so today, anyone who speaks the Basque language, Euskara, is considered a "Basque."

Euskara, related to no other surviving tongue, has been used since Neolithic times—making it, very likely, the oldest European language that's still spoken. With its seemingly impossible-to-pronounce words filled with k's, tx's, and z's (restrooms are *komunak: gizonak* for men and *emakumeak* for women), Euskara makes speaking French suddenly seem easy. (Some tips: *tx* is pronounced "ch" and *tz* is pronounced "ts." Other key words: *kalea* is "street," and *ostatua* is a cheap hotel.) Kept alive as a symbol of Basque cultural identity, Euskara typically is learned proudly as a second or third language. Many locals can switch effortlessly from Euskara to Spanish or French. Basques wave their language like a flag—look for Euskara street signs, menus, and signs in shops.

The Basque economy has historically been shaped by three factors: the sea, agriculture, and iron deposits.

Basque sailors were some of the first and finest in Europe, as they built ever-better boats to venture farther and farther into the Atlantic in search of whales. (These long journeys were made possible by the invention of *bacalao*—dried, salted cod that could be preserved for months to sustain whalers.) By the year 1000, Basque sailors were chasing whales a thousand miles from home, in the Norwegian fjords. Despite lack of physical evidence, many historians surmise that the Basques must have sailed to the Americas before Christopher Columbus.

When the "Spanish" era of exploration began, Basques continued to play a key role, as sailors and shipbuilders. Columbus' *Santa María* was likely Basque-built, and his crew included many Basques. History books teach that Ferdinand Magellan was the first to circumnavigate the globe, with the footnote that he was killed partway around. Who took over the helm for the rest of the journey, completing the circle? The Basque sailor Juan Sebastián de Elcano. And a pair of well-traveled Catholic priests, known for their far-reaching missionary trips that led to founding the Jesuit order, were also Basques: St. Ignatius of Loyola and St. Francis Xavier.

Later, the Industrial Age swept Europe, gaining a foothold in Iberia when the Basques began using their rich iron deposits to make steel. Pioneering Basque industrialists set the tempo as they dragged Spain into the modern world. Cities such as Bilbao were heavily industrialized, sparking an influx of workers from around Spain (which gradually diluted Basque blood in the Basque Country).

The independence-minded Basques are notorious for their stubbornness. In truth, as a culturally and linguistically unique

island surrounded by bigger and stronger nations, the Basques have learned to compromise. Historically Basques have remained on good terms with outsiders, so long as their traditional laws, the *Fueros,* were respected. Though outdated, the *Fueros* continue to symbolize a self-governance that the Basques hold dear. It is only when foreign law has been placed above the *Fueros*—as many of today's Basques feel Spanish law is—that the people become agitated.

In recent years, much of the news of the Basques—especially in Spain—was made by the terrorist organization ETA, whose goal has been to establish an independent Basque state. (ETA stands for the Euskara phrase "Euskadi Ta Askatasuna," or "Basque Country and Freedom.") ETA has been blamed for more than 800 deaths since 1968, but in late 2011, the group declared an end to its campaign of violence (but not its call for independence). While many people in the Basque Country would like a greater degree of autonomy from Madrid, only a tiny minority of the population supports ETA, and the vast majority rejects violence.

Throughout the Basque Country—in both Spain and France—the Basque spirit remains strong. Basque nationalists with websites prefer the suffix .eh (for *Euskal Herria*) or the more generic .com to .es (for *España*) or .fr (for France).

This is only a first glimpse into the important, quirky, and fascinating Basque people. To better understand the Basques, there's no better book than Mark Kurlansky's *The Basque History of the World*—essential pre-trip reading for historians. And various museums in this region also illuminate Basque culture and history, including the Museum of San Telmo in San Sebastián (see page 574), the Assembly House and Basque Country Museum in Guernica (page 594), and the Museum of Basque Culture in Bayonne (page 553).

and A-8 in Spain (rough timings: Bayonne to St-Jean-de-Luz, 30 minutes; St-Jean-de-Luz to San Sebastián, 45 minutes; San Sebastián to Bilbao, 1.25 hours).

Language Warning: For the headers throughout this chapter, I've listed place names using the French or Spanish spelling first and the Euskara spelling second. In the text, I use the spelling that prevails locally. While most people refer to towns by their French or Spanish names, many road signs list places in Euskara. (In less separatist-minded France, signs are often only in French. But in Spain, signs are usually posted in both Euskara and Spanish, either on the same sign or with dual signage on opposite sides of the street.) The French or Spanish version is sometimes scratched out by locals, so you might have to navigate by Euskara names.

Also note that in terms of linguistic priority (e.g., museum information), Euskara comes first, French and Spanish tie for second, and English is a distant fourth...when it makes the cut at all.

Cuisine Scene in the Basque Country

Mixing influences from the mountains, sea, France, and Spain, Basque food is reason enough to visit the region. The local cui-

sine—dominated by seafood, tomatoes, and red peppers—offers some spicy dishes, unusual in most of Europe. And though you'll find similar specialties throughout the Basque lands, France is still France and Spain is still Spain. Here are some dishes you're most likely to find in each area.

French Basque Cuisine: The red peppers (called *piments d'Espelette*) hanging from homes in small villages give foods a distinctive flavor and often end up in *piperade*, a dish that combines peppers, tomatoes, garlic, ham, and eggs. Peppers are also dried and used as condiments. Look for them with the terrific Basque dish *axoa* (a veal or lamb stew on mashed potatoes). Look also for anything "Basque-style" *(basquaise)*—cooked with tomato, eggplant, red pepper, and garlic. Don't leave without trying *ttoro* (tchoo-roh), a seafood stew that is the Basque Country's answer to bouillabaisse and cioppino. *Marmitako* is a hearty tuna stew. Local cheeses come from Pyrenean sheep's milk *(pur brebis)*, and the local ham *(jambon de Bayonne)* is famous throughout France. After dinner try a shot of *izarra* (herbal-flavored brandy). To satisfy your sweet tooth, look for *gâteau basque*, a local tart filled with cream or crème with cherries from Bayonne. Hard apple cider is a tasty and local beverage. The regional wine, Irouléguy, comes in red, white, and rosé, and is the only wine produced in the French part of Basque Country (locals like to say that it's made from the smallest vineyard in France but the biggest in the Northern Basque Country).

Spanish Basque Cuisine: Hopping from bar to bar sampling *pintxos*—the local term for tapas—is a highlight of any trip (for details, see the sidebar on page 584). Local brews include *sidra* (hard apple cider) and *txakolí* (cha-koh-LEE, a light, sparkling white wine—often theatrically poured from high above the glass for aeration). You'll want to sample the famous *pil-pil*, made from emulsifying the skin of *bacalao* (dried, salted cod) into a mayonnaise-like substance with chili and garlic. Another tasty dish is *kokotxas*, usually made from hake *(merluza)* fish cheeks, prepared like *pil-pil*, and cooked slowly over a low heat so the natural gelatin is released, turning it into a wonderful sauce—*¡qué bueno!* Look also for white asparagus from Navarra. Wine-wise, I prefer the reds and rosés from Navarra. Finish your dinner with *cuajada*, a yogurt-like, creamy milk dessert that's sometimes served with honey and nuts. Another specialty, found throughout Spain, is *membrillo*, a sweet and *muy* dense quince jelly. Try it with cheese for a light dessert, or look for it at breakfast.

French Basque Country (Le Pays Basque)

Compared to their Spanish cousins across the border, the French Basques seem French first and Basque second. You'll see less Euskara writing here than in Spain, but these destinations have their own special spice, mingling Basque and French influences with beautiful rolling countryside and gorgeous beaches.

My favorite home base here is the central, comfy, and manageable resort village of St-Jean-de-Luz. It's a stone's throw to Bayonne (with its "big-city" bustle and good Basque museum) and the snazzy beach town of Biarritz. A drive inland rewards you with a panoply of adorable French Basque villages. And St-Jean-de-Luz is a relaxing place to "come home" to, with its mellow ambience, fine strolling atmosphere, and good restaurants.

St-Jean-de-Luz / Donibane Lohizune

St-Jean-de-Luz (san zhahn-duh-looz) sits cradled between its small port and gentle bay. The days when whaling, cod fishing, and piracy made it wealthy are long gone, but don't expect a cute Basque backwater. Tourism has become the economic mainstay, and it shows. Pastry shops serve Basque specialties, and store windows proudly display berets (a Basque symbol). Ice-cream lickers stroll traffic-free streets, while soft, sandy beaches tempt travelers to toss their itineraries into the bay. The knobby little mountain, La Rhune, towers above the festive scene. Locals joke that if it's clear enough to see La Rhune's peak, it's going to rain, but if you can't see it, it's raining already.

The town has little of sightseeing importance, but it's a good base for exploring the Basque Country and a convenient beach and port town that provides the most enjoyable dose of Basque culture in France. The town fills with French tourists in July and August—especially the first two weeks of August, when it's practically impossible to find a room without a reservation made long in advance.

Orientation to St-Jean-de-Luz

St-Jean-de-Luz's old city lies between the train tracks, the Nivelle River, and the Atlantic. The main traffic-free street, Rue Gambetta, channels walkers through the center, halfway between the train tracks and the ocean. The small town of Ciboure, across the river, holds nothing of interest.

The only sight worth entering in St-Jean-de-Luz is the church where Louis XIV and Marie-Thérèse tied the royal knot (Eglise St. Jean-Baptiste, described later). St-Jean-de-Luz is best appreciated along its pedestrian streets, lively squares, and golden, sandy beaches. With nice views and walking trails, the park at the far eastern end of the beachfront promenade at Pointe Ste. Barbe makes a good walking destination.

Tourist Information

The helpful TI is next to the big market hall, along the busy Boulevard Victor Hugo (July-Aug Mon-Sat 9:00-19:30, Sun 10:00-13:00 & 15:00-19:00; Sept-June Mon-Sat 9:00-12:30 & 14:00-18:00, Sun 10:00-13:00—except Jan-March, when it's closed Sun; 20 Boulevard Victor Hugo, tel. 05 59 26 03 16, town info: www .saint-jean-de-luz.com, regional info: www.terreetcotebasques .com).

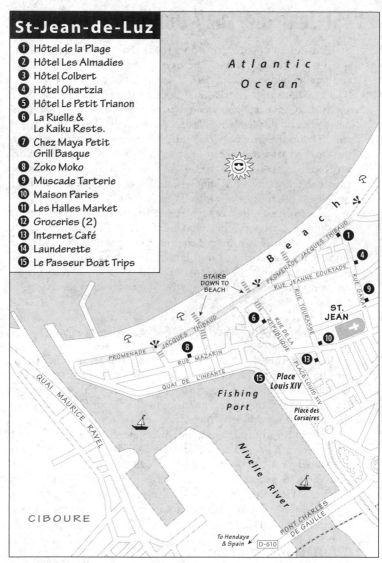

St-Jean-de-Luz

1. Hôtel de la Plage
2. Hôtel Les Almadies
3. Hôtel Colbert
4. Hôtel Ohartzia
5. Hôtel Le Petit Trianon
6. La Ruelle & Le Kaiku Rests.
7. Chez Maya Petit Grill Basque
8. Zoko Moko
9. Muscade Tarterie
10. Maison Paries
11. Les Halles Market
12. Groceries (2)
13. Internet Café
14. Launderette
15. Le Passeur Boat Trips

Atlantic Ocean

Beach

PROMENADE JACQUES THIBAUD

RUE JEANNE COURTADE

STAIRS DOWN TO BEACH

RUE GARAT

ST. JEAN

PROMENADE JACQUES THIBAUD

RUE TOURASSE

RUE DE LA RÉPUBLIQUE

RUE MAZARIN

QUAI DE L'INFANTE

PLACE LOUIS XIV

Place Louis XIV

Place des Corsaires

QUAI MAURICE RAVEL

Fishing Port

Nivelle River

CIBOURE

PONT CHARLES DE GAULLE

To Hendaye & Spain   D-610

Arrival in St-Jean-de-Luz

By Train or Bus: From the station, the pedestrian underpass leads toward the TI and the center of Old Town (just a few blocks away—see map).

By Car: Follow signs for *Centre-Ville*, then *Gare* and *Office de Tourisme*. The Old Town is not car-friendly—your best bet may be paying to park in the big underground garage behind the TI (€1.20/hour, €11/day). Hotels or the TI can advise you.

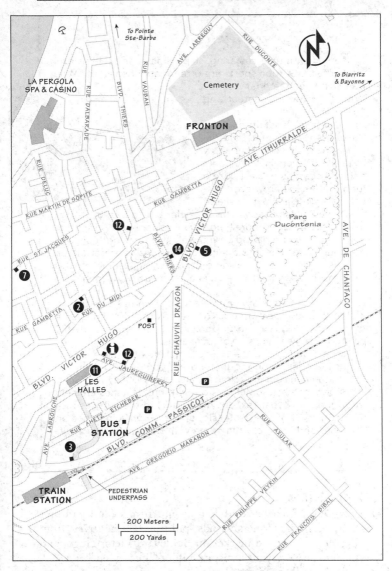

By Plane: The nearest airport is Biarritz-Anglet-Bayonne Airport, 10 miles to the northeast near Biarritz. The tiny airport is easy to navigate, with a useful TI desk (airport code: BIQ, airport tel. 05 59 43 83 83, www.biarritz.aeroport.fr). To reach St-Jean-de-Luz, you can take a public bus (€3, 7/day, 30 minutes, tel. 05 59 26 06 99, www.transdev-atcrb.com) or a 20-minute taxi ride (about €30).

Pelota

In keeping with their seafaring, shipbuilding, and metalworking heritage, Basque sports are often feats of strength: Who
can lift the heaviest stone?
Who can row the fastest and
farthest?

But the most important
Basque sport of all is *pelota*—
similar to what you might know
as jai alai. Players in white pants
and red scarves or shirts use a
long, hook-shaped wicker basket (called a *txistera* in Euskara)
to whip a ball (smaller and far bouncier than a baseball) back
and forth off walls at more than 150 miles per hour. This men's-
only game can be played with a wall at one or both ends of
the court. Most matches are not professional, but betting on
them is common. It can also be played without a racket—this
slow-motion handball version is used as a starter game for
kids.

It seems that every small Basque town has two things:
a church and a *pelota* court (called *frontón*). While some
frontóns are simple and in poor repair, others are freshly
painted as a gleaming sign of local pride.

The TI in St-Jean-de-Luz sells tickets and has a schedule of matches throughout the area; you're more likely to
find a match in summer (almost daily at 21:00 July-mid-Sept,
afternoon matches sometimes on Sat-Sun). Matches are held
throughout the year (except for winter) in the villages (ask
for details at TI). The professional *cesta punta* matches on
Tuesdays and Fridays often come with Basque folkloric halftime shows.

Helpful Hints

Market Days: Tuesday and Friday mornings (and summer
Saturdays), the farmers' stands spill through the streets from
Les Halles' covered market on Boulevard Victor Hugo, and
seem to give everyone a rustic whiff of "life is good."

Supermarkets: There are two **Petit Casino** groceries. One is across
from the market hall, next to the TI (Mon-Tue and Thu-Sat
8:30-13:00 & 15:30-19:30, Sun 9:00-13:00 & 16:30-19:30,
closed Wed). The other, at the east end of Rue Gambetta, is
smaller (open Wed but closed Sun).

Internet Access: Run by friendly Irish expats Margaret and Peter,
Internet World is best (July-Aug Mon-Sat 10:00-24:00,
closed Sun; Sept-June daily 10:00-18:00; 7 Rue Tourasse, tel.
05 59 26 86 92). The TI also has free Wi-Fi.

Laundry: Laverie Automatique du Port is at 4 Boulevard Thiers (self-service €4.80/load, daily 7:00-21:00, change machine; full-service available Tue-Fri 9:30-12:30 & 14:30-18:00; tel. 06 80 06 48 36).

Car Rental: Avis, at the train station, is handiest (Mon-Fri 8:00-18:00, Sat 9:00-18:00, closed Sun, tel. 05 59 26 79 66).

Tours in St-Jean-de-Luz

Tourist Train—A little tourist train does a 30-minute trip around town (€5.50, departs every 45 minutes from the port, runs April-Nov 10:30-19:00, no train Dec-March). It's only worth the money if you need to rest your feet.

Bus Excursions—**Le Basque Bondissant** runs popular day-trip excursions, including a handy jaunt to the Guggenheim Bilbao (€35 round-trip, includes €13 museum admission, Wed only, departs 9:30 from green bus terminal across the street from train station, returns 19:30). Other itineraries include Ainhoa, Espelette, St-Jean-Pied-de-Port, Loyola and the Cantabrian coast, San Sebastián, and a trip to the *ventas* (see sidebar on page 563). You can get information and buy tickets at the TI, or visit the Le Basque Bondissant office in the bus station (Mon-Fri 8:45-12:00 & 13:30-17:30 except closed Wed afternoon, closed Sat-Sun, tel. 05 59 26 30 74, www.basque-bondissant.com). Advance reservations are recommended in winter, when trips are canceled if not enough people sign up.

Boat Trips—**Le Passeur,** at the port, offers mini-Atlantic cruises and fishing excursions (May-Sept, no guides; cruises-€9/45 minutes, €15/1.75 hours; fishing trips-€30; tickets sold on boat, mobile 06 11 69 56 93).

Self-Guided Walk

Welcome to St-Jean-de-Luz

To get a feel for the town, take this hour-long self-guided stroll. You'll start at the port and make your way to the historic church.

    Port: Begin at the little working port (at Place des Corsaires, just beyond the parking lot). Pleasure craft are in the next port over. Whereas fishing boats used to catch lots of whales and anchovies, now they take in sardines and tuna—and take out tourists on joyrides. Anchovies, once a big part of the fishing business, were overfished nearly into extinction, so they've been protected by the EU for the last few years (though now some limited fishing is permitted).

    St-Jean-de-Luz feels cute and nonthreatening now, but in the 17th century it was home to the Basque Corsairs. With the French government's blessing, these pirates who worked the sea—and enriched the town—moored here.

• *After you walk the length of the port, on your right is the tree-lined...*

Place Louis XIV: The town's main square, named for the king who was married here, is a hub of action that serves as the town's communal living room. During the summer, the bandstand features traditional Basque folk music and dancing at 21:00 (almost nightly July-Aug, otherwise Sun and Wed). Facing the square is the City Hall (Herriko Etchea) and the "House of Louis XIV" (he lived here for 40 festive days in 1660). A visit to this house is worthwhile only if you like period furniture, though it's only open for part of the year; the rest of the time the privately owned mansion is occupied by the same family that's had it for over three centuries (€5, June-mid-Oct Wed-Mon, closed Tue and mid-Oct-July, visits by 40-minute guided tour only, 2-4/day, in French with English handouts, tel. 05 59 26 27 58, www.maison-louis-xiv.fr). The king's visit is memorialized by a small black equestrian statue at the entrance of the City Hall (a miniature of the huge statue that marks the center of the Versailles courtyard). The plane trees, with truncated branches looking like fists, are cut back in the winter so that in the summer they'll come back with thick, shady foliage.

• *Opposite the port on the far side of the square is...*

Rue de la République: This historic lane leads from Place Louis XIV to the beach. Once the home of fishermen, today it's lined with mostly edible temptations. Facing the square, **Maison Adam** still uses the family recipe to bake the *macarons* Louis XIV enjoyed during his visit (at #6; look for the gigantic display of plastic red peppers, and then go next door for their sweets). You can buy one (€1), or sample a less historic but just as tasty *gâteau basque,* a baked tart with a cream or cherry filling.

Don't eat your dessert just yet, though, because farther down Rue de la République you'll find **Pierre Oteiza,** stacked with rustic Basque cheeses and meats from mountain villages (with a few samples generally out for the tasting, and handy €3.50 paper cones of salami or cheese slices—perfect for munching during this walk; closed 12:30-14:00).

You'll likely eat on this lane tonight. The recommended **Le Kaiku,** the town's top restaurant, fills the oldest building in St-Jean-de-Luz (with its characteristic stone lookout tower), dating from the 1500s. This was the only building on the street to survive a vicious 1558 Spanish attack. Each end of the street is flanked by cannon, which may be from Basque pirate ships. At the upper end of the street, notice the photo of fisherwomen with baskets on their heads, who would literally run to Bayonne to sell their fresh fish.

• *Continue to the...*

Beach: A high embankment protects the town from storm waters, but generally the Grande Plage—which is lovingly groomed daily—is the peaceful haunt of sun-seekers and happy children. Walk the elevated promenade (to the right). Various tableaux tell history in French. Storms (including a particularly disastrous one in 1749) routinely knocked down buildings. Repeated flooding around 1800 drove the population down by two-thirds. Finally, in 1854, Napoleon III—who had visited here and appreciated the town—began building the three breakwaters you see today. Decades were spent piling 8,000 fifty-ton blocks, and by 1895 the town was protected. To develop their tourist trade, they built a casino and a fine hotel, and even organized a special getaway train from Paris. During those days there were as many visitors as residents (3,000).

• *Stroll through the seaside shopping mall fronting the late-Art-Deco-style La Pergola, which houses a casino and the Hélianthal spa center (entrance around back) and overlooks the beach. Anyone in a white robe strolling the beach is from the spa. Beyond La Pergola is the pink, Neo-Romantic Grand Hôtel (c. 1900), with an inviting terrace for an expensive coffee break (€7 cappuccino). From here circle back into town along Boulevard Thiers until you reach the bustling...*

Rue Gambetta: Turn right and circle back to your starting point, following the town's lively pedestrian shopping street. You'll notice many stores selling the renowned *linge Basque*—cotton linens such as tablecloths, napkins, and dishcloths, in the characteristic Basque red, white, and green.

• *Just before Place Louis XIV, you'll see the town's main church.*

Eglise St. Jean-Baptiste: The marriage of Louis XIV and Marie-Thérèse put St-Jean-de-Luz on the map, and this church is where it all took place. The ultimate in political marriages, the knot tied between Louis XIV and Marie-Thérèse in 1660 also cinched a reconciliation deal between Europe's two most powerful countries. The king of Spain, Philip IV—who lived in El Escorial palace—gave his daughter in marriage to the king of France, who lived in Versailles. This marriage united Europe's two largest palaces, which helped end a hundred years of hostility and forged an alliance that enabled both to focus attention on other matters (like England). Little St-Jean-de-Luz was selected for its 15 minutes of fame because it was roughly halfway between Madrid and Paris, and virtually on the France-Spain border. The wedding cleared out both Versailles and El Escorial palaces, as anyone who was anyone attended this glamorous event.

The church, centered on the pedestrian street Rue Gambetta, seems modest enough from the exterior...but step inside (Mon-Sat 8:00-12:00 & 14:00-18:30, Sun 8:00-11:30 & 15:00-19:30). The local expertise was in shipbuilding, so the ceiling resembles the hull of a ship turned upside down. The dark wood balconies running along the nave segregated the men from the women and children (men went upstairs until the 1960s, as they still do in nearby villages) and were typical of Basque churches. The number of levels depended on the impor-

tance of the church, and this church, with three levels, is the largest Basque church in France.

The three-foot-long paddle-wheel ship hanging in the center was a gift from Napoleon III's wife, Eugènie. It's a model of an ill-fated ship that had almost sunk just offshore when she was on it. The 1670 Baroque altar feels Franco-Spanish and features 20 French saints. Locals of this proud and rich town call it the finest in the Basque Country. The box across from the pulpit was reserved for leading citizens, who were expected to be seen in church and set a good example. Today the mayor and city council members sit here on festival Sundays. The place has great acoustics, and the 17th-century organ is still used for concerts (around €10, mostly in summer, get schedule at TI or online at www.orgueluz.c.la, tickets available at door and possibly in advance at the TI).

As you leave the church, turn left to find the bricked-up doorway—the church's original entrance. According to a quaint but untrue legend, it was sealed after the royal marriage (shown on the wall to the right in a photo of a painting) to symbolize a permanent closing of the door on troubles between France and Spain.

Sleeping in St-Jean-de-Luz

Hotels are a good value here. The higher prices are for peak season (generally July-Sept). In winter, some prices drop below those I've listed. Most hoteliers speak English, and breakfast costs extra. Those wanting to eat and sleep for less will do slightly better just over the border, in San Sebastián.

$$$ Hôtel de la Plage*** has the best location, right on the ocean. Its 22 rooms, 16 with ocean views, have a lively yellow-and-blue modern nautical decor (Db-€89-119, ocean view Db-€119-169, family rooms for up to 5-€30 per extra person, breakfast-€11 but free for kids, air-con, elevator, free Wi-Fi, garage-€15, 33 Rue Garat, tel. 05 59 51 03 44, fax 05 59 51 03 48, www.hoteldelaplage .com, reservation@hoteldelaplage.com, run by friendly Pierre, Laurent, and Frederic).

$$$ Hôtel Les Almadies***, on the main pedestrian street, is a bright boutique hotel with seven flawless rooms, comfy pub-

Sleep Code

(€1 = about $1.30, France country code: 33, Spain country code: 34, * = French hotel rating system, 0-5 stars)

S = Single, **D** = Double/Twin, **T** = Triple, **Q** = Quad, **b** = bathroom, **s** = shower only. Unless otherwise noted, credit cards are accepted and English is spoken, but breakfast is generally not included. This code applies to this chapter's listings in both France and Spain. The word *ostatua* (which you'll see throughout the Basque Country) means "pension."

To help you sort easily through these listings, I've divided the accommodations into three categories based on the price for a standard double room with bath in peak season:

$$$ Higher Priced—Most rooms €90 or more.
$$ Moderately Priced—Most rooms €60-90.
$ Lower Priced—Most rooms €60 or less.

Prices can change without notice; verify the hotel's current rates online or by email.

lic spaces with clever modern touches, a pleasant breakfast room and lounge, an inviting sun deck, and a caring owner (Db-€85-135, higher prices are for rooms with tubs, buffet breakfast-€12, free Wi-Fi, parking-€10, 58 Rue Gambetta, tel. 05 59 85 34 48, fax 05 59 26 12 42, www.hotel-les-almadies.com, hotel.lesalmadies @wanadoo.fr, Monsieur and Madame Hargous will charm you with their Franglish).

$$$ Hôtel Colbert*, a Best Western, has 34 modern, tastefully appointed rooms across the street from the train station (Sb-€80-133, Db-€96-162, extra bed-€15, family room-€241-339, breakfast-€14, air-con, elevator, free Wi-Fi, private parking-€20, 3 Boulevard du Commandant Passicot, tel. 05 59 26 31 99, fax 05 59 51 05 61, www.hotelcolbertsaintjeandeluz.com, contact@hotel colbertsaintjeandeluz.com).

$$ Hôtel Ohartzia** ("Souvenir"), one block off the beach, is comfortable, clean, and peaceful, with the most charming facade I've seen. It comes with 17 simple but well-cared-for rooms, generous and homey public spaces, and a delightful garden. Higher prices are for the four rooms with tubs (mid-July-Sept Db-€81-91, April-mid-July Db-€71-76, Oct-March Db-€69-74, extra bed-€15, breakfast-€8, free Wi-Fi, 28 Rue Garat, tel. 05 59 26 00 06, fax 05 59 26 74 75, www.hotel-ohartzia.com, hotel.ohartzia@wanadoo .fr). Their front desk is technically open only 8:00-21:00, but owners Madame and Monsieur Audibert (who speak little English) live in the building; their son Benoît speaks English well.

BASQUE COUNTRY

$$ Hôtel Le Petit Trianon,** on a major street a couple of blocks above the Old Town's charm, is simple and traditional, with 25 tidy rooms and an accommodating staff (July-Sept Db-€85-89, Tb-€115, Qb-€150; April-June and Oct-mid-Nov Db-€70-75, Tb-€95, Qb-€120; even less off-season, air-con in most rooms, breakfast-€8, free Wi-Fi, limited parking-€10, 56 Boulevard Victor Hugo, tel. 05 59 26 11 90, fax 05 59 26 14 10, www.hotel-lepetit trianon.com, lepetittrianon@wanadoo.fr). To get a room over the quieter courtyard, ask for *côté cour* (koh-tay koor).

Eating in St-Jean-de-Luz

St-Jean-de-Luz restaurants are known for offering good-value, high-quality cuisine. You can find a wide variety of eateries in the old center. For forgettable food with unforgettable views, choose from several places overlooking the beach. Most places serve from 12:15 to 14:00, and from 19:15 on.

The traffic-free Rue de la République, which runs from Place Louis XIV to the ocean promenade, is lined with hardworking restaurants (two of which are recommended below). Places are empty at 19:30, but packed at 20:30. Making a reservation, especially on weekends or in summer, is wise. Consider a fun night of bar-hopping for dinner in San Sebastián instead (an hour away in Spain, described on page 565).

La Ruelle serves good, traditionally Basque cuisine—mostly seafood—in a convivial dining room packed with tables, happy eaters, and kitschy Basque decor. André and his playful staff obviously enjoy their work, which gives this popular spot a relaxed and fun ambience. They offer a free sangria to diners with this book. Portions are huge; their €20 *ttoro* (seafood stew) easily feeds two—splitting is okay if you order two starters (€20-25 *menus*, closed Tue-Wed Oct-May, 19 Rue de la République, tel. 05 59 26 37 80).

Le Kaiku is *the* gastronomic experience in St-Jean-de-Luz. They serve modern, creatively presented cuisine, and specialize in wild seafood (rather than farmed). This dressy place is the most romantic in town, but manages not to be stuffy (€25 lunch *menus*, €30 dinner *menus*, closed Tue-Wed except July-Aug, 17 Rue de la République, tel. 05 59 26 13 20, Serge and Julie). For the best experience, talk with Serge about what you like best and your price limits (about €55 will get you a three-course meal *à la carte* without wine).

Chez Maya Petit Grill Basque serves hearty traditional Basque cuisine. Their €18 *ttoro* was a highlight of my day. They have €21 and €30 *menus*, but à la carte is more interesting. If you stick around in warm weather, you'll see the clever overhead fan system kick into action (closed for lunch Mon and Thu and all day Wed, 2 Rue St. Jacques, tel. 05 59 26 80 76).

Zoko Moko offers Mediterranean *nouveau* cuisine, with small portions on big plates. Get an *amuse-bouche* (an appetizer chosen by the chef) and a *mignardise* (a fun bite-sized dessert) with each main plate ordered (€25 lunchtime *plats*, €43 evening *menu*, closed Mon, 6 Rue Mazarin, tel. 05 59 08 01 23, owner Charles).

Fast and Cheap: Consider the take-away crêpe stands on Rue Gambetta. For a sit-down salad or a tart—either sweet or savory— consider **Muscade Tarterie** (€7-12 per slice; closed Mon; 20 Rue Garat, tel. 05 59 26 96 73).

Sweets: **Maison Paries** is a favorite for its traditional sweets. Locals like their fine chocolates, *tartes, macarons,* fudge *(kanou-gas),* and *touron* (like marzipan, but firmer and made of sugar), which comes in a multitude of flavors—brought by Jews who stopped here just over the border in 1492 after being expelled from Spain. The delectable chocolate version of the *gâteau basque* is also worth a try (9 Rue Gambetta, tel. 05 59 26 01 46).

St-Jean-de-Luz Connections

The train station in St-Jean-de-Luz is called St-Jean-de-Luz-Ciboure. Its handy departure board displays lights next to any trains leaving that day. Buses leave from the green building across the street. There is reduced bus and rail service on Sundays and off-season.

From St-Jean-de-Luz by Train to: Bayonne (hourly, 25 minutes), **St-Jean-Pied-de-Port** (3/day, 6/day in summer, 2 hours with transfer in Bayonne), **Paris** (4 TGV connections per day via Bordeaux, 6-7 hours; more with bus transfer in Dax, 8 hours), **Bordeaux** (11/day, 2.5 hours), **Sarlat** (4/day, 6-8 hours, transfer in Bordeaux), **Carcassonne** (5/day, 6 hours, transfers likely in Bayonne and Toulouse).

By Train to San Sebastián: First, take the 10-minute train to the French border town of Hendaye (Gare SNCF stop, about 10/day). Or get to Hendaye by bus (3/day, 35 minutes); check the schedule to see which leaves first.

Leave the Hendaye SNCF train station to the right, and look for the light-blue EuskoTren building, where you'll catch the commuter EuskoTren into San Sebastián (2/hour, generally at :03 and :33 after the hour 7:00-22:33, 35 minutes). This slow, milk-run train is known as the Topo ("Mole"), because it goes underground part of the time.

By Bus: Buses leave from both sides of the road in front of the train station. Be sure you are on the correct side of the road for your bus (you can only cross the road by using the pedestrian underpass). All tickets are bought on the bus. Local bus #26 connects St-Jean-de-Luz either to **Bayonne** or **Biarritz** almost hourly. Confusingly, this one bus can run two different routes (one to Bayonne, the other to Biarritz Centre, 45 minutes to either one)—check the destination carefully. Bus #24 connects St-Jean-de-Luz to **Sare** (Mon-Fri 5/day, Sat 2/day, none Sun, 30 minutes). A Spanish bus runs to **San Sebastián** (Mon-Sat only, 2/day direct—likely at 12:45 and 19:15, none on Sun, 1 hour, only 1/week off-season, info in Spain toll tel. 902-101-210).

By Excursion: If you're without a car, consider using **Le Basque Bondissant**'s day-trip excursions to visit otherwise difficult-to-reach destinations, such as the Guggenheim Bilbao (see "Tours in St-Jean-de-Luz," earlier).

By Taxi to San Sebastián: This will cost you about €75 for up to four people, but it's convenient (tel. 05 59 26 10 11 or mobile 06 25 76 97 69).

Route Tips for Drivers

A one-day side-trip to both Bayonne and Biarritz is easy from St-Jean-de-Luz. These three towns form a sort of triangle (depending on traffic, each one is less than a 30-minute drive from the other). Hop on the autoroute to Bayonne, sightsee there, then take the N-10 road into Biarritz. Leaving Biarritz, continue along the coastal N-10. In Bidart, watch (on the right) for the town's proud *frontón* (*pelota* court). Consider peeling off to go into the village center of Guéthary, with another *frontón*. If you're up for a walk on the beach, cross the little bridge in Guéthary, park by the train station, and hike down to the walkway along the surfing beach (lined with cafés and eateries). When you're ready to move on, you're a very short drive from St-Jean-de-Luz.

Bayonne / Baiona

To feel the urban pulse of French Basque Country, visit Bayonne—modestly but honestly nicknamed "your anchor in the Basque Country" by its tourist board. With frequent, fast connections with St-Jean-de-Luz (25 minutes by train, 40 minutes by bus), Bayonne makes an easy half-day side-trip.

Come here to browse through Bayonne's atmospheric and well-worn-yet-lively Old Town, and to admire its impressive Museum of Basque Culture.

Known for establishing Europe's first whaling industry and for inventing the bayonet, Bayonne is more famous today for its ham *(jambon de Bayonne)* and chocolate.

Get lost in Bayonne's Old Town. In pretty Grand Bayonne, tall, slender buildings, decorated in Basque fashion with green-and-red shutters, climb above cobbled streets. Be sure to stroll the streets around the cathedral and along the banks of the smaller Nive River, where you'll find the market (Les Halles).

Orientation to Bayonne

Bayonne's two rivers, the grand Adour and the petite Nive, divide the city into three parts: St-Esprit, with the train station; and the more interesting Grand Bayonne and Petit Bayonne, which together make up the Old Town.

Tourist Information

The TI is in a modern parking lot a block off the mighty Adour River, on the northeastern edge of Grand Bayonne. They have very little in English other than a map and a town brochure (Mon-Fri 9:00-18:30, Sat 10:00-18:00, closed Sun except July-Aug 10:00-13:00, Place des Basques, tel. 08 20 42 64 64, www.bayonne -tourisme.com).

Arrival in Bayonne

By Train: The TI and Grand Bayonne are a 15-minute walk from the train station: Walk straight out of the station, cross the traffic circle, and then cross the imposing bridge (Pont St. Esprit). Once past the big Adour River, continue across a smaller bridge (Pont Mayou), which spans the smaller Nive River. Stop on Pont Mayou to orient yourself: You just left Petit Bayonne (left side of Nive River); ahead of you is Grand Bayonne (spires of cathedral straight ahead, TI a few blocks to the right). The Museum of Basque Culture is in Petit Bayonne, facing the next bridge up the Nive River.

By Car and Bus: The handiest parking is also where buses arrive in Bayonne: next to the TI at the modern parking lot on the edge of Grand Bayonne. To reach the town center from here, first walk with the busy road on your left to the big park and the war memorial. Then turn right and walk with the park on your left-hand side. After a few blocks, you'll see atmospheric streets leading up to the cathedral on your right; if you continue straight, you'll reach the bridge over the Nive River called Pont Mayou (described above).

To reach this parking lot, **drivers** take the *Bayonne Sud* exit from the autoroute, then follow green *Bayonne Centre* signs, then

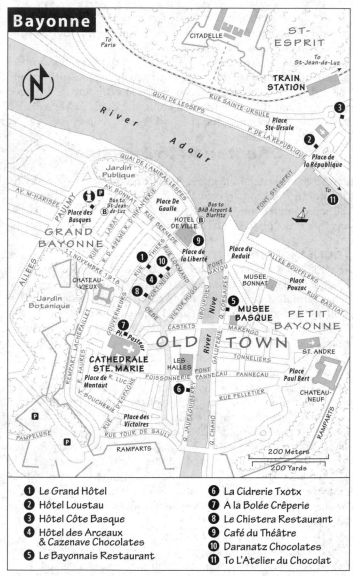

Bayonne

- ① Le Grand Hôtel
- ② Hôtel Loustau
- ③ Hôtel Côte Basque
- ④ Hôtel des Arceaux
  & Cazenave Chocolates
- ⑤ Le Bayonnais Restaurant
- ⑥ La Cidrerie Txotx
- ⑦ A la Bolée Crêperie
- ⑧ Le Chistera Restaurant
- ⑨ Café du Théâtre
- ⑩ Daranatz Chocolates
- ⑪ To L'Atelier du Chocolat

white *Centre-Ville* signs (with an *i* for tourist information). You'll see the lot on your right. In high season, when this lot can be full, use one of the lots just outside the center (follow signs to *Glain* or *Porte d'Espagne* as you arrive in town), then catch the little orange *navette* (shuttle bus) to get into the center (free, find route maps posted at stops in town, every 7 minutes, Mon-Sat 7:30-19:30, closed Sun).

BASQUE COUNTRY

Helpful Hints

Loaner Bikes: Although Bayonne's sights are easily reached on foot (except the chocolate workshop), pedaling about by bike is simple and relaxing. The TI lends a limited number of bikes for free to adults during office hours (must leave passport or driver's license and a €150 deposit, same hours and contact information as TI, www.cyclocom.fr).

Laundry: Laverie is just blocks from the cathedral (self-service €4/load, daily 7:00-20:00, 6 Rue d'Espagne, tel. 05 59 59 54 03).

Sights in Bayonne

▲**Museum of Basque Culture (Musée Basque)**—This museum (in Petit Bayonne, facing the Nive River at Pont Marengo) explains French Basque culture from cradle to grave—in French, Euskara, and Spanish. The only English you'll read is "do not touch" (unless you buy their informative €5 English booklet). Artifacts and videos take you into traditional Basque villages and sit you in the front row of time-honored festivals, letting you envision this otherwise hard-to-experience culture.

Cost and Hours: €6.50, free first Sun of month; open July-Aug daily 10:00-18:30, Thu until 20:30; Sept-June Tue-Sun 10:00-18:30, closed Mon; last entry one hour before closing, 37 Quai des Corsaires, tel. 05 59 59 08 98, www.museebasque.com.

Visiting the Museum: On the ground floor, you'll begin by walking past some 16th-century gravestones, then see a display of carts and tools used in rural life. Look for the *laiak*—distinctive forked hoes used to work the ground. At the end of this section you'll watch a grainy film on Basque rural lifestyles.

The next floor up begins by explaining that the house *(etxea)* is the building block of Basque society. More than just a building, it's a social institution—Basques are named for their house, not vice versa. You'll see models and paintings of Basque houses, then domestic items, a giant door, kitchen equipment, and furniture (including a combination bench-table, near the fireplace). After an exhibit on Basque clothing, you'll move into the nautical life, with models, paintings, and actual boats. The little door leads to a model of the port of Bayonne in 1805, back when it was a strategic walled city.

Upstairs you'll learn that the religious life of the Basques was strongly influenced by the Camino de Santiago pilgrim trail, which passes through their territory. One somber room explains Basque funeral traditions. The section on social life includes a video of Basque dances (typically accompanied by flute and drums). These are improvised, but according to a clearly outlined structure—not unlike a square dance.

The prominence given to the sport of *pelota* (see sidebar on page 542) indicates its importance to these people. One dimly lit room shows off several types of *txistera* baskets (*chistera* in French), gloves, and balls used for the game; videos show you how these items are made. The museum wraps up with a brief lesson on the region's history from the 16th to the 20th centuries, including exhibits on the large Jewish population here (who had fled from a hostile Spain) and the renaissance of Basque culture in the 19th century.

Cathédrale Ste. Marie—Bankrolled by the whaling community, this cathedral sits dead-center in

Grand Bayonne and is worth a peek. Find the unique keystones on the ceiling along the nave, then circle behind the church to find the peaceful 13th-century cloisters.

Cost and Hours: Cathedral—free, Mon-Sat 10:00-11:45 & 15:00-17:45, Sun 15:30-18:00; cloisters—free, daily 9:00-12:30 & 14:00-17:00, until 18:00 mid-May-mid-Sept.

Sweets Shops—With no more whales to catch, Bayonne turned to producing mouthwatering chocolates and marzipan; look for shops on the arcaded Rue du Port Neuf (running between the cathedral and the Adour River). **Daranatz** is Bayonne's best chocolate shop, with bars of chocolate blended with all kinds of flavors—one with a general mix of spices (lots of cardamom), one with just cinnamon, and another with *piments d'Espelette* (15 arceaux Port Neuf, tel. 05 59 59 03 55, www.chocolat-bayonne-daranatz.fr). **Cazenave** is a fancy *chocolaterie* with a small café in the back. Try their foamy hot chocolate with fresh whipped cream on the side, served with buttered toast for €9 (closed Sun-Mon, 19 Arceaux Port Neuf, tel. 05 59 59 03 16, www.chocolats-bayonne-cazenave.fr).

Chocolate Workshop—L'Atelier du Chocolat is a chocolate factory and boutique in an industrial part of town. You'll see a detailed exhibit on the history and making of chocolate, some workers making luscious goodies (9:30-11:00 only), and a video. The generous chocolate tasting at the end is worth the ticket price for chocoholics.

Cost and Hours: €5.90, Mon-Sat 9:30-12:30 & 14:00-18:00, closed Sun, last entry 1.5 hours before closing; take city bus #A1 from the TI or the Mairie stop, buy €1 ticket on board, get off at the Jean-Jaurès stop, walk under railway bridge past the roundabout, and follow signs to 7 Allée de Gibéléou; tel. 05 59 55 70 23, www.atelierduchocolat.fr.

Ramparts—The ramparts around Grand Bayonne are open for walking and great for picnicking (access from park at far end of TI parking lot). However, the ramparts do not allow access to either of Bayonne's castles—both are closed to the public.

Sleeping in Bayonne

(€1 = about $1.30, country code: 33)

$$$ **Le Grand Hôtel***** is the best of the limited options in Bayonne—it's well-located in Grand Bayonne, with all the comforts and a pleasant staff. While renovating their old building, the owners took care to maintain the original, classic decor (Sb-€75-160, Db-€81-166, breakfast-€13, elevator, free Wi-Fi, parking-€13, 21 Rue Thiers, tel. 05 59 59 62 00, fax 05 59 59 62 01, www.legrandhotelbayonne.com, info@legrandhotelbayonne.com, Caroline).

$$$ **Hôtel Loustau***** sits next to the Pont Saint Esprit near the train station. Some of its 45 respectable rooms overlook the river (Sb-€86-116, Db-€96-135, Tb-€99-145, includes breakfast, elevator, parking-€8, 1 Place de la République, tel. 05 59 55 08 08, fax 05 59 55 69 36, www.hotel-loustau.com, info@loustau.com).

$$ **Hôtel Côte Basque**** is conveniently located by the train station in the Saint Esprit neighborhood, just across the river from the Old Town. It's on a busy street, but the small-but-comfortable rooms have double-paned windows to cut the noise (Sb-€60-65, Db-€65-75, breakfast-€8, elevator, free Wi-Fi, 2 Rue Maubec, tel. 05 59 55 10 21, www.hotel-cotebasque.fr, hotelcotebasque @orange.fr).

$$ **Hôtel des Arceaux**** is a family-run B&B-style establishment with 16 rooms on a small pedestrian street in Grand Bayonne. It's just around the corner from the cathedral (Db-€66-76, breakfast-€7, free Wi-Fi, 26 Rue Port Neuf, tel. 05 59 59 15 53, fax 05 59 25 64 75, www.hotel-arceaux.com, hotel.arceaux@wanadoo.fr).

Eating in Bayonne

The Grand Bayonne riverside has several tapas restaurants, a couple of easy *bistrots*, and a pizza place. The Petit Bayonne riverside has some *bistrots* and a few more proper sit-down restaurants. The pedestrian streets surrounding the cathedral in Grand Bayonne offer casual dining spots serving crêpes, tartines, quiches, and salads. Most places have outdoor tables in nice weather.

Le Bayonnais, next door to the Museum of Basque Culture, serves traditional Basque specialties à la carte. Sit in the blue-tiled interior or out along the river (€18 lunch and dinner *menu* on weekdays, closed Sun-Mon, Quai des Corsaires 38, tel. 05 59 25 61 19).

BASQUE COUNTRY

La Cidrerie Txotx (pronounced "choch") has a Spanish-bodega ambience under a chorus line of hams. You can also sit outside, along the river, just past the market hall (€8-10 Basque tapas or €12-19 *plats*, daily, 49 Quai Jauréguiberry, tel. 05 59 59 16 80).

A la Bolée serves up inexpensive sweet and savory crêpes in a cozy atmosphere along the side of the cathedral (daily, 10 Place Pasteur, tel. 05 59 59 18 75).

Le Chistera, run by a family that's spent time in the US, proudly serves traditional Basque dishes made with market-fresh ingredients. Try the *poulet* with Basque sauce or one of their soups, and polish off your meal with homemade *gâteau basque* (€25-30 dinners, Tue-Wed 12:00-14:00, Thu-Sun 12:00-14:00 & 19:30-21:00, closed Mon, 42 Rue Port Neuf, tel. 05 59 59 25 93).

Café du Théâtre has pleasant outdoor tables by the river. Try it for a simple early breakfast (Place de la Liberté, tel. 05 59 59 09 31).

If the weather is good, consider gathering a picnic from the shops along the pedestrian streets, at Les Halles market (only open in the mornings), in the Casino minimart (Mon-Sat 8:00-13:00 & 15:30-20:00, closed Sun, 38 Rue Port Neuf), or at the Monoprix (Mon-Sat 8:30-20:30, closed Sun, 8 Rue Orbe). Don't forget the chocolate, then head for the park around the ramparts below the *Jardin Botanique* (benches galore).

Bayonne Connections

Chronoplus buses run throughout the area regularly. Most lines run two to three times an hour from about 7:00 to 20:00, but are noticeably less frequent on Saturdays and even sparser on Sundays. Buy a €1 ticket on the bus; if you plan to ride twice or more in one day, buy the 24-hour ticket for €2 (tel. 05 59 52 59 52, www.chronoplus.eu).

From Bayonne by Bus to: BAB (Biarritz-Anglet-Bayonne) Airport (2-3/hour, 15 minutes, line #C is best option), Biarritz (2-3/hour, fewer on Sun, 30 minutes, lines #A1 and #A2), and St-Jean-de-Luz (almost hourly, 45 minutes, line #26, €3). Pick up BAB and Biarritz buses by the Mairie/Théâter stop on the riverside; catch the St-Jean-de-Luz bus from Place des Basques by the TI. Buses to the inland Basque villages of Espelette and Ainhoa are impractical.

By Train to: St-Jean-Pied-du-Port (4/day, 6/day in summer, 1.25 hours).

By Taxi to: Biarritz (15 minutes, about €25) and St-Jean-de-Luz (30 minutes, about €50, tel. 05 59 59 48 48).

It Happened at Hendaye

If taking the train between the Spanish and French Basque regions, you'll change trains at the nondescript little Hendaye Station. While it seems innocent enough, this was a site of a fateful meeting between two of Europe's most notorious 20th-century dictators.

In the days before World War II, Adolf Hitler and Francisco Franco maintained a diplomatic relationship. But after the fall of France, they decided to meet secretly in Hendaye to size each other up. On October 23, 1940, Hitler traveled through Nazi-occupied France, then waited impatiently on the platform for Franco's delayed train. The over-eager Franco hoped the Führer would invite him to join in a military alliance with Germany (and ultimately share in the expected war spoils).

According to reports of the meeting, Franco was greedy, boastful, and misguided, leading Hitler to dismiss him as a buffoon. Franco later spun the situation by claiming that he had cleverly avoided being pulled into World War II. In fact, his own incompetence is what saved Spain. Had Franco made a better impression on Hitler here at Hendaye, it's possible that Spain would have entered the war, which could have changed the course of Spanish, German, and European history.

Biarritz / Biarritz

A glitzy resort town steeped in the belle époque, Biarritz (bee-ah-ritz) is where the French Basques put on the ritz. In the 19th century, this simple whaling harbor became, almost overnight, a high-class aristocrat-magnet dubbed the "beach of kings." Although St-Jean-de-Luz and Bayonne are more fully French and more fully Basque, the made-for-inter-

national-tourists, jet-set scene of Biarritz is not without its charms. Perched over a popular surfing beach, anchored by grand hotels and casinos, hemmed in by jagged and picturesque rocky islets at either end, and watched over by a lighthouse on a distant promontory, Biarritz is a striking beach resort. However, for sightseers with limited time, it's likely more trouble than it's worth.

Orientation to Biarritz

Biarritz feels much bigger than its population of 30,000. The town sprawls, but virtually everything we're interested in lines up along the waterfront: the beach, the promenade, the hotel and shopping zone, and the TI.

Tourist Information

The TI is in a little pink castle two blocks up from the beach (just above the beach and casino, hiding behind the City Hall/*hôtel de ville*—look for signs). Pick up the free map and get details on any sightseeing that interests you (July-Aug daily 9:00-19:00; Sept-June Mon-Fri 9:00-18:00, Sat-Sun 10:00-17:00; Square d'Ixelles, tel. 05 59 22 37 00, www.biarritz.fr).

Arrival in Biarritz

By Car: Drivers follow signs for *Centre-Ville*, then carefully track signs for specific parking garages. The most central garages are called Grande Plage, Casino, Bellevue, and St. Eugénie (closest to the water). Signs in front of each tell you whether it's full *(complet)*, in which case move on to the next one.

By Bus: Buses stop at "Biarritz Centre," a parking lot next to the TI (buses to/from Bayonne stop along the side of the lot; buses to/from St-Jean-de-Luz stop at the end of the lot). If you're taking a bus, be aware that some stop at the outskirts of town—only take one to "Centre."

Don't bother taking the **train** to or from Biarritz, as the station is about two miles from the tourist area (buses #2 and #9 connect the train station to the city center).

There is no baggage storage in Biarritz.

Sights in Biarritz

There's little of sightseeing value in Biarritz. The TI can fill you in on the town's four museums (Marine Museum—described below; Chocolate Planet and Museum—intriguing, but a long walk from the center; Oriental Art Museum—large, diverse collection of art from across Asia; and Biarritz Historical Museum—really?).

Your time is best spent strolling along the various levels that climb up from the sea. From the TI you can do a loop: First head west on the lively **pedestrian streets** that occupy the plateau above the water, which are lined with restaurants, cafés, and high-class, resorty "window-licking." (Place Georges Clemenceau is the grassy "main square" of this area.)

Work your way out to the point with the **Marine Museum** (Musée de la Mer). The most convenient of Biarritz's attractions, this pricey Art Deco museum/aquarium wins the "best rainy-day option" award, with a tank of seals and a chance to get face-to-teeth with live sharks (€13, daily 9:30-19:00, July-Aug until 24:00, last entry one hour before closing, tel. 05 59 22 33 34, www .museedelamer.com).

Whether or not you're visiting the museum, it's worth hiking down to the entrance, then wandering out on the walkways that

connect the big offshore rocks. These lead to the so-called **Virgin Rock** (Rocher de la Vierge), topped by a statue of Mary. Spot any surfers?

From here, stick by the water as you head back toward the TI. After a bit of up and down over the rocks, don't miss the trail down to **Fishermen's Wharf** (Port des Pêcheurs), a little pocket of salty authenticity that clings like barnacles to the cliff below the hotels. The remnants of an aborted construction project from the town's glory days, this little fishing settlement of humble houses and rugged jetties seems to faintly echo the Basque culture that thrived here before the glitz hit. Many of the houses have been taken over by the tourist trade (gift shops and restaurants).

Continuing along the water (and briefly back up to street level), make your way back to the town's centerpiece, the **big beach** (Grande Plage). Dominating this inviting stretch of sand is the Art Deco casino, and the TI is just above that. If you haven't yet taken the time on your vacation to splash, wade, or stroll on the beach...now's your chance.

Biarritz Connections

From Biarritz by Bus to: St-Jean-de-Luz (nearly hourly, fewer on Sundays, 45 minutes, line #26) and **Bayonne** (2-3/hour, fewer on Sundays, 30 minutes, lines #A1 and #A2).

Villages in the French Basque Country

Traditional villages among the green hills, with buildings colored like the Basque flag, offer the best glimpse of Basque culture. Cheese, hard cider, and *pelota* players are the primary products of these villages, which attract few foreigners but many French summer visitors. Most of these villages have welcomed pilgrims bound for Santiago de Compostela since the Middle Ages. Today's hikers trek between local villages or head into the Pyrenees. The most appealing villages lie in the foothills of the Pyrenees, spared from beach-scene development.

Use St-Jean-de-Luz as your base to visit the Basque sights described below. You can reach some of these places by public transportation, but the hassle outweighs the rewards. Do a circuit of these towns in the order they're listed here. Assuming you're driving, I've included route instructions as well.

• *From St-Jean-de-Luz, follow signs for* Ascain, *then* Sare. *On the road toward Sare, you'll pass the station for the train up to...*

La Rhune / Larrun

Between the villages of Ascain and Sare, near the border with Spain, a small cogwheel train takes tourists to the top of La Rhune, the region's highest peak (2,969 feet). You'll putt-putt up the hillside for 35 minutes in an open-air train car to reach panoramic views of land and sea (adults-€15 round-trip, kids-€8, all pay €2-3 more in summer, runs March-mid-Nov daily, closed mid-Nov-Feb, departures weather-dependent—the trip is worthless if it's not clear, goes every 35 minutes when busiest July-Aug, tel. 05 59 54 20 26, www.rhune.com).

• *Continue along the same road to...*

Sare / Sara

Sare, which sits at the base of the towering mountain La Rhune, is among the most picturesque villages—and the most touristed. It's easily reached from St-Jean-de-Luz by bus or car. The small TI is on the main square (Mon-Fri 9:30-12:30 & 13:30-17:30, Sat 9:30-12:30, closed Sun year-round and Sat Nov-March, tel. 05 59 54 20 14). Nearby is a cluster of hotels and the town church (which has an impressive interior, with arches over the altar and Basque-style balconies lining the nave). At the far end of the square is the town's humble *frontón* (*pelota* court).

• *Leaving Sare, first follow signs for* St-Pée, *then watch for the turnoff to...*

Ainhoa / Ainhoa

Ainhoa is a colorful, tidy, picturesque one-street town that sees fewer tourists (which is a good thing). Its chunks of fortified walls and gates mingle with red-and-white half-timbered buildings. The 14th-century church—with a beautiful golden *retable* (screen behind the altar)—and the *frontón* share center stage.

Ainhoa is also a popular starting point for hikes into the hills. For a spectacular village-

and-valleys view, drive five minutes (or walk 90 sweaty minutes) up the steep dirt road to the Chapelle de Notre-Dame d'Aranazau ("d'Aubepine" in French). Start in the parking lot directly across the main street from the church, then head straight uphill. Follow signs for *oratoire*, then count the giant white crosses to the top.
• *As you leave Ainhoa, you'll have to backtrack the way you came in to find the road to...*

Espelette / Ezpeleta

Espelette won't let you forget that it's the capital of the region's AOC red peppers *(piments d'Espelette)*, with strands of them dan- gling like good-luck charms from many houses and storefronts. After strolling the charming, cobbled center, wander downhill at the end of town to find the town church and the well-restored château and medieval tower, which now houses the town hall, an exhibition, and the TI (Mon-Fri 8:30-12:30 & 14:00-18:00, Sat 9:30-12:30, closed Sun, tel. 05 59 93 95 02).

Sleeping and Eating: For a good regional meal, consider the **$$ Hôtel Euzkadi**** restaurant, with a *muy* Spanish ambience (€18-35 *menus*, daily 12:30-14:00 & 19:30-21:00, July-Aug closed Mon, Sept-June closed Mon-Tue, 285 Karrika Nagusia, tel. 05 59 93 91 88). The hotel has 27 rooms with modern touches and a swimming pool (Db-€62-82, €10 more in July-Aug, air-con, elevator, free Wi-Fi, www.hotel-restaurant-euzkadi.com).
• *From Espelette, if you have time, you can follow signs to Cambo les Bains, then St-Jean-Pied-de-Port (40 minutes).*

St-Jean-Pied-de-Port / Donibane Garazi

Just five miles from the Spanish border, the walled town of St-Jean-Pied-de-Port (san zhahn-pee-ay-duh-por) is the most

popular village in all the French Basque countryside. Traditionally, St-Jean-Pied-de-Port has been the final stopover in France for pilgrims undertaking the Camino de Santiago ("Way of Saint James")—the medieval pilgrimage route that runs from here 500 miles across the north of Spain to the city of Santiago de Compostela. After centuries of obscurity, the pilgrimage has become more popular again recently, as

thousands of modern travelers each year follow that ancient trail on foot, bike, or horseback. From St-Jean-Pied-de-Port, Santiago-bound pilgrims cross the Pyrenees together and continue their march through Spain. The scallop shell of "St. Jacques" (French for "James") is etched on walls throughout the town.

Visitors to this town are equal parts pilgrims and French tourists. Gift shops sell a strange combination of pilgrim gear (such as quick-drying shirts and shorts) and Basque souvenirs. This place is packed in the summer (so come early or late).

Tourist Information: The TI, on the main road along the outside of the walled Old Town, can give you a town map (hours vary, generally July-Aug Mon-Sat 9:00-19:00, Sun 10:00-12:00; Sept-June Mon-Sat 9:00-12:00 & 14:00-18:00, Sun 10:00-12:00; maybe less in winter; tel. 08 10 75 36 71). Ask the TI about weekly *pelota vasca* games (usually Mon at 16:00 or 17:00 at Trinquet court on Place du Trinquet).

Arrival in St-Jean-Pied-de-Port: Parking is ample and well-signed from the main road. If arriving by **train,** exit the station to the left, then follow the busy road at the traffic circle toward the city wall.

Sights: There's little in the way of sightseeing here, other than pilgrim-spotting. Many modern pilgrims begin their Camino in this traditional spot because of its easy train connection to Bayonne, and because—as its name implies ("St. John at the Foot of the Pass")—it offers a very challenging but rewarding first leg: up, over, and into Spain.

Cross the old bridge over the Nive River (the same one that winds up in Bayonne) to the **Notre-Dame Gate,** which was once a drawbridge. Then head up the main walking drag, **Rue de la Citadelle.** With its rosy-pink buildings and ancient dates above its doorways, this lane simply feels old. Notice lots of signs for *chambres* (rooms) and *refuges*—humble, hostel-like pilgrim bunkhouses.

Partway up, on the left at #39, look for the **Pilgrim Friends Office** (Les Amis du Chemin de Saint-Jacques, daily 7:30-12:00 & 13:30-20:00 & 21:15-22:00, tel. 05 59 37 05 09). This is where pilgrims check in before their long journey to Santiago; about 19,000 pilgrims started out here in 2011 (compared with just 4,000 about a decade ago). For €2 a pilgrim can buy the official credential *(credenciel)* that she'll get stamped at each stop between here and Santiago to prove she walked the whole way and earn her *compostela* certificate. Pilgrims also receive a warm welcome, lots of advice, and help finding a bunk (the well-

Ventas Shops

Scattered between France and Spain and along the foothills of the Pyrenees, you'll see many signs for *ventas* (from the Spanish *vender,* "to sell"). Follow one of these signs to a cultural detour. Originally used as contraband outposts, *ventas* operate as cafés, bars, restaurants, grocery stores, gas stations, cheap boutiques, and more. Most are lost in the hills and hard to find, and many still don't have signs—locals just know where they are. Today they are legal in a borderless Europe, and they still offer inexpensive products. Customers are mostly the French Basque, who cause traffic jams on weekends driving to the border to do cheap shopping or fill the gas tank. In most *ventas,* gas is cheaper by 25 percent, cigarettes and alcohol leave by the case, and the Spanish, French, and Euskara languages mingle as locals enjoy a coffee or beer among hanging garlands of cheap hams. You can take a bus tour to some *ventas* from St-Jean-de-Luz (see page 539).

traveled staff swears that no pilgrim ever goes without a bed in St-Jean-Pied-de-Port).

A few more steps up, on the left, you'll pass the skippable €3 Bishop's Prison (Prison des Evêques, sometimes closed in winter). Continue on up to the **citadel,** dating from the mid-17th century—when this was a highly strategic location, keeping an eye on the easiest road over the Pyrenees between Spain and France. Although not open to the public (as it houses a school), the grounds around this stout fortress offer sweeping views over the French Basque countryside.

Sleeping in St-Jean-Pied-de-Port: Lots of humble pilgrim dwellings line the main drag, Rue de la Citadelle. If you're looking for a bit more comfort, consider these options. **$$ Hotel Ramuntcho**** is the only real hotel option in the Old Town, located partway up Rue de la Citadelle. Its 16 rooms above a restaurant are straightforward but modern (Db-€60-89, breakfast-€9, free Wi-Fi, 1 Rue de France, tel. 05 59 37 03 91, fax 05 59 37 35 17, http://hotel.ramuntcho.pagesperso-orange.fr, hotel.ramuntcho @wanadoo.fr). **$$ Itzalpea,** a café and tea house, rents five rooms along the main road just outside the Old Town (Sb-€55-58, Db-€65-80 depending on size, includes breakfast, closed Sat off-season, air-con, 5 Place du Trinquet, tel. 05 59 37 03 66, fax 05 59 37 33 18, www.maisondhotes-itzalpea.com, itzalpea@wanadoo .fr). **$ Chambres Chez l'Habitant** has five old-fashioned, pilgrim-perfect rooms along the main drag. Welcoming Maria and Jean Pierre speak limited English, but their daughter can help translate (€20-25 per person in D, Db, Q, or Qb, includes breakfast, 15 Rue de la Citadelle, tel. 05 59 37 05 83).

Eating in St-Jean-Pied-de-Port: Tourists, pilgrims, and locals alike find plenty of places to eat along Rue de la Citadelle and also off Rue du Trinquet, the main drag into town. Consider **Café Navarre** (1 Place Juan de Huarte, tel. 05 59 37 01 67) or **Cafe Ttipia** (2 Place Charles Floquet, tel. 05 59 37 11 96). If you want a **picnic** and are lucky enough to land here on a Monday morning, shop at the weekly market. Farmers, cheesemakers, and winemakers bring their products in from the countryside.

St-Jean-Pied-de-Port Connections: A scenic train conveniently links St-Jean-Pied-de-Port to **Bayonne** (€9, 4/day, 6/day in summer, 1.5 hours), and from there to **St-Jean-de-Luz** (about 30 minutes beyond Bayonne, www.sncf.fr). By car, it's about a 1.25-hour drive to St-Jean-de-Luz.

Spanish Basque Country (El País Vasco)

Four of the seven Basque territories lie within Spain. Many consider Spanish Basque culture to be feistier and more colorful than that of the relatively assimilated French Basques—you'll hear more Euskara spoken here than in France.

For 40 years, beginning in 1939, the figure of Generalísimo Franco loomed large over the Spanish Basques. Franco depended upon Basque industry to keep the floundering Spanish economy afloat. But even as he exploited the Basques economically, he so effectively blunted Basque culture that the language was primarily Spanish by default. Franco kicked off his regime by offering up the historic Basque town of Guernica as target practice to his ally Hitler's air force. The notorious result—the wholesale slaughter of innocent civilians—was immortalized by Pablo Picasso's mural *Guernica*.

But Franco is long gone, and today's Basques are looking to the future. The iron deposits have been depleted, prompting the Basques to re-imagine their rusting cities for the 21st century. True to form, they're rising to the challenge. Perhaps the best example is Bilbao, whose iconic Guggenheim Museum—built on the former site of an industrial wasteland—is the centerpiece of a bold new skyline.

San Sebastián is the heart of the tourist's *País Vasco*, with its sparkling, picturesque beach framed by looming green mountains and a charming Old Town with gourmet *pintxos* (tapas) spilling out of every bar. On-the-rise Bilbao is worth a look for its land-mark Guggenheim and its atmospheric Old Town. For small-town fun, drop by the fishing village of Lekeitio (near Bilbao). And for history, Guernica has some intriguing museums.

San Sebastián / Donostia

Shimmering above the breathtaking Concha Bay, elegant and pros-perous San Sebastián (Donostia in Euskara) has a favored location

with golden beaches, capped by twin peaks at either end, and with a cute little island in the center. A delightful beachfront promenade runs the length of the bay, with an intriguing Old Town at one end and a smart shopping district in the center. It has 183,000 residents and almost that many tourists in

high season (July-Sept). With a romantic setting, a soaring statue of Christ gazing over the city, and a late-night lively Old Town, San Sebastián has a mini-Rio de Janeiro aura. Though the actual "sightseeing" isn't much, the scenic city itself provides a pleasant introduction to Spain's Basque Country. And as a culinary capital of Spain, it dishes up some of the top tapas anywhere.

In 1845 Queen Isabel II's doctor recommended she treat her skin problems by bathing here in the sea. (For modesty's sake, she would go inside a giant cabana that could be wheeled into the surf—allowing her to swim far from prying eyes, never having to set foot on the beach.) Her visit mobilized Spain's aristocracy, and soon the city was on the map as a seaside resort. By the turn of the 20th century, San Sebastián was the toast of the belle époque, and a leading resort for Europe's beautiful people. Before World War I, Queen María Cristina summered here and held court in her Miramar Palace overlooking the crescent beach (the turreted, red-brick building partway around the bay). Hotels, casinos, and theaters flourished. Even Franco enjoyed 35 summers in a place he was sure to call San Sebastián, not Donostia.

Planning Your Time

San Sebastián's sights can be exhausted in a few hours, but it's a great place to be on vacation for a full, lazy day (or longer). Stroll the two-mile-long promenade and scout the place you'll grab to work on a tan. The promenade leads to a funicular that lifts you to the Monte Igueldo viewpoint. After exploring the Old Town and port, walk up to the hill of Monte Urgull. If you have more time, enjoy the delightful aquarium. Museum-goers find it worthwhile

Dipping into Spain

If you're heading from France to Spain, you don't have to worry about border stops or currency changes (both countries use the euro). But here are a few other practicalities:

Phones: Spain's telephone country code is 34. Remember that French phone cards and stamps will not work in Spain.

Hours: Most Spanish sights and stores close for a "siesta" from about 13:00 to 16:00, and dinner doesn't begin until 21:00 or 22:00 (though tapas are always available).

Eating Tips: Most Spaniards have their big meal at lunch, then build a light dinner out of appetizer portions called tapas (or, in Basque Country, *pintxos*). Rather than choosing one restaurant for the evening, eaters hop from bar to bar sampling these tasty snacks. For tips on this ritual, see "Do the *Txikiteo*—Tapas Cheat Sheet" on page 584.

Spanish Survival Phrases: While many Spanish Basques speak Euskara, most speak Spanish in everyday life. You'll find these phrases useful:

English	Spanish	Pronounced
Good day.	*Buenos días.*	**bway**-nohs **dee**-ahs
Mr. / Mrs.	*Señor / Señora*	sayn-**yor** / sayn-**yor**-ah
Please.	*Por favor*	por fah-**bor**
Thank you.	*Muchas gracias.*	**moo**-chahs **grah**-thee-ahs
You're welcome.	*De nada.*	day **nah**-dah
Excuse me.	*Perdone.*	pehr-**doh**-nay
Yes. / No.	*Sí. / No*	see / noh
Cheers!	*¡Salud!*	sah-**lood**
men	*hombres, caballeros*	**ohm**-brays, kah-bah-**yay**-rohs
women	*mujeres, damas*	moo-**hehr**-ays, **dah**-mahs
one / two / three	*uno / dos / tres*	**oo**-noh / dohs / trays
coffee with milk	*café con leche*	kah-**feh** kohn **lay**-chay
sandwich	*bocadillo*	boh-kah-**dee**-yoh
Where is...?	*¿Donde está...?*	**dohn**-day ay-**stah**
tourist office	*turismo*	too-**rees**-moh
city center	*centro ciudad*	**thehn**-troh thee-oo-**dahd**
Do you speak English?	*¿Habla usted inglés?*	**ah**-blah oo-**stehd** een-**glays**

to visit the Museum of San Telmo, the largest of its kind on Basque culture. A key ingredient of any visit to San Sebastián is enjoying tapas in the Old Town bars.

Orientation to San Sebastián

The San Sebastián that we're interested in surrounds Concha Bay (Bahía de la Concha). It can be divided into three areas: Playa de la

Concha (best beaches), the shopping district (called Centro), and the skinny streets of the grid-planned Old Town (called Parte Vieja, to the north of the shopping district). Centro, just east of Playa de la Concha, has beautiful turn-of-the-20th-century architecture, but no real sights. A busy drag called Alameda del Boulevard (or just "Boulevard") stands where the city wall once ran, and separates the Centro from the Old Town.

It's all bookended by mini-mountains: Monte Urgull to the north and east, and Monte Igueldo to the south and west. The river (Río Urumea) divides central San Sebastián from the district called Gros, which—contrary to its name—is actually quite nice, with a lively night scene and surfing beach.

Tourist Information

San Sebastián's TI, conveniently located right on the Boulevard, has information on city and regional sights, bike rentals (see "Helpful Hints," later), and bus and train schedules. Pick up the free map and various pamphlets with English descriptions of three self-guided walking tours—the Old Town/Monte Urgull walk is best. The TI also offers guided walking tours—see page 570 (July-Sept Mon-Sat 9:00-20:00, Sun 10:00-19:00; Oct-June Mon-Thu 9:00-13:30 & 15:30-19:00, Fri-Sat 10:00-19:00, Sun 10:00-14:00; Boulevard 8, tel. 943-481-166, www.sansebastianturismo .com).

Arrival in San Sebastián

By Train: The town has two train stations (neither has luggage storage, but you can leave bags at Zarranet Internet café downtown—see "Helpful Hints," page 569).

If you're coming on a regional Topo train from Hendaye/Hendaia on the French border, get off at the **EuskoTren Station** (end of the line, called Amara). It's a level 15-minute walk to the center: Exit the station and walk across the long plaza, then veer right and walk eight blocks down Calle Easo (toward the statue of Christ hovering on the hill) to the beach. The Old Town will be ahead on your right, with Playa de la Concha to your left. To speed things up, catch bus #21, #26, or #28 along Calle Easo and take it to the Boulevard stop, near the TI at the bottom of the Old Town.

If you're arriving by train from elsewhere in Spain (or from France after transferring in Irún), you'll get off at the main **RENFE Station.** It's just across the river from the Centro shopping district. There are no convenient buses from the station—to get to the Old Town and most recommended hotels, catch a taxi (they wait out front, €6 to downtown). Or just walk (about 10-15 minutes)—cross the fancy dragon-decorated María Cristina Bridge, turn right onto the busy avenue called Paseo de los Fueros, and follow the Urumea River until the last bridge.

By Bus: A few buses—such as those from Hondarribia and the airport—can let you off at pretty Plaza de Gipuzkoa (first stop after crossing the river, in Centro shopping area, one block from the Boulevard, TI, and Old Town). But most buses—including those from Bilbao—take you instead to San Sebastián's makeshift "bus station" (dubbed Amara) at a big roundabout called Plaza Pío XII. It's basically a parking lot with a few bus shelters and a TI kiosk (open July-Aug only). At the end of the lot nearest the big roundabout, you'll see directional signs pointing you toward the town center (about a 30-minute walk). To save time and energy, catch local bus #21, #26, or #28 from the bus stop at the start of Avenida de Sancho el Sabio and get off at the Boulevard stop, near the TI at the start of the Old Town.

By Plane: San Sebastián Airport (code: EAS) is beautifully situated along the harbor in the nearby town of Hondarribia, 12 miles east of the city (just across the bay from France). An easy bus (#E21) connects the airport to San Sebastián's Plaza de Gipuzkoa, just a block south of the Boulevard and TI (€2, about hourly Mon-Sat 6:00-20:15, Sun 9:40-20:55, 35 minutes, timetable at TI). A taxi into town costs about €30. For flight information, call 943-668-500 (airport info: www.aena.es).

If you arrive at **Bilbao Airport,** go out front and take the Pesa bus directly to San Sebastián (€15.40, pay driver, runs hourly, 1 hour, drops off at Plaza Pío XII; buy ticket *to* the airport at Pesa office in San Sebastián at Avenida de Sancho el Sabio 33; www.pesa.net).

By Car: Take the Amara freeway exit, follow *centro ciudad* signs into the city center, and park in a pay lot (many are well-signed). If you're picking up or returning a rental car, you'll find **Europcar** at the RENFE train station (tel. 943-322-304). Less centrally located are **Hertz** (Centro Comercial Garbera, Travesía

de Garbera 1, bus #16 connects with downtown, tel. 943-392-223)
and **Avis** (a taxi ride away at Hotel Barceló Costa Vasca, Pío Baroja
15, tel. 943-461-556).

Helpful Hints

Internet Access: A half-dozen Internet cafés are well-advertised
throughout the Old Town, most offering fast access for about
€2/hour; try **Zarranet** (Mon-Sat 10:00-22:00, Sun 16:00-
22:00, closed for lunch in winter, Calle San Lorenzo 6, tel.
943-433-381, helpful Juan). These days, government-subsi-
dized Wi-Fi access is available just about everywhere (including at most hotels).

Bookstore: Elkar, an advocate of Basque culture and literature,
has two branches on the same street in the Old Town. Both
have a collection of Basque literature, and one has a wide
selection of guidebooks, maps, and books in English (Mon-
Sat 10:00-14:00 & 16:00-20:00, Sun 11:00-14:00 & 16:30-
20:30, Calle Fermín Calbetón 21 and 30, tel. 943-420-080).

Baggage Storage: There's no baggage storage at the train or bus
stations. **Zarranet** Internet café, listed above, has space for
about 80 bags (first-come, first-served; €0.50/hour, €5/over-
night, €10/24 hours).

Laundry: Wash & Dry is in the Gros neighborhood, across the
river (self-service €14/load, daily 8:00-22:00; drop-off service
€22/load, Mon-Fri 9:30-13:00 & 16:00-20:00; Iparragirre 6,
tel. 943-293-150).

Bike Rental: The city has some great bike lanes and is a good
place to enjoy on two wheels. Like many cities in Europe, San
Sebastián has an automated bike-sharing program. Purchase
a dBizi Card from the **TI** and use it to unlock your bike—
there are nine stands spread around the city. Bikes must be
returned to any stand within four hours, but you can pick up
another one after 30 minutes (€8/day, €15/3 days, €20 cash-
only deposit, return dBizi Card to TI during office hours
to retrieve deposit; rental office hours Mon-Sat 10:00-13:00
& 15:30-18:00, Sun 10:30-13:00, longer in summer; TI at
Boulevard 8; tel. 943-481-166). The TI also offers an English
bike tour of the city in the summer (€14, July-Aug at 11:00
and 17:00, 1.5 hours, includes bike).

For longer-term bike rentals, try **Bici Rent Donosti** (also
rents scooters in summer, Avenida de Zurriola 22, 3 blocks
across river from TI, mobile 639-016-013) or **Sanse Bikes**
(across from TI at Boulevard 25, tel. 943-045-229).

Marijuana: While Spain is famously liberal about marijuana laws,
the Basque Country is even more so. Walking around San
Sebastián, you'll see "grow shops" sporting the famous green

leaf (shopkeepers are helpful if you have questions). The sale of marijuana is still illegal, but the consumption of marijuana is decriminalized and people are allowed to grow enough for their personal use at home. With the town's mesmerizing aquarium and delightfully lit bars filled with enticing munchies, it just makes sense here.

Getting Around San Sebastián

By Bus: Along the Boulevard at the bottom edge of the Old Town, you'll find a line of public buses ready to take you anywhere in town; give any driver your destination, and he or she will tell you the number of the bus to catch (€1.45, pay driver).

Some handy bus routes: #21, #26, and #28 connect the Amara bus and EuskoTren stations to the TI (get off at the Boulevard stop); #16 begins at the Boulevard/TI stop, goes along Playa de la Concha and through residential areas, and eventually arrives at the base of the Monte Igueldo funicular. The TI has a bus-route map (or see www.dbus.es).

By Taxi: Taxis start at €6, which covers most rides in the center. You can't hail a taxi on the street—you must call one (tel. 943-404-040 or 943-464-646) or find a taxi stand (most convenient along the Boulevard).

By Metro: A new Metro system is currently under construction in San Sebastián—it will connect the main areas of the city and eventually extend to the airport.

Tours in San Sebastián

Walking Tours—The TI runs English-language walking tours. Options include Essential San Sebastián (€10, 2 hours), Flavors of San Sebastián (€18, 2 hours, includes three *pintxos* and three drinks), and San Sebastián—A Film City (€14, 2 hours, includes one *pintxo* and one drink). Schedules vary—ask at the TI, call 943-217-717, or check www.sansebastianreservas.com for info and reservations.

Local Guides—**Itsaso Petrikorena** is good (mobile 647-973-231, betitsaso@yahoo.es). **Gabriella Ranelli,** an American who's lived in San Sebastián for over 20 years, specializes in culinary tours. She can take you on a sightseeing spin around the Old Town, along with a walk through the market and best *pintxo* bars (€160/half-day, €210/day, more for driving into the countryside, mobile 609-467-381, www.tenedortours.com, info@tenedortours.com). Gabriella also organizes cooking classes—where you shop at the market, then join a local chef to cook up some tasty *pintxos* of your own (€120/person for a small group)—as well as wine-tastings (€50-130/person).

Gastronomic Tours—San Sebastián Food offers travelers the opportunity to enter one of San Sebastián's exclusive "private eating clubs" (described on the next page) and even participate in preparing a gourmet meal. Prices start around €145 per person (4-person minimum), including ingredients and wine. They also organize €85 *pintxo* tours that have you hopping from bar to bar (includes food and wine) and €75 Iberian ham-cutting courses with sherry tasting (Calle Aldamar 30, mobile 634-759-503, www .sansebastianfood.com, info@sansebastianfood.com).

Tours on Wheels—Two tour options on wheels (following a similar route around the bay) are available, but most travelers won't find them necessary in this walkable city: the **"txu-txu"** tourist train (€5, daily July-mid-Sept 10:30-21:00, mid-Sept-June 11:00-18:30, closed Jan-Feb and Mon off-season, 40-minute round-trip, tel. 943-422-973, www.txu-txu.com) and the **Donosti Tours** hop-on, hop-off bus tour along the bay and around the city (€12, full loop takes about one hour, ticket good for 24 hours, leaves from Victoria Eugenia theater on the Boulevard, tel. 943-441-828, www .busturistikoa.com, Raquel).

Basque Excursions—Based in San Sebastián, **Agustin Ciriza** leads minibus tours for up to eight people through the Spanish and French Basque Country, with destinations including Bilbao, Hondarribia, Biarritz, the Biscay Coast, Bayonne, and Pamplona (even during the running of the bulls). He also offers guided kayaking expeditions, pilgrimages, mountain treks, surf lessons, surfing trips, wine tours to the Rioja region, and wine tastings, food tours, and cooking classes in town. Prices start at €65 per person for a half-day excursion (minimum two people, mobile 686-117-395, www.gorilla-trip.com, agus@gorilla-trip.com).

Sights in San Sebastián

▲▲Old Town (Parte Vieja)

Huddled in the shadow of its once-protective Monte Urgull, the Old Town is where San Sebastián was born about 1,000 years ago. Because the town burned down in 1813 (as Spain, Portugal, and England fought the French to get Napoleon's brother off the Spanish throne), the architecture you see is generally Neoclassical and uniform. Still, the grid plan of streets hides heavy Baroque and Gothic churches, surprise plazas, and fun little shops, including venerable pastry stores, rugged produce markets, Basque-independence souvenir shops, and seafood-to-go delis. The highlight of the Old Town is its array of incredibly lively tapas bars—though here these snacks are called *pintxos* (PEEN-chohs; see "Eating in San Sebastián" on page 582). To see the fishing industry in action, wander out to the port (described later).

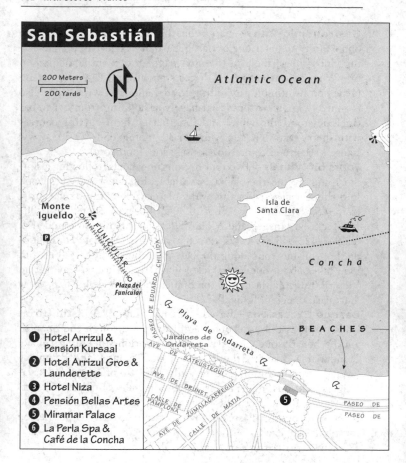

San Sebastián

200 Meters
200 Yards

Atlantic Ocean

Monte Igueldo

FUNICULAR

Plaza del Funicular

Isla de Santa Clara

Concha

Playa de Ondarreta

Jardines de Ondarreta

AVE. DE SATRUSTEGUI

AVE. DE BRUNET

CALLE DE PAMPLONA

AVE. DE ZUMALACARREGUI

CALLE DE MATIA

PASEO DE EDUARDO CHILLIDA

B E A C H E S

PASEO DE

PASEO DE

❶ Hotel Arrizul & Pensión Kursaal

❷ Hotel Arrizul Gros & Launderette

❸ Hotel Niza

❹ Pensión Bellas Artes

❺ Miramar Palace

❻ La Perla Spa & Café de la Concha

Although the struggle for Basque independence is currently in a relatively calm stage, with most people opposing violent ETA tactics, there are still underlying tensions between Spain and the Basque people. In the middle of the Old Town, **Calle Juan de Bilbao** is the political-action street. Here you'll find people more sympathetic to the struggle (whereas for others, it's a street to avoid). Speaking Basque is encouraged.

Flagpoles mark **"private eating clubs"** throughout the Old Town (otherwise unmarked). Basque society is matrilineal and very female-oriented. A husband brings home his paycheck and hands it directly to his wife, who controls the house's purse strings (and everything else). Basque men felt they needed a place where they could congregate and play "king of the castle," so they formed these clubs where members could reserve a table and cook for their friends. The clubs used to be exclusively male; women are now allowed as invited guests...but never in the kitchen, which remains

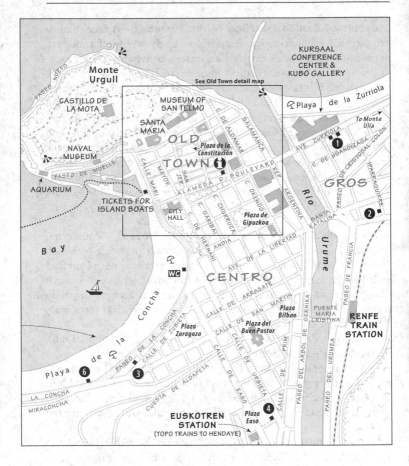

the men's domain.

▲**Plaza de la Constitución**—The Old Town's main square is where bullfights used to be held. Notice the seat numbering on the

balconies: Even if you owned an apartment here, the city retained rights to the balconies, which it could sell as box seats. (Residents could peek over the paying customers' shoulders.) Above the clock, notice the seal of San Sebastián: a merchant ship with sails billowing in the wind. The city was granted trading rights by the crown—a reminder of the Basque Country's importance in Spanish seafaring. Inviting café tables spill into the square from all corners.

BASQUE COUNTRY

Museum of San Telmo (San Telmo Museoa)—A recent addition to this fascinating museum innovatively wrapped a modern facade around a 16th-century Dominican convent and its peaceful cloister. It's now the largest museum of Basque culture in the country. Exhibits of archaeological and ethnographic artifacts demonstrate the traditional folkways of Basque life and vividly tell the history of the region. An art historical painting collection features a few gems (El Greco, Rubens, Tintoretto), while 19th- and 20th-century paintings by Basque artists offer an interesting peek into the spirit, faces, and natural beauty of these fiercely independent people (other featured artists include El Greco and Rubens).

Cost and Hours: €5, free on Tue, open Tue-Sun 10:00-20:00, closed Mon, Plaza Zuloaga 1, tel. 943-481-580, www.santelmo museoa.com.

▲**Bretxa Public Market (Mercado de la Bretxa)**—Wandering through the public market is a fun way to get in touch with San Sebastián and Basque culture. Although the big, white market building facing the Boulevard has been converted into a modern shopping mall, the farmers' produce market thrives here (lined up along the left side of the building), as does the fish and meat market (behind it and underground).

Hours: Mon-Fri 8:00-14:00 & 17:00-20:00, Sat 8:00-14:00, closed Sun, Plaza de Sarriegi.

Visiting the Market: To get to the fish and meat market, walk past the produce vendors (look under the eaves of the modern building to see what the farmers are selling), and find a big glass cube in the square, where an escalator will take you down into the market.

At the bottom of the escalator, notice the **fish stall** on the left (marked *J. Ma. Mujika*). In the case, you'll see different cuts of *bacalao* (cod). Entire books have been written about the importance of cod to the evolution of seafaring in Europe. The fish could be preserved in salt to feed sailors on ever-longer trips into the North Atlantic, allowing them to venture beyond the continental shelf (into deeper waters where they couldn't catch fresh fish). Cod was also popular among Catholic landlubbers on Fridays. Today cod remains a Basque staple. People still buy the salted version, which must be soaked for 48 hours (and the water changed three times) to become edible. If you're in a rush, you can buy de-salted cod...but at a cost in flavor. Stroll behind this stall to explore the fresh fish market—often with the catch of the day set up in cute little scenes. There's a free **WC** in the market—just ask *"¿Dónde está el servicio, por favor?"*

When you're done exploring, take the escalator up and cross the busy street to the **Aitor Lasa** cheese shop (Mon-Fri 8:30-14:00 & 17:15-20:00, Sat 8:30-14:30, closed Sun, Aldamar 12, tel. 943-

430-354). Pass the fragrant piles of mushrooms at the entrance and head back to the display case, showing off the Basque specialty of *idiazábal*—raw sheep's milk cheese. Notice the wide variety, which depends on the specific region it came from, whether it's smoked or cured, and for how long it's been cured *(curación)*. If you're planning a picnic, this is a very local (and expensive) ingredient. To try the cheese that won first prize a few years back in the Ordizia International Cheese Competition, ask for *"El queso con el premio de Ordizia, por favor."* The owners are evangelical about the magic of combining the local cheese with walnuts and *casero* (homemade) apple jam.

The Port

At the west end of the Old Town, protected by Monte Urgull, is the port. Take the passage through the wall at the appropriately

named Calle Puerto, and jog right along the level, portside promenade, Paseo del Muelle. You'll pass fishing boats unloading the catch of the day (with hungry locals looking on), salty sailors' pubs, and fishermen mending nets. Also along this strip are the skippable Naval Museum and the entertaining aquarium. Trails to the top of Monte Urgull are just above this scene, near Santa María Church (or climb the stairs next to the aquarium).

Cruises—Small boats cruise from the Old Town's port to the island in the bay (Isla Santa Clara), where you can hike the trails and have lunch at the lone café, or pack a picnic before setting sail (€3.80 round-trip, small ferry departs June-Sept only, on the hour 10:00-20:00). The *City of San Sebastián* catamaran gives 30-minute tours of the bay for €8.50.

Naval Museum (Museo Naval)—This museum's two floors of exhibits describe the seafaring city's history, revealing the intimate link between the Basque culture and the sea.

    Cost and Hours: €1.20, free on Thu, borrow English description at entry, Tue-Sat 10:00-13:30 & 16:00-19:30, Sun 11:00-14:00, closed Mon, Paseo del Muelle 24, tel. 943-430-051.

    ▲▲**Aquarium**—San Sebastián's aquarium is surprisingly good. Exhibits are thoughtfully described in English and include a history of the sea, a collection of naval vessels, and models showing various drift-netting techniques. You'll see a petting tank filled with nervous fish; a huge whale skeleton; a trippy, illuminated, slowly tumbling tank of jellyfish; and a mesmerizing 45-foot-long tunnel that lets you look up into a wet world of floppy rays, menacing sharks, and local fish. The local section ends with a tank of shark fetuses safely incubating away from hungry predators. Local kids see the tropical wing and holler, "Nemo!"

Cost and Hours: €12, €6 for kids under 13; July-Aug daily 10:00-21:00; Sept-June Mon-Fri 10:00-19:00, Sat-Sun 10:00-20:00; last entry one hour before closing, at the end of Paseo del Muelle, tel. 943-440-099, www.aquariumss.com.

▲**Monte Urgull**—The once-mighty castle (Castillo de la Mota) atop the hill deterred most attackers, allowing the city to prosper in the Middle Ages. The free museum within the castle, featuring San Sebastián history, is mildly interesting. The best views from the hill are not from the statue of Christ, but from the ramparts on the left side (as you face the hill), just above the port's aquarium. **Café El Polvorín,** nestled in the park, is a free-spirited place with salads, sandwiches, and good sangria.

A walkway allows you to stroll the mountain's entire perimeter near sea level. This route is continuous from Hotel Parma to the aquarium, and offers an enjoyable after-dinner wander. You can also walk a bit higher up over the port (along the white railing)—called the *paseo de las curas,* or "priest's path," where the clergy could stroll unburdened by the rabble in the streets below. These paths are technically open only from sunrise to sunset (daily May-Sept 8:00-21:00, Oct-April 8:00-19:00), but you can often access them later.

The Beach and Beyond

▲▲**La Concha Beach and Promenade**—The shell-shaped Playa de la Concha, the pride of San Sebastián, has one of Europe's loveliest stretches of sand. Lined with a two-mile-long promenade, it allows even backpackers to feel aristocratic. Although it's pretty empty off-season, sunbathers pack its shores in summer. But year-round it's surprisingly devoid of eateries and money-grubbing businesses.

There are free showers, and *cabinas* provide lockers, showers, and shade for a fee. For a century, the lovingly painted wrought-iron balustrade that stretches the length of the promenade has been a symbol of the city; it shows up on everything from jewelry to headboards. It's shaded by tamarisk trees, with branches carefully pruned into knotty bulbs each winter that burst into leafy shade-giving canopies in the summer—another symbol of the city. **Café de la Concha** serves reasonably priced, mediocre food, but you can't beat the location of its terrace overlooking the beach (€14 weekday lunch special, tel. 943-473-600).

The **Miramar palace and park,** which divides the crescent beach in the middle, was where Queen María Cristina held court when she summered here. Her royal changing rooms are used today as inviting cafés, restaurants, and a fancy spa. You can walk in the park, although the palace, used as a music school, is closed to the public.

La Perla Spa—The spa overlooking the beach attracts a less royal crowd today and appeals mostly to visitors interested in sampling "the curative properties of the sea." You can enjoy its Talasso Fitness Circuit, featuring a hydrotherapy pool, a relaxation pool, a panoramic Jacuzzi, cold-water pools, a seawater steam sauna, a dry sauna, and a relaxation area.

Cost and Hours: €26 for 2-hour fitness circuit, €31 for 3-hour circuit, daily 8:00-22:00, €3 caps and €1 rental towels, bring a swimsuit or buy one for €33, on the beach at the center of the crescent, Paseo de la Concha, tel. 943-458-856, www.la-perla.net.

Monte Igueldo—For commanding city views (if you ignore the tacky amusements on top), ride the funicular up Monte Igueldo,

a mirror image of Monte Urgull. The views over San Sebastián, along the coast, and into the distant green mountains are sensational day or night. The entrance to the funicular is on the road behind the tennis club on the far western end of Playa de Ondarreta, which extends from Playa de la Concha to the west.

Cost and Hours: Funicular—€2.80 round-trip; changeable hours but roughly April-Sept Mon-Tue and Thu-Sun 10:00-22:00, closed Wed; Oct-March Mon-Tue and Thu-Fri 11:00-18:00, Sat-Sun 11:00-20:00, closed Wed. If you drive to the top, you'll pay €1.90 to enter. Bus #16 takes you from the Old Town to the base of the funicular in about 10 minutes.

In Gros

Gros and Zurriola Beach—The district of Gros, just east across the river from the Old Town, offers a distinct Californian vibe. Literally a dump a few years ago, today it has a surfing scene on Zurriola Beach (popular with students and German tourists) and a futuristic conference center (described next). Long-term plans call for a new promenade that will arc over the water and under Monte Ulía.

▲Kursaal Conference Center and Kubo Gallery—These two Lego-like boxes (just east and across the river from the Old Town, in Gros) mark the spot of what was once a grand casino, torn down by Franco to discourage gambling. Many locals wanted to rebuild it as it once was, in a similar style to the turn-of-the-20th-century buildings in the Centro, but—in an effort to keep up with the postmodern trends in Bilbao—city leaders opted instead for Rafael Moneo's striking contemporary design. The complex is supposed to resemble the angular rocks that make up the town's breakwater. The Kursaal houses a theater, conference facilities, some gift shops and travel agencies, a restaurant, and the Kubo Gallery. The gallery offers temporary exhibits by international artists and promotes contemporary Basque artists. Each exhibit is complemented by a 10-minute video that plays continuously in the gallery theater.

Cost and Hours: Free, Kubo Gallery open daily 11:30-13:30 & 17:00-21:00.

Sleeping in San Sebastián

(€1 = about $1.30, country code: 34)
Rates in San Sebastián fluctuate with the season. When you see a range of prices in these listings, the top end is for summer (roughly July-Sept), and the low end is for the shoulder season (May-June and Oct); outside of these times, you'll pay even less. Since breakfast is often not included, I've recommended some good options elsewhere in town (see "Eating in San Sebastián," later).

In or near the Old Town

$$$ Hotel Parma is a business-class place with 27 fine rooms and family-run attention to detail and service. It stands, stately, on the edge of the Old Town, away from the bar-scene noise, and overlooks the river and a surfing beach (Sb-€70-99, windowless interior Db-€103-151, view Db-€124-165, breakfast-€10.50, air-con, modern lounge, free Wi-Fi, Paseo de Salamanca 10, tel. 943-428-893, fax 943-424-082, www.hotelparma.com, hotelparma@hotelparma .com; Iñaki, Pino, Maria Eugenia, and Ana).

$$ Pensión Edorta ("Edward"), deep in the Old Town, elegantly mixes wood, brick, and color into nine modern, stylish rooms (D-€40-70, Db-€60-90, extra bed-€20-25, free Wi-Fi, elevator, Calle Puerto 15, tel. 943-423-773, fax 943-433-570, www .pensionedorta.com, info@pensionedorta.com, Javier).

$ Pensión Amaiur is a flowery place with long, narrow halls and great-value rooms within the Old Town. Kind Virginia gives the justifiably popular *pensión* a homey warmth. All but one of her 13 colorful, cozy rooms share six clean bathrooms (S-€34-42, quiet interior D-€44-50, exterior D-€54-60, Db-€69-75, T-€69-75, family room €84-90, kitchen facilities, pay Internet access, free Wi-Fi, next to Santa María Church at Calle 31 de Agosto 44, tel. 943-429-654, www.pensionamaiur.com, amaiur@telefonica.net).

Across the River, in Gros

The pleasant Gros district—San Sebastián's "uptown"—is marked by the super-modern, blocky Kursaal conference center. The nearby Zurriola Beach is popular with surfers. These hotels are less than a five-minute walk from the Old Town. For locations, see the map on page 572.

$$$ Hotel Arrizul is bright and fresh, with mod, minimalist decor in each of its 12 rooms (Sb-€62-105, Db-€90-142, Db suite-€110-178, Qb-€140-225, breakfast-€7, air-con, elevator, free Wi-Fi, parking-€17, Peña y Goñi 1, tel. 943-322-804, fax 943-326-701, www.arrizul.com, info@arrizulhotel.com). Its sister hotel, **Hotel Arrizul Gros,** is about five blocks away and has 17 rooms with similar decor (slightly lower rates, includes small breakfast) plus seven apartments (apartments: €145-189/2 people, €185-229/4 people, €215-249/6 people; Iparraguirre 3, same contact info as main Hotel Arrizul).

$$ Pensión Kursaal has 21 basic but colorful and modern rooms in a historic building, with white and beige decor (Db-€50-89, family room, elevator, pay Internet access, free Wi-Fi, parking-€12, Peña y Goñi 2, tel. 943-292-666, fax 943-297-536, www.pensionesconencanto.com, kursaal@pensionesconencanto.com).

On the Beach

$$$ Hotel Niza, set in the middle of Playa de la Concha, is often booked well in advance. Half of its 40 rooms (some with balconies) overlook the bay. From its chandeliered and plush lounge, a classic elevator takes you to comfortable pastel rooms with wedding-cake molding (tiny interior Sb-€55-68, Db-€132-157, view rooms cost the same—request one when you reserve...but no promises, extra bed-€22, only streetside rooms have air-con, fans on request, great buffet breakfast-€11, free Internet access and Wi-Fi, parking-€15/day—must reserve in advance, Zubieta 56, see map on page 572 for location, tel. 943-426-663, fax 943-441-251, www.hotelniza.com, niza@hotelniza.com). The breakfast room has a sea view and doubles as a bar with light snacks throughout the day (Bar Biarritz, daily 7:30-24:00).

Between the Beach and EuskoTren Station

$$$ Pensión Bellas Artes, while farther from the Old Town than my other listings, is worth the 15-minute walk. Lively Leire, who lived in New York and runs her *pensión* with pride, rents 10 small, well-appointed, tidy rooms with thoughtful extra touches like fresh flowers in each room and a free loaner laptop. Leire loves to give her guests sightseeing and dining tips. She can also tell you about apartment rentals in the area (Sb-€69-89, Db-€89-109, extra bed for 20 percent more, elevator, free Internet access and Wi-Fi,

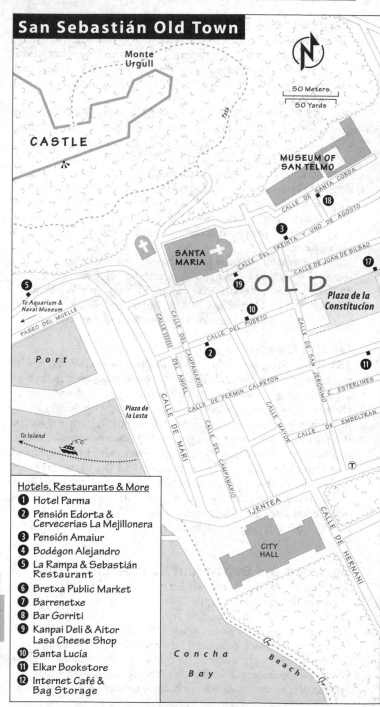

San Sebastián Old Town

Monte Urgull

N

50 Meters

50 Yards

CASTLE

MUSEUM OF SAN TELMO

CALLE DE SANTA CORDA

18

3

SANTA MARIA

CALLE DEL TREINTA Y UNO DE AGOSTO

CALLE DE JUAN DE BILBAO

17

5

O L D

19

To Aquarium & Naval Museum

PASEO DEL MUELLE

Plaza de la Constitucíon

10

CALLE DEL PUERTO

Port

CALLE DEL CAMPANARIO

CALLE DEL ANGEL

2

CALLE DE SAN JERONIMO

11

C. ESTERLINES

Plaza de la Lasta

CALLE DE FERMIN CALBETON

CALLE DE MARI

CALLE DEL CAMPANARIO

CALLE MAYOR

CALLE DE EMBELTRAN

To Island

T

IJENTEA

CITY HALL

CALLE DE HERNANI

Hotels, Restaurants & More

1 Hotel Parma

2 Pensión Edorta & Cervecerias La Mejillonera

3 Pensión Amaiur

4 Bodégon Alejandro

5 La Rampa & Sebastián Restaurant

6 Bretxa Public Market

7 Barrenetxe

8 Bar Gorriti

9 Kanpai Deli & Aitor Lasa Cheese Shop

10 Santa Lucía

11 Elkar Bookstore

12 Internet Café & Bag Storage

Concha Bay

Beach

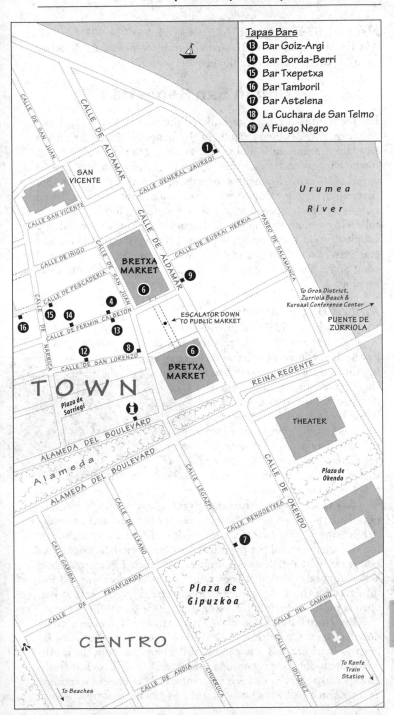

Tapas Bars
13 Bar Goiz-Argi
14 Bar Borda-Berri
15 Bar Txepetxa
16 Bar Tamboril
17 Bar Astelena
18 La Cuchara de San Telmo
19 A Fuego Negro

SAN VICENTE

Urumea River

CALLE DE SAN JUAN
CALLE DE ALDAMAR
CALLE GENERAL JAUREGI
CALLE SAN VICENTE
CALLE DE INIGO
CALLE DE EUSKAI HERRIA
PASEO DE SALAMANCA

BRETXA MARKET

To Gros District,
Zurriola Beach &
Kursaal Conference Center

CALLE DE PESCADERIA
CALLE DE SAN JUAN
CALLE DE FERMIN CALBETON
ESCALATOR DOWN
TO PUBLIC MARKET

PUENTE DE ZURRIOLA

CALLE DE NARRICA
CALLE DE SAN LORENZO

BRETXA MARKET

T O W N

Plaza de Sarriegi

REINA REGENTE

THEATER

ALAMEDA DEL BOULEVARD

Alameda

ALAMEDA DEL BOULEVARD

Plaza de Okendo

CALLE TEGAZPI
CALLE DE ELKANO
CALLE BENGOETXEA
CALLE DE OKENDO

Plaza de Gipuzkoa

CALLE GARIBAL
CALLE DE PENAFLORIDA

CENTRO

CALLE DEL CAMINO

CALLE DE ANOIA
C. CHURRUCA
CALLE DE IDIAQUEZ

To Renfe Train Station

To Beaches

near EuskoTren Station at Urbieta 64, tel. 943-474-905, fax 943-463-111, www.pension-bellasartes.com, info@pension-bellasartes .com). For the location, see the map on page 572.

Eating in San Sebastián

Basque food is regarded as some of the best in Spain, and San Sebastián is the culinary capital of the Basque Country. What the city lacks in museums and sights, it more than makes up for in food. (For tips on Basque cuisine, see page 536.) San Sebastián is proud of its many Michelin-rated fine-dining establishments, but they require a big commitment of time and money. Most casual visitors will prefer to hop from pub to pub through the Old Town, following the crowds between Basque-font signs. I've listed a couple of solid traditional restaurants, but for the best value and memories, I'd order top-end dishes with top-end wine in top-end bars. Some places close for siesta in the late afternoon and early evening.

Pintxo Bar-Hopping

San Sebastián's Old Town provides the ideal backdrop for tapas-hopping; just wander the streets and sidle up to the bar in the live-

liest spot. Calle Fermín Calbetón has the best concentration of bars; the streets San Jerónimo and 31 de Agosto are also good. I've listed these top-notch places in order as you progress deeper into the Old Town. Note that there are plenty of other options along the way. Before you begin, study the sidebar on page 584.

Bar Goiz-Argi ("Morning Light"), every local's top recommendation, serves its tiny dishes with pride and attitude. Advertising *pintxos calientes,* they cook each treat for you, allowing you a montage of petite gourmet snacks. Try their *tartaleta de txangurro* (spider-crab spread on bread) or their signature shrimp kebab. A good selection of open wine bottles are clearly priced and displayed on the shelf (great prices, no chairs, congregate at bar, open daily, Calle Fermín Calbetón 4, tel. 943-425-204).

Bar Borda-Berri (loosely, "Mountain Hut"), a couple doors down, features a more low-key ambience and top-quality €3 *pintxos.* There are only a few items at the bar; check out the chalkboard menu for today's options, order, and they'll cook it fresh. The specialty here is melt-in-your-mouth beef cheeks *(carrillera de tenera)* in a red-wine sauce, risotto with wild mushrooms, and foie gras (grilled goose liver) with apple jelly, which is even better paired with a glass of their best red wine (closed Mon, Calle Fermín Calbetón 12, tel. 943-430-342).

Bar Txepetxa is *the* place for anchovies. A plastic circle displaying a variety of *antxoas* tapas makes choosing your anchovy treat easy. These fish are fresh—not cured and salted like those most Americans hate (€2.20/*pintxo*, Tue lunch only, closed Sun-Mon, Calle Pescaderia 5, tel. 943-422-227).

Bar Tamboril is a traditional spot right on the main square favored for its seafood, mushrooms *(txampis tamboril),* and anchovy tempura along with its good prices. Their list of hot *pintxos* (grab the little English menu on the bar) makes you want to break the one-tapa-per-stop rule (Calle Pescaderia 2, tel. 943-423-507).

Bar Astelena, across the square from Tamboril, serves a delicious blend of traditional and modern plates, all thoughtfully presented. Try any of the specials, particularly the *solomillo a lo pobre* (small sirloin fillet with mini-fries and a fried egg). Other standouts include *rabo de buey* (oxtail) and capellini-wrapped prawns. There's no English menu, but the staff is happy to help translate (€3-4 *pintxos*, Calle de Iñigo 1, tel. 943-425-245).

La Cuchara de San Telmo, with cooks taught by a big-name Basque chef, Alex Mondiel, is a cramped place that devotes as much space to its thriving kitchen as its bar. It has nothing precooked and set on the bar—order your mini-gourmet plates with a spirit of adventure from the constantly changing blackboard. Their foie gras with apple jelly is rightfully famous (€3 *pintxos,* closed Mon, tucked away on a lonely alley called Santa Corda behind Museum of San Telmo at 31 de Agosto #28, tel. 943-435-446).

A Fuego Negro is cool and upscale compared with the others, with a hip, slick vibe and a blackboard menu of *pintxos* and drinks (there's an English translation sheet). They have a knack for mixing gourmet pretentiousness with whimsy here: Try their *arroz, tomate, y un huevo* (risotto with tomato and egg); *bakailu* (cod); and *regaliz* (licorice ice cream) trio for a unique taste-bud experience (€3.60). Enjoy their serious and extensive wine selection (closed Mon, 31 de Agosto #31, tel. 650-135-373). An inviting little section in the back makes this a sit-down dining opportunity.

Cervecerias La Mejillonera is famous among students for its big, cheap beers, *patatas bravas,* and mussels (*"tigres"* are the spicy favorites). A long, skinny stainless-steel bar and lots of photos make ordering easy—this is the only place in town where you pay when served (Calle Puerto 15, tel. 943-428-465).

Restaurants

Bodégon Alejandro is a good spot for modern Basque cuisine in a traditional cellar setting (three-course fixed-price lunch-€15,

Do the *Txikiteo:* A Tapas Cheat Sheet

Txikiteo (chih-kee-TAY-oh) is the Basque word for hopping from bar to bar, enjoying small sandwiches and tiny snacks (*pintxos,* PEEN-chohs) and glasses of wine. Local competition drives small bars to lay out the most appealing array of *pintxos.* The selection is amazing, but the key to eating well here is going for the *pintxos calientes*—the hot tapas advertised on blackboards and cooked to order. Tapas are best, freshest, and accompanied by the most vibrant crowd from 12:00 to 14:00 and from 20:00 to 22:30. Watch what's being served—the locals know each bar's specialty. No matter how much you like a place, just order one dish; you want to be mobile.

Later in the evening, bars get more crowded and challenging for tourists. To get service amid the din, speak loudly and directly (little sweet voices get ignored), with no extra words. Expect to share everything. Double-dipping is encouraged. It's rude to put a dirty napkin on the table; it belongs on the floor.

If you can't get the bartender's attention to serve you a particular *pintxo,* don't be shy—just grab it and a napkin, and munch away. Basque tapas bars distinguish themselves by laying out big platters of help-yourself goodies. This user-friendly system lets you simply grab what looks good, rather than navigating a menu. This system works so well, it's becoming popular in other parts of Spain (for example, some of Barcelona's trendiest eateries now are Basque-style bars). You pay when you leave; just keep a mental note of the tapas you've eaten. There's a code of honor. Everyone is part of the extended Basque family.

If you want a meal instead of *pintxos,* some bars—even ones that look only like bars from the street—have attached dining rooms, usually in the back.

Pintxos

antxoas	anchovies (not the cured, heavily salted kind you always hated)
bocadillos	baguette sandwiches
bacalao	cod (served lots of ways)
txampis (chahm-pees)	mushrooms
gambas	shrimp
patatas bravas	crisp potato cubes served with a spicy sauce

tortilla	big, round omelet pie served by the slice (many varieties)
txangurro (chang-GOO-roh)	spider crab, a delicacy, often mixed with onions, tomatoes, and wine, served hot or made into a spread to put on bread

Descriptions

brocheta	anything on a stick
calientes	served hot and cooked to order (listed on chalkboard, not already on the bar)
cazuelas	hot meal-size servings (like *raciones* in Spanish)
plancha	anything grilled

Drinks

caña (KAHN-yah)	draft beer
mosto	non-alcoholic grape juice that comes in red or white (for when you've had enough beer and wine)
Rioja	better wine
sidra	dry cider that's a bit more alcoholic than beer
sin (seen)	non-alcoholic beer (literally means "without")
tinto	red house wine
txakoli (chah-koh-LEE)	fresh white wine, poured from high to "break against the glass" and aerate it to add sparkle. Good with seafood, and therefore fits the local cuisine well.
un crianza	a glass of nicely aged wine. It's smart to ask for this instead of "*un tinto*" to get better quality for nearly the same price.
vaso de agua	glass of tap water (they'll ask you "bottled?"—*embotellada?*—and you say no)
zurito (thoo-REE-toh)	small beer

Paying the Bill

Zenbat da?	"How much?"
Me cobras?	"What's the damage?" (a fun way to say "The bill, please")

Tue-Sun 13:00-15:30 & 20:30-22:30 except closed Sun night, closed Mon, in Old Town on Calle Fermín Calbetón 4, tel. 943-427-158).

Seafood Along the Port: For seafood with a salty sailor's view, check out the half-dozen hardworking, local-feeling restaurants that line the harbor on the way to the aquarium. **La Rampa** is an upscale eatery, specializing in crab *(txangurro)* and lobster dishes and seafood *parillada* (€30-50 for dinner, closed Tue-Wed, Paseo Muelle/Kaiko Pasealekua 26-27, tel. 943-421-652). Also along here, locals like **Sebastián** (more traditional, closed Tue).

Picnics and Takeout

A picnic on the beach or atop Monte Urgull is a tempting option. You can assemble a bang-up spread at the **Bretxa Public Market** at Plaza de Sarriegi (described earlier).

Upscale **Barrenetxe** has an amazing array of breads, prepared foods, and some of the best desserts in town. In business since 1699, their somewhat formal service is justified (daily 8:00-20:00, Plaza de Guipúzcoa 9, tel. 943-424-482).

Kanpai, a high-quality deli serving Basque and international cuisine, is run by Davíd and his mother. Step up to the display case and get something "to go" for an easy and tasty picnic (daily 10:00-15:00 & 17:00-20:30, shorter hours off-season, Calle Aldamar 10, tel. 943-428-334).

Breakfast

If your hotel doesn't provide breakfast—or even if it does—consider one of these places. The first is a traditional stand-up bar; the second is a greasy spoon.

Bar Gorriti, delightfully local, is packed with market workers and shoppers starting their day. You'll stand at the bar and choose a hot-off-the-grill *francesca jamon* omelet (fluffy mini-omelet sandwich topped with a slice of ham) and other goodies (€2 each). This and a good cup of coffee makes for a very Basque breakfast. By the time you get there for breakfast, many market workers will be taking their mid-morning break (daily, breakfast served 7:00-10:00, facing the side of the big white market building at San Juan 3, tel. 943-428-353).

Santa Lucía, a 1950s-style diner, is ideal for a cheap Old Town breakfast or *churros* break (*churros* are like deep-fried doughnut sticks that can be dipped in pudding-like hot chocolate). Photos of two dozen different breakfasts decorate the walls, and plates of fresh *churros* keep patrons happy. Grease is liberally applied to the grill...from a squeeze bottle (daily 8:30-21:30, Calle Puerto 6, tel. 943-425-019).

San Sebastián Connections

By Train

San Sebastián has two train stations: RENFE and EuskoTren (described under "Arrival in San Sebastián" on page 567). The station you use depends on your destination.

EuskoTren Station: If you're going into France, take the regional Topo train (which leaves from the EuskoTren Station) over the French border into **Hendaye** (2/hour, 35 minutes, departs EuskoTren Station at :15 and :45 after the hour 6:15-21:45). From Hendaye, connect to France's SNCF network (www.sncf.com), where connections include **Paris** (4/day direct, 5.5-6 hours, or 8.5-hour night train, reservations required). Unfortunately, San Sebastián's EuskoTren Station doesn't have information on Paris-bound trains from Hendaye. Don't buy the Spanish ticket too far in advance—EuskoTren tickets to Hendaye must be used within two hours of purchase (or else they expire).

Also leaving from San Sebastián's EuskoTren Station are slow regional trains to destinations in Spain's Basque region, including **Bilbao** (hourly, 2.5 hours—the bus is faster, €8.50 round-trip ticket saves €1.50; EuskoTren info: toll tel. 902-543-210, www.euskotren.es). Although the train ride from San Sebastián to Bilbao takes twice as long as the bus, it passes through more interesting countryside. The Basque Country shows off its trademark green and gray: lush green vegetation and gray clouds. It's an odd mix of heavy industrial factories, small homegrown veggie gardens, streams, and every kind of livestock you can imagine.

RENFE Station: This station handles long-distance destinations within Spain (most of which require reservations). Connections include **Irún** (8/day, 25 minutes), **Hendaye,** France (4/day, 30 minutes), **Madrid** (4/day, 5-6 hours), **Burgos** (6/day, 3-3.5 hours), **León** (1/day, 5 hours), **Pamplona** (2/day, 1.75 hours), **Salamanca** (4/day, 6 hours), **Vitoria** (8/day, 1.75 hours), **Barcelona** (2/day, 5.5 hours), and **Santiago de Compostela** (1/day direct, 11 hours, final destination A Coruña).

By Bus

San Sebastián's "bus station," called Amara for the neighborhood, is a congregation of bus parking spots next to the big Hotel Amara Plaza, at the roundabout called Plaza Pío XII (on the river, four blocks south of EuskoTren Station; take bus #21, #26, or #28 from Boulevard). Some schedules are posted at various stops, but confirm departure times. You must buy your tickets in advance at the bus companies, with offices on either side of the block north of the station area (toward downtown, along Avenida de Sancho el

Sabio and Paseo de Vízcaya). Bus tickets are not available from the driver. The Pesa office, which serves St-Jean-de-Luz and Bilbao, is located at Avenida de Sancho el Sabio 33 (toll tel. 902-101-210, www.pesa.net). The Alsa office—which serves Madrid, Burgos, and León—is just beyond Pesa at Sancho el Sabio 31 (toll tel. 902-422-242, www.alsa.es). The Roncalesa office is in the same office as Alsa (tel. 943-461-064, www.condasa.com). The Vibasa office—which serves Burgos, Pamplona, and Barcelona—is on the other side of the block, at Calle Vizcaya 15 (closed 13:30-15:00, toll tel. 902-101-363, www.vibasa.es).

From San Sebastián, buses go to **Bilbao** (2/hour, hourly on weekends, 6:30-22:00, 1.25 hours, €10, get ticket from Pesa office, departs from Amara; morning buses fill with tourists, commuters, and students, so consider buying your ticket the day before; once in Bilbao, buses leave you at Termibús stop with easy tram connections to the Guggenheim modern-art museum); **Bilbao Airport** (a Pesa bus leaves directly from Plaza Pío XII, hourly, 1.25 hours, €15.40, get tickets from Pesa office), **Pamplona** (almost hourly, 1 hour, €7, Roncalesa office), **León** (1/day, 6 hours, €30, Alsa office), **Madrid** (8/day, 6 hours direct, otherwise 7 hours, €34-50, Alsa office), **Burgos** (6/day, 3-3.5 hours, €16, Alsa or Vibasa office), and **Barcelona** (2/day and 1/night, 7 hours, €30, Vibasa office).

To visit **Hondarribia** (described next), you can catch bus #E21 or #E23 much closer to the center at Plaza de Gipuzkoa (1 block south of TI; about 3/hour, 35 minutes, #E21 goes to airport en route to Hondarribia, €2).

Buses to French Basque Country: A bus goes from San Sebastián's Amara bus station to **St-Jean-de-Luz** (Mon-Sat only, 2/day at 9:00 and 14:30, none on Sun, 1 hour, return trips at 12:45 and 19:15, only 1/week off-season, €4.50, get ticket from Pesa office), then continues directly to **Biarritz** (1.25 hours from San Sebastián, €6.60) and **Bayonne** (1.5 hours from San Sebastián, €7.75).

Between San Sebastián and St-Jean-de-Luz

Just 45 minutes apart by car, San Sebastián and St-Jean-de-Luz bridge the Spanish and French Basque regions. Between them you'll find the functional towns of Irún (Spain) and Hendaye (France), and the delightful hill town of Hondarribia, which is worth a visit if you have time to spare.

Fuenterrabía / Hondarribia

For a taste of small-town *País Vasco*, dip into this enchanting, seldom-visited town (more commonly known by its Euskara name

rather than the Spanish version, Fuenterrabía). Much smaller and easier to manage than San Sebastián, and also closer to France (across the picturesque Bay of Txingudi from Hendaye), Hondarribia allows travelers a stress-free opportunity to enjoy Basque culture. While it's easy to think of this as a border town (between France and Spain), culturally it's in the middle of the Basque Country.

The town comes in two parts: the lower port town and the historic, balcony-lined streets of the hilly and walled upper town. The upper town, which feels quite manicured, is a delightful place to poke around if you have time. The main square is fronted by Charles V's austere, oddly squat castle (now a parador inn—see below). You can follow the TI's self-guided tour of the Old Town (English brochure available) or just lose yourself within the walls to explore the plazas.

In the modern lower town, straight shopping streets serve a local clientele, and a pleasant walkway takes strollers along the beach.

Tourist Information: There are two TIs—one is located on the main square, Plaza de Armas, across from the parador; the other is at Minatera 9 near the port (both July-Sept daily 10:30-13:30 & 15:30-20:00; Oct-June Tue-Sat 10:00-13:30 & 15:30-18:30, Sun 10:00-14:00, closed Mon; tel. 943-645-458, www.bidasoa turismo.com).

Arrival in Hondarribia: Drivers can use the metered parking by the port (marked with blue lines, prepay for parking at machine). Buses into town stop near the main square.

Sleeping in Hondarribia: Accommodations are pricey here, but it's a nice small-town alternative to San Sebastián. **$$$ Parador El Emperador,** with 36 rooms housed in a former imperial fortress, is the town's splurge. Tourists are allowed to have sangria in the *muy* cool bar, though the terraces are for guests only (Sb-€168, Db-€240, elevator, free Wi-Fi, Plaza de Armas 14, tel. 943-645-500, fax 943-642-153, www.parador.es, hondarribia@parador.es). **$$ Hotel San Nikolas,** facing the parador from across the square, offers a more affordable alternative, with 17 nicely appointed rooms (many with views) above a local café (Sb-€35-60, Db-€45-75, Db with sea view-€50-90, higher price is for mid-July-mid-Sept, can be even cheaper Mon-Thu off-season, elevator, free Wi-Fi, Plaza de Armas 6, tel. 943-644-278, fax 943-646-217, www.hotelsan nikolas.es, info@hotelsannikolas.es).

BASQUE COUNTRY

Hondarribia Connections: Buses go from Hondarribia to **San Sebastián** (about 3/hour, 30 minutes on express buses #E23 or #E21, departs near main square—#E21 also stops at airport; or twice as long on local public buses #E26 and night bus #E77), and **Irún** near the French border (2/hour, 20 minutes, buses #E25 and night bus #E77). A boat goes to **Hendaye** (4/hour in summer, 2/hour off-season, 10 minutes, runs about 11:00-19:00 or until dark).

Between San Sebastián and Bilbao: The Bay of Biscay

Between the two Spanish Basque cities of San Sebastián and Bilbao is a beautiful countryside of rolling green hills and a scenic, jagged coastline that looks almost Celtic. Aside from a scenic joyride, this area merits a visit for the cute fishing and resort town of Lekeitio.

Route Tips for Drivers

San Sebastián and Bilbao are connected in about an hour and a quarter by the A-8 expressway (€9 toll). While speedy and scenic, this route is nothing compared to some of the free, but slower, back roads connecting the two towns.

If side-tripping from San Sebastián to Bilbao, you can drive directly there on A-8 in the morning. But coming home to San Sebastián, consider this more scenic route: Take A-8 until the turnoff for Guernica (look for *Gernika-Lumo* sign), then head up into the hills on BI-635. After visiting Guernica, follow signs along the very twisty road to Lekeitio (about 40 minutes). Leave Lekeitio on the road just above the beach; after crossing the bridge, take the left fork and follow BI-3438 to Ondarroa (with a striking modern bridge and nice views back into the steep town), Mutriku, and Deba to hug the coastline east to San Sebastián. There's a good photo-op pullout as you climb along the coast just after Deba. Soon after you'll have two opportunities to get on the A-8 (blue signs) for a quicker approach to San Sebastián; but if you've enjoyed the scenery so far, stick with the coastal road (white signs, N-634) through Zumaia and Getaria, rejoining the expressway at Zarautz.

Lequeitio / Lekeitio

More commonly known by its Euskara name, Lekeitio (leh-KAY-tee-oh)—rather than the Spanish version, Lequeitio—this small

fishing port has an idyllic harbor and a fine beach. It's just over an hour by bus from Bilbao and an easy stop for drivers, and is protected from the Bay of Biscay by a sand spit that leads to the lush and rugged little San Nicolás Island. Hake boats fly their Basque flags, and proud Basque locals black out the Spanish translations on street signs.

Lekeitio is a teeming resort during July and August (when its population of 7,000 triples as big-city Basque folks move into their vacation condos). Isolated from the modern rat race by its location down a long, windy little road, it's a backwater fishing village the rest of the year.

Sights here are humble, though the 15th-century St. Mary's Parish Church is a good example of Basque Gothic, with an impressive altarpiece (Mon-Sat 8:00-12:00 & 17:00-19:30, closed Sun). The town's back lanes are reminiscent of old days when fishing was the only industry. Fisherwomen sell their husbands' catches each morning from about 10:30 along the port. The golden crescent beach is as inviting as the sandbar, which—at

low tide—challenges you to join the seagulls out on San Nicolás Island.

The best beach in the area for surfers and sun-lovers is Playas Laga (follow signs off the road from Bilbao to Lekeitio). Relatively uncrowded, it's popular with body-boarders.

Getting There: Buses connect Lekeitio with **Bilbao** (hourly, 1.25 hours; same bus stops at **Guernica,** 40 minutes) and **San Sebastián** (4/day Mon-Fri, 2/day Sat-Sun, 1.25 hours). But this stop is most logical for those with a car. Drivers can park most easily in the lot near the bus station. Exit the station left, walk along the road, then take the first right (down the steep, cobbled street) to reach the harbor. There is no luggage storage in town.

Tourist Information: The TI faces the fish market next to the harbor (July-Aug daily 10:00-14:00 & 16:00-20:00; Sept-June Tue-Sat 10:30-13:30 & 16:00-19:00, Sun 10:00-14:00, closed Mon; tel. 946-844-017, www.lekeitio.com).

Sleeping in Lekeitio: **$$ Emperatriz Zita Hotel** is the obvious best bet for your beach-town break. It's named for Empress Zita (who lived here in exile after her Habsburg family lost World War I and was booted from Vienna). Zita's mansion burned down, but this 1930s rebuild still has a belle époque aristocratic charm, solid classy furniture in 42 spacious rooms, real hardwood floors, and an elegant spa in the basement. Located on the beach a few steps from the harbor, with handy free parking and a view restaurant, it's a fine value (Sb-€60-76, Db-€70-99, Db suite-€103-132, views—ask for *vistas del mar*—are worth it, prices can be higher July-Aug and Fri-Sat all year, extra bed-€25, breakfast-€10, elevator, free Wi-Fi, Santa Elena Etorbidea, tel. 946-842-655, fax 946-243-500, www .aisiahoteles.com, lekeitio@aisiahoteles.com). The hotel also has a thermal seawater pool, a Jacuzzi, and a full-service spa (all available at reasonable prices).

Eating in Lekeitio: Although it's sleepy in the off-season, the harbor promenade is made-to-order in summer for a slow meal or a tapas crawl. **Restaurante Kaia** offers a mostly seafood menu, with a €15 fixed-priced lunch (Tue-Sat lunch and dinner, Sun dinner only, closed Mon, on the harbor at Txatxo Kaia 5, tel. 946-840-284).

Guernica / Gernika

The workaday market town of Guernica (GEHR-nee-kah) is

near and dear to Basques and pacifists alike. This is the site of the Gernikako Arbola (oak tree of Gernika), which marked the assembly point where the regional Basque leaders, the Lords of Bizkaia, met through the ages to assert their people's freedom. Long the symbolic heart of Basque separatism, it was also a natural target for Franco (and his ally Hitler) in the Spanish Civil War—resulting in an infamous bombing raid that left the town in ruins (see "The Bombing of Guernica" sidebar), as immortalized by Picasso in his epic work *Guernica.*

Today's Guernica, rebuilt after being bombed flat in 1937 and nothing special at first glance, holds some of the Basque Country's more compelling museums. And Basque bigwigs have reclaimed the town as a meeting point—they still elect their figurehead leader on that same ancient site under the oak tree.

Orientation to Guernica

Guernica is small (about 17,000 inhabitants) and compact, focused on its large market hall (Monday market 9:00-14:00).

Tourist Information: The TI is in the town center (Mon-Sat 10:00-14:00 & 16:00-19:00—no lunch break July-Aug, Sun 10:00-14:00, Artekalea 8, tel. 946-255-892, www.gernika-lumo.net). Pick up the free, good town map. If you'll be visiting both the Peace Museum and the Basque Country Museum, buy the €5.25 combo-ticket here.

Arrival in Guernica: Drivers will find a handy parking lot near the train tracks at the end of town. Buses drop off passengers along the main road skirting the town center. No matter where you enter, the TI is well-signed (look for yellow *i* signs)—head there first to get your bearings.

Sights in Guernica

I've arranged Guernica's sights in the order of a handy sightseeing loop from the TI.

• *Exit the TI to the left, cross the street, and walk up the left side of the square, where you'll find the...*

▲**Gernika Peace Museum**—Because of the brutality of the Guernica bombing, and the powerful Picasso painting that documented the atrocities of war, the name "Guernica" has become synonymous with pacifism. This thoughtfully presented exhibit has taken a great tragedy of 20th-century history and turned it into a compelling cry for peace in our time. Borrow the English translations at the entry, request an English showing of the movie upstairs, and head up through the two-floor exhibit. The first floor begins by considering different ways of defining "peace." You'll then enter an apartment and hear Begoña describe her typical Guernica life in the 1930s...until the bombs dropped (a mirror effect shows you the devastating aftermath). You'll exit into an exhibit about the town's history, with a special emphasis on the bombing. Finally, a 10-minute movie shows grainy footage of the destruction, and ends with a collage of peaceful reconciliations in recent history—in Ireland, South Africa, Guatemala, Australia, and Berlin. On the second floor, Picasso's famous painting is superimposed on three transparent panels to highlight different themes. The exhibit concludes with a survey of the recent history of conflicts in the Basque Country.

Cost and Hours: €5; Tue-Sat 10:00-14:00 & 16:00-19:00, Sun 10:00-14:00, closed Mon; Foru Plaza 1, tel. 946-270-213, www.peacemuseumguernica.org.

The Bombing of Guernica

During the Spanish Civil War, Guernica was the site of one of history's most reviled wartime acts.

Monday, April 26, 1937, was market day, when the town was filled with farmers and peasants from the countryside selling their wares. At about 16:40 in the afternoon, a German warplane appeared ominously on the horizon, and proceeded to bomb bridges and roads surrounding the town. Soon after, more planes arrived. Three hours of relentless saturation bombing followed, as the German and Italian air forces pummeled the city with incendiary firebombs. People running through the streets or along the green hillsides were strafed with machine-gun fire. As the sun fell low in the sky and the planes finally left, hundreds—or possibly thousands—had been killed, and many more wounded. (Because Guernica was filled with refugees from other besieged towns, nobody is sure how many perished.)

Hearing word of the attack in Paris, Pablo Picasso—who had been commissioned to paint a mural for the 1937 world's fair—was devastated at the news of what had gone on in Guernica. Inspired, he painted what many consider the greatest work of antiwar art, ever.

Why did the bombings happen? Reportedly, Adolf Hitler wanted an opportunity to try out his new saturation-bombing attack strategy. Spanish dictator Francisco Franco, who was fed up with the independence-minded Basques, offered up their historic capital as a candidate for the experiment.

There's no doubt that Guernica, a gateway to Bilbao, was strategically located. But historians believe most of the targets here were far from strategic. Why attack so mercilessly, during the daytime, on market day, when innocent casualties would be maximized? Like the famous silent scream of Picasso's *Guernica* mother, this question haunts pacifists everywhere to this day.

• *Continue uphill to the big church. At the road above the church, you can turn right and walk a block and a half to find an underwhelming tile replica of* **Picasso's** **Guernica** *(left-hand side of the street). Or you can head left to find the next two attractions.*

▲**Basque Country Museum (Euskal Herria Museoa)**—This well-presented exhibit offers a good overview of Basque culture and history. Start in the ground-floor theater and see the overview video (request English). Follow the suggested route and climb chronologically up through Basque history, with the necessary help of an included audioguide. You'll find exhibits about traditional Basque architecture and landscape, and a region-by-region rundown of the Basque Country's seven territories. One interesting map shows Basque emigration over the centuries—including to the US. The top floor is the most engaging, highlighting Basque culture: sports, dances, cuisine, myths and legends, music, and language, plus a wraparound movie featuring images of a proud people living the Basque lifestyle.

Cost and Hours: €3, free on Sat, includes audioguide, open Tue-Sat 10:00-14:00 & 16:00-19:00, Sun 10:30-14:30, closed Mon, Allendesalazar 5, tel. 946-255-451.

▲▲Gernika Assembly House and Oak Tree—In the Middle Ages, the meeting point for the Basque general assembly was under the old oak tree on the gentle hillside above Guernica. The tradition continues today, as the tree stands at the center of a modest but interesting complex celebrating Basque culture and self-government.

Cost and Hours: Free, daily 10:00-14:00 & 16:00-18:00, June-Sept until 19:00, on Allendesalazar, tel. 946-251-138.

⊙ Self-Guided Tour: As you enter the grounds, you'll see an **old trunk** in the small colonnade dating from the 1700s. Basque traditions have lived much, much longer than a single tree's life span. When one dies, it's replaced with a new one. This is the oldest surviving trunk.

The exhibit has four parts: a stained-glass window room, the oak-tree courtyard, the assembly chamber, and a basement theater (request the 10-minute video in English that extols the virtues and beauties of the Basque Country).

Inside the first building, find the impressive **stained-glass window room.** The computer video here gives a good six-minute

overview of the exhibit (plays in English when you click). The gorgeous stained-glass ceiling is rife with Basque symbolism. The elderly leader stands under the oak holding a book with the "Old Law" *(Lege Zarra),* which are the laws by which the Basques lived for centuries. Below him are groups representing the three traditional career groups of this industrious people: sailors and fishermen; miners and steelworkers; and farmers. Behind them all is a classic Basque landscape: on the left is the sea, and on the right are rolling green hills dotted with red-and-white homes.

Out back, a tribune surrounds the fateful **oak tree.** This little fella is from 2005, planted here when the earlier one "finished out its life cycle" after standing here for nearly a century and a half. This tree is a descendant of that one, and (supposedly) of all the trees here since ancient times. This location is where Basque leaders have met in solidarity across the centuries.

In the Middle Ages, after Basque lands became part of Castile, Castilian kings came here to pledge respect to the old Basque laws. When Basque independence came under fire in the 19th century, patriots rallied by singing a song about this tree ("Ancient and holy symbol / Let thy fruit fall worldwide / While we gaze in adoration / Upon thee, our blessed tree"). After the 1937 bombing, in which this tree's predecessor was left miraculously unscathed, hundreds of survivors sought refuge under its branches. Today, although official representatives in the Spanish government are elected at the polls, the Basques choose their figurehead leader, the Lehendakari ("First One"), in this same spot.

Step back inside and enter the **assembly chamber**—like a mini-parliament for the region of Bizkaia ("Vízcaya" in Spanish, "Biscay" in English; one of the seven Basque territories). Notice the holy water and the altar—a sign that there's no separation of church and state in Basque politics. The paintings show the Lords of Bizkaia swearing allegiance to the Old Law.

Guernica Connections

Guernica is well-connected to **Bilbao** (1-2 trains/hour, 50 minutes, arrive at Bilbao's Atxuri Station; also 4 buses/hour, 40 minutes) and to **Lekeitio** (hourly buses, 40 minutes). Connections are sparser on weekends. The easiest way to connect to San Sebastián is via Bilbao, though you can also get there on the slow "Topo" EuskoTren train (transfer in Lemoa, about 3-4 hours).

Bilbao / Bilbo

In recent years, Bilbao (bil-BOW, rhymes with "cow") has seen a transformation like no other Spanish city. Entire sectors of the industrial city's long-depressed port have been cleared away to allow construction of a new opera house, a convention center, and the stunning Guggenheim Museum.

Bilbao feels at once like a city of the grim industrial past...and of an exciting new future. It mingles beautiful but crumbling old buildings; eyesore high-rise apartment blocks; brand-new super-modern additions to the skyline (such as the Guggenheim); and, scattered in the lush green hillsides all around the horizon, typical whitewashed Basque homes with red roofs. Bilbao enjoys a vitality and well-worn charm befitting its status as a regional capital of culture and industry.

Planning Your Time

For most visitors, the Guggenheim is the main draw (and many could spend the entire day there). But with a little more time, it's also worth hopping on a tram to explore the atmospheric Old Town (Casco Viejo). Don't bother coming to Bilbao on Monday, when virtually all its museums—including the almighty Guggenheim—are closed (except in July-Aug).

Orientation to Bilbao

When you're in the center, Bilbao feels smaller than its population of 350,000. The city, nestled amidst green hillsides, hugs the

Bilbao River as it curves through town. The Guggenheim is more or less centrally located near the top of that curve; the bus station is to the west; the Old Town (Casco Viejo) and train stations are to the east; and a super-convenient and fun-to-ride green tram called the EuskoTran ties it all together.

Tourist Information

Bilbao's handiest TI is next to the Guggenheim (look for the *i* sign on top of a pole). Pick up a city map and the bimonthly *Bilbao Guide*. If you're interested in something beyond the Guggenheim, ask about walking tours in English (€4.50, Tue, Thu, and Sat-Sun in summer, Sat-Sun only in off-season) and grab the Bilbao museums brochure, describing museums dedicated to everything from bullfighting and seafaring to sports and Holy Week processionals (July-Aug Mon-Sat 10:00-19:00, Sun 10:00-18:00; Sept-June Tue-Fri 11:00-18:00, Sat 11:00-19:00, Sun 11:00-15:00, closed Mon; tel. 944-795-760, www.bilbao.net). For now, convenient TI branches are open daily at the airport and at Arriaga Theater (at Plaza de Arriaga, near the Old Town)—but these might be closed or relocated in 2013.

Arrival in Bilbao

Most travelers—whether arriving by train, bus, or car—will want to go straight to the Guggenheim. Thanks to a perfectly planned tram system (EuskoTran), this couldn't be easier. From any point of entry, simply buy a €1.40 single-ride ticket at a user-friendly

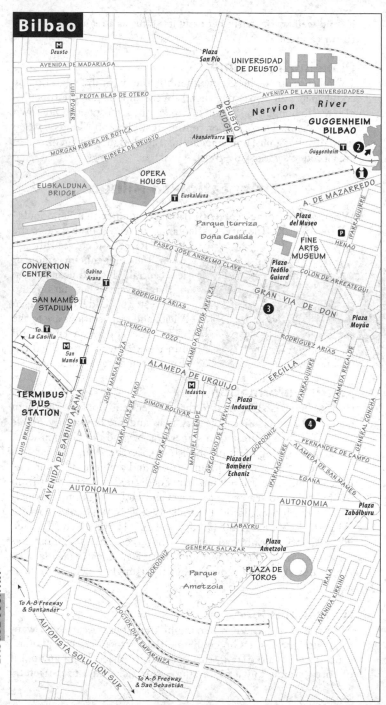

Bilbao

M Deusto

AVENIDA DE MADARIAGA

Plaza San Pío

UNIVERSIDAD DE DEUSTO

LUIS POWER

PEOTA BLAS DE OTERO

AVENIDA DE LAS UNIVERSIDADES

MORGAN RIBERA DE BOTICA

RIBERA DE DEUSTO

DEUSTO BRIDGE

Nervion River

Abandoibarra T

GUGGENHEIM BILBAO

Guggenheim T ②

ⓘ

EUSKALDUNA BRIDGE

OPERA HOUSE

T Euskalduna

A. DE MAZARREDO

Parque Iturriza Doña Casilda

Plaza del Museo

FINE ARTS MUSEUM

P IPARRAGUIRRE

HENAO

PASEO JOSE ANSELMO CLAVE

CONVENTION CENTER

Sabino Arana T

Plaza Teófilo Guiard

COLON DE ARREATEGUI

SAN MAMÉS STADIUM

RODRIGUEZ ARIAS

GRAN VIA DE DON

③

Plaza Moyúa

To La Casilla T

LICENCIADO POZO

ALAMEDA DOCTOR AREILZA

RODRIGUEZ ARIAS

M San Mamés T

JOSE MARIA ESCUZA

ALAMEDA DE URQUIJO

ERCILLA

ALAMEDA RECALDE

AVENIDA DE SABINO ARANA

MARIA DIAZ DE HARO

DOCTOR AREILZA

SIMON BOLIVAR

M Indautxu

Plaza Indautxu

IPARRAGUIRRE

GENERAL CONCHA

TERMIBUS BUS STATION

LUIS BRIÑAS

MANUEL ALLENDE

GREGORIO DE LA REVILLA

GORDONIZ

④

FERNANDEZ DE CAMPO

ALAMEDA DE SAN MAMES

Plaza del Bombero Echaniz

EGAÑA

AUTONOMIA

AUTONOMIA

Plaza Zabálburu

LABAYRU

Plaza Ametzola

GENERAL SALAZAR

GORDONIZ

Parque Ametzoia

PLAZA DE TOROS

IRALA

To A-8 Freeway & Santander

DOCTOR DIAZ EMPARANZA

AVENIDA KIRIKIÑO

AUTOPISTA SOLUCION SUR

To A-8 Freeway & San Sebastián

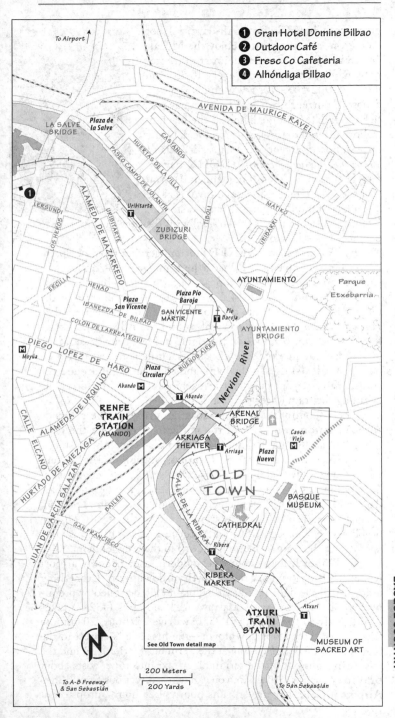

1. Gran Hotel Domine Bilbao
2. Outdoor Café
3. Fresc Co Cafeteria
4. Alhóndiga Bilbao

To Airport

LA SALVE BRIDGE

Plaza de la Salve

AVENIDA DE MAURICE RAVEL

CASTAÑOS

HUERTAS DE LA VILLA

PASEO CAMPO DE VOLANTÍN

LERSUNDI

LOS HEROS

ALAMEDA DE MAZARREDO

URIBITARTE

Uribitarte

ZUBIZURI BRIDGE

MATIKO

URIBARRI

URIBARRI

ERCILLA

HENAO

IBAÑEZDA DE BILBAO

COLON DE LARREATEGUI

Plaza San Vicente

Plaza Pío Baroja

SAN VICENTE MÁRTIR

AYUNTAMIENTO

Parque Etxebarría

DIEGO LOPEZ DE HARO

Moyúa

BUENOS AIRES

Pío Baroja

AYUNTAMIENTO BRIDGE

Nervion River

Plaza Circular

Abando

Abando

CALLE ELCANO

ALAMEDA DE URQUIJO

HURTADO DE AMEZAGA

JUAN DE GARCÍA SALAZAR

RENFE TRAIN STATION (ABANDO)

ARENAL BRIDGE

ARRIAGA THEATER

Arriaga

Plaza Nueva

Casco Viejo

OLD TOWN

BASQUE MUSEUM

BAILEN

SAN FRANCISCO

CALLE DE LA RIBERA

CATHEDRAL

Ribera

LA RIBERA MARKET

ATXURI TRAIN STATION

Atxuri

MUSEUM OF SACRED ART

See Old Town detail map

N

200 Meters
200 Yards

To A-8 Freeway & San Sebastián

To San Sebastián

BASQUE COUNTRY

green machine (€3.80 for an all-day pass), hop on a green-and-gray tram, enjoy the Muzak, and head for the Guggenheim stop (there's only one line, trams come every 10-15 minutes, tel. 902-543-210, www.euskotren.es—choose "Tranvía Bilbao"). When you buy your ticket, validate it immediately at the machine (follow the red arrow), since you can't do it once onboard. If you get lost, ask: *"¿Dónde está el museo Guggenheim?"* (DOHN-day ay-STAH el moo-SAY-oh "Guggenheim"). Note that the only luggage storage in town is at the Termibús Station (not at either train station). Don't confuse the tram (Eusko*Tran*) with the slow, scenic train to San Sebastián (Eusko*Tren*).

By Train: Bilbao's **RENFE Station** (serving most of Spain) is on the river in central Bilbao. The train station is on top of a small shopping mall (a Europcar rental office is by the train-station ticket office, tel. 944-239-390). To reach the tram to the Guggenheim, descend into the stores. Leave from the exit marked *Hurtado de Amézaga*, and go right to find the BBK bank. Enter, find the *Automatikoa* door on the right, and buy your ticket at the green machine marked *Abando* (the machine is mixed in with a bunch of ATMs). Leave the bank and continue right around the corner. Validate your ticket at the machines at the tram stop before boarding the tram (direction: La Casilla).

Trains coming from San Sebastián arrive at the riverside **Atxuri Station,** southeast of the museum. From here the tram (direction: La Casilla) follows the river to the Guggenheim stop.

By Bus: Buses stop at the **Termibús Station** on the western edge of downtown, about a mile southwest of the Guggenheim. The station has luggage lockers and a left-luggage desk (€2/bag, daily 7:00-22:00, ring bell to enter). The tram (San Mamés Station) is on the road just below the station—look for the steel *CTB* sign or follow the *Tran* signs. Buy and validate a ticket at the machine, and hop on the tram (direction: Atxuri) to the Guggenheim.

By Plane: Bilbao's compact, modern, user-friendly airport (code: BIO) is about six miles north of downtown. Everything branches off the light-and-air-filled main hall, designed by prominent architect Santiago Calatrava. A handy bus (#3247) takes you directly to the center (€1.35, pay driver, 2/hour, 20-minute trip, makes three stops downtown—the first one is closest to the Guggenheim—before ending at the Termibús Station). To find the bus, turn right out of the terminal. A taxi into town costs about €25. To get to San Sebastián, you can take a direct bus from Bilbao Airport (€15.40, pay driver, runs hourly, 1.25 hours, drops off at

Plaza Pío XII in San Sebastián, www.pesa.net). A taxi directly to San Sebastián will run you €150.

By Car: A big underground car park is near the museum; if you have a car, park it here and use the tram. From the freeway, take the exit marked *Centro* (with bull's-eye symbol), follow signs to *Guggenheim* (you'll see the museum), and look for the big *P* that marks the garage.

Tours in Bilbao

Walking Tours—**Bilbao Walking Tours** offers 1.5-hour tours Saturday and Sunday only: an Old Town tour (starts at the Arriaga TI at 10:00—but confirm where tour begins with main TI, as this location may close in 2013), and a modern-city tour showing the city's history since the 19th century (starts at the Guggenheim TI at 12:00). Tours are in Spanish and English, and you must call ahead to reserve (€4.50, tel. 944-795-760, www.bilbao.net/bilbao turismo, informacion@bilbaoturismo.bilbao.net).

Tram Tour—Riding the EuskoTran round-trip between the Atxuri and Euskalduna stops is a great way to see the city's oldest and newest neighborhoods, especially on rainy days. For more on this tram, see "Arrival in Bilbao," earlier.

Bus Tour—The TI runs a decent hop-on, hop-off bus tour around the city. The hour-long trip picks up on the hour outside the Guggenheim TI, and has stops in the Old Town and across the river (€14, ticket good for 24 hours, buy at TI or from driver at any stop, July-Aug daily 11:00-18:00, shorter hours rest of year, no buses Jan-March or Tue in shoulder season, tel. 696-429-848, www.busturistikoa.com).

Boat Tour—For a different view of the city, try the **Bilboats** one-hour tour along the river, offering plenty of architectural Kodak moments (€10, Mon-Sat in summer at 13:00, 16:00, 17:30, and 19:00, fewer departures off-season; reserve ahead as trips are canceled if less than 10 people; tour begins near City Hall bridge, tram stop: Pío Baroja, Metro stop: Abando; Plaza de Pío Baroja, tel. 946-424-157, www.bilboats.com).

Local Guide—Knowledgeable Bilbao resident **Iratxe Muñoz** offers tours of the city, including the Guggenheim and the Basque region (rates vary, mobile 607-778-072, www.apite.eu/iratxe munoz, iratxe.m@apite.eu).

Sights in Bilbao

▲▲▲Guggenheim Bilbao
Although the collection of art in this museum is no better than those in Europe's other great modern-art museums, the building

itself—designed by Frank Gehry
and opened in 1997—is reason
enough for many travelers to happily splice Bilbao into their itineraries. Even if you're not turned
on by contemporary art, the
Guggenheim is a must-see experience. Its 20 galleries, on three
floors, are full of surprises, and it's

well worth the entry fee just to appreciate the museum's structural
design, which is a masterpiece in itself.

Cost and Hours: €13, includes excellent audioguide; July-
Aug daily 10:00-20:00; Sept-June Tue-Sun 10:00-20:00, closed
Mon; same-day re-entry allowed—get wristband on your way out;
café, no photos inside galleries, tram stop: Guggenheim, Metro
stop: Moyúa, Avenida Abandoibarra 2, tel. 944-359-080, www
.guggenheim-bilbao.es.

Tours: Free, one-hour guided tours in Spanish generally run
4/day—always at 11:00 and 12:30, sometimes at 18:00, other times
vary. Show up at least 30 minutes early to put your name on the list
at the tour desk (to the left as you enter). Guided tours in English
are available only by advance reservation and with a fee (€95 for up
to 20 people).

Background: Frank Gehry's groundbreaking triumph offers
a fascinating look at 21st-century architecture. Using cutting-edge
technologies, unusual materials, and daring forms, he created a
piece of sculpture that smoothly integrates with its environment
and serves as the perfect stage for some of today's best art. Clad
in limestone and titanium, the building connects the city with its
river. Gehry meshed many visions. To him, the building's multiple
forms jostle like a loose crate of bottles. The building is inspired by
a silvery fish...and also evokes wind-filled sails heading out to sea.
Gehry keeps returning to his fish motif, reminding visitors that, as
a boy, he was inspired by carp...even taking them into the bathtub
with him.

❍ Self-Guided Tour: The audioguide will lead you room-
by-room through the collection, but this information will get you
started.

Guarding the main entrance is artist Jeff Koons' 42-foot-tall
West Highland Terrier. Its 60,000 plants and flowers, which
blossom in concert, grow through steel mesh. A joyful structure, it
brings viewers back to their childhoods—perhaps evoking human-
kind's relationship to God—or maybe it's just another notorious
Koons hoax. One thing is clear: It answers to "Puppy." Although
the sculpture was originally intended to be temporary, the people

of Bilbao fell in love with *Puppy*—so they bought it.

Descend to the **main entrance.** After buying your ticket, be sure to pick up the free exhibit audioguide. At the information desk, pick up the small English brochure explaining the architecture and museum layout, and the seasonal *Guggenheim Bilbao* magazine that details the art currently on display.

After presenting your ticket, enter the **atrium.** This acts as the heart of the building, pumping visitors from various rooms on three levels out and back, always returning to this central area before moving on to the next. The architect invites you to caress the sensual curves of the walls. There are virtually no straight lines (except the floor). Notice the sheets of glass that make up the elevator shaft—overlapping each other like a fish's scales. Each glass and limestone panel is unique, designed by a computer and shaped by a robot...as will likely be standard in constructing the great buildings of the future.

From the atrium, step out onto the riverside **terrace.** The "water garden" lets the river symbolically lap at the base of the building. This pool is home to two unusual sculptures (which appear occasionally throughout the day): a five-part "fire fountain" (notice the squares in the pool to the right) and a "fog sculpture" that billows up from below.

Still out on the terrace, notice the museum's commitment to public spaces: On the right a grand **staircase** leads under a big green bridge to a tower; the effect wraps the bridge into the museum's grand scheme. The 30-foot-tall **spider,** called *Maman* ("Mommy"), is French artist Louise Bourgeois' depiction of her mother: She spins a beautiful and delicate web of life...which is used to entrap her victims. (It makes a little more sense if you understand that the artist's mother was a weaver. Or maybe not.)

Gehry designed the vast **ground floor** mainly to house often-huge modern-art installations. Computer-controlled lighting adjusts for different exhibits. Surfaces are clean and bare, so you can focus on the art. While most of the collection comes and goes, Richard Serra's huge *Matter of Time* sculpture in the largest gallery is permanent (who would want to move those massive metal coils?). The intent is to have visitors walk among these metal walls—the "art" is experiencing this journey.

Because this museum is part of the Guggenheim "family" of museums, the **collection** perpetually rotates among the sister Guggenheim galleries in New York, Venice, and Berlin. The best approach to your visit is simply to immerse yourself in a modern-art happening, rather than to count on seeing a particular piece or a specific artist's works.

You can't fully enjoy the museum's architecture without

taking a circular stroll up and down each side of the river along the handsome promenade and over the two modern **pedestrian bridges.** (After you tour the museum, you can borrow a free "outdoor audioguide" to learn more—ID required—but it doesn't say much or take you across the river.) The building's skin—shiny and metallic, with a scale-like texture—is made of thin titanium, carefully created to give just the desired color and reflective quality. The external appearance tells you what's inside: the blocky limestone parts contain square-shaped galleries, and the titanium sections hold nonlinear spaces.

As you look out over the rest of the city, think of this: Gehry designed his building to reflect what he saw here in Bilbao. Now other architects are, in turn, creating new buildings that complement his. It's an appealing synergy for this old city.

Leaving the Museum: To get to the Old Town from the Guggenheim, take the tram that leaves from the river level beside the museum, just past the kid-pleasing fountain (ride it in direction: Atxuri). Hop off at the Arriaga stop, near the dripping-Baroque riverfront theater of the same name. From here it's a short walk into the twisty Old Town.

Near the Guggenheim

Fine Arts Museum (Museo de Bellas Artes)—Often overshadowed by the Guggenheim, the Fine Arts Museum contains a thoughtfully laid out collection arranged chronologically from the 12th century to the present. Find minor works by many Spanish artists such as Goya, El Greco, Picasso, Murillo, Zurbarán, Sorolla, Chillida, Tàpies, and Barceló—along with a handful of local painters. Other international artists in the collection include Gauguin, Klee, Bacon, Cassatt, and more. The museum is at the edge of the lovely Doña Casilda Iturrizar Park, perfect for a stroll after your visit.

Cost and Hours: €6, Tue-Sun 10:00-20:00, closed Mon, last entry 15 minutes before closing, a short walk from the Guggenheim at Museo Plaza 2, Metro stop: Moyúa, tel. 944-396-060, www.museobilbao.com.

Alhóndiga Bilbao—Bilbao's new culture and leisure center, designed by French architect Philippe Starck, is worth a quick visit or a lazy afternoon. Not one of the 43 interior columns is alike—the designs are meant to represent the entirety of materials and styles from antiquity to today. The center houses a cinema, auditorium, exhibition spaces, and restaurant. Most impressive is its glass-bottomed rooftop pool—from the atrium below, visitors can gaze up at backstrokers in the water above.

Cost and Hours: Entry to the Alhóndiga itself is free; a €5 day pass gives you access to the pool and sundeck. Mon-Fri 7:00-23:00, Sat-Sun 8:30-23:00, 10-minute walk from the Guggenheim at Plaza Arriquibar 4, tel. 944-014-014, www.alhondigabilbao.com.

Old Town (Casco Viejo)

Bilbao's Old Town, with tall, narrow lanes lined with thriving shops and tapas bars, is worth a stroll. Because the weather is wetter here than in many other parts of Spain (hence the green hillsides), the little balconies that climb the outside walls of buildings are glassed in, creating cozy little breakfast nooks.

Whether you want to or not, you'll eventually wind up at Old Bilbao's centerpiece, the **Santiago Cathedral,** a 14th-century Gothic church with a tranquil interior that has been scrubbed clean inside and out (free, €1 to dip into cloister, Mon-Fri 10:00-13:00 & 17:00-19:30, closed Sat-Sun, tel. 944-153-627).

Various museums (including those dedicated to diocesan art and the Holy Week processions) are in or near the Old Town, but on a quick visit only one is worth considering...

Basque Museum (Euskal Museoa)—It's fitting that Bilbao, a leading city of Spain's Basque region, would have a museum dedicated to its unique culture. Unfortunately, the almost complete lack of English leaves the exhibits shrouded in mystery—much like the Basques themselves. Around a ground-floor cloister, you'll see old stone monuments. The first floor delves into the Basque cultural heritage, displaying ceramics, guns, looms, and other tools. Special emphasis is given to nautical artifacts from this seafaring people, Basque settlers in the American West, and the pastoral lifestyles of rural Basques. The top floor is dedicated to archaeology, with exhibits about old tools and settlements.

Cost and Hours: €3, Tue-Sat 11:00-17:00, Sun 11:00-14:00, closed Mon, Miguel de Unamuno Plaza 4, tel. 944-155-423, www.euskal-museoa.org.

Sleeping in Bilbao

(€1 = about $1.30, country code: 34)

Bilbao merits an overnight stay. Even those who are interested only in the Guggenheim find that there's much more to see in this historic yet quickly changing city. Unless otherwise noted, the IVA hotel tax is not included in the prices listed below.

BASQUE COUNTRY

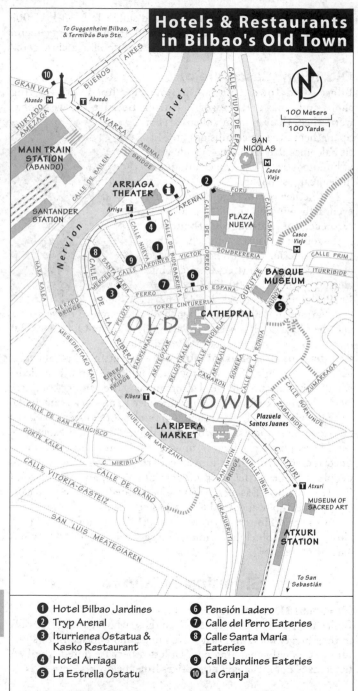

Hotels & Restaurants in Bilbao's Old Town

To Guggenheim Bilbao, & Termibús Bus Stn.

100 Meters
100 Yards

MAIN TRAIN STATION (ABANDO)

SANTANDER STATION

ARRIAGA THEATER

SAN NICOLAS

PLAZA NUEVA

Casco Viejo

Casco Viejo

CALLE PRIM
ITURRIBIDE

BASQUE MUSEUM

OLD

CATHEDRAL

TOWN

Plazuela Santos Juanes

LA RIBERA MARKET

MUSEUM OF SACRED ART

ATXURI STATION

To San Sebastián

BASQUE COUNTRY

1 Hotel Bilbao Jardines
2 Tryp Arenal
3 Iturrienea Ostatua & Kasko Restaurant
4 Hotel Arriaga
5 La Estrella Ostatu
6 Pensión Ladero
7 Calle del Perro Eateries
8 Calle Santa María Eateries
9 Calle Jardines Eateries
10 La Granja

Near the Guggenheim Museum

$$$ Gran Hotel Domine Bilbao is *the* place for wealthy modern-art fans looking for a splurge close to the museum. It's right across the street from the main entrance to the Guggenheim and Jeff Koons' *Puppy*. The hotel is gathered around an atrium with a giant "stone tree" and other artsy flourishes, and its decor (by a prominent Spanish designer) was clearly inspired by Gehry's masterpiece. The 145 plush rooms are distinctly black, white, steel, and very postmodern (standard Db-€130-200, museum-view "executive" rooms for €20 more, rates vary widely with events and demand, breakfast-€25, air-con, elevator, free Internet access and Wi-Fi, great museum-view breakfast terrace, free gym with wet and dry saunas, Alameda Mazarredo 61, tel. 944-253-300, fax 944-253-301, www.granhoteldominebilbao.com, recepcion.domine @hoteles-silken.com). If arriving by tram, take the main museum steps up by the fountains to reach the hotel.

In the Old Town

To reach the Old Town, take the tram to the Arriaga stop.

$$ Hotel Bilbao Jardines is a fresh new place buried in the Old Town with 32 modern but basic rooms (Sb-€58, Db-€75, cheaper off-season, breakfast-€5, quieter rooms in back, air-con, elevator, free Wi-Fi, Calle Jardines 9, tel. 944-794-210, fax 944-794-211, www.hotelbilbaojardines.com, info@hotelbilbaojardines .com, Marta, Felix, and Monica).

$$ Tryp Arenal is a chain hotel with simple, business-class rooms and helpful staff in a great location across from the Arriaga Theater (Db-€60-80, breakfast-€7, air-con, elevator, free Wi-Fi, Calle Los Fueros 2, tel. 944-153-100, fax 944-156-395, www.melia .com, tryp.arenal@melia.com).

$ Iturrienea Ostatua, next door to the recommended Kasko restaurant on a pedestrian street in the Old Town, is a tidy, B&B-style accommodation renting 21 rooms packed with brick, stone, and antiques (Sb-€50, Db-€60, twin Db-€66, Tb-€80, prices include tax, breakfast-€6, free Wi-Fi, near the river at Santa María 14, tel. 944-161-500, fax 944-158-929, www.iturrieneaostatua.com, info@iturrieneaostatua.com, friendly Igone).

$ Hotel Arriaga offers 21 traditional but well-maintained rooms and a spirited reception (Sb-€45, Db-€54, extra bed-€16, some rooms overlook a busy street—request a quiet back room, free Internet access and Wi-Fi, lounge, parking-€8, Ribera 3, tel. 944-790-001, fax 944-790-516, www.hotelarriaga.es, info@hotel arriaga.es, Jon). As you cross the bridge from the station, it's just behind the big theater of the same name.

$ La Estrella Ostatu is a family-run establishment with 26 simple but neat rooms up a twisty staircase near the Basque

Museum (Sb-€35, Db-€60 in summer, cheaper off-season, breakfast-€3-4, María Muñoz 6, tel. 944-164-066, fax 944-150-731, www.la-estrella-ostatu.com, laestrellabilbao@yahoo.es, just enough English spoken, Jesus and Begoña).

$ Pensión Ladero, renting 18 ramshackle but clean and cheap rooms, is a fine budget option in the Old Town. They don't accept reservations, so call upon arrival to check availability (S-€25, D-€35, T-€50, Q-€60, up 4 flights of stairs; 7 rooms up a very tight spiral staircase—watch your head—share 1 bathroom, while 11 rooms use the other 3 bathrooms on the main floor; cash only, Lotería 1, tel. 944-150-932, www.pensionladero.es, Margarita). You'll find the *pensión* just before the cathedral at the center of the Old Town. This is a better value than the more prominent Pensión Roquefer across the street.

Eating in Bilbao

Near the Guggenheim Museum

The easiest choice is the good **cafeteria** in the museum itself (upper level, separate entry above museum entry; Tue-Sun 9:00-20:30, closed Mon, €20 lunch deal offered 13:00-15:15, reservations smart, tel. 944-239-333).

The circular structure outside the museum by the playgrounds and fountains is a pleasant **outdoor café** serving €2.50 tapas (point at the ones you like on the bar). If the tables are full, you can take your food to one of the stone benches nearby. In the evenings, they sometimes have live music.

The streets in front of the museum have a handful of both sit-down and carry-out eateries (cafés, pizzerias, sandwich shops) to choose from. **Fresc Co** is a healthy and cheap option for lunch or dinner, with an all-you-can-eat salad buffet including some hot dishes, dessert, and coffee for less than €10 (daily 12:30-24:00, 10-minute walk from the Guggenheim, three blocks to the left of Plaza Moyúa at Gran Vía 55).

In the Old Town

Bilbao has a thriving restaurant and tapas-bar scene. For pointers on Basque food, see page 536. You'll find plenty of options on the lanes near the cathedral. Most restaurants around the Old Town advertise a fixed-price lunch for around €12; some close for siesta between 16:00 and 20:00.

The street called **Calle del Perro** is tops for the tasty little tapas called *pintxos* (PEEN-chohs). **Xukela Bar** is my favorite, with its inviting atmosphere, good wines, and addictive array of €1.60 tapas spread along its bar (tables only for clients eating hot dishes, Calle del Perro 2, tel. 944-159-772). Calle del Perro is also good for sit-down restaurants. Browse the menus and interiors and choose your favorite. Well-regarded options include three places virtually next door to each other: **Egiluz** (€11 meals served in small restaurant up steep spiral staircase in the back); **Río-Oja** (€8 specialties, focus on shareable traditional dishes called *cazuelitas*); and **Rotterdam** (€10-15 plates, also has *cazuelitas;* try the *chipirones en su tinta*—squids in their own ink, served with a glass of house red for €11).

The street called **Calle Santa María** caters to a younger crowd, with softer lighting and a livelier atmosphere, and has three bars worth considering: Gatz, Santa María, and Kasko. **Kasko** is the most upscale option, with stuffy service, a pianist, and an interesting fixed-price dinner (starter, main course, dessert, and good wine served 20:30-23:00 for €25 Mon-Thu and €32 Fri-Sun, Santa Maria 16, tel. 944-160-311).

Eateries also abound on **Jardines** street, including the popular **Berton** (meals and *pintxos*, at #11, closed Mon).

Near the RENFE Train Station

There's not much on the main facade to distinguish it, but stepping through **La Granja**'s revolving doors is like entering a time machine. Founded in 1926, the interior seems more like a dusty gentlemen's club than a restaurant. The food is simply presented with oh-so-correct waiters and classic white tablecloths. It's a good spot to fuel up on coffee before hopping on the tram to the Guggenheim (€13.50 fixed-price lunch, daily, at Plaza Circular 3 but look for rear entrance on Calle Ledesma, tel. 944-230-813).

Bilbao Connections

From Bilbao by Bus to: San Sebastián (2/hour, hourly on weekends, 6:00-22:30, 1.25 hours, arrives at San Sebastián's Amara Station), **Guernica** (4/hour, 40 minutes), **Lekeitio** (hourly, 1.25 hours), **Pamplona** (6/day, 2 hours), **Burgos** (4/day, 2 hours), **Santander** (hourly, 1.5 hours, transfer there to bus to **Santillana del Mar** or **Comillas**). These buses depart from Bilbao's Termibús Station (www.termibus.es).

By EuskoTren to: San Sebastián (hourly, long and scenic 2.5-hour trip to San Sebastián's EuskoTren Station, €8.50 round-trip ticket saves €1.50, EuskoTren info: toll tel. 902-543-210, www.euskotren.es), **Guernica** (1-2/hour, 50 minutes). These trains depart from Bilbao's Atxuri Station, just beyond the Old Town past the Ribera Market.

By RENFE Train to: Madrid (2/day, 5 hours, €49), **Barcelona** (2/day, 6.5 hours, €65), **Burgos** (4/day, 2.5-3 hours, €23), **Salamanca** (1/day, 5.5 hours, €35), **León** (1/day, 5 hours, €30),

Santiago de Compostela (1/day direct, 11 hours, €47). Remember, these trains leave from the RENFE Station, across the river from the Old Town (tram stop: Abando). A planned new train line (coming in 2017) will connect Bilbao to other cities in a snap (30 minutes to San Sebastián, 2.25 hours to Madrid, 5.5 hours to Paris)—but trains are still slow for now.

LANGUEDOC

Albi • Carcassonne • Collioure

From the 10th to the 13th centuries, this mighty and independent region controlled most of southern France. The ultimate in mean-spirited crusades against the Cathars (or Albigensians) began here in 1208, igniting Languedoc's meltdown and eventual incorporation into the state of France.

The name *languedoc* comes from the *langue* (language) that its people spoke: *Langue d'oc* ("language of Oc," *Oc* for the way they said "yes") was the dialect of southern France; *langue d'oïl* was the dialect of northern France (where *oïl* later became *oui*, or "yes"). Languedoc's language faded with its power. The region was historically known as Languedoc-Roussillon, with the Roussillon part corresponding closely with its Catalan corner, near the border with Spain.

The Moors, Charlemagne, and the Spanish have all called this area home. The Spanish influence is still *muy* present, particularly in the south, where restaurants serve paella and the siesta is still respected.

While sharing many of the same attributes as Provence (climate, wind, grapes, and sea), this sunny, intoxicating, southwesternmost region of France is allocated little time by most travelers. Lacking Provence's cachet and sophistication, Languedoc feels more real. Pay homage to Henri de Toulouse-Lautrec in Albi; spend a night in Europe's greatest fortress city, Carcassonne; scamper up to a remote Cathar castle; and sift through sand in Collioure. That wind you feel is called *la tramontane* (trah-mohn-tahn-yuh), Languedoc's version of Provence's mistral wind.

Planning Your Time

Albi makes a good day or overnight stop between the Dordogne region and Carcassonne (figure about two autoroute hours from Albi to either place). Plan your arrival in popular Carcassonne carefully: Get there late in the afternoon, spend the night, and leave by 11:00 the next morning to miss most day-trippers. Collioure lies a few hours from Carcassonne and is your Mediterranean beach-town vacation from your vacation, where you'll want two nights and a full day. To find the Cathar castle ruins and the village of Minerve, you'll need wheels of your own and a good map. If you're driving, the most exciting Cathar castles—Peyrepertuse and Quéribus—work well as day stops between Carcassonne and Collioure. And if nature beckons, the Gorges du Tarn make an idyllic joyride a few hours east of Albi. No matter what kind of transportation you use, Languedoc is a logical stop between the Dordogne and Provence—or on the way to Barcelona, which is just over the border.

Getting Around Languedoc

Albi, Carcassonne, and Collioure are all accessible by train, but a car is essential for seeing the remote sights. Pick up your rental car in Albi or Carcassonne, and buy Michelin Local maps #344 and #338. Roads can be pencil-thin, and traffic slow.

For a scenic one-hour detour route connecting Albi and points north (such as the Dordogne), take D-964 between Caussade (30 minutes south of Cahors), Bruniquel, Gaillac, and Albi. With a bit more time, link Caussade, Saint-Antonin-Noble-Val (D-5 and D-926), Bruniquel, Castelnau-de-Montmiral, Gaillac, and Albi (using D-115 and D-964; see "Route of the *Bastides*" on page 625). If you really want to joyride, take a half-day drive through the glorious Lot River Valley via Villefranche-de-Rouergue, Cajarc, and St-Cirq Lapopie (see the "Dordogne" chapter). If speed is of the essence, connect the Dordogne with Albi on the autoroute to Montauban.

Languedoc's Cuisine Scene

Hearty peasant cooking and full-bodied red wines are Languedoc's tasty trademarks. Be adventurous. Cassoulet, an old Roman concoction of goose, duck, pork, mutton, sausage, and white beans, is the main-course specialty. You'll also see *cargolade,* a satisfying stew of snail, lamb, and sausage. Local cheeses are Roquefort and Pelardon (a nutty-tasting goat cheese). Corbières, Minervois, and Côtes du Roussillon are the area's good-value red wines. The locals distill a fine brandy, Armagnac, which tastes just like cognac and costs less.

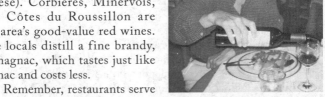

Remember, restaurants serve only during lunch (11:30-14:00) and dinner (19:00-21:00, later in bigger cities); some cafés serve food throughout the day.

Albi

Albi, an enjoyable river town of sienna-tone bricks, half-timbered buildings, and a marvelous traffic-free center, is worth a stop for two world-class sights: its towering cathedral and the Toulouse-Lautrec Museum. Lost in the Dordogne-to-Carcassonne shuffle and overshadowed by its big brother Toulouse, unpretentious Albi rewards the stray tourist well.

Orientation to Albi

Albi's cathedral is home base. For our purposes, all sights, pedestrian streets, and hotels fan out from here and are less than a five-minute walk away. The Tarn River hides below and behind the cathedral. The best city view is from the 22 Août 1944 bridge. Albi is dead quiet on Sundays and Monday mornings.

Tourist Information

The TI is on the square in front of the cathedral, next to the Toulouse-Lautrec Museum (mid-June-Sept Mon-Sat 9:00-19:00, Sun 10:00-12:30 & 14:30-18:30; Oct-mid-June Mon-Sat 9:00-12:30 & 14:30-18:00, Sun 10:00-12:30 & 14:30-17:00; tel. 05 63 49 48 80, www.albi-tourisme.fr). They sell a combo-ticket that includes the museum and the cathedral choir for €8 (saves €1). Ask about concerts, and pick up a map of the city center, the walking-tour brochure, and the map of *La Route des Bastides Albigeoises* (hill towns near Albi). You can download a free, 19-minute English audioguide of the city's monuments and old town from the TI website.

Arrival in Albi

By Train: There are two stations in Albi; you want Albi-Ville (no baggage storage). It's a level 15-minute walk to the town center: Exit the station, take the second left onto Avenue Maréchal Joffre, and then take another left on Avenue du Général de Gaulle. Go straight across Place Lapérouse and find the traffic-free street to the left that leads into the city center. This turns into Rue Ste. Cécile, which takes you to my recommended hotels and the cathedral.

By Car: Follow *Centre-Ville* and *Cathédrale* signs (if you lose your way, follow the tall church tower). For the lot closest to the old city, follow signs for *Cathédrale* parking along Boulevard Général

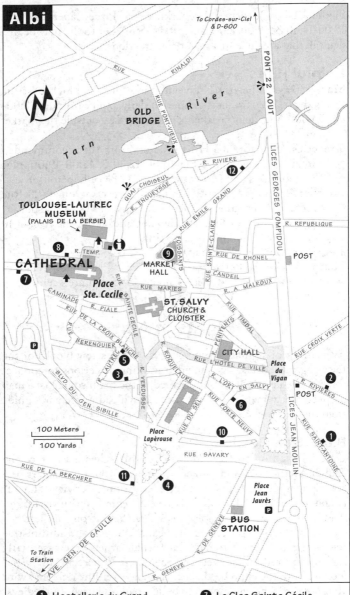

Albi

To Cordes-sur-Ciel & D-600

Tarn River

OLD BRIDGE

PONT 22 AOÛT

RUE RINALDI

RUE

RUE PONTVIEUX

R. RIVIERE

LICES GEORGES POMPIDOU

R. REPUBLIQUE

QUAI CHOISEUL

R. ENGUEYSSE

TOULOUSE-LAUTREC MUSEUM (PALAIS DE LA BERBIE)

RUE EMILE GRAND

FOISSANTS

RUE SAINTE-CLAIRE

RUE DE RHONEL

POST

R. TEMP.

CATHEDRAL

❽

❶

❾ **MARKET HALL**

RUE CANDEIL

R. A. MALROUX

❼

Place Ste. Cecile

CAMINADE

R. PIALE

RUE DE LA CROIX BLANCHE

RUE MARIES

RUE SAINTE CECILE

ST. SALVY CHURCH & CLOISTER

RUE TIMBAL

RUE CROIX VERTE

RUE BERENGUIER

RUE LAUTREC

❺

❸

RUE VERDUSSE

RUE ROQUELAURE

R. PENITENTS

CITY HALL

RUE L'HOTEL DE VILLE

Place du Vigan

❷ R. RIVIERES

POST

❶

P

BLVD DU GEN. SIBILLE

R. L'ORT EN SALVY

❻

RUE PORTE NEUVE

RUE DU SEL

100 Meters
100 Yards

Place Lapérouse

❿

LICES JEAN MOULIN

RUE SAINT-ANTOINE

RUE SAVARY

RUE DE LA BERCHERE

❶❶

❹

Place Jean Jaurès

P

BUS STATION

To Train Station

AVE. GEN. DE GAULLE

R. DE GENEVE

R. GENEVE

❶❷

R. RIVIERE

❶ Hostellerie du Grand Saint Antoine
❷ Hôtel Chiffre
❸ Le Vieil Alby Hôtel-Rest.
❹ Hôtel Lapérouse
❺ Le Papillon Restaurant
❻ Le Tournesol Restaurant

❼ Le Clos Sainte Cécile
❽ Restaurant Stéphane Laurens (La Pause)
❾ Market Hall
❿ Internet Café
❶❶ 8 à Huit Grocery
❶❷ Launderette

Sibille (€1/hour); there's also parking near Place Lapérouse (free 12:00-14:00 & 19:00-8:00, and all day Sun), but traffic may be difficult in that area due to a major construction project.

Helpful Hints

Market Days: The Art Nouveau market hall, a block past the cathedral square, hosts a market daily except Monday (8:00-14:00). A farmers' market is held Saturdays outside the market hall.

Groceries: The store **8 à Huit** is across from the recommended Hôtel Lapérouse (Tue-Sat 10:00-12:30 & 15:00-19:00, plus Sun mornings and Mon afternoons, 14 Place Lapérouse).

Internet Access: Leader PC is near Place Lapérouse (28 Rue Docteur Camboulives). The TI has a list of Wi-Fi hotspots.

Laundry: Do your washing at **Lavomatique,** above the river at 10 Rue Emile Grand (daily 7:00-21:00).

Taxi: Call **Albi Taxi Radio** at 05 63 54 85 03.

Tourist Train: Le Petit Train leaves from Place Ste. Cécile in front of the cathedral and makes a 45-minute scenic loop around Albi (€6, buy tickets at TI, 6/day).

Sights in Albi

Everything of sightseeing interest is within a few blocks of the towering cathedral. (I've included walking directions to connect some of the key sights.) Get oriented in the main square (see map on page 615; remember that you can download a free audioguide from the TI's website).

Place Ste. Cécile

Grab a bench on the far side of Place Ste. Cécile and face the church. With the church directly in front of you, the bishop's palace (along with the Toulouse-Lautrec Museum, river view, and TI) is a bit to the right. The market is a block behind you on your right. And the sleepy St. Salvy cloister is a block behind on your left.

Why the big church? At its peak, Albi was the administrative center for 465 churches. Back when tithes were essentially legally required taxes, everyone gave their 10 percent, or *"dime"* (dee-may), to the church. The local bishop was filthy rich, and with all those *dimes*, he had money to build a dandy church. In medieval times, there was no interest in making a space so people could step back and get a perspective on such a beautiful building. A clutter of houses snuggled right up to the church's stout walls, and only in the 19th century were things cleared away. Just in the last few years the cars were cleared out (another triumph for the European pedestrian).

Why so many bricks? Because there were no stone quarries nearby. Albi is part of a swath of red-brick towns from here to Toulouse (nicknamed "the pink city" for the way its bricks dominate that townscape). Notice on this square the buffed brick addresses next to the sluggish stucco ones. As late as the 1960s, the town's brickwork was considered low-class and was covered by stucco. Today, the stucco is being peeled away, and Albi has that brick pride going on again.

▲▲Ste. Cécile Cathedral (Cathédrale Ste. Cécile)

When the heretical Cathars were defeated in the 13th century, this massive cathedral was the final nail in their coffin. Big and bold, it made it clear who was in charge.

The imposing exterior and the stunning interior drive home the message of the Catholic (read: "universal") Church in a way that would have stuck with any medieval worshipper. This place oozes power—get on board, or get run over.

Cost and Hours: Free, daily June-Sept 9:00-18:00, Oct-May 9:00-12:00 & 14:00-18:00. Once inside, you'll pay €2 to enter the choir (worthwhile). The treasury (a single room of reliquaries and church art) is not worth the €2 fee or the climb (€3 for both with audioguide).

Organ Concerts: The cathedral hosts frequent concerts (the TI has a schedule); free organ concerts usually are offered in July and August (Sun at 16:00 and Wed at 17:00).

○ Self-Guided Tour: Visit the cathedral using the following self-guided commentary.

• *Begin facing the...*

Exterior: The cathedral looks less like a church and more like a fortress. In fact, it was a central feature of the town's defensive walls. Notice how high the windows are (out of stone-tossing range). The simple Gothic style was typical of this region—designed to be sensitive to the anti-materialistic tastes of the local Cathars.

The top (from the gargoyles and newer, brighter bricks upward) is a fanciful, 19th-century, Romantic-era renovation. The church was originally as plain and austere as the bishop's palace (the similar, bold brick building to the right, now housing the Toulouse-Lautrec Museum). Imagine the church with a rooftop more like that of the bishop's palace.

• *Climb up to the extravagant Flamboyant Gothic...*

The Cathars

The Cathars were a heretical group of Christians who grew in numbers from the 11th through the 13th centuries under tolerant rule in Languedoc. They saw life as a battle between good (the spiritual) and bad (the material), and they considered material things evil and of the devil. Although others called them "Cathars" (from the Greek word for "pure") or "Albigensians" (for their main city, Albi), they called themselves simply "friends of God." Cathars focused on the teachings of St. John, and recognized only baptism as a sacrament. Because they believed in reincarnation, they were vegetarians.

Travelers encounter traces of the Cathars in their Languedoc sightseeing because of the Albigensian Crusades (1209-1240s). The king of France wanted to consolidate his grip on southern France. The pope needed to make a strong point that the only acceptable Christianity was Roman style. Both found self-serving reasons to wage a genocidal war against the Cathars, who never amounted to more than 10 percent of the local population and coexisted happily with their non-Cathar neighbors. After a terrible generation of torture and mass burnings, the Cathars were wiped out. The last Cathar was burned in 1321.

Today, tourists find haunting castle ruins (once Cathar strongholds) high in the Pyrenees, and eat meaty, if misnamed, *salades Cathar*.

Entry Porch: The entry was built about two centuries after the original plain church (1494), when concerns about Cathar sensitivities were long passé. Originally colorfully painted, it provided one fancy entry.

• *Head into the cathedral's...*

Interior: The inside of the church—also far from plain—looks essentially as it did in 1500. The highlights are the vast *Last Judgment* painting (west wall, under the organ) and the ornate choir (east end).

• *Walk to the front of the altar and face the...*

Last Judgment: The oldest art in the church (1474), this is also the biggest Last Judgment painting from the Middle Ages. The dead come out of the ground, then line up (above) with a printed accounting of their good and bad deeds displayed in ledgers on their chests. Judgment, here we come. Those on the left (God's right) look confident and comfortable. Those on the right—the hedonists—look edgy. Get closer. Below, on both sides of the arch, are seven frames illustrating a wonderland of gruesome punishments sinners could suffer through while attempting to earn a second chance at salvation. Those who fail end up in the black clouds of Hell (upper right). But where's Jesus—the key figure in any Judgment Day painting? The missing arch in the middle (cut out in late-Renaissance times to open the way to a new chapel) once featured Christ overseeing all the action. Go back to the last pew and find the black-and-white image on a small stand. The picture provides a good guess at how this painting would have looked—though no one knows for sure. The assembly above (on the left) shows the heavenly hierarchy: The pope and bishops sit closest to (the missing) Jesus; then more bishops and priests—before kings—followed by monks; and then, finally, commoners like you and me. To learn more about the *Last Judgment*, tour the choir (described later), which includes an audioguide with commentary on the painting.

The **altar** is the newest art in the church. But this is not the front of the church at all—you're facing west. Turn 180 degrees and head east, for Jerusalem (where most medieval churches point).

• *Stop first at the choir—a fancy, more intimate room within the finely carved stone "screen."*

The Choir: In the Middle Ages, nearly all cathedrals had ornate Gothic choir screens like this one. These highly decorated walls divided the church into a private place for clergy and a general zone for the common rabble. The screen enclosed the altar and added mystery to the Mass. In the 16th century, with the success of the Protestant movement and the Catholic Church's Counter-Reformation, choir screens were removed. (In the 20th century, the Church took things one step further, and priests actually turned and faced their parishioners.) Later, French Revolutionary atheists destroyed most of the choir screens that remained—Albi's is a rare survivor.

Pay €2 to stroll around the choir (excellent audioguide included, follow the English diagram). You'll see Old Testament figures in the Dark Ages exterior and New Testament figures in the enlightened interior. Stepping inside, marvel at the fine limestone carving. Scan each of the 72 unique little angels just above the wood-paneled choir stalls. Check out the brilliant ceiling, which hasn't been touched or restored in 500 years. A bishop, impressed by the fresco technique of the Italian Renaissance, invited seven Florentine artists to do the work. Good call.

• *Exit through the side door, next to where you paid for the choir. You'll pass a WC on your way to the...*

▲▲Toulouse-Lautrec Museum (Musée Toulouse-Lautrec)

The Palais de la Berbie (once the fortified home of Albi's archbishop) has the world's largest collection of Henri de Toulouse-Lautrec's paintings, posters, and sketches. The museum was completely reorganized and expanded in 2012. The information below won't help you navigate the new layout, but it will give you some helpful background.

Cost and Hours: €8, audioguide-€3 (for most, the printed English explanations are sufficient); July-Sept daily 9:00-18:00; June daily 9:00-12:00 & 14:00-18:00; April-May and Oct daily 10:00-12:00 & 14:00-18:00—but closed Tue in Oct; Feb-March and Nov-Dec Wed-Mon 10:00-12:00 & 14:00-17:30, closed Tue; Jan Wed-Mon 10:00-12:00 & 14:00-17:00, closed Tue; Place Ste. Cécile, tel. 05 63 49 48 70, www.museetoulouselautrec.net.

Background: Henri de Toulouse-Lautrec, born here in 1864, was crippled from youth. After he broke his right leg at age 13 and then his left leg the next year (probably due to a genetic disorder), the lower half of his body stopped growing. His father, once very engaged in parenting, lost interest in his son. Henri moved to the fringes of society, where he gained an affinity for people who didn't quite fit in. He later made his mark painting the dregs of the Parisian underclass with an intimacy only made possible by a man with his life experience.

Visiting the Museum: The museum displays more than 1,000 of Toulouse-Lautrec's pieces, mostly in chronological order and often around themes (for example, close friends, family members, horses, and scenes from daily life). As you tour, use the dates of the paintings (always indicated) to tie Henri's evolution as an artist to his work. *Suite de la Visite* signs guide you through the collection, and English information sheets—available in most rooms—give plenty of background for your visit.

You'll find rooms dedicated to the artist's **early years,** including a small collection of portraits by Toulouse-Lautrec and others. In the 1880s, Henri was stuck in Albi, far from any artistic action. During these years, he found inspiration in nature, in the pages of magazines, and by observing people. This was his Impressionistic stage. Look for works from his youth *(jeunesse)* in a glass case—the impressive doodles of a kid just 11 to 15 years young (1870s).

In 1882, Henri moved to the big city to pursue his passion. In his early **Paris** works, we see his trademark shocking colors; down-and-dirty, street-life scenes emerge. Compare his art-school work and his street work: Henri augmented his classical training with vivid life experience. His subjects were from bars, brothels, and cabarets...Toto, we're not in Albi anymore. Henri was fascinated by cancan dancers (whose legs moved with an agility he'd never experience), and he captured them expertly. In these exploratory years, he dabbled in any style he encountered. The naked body emerged as one of his fascinations.

Henri started making some money in the 1890s by selling

illustrations to magazines and newspapers. Back then, his daily happy hour included brothel visits—1892-1894 was his prostitution period. He respected the ladies, feeling both fascination and empathy toward them. The **prostitutes** accepted him the way he was and let him into their world...which he sketched brilliantly. Notice how he shows the prostitutes as real humans—they are neither glorified nor vulgarized in his works.

Find the big *Au Salon de la Rue des Moulins* (1894). There are two versions: the quick sketch, then the finished studio version. With this piece, Toulouse-Lautrec arrived—no more sampling.

The artist has established his unique style, oblivious to society's norms: colors (strong), subject matter (hidden worlds), and moralism (none). Henri's trademark use of cardboard was simply his quick, snapshot way of working: He'd capture these slice-of-life impressions on the fly on cheap, disposable material, intending to convert them to finer canvas paintings later, in his studio. But the cardboard quickies survive as Toulouse-Lautrec masterpieces.

Toulouse-Lautrec's bread and butter were his **advertising posters.** He was an innovative advertiser, creating simple, bold, and powerful lithographic images. You'll find displays of his original lithograph blocks (simply prepare the stone with a backward image, apply ink—which sticks chemically to the black points—and print posters).

Four-color posters meant creating four different blocks. The **Moulin Rouge** poster established his business reputation in Paris—strong symbols, bold and simple: just what, where, and when. Cabaret singer and club owner Aristide Bruant (*dans son cabaret*—"in his cabaret") is portrayed as bold and dashing.

Toulouse-Lautrec's **cane** offers more insight into this tortured artistic genius (if you can't find it, ask a guard). To protect him from his self-destructive lifestyle, loved ones had him locked up in a psychiatric hospital. But, with the help of this clever hollow cane, he still got his booze. Friends would drop by with hallucinogenic absinthe, his drink of choice—also popular among many other artists of the time. With these special deliveries, he'd restock his cane, which even came equipped with a fancy little glass.

In 1901, at age 37, alcoholic, paranoid, depressed, and syphilitic, Henri de Toulouse-Lautrec returned to his mother—the only woman who ever really loved him—and died in her arms. The art world didn't mourn. Obituaries, speaking for the art establishment, basically said good riddance to Toulouse-Lautrec and his ugly art. Although no one in the art world wanted Henri's pieces, his mother and his best friend—a boyhood pal and art dealer named Maurice Joyant—recognized his genius and saved his work. They first offered it to the Louvre, which refused. Finally, in 1922, the mayor of Albi accepted the collection and hung Toulouse-Lautrec's work here in what, for more than a century, had been a boring museum of archaeology.

• *Leave the Toulouse-Lautrec Museum courtyard and turn right, then follow the cobbled path to the gardens for a good city view over the Tarn River (described next).*

More Sights in Albi

▲**Albi Town View**—Albi was situated here because of its river access to Bordeaux (which connected the town to the global market). In medieval times, the fastest, most economical way to transport goods was down rivers like this. The lower, older bridge (Pont Vieux) was first built in 1020. Prior to its construction, the weir (look just beyond this first bridge) provided a series of stepping stones that enabled people to cross the river. Look at the bishop's palace. The garden below dates from the 17th century (when the palace at Versailles inspired the French to create fancy gardens). The palace itself grew from the 13th century until 1789, when the French Revolution ended the power of the bishops and the state confiscated the building. Since 1905, it's been a museum.

• *The last two sights are right in the town center, roughly behind the cathedral.*

St. Salvy Church and Cloister (Eglise St. Salvi et Cloître)— Although this church (the oldest in town) is nothing special, the cloister creates a delightful space. Delicate arches surround an enclosed courtyard (open all day), providing a peaceful interlude from the shoppers that fill the pedestrian streets. Notice the church wall from the courtyard. It was the only stone building in Albi in the 11th century; the taller parts, added later, are made of brick. This is one of many little courtyards hiding throughout town. In the rough-and-tumble Middle Ages, most buildings faced inward. If doors are open, you're welcome to pop into courtyards. The Hôtel Décazes (8 Rue Toulouse-Lautrec, across from La Viguière restaurant) is another good example.

Market Hall (Marché Couvert)—Albi's quiet Art Nouveau market is good for picnic-gathering and people-watching (Tue-Sun 8:00-14:00, closed Mon, 2 blocks from cathedral). On Saturday, a farmer's market sets up outside the market hall.

Sleeping in Albi

$$$ Hostellerie du Grand Saint Antoine** is Albi's oldest hotel (established in 1784), and the most comfortable and traditional place I list. Guests enter an inviting, spacious lobby that opens onto an enclosed garden. Rooms are Old World cozy, with all the comforts (Db-€130-150, big Db-€170-200, suites-€190-260, breakfast-€15, Wi-Fi, parking-€7, a block above big Place du Vigan at 17 Rue Sainte-Antoine, tel. 05 63 54 04 04, fax 05 63 47 10 47, www.hotel -saint-antoine-albi.com, courriel@hotel-saint-antoine-albi.com).

$$ Hôtel Chiffre** is a safe bet, with 38 well-appointed rooms (Db-€78, bigger Db-€96-126, family rooms-€145, some with queen-size beds, check website for deals, air-con, elevator, pay Wi-Fi, garage-€9, traditional restaurant, near Place du Vigan at 50 Rue Séré de Rivières, tel. 05 63 48 58 48, fax 05 63 47 20 61, www.hotelchiffre.com, contact@hotelchiffre.com).

$$ Le Vieil Alby Hôtel-Restaurant**,** in the heart of Albi's pedestrian area, has simple, well-maintained, non-smoking rooms (Db-€50-68, Tb-€72, garage-€7, 25 Rue Toulouse-Lautrec, tel. 05 63 54 14 69, fax 05 63 54 96 75, www.levieilalby.com, levieilalby @live.fr).

$ Hôtel Lapérouse** is a work in progress, one block from the old city and a 10-minute walk to the train station. The family-run hotel offers simple rooms; some are renovated and cheery, though I'd skip the rooms facing the busy street. It comes with a quiet garden, a big pool, and *très* friendly English-speaking owners. Spring for a room with a balcony over the garden and pool (Db on street-€50, Db on garden-€63, Db on garden with deck-€73,

---

Sleep Code

(€1 = about $1.30, country code: 33)

S = Single, **D** = Double/Twin, **T** = Triple, **Q** = Quad, **b** = bathroom, **s** = shower only, ***** = French hotel rating system (0-5 stars). Unless otherwise noted, credit cards are accepted and English is spoken.

To help you sort easily through these listings, I've divided the accommodations into three categories based on the price for a standard double room with bath:

$$$ Higher Priced—Most rooms €90 or more.

$$ Moderately Priced—Most rooms between €60-90.

$ Lower Priced—Most rooms €60 or less.

Prices can change without notice; verify the hotel's current rates online or by email.

Internet access and Wi-Fi, 21 Place Lapérouse, tel. 05 63 54 69 22, fax 05 63 38 03 69, www.hotel-laperouse.com, hotel.laperouse @wanadoo.fr).

Eating in Albi

Albi is filled with reasonable restaurants that serve a rich local cuisine. Be warned: "Going local" here is likely to get you tripes (cow intestines), andouillette (sausages made from pig intestines), *foie de veau* (calf liver), and *tête de veau* (calf's head). Choose a restaurant or select one of the many cafés on the lively Place du Vigan. For a choice of traditional restaurants, survey the places along Rue Toulouse-Lautrec (2 blocks from Hôtel St. Clair).

Le Papillon Restaurant, an inviting, Cathar-cool eatery under medieval stones and timbers, fuses Californian and French cuisines. It's the dream come true for two guys from California— while Michael Gabel cooks, his partner, Rick Perry, serves. Seafood is their forte, though their meat dishes are tasty, too. There are also good vegetarian options, and the salads are tops (€19-29 *menus,* €15-20 evening *plats,* open Thu-Sat for dinner, Tue-Sat for lunch, 1 Rue Toulouse-Lautrec, tel. 05 63 43 10 77).

Le Tournesol is a good lunch option for vegetarians, since that's all they do. The food is organic and delicious, the setting is bright with many windows, and the service is friendly. Try the wonderful homemade tarts (€10 *plats,* open for lunch only, closed Sun-Mon, 11 Rue de l'Ort en Salvy, tel. 05 63 38 38 14).

Le Clos Sainte Cécile, hidden behind the cathedral, is an old school transformed into a family-run restaurant. Friendly waiters serve delicious dishes in their large, shady garden—at a French pace (€17-23 *menus,* closed Tue-Wed, 3 Rue du Castelviel, tel. 05 63 38 19 74).

Restaurant Stéphane Laurens (La Pause) sits alone in a quiet pedestrian area immediately north of the cathedral. It has a handsome interior along with a peaceful terrace offering point-blank views of the cathedral. The focus here is on wines (€10 lunch *plats,* €20-26 dinner *menus,* closed Sun-Mon, 10 Place Monseigneur Mignot, tel. 05 63 43 62 41).

Albi Connections

You'll connect to just about any destination through Toulouse.

From Albi by Train to: Toulouse (11/day, 70 minutes), **Carcassonne** (12/day, 3 hours, change in Toulouse), **Sarlat** (6/day, 5-7 hours with 2-3 changes, some require bus from Souillac to Sarlat), **Paris** (6/day, 6.5-9 hours, change in Toulouse, also night train).

Near Albi

▲Route of the Bastides
(La Route des Bastides Albigeoises)

The hilly terrain north of Albi was tailor-made for medieval villages to organize around for defensive purposes. Here, scores of fortified villages *(bastides)* spill over hilltops, above rivers, and between wheat fields, creating a worthwhile detour for drivers. These planned communities were the medieval product of community efforts organized by local religious or military leaders. Most *bastides* were built during the Hundred Years' War (see sidebar on page 269) to establish a foothold for French or British rule in this hotly contested region, as well as to provide stability to benefit trade. Unlike other French hill towns, *bastides* were not the product of a safe haven provided by a castle. Instead, they were a premeditated effort by a community to collectively construct houses as a planned defensive unit, *sans* castle.

Connect these *bastides* as a day trip from Albi, or as you drive between Albi and the Dordogne. I've described the top *bastides* in the order you'll reach them on these driving routes.

Day Trip from Albi: For a good loop route northwest from Albi, cross the 22 Août 1944 bridge and follow signs to *Cordes-sur-Ciel* (allow 30 minutes). The view of Cordes as you approach is memorable. From Cordes, follow signs to *Saint-Antonin-Noble-Val*, an appealing, flat "hill town" on the river, with few tourists. Then pass vertical little Penne, Bruniquel (signed from Saint-Antonin-Noble-Val), Larroque, Puycelci (my favorite), and, finally, Castelnau-de-Montmiral (with a lovely main square), before returning to Albi. Each of these places is worth exploring if you have the time.

On the Way to the Dordogne: For a one-way scenic route north to the Dordogne that includes many of the same *bastides*, leave Albi, head toward Toulouse, and make time on the free A-68. Exit at Gaillac, go to its center, and track D-964 to Castelnau-de-Montmiral, Puycelci, and on to Bruniquel. From here you can head directly to Caussade on D-118 and D-964, then to Cahors on A-20 or D-820 (and on to Sarlat if that or the river villages are your destination). Or, if you're into this scenic drive and not pushed for time, continue north on D-115 through the beautiful Gorges de l'Aveyron to Saint-Antonin-Noble-Val, making time to explore this fine town. From Saint-Antonin, you can follow D-5 and D-926 to Caussade, then take N-20 to Cahors.

Cordes-sur-Ciel—It's hard to resist this brilliantly situated hill town just 15 miles north of Albi, but I would (in high season, at least). Enjoy the fantastic view on the road from Albi, and consider a detour up into town only if the coast looks clear (read:

off-season). Cordes, once an important Cathar base, has slipped over the boutique-filled edge to the point where it's hard for me to find the medieval town. But it's a dramatic setting filled with steep streets, half-timbered buildings, and great views. Small buses shuttle visitors to the top from near the TI (tel. 05 63 56 00 52, www.cordessurciel.fr).

Bruniquel—This overlooked, *très* photogenic, but less-tended village will test your thighs as you climb the lanes upward to the château (€2.50, April-Sept daily 10:00-12:30 & 14:00-18:00, closed Oct-March). Don't miss the dramatic view up to the village from the river below as you drive along D-964. **$$ L'Etape du Château** rents very comfortable rooms at good rates (Db-€80, extra person-€25, includes breakfast, Wi-Fi, sauna, tel. 05 63 67 25 00, www.etapeduchateau.com, etapeduchateau@gmail.com). They also serve meals featuring organic foods.

▲**Puycelci**—This town crowns a bluff surrounded only by green (20 minutes north of Gaillac). Drive to the top, where you'll find easy parking and an unspoiled, level village with a couple of cafés, one real restaurant, a small grocery, a happy bakery (selling great cookies and small cartons of the local sorbet), a few *chambres d'hôtes*, and one sharp little hotel.

Stroll through the village, starting at the parking lot. Enter the village, passing the recommended Puycelci Roc Café, and make your way through town. At the opposite side of the village, a rampart walk circles counterclockwise back to the parking lot, where an orientation table explains what's in the distance. The park-like ramparts come with picnic benches and grand vistas. It's a good place to listen to the birds and feel the wind.

As you wander, consider the recent history of an ancient town like this. In 1900, 2,000 people lived here with neither running water nor electricity. Then things changed. Half of all French men lost their lives in World War I; Puycelci didn't escape this fate, as the monument (by the parking lot) attests. By 1968 the village was down to three families. But then running water replaced the venerable cisterns, and things started looking up. Today, there is still almost no commercial activity, but the town has a stable population of 110, all marveling at how the value of their land has skyrocketed.

Eating and Sleeping in Puycelci: **Puycelci Roc Café,** at the parking lot, has café fare, a warm interior, and pleasant outdoor tables (daily for dinner, Sat-Wed for lunch, tel. 05 63 33 13 67). A night in Puycelci is my idea of a vacation.

$$ L'Ancienne Auberge is *the* place to eat and sleep, with eight surprisingly smart and comfortable rooms, a country-classy restaurant, a cozy *bistrot* with a fireplace you could walk into, and two outdoor patios (€11.50 lunch *menu*, dinner *plats* from €13, dinner *menus* from €24). Owner/chef Dorothy moved here from New Jersey many years ago and is eager to share her cuisine and her passion for this region (Db-€70-125, air-con, Wi-Fi, Place de l'Eglise, tel. 05 63 33 65 90, fax 05 63 33 21 12, www.ancienne-auberge.com, contact@ancienne-auberge.com). They also run **$ Le Rempart,** a good-value *chambre d'hôte* (Db-€60, www.puycelsi-le-rempart.fr).

$$ Delphine de Laveleye Chambres is another solid choice, with three homey rooms around a small garden and pool, and a three-room *gîte* (Db-€60-75, Tb-€90-125, *gîte*-€600/week, cash only, Wi-Fi, tel. 05 63 33 13 65, mobile 06 72 92 69 59, www.chez delphine.com, delphine@chezdelphine.com).

Castelnau-de-Montmiral—This overlooked village has quiet lanes leading to a perfectly preserved *bastide* square surrounded by fine arcades and filled with brick half-timbered facades. Ditch your car below and wander up to the square, where a restaurant, a café, and a small *patisserie* await. Have a drink or lunch on the square at the simple **Auberge des Arcades** café (open daily, tel. 05 63 33 20 88).

East of Albi

Two hours east of Albi lies a hauntingly beautiful region unknown to most Americans. Mountains, rivers, and *Brigadoon*-like villages conspire to give the adventurous nature-lover a true experience of *la France profonde*.

▲**Gorges du Tarn**—You can canoe, hike, or drive the beautiful Tarn River Gorge by heading east from Albi to Millau, then following the gorge all the way to St. Enimie. Roads are slow but spectacular.

The best base for canoeing is from tiny La Malène (on the way to St-Enimie, 25 miles northeast of Millau). In La Malène, **Company Canoë 2000** rents what you need to run the mellow river (down the path to the right of bridge, tel. 04 66 48 57 71); the 8- or 11-kilometer trips (about 5 or 7 miles) have the best views (€34 per canoe). Take your lunch and picnic along the way. If you'd rather not paddle a canoe, you can take a Batelier boat (leaves from bridge, seats 5-6 people, ask for a boatman who speaks a leetle English).

Sleeping in La Malène: Stay at the simple but comfortable **$ Auberge de l'Embarcadère** (Db-€45, Tb-€52, tel. 04 66 48 51 03, fax 04 66 48 58 94) or in the rustic-luxurious **$$$ Manoir de Montesquiou,** run entirely by one family. Dad manages the hotel, Mom is the head chef, and the three sisters serve your meals and run the bar (Db-€80-119, suites fit for a queen-€150, extra bed-€18, Wi-Fi, you'll be expected to dine at its great restaurant, *menus* from €29-39, tel. 04 66 48 51 12, fax 04 66 48 50 47, www.manoir-montesquiou.com, montesquiou@demeures-de-lozere.com).

▲**Millau Bridge (Viaduc de Millau)**—Completed in 2005, this sleek, futuristic 1.5-mile-long suspension bridge, which shoots across the Tarn River Valley, is the world's highest at 885 feet. A modern-day Pont du Gard, the Millau Bridge was built as a critical link in the A-75 autoroute, which connects Paris with the Mediterranean and Barcelona. A quarter-million tons of concrete were used to set the supporting pillars, with the tallest rising 1,125 feet—taller than the Eiffel Tower (in fact, it was built by the same construction company that erected the Eiffel Tower in 1889). The bridge's British architect, Lord Norman Foster, also designed London's egg-shaped City Hall, as well as Berlin's equally glassy Reichstag Parliament dome. There's a visitor center on the northern end of the bridge with sensational views, and another below the bridge, at the southern end (both open daily, tel. 05 65 59 42 86, current car toll about €6, or €7.50 in July-Aug; bridge is 70 miles northeast of Albi on A-75).

Carcassonne

Medieval Carcassonne is a 13th-century world of towers, turrets, and cobblestones. Europe's ultimate walled fortress city, it's also stuffed with too many tourists. At 10:00, salespeople stand at the doors of their main-street shops, a gauntlet of tacky temptations poised and ready for their daily ration of customers—consider yourself warned. But early, late, or off-season, a quieter Carcassonne is an evocative playground for any medievalist. Forget midday—spend the night.

Locals like to believe that Carcassonne got its name this way: 1,200 years ago, Charlemagne and his troops besieged this fortress-town (then called La Cité) for several years. A cunning townsperson named Madame Carcas saved the town. Just as food was running out, she fed the last few bits of grain to the last pig and tossed him over the  wall. Splat. Charlemagne's bored and frustrated forces, amazed that the town still had enough food to throw fat party pigs over the wall, decided they would never succeed in starving the people out. They ended the siege, and the city was saved. Madame Carcas

LANGUEDOC

sonne-d (sounded) the long-awaited victory bells, and La Cité had a new name: Carcas-sonne. It's a cute story...but historians suspect that Carcassonne is a Frenchified version of the town's original name (Carcas).

As a teenager on my first visit to Carcassonne, I wrote this in my journal: "Before me lies Carcassonne, the perfect medieval city. Like a fish that everyone thought was extinct, somehow Europe's greatest Romanesque fortress city has survived the centuries. I was supposed to be gone yesterday, but here I sit imprisoned by choice—curled in a cranny on top of the wall. The wind blows away the sounds of today, and my imagination 'medievals' me. The moat is one foot over and 100 feet down. Small plants and moss upholster my throne." Avoid the midday mobs and let this place make you a kid on a rampart.

Orientation to Carcassonne

Contemporary Carcassonne is neatly divided into two cities: The magnificent La Cité (the fortified old city, with 200 full-time residents taking care of lots more tourists) and the local-feeling and lively Ville Basse (modern lower city). Two bridges, the busy Pont Neuf and the traffic-free Pont Vieux, both with great views, connect the two parts.

Tourist Information

Carcassonne's TI has three locations. The main TI, in **Ville Basse,** is useful only if you're walking to La Cité (28 Rue de Verdun). A far more convenient branch is in **La Cité,** to your right as you enter the main gate (Narbonne Gate—or Porte Narbonnaise). Both TIs have the same hours and telephone number (April-Oct daily 9:00-18:00, until 19:00 in July-Aug; Nov-March Mon-Sat 9:00-17:00, Sun 14:00-18:00; tel. 04 68 10 24 30). If you're arriving by train, the most convenient TI is the small kiosk across the canal from the **train station** (unpredictable hours, generally daily July-Sept 9:15-13:00 & 14:15-18:00, usually closed Oct-June...but you never know, tel. 04 68 25 94 81).

At any of the TI locations, pick up the map of La Cité, which includes a fine self-guided tour. Walking tours in English depart from La Cité TI (€9, daily at 9:30 April-Oct). The TI's €15 City Pass bundles the walking tour with a canal cruise, plus discounts

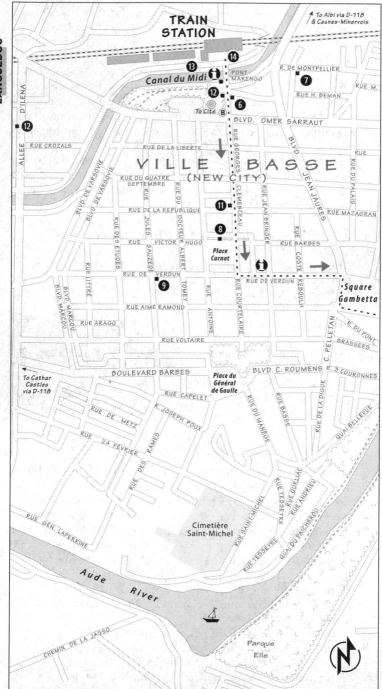

LANGUEDOC

TRAIN STATION

To Albi via D-118 & Caunes-Minervois

13

Canal du Midi

14

PONT MARENGO

R. DE MONTPELLIER

7

RUE H. BEMAN

RUE M.

12

To Cité

B

6

BLVD. OMER SARRAUT

12

ALLEE D'ILENA

RUE CROZALS

RUE DE LA LIBERTE

VILLE BASSE
(NEW CITY)

BLVD. DE VARSOVIE

BLVD. DE VARSOVIE

RUE DU QUATRE SEPTEMBRE

RUE DE LA REPUBLIQUE

RUE DES ETUDES

RUE JULES SAUZEDE

RUE DU DOCTEUR ALBERT

RUE GEORGES CLEMENCEAU

RUE JEAN BRINGER

RUE JEAN JAURES

RUE DU PALAIS

RUE MAZAGRAN

11

8

RUE VICTOR HUGO

Place Carnot

RUE BARBES

RUE COSTE

RUE LITTRE

BLVD. MARCOU

BLVD. MARCOU

RUE ARAGO

RUE DE VERDUN

9

TOMEY

RUE ANTOINE

RUE AIMÉ RAMOND

RUE VOLTAIRE

RUE COURTEJAIRE

RUE REBOULH

RUE DE VERDUN

i

Square Gambetta

R. DU PONT

BRASSERS

To Cathar Castles via D-118

BOULEVARD BARBES

Place du Général de Gaulle

BLVD. C. ROUMENS

C. PELLETAN

R. 3 COURONNES

RUE CAPELET

RUE DE METZ

R. JOSEPH POUX

RUE DU MANEGE

RUE BASSE

RUE DE LA DIGUE

QUAI BELLEVUE

RUE 24 FEVRIER

RUE DES RAMES

RUE GEN LAPERRINE

Cimetière Saint-Michel

RUE SAINT-MICHEL

RUE TESSEYRE

RUE OURLIAC

RUE ANDRIEU

QUAI DU PAICHEROU

CHEMIN DE LA JASSO

Aude River

Parque Elle

N

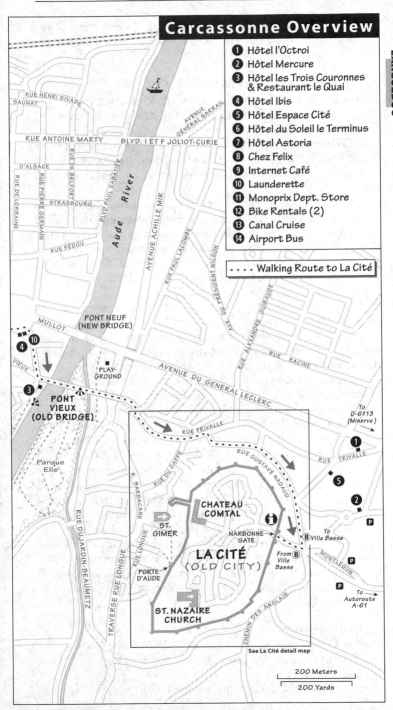

Carcassonne Overview

1. Hôtel l'Octroi
2. Hôtel Mercure
3. Hôtel les Trois Couronnes & Restaurant le Quai
4. Hôtel Ibis
5. Hôtel Espace Cité
6. Hôtel du Soleil le Terminus
7. Hôtel Astoria
8. Chez Felix
9. Internet Café
10. Launderette
11. Monoprix Dept. Store
12. Bike Rentals (2)
13. Canal Cruise
14. Airport Bus

- - - - Walking Route to La Cité

at Cathar sights. Also ask about festivals (www.carcassonne
-tourisme.com) and guided excursions to sights near Carcassonne
(described later, under "Helpful Hints").

Arrival in Carcassonne

By Train: The train station (no bag storage) is located in the Ville
Basse, a 30-minute walk from La Cité. You have three basic options
for reaching La Cité: taxi, various shuttles, or on foot.

Taxis charge €8 for the short trip to La Cité but cannot enter
the city walls. Taxis wait in front of the train station, or you can
find the taxi stand one block from the station (after crossing the
canal).

Two different, cheaper options run from the Chénier stop
(on Boulevard Omer Sarraut, a block from the station) to La Cité:
public bus #4 (€1, hourly, Mon-Sat, none Sun) and the *navette/
shuttle* (which can be a bus or a *petit train;* €2 one-way, €3 round-
trip, hourly 9:30-19:30, July-Aug daily, June and Sept-mid-Oct
Mon-Sat only, does not run off-season). Schedules for both bus #4
and the *navette* are posted in the bus shelter.

An **airport bus** departs from in front of the station and runs
about hourly to Carcassonne's airport (€5).

The 30-minute **walk** through the new city to La Cité ends
with a good uphill climb. Walk straight out of the station, cross
the canal, then cross the busy ring road, and keep straight on Rue
Clemenceau for about seven blocks. After Place Carnot (frequent
markets), turn left on Rue de Verdun, walk three blocks, and turn
right on the vast Square Gambetta. Angle across the square, turn
right after Hôtel Ibis, then cross Pont Vieux (great views). Signs
will guide you up Rue Trivalle and Rue Nadaud to La Cité.

By Car: Follow signs to *Centre-Ville*, then *La Cité*. You'll
come to several large parking lots at the entry to the walled city
(first hour free, €5/1-6 hours, then €1/hour after that) and a drawbridge at the Narbonne Gate, at the walled city's entrance. If staying inside the walls, you can park for free in the castle moat (facing
the Narbonne Gate, turn left, then right after the small cemetery).
You must show your reservation or have the attendant call your
hotel. (Verbal assurances won't do.) Allow 15 minutes on foot over
uneven surfaces to hotels (the recommended Hôtels le Donjon and
de la Cité will pick you up). Theft is common—leave nothing in
your car at night.

Helpful Hints

Market Days: Pleasing Place Carnot in Ville Basse hosts a non-
touristy open market (Tue, Thu, and Sat mornings until 13:00;
Sat is the biggest).

Summer Festivals: Carcassonne becomes colorfully medieval during many special events each July and August. Highlights are the *spectacle équestre* (jousting matches) and July 14 (Bastille Day) fireworks. The TI has details.

Internet Access: Most hotels have Internet access. In the Ville Basse, **Alerte Rouge** is good, with 10 computers, Wi-Fi, a call center, and a snack bar (daily 9:00-22:00, 73 Rue de Verdun, tel. 04 68 25 20 39).

Laundry: Try **Laverie Express** (daily 8:00-22:00, 5 Square Gambetta at Hôtel Ibis; from La Cité, cross Pont Vieux and turn right).

Department Store: there's a **Monoprix** where Rues Clemenceau and de la République cross, a few blocks from the train station.

Tourist Train: Hop on at the Narbonne Gate for a 45-minute loop around La Cité (€7).

Bike Rental: Bike riding is very popular thanks to the scenic towpath that follows the canal (at the train station). **Génération VTT** rents bikes (get the free English map, daily 9:30-12:30 & 13:30-18:30, just beneath the train station TI kiosk, mobile 06 09 59 30 85, www.generation-vtt.com). **Evasion 2 Roues** also rents bikes, and has tandems (closed Sun-Mon, 85 Allée d'Iéna, tel. 04 68 11 90 40, www.evasion2roues.eu).

Taxi: Call 04 68 71 50 50 or 04 68 71 36 36.

Car Rental: Avis is at the train station (tel. 04 68 25 05 84). The airport has all the rental companies, but it's a lousy place to pick up a car—it's 30 minutes from Carcassonne and offices tend to be understaffed.

Guided Excursions from Carcassonne: Capable and fun English expat **Wendy Gedney,** based in Caunes-Minervois, runs day-long tours that mix sightseeing with wine-tasting and cultural experiences. She's thrilled to show you her adopted region (€90-95/person for full-day tours that usually include two wine-tastings, lunch, and visits to key sights such as the Cathar castles; tel. 04 68 76 27 57, mobile 06 42 33 34 09, www .vinenvacances.com, info@vinenvacances.com).

Minivan Service: Friendly **Didier** provides comfortable transportation for up to eight passengers to all area châteaux and sights. He's not a guide, so you can decide the itinerary (about €280/half-day, €400/day, mobile 06 03 18 39 95, bod.aude11 @orange.fr).

Self-Guided Walk

▲▲▲Carcassonne's Medieval Walls and La Cité

While the tourists shuffle up the main street, this walk introduces you to the city with history and wonder, rather than tour groups and plastic swords. We'll sneak into the town on the other side of the wall...through the back door (see map on the opposite page). This walk is wonderfully peaceful and scenic early or late in the day, when the sun is low.

Start on the asphalt outside La Cité's main entrance, the Narbonne Gate (Porte Narbonnaise). You're welcomed by a contemporary-looking bust of Madame Carcas—which is actually modeled after a 16th-century original of the town's legendary first lady (for her story, see page 628).

• *Cross the bridge toward the...*

Narbonne Gate: Pause at the drawbridge and survey this immense fortification. When forces from northern France finally conquered Carcassonne, it was a strategic prize. Not taking any chances, they evicted the residents, whom they allowed to settle in the lower town (Ville Basse)—as long as they stayed across the river. (Though it's called "new," this lower town actually dates from the 13th century.) La Cité remained a French military garrison until the 18th century.

The drawbridge was made crooked to slow any attackers' rush to the main gate and has a similar effect on tourists today.

• *After crossing the drawbridge, lose the crowds and walk left between the walls. At the first short set of stairs, climb to the outer-wall walkway and linger while facing the inner walls.*

Wall View: The Romans built Carcassonne's first wall, upon which the bigger medieval wall was constructed. Identify the ancient Roman bits by looking about one-third of the way up and finding the smaller rocks mixed with narrow stripes of red bricks (and no arrow slits). The outer wall that you're on was not built until the 1300s, more than a thousand years after the Roman walls went up. The massive walls you see today—nearly two miles around, with 52 towers—defended an important site near the intersection of north-south and east-west trade routes.

Look over the wall and down at the moat below (now mostly used for parking). Like most medieval moats, it was never filled with water (or even alligators). A ditch like this—which was originally even deeper—effectively stopped attacking forces from rolling up against the wall in their mobile towers and spilling into the city. Another enemy tactic was to "undermine" (tunnel underneath) the wall, causing a section to cave in. Notice the small, square holes at foot level along the ramparts. Wooden extensions of the rampart walkways (which we'll see later at the castle) once plugged into these holes so that townsfolk could drop nasty, sticky things on anyone tunneling in. In peacetime this area between the two walls *(les lices)* was used for medieval tournaments, jousting practice, and markets.

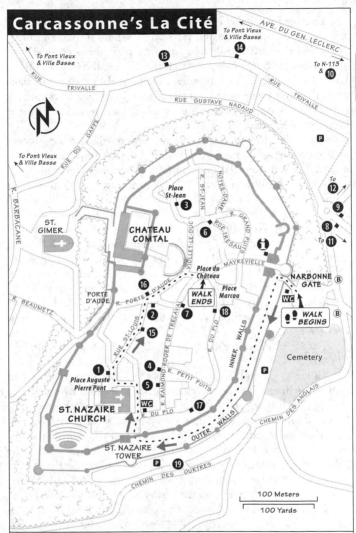

Carcassonne's La Cité

To Pont Vieux & Ville Basse
AVE. DU GEN. LECLERC
To Pont Vieux & Ville Basse

⑬

⑭

To N-113 & ⑩

RUE TRIVALLE

RUE GUSTAVE NADAUD

RUE TRIVALLE

To Pont Vieux & Ville Basse

RUE DU GAFFE

R. BARBACANE

ST. GIMER

CHATEAU COMTAL

Place St-Jean

③

⑥

R. ST-JEAN

NOTRE-DAME

R. GRAND PUITS

RUE TRESAUS

VIOLLET-LE-DUC

To ⑫

⑨

⑧

To ⑪

P

Place du Château

WALK ENDS

Place Marcou

NARBONNE GATE

B

WC

WALK BEGINS

B

R. BEAUMETZ

PORTE D'AUDE

R. PORTE D'AUDE

⑯

②

⑦

⑮

⑱

MAYREVIELLE

R. RAIMOND ROGER DE TRECAVAL

INNER WALLS

Cemetery

RUE ST-LOUIS

④

⑤

R. DU PLO

R. PETIT PUITS

①

Place Auguste Pierre Pont

WC

⑰

ST. NAZAIRE CHURCH

R. DU PLO

P

CHEMIN DES ANGLAIS

ST. NAZAIRE TOWER

OUTER WALLS

P

⑲

CHEMIN DES OURTRES

100 Meters

100 Yards

① Hôtel de la Cité & Barbacane Restaurant
② Best Western Hôtel le Donjon
③ Maison des Remparts, Le St. Jean & Restaurant Adelaide
④ Chambres l'Echappée Belle
⑤ Auberge des Lices Rooms & Restaurant
⑥ Chambres le Grand Puits
⑦ Hostel Carcassonne
⑧ Hôtel du Château
⑨ Hôtel le Montmorency

⑩ To Hôtel l'Octroi
⑪ To Hôtel Mercure
⑫ To Hôtel Espace Cité
⑬ Chambres les Florentines
⑭ Notre-Dame de l'Abbaye Rooms
⑮ Au Comte Roger Restaurant
⑯ Le Jardin de la Tour Restaurant
⑰ Le Bar à Vins Café & Jazz Bar
⑱ Gérard Sion Galerie (Photos)
⑲ Hotel Parking Entrance (Daytime Only)

During La Cité's Golden Age, the 1100s, independent rulers with open minds allowed Jews and Cathars to live and prosper within the walls, while troubadours wrote poems of ideal love. This liberal attitude made for a rich intellectual life but also led to La Cité's downfall. The Crusades aimed to rid France of the dangerous Cathar movement (and their liberal sympathizers), which led to Carcassonne's defeat and eventual incorporation into the kingdom of France.

The walls of this majestic fortress were partially reconstructed in 1855 as part of a program to restore France's important monuments. The tidy crenellations and the pointy tower roofs are generally from the 19th century. As you continue your wall walk to higher elevations, the lack of guardrails is striking. This would never happen in the US; in France, if you fall, it's your own fault (so be careful). Note the lights embedded in the walls. This fortress, like most important French monuments, is beautifully illuminated every night (for directions to a good nighttime view, see "Night Wall Walk to Pont Vieux" on page 638).

• *You could keep working your way around the walls, and finish with the five Roman towers just before you return to the starting point. Walking the entire circle between the inner and outer gate is a terrific 30-minute stroll (and fantastic after dark).*

But for this tour, we'll stop at the first entrance possible into La Cité, the...

Inner Wall Gate: The wall has the same four gates it had in Roman times. Before entering, notice the squat tower on the outer wall—this was a "barbican" (placed opposite each inner gate for extra protection). Barbicans were always semicircular—open on the inside to expose anyone who breached the outer defenses. Invading today is far easier than in the good old days. Notice the holes in the barbican for supporting a wooden catwalk. Breach the walls and enter the square gate—look up to see a slot for the portcullis (the big iron grate), and the frame for a heavy wooden door.

Once safely inside, look back up at the inner wall tower to view *beaucoup de* narrow arrow slits—even if enemies got this far, they still weren't home free.

• *Opposite the tower, work your way around to the entry of the...*

St. Nazaire Church (Basilique St. Nazaire): This was a cathedral until the 18th century, when the bishop moved to the lower town. Today, due to the depopulation of the basically dead-except-for-tourism Cité, it's not even a functioning parish church. Notice the Romanesque arches of the nave and the delicately vaulted Gothic arches over the altar and transepts. After its successful conquest of this region in the 13th-century Albigensian Crusades, France set out to destroy all the Romanesque churches and replace them with Gothic ones—symbolically asserting its northern rule with this more northern style of church. With the start of the Hundred Years' War in 1337, the expensive demolition was abandoned. Today, the Romanesque remainder survives, and the destroyed section has been rebuilt Gothic, which makes it one of the best examples of Gothic architecture in southern France. When the lights are off (as they often are), the interior—lit only by candles and 14th-century stained glass—is evocatively medieval. A plaque near the door tells that St. Dominique (founder of the Dominican order) preached at this church in 1213 (Mon-Sat 9:00-11:45 & 13:45-18:00, Sun 9:00-10:45 & 14:00-18:00, Sun Mass at 11:00).

Hôtel de la Cité: Located 50 steps from St. Nazaire Church, this beyond-posh hotel sits where the Bishop's Palace did 700 years ago. Today, it's a worthwhile detour to see how the privileged few travel. You're free to wander, so find the library-cozy bar (€8 beer and wine), then find the rear garden and turn right for super wall views that you can't see from anywhere else.

• *From here, follow Rue St. Louis (passing Chez Saskia on your left) for several blocks, merge right onto Rue Port d'Aude, then look for a small castle-view terrace on your left a block up.*

Château Comtal: Originally built in 1125, Carcassonne's third layer of defense was completely redesigned in later reconstructions. From this impressive viewpoint you can see the wooden rampart extensions that once circled the entire city wall. (Notice the empty peg holes to the left of the bridge.) When *Robin Hood: Prince of Thieves,* starring Kevin Costner, was filmed here in 1990, the entire city was turned into a film set. Locals enjoyed playing bit parts and seeing their château labeled "Nottingham Castle" in the fanciful film.

Château Comtal is open to the public and makes for a worthwhile visit. An intro film—well-done, with big sound—sets the table for your visit (sit on the left to read English subtitles). Next is a room-size model of La Cité, after which a self-guided tour leads you around the inner ramparts of Carcassonne's defenses, allowing you to see the underpinnings of towers and catwalks that hung from the walls. The views are terrific. Your visit ends with a museum showing bits of St. Nazaire Church and fragments from important homes (€8.50, audioguide-€4.50 or €6/2 people, daily 10:00-18:00, last entry 45 minutes before closing, tel. 04 68 11 70 77).

• *Fifty yards away, opposite the entrance to the castle, is...*

Place du Château: This busy little square sports a modest statue honoring the man who saved the city from deterioration and neglect in the 19th century. The bronze model circling the base of the statue shows Carcassonne's walls as they looked before the 1855 reconstruction by Eugène Viollet-le-Duc.

• *Facing the château entry, Place du Grand Puits lies a block to your right. It's named for the oldest of Carcassonne's 22 wells that served the city in the Middle Ages. Behind you, the main drag leads down to the Narbonne Gate, where you began this walk.*

Sights in Carcassonne

▲▲▲**Night Wall Walk to Pont Vieux**—Save some post-dinner energy for a don't-miss walk around the same walls you visited today (great dinner picnic sites as

well). The effect at night is mesmerizing: The embedded lights become torches and unfamiliar voices become the enemy. End at Pont Vieux for a floodlit fantasy. The best route is a partial circumnavigation clockwise between the walls. Start at the Narbonne Gate, and follow my self-guided walk (described earlier) to the Inner Wall Gate. Don't enter La Cité through this gate; instead, continue your walk between the walls (this section is occasionally closed; if so, you'll have to make your way through the village and out the rear along Rue de la Porte d'Aude to meet up with the route described from here).

The path narrows as you walk behind Château Comtal. When you come to a ramp leading down (after about five minutes), make a U-turn to the left, just before the path rises back up. This ramp leads down the hill; make a left when you come to the church (St. Gimer), then a right on Rue de la Barbacane (follow the *Centre-Ville* sign). Go straight to reach Pont Vieux and exceptional views of floodlit Carcassonne. Return from the bridge the same way you came, and complete your clockwise walk between the walls back to the Narbonne Gate, or take Rue Trivalle to Rue Gustave Nadaud for a quicker return.

Riverside Walk—Two scenic paths running southwest along each side of the Aude River below La Cité offer occasional views to the fortress and a verdant escape for runners and walkers. Both paths can be accessed from below the Pont Vieux.

Canal du Midi—Completed in 1681, this sleepy 155-mile canal connects France's Mediterranean and Atlantic coasts and runs right by the train station in Carcassonne. Before railways, Canal du Midi was clogged with commercial traffic; today, it entertains only pleasure craft. Look for the slow-moving hotel barges strewn with tanned and well-fed vacationers. Small boats that ferry tourists along the canal leave from in front of the train station (€9/1.5

hours, €11.50/2.5 hours, 3-5/day, April-Oct, closed Mon, mobile 06 80 47 54 33, www.carcassonne-croisiere.com). The boat company on the other side of the canal has the same prices (closed Tue, mobile 06 07 74 04 57). A better way to experience the canal is on a relaxed bike ride along the level towpath (for bike rental, see "Helpful Hints," earlier).

Gérard Sion Galerie—Duck into this impressive photo gallery before selecting which Cathar castles you want to visit (brilliant shots of many monuments in Languedoc, generally open daily 10:00-19:00, just up from Place Marcou at 27 Rue du Plô).

Nightlife in Carcassonne

For relief from all the medieval kitsch, savor a drink in four-star, library-meets-bar ambience at the **Hôtel de la Cité** bar (€8 beer and wine, Place de l'Eglise). To taste the liveliest square, with loads of tourists and strolling musicians, sip a drink or nibble a dessert on **Place Marcou.** To be a medieval poet, share a bottle of wine in your own private niche somewhere remote on the ramparts.

Le Bar à Vins (also recommended later, under "Eating in Carcassonne") offers jazz, good wines by the glass for €2.30, and a young crowd enjoying a garden in the moonshadow of the wall... without any tourists (open daily until 2:00 in the morning during high season).

For a fine before- or after-dinner drink and floodlit wall views, stop by the recommended **Hotel du Château**'s broad terrace, below the Narbonne Gate (2 Rue Camille Saint-Saëns).

Sleeping in Carcassonne

(€1 = about $1.30, country code: 33)
Sleep within or near the old walls, in La Cité. I've also listed a pair of hotels near the train station. In the summer, when La Cité is jammed with tourists, think of sleeping in quieter Caunes-Minervois (you'll find my suggestions on page 643). Top prices listed are for July and August, when the town is packed. At other times of the year, prices drop and there are generally plenty of rooms.

In La Cité

Two pricey hotels, three good B&Bs, and an excellent youth hostel offer a full range of rooms inside the walls.

$$$ Hôtel de la Cité***** offers 61 rooms with deluxe everything in a beautiful building next to St. Nazaire Church. Peaceful gardens, a swimming pool, royal public spaces, the elegant Barbacane restaurant, and reliable luxury are yours—for a price (deluxe Db-€320-480, suites-€425-900, extra adult-€80, breakfast-€28, air-con, garage-€21, Place Auguste-Pierre Pont, tel. 04 68 71 98 71, fax 04 68 71 50 15, www.hoteldelacite.com, reservations @hoteldelacite.com).

$$$ Best Western Hôtel le Donjon*** has 62 well-appointed rooms, a polished lobby with a full bar, and a great location inside the walls. Rooms are split between two different buildings in La Cité (the main building and the cheaper Maison des Remparts a few blocks away). The main building is more appealing, and the rooms with terraces on the garden are delightful (main building: Db-€130-175, Db suite-€180-300, extra person-€20; Maison des Remparts: Db-€115-170; check website for deals, air-con, elevator, Internet access and Wi-Fi, private parking-€15, 2 Rue Comte Roger, tel. 04 68 11 23 00, fax 04 68 25 06 60, www.hotel-donjon .fr, info@bestwestern-donjon.com).

$$$ Chambres l'Echappée Belle, in the center of La Cité, is run by serious owners Johanna and Bruce. Four traditional rooms have wood floors, queen-size beds, jet showers, and air-conditioning (Db-€105-145, includes breakfast, two-night minimum at busy times, check-in between 15:00 and 18:00, Wi-Fi, near St. Nazaire Church, just off Rue du Plô at 5 Rue Raymond Roger Trencavel, tel. 04 68 25 33 40, www.lechappeebelle.co.uk, info@lechappeebelle.co.uk).

$$ Auberge des Lices hides two lovely rooms above its restaurant, with high ceilings, exposed beams, and stone walls (Db with basilica views-€80, larger Db with rampart views-€140, €20/ extra person up to five, air-con, 3 Rue Raymond Roger Trencavel, tel. 04 68 72 34 07, fax 04 68 72 61 55, www.blasco.fr, leslices @blasco.fr).

$$ Chambres le Grand Puits, across from Hôtel des Remparts, is a splendid value. It has one cute double room and two cavernous apartment-like rooms that could sleep five, with kitchenette, private terrace, and sweet personal touches. Inquire in the small boutique, and say *bonjour* to happy-go-lucky Nicole (Sb/Db-€52-74, Tb-€70-84, Qb-€80-94, includes self-serve breakfast, cash only, 8 Place du Grand Puits, tel. 04 68 25 16 67, mobile 06 20 47 02 31, http://legrandpuits.free.fr, nicole.trucco@club-internet.fr).

$ Hostel Carcassonne is big, clean, and well-run, with an outdoor garden courtyard, a self-service kitchen, a TV room, bar, a washer/dryer, bike rental, Internet access and Wi-Fi, and a welcoming ambience. If you ever wanted to bunk down in a hostel, do it here—all ages are welcome. Only summer is tight; reserve ahead (bunk in 4- to 6-bed dorm-€23/bed, 2-bed private room-€46, includes sheets and breakfast, open all day, Rue du Vicomte Trencavel, tel. 04 68 25 23 16, www.fuaj.org or www.hihostels .com, carcassonne@fuaj.org).

Just Outside La Cité

Sleeping just outside La Cité offers the best of both worlds: quick access to the ramparts, less claustrophobic surroundings, and easy parking.

The first three hotels are run by the same family and offer travelers a full range of price options. An easy walk to La Cité, the rooms all have air-conditioning, offer free Internet access and Wi-Fi, and charge €12 for a forgettable breakfast and €10 for parking. The first two come with a snazzy pool (heated all year), a Jacuzzi and spa, view terraces to the walls of Carcassonne, two lazy hounds, and a sweet cat who hangs out in the lobby (www .hotels-carcassonne.net, contact@hotels-carcassonne.net).

$$$ Hôtel du Château*** is the mothership, occupying the main building just across from La Cité's walls. It offers four-star comfort at three-star prices, with 17 sumptuous rooms, a welcoming terrace, and an elaborate spa (standard Db-€140-180, superior Db-€180-200, Db with terrace on pool-€200-250, 2 Rue Camille Saint-Saëns, tel. 04 68 11 38 38, www.hotelduchateau.net).

$$$ Hôtel le Montmorency**, a block behind the Hôtel du Château (same reception), has a split personality. Half the rooms are neon-colored-mod (Db-€100-180), and half are purely *Provençal* and a bit smaller (Db-€75-110, extra person-€15). Several rooms have views to the ramparts, and many come with pleasing private decks or terraces (2 Rue Camille Saint-Saëns, tel. 04 68 11 96 70, www.lemontmorency.com).

$$ Hôtel l'Octroi* hunkers three blocks below its fancier sister hotels. It delivers solid, contemporary comfort at reasonable rates (Db-€65-95, extra person-€10, several family suites for up to 6-€170-210, small stylish pool, 106 Avenue du Général Leclerc, tel. 04 68 25 29 08, www.hoteloctroi.com).

$$$ Hôtel Mercure*** hides a block behind the Hôtel le Montmorency, a five-minute walk to La Cité. It rents 80 overpriced, snug-but-comfy, air-conditioned rooms and has a refreshing garden, a good-sized pool, big elevators, and a warm bar-lounge. A few rooms have views of La Cité (small Db-€105-170, bigger Db-€135-200, free Internet access and Wi-Fi, includes parking, 18 Rue Camille Saint-Saëns, tel. 04 68 11 92 82, fax 04 68 71 11 45, www.mercure.com, h1622@accor.com).

$$$ Hôtel les Trois Couronnes*** offers 44 good rooms with terrific views up to La Cité (and 26 non-view rooms that you don't want), housed in a modern shell. It's a 15-minute walk below La Cité, and 20 minutes on foot from the train station (Db with view-€130-155, €20 less for no view, air-con, elevator, Wi-Fi, indoor pool with views, garage-€9, 2 Rue des Trois Couronnes—see map on page 630, tel. 04 68 25 36 10, fax 04 68 25 92 92, www.hotel -destroiscouronnes.com, hotel3couronnes@wanadoo.fr). Their reasonably priced restaurants also have good views (see "Eating in Carcassonne," later).

$$ Hôtel Ibis**, halfway between the train station and La Cité, delivers reliable two-star comfort at fair prices (Db-€78-98, request a room off the square, air-con, Internet access and Wi-Fi, 5 Square Gambetta, tel. 04 68 72 37 37, www.ibishotel.com, ibis centre.carcassonne@wanadoo.fr).

On Rue Trivalle

These places are 10 minutes below La Cité and 20 minutes from the train station on foot.

$$ Hôtel Espace Cité**, two blocks downhill from Hôtel le Montmorency (described earlier), is a good value. With 48 small but sharp rooms, this place is well-run and handy for drivers (Db-€65-90, Tb-€78-95, Qb-€93-130, breakfast buffet-€8, air-con, Internet access and Wi-Fi, includes parking, 132 Rue Trivalle, tel. 04 68 25 24 24, fax 04 68 25 17 17, www.hotelespacecite.fr, espace-cite@inter-hotel-carcassonne.fr).

$$ Chambres les Florentines is a good-value bed-and-breakfast run by welcoming Madame Mistler. The five rooms are spacious, homey, and affordable. One room comes with a big deck and million-dollar views of La Cité (Db-€75-85, view Db-€115, Tb-€130, Qb-€140, includes breakfast, Wi-Fi, parking-€4, 71 Rue Trivalle, tel. 04 68 71 51 07, mobile 06 88 89 33 42, www.les florentines.net, lesflorentines11@gmail.com).

$ At Notre-Dame de l'Abbaye, you can sleep like a monk (with about the same level of comfort). This hostel-like abbey rents basic, spotless rooms—some with good views to the ramparts—that surround a quiet cloister. Lots of school groups stay here, but they're kept in the other wing (dorm bed-€18, S/D-€47, Db with tiny bathroom-€59, Tb/Qb-€79, breakfast-€5, dinner-€12, credit cards OK, Wi-Fi, 103 Rue Trivalle, tel. 04 68 25 16 65, fax 04 68 11 47 01, www.abbaye-carcassonne.com, ndaa@wanadoo.fr).

Near the Train Station

$$$ Hôtel du Soleil le Terminus***, across from the train station, is turn-of-the-century faded-grand. The lobby reminds me of a train-station waiting hall. Rooms are big and comfortable, with high ceilings and prices (Db-€120-145, pricier rooms have better views, check website for Internet deals, air-con, elevator, pay Internet access and Wi-Fi, basement pool, secure parking-€10, lots of groups, rental bikes, 2 Avenue Maréchal Joffre, tel. 04 68 25 25 00, fax 04 68 72 53 09, www.soleilvacances.com, reservation @soleilvacances.com).

$$ Hôtel Astoria**, run by delightful Marc and Sevrine, offers some of the cheapest hotel beds that I list in town, divided between a main hotel and an annex across the street. The shiny, tiled, and colorful rooms are modern and clean. Call ahead; it's popular (D-€35-49, Ds-€45-58, Db-€55-72, Tb/Qb-€60-90, 6 rooms have air-con, Wi-Fi, parking-€4; from the train station, walk across the canal, turn left, and go two blocks to 18 Rue Tourtel; tel. 04 68 25 31 38, fax 04 68 71 34 14, www.astoria carcassonne.com, hotel-astoria@wanadoo.fr).

Near Carcassonne, in Caunes-Minervois

To experience unspoiled, tranquil Languedoc, sleep surrounded by vineyards in the authentic-feeling village of Caunes-Minervois. Comfortably nestled in the foothills of the Montagne Noire, Caunes-Minervois—a 25-minute drive from Carcassonne (take route D-118 to a big roundabout and exit onto D-620)—offers an eighth-century abbey (complete with Internet access), two cafés, a good pizzeria, a handful of wineries, and very few tourists. The friendly staff at the town's TI is eager to help you explore the region.

$$ Hôtel d'Alibert, in a 15th-century home with ambience galore, sits in the heart of the village. It has a mix of nicely renovated, Old World traditional rooms. It's managed with a relaxed *je ne sais quoi* by Frédéric "call me Fredo" Dalibert (standard Db-€80, huge Db-€90, extra person-€10, includes breakfast and bottle of local wine on arrival, Wi-Fi, Place de la Mairie, tel. 04 68 78 00 54, frederic.dalibert@wanadoo.fr). Eat lunch or dinner in his terrific restaurant (closed Sun-Mon).

Nearby, in Le Somail: Drivers who want to experience the Canal du Midi boating scene sleep in Le Somail, a picturesque hamlet that has changed little since the construction of the canal in the 1600s. The town has an impressive bookshop, three art galleries, and two restaurants. Sleep at **$$ La Maison des Escalliers,** where Tina and Ruud have created a beautiful B&B with five stylish and comfortable rooms in their restored 19th-century house. Breakfast is served by the pool with views of the vineyards (D-€70, Db-€80-90, 6 Rue Paul Riquet, tel. 04 68 48 44 23, mobile 06 79 55 33 37, www.patiasses.com, mail@patiasses.com). They also rent a *gîte* (€450-850/week).

Eating in Carcassonne

For a social outing in La Cité, take your pick from a food circus of basic eateries on a leafy courtyard—often with strolling musicians in the summer—on lively **Place Marcou** (just inside the front gate and up to the left). If rubbing elbows with too many tourists gives you hives, go local and dine below in La Ville Basse (the new city). Cassoulet (described on page 613) is the traditional must (tip: a dash of vinegar helps the digestion); big salads provide a lighter alternative. For a local before-dinner drink, try a glass of Muscat de Saint-Jean-de-Minervois.

On Place St. Jean: My favorite place for dinner in La Cité is on Place St. Jean, where two good eateries sit side by side, with view tables from their outside terraces to the floodlit Château Comtal. **Restaurant Adelaide** attracts a lively, loyal following with its well-presented bistro fare at reasonable prices; they serve a good €15, three-course *menu* with cassoulet, as well as good €12-18 *plats* and big €15 salads in an orange-walled, beamed interior (daily June-Aug, closed Mon Sept-May, tel. 04 68 47 66 61). **Le St. Jean** sits next door with similar prices and choices (€15-25 *menus*, €8 kid *menu,* daily, tel. 04 68 47 42 43).

Hôtel de la Cité's **Barbacane Restaurant** owns La Cité's only Michelin star (€80-160 *menus;* see "Sleeping in Carcassonne," earlier).

Au Comte Roger's quiet elegance seems out of place in this touristy town. For half the price of the Barbacane, you can celebrate a special occasion. Chef Pierre specializes in fresh products and Mediterranean cuisine. Ask for a table in the vine-covered courtyard, or eat inside in their stylish dining room. Book ahead in high season (€38 dinner *menus,* massive cassoulet-€30, closed Sun-Mon, 14 Rue St. Louis, tel. 04 68 11 93 40).

Auberge des Lices, a shy yet popular place hidden down a quiet lane, has a feminine interior and a peaceful courtyard. It manages a delicate balance of price and quality for traditional cuisine, though service can be spotty (€20-39 *menus,* daily July-Aug, closed Tue-Wed Sept-June, 3 Rue Raymond Roger Trencavel, tel. 04 68 72 34 07). They also rent two rooms (see "Sleeping in Carcassonne," earlier).

Le Jardin de la Tour, run by Elodie for more than 20 years, has cool outdoor seating in the garden and cozy indoor tables with a jazzy ambience (€15-25 *plats*, try the *salade Languedocienne,* open Tue-Sat, closed Sun-Mon, 11 Rue Porte-d'Aude, tel. 04 68 25 71 24).

Restaurant les Trois Couronnes, just outside La Cité in Hôtel les Trois Couronnes (described earlier, under "Sleeping in Carcassonne"), gives you a panorama of Carcassonne from the top floor of a concrete hotel (€29 *menus,* open daily Sept-June for dinner only, closed July-Aug, call ahead, 2 Rue des Trois Couronnes, tel. 04 68 25 36 10). Their peaceful riverfront restaurant, **Le Quai,** also has views of the old city (€14 lunch *menu,* open daily 12:00-14:00 & 19:00-22:00, closed in bad weather, call before making the walk).

Le Bar à Vins, popular with the twenty- and thirtysomething set at night, is tucked away in a pleasant garden just inside the wall but away from the crowds. It serves an enticing selection of open wines (€2.30 a glass), €9-13 appetizers and tapas, and €6 sandwiches (daily 10:00-2:00 in the morning, closes earlier off-season, closed Nov-Jan, 6 Rue du Plô, tel. 04 68 47 38 38).

Picnics: Basic supplies can be gathered at the shops along the main drag (generally open until at least 19:30). For your beggar's banquet, picnic on the city walls.

Eating in the Ville Basse: **Chez Felix** has good seats on the main square, is family-run, and serves traditional cuisine (closed Sun, 11 Place Carnot, tel. 04 68 25 17 01).

Carcassonne Connections

From Carcassonne by Train to: Albi (12/day, 3 hours, change in Toulouse), **Collioure** (8/day, 2 hours, most require change in Narbonne), **Sarlat** (5/day, 5.5-7 hours, 1-3 changes, some require bus from Souillac to Sarlat), **Arles** (8/day, 2.5-3.75 hours, most with transfer in Narbonne or Nîmes), **Nice** (7/day, 6-7 hours), **Paris** (Gare de Lyon: 8/day, 7-8 hours, 1 change; Gare d'Austerlitz: 1/day direct, 7.5 hours; 1 night train, 7.75 hours; note that Intercité trains to Paris require a reservation), **Toulouse** (nearly hourly, 1 hour), **Barcelona** (4/day, 4-6 hours, change in Narbonne and Port Bou—the border town).

Near Carcassonne

The land around Carcassonne is carpeted with vineyards and littered with romantically ruined castles, ancient abbeys, and photogenic villages. The castle remains of Peyrepertuse and Quéribus make terrific stops between Carcassonne and Collioure (allow 1.5-2 hours from Carcassonne on narrow, winding roads). The gorge-sculpted village of Minerve, 40 minutes northeast of Carcassonne, works well for Provence-bound travelers.

Getting There: Public transportation is hopeless; taxis for up to six people cost €150-200 for a day-long excursion (taxi tel. 04 68 71 50 50). See page 633 for excursion bus and minivan tours to these places.

▲▲▲Châteaux of Hautes Corbières

About two hours south of Carcassonne, in the scenic foothills of the Pyrenees, you'll find a series of surreal, mountain-capping castle ruins. Like a Maginot Line of the 13th century, these sky-high castles were strategically located between France and the Spanish kingdom of Roussillon. As you can see by flipping through the picture books in Carcassonne tourist shops, these castles' crumbled ruins are an impressive contrast to the restored walls of La

Near Carcassonne

Cité. Bring a good map (lots of tiny roads) and sturdy walking shoes—prepare for a vigorous climb, and be wary of slick stones. The Carcassonne TI's City Pass saves a little on each entry (see page 629).

The most spectacular is the château of **Peyrepertuse,** where the ruins seem to grow right out from the narrow splinter of cliff. The views are sensational—you can almost reach out and touch Spain. Let your imagination soar, but watch your step as you try to reconstruct this eagle's nest (€8.50 in July-Aug, €6 at other times, open daily April-Sept-9:00-19:00—until 20:00 July-Aug, Oct-March 10:00-17:00, closed Jan, tel. 04 82 53 24 07, www .chateau-peyrepertuse.com). Canyon lovers will enjoy the detour to the nearby and narrow **Gorges de Galamus,** just north of St-Paul de Fenouillet. Closer to D-117, impressive **Quéribus** towers above the road and requires a steep hike. It's famous as the last Cathar castle to fall, and was left useless after 1659, when the border between France and Spain was moved farther south into the high Pyrenees (€5, daily April-Sept 9:30-19:00—until 20:00 July-Aug, Oct and March 10:00-18:00, Nov-Feb 10:00-17:00).

Sleeping and Eating near Peyrepertuse and Quéribus: To really get away (and I mean really), sleep in the lovely little village of Cucugnan, located between the castles. **$$ L'Ecurie de Cucugnan** is a friendly bed-and-breakfast with five comfortable rooms at great rates, a view pool, and a shady garden (Sb-€55, Db-€60-66, includes breakfast, free Wi-Fi, 2-room house-€500/week, 10 Rue Achille Mir, tel. 04 68 33 37 42, mobile 06 76 86 38 52, ecurie.cucugnan@orange.fr). For a light meal, find the *boulangerie* at the 17th-century windmill, where they mill their own flour and prepare delicious breads and pasta (daily 8:00-19:00, closed Mon Nov-April, Moulin du Village de Cucugnan, tel. 04 68 33 55 03).

Near Caunes-Minervois

The next two Cathar sights tie in well with a visit to Caunes-Minervois (where I recommend accommodations—see page 643) and provide an easy excursion from Carcassonne, offering you a taste of this area's appealing countryside.

Châteaux of Lastours

Ten miles north of Carcassonne, these four ruined castles cap a barren hilltop and give drivers a handy (if less dramatic) look

at the region's Cathar castles. From Carcassonne, follow signs to *Mazamet,* then *Conques-sur-Orbiel,* then *Lastours.* In Lastours you can hike to the castle or drive to a viewpoint.

Hikers park at the lot as they enter the village, walk five minutes upriver to the glass entry, then walk 20 minutes uphill to the castles (allow at least an hour for a reasonable tour, wear sturdy walking shoes). The castles, which once surrounded a fortified village, date from the 11th century. The village welcomed Cathars (becoming a bishop's seat at one point) but paid for this "tolerance" with destruction by French troops in 1227. Everyone should make the short drive to the belvedere for a smashing panorama over the castles.

Cost and Hours: €5 for access to castles and belvedere viewpoint, €2 for viewpoint only; July-Aug daily 9:00-20:00; April-June and Sept daily 10:00-18:00—until 17:00 in Oct; Nov-Dec and Feb-March Sat-Sun only 10:00-17:00, closed Mon-Fri; closed Jan; tel. 04 68 77 56 02.

Eating: An idyllic lunch awaits near the lower entry at **Le Moulin de Lastours,** where a small bakery has arranged a few tables serenely overlooking the river (good quiche, sandwiches, drinks, closed Tue).

▲Minerve

A onetime Cathar hideout, the spectacular village of Minerve is sculpted out of a deep canyon that provided a natural defense.

Strong as it was, it couldn't keep out the Pope's armies, and the village was razed during the vicious Albigensian Crusades. Follow the *P* signs to the new parking lot above the village (€3), then walk down to a ruined tower and into the village. (A worthwhile path leads from the left of the tower, around the vil-

lage, and down to the river—watch your step as you descend; you can re-enter the village from the riverbed at its lower end.)

Minerve has two cool cafés, one hotel, a nifty little bookshop, a few wine shops, and a smattering of art galleries. You'll also find two small museums: a prehistory museum and the compact **Hurepel de Minerve,** with models from the Cathar era that effectively describe this terrible time (€3, free for children under 14, excellent English explanations, interesting for kids, daily April-Oct 10:00-13:00 & 14:00-18:00, closed Nov-March, Rue des Martyrs, tel. 04 68 91 12 26).

Getting to Minerve: Located between Carcassonne and Béziers, Minerve is nine miles north of Olonzac and 40 minutes by car from Carcassonne. It makes for a good stop between Provence and Carcassonne.

Sleeping and Eating in Minerve: Stay here and melt into southern France (almost literally, if it's summer). **$ Relais Chantovent**'s unpretentious and spotless rooms are designed for those who come to get away from it all, with no phones or TV... and ample quiet (Sb-€39, Db-€46, breakfast-€7, free Wi-Fi, tel. 04 68 91 14 18, www.relaischantovent-minerve.fr, sandra.bru@orange

.fr). Its sharp restaurant deserves your business and is popular, so reserve ahead (*menus* from €19, closed Wed year-round, closed Sun and Tue for dinner in winter).

Collioure

Surrounded by less-appealing resorts, lovely Collioure is blessed with a privileged climate and a romantic setting. By Mediterranean

standards, this seaside village should be slammed—it has everything. Like an ice-cream shop, Collioure offers 31 flavors of pastel houses and 6 petite, scooped-out, pebbled beaches sprinkled with visitors. This sweet scene, capped by a winking lighthouse, sits under a once-mighty castle in the shade of the Pyrenees.

Just 15 miles from the Spanish border, Collioure (Cotlliure in Catalan) shares a common history and independent attitude with its Catalan siblings across the border. Undeniably French yet proudly Catalan, it flies the yellow-and-red flag of Catalunya, displays street names in French and Catalan, and sports business names with *el* and *els,* rather than *le* and *les.* Sixty years ago, most villagers spoke Catalan; today that language is enjoying a resurgence as Collioure rediscovers its roots.

Come here to unwind and regroup. Even with its crowds of vacationers in peak season (July and August are jammed), Collioure is what many look for when they head to the Riviera—a sunny, relaxing splash in the Mediterranean.

Planning Your Time

Check your ambition at the station. Enjoy a slow coffee on *le Med,* lose yourself in the old town's streets, compare the *gelati* shops on Rue Vauban, sample the excellent wines, and relax on a pebble-sand beach (waterproof shoes are helpful). And if you have a car, don't miss a drive into the hills above Collioure.

Orientation to Collioure

Most of Collioure's shopping, sights, and hotels are in the old town, across the drainage channel from Château Royal. There are good views of the old town from across the bay near the recommended Hôtel Boramar and brilliant views from the hills above.

LANGUEDOC

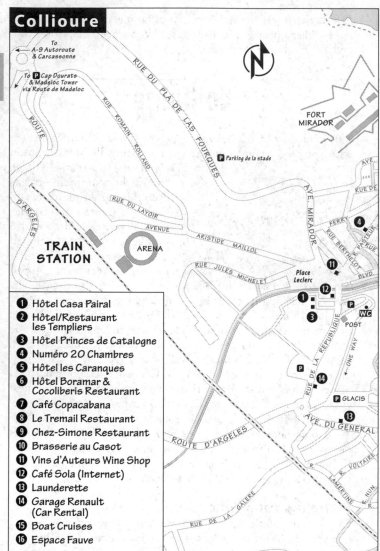

Collioure

To
← A-9 Autoroute
& Carcassonne

To 🅿 Cap Dourats
& Madeloc Tower
via Route de Madeloc

RUE DU PLA DE LAS FOURQUES

RUE ROMAIN ROLLAND

ROUTE

D'ARGELES

RUE DU LAVOIR

AVENUE

ARISTIDE MAILLOL

🅿 Parking de la stade

FORT
MIRADOR

AVE.

RUE DE

AVE. MIRADOR

FERKY

RUE PASTEUR

❹

RUE BERTHELOT

BLVD.

TRAIN
STATION

ARENA

RUE JULES MICHELET

Place
Leclerc

❶

❸

❶❶

❶❷

🅿

WC

POST

🅿

❶❹

RUE DE LA REPUBLIQUE

ONE WAY

🅿 GLACIS

AVE. DU GENERAL

❶❸

ROUTE D'ARGELES

R. VOLTAIRE

R. LAMERTINE

R. NUN

RUE DE LA GALERE

❶ Hôtel Casa Pairal
❷ Hôtel/Restaurant
   les Templiers
❸ Hôtel Princes de Catalogne
❹ Numéro 20 Chambres
❺ Hôtel les Caranques
❻ Hôtel Boramar &
   Cocoliberis Restaurant
❼ Café Copacabana
❽ Le Tremail Restaurant
❾ Chez-Simone Restaurant
❿ Brasserie au Casot
⓫ Vins d'Auteurs Wine Shop
⓬ Café Sola (Internet)
⓭ Launderette
⓮ Garage Renault
   (Car Rental)
⓯ Boat Cruises
⓰ Espace Fauve

Tourist Information

The TI hides behind the main beachfront cafés at 5 Place du 18 Juin (July-Aug Mon-Sat 9:00-20:00, Sun 10:00-18:00; April-June and Sept Mon-Sat 9:00-12:00 & 14:00-19:00, Sun 10:00-12:00 & 14:00-18:00; Oct-March Mon-Sat 9:00-12:00 & 14:00-18:00, closed Sun; tel. 04 68 82 15 47, www.collioure.com).

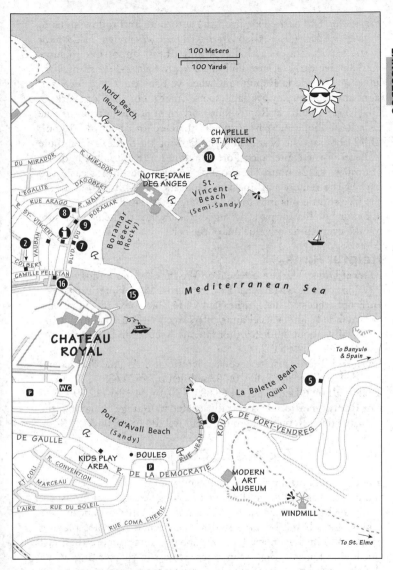

Arrival in Collioure

By Train: Walk out of the station (no baggage storage), turn right, and follow Rue Aristide Maillol downhill for about 10 minutes until you see Hôtel Fregate (directions to hotels are listed from this reference point—see "Sleeping in Collioure," later). Pick up a schedule for Spanish side-trips or for your next destination (station staffed 9:00-13:30 & 14:40-18:00).

By Car: Collioure is 16 miles south of Perpignan. Take the

Perpignan-Sud Sortie exit from the autoroute and follow signs to *Argelès-sur-Mer* (also called *Argelès*), then *Collioure par la Corniche* (*sortie* 13). Parking is a challenge and almost impossible in summer—arrive early or late. Follow *Collioure Centre-Ville* signs, turn left onto Rue de la République when you see the *Garage Renault* sign, and look for any available spots. There's a big pay lot (Parking Glacis) off Rue de la République (stay right at the bottom of Rue de la République and pass through a metered lot, about €1.50/hour, €10/24 hours). The best deal is the Parking du Stade, a 15-minute walk from the center past Fort Miradou (on Route du Pla de las Fourques, €2/24 hours year-round). In high season, it's easiest to park at the remote Parking Cap Dourats (€6/24 hours) and take the free shuttle bus into town (3/hour, 10:00-24:00). You can also ask your hotelier for parking suggestions. Once parked, make sure to take everything of value out of the car.

Helpful Hints

Market Days: Markets are held on Wednesday and Sunday mornings on Place Maréchal Leclerc, across from Hôtel Fregate.

Internet Access: The lighthearted **Café Sola,** next to the recommended Hôtel Casa Pairal, offers free Wi-Fi if you buy a drink (daily, about 7:00-21:00 or later, 2 Avenue de la République, tel. 04 68 82 55 02).

Laundry: There's a self-serve launderette at 8 Avenue du Général de Gaulle (daily 7:00-20:00, mobile 06 74 57 17 39).

Taxi: Call 04 68 82 27 80, 04 68 82 09 30, or 04 68 82 12 89.

Car Rental: National is centrally located in Garage Renault at the Rue de la République roundabout (tel. 04 68 82 08 34).

Sights in Collioure

There's no important sight here except what lies on the beach and the views over Collioure. Indulge in a long seaside lunch, inspect the colorful art galleries, catch up on your postcards, and maybe take a hike. Don't be surprised to see French Marines playing commando in their rafts; Collioure's bay caters to more than just sun-loving tourists. Sightseeing here is best in the evening, when the sky darkens, and yellow lamps reflect warm pastels and deep blues.

▲**View from the Beach**—Walk out to the jetty's end, past the church and the little chapel, and find a spot along the rail. Collioure has been a popular place since well before your visit. For more than 2,500 years, people have fought to control its enviable position on the Mediterranean at the foot of the Pyrenees. The mountains that rise behind Collioure provide a natural defense, and its port gives it a commercial edge, making Collioure an irre-

LANGUEDOC

sistible target. A string of forts defended Collioure's landlocked side. To the left, you can see the still-standing Fort St. Elme (built by powerful Spanish king Charles V, the same guy who built El Escorial near Madrid). The 2,100-foot-high observation tower of Madeloc rises way above, front and center, and scattered ruins crown several other hilltops. Topping the village to the far right is the 18th-century *citadelle*, Fort Mirador, now home to a French Marine base. Back to the left, that ancient windmill (1344) was originally used for grain; today it grinds out olive oil. The stony soil and ideal weather conditions in the hills above Collioure allow grapes to prosper. Those beautiful terraced vineyards, averaging 250 days of sunshine a year, grow primarily Grenache, Syrah, and Mourvèdre grapes, which make terrific reds and rosés.

Collioure's medieval town gathers between its church and royal château, sandwiched defensively and spiritually between the two. The town was batted back and forth between the French and Spanish for centuries. Locals just wanted to be left alone—as Catalans, and most still do (notice the yellow-and-red Catalan flag flying above the château). It was Spanish for nearly 400 years before becoming definitively French in 1659 (*merci* to Louis XIV). After years of neglect, Collioure was rediscovered by artists drawn to its pastel houses and lovely setting. Henri Matisse, André Derain, Pablo Picasso, Georges Braque, Raoul Dufy, and Marc Chagall all dipped their brushes here at one time or another. You're likely to recognize Collioure in paintings in many museums across Europe.

Château Royal (Royal Castle)—The 800-year-old castle, built over Roman ruins, served as home over the years to Majorcan kings, Crusaders, Dominican monks, and Louis XIV (who had the final say on the appearance we see now). Today it serves tourists, offering great rampart walks, views, and mildly interesting local history exhibits.

Cost and Hours: €4, daily June-Sept 10:00-18:00, Oct-May 9:00-17:00, last entry 45 minutes before closing, tel. 04 68 82 06 43.

Notre-Dame des Anges (Our Lady of the Angels Church)—This waterfront church is worth a gander (daily 9:00-18:00). Find a pew and listen to the waves while searching your soul. Supporting a guiding light (in more than one way), the church's foundations are built into the sea, and its one-of-a-kind lighthouse-bell tower helped sailors return home safely. The highlight is its over-the-top golden altar, unusual in France but typical of Catalan churches

across the border. Drop €1 in the box to the left of the altar: lights, cameras, reaction—ooh la la!

Path of Fauvism (Chemin du Fauvisme)—As you stroll Collioure's lanes, you'll occasionally see prints hanging on the walls. You're on the "Chemin du Fauvisme," where you'll find 20 copies of Derain's and Matisse's works, inspired by their stays in Collioure in 1905. The **Espace Fauve** office, across from the château at the foot of the footbridge, has French-only fliers that identify where the copies are mounted in Collioure. As with Arles and Vincent van Gogh, there are no original paintings by Derain or Matisse here for the public to enjoy. However, the museum in Céret has a good collection (see page 656), as does the recommended Hôtel les Templiers.

Beaches (Plages)—You'll usually find the best sand-to-stone ratio at Plage de Port d'Avall or Plage St. Vincent (paddleboat/kayak rentals-€14-20/hour, summer only). The tiny Plage de la Balette is quietest, with views of Collioure.

Wine-Tasting—Collioure and the surrounding area produce well-respected wines, and many shops offer informal tastings of the sweet Banyuls and Collioure reds and rosés. Try **Vins d'Auteurs,** with a good selection from many wineries and fair prices (next to Hôtel Fregate at 6 Place Maréchal Leclerc, tel. 04 68 55 45 22).

Cruise—Mildly interesting **Promenade sur Mer** boat excursions provide views of Collioure from the Mediterranean as they cruise toward Spain and back (€12-16, 3-5/day, 1 hour, Easter-Sept weather permitting, leaves from breakwater near château, commentary in French only, mobile 06 33 61 97 44). **Roussillon Crosières** offers boat service to Argelès sur Mer, allowing you to boat one way and take the train back (€6, 4/day, daily, www.roussillon-croisieres.com).

Hikes

The three views described here offer different perspectives of this splendid area.

▲**Stone Windmill**—Stone steps lead 10 minutes up behind Collioure's museum to a 13th-century windmill with good views that are positively peachy at sunset. Find the museum behind Hôtel Triton, walk through its stony backyard, follow the paved path marked with yellow dashes, and climb about 140 steps. Bring your own beverage.

▲**Hike to Fort St. Elme**—This vertical hike is best done early or late (there's no shade) and is worth the sweat, even if you don't make it to the top (trail starts from windmill described above, allow 30 minutes each way). You can't miss the square castle lurking high above Collioure, with a grand view from the top. The privately owned castle has medieval exhibits—pick up the English booklet that explains them (€6, daily April-Sept 10:30-19:00, Oct 14:30-17:00, closed Nov-March, mobile 06 64 61 82 42, www.fort saintelme.com).

Cheaters can just **drive** there: Head to Port Vendres, then follow the higher road to Perpignan and the small sign marked *Fort St. Elme* on the right just before leaving the port (the road also leads to the supermarket). Continue on the small road that leads up from the train station. Port Vendres' *petit train* also gets you there (€7 round-trip, leaves from the post office).

▲▲▲**Drive/Hike Through Vineyards to Madeloc Tower (Tour de Madeloc)**—Check your vertigo at the hotel, fasten your seatbelt, and take this drive-and-hike combination high above Collioure. The narrow road, hairpin turns, and absence of guardrails only add to the experience, as Collioure shrinks to Lego-size and the clouds become your neighbors.

Leave Collioure, heading toward Perpignan, and look for signs reading *Tour de Madeloc* at the roundabout above the town. Climb through steep and rocky terraced vineyards, following *Tour* signs. After 10 kilometers (6 miles, or about 20 minutes), you'll come to a fork in the road with a paved path (marked by a "no entry" symbol that applies to cars) and a road leading downhill. Park at the fork in the road, and walk up the paved path. The views everywhere are magnificent—the Pyrenees on one side, and the beach towns of Port Vendres and Collioure on the other. Allow 30 minutes at a slow-yet-steady pace along the splintered ridgetop to reach the eagle's-nest setting of the ancient tower (La Tour), now fitted with communication devices. Here you can commune with the gods, but beware—there's no shade, so do this hike early or late in the day. Once you're back down among mortals, you can return to Collioure following *La Route des Vignobles* along a narrow road to Banyuls-sur-Mer, then take coastal N-114 to Collioure and your hotel (skip D-914 in July and August, when it's too crowded).

Near Collioure

Day Trip to Spain—The 15-mile, 40-minute coastal drive via the Col de Banyuls into Spain is beautiful and well worth the countless curves, even if you don't venture past the border.

To visit the wild **Salvador Dalí museum,** take the autoroute to Figueres, which takes about an hour each way (museum: €12; July-Sept daily 9:00-20:00; March-June and Oct Tue-Sun 9:30-18:00, closed Mon; Nov-Feb Tue-Sun 10:30-18:00, closed Mon; last entry 45 minutes before closing, Spanish tel. 972-677-500, www.salvador-dali.org).

Train travelers can also day-trip to Spain, either to Barcelona (4/day, 3-4 hours, 1-2 transfers) or to the closer Figueres (4-6/day, 1-2 hours, 1 transfer). Get train schedules at the station.

Céret—To see the art that Collioure inspired, you'll have to drive 25 windy miles inland to this pleasing town, featuring fountains and mountains at its doorstep. Céret's claim to fame is its modern-art museum, with works by some of Collioure's more famous visitors, including Picasso, Joan Miró, Chagall, and Matisse (€8, daily July-mid-Sept 10:00-19:00, mid-Sept-June 10:00-18:00, closed Tue Oct-March, tel. 04 68 87 27 76, www.musee-ceret .com). Allow 40 minutes to Céret by car, or ride the bus—ask at Collioure's TI.

Sleeping in Collioure

(€1 = about $1.30, country code: 33)
Collioure has a fair range of hotels at favorable rates. You have two good choices for your hotel's location: central, in the old town (closer to train station); or across the bay, with views of the old town (10-minute walk from the central zone, with easier parking).

In the Old Town

Directions to the following places are given from the big Hôtel Fregate, at the edge of the old town, a 10-minute walk down from the train station. Price ranges reflect low versus high season.

$$$ Hôtel Casa Pairal***, opposite Hôtel Fregate and hiding down a short alley (behind Café Sola), is Mediterranean-elegant and Collioure's best splurge. Enter to the sounds of a fountain gurgling in the flowery courtyard. Reclining lounges await in the garden and by the pool. The rooms are quiet, comfortable, and tastefully designed. "Privilege" rooms, on the first floor, have high ceilings and small balconies over a courtyard (standard Db-€100-125, "privilege" Db-€141-189, big Db suite with terrace-€189-289, extra bed-€25, air-con, free Wi-Fi, parking-€14, Impasse des Palmiers, tel. 04 68 82 05 81, fax 04 68 82 52 10, www.hotel-casa -pairal.com, contact@hotel-casa-pairal.com, reserve ahead for room and parking).

$$ Hôtel les Templiers**, in the heart of the old town, has wall-to-wall paintings squeezed in every available space, a perennially popular café-bar, low-key management, and good-value rooms. The paintings are payments in kind and thank-yous from artists who have stayed here—find the black-and-white photo in the bar of the hotel's owner with Picasso. The rooms—some of which have views—are either new and modern, or older and charming. Those in the main building above the bar are best (standard Db-€68-95, bigger Db-€90-130, pass on the annex rooms unless they're next to main hotel block, air-con in main building, Wi-Fi, elevator, a block toward beach from Hôtel Fregate along drainage canal at 12 Quai de l'Amirauté, tel. 04 68 98 31 10, fax 04 68 98 01 24, www.hotel-templiers.com, info@hotel-templiers .com).

$$ Hôtel Princes de Catalogne*** offers 30 comfortable, spacious, contemporary rooms. Get a room on the mountain side, or *côté montagne* (koh-tay mon-tan-yah), for maximum quiet (Db without view-€70-80, superior Db with view-€80-90, family room-€135-155, air-con, next to Casa Pairal, Rue des Palmiers, tel. 04 68 98 30 00, fax 04 68 98 30 31, www.hotel-princescatalogne .com, contact@hotel-princescatalogne.com).

$ Numéro 20 Chambres, with eager-to-help hosts Véronique and Noel, is a good budget value. The rooms are simple, clean, spacious, and suitable for families, with small fridges, coffeemakers, and microwaves (Db-€60, Tb-€80, Qb-€100, cash only, on the pedestrian street two blocks past Hôtel Fregate at 20 Rue Pasteur, tel. 04 68 82 15 31, mobile 06 17 50 16 89, www.collioure-chambre -peroneille.fr, numero20ruepasteur@gmail.com).

Across the Bay

$$$ Hôtel les Caranques**, a few curves toward Spain from Collioure's center, tumbles down the cliffs and showcases million-dollar sea views from each of
its rooms, which all have balconies.
Enjoy the sensational view decks
scattered about and the stylish bar
serving reasonably priced tapas and
drinks (smallish Db-€90-110, razzle-
dazzle Db-suite-€180-250, Route de
Port Vendres, 30-minute walk from
train station, tel. 04 68 82 06 68, fax
04 68 82 00 92, www.les-caranques
.com, contact@les-caranques.com).

For a scenic walk to Collioure's center,
follow the sidewalk, then turn right
down the steps just after the *Relais des Trois Mas* sign.

$$ Hôtel Boramar**, across the bay from Collioure's center, is understated and modest (like its owner Thierry), but well-maintained (also like Thierry) and a solid value. Get a room with a terrace facing the sea and smile...or sleep elsewhere (Db without view-€65, Db with view-€75, Tb with view-€80, breakfast-€6.50, Rue Jean Bart, tel. 04 68 82 07 06, www.hotel-boramar.fr).

Eating in Collioure

Test the local wine and eat anything Catalan, including the fish and anchovies (hand-filleted, as no machine has ever been able to accomplish this precise task). Consistency is elusive with restaurants in Collioure, but those listed below have been reliable. All of my recommended restaurants have indoor and outdoor tables, and most are in the old town. Your task is to decide whether you want to eat well or with a view. Several delicious *gelati* shops and a Grand Marnier crêpe stand next to the Café Copacabana fuel after-dinner strollers with the perfect last course. If you're traveling off-season, call ahead—many restaurants here are closed December through February.

Café Copacabana, on the main beach (Boramar), offers big salads and a few seafood dishes in its sandy café. Skip their sidewalk-bound restaurant (which has a bigger selection but smaller view) and find a chair beachside. The quality is good enough, considering the view, and it's family-friendly—kids can play on the beach while you dine (€9 cheeseburgers and wraps, €15 salads and *plats*, daily mid-March-mid-Dec, Plage Boramar, tel. 04 68 82 06 74, best at sunset).

Le Tremail is good for contemporary seafood and Catalan specialties served outside or in. It's a small, popular place one block from the bay, where Rue Arago and Rue Mailly meet. Reserve ahead if you can (€25-35 *menus,* open daily year-round, 16 bis Rue Mailly, tel. 04 68 82 16 10).

The restaurant at the recommended **Hôtel les Templiers** is popular with locals and dishes up reliable value (daily, 12 Quai de l'Amirauté, tel. 04 68 98 31 10).

Chez-Simone, a lighthearted budget place, serves €3-5 tapas and *tartines* and €12 *plats* with a smile (daily for lunch, Thu-Sun for dinner, Boulevard Boramar, tel. 04 68 82 12 56).

Cocoliberis, a 10-minute stroll around the bay, is a simple, seaside place with a local following, a reliable seafood-focused cuisine, and terrific views (€15-18 *plats*, next to the recommended Hôtel Boramar at 17 Rue Jean Bart, tel. 04 68 88 86 65).

Brasserie au Casot owns the best setting away from the crowds, past the church on Plage St. Vincent, and serves salads and *plats* with views for a fair price. Matisse would dig the decor. Ask owner Alix about his homemade sangria (€13-16 *plats,* June-Sept daily 11:00-20:00 weather permitting, lunch only Oct and May, Plage St. Vincent, tel. 04 68 22 42 46).

Eating Cheaply: Small places sell a variety of meals to go (*à emporter;* ah em-pohr-tay) for budget-minded romantics wanting to dine on the bay.

After Hours: For post-dinner fun, head to one of the bayfront cafés on **Plage Boramar,** or try the bar at the recommended **Hôtel les Templiers** and get down with the locals.

Collioure Connections

Collioure's tiny station is staffed from 9:00-13:30 and 14:40-18:00. If you need to buy tickets, do so during those hours (tel. 04 68 82 05 89).

    From Collioure by Train to: Carcassonne (8/day, 2 hours, most require change in Narbonne), **Paris** (10/day, 6 hours, 1-2 changes, one direct night train to Gare d'Austerlitz in 11 hours), **Barcelona,** Spain (4/day, 3-4 hours, most change in Figueres or Port Bou), **Figueres,** Spain (3/day, 1-2 hours, most change in Port Bou), **Avignon/Arles** (8/day, 3.5-4.5 hours, several transfer points possible). Consider the handy night trains to Paris, key Italian destinations, and Geneva (Switzerland).

PROVENCE

Arles • Avignon • Pont du Gard • Les Baux •
Orange • Villages of the Côtes du Rhône •
Hill Towns of the Luberon

This magnificent region is shaped like a giant wedge of quiche. From its sunburned crust, fanning out along the Mediterranean coast from the Camargue to Marseille, it stretches north along the Rhône Valley to Orange. The Romans were here in force and left many ruins—some of the best anywhere. Seven popes, artists such as Vincent van Gogh and Paul Cézanne, and author Peter Mayle all enjoyed their years in Provence. This destination features a splendid recipe of arid climate, oceans of vineyards, dramatic scenery, lively cities, and adorable hill-capping villages.

Explore the ghost town that is ancient Les Baux, and see France's greatest Roman ruins, the Pont du Gard aqueduct and the theater in Orange. Admire the skill of ball-tossing *boules* players in small squares in every Provençal village and city. Spend a few Van Gogh-inspired starry, starry nights in Arles. Youthful but classy Avignon bustles in the shadow of its brooding Palace of the Popes. It's a short hop from Arles or Avignon into the splendid scenery and villages of the Côtes du Rhône and Luberon regions.

The main city of Provence, Marseille, has been selected as a European Capital of Culture for 2013—meaning that the EU believes it to have an established culture worthy of showing off to the world. This designation is bringing various cultural exhibits to cities in the Marseille area; of the towns I cover in this chapter, Arles will feel the impact most directly.

Planning Your Time

Make Arles or Avignon your sightseeing base—particularly if you have no car. Italophiles prefer smaller Arles, while poodles pick

Provence

To Lyon & Burgundy
Grignan
Vallreas
Ardèches Gorges
Bollene
Nyons
Buis-les-Baronnies
Ste-Cecile
To Chamonix & Alps
Rhône
Rasteau
Vaison la Romaine
Sablet · Séguret
Dentelles de Montmirail
Orange · Gigondas
Suzette
Malaucène
Vacqueyras
Beaumes de Venise
Châteauneuf-du-Pape
COTES DU RHONE
Mont Ventoux
Uzès
To Gorges du Tarn
Gard
PONT DU GARD · Remoulins
Avignon
L' Isle-sur-la-Sorgue
Gordes · Joucas
Roussillon
Nîmes ·
Durance
Tarascon
Cavaillon
Oppède
Apt
Beaucaire
Les Baux · St-Rémy
LUBERON
Petit Rhône
Fontvieille
Alpilles
Lourmarin
Arles
Pertuis
Aigues-Mortes
CAMARGUE
Rhône
To Gorges du Verdon
Saintes-Maries-de-la-Mer
Aix-en-Provence
· Palette
Martigues
To Nice & Côte d'Azur
Marseille
Aubagne
Paris
FRANCE
Mediterranean Sea Les Calanques
· Cassis
100 Miles
20 Kilometers
20 Miles

PROVENCE

urban Avignon. Arles has a blue-collar quality; the entire city feels like Van Gogh's bedroom. Avignon—double the size of Arles—feels sophisticated, with more nightlife and shopping, and makes a good base for non-drivers thanks to its convenient public-transit options. To measure the pulse of rural Provence, spend at least one night in a smaller town (such as Vaison la Romaine or Roussillon), or in the countryside.

When budgeting your time, you'll want a full day for sightseeing in Arles and Les Baux (best on Wed or Sat, when it's market day); a half-day for Avignon; and a day or two for the villages and sights in the countryside.

Pont du Gard is a short hop west of Avignon and on the way to/from Languedoc for drivers. Les Baux works well by car from Avignon or Arles, and in summer by bus from Arles (daily

July-Aug, Sat-Sun only June and Sept). The town of Orange ties in tidily with a trip to the Côtes du Rhône villages. The Côtes du Rhône is ideal for wine connoisseurs and an easy stop for those heading to or from the north. Vaison la Romaine is also ideal for those heading to or from the north, and Isle-sur-la-Sorgue (the most accessible small town by train) is conveniently located between Avignon and the Luberon.

Getting Around Provence

By Bus or Train: Public transit is good between cities and decent to some towns, but marginal at best to the smaller villages. Frequent trains link Avignon and Arles (no more than 30 minutes between each). Avignon has good train connections with Orange and adequate service to Isle-sur-la-Sorgue.

Buses connect many smaller towns, though service can be sporadic. From Avignon, you can bus to Pont du Gard, Isle-sur-la-Sorgue (also by train), and to some Côtes du Rhône villages. From Arles, buses run to Les Baux (in high season only), St-Rémy, the Camargue, and Nîmes. Excellent minivan tours and basic bus excursions are available from both Avignon and Arles to Côtes du Rhône villages. (TIs in both cities also have information on excursions to regional sights; see "Tours of Provence," below.)

By Car: The region is made to order for a car, though travel time between some sights will surprise you—thanks, in part, to narrow roads and endless roundabouts (for example, figure an hour from Les Baux to Pont du Gard, and two hours from Arles to Vaison la Romaine). The yellow Michelin maps #332 (Luberon and Côtes du Rhône) and #340 (Arles area) are worth considering; the larger-scale orange Michelin map #527 also includes the Riviera. Avignon (pop. 110,000) is a headache for drivers. Arles (pop. 52,000) is easier but still challenging. Be wary of thieves—this is France's worst area for car break-ins. Park only in well-monitored spaces and leave nothing valuable in your car. If you're heading north from Provence, consider a three-hour detour through the spectacular Ardèche Gorges (see page 746).

Tours of Provence

Wine Safari—Dutchman Mike Rijken runs a one-man show, taking travelers through the region he adopted more than 20 years ago. Mike came to France to train as a chef, later became a wine steward, and has now found his calling as a driver/guide. His English is fluent, and though his focus is on wine and wine villages, Mike knows the region thoroughly and is a good teacher of its history (€60/half-day, €110/day, priced per person, group size varies from 2 to 6; pickups possible in Arles, Avignon, Lyon, Marseille, or Aix-en-Provence; tel. 04 90 35 59 21, mobile 06 19 29

Public Transportation in Provence

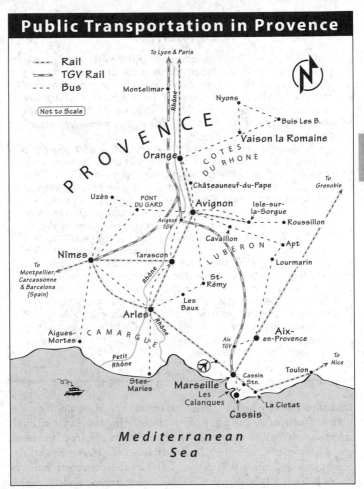

50 81, www.winesafari.net, mikeswinesafari@orange.fr).

Local Guides—Celine Viany is a retired wine sommelier turned charming tour guide. She's an easy-to-be-with expert on her region and its chief product (tel. 04 90 46 90 80, mobile 06 76 59 56 30, www.levinalabouche.com, contact@degustation-levinalabouche .com).

Avignon Wine Tour—For a playful and distinctly French perspective on wines of the Côtes du Rhône region, contact François Marcou, who runs his tours with passion and energy, offering different itineraries every day (€80/person for all-day wine tours that include 4-5 tastings, €350 for private groups, mobile 06 28 05 33 84, www.avignon-wine-tour.com, avignon.wine.tour@modulo net.fr).

Le Mistral

Provence lives with its vicious mistral winds, which blow 30-60 miles per hour, about 100 days out of the year. Locals say it blows in multiples of threes: three, six, or nine days in a row. The mistral clears people off the streets and turns lively cities into ghost towns. You'll likely spend a few hours or days taking refuge—or searching for cover. The winds are strongest between noon and 15:00.

When the mistral blows, it's everywhere, and you can't escape. Author Peter Mayle said it could blow the ears off a donkey (I'd include the tail). According to the natives, it ruins crops, shutters, and roofs (look for stones holding tiles in place on many homes). They'll also tell you that this pernicious wind has driven many people crazy (including young Vincent van Gogh). A weak version of the wind is called a *mistralet*.

The mistral starts above the Alps and Massif Central mountains and gathers steam as it heads south, gaining momentum as it screams over the Rhône Valley (which acts like a funnel between the Alps and the Cévennes mountains) before exhausting itself when it hits the Mediterranean. And though this wind rattles shutters throughout the Riviera and Provence, it's strongest over the Rhône Valley...so Avignon, Arles, and the Côtes du Rhône villages bear its brunt. While wiping the dust from your eyes, remember the good news: The mistral brings clear skies.

Imagine Tours—Unlike most tour operators, this nonprofit organization focuses on cultural excursions, offering low-key, personalized tours that allow visitors to discover the "true heart of Provence and Occitania." The itineraries are adapted to your interests, and the guides will meet you at your hotel or the departure point of your choice (€170/half-day, €295/day, prices are for up to 4 people starting from the region around Avignon or Arles, mobile 06 89 22 19 87, fax 04 90 24 84 26, www.imagine-tours.net, imagine.tours @gmail.com). They are also happy to help you plan your itinerary, book hotel rooms, or address other travel issues.

Wine Uncovered—Passionate and engaging Englishman Olivier Hickman takes small groups on focused tours of selected wineries in Châteauneuf-du-Pape and in the villages near Vaison la Romaine. Olivier is serious about French wine and knows his subject matter inside and out. His in-depth tastings include a half-day tour of two or three wineries; the Châteauneuf-du-Pape tour is especially popular. He also offers multiday tours with food and wine tastings, and if you need transportation, he can help arrange it (€35-70/person for half-day to full-day tours, prices subject to minimum tour fees, see website for details, mobile 06 75 10 10

01, www.wine-uncovered.com, olivier.hickman@wine-uncovered
.com).

Tours du Rhône—American Doug Graves, who owns a small wine domaine in the Côtes du Rhône, shares his passion for his adopted region, its people, and its wines on his guided tours of Châteauneuf-du-Pape, the villages of the Côtes du Rhône, and the Luberon Valley (€100/person, 4-person max, mobile 06 37 16 04 56, www.toursdurhone.com, doug@masdelalionne.com).

Visit Provence—This company runs day tours from Avignon and Arles. Tours from Avignon run year-round and include a great variety of destinations; tours from Arles run April through September only and are more limited (check their website for current destinations). While these tours provide introductory commentary to what you'll see, there is no guiding at the actual sights. They use eight-seat, air-conditioned minivans (about €60-80/half-day, €100-120/day; they'll pick you up at your hotel in Avignon or at the main TI in Arles). Ask about their cheaper big-bus excursions, or consider hiring a van and driver for your private use (plan on €220/half-day, €490/day, tel. 04 90 14 70 00, www.provence-reservation.com).

Provence's Cuisine Scene

The almost extravagant use (by French standards) of garlic, olive oil, herbs, and tomatoes makes Provence's cuisine France's liveliest. To sample it, order anything *à la provençal*. Among the area's spicy specialties are ratatouille (a mixture of vegetables in a thick, herb-flavored tomato sauce), aioli (a rich, garlicky mayonnaise spread over vegetables, potatoes, fish, or whatever),

tapenade (a paste of pureed olives, capers, anchovies, herbs, and sometimes tuna), *soupe au pistou* (thin yet flavorful vegetable soup with a sauce—called *pistou*—of basil, garlic, and cheese), and *soupe à l'ail* (garlic soup, called *aigo bouido* in the local dialect). Look for *riz de Camargue* (the reddish, chewy, nutty-tasting rice that has taken over the Camargue area) and *taureau* (bull's meat). The native goat cheeses are *banon de banon* or *banon à la feuille* (wrapped in chestnut leaves) and spicy *picodon*. Provence also produces some of France's great wines at relatively reasonable prices. Look for Gigondas, Sablet, Côtes du Rhône Villages, and Côte de Provence. If you like rosé, try the Tavel. This is the place to splurge for a bottle of Châteauneuf-du-Pape.

Remember, restaurants serve only during lunch (11:30-14:00)

and dinner (19:00-21:00, later in bigger cities), but some cafés serve food throughout the day.

Provence Market Days

Provençal market days offer France's most colorful and tantalizing outdoor shopping. The best markets are on Monday in Cavaillon, Tuesday in Vaison la Romaine, Wednesday in St-Rémy, Thursday in Nyons, Friday in Lourmarin, Saturday in Arles, Uzès, and Apt, and, best of all, Sunday in Isle-sur-la-Sorgue. Crowds and parking problems abound at these popular events—arrive by 9:00, or, even better, sleep in the town the night before.

Monday:	Cavaillon, Bedoin (between Vaison la Romaine and Mont Ventoux)
Tuesday:	Vaison la Romaine, Gordes, and Lacoste
Wednesday:	St-Rémy, Arles, Uzès, Sault, and Malaucène (near Vaison la Romaine)
Thursday:	Nyons, Vacqueyras, Roussillon, and Isle-sur-la-Sorgue
Friday:	Lourmarin, Carpentras, Bonnieux, and Châteauneuf-du-Pape
Saturday:	Arles, Uzès, Apt, and Sainte-Cécile-les-Vignes (near Vaison la Romaine)
Sunday:	Isle-sur-la-Sorgue, Coustellet

How About Them Romans?

Provence is littered with Roman ruins. Many scholars claim the best-preserved ancient Roman buildings are not in Italy, but in France. These ancient stones will compose an important part of your sightseeing agenda in this region, so it's worth learning about how they came to be.

Classical Rome endured from about 500 B.C. through A.D. 500—spending about 500 years growing, 200 years peaking, and 300 years declining. In 49 B.C., Julius Caesar defied the Republic by crossing the Rubicon River in northern Italy, conquering Provence (and ultimately all of France)—and killing about a third of its population in the process. He erected a temple to Jupiter on the future site of Paris' Notre-Dame Cathedral.

The concept of one-man rule lived on with his grandnephew, Octavian (whom he had also adopted as his son). Octavian killed Brutus, eliminated his rivals (Mark Antony and Cleopatra), and united Rome's warring factions. He took the title "Augustus" and became the first in a line of emperors who would control Rome for the next 500 years—ruling like a king, with the backing of the army and the rubber-stamp approval of the Senate. Rome morphed from a Republic into an Empire: a collection of many diverse territories ruled by a single man.

Augustus' reign marked the start of 200 years of peace, prosperity, and expansion known as the *Pax Romana*. At its peak (c. A.D. 117), the Roman empire had 54 million people and stretched from Scotland in the north to Egypt in the south, as far west as Spain and as far east as modern-day Iraq. To the northeast, Rome was bounded by the Rhine and Danube Rivers. On Roman maps, the Mediterranean was labeled *Mare Nostrum* ("Our Sea"). At its peak, "Rome" didn't just refer to the city, but to the entire civilized Western world.

The Romans were successful not only because they were good soldiers, but also because they were smart administrators and businessmen. People in conquered territories knew they had joined the winning team and that political stability would replace barbarian invasions. Trade thrived. Conquered peoples were welcomed into the fold of prosperity, linked by roads, education, common laws and gods, and the Latin language.

Provence, with its strategic location, benefited greatly from Rome's global economy and grew to become an important part of

its worldwide empire. After Julius Caesar conquered Gaul, Emperor Augustus set out to Romanize it, building and renovating cities in the image of Rome. Most cities had a theater (some had several), baths, and aqueducts; the most important cities had sports arenas. The Romans also erected an elaborate infrastructure of roads, post offices, schools (teaching in Latin), police stations, and water-supply systems.

With a standard language and currency, Roman merchants were able to trade wine, salt, and olive oil for foreign goods. The empire invested heavily in cities that were strategic for trade. For example, the Roman-built city of Arles was a crucial link in the trade route from Italy to Spain, so they built a bridge across the Rhône River and fortified the town.

A typical Roman city (such as Arles, Orange, Vaison la Romaine, or Nîmes) was a garrison town, laid out on a grid plan with two main roads: one running north-south (the *cardus*), the other east-west (the *decumanus*). Approaching the city on your chariot, you'd pass by the cemetery, which was located outside of town for hygienic reasons. You'd enter the main gate and speed past warehouses and apartment houses to the town square (forum). Facing the square were the most important temples, dedicated to the patron gods of the city. Nearby, you'd find bathhouses; like today's fitness clubs, these served the almost sacred dedication to personal vigor. Also close by were businesses that catered to the citizens' needs: the marketplace, bakeries, banks, and brothels.

Aqueducts brought fresh water for drinking, filling the baths, and delighting the citizens with bubbling fountains. Men flocked to the stadiums in Arles and Nîmes to bet on gladiator games; eager couples attended elaborate plays at theaters in Orange, Arles, and Vaison la Romaine. Marketplaces brimmed with exotic fruits, vegetables, and animals from the far reaches of the empire. Some cities in Provence were more urban 2,000 years ago than they are today. For instance, Roman Arles had a population of 100,000—double today's size. Think about that when you visit.

In these cities, you'll see many rounded arches. These were constructed by piling two stacks of heavy stone blocks, connecting them with an arch (supported with wooden scaffolding), then inserting an inverted keystone where the stacks met. *Voilà!* The heavy stones were able to support not only themselves, but also a great deal of weight above the arch. The Romans didn't invent the rounded arch, but they exploited it better than their predecessors, stacking arches to build arenas and theaters, stringing them side by side for aqueducts, stretching out their legs to create barrel-vaulted ceilings, and building freestanding "triumphal" arches to celebrate conquering generals.

When it came to construction, the Romans' magic building ingredient was concrete. A mixture of volcanic ash, lime, water, and small rocks, concrete—easier to work than stone, longer-lasting than wood—served as flooring, roofing, filler, glue, and support. Builders would start with a foundation of brick, then fill it in with poured concrete. They would then cover important structures, such as basilicas, in sheets of expensive marble (held on with nails), or decorate floors and walls with mosaics—proving just how talented the Romans were at turning the functional into art.

Arles

By helping Julius Caesar defeat Marseille, Arles (pronounced "arl") earned the imperial nod and was made an important port city. With the first bridge over the Rhône River, Arles was a key stop on the Roman road from Italy to Spain, the Via Domitia (a model of this bridge is at the Ancient History Museum). After reigning as the seat of an important archbishop and as a trading center for centuries, the city became a sleepy backwater of little importance in the 1700s. Vincent van Gogh settled here in the late 1800s, but left only a chunk of his ear (now long gone). American bombers destroyed much of Arles in World War II as the townsfolk hid out in its underground Roman galleries. But today Arles thrives again, with its evocative Roman ruins, an eclectic assortment of museums, made-for-ice-cream pedestrian zones, and squares that play hide-and-seek with visitors.

The city's unpolished streets and squares are not to everyone's taste. This workaday city has not sold out to tourism, so you won't see dolled-up lanes and perfectly preserved buildings. But to me, that's part of its charm. And in 2013, Arles is receiving special attention thanks to big brother Marseille's reign as a European Capital of Culture—there's talk that several Van Gogh paintings will be on display here (see www.mp2013.fr or ask the TI for details).

Orientation to Arles

Arles faces the Mediterranean, turning its back on Paris. And though the town is built along the Rhône, it largely ignores the river. Landmarks hide in Arles' medieval tangle of narrow, winding streets. Virtually everything is close—but first-timers can walk forever to get there. Hotels have good, free city maps, and Arles provides helpful street-corner signs that point you toward sights and hotels. Speeding cars enjoy Arles' medieval lanes, turning sidewalks into tightropes and pedestrians into leaping targets.

Tourist Information

The **main TI** is on the ring road Boulevard des Lices, at Esplanade Charles de Gaulle (April-Sept daily 9:00-18:45; Oct-March Mon-Sat 9:00-16:45, Sun 10:00-13:00; tel. 04 90 18 41 20, www.arles tourisme.com). There's also a **train station TI** (Mon-Fri 9:30-13:00

PROVENCE

Arles

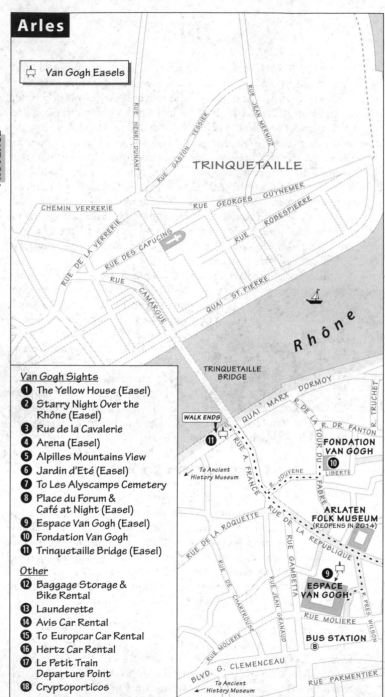

⌂ Van Gogh Easels

TRINQUETAILLE

RUE HENRI DUNANT

RUE GASTON TESSIER

RUE JEAN MERMOZ

CHEMIN VERRERIE

RUE GEORGES GUYNEMER

RUE ROBESPIERRE

RUE DE LA VERRERIE

RUE DES CAPUCINS

RUE

RUE CAMARGUE

QUAI ST. PIERRE

Rhône

TRINQUETAILLE
BRIDGE

QUAI MARX DORMOY

R. TRUCHET

R. DR. FANTON

R. DE LA TOUR DU FABRE

WALK ENDS

11

RUE A. FRANCE

FONDATION
VAN GOGH

10

To Ancient
History Museum

R. JOUVENE

LIBERTE

ARLATEN
FOLK MUSEUM
(REOPENS IN 2014)

RUE DE LA ROQUETTE

RUE DE LA REPUBLIQUE

RUE DE LA

RUE GAMBETTA

ESPACE
VAN GOGH

9

R. PRES. WILSON

RUE DE CHARTROUSE

RUE JEAN GRANAUD

RUE MOLIERE

BUS STATION
B

RUE MOLIERE

BLVD. G. CLEMENCEAU

To Ancient
History Museum

RUE PARMENTIER

Van Gogh Sights
1 The Yellow House (Easel)
2 Starry Night Over the Rhône (Easel)
3 Rue de la Cavalerie
4 Arena (Easel)
5 Alpilles Mountains View
6 Jardin d'Eté (Easel)
7 To Les Alyscamps Cemetery
8 Place du Forum & Café at Night (Easel)
9 Espace Van Gogh (Easel)
10 Fondation Van Gogh
11 Trinquetaille Bridge (Easel)

Other
12 Baggage Storage & Bike Rental
13 Launderette
14 Avis Car Rental
15 To Europcar Car Rental
16 Hertz Car Rental
17 Le Petit Train Departure Point
18 Cryptoporticos

PROVENCE

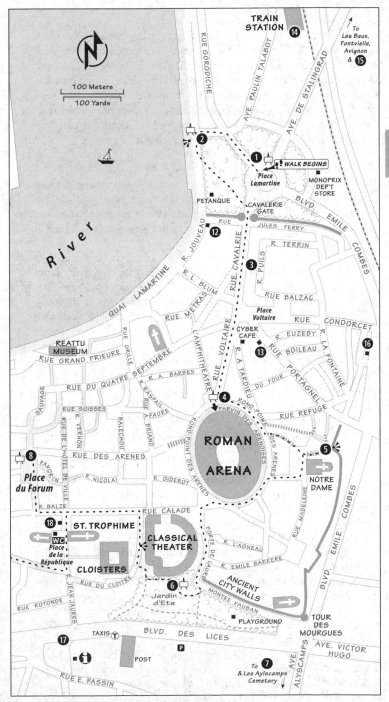

N

100 Meters
100 Yards

TRAIN STATION **14**

To Les Baux, Fontvielle, Avignon & **15**

RUE GORDICHE

AVE. PAULIN TALABOT

AVE. DE STALINGRAD

2

1 ⚓ WALK BEGINS

Place Lamartine

MONOPRIX DEP'T STORE

PETANQUE

CAVALERIE GATE

BLVD. EMILE COMBES

RUE JOUVEAU

RUE

RUE CAVALRIE

JULES FERRY

R. PUILS

R. TERRIN

12

3

RUE BALZAC

Place Voltaire

RUE CONDORCET

R i v e r

QUAI LAMARTINE

R.L. BLUM

RUE METRAS

RUE VOLTAIRE

CYBER CAFE

R. EUZEBY

R. A. TARDIEU

13

RUE BOILEAU

LA FONTAINE

16

REATTU MUSEUM

RUE GRAND PRIEURE

RUE GRILLE

L'AMPHITHEATRE

RUE PORTAGNEL

DU FOUR

RUE DU QUATRE SEPTEMBRE

R. A. BARBES

FOND-ROND-POINT DES ARENES

RUE REFUGE

SAUVAGE

RUE RASPAIL

R. A. FAURE

RUE SUISSES

RUE DE L'HOTEL DE VILLE

R. VERNON

BALECHOU

R. A. BRIAND

4

PARVIS DES ARENOISES

ROMAN ARENA

ROND-POINT DES ARENES

RUE DES ARENES

5

NOTRE DAME

8

Place du Forum

FAVORIN

R. NICOLAI

R. DIDEROT

RUE MADELEINE

BLVD. EMILE COMBES

R. BALZE

RUE CALADE

18

ST. TROPHIME

WC

Place de la République

CLASSICAL THEATER

PORTE DE LAURE

R. L'AGNEAU

R. EMILE BARRERE

CLOISTERS

RUE DU CLOITRE

JEAN JAURES

6

Jardin d'Ete

ANCIENT CITY WALLS

MONTEE VAUBAN

TOUR DES MOURGUES

RUE ROTONDE

PLAYGROUND

17

TAXIS Ⓣ

BLVD. DES LICES

P

POST

AVE. VICTOR HUGO

7

To & Les Alyscamps Cemetery

AVE. ALYSCAMPS

RUE E. FASSIN

& 14:00-18:00, closed Sat-Sun).

At either TI, pick up the city map, get the bus schedules you need, and ask for English information on nearby destinations such as the Camargue wildlife area (described on page 686). Ask about "bullgames" in Arles and nearby towns (Provence's more humane version of bullfights—see page 688). Skip the useless €1 brochure describing several walks in Arles, including one that locates Van Gogh's "easels" (better explained on page 681). Both TIs can help you reserve hotel rooms (credit card required for deposit).

Arrival in Arles

By Train: The train station is on the river, a 10-minute walk from the town center. Before heading into town, get what you need at the train station TI. There's no baggage storage at the station, but you can walk 10 minutes to stow it at Hôtel Régence (see "Helpful Hints," later).

To reach the town center or Ancient History Museum, wait for the free **Envia minibus** at the glass shelter facing away from the station (cross the street and veer left, 3/hour Mon-Sat 7:00-19:00, none Sun). The bus makes a loop around Arles, stopping near most of my recommended hotels. It's a 15-minute **walk** into town (turn left out of the train station). **Taxis** usually wait in front of the station, but if you don't see any, call the posted telephone numbers, or dial 04 89 73 36 00. If the train station TI is open, you can ask them to call. Taxi rates are fixed—allow about €10 to any of my recommended hotels.

By Bus: All buses stop at the Centre-Ville bus station, a few blocks below the main TI, on the ring road at 16-24 Boulevard Georges Clemenceau. Buses to Les Baux and Avignon's TGV station also stop at the train station.

By Car: Most hotels have parking nearby—ask for detailed directions (€2.80/8 hours at most meters; free 12:00-14:00 & 19:00-9:00, and all day on Sundays; some meters limited to 2.5 hours). For most hotels, first follow signs to *Centre-Ville*, then *Gare SNCF* (train station). You'll come to a big roundabout (Place Lamartine) with a Monoprix department store to the right. You can park along the city wall and find your hotel on foot; the hotels I list are no more than a 10-minute walk away (best not to park here overnight due to theft concerns and markets on Wed and Sat). Fearless drivers can plunge into the narrow streets between the two stumpy towers via Rue de la Calade, and follow signs to their hotel. Again, theft is a problem—leave nothing in your car, and trust your hotelier's advice on where to park.

If you can't find parking near your hotel, Parking des Lices (Arles' only parking garage), near the TI on Boulevard des Lices, is a good fallback (€2.20/hour, €15/24 hours).

Helpful Hints

Market Days: The big markets are on Wednesdays and Saturdays. For all the details, see page 687.

Crowds: An international photo event jams hotels the second weekend of July. The let-'er-rip, twice-yearly Féria draws crowds over Easter and in mid-September (see www.arles tourisme.com for dates).

Internet Access: There's an Internet café near Place Voltaire at 31 Rue Augustin Tardieu (daily, tel. 04 90 18 87 40).

Baggage Storage and Bike Rental: The recommended **Hôtel Régence** will store your bags for €3 (daily 7:30-22:00 mid-March-mid-Nov, closed in winter, 5 Rue Marius Jouveau). They also rent bikes (€7/half-day, €14/day, one-way rentals within Provence possible, same hours as baggage storage) and may have electric bikes—ask. From Arles, you could ride to Les Baux (20 miles round-trip), but it's a dang steep climb getting there (consider busing up there and gliding back, regional buses have bike racks). Those in great shape can consider biking into the Camargue (40 miles round-trip, forget it in the wind).

Laundry: A launderette is at 12 Rue Portagnel (daily 7:00-21:30, you can stay later to finish if you're already inside, English instructions).

Car Rental: Avis is at the train station (tel. 08 20 05 05 05); **Europcar** and **Hertz** are downtown (Europcar is at 61 Avenue de Stalingrad, tel. 04 90 93 23 24; Hertz is closer to Place Voltaire at 10 Boulevard Emile Combes, tel. 04 90 96 75 23).

Local Guide: Charming **Agnes Barrier** is a good guide, knows Arles and nearby sights intimately, and loves her work. Her tours of Arles cover Van Gogh and Roman history (€130/3 hours, mobile 06 11 23 03 73, agnes.barrier@hotmail.fr).

English Book Exchange: A small exchange is available at the recommended **Soleileis** ice-cream shop.

Public Pools: Arles has three public pools (indoor and outdoor). Ask at the TI or your hotel.

Boules: The local "*boul*ing alley" is by the river on Place Lamartine. After their afternoon naps, the old boys congregate here for a game of *pétanque* (see page 1141 for more on this popular local pastime).

Getting Around Arles

In this flat city, everything's within **walking** distance. Only the Ancient History Museum requires a healthy walk (or you can take a taxi or bus). The elevated riverside promenade provides Rhône views and a direct route to the Ancient History Museum (to the southwest) and the train station (to the northeast). Keep your head up for *Starry Night* memories, but eyes down for decorations by dogs with poorly trained owners.

Arles' **taxis** charge a set fee of about €10, but nothing except the Ancient History Museum is worth a taxi ride. To call a cab, dial 04 89 73 36 00 or 04 90 96 90 03.

The free **Envia minibus** circles the town (3/hour, Mon-Sat 7:00-19:00, none Sun), useful for access to the train station and the Ancient History Museum.

Le Petit Train d'Arles, a typical tourist train, gives you the lay of the land—if you prefer sitting to walking (€7, 35 minutes, stops in front of the main TI and at the Roman Arena).

Sights in Arles

Most sights cost €3.50-7, and though any sight warrants a few minutes, many aren't worth their individual admission price. The TI sells two different monument passes (called "Passeports"). **Le Passeport Avantage** covers almost all of Arles' sights (€13.50, under 18-€12); **Le Passeport Liberté** (€9) lets you choose any five monuments (one must be a museum). Depending on your interests, the €9 Passeport is probably best.

Start at the Ancient History Museum (closed Tue) for a helpful overview (drivers should try to do this museum on their way into Arles), then dive into the city-center sights. Remember, many sights stop selling tickets one hour before closing (both before lunch and at the end of the day). To make the most of Arles' Roman history, see page 666.

▲▲Ancient History Museum (Musée de l'Arles et de la Provence Antiques)

Begin your town visit here, for Roman Arles 101. Located on the site of the Roman chariot racecourse (the arc of which is built into the parking lot), this air-condi-tioned, all-on-one-floor museum is just west of central Arles along the river. Models and original sculptures (with almost no posted English translations but a decent handout) re-create the Roman city, making workaday life and culture easier to imagine.

Cost and Hours: €6, Wed-Mon 10:00-18:00, closed Tue, Presqu'île du Cirque Romain, tel. 04 13 31 51 03, www.arles -antique.cg13.fr. Ask for the English booklet, which provides a helpful if not in-depth background on the collection.

Getting There: To reach the museum, take the free **Envia**

minibus (stops at the train station and along Rue du 4 Septembre, then along the river, 3/hour Mon-Sat, none Sun). If you're coming **on foot** from the city center (a 20-minute walk), turn left at the river and take the scruffy riverside path under two bridges to the big, blue, modern building. As you approach the museum, you'll pass the verdant Hortus Garden—designed to recall the Roman circus and chariot racecourse that were located here. A **taxi** ride costs €10 (museum can call a taxi for your return).

◑ Self-Guided Tour: The collection is housed in one large room separated by dividers and exhibits. Tour the room moving basically counterclockwise.

A big **map** of the Roman Arles region greets visitors and shows the key Roman routes accessible to Arles. You'll then pass a model of a small **pre-Roman village** (allowing you to compare pre- and post-Roman life in Arles), and see maps showing Arles' expanding city limits during its Roman era.

Next you'll see **models** of every Roman structure in (and near) Arles. These are the highlight for me, as they breathe life into

the buildings, showing them as they looked 2,000 years ago. Start with the model of Roman Arles, and imagine the city's splendor. Find the Forum—still the center of town today, though only two columns survive. Look at the space Romans devoted to their arena and huge racecourse—a reminder that an emphasis on sports is not unique to modern civilizations. The model also illustrates how little Arles seems to have changed over two millennia, with its houses still clustered around the city center, and warehouses still located on the opposite side of the river.

Look for individual models of important buildings shown in the city model: the elegant forum; the floating bridge that gave Arles a strategic advantage (over the widest, and therefore slowest, part of the river); the theater (with its magnificent stage wall); the arena (with its movable stadium cover to shelter spectators from sun or rain); the hydraulic mill of Barbegal (with its 16 waterwheels powered by water cascading down a hillside); and the circus (a.k.a. chariot racecourse). Part of the original racecourse was just outside the windows, and though long gone, it must have resembled Rome's Circus Maximus in its day—its obelisk is now the centerpiece of Arles' Place de la République.

You'll also pass displays of pottery, jewelry, metal and glass artifacts, and well-crafted mosaic floors that illustrate how Roman Arles was a city of art and culture. The many **statues** that you see are all original, except for the greatest—the *Venus of Arles*, which

Louis XIV took a liking to and had moved to Versailles. It's now in the Louvre—and, as locals say, "When it's in Paris...bye-bye."

Preparations are well under way for the installation of a **Gallo-Roman vessel** and much of its cargo, to be displayed in a large new room facing the Hortus Garden (opening in late 2013). This almost 100-foot-long Roman barge was pulled out of the Rhône in 2010, along with some 280 amphorae and 3,000 ceramic artifacts. It was typical of flat-bottomed barges used to shuttle goods between Arles and ports along the Mediterranean (vessels were manually towed upriver).

Just before leaving, you'll pass an impressive row of pagan and early-Christian **sarcophagi** (from the second to fifth centuries A.D.). These would have lined the Via Aurelia outside the town wall. In the early days of the Church, Jesus was often portrayed beardless and as the good shepherd, with a lamb over his shoulder.

In Central Arles

Ideally, visit these sights in the order listed below. I've included some walking directions to connect the dots (see the Arles map on page 670).

▲▲**Forum Square (Place du Forum)**—Named for the Roman forum that once stood here, Place du Forum was the political and religious center of Roman Arles. Still lively, this café-crammed square is a local watering hole and popular for a *pastis* (anise-based apéritif). The bistros on the square, though no place for a fine dinner, can put together a good-enough salad or *plat du jour*—and when you sprinkle on the ambience, that's €12 well spent.

At the corner of Grand Hôtel Nord-Pinus (a favorite of Pablo Picasso), a plaque shows how the Romans built a foundation of galleries to make the main square level in order to compensate for Arles' slope down to the river. The two columns are all that survive from the upper story of the entry to the Forum. Steps leading to the entrance are buried—the Roman street level was about 20 feet below you (you can get a glimpse of it by peeking through the street-level openings under the Hôtel d'Arlatan, two blocks below Place du Forum on Rue du Sauvage). To see the underground arches, visit the Cryptoporticos (see next page).

The statue on the square is of **Frédéric Mistral** (1830-1914). This popular poet, who wrote in the local dialect rather than in French, was a champion of Provençal culture. After receiving the Nobel Prize in Literature in 1904, Mistral used his prize money to preserve and display the folk identity of Provence. He founded the regional folk museum (the Arlaten Folk Museum, described later) at a time when France was rapidly centralizing. (The local mistral wind—literally "master"—has nothing to do with his name.)

The **bright-yellow café**—called Café la Nuit—was the subject of one of Vincent van Gogh's most famous works in Arles. Although his painting showed the café in a brilliant yellow from the glow of gas lamps, the facade was bare limestone, just like the other cafés on this square. The café's current owners have painted it to match Van Gogh's version...and to cash in on the Vincent-crazed hordes who pay too much to eat or drink here.

• *Facing Café la Nuit, walk right one block (past Grand Hôtel Nord Pinus) and turn left. Walk through the Hôtel de Ville's vaulted entry (or take the next right if it's closed), and pop out onto the big...*

Republic Square (Place de la République)—This square used to be called "Place Royale"...until the French Revolution. The obelisk was the former centerpiece of Arles' Roman Circus. The lions at its base are the symbol of the city, whose slogan is (roughly) "the gentle lion." Find a seat and watch the peasants—pilgrims, locals, and street musicians. There's nothing new about this scene.

• *Return to the Hôtel de Ville (where you came in) and look for the entrance to...*

Cryptoporticos (Cryptoportiques)—This dark, drippy underworld of Roman arches was constructed to support Forum Square. Two thousand years ago, most of this gallery of arches was at or above street level—modern Arles has buried about 20 feet of its history over the millennia. Pick up the minimalist English flier and read it before you descend into the dark.

Cost and Hours: €3.50, daily May-Sept 9:00-12:00 & 14:00-19:00, March-April and Oct 9:00-12:00 & 14:00-18:00, Nov-Feb 10:00-12:00 & 14:00-17:00.

• *Just outside the Hôtel de Ville, back in Place de la République, find...*

▲▲**St. Trophime Church**—Named after a third-century bishop of Arles, this church sports the finest Romanesque main entrance I've seen anywhere.

Cost and Hours: Church—free, daily April-Sept 9:00-12:00 & 14:00-18:30, Oct-March 9:00-12:00 & 14:00-17:00; cloisters—€3.50, daily May-Sept 9:00-19:00, March-April and Oct 9:00-18:00, Nov-Feb 10:00-17:00.

➋ **Self-Guided Tour:** Like a Roman triumphal arch, the church facade trumpets the promise of Judgment Day. The tympanum (the semicircular area above the door) is filled with Christian symbolism. Christ sits in majesty, surrounded by symbols of the four evangelists: Matthew (the winged man), Mark (the winged lion), Luke (the ox), and John (the eagle). The 12 apostles are lined up below Jesus. It's Judgment Day...some are saved, and others aren't. Notice the condemned (on the right)—a chain gang doing a sad bunny-hop over the fires of hell. For them, the tune trumpeted by the three angels above Christ is not a happy one. Below the chain gang, St. Stephen is being stoned to death, with his soul leaving through his mouth and instantly being welcomed by

angels. Ride the exquisite detail back to a simpler age. In an illiterate medieval world, long before the vivid images of our Technicolor time, this was a neon billboard over the town square.

Interior: Just inside the door on the right, a chart locates the interior highlights and helps explain the carvings you just saw on the tympanum.

Tour the church counterclockwise. The tall 12th-century Romanesque nave is decorated by a set of tapestries showing scenes from the life of Mary (17th century, from the French town of Aubusson). Amble around the Gothic apse. Two-thirds of the way around, find the relic chapel behind the ornate wrought-iron gate, with its fine golden boxes that hold long-venerated bones of obscure saints. The next chapel houses the skull of St. Anthony of the Desert, with good English explanations of this saint's importance. Several chapels down, look for the early-Christian sarcophagus from Roman Arles (dated about A.D. 300) under the black columns. The heads were lopped off during the French Revolution.

This church is a stop on the ancient pilgrimage route to Santiago de Compostela in northwest Spain. For 800 years pilgrims on their way to Santiago have paused here...and they still do today. Notice the modern-day pilgrimages advertised on the far right near the church's entry.

Cloisters: Leaving the church, turn left, then left again through a courtyard to enter the adjacent cloisters.

The cloisters are worth a look only if you have a pass (enter at the far end of the courtyard). The many small columns were scavenged from the ancient Roman theater. Enjoy the sculpted capitals, the rounded 12th-century Romanesque arches, and the pointed 14th-century Gothic ones. The pretty vaulted hall exhibits 17th-century tapestries showing scenes from the First Crusade to the Holy Land. On the second floor, you'll walk along an angled rooftop designed to catch rainwater—notice the slanted gutter that channeled the water into a cistern and the heavy roof slabs covering the tapestry hall below.

• *Turn right out of the church cloisters, then take the first right on Rue de la Calade to reach the…*

Classical Theater (Théâtre Antique)—This first-century B.C. Roman theater once seated 10,000…just like the theater in Orange.

But unlike Orange, here in Arles there was no hillside to provide support. This theater was an elegant, 3-level structure with 27 arches radiating out to the street level. From the outside, it looked much like a halved version of Arles' Roman Arena. Budget travelers can peek over the fence from Rue du Cloître and see just about everything for free.

Cost and Hours: €6.50, daily May-Sept 9:00-19:00, March-April and Oct 9:00-18:00, Nov-Feb 10:00-17:00.

Visiting the Theater: Start with the video outside, which provides helpful background information and images that make it easier to put the scattered stones back in place (crouch in front to make out the small English subtitles). Next, walk to a center aisle and pull up a stone seat. To appreciate the theater's original size, look left (about 9:00) to the upper-left side of the tower and find the protrusion that supported the highest seating level. The structure required 33 rows of seats covering three levels to accommodate demand. During the Middle Ages, the old theater became a convenient town quarry—St. Trophime Church was built from theater rubble. Precious little of the original theater survives—though it still is used for events, with seating for 3,000 spectators.

Two lonely Corinthian columns are all that remain of a three-story stage wall that once featured more than 100 columns and statues painted in vibrant colors. The orchestra section is defined by a semicircular pattern in the stone in front of you. Stepping up onto the left side of the stage, look down to the slender channel that allowed the brilliant-red curtain to disappear below, like magic. The stage, which was built of wood, was about 160 feet across and 20 feet deep. The actors' changing rooms are backstage, down the steps.

• A block uphill is the…

▲▲▲Roman Arena (Amphithéâtre)—Nearly 2,000 years ago, gladiators fought wild animals here to the delight of 20,000 screaming fans. Today local daredevils still fight wild animals here—"bullgame" posters around the arena advertise upcoming spectacles (described later, under "Experiences in Arles"). A lengthy restoration process is almost complete, giving the amphitheater an almost bleached-teeth whiteness. After the ticket kiosk is a helpful English information display that describes the arena's history and renovation.

Cost and Hours: €6.50, daily May-Sept 9:00-19:00, March-April and Oct 9:00-18:00, Nov-Feb 10:00-17:00, Rond-point des Arènes, tel. 08 91 70 03 70, www.arenes-arles.com.

Visiting the Arena: Find a seat in the upper deck. In Roman times, games were free (sponsored by city bigwigs), and fans were seated by social class. Thirty-four rows of stone bleachers extended all the way to the top of those vacant arches that circle the arena. There were no gates, just welcoming arches, numbered to allow entertainment-seekers to come and go freely. The purpose was to create a populace that was thoroughly Roman—enjoying the

same activities and entertainment, all thinking as one (not unlike Americans' nationwide obsession with the same reality-TV shows). The many passageways you'll see (called *vomitoires*) allowed for rapid dispersal after the games—fights would break out among frenzied fans if they couldn't leave quickly. Through medieval times and until the early 1800s, the arches were bricked up and the stadium became a fortified town—with 200 humble homes crammed within its circular defenses. Parts of three of the medieval towers survive (the one above the ticket booth is open and rewards those who climb it with terrific views). To see two still-sealed arches—complete with cute medieval window frames—turn right as you leave, walk to the L'Andaluz Restaurant, and look back to the second floor.

• *The next three sights are back across town. The Arlaten Folk Museum (closed until 2014) and Fondation Van Gogh (closed until summer 2013) are close to Place du Forum, and the Réattu Museum is near the river.*

▲Arlaten Folk Museum (Musée Arlaten/Museon Arlaten)—This museum, which explains the ins and outs of daily Provençal life, is closed for renovation until 2014. Ask at the TI or check the museum's website for the latest (www.museonarlaten.fr, French only).

▲Fondation Van Gogh—In the summer of 2013, this art gallery should reopen in its new location in the Hôtel Léautaud de Donines, a 15th-century townhouse (5 Place Honoré Clair, between Place du Forum and Trinquetaille Bridge). A good variety of Van Gogh souvenirs, prints, and postcards will be available in the gift shop. The following description assumes the collection will stay intact (for details, call 04 90 93 08 08 or visit www.fondation-vincentvangogh-arles.org).

The foundation offers a refreshing stop for modern-art lovers and Van Gogh fans (but be warned that the collection contains no Van Gogh originals). Contemporary artists, including Roy Lichtenstein and Robert Rauschenberg, pay homage to Vincent through thought-provoking interpretations of his works (for more on Vincent, see below). The black-and-white photographs (both art and shots of places that Vincent painted) complement the paintings. Unfortunately, this collection is often on the road from July through September, when material not related to Van Gogh is displayed.

Réattu Museum (Musée Réattu)—Housed in the former Grand Priory of the Knights of Malta, this modern-art collection is always changing. The permanent collection usually includes a series of works by homegrown Neoclassical artist Jacques Réattu, along with at least one Picasso painting and a roomful of his drawings (donated by the artist, some two-sided and all done in a flurry of creativity). The museum shuffles its large Picasso collection around regularly (they have more works than space to display them), and many of Picasso's works are likely to be moved during 2013 as a part of Marseille's European Capital of Culture program. Most of the three-floor museum houses temporary exhibits of modern artists—check the website to see who's playing.

Cost and Hours: €7, free first Sun of each month, open July-Sept Tue-Sun 10:00-19:00, Oct-June Tue-Sun 10:00-12:30 & 14:00-18:30, closed Mon year-round, last entry 30 minutes before closing for lunch or at end of day, 10 Rue du Grand Prieuré, tel. 04 90 49 37 58, www.museereattu.arles.fr.

Van Gogh Sights in Arles

In the dead of winter in 1888, 35-year-old Dutch artist Vincent van Gogh left big-city Paris for Provence, hoping to jump-start his floundering career and personal life. He was inspired, and he was lonely. Coming from the gray skies and flat lands of the north, Vincent was bowled over by everything Provençal—the sun, bright colors, rugged landscape, and unspoiled people. For the next two years he painted furiously, cranking out a masterpiece every few days.

None of the 200-plus paintings that Van Gogh did in the south can be found today in the city that so moved him. But you can walk the same streets he knew and see places he painted, marked by about a dozen steel-and-concrete "**easels**," with photos of the final paintings for then-and-now comparisons. The TI has a €1 brochure that locates all the easels (those described in this book are easily found without the brochure—see the map on page 670). Small stone markers with yellow accents embedded in the pavement lead to the easels.

• *Take a walk in Vincent's footsteps (roughly north to south through*

Arles' center) and watch his paintings come to life by putting yourself in his shoes. Start at **Place Lamartine** *and find the stone easel across the grass from the Civette Crêperie-Brasserie.*

❶ **The Yellow House Easel:** Vincent arrived in Arles on February 20, 1888, to a foot of snow. He rented a small house on the north side of Place Lamartine. The house was destroyed in 1944 by an errant bridge-seeking bomb, but the four-story building behind it—where you see the Civette Arlesienne—still stands (find it in the painting). The house had four rooms, including a small studio and the cramped trapezoid-shaped bedroom made famous in paint-

ings. It was painted yellow inside and out, and Vincent named it..."The Yellow House." In the distance, the painting shows the same bridges you see today, as well as a steam train—which was a rather recent invention in France, allowing people like Vincent to travel greater distances and be jarred by new experiences. (Today's TGV system continues that trend.)

Freezing Arles was buttoned up tight when Vincent arrived, so

he was forced to work inside, where he painted still-lifes and self-portraits—anything to keep his brush moving. In late March, spring finally arrived. In those days, a short walk from Place Lamartine led to open fields. Donning his straw hat, Vincent set up his easel outdoors and painted quickly, capturing what he saw and felt—the blossoming fruit trees, gnarled olive trees, peasants sowing and reaping, jagged peaks, and windblown fields, all lit by

a brilliant sun that drove him to use ever-brighter paints.

• *Walk to the river, passing a monument in honor of two WWII American pilots killed in action during the liberation of Arles. The monument was erected in 2002 as a post-9/11 sign of solidarity with Americans. Find the easel in the wall where ramps lead down to the river.*

❷ *Starry Night over the Rhône* **Easel:** One night, Vincent set up shop along the river and painted the stars boiling above the city skyline. Vincent looked to the night sky for the divine and was the first to paint outside after dark, adapting his straw hat to hold candles (which must have blown the minds of locals back then). As his paintings progressed, the stars became larger and more animated (like Vincent himself). The lone couple in the painting pops up again and again in his work. Experts say that Vincent was desperate for a close relationship with another being...someone to stroll the riverbank with under a star-filled sky. (Note: This painting is not the *Starry Night* you're thinking of—that one was painted later in St-Rémy.)

To his sister Wilhelmina, Van Gogh wrote, "At present I absolutely want to paint a starry sky. It often seems to me that night is still more richly colored than the day; having hues of the most intense violets, blues, and greens. If only you pay attention to it, you will see that certain stars are lemon-yellow, others pink or a green, blue, and forget-me-not brilliance." Vincent painted this scene on his last night in Arles. Come back at night to match his painting with today's scene.

• *Turn around and walk through the small park, then go into town between the stone towers along ❸ Rue de la Cavalerie, which becomes Rue Voltaire.*

Van Gogh walked into town the same way, underneath the arch and along this street. Arles' 19th-century red light district was just east of Rue de la Cavalerie, and the far-from-home Dutchman spent many lonely nights in its bars and brothels.

• *Pass through Place Voltaire, continue walking up Rue Voltaire to the Roman Arena, and then find the easel at the top of the arena steps, to the right.*

❹ **Arena Easel:** All summer long, fueled by sun and alcohol, Vincent painted the town. He loved the bullfights in the arena and sketched the colorful surge of the crowds, spending more time studying the people than watching the bullfights (notice how the bull is barely visible). Vincent had little interest in Arles' antiquity—it was people and nature that fascinated him.

• *Walk clockwise around the arena, then up the cobbled lane next to L'Andaluz Restaurant. Keep left in the parking lot to find a viewpoint.*

❺ **Alpilles Mountains View:** This view (no easel) pretty much matches what Vincent would have seen (be here late in the day for the best light). Vincent was an avid walker. Imagine him hauling his easel into those fields under intense sun, leaning against a ferocious wind, struggling to keep his hat on. He did this about 50 times during his stay in Arles, just to paint the farm workers. Vincent venerated but did not glorify peasants. Wanting to show their lives and their struggles, he reproached Renoir and Monet for elevating them in their works.

Vincent carried his easel as far as the medieval abbey of Montmajour, that bulky structure three miles straight ahead. The St. Paul Hospital, where he was eventually treated in St-Rémy, is on the other side of the Alpilles, several miles beyond Montmajour. On a clear day, you can make out the hill town of Les Baux at about 2 o'clock (with Montmajour at high noon).

• *Continue past the upper end of the arena, turn left before the Classical Theater, and walk out Rue de Porte de Laure. At the end of the street, walk down the curved staircase into the park and find the easel on the last path before the end of the park to the right.*

❻ Jardin d'Eté Easel: Vincent spent many a sunny day painting the leafy Jardin d'Eté. In another letter to his sister, Vincent wrote, "I don't know whether you can understand that one may make a poem by arranging colors.... In a similar manner, the bizarre lines, purposely selected and multiplied, meandering all through the picture may not present a literal image of the garden, but they may present it to our minds as if in a dream."

Vincent never made real friends, though he desperately wanted to. The son of disinterested parents, he never found the social skills necessary to sustain close friendships. He palled around with (and painted) his mailman and a Foreign Legionnaire. (The fact that locals pronounced his name "vahn-saw van gog" had nothing to do with his psychological struggles here.)

Packing his paints and a picnic in a rucksack, he day-tripped to the old Roman cemetery of **❼ Les Alyscamps,** a 10-minute detour from this route (across the busy street and to the left).

• *Continue through the gardens and exit at the far upper-right corner. Work your way past the Classical Theater on Rue du Cloître, and take the first left on Rue de la Calade. Turn right on Rue du Palais to find* **Place du Forum;** *locate an easel one café down from the yellow Café la Nuit.*

❽ Café at Night Easel: In October, lonely Vincent—who dreamed of making Arles a magnet for fellow artists—persuaded his friend Paul Gauguin to come. He decorated Gauguin's room with several humble canvases of sunflowers (now some of the world's priciest paintings), knowing that Gauguin had admired a similar painting he'd done in Paris. Their plan was for Gauguin to be the "dean" of a new art school in Arles, and Vincent its instructor-in-chief. At first, the two got along well. They spent days side by side, rendering the same subject in their two distinct styles. At night they hit the bars and brothels. Van Gogh's well-known *Café at Night* captures the glow of an absinthe buzz at Café la Nuit on Place du Forum.

After two months together, the two artists clashed over art and personality differences (Vincent was a slob around the house, whereas Gauguin was meticulous). The night of December 23, they were drinking absinthe at the café when Vincent suddenly went ballistic. He threw his glass at Gauguin. Gauguin left. Walking through Place Victor Hugo, Gauguin heard footsteps behind him and turned to see Vincent coming at him, brandishing a razor.

Gauguin quickly fled town. The local paper reported what happened next: "At 11:30 p.m., Vincent Vaugogh [*sic*], painter from Holland, appeared at the brothel at no. 1, asked for Rachel, and gave her his cut-off earlobe, saying, 'Treasure this precious object.' Then he vanished." He woke up the next morning at home with his head wrapped in a bloody towel and his earlobe missing. Was Vincent emulating a successful matador, whose prize is cutting off the bull's ear?

• *From here, retrace your steps a bit: Turn right to walk through the Place de la République, turn right in the far corner, and find the Arlaten Folk Museum. Turn left on Rue Président Wilson, and find Espace Van Gogh (on the right). There's an easel in the center of the courtyard.*

❾ **Espace Van Gogh Easel:** Vincent was checked into the local hospital—today's Espace Van Gogh cultural center (the Espace is free, but only the courtyard is open to the public). It surrounds a flowery courtyard that the artist loved and painted when he was being treated for blood loss as well as for hallucinations and severe depression that left him bedridden for a month. The citizens of
Arles circulated a petition demanding that the mad Dutchman be kept under medical supervision. Félix Rey, Vincent's kind doctor, worked out a compromise: The artist could leave during the day so that he could continue painting, but he had to sleep at the hospital at night. Look through the postcards sold in the courtyard and find a painting of Vincent's ward showing nuns attending to patients in a gray hall *(Ward of Arles Hospital)*.

In the spring of 1889, the bipolar genius (a modern diagnosis) admitted himself to the St. Paul Monastery and Hospital in St-Rémy, where he spent a year, thriving in the care of nurturing doctors and nuns. Painting was part of his therapy, so they
gave him a studio to work in, and he produced more than 100 paintings. Alcohol-free and institutionalized, he did some of his wildest work. With thick, swirling brushstrokes and surreal colors, he made his placid surroundings throb with restless energy. Today, at the hospital in St-Rémy, you can see a replica of his room and his studio, plus

many scenes he painted *in situ* like these in Arles—the courtyard, the plane trees, the view out the upstairs window of nearby fields, and the rugged Alpilles Mountains.

In the spring of 1890, Vincent left Provence to be cared for by a doctor in Auvers-sur-Oise, north of Paris. On July 27, he wandered into a field and shot himself. He died two days later.

• *To see paintings by artists inspired by Van Gogh, return to Rue de la République. Follow it to Rue Jouvène, turn right, then take a left on Rue Tour du Fabre. You'll be in Place Honoré Clair, where the ❿ Fondation Van Gogh is at #5 (reopens in the summer of 2013; described on page 680).*

The final easels are less central, but easily located and worth the effort for Van Gogh fans.

Bridge Easels: The ⓫ **Trinquetaille Bridge** is on the river walkway toward the Ancient History Museum (the current bridge is a 1951 replacement). Most famous, the **Langlois Drawbridge** is 1.5 miles south of town, along a Rhône canal (today's bridge is a 1926 duplicate of the original).

Near Arles

The Camargue—Knocking on Arles' doorstep, this is one of the few truly "wild" areas of France, where pink flamingos, wild bulls, nasty boars, nastier mosquitoes (in every season but winter—come prepared), and the famous white horses wander freely through lagoons and tall grass. It's a ▲▲ sight for nature lovers, but underwhelming for others. While possible by public transportation, it's ideal by car. The best route to follow is toward **Salin de Giraud:** Leave Arles on D-570 toward Stes-Maries-de-la-Mer, passing the D-36 turnoff to Salin de Giraud (you'll return along this route). After about 10 kilometers (6 miles), consider a stop at the Camarguais Museum. Next, continue along D-570, then turn left on D-37 toward Salin de Giraud and follow it as it skirts the Etang de Vaccarès lagoon. The lagoon itself is off-limits, but this area has views and good opportunities to get out of the car and smell the marshes. Turn right off D-37 onto the tiny road at Villeneuve, following signs for *C-134* to La Capelière and La Fiélouse. The best part of the Camargue (particularly in spring) awaits at **La Digue de la Mer,** about 10 scenic kilometers (6 miles) past La Capelière. A rough dirt road rising above water on both sides greets travelers; it's time to get out of your car and stroll (though you can drive on for about 5 kilometers/3 miles to Phare de la Gacholle). This is a critical reproduction area for flamingos (about 5,000 offspring annually), so it's your best chance to see groups of mamas and papas up close and personal.

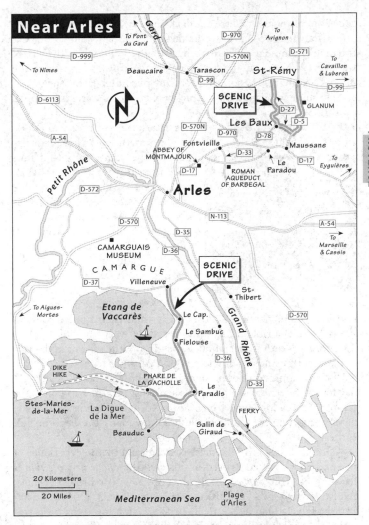

Experiences in Arles

▲▲**Markets**—On Wednesday and Saturday mornings, Arles' ring road erupts into an open-air festival of fish, flowers, produce, and you-name-it. The main event is on Saturday, with vendors jamming the ring road from Boulevard Emile Combes to the east, along Boulevard des Lices near the TI (the heart of the market), and continuing down Boulevard Georges Clemenceau to the west. Wednesday's market runs only along Boulevard Emile Combes, between Place Lamartine and bis Avenue Victor Hugo;

the segment nearest Place Lamartine is all about food, and the upper half features clothing, tablecloths, purses, and so on. On the first Wednesday of the month, a flea market doubles the size of the usual Wednesday market along Boulevard des Lices near the main TI. Join in: Buy some flowers for your hotelier, try the olives, sample some wine, and swat a pickpocket. Both markets are open until 12:30.

▲▲**Bullgames (Courses Camarguaises)**—Provençal "bull-games" are held in Arles and in neighboring towns. Those in Arles

occupy the same seats that fans have used for nearly 2,000 years, and take in Arles' most memorable experience—the *courses camarguaises* in the ancient arena. The nonviolent bullgames are more sporting than bloody bullfights (though traditional Spanish-style bullfights still take place on occasion). The bulls of Arles (who, locals stress, "die of old age") are promoted in posters even more boldly than their human foes. In the bullgame, a ribbon *(cocarde)* is laced between the bull's horns. The *razeteur,* with a special hook, has 15 minutes to snare the ribbon. Local businessmen encourage a *razeteur* (dressed in white with a red cummerbund) by shouting out how much money they'll pay for the *cocarde.* If the bull pulls a good stunt, the band plays the famous "Toreador" song from *Carmen.* The following day, newspapers report on the games, including how many *Carmens* the bull earned.

Three classes of bullgames—determined by the experience of the *razeteurs*—are advertised in posters: The *course de protection* is for rookies. The *trophée de l'Avenir* comes with more experience. And the *trophée des As* features top professionals. During Easter and the fall rice-harvest festival *(Féria du Riz),* the arena hosts traditional Spanish bullfights as it has for 150 years (look for *corrida*) with outfits, swords, spikes, and the whole gory shebang.

Don't pass on a chance to see *Toro Piscine,* a silly spectacle for warm summer evenings where the bull ends up in a swimming pool (uh-huh...get more details at TI). Nearby villages stage *courses camarguaises* in small wooden bullrings nearly every weekend; TIs have the latest schedule, or check online at www.ffcc.info.

Cost and Hours: Arles' bullgame tickets usually run €5-15; bullfights are pricier (€14-80). Schedules vary (usually July-Aug on Wed and Fri)—ask at the TI or check online at www.arenes-arles .com.

Sleeping in Arles

Hotels are a great value here—many are air-conditioned, though few have elevators. The Calendal, Musée, and Régence hotels offer exceptional value.

$$$ Hôtel le Calendal*** is a seductive place located between the Roman Arena and Classical Theater. Enter an expertly run hotel with airy lounges and a lovely palm-shaded courtyard. Enjoy the elaborate €12 buffet breakfast, have lunch in the courtyard or at the inexpensive sandwich bar (daily 12:00-15:00), and take advantage of their four free laptops for guests. You'll also find a Jacuzzi and a spa with a Turkish bath, hot pool, and massages at good rates. The comfortable rooms sport Provençal decor and come in all shapes and sizes (standard Db-€119, larger or balcony Db-€139, spacious Db-€169, Tb/Qb-€169, air-con, Wi-Fi, reserve ahead for parking-€8, just above arena at 5 Rue Porte de Laure, tel. 04 90 96 11 89, fax 04 90 96 05 84, www.lecalendal.com, contact@le calendal.com). Ask about their studio apartments. They also run the nearby, budget La Maison du Pelerin, described later.

$$$ Hôtel d'Arlatan***, built on the site of a Roman basilica, offers faded elegance in a classy shell. It has comfy public spaces, a tranquil terrace, a pool, and a range of rooms, many with high, wood-beamed ceilings and stone walls (a newer wing has more modern rooms). In the lobby of this 15th-century building, a glass floor looks down into Roman ruins. Hallway carpets are worn, and some rooms could use some TLC, but the place is still a fair value if Old World charm trumps updated amenities (standard

---

Sleep Code

(€1 = about $1.30, country code: 33)
S = Single, **D** = Double/Twin, **T** = Triple, **Q** = Quad, **b** = bathroom, **s** = shower only, ***** = French hotel rating system (0-5 stars). Unless otherwise noted, credit cards are accepted and English is spoken.

To help you sort easily through these listings, I've divided the accommodations into three categories based on the price for a standard double room with bath:

$$$ Higher Priced—Most rooms €90 or more.
$$ Moderately Priced—Most rooms between €65-90.
$ Lower Priced—Most rooms €65 or less.

Prices can change without notice; verify the hotel's current rates online or by email.

PROVENCE

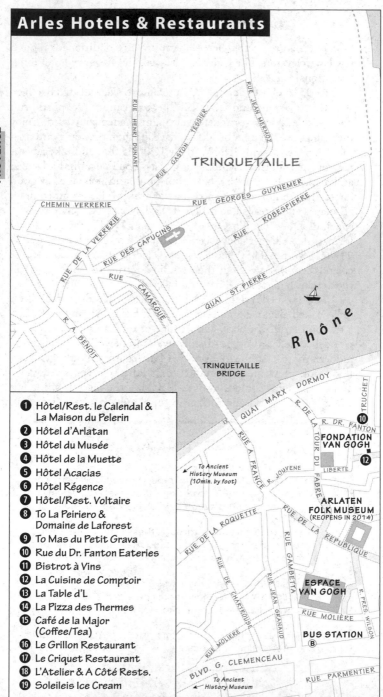

Arles Hotels & Restaurants

TRINQUETAILLE

RUE HENRI DUNANT

RUE GASTON TESSIER

RUE JEAN MERMOZ

CHEMIN VERRERIE

RUE GEORGES GUYNEMER

RUE DES CAPUCINS

RUE ROBESPIERRE

RUE DE LA VERRERIE

RUE CAMARGUE

QUAI ST. PIERRE

R. A. BENOIT

Rhône

TRINQUETAILLE BRIDGE

QUAI MARX DORMOY

RUE A. FRANCE

RUE DE LA TOUR DU FABRE

R. DE LA FANTON

R. DR. FANTON

TRUCHET

FONDATION VAN GOGH

To Ancient History Museum (10min. by foot)

R. JOUVENE

LIBERTE

ARLATEN FOLK MUSEUM (REOPENS IN 2014)

RUE DE LA ROQUETTE

RUE DE LA REPUBLIQUE

RUE DE CHARTROUSE

RUE GAMBETTA

RUE JEAN GRANAUD

ESPACE VAN GOGH

RUE MOLIERE

R. PRES. WILSON

RUE MOLIERE

BUS STATION (B)

BLVD. G. CLEMENCEAU

RUE PARMENTIER

To Ancient History Museum

1. Hôtel/Rest. le Calendal & La Maison du Pelerin
2. Hôtel d'Arlatan
3. Hôtel du Musée
4. Hôtel de la Muette
5. Hôtel Acacias
6. Hôtel Régence
7. Hôtel/Rest. Voltaire
8. To La Peiriero & Domaine de Laforest
9. To Mas du Petit Grava
10. Rue du Dr. Fanton Eateries
11. Bistrot à Vins
12. La Cuisine de Comptoir
13. La Table d'L
14. La Pizza des Thermes
15. Café de la Major (Coffee/Tea)
16. Le Grillon Restaurant
17. Le Criquet Restaurant
18. L'Atelier & A Côté Rests.
19. Soleileis Ice Cream

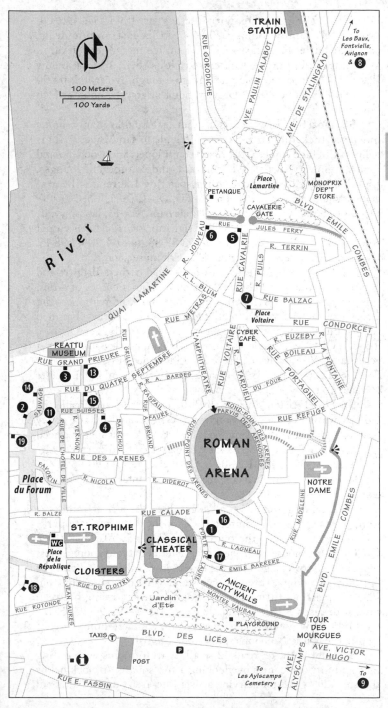

TRAIN STATION

To Les Baux, Fontvielle, Avignon & 8

Place Lamartine

PETANQUE

MONOPRIX DEP'T STORE

CAVALERIE GATE

BLVD. EMILE COMBES

100 Meters
100 Yards

R i v e r

RUE GORODICHE

AVE. PAULIN TALABOT

AVE. DE STALINGRAD

RUE JULES FERRY

R. JOUVEAU

RUE CAVALRIE

R. TERRIN

R. PUILS

RUE BALZAC

RUE

CONDORCET

RUE

6 5

7

Place Voltaire

QUAI LAMARTINE

RUE L. BLUM

RUE METRASSN

RUE DU QUATRE SEPTEMBRE

CYBER CAFÉ

R. EUZEBY

LA FONTAINE

RUE BOILEAU

RUE PORTAGNEL

DU FOUR

RUE VOLTAIRE

L'AMPHITHEATRE

RUE GRILLE

RUE GRAND PRIEURE

REATTU MUSEUM

3   13

14

2

11   15

19   4

SAUVAGE

RUE SUISSES

R. VERNON

BALECHOU

R. A. BARBES

R. RASPAIL

R. BRIAND

R. FAURE

RUE DES ARENES

RUE DE L'HOTEL DE VILLE

FAVORIN

R. NICOLAI

R. BALZE

Place du Forum

R. TARDIEU

ROND-POINT DES ARENES

PARVIS DES ARENES

ROND-POINT DES ARENOISES

ROMAN ARENA

RUE REFUGE

RUE MADELEINE

NOTRE DAME

ST. TROPHIME

WC

Place de la République

CLOISTERS

RUE DU CLOITRE

R. JEAN JAURES

RUE ROTONDE

18

RUE CALADE

CLASSICAL THEATER

PORTE DE LAURE

R. L'AGNEAU

R. EMILE BARRERE

1   16

17

R. DIDEROT

Jardin d'Ete

MONTEE VAUBAN

ANCIENT CITY WALLS

PLAYGROUND

BLVD. EMILE COMBES

TOUR DES MOURGUES

TAXIS

POST

P

BLVD. DES LICES

To Les Alyscamps Cemetery

AVE. ALYSCAMPS

AVE. VICTOR HUGO

To 9

RUE E. FASSIN

Db-€85-137, bigger Db with terrace or Tb-€157, Db/Qb suites-€180, family rooms-€200-247, killer last-minute deals, excellent buffet breakfast-€15, air-con, ice machines, elevator, Wi-Fi, parking garage-€15, closed Nov-April, 1 block below Place du Forum at 26 Rue du Sauvage—tough by car, tel. 04 90 93 56 66, fax 04 90 49 68 45, www.hotel-arlatan.fr, hotel-arlatan @wanadoo.fr).

PROVENCE

$$ Hôtel du Musée** is a quiet, affordable manor-home hideaway tucked deep in Arles (difficult to find by car). This delightful refuge comes with 28 air-conditioned and wood-floored rooms, a flowery two-tiered courtyard, and comfortable lounges. Lighthearted Claude and English-speaking Laurence, the gracious owners, are eager to help (Sb-€65, Db-€70-85, Tb-€90-100, Qb-€140, buffet breakfast-€8.50, no elevator, Wi-Fi, laptop available for guests, garage-€10, follow signs to *Réattu Museum* to 11 Rue du Grand Prieuré, tel. 04 90 93 88 88, fax 04 90 49 98 15, www.hoteldumusee.com, contact@hoteldumusee.com). ·

$$ Hôtel de la Muette**, with reserved owners Brigitte and Alain, is another good choice. Located in a quiet corner of Arles, this low-key hotel is well kept, with stone walls, brown tones, and a small terrace in front. You'll pay a bit more for the upgraded rooms, but it's money well spent (most Db-€66, bigger Db-€75, Tb-€77, Qb-€92, buffet breakfast-€8, air-con, no elevator, Internet access and Wi-Fi, private garage-€8, 15 Rue des Suisses, tel. 04 90 96 15 39, fax 04 90 49 73 16, www.hotel-muette.com, hotel.muette @wanadoo.fr).

$$ Hôtel Acacias**, just off Place Lamartine and inside the old city walls, is a modern hotel with less personality. The pretty pastel rooms are on the small side, but they're reasonably priced (standard Sb-€55, Db-€65-74, extra bed-€15, breakfast-€6, air-con, elevator, Wi-Fi, 2 Rue de la Cavalerie, tel. 04 90 96 37 88, fax 04 90 96 32 51, www.hotel-acacias.com, contact@hotel-acacias .com).

$ Hôtel Régence**, a top budget deal, has a riverfront location, immaculate and comfortable Provençal rooms, safe parking, and easy access to the train station (Db-€55-70, Tb-€70-85, Qb-€80-100, choose river view or quieter courtyard rooms, most rooms have showers, good buffet breakfast-€7, air-con, no elevator but only two floors, Internet access and Wi-Fi, garage-€6; from Place Lamartine, turn right immediately after passing between towers to reach 5 Rue Marius Jouveau; tel. 04 90 96 39 85, fax 04 90 96 67 64, www.hotel-regence.com, contact@hotel-regence .com). The gentle Nouvions speak some English.

$ Hôtel Voltaire* rents 12 small, spartan rooms with ceiling fans and nifty balconies overlooking a fun square. A block below the arena, it's good for starving artists who aren't particular about cleanliness. Smiling owner "Mr." Ferran (fur-ran) loves the States, and hopes you'll add to his postcard collection (D-€30, Ds-€35, Db-€40, 1 Place Voltaire, tel. 04 90 96 49 18, fax 04 90 96 45 49, levoltaire13@aol.com). They also serve a good-value lunch and dinner in their recommended restaurant.

$ La Maison du Pelerin offers spotless dorm rooms with three to six beds per room. It's a great value, just above the Roman Arena and Classical Theater, with a shared kitchen and homey living area. Book in advance by phone or email and get the door code. You can also check in next door at the recommended Hôtel le Calendal (they own the place). Sheets are included (€25/person, shared bath, must pay in advance, Wi-Fi, 26 Place Pomme, mobile 06 99 71 11 89, www.arles-pelerins.fr).

PROVENCE

Near Arles

Many drivers, particularly those with families, prefer staying outside Arles in the peaceful countryside, with easy access to the area's sights. See also "Sleeping in and near Les Baux," on page 733.

$$$ La Peiriero*, 15 minutes from Arles in the town of Fontvieille, is a pooped parent's dream come true, with a grassy garden, massive heated pool, table tennis, badminton, massage parlor, indoor children's play area, and even a few miniature golf holes. The spacious family-loft rooms, capable of sleeping up to five, have full bathrooms on both levels. This complete retreat also comes with a terrace café and a well-respected restaurant, and helpful owners, the Levys (streetside Sb or Db-€100, garden-side Db-€120, Db with terrace-€141, loft-€218, dinner *menu*-€31, breakfast and dinner-€38, air-con, Wi-Fi, free parking, just east of Fontvieille on road to Les Baux, 34 Avenue des Baux, tel. 04 90 54 76 10, fax 04 90 54 62 60, www.hotel-peiriero.com, info@hotel-peiriero.com). Just a short drive from Arles and Les Baux (and 20 minutes from Avignon), little Fontvieille slumbers in the shadows of its big-city cousins—though it has its share of restaurants and boutiques.

$$$ Mas du Petit Grava is a vintage Provençal farmhouse 15 tree-lined minutes east of Arles. Here California refugees Jim and Ike offer four large and well-cared-for rooms with tubs, tiles, and memories of Vincent (Jim is an expert on Van Gogh's life and art—ask him anything). A lovely garden surrounds a generously sized pool, but what draws most here are Jim and Ike. Book this place early (Db-€110-130, includes a fine breakfast, no air-con, free Wi-Fi, tel. 04 90 98 35 66, www.masdupetitgrava.net, masdupetit grava@masdupetitgrava.net). From Arles, drive east on D-453 toward St-Martin de Crau (2.5 kilometers/1.5 miles), then turn left on Route St. Hippolyte to the right of the large building (Massa Autopneu).

$$ Domaine de Laforest is ideally located a few minutes below Fontvieille, near the aqueduct of Barbegal. It's a big 320-acre spread engulfed by vineyards, rice fields, and swaying trees. The sweet owners (Sylvie and mama Mariette) have eight two-bedroom apartments with great weekly rates, though they may be rented for fewer days when available (€310, €400, or €700 per week, air-con, washing machines, Wi-Fi in all apartments, pool, big lawn, swings, 1000 Route de l'Aqueduc Romain, tel. 04 90 54 70 25, fax 04 90 54 60 50, www.domaine-laforest.com, contact @domaine-laforest.com).

Eating in Arles

You can dine well in Arles on a modest budget—in fact, it's hard to blow a lot on dinner here (most of my listings have *menus* for under €25). The bad news is that restaurants change regularly, so double-check my suggestions. Before dinner, go local on Place du Forum and enjoy a *pastis*. This anise-based apéritif is served straight in a glass with ice, plus a carafe of water—dilute to taste. Sunday is a quiet night for restaurants, though most eateries on Place du Forum are open.

For **picnics,** a big, handy Monoprix supermarket/department store is on Place Lamartine (Mon-Thu 8:30-19:30, Fri-Sat 8:30-20:00, closed Sun).

On or near Place du Forum

Great atmosphere and mediocre food at fair prices await on Place du Forum. By all accounts, the garish yellow Café la Nuit is worth avoiding. Most other cafés on the square deliver acceptable quality and terrific ambience. For better cuisine, wander away from the square.

On Rue du Dr. Fanton

A half-block below the Forum, on Rue du Dr. Fanton, lies a terrific lineup of restaurants. Come here to peruse your options side by side. You can't go wrong—all offer good value and have appealing indoor and outdoor seating.

Le 16 is a warm, affordable place to enjoy a fresh salad (€10) or a fine two- or three-course dinner (€20-€25). The choices are limited, so check the selection before sitting down. The goat cheese *croustillant* salad and *taureau* (bull's meat) in a tasty sauce make a fine combination (closed Sat-Sun, 16 Rue du Dr. Fanton, tel. 04 90 93 77 36).

Le Gaboulet is a popular local spot, blending a cozy interior, classic French cuisine, and service with a smile (thanks to owner

Frank). It's the most expensive of the places I list on this street, but it's still busy. If it's cold out, the huge chimney should be lit (€27 *menu*, great fries, closed Sun-Mon, 18 Rue du Dr. Fanton, tel. 04 90 93 18 11).

Au Brin du Thym, next door, offers a reliable blend of traditional French and Provençal cuisine at very fair prices. Arrive early for an outdoor table or call ahead, and let hardworking and formal Monsieur and Madame Colombaud and their daughter take care of you. Monsieur does *le cooking* while Madame does *le serving* (€14 lunch *menu;* excellent à la carte choices: €9 starters, €16 *plats;* closed Tue, 22 Rue du Dr. Fanton, tel. 04 90 49 95 96).

Le Plaza, next to Au Brin, features tasty Provençal cuisine served in a fine setting at good prices (€22 *menu,* closed Wed, 28 Rue du Dr. Fanton, tel. 04 90 96 33 15).

Bistrot à Vins suits wine lovers who enjoy pairing food and drink, and those in search of a good glass of *vin.* Sit at a convivial counter or at one of five tables while listening to light jazz (book ahead for a table). Affable Ariane speaks enough English and offers a limited selection of simple, tasty dishes. Her savory tarts and fresh green salad make a great meal (€10-16), and the wines—many available by the glass—are well priced (indoor dining only from 18:30 to 22:00, closed Mon-Tue, 2 Rue du Dr. Fanton, tel. 04 90 52 00 65).

Other Places near Place du Forum

At **La Cuisine de Comptoir,** a cool little bistro, locals of all ages abandon Provençal decor. Welcoming owners Alexandre and Vincent offer light *tartine* dinners—a delicious cross between pizza and bruschetta, served with soup or salad for just €11 (a swinging deal—the *brandada* is tasty and filling). Sit at the counter and watch *le chef* at work as you sip your €2 glass of rosé in fine glassware (closed Sun, mostly indoor dining, just off Place du Forum's lower end at 10 Rue de la Liberté, tel. 04 90 96 86 28).

La Table d'L has mod decor and is warmly run by eager-to-please waitress Ellie and chef Jay. Relatively new to Arles, Jay worked in a restaurant in New York for 17 years. The selection is limited but the quality is not. Jay loves her lamb and fish, and so will you (€8-21 starters, €24-34 *plats,* reasonably priced wine list, closed Mon, 1 bis Rue Réattu, tel. 04 90 96 32 53).

La Pizza des Thermes is a welcoming eatery with comfortable indoor and outdoor seating a few blocks north of Place du Forum. It serves good pizza and pasta for €9-12 (daily, 6 Rue du Sauvage, tel. 04 90 49 60 64).

Café de la Major is *the* place to go to recharge with some serious coffee or tea (closed Sun, 7 bis Rue Réattu, tel. 04 90 96 14 15).

Near the Roman Arena

For about the same price as on Place du Forum, you can enjoy regional cuisine with a point-blank view of the arena. Because they change regularly, the handful of (mostly) outdoor eateries that overlook the arena are pretty indistinguishable.

Le Grillon, with the best view above the arena, offers friendly service (say *bonjour* to smiling Nordine) and good-enough salads (the *camarguaise* is a riot of color), pizza and tasty *tartines* for €10 (including small salad), and *plats du jour* for €10-14 (closed all day Wed and Sun nights, at the top of the arena on Rond-point des Arènes, tel. 04 90 96 70 97).

Le Criquet is a sweet little place serving Provençal classics with joy at good prices two blocks above the arena. If you're really hungry, try the €25 *bourride*—a creamy fish soup thickened with aioli and garlic and stuffed with mussels, clams, calamari, and more (good €19-26 three-course *menus,* indoor and outdoor dining, 21 Rue Porte de Laure, tel. 04 90 96 80 51).

For details on the next two places, see their listings under "Sleeping in Arles," earlier: **Hôtel le Calendal** serves lunch in its lovely courtyard (€12-18, daily 12:00-15:00) or delicious little sandwiches for €2.50 each at its small café. **Hôtel Voltaire,** well-situated on a pleasing square, serves simple three-course lunches and dinners at honest prices to a loyal clientele (€13 *menus*; hearty *plats* and filling salads for €10—try the *salade fermière, salade Latine,* or the filling *assiette Provençale;* closed Sun evening).

A Gastronomic Dining Experience

One of France's most recognized chefs, Jean-Luc Rabanel, has created a sensation with two very different options 50 yards from Place de la République (at 7 Rue des Carmes). They sit side by side, both offering indoor and terrace seating.

L'Atelier is so intriguing that people travel great distances just for the experience. Diners fork over €95 (at lunch, you'll spoon out €55) and trust the chef to create a memorable meal...which he does. There is no menu, just an onslaught of delicious taste sensations served in artsy dishes. Don't plan on a quick dinner, and don't come for the setting—it's a contemporary, shoebox-shaped dining room, but several outdoor tables are also available. The get-to-know-your-neighbor atmosphere means you can't help but join the party. You'll probably spot the famous chef (hint: he has long brown hair), as he is very hands-on with his waitstaff (closed

Mon-Tue, best to book ahead, friendly servers will hold your hand through this palate-widening experience, tel. 04 90 91 07 69, www.rabanel.com).

A Côté saddles up next door, offering a smart wine bar/bistro ambience and top-quality cuisine for far less. Here you can sample the famous chef's talents for as little as €18 (daily *plat*) or as much as €38 (three-course *menu*, smallish servings, reasonably priced wines, open daily, tel. 04 90 47 61 13).

And for Dessert...

Soleileis has Arles' best ice cream, with all-natural ingredients and unusual flavors such as *fadoli*—olive oil mixed with nougatine. There's also a shelf of English books for exchange (open daily 14:00-18:30, across from recommended Le 16 restaurant at 9 Rue du Dr. Fanton).

Arles Connections

Some trains in and out of Arles require a **reservation**. These include connections with Nice to the east and Bordeaux to the west (including intermediary stops). Ask at the station.

From Arles by Train to: Paris (11/day, 2 direct TGVs—4 hours, 9 with transfer in Avignon—5 hours), **Avignon Centre-Ville** (roughly hourly, 20 minutes, less frequent in the afternoon), **Nîmes** (9/day, 30 minutes), **Orange** (4/day direct, 35 minutes, more frequent with transfer in Avignon), **Aix-en-Provence Centre-Ville** (10/day, 2.25 hours, transfer in Marseille, train may separate midway—be sure you're in section going to Aix-en-Provence), **Marseille** (11/day, 1.5 hours), **Cassis** (7/day, 2 hours), **Carcassonne** (8/day, 2.5-3.75 hours, most with transfer in Nîmes or Avignon, direct trains may require reservations), **Beaune** (10/day, 4.5-5 hours, 9 with transfer in Lyon and Nîmes or Avignon), **Nice** (11/day, 3.75-4.5 hours, most require transfer in Marseille), **Barcelona** (2/day, 6 hours,), **Italy** (3/day transfer in Marseille and Nice; from Arles, it's 4.5-5 hours to Ventimiglia on the border, 8 hours to Milan, 9.5 hours to Cinque Terre, 11-12 hours to Florence, and 13 hours to Venice or Rome).

From Arles Train Station to Avignon TGV Station: If you're going to the TGV station in Avignon, it's easiest to take the SNCF bus directly there from Arles' train station (10/day, 1 hour, €7, included with railpass). Another option—which takes the same amount of time, but adds more walking—is to take the regular train from Arles to Avignon's Centre-Ville Station, then catch the *navette* (shuttle bus) to the TGV Station from there.

From Arles by Bus to: Nîmes (bus #C30, 6/day, 1 hour, €1.50), **St-Rémy-de-Provence** (bus #54, 3/day Mon-Sat, none on Sun, 50 minutes; bus #59 also goes to St-Rémy via Les Baux—see below, €2.20), **Fontvieille** (6/day, 10 minutes), **Camargue/Stes-Maries-de-la-Mer** (bus #20, 6/day including Sun, 1 hour). The bus station is at 16-24 Boulevard Georges Clemenceau (2 blocks below main TI, next to Café le Wilson). Bus info: tel. 04 90 49 38 01 (unlikely to speak English).

From Arles by Bus to Les Baux and St-Rémy: Bus #59 connects Arles to **Les Baux** and **St-Rémy** (6/day daily July-Aug, Sat-Sun only in June and Sept; 35 minutes to Les Baux, 50 minutes to St-Rémy, then runs between St-Rémy and Avignon as bus #57). Bus #54 (see above) also goes to St-Rémy but not via Les Baux. Buses to Les Baux and St-Rémy depart from Arles' central bus station and from the train station. For other ways to reach Les Baux and St-Rémy, see page 727.

Avignon

Famous for its nursery rhyme, medieval bridge, and brooding Palace of the Popes, contemporary Avignon (ah-veen-yohn) bustles and prospers behind its mighty walls. During the 94 years (1309-1403) that Avignon starred as the *Franco Vaticano* (the temporary residence of the popes) and hosted two antipopes, it grew from a quiet village into a thriving city. With its large student population and fashionable shops, today's Avignon is an intriguing blend of medieval history, youthful energy, and urban sophistication. Street performers entertain the international throngs who fill Avignon's ubiquitous cafés and trendy boutiques. If you're here in July, be prepared for big crowds and higher  prices, thanks to the rollicking theater festival. (Reserve your hotel far in advance.) Clean, lively, and popular with tourists, Avignon is more impressive for its outdoor ambience than for its museums and monuments.

Orientation to Avignon

Cours Jean Jaurès, which turns into Rue de la République, runs straight from the Centre-Ville train station to Place de l'Horloge and the Palace of the Popes, splitting Avignon in two. The larger eastern half is where the action is. Climb to the Jardin du Rochers des Doms for the town's best view, consider touring the pope's immense palace, lose yourself in Avignon's back streets (you can follow my "Discovering Avignon's Back Streets" self-guided walk), and find a shady square to call home. Avignon's shopping district fills the traffic-free streets near where Rue de la République meets Place de l'Horloge. As you wander, look for signs in Occitan—the language of the Occitania region; you might see the name of the city written as "Avinhon" or "Avignoun."

Tourist Information

The **main TI** is between the Centre-Ville train station and the old town, at 41 Cours Jean Jaurès (April-Oct Mon-Sat 9:00-18:00—until 19:00 in July, Sun 9:45-17:00; Nov-March Mon-Fri 9:00-18:00, Sat 9:00-17:00, Sun 10:00-12:00; tel. 04 32 74 32 74, www.avignon-tourisme.com). From April through mid-October, a branch TI office is open inside **Les Halles market** (Fri-Sun 10:00-13:00, closed Mon-Thu). At any TI, get the helpful map. If you're staying awhile, pick up the free *Guide Pratique* (info on bike rentals, hotels, apartment rentals, events, and museums).

Sightseeing Pass: Everyone should pick up the free **Avignon Passion Pass** (valid 15 days, for up to five family members). Get the pass stamped when you pay full price at your first sight, and then receive reductions at the others (for example, €2 less at the Palace of the Popes and €3 less at the Petit Palais). The discounts add up—always show your Passion Pass when buying a ticket. The pass comes with the Avignon "Passion" map and guide, which includes several good (but tricky-to-follow) walking tours.

Arrival in Avignon

By Train

Avignon has two train stations: TGV (linked to downtown by frequent shuttle buses) and Centre-Ville. While most TGV trains serve only the TGV Station, some also stop at Centre-Ville—verify your station in advance.

TGV Station (Gare TGV): This shiny new station, on the  outskirts of town, has no baggage storage (bags can be stored only at the Centre-Ville train station).

To get to the city center, take the *navette*/**shuttle bus** (marked *Navette/Avignon Centre;* €1.20, buy ticket from driver, 3/hour, 15 minutes). To find the bus stop, leave the station by the north exit *(sortie nord)*, walk down the stairs, and find the long bus shelter to the left. In downtown Avignon, you'll arrive at a stop just

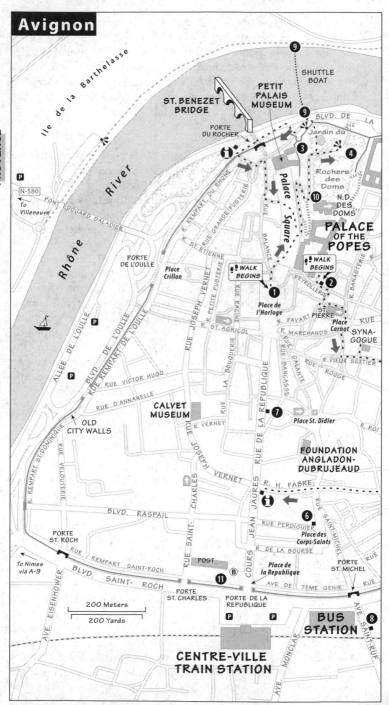

Avignon

PROVENCE

Ile de la Barthelasse

Rhône River

ST. BENEZET BRIDGE

PETIT PALAIS MUSEUM

SHUTTLE BOAT

9

PORTE DU ROCHER

BLVD. DE LA

Jardin du

9

3

4

Rochers des Doms

10

N.D. DES DOMS

PALACE OF THE POPES

N-580
To Villeneuve

PONT EDOUARD DALADIER

R. REMPART DU RHÔNE

R. RUE GRANDE FUSTERIE

R. ST. ETIENNE

Palace Square

RUE BALANCE

PORTE DE L'OULLE

Place Crillon

R. PETITE FUSTERIE

RUE RACINE

WALK BEGINS

1

WALK BEGINS

2

PEYROLLERIE

R. BANASTERIE

ALLÉE DE L'OULLE

BLVD. DE L'OULLE

RUE REMPART DE L'OULLE

RUE JOSEPH VERNET

R. ST. AGRICOL

Place de l'Horloge

R. FAVART

ST PIERRE

Place Carnot

RUE

P

RUE VICTOR HUGO

RUE LA BOUQUERIE

R. MARCHANDS

RUE GALANTE

RUE BANCASSE

RUE ROUGE

R.VIEUX SEXTIER

SYNA-GOGUE

RUE D'ANNANELLE

CALVET MUSEUM

R. VERNET

RUE DE LA REPUBLIQUE

7

Place St. Didier

R. ROI

OLD CITY WALLS

RUE VELOUTERIE

RUE JOSEPH VERNET

FOUNDATION ANGLADON-DUBRUJEAUD

R. REMPART ST-DOMINIQUE

RUE CHARLES VERNET

R. H. FABRE

i

6

RUE SAINT-MICHEL

P

BLVD. RASPAIL

RUE PERDIGUIER

Place des Corps-Saints

PORTE ST. ROCH

RUE SAINT-

COURS JEAN JAURES

RUE DE LA BOURSE

PORTE ST. MICHEL

To Nimes via A-9

RUE REMPART SAINT-ROCH

POST

B

11

Place de la République

AVE. DE 7EME GENIE

RUE

AVE. EISENHOWER

BLVD. SAINT- ROCH

PORTE ST. CHARLES

PORTE DE LA REPUBLIQUE

P

P

BUS STATION

8

AVE. SAINT-RUE

AVE. MONCLAR

CENTRE-VILLE TRAIN STATION

200 Meters
200 Yards

PROVENCE

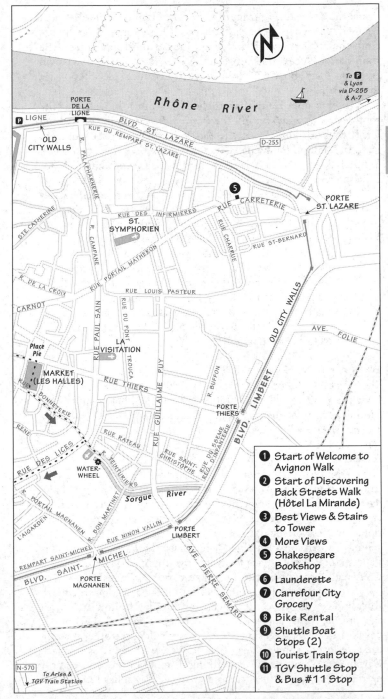

To **P** & Lyon via D-255 & A-7

Rhône River

PORTE DE LA LIGNE

P LIGNE

OLD CITY WALLS

BLVD. ST. LAZARE

RUE DU REMPART ST. LAZARE

D-255

R. PALAPHARNERIE

STE. CATHERINE

RUE DES INFIRMIERES

5

RUE CARRETERIE

PORTE ST. LAZARE

ST. SYMPHORIEN

R. CAMPANE

RUE CHARRUE

RUE ST-BERNARD

R. DE LA CROIX

RUE PORTAIL MATHERON

RUE LOUIS PASTEUR

OLD CITY WALLS

CARNOT

RUE PAUL SAIN

RUE DU PONT TROUCA

AVE. FOLIE

Place Pie

LA VISITATION

MARKET (LES HALLES)

RUE THIERS

RUE GUILLAUME PUY

R. BUFFON

PORTE THIERS

BONNETERIE

RENE

RUE RATEAU

RUE SAINT-CHRISTOPHE

RUE DU 58EME RÉGT. D'INFANTERIE

BLVD. LIMBERT

RUE DES LICES

R. JEINTURIERS

WATER-WHEEL

Sorgue River

L'AIGARDEN

R. PORTAIL MAGNANEN

R. BON MARTINET

RUE NINON VALLIN

PORTE LIMBERT

REMPART SAINT-MICHEL

BLVD. SAINT-MICHEL

PORTE MAGNANEN

AVE. PIERRE SEMARD

N-570

To Arles & TGV Train Station

1 Start of Welcome to Avignon Walk

2 Start of Discovering Back Streets Walk (Hôtel La Mirande)

3 Best Views & Stairs to Tower

4 More Views

5 Shakespeare Bookshop

6 Launderette

7 Carrefour City Grocery

8 Bike Rental

9 Shuttle Boat Stops (2)

10 Tourist Train Stop

11 TGV Shuttle Stop & Bus #11 Stop

inside the city walls, in front of the post office on Cours Président Kennedy (see map on page 700). From here you're three blocks from the city's main TI and two blocks from the Centre-Ville train station. A **taxi** ride between the TGV Station and downtown Avignon costs about €20 (to find taxis, exit the TGV Station via *sortie nord*).

To pick up a **rental car** at the TGV Station, walk out the south exit *(sortie sud)* to find the *location de voitures* in the parking lot. If you're driving directly to Arles, Les Baux, or the Luberon, leave the station, following signs to *Avignon Sud*, then *La Rocade*. You'll soon see exits to Arles (best for Les Baux) and Cavaillon (for Luberon villages).

If you're heading from the Avignon TGV Station to the **Arles train station,** catch the direct SNCF bus from the TGV Station's bus stop (10/day, 1 hour, €7, schedule posted on the shelter and available at any information booth inside the TGV Station).

Centre-Ville Station (Gare Avignon Centre-Ville): All non-TGV trains (and a few TGV trains) serve the central station. You can stash your bags here—exit the station to the left and look for the *consignes* sign (confirm closing time when you leave your bag). To reach the town center, cross the busy street in front of the station and walk through the city walls onto Cours Jean Jaurès. The TI is three blocks down, at #41.

By Bus

The dingy bus station *(gare routière)* is 100 yards to the right as you leave the Centre-Ville train station, beyond and below Hôtel Ibis (info desk open Mon-Sat 8:00-19:30, closed Sun, tel. 04 90 82 07 35, staff speaks a little English).

By Car

Drivers entering Avignon follow *Centre-Ville* and *Gare SNCF* (train station) signs. You'll find central pay lots (about €10/half-day, €15/day) in the garage next to the Centre-Ville train station, at the Parking Jean Jaurès under the ramparts across from the station. Two less pricey options are the Parking Les Halles in the center of town, on Place Pie ("pee"), and the Parking Palais des Papes. Hotels have advice for smart overnight parking, and some offer small discounts in the municipal parking garages.

Free or Cheap Parking: Two free lots have complimentary shuttle buses to the center except on Sunday (follow *P Gratuit* signs): One is just across Daladier Bridge (Pont Daladier) on Ile de la Barthelasse, with shuttles to Place Crillon; the other is along the river east of the Palace of the Popes, with shuttles to Place Carnot (both lots are within walking distance of the city center if need be). Parking on the street is free in the *bleu* zones 12:00-14:00

and 19:00-9:00. It's €2 for about three hours 9:00-12:00 and 14:00-19:00 (hint: if you put €2 in the meter after 19:00, it's good until 14:00 the next day). No matter where you park, leave nothing in your car.

Helpful Hints

Book Ahead for July: During the July theater festival, rooms are sparse—reserve very early, or stay in Arles.

Local Help: David at **Imagine Tours** (a nonprofit group whose goal is to promote this region) can help with hotel emergencies or tickets to special events (mobile 06 89 22 19 87, www .imagine-tours.net, imagine.tours@gmail.com). If you get no answer, leave a message.

Internet Access: The TI has a current list of Internet cafés, or you can ask your hotelier. Many bigger cafés provide free Wi-Fi to anyone who buys a drink.

English Bookstore: Try **Shakespeare Bookshop** (Tue-Sat 9:30-12:00 & 14:00-18:30, closed Sun-Mon, 155 Rue Carreterie, in Avignon's northeast corner, tel. 04 90 27 38 50).

Baggage Storage: You can leave your bags at Centre-Ville train station (see "Arrival in Avignon," earlier).

Laundry: The launderette at 66 Place des Corps-Saints, where Rue Agricol Perdiguier ends, has English instructions and is handy to most hotels (daily 7:00-20:00).

Grocery Store: Carrefour City is central and has long hours (Mon-Sat 7:00-22:00, Sun 9:00-12:00, next to McDonald's, 2 blocks from the TI, toward Place de l'Horloge on Rue de la République).

Bike Rental: You can rent bikes and scooters at **Provence Bike** (7 Avenue St. Ruf, tel. 04 90 27 92 61, www.provence-bike.com) You'll enjoy riding on the Ile de la Barthelasse, but biking is better in Isle-sur-la-Sorgue and Vaison la Romaine.

Car Rental: The TGV Station has car-rental agencies (open long hours daily).

Shuttle Boat: A free shuttle boat, the *Navette Fluviale,* plies back and forth across the river (as it did in the days when the town had no functioning bridge) from near St. Bénezet Bridge (daily July-Aug 11:00-21:00, Sept-June roughly 10:00-12:30 & 14:00-18:00, 3/hour). It drops you on the peaceful Ile de la Barthelasse, with its recommended riverside restaurant, grassy walks, and bike rides with terrific city views. If you stay on the island for dinner, check the schedule for the last return boat—or be prepared for a taxi ride or a pleasant 25-minute walk back to town.

Commanding City Views: For great views of Avignon and the river, walk or drive across Daladier Bridge, or ferry across the

Rhône on the *Navette Fluviale* (described above). I'd take the boat across the river, walk the view path to Daladier Bridge, and then cross back over the bridge (45-minute walk over mostly level ground). You can enjoy other impressive vistas from the top of the Jardin du Rochers des Doms, from the tower in the Palace of the Popes, from the end of the famous, broken St. Bénezet Bridge, and from the entrance to Fort St. André, across the river in Villeneuve-lès-Avignon.

Tours in Avignon

Walking Tours—On mid-season Mondays and Saturdays, the TI offers informative English walking tours of Avignon, which include a visit to the Palace of the Popes (€17, discounted with Avignon Passion Pass, April-June and Aug-Oct Mon at 10:30 and Sat at 14:30, no tours in July or Nov-March).

Tourist Trains—The little train leaves regularly from in front of the Palace of the Popes and offers a decent overview of the city, including the Jardin du Rochers des Doms and St. Bénezet Bridge (€7, 2/hour, 40 minutes, mid-March-mid-Oct daily 10:00-18:00, until 19:00 July-Aug, English commentary).

Guided Excursions—Several minivan tour companies based in Avignon offer transportation to destinations described in this chapter, including Pont du Gard, the Luberon, and the Camargue (about €65-80/person for all-day tours). See "Tours of Provence" on page 662 (note that guide François Marcou and Imagine Tours are both based in Avignon).

Self-Guided Walks

For a fine overview of the city, combine these two walks. "Welcome to Avignon" covers the major sights, while "Discovering Avignon's Back Streets" leads you along the lanes less taken, delving beyond the surface of this historic city.

▲▲Welcome to Avignon

Before starting this walk—which connects the city's top sights—be sure to pick up the Avignon Passion Pass at the TI, then show it when entering each attraction to receive discounted admission (explained earlier, under "Tourist Information").

• *Start your tour where the Romans did, on Place de l'Horloge, in front of City Hall (Hôtel de Ville).*

Place de l'Horloge

This café square was the town forum during Roman times and the market square through the Middle Ages. (Restaurants here offer good people-watching, but they also have less ambience and low-quality meals—you'll find better squares elsewhere to hang your beret in.) Named for a medieval clock tower mostly hidden behind City Hall (find plaque in English), this square's present popularity arrived with the trains in 1854. Walk a few steps to the center of the square, and look down the main drag, Rue de la République. When the trains came to Avignon, proud city fathers wanted a direct, impressive way to link the new station to the heart of the city (just like in Paris)—so they plowed over homes to create Rue de la République and widened Place de l'Horloge. This main drag's Parisian feel is intentional—it was built not in the Provençal manner, but in the Haussmann style that is so dominant in Paris (characterized by broad, straight boulevards lined with stately buildings).

• Walk uphill past the carousel (public WCs behind). Look up and follow the golden statue of Mary, floating high above the buildings. Veer right at the street's end, and continue into...

Palace Square (Place du Palais)

This grand square is lined with the Palace of the Popes, the Petit Palais, and the cathedral. In the 1300s, the entire headquarters of the Catholic Church was moved to Avignon. The Church bought Avignon and gave it a complete makeover. Along with clearing out vast spaces like this square and building this three-acre palace, the Church erected more than three miles of protective wall (with 39 towers), "appropriate" housing for cardinals (read: mansions), and residences for its entire bureaucracy. The city was Europe's largest construction zone. Avignon's population grew from 6,000 to 25,000 in short order. (Today, 13,000 people live within the walls.) The limits of pre-papal Avignon are outlined on city maps: Rues Joseph Vernet, Henri Fabre, des Lices, and Philonarde all follow the route of the city's earlier defensive wall.

The Petit Palais (Little Palace) seals the uphill end of the square and was built for a cardinal; today it houses medieval paintings (museum described later). The church just to the left of the Palace of the Popes is Avignon's cathedral. It predates the Church's purchase of Avignon by 200 years. Its small size reflects Avignon's modest, pre-papal population. The gilded Mary was added in 1854, when the Vatican established the doctrine of her Immaculate Conception. Mary is taller than the Palace of the Popes by design: The Vatican never accepted what it called the "Babylonian Captivity" and had a bad attitude about Avignon long after the pope was definitively back in Rome. There hasn't been a French pope since the Holy See returned to Rome—over 600 years ago. That's what I call a grudge.

Directly across the square from the palace's main entry stands a cardinal's residence, built in 1619 (now the Conservatoire National de Musique). Its fancy Baroque facade was a visual counterpoint to the stripped-down Huguenot aesthetic of the age. During this time, Provence was a hotbed of Protestantism—but, buried within this region, Avignon was a Catholic stronghold. Notice the stumps in front and nearby. Nicknamed *bites* (slang for the male anatomy), they effectively keep cars from double-parking in areas designed for people. Many of the metal ones slide up and down by remote control to let privileged cars come and go.

• *You can visit the massive **Palace of the Popes** (described on page 708) now, but it works better to visit that palace at the end of this walk, then continue directly to the "Discovering Avignon's Back Streets" walk, described later.*

Now is a good time to take in the...

Petit Palais Museum (Musée du Petit Palais)

This former cardinal's palace now displays the Church's collection of mostly medieval Italian painting (including one delightful Botticelli) and sculpture. All 350 paintings deal with Christian themes. A visit here before going to the Palace of the Popes helps furnish and populate that otherwise barren building, and a quick peek into its courtyard (even if you don't tour the museum) shows the importance of cardinal housing.

Cost and Hours: €6, €3 English brochure, some English explanations posted; Wed-Mon 10:00-13:00 & 14:00-18:00, closed Tue; at north end of Palace Square, tel. 04 90 86 44 58.

• *From Palace Square, we'll head up to the rocky hilltop where Avignon was first settled, then drop down to the river. With this short loop, you can enjoy a small park, hike to a grand river view, and visit Avignon's beloved broken bridge—an experience worth* ▲▲.

Start by climbing to the church level (you can fill your bottle with cold water here), then continue up to...

▲▲Jardin du Rochers des Doms

Though the park itself is a delight—with a sweet little café (good prices for food and drinks) and public WCs—don't miss the climax: a panoramic view of the Rhône River Valley and the broken bridge. For the best views (and the  favorite make-out spot for local teenagers later in the evening), find the terrace behind the odd zodiac display (across the grass from the pond-side park café, near the statue of Jean Althen). If the green fence is ruining it for you, stand on the short wall behind you, or detour a few minutes through the park (to the right, with the river on your left) to find a bigger terrace.

On a clear day, the tallest peak you see, with its white limestone cap, is Mont Ventoux ("Windy Mountain"). Below and just to the right, you'll spot free passenger ferries shuttling across the river (great views from path on other side of the river), and—tucked amidst the trees on the far side of the river—a fun, recommended restaurant, Le Bercail. The island in the river is the Ile de la Barthelasse, a nature preserve where Avignon can breathe.

Fort St. André (across the river on the hill; see the info plaque to the left) was built by the French in 1360, shortly after the pope moved to Avignon, to counter the papal incursion into this part of Europe. The castle was across the border, in the kingdom of France. Avignon's famous bridge was a key border crossing, with towers on either end—one was French, and the other was the pope's. The French one, across the river, is the Tower of Philip the Fair (described later, under "More Sights in Avignon").

Cost and Hours: Free, park gates open daily April-Sept 7:30-20:00, Oct-March 7:30-18:00.

• *From the smaller viewpoint (with the zodiac), take the stairs to the left (closed at night) down to the tower. You'll catch glimpses of the...*

Ramparts

The only bit of the rampart you can walk on is accessed from St. Bénezet Bridge (pay to enter—see next). Just after the papacy took control of Avignon, the walls were extended to take in the convents and monasteries that had been outside the city. What you see today was restored in the 19th century.

• *When you come out of the tower on street level, take the right-side exit and walk left along the wall to the old bridge. Pass under the bridge to find its entrance shortly after.*

▲▲St. Bénezet Bridge (Pont St. Bénezet)

This bridge, whose construction and location were inspired by a shepherd's religious vision, is the "Pont d'Avignon" of nursery-rhyme fame. The ditty (which you've probably been humming all day) dates back to the 15th century: *Sur le Pont d'Avignon, on y danse, on y danse, sur le Pont d'Avignon, on y danse tous en rond* ("On the bridge of Avignon, we will dance, we will dance, on the bridge of Avignon, we will dance all in a circle").

But the bridge was a big deal even outside of its kiddie-tune fame. Built between 1171 and 1185, it was the only bridge crossing the mighty Rhône in the Middle Ages—important to pilgrims, merchants, and armies. It was damaged several times by floods and subsequently rebuilt, until 1668, when most of it was knocked down by a disastrous icy flood. Lacking a government stimulus package, the townsfolk decided not to rebuild this time, and for more than a century, Avignon had no bridge across the Rhône. While only four arches survive today, the original bridge was huge: Imagine a 22-arch, 3,000-foot-long bridge extending from Vatican territory to the lonely Tower of Philip the Fair, which marked the beginning of France (see displays of the bridge's original length).

Cost and Hours: €4.50, includes audioguide, €13 combo-ticket includes Palace of the Popes, same hours as the Palace of the Popes (described next), tel. 04 90 27 51 16.

Visiting the Bridge: The ticket booth is housed in what was a medieval hospital for the poor (funded by bridge tolls). Admission includes a small room dedicated to the song of Avignon's bridge and your only chance to walk a bit of the ramparts (enter both from the tower). A Romanesque chapel on the bridge is dedicated to St. Bénezet. Though there's not much to see on the bridge, the audioguide included with your ticket tells a good enough story. It's also fun to be in the breezy middle of the river with a sweeping city view.

• *To get to the Palace of the Popes from here, exit left, then turn left again back into the walls. Walk to the end of the short street, then turn right following signs to* Palais des Papes. *Next, look for brown signs leading left under the passageway. After a block of uphill walking, find the stairs to the palace square.*

▲Palace of the Popes (Palais des Papes)

In 1309, a French pope was elected (Pope Clément V). At the urging of the French king, His Holiness decided that danger-ous Italy was no place for a pope, so he moved the whole operation to Avignon for a secure rule under a sup-portive king. The Catholic Church lit-erally bought Avignon (then a two-bit town), and popes resided here until 1403. Meanwhile, Italians demanded a Roman pope, so from 1378 on, there were twin popes—one in Rome and one in Avignon—causing a schism in the Catholic Church that wasn't fully resolved until 1417.

Cost and Hours: €10.50 (more for special exhibits), includes audioguide, €13 combo-ticket includes St. Bénezet Bridge, daily mid-March-Oct 9:00-19:00, until 20:00 in July-Sept, until 21:00 in Aug, Nov-mid-March 9:30-17:45, last entry one hour before closing, tel. 04 90 27 50 74, www.palais-des-papes.com.

Visiting the Palace: A visit to the mighty yet barren papal palace comes with a slick multimedia audioguide that leads you along a one-way route and does a decent job of overcoming the complete lack of furnishings. It teaches the basic history while allowing you to tour at your own pace. A small museum inside the palace also helps add context. Still, touring the palace is pretty anticlimactic, given its historic importance.

As you wander, ponder that this palace—the largest surviving Gothic palace in Europe—was built to accommodate 500 people as the administrative center of the Holy See and home of the pope. This was the most fortified palace of the age (remember, the pope left Rome to be more secure). Nine popes ruled from here, making this the center of Christianity for nearly 100 years. You'll walk through the pope's personal quarters (frescoed with happy hunting scenes), see many models of how the various popes added to the building, and learn about its state-of-the-art plumbing. The rooms are huge. The "pope's chapel" is twice the size of the adjacent Avignon cathedral.

The last pope (or, technically, antipope, since by then Rome also had its own rival pope) checked out in 1403 (escaping a siege), but the Church owned Avignon until the French Revolution in 1789. During this interim period, the pope's "legate" (official representative, normally a nephew) ruled Avignon from this palace. Avignon residents, many of whom had come from Rome, spoke Italian for a century after the pope left, making it a linguistic ghetto within France. In the Napoleonic age, the palace was a barracks, housing 1,800 soldiers. You can see cuts in the wall where high ceilings gave way to floor beams. Climb the tower (Tour de la Gâche) for grand views and a rooftop café with surprisingly good food at very fair prices.

Wine Room: A room at the end of the tour (called *la boutellerie*) is dedicated to the region's wines, of which they claim the pope was a fan. Sniff "Le Nez du Vin"—a black box with 54 tiny bottles designed to develop your "nose." (Blind-test your travel partner.) The nearby village of Châteauneuf-du-Pape is where the pope summered in the 1320s. Its famous wine is a direct descendant of his wine. You're welcome to taste here (€6 for three to five fine wines and souvenir tasting cup). If it's only wine you want, go directly to the back entrance of the palace and enter the boutique.

• *You'll exit at the rear of the palace, where my "Back Streets" walking tour begins (described next). Or, to return to Palace Square, make two rights after exiting the palace.*

PROVENCE

▲▲Discovering Avignon's Back Streets

Use the map in this chapter or the TI map to navigate this easy, level, 30-minute walk. This self-guided tour begins in the small square (Place de la Mirande) behind the Palace of the Popes. If you've toured the palace, this is where you exit. Otherwise, from the front of the palace, follow the narrow, cobbled Rue de la Peyrollerie—carved out of the rock—around the palace on the right side as you face it.

• *Our walk begins at the...*

Hôtel La Mirande: Located on the square, Avignon's finest hotel welcomes visitors. Find the atrium lounge and consider a coffee break amid the understated luxury (€13 afternoon tea served daily 15:00-18:00, includes a generous selection of pastries). Inspect the royal lounge and recommended dining room; cooking demos are offered in the basement below. Rooms start at about €425 in high season.

• *Turn left out of the hotel and left again on Rue de la Peyrollerie ("Coppersmiths Street"), then take your first right on Rue des Ciseaux d'Or. On the small square ahead you'll find the...*

Church of St. Pierre: The original chestnut doors were carved in 1551, when tales of New World discoveries raced across Europe. (Notice the Indian headdress, top center of left-side door.) The fine Annunciation (eye level on right-side door) shows Gabriel giving Mary the exciting news in impressive Renaissance 3-D. Now take 10 steps back from the door and look way up. The tiny statue breaking the skyline of the church is the pagan god Bacchus, with oodles of grapes. What's he doing sitting atop a Christian church? No one knows. The church's interior holds a beautiful Baroque altar. (For recommended restaurants near the Church of St. Pierre, see "Eating in Avignon," later.)

• *With your back to the church, follow the alley to the right, which was covered and turned into a tunnel during the town's population boom. It leads into...*

Place des Châtaignes: The cloister of St. Pierre is named for the chestnut *(châtaigne)* trees that once stood here (now replaced by plane trees). The practical atheists of the French Revolution destroyed the cloister, leaving only faint traces of the arches along the church side of the square.

• *Continue around the church and cross the busy street to the Banque Chaix. Across little Rue des Fourbisseurs find the classy...*

15th-Century Building: With its original beamed eaves showing, this is a rare vestige from the Middle Ages. Notice how this building widens the higher it gets. A medieval loophole based taxes on ground-floor square footage—everything above was tax-free. Walking down Rue des Fourbisseurs ("Street of the Animal Furriers"), notice how the top floors almost meet. Fire was a constant danger in the Middle Ages, as flames leapt easily from one home to the next. In fact, the lookout guard's primary responsibility was watching for fires, not the enemy. Virtually all of Avignon's medieval homes have been replaced by safer structures.

• Walk down Rue des Fourbisseurs and turn left onto the traffic-free Rue du Vieux Sextier ("Street of the Old Balance," for weighing items); another left under the first arch leads 10 yards to Avignon's...

Synagogue: Jews first arrived in Avignon with the Diaspora (exile) of the first century. Avignon's Jews were nicknamed "the Pope's Jews" because of the protection that the Vatican offered to Jews expelled from France. Although the original synagogue dates from the 1220s, in the mid-19th century it was completely rebuilt in a Neoclassical Greek-temple style by a non-Jewish architect. This is the only synagogue under a rotunda that you'll see anywhere. It's an intimate, classy place dressed with white colonnades and walnut furnishings. To enter the synagogue, you'll have to email in advance of your visit (free, closed Sat-Sun, 2 Place Jerusalem, tel. 04 90 55 21 24, rabinacia@hotmail.fr).

• Retrace your steps to Rue du Vieux Sextier and turn left, then continue to the big square and find the big, boxy...

Market (Les Halles): In 1970, the town's open-air market was replaced by this modern one. The market's jungle-like green wall reflects the changes of seasons and helps mitigate its otherwise stark exterior (open Tue-Sun until 13:00, closed Mon, small TI inside open Fri-Sun). Step inside for a sensual experience of organic breads, olives, and festival-of-mold cheeses. Rue des Temptations cuts down the center. Cafés and cheese shops are on the right—as far as possible from the stinky fish stalls on the left. Follow your nose away from the fish and have a coffee with the locals.

• Exit out the back door of Les Halles, turn left on Rue de la Bonneterie ("Street of Hosiery"), and track the street for five minutes to the plane trees, where it becomes...

Rue des Teinturiers: This "Street of the Dyers" is a tie-dyed, tree- and stream-lined lane, home to earthy cafés and galleries. This was the cloth industry's dyeing and textile center in the 1800s. The stream is a branch of the Sorgue River. Those stylish Provençal fabrics and patterns you see for sale everywhere were first made here, after a pattern imported from India.

About three small bridges down, you'll pass the Grey Penitents chapel on the right. The upper facade shows the GPs,

PROVENCE

who dressed up in robes and pointy hoods to do their anonymous good deeds back in the 13th century (long before the KKK dressed this way). As you stroll on, you'll see the work of amateur sculptors, who have carved whimsical car barriers out of limestone.

Fun restaurants on this atmospheric street are recommended later, under "Eating in Avignon."

• *Farther down Rue des Teinturiers, you'll come to the...*

Waterwheel: Standing here, imagine the Sorgue River— which hits the mighty Rhône in Avignon—being broken into several canals in order to turn 23 such wheels. In about 1800, waterwheels powered the town's industries. The little cogwheel above the big one could be shoved into place, kicking another machine into gear behind the wall.

• *To return to the real world, double back on Rue des Teinturiers and turn left on Rue des Lices, which traces the first medieval wall. (Lice is the no-man's-land along a wall.) After a long block, you'll pass a striking four-story building that was a home for the poor in the 1600s, an army barracks in the 1800s, a fine-arts school in the 1900s, and is a deluxe condominium today (much of this neighborhood is going high-class residential). Eventually you'll return to Rue de la République, Avignon's main drag.*

More Sights in Avignon

Most of Avignon's top sights are covered earlier by my self-guided walks. With more time, consider these options.

Fondation Angladon-Dubrujeaud—Visiting this museum is like being invited into the elegant home of a rich and passionate art collector. It mixes a small but enjoyable collection of art from Post-Impressionists to Cubists (including Paul Cézanne, Vincent van Gogh, Honoré Daumier, Edgar Degas, and Pablo Picasso), with re-created art studios and furnishings from many periods. It's a quiet place with a few superb paintings.

Cost and Hours: €6, Tue-Sun 13:00-18:00, closed Mon, 5 Rue Laboureur, tel. 04 90 82 29 03, www.angladon.com.

Calvet Museum (Musée Calvet)—This fine-arts museum impressively displays its collection, highlighting French Baroque works. This museum goes ignored by most, but you'll find a few diamonds in the rough upstairs: Géricault, Soutine, and one painting each from Manet, Sisley, Bonnard, Dufy, and Vlaminck.

Cost and Hours: €6, includes audioguide, Wed-Mon 10:00-13:00 & 14:00-18:00, closed Tue, in the quieter western half of town at 65 Rue Joseph Vernet, antiquities collection a few blocks away at 27 Rue de la République—same hours and ticket, tel. 04 90 86 33 84, www.musee-calvet.org.

Near Avignon, in Villeneuve-lès-Avignon

▲Tower of Philip the Fair (Tour Philippe-le-Bel)—Built to protect access to St. Bénezet Bridge in 1307, this massive tower offers a terrific view over Avignon and the Rhône basin. It's best late in the day.

Cost and Hours: €2.10; April-Sept daily 10:00-12:30 & 14:00-18:30; Oct-Nov Tue-Sat 10:00-12:30 & 14:00-17:00, closed Sun-Mon; closed Dec-March.

Getting There: To reach the tower from Avignon, drive 5 minutes (cross Daladier Bridge, follow signs to *Villeneuve-lès-Avignon*), or take bus #11 (2/hour, catch bus in front of post office on Cours Président Kennedy—see map on page 700).

Sleeping in Avignon

(€1 = about $1.30, country code: 33)
Hotel values are better in Arles, though I've found some good values in Avignon and have listed them below. Avignon is crazy during its July festival, when you must book long ahead (expect inflated prices). Drivers should ask about parking deals.

Near Avignon's Centre-Ville Station

These listings are a five- to ten-minute walk from the Centre-Ville train station.

$$$ Hôtel Bristol* is a big, professionally run place on the main drag, offering predictable "American" comforts, including spacious public spaces, large rooms decorated in neutral tones, duvets on the beds, a big elevator, air-conditioning, and a generous buffet breakfast (standard Db-€96-€116, bigger Db-€140, Tb/Qb-€168, breakfast-€12, parking-€12, 44 Cours Jean Jaurès, tel. 04 90 16 48 48, fax 04 90 66 22 72, www.bristol-hotel-avignon.com, contact@bristol-avignon.com).

$$ Hôtel Ibis Centre Gare offers no surprises—just predictable two-star comfort at the central train and bus stations. This well-priced place offers generous public spaces, a café, an elevator, and a bar (Db-€75-90, Internet access and Wi-Fi, 42 Boulevard St. Roch, tel. 04 90 85 38 38, fax 04 90 86 44 81, www.ibishotel.com, h0944@accor.com).

$$ Hôtel Colbert is a solid two-star hotel and a good midrange bet, with richly colored, comfortable rooms in many sizes. Your hardworking hosts—Patrice, Annie, and *le chien* Brittany—care for this restored manor house, with its warm public spaces and

PROVENCE

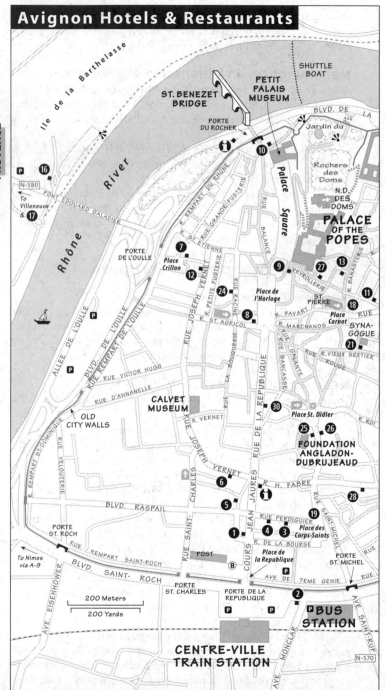

Avignon Hotels & Restaurants

SHUTTLE BOAT

Ile de la Barthelasse

Rhône River

ST. BENEZET BRIDGE

PETIT PALAIS MUSEUM

PORTE DU ROCHER

Jardin du

BLVD. DE LA

Rochers des Doms

N.D. DES DOMS

PALACE OF THE POPES

Palace Square

16

P

N-580

To Villeneuve & **17**

PONT EDOUARD DALADIER

PORTE DE L'OULLE

Place Crillon

7

12

R. ST. ETIENNE

RUE GRANDE FUSTERIE

RUE REMPART DU RHÔNE

RUE BALANCE

9

PEYROLLERIE

ST. PIERRE

27

13

R. BANASTERIE

11

18

RUE

SYNA-GOGUE

Place Carnot

R. FAVART

RUE MARCHANDS

RUE GALANTE

RUE BANCASSE

R.VIEUX SEXTIER

ROUGE

21

Place de l'Horloge

24

RUE JOSEPH VERNET

RUE PETITE FUSTERIE

RUE RACINE

R. ST. AGRICOL

LA BOUQUERIE

8

ALLÉE DE L'OULLE

BLVD. DE L'OULLE

RUE REMPART DE L'OULLE

RUE VICTOR HUGO

RUE D'ANNANELLE

CALVET MUSEUM

R. VERNET

RUE JOSEPH VERNET

RUE DE LA REPUBLIQUE

30

Place St. Didier

25

26

FOUNDATION ANGLADON-DUBRUJEAUD

R. ROI

OLD CITY WALLS

R. REMPART ST-DOMINIQUE

RUE VELOUTERIE

BLVD. RASPAIL

RUE SAINT-CHARLES

6

5

JEAN JAURES

R. H. FABRE

28

RUE SAINT-MICHEL

RUE

PORTE ST. ROCH

To Nimes via A-9

AVE. EISENHOWER

RUE REMPART SAINT-ROCH

1

POST

B

4 **3**

19

RUE PERDIGUIER

Place des Corps-Saints

R. DE LA BOURSE

Place de la Republique

COURS

P

AVE. DE

PORTE ST. MICHEL

AVE. SAINT-RUF

BLVD. SAINT-ROCH

PORTE ST. CHARLES

PORTE DE LA REPUBLIQUE

7EME GENIE

2

P BUS STATION

200 Meters

200 Yards

P

P

CENTRE-VILLE TRAIN STATION

AVE. MONCLAR

N-570

10

PROVENCE

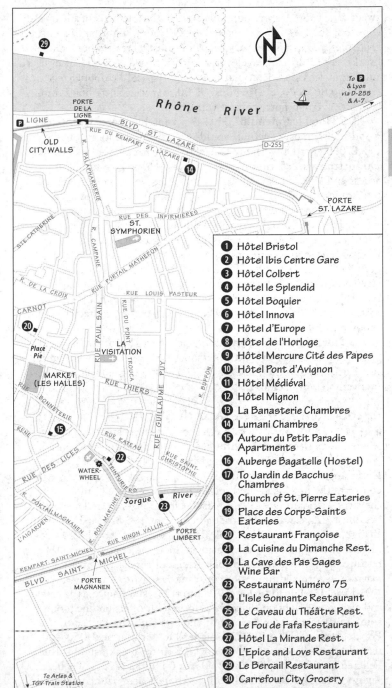

1 Hôtel Bristol
2 Hôtel Ibis Centre Gare
3 Hôtel Colbert
4 Hôtel le Splendid
5 Hôtel Boquier
6 Hôtel Innova
7 Hôtel d'Europe
8 Hôtel de l'Horloge
9 Hôtel Mercure Cité des Papes
10 Hôtel Pont d'Avignon
11 Hôtel Médiéval
12 Hôtel Mignon
13 La Banasterie Chambres
14 Lumani Chambres
15 Autour du Petit Paradis Apartments
16 Auberge Bagatelle (Hostel)
17 To Jardin de Bacchus Chambres
18 Church of St. Pierre Eateries
19 Place des Corps-Saints Eateries
20 Restaurant Françoise
21 La Cuisine du Dimanche Rest.
22 La Cave des Pas Sages Wine Bar
23 Restaurant Numéro 75
24 L'Isle Sonnante Restaurant
25 Le Caveau du Théâtre Rest.
26 Le Fou de Fafa Restaurant
27 Hôtel La Mirande Rest.
28 L'Epice and Love Restaurant
29 Le Bercail Restaurant
30 Carrefour City Grocery

sweet little patio. It's a popular place, so it's best to book in advance (Sb-€68, small Db-€78, bigger Db-€90, some tight bathrooms, no triples, rooms off the patio are a bit musty, creative homemade breakfast-€12, air-con, no elevator, Wi-Fi, closed Nov-mid-March, turn right off Cours Jean Jaurès on Rue Agricol Perdiguier to #7, tel. 04 90 86 20 20, fax 04 90 85 97 00, www.lecolbert-hotel.com, contact@avignon-hotel-colbert.com).

$$ Hôtel le Splendid* rents 17 acceptable rooms with faux-wood floors, most of which could use a little attention (Sb-€50, Db-€70, bigger Db with air-con-€80, Tb with air-con-€88, three Db apartments-€95, continental breakfast-€9, no elevator, Internet access and Wi-Fi, turn right off Cours Jean Jaurès on Rue Agricol Perdiguier to #17, tel. 04 90 86 14 46, fax 04 90 85 38 55, www.avignon-splendid-hotel.com, splendidavignon@gmail.com).

$ Hôtel Boquier**, run by engaging managers Madame Sendra and husband Pascal, has 12 quiet, good-value, and homey rooms under wood beams in a central location (small Db-€61, bigger Db-€73, Tb-€81, Qb-€92, air-con, Internet access and Wi-Fi, steep and narrow stairways to some rooms and no elevator, parking-€12, near the TI at 6 Rue du Portail Boquier, tel. 04 90 82 34 43, fax 04 90 86 14 07, www.hotel-boquier.com, contact@hotel-boquier.com).

$ Hôtel Innova is a shy little place with 11 spotless rooms at good rates (Db-€50-60, extra person-€7, no air-con, no elevator, 100 Rue Joseph Vernet, tel. 04 90 82 54 10, www.hotel-innova.fr, innova.hotel@wanadoo.fr).

In the Center, near Place de l'Horloge

$$$ Hôtel d'Europe****, with Avignon's most prestigious address, lets peasants sleep royally without losing their shirts—but only if you land one of the 10 surprisingly reasonable "classique" rooms. Enter a shady courtyard, linger in the lounges, and savor every comfort. The hotel is located on the handsome Place Crillon, near the river (standard Db-€195, superior Db-€365, prestige Db-€550, breakfast-€21, elevator, Internet access, garage-€18, near Daladier Bridge at 12 Place Crillon, tel. 04 90 14 76 76, fax 04 90 14 76 71, www.heurope.com, reservations@heurope.com). The hotel's restaurant is Michelin-rated (one star) and serves an upscale €48 *menu* in its formal dining room or front courtyard.

$$$ Hôtel de l'Horloge***, a top three-star choice, is as central as it gets—right on Place de l'Horloge. It offers 66 fine rooms, some with terraces and views of the city and the Palace of the Popes (standard Db-€100-120, bigger Db with terrace-€150-200, terrace rooms also work as Tb or Qb, buffet breakfast-€14, Rue Félicien David, tel. 04 90 16 42 00, fax 04 90 82 17 32, www.hotel-avignon-horloge.com, hotel.horloge@hotels-ocre-azur.com).

$$$ Hôtel Mercure Cité des Papes*** is a modern chain hotel within spitting distance of the Palace of the Popes. It has 89 small, smartly designed rooms (Sb-€135-150, Db-€170-190, breakfast-€13, promotional deals best if booked 15 days ahead, many rooms have views over Place de l'Horloge, air-con, elevator, 1 Rue Jean Vilar, tel. 04 90 80 93 00, fax 04 90 80 93 01, www.mercure .com, h1952@accor.com).

$$$ Hôtel Pont d'Avignon***, just inside the walls near St. Bénezet Bridge, is part of the same chain as the Hôtel Mercure Cité des Papes, with the same prices for its 87 rooms (direct access to a garage makes parking easier than at the other Mercure hotel, elevator, on Rue Ferruce, tel. 04 90 80 93 93, fax 04 90 80 93 94, www.mercure.com, h0549@accor.com).

$$ Hôtel Médiéval** is burrowed deep a few blocks from the Church of St. Pierre. Built as a cardinal's home, this massive stone mansion has a small garden and 35 wood-paneled, air-conditioned, unimaginative rooms, with friendly-as-they-get Régis at the helm. Big renovation plans in 2013 may change the layout—and increase prices (Sb-€51, Db-€65-81, bigger Db or Tb-€90-97, breakfast-€8, kitchenettes available but require 3-night minimum stay, no elevator, Wi-Fi, 5 blocks east of Place de l'Horloge, behind Church of St. Pierre at 15 Rue Petite Saunerie, tel. 04 90 86 11 06, fax 04 90 82 08 64, www.hotelmedieval.com, hotel.medieval@wanadoo.fr).

$$ Hôtel Mignon* is a good-enough, one-star place with basic comfort and tiny bathrooms (Db-€70-75, Tb-€85, Qb-€116, air-con, Internet access and Wi-Fi, 12 Rue Joseph Vernet, tel. 04 90 82 17 30, www.hotel-mignon.com, reservation@hotel-mignon.fr).

Chambres d'Hôtes and Apartments

$$$ La Banasterie, a well-located refuge in a historic building a block behind the Palace of the Popes, has five spacious rooms—two with decks (Db-€100-190, cash only, includes breakfast, air-con, 11 Rue de la Banasterie, mobile 06 87 72 96 36, www.labanasterie .com, labanasterie@labanasterie.com).

$$$ Lumani provides the ultimate urban refuge just inside the city walls, a 15-minute walk from the Palace of the Popes. In this graceful old manor house, gentle Elisabeth and Jean welcome guests to their art-gallery-cum-bed-and-breakfast that surrounds a fountain-filled courtyard with elbow room. She paints, he designs buildings, and both care about your experience in Avignon. The five rooms are decorated with flair; no two are alike, and all overlook the shady garden (small Db-€100, big Db-€140, Db suites-€170, extra person-€30, includes breakfast, Internet access and Wi-Fi, music studio, parking-€10 or easy on street, 37 Rue de Rempart St. Lazare, tel. 04 90 82 94 11, www.avignon-lumani.com, lux @avignon-lumani.com).

$$$ At **Autour du Petit Paradis Apartments,** owners Sabine and Patrick welcome visitors into their four well-furnished apartments with everything you need. They are conveniently located in the city center (€750-1,000/week, 5 Rue Noel Biret, tel. 04 90 81 00 42, www.autourdupetitparadis.com; contact@autourdupetit paradis.com).

On the Outskirts of Town

$ **Auberge Bagatelle's hostel** offers dirt-cheap beds, lively atmosphere, café, grocery store, launderette, great views of Avignon, and campers for neighbors (Ds-€44, Ts-€73, Tb-€82, Q-€73, Qb-€100, dorm bed-€18, includes breakfast, across Daladier Bridge on Ile de la Barthelasse, bus #10 from main post office, tel. 04 90 86 71 31, fax 04 90 27 16 23, www.campingbagatelle.fr, auberge.bagatelle@wanadoo.fr).

Near Avignon

$$$ At **Jardin de Bacchus,** just 15 minutes northwest of Avignon and convenient to Pont du Gard, enthusiastic and English-speaking Christine and Erik offer three rooms in their rural farmhouse, which overlooks the famous rosé vineyards of Tavel (Db-€90-120, €30 extra for one-night stays, includes breakfast, fine dinner possible, Wi-Fi, swimming pool, tel. 04 66 90 28 62, www.jardindebacchus.fr, jardindebacchus@free.fr). To learn about their small-group food and wine tours, check their website. For bus connections, see www.edgard-transport.fr.

Eating in Avignon

Dining on a Square

Skip the overpriced, underwhelming restaurants on Place de l'Horloge and find a more intimate location for your dinner. Avignon is riddled with delightful squares filled with tables ready to seat you.

Near the Church of St. Pierre

The church stands between two enchanting squares: Quiet and intimate Place St. Pierre (where L'Epicerie sits alone), and, just under the nearby arch, lively and enchanting Place des Châtaignes, with a fun commotion of tables—peruse your options.

La Vache à Carreaux venerates cheese and wine (while offering a full range of cuisine). The colorful decor is fun, and the wine list is extensive and reasonable. This place is a hit with locals, who gather around outside, sipping €4 glasses of good wine, reluctant to leave (€12-18 *plats*, open daily, just off Place des Châtaignes at 14 Rue de la Peyrollerie, tel. 04 90 80 09 05).

L'Epicerie, homey inside and out, serves top cuisine with a focus on products from the south of France—expect lots of color and a dash of spice (€35 *menu*, €18-25 *plats*, daily, 10 Place St. Pierre, tel. 04 90 82 74 22).

Other Place des Châtaignes Options: The **Crêperie du Cloître** makes mediocre dinner crêpes and salads (daily, cash only). Next door and across from La Vache à Carreaux is the family-run Vietnamese **Restaurant Nem** (*menus* from €12, cash only). **Coin Caché** is lighthearted, with decidedly French fare (€6 starters and desserts, €15 *plats*, closed Tue). **Pause Gourmande** is a small, lunch-only eatery with €9 *plats du jour,* and always has a veggie option (closed Sun, around the corner and behind the church).

Place des Corps-Saints: This untouristy yet welcoming square is my favorite place for simple outdoor dining in Avignon. You'll find several youthful and reasonable eateries with tables sprawling under big plane trees. **Bistrot à Tartines** specializes in—you guessed it—*tartines* (big slices of toast smothered with toppings), and has the coziest interior and best desserts on the square (€8 *tartines* and salads, €10 lunch *menu,* daily, tel. 04 90 85 58 70). **Zeste** is a friendly, modern deli offering fresh soups, pasta salads, wraps, smoothies, and more. Get it to go, or eat inside or on the scenic square—all at unbeatable prices (closed Sun, tel. 09 51 49 05 62). **Boulangerie Olivero** makes a fine setting for a budget breakfast, lunch, or a light (and early) dinner. Monsieur Olivero makes a mean baguette and offers anyone showing this book a free croissant with any purchase. Enjoy your coffee, croissant, sandwich, or quiche at the outside tables (on the square near Rue des Lices, daily until 20:00).

By the Market (Les Halles)

Here you'll find a good selection of eateries with good prices.

Restaurant Françoise is a pleasant café and tea salon, where fresh-baked tarts—savory and sweet—and a variety of salads and soups make a healthful meal, and vegetarian options are plentiful (€7-12 dishes, Mon-Sat 8:00-19:00, closed Sun, free Wi-Fi, 6 Rue Général Leclerc, tel. 04 32 76 24 77).

La Cuisine du Dimanche offers an appealing stone interior with an atrium courtyard. They get rave reviews for the quality of their cuisine—but not for the service (€18-25 *plats*, daily, 31 Rue de la Bonneterie, tel. 04 90 82 99 10).

Rue des Teinturiers

This "Tie-Dye Street" has a wonderful concentration of eateries popular with the natives, and justifies the long walk. It's a trendy, youthful area, spiffed up with a canalside ambience and little hint of tourism.

La Cave des Pas Sages makes a colorful pause before dinner. The owners enjoy serving you a fragrant and cheap glass of regional wine. Choose from the blackboard by the bar that lists all the bottles open today, then join the gang outside by the canal. In the evening, this place is a hit with the young local crowd for its wine and weekend concerts (Mon-Sat 10:00-1:00 in the morning, closed Sun, no food in evening, across from waterwheel at 41 Rue des Teinturiers).

Restaurant Numéro 75 is worth the walk (just past where the cobbles end on Rue des Teinturiers). It fills the Pernod mansion (of *pastis* liquor fame) and a large, romantic courtyard with outdoor tables. The selection is limited to Mediterranean cuisine, but everything's *très* tasty. It's best to go with the options offered by your young black-shirted server (€30 lunch *menu*; dinner *menus:* €29/appetizer and main course or main course and dessert, €35/three courses; Mon-Sat 12:00-14:00 & 20:00-22:00, closed Sun, 75 Rue Guillaume Puy, tel. 04 90 27 16 00).

Elsewhere in Avignon

At **L'Isle Sonnante,** join chef Boris and wife Anne to dine intimately in their formal and charming one-room *bistrot*. You'll choose from a small selection offering only fresh products and be served by owners who care (*menus* from €35, closed Sun-Mon, 100 yards from the carousel on Place de l'Horloge at 7 Rue Racine, tel. 04 90 82 56 01, best to book ahead).

Le Caveau du Théâtre is a welcoming place where Richard invites diners to have a glass of wine or dinner at a sidewalk table, or inside in one of two carefree rooms (€15 *plats*, €20-24 *menus*, fun ambience for free, closed for lunch Sat and all day Sun, 16 Rue des Trois Faucons, tel. 04 90 82 60 91).

Le Fou de Fafa sits across from Le Caveau du Théâtre. Its friendly British owners are making a splash with locals, serving top-notch crêpes and inexpensive dishes in a warm setting (closed Mon, 17 Rue des Trois Faucons, tel. 04 32 76 35 13).

Hôtel La Mirande is the ultimate Avignon splurge. Reserve ahead here for understated elegance and Avignon's finest cuisine (€35 lunch *menu*, €105 dinner tasting *menu*; closed Tue-Wed—but for a price break, dine in the kitchen with the chef on these "closed" days for €92 including wine; behind Palace of the Popes, 4 Place de la Mirande, tel. 04 90 14 20 20, www.la-mirande.fr).

At **L'Epice and Love** (the name is a fun French-English play on words, pronounced "lay peace and love"), English-speaking owner Marie creates a playful atmosphere in her inviting restaurant, where the few colorfully decorated tables (inside only) greet the hungry traveler. The limited selection changes daily, and Marie cooks it all: tasty meat, fish, and vegetarian dishes, some with a North African touch, all served at good prices (€16 *menus*, closed Sun, 30 Rue des Lices, tel. 04 90 82 45 96).

Across the River

Le Bercail offers a fun opportunity to get out of town (barely) and take in *le fresh air* with a terrific riverfront view of Avignon, all while enjoying fun Provençal cooking served in big portions (*menus* from €26, serves late, daily April-Oct, tel. 04 90 82 20 22). Take the free shuttle boat (located near St. Bénezet Bridge) to the Ile de la Barthelasse, turn right, and walk five minutes. As the boat usually stops running at about 18:00 (except in July-Aug, when it runs until 21:00), you can either taxi home or walk 25 minutes along the pleasant riverside path and over Daladier Bridge.

Avignon Connections

By Train

Remember, there are two train stations in Avignon: the suburban TGV Station and the Centre-Ville Station in the city center (€1.20 shuttle buses connect to both stations, buy ticket from driver, 3/hour, 15 minutes). TGV trains usually serve the TGV Station only, though a few depart from Centre-Ville Station (check your ticket). Only Centre-Ville has baggage storage (see "Arrival in Avignon," page 699). Car rental is available only at the TGV Station. Some cities are served by slower local trains from Centre-Ville Station as well as by faster TGV trains from the TGV Station; I've listed the most convenient stations for each trip.

From Avignon's Centre-Ville Station to: Arles (roughly hourly, 20 minutes, less frequent in the afternoon), Orange (15/day, 15 minutes), Nîmes (14/day, 30 minutes), Isle-sur-la-Sorgue (10/day on weekdays, 5/day on weekends, 30 minutes), Lyon (10/day, 2 hours, also from TGV Station in 1 hour—see below), Carcassonne (8/day, 7 with transfer in Narbonne, 3 hours), Barcelona, Spain (2/day, 5.75 hours with changes in Nîmes and Figueres-Vilafant; more frequent but slower with a change in Cerbère).

From Avignon's TGV Station to: Nice (20/day, most by TGV, 4 hours, most require transfer in Marseille), Marseille (10/day, 35 minutes), Cassis (7/day, 2 hours), Aix-en-Provence TGV (10/day, 25 minutes), Lyon (12/day, 1.5 hour, also from Centre-Ville Station—see above), Paris' Gare de Lyon (9/day direct, 2.5

hours; more connections with transfer, 3-4 hours), **Paris'** Charles de Gaulle Airport (7/day, 3 hours).

By Bus

The bus station *(gare routière)* is just past and below Hôtel Ibis, to the right as you exit the train station. Nearly all buses leave from this station (a few leave from the ring road outside the station—ask, buy tickets on bus, small bills only). Service is reduced or nonexistent on Sundays and holidays. Check your departure time beforehand, and make sure to verify your destination with the driver.

From Avignon to Pont du Gard: Buses go to this famous old aqueduct (3/day, 50 minutes, departs from bus station, usually from stall #11, also from TGV Station); I'd also consider a taxi one-way and bus back.

By Bus to Other Regional Destinations: Arles (10/day, 1 hour, leaves from TGV Station); **Uzès** (3-5/day, 60-80 minutes, stops at Pont du Gard); **St-Rémy-de-Provence** (bus #57, 6/day, 45 minutes, stall #2, handy way to visit its Wed market); **Orange** (Mon-Sat hourly, none Sun, 45 minutes—take the train instead); **Isle-sur-la-Sorgue** (6-8/day Mon-Sat, 3-4/day Sun, 45 minutes, stall #13, some leave from ring road); **Châteauneuf-du-Pape** (2/day Mon-Sat, none Sun, 45 minutes). For the **Côtes du Rhône** area, the bus runs to **Vaison la Romaine, Nyons, Sablet,** and **Séguret** (5/day during the school year—called *période scolaire,* 3/day otherwise, and 1/day from TGV Station; 1.5 hours, all buses pass through Orange—faster to take train to Orange and transfer to bus there). For the **Luberon** area—including **Lourmarin, Roussillon,** and **Gordes**—take the bus to Cavaillon, then take bus #8 toward Pertuis for Lourmarin (3/day) or bus #15 for Gordes/Roussillon (only 1/day).

Pont du Gard

Throughout the ancient world, aqueducts were like flags of stone that heralded the greatness of Rome. A visit to this sight still works to proclaim the wonders of that age. This perfectly preserved Roman aqueduct was built in about 19 B.C. as the critical link of a 30-mile canal that, by dropping one inch for every 350 feet, supplied nine million gallons of water per day (about 100 gallons per second) to Nîmes—one of ancient Europe's largest cities. Though most of the aqueduct is on or below the ground, at Pont du Gard it spans a canyon on a massive bridge—one of the most remarkable surviving Roman ruins anywhere. Wear sturdy shoes if you

Pont du Gard

Not to scale:
Museum to Pont du Gard
is a 5-minute walk

N

TRAIL
ALONG CANAL

BEST
VIEW

**PONT DU
GARD**

WOW!

To
Canal
Ruins

CANAL TUNNEL

PROVENCE

Garrigue
Natural Area

Gardon River

P Rive Droite
DON'T PARK
HERE

To
Remoulins
& Nîmes

3

MUSEUM COMPLEX
CINEMA, LUDO (KID'S SPACE),
INFO, SHOP, WC &
RESTAURANT

P Rive Gauche
PARK HERE

D-981

2

To Uzés

D-981

ROUNDABOUT

1

To Remoulins,
Nîmes, Avignon,
Arles & A-9
Freeway

❶ Bus Stop from Avignon & Nîmes
❷ Bus Stop to Avignon & Nîmes
❸ Bus Stop (Summer & Weekends)

want to climb around the aqueduct (footing is tricky), and bring swimwear and flip-flops if you plan to backstroke with views of the monument.

Getting to Pont du Gard

The famous aqueduct is between Remoulins and Vers-Pont du Gard on D-981, 13 miles from Avignon.

By Car: Pont du Gard is a 25-minute drive due west of Avignon (follow N-100 from Avignon, tracking signs to *Nîmes* and *Remoulins,* then *Pont du Gard* and *Rive Gauche*), and 45 minutes northwest of Arles (via Tarascon on D-15). If going to Arles from Pont du Gard, follow signs to *Nîmes* (not *Avignon*), then follow D-986 and then D-15 to Arles.

By Bus: Buses run to Pont du Gard (on the Rive Gauche side) from Avignon (3/day, 50 minutes), Nîmes, and Uzès. Consider this plan: Take a morning bus from Avignon's bus or TGV Station (leaves bus station at about 8:45 or 11:40, leaves TGV Station at 8:30 or 11:25). To return to Avignon, the bus leaves Pont du Gard at 13:20 or 17:30. Confirm all of these times at a TI or at www.pontdugard.fr. The 8:45 trip out and 13:20 trip back works best for most. Allow about four or five hours for visiting Pont du Gard, including transportation time from Avignon.

Buses stop at the traffic roundabout 300 yards from the aqueduct (see Pont du Gard map). In summer and on weekends, however, buses usually drive into the Pont du Gard site and stop at the parking lot's ticket booth. Confirm where the bus stops at the parking booth inside the Pont du Gard site.

At the roundabout, the stop for buses coming from Avignon and Nîmes (and going to Uzès) is on the side opposite Pont du Gard; the stop for buses to Nîmes and to Avignon is on the same side as Pont du Gard (a block to your left as you exit Pont du Gard onto the main road). Make sure you're waiting for the bus on the correct side of the traffic circle (stops have schedules posted), and wave your hand to signal the bus to stop for you (otherwise, it'll chug on by). Buy your ticket when you get on and verify your destination with the driver.

By Taxi: From Avignon, it's about €50 for a taxi to Pont du Gard (allow €64 after 19:00 and on Sun). If you're staying in Avignon and have limited time to see Pont du Gard, take the first bus there, and splurge on a taxi back (arrange in advance or ask the staff at Pont du Gard to call one for you).

Orientation to Pont du Gard

There are two riversides to Pont du Gard: the Left Bank (Rive Gauche) and Right Bank (Rive Droite). Park on the Rive Gauche, where you'll find the museums, ticket booth, ATM, cafeteria, WCs, and shops—all built into a modern plaza. You'll see the aqueduct in two parts: first the fine museum complex, then the actual river gorge spanned by the ancient bridge.

Cost and Hours: €18 per car (no matter how few or many; €23 for an annual pass). If arriving on foot, by bus, or by bike, you'll pay €10 for one person or €15 for groups of up to five (consider gathering a gang of fellow sightseers at the entrance before buying your ticket). This gives you access to the aqueduct, museum, film, and outdoor *garrigue* nature area. The museum is open daily May-Sept 9:00-19:00, Oct-April 9:00-17:00, closed two weeks in Jan. The aqueduct itself is open until 1:00 in the morning, as is the parking lot. The *garrigue* is always open. Tel. 04 66 37 50 99, www.pontdugard.fr.

Tours: Call ahead or visit the website for information on infrequent guided walks on top of the aqueduct (about €10).

Canoe Rental: Floating under Pont du Gard by canoe is an experience you won't soon forget. Collias Canoes will pick you up at Pont du Gard (or elsewhere, if pre-arranged) and shuttle you to the town of Collias. You'll float down the river to the nearby town of Remoulins, where they'll pick you up and take you back to Pont du Gard (€21/person, €12/child under 12, usually 2 hours—though you can take as long as you like, good idea to reserve the day before in July-Aug, tel. 04 66 22 85 54).

Plan Ahead for Swimming and Hiking: Pont du Gard is perhaps best enjoyed on your back and in the water—bring along a swimsuit and flip-flops for the rocks. The best Pont du Gard viewpoints are up steep hills with uneven footing—bring good shoes.

Sights at Pont du Gard

▲**Museum**—In this state-of-the-art museum (well-presented in English), you'll enter to the sound of water and understand the critical role fresh water played in the Roman "art of living." You'll see examples of lead pipes, faucets, and siphons; walk through a mock rock quarry; and learn how they moved those huge rocks into place and how those massive arches were made. While actual artifacts from the aqueduct are few, the exhibit shows the immensity of the undertaking as well as the payoff. Imagine the excitement as this extravagant supply of water finally tumbled into Nîmes. A relaxing highlight is the scenic video of a helicopter ride along the entire 30-mile course of the structure, from its start at Uzès all the way to the Castellum in Nîmes.

Other Activities—Several additional attractions are designed to give the sight more meaning—and they do (but for most visitors, the museum is sufficient). A corny, romancing-the-aqueduct 25-minute film plays in the same building as the museum and offers good information in a flirtatious French-Mediterranean style...and a cool, entertaining, and cushy break. The nearby kids' museum, called *Ludo,* offers a scratch-and-sniff teaching experience (in English) of various aspects of Roman life and the importance of water. The extensive outdoor *garrigue* natural area, closer to the aqueduct, features historic crops and landscapes of the Mediterranean.

▲▲▲**Viewing the Aqueduct**—A park-like path leads to the aqueduct. Until a few years ago, this was an actual road—adjacent to the aqueduct—that had spanned the river since 1743. Before you cross the bridge, pass under it and hike about 300 feet along the riverbank for a grand viewpoint from which to study the world's second-highest standing Roman structure. (Rome's Colosseum is only 6 feet taller.)

This was the biggest bridge in the whole 30-mile-long aqueduct. It seems exceptional because it is: The arches are twice the width of standard aqueducts, and the main arch is the largest the Romans ever built—80 feet (so it wouldn't get its feet wet).

The bridge is about 160 feet high and was originally about 1,100 feet long. Today, 12 arches are missing, reducing the length to 790 feet.

Though the distance from the source (in Uzès) to Nîmes was only 12 miles as the eagle flew, engineers chose the most economical route, winding and zigzagging 30 miles. The water made the trip in 24 hours with a drop of only 40 feet. Ninety percent of the aqueduct is on or under the ground, but a few river canyons like this required bridges. A stone lid hides a four-foot-wide, six-foot-tall chamber lined with waterproof mortar that carried the stream for more than 400 years. For 150 years, this system provided Nîmes with good drinking water. Expert as the Romans were, they miscalculated the backup caused by a downstream corner, and had to add the thin extra layer you can see just under the lid to make the channel deeper.

The bridge and the river below provide great fun for holiday-goers. While parents suntan on rocks, kids splash into the gorge from under the aqueduct. Some daredevils actually jump from the aqueduct's lower bridge—not knowing that crazy winds scrambled by the structure cause painful belly flops (and sometimes even accidental deaths). For the most refreshing view, float flat on your back underneath the structure.

The appearance of the entire gorge changed in 2002, when a huge flood flushed lots of greenery downstream. Those floodwaters put Roman provisions to the test. Notice the triangular-shaped buttresses at the lower level—designed to split and divert the force of any flood *around* the feet of the arches rather than *into* them. The 2002 floodwaters reached the top of those buttresses. Anxious park rangers winced at the sounds of trees crashing onto the ancient stones...but the arches stood strong.

The stones that jut out—giving the aqueduct a rough, unfinished appearance—supported the original scaffolding. The protuberances were left, rather than cut off, in anticipation of future repair needs. The lips under the arches supported wooden templates that allowed the stones in the round arches to rest on something until the all-important keystone was dropped into place. Each stone weighs four to six tons. The structure stands with no mortar (except at the very top, where the water flowed)—taking full advantage of the innovative Roman arch, made strong by gravity.

Hike over the bridge for a closer look and the best views. Steps lead up a high trail (marked *panorama*) to a superb view-

point (go right at the top; best
views are soon after the trail
starts descending). You'll also see
where the aqueduct meets a rock
tunnel. Walk through the tunnel
and continue for a bit, following
a trail that meanders along the
canal's path.

Back on the museum side,
steps lead up to the Rive Gauche
(parking lot) end of the aqueduct, where you can follow the
canal path along a trail (marked
with red-and-white horizontal lines) to find some remains of the
Roman canal. You'll soon reach another *panorama* with great
views of the aqueduct. Hikers can continue along the path, following the red-and-white markings that lead through a forest,
after which you'll come across more remains of the canal (much
of which are covered by vegetation). There's not much left to see
because of medieval cannibalization—frugal builders couldn't
resist the precut stones as they constructed area churches (stones
along the canal were easier to retrieve than those high up on the
aqueduct). The path continues for about 15 miles, but there's little
reason to go farther. However, there is talk of opening the ancient
quarry...someday.

Les Baux

The hilltop town of Les Baux crowns the rugged Alpilles (ahl-pee)
Mountains, evoking a tumultuous medieval history. Here, you can
imagine the struggles of a strong community that lived a rough-
and-tumble life—thankful more for their top-notch fortifications
than for their dramatic views. It's mobbed with tourists most of
the day, but Les Baux rewards those who arrive by 9:00 or after
17:30. (Although the hilltop citadel's entry closes at the end of the
day, once you're inside, you're welcome to live out your medieval
fantasies all night long.) Sunsets are dramatic, the castle is brilliantly illuminated after dark, and nights in Les Baux are pin-drop
peaceful.

Getting to Les Baux

By Car: Les Baux is a 20-minute drive from Arles: Follow signs
for *Avignon*, then *Les Baux*.

By Bus: From Arles, bus #59 runs to Les Baux daily July

through August and Saturday-Sunday in June and September (6/day, 35 minutes, via Abbey of Montmajour, Fontvieille, and Le Paradou).

The appealing town of St-Rémy, about seven miles north of Les Baux, is a workable transit point for those home-basing in Avignon: Ride the #57 bus from Avignon to St-Rémy (6/day, 45 minutes); on summer weekends or daily July-August, you can continue to Les Baux on the same bus, renumbered as #59. Or travel from St-Rémy to Les Baux by taxi (€18, mobile 06 80 27 60 92—handy for off-season days when the #59 bus doesn't run).

By Taxi: Figure €40 for a taxi one-way from Arles to Les Baux (€50 after 19:00).

By Minivan Tour: The best option for many is a minivan tour, which can be both efficient and economical (easiest from Avignon; see "Tours of Provence" on page 662).

Orientation to Les Baux

Les Baux is actually two visits in one: castle ruins perched on an almost lunar landscape, and a medieval town below. Savor the castle, then tour—or blitz—the lower streets on your way out. While the town, which lives entirely off tourism, is packed with shops, cafés, and tourist knickknacks, the castle above stays manageable because crowds are dispersed over a big area. The lower town's polished-stone gauntlet of boutiques is a Provençal dream come true for shoppers.

Tourist Information

The TI is immediately on the left as you enter the village (daily 9:30-17:30, later in summer, tel. 04 90 54 34 39, www.lesbauxdeprovence .com). Ask (or check their website) about their "Passes," which can save you money provided you visit all the sights. You'll also see deals combining Les Baux with other sights in the region (such as the theater in Orange). The TI can also call a cab for you.

Arrival in Les Baux

Drivers pay €5 to park at the foot of the village (behind the barrier), or €4 to park several blocks below (you'll pass the parking lot on your way in; the ticket is good for the day). Pay at the machine just below the town entry (next to the pay phone, WC, and bakery) before you return to your car—you'll need the validated ticket to exit the lot.

Walk up the cobbled street into town, where you're greeted first by the TI. From here the main drag leads directly to the castle—just keep going uphill (a 10-minute walk).

Sights in Les Baux

▲▲▲The Castle Ruins (The "Dead City")

The sun-bleached ruins of the "dead city" of Les Baux are carved into, out of, and on top of a rock 650 feet above the valley floor.

Many of the ancient walls of this striking castle still stand as a testament to the proud past of this once-feisty village.

Cost and Hours: €9 (ask about family rates), includes excellent audioguide available up to one hour before closing, daily July-Aug 9:00-20:00, Easter-June 9:00-19:00, Sept-Oct 9:30-18:00, Nov-Easter 10:00-17:00. If you're inside the castle when the entry closes, you can stay as long as you like.

Entertainment: On weekends from April through September, the castle presents medieval pageantry, tournaments, demonstrations of catapults and crossbows, and jousting matches (schedule in English at www.chateau-baux-provence.com). If you bring your lunch, enjoy the picnic tables.

Background: Imagine the importance of this citadel in the Middle Ages, when the Lords of Baux were notorious warriors. (How many feudal lords could trace their lineage back to one of the "three kings" of Christmas carol fame, Balthazar?) In the 11th century, Les Baux was a powerhouse in southern France, controlling about 80 towns. The Lords of Baux fought the counts of Barcelona for control of Provence...and eventually lost. But while in power, these guys were mean. One ruler enjoyed forcing unransomed prisoners to jump off his castle walls.

In 1426, Les Baux was incorporated into Provence and France. Not accustomed to subservience, Les Baux struggled with the French king, who responded by destroying the fortress in 1483. Later, Les Baux regained some importance and emerged as a center of Protestantism. Arguing with Rome was a high-stakes game in the 17th century, and Les Baux's association with the Huguenots brought destruction again in 1632, when Cardinal Richelieu (under King Louis XIII) demolished the castle. Louis rubbed salt in the wound by billing Les Baux's residents for his demolition expenses. The once-powerful town of 4,000 was forever crushed.

Visiting the Castle: Buy your ticket in the old olive mill, inspect the models of Les Baux before its 17th-century destruction, and then pick up your audioguide after entering the sight. The audioguide follows posted numbers counterclockwise around the rocky spur. Take full advantage of this tool—as you wander

PROVENCE

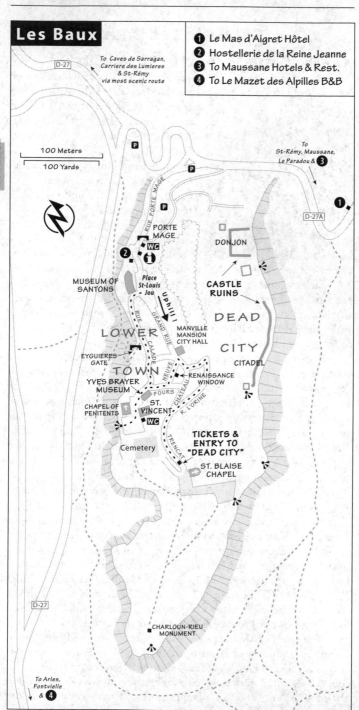

Les Baux

1 Le Mas d'Aigret Hôtel
2 Hostellerie de la Reine Jeanne
3 To Maussane Hotels & Rest.
4 To Le Mazet des Alpilles B&B

PROVENCE

To Caves de Sarragan,
Carriere des Lumieres
& St-Rémy
via most scenic route

D-27

100 Meters
100 Yards

To
St-Rémy, Maussane,
Le Paradou & 3

D-27A

1

P

P

P

RUE PORTE MAGE

PORTE
MAGE

WC

2 i

MUSEUM OF
SANTONS

Place
St-Louis-
Jou

Uphill!

DONJON

CASTLE
RUINS

DEAD

CITY

LOWER

RUE CALADE

GRAND RUE

MANVILLE
MANSION
CITY HALL

EYGUIERES GATE

TOWN

NEUVE

RENAISSANCE
WINDOW

CITADEL

YVES BRAYER
MUSEUM

FOURS

CHATEAU

R. L'ORME

CHAPEL OF
PENITENTS

ST.
VINCENT

WC

TICKETS &
ENTRY TO
"DEAD CITY"

Cemetery

TRENCAT

ST. BLAISE
CHAPEL

CHARLOUN-RIEU
MONUMENT

To Arles,
Fontvielle
& 4

D-27

around, key in the number for any of the 30 narrated stops that interest you.

As you walk on the windblown spur (*baux* in French), you'll pass kid-thrilling medieval siege weaponry (go ahead, try the battering ram). Good displays in English and images help reconstruct the place. Try to imagine 4,000 people living up here. Notice the water-catchment system (a slanted field that caught rainwater and drained it into cisterns—necessary during a siege) and find the reservoir cut into the rock below the castle's highest point. Look for post holes throughout the stone walls that reveal where beams once supported floors.

For the most sensational views, climb to the blustery top of the citadel. Hang on. The mistral wind just might blow you away.

The St. Blaise chapel across from the entry/exit runs videos with Provençal themes (plays continuously; just images and music, no words).

▲Lower Town

After your castle visit, you can shop and eat your way back through the new town. Or you can escape some of the crowds by following my walking short tour, below, which covers these minor but worthwhile sights as you descend (all stay open at lunch except the Yves Brayer Museum).

• *Follow the main drag (grand Rue Frédéric Mistral) downhill. On the right a few short blocks below the castle exit, find the flags.*

Manville Mansion City Hall—The 15th-century city hall occasionally flies the red-and-white flag of Monaco amid several others, a reminder that the Grimaldi family (which has long ruled the tiny principality of Monaco) owned Les Baux until the French Revolution (1789). In fact, in 1982, Princess Grace Kelly and her royal husband, Prince Rainier Grimaldi, came to Les Baux to receive the key to the city.

Exit left out of the city hall and walk to the empty 1571 **Renaissance window frame,** marking the site of a future Calvinist museum. This beautiful stone frame stands as a reminder of this town's Protestant history. This was probably a place of Huguenot worship—the words carved into the lintel, *Post tenebras lux,* were a popular Calvinist slogan: "After the shadow comes the light."

• *Continue walking uphill, and turn right on Rue des Fours to find the...*

Yves Brayer Museum (Musée Yves Brayer)—This enjoyable museum lets you peruse three floors of paintings (Van Gogh-like

Expressionism, without the tumult) by Yves Brayer (1907-1990), who spent his final years here in Les Baux. Like Van Gogh, Brayer was inspired by all that surrounded him. Brayer picked up inspiration from his travels through Morocco, Spain, and the rest of the Mediterranean world. Pick up the descriptive English sheet at the entry.

Cost and Hours: €5, daily April-Sept 10:00-12:30 & 14:00-18:30, Oct-March 10:00-11:30 & 15:00-17:00, tel. 04 90 54 36 99.

• *Next door is...*

St. Vincent Church—This 12th-century Romanesque church was built short and wide to fit the terrain. The center chapel on the right (partially carved out of the rock) houses the town's traditional Provençal processional chariot. Each Christmas Eve, a ram pulled this cart—holding a lamb, symbolizing Jesus, and surrounded by candles—through town to the church.

• *Around the corner to the left as you leave the church are public WCs. Directly in front of the church is a vast view, making clear the strategic value of this rocky bluff's natural fortifications. A few steps away is the...*

Chapel of Penitents—Inside, notice the nativity scene painted by Yves Brayer, illustrating the local legend that says Jesus was born in Les Baux. On the opposite wall, find his version of a starry night. Leaving the chapel, turn left.

• *As you leave the church, wash your shirt in the old town "laundry"—with a pig-snout faucet and 14th-century stone washing surface designed for short women.*

Continue down steep Rue de la Calade, passing cafés with wonderful views, the town's fortified wall, and one of its two gates. Before long, you'll run into the...

Museum of Santons—This free "museum" displays a collection of *santons* ("little saints"), popular folk figurines that decorate local Christmas mangers. Notice how the nativity scene "proves" once again that Jesus was born in Les Baux. These painted clay dolls show off local dress and traditions (with good English descriptions). Find the old couple leaning heroically into the mistral.

Near Les Baux

Best Views—A half-mile beyond Les Baux, D-27 (toward Maillane) leads to dramatic views of Les Baux. Pull into the Caves de Sarragan parking lot for terrific views of Les Baux. These cavernous caves are in former limestone quarries and date back to the Middle Ages. (The limestone is easy to cut, but gets hard and nicely polished when exposed to the weather.) Speaking of quarries, in 1821, the rocks and soil of this area were found to contain an important mineral for making aluminum. It was named after the town: bauxite.

For still better views, continue driving up. After several switchbacks you'll reach the top—turn right on the paved lane where you see a red kilometer marker and find the views. You'll find walking trails nearby (ask at TIs for info on hikes in the Alpilles; Les Baux to St-Rémy is a 2.5-hour hike).

▲▲**Carrière des Lumières**—This nearby cave (north of Les Baux on D-27) offers a mesmerizing sound-and-slide show, with 48 projectors flashing countless images on quarry walls set to music. The show lasts 40 minutes (dress warmly, as the cave is cool), and there's a different program every year. In 2013, the show celebrates artists—from Impressionists to Fauvists—who have been drawn to the Mediterranean.

Cost and Hours: €8.50, March-Dec daily 10:00-18:00, until 19:00 April-Sept, closed Jan-Feb, tel. 04 90 54 47 37, www.culture spaces.com/en/carrieres.

Sleeping in and near Les Baux

(€1 = about $1.30, country code: 33)

In Les Baux

$$$ Le Mas d'Aigret***, a 10-minute walk east of Les Baux on the road to St-Rémy (D-27), is a lovely refuge that crouches under Les

Baux. Lie on your back and stare up at the castle walls rising beyond the swimming pool, or enjoy valley views from the groomed terraces (viewless Db-€120, larger Db with balcony and view-€160, Tb/Qb-€205-240, two cool troglodyte rooms-€205, half-pension option with big breakfast and good dinner-about €45/person, air-con, rooms have some daytime road noise, tel. 04 90 54 20 00, fax 04 90 54 44 00, www.masdaigret.com, contact@masdaigret .com, Dutch Marieke and French Eric).

$$ Hostellerie de la Reine Jeanne**, warmly run by Gaelle (speaks English) and Marc (speaks French), offers a handful of rooms above a busy (and good-value) restaurant. The rooms are scheduled to be renovated, so these prices may change (standard Db-€65, Db with view deck-€90, Tb-€105, cavernous family suite-€120, air-con in half the rooms, for view deck ask for *chambre avec terrasse*, good *menus* from €16, 150 feet to your right after entry to the village of Les Baux, tel. 04 90 54 32 06, fax 04 90 54 32 33, www.la-reinejeanne.com, marc.braglia@wanadoo.fr).

PROVENCE

In Maussane

The appealing village of Maussane lies a few minutes' drive south of Les Baux. It has some hotels, a handful of restaurants, and a fine square lined with cafés and atmosphere. There's also bike rental and a small TI (tel. 04 90 54 33 60, www.maussane.com). The following two Maussane accommodations are well worth considering.

$$ Hôtel les Magnanarelles**, in the center of Maussane, gives solid two-star value in its 18 tastefully designed rooms above a handsome restaurant. Enjoy the generously sized pool (Db-€68-78, extra person-€17, ask for a room off the street, no air-con, 104 Avenue de la Vallée des Baux, tel. 04 90 54 30 25, www.hotel-magnanarelles.com, hotel.magnanarelles@wanadoo.fr).

$$ Le Mas de l'Esparou *chambre d'hôte* is welcoming and kid-friendly, with three simple-yet-spacious rooms, a big swimming pool, table tennis, and distant views of Les Baux. Jacqueline loves her job, and her lack of English only makes her more animated (Db-€74, Tb/Qb-€120-142, includes breakfast, cash only, no air-con, between Les Baux and Maussane on D-5, look for white sign with green lettering, tel. & fax 04 90 54 41 32).

In Le Paradou

$ Le Mazet des Alpilles is a small home with three tidy, air-conditioned rooms around a lovely garden, located just outside the sleepy village of Le Paradou (five minutes south of Les Baux). Sweet Annick is happy to share her knowledge of the area with you (Db-€65, ask for largest room, includes breakfast, cash only, air-con, child's bed available, drive into Le Paradou and look for signs, Route de Brunelly, tel. 04 90 54 45 89, www.alpilles.com/mazet.htm, lemazet@wanadoo.fr).

Eating in and near Les Baux

You'll find quiet cafés with views along my self-guided tour route.

The recommended **Hostellerie de la Reine Jeanne** offers friendly service and good-value meals indoors or out (€12 salads, €16 *menus,* try the *salade Estivale,* open daily).

You'll also find several worthwhile places in Maussane, south of Les Baux. Place de la Fontaine is the town's central square and makes a good stop for café fare. **Pizza Brun** has the region's best pizza (1 Rue Edouard Foscalina, tel. 04 90 54 40 73). **La Place** is a good choice for a real restaurant (*menus* from €22, daily, 65 Avenue de la Vallée des Baux, tel. 04 90 54 23 31).

Orange

Orange, called *Arausio* in Roman times, is notable for its Roman arch and grand Roman Theater. Orange was a thriving city in ancient times—strategically situated on the Via Agrippa, connecting the important Roman cities of Lyon and Arles. It was actually founded as a comfortable place for Roman army officers to enjoy their retirement. Even in Roman times, professional military men retired with time for a second career. Did the emperor want thousands of well-trained, relatively young guys hanging around Rome? No way. What to do? "How about a nice place in the south of France...?"

Today's Orange works well as a base for non-drivers, thanks to its quick rail link to Avignon and Arles, and just enough bus service to wine villages of the Côtes du Rhône.

Orientation to Orange

Tourist Information

The unnecessary TI is located next to the fountain and parking area at 5 Cours Aristide Briand (April-Sept Mon-Sat 9:00-18:30, Sun 10:00-13:00 & 14:00-18:30; Oct-March Mon-Sat 10:00-13:00 & 14:00-17:00, closed Sun; tel. 04 90 34 70 88, www.otorange.fr).

Arrival in Orange

By Train: Orange's **train station** is a level 20-minute walk from the Roman Theater (or an €8 taxi ride, mobile 06 09 51 32 25). The recommended Hôtel de Provence, across from the station, will keep your bags (see "Sleeping in Orange," later). To walk into town from the train station, head straight out of the station (down Avenue Frédéric Mistral), merge left onto Orange's main shopping street (Rue de la République), then turn left on Rue Caristie; you'll run into the Roman Theater's massive stage wall.

By Bus: Buses stop at the train station (Gare SNCF) and at Place Pourtoules, two blocks from the Roman Theater (walk to the hill and turn right to reach the theater, bus station tel. 04 90 34 15 59, www.vaucluse.fr/86-reseau-departemental.htm).

By Car: Follow *Centre-Ville* signs, then *Théâtre Antique* signs, and park as close to the Roman Theater's huge wall as possible—the easiest option is labeled *Parking Office du Tourisme* (by the fountain and the TI). Those coming from the autoroute will land here by following *Centre-Ville* signs; others should follow *Centre-Ville* signs, then *Office du Tourisme* signs, to find this parking lot. To reach the theater, walk to the hill and turn left.

Sights in Orange

▲▲Roman Theater (Théâtre Antique)—Orange's ancient theater is the best-preserved in existence, and the only one in Europe with its acoustic wall still standing. (Two others in Asia Minor also survive.)

Cost and Hours: €8.50, drops to €7.50 one hour before closing; ticket includes film, multimedia show, and entry to small museum across the street; good audioguide-€2, daily April-Sept 9:00-18:00, until 19:00 in summer, Oct-March 9:30-17:30 except Nov-Feb until 16:30, tel. 04 90 51 17 60, www.theatre-antique .com.

Cheap Trick: Vagabonds wanting a partial but free view of the theater can see it from the bluff high above in the Parc de la Colline St-Eutrope. Find the *escalier est* (east staircase) off Rue Pourtoules and start climbing—it's several hundred steps to the top. At the sign for *Promenade Botanique,* keep left, and at the next fork, follow the stairs up to the right. When you see the playground, head to the right to find the view. Benches and grassy areas make this a good picnic spot (no WCs).

Museum: Pop into the museum across the street (Musée d'Art et d'Histoire, included with ticket) to see a few theater details and a rare grid used as the official property-ownership registry—each square represented a 120-acre plot of land.

Eating: The café in the theater, La Grotte d'Auguste (closed Sun year-round, closed Mon in off-season), has reasonably priced snacks and lunches and great views. A shaded café-filled square (Place de la République) is two blocks from the theater up Rue Ségond Weber.

❍ Self-Guided Tour: After you enter (to the right of the actual theater), you'll see a huge dig—the site of the Temple to the Cult of the Emperor (English explanations posted). *Arausio* is the Roman name for the town.

Look for signs to the worthwhile film and multimedia show (near the ticket office). The 15-minute **film** is in French with English subtitles (ask at front desk if subtitles aren't on). *The Ghosts of the Theatre* **multimedia show** covers four different periods of performance history. Both run continuously and can help you gain a good visual sense of how the theater looked to the Romans.

Next, enter the theater, then climb the steep stairs to find a seat high up to appreciate the acoustics (eavesdrop on people by the stage). Contemplate the idea that 2,000 years ago, Orange residents enjoyed grand spectacles with high-tech sound and lighting effects—such as simulated thunder, lightning, and rain.

A grandiose **Caesar** overlooks everything, reminding attendees of who's in charge. If it seems like you've seen this statue

PROVENCE

PROVENCE

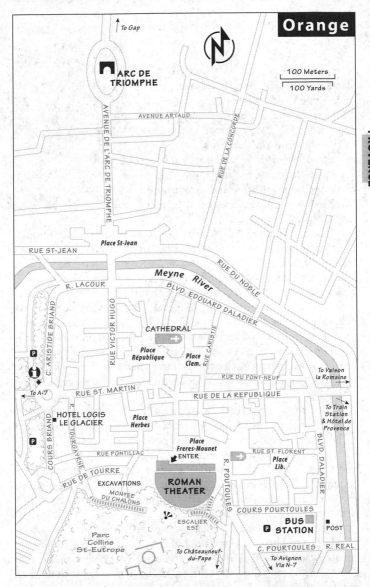

before, you probably have. Countless sculptures identical to this one were mass-produced in Rome and shipped throughout the empire to grace buildings like this theater for propaganda purposes. To save money on shipping and handling, only the heads of these statues were changed with each new ruler. The permanent body wears a breastplate emblazoned with the imperial griffon (body of a lion, head and wings of an eagle) that only the emperor could wear. When a new emperor came to power, new heads were made in Rome and shipped off throughout the empire to replace the pop-off heads on all these statues. (Imagine Barack Obama's head on George W. Bush's body.)

Archaeologists believe that a puny, vanquished Celt was included at the knee of the emperor, touching his ruler's robe respectfully—a show of humble subservience to the emperor. It's interesting to consider how an effective propaganda machine can con the masses into being impressed by their leader.

The horn has blown. It's time to find your **seat**: row 2, number 30. Sitting down, you're comforted by the "EQ GIII" carved into the seat (*Equitas Gradus* #3...three rows for the Equestrian order). You're not comforted by the hard limestone bench (thinking it'll probably last 2,000 years). The theater is filled with 10,000 people. Thankfully, you mix only with your class, the nouveau riche—merchants, tradesmen, and city big shots. The people seated above you are the working class, and way up in the "chicken roost" section is the scum of the earth—slaves, beggars, prostitutes, and youth hostellers. Scanning the orchestra section (where the super-rich sit on real chairs), you notice the town dignitaries hosting some visiting VIPs.

OK, time to worship. They're parading a bust of the emperor from its sacred home in the adjacent temple around the **stage**. Next is the ritual animal sacrifice called *la pompa* (so fancy, future generations will use that word for anything full of such...pomp). Finally, you settle in for an all-day series of spectacles and dramatic entertainment. All eyes are on the big stage door in the middle—where the Angelina Jolies and Brad Pitts of the day will appear. (Lesser actors come out of the side doors.)

The play is good, but many come for the halftime shows—jugglers, acrobats, and striptease dancers. In Roman times, the theater was a festival of immorality. An ancient writer commented, "The vanquished take their revenge on us by giving us their vices through the theater."

With an audience of 10,000 and no amplification, **acoustics** were critical. A roof made of linen (called the velarium) originally covered the stage, somewhat like the glass-and-iron roof you see today (installed to protect the stage wall). The original was designed not to protect the stage from the weather, but to project the voices of the actors into the crowd. For further help, actors wore masks with leather caricature mouths that functioned as megaphones. The theater's side walls originally rose as high as the stage wall and supported a retractable roof that gave the audience some protection from the sun or rain. After leaving the theater, look up to the stage wall from the outside and notice the supports for poles that held the velarium in place, like the masts and sails of a ship.

The Roman Theater was all part of the "give them bread and circuses" approach to winning the support of the masses (not unlike today's philosophy of "give them tax cuts and *American Idol*"). The spectacle grew from 65 days of games per year when the theater was first built (and when Rome was at its height) to about 180 days each year by the time Rome finally fell.

▲**Roman "Arc de Triomphe"**—Technically the only real Roman arches of triumph are in Rome's Forum, built to commemorate various emperors' victories. The great Roman arch of Orange is actually a municipal arch erected (in about A.D. 19) to commemorate a general named Germanicus, who protected the town. The 60-foot-tall arch is on a noisy traffic circle (north of city center, on Avenue Arc de Triomphe).

Sleeping in Orange

(€1 = about $1.30, country code: 33)

$$ **Hôtel de Provence****, at the train station, is air-conditioned, quiet, comfortable, and affordable. Friendly Madame Verbe runs this traditional place with grace (Db-€62-82, Tb-€84-98, Qb-€89-109, small rooftop pool, café, 60 Avenue Frédéric Mistral, tel. 04 90 34 00 23, fax 04 90 34 91 72, www.hotelprovence-orange.com, hoteldeprovence84@orange.fr).

$ **Hôtel Logis Le Glacier**** is a sweet hotel with nice touches in the center of town, two blocks from the Roman Theater. It has easy parking and very fair rates (small Db-€50, bigger Db-€70, still bigger Db-€95, 46 Cours Aristide Briand, tel. 04 90 34 02 01, fax 04 90 51 13 80, www.le-glacier.com, info@le-glacier.com).

Orange Connections

From Orange by Train to: Avignon (15/day, 15 minutes), **Arles** (4/day direct, 35 minutes, more frequently with transfer in Avignon), **Lyon** (16/day, 2 hours).

By Bus to: Châteauneuf-du-Pape (2/day, none Sun, 30 minutes), **Vaison la Romaine** (3-5/day, 45 minutes), **Avignon** (Mon-Sat hourly, none Sun, 45 minutes—take the train instead). Buses to Vaison la Romaine and other wine villages depart from the Gare SNCF and from Place Pourtoules (turn right out of the Roman Theater, and right again onto Rue Pourtoules).

Villages of the Côtes du Rhône

The sunny Côtes du Rhône wine road—one of France's best—starts at Avignon's doorstep. It winds north through a mountainous landscape carpeted with vines, studded with warm stone villages, and presided over by the Vesuvius-like Mont Ventoux. The wines of the Côtes du Rhône (grown on the *côtes,* or hillsides, of the Rhône River Valley) are easy on the palate and on your budget. But this hospitable place offers more than famous wine—its hill-capping villages inspire travel posters, its Roman ruins inspire awe, and the people you'll meet are welcoming...and, often, as excited about their region as you are. Yes, you'll have good opportunities for enjoyable wine-tasting, but there is also a soul to this area...if you take the time to look.

Planning Your Time

Vaison la Romaine is the small hub of this region, offering limited bus connections with Avignon and Orange, bike rental, and a mini-Pompeii in the town center. Nearby, you can visit the impressive Roman Theater in Orange (described earlier), follow my self-guided "Côtes du Rhône Wine Road" driving tour, or pedal to nearby towns for a breath of fresh air. The vineyards' centerpiece, the Dentelles de Montmirail mountains, are laced with a variety of trails ideal for hikers.

To explore this area, allow two nights for a good start. Drivers should head for the hills. Those without wheels find that Vaison la Romaine or Orange make the only practical home bases (or, maybe better, consider a minivan tour for this area).

Getting Around the Côtes du Rhône

By Car: Pick up Michelin maps #332 or #527 to navigate your way around the Côtes du Rhône. (Landmarks like the Dentelles de Montmirail and Mont Ventoux make it easy to get your bearings.) I've described my favorite driving route on page 749. If your plan is to connect the Côtes du Rhône with the scenic **Luberon,** you can do it via Mont Ventoux (follow signs to *Malaucène,* then to *Mont Ventoux,* allowing 2 hours to Roussillon). This route is one of the most spectacular in Provence. If continuing north toward Lyon, consider the worthwhile detour via the Ardèche Gorges (described on page 746).

By Bus: Buses run to Vaison la Romaine from Orange and Avignon (3-5/day, 45 minutes from Orange, 1.5 hours from Avignon) and connect several wine villages with Vaison la Romaine and Nyons to the north. (From Avignon, you can save time by taking the 15-minute train to Orange, then connecting by bus to Vaison la Romaine.) Another bus line runs from Vaison la Romaine to Carpentras, serving Crestet (below Le Crestet), Malaucène, and Le Barroux (Mon-Sat 3/day, none on Sun, tel. 04 90 36 09 90). Both routes provide scenic rides through this area.

By Train: Trains get you as far as Orange (from Avignon: 15/day, 15 minutes).

By Minivan Tour: Various all-day minivan excursions leave from Avignon. For a wine-focused tour, I recommend several individuals who can expertly guide you through the region. For all tours to this area, see "Tours of Provence" on page 662.

PROVENCE

Vaison la Romaine

With quick access to vineyards, villages, and Mont Ventoux, this lively little town of 6,000 makes a handy base for exploring the Côtes du Rhône region by car, by bike, or on foot. You get two villages for the price of one: Vaison la Romaine's "modern" lower city has worthwhile Roman ruins, a lone pedestrian street, and a lively main square: café-studded Place Montfort. The car-free medieval hill town looms above, with meandering cobbled lanes, a dash of art galleries and cafés, and a ruined castle with a fine view from its base. (Vaison la Romaine is also a good place to have your hair done, since there are more than 20 hairdressers in this small town.)

Orientation to Vaison la Romaine

The city is split in two by the Ouvèze River. The Roman Bridge connects the more modern lower town (Ville-Basse) with the hill-capping medieval upper town (Ville-Haute).

Tourist Information

The superb TI is in the lower city, between the two Roman ruin sites, at Place du Chanoine Sautel (June-Aug Mon-Fri 9:00-18:45, Sat-Sun 9:00-12:30 & 14:00-18:45; Sept-May Mon-Sat 9:30-12:00 & 14:00-17:45, Sun 9:00-12:00—except closed Sun mid-Oct-March;

tel. 04 90 36 02 11, www.vaison-ventoux-tourisme.com). S
jour to *charmante* and ever-so-patient Valerie. Get bus sch
ask about festivals and evening programs, and pick up infor
on walks from Vaison la Romaine. Find the big wall map s
hiking trails, and try the slick computer terminals that all
to download hikes and bike rides with English instructio
can also pick up English pamphlets on biking and hikin
instructions for several loop trails, ranging from easy half-d
to all-day affairs.

Arrival in Vaison la Romaine

By Bus: The unmarked bus stop to Orange and Avigno
front of the Cave la Romaine winery (by the driveway closer
roundabout). Buses from Orange or Avignon drop you acr
street (3-5/day, 45 minutes from Orange, 1.5 hours from Av
best from Orange and just €3). Tell the driver you want th
for the *Office de Tourisme*. When you get off the bus, walk five
utes down Avenue Général de Gaulle to reach the TI and r
mended hotels.

By Car: Follow signs to *Centre-Ville*, then *Office de Tou*
parking is free across from the TI—most parking is free in
la Romaine as well.

Helpful Hints

Market Day: Sleep in Vaison la Romaine on Monday night
you'll wake to an amazing Tuesday market. But be wa
Mondays are quiet during the day, as many shops clos
sights are open). If you spend a Monday night, avoid pa
at market sites, or you won't find your car where you
(if signs indicate *Stationnement Interdit le Mardi*, don't
there—ask your hotel where you can park).

Internet Access: Try **Vaison 2 Mils** at 51 Cours Taulignan (te
90 36 23 24). For Wi-Fi, head to **Café Universal** on atmosp
Place Montfort. For other choices, the TI has a good list.

Laundry: The self-service **Laverie la Lavandière** is on
Taulignan, near Avenue Victor Hugo (daily 8:00-22:00)
friendly owners, who work next door at the dry cleaners
do your laundry while you sightsee—when you pick up
laundry, thank them with a small tip (dry cleaners open N
Sat 9:00-12:00 & 15:00-19:00, closed Sun).

Supermarket: A handy **Casino** is on Place Montfort in the
of the cafés.

Bike Rental: The TI has a list. The most central shop, C
Chaves, gets complaints for poor bike service and bike qu
Vélo Speed is less than a mile from the center on the Rout
Nyons (tel. 04 90 28 17 84).

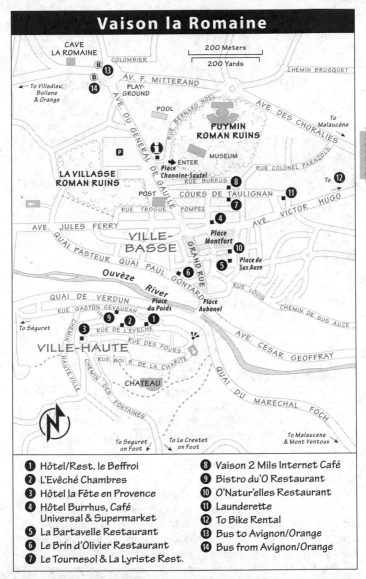

Vaison la Romaine

CAVE LA ROMAINE
COLOMBIER
AV. F. MITTERAND
CHEMIN BRUSQUET
← To Villedieu, Bollene & Orange
PLAY-GROUND
POOL
RUE BERNARD NOEL
AVE. DES CHORALIES
To Malaucène →
PUYMIN ROMAN RUINS
MUSEUM
AVE. DU GENERAL DE GAULLE
P
ENTER
Place Chanoine-Sautel
LA VILLASSE ROMAN RUINS
RUE COLONEL PARAZOLS
RUE BURRUS
To →
POST
COURS DE TAULIGNAN
RUE TROGUE POMPEE
AVE. VICTOR HUGO
AVE. JULES FERRY
VILLE-BASSE
QUAI PASTEUR
QUAI PAUL GONTARD
Place Montfort
Place de Sus Auze
GRAND RUE
RUE LOUIS
Ouvèze River
QUAI DE VERDUN
RUE GASTON GEVAUDAN
Place du Poids
Place Aubanel
CHEMIN DE SUS AUZE
← To Séguret
CHEMIN
RUE DE L'EVECHE
RUE DES FOURS
AVE. CESAR GEOFFRAY
VILLE-HAUTE
HAUTE VILLE
RUE ROI R. DE LA CHARITE
CHATEAU
QUAI DU MARECHAL FOCH
CHEMIN DES FONTAINES
N
To Séguret on Foot ↓
To Le Crestet on Foot ↓
To Malaucene & Mont Ventoux →

200 Meters
200 Yards

PROVENCE

❶ Hôtel/Rest. le Beffroi	❽ Vaison 2 Mils Internet Café
❷ L'Evêché Chambres	❾ Bistro du'O Restaurant
❸ Hôtel la Fête en Provence	❿ O'Natur'elles Restaurant
❹ Hôtel Burrhus, Café Universal & Supermarket	⓫ Launderette
❺ La Bartavelle Restaurant	⓬ To Bike Rental
❻ Le Brin d'Olivier Restaurant	⓭ Bus to Avignon/Orange
❼ Le Tournesol & La Lyriste Rest.	⓮ Bus from Avignon/Orange

Taxi: Call 04 90 36 00 04 or 06 22 28 24 49.

Car Rental: You can rent cars by the day that must be returned to Vaison; ask at the TI for locations.

Local Guide: Let sincere and knowledgeable **Anna-Marie Melard** bring those Roman ruins to life for you (tel. 04 90 36 50 48).

Cooking Classes: Charming **Barbara Schuerenberg** offers reasonably priced cooking classes from her home in Vaison la

Romaine (€80, includes lunch, 4-person maximum, tel. 04 90 35 68 43, www.cuisinedeprovence.com, barbara@cuisine deprovence.com).

Sights in Vaison la Romaine

PROVENCE

Roman Ruins—Ancient Vaison la Romaine had a treaty that gave it the preferred "federated" relationship with Rome (rather

than simply being a colony). This, along with a healthy farming economy (olives and vineyards), made it a most prosperous place...as a close look at its sprawling ruins demonstrates. About 6,000 people called Vaison la Romaine home 2,000 years ago. When the barbarians arrived, the Romans were forced out, and the townspeople fled into the hills. The town has only recently reached the same population it had during its Roman era.

Cost and Hours: €8 Roman ruins combo-ticket includes both ruins, helpful audioguide, and cloister at the Notre-Dame de Nazareth Cathedral (described later); daily April-Sept 9:30-18:00, Oct-March 10:00-12:00 & 14:00-17:00.

Visiting the Ruins: Vaison la Romaine's Roman ruins are split by a modern road into two sites: Puymin and La Villasse. Each is well-presented thanks to the audioguide and some English information panels, offering a good look at life during the Roman Empire. The Roman town extended all the way to the river, and its forum still lies under Place Montfort. What you can see is only a small fraction of the Roman town's extent—most is still buried under today's city.

Visit **Puymin** first. Nearest the entry are the scant but impressive ruins of a sprawling mansion. Find the faint remains of a colorful frescoed wall. Climb the hill to the good little **museum** (pick up your audioguide here; exhibits also explained in English loaner booklet). Don't miss the **3-D film** that takes you inside the home

of a wealthy Vaison resident and explores daily life some 2,000 years ago.

Behind the museum is a still well-used, 6,000-seat theater, with just enough seats for the whole town (of yesterday and today).

Back across the modern road in **La Villasse,** you'll explore a "street of

Romaine (€80, includes lunch, 4-person maximum, tel. 04 90 35 68 43, www.cuisinedeprovence.com, barbara@cuisine deprovence.com).

Sights in Vaison la Romaine

Roman Ruins—Ancient Vaison la Romaine had a treaty that gave it the preferred "federated" relationship with Rome (rather

than simply being a colony). This, along with a healthy farming economy (olives and vineyards), made it a most prosperous place...as a close look at its sprawling ruins demonstrates. About 6,000 people called Vaison la Romaine home 2,000 years ago. When the barbarians arrived, the Romans were forced out, and the townspeople fled into the hills. The town has only recently reached the same population it had during its Roman era.

Cost and Hours: €8 Roman ruins combo-ticket includes both ruins, helpful audioguide, and cloister at the Notre-Dame de Nazareth Cathedral (described later); daily April-Sept 9:30-18:00, Oct-March 10:00-12:00 & 14:00-17:00.

Visiting the Ruins: Vaison la Romaine's Roman ruins are split by a modern road into two sites: Puymin and La Villasse. Each is well-presented thanks to the audioguide and some English information panels, offering a good look at life during the Roman Empire. The Roman town extended all the way to the river, and its forum still lies under Place Montfort. What you can see is only a small fraction of the Roman town's extent—most is still buried under today's city.

Visit **Puymin** first. Nearest the entry are the scant but impressive ruins of a sprawling mansion. Find the faint remains of a colorful frescoed wall. Climb the hill to the good little **museum** (pick up your audioguide here; exhibits also explained in English loaner booklet). Don't miss the **3-D film** that takes you inside the home

of a wealthy Vaison resident and explores daily life some 2,000 years ago.

Behind the museum is a still well-used, 6,000-seat theater, with just enough seats for the whole town (of yesterday and today).

Back across the modern road in **La Villasse,** you'll explore a "street of

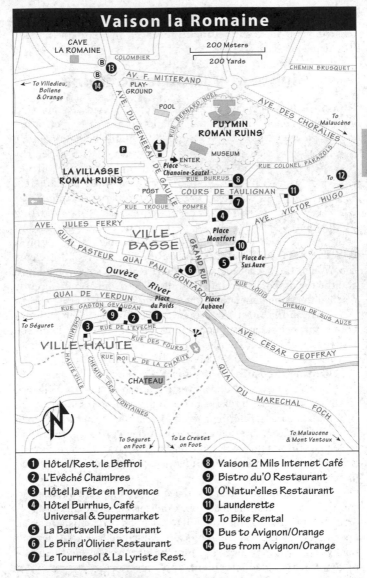

Vaison la Romaine

① Hôtel/Rest. le Beffroi
② L'Evêché Chambres
③ Hôtel la Fête en Provence
④ Hôtel Burrhus, Café Universal & Supermarket
⑤ La Bartavelle Restaurant
⑥ Le Brin d'Olivier Restaurant
⑦ Le Tournesol & La Lyriste Rest.

⑧ Vaison 2 Mils Internet Café
⑨ Bistro du'O Restaurant
⑩ O'Natur'elles Restaurant
⑪ Launderette
⑫ To Bike Rental
⑬ Bus to Avignon/Orange
⑭ Bus from Avignon/Orange

Taxi: Call 04 90 36 00 04 or 06 22 28 24 49.

Car Rental: You can rent cars by the day that must be returned to Vaison; ask at the TI for locations.

Local Guide: Let sincere and knowledgeable **Anna-Marie Melard** bring those Roman ruins to life for you (tel. 04 90 36 50 48).

Cooking Classes: Charming **Barbara Schuerenberg** offers reasonably priced cooking classes from her home in Vaison la shops" and the foundations of more houses. You'll also see a few wells, used before Vaison's two aqueducts were built.

Lower Town (Ville-Basse)—Vaison la Romaine's modern town centers on café-friendly Place Montfort. Tables grab the north side of the square, conveniently sheltered from the prevailing mistral wind while enjoying the generous shade of the ubiquitous plane *(platane)* trees, which are cut back each year to form a leafy canopy.

A 10-minute walk below Place Montfort, the stout **Notre-Dame de Nazareth Cathedral**—with an evocative cloister—is a good example of Provençal Romanesque (cloister entry-€1.50, or covered by Roman ruins combo-ticket, daily 15:00-19:00). The pedestrian-only Grand Rue is a lively shopping street leading to the small river gorge and the Roman Bridge.

Roman Bridge—The Romans cut this sturdy, no-nonsense vault into the canyon rock 2,000 years ago, and it has survived ever since. Find the information panel at the new town end of the bridge. Until the 20th century, this was the only way to cross the Ouvèze River. The stone plaque on the rock wall *(Septembre 22-92...)* shows the high-water mark of the record flood that killed 30 people and washed away the valley's other bridges. The flood swept away the modern top of this bridge...but couldn't budge the 55-foot Roman arch.

Upper Town (Ville-Haute)—Although there's nothing of particular importance to see in the fortified medieval old town atop the hill, the cobbled lanes and enchanting fountains make you want to break out a sketchpad. Vaison la Romaine had a prince-bishop since the fourth century. He came under attack by the Count of Toulouse in the 12th century. Anticipating a struggle, the prince-bishop abandoned the lower town and built a château on this rocky outcrop (about 1195). Over time, the rest of the townspeople followed, vacating the lower town and building their homes at the base of the château behind the upper town's fortified wall.

To reach the upper town, hike up from the Roman Bridge (passing memorials for both world wars) through the medieval gate, under the lone tower crowned by an 18th-century wrought iron bell cage. The château is closed, but a steep, uneven trail to its base rewards hikers with a sweeping view.

▲▲**Market Day**—In the 16th century, the pope gave Vaison la Romaine market-town status. Each Tuesday morning since then, the

PROVENCE

town has hosted a farmers market. Today merchants gather with gusto, turning the entire place into a festival of produce and Provençal products. This market is one of France's best, but it can challenge claustrophobes. Be warned that parking is a real headache unless you arrive early (see "Helpful Hints," earlier).

Wine Tasting—**Cave la Romaine,** a five-minute walk up Avenue Général de Gaulle from the TI, offers a big variety of good-value wines from nearby villages in a pleasant, well-organized tasting room (free tastes, Mon-Sat 8:30-18:30, Sun 9:00-12:00, Avenue St. Quenin, tel. 04 90 36 55 90, www.cave-la-romaine.com).

▲Hiking—The TI has good information on relatively easy hikes into the hills above Vaison la Romaine. It's about 1.25 hours to the quiet hill town of Le Crestet, though views begin immediately. To find this trail, drive or walk on the road past the upper town (with the rock base and castle just on your left), continue on Chemin des Fontaines (blue signs), and stay the course as far as you like (follow yellow *Crestet* signs). Cars are not allowed on the road after about a mile. To find the 8.5-mile walk to Séguret, take the same road above Vaison la Romaine and look for a yellow sign (walk takes about 2.5 hours). In both cases, consider the value of hiking one way and taking a taxi back (see "Helpful Hints," earlier, for taxi contact info).

Biking—This area is not particularly flat, and if it's hot and windy, bike-riding is a dicey option. But if the air's calm, the five-mile ride to cute little Villedieu (recommended restaurant listed on page 755) is a delight. The bike route is signed along small roads; you'll find signs from Vaison la Romaine to Villedieu at the roundabout past Cave La Romaine toward Orange (see map on page 743). With a bit more energy, you can pedal beyond Villedieu on the lovely road to Mirabel (from Villedieu, follow signs to *Nyons*) and loop back on a busier road to Vaison (figure about 18 miles total). Or get a good map and connect the following villages for an enjoyable 11-mile loop ride: Vaison la Romaine, St-Romain-en-Viennois, Puyméras (with a recommended restaurant—see page 755), Faucon, and St-Marcellin-lès-Vaison. The TI and bike shop have good information on mountain-biking trails.

Near Vaison la Romaine

▲Ardèche Gorges (Gorges de l'Ardèche)—These gorges, which wow visitors with abrupt chalky-white cliffs, follow the Ardèche River through immense canyons and thick forests. To reach the gorges from Vaison la Romaine, drive west 45 minutes, passing through Bollène and Pont Saint-Esprit to Vallon Pont d'Arc (the tourist hub of the Ardèche Gorges). From Vallon Pont d'Arc, you can canoe along the peaceful river through some of the canyon's most spectacular scenery and under the rock arch of Pont d'Arc (half-day, all-day, and 2-day trips possible; less appealing in summer, when the river is crowded and water levels are low), and learn about hiking trails that get you above it all (**TI** tel. 04 75 88 04 01, www.vallon-pont-darc.com). If continuing north toward Lyon, connect Privas and Aubenas, then head back on the autoroute. Endearing little **Balazuc**—a village north of the gorges, with narrow lanes, flowers, views, and a smattering of cafés and shops—makes a great stop.

Sleeping in Vaison la Romaine

(€1 = about $1.30, country code: 33)
Hotels in Vaison la Romaine are a good value. Those in the medieval upper town (Ville-Haute) are quieter, cozier, and cooler, but require a 15-minute walk to the town center and Roman ruins. If staying at one of the first three places, follow signs to *Cité Médiévale* and park just outside the upper village entry (driving into the Cité Médiévale itself is a challenge, with tiny lanes and nearly impossible parking). If you have a car, consider staying in one of the Côtes du Rhône villages near Vaison la Romaine (see "Sleeping Along the Côtes du Rhône" on page 754).

$$$ Hôtel le Beffroi*** hides deep in the upper town, just above a demonstrative bell tower (you'll hear what I mean). It offers 16th-century red-tile-and-wood-beamed-cozy lodgings with nary a level surface. The rooms—split between two buildings a few doors apart—are Old World comfy, and some have views. You'll also find tasteful public spaces, a garden with view tables (light meals available in the summer), a small pool with more views, and animated Nathalie at the reception (standard Db-€95-120, superior Db-€150, Tb-€175, Rue de l'Evêché, tel. 04 90 36 04 71, fax 04 90 36 24 78, www.le-beffroi.com, info@le-beffroi.com). The hotel's restaurant offers *menus* from €28.

$$ L'Evêché Chambres, almost next door to le Beffroi in the upper town (look for the ivy), is a five-room melt-in-your-chair B&B. The owners (the Verdiers) have an exquisite sense of interior design, and are passionate about books, making this place feel like a cross between a library and an art gallery (Sb-€85, standard Db-€92, Db suite-€115-140, the *solanum* suite is worth every euro, Tb-€120-160, Internet access and Wi-Fi, Rue de l'Evêché, tel. 04 90 36 13 46, fax 04 90 36 32 43, http://eveche.free.fr, eveche @aol.com).

$$ Hôtel la Fête en Provence, conveniently located for drivers at the entry to the medieval upper town, has a variety of room shapes and sizes. All the rooms are chiffon-comfortable, and several have small kitchenettes. Rooms are located around a calming courtyard, and there's a pool and Jacuzzi next door (standard Db-€75, bigger Db with king-size bed and bath-€110, extra person-€15, Cité Médiévale, tel. & fax 04 90 36 36 43, www .hotellafete-provence.com, fete-en-provence@wanadoo.fr). Their apartments (€155) sleep up to six people, and come with a kitchen-ette and sitting area.

$ Hôtel Burrhus** is part art gallery, part simple, funky hotel—and the best value in the lower town. It's a central, laid-back, go-with-the-flow place, with a broad terrace over the rau-cous Place Montfort (the double-paned windows are effective, but for maximum quiet, request a back room). Its floor plan will con-found even the ablest navigator. The bigger, newer rooms—with contemporary decor, bigger bathrooms, and air-conditioning—are worth the extra euros (Db-€57-67, newer Db-€78-95, Qb apart-ment-€140, extra bed-€15, air-con, Internet access and Wi-Fi, 1 Place Montfort, tel. 04 90 36 00 11, fax 04 90 36 39 05, www .burrhus.com, info@burrhus.com).

Eating in Vaison la Romaine

Vaison la Romaine offers a handful of excellent places—arrive by 19:30 or reserve ahead, particularly on weekends. And while you can eat very well on a moderate budget in Vaison, it's well worth venturing to nearby Côtes du Rhône villages to eat (see "Eating Along the Côtes du Rhône" on page 755). Wherever you dine, begin with a fresh glass of Muscat from the nearby village of Beaumes de Venise.

La Bartavelle is a good place to savor traditional French cuisine in the lower town, with a tourist-friendly mix-and-match choice of local options. The €29 *menu* gets you four courses; the €22 *menu* gives you access to all the top-end selections but fewer courses. Be sure to reserve ahead (closed Mon, small terrace out-side, air-con interior, 12 Place de Sus Auze, tel. 04 90 36 02 16).

Le Brin d'Olivier is the most romantic place I list, with soft lighting, hushed conversations, earth tones, and a semi-gastro-nomic range of food that celebrates Provence (no-choice €29 and €36 *menus,* €22-26 à la carte *plats,* closed Wed except July-Aug, 4 Rue du Ventoux, tel. 04 90 28 74 79).

Le Tournesol offers a decent €19 *menu,* mostly Provençal dishes, and friendly service. Show this book to get a free *kir* (daily, 30 Cours Taulignan, tel. 04 90 36 09 18, owner Patrick speaks a little English).

La Lyriste, named for the loudest "singing" *cigale* (cicada), puts cuisine above decor. Marie serves what hubby Benoît cooks. Both are shy, yet proud of their restaurant. There's a fine *menu* for €19, but go for the slightly pricier *menus,* which are inventive and *très delectable* (closed Mon, indoor and outdoor seating, 45 Cours

Taulignan, tel. 04 90 36 04 67).

Bistro du'O, in the upper village, is popular with Vaison's yuppie crowd. Reserve ahead to dine on soft leather chairs under tall stone arches. You'll enjoy mouthwatering cuisine that is creatively presented yet affordable. Try the chef's beefy *noix de St. Jacques* (*menus* from €29, closed Sun-Mon, Rue du Château, tel. 04 90 41 72 90).

O'Natur'elles is ideal for vegetarians, since its all-organic dishes are served with or without meat (€14-20 *plats,* daily, 36 Place Montfort, tel. 04 90 65 81 67).

The recommended **Hôtel le Beffroi's** garden is just right for a light dinner in the summer (*menus* from €28).

Vaison la Romaine Connections

The most central **bus stop** is a few blocks up Avenue Général de Gaulle from the TI at the main winery, Cave la Romaine.

From Vaison la Romaine by Bus to: Avignon (5/day during school year—called *période scolaire,* otherwise 3/day, all buses pass through Orange, 1.5 hours; faster to bus to Orange and train from there), **Orange** (3-5/day, 45 minutes), **Nyons** (3-5/day, 45 minutes), **Crestet** (lower village below Le Crestet, 2/day, 5 minutes), **Carpentras** (2/day, 45 minutes). Bus info: tel. 04 90 86 36 75, www.cars-lieutaud.fr.

Côtes du Rhône Sights near Vaison la Romaine

▲▲▲The Côtes du Rhône Wine Road

This self-guided driving tour introduces you to the characteristic best of the Côtes du Rhône wine road. While circling the rugged Dentelles de Montmirail mountain peaks, you'll experience all that's unique about this region: its natural beauty, glowing limestone villages, inviting wineries, and rolling hills of vineyards. As you drive, notice how some vineyards grow at angles—they're planted this way to compensate for the strong effect of the mistral wind.

The many fine restaurants along the way are another highlight of the route. I've mentioned some of my favorites; you'll find much more detail about these later, under "Eating Along the Côtes du Rhône."

Our tour starts just south of Vaison la Romaine in little Séguret. This town is best for a visit early or late, when it's quieter. (If you get a late start or prefer ending your tour here, begin the tour in Le Crestet—stop #3—and save the first two stops for last.)

PROVENCE

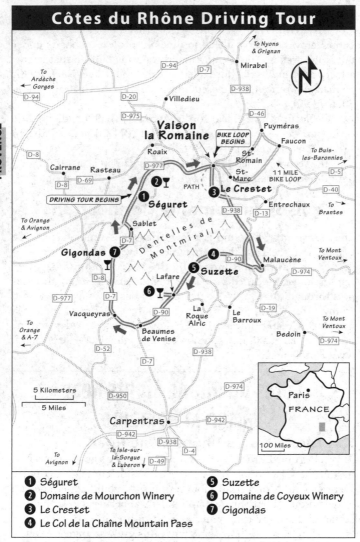

Côtes du Rhône Driving Tour

1 Séguret
2 Domaine de Mourchon Winery
3 Le Crestet
4 Le Col de la Chaîne Mountain Pass
5 Suzette
6 Domaine de Coyeux Winery
7 Gigondas

• *From Vaison la Romaine, the easiest way to reach Séguret is to follow signs for* Orange, *then look for the turnoff to Séguret in a few minutes.*

❶ Séguret

Blending into the hillside with a smattering of shops, two cafés, made-to-stroll lanes, and a natural spring, this hamlet is understandably popular. Séguret makes for a good coffee or dinner stop (see recommended restaurants on page 755).

Séguret's name comes from the Latin word *securitas* (meaning "security"). The bulky entry arch came with a massive gate, which drilled in the message of the village's name. In the Middle Ages, Séguret was patrolled 24/7—they never took their *securitas* for granted. Walk through the arch. To appreciate how the homes' outer walls provided security in those days, drop down the first passage on your right (near the fountain). These exit passages, or *poternes*, were needed in periods of peace to allow the town to expand below. Wander deep. Rue Calade leads to an unusual 12th-century church and views (the circular village you see below is Sablet).

• *Signs near Séguret's parking will lead you up, up, and away to our next stop, Domaine de Mourchon.*

❷ Domaine de Mourchon

This high-flying winery has become the buzz of the Côtes du Rhône by blending state-of-the-art technology with traditional

winemaking methods (a dazzling ring of stainless-steel vats holds wines grown on land plowed by horses). The wines are winning the respect of international critics, yet the (Scottish) owners seem eager to help anyone understand Rhône Valley wines. Language is not an issue here, nor is a lack of stunning views. Free and informative English tours of the vineyards are offered once a week.

Cost and Hours: Winery open Mon-Fri 8:00-12:00 & 14:00-18:00, plus April-Sept Sat 14:00-18:00, closed Sun year-round; free English tour and tasting Easter-Sept Wed only at 17:00, check website or call to verify; tel. 04 90 46 70 30, www.domainede mourchon.com.

• *Next, return to Vaison la Romaine and follow signs toward* Carpentras/Malaucène. *After passing through Crestet, you'll come to Le Crestet (on D-938). Look for signs leading up to Le Village and park at its entry.*

❸ Le Crestet

This village—founded after the fall of the Roman Empire, when people banded together in high places like this for protection from marauding barbarians—followed the usual hill-town evolution. The outer walls of the village did double duty as ramparts and house walls. The castle above (from about A.D. 850) provided a final safe haven when the village was attacked.

The Bishop of Vaison la Romaine was the first occupant,

lending little Le Crestet a certain prestige. With about 500 residents in 1200, Le Crestet was a big deal in this region, reaching its zenith in the mid-1500s, when 660 people called it home. Le Crestet's gradual decline started when the bishop moved to Vaison la Romaine in the 1600s, though the population remained fairly stable until World War II. Today, about 35 people live within the walls year-round (about 55 during the summer boom).

The village's only business, the recommended café-restaurant **Le Panoramic,** has an upstairs terrace with a view that justifies the name...even if the food is mediocre.

• *Reconnect with the road below, following signs to* Malaucène. *As you near Malaucène, look for the huge* boules *courts separated by logs (on your left). Entering Malaucène, turn right on D-90 (direction: Suzette) just before the gas station. After a few minutes, you'll approach a pass. Look for signs on the left to* Le Col de la Chaîne *("Chain Pass"). From this point on, the scenery gets better fast.*

❹ Le Col de la Chaîne Mountain Pass

Get out of your car at the pass (about 1,500 feet) and enjoy the breezy views. Wander about. The peaks in the distance—thrusting up like the back of a stegosaurus or a bad haircut (you decide)—are the Dentelles de Montmirail, a small range running just nine miles basically north to south and reaching 2,400 feet in elevation. This region's land is constantly shifting. Those rocky tops were the result of a gradual uplifting of the land, then were blown bald by the angry mistral wind. Below, pine and oak trees mix with the shrub Scotch broom, which blooms brilliant yellow in May and June. You may see rich yellow-to-reddish patches of land—the result of deposits of ochre located deep below. The village below the peaks is Suzette (you'll be there soon). The yellow-signed hiking-only trail leads to the castle-topped village of Le Barroux (3.5 miles, mostly downhill).

Now turn around and face Mont Ventoux. Are there clouds in the horizon? You're looking into the eyes of the Alps (behind Ventoux), and those "foothills" help keep Provence sunny.

• *Time to push on. You'll pass yellow trail signs along this drive. (The Dentelles provide fertile ground for walking trails.) With the medieval castle of Le Barroux topping the horizon in the distance (off to the left), drive on to little...*

❺ Suzette

Tiny Suzette floats on its hilltop, with a small 12th-century chapel, one café, a handful of residents, and the gaggle of houses where they live. Park in Suzette's lot below, then find the big orientation board above the lot (Rome is 620 kilometers—385 miles—away). Look out to the broad shoulders of Mont Ventoux. At 6,000 feet, it always seems to have some clouds hanging around. If it's clear, the top looks like it's snow-covered; if you drive up there, you'll see it's actually white stone. If it's very cloudy, the mountain takes on a dark, foreboding appearance.

Look to the village. A sign asks you to *Respectez son Calme* (respect its peace). Suzette's homes once lived in the shadow of an imposing castle, destroyed during the religious wars of the mid-1500s. The recommended **Les Coquelicots** café makes a good lunch or drink stop. Good picnic tables lie just past Suzette on our route. Back across the road from the orientation table is a tasting room for **Château Redortier** wines (unreliable hours, English brochure and well-explained wine list provided).

• *Continue from Suzette in the direction of Beaumes de Venise. You'll drop down into the lush little village of La Fare. La Fare's best wine-tasting opportunity is back on our route just after leaving the village, at...*

❻ Domaine de Coyeux

A private road winds up and up to this impossibly beautiful setting, with the best views of the Dentelles I've found. Olive trees frame

the final approach, and *Le Caveau* signs lead to a modern tasting room (you may need to ring the buzzer). The owners and staff (mainly Marion) are formal but sincere, and take your interest in their wines seriously—pass on by if you only want a quick taste or are not interested in buying. These wines have earned their excellent reputation (and are now available in the US). Start with their two delectable reds (a Gigondas and a smashing Beaumes de Venise) and finish with their trademark dry and sweet Muscats. After tasting, take time to wander about the vineyards.

Cost and Hours: Wines-€7-14/bottle, Mon-Sat 10:00-12:00 & 14:00-18:00, no midday closure July-Aug, closed Sun, tel. 04 90 12 42 42, some English spoken.

• *Drive on toward Beaumes de Venise. You'll soon pass the recommended* **Côté Vignes**, *a good stop for lunch or dinner. Next, you'll drop out of the hills. Navigate through Beaumes de Venise, following signs for* Gigondas *and* Vaison par la route touristique. *As you enter Gigondas, follow signs to the TI and park on or near the tree-shaded square.*

❼ Gigondas

This town produces some of the region's best reds and is ideally situated for hiking, mountain-biking, and driving into the mountains.

PROVENCE

The **TI** has a list of wineries, *chambres d'hôtes,* and good hikes or drives (Mon-Sat 10:00-12:30 & 14:00-18:00, likely closed Sun, Place du Portail, tel. 04 90 65 85 46, www.gigondas-dm.fr). Take a short walk through the village lanes above the TI—the church is an easy destination with good views over the heart of the Côtes du Rhône vineyards.

You'll find several good tasting opportunities on the main square. **Le Caveau de Gigondas** is best, where Sandra and Barbara await your visit with a large and free selection of tiny bottles for sampling, filled directly from the barrel (daily 10:00-12:00 & 14:00-18:30, across from TI under the post office, tel. 04 90 65 82 29). They pride themselves on attentive service, so be patient if they are with someone when you arrive. Here you can compare wines from a variety of private producers in an intimate, low-key surrounding.

You'll find a small grocery store and several eating options in the village. Diagonally across from the TI, the shaded red tables of **Du Verre à l'Assiette** ("From Glass to Plate") entice lunch-time eaters (also good interior ambience, €11 salads, €14-20 *plats,* closed Wed year-round, off-season open for lunch daily and Fri-Sat nights only, Place du Village, tel. 04 90 12 36 64). To dine very well or sleep nearby, find the recommended **Hôtel les Florets,** a half-mile above town (restaurant closed Wed).

• *From Gigondas, follow signs to the circular wine village of Sablet— with generally inexpensive yet tasty wines (the TI and wine cooperative share a space in the town center)— then past Séguret and back to Vaison la Romaine, where our tour ends.*

Sleeping Along the Côtes du Rhône

(€1 = about $1.30, country code: 33)
These accommodations are along the self-guided driving tour route described above. They offer a great opportunity for drivers who want to experience rural France and get better values.

Near Vaison la Romaine
These accommodations are within a 10-minute drive of Vaison la Romaine.

$$$ Hôtel les Florets**, a lovely spread a half-mile above Gigondas, is buried in the foothills of the Dentelles de Montmirail. It comes with a vast terrace with views and hiking trails into the mountains, tastefully designed rooms, and a fine restaurant (standard Db-€115-130, superior Db-€140-175, annex rooms have front patios but I prefer rooms in the main building, Wi-Fi, tel. 04 90 65 85 01, fax 04 90 65 83 80, www.hotel-lesflorets.com, accueil @hotel-lesflorets.com).

$$$ Domaine des Tilleuls***, 10 minutes from Vaison la Romaine in workaday Malaucène, is a well-priced refuge, and the most family-friendly place I list. (Welcoming owners Arnould and Dominique have three kids.) Its 20 country-modern rooms fill an old farmhouse overlooking lovely grounds with namesake linden trees *(tilleuls)*, a sandbox, toys, and a large pool. If you missed market day in Vaison la Romaine, sleep here Tuesday night and wake to a bustling market (Db-€85-100, Tb/Qb-€120, breakfast-€13, Wi-Fi, well-signed in Malaucène on the route to Mont Ventoux, tel. 04 90 65 22 31, fax 04 90 65 16 77, www.hotel-domainedes tilleuls.com, info@hotel-domainedestilleuls.com).

$$ L'Ecole Buissonnière Chambres is run by an engaging Anglo-French team, Monique and John, who share their peace and quiet 10 minutes from Vaison la Romaine. This creatively restored farmhouse has three character-filled half-timbered rooms, and convivial public spaces. Getting to know John, who has lived all over the south of France and even worked as a *gardian* (cowboy) in the Camargue, is worth the price of the room; he's also generous with his knowledge of the area. The outdoor kitchen allows guests to picnic in high fashion in the tranquil garden (Db-€62-74, Tb-€78-89, Qb-€94-99, cash only, includes breakfast, Wi-Fi; between Villedieu and Buisson on D-75—leave Vaison following signs to *Villedieu*, then follow D-51 toward Buisson and turn left onto D-75; tel. 04 90 28 95 19, ecole.buissonniere@wanadoo.fr).

$$ Domaine le Puy du Maupas Chambres, three miles from Vaison la Romaine in the village of Puyméras, is a good-value B&B with five rooms, views over vineyards to Mont Ventoux, and a pool (Db-€68-80, Tb-€80, includes breakfast, cash only, Wi-Fi, on D-938, Route de Nyons, tel. 04 90 46 47 43, www.puy-du -maupas.com, sauvayre@puy-du-maupas.com).

Eating Along the Côtes du Rhône

Many of these eateries are described in my self-guided driving tour route (earlier); I've listed them by distance from Vaison la Romaine (nearest to farthest). Most are within a 10-minute drive of Vaison la Romaine. All have some outdoor seating and should be considered for lunch or dinner.

La Girocedre is an enchanting place to eat lunch or dinner if you have a car and it's nice outside. Just three picturesque miles from Vaison la Romaine in adorable Puyméras, this place offers a complete country-Provençal package: outdoor tables placed just-so in a lush garden, warm interior decor, and real Provençal cuisine (€19 three-course lunch *menus*, €27 dinner *menus*, closed all day Mon, closed for lunch Tue, tel. 04 90 46 50 67).

Auberge d'Anaïs, at the end of a dirt road 10 minutes from Vaison la Romaine, is another find—and a true Provençal experience. Outdoor tables gather under cheery lights with views and reliable cuisine. Ask for a table *sur la terrasse* (€11 lunch *menu*, good three-course dinner *menus* from €17, closed Mon, tel. 04 90 36 20 06). From Vaison la Romaine, follow signs to *Carpentras,* then *St. Marcellin;* signs will guide you from there.

Le Panoramic, in hill-capping Le Crestet, serves average salads and *plats* at what must be Provence's greatest view tables. Drink in the view, but if cuisine is important, eat elsewhere (€12 *plats du jour,* €28 *menus,* daily 10:30-22:00, tel. 04 90 28 76 42). Drivers should pass by the first parking lot in Le Crestet and keep climbing to park at Place du Château. The restaurant is well-signed at the top of the village.

Hôtel les Florets, just above Gigondas, is a traditional, family-run place that's well worth the drive—particularly if you dine on the magnificent terrace. Dinners are a sumptuous blend of classic French cuisine and Provençal accents, served with class by English-speaking Thierry. The weighty wine list is (literally) encyclopedic (€31 and €46 *menus,* €14 lunch *plat du jour,* restaurant closed Wed, service can be slow). See hotel listing, earlier.

La Maison Bleue, on Villedieu's delightful little square, is a pizza-and-salad place with great outdoor ambience. Skip it if the weather forces you inside (open for lunch and dinner, closed Mon, tel. 04 90 28 97 02).

Les Coquelicots, a tiny eatery surrounded by vines and views in minuscule Suzette, is a sweet spot. The food is scrumptious (owner/chef Frankie insists on fresh products), and the setting is memorable. Try the *Assiette Provençale,* his omelets with herbs, or any of his grilled meats and fish (May-Sept usually closed Tue evening and all day Wed, Oct-April open weekends only, tel. 04 90 65 06 94).

Côté Vignes, off a short dirt road between Suzette and Beaumes de Venise, is a lighthearted, wood-fired-everything place with outdoor tables flanked by fun interior dining. Young Corrine runs the restaurant with enthusiasm; try the Camembert cheese flambé with lettuce, potatoes, and ham (€10 salads and good pizza, *menus* from €18.50, closed Wed year-round, Oct-April also closed Mon-Tue evenings, tel. 04 90 65 07 16).

Hill Towns of the Luberon

Just 30 miles east of Avignon, the Luberon region hides some of France's most captivating hill towns and sensuous landscapes.

Those intrigued by Peter Mayle's books love joyriding through the region, connecting I-could-live-here villages, crumbled castles, and meditative abbeys. Mayle's bestselling *A Year in Provence* describes the ruddy local culture from an Englishman's perspective as he buys a stone farmhouse, fixes it up, and adopts the region as his new home.

The Luberon terrain in general (much of which is a French regional natural park) is as enticing as its villages. Gnarled vineyards and wind-sculpted trees separate tidy stone structures from abandoned buildings—little more than rock piles—that challenge city slickers to fix them up. Mountains of limestone bend along vast ridges, while colorful hot-air balloons survey the scene from above.

There are no obligatory museums, monuments, or vineyards in the Luberon. Treat this area like a vacation from your vacation. Downshift your engine. Brake for the views, and lose your car to take a walk. Get on a first-name basis with a village.

What follows is a rundown of my favorite villages and stops in this beautiful area. The D-900 highway cuts the Luberon in half like an arrow. The first four places I describe are north of it; the last three sit south of it.

Getting Around the Luberon

By Car: Luberon roads are scenic and narrow. With no major landmarks, it's easy to get lost in this area—and you will get lost, trust me—but getting lost is the point. Pick up Michelin map #332 or #527 to navigate.

By Bus: Isle-sur-la-Sorgue is accessible by bus from Avignon, with several daily trips and a central stop at the post office (6-8/day Mon-Sat, 3-4/day Sun, 45 minutes). Without a car or minivan tour, skip the more famous hill towns of the Luberon.

By Train: Trains get you to Isle-sur-la-Sorgue (station called "L'Isle-Fontaine de Vaucluse") from Avignon (10/day on weekdays, 5/day on weekends, 30 minutes). If you're day-tripping by train, check return times before leaving the station.

By Minivan Tour: Dutchman Mike Rijken, who runs **Wine Safari,** offers tours of this area, as do several other Avignon-based companies (see "Tours of Provence" on page 662).

By Taxi: Contact **Luberon Taxi** (based in Maubec off D-3, mobile 06 08 49 40 57, www.luberontaxi.com, contact@luberon taxi.com).

By Bike: Hardy bikers can ride from Isle-sur-la-Sorgue to Gordes, then to Roussillon, connecting other villages in a full-day loop ride (30 miles round-trip to Roussillon and back, with lots of hills). Many appealing villages are closer to Isle-sur-la-Sorgue and offer easier biking options.

Isle-sur-la-Sorgue

This sturdy market town—literally, "Island on the Sorgue River"—sits within a split in its crisp, happy little river. It's a workaday

town, with a gritty charm that feels refreshingly real after so many adorable villages. It's also one of the only smaller towns in this region accessible by train and bus.

In Isle-sur-la-Sorgue—a.k.a. the "Venice of Provence"—the Sorgue River's extraordinarily clear and shallow flow divides like cells, producing water, water everywhere. The river has long nourished the region's economy. Today, antiques shops power the town's economy—every other shop seems to sell some kind of antique. Although Isle-sur-la-Sorgue is renowned for its market days (Sun and Thu), it's an otherwise pleasantly average town with no important sights and a steady trickle of tourism. It's calm at night and dead on Mondays.

Navigate by the town's splintered streams and nine mossy **waterwheels,** which, while still turning, power only memories of the town's wool and silk industries. At its peak, Isle-sur-la-Sorgue had 70 waterwheels; in the 1800s, the town competed with Avignon as Provence's cloth-dyeing and textile center. Find **le Bassin,** where the Sorgue River crashes into the town and separates into many branches (carefully placed lights make this a beautiful sight after dark). With its source (a spring) a mere five miles away, the Sorgue River never floods and has a constant flow and temperature in all seasons. Despite its exposed (flat) location, Isle-sur-la-Sorgue prospered in the Middle Ages, thanks to the natural protection this river provided.

The town erupts into a carnival-like **market** frenzy each Sunday and Thursday, with hardy crafts and local produce. The Sunday market is astounding and famous for its antiques; the Thursday market is more intimate. Landing a seat at the **Café de**

France across from the Church of Notre-Dame des Anges and watching the scene is my idea of good travel.

The **TI** has information on hiking, biking itineraries, and a line on rooms in private homes, all of which are outside of town (Mon-Sat 9:00-12:30 & 14:30-18:00, Sun 9:00-12:30, in town center next to church, tel. 04 90 38 04 78, www.oti-delasorgue.fr).

Isle-sur-la-Sorgue is well-situated for short **biking** forays into the mostly level terrain nearby. Pick up biking information at the TI and rent your bike at **Isles 2 Roues** (by the train station at 10 Avenue de la Gare, closed Sun-Mon, tel. 04 90 38 19 12). These towns make easy biking destinations: Velleron (5 flat miles north, a tiny version of Isle-sur-la-Sorgue with waterwheels, fountains, and an evening farmer's market Mon-Sat 18:00-20:00); Lagnes (3 miles east, a pretty and well-restored hill town with views from its ruined château); and Fontaine-de-Vaucluse (5 gently uphill miles northeast, a touristy village at the source of the Sorgue River).

Sleeping and Eating in Isle sur la Sorgue

(€1 = about $1.30, country code: 33)

$$ Hôtel les Névons**, two blocks from the center (behind the post office), is concrete-motel-modern outside, but a fair value inside, with several family suites and a roof deck with 360-degree views around a small pool (old wing—Db-€61; new wing—big Db-€70, Tb-€90, Qb-€95; air-con, Internet access, Wi-Fi in lobby, easy parking, 205 Chemin des Névons, push and hold the gate button a bit on entry, tel. 04 90 20 72 00, fax 04 90 20 56 20, www.hotel-les-nevons.com, info@hotel-les-nevons.com).

$ Hôtel les Terrasses du Bassin rents eight spotless rooms with designer touches over a good restaurant on Le Bassin, where the river waters separate before running through town. Several rooms look out over Le Bassin, most have some traffic noise (Db-€64, extra bed-€10, air-con, Wi-Fi, 2 Avenue Charles de Gaulle, tel. 04 90 38 03 16, fax 04 90 38 65 61, www.lesterrassesdubassin .com, corinne@lesterrassesdubassin.com).

Inexpensive restaurants are easy to find in Isle-sur-la-Sorgue, but consistent quality is another story. For inexpensive meals, troll the riverside cafés for today's catch.

Les Terrasses du Bassin is your best riverfront option, with moderate prices and tasty choices (eat on the terrace). Come for a full meal or just a *plat* (€10 lunch salads and starters, €16 dinner *plats*, €24-34 dinner *menu*, closed Tue-Wed Oct-May, 2 Avenue Charles de Gaulle, tel. 04 90 38 03 16).

The **Fromenterie** bakery next to the post office (PTT) sells decadent quiches, monster sandwiches, desserts, wine, and other drinks—in other words, everything you need to picnic (open daily until 20:00).

Roussillon

With all the trendy charm of Santa Fe on a hilltop, photogenic Roussillon requires serious camera and café time. An enormous deposit of ochre gives the earth and its buildings that distinctive red color. Climb a few minutes— passing the Hollywood-set-like square under the bell tower and the church—and find the orientation plaque and the dramatic **viewpoint** at the top of the village. Roussillon sits atop Mont Rouge ("Red Mountain") at about

1,000 feet above sea level. During the Middle Ages, a castle stood where you are. On your way down, duck into the pretty 11th-century Church of St. Michel, then linger over *un café,* or—if it's later in the day—*un pastis,* in what must be the most picturesque village square in Provence **(Place de la Mairie).** While Roussillon receives its share of day-trippers, mornings and evenings are romantically peaceful on this square.

Roussillon was Europe's capital for ochre production until World War II. A stroll to the south end of town, beyond the upper parking lot, shows you why: Roussillon sits on the world's largest known ochre deposit. A radiant orange path leads through the richly colored **ochre cliffs,** explaining the hue of this village and making me think I'm in Bryce Canyon (€2.50, €7 combo-ticket with Ochre Conservatory, daily 9:30-18:30, until 19:30 in summer; beware—light-colored clothing and orange powder don't mix).

For a helpful introduction to the history and uses of ochre, visit the **Ochre Conservatory** (Conservatoire des Ocres et Pigments Appliqués), a reconstructed ochre factory. Grab a pamphlet and follow their well-done self-guided tour, which shows how ochre is converted from an ore to a pigment (€6, €7 combo-ticket with ochre cliffs, daily 9:00-18:00, July-Aug until 19:00, about a half-mile below Roussillon toward Apt on D-104, tel. 04 90 05 66 69, www.okhra.com).

The little **TI** is in the village center, across from the David restaurant. Walkers should get info on trails from Roussillon to nearby villages (TI open April-Oct Mon-Sat 9:30-12:00 & 13:30-18:00, closed Sun except in summer; Nov-March Mon-Sat 14:00-17:30, closed Sun; tel. 04 90 05 60 25, www.roussillon-provence .com).

Sleeping and Eating in Roussillon

(€1 = about $1.30, country code: 33)

The TI posts a list of hotels and *chambres d'hôtes;* also see "Sleeping and Eating in Joucas" on the following page.

$$ Hôtel Rêves d'Ocres** is a good two-star value, run by friendly Sandrine and Yvan. It's ochre-colored, warm, and sufficiently comfortable, with 16 tastefully designed rooms—some with musty bathrooms. Eight smaller rooms have view terraces (Sb-€60, Db without balcony-€80, Db with balcony-€85, Tb-€100, Qb-€120, meek air-con, Internet access, Wi-Fi, Route de Gordes, tel. 04 90 05 60 50, fax 04 90 05 79 74, www.hotel-revesdocres .com, hotelrevesdocres@wanadoo.fr). Coming from Gordes and Joucas, it's the first building you pass in Roussillon.

$ Madame Cherel rents bare-bones rooms with firm beds and a shared view terrace at fair rates (D-€45-49, family suite available, cash only, includes basic breakfast, Wi-Fi, access to kitchenette, 3 blocks from upper parking lot, between Casino store and school, La Burlière, tel. 04 90 05 71 71, mulhanc@hotmail.com). Chatty and sincere Cherel speaks English and offers a wealth of regional travel tips.

When restaurant-hunting, choose ambience over cuisine if dining in Roussillon, and enjoy any of the eateries on the main square. The following places share the same square and offer similar values. At least one should be open.

At **Le Bistrot de Roussillon,** Johan offers the most consistent value on the square, with excellent salads (try the *salad du bistrot*) and *plats* for the right price. There's a breezy terrace in back and a comfy interior (€15 for a filling salad and dessert, €13-18 *plats,* daily, tel. 04 90 05 74 45).

Café Couleur and **Le Castrum** flank Le Bistrot de Roussillon, offering similar atmosphere and prices, but less-steady quality.

More Luberon Hill Towns and Sights

Gordes

In the 1960s, Gordes was a virtual ghost town of derelict build-

ings. But now it's thoroughly renovated and filled with people who live in a world without calluses. Many Parisian big shots and wealthy foreigners have purchased and restored older homes here, putting property values out of sight for locals— and creating gridlock and parking headaches (come early). As you approach Gordes, make a hard right at the impressive viewpoint (you'll find some parking along the small road). Beyond here, the village has little of interest, except its many boutiques and its Tuesday market (which ends at 13:00). The town's 11th-century castle houses contemporary art exhibits. The more interesting Abbey Notre-Dame de Sénanque is nearby and well-marked from Gordes.

Abbey Notre-Dame de Sénanque

This still-functioning and beautifully situated Cistercian abbey was built in 1148 as a back-to-basics reaction to the excesses of Benedictine abbeys. The abbey is best appreciated from the outside, and is worth the trip for its splendid and remote setting alone. Come early or late, stop at a pull-out for a bird's-eye view as you descend, then wander the abbey's perimeter. The abbey church (Eglise Abbatiale) is open (and free) and highlights the utter simplicity sought by these monks. In late June through much of July, the lavender fields that surround the abbey make for breathtaking pictures and draw loads of visitors. The abbey itself can only be visited on a skippable 50-minute, French-only tour with an English handout.

Cost and Hours: €7, includes mandatory French-only tour—Mon-Sat usually at 10:00, 10:30, 14:30, 15:30, and 16:30; Sun at 14:30, 15:30, and 16:30; tel. 04 90 72 05 72, www.senanque.fr. You can also attend Mass (check website or call to confirm).

Joucas

This understated, quiet, and largely overlooked village slumbers below the Gordes buzz. Vertical stone lanes with carefully arranged flowers and well-restored homes play host to aspiring Claude Monets and a smattering of locals. Joucas has one tiny grocery, a view café, one pharmacy, and a good kids' play area. Sleep here for a central Luberon location and utter silence. For views, walk past the little fountain in the center and up the steep lanes as high as you want. Several **hiking** trails leave from Joucas. Gordes and Roussillon are each three miles away, uphill. The three-mile hike up to the attractive village of Murs (which has several cafés/restaurants) is more scenic, though it's easier in the other direction (yellow signs point the way from the top of the village). You don't have to go far to enjoy the natural beauty on this trail.

Sleeping and Eating in Joucas: **$$$ La Ferme de la Huppe***
is a small farmhouse-elegant hacienda that makes an excellent

mini-splurge. Ten low-slung rooms gather on two levels behind the stylish pool. The decor is tasteful, understated, and rustic (small Db-€140, bigger Db-€170, much bigger Db-€200, includes good breakfast, mini-fridges, air-con, Wi-Fi; between Joucas and Gordes on D-156 road to Goult, just off D-2; tel. 04 90 72 12 25, fax 04 90 72 25 39, www.lafermedelahuppe.com, info@laferme delahuppe.com). Dine poolside or in the smart dining room (€42 three-course *menu* or €62 five-course tasting *menu*).

$$ Hostellerie des Commandeurs**, run by soft Anne-Sophie and Gérard, has modern, comfortable, and clean rooms in the center of Joucas. It's kid-friendly, with a big pool and a sports field/play area next door. Ask for a south-facing room *(coté sud)* for the best views, or a north-facing room *(coté nord)* if it's hot. All rooms have showers (Db-€68-74, extra bed-€16, mini-fridges, above park at village entrance, tel. 04 90 05 78 01, fax 04 90 05 74 47, http://lescommandeurs.free.fr, hostellerie@lescommandeurs .com). The simple restaurant offers tasty cuisine at fair prices (three-course *menus* from €23, succulent lamb, memorable crème brûlée with lavender, restaurant closed Wed).

Julien Bridge (Pont Julien)

Due south of Roussillon, just below D-900, this delicate three-arched bridge survives as a testimony to Roman engineers—and

to the importance of this rural area 2,000 years ago. It's the only surviving bridge on what was the main road from northern Italy to Provence—the primary route used by Roman armies. The 215-foot-long Roman bridge was under construction from 27 B.C. to A.D. 14. Mortar had not yet been invented, so (as with Pont du Gard) stones were carefully set in place. Amazingly, the bridge survives today, having outlived Roman marches, hundreds of floods, and decades of automobile traffic. A new bridge finally rerouted traffic from this beautiful structure in 2005.

Lacoste

Little Lacoste slumbers across the valley from Bonnieux in the shadow of its looming castle. Climb through this photogenic village of arches and stone paths, passing American art students (from the Savannah College of Art and Design) showing their work. The view of Bonnieux from the base of Lacoste's castle is as good as it gets. The Marquis de Sade (1740-1814) lived in this **castle** for more than 30 years. Author of dirty novels, he was notorious for hosting orgies behind these walls, and for kidnapping peasants

PROVENCE

for scandalous purposes. He was eventually arrested and imprisoned for 30 years, and thanks to him, we have a word to describe his favorite hobby—sadism. Today, fashion designer Pierre Cardin lives in the lower part of the castle, having spent a fortune shoring up the protective walls and sponsoring a high-priced summer opera series.

Eating in Lacoste: If it's time for lunch, find the **Bar/Restaurant de France**'s outdoor tables overlooking Bonnieux and savor the view (inexpensive, good omelets, daily, lunch only off-season, tel. 04 90 75 82 25).

Ménerbes

Ménerbes, now (in)famous as the village that drew author Peter Mayle's attention to this region, is also noteworthy for its truffle center and a smattering of pleasing buildings. The town lies 10 minutes east of Lacoste. To explore Ménerbes, stash your car, then follow *Eglise* signs to the end of the village. At the end of Rue Corneille you'll pass the **citadel,** built in 1584 (after the Protestants of Ménerbes were defeated in the religious wars of 1577)—and never tested. Further on, find the heavy Romanesque church (closed and under renovation) and **graveyard** (good views in all directions). Nearby, foodies can duck into the snazzy **Maison de la Truffe et du Vin,** which houses a cute tasting room full of Luberon wines (sold at good prices). Their small restaurant serves a killer €24 *truffe d'été menu* (summer truffle, available June-Sept), best enjoyed in the garden's lovely setting (daily 12:30-17:00, tel. 04 90 72 38 37).

Oppède-le-Vieux

This windy barnacle of a town clings with all its might to its hillside. There's one boutique, two cafés, and a dusty little square at the base of a short, ankle-twisting climb  to a pretty little church and ruined castle. This off-the-beaten-path fixer-upper of a village was completely abandoned in 1910, and today has a ghost town-like feel (it once housed 200 people). The inhabited village below has a rugged character and is ideal for those looking to perish in Provence. It's a 20 minute climb straight up to the **ruined castle,** but the Luberon views justify the effort. Walk under the central arch of the building across from Le Petit Café to where the path splits and climb (either direction works). Find the little church terrace. From here, tiled rooftops paint a delightful picture with the grand panorama; the flat plain of the Rhône delta is visible off to the left. There's been a church on this site for 1,000 years—the colorful **Notre-Dame d'Alidon church** (1588) is generally open 9:30-18:30 (depending on availability of village volunteers, who are eager to answer questions).

Eating and Sleeping in Oppède-le-Vieux: Once you're back down, consider a cheap and tasty lunch with views of the castle ruins at **Petit Café,** where friendly Jean-Marie is in charge (closed Wed, also closed for dinner on Tue night and Nov-April). **$$ Petit Café** also offers simple but comfy rooms (Db-€65-75, big Db-€95, includes breakfast, Jacuzzi, sauna, rooftop terrace, tel. 04 90 76 74 01, www.petitcafe.fr).

THE FRENCH RIVIERA

La Côte d'Azur: Nice • Villefranche-sur-Mer • The Three Corniches • Monaco • Antibes • Inland Riviera

A hundred years ago, celebrities from London to Moscow flocked to the French Riviera to socialize, gamble, and escape the dreary weather at home. Today, budget vacationers and heat-seeking Europeans fill belle-époque resorts at France's most sought-after fun-in-the-sun destination.

Some of the Continent's most stunning scenery and intriguing museums lie along this strip of land—as do millions of sun-worshipping tourists. Nice has world-class museums, a splendid beachfront promenade, a seductive old town, and all the drawbacks of a major city (traffic, crime, pollution, and so on). The day-trip possibilities are easy and exciting: Monte Carlo welcomes everyone with money to spend; Antibes has a thriving port and silky sand beaches; and the inland hill towns present a breezy and photogenic alternative to the beach scene. Evenings on the Riviera, a.k.a. la Côte d'Azur, were made for a promenade and outdoor dining.

Choose a Home Base

My favorite home bases are Nice, Antibes, and Villefranche-sur-Mer.

Nice is the region's capital and France's fifth-largest city. With convenient train and bus connections to most regional sights, this is the most practical base for train travelers. Urban Nice also has a full palette of museums (most of which are free), a beach scene that rocks, the best selection of hotels in all price ranges, and good nightlife options. A car is a headache in Nice, though it's easily stored at one of the many pricey parking garages or for free at an outer tram station.

Nearby **Antibes** is smaller, with a bustling center, a lively

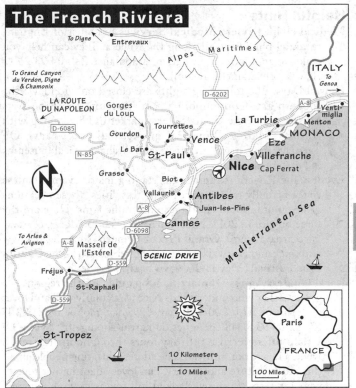

The French Riviera

To Digne
Entrevaux

Alpes   Maritimes

To Grand Canyon
du Verdon, Digne
& Chamonix

ITALY
To
Genoa

D-6202

A-8   Venti-
miglia

LA ROUTE
DU NAPOLEON

Gorges
du Loup

La Turbie   Menton

D-6085

Tourrettes   MONACO

Gourdon   Vence   Eze

Le Bar   St-Paul   Villefranche

N-85   Nice   Cap Ferrat

Grasse   Biot

Vallauris   Antibes

A-8   Juan-les-Pins

Cannes

D-6098

To Arles &
Avignon

A-8   Masseif de
l'Estérel

D-559

SCENIC DRIVE

Mediterranean Sea

Fréjus

St-Raphaël

D-559

St-Tropez

10 Kilometers

10 Miles

Paris

FRANCE

100 Miles

THE FRENCH RIVIERA

night scene, great sandy beaches, grand vistas, good walking trails, and a much-admired Picasso Museum. Antibes has frequent train service to Nice and Monaco, and it's easy for drivers, with light traffic and easy hotel parking.

Villefranche-sur-Mer is the romantic's choice, with a serene setting and small-town warmth. It has finely ground pebble beaches; quick public transportation to Nice and Monaco; easy parking; and a small selection of hotels in most price ranges.

Planning Your Time

Ideally, allow a full day for Nice, a day for Monaco and the Corniche route that connects it with Nice, and a half-day for Villefranche-sur-Mer or Antibes. Monaco and Villefranche-sur-Mer have good energy at night (sights are closed, but crowds are few; consider dinner there), and Antibes works well by day (good beaches and hiking) and night (fine choice of restaurants and a lively after-hours scene). Hill town-loving naturalists should allow a day to explore the hill-capping hamlets near Vence (but for most, these are a lower priority).

Helpful Hints

Medical Help: Riviera Medical Services has a list of English-speaking physicians all along the Riviera. They can help you make an appointment or call an ambulance (tel. 04 93 26 12 70, www.rivieramedical.com).

Closed Days: The following sights are closed on Mondays: the Modern and Contemporary Art Museum, the Fine Arts Museum, and the Cours Saleya market in Nice, along with Antibes' Marché Provençal market hall (Sept-May). On Tuesdays the Chagall, Matisse, and Archaeological museums in Nice are closed.

Events: The Riviera is famous for staging major events. Unless you're actually taking part in the festivities, these occasions give you only room shortages and traffic jams. Here are the three biggies in 2013: **Nice Carnival** (Feb 15-March 6, www.nicecarnaval.com), **Grand Prix of Monaco** (May 23-26, www.acm.mc), and Festival de Cannes, better known as the **Cannes Film Festival** (May 15-26, www.festival-cannes.com).

Local Guides: Agnès Dumartin, a top guide for the region, is a good teacher who understands Nice particularly well and loves all forms of art (€200/half-day, €295/day, mobile 06 81 82 17 67, fax 04 93 51 48 63, agnes.dumartin@orange.fr). **Sylvie Di Cristo** offers terrific full-day tours throughout the French Riviera in a car or minivan. She adores educating people about this area's culture and history, and loves adapting her tour to your interests, from overlooked hill towns to wine, cuisine, art, or perfume (€200/person for 2-3 people, €130-150/person for 4-6 people, €90/person for 7-8 people, 2-person minimum, mobile 06 09 88 83 83, www.frenchrivieraguides.net, dicristo sylvie@gmail.com). Lovely **Sofia Villavicencio** is a pleasant guide with a passion for art (€145/half-day, €200/day, tel. 04 93 32 45 92, mobile 06 68 51 55 52, sofia.villavicencio@laposte.net).

Cooking Tours: Canadian **Rosa Jackson** caters to foodies (see listing on page 784).

Minivan Tours: The TI and most hotels have information on minivan excursions from Nice (roughly €50/half-day, €80-110/day). **Revelation Tours** takes pride in its guides (tel. 04 93 53 69 85, www.revelation-tours.com). **Med-Tour** is one of many (tel. 04 93 82 92 58, mobile 06 73 82 04 10, www.med-tour.com); **Tour Azur** is another (tel. 04 93 44 88 77, www.tourazur.com). All also offer private tours by the day or half-day (check with them for their outrageous prices, about €90/hour).

Longer-Stay Rentals: Renting an apartment, house, or villa can be a cost-effective way to explore the Côte d'Azur. Rentals

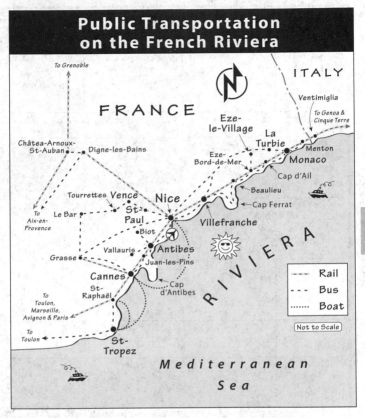

Public Transportation on the French Riviera

To Grenoble

ITALY

N

FRANCE

Ventimiglia

To Genoa & Cinque Terre

Eze-le-Village

La Turbie

Menton

Châtea-Arnoux-St-Auban

Digne-les-Bains

Eze-Bord-de-Mer

Monaco

Cap d'Ail

Beaulieu

Tourrettes

Vence

Nice

Cap Ferrat

To Aix-en-Provence

Le Bar

St-Paul

Villefranche

Biot

RIVIERA

Vallauris

Antibes

Grasse

Juan-les-Pins

Rail

Bus

Boat

Cannes

St-Raphaël

Cap d'Antibes

To Toulon, Marseille, Avignon & Paris

Not to Scale

To Toulon

St-Tropez

Mediterranean Sea

THE FRENCH RIVIERA

are typically by the week, giving you time to take advantage of day-trip possibilities. **Riviera Pebbles** offers a wide range of rental apartments throughout the Riviera and gets good reviews from happy clients (www.rivierapebbles.com). **VRBO,** an international network of vacation rentals (houses, apartments, and *gîtes*), cuts out the middleman and puts you directly in touch with the owner (www.vrbo.com).

Cruise-Ship Sightseeing: The French Riviera is a popular cruise destination. Arriving ships are divided about evenly between three ports: Nice, Villefranche-sur-Mer, and Monaco. I've provided arrival instructions in the "Connections" section for these three ports. If your cruise includes destinations beyond the French Riviera, consider my guidebook, *Rick Steves' Mediterranean Cruise Ports.*

Getting Around the Riviera

If taking the train or bus, have coins handy. Ticket machines don't take US credit cards or paper money, smaller train stations may be

Public Transportation on the French Riviera

From	To Cannes	To Antibes	To Nice	
Cannes by Train	N/A	2/hr, 15 min	2/hr, 30-40 min	
Cannes by Bus	N/A	#200, 2-4/hr, 35 min	#200, 2-4/hr, 1.5-1.75 hrs	
Antibes by Train	2/hr, 15 min	N/A	2/hr, 15-30 min	
Antibes by Bus	#200, 2-4/hr, 35 min	N/A	#200, 2-4/hr, 1-1.5 hrs	
Nice by Train	2/hr, 30-40 min	2/hr, 15-30 min	N/A	
Nice by Bus	#200, 2-4/hr, 1.5-1.75 hrs	#200, 2-4/hr, 1-1.5 hrs	N/A	
Villefranche-sur-Mer by Train	2/hr, 50 min	2/hr, 40 min	2/hr, 10 min	
Villefranche-sur-Mer by Bus	Not recommended	Not recommended	#100, 3-4/hr, 20 min; also #81, 2-4/hr, 20 min	

unstaffed, and bus drivers cannot change large bills.

By Public Transportation: Trains and buses do a good job of connecting places along the coast, with bonus views along many routes. Buses also provide reasonable service to some inland hill towns. Choose the bus for convenience and economy, or the pricier but faster train when you want to save time.

Buses are an amazing deal. The Côte d'Azur has one regional transportation network—Lignes d'Azur (www.lignesdazur.com). Any one-way bus ride costs €1 (except on express airport buses),

(Note: Not all destinations are covered in detail in this book.)			
To Villefranche-sur-Mer	To Cap Ferrat	To Eze-le-Village	To Monaco
2/hr, 50 min	2/hr, 1 hr to Beaulieu-sur-Mer; then bus #81 to Cap Ferrat (2-4/hr, 10 min)	2/hr, 1 hr to Eze-Bord-de-Mer; then bus #83 to Eze (8/day, 15 min)	2/hr, 1 hr
Not recommended	Not recommended	Not recommended	Not recommended
2/hr, 40 min	2/hr, 40 min to Beaulieu-sur-Mer; then bus #81 to Cap Ferrat (2-4/hr, 10 min)	2/hr, 45 min to Eze-Bord-de-Mer; then bus #83 to Eze (8/day, 15 min)	2/hr, 50 min
Not recommended	#200 to Nice (2-4/hr, 1-1.5 hrs); then #81 to Cap Ferrat (2-4/hr, 10 min)	Not recommended	Not recommended
2/hr, 10 min	Not recommended	2/hr, 15 min to Eze-Bord-de-Mer; then bus #83 to Eze (8/day, 15 min)	2/hr, 20 min
#100, 3-4/hr, 20 min; also #81, 2-4/hr, 20 min	#81, 2-4/hr, 35 min	#82/#112, 8-16/day, 40 min	#100, 3-4/hr, 1.25 hrs
N/A	N/A	2/hr, 10 min to Eze-Bord-de-Mer; then bus #83 to Eze (8/day, 15 min)	2/hr, 10 min
N/A	#81, 2-4/hr, 15 min	#80 to upper Villefranche; then bus #82/#112 (8-16/day, 25 min)	#100, 3-4/hr, 25 min

(continued on next page)

whether you're riding 20 minutes from Nice to Villefranche-sur-Mer, 45 minutes to Monaco, or an hour to Antibes. The €1 ticket is good for 74 minutes of travel in one direction anywhere within the bus system (can't be used for a round-trip), and also covers the tram in Nice. Buy your bus ticket from the driver (or from the machines at tram stops), and validate your ticket in the machine on board. You can even transfer between the buses of the Lignes d'Azur and the smaller TAM (Transports Alpes-Maritimes) system; if you board a TAM bus and need a transfer, ask for *un ticket correspondance*. A €4 all-day ticket is good on Nice's city buses, tramway, and airport express bus, plus selected buses serving nearby destinations (such as Villefranche and Eze-le-Village).

The **train** is more expensive, but there's no quicker way to move about the Riviera (www.sncf.com). Speedy trains link the Riviera's

Public Transportation on the French Riviera

From	To Cannes	To Antibes	To Nice
(continued from previous page)			
Cap Ferrat by Train	Bus #81 to Beaulieu-sur-Mer (2-4/hr, 10 min); then train to Cannes (2/hr, 1 hr)	Bus #81 to Beaulieu-sur-Mer (2-4/hr, 10 min); then train to Antibes (2/hr, 40 min)	N/A
Cap Ferrat by Bus	Not recommended	#81 to Cap Ferrat (2-4/hr, 10 min); then #200 to Nice (2-4/hr, 1-1.5 hrs)	#81, 2-4/hr, 35 min
Eze-le-Village by Train	Bus #83 to Eze-Bord-de-Mer (8/day, 15 min); then train to Cannes (2/hr, 1 hr)	Bus #83 to Eze-Bord-de-Mer (8/day, 15 min); then train to Antibes (2/hr, 45 min)	Bus #83 to Eze-Bord-de-Mer (8/day, 15 min); then train to Nice (2/hr, 15 min)
Eze-le-Village by Bus	Not recommended	Not recommended	#82/#112, 8-16/day, 40 min
Monaco by Train	2/hr, 1 hr	2/hr, 50 min	2/hr, 20 min
Monaco by Bus	Not recommended	Not recommended	#100, 3-4/hr, 1.25 hrs

beachfront destinations—Cannes, Antibes, Nice, Villefranche-sur-Mer, Monaco, and Menton. If in Nice, Villefranche, or Monaco, you can assume trains marked *Vintimille* or *Menton* are going east, and those marked *Grasse* or *Nice* are going west. Never board a train without a ticket or valid pass—fare inspectors don't accept any excuses, and the minimum fine is €70.

Nice makes the most convenient base for day trips, though public transport also works well from smaller Riviera towns such as Antibes and Villefranche-sur-Mer. Details are provided under each destination's "Connections" section. For a scenic inland train ride, take the narrow-gauge train into the Alps (see page 864).

And a final tip: No matter where you go, bring along a swimsuit if the weather's sunny—good beaches are plentiful.

By Boat: Trans Côte d'Azur offers boat service from Nice to Monaco or to St-Tropez from June into September (tel. 04 92 98 71 30, www.trans-cote-azur.com). For details, see page 783.

(Note: Not all destinations are covered in detail in this book.)

To Villefranche-sur-Mer	To Cap Ferrat	To Eze-le-Village	To Monaco
N/A	N/A	N/A	N/A
#81, 2-4/hr, 15 min	N/A	#100 direction: Monaco to Gare d'Eze stop (3-4/hr); then bus #83 to village (8/day, 15 min,)	#100, 3-4/hr, 20 min
Bus #83 to Eze-Bord-de-Mer (8/day, 15 min); then train to Villefranche (2/hr, 10 min)	N/A	N/A	N/A
#82/#112 to upper Villefranche (8-16/day, 25 min), then bus #80 to Villefranche	#83 to Gare d'Eze stop (8/day, 15 min); then bus #100 direction: Nice	N/A	#112, 6/day Mon-Sat, none on Sun, 20 min
2/hr, 10 min	N/A	N/A	N/A
#100, 3-4/hr, 25 min	#100, 3-4/hr, 20 min	#112, 6/day Mon-Sat, none on Sun, 20 min	N/A

The Riviera's Art Scene

The list of artists who have painted the Riviera reads like a Who's Who of 20th-century art. Pierre-Auguste Renoir, Henri Matisse, Marc Chagall, Georges Braque, Raoul Dufy, Fernand Léger, and Pablo Picasso all lived and worked here—and raved about the region's wonderful light. Their simple, semi-abstract, and—most importantly—colorful works reflect the pleasurable atmosphere of the Riviera. You'll experience the same landscapes they painted in this bright, sun-drenched region, punctuated with views of the "azure sea." Try to imagine the Riviera with a fraction of the people and development you see today.

But the artists were mostly drawn to the uncomplicated lifestyle of fishermen and farmers that has reigned here since time began. As the artists grew older, they retired in the sun, turned their backs on modern art's "isms," and painted with the wide-eyed wonder of children, using bright primary colors, basic outlines, and simple subjects.

A dynamic concentration of well-organized modern- and contemporary-art museums (many described in this chapter) litter the Riviera, allowing art lovers to appreciate these masters' works while immersed in the same sun and culture that inspired them. Many of the museums were designed to blend pieces with the surrounding views, gardens, and fountains, thus highlighting that modern art is not only stimulating, but sometimes simply beautiful.

The Riviera's Cuisine Scene

While many of the same dishes served in Provence are available throughout the Riviera (see "Provence's Cuisine Scene" on page 665), the Riviera adds an Italian-Mediterranean flair, with plenty of pasta dishes and seafood.

Local specialties are bouillabaisse (the spicy seafood stew that seems worth the cost only for those with a seafood fetish), *bourride* (a creamy fish soup thickened with aioli, a garlic sauce), and *salade niçoise* (nee-swaz). This salad has many variations, though most include a base of green salad topped with green beans, boiled potatoes (sometimes rice), tomatoes (sometimes corn), anchovies, olives, hard-boiled eggs, and lots of tuna. You'll also find these tasty bread treats: *pan bagnat* (like a *salade niçoise* stuffed into a hollowed-out soft roll), *pissaladière* (bread dough topped with onions, olives, and anchovies), *fougasse* (a spindly, lace-like bread sometimes flavored with nuts, herbs, olives, or ham), and *socca* (a thin chickpea crêpe, seasoned with pepper and olive oil and often served in a paper cone by street vendors).

Italian cuisine is native (ravioli was first made in Nice), easy to find, and generally a good value (*pâtes fraîches* means "fresh pasta"). For wine, Bandol (red) and Cassis (white) are popular and from a region nearly on the Riviera. The only wines made in the Riviera are Bellet rosé and white.

Remember, restaurants serve only during lunch (11:30-14:00) and dinner (19:00-21:00, later in bigger cities); cafés—except for the smaller ones—serve food throughout the day.

Nice

Nice (sounds like "niece"), with its spectacular Alps-to-Mediterranean surroundings, is an enjoyable big-city highlight of the Riviera. Its traffic-free old city mixes Italian and French flavors to create a spicy Mediterranean dressing, while its big squares, broad seaside walkways, and long beaches invite lounging and people-watching. Nice may be nice, but it's hot and jammed in July and August—reserve ahead and get a room with air-conditioning *(une chambre avec climatisation)*. Everything you'll want to see in Nice is either within walking distance or a short bus or tram ride away.

THE FRENCH RIVIERA

Orientation to Nice

The main points of interest lie between the beach and the train tracks (about 15 blocks apart—see map on the next page). The city

revolves around its grand Place Masséna, where pedestrian-friendly Avenue Jean Médecin meets Vieux (Old) Nice and the Albert 1er parkway (with quick access to the beaches). It's a 20-minute walk (or a €15 taxi ride) from the train station to the beach, and a 20-minute walk along the promenade from the fancy Hôtel Negresco to the heart of Vieux Nice.

A 10-minute ride on the smooth-as-silk tramway through the center of the city connects the train station, Place Masséna, Vieux Nice, and the port (from nearby Place Garibaldi). The tram and all city and regional buses cost only €1 per trip, making this one of the cheapest and easiest cities in France to get around in (see "Getting Around Nice," later). In 2013, work may begin on a new tramway line along the Promenade des Anglais—prepare for detours and traffic delays.

Tourist Information

Nice's helpful TIs share a phone number and website (tel. 08 92 70 74 07, www.nicetourisme.com). There are TI branches at the

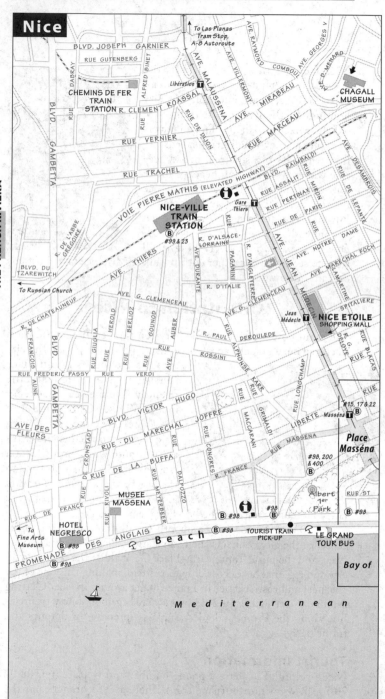

Nice

THE FRENCH RIVIERA

BLVD. JOSEPH GARNIER

RUE GUTENBERG

To Las Planas
Tram Stop,
A-8 Autoroute

RUE D'ABRAY

RUE ALFRED BINET

Libération

CHEMINS DE FER
TRAIN
STATION

R. CLEMENT ROASSAL

RUE DE DIJON

AVE. MALAUSSENA

AVE. RAYMOND

AVE. VILLERMONT

COMBOUL

AVE. D-MENARD

AVE. GEORGES V

CHAGALL
MUSEUM

AVE. MIRABEAU

AVE. MARCEAU

RUE MARCEAU

BLVD. GAMBETTA

RUE

RUE VERNIER

RUE TRACHEL

BLVD. RAIMBALDI

RUE DE LEPANTE

RUE DESAMBROIS

VOIE PIERRE MATHIS (ELEVATED HIGHWAY)

RUE ASSALIT

RUE PERTINAX

RUE MIRON

AVE. THIERS

NICE-VILLE
TRAIN
STATION

Gare
Thiers

R. D'ALSACE-
LORRAINE

RUE DE PARIS

AVE. JEAN MÉDECIN

RUE

AVE. NOTRE-DAME

#99 & 23

R. D'ANGLETERRE

AVE. DURANTE

R. PAGANINI

R. D'ITALIE

AVE. MARECHAL FOCH

AVE. MARMARTINE

SPITALIERE

R. DE L'ABBE
GREGOIRE

BLVD. DU
TZAREWITCH

To Russian Church

R. DE CHATEAUNEUF

AVE. G. CLEMENCEAU

AVE. G. CLEMENCEAU

Jean
Médecin

NICE ETOILE
SHOPPING MALL

R. G. DELOYE

RUE BLACAS

BLVD. FRANCOIS GAUNE

AVE. GIUGLIA

RUE HEROLD

RUE BERLIOZ

RUE GOUNOD

AVE. AUBER

R. PAUL DEROULEDE

RUE ALPHONSE KARR

RUE LONGCHAMP

RUE FREDERIC PASSY

RUE VERDI

ROSSINI

RUE

BLVD. VICTOR HUGO

RUE DU MARECHAL JOFFRE

RUE

RUE GRIMALDI

RUE MACCARANI

#15, 17 & 22

Masséna

Place
Masséna

AVE. DES
FLEURS

RUE DE CRONSTADT

RUE DE LA BUFFA

RUE CONGRES

RUE DALPOZZO

R. FRANCE

RUE MASSENA

LIBERTE

RUE MASSENA

#98, 200
& 400

RUE

RUE DE FRANCE

MUSEE
MASSENA

RUE MEYERBEER

Albert
1er
Park

RUE ST

To
Fine Arts
Museum

HOTEL
NEGRESCO

#98

PROMENADE DES ANGLAIS

#98

#98

#98

TOURIST TRAIN
PICK-UP

LE GRAND
TOUR BUS

#98

Beach

Bay of

M e d i t e r r a n e a n

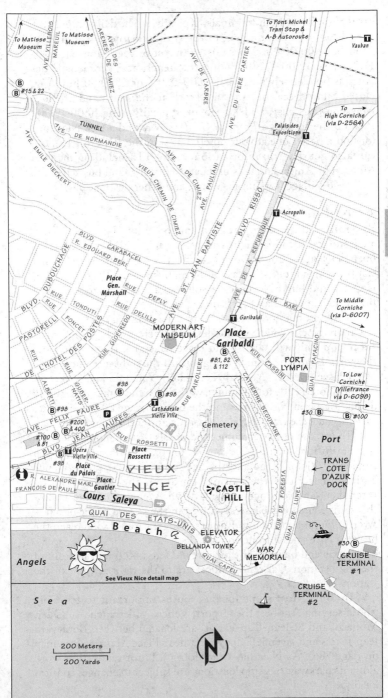

airport (desks in both terminals, typically quiet, daily 8:00-21:00, closed Sun off-season); next to the **train station** (busy, summer Mon-Sat 8:00-20:00, Sun 9:00-19:00; rest of year Mon-Sat 9:00-19:00, Sun 10:00-17:00); facing the **beach** at 5 Promenade des Anglais (moderately busy, daily 9:00-18:00, until 20:00 July-Aug, closed Sun off-season); and in a kiosk at the south end of **Place Masséna** (less busy, mid-June-Sept, typically daily 10:00-19:00). Pick up the thorough *Practical Guide to Nice* and a free Nice map (or find a better one at your hotel), but skip the Riviera Pass. You can also get day-trip information at any TI (including maps of Monaco or Antibes, details on boat excursions, and bus schedules to Eze-le-Village, La Turbie, Vence, and other destinations).

Arrival in Nice

By Train: All trains stop at Nice's main station, Nice-Ville (baggage storage at the far right with your back to the tracks, lockers open daily 8:00-21:00). (Don't get off at the suburban Nice-Riquier station, which is one stop east of the main station.) The station area is gritty and busy: Never leave your bags unattended, and don't linger here longer than necessary.

Turn left out of the station to find a **TI** next door. Continue a few more blocks down Avenue Jean Médecin for the Gare Thiers **tram stop** (this will take you to Place Masséna, the old city, and the port). Board the tram heading toward the right (direction: Pont Michel; see "Getting Around Nice," later). You'll find many recommended hotels a 10- to 20-minute walk down the same street (listed under "Between Nice Etoile and the Sea" on page 801), though it's easier to take the tram to Place Masséna and walk from there.

To walk to other recommended hotels (listed under "Between the Train Station and Nice Etoile" on page 800, and "Between Boulevard Victor Hugo and the Sea" on page 805), cross Avenue Thiers in front of the station, go down the steps by Hôtel Interlaken, and continue walking down Avenue Durante. Follow this same route for the fastest path from the station to the beach—Avenue Durante turns into Rue des Congrés. You'll soon reach the heart of Nice's beachfront promenade.

Taxis and **buses to the airport** (#23 and #99) wait in front of the train station. **Car rental** offices are to the right as you exit the station.

By Bus: Most stops for bus routes important to travelers (those serving Antibes, the airport, Vence, Villefranche-sur-Mer, Monaco, and St-Jean-Cap-Ferrat) are located between Boulevard Jean Jaurès and Avenue Félix Faure, near Place Masséna (see map on page 786). As Nice has been doing a lot of renovation work along its parkway, bus stop locations are subject to change; confirm locally.

By Car: To reach the city center on the autoroute from the west, take the first Nice exit (for the airport—called Côte d'Azur, Central) and follow signs for *Nice Centre* and *Promenade des Anglais* (expect detours if tramway construction is underway). Avoid arriving at rush hour (usually Mon-Fri 8:00-9:30 & 17:00-19:30), when Promenade des Anglais grinds to a halt. Hoteliers know where to park (allow €15-26/day; some hotels offer special deals, but space is limited, so reserve ahead). The parking garage at the Nice Etoile shopping center on Avenue Jean Médecin is pricey but near many recommended hotels (ticket booth on third floor, about €20/day, €12 overnight—20:00-8:00). The garage next to the recommended Hôtel Ibis at the train station has better rates. All on-street parking is metered (9:00-18:00 or 19:00), but usually free all day Sunday.

You can avoid driving in the center—and park for free during the day (no overnight parking)—by ditching your car at a parking lot at a remote tram stop (Las Planas is best) and taking the tram into town (10/hour, 15 minutes, €1, don't leave anything in your car; tramway described later, under "Getting Around Nice"). To find the Las Planas tram station from the A-8 autoroute, take the *Nice Nord* exit (see map on page 776).

By Plane or Cruise Ship: For information on Nice's airport and cruise-ship port, see pages 814 and 816.

Helpful Hints

Theft Alert: Nice has its share of pickpockets. Thieves target fanny packs: Have nothing important on or around your waist, unless it's in a money belt tucked out of sight. Don't leave things unattended on the beach while swimming, and stick to main streets in Vieux Nice after dark.

Museums: Some Nice museums (Chagall, Matisse, Archaeological) are closed on Tuesdays, while others (Modern and Contemporary Art, Fine Arts) close on Mondays. All of the sights in Nice—except the Chagall Museum and the Russian Cathedral—cost zilch to enter, making rainy-day options a swinging deal here.

Internet Access: There's no shortage of places to get online. Almost all of the hotels I list have free Wi-Fi, and some have computers for guests. For other access points, ask at your hotel or look for one of these establishments, all with free Wi-Fi: Quick Hamburger, Häagen Dazs, and McDonald's (multiple locations), or the Nice Etoile shopping center and Virgin Megastore (on Avenue Jean Médecin).

Laundry: You'll find launderettes everywhere in Nice—ask your hotelier for the nearest one.

Grocery Store: The big **Monoprix** on Avenue Jean Médecin and Rue Biscarra has it all, including deli counter, bakery, and cold drinks (Mon-Sat 8:30-21:00, closed Sun, see map on page 808). You'll also find many small grocery stores (some open Sun and/or until late hours) near my recommended hotels.

Boutique Shopping: The chic streets where Rue Alphonse Karr meets Rue de la Liberté and then Rue de Paradis are known as the "Golden Square." If you need pricey stuff, shop here.

SNCF Boutique: There's a handy French rail ticket office a half-block west of Avenue Jean Médecin at 2 Rue de la Liberté (Mon-Fri 10:00-18:00, closed Sat-Sun).

Renting a Bike (and Other Wheels): Roller Station rents bikes (*vélos*, can be taken on trains, €5/hour, €10/half-day, €15/day), rollerblades, skateboards, and Razor-type scooters (*trotinettes*, €7/half-day, €9/day). You'll need to leave your ID as a deposit (daily March-May and Sept-Oct 10:00-17:00, June-Aug 10:00-22:00, Nov-Feb 10:00-18:00, next to yellow awnings of Pailin's Asian restaurant at 49 Quai des Etats-Unis—see map on page 786, tel. 04 93 62 99 05, owner Eric). If you need more power, the TI has a list of places renting electric scooters.

You'll notice blue bikes **(Vélos Bleu)** stationed at various points in the city. A thousand of these bikes, available for locals to use when running errands, rent cheaply for short-term use (first 30 minutes free, requires European-style chip-and-PIN credit card, American Express cards should work).

Car Rental: Renting a car is easiest at Nice's airport, which has offices for all the major companies. You'll also find most companies represented at Nice's train station and near Albert 1er Park.

English Radio: Tune in to Riviera-Radio at FM 106.5.

Views: For panoramic views, climb Castle Hill (see page 791), or take a one-hour boat trip (described later, under "Tours in Nice").

Beach Gear: To make life tolerable on the rocks, swimmers should buy a pair of the cheap plastic beach shoes sold at many shops (flip-flops fall off in the water). **Go Sport** at #13 on Place Masséna sells beach shoes, flip-flops, and cheap sunglasses (daily 10:00-20:00—see map on page 786).

Getting Around Nice

Although you can walk to most attractions in Nice, smart travelers make good use of the buses and tram. Both are covered by the same €1 single-ride ticket (good for 74 minutes in one direction, including transfers between bus and tram; can't be used for a round-trip). The **bus** is particularly handy for reaching the Chagall and Matisse museums and the Russian Cathedral. Pick up timetables at Nice's TIs (or view them online at www.lignesdazur.com) and buy tickets from the driver. Make sure to validate your ticket in the machine just behind the driver—watch locals do it and imitate.

The €4 all-day pass is valid on city buses and trams, as well as buses to some nearby destinations. The all-day ticket makes sense if you plan to take the bus to museums, use the tramway several times, or are going to the airport (you must validate your ticket on every trip). Express buses to and from the airport (#98 and #99) require the €4 all-day ticket, so savvy riders pack in other bus and/or tram rides on the day of their flight.

Nice's **tramway** makes an "L" along Avenue Jean Médecin and Boulevard Jean Jaurès, and connects the main train station (Gare Thiers stop), Place Masséna (Masséna stop, near many regional bus stops and a few blocks' walk from the sea), Vieux Nice (Opéra-Vieille Ville, Cathédrale-Vieille Ville), and the Modern and Contemporary Art Museum and port (Place Garibaldi). It also comes within a few blocks of the Chemins de Fer de Provence train station (Libération stop)—the departure point for the scenic narrow-gauge rail journey (see page 864).

Boarding the tram in the direction of Pont Michel takes you from the train station toward the beach and Vieux Nice (direction: Las Planas goes the other way). Buy tickets at the machines on the platforms (coins only, no credit cards). Choose the English flag to change the display language, turn the round knob and push the green button to select your ticket, press it twice at the end to get your ticket, or press the red button to cancel. Once you're on the tram, validate your ticket by inserting it into the top of the white box, then reclaiming it (http://tramway.nice.fr).

Taxis are useful for getting to Nice's less-central sights, and worth it if you're nowhere near a bus or tram stop (figure €15 from Promenade des Anglais). Cabbies normally only pick up at taxi stands *(tête de station)*, or you can call 04 93 13 78 78.

The hokey **tourist train** gets you up Castle Hill (see "Tours in Nice," later).

Getting Around the Riviera from Nice

By Train and Bus: Nice is perfectly situated for exploring the Riviera by public transport. Monaco, Eze-le-Village, Villefranche-sur-Mer, Antibes, Vence, and St-Paul-de-Vence are all within about a one-hour bus or train ride. The train is pricier (fares range from €2 to nearby Villefranche-sur-Mer to €8.50 to farther-away Grasse) than the bus (€1 for most destinations), but will often save you time. Both modes of transportation work well (see the map on pages 776-777 for key bus locations).

All trains serving Nice arrive at and depart from the Nice-Ville Station. Most regional buses stop near Place Masséna (look for the J.C. Bermond stop, between Boulevard Jean Jaurès and Avenue Félix Faure), along Boulevard Jean Jaurès, or near Place Garibaldi (near Vieux Nice; see map on page 786 for stop locations, www.lignesdazur.com).

With a little planning, you can link locations into an all-day circuit. For example, you can triangulate Nice, Monaco, and Eze-le-Village or La Turbie in a loop that ends up back in Nice (see page 843 for details). For a summary of train and bus connections, see "Nice Connections" on page 813.

By Boat: From June to mid-September, Trans Côte d'Azur offers scenic trips several days a week from Nice to Monaco and Nice to St-Tropez. Boats leave in the morning and return in the evening, giving you all day to explore your destination. Drinks and WCs are available on board.

Boats to **Monaco** depart at 9:30 and 16:00, and return at 11:00 and 18:00 (€34 round-trip, €28 if you don't get off in Monaco, 45 minutes each way, June-mid-Sept Tue, Thu, and Sat only).

Boats to **St-Tropez** depart at 9:00 and return at 19:00 (€60 round-trip, 2.5 hours each way; July-mid-Sept Tue-Sun, no boats Mon; June and late Sept Tue, Thu, Sat, and Sun only).

Reservations are required for both boats, and tickets for St-Tropez often sell out, so book a few days ahead (tel. 04 92 98 71 30 or 04 92 00 42 30, www.trans-cote-azur.com, croisieres @trans-cote-azur.com). The boats leave from Nice's port, Bassin des Amiraux, just below Castle Hill—look for the ticket booth *(billeterie)* on Quai de Lunel (see map on page 776). The same company also runs one-hour round-trip cruises along the coast to Cap Ferrat (see "Tours in Nice," next).

Tours in Nice

Bus Tour—Le Grand Tour Bus provides a 11-stop, hop-on, hop-off service on an open-deck bus with headphone commentary (2/hour, 1.5-hour loop) that includes the Promenade des Anglais, the old port, Cap de Nice, and the Chagall and Matisse Museums on Cimiez Hill (€20/1-day pass, €23/2-day pass, cheaper for seniors and students, €12 for last tour of the day at about 18:00, some hotels offer small discounts, buy tickets on bus, main stop is near where Promenade des Anglais and Quai des Etats-Unis meet, across from the Plage Beau Rivage lounge, tel. 04 92 29 17

THE FRENCH RIVIERA

Nice at a Glance

▲▲▲**Chagall Museum** The world's largest collection of Marc Chagall's work, popular even with people who don't like modern art. **Hours:** Wed-Mon 10:00-17:00, May-Oct until 18:00, closed Tue year-round. See page 792.

▲▲▲**Promenade des Anglais** Nice's four-mile sunstruck seafront promenade. **Hours:** Always open. See page 789.

▲▲**Vieux Nice** Charming old city offering enjoyable atmosphere and a look at Nice's French-Italian cultural blend. **Hours:** Always open. See page 785.

▲**Matisse Museum** Small but worthwhile collection of Henri Matisse's paintings, sketches, paper cutouts, and more. **Hours:** Wed-Mon 10:00-18:00, closed Tue. See page 794.

▲**Modern and Contemporary Art Museum** Ultramodern museum with enjoyable collection from the 1960s-1970s, including Warhol and Lichtenstein. **Hours:** Tue-Sun 10:00-18:00, closed Mon. See page 795.

▲**Russian Cathedral** Finest Orthodox church outside of Russia. **Hours:** Mon-Sat 9:00-12:00 & 14:30-18:00, Sun 14:30-18:00, until 17:00 off-season. See page 797.

▲**Castle Hill** Site of an ancient fort boasting great views—especially in early mornings and evenings. **Hours:** Park closes at 20:00 in summer, earlier off-season. Free elevator runs daily 10:00-19:00, until 20:00 in summer. See page 791.

Fine Arts Museum Lush villa shows off impressive paintings by Monet, Sisley, Bonnard, and Raoul Dufy. **Hours:** Tue-Sun 10:00-18:00, closed Mon. See page 796.

Molinard Perfume Museum Two-room museum in storefront boutique tracing the history of perfume. **Hours:** Daily April-Sept 10:00-19:00, Oct-March 10:00-13:00 & 14:00-18:30, sometimes closed Sun off-season. See page 796.

THE FRENCH RIVIERA

00, www.nicelegrandtour.com). This tour is a pricey way to get to the Chagall and Matisse Museums, but it's an acceptable option if you also want a city overview. Check the schedule if you plan to use this bus to see the Russian Cathedral, as it may be faster to walk there.

▲**Boat Cruise**—Here's your chance to view Nice from the water. On this one-hour star-studded tour run by Trans Côte d'Azur, you'll cruise in a comfortable yacht-size vessel to Cap Ferrat and past Villefranche-sur-Mer, then return to Nice with a final lap along Promenade des Anglais. It's a scenic trip; the best views are from the seats on top.

French (and sometimes English-speaking) guides play Robin Leach, pointing out mansions owned by some pretty famous people, including Elton John (just as you leave Nice, it's the soft-yellow square-shaped place right on the water), Sean Connery (on the hill above Elton, with rounded arches and tower), and Microsoft co-founder Paul Allen (in saddle of Cap Ferrat hill, above yellow-umbrella beach with sloping red-tile roof). I wonder if this gang ever hangs out together. Guides also like to point out the mansion (between Villefranche-sur-Mer and Cap Ferrat) where the Rolling Stones recorded *Exile on Main Street* (€16; April-Oct Tue-Sun 2/day, usually at 11:00 and 15:00, no boats Mon or in off-season, call ahead to verify schedule, arrive 30 minutes early to get best seats, drinks and WCs available). For directions to the dock and contact information, see "Getting Around the Riviera From Nice—By Boat," earlier.

Tourist Train—For €8 (€4 for children under age 9), you can spend 45 embarrassing minutes on the tourist train tooting along the promenade, through the old city, and up to Castle Hill. This is a sweat-free way to get to the top of the hill—but so is the elevator, which is free (train runs every 30 minutes, daily 10:00-18:00, June-Aug until 19:00, recorded English commentary, meet train near Le Grand Tour Bus stop on Quai des Etats-Unis, next departure posted, tel. 02 99 88 47 07, www.ttdf.com).

Walking Tours—The TI on Promenade des Anglais organizes weekly walking tours of Vieux Nice in French and English (€12, May-Oct only, usually Sat morning at 9:30, 2.5 hours, reservations necessary, depart from TI, tel. 08 92 70 74 07). They also have evening art walks on Fridays at 19:00.

Local Guides—**Agnès Dumartin, Sylvie Di Cristo,** and **Sofia Villavicencio** all give enjoyable tours of Nice (for contact info, see page 768).

Cooking Tour and Classes—Charming Canadian Francophile Rosa Jackson, a food journalist, Cordon Bleu-trained cook, and longtime resident of France, runs **Les Petits Farcis,** which offers three-hour "Taste of Nice" food tours for €90. She also teaches popular cooking classes in Vieux Nice, which include a morning trip to the open-air market on Cours Saleya to pick up ingredients, and an afternoon session spent creating an authentic Niçois meal from your purchases (€195/person, mobile 06 81 67 41 22, www.petitsfarcis.com).

Self-Guided Walk

▲▲A Scratch-and-Sniff Walk Through Vieux Nice

This approximately hour-long walk leads you through the delights of Vieux (Old) Nice.

• *See the map on the next page, and start at Nice's main market square...*

Cours Saleya (koor sah-lay-yuh): Named for its broad exposure to the sun *(soleil)*, this commotion of color, sights, smells,

and people has been Nice's main market square since the Middle Ages (produce market held Tue-Sun until 13:00—on Mon, an antiques market takes center stage). Amazingly, part of this square was a parking lot until 1980, when the mayor of Nice had an underground garage built.

The first section is devoted to the Riviera's largest flower market (all day Tue-Sun and in operation since the 19th century). Here you'll find plants and flowers that grow effortlessly and ubiquitously in this climate, including the local favorites: carnations, roses, and jasmine. Not long ago, this region supplied all of France with its flowers; today, many are imported from Africa (the glorious orchids are from Kenya). Still, fresh flowers are perhaps the best value in this city.

The boisterous produce section trumpets the season with mushrooms, strawberries, white asparagus, zucchini flowers, and more—whatever's fresh gets top billing. Find your way down the center and buy something healthy.

The market opens up at Place Pierre Gautier (also called Plassa dou Gouvernou—bilingual street signs include the old Niçoise language, an Italian dialect). This is where farmers set up stalls to sell their produce and herbs directly.

Continue down the center of Cours Saleya, stopping when you see La Cambuse restaurant on your left. In front, hovering over the black-barrel fire with the paella-like pan on top, is the self-proclaimed **Queen of the Market,** Thérèse. She's cooking *socca,* Nice's chickpea crêpe specialty (until about 13:00). Spend €3 for a wad (careful—it's hot, but good). If Thérèse doesn't have a pan out, that means it's on its way (watch for the frequent scooter deliveries). Wait in line...or else it'll be all gone when you return.

• *Continue down Cours Saleya. The fine golden building that seals the end of the square is where Henri Matisse spent 17 years with a brilliant view onto Nice's world. The **Café les Ponchettes** is perfectly positioned for a people-watching break. Turn at the café onto...*

THE FRENCH RIVIERA

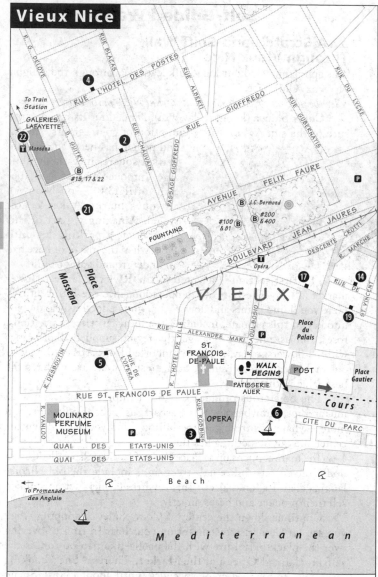

Vieux Nice

1 Hôtel la Perouse & Hôtel Suisse
2 Hôtel Masséna
3 Hôtel Mercure Marché aux Fleurs
4 Hôtel Lafayette
5 Hôtel de la Mer
6 La Voglia Restaurant
7 Le Safari Restaurant
8 Palmyre Restaurant
9 La Festival de la Moule
10 Le Bistrot du Fromager
11 Oliviera Shop/Restaurant
12 Restaurant Castel
13 L'Acchiardo Restaurant
14 Ville de Siena Restaurant
15 Lou Pilha Leva Restaurant
16 Fenocchio's Gelato (2)

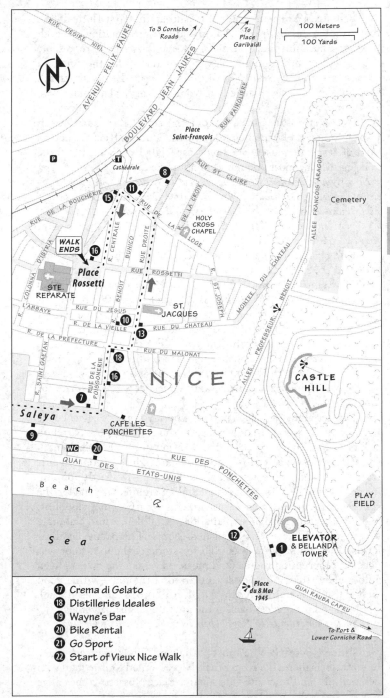

THE FRENCH RIVIERA

⑰ Crema di Gelato
⑱ Distilleries Ideales
⑲ Wayne's Bar
⑳ Bike Rental
㉑ Go Sport
㉒ Start of Vieux Nice Walk

Rue de la Poissonnerie: Look up at the first floor of the first building on your right. **Adam and Eve** are squaring off, each holding a zucchini-like gourd. This scene (post-apple) represents the annual rapprochement in Nice to make up for the sins of a too-much-fun Carnival (Mardi Gras, the pre-Lenten festival). Residents of Nice have partied hard during Carnival for more than 700 years.

A few steps ahead, check out the small **Baroque church** (Notre-Dame-de-l'Annonciation) dedicated to St. Rita, the patron saint of desperate causes. She holds a special place in locals' hearts, making this the most popular church in Nice.

• *Turn right on the next street, where you'll pass Vieux Nice's most happening café/bar,* **Distilleries Ideales,** *with a lively happy hour (18:00-20:00) and a* Pirates of the Caribbean-*style interior.*

Now turn left on "Right" Street (Rue Droite), and enter an area that feels like a Little Naples.

Rue Droite: In the Middle Ages, this straight, skinny street provided the most direct route from wall to wall, or river to sea. Stop at **Esipuno's bakery** (at Place du Jésus, closed Mon-Tue) and say *bonjour* to the friendly folks. Decades ago, this baker was voted the best in France—the trophies you see were earned for bread-making, not bowling. His son now runs the place. Notice the firewood stacked behind the oven. Try the house specialty, *tourte aux blettes*—a Swiss chard tart. It's traditionally made with jam (a sweet, tasty breakfast treat), but there's also a savory version, stuffed with pine nuts, raisins, and white beets (my favorite for lunch).

Farther along, at #28, Thérèse (whom you met earlier) cooks her *socca* in the wood-fired oven before she carts it to her barrel on Cours Saleya. The balconies of the mansion in the next block mark the **Palais Lascaris** (c. 1647, gorgeous at night), a rare souvenir from one of Nice's most prestigious families. It's worth popping inside (handy WCs) for its Baroque Italian architecture and terrific collection of antique musical instruments—harps, guitars, violins, and violas (good English explanations). You'll also find elaborate tapestries and a few well-furnished rooms. The palace has four levels: The ground floor was used for storage, the first floor was devoted to reception rooms (and musical events), the owners lived a floor above that, and the servants lived at the top—with a good view but lots of stairs (free, Wed-Mon 10:00-18:00, closed Tue). Look up and make faces back at the guys under the balconies.

• *Turn left on Rue de la Loge, then left again on Rue Centrale, to reach...*

Place Rossetti: The most Italian of Nice's piazzas, Place Rossetti feels more like Roma than Nice. Named for the man who donated his land to create this square, Place Rossetti comes alive after dark. The recommended Fenocchio gelato shop is popular for its many flavors, ranging from classic to innovative.

Walk to the fountain and stare back at the church. This is the **Cathedral of St. Réparate**—an unassuming building for a major city's cathedral. It was relocated here in the 1500s, when Castle Hill was temporarily converted to military use only. The name comes from Nice's patron saint, a teenage virgin named Réparate whose martyred body floated to Nice in the fourth century accompanied by angels. The interior of the cathedral gushes Baroque, a response to the Protestant Reformation. With the Catholic Church's Counter-Reformation, the theatrical energy of churches was cranked up with re-energized, high-powered saints and eye-popping decor.

• *Our walk is over. Castle Hill is straight up the stepped lane opposite the cathedral.*

Sights in Nice

Walks and Beach Time

▲▲▲**Promenade des Anglais and Beach**—Welcome to the Riviera. There's something for everyone along this four-mile-long

seafront circus. Watch Europeans at play, admire the azure Mediterranean, anchor yourself on a blue seat, and prop your feet up on the made-to-order guardrail. Later in the day, come back to join the evening parade of tans along the promenade.

The broad sidewalks of the Promenade des Anglais ("walkway of the English") were financed by upper-crust English tourists who wanted a secure and comfortable place to stroll and admire the view. The walk was done in marble in 1822 for aristocrats who didn't want to dirty their shoes or smell the fishy gravel.

Stroll like the belle-époque English aristocrats for whom the promenade was paved. Start at the pink-domed Hôtel Negresco, then cross to the sea and end your promenade at Castle Hill. The following sights are listed in the order you'll pass them. This walk is ideally done at sunset (as a pre-dinner stroll).

Hôtel Negresco—Nice's finest hotel is also a historic monument, offering up the city's most expensive beds (see "Sleeping in Nice," later) and a free "museum" interior (always open, provided you're dressed decently—absolutely no beach attire).

March straight through the lobby (as if you're staying here)

THE FRENCH RIVIERA

into the exquisite **Salon Royal,** an elegant place for a drink and a frequent host to modern art exhibits (opens at 11:00). The chandelier hanging from the Eiffel-built dome is made of 16,000 pieces of crystal. It was built in France for the Russian czar's Moscow palace...but thanks to the Bolshevik Revolution in 1917, he couldn't take delivery (portraits of Czar Alexander III and his wife, Maria Feodorovna—who returned to her native Denmark after the revolution—are to the right, under the dome). Saunter around the perimeter counterclockwise. If the bar door is open (after about 15:00), wander up the marble steps for a look. Farther along, nip into the toilets for either an early 20th-century powder room or a Battle of Waterloo experience. The chairs nearby were typical of the age (cones of silence for an afternoon nap sitting up).

Bay of Angels (Baie des Anges)—Grab a blue chair and face the sea. The body of Nice's patron saint, Réparate, was supposedly escorted into this bay by angels in the fourth century. To your right is where you might have been escorted into France—Nice's airport, built on a massive landfill. On that tip of land way beyond the runway is Cap d'Antibes. Until 1860, Antibes and Nice were in different countries—Antibes was French, but Nice was a protectorate of the Italian kingdom of Savoy-Piedmont, a.k.a. the Kingdom of Sardinia. In 1850, the people here spoke Italian and ate pasta. As Italy was uniting, the region was given a choice: Join the new country of Italy or join good old France (which was enjoying good times under the rule of Napoleon III). The vast majority voted in 1860 to go French...and voilà!

The lower green hill to your left is Castle Hill (described later). Farther left lies Villefranche-sur-Mer (marked by the tower at land's end, and home to lots of millionaires), then Monaco (which you can't see, with more millionaires), then Italy (with lots of, uh, Italians). Behind you are the foothills of the Alps (Alpes-Maritimes), which trap threatening clouds, ensuring that the Côte d'Azur enjoys sunshine more than 300 days each year. While half a million people live here, pollution is carefully treated—the water is routinely tested and very clean.

Stroll the promenade with the sea starboard, and contemplate beach time (see next) on your way to the Albert 1er Park.

Beaches—Settle in on the smooth rocks or find a section with imported sand, and consider your options: You can play beach volleyball, table tennis, or *boules;* rent paddleboats, personal watercraft, or windsurfing equipment; explore ways to use your zoom lens for some revealing people-watching; or snooze on a comfy beach bed.

To rent a spot on the beach, compare rates, as prices vary—beaches on the east end of the bay are usually cheaper (chair and mattress—*chaise longue* and *transat*—about €15, umbrella-€5, towel-€4). Some hotels have special deals with certain beaches for discounted rentals (check with your hotel for details). Have lunch in your bathing suit (€12 salads and pizzas in bars and restaurants all along the beach). Or, for a peaceful café au lait on the Mediterranean, stop here first thing in the morning before the crowds hit. *Plage Publique* signs explain the 15 beach no-nos (translated into English).

Albert 1er Park—The park is named for the Belgian king who enjoyed wintering here—these were his private gardens. While the English came first, the Belgians and Russians were also big fans of 19th-century Nice. That tall statue at the edge of the park commemorates the 100-year anniversary of Nice's union with France.

If you detour from the promenade into the park and continue down the center of the grassy strip, you'll be walking over Nice's river, the Paillon (covered since the 1800s). For centuries, this river was Nice's natural defense to the north and west (the sea protected the south, and Castle Hill defended the east). Imagine the fortified wall that ran along its length from the hills behind you to the sea. With the arrival of tourism in the 1800s, Nice expanded over and beyond the river.

▲Castle Hill (Colline du Château)—This hill—in an otherwise flat city center—offers sensational views over Nice, the port (to the east), the foothills of the Alps, and the Mediterranean. The views are best early or at sunset, or whenever the weather's clear (park closes at 20:00 in summer, earlier off-season). The city of Nice was first settled here by Greeks circa 400 B.C. In the Middle Ages, a massive castle stood here, with turrets, high walls, and soldiers at the ready. With the river guarding one side and the sea the other, this mountain fortress seemed strong—until Louis XIV leveled it in 1706. Nice's medieval seawall ran along the lineup of two-story buildings below. Today you'll find a waterfall, a playground, two cafés (with fair prices), and a cemetery—but no castle—on Castle Hill. Nice's port is just below on the east edge of Castle Hill.

Getting There: You can get to the top of Castle Hill by foot, by elevator (free, runs daily 10:00-19:00, until 20:00 in summer, next to beachfront Hôtel Suisse), or by pricey tourist train (described under "Tours in Nice," earlier).

Bike Routes—Meandering along Nice's seafront on foot or by bike is a must. To rev up the pace of your saunter, rent a bike and glide along the coast in either or both directions (about 30 minutes each way; for rental info see "Helpful Hints," earlier). Both of the following paths start along Promenade des Anglais.

The path to the **west** stops just before the airport at perhaps the most scenic *boules* courts in France. Pause here to watch the old-timers while away the afternoon tossing shiny metal balls (for more on this game, see page 1141). If you take the path heading **east**, you'll round the hill—passing a scenic cape and the town's memorial to both world wars—to the harbor of Nice, with a chance to survey some fancy yachts. Pedal around the harbor and follow the coast past the Corsica ferry terminal (you'll need to carry your bike up a flight of steps). From there the path leads to an appealing tree-lined residential district.

Museums and Monuments

To bring culture to the masses, the city of Nice has nixed entry fees to all municipal museums—so it's free to enter all the following sights except the Chagall Museum and the Russian Cathedral. Cool.

The first two museums (Chagall and Matisse) are a long walk northeast of Nice's city center. Because they're in the same direction and served by the same bus line (buses #15 and #22 stop at both museums), it makes sense to visit them on the same trip. From Place Masséna, the Chagall Museum is a 10-minute bus ride or a 30-minute walk, and the Matisse Museum is a 20-minute bus ride or a one-hour walk.

▲▲▲Chagall Museum (Musée National Marc Chagall)— Even if you're suspicious of modern art, this museum—with the

world's largest collection of Marc Chagall's work in captivity—is a delight. After World War II, Marc Chagall (1887-1985) returned from the United States to settle in Vence, not far from Nice. Between 1954 and 1967 he painted a cycle of 17 large murals designed for, and donated to, this museum. These paintings, inspired by the biblical books of Genesis, Exodus, and the Song of Songs, make up the "nave," or core, of what Chagall called the "House of Brotherhood."

Each painting is a collage of images that draws from Chagall's Russian folk-village youth, his Jewish heritage, biblical themes, and his feeling that he existed somewhere between heaven and earth. He believed that the Bible was a synonym for nature, and that color and biblical themes were key for understanding God's love for his creation. Chagall's brilliant blues and reds celebrate nature, as do his spiritual and folk themes. Notice the focus on

Chagall's Style

Chagall uses a deceptively simple, almost childlike style to paint a world that's hidden to the eye—the magical, mystical world below the sur-face. Here are some of the characteristics of his paintings:

- **Deep, radiant colors,** inspired by Expressionism and Fauvism (an art movement pioneered by Matisse and other French painters).
- **Personal imagery,** particularly from his childhood in Russia—smiling barn-yard animals, fiddlers on the roof, flower bouquets, huts, and blissful sweethearts.
- **A Hasidic Jewish perspective,** the idea that God is every-where, appearing in everyday things like nature, animals, and humdrum activities.
- **A fragmented Cubist style,** multifaceted and multidi-mensional, a perfect style to mirror the complexity of God's creation.
- **Overlapping images,** like double-exposure photogra-phy, with faint imagery that bleeds through, suggesting there's more to life under the surface.
- **Stained-glass-esque technique** of dark, deep, earthy, "potent" colors, and simplified, iconic, symbolic figures.
- **Gravity-defying compositions,** with lovers, animals, and angels twirling blissfully in midair.
- **Happy (not tragic) mood** depicting a world of personal joy, despite the violence and turmoil of world wars and revolution.
- **Childlike simplicity,** drawn with simple, heavy outlines, filled in with Crayola colors that often spill over the lines. Major characters in a scene are bigger than the lesser characters. The grinning barnyard animals, the bright colors, the magical events presented as literal truth...Was Chagall a lightweight? Or a lighter-than-air-weight?

couples. To Chagall, humans loving each other mirrored God's love of creation.

Although Chagall would suggest that you explore his works without help, the free audioguide gives you detailed explanations of his works and covers temporary exhibits. The free *Plan du Musée* helps you locate the rooms, though you can do without, as the museum is pretty simple.

Cost and Hours: €7.50, €1-2 more with (frequent) special exhibits, free first Sun of the month (but crowded), open Wed-Mon 10:00-17:00, May-Oct until 18:00, closed Tue year-round, Avenue Docteur Ménard, tel. 04 93 53 87 20, www.musee-chagall.fr.

Getting to the Chagall Museum: You can reach the museum, located on Avenue Docteur Ménard, by bus or on foot.

Buses #15 and #22 serve the Chagall Museum from the Masséna Guitry stop, near Place Masséna (5/hour Mon-Sat, 3/hour Sun, €1, immediately behind Galeries Lafayette department store—see map on page 786). The museum's bus stop (called Musée Chagall, shown on the bus shelter) is on Boulevard de Cimiez (walk uphill from the stop to find the museum).

To **walk** from central Nice to the Chagall Museum (30 minutes), go to the train-station end of Avenue Jean Médecin and turn right onto Boulevard Raimbaldi. Walk four long blocks along the elevated road, then turn left onto Avenue Raymond Comboul, and follow *Musée Chagall* signs.

Cuisine Art and WCs: An idyllic café (€10 salads and *plats*) awaits in the corner of the garden. A spick-and-span WC is next to the ticket desk (there's one inside, too).

Leaving the Museum: To take **buses** #15 or #22 back to downtown Nice, turn right out of the museum, then make another right down Boulevard de Cimiez, and catch the bus heading downhill. To continue on to the Matisse Museum, catch buses #15 or #22 using the uphill stop located across the street. **Taxis** usually wait in front of the museum. It's about €12 for a ride to the city center.

To **walk** to the train station area from the museum (20 minutes), turn left out of the museum grounds on Avenue Docteur Ménard, and follow the street to the left at the first intersection, continuing to hug the museum grounds. Where the street curves right (by #32), take the ramps and staircases down on your left, turn left at the bottom, cross under the freeway and the train tracks, then turn right on Boulevard Raimbaldi to reach the station.

▲**Matisse Museum (Musée Matisse)**—This small museum contains a sampling of works from the various periods of Henri Matisse's long artistic career. The museum offers a painless introduction to the artist's many styles and materials, both shaped by Mediterranean light and by fellow Côte d'Azur artists Pablo Picasso and Pierre-Auguste Renoir. The collection is scattered throughout several rooms with a few worthwhile works, though it lacks a certain *je ne sais quoi* when compared to the Chagall Museum.

Henri Matisse (1869-1954), the master of leaving things out, could suggest a woman's body with a single curvy line—letting the viewer's mind fill in the rest. Ignoring traditional 3-D perspective, he expressed his passion for life through simplified but recognizable scenes in which dark outlines and saturated, bright blocks of color create an overall decorative pattern. You don't look "through" a Matisse canvas, like a window; you look "at" it, like wallpaper.

Matisse understood how colors and shapes affect us emotionally. He could create either shocking, clashing works (early Fauvism) or geometrical, balanced, harmonious ones (later cutouts). Whereas other modern artists reveled in purely abstract design, Matisse (almost) always kept the subject matter at least vaguely recognizable. He used unreal colors and distorted lines not just to portray what an object looks like, but to express its inner nature (even inanimate objects). Meditating on his paintings helps you connect with life—or so Matisse hoped.

Cost and Hours: Free, Wed-Mon 10:00-18:00, closed Tue, 164 Avenue des Arènes de Cimiez, tel. 04 93 81 08 08, www.musee-matisse-nice.org. The museum is housed in a beautiful Mediterranean mansion set in an olive grove amid the ruins of the ancient Roman city of Cemenelum.

Getting to the Matisse Museum: It's a long uphill walk from the city center. Take the bus (details follow) or a cab (€20 from Promenade des Anglais). Once here, walk into the park to find the pink villa. **Buses #15, #17,** and **#22** offer regular service to the Matisse Museum from just off Place Masséna on Rue Sacha Guitry (Masséna Guitry stop, at the east end of the Galeries Lafayette department store—see map on page 786, 20 minutes; note that bus #17 does not stop at the Chagall Museum). **Bus #20** connects the port to the museum. On any bus, get off at the Arènes-Matisse bus stop (look for the crumbling Roman wall).

Leaving the Museum: When leaving the museum, find the stop for buses #15 and #22 (frequent service downtown and stops en route at the Chagall Museum): Turn left from the Matisse Museum into the park and keep straight on Allée Barney Wilen, exiting the park at the Archaeological Museum, then turn right. Pass the bus stop across the street (#17 goes to the city center but not the Chagall Museum, and #20 goes to the port), and walk to the small roundabout. Cross the roundabout to find the shelter (facing downhill) for buses #15 and #22.

▲**Modern and Contemporary Art Museum (Musée d'Art Moderne et d'Art Contemporain)**—This ultramodern museum features an explosively colorful, far-out, yet manageable collection focused on American and European-American artists from the 1960s and 1970s (Pop Art and New Realism styles are highlighted). The exhibits cover three floors and include a few works by Andy Warhol, Roy Lichtenstein, and Jean Tinguely, and small models of Christo's famous wrappings. You'll find rooms dedicated to Robert Indiana, Yves Klein, and Niki de Saint Phalle (my favorite). The temporary exhibits can be as appealing to modern-art lovers as the permanent collection: Check the museum website for what's playing. Don't leave without exploring the rooftop terrace.

Cost and Hours: Free, Tue-Sun 10:00-18:00, closed Mon, about a 15-minute walk from Place Masséna, near Vieux Nice on Promenade des Arts, tel. 04 93 62 61 62, www.mamac-nice.org.

Fine Arts Museum (Musée des Beaux-Arts)—Housed in a sumptuous Riviera villa with lovely gardens, this museum holds 6,000 artworks from the 17th to 20th centuries. Start on the first floor and work your way up to experience an appealing array of paintings by Monet, Sisley, Bonnard, and Raoul Dufy, as well as a few sculptures by Rodin and Carpeaux.

Cost and Hours: Free, Tue-Sun 10:00-18:00, closed Mon, inconveniently located at the western end of Nice, take bus #12 or #23 from the train station to the Rosa Bonheur stop and walk to 3 Avenue des Baumettes, tel. 04 92 15 28 28, www.musee-beaux -arts-nice.org.

Molinard Perfume Museum—The Molinard family has been making perfume in Grasse (about an hour's drive from Nice) since 1849. Their Nice store has a small museum in the rear that illustrates the story of their industry. Back when people believed water spread the plague (Louis XIV supposedly bathed less than once a year), doctors advised people to rub fragrances into their skin and then powder their body. At that time, perfume was a necessity of everyday life.

Cost and Hours: Free, daily April-Sept 10:00-19:00, Oct-March 10:00-13:00 & 14:00-18:30, sometimes closed Sun off-season, just between beach and Place Masséna at 20 Rue St. François de Paule, see map on page 786, tel. 04 93 62 90 50, www .molinard.com.

Visiting the Museum: The tiny first room shows photos of the local flowers, roots, and other plant parts used in perfume production. The second, main room explains the earliest (18th-century) production method. Petals were laid out in the sun on a bed of animal fat, which would absorb the essence of the flowers as they baked. For two months, the petals were replaced daily, until the fat was saturated. Models and old photos show the later distillation process (660 pounds of lavender produced only a quarter-gallon of essence). Perfume is "distilled like cognac and then aged like wine." The bottles on the tables demonstrate the role of the "blender" and the perfume mastermind called the "nose" (who knows best); clients are allowed to try their hand at mixing scents. Of the 150 real "noses" in the world, more than 100 are French. Notice the photos of these lab-coat-wearing perfectionists. You are welcome to enjoy the testing bottles.

▲**Russian Cathedral (Cathédrale Russe)**—Nice's Russian Orthodox church, claimed by some to be the finest outside Russia, is worth a visit.

Cost and Hours: Free, Mon-Sat 9:00-12:00 & 14:30-18:00, Sun 14:30-18:00, until 17:00 off-season; chanted services Sat at 17:30 or 18:00, Sun at 10:00; no tourist visits during services, no short shorts, 17 Boulevard du Tzarewitch, tel. 04 93 96 88 02, www.acor-nice.com. The park around the church stays open at lunch and makes a fine setting for picnics.

Getting to the Russian Cathedral: It's at 17 Boulevard du Tzarewitch, a 10-minute walk from the train station. Head west on Avenue Thiers, turn right on Avenue Gambetta, go under the freeway, and turn left following *Eglise Russe* signs. Or, from the station, take any bus heading west on Avenue Thiers and get off at Avenue Gambetta (then follow the previous directions).

Background: Five hundred rich Russian families wintered in Nice in the late 19th century, and they needed a worthy Orthodox house of worship. Czar Nicholas I's widow provided the land (which required tearing down her house), and Czar Nicholas II gave this church to the Russian community in 1912. (A few years later, Russian comrades who *didn't* winter on the Riviera assassinated him.) Here in the land of olives and anchovies, these proud onion domes seem odd. But, I imagine, so did those old Russians.

Visiting the Cathedral: The one-room interior is filled with icons and candles, and old Russian music adds to the ambience. The wall of icons (iconostasis) divides things between the spiritual realm and the temporal world of the worshippers. Only the priest can walk between the two worlds, by using the "Royal Door." The items lining the front are interesting (described in order from left corner). The angel with red boots and wings—the protector of the Romanov family—stands over a symbolic tomb of Christ. The tall, black, hammered-copper cross commemorates the massacre of Nicholas II and his family in 1918. A Jesus icon is to the right of the Royal Door. According to a priest here, as worshippers meditate, staring deep into the eyes of Jesus, they enter a lake where they find their soul. Surrounded by incense, chanting, and your entire community...it could happen. Farther to the right, the icon of the unhappy-looking Virgin and Child is decorated with semiprecious stones from the Ural Mountains. Artists worked a triangle into each iconic face—symbolic of the Trinity.

Other Nice Museums

Both of these museums are acceptable rainy-day options, and free of charge.

Archaeological Museum (Musée Archéologique)—This museum displays various objects from the Romans' occupation of this region. It's convenient—just below the Matisse Museum—but has little of interest to anyone but ancient Rome aficionados. You also get access to the Roman bath ruins...which are, sadly, overgrown with weeds.

Cost and Hours: Free, very limited information in English, Wed-Mon 10:00-18:00, closed Tue, near Matisse Museum at 160 Avenue des Arènes de Cimiez, tel. 04 93 81 59 57, www.musee -archeologique-nice.org.

Masséna Museum (Musée Masséna)—Like Nice's main square, this museum was named in honor of Jean-André Masséna, a highly regarded commander during France's Revolutionary and Napoleonic wars. The beachfront mansion is worth a gander for its lavish decor and lovely gardens alone (pick up your free ticket at the boutique just outside; no English information available).

Cost and Hours: Free, Wed-Mon 10:00-18:00, closed Tue, last entrance 30 minutes before closing, 35 Promenade des Anglais, tel. 04 93 91 19 10, www.massena-nice.org.

Visiting the Museum: There are three levels. The elaborate reception rooms on the ground floor host occasional exhibits and give the best feeling for aristocratic Nice at the turn of the 19th century (find Masséna's portrait to the right after entering). The first floor up, offering a folk-museum-like look at Nice through the years, deserves most of your time. Moving counterclockwise around the floor, you'll find Napoleonic paraphernalia, Josephine's impressive cape and tiara, and Napoleon's vest (I'd look good in it). Next, antique posters promote vacations in Nice—look for the model and photos of the long-gone La Jetée Promenade and its casino, Nice's first. You'll see paintings of Russian nobility who appreciated Nice's climate, images of the city before its river was covered over by Place Masséna, and paintings honoring Italian patriot and Nice favorite Giuseppe Garibaldi. The top-floor painting gallery is devoted to the Riviera before World War II, with scenes of rural Villefranche-sur-Mer and other bucolic spots showing how the area looked before the tourist boom.

Nightlife in Nice

Promenade des Anglais, Cours Saleya, and Rue Masséna are all worth an evening walk. Nice's bars play host to a happening late-night scene, filled with jazz, rock, and trolling singles. Most activity focuses on Vieux Nice. Rue de la Préfecture and Place du Palais are ground zero for bar life, though Place Rossetti and Rue Droite are also good targets. **Distilleries Ideales** is a good place to start or end your evening, with a lively international crowd and a fun interior (where Rues de la Poissonnerie and Barillerie meet, happy hour 18:00-20:00). **Wayne's Bar** is a happening spot for the younger, English-speaking backpacker crowd (15 Rue Préfecture). Along the Promenade des Anglais, the plush bar at **Hôtel Negresco** is fancy-cigar old English.

Plan on a cover charge or expensive drinks where music is involved. If you're out very late, avoid walking alone. Nice is well known for its lively after-dark action, but if you need even more action, head for the town of Juan-les-Pins (page 856). For more relaxed and accessible nightlife, consider nearby Antibes (page 846).

Sleeping in Nice

Don't look for charm in Nice. Go for modern and clean, with a central location and in summer, air-conditioning. The rates listed here are for April through October. Prices generally drop €15-30 November through March, but go sky-high during the Nice Carnival (Feb 15-March 6), the Cannes Film Festival (May 15-26), and Monaco's Grand Prix (May 23-26). Between the film festival and the Grand Prix, the second half of May is very tight every year. Nice is also one of Europe's top convention cities, and June is convention month here. Reserve early if visiting from May through August, especially during these times. For parking, ask your hotelier (several hotels offer deals for stashing your car or have limited

---

Sleep Code

(€1 = about $1.30, country code: 33)
S = Single, **D** = Double/Twin, **T** = Triple, **Q** = Quad, **b** = bathroom, **s** = shower only, * = French hotel rating (0-5 stars). Hoteliers speak English; the hotels have elevators and accept credit cards unless otherwise noted.

To help you sort easily through these listings, I've divided the accommodations into three categories based on the price for a standard double room with bath:

  $$$ **Higher Priced**—Most rooms €200 or more.
   $$ **Moderately Priced**—Most rooms between €100-200.
    $ **Lower Priced**—Most rooms €100 or less.

Prices can change without notice; verify the hotel's current rates online or by email.

private parking; reserve early), or see "Arrival in Nice—By Car" on page 779.

I've divided my sleeping recommendations into three areas: between the train station and Nice Etoile shopping center (easy access to the train station and Vieux Nice via the tramway, 20-minute walk to Promenade des Anglais); between Nice Etoile and the sea (east of Avenue Jean Médecin, good access to Vieux Nice and the sea at Quai des Etats-Unis); and between Boulevard Victor Hugo and the sea (a somewhat classier and quieter area, offering better access to the Promenade des Anglais but longer walks to the train station and Vieux Nice). I've also listed a hostel on the outskirts, and a few hotel-chain options near the airport. Before reserving, check hotel websites for deals (more common at larger hotels).

Between the Train Station and Nice Etoile

This area offers Nice's cheapest sleeps, though most hotels near the station ghetto are overrun, overpriced, and loud. The following hotels are the pleasant exceptions (most are near Avenue Jean Médecin), and are listed in order of proximity to the train station, going toward the beach.

$$ At **Hôtel Durante****, you know you're on the Mediterranean as soon as you enter this cheery, way-orange building with rooms wrapped around a flowery courtyard. Every one of its quiet rooms overlooks a spacious, well-maintained patio/garden with an American-style Jacuzzi. The rooms are good enough (mostly big beds), the price is right enough, and the parking (limited spaces) is free (Sb-€85-105, Db-€100-115, Tb-€150-175, Qb-€180-200, breakfast-€10, air-con, Wi-Fi, 16 Avenue Durante, tel. 04 93 88 84 40, fax 04 93 87 77 76, www.hotel-durante.com, info@hotel-durante.com).

$$ **Hôtel St. Georges****, five blocks from the station toward the sea, is a basic place with reasonably clean, high-ceilinged rooms, orange tones, blue halls, fair rates, a backyard patio, and friendly Houssein at the reception (Sb-€95, Db-€115, Tb with 3 beds-€135, extra bed-€20, breakfast-€9, air-con, free Wi-Fi, 7 Avenue Georges Clemenceau, tel. 04 93 88 79 21, fax 04 93 16 22 85, www.hotelsaintgeorges.fr, contact@hotelsaintgeorges.fr).

$ **Hôtel Ibis Nice Centre Gare****, 100 yards to the right as you leave the station, gives those in need of train station access a secure refuge in this seedy area. It's big (200 rooms) and modern, but a good value with sharp rooms, a refreshing pool, and cheap €9 parking (Db-€93, big "Club" Db-€125, air-con, Internet access and Wi-Fi, bar, café, 14 Avenue Thiers, tel. 04 93 88 85 85, fax 04 93 88 58 00, www.ibishotel.com, h1396@accor.com).

$ **Hôtel Belle Meunière***, in a fine old mansion built for Napoleon III's mistress, offers cheap beds and private rooms a block below the train station. Lively and youth hostel-esque, this simple but well-kept place attracts budget-minded travelers of all ages with basic-but-adequate rooms and charismatic Mademoiselle Marie-Pierre presiding (with perfect English). Tables in the front yard greet guests and provide opportunities to meet other travelers (bunk in 4-bed dorm-€28 with private bath, €22 with shared bath; Db-€78, Tb-€93, Qb-€124, includes breakfast, Wi-Fi, laundry service, limited parking-€9, 21 Avenue Durante, tel. 04 93 88 66 15, fax 04 93 82 51 76, www.bellemeuniere.com, hotel.belle .meuniere@cegetel.net).

$ **Auberge de Jeunesse les Camélias** is a fun, laid-back youth hostel with a great location, modern facilities, and a fun evening atmosphere. Rooms accommodate between four and eight people of all ages in bunk beds (136 beds in all) and come with showers and sinks—WCs are down the hall. Reservations must be made on the website at least 3 days in advance. If you don't have a reservation, call by 10:00—or, better, try to snag a bunk in person. The place is popular but worth a try for last-minute availability (€26/bed, one-time €16 extra charge without hostel membership, includes breakfast, maximum 6-night stay, rooms closed 11:00-15:00 but can leave bags, Internet access, laundry, kitchen, safes, bar, 3 Rue Spitalieri, tel. 04 93 62 15 54, www.hihostels.com, nice -camelias@fuaj.org).

$ **B&B Nice Home Sweet Home** is a great value. Gentle Genevieve (a.k.a. Jennifer) Levert rents out three large rooms and one small single in her home. Her rooms are simply decorated, with high ceilings, big windows, lots of light, and space to spread out. One room comes with private bath; otherwise, it's just like at home...down the hall (S-€35-44, D-€61-75, Db-€65-78, Tb-€75-85, Q-€80-110, includes breakfast, air-con units available in summer, elevator, one floor up, washer/dryer-€6, kitchen access, 35 Rue Rossini at intersection with Rue Auber, mobile 06 19 66 03 63, www.nicehomesweethome.com, glevert@free.fr).

Between Nice Etoile and the Sea

These hotels are either on the sea or within an easy walk of it, and are the closest to Vieux Nice. For locations, see the map on page 786.

$$$ **Hôtel la Perouse****, built into the rock of Castle Hill at the east end of the bay, gets my vote for Nice's best splurge. This refuge-hotel is top-to-bottom flawless in every detail—from its elegant rooms (satin curtains, velour headboards) and attentive staff to its rooftop terrace with Jacuzzi, sleek pool, and lovely garden restaurant. Sleep here to be spoiled and escape the big city (garden-view Db-€325, seaview Db-€480, good family options and Web deals, free Wi-Fi, 11 Quai Rauba Capeu,

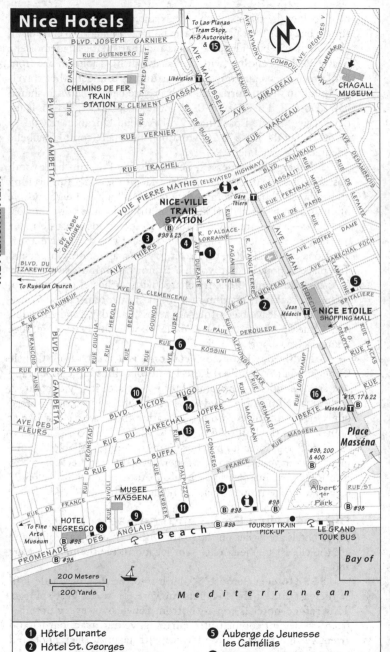

Nice Hotels

1. Hôtel Durante
2. Hôtel St. Georges
3. Hôtel Ibis Nice Centre Gare
4. Hôtel Belle Meunière
5. Auberge de Jeunesse les Camélias
6. B&B Nice Home Sweet Home
7. Hôtel Vendôme
8. Hôtel Negresco

THE FRENCH RIVIERA

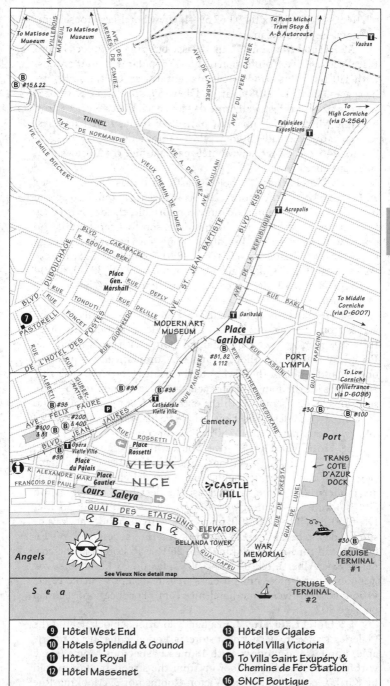

9 Hôtel West End	**13** Hôtel les Cigales
10 Hôtels Splendid & Gounod	**14** Hôtel Villa Victoria
11 Hôtel le Royal	**15** To Villa Saint Exupéry & Chemins de Fer Station
12 Hôtel Massenet	**16** SNCF Boutique

tel. 04 93 62 34 63, fax 04 93 62 59 41, www.hotel-la-perouse.com, lp@hotel-la-perouse.com).

$$$ Hôtel Masséna***, in a classy building two blocks from Place Masséna, is a "professional" hotel (popular with tour groups) with 110 rooms at almost-reasonable rates and way-mod public spaces (small Db-€199, larger Db-€289, still larger Db-€339, skip the €20 breakfast, call same day for special rates—prices drop big time when hotel is not full, sixth-floor rooms have balconies, reserve parking ahead-€30/day, 58 Rue Gioffredo, tel. 04 92 47 88 88, fax 04 92 47 88 89, www.hotel-massena-nice.com, info@hotel -massena-nice.com).

$$$ Hôtel Suisse***, below Castle Hill, has Nice's best sea and city views for the money, and is surprisingly quiet given the busy street below. Rooms are quite comfortable, the decor is tasteful, and the staff helpful. There's no reason to sleep here if you don't land a view, so I've listed prices only for view rooms—many of which have balconies (Db-€175-220, extra bed-€36, breakfast-€15, Wi-Fi, 15 Quai Rauba Capeu, tel. 04 92 17 39 00, fax 04 93 85 30 70, www.hotels-ocre-azur.com, hotel.suisse@hotels-ocre -azur.com).

$$ Hôtel Mercure Marché aux Fleurs**** is ideally situated across from the sea and behind Cours Saleya. Rooms are tastefully designed and well-maintained (some with beds in a loft). Prices are reasonable, though rates vary dramatically depending on demand—check their website for deals. Don't confuse this Mercure with the four other branches in Nice (standard Db-€170, superior Db-€200 and worth the extra euros, sea view-€50 extra, air-con, 91 Quai des Etats-Unis, tel. 04 93 85 74 19, fax 04 93 13 90 94, www.hotelmercure.com, h0962@accor.com).

$$ Hôtel Vendôme*** gives you a whiff of the belle époque, with pink pastels, high ceilings, and grand staircases in a mansion set off the street. Its public spaces are delightful. The rooms are modern and come in all sizes; the best have balconies (on floors 4 and 5)—request *une chambre avec balcon* (Sb-€115-130, Db-€150-180, Tb-€180-200, prices vary with demand, check website for deals, breakfast-€15, air-con, Internet access and Wi-Fi, book ahead for limited parking-€15, 26 Rue Pastorelli at the corner of Rue Alberti, tel. 04 93 62 00 77, fax 04 93 13 40 78, www .vendome-hotel-nice.com—useless website except to make reservation, contact@vendome-hotel-nice.com). For location, see map on page 802.

$$ Hôtel Lafayette***, in a handy location a block behind the Galeries Lafayette department store, is a good value. It's comfortable, homey, and modest, with 18 mostly spacious rooms (some with thin walls), all one floor up from the street. It's family-run by Kiril, George, and young Victor. Rooms not overlooking Rue de l'Hôtel des Postes are quieter and worth requesting (standard Db-€105-120, spacious Db-€115-130, preferential rates for Rick Steves readers, coffee service in rooms, breakfast-€10, air-con, no elevator, Internet access and Wi-Fi, 32 Rue de l'Hôtel des Postes, tel. 04 93 85 17 84, fax 04 93 80 47 56, www.hotellafayettenice .com, info@hotellafayettenice.com).

$$ Hôtel de la Mer** is a tiny place with an enviable position overlooking Place Masséna, just steps from Vieux Nice (it's among the closest of my listings to the old town). Half of the rooms are smartly renovated and worth the higher price; the other half are "old school" and priced that way (older Db-€110, newer Db-€130, Tb-€155, air-con, Wi-Fi, 4 Place Masséna, tel. 04 93 92 09 10, fax 04 93 85 00 64, www.hoteldelamernice.com, hotel.mer @wanadoo.fr).

Between Boulevard Victor Hugo and the Sea

These hotels are close to the Promenade des Anglais (and far from Vieux Nice). The Negresco, West End, and le Royal are big, vintage Nice hotels that open onto the sea from the heart of the Promenade des Anglais.

$$$ Hôtel Negresco**** owns Nice's most prestigious address on Promenade des Anglais and knows it. Still, it's the kind of place that if you were to splurge just once in your life.... Rooms are opulent (see page 802 for more description), and tips are expected (viewless Db-€380, seaview Db-€330-680, view suite-€770-2,200, breakfast-€30, Old World bar, 37 Promenade des Anglais, tel. 04 93 16 64 00, fax 04 93 88 35 68, www.hotel-negresco-nice.com, reservations@hotel-negresco.com).

$$$ Hôtel West End*** delivers formal service and decor, polished public spaces, and high prices. Its chic rooms come with effective blinds and all the comforts (viewless Db-€300, seaview Db-€340, check website for deals, Internet access and Wi-Fi, 31 Promenade des Anglais, tel. 04 92 14 44 00, fax 04 93 88 85 07, www.hotel-westend.com, reception@westsend3ahotels.com).

$$$ Hôtel Splendid**** is a worthwhile splurge if you miss your Marriott. The panoramic rooftop pool, bar/restaurant, and breakfast room almost justify the cost...but throw in plush rooms (all six floors are non-smoking), a free gym, spa services, and air-conditioning, and you're as good as home (Db-€235—some with decks, deluxe Db with terrace-€280, suites-€360-410, breakfast-€16, better prices available on website, parking-€24, 50 Boulevard Victor Hugo, tel. 04 93 16 41 00, fax 04 93 16 42 70, www.splendid-nice.com, info@splendid-nice.com).

$$ Hôtel le Royal*** is a relaxed resort hotel with 140 rooms, big lounges, and hallways that stretch forever. But the prices are reasonable considering the reliable air-conditioned comfort and

THE FRENCH RIVIERA

terrific location—and sometimes they have rooms when others don't (viewless Db-€145-189, seaview Db-€180-205, bigger view room-€200-225 and worth it, extra person-€25, 23 Promenade des Anglais, tel. 04 93 16 43 00, fax 04 93 16 43 02, www.hotel-royal -nice.cote.azur.fr, royal@vacancesbleues.com).

$$ Hôtel Massenet*** is tucked away a block off the Promenade des Anglais in a pedestrian zone. It has 29 tidy rooms (love the shag carpet) at good rates (small Db-€95, standard Db-€130-155, larger Db-€160, some rooms with decks, parking-€10, 11 Rue Massenet, tel. 04 93 87 11 31, fax 04 93 16 08 69, www.hotelmassenet.com, hotelmassenet@wanadoo.fr).

$$ Hôtel les Cigales***, a few blocks from the Promenade des Anglais, is a smart little pastel place with tasteful decor, 19 sharp rooms (those with showers are a tad small, most have tub-showers and are standard size), air-conditioning, and a nifty upstairs terrace, all well managed by friendly Mr. Valentino, with Veronique and Elaine. Rick Steves readers who book directly through the hotel get a 7 percent discount by typing this code: RICK (standard Db-€110-160, Tb-€130-180, free Wi-Fi, 16 Rue Dalpozzo, tel. 04 97 03 10 70, fax 04 97 03 10 71, www.hotel-lescigales.com, info @hotel-lescigales.com).

$$ Hôtel Gounod*** is behind Hôtel Splendid. Because the two share the same owners, Gounod's guests are allowed free access to Splendid's pool, Jacuzzi, and other amenities. Don't let the lackluster lobby fool you—most rooms are comfortable, with high ceilings (Db-€170, palatial 4-person suites-€270, air-con, parking-€17, 3 Rue Gounod, tel. 04 93 16 42 00, fax 04 93 88 23 84, www.gounod-nice.com, info@gounod-nice.com).

$$ Hôtel Villa Victoria*** is a fine place managed by cheery Marlena, who welcomes travelers into her spotless, classy old building with an open, attractive lobby overlooking a sprawling garden-courtyard. Rooms are traditional and well kept, with space to stretch out (streetside Db-€150, garden-side Db-€180, Tb-€160-185, suites-€210-235, breakfast-€15, air-con, minibar, Wi-Fi, parking-€18, 33 Boulevard Victor Hugo, tel. 04 93 88 39 60, fax 04 93 88 07 98, www.villa-victoria.com, contact@villa -victoria.com).

Barely Beyond Nice

$ Villa Saint Exupéry, a service-oriented hostel (they answer the phone in English) is a haven two miles north of the city center. Its amenities and 60 comfortable, spick-and-span rooms create a friendly climate for budget-minded travelers of any age. Often filled with energetic youth, the place can be noisy. There are units for one, two, and up to six people. Many have private bathrooms and views of the Mediterranean—some come with balconies.

You'll also find a laundry room, complete kitchen facilities, and a lively bar. There's easy Internet access with a wall of computers in the lobby and Wi-Fi in all the rooms (bed in dorm-€30/person, S-€50-70, Db-€60-90, Tb-€115, includes big breakfast, no curfew, 22 Avenue Gravier, tel. 04 93 84 42 83, toll-free tel. 08 00 30 74 09—works only within France, fax 04 92 09 82 94, www.villa hostels.com, reservations@vsaint.com). From the center of town, ride the tram (direction: Las Planas) to the Compte de Falicon stop, then either walk 10 minutes, or take the free shuttle from the Casino supermarket by the tram stop (no service 12:00-17:00).

Near the Airport

Several airport hotels offer a handy and cheap port-in-the-storm for those with early flights or who are just stopping in for a single night: Etap Hôtel (the cheapest, www.etaphotel.com), Hôtel Première Classe (www.premiereclasse.com), and Hôtel Ibis Nice Aéroport (www.ibisnice.com). Free shuttles connect these hotels with both airport terminals.

You'll find greater comfort at the airport for a bit more (and free private shuttle vans) at these hotels: Novotel (www.novotel .com), Holiday Inn (www.holidayinn.com), and Campanile (www .campanile.fr).

Eating in Nice

Remember, you're in a resort. Seek ambience and fun, and lower your palate's standards. Italian is a low-risk and regional cuisine. The listed restaurants are concentrated in neighborhoods close to my recommended hotels. Promenade des Anglais is ideal for picnic dinners on warm, languid evenings. Vieux Nice has the best and busiest dining atmosphere (and best range of choices), while the Nice Etoile area is more local, convenient, and also offers a good range of choices. To feast cheaply, eat on Rue Droite in Vieux Nice, or explore the area around the train station. For a more peaceful meal, head for nearby Villefranche-sur-Mer (later in this chapter). Allow yourself one dinner at a beachfront restaurant in Nice, and for terribly touristy trolling, wander the wall-to-wall eateries lining Rue Masséna. Yuck.

In Vieux Nice

Nice's dinner scene converges on Cours Saleya, which is entertaining enough in itself to make the generally mediocre food a good deal. It's a fun, festive spot to compare tans and mussels. Even if you're eating elsewhere, wander through here in the evening. For locations, see the map on page 786.

THE FRENCH RIVIERA

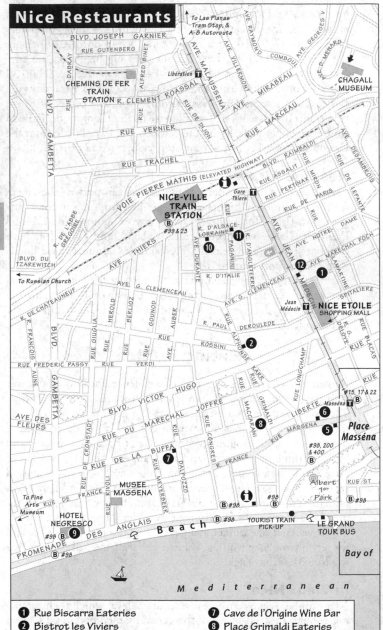

Nice Restaurants

1. Rue Biscarra Eateries
2. Bistrot les Viviers
3. L'Ovale Restaurant
4. Le Luna Rossa Restaurant
5. La Maison de Marie Rest.
6. Villa d'Este Restaurant
7. Cave de l'Origine Wine Bar
8. Place Grimaldi Eateries
9. Chantecler Restaurant
10. Voyageur Nissart Rest.
11. Zen Restaurant
12. Monoprix Grocery Store

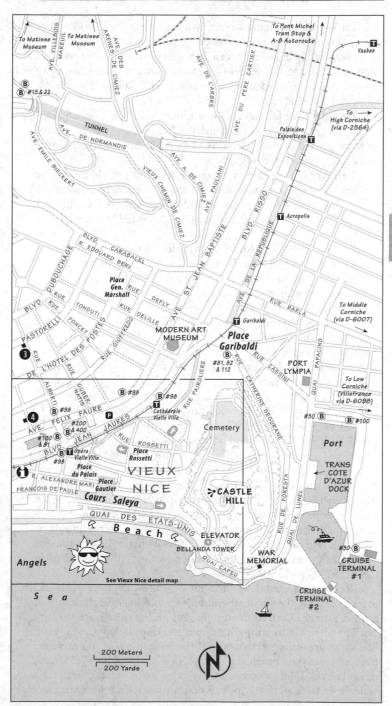

La Voglia has figured out a winning formula: Good food + ample servings + fair prices = good business. Come here early for top-value Italian cuisine, or plan on waiting for a table. There's fun seating inside and out (€12-14 pizza and pasta, €15-25 *plats,* open daily, at the western edge of Cours Saleya at 2 Rue St. Francois de Paule, tel. 04 93 80 99 16).

Le Safari is a fair option for outdoor dining on Cours Saleya, with a few more locals than tourists. The cuisine is Italo-*niçoise,* and the service is professional (€12-18 *plats,* open daily, 1 Cours Saleya, tel. 04 93 80 18 44).

Palmyre is the place to eat on a budget in the old town. The ambience is rustic but intimate, and the menu changes every two weeks. The three-course *menu* is only €15, and the food could not be more homemade (closed Sun, cash only, 5 Rue Droite, tel. 04 93 85 72 32).

La Festival de la Moule is a simple, touristy place for lovers of mussels (or for just plain hungry folks). For €15 you get all-you-can-eat fries and mussels (3 sauces included, 7 additional for €2.50 each) in a youthful outdoor setting (other bistro fare available, 20 Cours Saleya, tel. 04 93 62 02 12).

Le Bistrot du Fromager's owner, Hugo, is crazy about cheese and wine. Come here to escape the heat and dine in cozy, cool, vaulted cellars surrounded by shelves of wine. All dishes use cheese as their base ingredient, although you'll also find pasta, ham, and salmon (with cheese, of course). This is a good choice for vegetarians (€10-13 starters, €15-21 *plats,* €6 desserts, closed Sun, just off Place du Jésus at 29 Rue Benoît Bunico, tel. 04 93 13 07 83).

Oliviera venerates the French olive. This shop/restaurant sells a variety of oils, offers free tastings, and serves a menu of dishes paired with specific oils (think of a wine pairing). Welcoming owner Nadim, who speaks excellent English, knows all his producers and provides "Olive Oil 101" explanations with his tastings (best if you buy something afterward or have a meal). You'll learn how passionate he is about his products, and once you've had a taste, you'll want to stay and eat—so go early (or reserve ahead), as tables fill fast (allow €40 with wine, €16-24 main dishes, Tue-Sat 10:00-22:00, closed Sun-Mon, indoor seating only, 8 bis Rue du Collet, tel. 04 93 13 06 45).

Restaurant Castel is a fine eat-on-the-beach option, thanks to its location at the very east end of Nice looking over the bay. You almost expect Don Ho to step up and grab a mic. Lose the city hustle and bustle by dropping down the steps below Castle Hill. The views are unforgettable even if the cuisine is not; you can even have lunch at your beach chair if you've rented one here (€15/half-day, €18/day). Dinner here is best: Arrive before sunset and find a waterfront table perfectly positioned to watch evening swimmers get in their last laps as the sky turns pink and city lights flicker on. Linger long enough to justify the few extra euros the place charges (€17 salads and pastas, €20-26 main courses, 8 Quai des Etats-Unis, tel. 04 93 85 22 66).

Dining Cheap *à la Niçoise*

Try at least one of these places—not just because they're terrific budget options, but primarily because they offer authentic *niçoise* cuisine.

L'Acchiardo, hidden away in the heart of Vieux Nice, is a homey eatery that does a good job mixing a loyal clientele with hungry tourists. Its simple, hearty *niçoise* cuisine is served for fair prices by gentle Monsieur Acchiardo. The small plaque under the menu outside says it's been run by father and son since 1927 (€8 starters, €15 *plats,* €5 desserts, cash only, closed Sat-Sun, indoor seating only, 38 Rue Droite, tel. 04 93 85 51 16).

Ville de Siena draws young travelers who dig this place for its big portions, fair prices, open kitchen, and raucous atmosphere with tables crammed on a narrow lane. The food is Italian and hearty (€12-17 *plats,* closed Sun, 10 Rue St. Vincent, tel. 04 93 80 12 45).

Lou Pilha Leva delivers basic cheap lunch or dinner options with *niçoise* specialties and always busy outdoor-only picnic-table dining (open daily, located where Rues de la Loge and Centrale meet in Vieux Nice).

And for Dessert...

Gelato lovers should save room for the tempting ice-cream stands in Vieux Nice. **Fenocchio** is the city's favorite, with mouthwatering displays of 86 flavors ranging from tomato to lavender to avocado—all of which are surprisingly good (daily March-Nov until 24:00, two locations: 2 Place Rossetti and 6 Rue de la Poissonnerie). Gelato connoisseurs should head for **Crema di Gelato,** where the selection may be a fraction of Fenocchio's, but the quality is superior (5 Rue de la Préfecture, on Place du Palais).

Eating near Nice Etoile

If you're not up for eating in Vieux Nice, try one of these spots around the Nice Etoile shopping mall.

On Rue Biscarra: An appealing lineup of bistros overflowing with outdoor tables stretches along the broad sidewalk on traffic-free Rue Biscarra (just east of Avenue Jean Médecin behind Nice Etoile, all closed Sun). Come here to dine with area residents away from the tourists. These two places are both good choices, with good interior and exterior seating: **L'Authentic** has the most creative cuisine and comes with a memorable owner, burly

Philippe (€23 two-course *menus,* €27 three-course *menus,* reasonable pasta dishes, tel. 04 93 62 48 88). **Le 20 sur Vin** is a neighborhood favorite with a cozy, wine-bar-meets-café ambience. It offers *(bien sûr)* good wines at fair prices, and basic bistro fare (tel. 04 93 92 93 20).

Bistrot les Viviers attracts those who require attentive service and authentic *niçoise* cuisine with a big emphasis on fish. This classy splurge offers two intimate settings as different as night and day: a soft, formal restaurant, and a relaxed *bistrot* next door, both with the same menu (€55 *menu,* €28-38 *plats,* bouillabaisse-€45, bourride-€27, fish soup starter-€10). I'd reserve a table in the atmospheric *bistrot,* where some outdoor seating is available (restaurant closed Sun, *bistrot* open daily, 5-minute walk west of Avenue Jean Médecin at 22 Rue Alphonse Karr, tel. 04 93 16 00 48).

L'Ovale takes its name from the shape of a rugby ball. This welcoming, well-run bistro has quality food at respectable prices, with an emphasis on the cuisine of southwestern France. Dine inside on big *plats* for €10-13; consider their specialty, cassoulet (€17), or the *salade de manchons* (€13), with duck and walnuts (excellent €18 three-course *menu,* €13 big salads, daily, air-con, 29 Rue Pastorelli, tel. 04 93 80 31 65).

Le Luna Rossa is *molto* Italian, with a smart setting inside and out. It's also *molto* popular with locals. Come early or book ahead (€10 starters, €20-27 *plats,* just north of the parkway at 3 Rue Chauvain, tel. 04 93 85 55 66).

La Maison de Marie is a surprisingly good-quality refuge off touristy Rue Masséna, where most other restaurants serve mediocre food to tired travelers. Enter through a deep-red arch to a bougainvillea-draped courtyard, and enjoy the fair prices and excellent cuisine that draw neighborhood regulars and out-of-towners alike. The interior tables are as appealing as those in the courtyard, but expect some smokers outside. The €23 *menu* is a terrific value (€10-15 starters and €15-30 *plats,* great fruit-salad dessert, open daily, look for the square red sign at 5 Rue Masséna, tel. 04 93 82 15 93).

Villa d'Este has the same owners as the recommended La Voglia (listed earlier, under "In Vieux Nice"). The portions are big, the price is right, and the quality is tops (daily, on a busy pedestrian street at 6 Rue Masséna, tel. 04 93 82 47 77).

Near Promenade des Anglais

Worthwhile restaurants are few and far between in this area. Either head for Vieux Nice or try one of these good places.

Cave de l'Origine is a find, and would be even away from the tourist fray. Kind Isabelle and her English-speaking staff welcome you to their cozy wine shop/*bistrot.* Isabelle prepares fresh, homemade dishes and finds the perfect wines to match. She features original cuisine from many areas in France (especially the south-west), made with regional, fresh ingredients (€7-11 starters, €16-21 *plats*, open Tue-Sat for lunch and dinner, reservations smart, indoor seating only; wine shop open Tue-Sat 10:00-20:00, closed Sun-Mon; 3 Rue Dalpozzo, tel. 04 83 50 09 60).

On Place Grimaldi: This square nurtures a lineup of appealing restaurants with good indoor and outdoor seating along a broad sidewalk under tall, leafy sycamore trees. **Crêperie Bretonne** is the only *crêperie* I list in Nice (€8 dinner crêpes, closed Sun, 3 Place Grimaldi, tel. 04 93 82 28 47). **Le Grimaldi** is popular for its café fare (€14 pasta, €15-25 *plats*, closed Sun, 1 Place Grimaldi, tel. 04 93 87 98 13).

Chantecler has Nice's most prestigious address—inside the Hôtel Negresco. This is everything a luxury restaurant should be: elegant, soft, and top quality. If your trip is ending in Nice, call or email for reservations—you've earned this splurge (*menus* from €90, closed Mon-Tue, 37 Promenade des Anglais, tel. 04 93 16 64 00, chantecler@lenegresco.com).

Near the Train Station

Both of the following restaurants, a block below the train station, provide good indoor and outdoor seating as well as excellent value.

Voyageur Nissart has blended good-value cuisine with cool Mediterranean ambience and friendly service since 1908. Current owner Max is a great host, and the quality of his cuisine makes this a good choice for travelers on any budget—try the wonderful €14 *filet de rouget à la niçoise* or the fine €8 *salade niçoise* (€17 three-course *menus*, good *plats* from €11, inexpensive wines, closed Mon, 19 Rue d'Alsace-Lorraine, tel. 04 93 82 19 60).

Zen provides a Japanese break from French cuisine. Interior seating is arranged around the chef's stove, and the tasty specialties draw a strong following (€16 three-course *menu*, €8-13 sushi, open daily, 27 Rue d'Angleterre, tel. 04 93 82 41 20).

Nice Connections

By Train and Bus

Note that most long-distance train connections to other French cities require a change in Marseille. The Grande Ligne train to Bordeaux (serving Antibes, Cannes, Toulon, and Marseille—and connecting from there to Arles, Nîmes, and Carcassonne) requires a reservation. Remember that on regional buses (except on express airport buses), many one-way rides cost €1—regardless of length (the €1 ticket is good for up to 74 minutes of travel in one direction, including transfers).

From Nice by Train to: Cannes (2/hour, 30-40 minutes),

Antibes (2/hour, 15-30 minutes), **Villefranche-sur-Mer** (2/hour, 10 minutes), **Eze-le-Village** (2/hour, 15 minutes to Eze-Bord-de-Mer, then bus #83 to Eze, 8/day), **Monaco** (2/hour, 20 minutes) **Menton** (2/hour, 25 minutes), **Grasse** (15/day, 1.25 hours), **Marseille** (18/day, 2.5 hours), **Cassis** (14/day, 3 hours, transfer in Toulon or Marseille), **Arles** (11/day, 3.75-4.5 hours, most require transfer in Marseille or Avignon), **Avignon** (20/day, most by TGV, 4 hours, most require transfer in Marseille), **Paris'** Gare de Lyon (hourly, 5.75 hours, may require change; 11.5-hour night train goes to Paris' Gare d'Austerlitz), **Aix-en-Provence** TGV Station (10/day, 3.5 hours, usually change in Marseille), **Chamonix** (4/day, 10 hours, many change in St-Gervais and Lyon), **Beaune** (7/day, 7 hours, 1-2 changes), **Munich** (4/day, 12.5-14 hours with 2-4 transfers, longer night trains possible, some via Italy), **Interlaken** (6/day, 9-10 hours, 2-5 transfers), **Florence** (6/day, 7-9 hours, 1-3 transfers), **Milan** (7/day, 5-5.5 hours, all require transfers), **Venice** (5/day, 8-9 hours, all require transfers), **Barcelona** (1/day via Montpellier, 10 hours, more with multiple changes).

From Nice by Bus to: Cannes (#200, 4/hour Mon-Sat, 2-3/hour Sun, 1.5-1.75 hours), **Antibes** (#200, 4/hour Mon-Sat, 2-3/hour Sun, 1-1.5 hours), **Villefranche-sur-Mer** (#100, 4/hour Mon-Sat, 3/hour Sun, 20 minutes; or #81, 2-4/hour, 20 minutes), **St-Jean-Cap-Ferrat** (#81, 2-4/hour, 35 minutes), **Eze-le-Village** (#82 or #112, 16/day Mon-Sat, 8/day Sun, 40 minutes), **La Turbie** (#116 or #T-66, 5/day Mon-Sat, 7/day Sun, 45 minutes), **Monaco** (#100, 4/hour Mon-Sat, 3/hour Sun, 45 minutes), **Menton** (#100, 4/hour Mon-Sat, 3/hour Sun, 1.25 hours), **St-Paul-de-Vence** (#400, every 30-45 minutes, 45 minutes), **Vence** (#400, every 30-45 minutes, 50 minutes), **Grasse** (#500, every 30-45 minutes, 1.25 hours).

By Plane

Nice's easy-to-navigate airport (Aéroport de Nice Côte d'Azur; airport code: NCE) is on the Mediterranean, a 20- to 30-minute drive west of the city center. Planes leave roughly hourly for Paris (one-hour flight, about the same price as a train ticket, check www.easyjet.com for the cheapest flights to Paris' Orly airport). The two terminals (Terminal 1 and Terminal 2) are connected by frequent shuttle buses *(navettes)*. Both terminals have TIs (and Terminal 1 has an info desk just for Monaco), banks, ATMs, taxis, baggage storage (€6.50/day per piece, open daily 5:45-23:00), and buses to Nice (tel. 04 89 88 98 28, www.nice.aeroport.fr).

Getting from the Airport to the City Center

Taxis into the center are expensive considering the short distance (figure €35 to Nice hotels, €60 to Villefranche-sur-Mer, €70 to

Antibes, 10 percent more 19:00-7:00 and all day Sun). Taxis stop outside door *(Porte)* A-1 at Terminal 1 and outside *Porte* A-3 at Terminal 2. Notorious for overcharging, Nice taxis are not always so nice. If your fare for a ride into town is much higher than €35 (or €40 at night or on Sun), refuse to pay the overage. If this doesn't work, tell the cabbie to call a *gendarme* (police officer). It's always a good idea to ask for a receipt *(reçu)*.

Airport shuttle vans work with some of my recommended hotels, but they only make sense when going *to* the airport, not when arriving on an international flight. Unlike taxis, shuttle vans offer a fixed price that doesn't rise on Sundays, early mornings, or evenings. Prices are best for groups (figure €30 for one person, and only a little more for additional people). **Nice Airport Shuttle** is one option (1-2 people-€32, additional person-€14, mobile 06 60 33 20 54, www.nice-airport-shuttle.com), or ask your hotelier for recommendations.

Three bus lines connect the airport with the city center, offering good alternatives to high-priced taxis. **Bus #99** (airport express) runs from both terminals to Nice's main train station (€4, 2/hour, 8:00-21:00, 30 minutes, drops you within a 10-minute walk of many recommended hotels). To take this bus *to* the airport, catch it right in front of the train station (departs on the half-hour). If your hotel is within walking distance of the station, #99 is a breeze.

Bus #98 serves both terminals, and runs along Promenade des Anglais to the edge of Vieux Nice (€4, 3/hour, from the airport 6:00-23:00, to the airport until 21:00, 30 minutes, see map on page 808 for stops). The slower, cheaper local **bus #23** serves only Terminal 1, and makes every stop between the airport and train station (€1, 5/hour, runs 6:00-20:00, 40 minutes, direction: St-Maurice).

For all buses, buy tickets in the information office just outside either terminal, or from the driver. To reach the bus information office and stops at Terminal 1, turn left after passing customs and exit the doors at the far end. Buses serving Terminal 2 stop across the street from the airport exit (information kiosk and ticket sales to the right as you exit).

If you take bus #98 or #99, hang on to your €4 ticket—it's good all day on any public bus and the tramway in Nice, and for buses between Nice and some nearby towns.

Getting from the Airport to Nearby Destinations

To get to **Villefranche-sur-Mer** from the airport, take bus #98 to Place Masséna, then use the same ticket to transfer to bus #81 or #100 (4/hour on #100, 3/hour Sun; 2-4/hour on #81; 15 minutes; see map on page 808 for stop location).

To reach **Antibes**, take bus #250 from either terminal (about

2/hour, 40 minutes, €8). For **Cannes,** take bus #210 from either terminal (2/hour, 45 minutes on freeway, €16). Pricey express bus #110 runs from the airport directly to **Monaco** (2/hour, 50 minutes, €19); it's cheaper (€4)—but more time-consuming—to take bus #99 or #98 to Nice, then transfer to a Monaco-bound bus or train.

By Cruise Ship

Nice's port is at the eastern edge of the town center, separated from the old town and best beaches by Castle Hill. Cruise ships dock at either end of the mouth of this port: **Terminal 1** to the east (along the embankment called Quai du Commerce), or **Terminal 2** to the west (along Quai Infernet). At both terminals, TI kiosks (under pointy white tents) are timed to be open when cruises arrive.

A street called Place Ile de Beauté runs along the top of the port; here you'll find bus stops (including stops for the bus to Villefranche and Monaco) and easy access to Place Garibaldi, where you can hop on Nice's tramway (which you can ride to the train station). From either terminal, it's about a 10-minute walk to the top of the port, or you can ride the free shuttle bus *(navette).*

Taxis at the terminals charge about €15-20 to points within Nice (for example, the train station, or the Matisse or Chagall museums), €35-40 one-way to Villefranche-sur-Mer, or €80 one-way to Monaco. **Le Grand Tour Bus** hop-on, hop-off bus circuit has a stop at the top of the port (see "Tours in Nice," page 782).

Getting from the Port to the City Center

Nice's main promenade and old town are just on the other side of Castle Hill from the port. If your ship docks at Terminal 2, just walk around the base of the castle-topped hill (with the sea on your left), and you'll be at Vieux Nice in about 10-15 minutes. Terminal 1 is at the far end of the port from the old town. If you arrive here, it's slightly faster to circle around the back of Castle Hill: Walk or ride the shuttle bus to the top of the port, take the angled Rue Cassini to Place Garibaldi (described next), then walk into the old town from there (total walk: about 20-25 minutes).

The square called **Place Garibaldi** serves as a gateway between the port of Nice and the rest of the city. It's about a 15- to 20-minute walk from either cruise terminal: First, walk (or ride the shuttle bus) to the top-left corner of the port area, and head up the angled Rue Cassini toward the square with the palm trees.

After three short blocks, you'll pop out at Place Garibaldi.

Once in Place Garibaldi, to reach Vieux Nice, walk straight through the middle of the square and out the other side, then turn left and walk down the broad Boulevard Jean Jaurès; the old town sprawls to your left. To reach the tram stop from Place Garibaldi, walk along the right side of the square, then turn right on Avenue de la République and walk a half-block. From here, you can ride the tram to Place Masséna (where you can catch bus #15 or #22 to the Chagall or Matisse museums, or #17 to the Matisse Museum) and the train station (Gare Thiers stop).

Getting from the Port to Nearby Destinations

To go from Nice to Villefranche-sur-Mer, Monaco, or other destinations, you can take either a train or a bus. The train is faster, but the bus stop is closer to Nice's port. For specifics on bus and train connections, see page 813.

From Nice's cruise port, you can get to the **train station** by bus (#30, 2/hour, 15 minutes to Gare SNCF stop; catch it at the top-left corner of the port along Place Ile de Beauté; from Terminal 1, you can also catch it along Boulevard de Stalingrad, up the stairs) or by tram (follow directions to Place Garibaldi, described on the previous page, then ride the tramway to the Gare Thiers stop, cross the tracks, and walk straight one long block on Avenue Thiers).

Handy **bus #100**—which connects to points eastward including Villefranche and Monaco—stops along the top of the port (near the right end of Place Ile de Beauté).

In summer, a **boat** to Monaco departs from near the cruise terminals, but it's slow and inconvenient if you're short on time (see page 782).

Villefranche-sur-Mer

In the glitzy world of the Riviera, Villefranche-sur-Mer offers travelers an easygoing slice of small-town Mediterranean life.

From here, convenient day trips allow you to gamble in style in Monaco, saunter the Promenade des Anglais in Nice, or drink in immense views from Eze-le-Village. Villefranche-sur-Mer feels Italian, with soft-orange buildings; steep, narrow streets spilling into the sea; and pasta on most menus. Luxury sailing yachts glisten in the bay—an inspiration to those lazing along the harborfront to start saving when their trips are over. Cruise ships make occasional calls to Villefranche-sur-Mer's famously deep harbor, creating periodic rush hours of frenetic shoppers and happy boutique owners. Sand-pebble beaches and a handful of interesting sights keep other visitors just busy enough.

Orientation to Villefranche-sur-Mer

Tourist Information

The main TI is in the park named Jardin François Binon, below the main bus stop, labeled *Octroi* (mid-June-mid-Sept daily 9:00-18:30; mid-Sept-mid-June Mon-Sat 9:00-12:00 & 14:00-17:00, closed Sun; 20-minute walk or €10 taxi ride from train station, tel. 04 93 01 73 68, www.villefranche-sur-mer.com). Pick up regional bus schedules here (buses #80, #81, #82, #83, #100, #112, and #114). Also ask for the brochure detailing a self-guided walking tour of Villefranche-sur-Mer and information on boat rides (usually mid-June-Sept). A smaller TI is on the port (mid-May-mid-Sept Mon-Fri 10:00-17:00, Sat-Sun 10:00-16:00, closed off-season).

Arrival in Villefranche-sur-Mer

By Bus: Whether you've taken bus #100 or #81 from Nice, or bus #100 from Monaco, hop off at the Octroi stop, at the Jardin François Binon, just above the TI. To reach the old town, walk past the TI down Avenue Général de Gaulle, take the first stairway on the left, then make a right at the street's end.

By Train: Not all trains stop in Villefranche-sur-Mer (you may need to transfer to a local train in Nice or Monaco). Villefranche's train station is a 15-minute walk along the water from the old town and many of my recommended hotels. Find your way down toward the water, and turn right to walk into town. Taxis to my listed hotels cost €15, but they don't wait here, and they prefer longer rides—call instead, and pray the pay phone outside the station is working (for taxi telephone numbers, see the next page).

By Car: From Nice's port, follow signs for *Menton, Monaco,* and *Basse Corniche.* In Villefranche, turn right at the TI (first signal after Hôtel la Flore) for parking and hotels. For a quick visit to the TI, park at the pay lot just below the TI. A bit farther down, you may find free parking in the small lot off Avenue Verdun; otherwise, look elsewhere and pay the meter). There's a secure pay lot on the water across from Hôtel Welcome, and some hotels have their own parking.

By Plane: Allow an hour from Nice's airport to Villefranche (for details on this connection, see page 815).

By Cruise Ship: For information on arrival by cruise ship, see "Villefranche-sur-Mer Connections" on page 827.

Helpful Hints

Market Day: A fun bric-a-brac market enlivens Villefranche-sur-Mer on Sundays (on Place Amélie Pollonnais by Hôtel Welcome, and in Jardin François Binon by the TI). On Saturday mornings, a small food market sets up near the TI (only in Jardin François Binon). A small trinket market springs to action on Place Amélie Pollonnais whenever cruise ships grace the harbor.

Last Call: Villefranche-sur-Mer makes a great base for day trips, but the last bus back from Nice or Monaco is at about 20:00. After that, take the train or a cab.

Arts Festival: In 2013, Villefranche is celebrating its role "as an actor in film" and its most famous former resident, Jean Cocteau (ask about special events at the TI).

Internet Access: Two options sit side by side on Place du Marché. **Chez Net,** an "Australian International Sports Bar Internet Café," has American keyboards, whereas **L'X Café** has French keyboards. Both are open daily, have Wi-Fi, and let you enjoy a late-night drink while surfing the Internet.

Laundry: The town has two launderettes, both owned by Laura and located just below the main road on Avenue Sadi Carnot. At the upper *pressing moderne,* Laura does your wash for you—for a price (Tue-Sun 9:00-12:30 & 15:00-18:30, closes Sat at 17:00, closed Mon, next to Hôtel Riviera, tel. 04 93 01 73 71). The lower *laverie* is self-service only (daily 7:00-20:00, opposite 6 Avenue Sadi Carnot).

Electric Bike Rental: If you plan to explore nearby coastal sights but don't feel like walking, consider renting an electric bike from Henri at **Eco-Loc.** The adventurous can also try this as an alternative to taking the bus to Cap Ferrat, Eze-le-Village, or even Nice (although the road to Nice is awfully busy). You get about 25 miles on a fully charged battery (less on hilly terrain—after that you're pedaling; €7/hour, €20/half-day, €30/day, April-Sept daily 9:00-18:00, deposit and ID required, best to call for reservations 24 hours in advance; helmets, locks, baskets, and child seats available; pick up bike across from small TI on the port, mobile 06 66 92 72 41, www.eco loc06.fr).

Taxi: For a reliable taxi in Villefranche-sur-Mer, call or email **Didier** (mobile 06 15 15 39 15, taxididier.villefranchesurmer @orange.fr). If he's busy, beware of taxi drivers who overcharge—the normal weekday, daytime rate to central Nice is about €35-40; to the airport, figure €50-60; one-way to

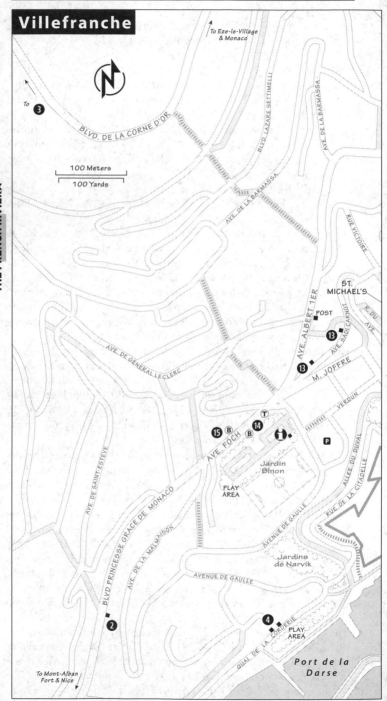

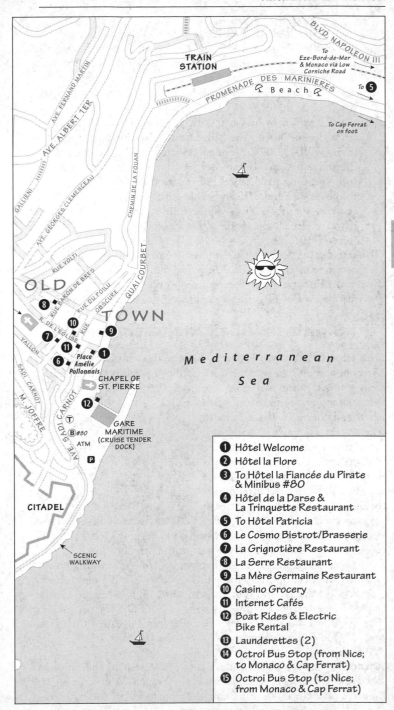

1 Hôtel Welcome

2 Hôtel la Flore

3 To Hôtel la Fiancée du Pirate & Minibus #80

4 Hôtel de la Darse & La Trinquette Restaurant

5 To Hôtel Patricia

6 Le Cosmo Bistrot/Brasserie

7 La Grignotière Restaurant

8 La Serre Restaurant

9 La Mère Germaine Restaurant

10 Casino Grocery

11 Internet Cafés

12 Boat Rides & Electric Bike Rental

13 Launderettes (2)

14 Octroi Bus Stop (from Nice; to Monaco & Cap Ferrat)

15 Octroi Bus Stop (to Nice; from Monaco & Cap Ferrat)

Cap Ferrat is about €20-25, to Eze-le-Village is about €35-40, and to Monaco is €50-60. The five-minute trip from the waterfront up to the main street level (to bus stops on the Low Corniche) should be less than €10. Ask your driver to write down the price before you get in, and get a receipt when you pay (mobile 06 09 33 36 12 or 06 39 32 54 09).

Minibus: Little **minibus #80** will save you the sweat of going from the harbor up the hill, but it only runs once per hour (daily 7:00-19:00, €1, schedule posted at stops and on www.lignedazur.com). It travels from the port to the top of the hill, stopping near Hôtel la Fiancée du Pirate and the stop for buses #82 and #112 to Eze-le-Village, before going to the outlying suburban Nice-Riquier train station (only convenient if you're already on minibus, must transfer to train to downtown Nice).

Tourist Train: Skip the useless white *petit train*, which goes nowhere interesting (€7, 20-minute ride).

Spectator Sports: Lively *boules* action takes place each evening just below the TI and the huge soccer field (see page 1141).

Sights in Villefranche-sur-Mer

The Harbor—Browse Villefranche-sur-Mer's minuscule harbor. Although the town was once an important fishing community, only a few families still fish here to make money. Find the footpath that leads beneath the citadel to the sea (by the port parking lot). Stop where the path hits the sea and marvel at the scene: a bay filled with beautiful sailing yachts. (You might see well-coiffed captains being ferried in by dutiful mates to pick up their statuesque call girls.)

Local guides keep a list of the world's 100 biggest yachts and talk about some of them as if they're part of the neighborhood.

Looking far to the right, that last apartment building on the sea was the headquarters for the US Navy's Sixth Fleet following World War II, and remained so until 1966, when de Gaulle pulled France out of the military wing of NATO. (The Sixth Fleet has been based in Naples ever since.) A wall plaque at the bottom of Rue de l'Eglise commemorates the US Navy's presence in Villefranche.

Citadel—The town's mammoth castle was built in the 1500s by the Duke of Savoy to defend against the French. When the region joined France in 1860, it became just a barracks. In the 20th century, the city had no military use for the space, and started using the citadel to house its police station, city hall, a summer outdoor theater, and two art galleries. There's still only one fortified entry to this huge complex.

Chapel of St. Pierre (Chapelle Cocteau)—This chapel, decorated by artist Jean Cocteau, is the town's cultural highlight. Cocteau was a Parisian transplant who adored little Villefranche-sur-Mer and whose career was distinguished by his work as an artist, poet, novelist, playwright, and filmmaker. Influenced by his pals Marcel Proust, André Gide, Edith Piaf, and Pablo Picasso, Cocteau was a leader among 20th-century avant-garde intellectuals. At the door, Marie-France—who is passionate about Cocteau's art—collects a €2.50 donation for a fishermen's charity. She then sets you free to enjoy the chapel's small but intriguing interior. She's happy to give some explanations if you ask.

In 1955 Jean Cocteau covered the barrel-vaulted chapel with heavy black lines and pastels. Each of Cocteau's surrealist works—the Roma (Gypsies) of Stes-Maries-de-la-Mer who dance and sing to honor the Virgin, girls wearing traditional outfits, and three scenes from the life of St. Peter—is explained in English. Is that Villefranche-sur-Mer's citadel in the scene above the altar?

Cost and Hours: Wed-Mon 10:00-12:00 & 15:00-19:00, usually closed Tue (varies with cruise-ship traffic) and when Marie-France is tired, below Hôtel Welcome, tel. 04 93 76 90 70.

Nearby: A few blocks north along the harbor (past Hôtel Welcome), Rue de May leads to the mysterious **Rue Obscure**—a covered lane running 400 feet along the medieval rampart. This street served as an air-raid shelter during World War II. Much of the lane is closed indefinitely for repair.

Boat Rides (Promenades en Mer)—Consider treating yourself to a seaborne perspective of this beautiful area. A relatively inexpensive option is to take a **cruise** (€18 for 2-hour cruise as far as Monaco—but doesn't actually stop there, departs at 15:00, June-Sept Wed and Sat, also on Thu in July-Aug, no trips Oct-May, boats depart from the harbor across from Hôtel Welcome, call to confirm ever-changing schedule, reservations a must, tel. 04 93 76 65 65, www.amv-sirenes.com). Or, to be your own skipper, rent a **motor boat** through Dark Pelican (€100/half-day, €165/day, deposit required, on the harbor at the Gare Maritime, tel. 04 93 01 76 54, www.darkpelican.com).

St. Michael's Church—The town church, a few blocks up Rue de l'Eglise from the harbor, features an 18th-century organ and a fine statue of a recumbent Christ—carved, they say, from a fig tree by a galley slave in the 1600s.

Seafront Walks—A seaside walkway originally used by customs agents to patrol the harbor leads under the citadel and connects the old town with the workaday harbor (Port de la Darse). At the port you'll find a few cafés, France's Institute of Oceanography (an outpost for the University of Paris oceanographic studies), and an 18th-century dry dock. This scenic walk turns downright romantic after dark. You can also wander the other direction along Villefranche's waterfront and continue beyond the train station for postcard-perfect views back to Villefranche (ideal in the morning—go before breakfast). You can even extend your walk to Cap Ferrat (the wooded peninsula across the bay).

Sleeping in Villefranche-sur-Mer

(€1 = about $1.30, country code: 33)

You have a handful of good hotels to choose from in Villefranche. The ones I list have sea views from at least half of their rooms—well worth paying extra for.

$$$ Hôtel Welcome**** easily has the best location in Villefranche, anchored right on the water in the old town, with all 35 balconied rooms overlooking the harbor. The lobby opens to the water, and the mellow wine bar lowers my pulse. You'll pay top price for all the comforts in this smart hotel (Sb-€105, "comfort" Db-€205, bigger "superior" Db-€235, suites-€340-390, air-con, elevator, parking garage-€45 with reservation, 3 Quai Amiral Courbet, tel. 04 93 76 27 62, fax 04 93 76 27 66, www.welcome hotel.com, resa@welcomehotel.com).

$$ Hôtel la Flore* is a good Villefranche value if your idea of sightseeing is to enjoy the view from your spacious bedroom deck (most rooms have one) or the pool. It's a 15-minute uphill walk from the old town, but the parking is free, and the bus stops for Nice and Monaco are close (Db with no view-€100-137, Db with view and deck-€140-150, larger Db with even better view and bigger deck-€170-212, Db mini-suite-€220, Qb loft with huge terrace-€220, extra bed-€34, breakfast-€12, 15 percent cheaper Oct-March, check website for deals, air-con, elevator; just off main road high above harbor—go 2 blocks from TI toward Nice to 5 Boulevard Princesse Grace de Monaco; tel. 04 93 76 30 30, fax 04 93 76 99 99, www.hotel-la-flore.fr, info@hotel-la-flore.fr).

$$ Hôtel la Fiancée du Pirate* is a family-friendly refuge that's best suited for drivers, as it's high above Villefranche on the Middle Corniche (although it is on bus lines #82 and #112 to Eze-le-Village and Nice, and also served by minibus #80 from the harbor). Don't let the streetside appearance deter you: Eager-to-please Eric and Laurence offer 15 bright and comfortable rooms, along with a large pool, a pleasant garden, a roomy lounge area (with board games), and a breakfast terrace with partial views of Cap Ferrat and the sea. Choose between rooms in the main building or below on the garden patio. Parking and Wi-Fi are free, the beds are firm, all rooms are air-conditioned, and the big breakfast features homemade crêpes. Light lunches, salads, and snacks are available during the day (Db-€128-148, Tb-€155-175, Qb-€185-205, laundry-€10/load, 8 Boulevard de la Corne d'Or, Moyenne Corniche/N-7, tel. 04 93 76 67 40, fax 04 93 76 91 04, www.fianceedupirate.com, info@fianceedupirate.com).

$ Hôtel de la Darse** is a shy, unassuming little hotel burrowed in the shadow of its highbrow neighbors. This low-profile alternative on the water at Villefranche's old port is a great budget option. It's less central—figure 10 minutes of level walking to the harbor, but a steep 15-minute walk up to the main road and buses. The rooms facing the sea are worth the extra few euros for their million-dollar-view balconies (view Db-€95, view Tb-€120, Qb-€120, most with air-con and some noise on weekend nights, book well ahead for these). Rooms on the quieter garden side are sharp and have air-con, but no view (Sb-€70, Db-€78, extra bed-€14, breakfast-€9, no elevator, good-value breakfast; from TI walk or drive down Avenue Général de Gaulle; walkers should turn left on Allée du Colonel Duval into the Jardins de Narvik and follow steps to bottom, then turn right at the old Port de la Darse; parking usually available nearby, tel. 04 93 01 72 54, fax 04 93 01 84 37, www.hoteldeladarse.com, info@hoteldeladarse.com).

$ Hôtel Patricia* sits across from Villefranche, at the start of Cap Ferrat. Helpful owners Joelle and Franck provide 12 simple, homey, and cheap rooms (Db-€64, Db with balcony and seaview-€89, parking available, near l'Ange Gardien bus stop at 310 Avenue de l'Ange Gardien, tel. 04 93 01 06 70, www.hotel-patricia.riviera.fr, hotelpatricia@free.fr). From the hotel, it's a 20-minute walk to Villefranche, and 10 minutes by foot into Beaulieu-sur-Mer.

Eating in Villefranche-sur-Mer

Comparison-shopping is half the fun of dining in Villefranche-sur-Mer. Make an event out of a pre-dinner stroll through the old city. Check what looks good on the lively Place Amélie Pollonnais (next to Hôtel Welcome), where the whole village seems to converge at night; saunter the string of pricey candlelit places lining the waterfront; and consider the smaller, wallet-friendlier eateries embedded in the old city's walking streets. Arm yourself with a gelato from any ice-cream shop

THE FRENCH RIVIERA

and enjoy a floodlit, post-dinner stroll along the sea.

Le Cosmo Bistrot/Brasserie takes center stage on Place Amélie Pollonnais with a great setting—a few tables have views to the harbor and to the Chapel of St. Pierre's facade (after some wine, Cocteau pops). Manager Arnaud runs a tight-but-friendly ship and offers well-presented, tasty meals with good wines (I love their red Bandol). Ask for the daily suggestions and consider the €13 *omelette niçoise* (€16 fine salads and pastas, €16-29 *plats*, open daily, Place Amélie Pollonnais, tel. 04 93 01 84 05).

Disappear into Villefranche's walking streets and find cute little **La Grignotière,** serving generous and delicious €21 *plats*, and plenty of other options. Gregarious Michel speaks English fluently and runs the place with his sidekick Brigitte. The mixed seafood grill is a smart order, as are the spaghetti and *gambas* (shrimp), and Michel's personal-recipe bouillabaisse (€22). They also offer a hearty €32 *menu*, but good luck finding room for it. Dining is primarily inside, making this a good choice for cooler days (daily April-Oct, closed Wed Nov-April, 3 Rue du Poilu, tel. 04 93 76 79 83).

La Serre, nestled in the old town below St. Michael's Church, is a simple place with a hardworking owner. Sylvie serves well-priced dinners to a loyal local clientele, always with a smile. Choose from the many pizzas (all named after US states and €10 or less), salads, and meats; or try the good-value, €17 three-course *menu* (open daily, evenings only, cheap house wine, 16 Rue de May, tel. 04 93 76 79 91).

La Mère Germaine, right on the harbor, is the only place in town classy enough to lure a yachter ashore. It's dressy, with formal service and a price list to match. The name commemorates the current owner's grandmother, who fed hungry GIs during World War II. Try the bouillabaisse, served with panache (€75/person with 2-person minimum, €48 mini-version for one, €43 *menu*, open daily, reserve harborfront table, tel. 04 93 01 71 39).

La Trinquette is a relaxed, low-key place away from the fray on the "other port," next to the recommended Hôtel de la Darse (a lovely 10-minute walk from the other recommended restaurants). The cuisine is good and weekends bring a cool live music scene (€11-17 *plats*, closed Wed, tel. 04 93 16 92 48).

There's a handy **Casino market/grocery store** a few blocks above Hôtel Welcome at 12 Rue du Poilu (Thu-Tue 7:30-12:30 & 15:00-19:30, Wed 7:30-13:00 only).

For Drivers: If you have a car and are staying a few nights, take the short drive up to Eze-le-Village or, better still, La Turbie (recommendations are listed under each destination, later in this chapter). If it's summer (June-Sept), the best option of all is to go across to Cap Ferrat's **Restaurant de la Plage Passable** for a before-dinner drink or a dinner you won't soon forget (50-minute walk, 10-minute drive, follow signs from near Villa Rothschild). Enjoy a surprisingly elegant dining experience to the sounds of children still at play on the beach. Notice the streetlights that illuminate the path of the Low and Middle Corniches (€12-16 starters, €18-27 *plats*, open for dinner daily late May-early Sept, tel. 04 93 76 06 17).

Villefranche-sur-Mer Connections

By Train
Trains run later than buses (until 24:00).

From Villefranche-sur-Mer by Train to: Monaco (2/hour, 10 minutes), **Nice** (2/hour, 10 minutes), **Antibes** (2/hour, 40 minutes).

By Bus
All buses in this area cost €1 per ride, regardless of your destination (buy ticket from driver). Tickets are good for 74 minutes in one direction and for transfers, but not round-trips. In Villefranche-sur-Mer, all bus stops are along the main drag; the most convenient is the Octroi stop, just above the TI.

These are the key routes: **Bus #81** follows a circular route from Nice through Villefranche-sur-Mer, Beaulieu-sur-Mer, then to all Cap Ferrat stops, ending at the port in the village of St-Jean (2-4/hour daily 7:00-19:50 from Nice, last return trip from St-Jean at 20:25, earlier on Sun). **Bus #100** runs along the coastal road between Nice and Menton, just beyond Monaco (4/hour Mon-Sat, 3/hour Sun). The last bus leaves Nice for Villefranche at about 20:00; the last bus from Villefranche to Nice departs at about 20:50.

From Villefranche-sur-Mer by Bus to: Monaco (#100, 25 minutes), **Nice** (#81 or #100, 20 minutes).

By Cruise Ship
Villefranche-sur-Mer hustles to impress its cruise passengers. Tenders deposit passengers at a slick terminal building (Gare Maritime) at the Port de la Santé, right in front of Villefranche-sur-Mer's old town. At the terminal TI, pick up the free town map that's tailor-made for arriving cruise passengers. The main road (with the main TI and bus stop) is a steep hike above, and the train station is a short stroll along the beach.

Taxis wait in front of the cruise terminal. Their exorbitant rates start with a minimum €10-20 charge for a ride to the train station, but many drivers will flat-out refuse such a short ride. For farther-flung trips, see the price estimates on page 819. For an all-day trip, you can try negotiating a flat fee (for example, €300 for a 4-hour tour).

It's easy to **walk** to various points in Villefranche. If you want to see the town itself, just walk straight ahead from the terminal into Villefranche's charming, restaurant-lined square and start poking into its twisty back lanes.

Little **minibus #80,** which departs from in front of the cruise terminal, saves you some hiking up to the main road and bus stop (see page 822).

To connect to other towns, choose between the bus (slower but more scenic) or train (fast). Leaving the terminal, you'll see directional sights pointing left, to *Town center/**bus*** (a 10- to 15-minute, steeply uphill walk to the Octroi bus stop with connections west to Nice or east to Monaco, both on bus #100 or #81); and right, to *Gare SNCF/**train** station* (a 10-minute, mostly level stroll with some stairs up at the end—just turn right and walk along the beach, with the sea on your right, until you see stairs up to the station on your left).

The Three Corniches: Villefranche to Monaco

Nice, Villefranche-sur-Mer, and Monaco are linked by three coastal routes: the Low, Middle, and High Corniches. The roads are nicknamed after the decorative frieze that runs along the top of a building (cornice). Each Corniche (kor-neesh) offers sensational views and a different perspective. You can find the three routes from Nice by driving up Boulevard Jean Jaurès past Vieux Nice. For the Low Corniche, follow signs to N-98 *(Monaco par la Basse Corniche)*, which leads past Nice's port. Shortly after the turnoff to the Low Corniche, you'll see signs for N-7 *(Moyenne Corniche)* leading to the Middle Corniche. Signs for the High *(Grande)* Corniche appear a bit after that; follow D-2564 to *Col des 4 Chemins* and the *Grande Corniche*.

Low Corniche: The Basse Corniche (also called "Corniche Inférieure") strings ports, beaches, and seaside villages together for a traffic-filled ground-floor view. It was built in the 1860s (along with the train line) to bring people to the casino in Monte Carlo. When this Low Corniche was finished, many hill-town villagers descended to the shore and started the communities that now line the sea. Before 1860, the population of the coast between Villefranche-sur-Mer and Monte Carlo was zero. Think about that

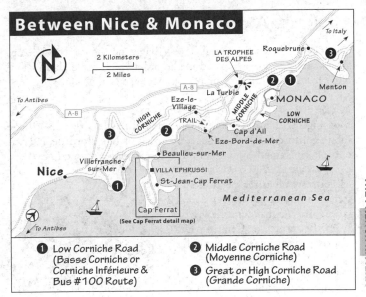

Between Nice & Monaco

2 Kilometers
2 Miles

To Italy

LA TROPHEE DES ALPES

Roquebrune

To Antibes

A-8

La Turbie

MONACO

Menton

HIGH CORNICHE

Eze-le-Village

MIDDLE CORNICHE

LOW CORNICHE

TRAIL

Cap d'Ail

Eze-Bord-de-Mer

Beaulieu-sur-Mer

Nice

Villefranche-sur-Mer

VILLA EPHRUSSI

St-Jean-Cap Ferrat

Mediterranean Sea

Cap Ferrat

(See Cap Ferrat detail map)

To Antibes

1 Low Corniche Road (Basse Corniche or Corniche Inférieure & Bus #100 Route)

2 Middle Corniche Road (Moyenne Corniche)

3 Great or High Corniche Road (Grande Corniche)

THE FRENCH RIVIERA

as you make the trip today.

Middle Corniche: The Moyenne Corniche is higher, quieter, and far more impressive. It runs through Eze-le-Village and provides breathtaking views over the Mediterranean, with several scenic pullouts. (The ones above Villefranche are the best.)

High Corniche: Napoleon's crowning road-construction achievement, the Grande Corniche caps the cliffs with staggering views from almost 1,600 feet above the sea. It is actually the Via Aurelia, used by the Romans to conquer the West.

Villas: Driving from Villefranche-sur-Mer to Monaco, you'll come upon impressive villas. A particularly grand entry leads to the sprawling estate built by King Leopold II of Belgium in 1902. Those driving up to the Middle Corniche from Villefranche can look down on this yellow mansion and its lush garden, which fill an entire hilltop. This estate was later owned by the Agnelli family (of Fiat fame and fortune), and then by the Safra family (Brazilian bankers).

The Best Route: For a ▲▲▲ route, **drivers** should take the Middle Corniche from Nice or Villefranche-sur-Mer to Eze-le-Village; from there, follow signs to the *Grande Corniche* and *La Turbie (La Trophée des Alpes)*, then finish by dropping down into Monaco. **Buses** travel each route; the higher the Corniche, the less frequent the buses (4/hour on Low, 12/day on Middle, and 5/day on High; get details at TIs, or check www.lignedazur.com). There are no buses between Eze-le-Village and La Turbie (45-minute walk), though buses do connect Nice and Monaco with La Turbie.

Sights Along the Three Corniches

The following two sights—Eze-le-Village and the La Trophée des Alpes monument—are listed in the order you'll reach them, traveling from Villefranche-sur-Mer to Monaco.

▲Eze-le-Village

Floating high above the sea, flowery and flawless Eze-le-Village (don't confuse it with the seafront town of Eze-Bord-de-Mer) is entirely consumed by tourism. This *village d'art et de gastronomie* (as it calls itself) nurtures perfume outlets, trendy boutiques, steep cobbled lanes, and magnificent views (best from the terrace at Château Eza). Touristy as this place certainly Eze, its stony state of preservation and magnificent hilltop setting over the Mediterranean may draw you away from the beaches. Day-tripping by bus to Eze-le-Village from Nice, Monaco, or Villefranche-sur-Mer works well, provided you know the bus schedules (ask at TIs or check www.lignedazur.com; Villefranche requires a transfer).

Bus stops and parking lots weld the town to the highway (Middle Corniche) that passes under its lowest wall. Eze-le-Village's main parking lot is a block below the town's entry. The stop for buses to Nice is across the road by the Avia gas station, and the stops for buses to Eze-Bord-de-Mer and Monaco are on the village side of the main road, near the Casino supermarket. The helpful **TI,** in the lot's far corner, has bus schedules (April-Oct daily 9:00-18:00, July-Aug until 19:00; Nov-March Mon-Sat 9:00-18:00, closed Sun; Place de Gaulle, tel. 04 93 41 26 00, www.eze-tourisme.com). English-language tours of the village and gardens are available for €8 (call to arrange in advance). Public WCs are located just behind the TI and in the village behind the church, though the cleanest and best-smelling are at the perfume showrooms.

At the **Jardins d'Eze** you'll find a prickly festival of cactus and a 360-degree view. Since 1949, these ruins have been home to 400 different plants 1,300 feet above the sea (€6, open daily, hours change frequently but usually May-Sept 9:00-19:00, Oct-April until dusk, well-described in English, tel. 04 93 41 10 30). At the top, you'll be treated to a commanding 360-degree view, with a helpful *table d'orientation.* On a crystal-clear day (they say...), you can see Corsica.

Trail to Eze-Bord-de-Mer—This steep trail leaves Eze-le-Village from the foot of the hill-town entry, near the fancy hotel gate (60 yards up from the main road), and descends 1,300 feet to the sea along a no-shade, all-view trail. The trail is easy to follow, but uneven—allow 45 minutes at a steady but manageable pace (good walking shoes are essential; expect to use all fours in certain sections). Once in Eze-Bord-de-Mer, you can catch a bus or train to all destinations between Nice and Monaco.

The **Fragonard perfume factory,** 350 feet below Eze-le-Village, is designed for tour groups, and cranks them through all day long. Drop in for an informative and free tour, which can last anywhere from 20 to 40 minutes depending on the walking ability of the group. You'll see how the perfume and scented soaps are made, before being herded into the gift shop. For a more personal and intimate (but unguided) look at perfume, cross the main road in Eze-le-Village to visit the **Gallimard** shop.

Eating in Eze-le-Village: To enjoy Eze-le-Village in relative peace, visit at sunset and stay for dinner. There's a handy **Casino** grocery store at the foot of the village by the bus stop (daily 8:00-20:00) and a wonderful picnic spot at the beginning of the trail to Eze-Bord-de-Mer. **Le Cactus** serves cheap crêpes, salads, and sandwiches at outdoor tables near the entry to the old town (daily, tel. 04 93 41 19 02). For a real splurge, dine at **Château Eza.** Its sensational view terrace is also home to an expensive-but-excellent restaurant. Reserve well ahead for dinner (€7 teas and beers, €10 glasses of wine, €55 lunch *menus,* allow €120 for dinner, open daily, tel. 04 93 41 12 24, www.chateaueza.com, info@chateaueza.com).

Getting to Eze-le-Village: There are two Ezes: Eze-le-Village (the spectacular hill town) and Eze-Bord-de-Mer (a

modern beach resort far below Eze-le-Village). Eze-le-Village is about 20 minutes east of Villefranche-sur-Mer on the Middle Corniche.

From Nice and upper Villefranche-sur-Mer, buses #82 and #112 provide 16 buses per day to Eze-le-Village (8 on Sun, 25 minutes from Villefranche). Take hourly minibus #80 from the center of Villefranche-sur-Mer uphill to the stop in front of Hôtel la Fiancée du Pirate to make this connection.

From Nice, Villefranche, or Monaco, you can also take the train or the Nice-Monaco bus to Eze-Bord-de-Mer, getting off at the Gare d'Eze stop. From here, take the #83 shuttle bus straight up to Eze-le-Village (8/day, daily 9:55-18:15,

THE FRENCH RIVIERA

schedule is posted at the stop but it's best to know schedule before you go).

To connect Eze-le-Village directly with Monte Carlo in Monaco, take bus #112 (6/day Mon-Sat, none on Sun, 20 minutes). There are no direct buses from Villefranche-sur-Mer's center to Eze-le-Village, and there are no buses between La Turbie (La Trophée des Alpes) and Eze-le-Village (40-minute walk).

You could take a pricey taxi between the two Ezes or from Eze-le-Village to La Turbie (allow €25 one-way, mobile 06 09 84 17 84).

▲▲La Trophée des Alpes (in La Turbie)

High above Monaco, on the Grande (High) Corniche in the overlooked village of La Turbie, lies one of this region's most evocative historical sights (with dramatic views over the entire country of Monaco as a bonus). Rising well above all other buildings, this massive Roman monument commemorates Augustus Caesar's conquest of the Alps' 44 hostile tribes. It's exciting to think that, in a way, La Trophée des Alpes celebrates a victory that kicked off the Pax Romana—joining Gaul and Germania, freeing up the main artery of the Roman Empire, and linking Spain and Italy. (It's depressing to think that it's closed on Mondays, if that's your only chance to visit.)

Walk around the monument and notice how the Romans built a fine, quarried-stone exterior, filled in with rubble and coarse concrete. Flanked by the vanquished in chains, the towering inscription tells the story: It was erected "by the senate and the people to honor the emperor." The monument later became a quarry before being restored in the 1930s and 1940s with money from the Tuck family of New Hampshire.

The one-room **museum** shows a reconstruction and translation of the dramatic inscription, which lists all the feisty alpine tribes that put up such a fight. Recently upgraded, it has good English explanations and modern exhibits.

Cost and Hours: €6, Tue-Sun mid-May-mid-Sept 9:30-13:00 & 14:30-17:30, off-season 10:00-13:00 & 14:30-17:00, closed Mon year-round, tel. 04 93 41 20 84.

La Turbie: The sweet old village of La Turbie sees almost no tourists, but it has plenty of cafés and restaurants. To stroll the old village, park in the main lot on Place Neuve (follow *Monaco* signs one block from the main road to find it), then walk behind the post office and find brick footpaths—they lead through a village with nary a shop. To eat very well, find **La Terrasse,** the Riviera's most welcoming restaurant (I'm not kidding—free calls are encouraged from their phone anywhere, anytime; there's a computer at your disposal; and the Wi-Fi is complimentary). Tables gather under sun shades and everyone seems to be on a first-name basis. Let Helen, Jacques, and Annette tempt you to return for dinner at sunset—book ahead for a table with a view (€8-12 salads, great €14 *plats du jour*, €20 three-course *menu* includes glass of wine, steak tartare is a specialty, daily, near the post office at the main parking lot, 17 Place Neuve, tel. 04 93 41 21 84).

Getting to and from La Trophée des Alpes: By **car,** take the High Corniche to La Turbie, ideally via Eze-le-Village (La Turbie is 10 minutes east of, and above, Eze-le-Village), then look for signs to *La Trophée des Alpes*. Once in La Turbie, park in the lot in the center of town (Place Neuve, follow *Monaco* signs for a short block) and walk from there (walk 5 minutes around the old village, with the village on your right); or drive to the site by turning right in front of La Régence Café. Those coming from farther afield can take the efficient A-8 to the La Turbie exit. To reach Eze-le-Village from La Turbie, follow signs to *Nice,* and then look for signs to *Eze-le-Village.*

You can also get here on **bus** #T-66 from Nice's Pont St. Michel stop (7/day, 45 minutes, last bus returns to Nice at about 18:00). In Nice, take the tram to the Pont St. Michel stop. From Monaco, bus #114 connects to La Turbie (6/day Mon-Sat, 5/day Sun, 30 minutes). La Turbie's bus stop is across from the post office (PTT) on Place Neuve (to reach La Trophée des Alps from here, walk 5 minutes around the old village, with the village on your right).

Monaco

Despite high prices, wall-to-wall daytime tourists, and a Disney-esque atmosphere, Monaco is a Riviera must. Monaco is on the go.

Since 1929, cars have raced around the port and in front of the casino in one of the world's most famous auto races, the Grand Prix de Monaco (May 23-26 in 2013). The modern breakwater—constructed elsewhere and towed in by sea—enables big cruise ships to dock here. The district of Fontvieille, reclaimed from the sea, bristles with luxury high-rise condos. But don't look for anything too deep in this glittering tax haven. Two-thirds of its 30,000 residents live here because there's no income tax—leaving fewer than 10,000 true Monegasques.

This minuscule principality (0.75 square mile) borders only

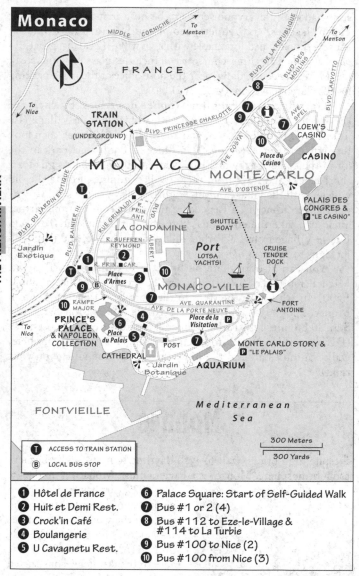

Monaco

- **1** Hôtel de France
- **2** Huit et Demi Rest.
- **3** Crock'in Café
- **4** Boulangerie
- **5** U Cavagnetu Rest.
- **6** Palace Square: Start of Self-Guided Walk
- **7** Bus #1 or 2 (4)
- **8** Bus #112 to Eze-le-Village & #114 to La Turbie
- **9** Bus #100 to Nice (2)
- **10** Bus #100 from Nice (3)

T ACCESS TO TRAIN STATION

B LOCAL BUS STOP

France and the Mediterranean. The country has always been tiny, but it used to be...less tiny. In an 1860 plebiscite, Monaco lost two-thirds of its territory when the region of Menton voted to join France. To compensate, France suggested that Monaco build a fancy casino and promised to connect it to the world with a road (the Low Corniche) and a train line. This started a high-class tourist boom that has yet to let up.

Although "independent," Monaco is run as a piece of France. A French civil servant appointed by the French president—with the blessing of Monaco's prince—serves as state minister and manages the place. Monaco's phone system, electricity, water, and so on, are all French.

The death of Prince Rainier in 2005 ended his 56-year career of enlightened rule. Today Monaco is ruled by Prince Rainier's unassuming son, Prince Albert Alexandre Louis Pierre, Marquis of Baux. Prince Albert had long been considered Europe's most eligible bachelor—until he finally married on July 2, 2011, at age 53. His bride, known as Princess Charlene, is a South African commoner twenty years his junior. Sadly for Monaco, this rare royal event was overshadowed by Prince William and Kate's London wedding.

A graduate of Amherst College, Albert is a bobsled enthusiast who raced in several Olympics, and an avid environmentalist who seems determined to clean up Monaco's tarnished tax-haven, money-laundering image. (Monaco is infamously known as a "sunny place for shady people.") Monaco is big business, and Prince Albert is its CEO. Its famous casino contributes only 5 percent of the state's revenue, whereas its 43 banks—which offer an attractive way to hide your money—are hugely profitable. The prince also makes money with a value-added tax (19.6 percent, the same as in France), plus real estate and corporate taxes.

The glamorous romance and marriage of the American actress Grace Kelly to Prince Rainier added to Monaco's fairy-tale mystique. Princess Grace (Prince Albert's mother) first came to Monaco to star in the 1955 Hitchcock movie *To Catch a Thief,* in which she was filmed racing along the Corniches. She married the prince in 1956 and adopted the country, but tragically, the much-loved princess died in 1982 after suffering a stroke while driving on one of those same scenic roads. She was just 52 years old.

Monaco is a special place: There are more people in Monaco's philharmonic orchestra (about 100) than in its army (about 80 guards). The princedom is well-guarded, with police and cameras on every corner. (They say you could win a million dollars at the casino and walk to the train station in the wee hours without a worry...and I believe it.) Stamps are so few that they increase in value almost as soon as they're printed. And collectors snapped up the rare Monaco versions of euro coins (with Prince Rainier's portrait) so quickly that many Monegasques have never even seen one.

Orientation to Monaco

The principality of Monaco consists of three distinct tourist areas: Monaco-Ville, Monte Carlo, and La Condamine. Monaco-Ville fills the rock high above everything else and is referred to by locals

THE FRENCH RIVIERA

as Le Rocher ("The Rock"). This is the oldest section, home to the Prince's Palace and all the sights except the casino. Monte Carlo is the area around the casino. La Condamine is the port (which lies between Monaco-Ville and Monte Carlo). From here, it's a 25-minute walk up to the Prince's Palace or to the casino, or three minutes by local bus (see "Getting Around Monaco," later). A fourth, less-interesting area, Fontvieille, forms the west end of Monaco and was reclaimed from the sea by Prince Rainier in the 1970s.

Tourist Information

The main TI is at the top of the park, above the casino (Mon-Sat 9:00-19:00, Sun 10:00-12:00, 2 Boulevard des Moulins, tel. 00-377/92 16 61 16 or 00-377/92 16 61 66, www.visitmonaco.com). Branch TIs may be open in the train station (Tue-Sat 9:00-17:00, closed Sun-Mon). From June to September, you might find information kiosks at the west exit (Nice end) of the train station, in the Monaco-Ville parking garage, and on the port. There is also a TI desk for Monaco in Terminal 1 of Nice's airport.

Arrival in Monaco

By Bus from Nice and Villefranche-sur-Mer: Bus riders need to pay attention, since stops are not announced. Cap d'Ail is the town before Monaco, so be on the lookout after that (the last stop before Monaco is called Cimetière). You'll enter Monaco through the modern cityscape of high-rises of the Fontvieille district. When you see the rocky outcrop of old Monaco, be ready to get off.

There are three stops in Monaco. Listed in order from Nice, they are Place d'Armes (in front of a tunnel at the base of Monaco-Ville's rock), Stade Nautique (closest stop to Monaco-Ville on the port), and Office de Tourisme (near the casino and the TI on Avenue d'Ostende). The Place d'Armes stop is the best starting point, and is the only signed stop (otherwise, verify with locals that you're at the right stop). From the Place d'Armes stop, you can walk up to Monaco-Ville and the palace (10 minutes straight up), or catch a quick local bus (line #1 or #2—see "Getting Around Monaco," later). To reach the bus stop and steps up to Monaco-Ville, cross the street right in front of the tunnel and walk with the rock on your right for about 200 feet (good WCs at the local-bus stop). To begin at the Casino stop, pass through the port, get off the bus when you see the Häagen-Dazs, walk past it, and turn right.

For directions on returning to Nice by bus, see "Monaco Connections," later.

By Train: This looooong underground train station is in central Monaco, about a 15-minute walk to the casino or to the port, and about 25 minutes to the palace. The station has no baggage storage.

The TI and ticket windows are up the escalator at the Italy end of the station. There are three exits from the train platform level (one at each end and one in the middle).

To reach Monaco-Ville and the palace from the station, take the platform-level exit at the Nice end of the tracks (signed *Sortie Fontvieille/Monaco Ville*), which leads through a long tunnel (TI annex at end); as you emerge from the tunnel, turn right, turn left at the end of the walkway, and cross the busy intersection. From here, it's a 15-minute hike up to the palace, or take the bus (#1 or #2).

To reach Monaco's port and the casino, take the mid-platform exit, closer to the Italy end of the tracks. Follow *Sortie la Condamine* signs down the steps and escalators, then follow *Accès Port* signs until you pop out at the port, where you'll see the stop for buses #1 and #2. It's a 25-minute walk from the port to the palace (to your right) or 20 minutes to the casino (up Avenue d'Ostende to your left), or a short trip via buses #1 or #2 to either.

If you plan to return to Nice by train after 20:30, when ticket windows close, buy your return tickets now or be sure to have about €4 in coins (the ticket machines only take coins).

To take the short-but-sweet coastal **walking path** into Monaco via its Fontvieille district, get off the train at Cap d'Ail, which is one stop before Monaco. Turn left out of the little station and walk 50 yards up the road, then turn left again, going down the stairs and under the tracks. Turn left onto the coastal trail, and hike the 20 minutes to Fontvieille. You'll end up at Plage Marquet. Once there, it's a 20-minute uphill hike to Monaco's sights (or hop on bus #100—walk up Avenue Marquet past the stadium, and make a left on Avenue de Fontvieille).

By Car: Follow *Centre-Ville* signs into Monaco (warning: traffic can be a problem), then watch for the red-letter signs to parking garages at *Le Casino* (for Monte Carlo) or *Le Palais* (for Monaco-Ville). You'll pay about €10 for four hours.

By Cruise Ship: For information on arrival by cruise ship, see "Monaco Connections," later.

Helpful Hints

Combo-Ticket: If you plan to see all three of Monaco's big sights (Prince's Palace, Napoleon Collection, and the Cousteau Aquarium), buy the €19 combo-ticket at the first sight you visit.

Telephone Tip: To call Monaco from France, dial 00, then 377 (Monaco's country code) and the eight-digit number. Within Monaco, simply dial the eight-digit number.

Minivan Tours from Nice: Several companies offer daytime and nighttime tours of Monaco, allowing you freedom to gamble without worrying about catching the last train or bus home (see "Helpful Hints" on page 768).

Loop Trip by Bus: You can visit Monaco by bus, then take a bus from Monaco directly to Eze-le-Village (#112, none on Sun) or La Turbie (#114), then return to Nice by bus from there. For details, see "Monaco Connections," later.

Getting Around Monaco

By Local Bus: Buses #1 and #2 link all areas with fast and frequent service (single ticket-€2, 10 tickets-€6, day pass-€5, pay driver or buy from machine, 10/hour, fewer on Sun, buses run until 21:00). You can split a 10-ride ticket with your travel partners (which is handy, since you're unlikely to take more than two or three rides in Monaco). Bus tickets are good for a free transfer if used within 30 minutes and are cheaper if purchased from a machine or online.

By Open Bus Tour: You could pay €18 for a hop-on, hop-off open-deck bus tour that makes 12 stops in Monaco, but I wouldn't. This tour doesn't go to the best view spot in the Jardin Exotique and, besides, most of Monaco is walkable. If you want a scenic tour of the principality that includes its best views, pay €2 to take local bus #2, and stay on board for a full loop (or hop on and off as you please).

By Tourist Train: "Monaco Tour" tourist trains are an efficient way to enjoy a blitz tour of Monaco. They begin at the aquarium and pass by the port, casino, and palace (€8, 2/hour, 40 minutes, recorded English commentary).

By Taxi: If you've lost all track of time at the casino, you can call the 24-hour taxi service (tel. 08 20 20 98 98)...provided you still have enough money to pay for the cab home.

Self-Guided Walk

Welcome to Monaco-Ville

All of Monaco's sights (except the casino) are in Monaco-Ville, packed within a few cheerfully tidy blocks. This walk makes a tight little loop, starting from the palace square.

• *To get from anywhere in Monaco to the palace square (Monaco-Ville's sightseeing center, home of the palace and the Napoleon Collection), take bus #1 or #2 to the end of the line at Place de la Visitation. Turn right as you step off the bus and walk five minutes down Rue Emile de Loth. You'll pass the post office, a worthwhile stop for its collection of valu-*

able Monegasque stamps. If you're walking up from the port, the well-marked lane leads you directly to the palace.

Palace Square (Place du Palais): This square is the best place to get oriented to Monaco. Facing the palace, go to the right and

look out over the city (er...principality). This rock gave birth to the little pastel Hong Kong look-alike in 1215, and it's managed to remain an independent country for most of its nearly 800 years. Looking beyond the glitzy port, notice the faded green roof above and to the right: It belongs to the casino that put Monaco on the map. The famous Grand Prix runs along the port, and then up the ramp to the casino. And Italy is so close, you can almost smell the pesto. Just beyond the casino is France again (which flanks Monaco on both sides)—you could walk one-way from France to France, passing through Monaco in about 60 minutes.

The odd statue of a woman with a fishing net is dedicated to **Prince Albert I**'s glorious reign (1889-1922). Albert was a Renaissance man with varied skills and interests. He had a Jacques Cousteau-like fascination with the sea (and built Monaco's famous aquarium), and was a determined pacifist who made many attempts to dissuade Germany's Kaiser Wilhelm II from becoming involved in World War I. It was Albert I's dad, Charles III, who built the casino.

• *Now walk toward the palace and find the statue of the monk grasping a sword.*

Meet **François Grimaldi,** a renegade Italian dressed as a monk, who captured Monaco in 1297 and began the dynasty that still rules the principality. Prince Albert is his great-great-great... grandson, which gives Monaco's royal family the distinction of being the longest-lasting dynasty in Europe.

• *Make your way to the...*

Prince's Palace (Palais Princier): A medieval castle sat where Monaco's palace is today. Its strategic setting has had a lot to do with Monaco's ability to resist attackers. Today, Prince Albert lives in the palace, while poor Princesses Stephanie and Caroline live down the street. The palace guards protect the prince 24/7 and still stage a **Changing of the Guard** ceremony with all the pageantry of an important nation (daily at 11:55, fun to watch but jam-packed). Audioguide tours take you through part of the prince's lavish palace in 30 minutes. The rooms are well-furnished and impressive, but interesting only if you haven't seen a château lately (€8 combo-ticket includes audioguide and Napoleon

Collection, €19 combo-ticket also includes Cousteau Aquarium; hours vary but generally April-Oct daily 10:00-18:00, last entry 30 minutes before closing, closed Nov-March; tel. 00-377/93 25 18 31).

• *Next to the palace entry is the...*

Napoleon Collection: Napoleon occupied Monaco after the French Revolution. This is the prince's private collection of items Napoleon left behind: military medals, swords, guns, letters, and—best—his hat. I found this collection more interesting than the palace (€4 includes audioguide, €8 combo-ticket includes Prince's Palace, €19 combo-ticket also includes Cousteau Aquarium; same hours as palace).

• *With your back to the palace, leave the square through the arch to the right side of the square (under the most beautiful police station I've ever seen) and find the...*

Cathedral of Monaco (Cathédrale de Monaco): The somber but beautifully lit cathedral, rebuilt in 1878, shows that Monaco cares for more than just its new casino. It's where centuries of Grimaldis are buried, and where Princess Grace and Prince Rainier were married. Circle slowly behind the altar (counterclockwise). The second tomb is that of Albert I, who did much to put Monaco on the world stage. The second-to-last tomb—inscribed *"Gratia Patricia, MCMLXXXII"*—is where Princess Grace was buried in 1982. Prince Rainier's tomb lies next to Princess Grace's (daily 8:30-18:45, until 18:00 in winter).

• *As you leave the cathedral, find the 1956 wedding photo of Princess Grace and Prince Rainier (keep an eye out for other photos of the couple as you walk), then dip into the immaculately maintained Jardin Botanique, with more fine views. In the gardens, turn left. Eventually you'll find the...*

Cousteau Aquarium (Musée Océanographique): Prince Albert I built this impressive, cliff-hanging aquarium in 1910 as a monument to his enthusiasm for things from the sea. The aquarium, which Captain Jacques Cousteau directed for 32 years, has 2,000 different specimens, representing 250 species. The bottom floor features Mediterranean fish and colorful tropical species (all nicely described in English). My favorite is the zebra lionfish, though I'm keen on eels too. Rotating exhibits occupy the entry floor. Upstairs, the fancy Albert I Hall houses a museum (included in entry fee, very little English information) and features ship models, whale skeletons, oceanographic instruments and tools, and scenes of Albert and his beachcombers hard at work. Find the display on Christopher Columbus with English explanations. Don't miss the elevator to the rooftop terrace view, where you'll also find convenient WCs and a reasonable café (aquarium entry-€14, kids-€7, €19 combo-ticket includes Prince's Palace and Napoleon

Collection; daily July-Aug 9:30-19:30, April-June and Sept 9:30-19:00, Oct-March 10:00-18:00; down the steps from Monaco-Ville bus stop, at the opposite end of Monaco-Ville from the palace; tel. 00-377/93 15 36 00, www.oceano.mc).

• *The red-brick steps, across from the aquarium and a bit to the right, lead up to stops for buses #1 and #2, both of which run to the port, the casino, and the train station. To walk back to the palace and through the old city, turn left at the top of the brick steps. For a brief movie break, as you leave the aquarium, take the escalator to the right and drop into the parking garage, then take the elevator down and find the...*

Monte Carlo Story: This informative 35-minute film gives an entertaining and informative account of Monaco's fairy-tale history, from fishing village to jet-set principality, and offers a comfortable, soft-chair break from all that walking. The last part of the film was added to the original version after the death of Prince Rainier, which is why your sound stops early (€8, headphone commentary in English; daily showings usually at 14:00, 15:00, 16:00, and 17:00; there may be a morning showing for groups that you can join—ask, tel. 00-377/93 25 32 33).

Sights in Monaco

Above Monaco-Ville

Jardin Exotique—This cliffside municipal garden, located above Monaco-Ville, has eye-popping views from France to Italy. It's a fascinating home to more than a thousand species of cacti (some giant) and other succulent plants, but probably worth the entry only for view-loving botanists (some posted English explanations provided). Your ticket includes entry to a skippable natural cave and an anthropological museum, as well as a not-to-be-missed view snack bar/café. Bus #2 runs here from any stop in Monaco, and makes for a worthwhile mini tour of the country, even if you don't visit the gardens. You can get similar views over Monaco for free from behind the souvenir stand at the Jardin's bus stop; or, for even grander vistas, cross the street and hike toward La Turbie.

Cost and Hours: €7, daily mid-May-mid-Sept 9:00-19:00, mid-Sept-mid-May 9:00-18:00 or until dusk, tel. 00-377/93 15 29 80, www.jardin-exotique.com.

In Monte Carlo

▲**Casino**—Monte Carlo, which means "Charles' Hill" in Spanish, is named for the prince who presided over Monaco's 19th-century makeover. Begin your visit opposite Europe's most famous casino, in the park above the pedestrian-unfriendly traffic circle. In the mid-1800s, olive groves stood here. Then, with the construction of the casino and spas, and easy road and train access, one of Europe's poorest countries was on the Grand Tour map—*the* place for the vacationing aristocracy to play. Today, Monaco has the world's highest per-capita income.

The casino is intended to make you feel comfortable while losing money. Charles Garnier designed the place (with an opera

house inside) in 1878, in part to thank the prince for his financial help in completing Paris' Opéra Garnier (which the architect also designed). The central doors provide access to private gaming rooms, and the opera house. The private gaming rooms occupy the left wing of the building.

The scene, flooded with camera-toting tourists during the day, is great at night—and downright James Bond-like in the private rooms. This is your chance to rub elbows with some high rollers—provided you're 18 or older (bring your passport for proof).

If paying an entrance fee to lose money is not your idea of fun, you can access all games for free in the plebeian, American-style Loews Casino, adjacent to the old casino.

Cost and Hours: The whole casino opens daily at 14:00 for gambling. The **first gaming rooms** (Salle Renaissance, Salon de l'Europe, and Salle des Amériques) are free to enter, with English roulette, blackjack, craps, and slot machines. (Or pay €10 to visit in the morning to gawk—but not gamble—in the same rooms, daily 9:30-12:30, no dress code.) The more glamorous **private game rooms** (Salons Touzet and Terrasse Salle Blanche) cost €10 to enter and have the same games as above, plus American roulette, Trente et Quarante, Ultimate Texas Hold 'Em poker, and Punto Banco—a version of baccarat (tel. 00-377/92 16 20 00, www .montecarlocasinos.com).

Dress Code: During gambling hours, men need to wear a jacket and slacks; dress standards for women are more relaxed—only tennis shoes and beach attire are definite no-nos.

Take the Money and Run: The stop for buses returning to Nice and Villefranche-sur-Mer, and for local buses #1 and #2, is at the top of the park, above the casino on Avenue de la Costa (under the arcade to the left). To get back to the train station from the casino, take bus #1 or #2 from this stop, or walk about 15 minutes down Avenue d'Ostende (just outside the casino) toward the port, and follow signs to *Gare SNCF* (see map).

Sleeping and Eating in Monaco

(€1 = about $1.30, country code: 377)

Sleeping in Monaco: **$$ Hôtel de France****, run by friendly Sylvie, is a centrally located, reasonably priced place. While basic, it should be entirely renovated in time for your visit (Db-about €130, Tb-about €150, includes breakfast, may have air-con, Wi-Fi, near west exit from train station at 6 Rue de la Turbie, tel. 00-377/93 30 24 64, fax 00-377/92 16 13 34, www.monte-carlo.mc/france, hotel -france@monte-carlo.mc).

Eating in Monaco: Several cafés serve basic, inexpensive fare (day and night) on the port. I prefer the eateries that line the flowery and traffic-free Rue de la Princesse Caroline, which runs between Rue Grimaldi and the port. The best this street has to offer is **Huit et Demi.** It has a white-tablecloth-meets-director's-chair ambience, mostly outdoor tables, and cuisine worth returning for (€15 salads, €15 pizzas, €18-24 *plats*, closed Sat for lunch and all day Sun, 7 Rue de la Princesse Caroline, tel. 00-377/93 50 97 02). For a simple and cheap salad or sandwich, find the **Crock'in** café farther down at 2 Rue de la Princesse Caroline (closed Sat, tel. 00-377/93 15 02 78).

In Monaco-Ville, you'll find incredible *pan bagnat* (*salade niçoise* sandwich), quiches, and sandwiches at the yellow-bannered **Boulangerie,** a block off Place du Palais (open daily until 21:00, 8 Rue Basse). Try a *barbajuan* (a spring roll-size beignet with wheat, rice, and parmesan), the *tourta de bléa* (pastry stuffed with pine nuts, raisins, and white beets), or the focaccia sandwich (salted bread with herbs, mozzarella, basil, and tomatoes, all drenched in olive oil). For dessert, order the *fougasse monégasque* (a soft-bread pastry topped with sliced almonds and anise candies). The best-value restaurant in Monaco-Ville is **U Cavagnetu**—and it's no secret. You'll dine very cheaply on specialties from Monaco just a block from Albert's palace (€13-17 *plats*, €26 *menu*, daily, 14 Rue Comte Félix Gastaldi, tel. 00-377/97 98 20 40). Monaco-Ville has other pizzerias, *crêperies,* and sandwich stands, but the neighborhood is dead at night.

Monaco Connections

By Train and Bus

From Monaco by Train to: Nice (2/hour, 20 minutes, €3.60), **Villefranche-sur-Mer** (2/hour, 10 minutes), **Antibes** (2/hour, 50 minutes), **Cannes** (2/hour, 1 hour).

By Bus to: Nice (#100, 4/hour Mon-Sat, 3/hour Sun, 45 minutes), **Nice Airport** (#110 express on the freeway, 2/hour, 50 minutes, €19), **Villefranche-sur-Mer** (#100, 4/hour Mon-Sat, 3/hour

Sun, 25 minutes), **Eze-le-Village** (#112, 6/day Mon-Sat, none on Sun, 20 minutes), **Cap Ferrat** (#100, 4/hour Mon-Sat, 3/hour Sun, 20 minutes plus 20-minute walk), **La Turbie** (#114, 6/day Mon-Sat, 5/day Sun, 30 minutes), **Menton** (#100, 4/hour Mon-Sat, 3/hour Sun, 40 minutes).

The Monaco-to-Nice bus (#100) is not identified at most stops—verify with a local by asking, *"A Nice?"* There's a handy stop below Monaco-Ville at Place d'Armes (on the main road to Nice in front of the Brasserie Monte Carlo). Another is a few blocks above the casino on Avenue de la Costa (under the arcade to the left of Barclays Bank).

Buses #112 (to Eze-le-Village) and #114 (to La Turbie) depart Monaco from Place de la Crémaillère, one block above the main TI and casino park. Walk up Rue Iris with Barclays Bank to your left, curve right, and find the bus shelter across the street at the green Costa à la Crémaillère café. Bus numbers for these routes are not posted, but this is the stop.

Last Call: The last bus leaves Monaco for Villefranche-sur-Mer and Nice at about 20:00; the last train leaves Monaco for Villefranche-sur-Mer and Nice at about 23:30. If you plan to leave Monaco by train after 20:30, buy your tickets in advance (since the window will be closed), or bring enough coins for the machines.

By Cruise Ship

Cruise ships tender passengers to the end of Monaco's yacht harbor, a short walk from downtown. *Très elegant!* There's a seasonal **TI** right next to the tender dock (open on busy days May-Sept). To summon a **taxi** (assuming none are waiting when you disembark), look for the grey taxi-call box near the tender dock—just press the button and wait for your cab to arrive.

Whether visiting the sights in Monaco itself, or heading to outlying destinations, the first step for most journeys is to walk from the cruise port to the little market square called **Place d'Armes.** It's an easy and level stroll: Head straight along the yacht harbor until you reach the busy street, which is Boulevard Albert 1er. Use the white overpass (with an elevator) to cross the street, then follow green *Gare S.N.C.F.* signs through a maze of skyscrapers, across the street, and up a charming lane lined with motorcycle shops. Continue straight into the peach-and-yellow building, and ride the free public elevator up to *Marché Place d'Armes* (level 0). You'll pop out into Place d'Armes. At the far end of this square is a roundabout and the busy Rue Grimaldi.

Getting into Town: To reach the cliff-top old town of **Monaco-Ville,** you can either hike steeply up to the top of the hill next to the harbor, or ride a bus up. By **foot,** the fastest, steepest ascent (with an elevator option partway) is near the tip of the

Monaco-Ville peninsula, just above where the tenders arrive: Climb up the stairs next to the Yacht Club de Monaco to the base of the hill, turn left, then curl around the tip of land (with the water on your left-hand side), following signs for *Palais/Musées*. At the parking garage, you can either keep hiking up through the manicured park, or enter the garage and ride up the elevator, then the escalator; either way, you'll emerge near the Cousteau Aquarium, close to the end of my self-guided walk. (It's a five-minute walk through town to Palace Square and the start of the walk.) To ride **bus #1 or #2** up to Monaco-Ville, first walk to the bus stop near Place d'Armes (described earlier). As you exit the elevator into Place d'Armes, turn left and cross the street, then continue up to the second, uphill street (which leads up to the hill-top). Cross this second street and bear right to find the bus stop.

The ritzy skyscraper zone of **Monte Carlo** is basically across the harbor from the tender dock (casino opens for gambling at 14:00). You can walk to the casino area in about 25 minutes—just go all the way around the harbor. To shave some time off the hike, ride the little "bateau bus" shuttle boat across the mouth of the harbor (to find the dock from your tender, walk toward town, then go right along the pier extending into the harbor; €2, €5/day pass, 3/hour). To reach the upper part of Monte Carlo—with the TI, views down over the casino gardens, and handy bus stops (including the one for Eze-le-Village)—catch bus #1 or #2 at the top of the yacht harbor, along Boulevard Albert 1er.

Getting to Sights Beyond Monaco: Monaco is connected to most nearby sights by both train and bus. Monaco's **train station** is about a 20-minute walk from the tender harbor. From Place d'Armes (described earlier), head up to the far end, cross the busy Rue Grimaldi, and take the narrow, angled, red-asphalt lane (Rue de la Turbie) in the middle of the block across the street. Go up the stairs (or ride the elevator) into the little plaza, where you'll see a small TI kiosk (open only in peak season). Turn left, walk up more stairs, and enter the train station (the big, pink building on your right; the easy-to-miss entrance is at the far end—look for *Acces Gare* signs).

The stop for **bus #100**—which conveniently connects Monaco along the Lower Corniche to Villefranche, Nice, and more—is near Place d'Armes. From Place d'Armes, head up to the far end, along Rue Grimaldi. The bus stop is across the roundabout on the left, on the right-hand side of the street (to get there, cross the street two times in either direction). To ride **bus #112** along the scenic Upper Corniche to Eze-le-Village (6/day Mon-Sat, none on Sun, 20 minutes), first ride bus #1 or #2 to the TI and casino (explained earlier), then follow the directions to the Place de la Crémaillère stop on page 844.

Near Monaco: Menton

If you wish the Riviera were less glitzy and more like a place where humble locals take their families to lick ice cream and make sand castles, visit Menton (15 minutes by bus beyond Monaco). Menton feels like a poor man's Nice. It's unrefined and unpretentious, with lower prices, fewer rentable umbrellas, and lots of Italians day-tripping in from just over the border (five miles away). There's not an American in sight.

Though a bit rough, the Menton beach is a joy. An inviting promenade lines the beach, and seaside cafés serve light meals and salads (much cheaper than in Nice). A snooze or stroll here is a lovely Riviera experience. From the promenade, a pedestrian street leads through town. Small squares are alive with jazz bands playing crowd-pleasers under palm trees.

Stepping into the old town—which blankets a hill capped by a fascinating cemetery—you're immersed in a pastel-painted, yet dark and tangled Old World scene with (strangely) almost no commerce. A few elegant restaurants dig in at the base of the towering, centuries-old apartment flats. The richly decorated Baroque St. Michael's Church (midway up the hill) is a reminder that, until 1860, Menton was a thriving part of the larger state of Monaco. Climbing past sun-grabbing flower boxes and people who don't get out much anymore, the steep stepped lanes finally deposit you at the ornate gate of a grand cemetery that fills the old castle walls. Explore the cemetery, which is the final resting place of many aristocratic Russians (buried here in the early 1900s) and offers breathtaking Mediterranean views.

Getting to Menton: While trains serve Menton regularly, the station is a 15-minute walk from the action. Buses are more convenient, as they drop visitors right on the beach promenade (#100, 4/hour Mon-Sat, 3/hour Sun, 1.25 hours from Nice, 40 minutes past Monaco, €1).

Antibes

Antibes has a down-to-earth, easygoing ambience that's rare in this area. Its old town is a maze of narrow streets and red-tile roofs rising above the blue Med, protected by twin medieval towers and wrapped in extensive ramparts. Visitors making the short trip from Nice can browse Europe's biggest yacht harbor, snooze on a sandy beach, loiter through an enjoyable old town, and hike along a sea-swept trail. The town's cultural claim to fame, the Picasso Museum, shows off its great collection in a fine old building.

Though much smaller than Nice, Antibes has a history that dates back just as far. Both towns were founded by Greek traders in the fifth century B.C. To the Greeks, Antibes was "Antipolis"—the town *(polis)* opposite *(anti)* Nice. For the next several centuries, Antibes remained in the shadow of its neighbor. By the turn of the 20th century, the town was a military base—so the rich and famous partied elsewhere. But when the army checked out after World War I, Antibes was "discovered" and enjoyed a particularly roaring '20s—with the help of party animals like Rudolph Valentino and the rowdy (yet silent) Charlie Chaplin. Fun-seekers even invented water-skiing right here in the 1920s.

Orientation to Antibes

Antibes' old town lies between the port and Boulevard Albert 1er and Avenue Robert Soleau. Place Nationale is the old town's hub of activity. The restaurant-lined Rue Aubernon connects the port and the old town. Stroll along the sea between the old port and Place Albert 1er (where Boulevard Albert 1er meets the water). The best beaches lie just beyond Place Albert 1er, and the walk is beautiful. Good play areas for children are along this path and on Place des Martyrs de la Résistance (close to recommended Hôtel Relais du Postillon).

Tourist Information

Antibes has three TIs: one in a kiosk at the **train station** (April-Sept only, Mon-Sat 9:00-18:00, closed Sun), one near the **port** at 32 Boulevard d'Aguillon (Mon-Sat 10:00-12:00 & 13:00-18:00, until 19:00 July-Aug, closed Sun), and the main TI on **Place Général de Gaulle** where the fountains squirt (July-Aug daily 9:00-19:00; Sept-June Mon-Sat 9:00-12:30 & 13:30-18:00, Sun 10:00-12:30 & 14:00-17:00; tel. 04 97 23 11 11, www.antibesjuanlespins.com). At any TI, pick up the excellent city map and the self-guided walking tour of old Antibes. The Nice TI has Antibes maps and the Antibes TI has Nice maps—plan ahead.

Arrival in Antibes

By Train: Bus #14 runs every 20 minutes from the train station (bus stop 50 yards to right as you exit station) to the *gare routière* (bus station; near the main TI and old town), and continues to the fine Plage de la Salis with quick access to the Phare de la Garoupe

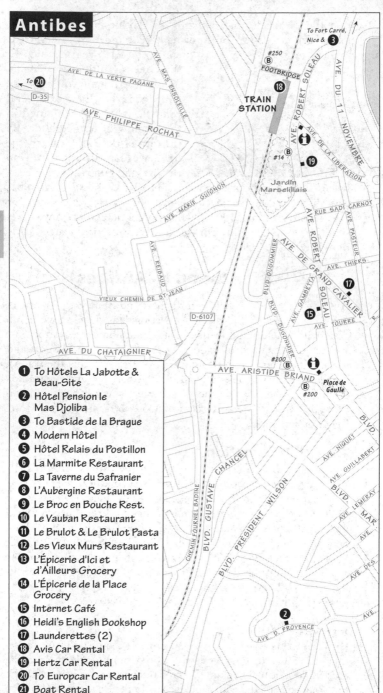

Antibes

To Fort Carré, Nice & **3**

#250 **B**
FOOTBRIDGE

18

TRAIN STATION

To **20**

D-35

AVE. DE LA VERTE PAGANE

AVE. MAS ENSOLEILLE

AVE. PHILIPPE ROCHAT

AVE. MARIE GUIGNON

AVE. REIBAUD

VIEUX CHEMIN DE ST-JEAN

D-6107

AVE. DU CHATAIGNIER

AVE. ROBERT SOLEAU

AVE. DU 11 NOVEMBRE

AVE. DE LA LIBERATION

#14 **B**   **19**

Jardín Marselillais

RUE SADI CARNOT

AVE. PASTEUR

AVE. ROBERT SOLEAU

AVE. DE GRAND CAVALIER

AVE. THIERS

BLVD. DUGOMMIER

BLVD. GAMBETTA

BLVD. DUGOMMIER

17

15

AVE. TOURRE

#200 **B**

AVE. ARISTIDE BRIAND

B #200

Place de Gaulle

BLVD.

AVE. NIQUET

AVE. GUILLABERT

BLVD. MAR

AVE. LEMERAY

CHEMIN FOURNEL BADINE

BLVD. GUSTAVE CHANCEL

BLVD. PRESIDENT WILSON

2

AVE. D. PROVENCE

AVE. DES

THE FRENCH RIVIERA

1 To Hôtels La Jabotte & Beau-Site
2 Hôtel Pension le Mas Djoliba
3 To Bastide de la Brague
4 Modern Hôtel
5 Hôtel Relais du Postillon
6 La Marmite Restaurant
7 La Taverne du Safranier
8 L'Aubergine Restaurant
9 Le Broc en Bouche Rest.
10 Le Vauban Restaurant
11 Le Brulot & Le Brulot Pasta
12 Les Vieux Murs Restaurant
13 L'Épicerie d'Ici et d'Ailleurs Grocery
14 L'Épicerie de la Place Grocery
15 Internet Café
16 Heidi's English Bookshop
17 Launderettes (2)
18 Avis Car Rental
19 Hertz Car Rental
20 To Europcar Car Rental
21 Boat Rental

trail. **Taxis** are usually waiting in front of the train station.

To **walk** to the port, the old town, and the Picasso Museum (15-20-minute walk), cross the street in front of the station, skirting left of the Piranha Café, and follow Avenue de la Libération downhill as it bends left. At the end of the street, head right along the port, and continue until you reach the end of the parking lots, then turn right into the old town.

To walk directly to my hotels and to the main TI (15-minute walk to TI), cross the street to the Piranha Café, turn right, and stay the course for about eight blocks on Avenue Robert Soleau until you reach the fountain-soaked Place Général de Gaulle.

The last train back to Nice leaves at about midnight.

By Bus: The airport bus (#250) drops you behind the train station (see "Helpful Hints," later). Buses from other destinations use the **bus station** at the edge of the old town on Place Guynemer, a block below the main TI on Place Général de Gaulle (info desk open Mon-Sat 7:30-19:00, closed Sun, www.envibus.fr).

By Car: Day-trippers follow signs to *Centre-Ville*, then *Port Vauban*, and park near the old town walls (first 30 minutes free, about €9/half-day). Walk into the old town through the last arch on the right. Street parking is free 12:00-14:00 and 19:00-8:00, and all day Sun.

If you're sleeping here, follow *Centre-Ville* signs, then signs to your hotel, and get advice from your hotelier on where to park. (Most hotels have free parking.) The most appealing hotels in Antibes are easiest by car. Antibes works well for drivers—compared to Nice, parking is easy, it's a breeze to navigate, and it's a convenient springboard for the Inland Riviera. Pay parking is usually available at Antibes' train station, so drivers can ditch their cars here and day-trip from Antibes by train.

Helpful Hints

Monday, Monday: Avoid Antibes on Mondays, when all sights are closed.

Internet Access: Centrally located **l'Outil du Web** is two blocks from the Place Général de Gaulle TI—walk toward the train station (Mon-Fri 9:30-18:30, Sat 9:30-13:00, closed Sun, 11 Avenue Robert Soleau, tel. 04 93 74 11 86).

English Bookstore: Heidi's English Bookshop has a welcoming vibe and a great selection of new and used books, with many guidebooks—including mine (Mon-Fri 10:00-19:00, Sat-Sun 11:00-18:00, 24 Rue Aubernon).

Laundry: There's a launderette above the market hall at 1 Rue de la Pompe (Mon-Fri 8:30-12:00 & 15:00-18:30, closed Sat-Sun), and another at 19 Avenue du Grand Cavalier (open daily).

Grocery Stores: Picnickers will appreciate **L'Épicerie d'Ici et**

d'Ailleurs on Cours Masséna, up the hill as you exit the Marché Provençal (daily until 23:00). **L'Épicerie de la Place** has a smaller selection (daily until 22:00 in summer, until 21:00 off-season, where Rue Sade meets Place Nationale).

Taxi: Call 08 25 56 07 07 or 04 93 67 67 67.

Car Rental: The big-name agencies have offices in Antibes (all close Mon-Sat 12:00-14:00 and all day Sun). The most central are **Avis** (at the train station, tel. 04 93 34 65 15) and **Hertz** (across from the train station at 46 Avenue Robert Soleau, tel. 04 92 91 28 00). **Europcar** is about a mile and a half northwest of town at 106 Route de Grasse (tel. 04 93 34 79 79).

Boat Rental: You can motor your own seven-person yacht thanks to **Antibes Bateaux Services** (€300/half-day, at the small fish market on the port, mobile 06 15 75 44 36, www.antibes -bateaux.com).

Airport Bus: Bus #250 runs from near the train station to Nice's airport (€8, 2/hour, 40 minutes; cross over the tracks on the pedestrian bridge—it's the last shelter to the right, stop from the airport is labeled *Vautrin,* stop going to the airport is labeled *Passerelle*).

Getting Around Antibes

Though most sights and activities are walkable, buses are a great value in Antibes, allowing one hour of travel for €1 (unlimited transfers including round-trip, www.envibus.fr). **Bus #2** provides access to the best beaches, the path to La Phare de la Garoupe, and the Cap d'Antibes trail (all described later). It runs from the bus station down Boulevard Albert 1er, with stops every few blocks (daily 7:00-19:00, every 40 minutes). **Bus #14** is also useful, linking the train station, bus station, old town, and Plage de la Salis. Pick up a schedule for return times for these and other regional buses at the bus station.

A **tourist train** offers circuits around old Antibes, the port, the ramparts, and to Juan-les-Pins (€7, departs from Place de la Poste, mobile 06 03 35 61 35).

Self-Guided Walk

Welcome to Antibes

This 40-minute walk will help you get your bearings, and works well day or night. Begin at the old port (Vieux Port) at the southern end of Avenue de Verdun. Stand at the port, across from the archway with the clock.

Old Port: Locals claim that this is Europe's first and biggest pleasure-boat harbor, with 1,600 stalls. The port was enlarged in the 1970s to accommodate ever-expanding yacht dimensions.

The work was financed by wealthy yacht owners (mostly Saudi Arabian) eager for a place to park their aircraft carriers. That old four-pointed structure crowning the opposite end of the port is **Fort Carré,** which protected Antibes from foreigners for more than 500 years. (For information on visiting the fort, see "Sights in Antibes," later.)

The pathetic remains of a once-hearty **fishing fleet** are moored in front of you. The Mediterranean is pretty much fished out. Most of the seafood you'll eat here comes from fish farms or the Atlantic.

Pass the sorry fleet and duck under the arches to the shell-shaped **Plage de la Gravette,** a normally quiet public beach tucked right in the middle of old Antibes. Wander up the ramp to the round lookout to better appreciate the scale of the ramparts that protected this town. Because Antibes was the last fort before the Italian border, the French king made sure the ramparts were top-notch. Those twin towers crowning the old town are the church's bell tower and the tower topping Château Grimaldi (today's Picasso Museum). Forested Cap d'Antibes is the point of land in the distance to the left.

Backtrack and enter Antibes' **old town** through the arch under the clock. Today, the town is the haunt of a large community of English, Irish, and Aussie boaters who help crew those giant yachts in Antibes' port. (That helps explain the Irish pubs and English bookstores.)

Continue straight and uphill (halfway up on the right, you'll pass Rue Clemenceau, which leads to the heart of the old town), and you'll arrive at Antibes' **market hall.** This hall does double duty—market by day, restaurants by night (a fun place for dinner).

Go left where the market starts (Rue Chessel) and find Antibes' pretty pastel **Church of the Immaculate Conception,** built on the site of a Greek temple (worth a peek inside). A church has stood on this site since the 12th century. This one served as the area's cathedral until the mid-1200s.

Looming above the church on prime real estate is the white-stone **Château Grimaldi,** where you'll find Antibes' prized **Picasso Museum** (described later). This site has been home to the acropolis of the Greek city of Antipolis, a Roman fort, and a medieval bishop's palace (once connected to the cathedral below). Later still, the château was the residence of the Grimaldi family (who still rule Monaco). Its proximity to the cathedral symbolized the sometimes too-cozy relationship between society's two dominant landowning classes: the Church and the nobility. (In 1789, the French Revolution changed all that.)

Find your way to the water and—heading right—follow the ramparts and views to the **History and Archaeology Museum** (described later). From the terrace above the museum, you'll get a clear view of **Cap d'Antibes,** crowned by its lighthouse and studded with mansions (a good place for a hike, described under "Walks and Hikes," later). The Cap was long the refuge of Antibes' rich and famous, and a favorite haunt of F. Scott Fitzgerald and Ernest Hemingway.

After taking a quick spin through the museum, continue hugging the shore past Place Albert 1er until you see the views back to old Antibes. Benches and soft sand await (a few copies of famous artists' paintings of Antibes are placed on bronze displays along the beach walkway). You're on your own from here—energetic walkers can continue to the view from the Phare de la Garoupe (see page 855); others can return to old Antibes and wander around in its peaceful back lanes.

Sights in Antibes

▲▲**Picasso Museum (Musée Picasso)**—Sitting serenely where the old town meets the sea, this compact three-floor museum offers

a manageable collection of Picasso's paintings, sketches, and ceramics.

Cost and Hours: €6, mid-June–mid-Sept Tue-Sun 10:00-18:00, July-Aug until 20:00, mid-Sept–mid-June Tue-Sun 10:00-12:00 & 14:00-18:00, closed Mon year-round, last entry 30 minutes before closing, tel. 04 92 90 54 20, www.antibes-juanlespins.com.

Visiting the Museum: Picasso lived in this castle for four months in 1946, when he cranked out an amazing amount of art. He was elated by the end of World War II, and his works show a celebration of color and a rediscovery of light after France's long nightmare of war. Picasso was also re-energized by his young and lovely companion, Françoise Gilot (with whom he would father two children). The resulting collection, donated by Picasso, put Antibes on the tourist map. You'll see many of his ceramics: plates with faces, bird-shaped vases, woman-shaped bottles, bull-shaped statues, and colorful tiles. But the highlight is his lively, frolicking, and big-breasted *La Joie de Vivre* painting (from 1946). This Greek bacchanal sums up the newfound freedom in a just-liberated France and sets the tone for the rest of the collection. You'll also see the colorless three-paneled *Satyr, Faun and Centaur with Trident* and several ceramic creations (the bull rocks).

As you tour the collection, you'll see both black-and-white and colorful ink sketches that challenge the imagination—these show off Picasso's skill as a cartoonist and caricaturist. Look also for the Basque fishermen and several Cubist-style nudes *(nus couchés)*, one painted on plywood—Picasso loved experimenting with materials and different surfaces (I particularly like the crayon sketches).

History and Archaeology Museum (Musée d'Histoire et d'Archéologie)—More than 2,000 years ago, Antibes was the center of a thriving maritime culture. It was an important Roman city with aqueducts, theaters, baths, and so on. This museum—the only place to get a sense of the city's ancient roots—displays Greek, Roman, and Etruscan odds and ends in two simple halls (no English descriptions, though the small museum brochure offers some background in English). Your visit starts at an 1894 model of Antibes and continues past displays of Roman coins, cups, plates, and scads of amphorae. The lanky lead pipe connected to a center box was used as a bilge pump; nearby is a good display of Roman anchors.

Cost and Hours: €3, mid-June-mid-Sept Tue-Sun 10:00-12:00 & 14:00-18:00, off-season Tue-Sun 10:00-13:00 & 14:00-17:00, closed Mon year-round, on the water between Picasso Museum and Place Albert 1er, tel. 04 93 34 00 39.

Market Hall (Marché Provençal)—The daily market bustles under a 19th-century canopy, with flowers, produce, Provençal products, and beach accessories. The market wears many hats: produce daily until 13:00, handicrafts Thursday through Sunday in the afternoon, and fun outdoor dining in the evenings (market closed Mon Sept-May, behind Picasso Museum on Cours Masséna).

Other Markets and Squares—Antibes' lively antiques/flea market fills Place Nationale and Place Audiberti (next to the port) on Thursdays and Saturdays (7:00-18:00). Its clothing market winds through the streets around the post office (Rue Lacan) on Thursdays (9:00-18:00). Place Général de Gaulle, a pleasing, palm-studded, and fountain-flowing square in Antibes' modern city, is the trendy place to be seen.

Fort Carré—This impressively situated citadel, dating from 1487, was the last fort inside France. It protected Antibes from Nice, which until 1860 was part of Italy. You can tour this unusual four-pointed fort for the fantastic views over Antibes, but there's little to see inside.

Cost and Hours: €3, includes tour in French, Tue-Sun 10:00-16:30, closed Mon, 30-minute walk from Antibes along Avenue du 11 Novembre, easy parking nearby.

▲**Beaches (*Plages*)**—The best beaches stretch between Antibes' port and Cap d'Antibes. The first you'll cross is Plage Publique

(no rentals required). Next are the groomed Plages de la Salis and du Ponteil, with mattress, umbrella, and towel rental. All are busy but manageable in summer and on weekends, with cheap snack stands and exceptional views of the old town. The closest beach to the old town is at the port (Plage de la Gravette), which seems calm in any season.

Walks and Hikes

From Place Albert 1er (where Boulevard Albert 1er meets the beach), you get a good view of Plage de la Salis and Cap d'Antibes. That tower on the hill is your destination for the first walk listed. The longer Cap d'Antibes hike begins on the next beach, just over that hill. The two hikes are easy to combine by bus, bike, or car.

▲▲**Chapelle et Phare de la Garoupe**—The territorial views—best in the morning, skippable if hazy—from this viewpoint more than merit the 20-minute uphill climb from Plage de la Salis (a few blocks after Maupassant Apartments, where the road curves left, follow signs and the rough, cobbled Chemin du Calvaire up to lighthouse tower). An orientation table explains that you can see from Nice to Cannes and up to the Alps.

Getting There: Take bus #2 or #14 to the Plage de la Salis stop and find the trail a block ahead. By car or bike, follow signs for *Cap d'Antibes*, then look for *Chapelle et Phare de la Garoupe* signs.

▲**Cap d'Antibes Hike (Sentier Touristique Piétonnier de Tirepoil)**—At the end of the mattress-ridden Plage de la Garoupe

(over the hill from Phare de la Garoupe lighthouse) lies a terrific trail around the tip of Cap d'Antibes. The beautiful path undulates above a splintered coastline splashed by turquoise water and peppered with exclusive mansions. You'll walk for two miles, then head inland along small streets, ending at the recommended Hôtel Beau-Site (and bus stop). You can walk as far as you'd like and then double back, or do the whole loop (allow 2.5 hours at most, use the TI's Antibes map). Bring good shoes, as the walkway is uneven and slippery in places. Sundays are busiest.

Getting There: Take bus #2 (catch it at the bus station, along Boulevard Albert 1er, or at Plage de la Salis) for about 15 minutes to the La Fontaine stop at Hôtel Beau-Site (return stop is 50 yards away on opposite side, get return times at station). Walk 10 minutes down to Plage de la Garoupe and start from there. By car or bike, follow signs to *Cap d'Antibes*, then to *Plage de la Garoupe*, and park there. The trail begins at the far-right end of Plage de la Garoupe.

Near Antibes

Juan-les-Pins—The low-rise town of Juan-les-Pins, sprawling across the Cap d'Antibes isthmus from Antibes, is where the action is...after hours. It's a modern waterfront resort with good beaches, plenty of lively bars and restaurants, and a popular jazz festival in July. The town is also famous for its clothing boutiques that stay open until midnight in high season (people are too busy getting tan to shop at normal hours). As locals say, "Party, sleep in, shop late, party more."

Buses, trains, and even a tourist train (see "Getting Around Antibes," earlier) make the 10-minute trip to and from Antibes constantly.

Sleeping in Antibes

(€1 = about $1.30, country code: 33)

My favorite Antibes hotels are best by car or taxi, though walkers and bus users can manage as well. Pickings are slim when it comes to centrally located hotels in this city, where restaurants are a dime a dozen but hotels play hard to get. Air-conditioning is rare.

Outside the Town Center

$$ Hôtel la Jabotte****, hidden along an ignored alley a block from the famous beaches and a 15-minute walk from the old town, is a cozy place that defies the rules. Yves, Claude, and dog Tommy have turned a small beach villa into a boutique hotel with personality: The colors are rich, the decor shows a personal touch, and most rooms have individual terraces facing a small, central garden where you'll get to know your neighbor. Rooms are not air-conditioned, but fans are provided (Db-€112-141, Db-suite €198, includes good breakfast and a few parking spots, Wi-Fi, 13 Avenue Max Maurey, take the third right after passing the big Hôtel Josse, tel. 04 93 61 45 89, fax 04 93 61 07 04, www.jabotte.com, info @jabotte.com).

$$ Hôtel Beau-Site*** is my only listing on Cap d'Antibes, a 10-minute drive from the old town. It's a terrific value if you want to get away...but not *too* far away. (But if you don't have a car, you may feel isolated.) This place is a sanctuary, with helpful Nathalie in charge as well as a pool, a comfy patio garden, and free parking. Rooms are spacious and comfortable, and several have balconies (standard Db-€90-100, bigger Db-€100-130, even bigger Db-€135-180, family rooms-€195-240; huge breakfast-€13, continental breakfast-€7.50, air-con, Wi-Fi, may have a few bikes available, 141 Boulevard Kennedy, tel. 04 93 61 53 43, fax 04 93 67 78 16, www.hotelbeausite.net, hbeausit@club-internet.fr). From the hotel, it's a 10-minute walk down to Plage de la Garoupe and a nearby hiking trail (described earlier, under "Walks and Hikes").

$$ Hôtel Pension le Mas Djoliba*** is a fair splurge that's better for drivers but also workable for walkers (10-minute walk from Plage de la Salis, 15 minutes to old Antibes, and 30 minutes to the train station). Reserve early for this traditional, bird-chirping, flower-filled manor house where no two rooms are the same. From May to September, they definitely prefer (but won't insist) that you dine here. It's hard to pass up once you see the setting: After a busy day of sightseeing, dinner by the pool is a treat. The cuisine is average but copious. Some rooms are small, but the bigger rooms are well worth the additional cost, and several come with small decks (Sb-€105, Db-€120-182, several good family rooms-€200-280, figure €95-120 per person with breakfast and dinner; air-con, Wi-Fi, cool *boules* court and loaner balls; 29 Avenue de Provence—from Boulevard Albert 1er, look for gray signs as you approach the beach and turn right onto Boulevard Général Maizière, then veer right again up Avenue Gaston Bourgeois; tel. 04 93 34 02 48, fax 04 93 34 05 81, www.hotel-djoliba.com, contact@hotel-djoliba.com).

$ Bastide de la Brague is an easygoing, seven-room bed-and-breakfast hacienda up a dirt road above Marineland (10-minute drive east of Antibes). It's run by a fun-loving family (wife Isabelle, who speaks English, hubby Franck, and Mama). Rooms are quite comfortable, air-conditioned, and affordable; several are made for families. Request the tasty €28 home-cooked dinner (less for kids; adult meal includes apéritif, wine, and coffee) and enjoy a family dining experience (Db-€90-110, Tb/Qb-€112-140, includes breakfast, free Wi-Fi and computer with printer for guests, 55 Avenue No. 6, tel. 04 93 65 73 78, www.bbchambreantibes.com, bastide bb06@gmail.com). Franck is happy to take guests on a private boat tour of the coast (allow €40/person for all afternoon, 4-person minimum). From Antibes, follow signs that read *Nice par Bord de la Mer*, turn left toward Brague and Marineland, then right at the roundabout (toward Groules), then take the first left and follow signs. Antibes bus #10 drops you five minutes away, and the

Biot train station and bus #200 are a 15-minute walk away (ask for details when you book). If arranged in advance, they can pick you up at the train station in Antibes or Biot.

In the Town Center

$ Modern Hôtel**, in the pedestrian zone near the bus station, is a solid value for budget-conscious travelers. The 17 standard-size rooms—each with air-conditioning, bright decor, and Wi-Fi—are simple, spick-and-span, and well-run by Laurence (Db-€85, 1 Rue Fourmillière, tel. 04 92 90 59 05, fax 04 92 90 59 06, www.modernhotel06.com, modern-hotel@wanadoo.fr).

$ Hôtel Relais du Postillon** is a mellow place on a central square above a peaceful café. There are a few cheap true singles and 12 well-designed doubles with small balconies but no air-conditioning (Sb-€57, Db-€80-100, price varies by room size, most have tight bathrooms, Wi-Fi, 8 Rue Championnet, tel. 04 93 34 20 77, fax 04 93 34 61 24, www.relaisdupostillon.com, relais@relaisdupostillon.com).

Eating in Antibes

Antibes is a fun place to dine out. You can eat on a budget, enjoy a good meal at an acceptable price, or join the party just inside the walls on Boulevard d'Aguillon, on Place Nationale, or—my favorite—under the festive Marché Provençal (all are filled with tables and tourists). The options are endless. Take a walk and judge for yourself, and be tempted by these suggestions. Romantics should picnic at the beach (**L'Épicerie d'Ici et d'Ailleurs** is open late; see "Helpful Hints" on page 850). Everyone should stroll along the ramparts after dinner.

La Marmite owner Patrick offers diners an honest, unpretentious budget value in old Antibes, with eight tables, charming decor, helpful service, and delicious seafood choices but no air-conditioning (*menus* from €16, closed Mon, 20 Rue James Close, tel. 04 93 34 56 79).

La Taverne du Safranier, hiding in a small square a block from the sea, feels right out of a movie. It's a cheery place away from the rest, where you'll order from colorful chalkboard menus and dine under grapevines and happy lights (seafood is their forte, €11 pasta, €14-24 *plats*, €28 three-course *menu*, closed Mon, Place du Safranier, tel. 04 93 34 80 50).

L'Aubergine delivers fine cuisine at fair prices—including good vegetarian options—served with no hurry in an intimate room rich with color. Arrive early to get a table (*menus* from €30, opens at 18:30, closed Wed, open for lunch on Sun only, 7 Rue Sade, tel. 04 93 34 55 93).

Le Broc en Bouche is part cozy wine bar, part bistro, and part collector's shop. Florence serves while her husband cooks; come early to get a seat at this cool little place and enjoy well-prepared dishes from a selective list (€23 *plats*, closed Tue-Wed, 8 Rue des Palmiers, tel. 04 93 34 75 60).

Le Vauban is run by a young couple who draw a local following with their handsome interior, smart tableware, and reliable cuisine at fair prices (€29 three-course *menu*, closed for lunch Mon and Wed, closed all day Tue, opposite 4 Rue Thuret, tel. 04 93 34 33 05).

Le Brulot is an Antibes institution with two restaurants—Le Brulot and Le Brulot Pasta—that sit almost side-by-side a short block below Marché Provençal on Rue Frédéric Isnard. Join Antibes residents at the very popular **Le Brulot,** known for its Provençal cuisine and meats cooked on an open fire. It's a small place, overflowing onto the street, with a few outside tables and a dining room below. Try the aioli (*menus* from €19, closed Sun, at #2, tel. 04 93 34 17 76). **Le Brulot Pasta** is family-friendly, with excellent pizza (the €11 *printanière* is tasty and huge) and big portions of pasta, served in air-conditioned comfort under stone arches (daily, at #3, tel. 04 93 34 19 19).

Les Vieux Murs is a romantic splurge with a candlelit, red-toned interior overlooking the sea. The outside tables are worth booking ahead—but pass on the upstairs room (€44 dinner *menu*, €30 lunch *menu*, closed Mon, also closed Sun evening off-season, valet parking available, along ramparts beyond Picasso Museum at 25 Promenade de l'Amiral de Grasse, tel. 04 93 34 06 73).

Antibes Connections

From Antibes by Train: TGV and local trains serve Antibes' little station. Trains go to **Cannes** (2/hour, 15 minutes), **Nice** (2/hour, 15-30 minutes), **Grasse** (1/hour, 40 minutes), **Villefranche-sur-Mer** (2/hour, 40 minutes), **Monaco** (2/hour, 50 minutes), and **Marseille** (16/day, 2.5 hours).

By Bus: Handy bus #200 ties everything together, but runs at a snail's pace when traffic is bad (Mon-Sat 4/hour, Sun 2-3/hour, any ride costs €1). This bus goes west to **Cannes** (35 minutes) and east to **Nice** (1-1.5 hours). Bus #250 links to **Nice Airport** (2/hour, 40 minutes, €8).

Inland Riviera

For a verdant, rocky, fresh escape from the beaches, head inland and upward. Some of France's most perfectly perched hill towns and splendid scenery hang, overlooked, in this region that's more famous for beaches and bikinis. Driving is the easiest way to get around, though the bus gets you to many of the places described. Vence and St-Paul-de-Vence are well-served by bus from Nice every 30-45 minutes (see "Nice Connections," page 813).

Vence

Vence is a well-discovered yet appealing town set high above the Riviera. While growth has sprawled beyond Vence's old walls, and cars jam its roundabouts, the mountains are front and center and the breeze is fresh. Vence bubbles with workaday life and ample tourist activity in the day but is quiet at night, with few visitors and cooler temperatures than along the coast. Vence makes a handy base for travelers wanting the best of both worlds: a hill-town refuge near the sea.

Orientation to Vence

Tourist Information

Vence's fully loaded and eager-to-help TI faces the main square at 8 Place du Grand Jardin, across from the tiny merry-go-round. They have bus schedules, brochures on the cathedral, and a city map with a well-devised self-guided walking tour (25 stops, incorporates informative wall plaques). They also publish a list of Vence art galleries, with English descriptions of the collections. To properly engage you in French culture, the TI has information on French-language classes and—even better—*pétanque* instructions with *boules* to rent for €3 per person (TI open July-Aug Mon-Sat 9:00-19:00, Sun 10:00-18:00; Sept-June Mon-Sat 9:00-18:00 but 10:00-17:00 in winter, Sun 10:00-17:00; tel. 04 93 58 06 38, www.ville-vence.fr).

Market day in the *cité historique* (old town) is on Friday mornings on Place Clemenceau. There's a big all-day antiques market on Place du Grand Jardin every Wednesday.

Arrival in Vence

By Bus: Buses #94 and #400 (from Nice and Cagnes-sur-Mer) drop you at the bus stop labeled *l'Ara*, which is on a roundabout at Place Maréchal Juin. It's a 10-minute walk to the town center along Avenue Henri Isnard or Avenue de la Résistance.

By Car: Follow signs to *cité historique,* and park where you can. Signs for parking are not well-marked, so keep your eyes peeled and be patient (you might only see a faded white *P* on the pavement). A central pay lot is under Place du Grand Jardin, across from the TI.

Sights in Vence

Explore the narrow lanes of the old town using the TI's worthwhile self-guided tour map. Connect the picturesque streets, enjoy a drink on a quiet square, inspect an art gallery, and find the small 11th-century cathedral with its colorful Chagall mosaic of Moses. If you're here later in the day, enjoy the *boules* action across from the TI (rent a set from the TI and join in).

Château de Villeneuve—This 17th-century mansion, adjoining an imposing 12th-century watchtower, bills itself as "one of the Riviera's high temples of modern art," with a rotating collection. Check with the TI to see what's playing in the temple.

　Cost and Hours: €5, Tue-Sun 10:00-12:30 & 14:00-18:00, closed Mon, tel. 04 93 58 15 78.

▲**Chapel of the Rosary (Chapelle du Rosaire)**—The chapel, a short drive or 20-minute walk from town, was designed by an

elderly and ailing Henri Matisse as thanks to the Dominican sister who had taken care of him (he was 81 when the chapel was completed). The modest chapel is a simple collection of white walls laced with yellow, green, and blue stained-glass windows and charcoal black-on-white tile sketches. The sunlight filters through the glass and does a cheery dance across the sketches. While the chapel is the ultimate pilgrimage for serious Matisse fans, the experience may underwhelm others. (If you've visited the Matisse Museum

in Nice, you'll remember that he was the master of leaving things out.) Decide for yourself whether Matisse met the goal he set himself: "Creating a religious space in an enclosed area of reduced proportions and to give it, solely by the play of colors and lines, the dimension of infinity."

　Cost and Hours: €4, Mon, Wed, and Sat 14:00-17:30, Tue and Thu 10:00-11:30 & 14:00-17:30, Sun only open for Mass at 10:00 followed by tour of chapel, closed Fri and mid-Nov-mid-Dec, 466 Avenue Henri Matisse, tel. 04 93 58 03 26, http://pagesperso-orange.fr/maison.lacordaire.

Getting There: It's about a 20-minute walk from the TI. After turning right out of the TI, take your first right and then a quick left to get onto Avenue Henri Isnard. Take this street all the way to the traffic circle (notice the colorful tiled roof of the Pénitents Blancs Chapel to your left). At the intersection, turn right across the one-lane bridge on Avenue Henri Matisse, following signs to *St-Jeannet.*

Eating in Vence

Tempting outdoor eateries litter the old town; they all look good to me. Lights embedded in the old-town cobbles illuminate the way after dark.

On Place Clemenceau: These two restaurants serve tasty Provençal cuisine a few doors apart on the charming Place Clemenceau: **La Cassolette,** at #10, is an intimate place with reasonable prices and a romantic terrace across from the floodlit church (€25-38 *menus,* €14-17 *plats,* closed Tue-Wed, tel. 04 93 58 84 15). **Les Agapes,** at #4, offers limited outdoor seating, a lovely upstairs dining room, and a terrific selection that stays fresh with each season (€27 and €35 *menus,* closed Mon year-round, also closed Sun Oct-May, tel. 04 93 58 50 64).

Nearby: At **La Peyra Brasserie,** enjoy a relaxed dinner salad or pasta dish outdoors to the sound of the town's main fountain (€16-20 *plats,* daily, 13 Place du Peyra, tel. 04 93 58 67 63).

Les Bacchanales and its talented young chef Christophe Dufau will treat you to an unforgettable €60 *menu* that showcases why he recently received a Michelin star (closed Tue-Wed, 100 yards before the Chapel of the Rosary, tel. 04 93 24 19 19).

Near Vence

St-Paul-de-Vence

The most famous of Riviera hill towns is also the most-visited village in France. And it feels that way—like an overrun and over-restored artist-shopping-mall. Its attraction is understandable, as every cobble and flower seems *just so,* and the setting is memorable. Avoid visiting between 11:00 and 18:00, particularly on weekends. Arriving early makes it easier to park near the village (cars are not allowed inside

St-Paul). Consider skipping breakfast at your hotel and instead eating at the local hangout, **Café de la Place,** where you can watch as waves of tourists crash into town.

The helpful **TI,** just through the gate into the old city on Rue Grande, has maps with minimal explanations of key buildings (daily 10:00-18:00, until 19:00 June-Sept). The TI offers five different themed walking tours with English translations, including tours focused on history, art, and *pétanque*. Call or email in advance to reserve (€5, tel. 04 93 32 86 95, www.saint-pauldevence .com, tourisme@saint-pauldevence.com). If the traffic-free lane leading to the old city is jammed, walk along the road that veers up and left just after Café de la Place, and enter the town through its side door. Meander deep into St-Paul-de-Vence's quieter streets to find panoramic views. See if you can locate the hill town of Vence at the foot of an impressive mountain.

▲**Fondation Maeght**—This inviting, pricey, and far-out private museum is situated a steep walk or short drive above St-Paul-

de-Vence. Fondation Maeght (fohn-dah-shown mahg) offers an excellent introduction to modern Mediterranean art by gathering many of the Riviera's most famous artists under one roof. The founder, Aimé Maeght, long envisioned the perfect exhibition space for the artists he supported and befriended as an art dealer. He purchased this arid hilltop, planted more than 35,000 plants, and hired an architect (José Luis Sert) with the same vision.

A sweeping lawn laced with amusing sculptures and bending pine trees greets visitors. On the right, a chapel designed by Georges Braque—in memory of the Maeghts' young son, who died of leukemia—features a moving purple stained-glass work over the altar. The unusual museum building is purposefully low-profile, to let its world-class modern-art collection take center stage. Works by Fernand Léger, Joan Miró, Alexander Calder, Georges Braque, and Marc Chagall are thoughtfully arranged in well-lit rooms. The backyard of the museum has views, a Gaudí-esque sculpture labyrinth by Miró, and a courtyard filled with the wispy works of Alberto Giacometti. The only permanent collection in the museum consists of the sculptures, though the museum tries to keep a good selection of paintings by the famous artists here year-round (see "The Riviera's Art Scene" on page 773). There's also a great gift shop and cafeteria.

Cost and Hours: €14, €5 to take photos, daily July-Sept 10:00-19:00, April-June 10:00-18:00, Oct-March 10:00-13:00 &

14:00-18:00, tel. 04 93 32 81 63, www.fondation-maeght.com.

Getting There: The museum is a steeply uphill but doable 20-minute walk from St-Paul-de-Vence and the bus stop. Blue signs indicate the way (parking is usually available at the top).

La Route Napoléon: North to the Alps

After getting bored in his toy Elba empire, Napoleon gathered his entourage, landed on the Riviera, bared his breast, and told his fellow Frenchmen, "Strike me down or follow me." France followed. But just in case, he took the high road, returning to Paris along the route known today as La Route Napoléon. (Waterloo followed shortly afterward.)

By Car: The route between the Riviera and the Alps is beautiful (from south to north, follow signs: *Digne, Sisteron,* and *Grenoble*). An assortment of pleasant villages with inexpensive hotels lies along this route, making an overnight easy. Little Entrevaux feels forgotten and still stuck in its medieval shell. Cross the bridge, meet someone friendly, and consider the steep hike up to the citadel (€3, TI tel. 04 93 05 46 73). Sisteron's Romanesque church and view from the citadel above make this town worth a quick leg-stretch.

By Narrow-Gauge Train (Chemins de Fer de Provence): Leave the tourists behind and take the scenic train that runs between Nice and Digne through canyons, along whitewater rivers, and through many tempting villages (Nice to Digne-les-Bains: €19, 25 percent discount with railpass, 4/day, 3.5 hours; departs Nice from Chemins de Fer de Provence Station—about 10 blocks behind the main train station, two blocks from the Libération tram stop, 4 Rue Alfred Binet; tel. 04 97 03 80 80, www.train provence.com). Ongoing track work may affect the schedule; be sure to double-check all departures, arrivals, and connections.

Start with an early-morning departure (look for an 8:30 train) and go as far as you want. Little **Entrevaux** is a good destination that feels forgotten and still stuck in its medieval shell (€10, 1.5 scenic hours from Nice). Climb high to the citadel for great views and appreciate the unspoiled character of the town. The train ends in **Digne-les-Bains** (a.k.a. simply Digne), where you can catch a bus (covered by railpasses) to other destinations such as Aix-en-Provence (4/day, 2 hours). Mainline rail service to Digne was recently eliminated, leaving travelers with few options other than limited bus connections. Most return to Nice, making a round-trip on the narrow-gauge train.

Sleeping along La Route Napoléon: To do the entire trip from Nice to Annecy in one day, you must leave Nice no later than 9:00, but I'd rather spend a night in one of the tiny villages en route. **$ Hôtel Beauséjour*** in little Annot, about two hours from Nice, makes a fun and reasonable getaway (Db-€55-70, Tb-€80, tel. 04 92 83 21 08, www.hotel-beausejour-annot.com). Farther along, in remote Clelles, you'll find **$ Hôtel Ferrat****, a basic family-run mountain hacienda at the base of Mont Aiguille, with a swimming pool and a good restaurant (room with half pension-€58-69 per person, tel. 04 76 34 42 70, fax 04 76 34 47 47, www.hotel-ferrat.fr, hotel.ferrat@wanadoo.fr).

THE FRENCH ALPS

Annecy • Chamonix

The Savoie region grows Europe's highest mountains and is the top floor of the French Alps (the lower Alpes-Dauphiné lie to the south). More than just a pretty-peaked face, stubborn Savoie maintained its independence from France until 1860, when mountains became targets, rather than obstacles, for travelers. Savoie's borders once extended south to the Riviera and far west across the Rhône River Valley. Home to skier Jean-Claude Killy and the first winter Olympics (1924, in Chamonix), today's Savoie is France's mountain-sports capital, featuring 15,771-foot Mont Blanc as its centerpiece. With wood chalets overflowing with geraniums and cheese fondue in every restaurant, Savoie feels more Swiss than French.

The scenery is drop-dead spectacular. Serenely self-confident Annecy is a postcard-perfect blend of natural and man-made beauty. In Chamonix, it's just you and Madame Nature—there's not a museum or important building in sight. If the weather's right, take Europe's ultimate cable-car ride to the 12,600-foot Aiguille du Midi in Chamonix.

Planning Your Time

Lakefront Annecy has boats, bikes, and hikes with mountain views for all tastes and abilities. Its trademark arcaded walking streets and good transportation connections (most trains to Chamonix pass through Annecy) make it a convenient stopover, but if you're

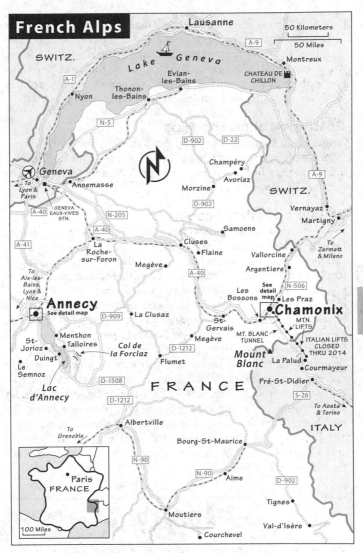

French Alps

SWITZ.

Lake Geneva

Lausanne

A-9

50 Kilometers

50 Miles

Montreux

CHATEAU DE
CHILLON

Evian-
les-Bains

A-1

Thonon-
les-Bains

Nyon

N-5

D-902   D-22

Champéry

Geneva

Annemasse

To
Lyon &
Paris

GENEVA
EAUX-VIVES
STN.

A-40

N-205

A-40

A-41

La
Roche-
sur-Foron

To
Aix-les-
Bains,
Lyon &
Nice

Morzine

Avoriaz

SWITZ.

Vernayaz

Martigny

Samoens

Cluses

Flaine

Megève

A-40

Vallorcine

Argentiere

To
Zermatt
& Milano

N-506

Les
Bossons

See
detail
map

Les Praz

Chamonix

MTN.
LIFTS

Annecy

See detail map

D-909   La Clusaz

St-
Gervais

Megève

ITALIAN LIFTS
CLOSED
THRU 2014

Menthon
Talloires

St-
Jorioz

Duingt

Col de
la Forclaz

D-1212

Flumet

*Mount
Blanc*

MT. BLANC
TUNNEL

La Palud

Courmayeur

Le
Semnoz

*Lac
d'Annecy*

D-1508

Pré-St-Didier

S-26

D-1212

F R A N C E

To Aosta
& Torino

ITALY

To
Grenoble

Albertville

Bourg-St-Maurice

N-90

Paris
FRANCE

N-90   Aime

D-902

Tignes

100 Miles

Moutiers

Courchevel

Val-d'Isère

pressed for time and antsy for Alps, park your sled in Chamonix. There you can skip along alpine ridges, glide over mountain meadows, zip down the mountain on a luge (wheeled bobsled), or meander along riverside paths on a mountain bike. Plan a minimum of two nights and one day in Chamonix, and try to work in an additional night in Annecy. Because weather is everything in this area, get the forecast by calling Chamonix's TI or checking online. If it looks good, make haste to Chamonix; if it's gloomy, Annecy offers more distraction. Both towns are mobbed with tourists in summer.

(If you're driving from here to the Riviera, see tips in "La Route Napoléon: North to the Alps," at the end of the previous chapter.)

The Alps have twin peaks: the summer and winter seasons, when hotels and trails or slopes are slammed. June and November are dead-quiet in Chamonix (many hotels and restaurants close) as locals recover from one high season and prepare for the next.

Getting Around the Alps

Annecy and Chamonix are well-connected by trains. Buses run from Chamonix to nearby villages, and the Aiguille du Midi lift takes travelers from Chamonix up, up, up and over to Europe's most scenic border crossing.

Savoie's Cuisine Scene

Savoie cuisine is mountain-hearty. Its Swiss-similar specialties include *fondue savoyarde* (melted Beaufort and Comté cheeses and local white wine, sometimes with a dash of Cognac), raclette (chunks of semi-melted cheese served with potatoes, pickles, sausage, and bread), *tartiflettes* (hearty scalloped potatoes with melted cheese), *poulet de Bresse* (the best chicken in France), Morteau (smoked pork sausage), *gratin savoyard* (a potato dish with cream, cheese, and garlic), and fresh fish. Local cheeses are Morbier (look for a charcoal streak down the middle), Comté (like Gruyère), Beaufort (aged for two years, hard and strong), Reblochon (mild and creamy), and Tomme de Savoie (mild and semi-hard). Evian water comes from Savoie, as does Chartreuse liqueur. Apremont and Crépy are two of the area's surprisingly good white wines. The local beer, Baton de Feu, is more robust than other French beers.

Remember, restaurants serve only during lunch (11:30-14:00) and dinner (19:00-21:00, later in bigger cities); some cafés serve food throughout the day.

Annecy

There's something for everyone in this lakefront city that knows how to be popular: mountain views, flowery lanes, romantic canals, a hovering château, and swimming in—or boating on, or biking around—the translucent lake. Sophisticated yet outdoors-oriented and bike-crazy, Annecy (ahn-see) is France's answer to

Switzerland's Luzern, and, though you may not have glaciers knocking at your door as in nearby Chamonix, the distant peaks paint a darn pretty picture with Annecy's lakefront setting. Annecy has a few museums, but none worth your time: You're here for the stunning setting and outdoor activities and sights. Annecy is also fun during the winter holidays, as Christmas markets and festive decorations animate the city throughout December.

Orientation to Annecy

Modern Annecy (pop. 50,000) sprawls for miles, but we're interested only in its compact old town, hunkered down on the northwest corner of the lake. The old town is split by the Thiou River and bounded by the château to the south, the TI and Rue Royale to the north, Rue de la Gare to the west, and the lake to the east.

Tourist Information

The TI is a few blocks from the old town, across from the big grass field, inside the brown-and-glass Bonlieu shopping center (mid-May-mid-Sept daily 9:00-18:30 except closed Sun 12:00-14:00; mid-Sept-mid-May Mon-Sat 9:00-12:30 & 13:45-18:30, Sun 10:00-13:00 except closed Sun mid-Nov-March; 1 Rue Jean Jaurès, tel. 04 50 45 00 33, www.lac-annecy.com). Get a city map, the *Town Walks* walking-tour brochure (describes four mildly interesting walks), the map of the lake showing the bike trail, and, if you're staying a few days, the helpful *Annecy Guide,* with everything a traveler needs to know. Ask about walking tours in English (€6, July-Aug only, normally Tue and Fri at 16:00). You'll also find TIs in most villages on the lake.

Arrival in Annecy

By Train: To reach the old town and TI, leave the station, veer left at street level, and cross the big road to the pinkish Hôtel des Alpes. Continue a few blocks down Rue de la Poste, then turn left on Rue Royale for the TI and some hotels, or continue straight to more recommended hotels. There is no baggage storage in Annecy, but day-trippers who rent bikes can leave their bags at the Roul' ma Poule bike-rental shop while they ride (see listing under "Helpful Hints," later).

By Car: Annecy is a traffic mess; in high season (July-Aug), try to arrive very early, during lunch, or late. Avoid most of the snarls by taking the Annecy Centre exit (#16) from the autoroute and following *Annecy/Albertville* signs. Upon entering Annecy, follow signs to *Le Lac,* and when you reach the lake, turn left at the roundabout for the city center. (Don't follow signs for *Annecy-le-Vieux,* which is another town entirely.)

Annecy

THE FRENCH ALPS

P
Carnot

AVE. DE BROGNY

19

TRAIN
STATION

Square
Verdun

RUE SOMMEILLER

RUE DE LA POSTE

5

RUE DE LANNOY

RUE VAUGELAS

RUE CARNOT

RUE PRESIDENT FAVRE

R. JEAN JAURES

i

Place de
la Libération

RUE DU PAQUIER

R. DES GLIERES

R. DE LA GARE

POST

RUE ROYALE

16

6

14

WC

PLAY
AREA
Place
Notre-Dame

NOTRE
DAME

10

15

1

RUE DU LAC

RUE JOSEPH BLANC

QUAI EUSTACHE

AVE.
CHAMBERY
← To A-41
Autoroute

RUE DE LA REPUBLIQUE

Q. CORDELIERS

O L D

R. FILATERIE

PROMENADE

LOUIS LACHENAL

Thiou River

4

RUE JEAN-JACQUES ROUSSEAU

QUAI DE L'EVECHE

R. GRENETTE

12

QUAI DE L'ISLE

21

3

RUE STE. CLAIRE

T O W N

LEVEC

11

MORENS

R. PERRIERE

2

9

18

FBG DE NEMOURS

8

7

RAMPE DU CHATEAU

CHATEAU

P
du Château

CHEMIN DE LA TOUR

AVE. DE LOVERCHY

FAUB. BALMETTES

100 Meters
100 Yards

Refer to the map of Annecy in this chapter to find these
pay parking lots: You can park right on the lake with the buses
opposite the boat dock at Parking Stade Nautique (few spaces for
cars, but this might be your lucky day), or follow signs to the big
underground Parking du Château (under the Hôpital-Clinique),
where you should find a spot. There are also handy lots near the
train station. If you're staying at a hotel in town, you can park
overnight for free at a public lot—but only if you ask at your
hotel. If you're staying at the recommended Hôtel du Château or
Maison d'Hôtes Les Jardins du Château, see my parking tips on
pages 876 and 877.

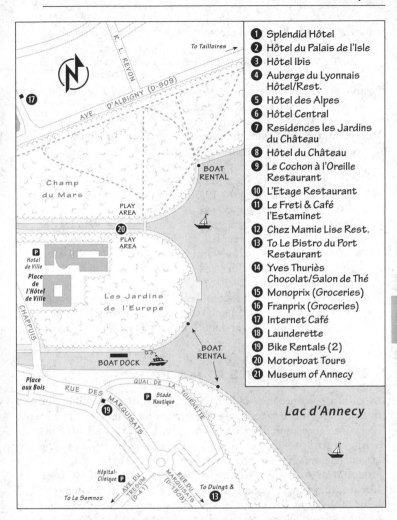

1. Splendid Hôtel
2. Hôtel du Palais de l'Isle
3. Hôtel Ibis
4. Auberge du Lyonnais Hôtel/Rest.
5. Hôtel des Alpes
6. Hôtel Central
7. Residences les Jardins du Château
8. Hôtel du Château
9. Le Cochon à l'Oreille Restaurant
10. L'Etage Restaurant
11. Le Freti & Café l'Estaminet
12. Chez Mamie Lise Rest.
13. To Le Bistro du Port Restaurant
14. Yves Thuriès Chocolat/Salon de Thé
15. Monoprix (Groceries)
16. Franprix (Groceries)
17. Internet Café
18. Launderette
19. Bike Rentals (2)
20. Motorboat Tours
21. Museum of Annecy

THE FRENCH ALPS

Helpful Hints

Market Days: A thriving outdoor food market occupies much of the old town center on Tuesday, Friday, and Sunday mornings until about 12:30. The biggest market in Annecy is on Saturday, but it's less central (food, clothes, and crafts; until 12:30, around Boulevard Taine—several blocks behind the TI).

Supermarkets: The **Monoprix** is at the corner of Rue du Lac and Rue Notre-Dame (Mon-Sat 8:30-19:50, closed Sun, supermarket upstairs). A smaller **Franprix** is on Rue de l'Annexion just off Rue Royale (Mon-Sat 8:00-20:30, Sun 9:00-13:00).

Internet Access: Planete Telcom is near the TI with long hours, lots of services (including fax), and helpful staff (Mon-Sat 10:00-19:00, Sun 14:30-19:00, 4 Rue Jean Jaurès, tel. 04 50 33 92 60).

Laundry: The launderette is at the western edge of the old town near where Rue de la Gare meets Rue Ste. Claire (daily 7:00-21:00, 6 Rue de la Gare).

Bike Rental: Across from the lake steamers, **Roul' ma Poule** rents all kinds of bikes—standard, tandem, and electric—and is near the lakefront bike path (€12/half-day, €18/day, includes helmet and basket, leave ID as deposit, mid-May-mid-Oct daily 9:00-12:30 & 14:00-19:00, closed mid-Oct-mid-May, 4 Rue Marquisats, tel. & fax 04 50 27 86 83, www.annecy-location-velo.com). You can also rent a bike at **Véloncey** at the train station (€15/day; less for students, seniors, and train travelers; includes helmet and basket, requires credit-card deposit, Tue 13:30-18:30, Wed-Sat 9:30-12:00 & 13:30-18:30, closed Sun-Mon, tel. 04 50 51 38 90).

Bad Weather: If it's raining, consider a day trip to Lyon (7 trains/day, 2 hours; see Lyon chapter). The last train back to Annecy usually leaves Lyon at about 20:00, allowing a full day in the big city.

Sights in Annecy

Strolling—Most of the old city is wonderfully traffic-free. The river, canals, and arcaded streets are made for ambling. The TI's *Town Walks* brochure describes Annecy with basic historical information. Get lost—the water is your boundary. Surrender to the luscious ice-cream shops and waterfront cafés.

Museum of Annecy (Palais de l'Isle)—This serenely situated 13th-century building cuts like the prow of a ship through the heart of the Thiou River. Once a prison, it held French Resistance fighters during World War II. Today it's a boring museum that holds rotating exhibits and a small section on local architecture.

Cost and Hours: €3.50, €6.60 combo-ticket includes Château Museum, June-Sept Wed-Mon 10:30-18:00, Oct-May Wed-Mon 10:00-12:00 & 14:00-17:00, closed Tue year-round, free English leaflet.

Château Museum (Musée-Château d'Annecy)—The castle was built in the late 1100s by aristocrats from nearby Geneva, and cuts an impressive figure as it hangs above the lake in the old city. But inside the château has little to offer. Many rooms house modern-art collections that rotate regularly, with a few rooms devoted to local folklore, anthropology, and natural history. Skip it.

Cost and Hours: €5, €6.60 combo-ticket includes Museum of

Annecy, same hours as Museum of Annecy.

▲**Boating**—This is one of Europe's cleanest, clearest lakes, and the water is warmer than you'd think (average summer water tem-

perature is 72 degrees Fahrenheit). To tool around the lake, rent a paddleboat (*pédalos,* some equipped with a slide, about €10/30 minutes, €15/hour) or a motorboat (*hors-bord,* no license needed; 2 people-about €30/30 minutes, €48/hour; each extra person-about €1, up to 7 people, several companies all have the same rates). Traditional open-air wood-hulled motorboats offer 35-minute loops around the lake (€10/person, up to about 10 people per boat).

Compagnie des Bateaux du Lac d'Annecy offers worthwhile lake cruises. The one-hour cruise makes no stops but has frequent departures (€13.10, 8-10/day May-Aug, 6-8/day April and Sept). The two-hour cruises, called Circuit Omnibus, make stops at several villages on a clockwise loop around the lake (€16.80 for the entire loop, 3-5/day); these are ideal for hikers and cyclists (see next two listings). The elaborate dinner and dancing cruises (€55-85) look like fun. Get schedules and prices for all boat trips at the TI or on the lake behind Hôtel de Ville (tel. 04 50 51 08 40, www .annecy-croisieres.com).

Scenic Walks—Get details on these walks from the TI. For a picturesque workout and a rewarding full-day excursion, take the 10:30 Omnibus boat to Menthon-St-Bernard (€5.60), hike 2.5 hours to lovely Talloires, then catch the 15:00 boat back to Annecy (€9.90). From the boat dock in Menthon-St-Bernard, walk to the right along the shore toward the large palace, and follow the signposts for *Roc de Chère.* The path leads up and over the Roc, passing the Golf de Talloires. The last stretch into Talloires is a steep drop—wear good shoes. Cross Talloires to the port and beach (swim and lunch there), then catch the boat back to Annecy (the last boat for Annecy from Talloires leaves at 17:30).

For an easy lakeside amble, take the Omnibus boat to Duingt (€9.50, 1.25 hours), then take the one-hour walk to St-Jorioz and return by boat to Annecy from there. The walk is mostly along a lakefront path called the *sentier Roselières.* To reach the path from Duingt's boat dock, follow the *piste cyclable* (bike path) to the right from the dock through the village, cross the main road, and find the foot trail near the lake. In St-Jorioz, catch the next boat back to Annecy (€5.90, 30 minutes). The 14:15 departure from Annecy leaves you in Duingt at 15:30, with 2.75 hours before the 18:15 boat from St-Jorioz back to Annecy (the first boat from Annecy gives you 4 hours for your walk to St-Jorioz).

▲▲**Biking**—Annecy was made for biking; it's an ain't-it-great-to-be-alive way to poke around the lake and test waterfront cafés and grassy parks. A popular bike trail runs along the southwest side of the lake (look for the green bike icon on white signs); it's smart to wear sunglasses and bring water. Even a short ride on the bike path is worth the effort. Ride as far as your legs take you, break for a lakefront café, then return to Annecy (the path is best after the town of Sévrier, where it leaves the roadside).

The small village of Duingt is seven level miles away and makes a terrific destination. Steady pedalers make it in 45 minutes; smell-the-roses cyclists need at least an hour. You can ride to Duingt and take the Omnibus boat back to Annecy (€7.30, 3 departures/day from Duingt; normally at 11:45, 15:30, and 18:00; more in summer, verify at boat dock or TI, bikes allowed).

To get to Duingt, leave Annecy on the main road toward Albertville (D-1508). Don't worry—you'll join the bike trail before long. Once the painted bike lane ends, you'll see a sign for the trail *(piste cyclable)* to the left. Follow it to Duingt (to reach the boat dock, exit the trail just before the tunnel for Duingt, ride down to the main road and turn right, then find the small, green boat-dock shelter just after the castle). The trail beyond Duingt is beautiful. Serious cyclists can make it all the way around the lake in about three hours (no bike path on opposite side of lake, just narrow roads, with one good hill). The bike path leaves the lake at its southern end and continues south for another seven miles, paralleling D-1508.

This route also works well in reverse: Take the Omnibus boat to Duingt and pedal back (turn right when you get off the boat and join the bike trail behind Duingt's tall church).

Driving Around the Lake—The road that links villages along the lake (D-1508) is busy, with little reward for drivers, but it does lead to a scenic route to Chamonix and to fantastic mountaintop views (described next).

Nearby Views—Several routes lead to remarkable views of this beautiful area. Go early for clearest skies, and skip it if it's hazy. For lovely mountain panoramas near Annecy that include Mont Blanc, take the summer-only bus or drive up...and up...and up to **Le Semnoz** (about 5,000 feet). Here you'll find cafés, a summer luge, and easy mountain walks (one leads to a cheese farm). Ligne d'été buses to Le Semnoz leave from the Annecy train station (6/day, 40 minutes, daily July-Aug, Sat-Sun only in June, none Sept-May, details at TI). To drive, follow D-41 from near the Hôpital-Clinique parking lot and allow 25 minutes (see this chapter's map of Annecy).

For drop-dead gorgeous views that take in the entire lake,

drive 18 miles from Annecy (allow 45 minutes one-way) to **Col de la Forclaz** (worth ▲▲ in clear weather). Start by taking D-1508 south along the lake past Duingt. A few miles after leaving the lake, turn left on D-42 (signed *Col de la Forclaz*), then wind your way up a narrow, windy lane for five miles past meadows and lovely scenery to the Col de la Forclaz (3,600 feet). Look out for cyclists on this climb. At the top you'll find a sensational viewpoint, cafés and restaurants, and paragliders galore. Several outfits offer a chance to jump off a cliff and sail over the lake, including the appropriately named Adrenaline Parapente (www.annecy -parapente.com). This trip ties in very well with the scenic route to Chamonix via D-1508.

Sleeping in Annecy

Annecy is popular, particularly on weekends and during the summer. Hotel rates drop from about mid-October through late April and generally increase in summer. Most hotels can help you find free overnight parking (in lots, usually after 19:00 until 9:00 in the morning). Unless otherwise noted, these hotels do not have elevators. For more hotel listings, try the site for Annecy's TI: www .lac-annecy.com.

In the Town Center
This part of town is pedestrian-friendly and comes with some noise.

$$$ **Splendid Hôtel***** makes an impression with its grand acade. This formal business hotel offers every comfort, and sits on

THE FRENCH ALPS

Sleep Code

(€1 = about $1.30, country code: 33)

S = Single, **D** = Double/Twin, **T** = Triple, **Q** = Quad, **b** = bathroom, **s** = shower only, ***** = French hotel rating system (0-5 stars). Unless otherwise noted, credit cards are accepted and English is spoken.

To help you sort easily through these listings, I've divided the accommodations into three categories based on the price for a standard double room with bath:

$$$ **Higher Priced**—Most rooms €100 or more.
$$ **Moderately Priced**—Most rooms between €70-100.
$ **Lower Priced**—Most rooms €70 or less.

Prices can change without notice; verify the hotel's current rates online or by email.

Annecy's busiest street across from the park and the TI. Rooms are handsome and well-appointed (Db-€135-150, suites-€160, extra person-€15, breakfast buffet-€14, air-con, elevator, big beds, Internet access and Wi-Fi, bar, terrace, 4 Quai Eustache Chappuis, tel. 04 50 45 20 00, fax 04 50 45 52 23, www.splendidhotel.fr, info @splendidhotel.fr).

$$$ Hôtel du Palais de l'Isle*** offers a romantic and pricey canalside location in the thick of the old town, and 33 contemporary and well-maintained rooms—several with canal or rooftop views, all with minibars. The wine bar/TV room doubles as a nice lounge (Db-€105-125, magnificent suites-€225-290, breakfast-€13, air-con, elevator, Internet access and Wi-Fi, 13 Rue Perrière, tel. 04 50 45 86 87, fax 04 50 51 87 15, www.palaisannecy.com, palisle @wanadoo.fr).

$$ Hôtel Ibis** is a cheery place and a good option in Annecy, with narrow rooms, a canalside lounge, and easy underground parking. It's well-situated on a modern courtyard on the edge of the old town, a few blocks from the train station (Sb/Db-€100, extra bed-€10, buffet breakfast-€10, air-con, elevator, Internet access and Wi-Fi, 12 Rue de la Gare, tel. 04 50 45 43 21, fax 04 50 52 81 08, www.ibishotel.com, h0538@accor.com).

$$ Auberge du Lyonnais** has 10 good-value, alpine-decorated rooms that play second fiddle to its bustling restaurant (recommended under "Eating in Annecy," later). It's as central as you can get, with adequately comfortable rooms—the rooms on the canal are worth the extra euros (Db-€65, canalside Db-€75, big Tb or Qb with deck over canal-€130, breakfast-€8, 9 Rue de la République, walk through the restaurant to the small reception, tel. 04 50 51 26 10, fax 04 50 51 05 04, www.auberge-du-lyonnais.com).

$$ Hôtel des Alpes**, a top value, has 32 immaculate, comfortable, and attractive rooms at a busy intersection just across from the train station. Rooms on the courtyard are quieter, but those on the street have effective double-pane windows (Sb-€58-65, Db-€70-90, Tb-€85-96, Qb-€98-108, Wi-Fi, 12 Rue de la Poste, tel. 04 50 45 04 56, fax 04 50 45 12 38, www.hotelannecy .com, info@hotelannecy.com).

$ Hôtel Central* is just that. This modest and homey place, behind an ivy-covered courtyard and dirty stairway off a big pedestrian street, makes a good bare-bones budget option (D-€45, Db-€60, Tb-€80, Qb-€100, breakfast-€6, Wi-Fi, 6 bis Rue Royale, tel. 04 50 45 05 37, fax 04 50 51 80 19, www.hotel centralannecy.com, hotelcentralannecy@orange.fr).

At the Foot of the Château

These places are in a quiet area a steep five-minute walk up from the old town on Rampe du Château. Drivers can pull up to the barrier at the Parking du Château, press the little button, and tell whoever answers that you are a hotel guest. They will raise the bar to let you drive in (staffed 24/7).

At **$$ Residences les Jardins du Château,** welcoming Anne-Marie and Jean-Paul have created Annecy's highest urban refuge (near the château entry). Their chalet comes with a small garden and eight modern yet comfy rooms—all with kitchenettes to prepare your own breakfast, and some with views and balconies. Jean-Paul doubles as a mountain guide and offers a wealth of information (Db-€60-120 depending on room size and season, good family rooms, cash only, no refunds, Wi-Fi, bike rental, 1 Place du Château, tel. 04 50 45 72 28, www.jardinduchateau.sitew .com, jardinduchateau@wanadoo.fr).

$$ Hôtel du Château**,** an unpretentious place barely below the château, comes with a view terrace and 15 simple, spotless rooms; about half have views. It's first-come, first-get for the precious few free parking spots (Db-€80, Tb-€90, Qb-€100, continental breakfast-€8, Internet access and Wi-Fi, 16 Rampe du Château, tel. 04 50 45 27 66, fax 04 50 52 75 26, www.annecy -hotel.com, hotelduchateau@noos.fr).

Eating in Annecy

Although the touristy old city is well-stocked with forgettable restaurants, I've found a few worthy places. And though you'll pay more to eat with views of the river or canal, the experience is uniquely Annecy. The ubiquitous and sumptuous *gelati* shops remind you how close Italy is. If it's sunny, assemble a gourmet picnic at the arcaded stores and dine lakeside. Annecy's coolest café tables hang opposite the entrance to the Palais de l'Isle Museum.

Le Cochon à l'Oreille ("The Pig's Ear") is a meat-lover's nirvana. Just off the Thiou canal, it welcomes you with a leafy courtyard and a raucous, higgledy-piggledy interior. Amicable owners "Fred" and Jean speak enough English (and fluent pig) and are serious about their cooking. The accent is on fresh products and meat dishes (particularly ham and pork). Melted cheese is not their thing (€18 *menu* changes weekly, daily for lunch and dinner, Quai du Perrière, tel. 04 50 45 92 51).

L'Etage is a good choice if you can't decide what you want. Regional specialties and a good range of standard brasserie fare are served at fair prices. Dine along the pedestrian street terrace or upstairs under wood beams around a big fireplace (€14 fondue, €18 three-course *menus*, daily, 13 Rue du Paquier, tel. 04 50 51 03 28).

Le Freti, with a lighthearted waitstaff, is the most reliable restaurant for local cuisine I've found in Annecy. It's *the* place to go for mouthwatering fondue, raclette, or anything with cheese.

THE FRENCH ALPS

Each booth comes with its own outlet for melting raclette (€12-14 fondue, good salads and onion soup and cheap wine, daily; walk through door at 12 Rue Ste. Claire, it's upstairs; tel. 04 50 51 29 52).

If Le Freti sounds too cheesy, go next door to **Café l'Estaminet** for some pub grub. You'll get salads, omelets, pasta, mussels, fries, and more for fair prices. A sliver of a backyard deck hangs over the river (daily in summer, closed Sun evening and Mon off-season, 8 Rue Ste. Claire, tel. 04 50 45 88 83).

Chez Mamie Lise is like eating in an alpine folk museum, with stuffed mountain animals, rusted tools, tourists, and knick-knacks everywhere. The cuisine—fondue, raclette, and other cheese dishes—is as alpine as the decor (€23 three-course *menu*, daily, 11 Rue Grenette, tel. 04 50 45 41 18).

Auberge du Lyonnais is a classy, well-respected riverfront eatery that specializes in seafood (indoor and outdoor seating). The outgoing owners love Americans; ask Dominique about his many trips to the States, and about his Ford pickup (€25-44 *menus*, cheaper on weeknights, daily, 9 Rue de la République, tel. 04 50 51 26 10).

Many cafés and restaurants ring Annecy's postcard-perfect lake. If you have a car and want views, prowl the many lakefront villages. **Le Bistro du Port,** a nautical place five minutes from Annecy by car, is beautifully situated at the boat dock at the southern end of Sévrier (daily, Port de Sévrier, tel. 04 50 52 45 00).

Dessert: Wherever you eat, don't miss an ice-cream-licking stroll along the lake after dark. But if it's chocolate you crave, head for **Yves Thuriès Chocolat/Salon de Thé** (closed Sun-Mon, 13 Rue Royale, tel. 04 50 52 28 58).

Annecy Connections

From Annecy by Train to: Chamonix (8/day, 2.5 hours, change in St-Gervais), **Lyon** (7/day, 2 hours, most change in Aix-les-Bains, some by bus), **Beaune** (7/day, 4-6 hours, change in Lyon), **Nice** (8/day, 7-9 hours, at least 3 changes), **Paris'** Gare de Lyon (hourly, 4 hours, many with change in Lyon).

Chamonix

Bullied by snow-dipped peaks, churning with mountain lifts, and littered with hiking trails, the resort of Chamonix (shah-moh-nee) is France's best base for alpine exploration. Officially called Chamonix-Mont Blanc, it's the largest of five villages at the base of Mont Blanc, with about 8,000 residents. Chamonix's purpose in life has always been to accommodate visitors with some of Europe's top alpine thrills—it's a busy place from early July through mid-August

and on winter holidays, but it's plenty peaceful at other times. Appropriately, Chamonix's sister city is Aspen, Colorado.

Planning Your Time

Summers bring huge crowds and long lift lines. You won't regret planning your trip to avoid the summer school break *(vacances scolaires)*, usually early July to late August. Ride the lifts early (crowds and clouds roll in later in the morning) and save your afternoons for lower altitudes.

If you have one sunny day, spend it this way: Start with the Aiguille du Midi lift (go early, reservations possible and recommended July-Aug), take it all the way to Helbronner (linger around the rock needle longer if you can't get to Helbronner), double back to Plan de l'Aiguille, hike to Montenvers and the Mer de Glace (only with good shoes and snow level permitting), explore there, then take the train down. End your day with a well-deserved drink at a view café in Chamonix. If the weather disappoints or the snow line's too low, hike the Petit Balcon Sud or Arve River trails.

Orientation to Chamonix

Eternally white Mont Blanc is Chamonix's southeastern limit; the Aiguilles Rouges mountains form the northwestern border. The frothy Arve River splits linear Chamonix in two. The thriving pedestrian zone, above and west of the river along Rues du Docteur Paccard and Joseph Vallot, is Chamonix's core. The TI is just above the pedestrian zone, and the train station is two long blocks below and east of the river. To get your bearings, head to the TI and find the big photo in front. With Switzerland and Italy as next-door neighbors, this town has always drawn an international crowd. Today about half of its foreign visitors are British—many have stayed and found jobs in hotels and restaurants.

Tourist Information

Visit the TI to prepare your attack. Get the weather forecast, pick up the free town and valley map and the "panorama" map of all the valley lifts, and consider the €4 hiking map called *Carte des Sentiers* (see "Chamonix Area Hikes" on page 892). Ask about hours of lifts and trains (critical), the Multipass for lifts, which is described later, under "Getting Around (and Up and Down) the Valley," biking information, and help with hotel reservations. Their helpful website has updated sightseeing info, weather forecasts, and more (July-Aug daily 9:00-19:00; Sept-June Mon-Sat 9:00-12:30 & 14:00-18:00, Sun 9:00-12:30; hours may vary—call ahead, tel. 04 50 53 00 24, fax 04 50 53 58 90, www.chamonix.com, info@chamonix.com). Pull up a beachy sling chair outside the TI and plan your hike, or check your email using their 24-hour Wi-Fi (free access outside, plus small cubicles inside to hole up in).

Arrival in Chamonix

By Train: Walk straight out of the station (no baggage check or WCs available) and up Avenue Michel Croz (see the "Chamonix Town" map on page 904). In three blocks, you'll reach the town center; turn left at the big clock, then right for the TI.

By Bus: The long-distance bus station is at the train station.

By Car: For most of my recommended hotels and the TI, take the Chamonix Nord turnoff—coming from Annecy, it's the second exit after you pass under the Aiguille du Midi cable car—and follow signs to *Centre-Ville*. Most parking is metered and well-signed, though your hotel can direct you to free parking.

The Mont Blanc tunnel (7.2 miles long, about a 12-minute drive) allows quick access between Chamonix and Italy (one-way-€39, round-trip-€49 with return valid for 1 week, about €400 if you're driving a truck, www.tunnelmb.com).

By Plane: The nearest international airports are in Lyon (linked by 10 trains/day, 4 hours; 3 hours by car) and in Geneva, Switzerland (hourly trains, 3.5-5 hours with two changes; 2 hours by shuttle van or bus—see "Chamonix Connections" on page 909; 1.5 hours by car).

Helpful Hints

Crowd-Beating Tips: In high season, take the first lift to beat the crowds and afternoon clouds. Consider breakfast at *le* top.

Plan Ahead: Snow abounds up high, making the glare unbearable, so bring your sunglasses. Be sure your camera has enough battery power and memory space for those perfect alpine shots.

Chamonix: A Quick History

1786 Jacques Balmat and Michel-Gabriel Paccard are the first to climb Mont Blanc (find the statue in Chamonix's pedestrian zone).

1818 First ascent of Aiguille du Midi.

1860 The Savoie region (including Chamonix) becomes part of France. After a visit by Napoleon III, the trickle of nature-loving visitors to Chamonix turns to a gush.

1901 Train service reaches Chamonix, unleashing its tourist appeal forever.

1908 The cogwheel train to Montenvers is completed.

1924 First Winter Olympics held in Chamonix.

1930 Le Brévent *téléphérique* (gondola lift) opens to tourists.

1955 Aiguille du Midi *téléphérique* opens to tourists.

2013 You visit Chamonix.

For Chamonix's weather, check at your hotel, the TI, or online at www.chamonix.com or www.chamonix-meteo.com. For current lift information and to book the Aiguille du Midi lift, head to the Compagnie du Mont Blanc website (www.compagniedumontblanc.com).

Open-Air Market: Chamonix's market is held Saturdays at Place Mont Blanc (until about 13:00).

Supermarkets: Little **Casino** markets are omnipresent in Chamonix. Supplement your run-of-the-mill groceries with gourmet local specialties from **Le Refuge Payot** (two locations: 166 Rue Joseph Vallot and 255 Rue du Docteur Paccard).

Inexpensive Mountain Gear: The best deals on sunglasses, day-packs, and the like are at **Technique Extrême** (daily 9:00-19:00, 200 Avenue de l'Aiguille du Midi).

Internet Access: The TI has free Wi-Fi and a good list of Internet cafés.

English Books: A small collection is kept at **Maison de la Presse** (101 Rue du Docteur Paccard).

Laundry: A self-service *laverie* is one block up from the Aiguille du Midi lift at 174 Avenue de l'Aiguille du Midi (daily 8:00-22:00, instructions in English).

Taxis: There's usually one at the train station (tel. 04 50 53 13 94 or mobile 06 07 26 36 62).

Car Rental: Europcar, the only game in town, is across from the train station and offers free airport pickup (36 Place de la Gare, tel. 04 50 53 63 40).

Getting Around (and Up and Down) the Valley

Lifts and cogwheel trains are named for their highest destination (for example, Aiguille du Midi, Montenvers, and Le Brévent). More details on individual lifts are described under "Sights in Chamonix," later. You can find current lift information and book the Aiguille du Midi lift on the Compagnie du Mont Blanc website (www.compagniedumontblanc.com).

By Lift: Gondolas *(téléphériques)* climb mountains all along the valley, but the best one—Aiguille du Midi—leaves from Chamonix. Though sightseeing is optimal from the Aiguille du Midi gondola, there are more hiking options from the Le Brévent and La Flégère gondolas.

The lift to Aiguille du Midi is open summer and winter (short closures possible in May, longer closures late Oct-early Dec). Due to ongoing construction, in 2013, the *télécabines* on the Panoramic Mont Blanc lift to Helbronner (atop the Italian border) run only from late June to early September, and even then only in good weather. (The lift on the Italian side of the mountain, from Helbronner down to La Palud, is closed through 2014.) Other area lifts are generally open from January to mid-April and from mid-June to late September. For all lifts, because maintenance closures can occur anytime, it's always smart to verify schedules at the TI.

The **Multipass** ticket option saves time and money for most visitors, particularly if you're spending two or more days in the Chamonix valley. It allows unlimited access to all the lifts and trains (except the Helbronner gondola to Italy—closed through 2014 anyway), and includes all reservation fees (both Aiguille du Midi and Montenvers) and the elevator at the top of Aiguille du Midi. You also get discounts for various activities in Chamonix, such as the Parc de Loisirs des Planards.

Best of all, it allows you to bypass lift-ticket lines after your first purchase. Your pass is a "smart card," valid all day, that allows you to scan your way to the top, letting you ride lifts you'd otherwise skip—hop on a lift just to have a drink from a view café at the top (€53/1 day, €66/2 days, €77/3 days, €92/4 days, €103/5 days, available for up to 15 days; days are consecutive, though you can buy a more expensive pass for nonconsecutive days; kids ages 4-15 pay about 15 percent less, kids under 4 may not be allowed, kids ages 16 and up pay adult fare; www.compagniedumontblanc.com). The one-day price is a good savings if you plan to do the round-trip lift from Chamonix to Aiguille du Midi plus the round-trip train from Chamonix to Montenvers (and not hike between the two).

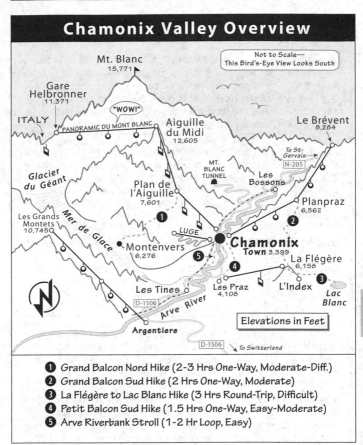

Chamonix Valley Overview

Not to Scale—
This Bird's-Eye View Looks South

Mt. Blanc
15,771

Gare
Helbronner
11,371

ITALY

"WOW!"

PANORAMIC DU MONT BLANC

Aiguille
du Midi
12,605

Le Brévent
8,284

To St-
Gervais
N-205

MT.
BLANC
TUNNEL

Les
Bossons

Glacier
du Géant

Plan de
l'Aiguille
7,601

❶

Planpraz
6,562

❷

Les Grands
Montets
10,745

Mer de Glace

LUGE

Montenvers
6,276

❺

Chamonix
Town 3,399

La Flégère
6,158

❹

Les Tines

D-1506

Arve River

Les Praz
4,108

L'Index

❸

Lac
Blanc

Argentiere

D-1506

To Switzerland

Elevations in Feet

❶ Grand Balcon Nord Hike (2-3 Hrs One-Way, Moderate-Diff.)
❷ Grand Balcon Sud Hike (2 Hrs One-Way, Moderate)
❸ La Flégère to Lac Blanc Hike (3 Hrs Round-Trip, Difficult)
❹ Petit Balcon Sud Hike (1.5 Hrs One-Way, Easy-Moderate)
❺ Arve Riverbank Stroll (1-2 Hr Loop, Easy)

THE FRENCH ALPS

Notice that a two-day pass costs only €13 more than a one-day pass.

Families can benefit from reduced fares by asking for family tickets (2 adults and 2 children ages 15 and under).

By Foot: See "Chamonix Area Hikes" on page 892.

By Bike: The peaceful river valley trail is ideal for bikes (and pedestrians). The TI has a brochure showing bike-rental shops and the best biking routes.

By Bus or Train: One road and one scenic rail line lace together the valley's towns and lifts. To help reduce traffic and pollution, your hotel will give you a free Chamonix Guest Card good for free travel during your stay. The cards are valid on all Chamonix-area buses (except the night bus) and the scenic valley train between Servoz and Vallorcine, and also give small discounts on a handful of area sights. This is a great value for those with time to explore the valley.

Chamonix Activities at a Glance

▲▲▲**Aiguille du Midi Gondola** The valley's most spectacular and popular lift, taking you to magnificent views at 12,600 feet. From here you can ride the cute *télécabines* over the Alps to the Italian border and back (summer only in 2013), take Chamonix's greatest hike to the Mer de Glace (from the halfway-up stop at Plan de l'Aiguille), or just enjoy the views.

▲▲▲**Train to Montenvers** Cogwheel train to the Mer de Glace, an eight-mile-long glacier where you can walk inside the glacier, admire jagged mountain peaks, have lunch with a view (or sleep) at the Montenvers hotel, and hike to the Aiguille du Midi lift (though the hike is best done in the other direction).

▲▲▲**Le Brévent Gondola** Second-most-spectacular lift from Chamonix, allowing access to the mountain range on the opposite side of the valley from Mont Blanc (closed late April-mid-June and Oct-Nov). Get off halfway at the Planpraz station for the Grand Balcon Sud hike to the La Flégère lift, or go all the way to Le Brévent for sky-high views and a restaurant.

▲▲▲**La Flégère Lift** Starting point for hikes to Lac Blanc and to the Grand Balcon Sud trail back to Planpraz (on the Le Brévent gondola). Refuge-Hôtel La Flégère, at the station, offers drinks, snacks, and accommodations, all with a view.

Arve Riverbank Stroll Several trails allow a level walk or bike ride in the woods between Chamonix and Les Praz. See paragliders make dramatic landings and enjoy mountain views outside Chamonix to the sound of the Arve River.

THE FRENCH ALPS

Local buses #1 and #2 run to valley villages (1-2/hour, main stops are 200 yards to the right when you leave the TI—past Hôtel Mont Blanc—look for the bus shelters, and on Rue Joseph Vallot where it crosses Avenue du Mont Blanc). Direction "Le Tour" on bus #1 and "Les Praz/Flégère" on bus #2 takes you toward Les Praz (for Hikes #2 and #3) and Switzerland (see map on page 894).

Le Mulet minibuses circulate around Chamonix village and are lifesavers for pooped hikers; they're especially handy to or from the Aiguille du Midi lift, which is a 15-minute walk from many hotels (free, run every 10 minutes 8:30-18:30).

The train ride toward **Martigny** in Switzerland is gorgeous, and villages such as Les Praz and Tines (10 minutes by bus) offer quiet village escapes from busy Chamonix.

By Excursion Tour: British-run **Chamexcursions** offers trips in English to top area sights, including a half-day tour of Chamonix or the Parc de Merlet animal park, and day trips to Annecy or Geneva (€40/half-day, €50-80/day, cheaper for kids, tel. 04 50 54 73 72, www.chamexcursions.com).

Sights in Chamonix

▲▲▲Aiguille du Midi

This is easily the valley's (and, arguably, Europe's) most spectacular and popular lift. If the weather's clear, the price doesn't matter.

Pile into the *téléphérique* (gondola) and soar to the tip of a rock needle 12,600 feet above sea level (you'll be packed into the gondola like sardines). Chamonix shrinks as trees fly by, soon replaced by whizzing rocks, ice, and snow. Change gondolas at Plan de l'Aiguille to reach the top. No matter how sunny it is, it's cold and the air is thin. People are giddy with delight (those prone to altitude sickness or agoraphobia are less so). Fun things can happen at Aiguille du Midi (ay-gwee doo mee-dee) if you're not too winded to join the locals in the halfway-to-heaven tango.

From the top of the lift station, you have several options. Follow *ascenseur* signs through a tunnel, then ride the elevator through the rock to the summit of this pinnacle (€3 in high season, free off-season and when the *télécabines* to Helbronner are not running). Missing the elevator is a kind of Alpus-Interruptus I'd rather not experience. The Alps spread out before you. Find the orientation posters to identify key peaks. If it's really clear, you can see the bent little Matterhorn—the tall, shady pyramid listed in French on the observation table as "Cervin—4,505 meters" (14,775 feet). And looming on the other side is **Mont Blanc,** the Alps' highest point, at 4,810 meters (15,771 feet). Use the telescopes to spot mountain climbers; more than 2,000 scale this mountain each year. That rusty tin-can needle above you serves as a communications tower. Check the temperature next to the elevator. Plan on 32 degrees Fahrenheit, even on a sunny day. Sunglasses are essential.

Back down, explore Europe's tallest lift station. More than 150 yards of tunnels *(galeries)* lead to various view *terrasses,* a cafeteria (fair prices—have lunch or coffee with a view), a restaurant (not such fair prices), WCs, a gift shop, and an icicle-covered gateway to the glacial world. A right turn out of the elevator leads you through a tunnel to the Mont Blanc Terrace, a small deck with more views.

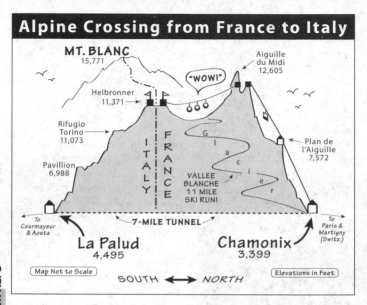

Alpine Crossing from France to Italy

MT. BLANC
15,771

"WOW!"

Aiguille
du Midi
12,605

Helbronner
11,371

Rifugio
Torino
11,073

Plan de
l'Aiguille
7,572

Pavillion
6,988

ITALY / FRANCE

VALLÉE
BLANCHE
11 MILE
SKI RUN!

GLACIER

7-MILE TUNNEL

To
Courmayeur
& Aosta

La Palud
4,495

Chamonix
3,399

To
Paris &
Martigny
(Switz.)

Map Not to Scale

Elevations in Feet

SOUTH ⟷ NORTH

THE FRENCH ALPS

Follow *la Vallée Blanche* signs to a drippy "ice tunnel" where skiers and mountain climbers make their exit. The views are sensational; merely observing is exhilarating. Peek down the icy cliff and ponder the value of an ice ax. Skiers make the 11-mile run to the Mer de Glace (described later) in about half a day (in winter they can ski 13 miles all the way back to the valley at Argentière). The Belvedere Rébuffet walkway

leads to bird's-eye views of the *télécabines* to Helbronner and to more amazing mountain views.

Go back through the tunnel to the main building, where gondolas return to Chamonix and climb metal stairs to more great view terraces, WCs, and the cafeteria/gift shop. Inside you'll see posters describing the 1950s construction of the lift station and the gondola line (the first cable was destroyed during construction by an avalanche). The photos are fascinating.

For your own private glacial dream world, get into the little red *télécabine* (called Panoramic Mont Blanc) and sail south to **Helbronner Point,** the Italian border station (in 2013, this runs only late June-early Sept). This line stretches three miles with no solid pylon. (It's propped by a "suspended pylon," a line stretched between two peaks 1,300 feet from the Italian end.) In a gondola for four, you'll dangle silently for 40 minutes as you glide over glaciers and past a forest of peaks to Italy. Hang your head out the window and explore every corner of your view. From Helbronner Point, you'll turn around and return to Aiguille du Midi (as construction currently prevents access down into Italy from Helbronner Point).

From Aiguille du Midi, you can ride all the way back to Chamonix; or—way, way better—get off halfway down at **Plan de l'Aiguille,** where you'll find a scenic café with sandwiches, drinks, and outdoor tables, paragliders jumping off cliffs (except in July-Aug), and hiking trails. But the best reason to get off here is to follow the wonderful trail to the Mer de Glace, then catch the train back into Chamonix (for details, see "Chamonix Area Hikes—Hike #1" on page 893).

Even if you don't do the hike, take a 15-minute walk below the lift station to the ignored and peaceful **Refuge-Plan de l'Aiguille** for reasonable meals (good omelets) and drinks inside or out (open daily May-Oct, may be open off-season—ask, mobile 06 65 64 27 53). This makes an easy mini-hike for hurried travelers. The short but steep climb back up to the lift will be your exercise for the day.

Whatever you do, don't hike all the way down to Chamonix from Plan de l'Aiguille or Montenvers-Mer de Glace; it's a long, steep walk through thick forests with few views.

Cost: From Chamonix to: Plan de l'Aiguille—round-trip-€27 (one-way-€13); Aiguille du Midi—round-trip-€46 (one-way-€40, not including parachute); the Panoramic Mont Blanc *télécabine* to Helbronner—round-trip-€70. If you are planning to stop at Plan de l'Aiguille on the way back down and hike to Montenvers, ask about a *"spécial randonée"* ticket for about €40. Tickets just for the stretch from Aiguille du Midi to Helbronner are sold at both base and summit lift stations with no difference in price (round-trip-€25).

Discounts: The prices listed above are for those ages 16 and over; kids ages 4-15 cost 15 percent less (family rates for 2 adults and 2 children ages 15 and under are also available).

Hours: Lifts are weather- and crowd-dependent, but generally run daily July-Aug 6:00 or 7:00-16:30, late May-June and Sept 7:00 or 8:00-16:30, and Oct-late May 8:00-15:30. Gondolas run every 10 minutes during busy times; the last return from Aiguille du Midi is generally one hour after the last ascent. The last *télécabine* departure to Helbronner Point is about 14:00-15:00, and the last train down from Montenvers (for hikers) is about 17:00-18:00.

Strategy: To beat the hordes and clouds, ride the Aiguille du Midi lift (up and down) as early as you can. To beat major delays in summer, leave no later than 7:00 or reserve ahead (first lift departs at 6:00 or 7:00, easy to verify in advance). If the weather has been bad and turns good, expect big crowds in any season (even worse on weekends). If it's clear, don't dillydally.

Understanding the Alps

The Alps were formed by the collision of two continents: About 100 million years ago, the African plate began pushing north against the stable plates of Europe and Asia. In the process, the sediments of the ancient Tethys Ocean (which occupied the general real estate of the modern Mediterranean) became smooshed between the landmasses. Shoving all this material together made the rocks and sediments fold, shatter, and pile on top of each other; over millennia this growing jumble built itself up into today's Alps. Up in the mountains, look for folds and faults in the rocks that hint at this immense compression, which is still happening today: The Alps continue to rise by at least a millimeter each year (while erosion wears them down at about the same rate).

The current shape of the mountains and valleys is the handiwork of at least five ice ages over the last two million years. Glaciers flowed down the mountain valleys, scooped out beautiful alpine lakes, and carried rocks far away from where they formed. The Alps were the first mountains extensively studied by geologists, and many of the geological terms that describe mountains originated here. Once you learn how to recognize a few of the landforms shaped by glaciers, you can easily spot these features when you visit other alpine areas. Study glacier exhibits to train your eye to recognize what you're seeing.

Glaciers are big and blunt, so they make simple, large-scale marks on the landscape. If a valley is U-shaped, like Chamonix's (with steep sides and a rounded base), it's probably been scoured out by a glacier. (California's Yosemite Valley is another classic example.)

A **cirque** (French for "circus") is the amphitheater-like depression carved out at the upper part of a valley by a glacier. If two adjacent cirques erode back close to each other, a sharp steep-sided ridge forms, called an **arête** (French for "fishbone"). Cirques and arêtes are common

From July to August, smart travelers reserve the Aiguille du Midi lift in advance (€2 fee). You can reserve at the information booth next to the lift (open mid-June–mid-Sept), online at www.compagniedumontblanc.com, or by phone (year-round, tel. 04 50 53 22 75, automated reservations in English). Reservations are taken up to 10 days in advance (6 days in winter); pick tickets up at the lift station at least 30 minutes before departure (the information booth at the Aiguille du Midi lift tells you which window to

in mountains that have had glaciers. More rarely, when three or
more cirques erode toward one
another, a pyramidal peak is created—called a **horn.** Switzerland's
Matterhorn (visible—barely—
from the Aiguille du Midi) is the
world's most famous example.
Glaciers flowed down all sides of
this mountain, scooping material
away as they went to leave its
distinctive sharp peak.

A common feature left behind by retreating glaciers is a
moraine, a pile of dirt and rocks that was carried along on the
glacier as it advanced, then was dumped as the glacier melted
(plainly visible around the Mer de Glace).

Alpine glaciers can only originate above the snowline, so if
you see any of these landforms (U-shaped valleys, cirques, horns,
or moraines) in lower elevations, you know that the climate there
used to be colder. The effects of a warming climate have pro-
foundly hit the glaciers of the Alps, which have lost at least a
third of their volume since the 1950s. At that rate, some studies project that most here could virtually disappear by the end
of the century, affecting water storage and hydroelectric power
generation, and making mountainsides less stable (for example,
a heat wave in the summer of 2003 caused several rockfalls on
the Matterhorn, resulting in trail closures and the evacuation of
dozens of climbers trapped on the summit).

Another consequence of the warming climate is that winter
weather no longer reliably produces snow at altitudes that it did
in the past—which is bad news for Europe's huge ski industry.
Seeing a future of ever-warmer winters, alpine resorts are putting their ingenuity to the test. This goes beyond snow machines:
Many resorts are investing hugely in new spas, convention centers, and other attractions that don't require snow. Meanwhile,
European governments strive to invest in environmentally
friendly technologies in hopes of keeping their mountains white
and their valleys green.

use). Reservations are free with a Multipass (described on page
882) and are not possible for the *télécabines* to Helbronner.

Time to Allow: Chamonix to Aiguille du Midi—20 minutes
one-way, two hours round-trip, three to four hours in peak season;
Chamonix to Helbronner—1.5 hours one-way, three to four hours
round-trip, longer in peak season. On busy days, minimize delays
by making a reservation for your return lift time upon arrival at the
top. (For information on Aiguille du Midi, call 04 50 53 30 80.)

▲▲▲Mer de Glace (Montenvers)

From Gare de Montenvers (the little station over the tracks from Chamonix's main train station), the cute cogwheel Train du Montenvers toots you up to tiny Montenvers (mohn-tuh-vehr). There you'll see a dirty, rapidly receding glacier called the Mer de Glace (mayr duh glahs, "Sea of Ice") and fantastic views up the white valley (Vallée Blanche) of splintered, snow-capped peaks (2-3/hour, 20 minutes, round-trip-€27, one-way-€21, family rates available, prices include gondola and ice caves entry, daily 8:30-17:00, July-Aug 8:00-18:00, confirm times with TI or call 04 50 53 12 54).

Find the **view deck** across from the train station. France's largest glacier, at eight miles long, is impressive from above and below. The swirling glacier extends under the dirt about a half-mile downhill to the left. Imagine that it recently reached as high as the vegetation below (see the dirt cliffs—called moraines—left behind in its retreat). In 1860, this glacier stretched all the way down to the valley floor. They say this fast-moving glacier is just doing its cycle thing, growing and shrinking—a thousand years ago, cows grazed on grassy fields here. Al Gore thinks people are speeding up the process.

Use the **orientation table** as you look up to the peaks. **Monsieur Dru**'s powerful spire, at about 11,700 feet, makes an irresistible target for climbers. It was first scaled in 1860 (long before the train you took here was built) and was recently free-climbed (no ropes, belays, etc.); see the colored lines indicating different routes taken—one by an *Américain*. Those guys are nuts. The smooth snow field to the left of Dru's spire (Les Grands Montets) is the top of Chamonix's most challenging ski run, with a vertical drop of about 6,500 feet (down the opposite side).

The glacier's **ice caves** are beneath you. Take the small gondola down and prepare to walk about 400 steps each way. (Several years ago, it was 280 steps; this glacier is beating a hasty retreat.) If you've already seen a glacier up close, you might skip this one, though I found it a relevant trip given the attention being paid to global warming *(le rechauffement climatique)*. This is also where skiers end their run from the Aiguille du Midi (you might recognize someone if you rode that lift earlier). The path to the right (as you face the glacier) leads to a fine view café and a reconstruction of a crystal cave.

The **Refuge-Hôtel du Montenvers,** a few minutes' walk

toward Chamonix, offers a full-service restaurant, view tables (fair prices, limited selection), and a warm interior (you can even bunk here—see "Sleeping in Chamonix," later). The five-room museum upstairs describes the history of the Montenvers train (no English but good exhibits). The hotel was built in 1880, when "tourists" arrived on foot or by mule.

The three-hour trail to **Plan de l'Aiguille** begins from above the hotel. For terrific views, hike toward Plan de l'Aiguille—via the trail that veers left—even just a short distance. The views get better fast, and the higher you climb, the better the view (follow signs on the stone building opposite the hotel; you want *sentier gauche* to *Signal Montenvers*). Bring a picnic.

▲▲▲Gondola Lifts *(Téléphériques)* to Le Brévent and La Flégère

Though Aiguille du Midi gives a more spectacular ride, the Le Brévent and La Flégère lifts offer worthwhile hiking and viewing options, with unobstructed panoramas across to the Mont Blanc range. The Le Brévent (luh bray-vahn) lift is in Chamonix; the La Flégère (lah flay-zhair) lift is in nearby Les Praz (lay prah). The lifts are connected by a scenic hike, or by bus along the valley floor (free with Chamonix Guest Card, see Hike #2 in the next section); both have sensational view cafés. Both lifts are closed from late April to mid-June and from October until ski season starts, usually in November.

Le Brévent lift is a steep 10-minute walk up the road above Chamonix's TI. It takes two lifts to reach **Le Brévent**'s top. The first lift to Planpraz, with automated eight-person *télécabines*, runs every minute. Sit backward and watch Chamonix shrink below. Notice supports for the old lift, which was replaced with this *très moderne* one (round-trip to Planpraz-€14, one-way-€12.50, nice restaurant, great views and good hiking options, see Hike #2 in the next section). The second, less impressive gondola to Le Brévent station needs a facelift. It leaves from Planpraz and runs less often (about 2-3/hour). At the top you get 360-degree views, more hikes, and a good view restaurant, but few visitor services. For most, Planpraz is high enough (round-trip from Chamonix to Le Brévent-€27, one-way-€20.50; mid-June-Sept and Nov-late April daily 8:45-16:30, July-Aug 8:00-17:30, last return from Planpraz one hour after last ascent, closed late April-mid-June and Oct, tel. 04 50 53 13 18).

La Flégère lift runs from the neighboring village of Les Praz, with just one stop at La Flégère station (round-trip-€14.50, one-way-€12.50, mid-June-mid-Sept and Nov-late April daily 8:15-16:30, summer 8:00-17:30, last return from La Flégère 15 minutes after last ascent, closed late April-mid-June and mid-Sept-Oct, tel.

THE FRENCH ALPS

Kids' Activities

Chamonix provides a wealth of fun opportunities for kids. The TI can suggest family-friendly hikes and activities (such as mini-golf, swimming pools with big slides, and more). Here are a few kid-pleasing activities to consider.

Parc de Loisirs des Planards—Chamonix's fun park for kids of all ages. It includes a luge (summer only) and a Parc d'Aventure with tree courses, Tarzan swings, trampolines, electric motorbikes, Jet Skis, and more (for details, see "Luge" listing on page 900).

Le Paradis des Praz Pleasant—Activity park fun for 4- to 10-year-olds, with pony rides, zip-wire rides, and more. It's in the small village of Les Praz, by the lift to La Flégère. Rent a bike in Chamonix and ride along the level Arve River trail to this park, or take the free bus (described on page 883).

   Cost and Hours: Pony rides-€4, otherwise free, July-Aug daily 10:00-18:00, otherwise Wed and weekend afternoons and holidays only, mobile 06 61 73 23 00.

Parc de Merlet—Animal sanctuary with trails that let you discover mountain animals (marmots, mountain goats, llamas, deer, and more). It's located in Coupeau above Les Houches, and comes with exceptional views (so parents get some scenery while kids get to see animals). You can get there by car (20-minute drive) or hike for two beautiful hours from Chamonix (too much for most kids). If you drive, head to the very top parking lot, as you'll be hiking uphill for 20-30 minutes just to reach the entry. There's a lot more walking inside the park to find the animals—bring good shoes and water.

   Cost and Hours: €6, kids ages 4-12-€4, view café with salads and regional dishes, no picnics allowed; May-June and Sept Tue-Sun 10:00-18:00, closed Mon; July-Aug daily 9:30-19:30; tel. 04 50 53 47 89, www.parcdemerlet.com.

04 50 53 18 58). Hikes to Planpraz and Lac Blanc leave from the top of this station (see Hikes #2 and #3 in the next section).

Chamonix Area Hikes

A good first stop is the full-service **Maison de la Montagne** across from the TI. On the second floor, the **Office of the High Mountain** (Office de Haute-Montagne) can help you plan your hikes and tell you about trail and snow conditions (daily 9:00-12:00 & 15:00-18:00, tel. 04 50 53 22 08, www.ohm-chamonix .com). The staff speaks enough English and has vital weather reports and maps, as well as some English hiking guidebooks (you can photocopy key pages). Ask to look at the trail guidebook (sold in many stores and at the TI but not here, includes the helpful €4 *Carte des Sentiers*, the region's hiking map). You can also use the handy restroom here on the second floor.

At **Compagnie des Guides de Chamonix** on the ground floor, you can hire a guide to take you hiking (about €185/half-day, €305/day, less per person for groups), help you scale Mont Blanc, or hike to the Matterhorn and Zermatt (open daily 9:00-12:00 & 15:30-19:00, closed Sun-Mon off-season, tel. 04 50 53 00 88, fax 04 50 53 48 04, www.chamonix-guides.com).

I describe three big hikes (Hikes #1, #2, and #3) and two easier walks (Hikes #4 and #5); see the map on the next page. These hikes give nature-lovers of any ability good options for enjoying the valley in most seasons. Start early, when the weather's generally best. This is critical in summer—if you don't get to the lifts by 8:30, you'll meet a conveyor belt of hikers. If starting later or walking longer, confirm lift closing hours, or prepare for a long, steep hike down. No matter when you're here, come ready for a lot of hikers on the trails and be prepared to wait it out if the weather gets rough—lifts don't run during electrical storms.

For your hike, pack sunglasses, sunscreen, rain gear, water, and snacks. Bring warm layers (mountain weather can change in a moment) and good shoes (trails are rocky and uneven). Take your time, watch your footing, don't take shortcuts, and say *"Bonjour!"* to your fellow hikers. Note that there's no shade on Hikes #1, #2, and #3.

▲▲▲Hike #1: Plan de l'Aiguille to Montenvers-Mer de Glace (Grand Balcon Nord)—This is the most efficient way

to incorporate a high-country hike into your ride down from the valley's greatest lift, and check out a world-class glacier to boot. The well-used trail rises but mostly falls (dropping 1,500 feet from Plan de l'Aiguille to Montenvers and the Mer de Glace) and is moderately difficult, provided the snow is melted (generally covered by snow until June; get trail details at the Office of the High Mountain, listed earlier). Some stretches are steep and strenuous, with uneven footing and slippery rocks. Take your time. Note the last train time from Montenvers-Mer de Glace back to Chamonix, or you'll be hiking another hour and a half straight down.

Here is an overview of this 2.5-hour hike: From the Aiguille du Midi lift, get off halfway down at Plan de l'Aiguille, *sortie* to the café, then find signs leading down to *Montenvers–Mer de Glace*. You'll drop steadily for 15 minutes down to a small refuge (good prices for meals and drinks), then go right, hiking the spectacularly scenic, undulating, and (for short periods) strenuous trail to

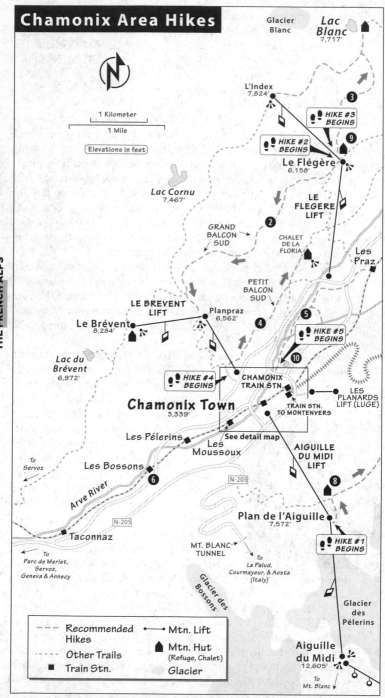

Chamonix Area Hikes

Glacier
Blanc

Lac Blanc
7,717'

L'Index
7,824'

HIKE #3 BEGINS

3

9

HIKE #2 BEGINS

Le Flégère
6,158'

1 Kilometer

1 Mile

Elevations in feet

Lac Cornu
7,467'

LE FLEGERE LIFT

GRAND BALCON SUD

CHALET DE LA FLORIA

Les Praz

PETIT BALCON SUD

LE BREVENT LIFT

Planpraz
6,562'

5

HIKE #5 BEGINS

Le Brévent
8,284'

4

10

Lac du Brévent
6,972'

HIKE #4 BEGINS

CHAMONIX TRAIN STN.

LES PLANARDS LIFT (LUGE)

Chamonix Town
3,339'

TRAIN STN. TO MONTENVERS

To Servoz

Les Pélerins

Les Moussoux

See detail map

AIGUILLE DU MIDI LIFT

Les Bossons

6

N-205

8

Arve River

N-205

Plan de l'Aiguille
7,572'

HIKE #1 BEGINS

Taconnaz

To Parc de Merlet, Servoz, Geneva & Annecy

MT. BLANC TUNNEL

To La Palud, Courmayeur, & Aosta (Italy)

Glacier des Pélerins

Glacier des Bossons

Aiguille du Midi
12,605'

To Mt. Blanc

Legend

--- Recommended Hikes

---•--- Mtn. Lift

····· Other Trails

▲ Mtn. Hut (Refuge, Chalet)

■ Train Stn.

Glacier

THE FRENCH ALPS

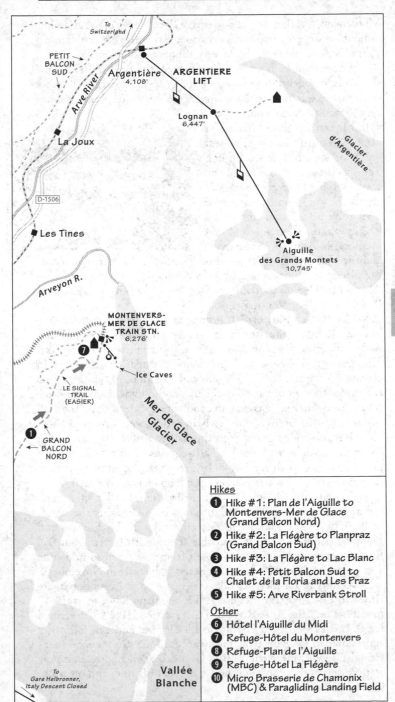

THE FRENCH ALPS

Hikes

1 Hike #1: Plan de l'Aiguille to Montenvers-Mer de Glace (Grand Balcon Nord)

2 Hike #2: La Flégère to Planpraz (Grand Balcon Sud)

3 Hike #3: La Flégère to Lac Blanc

4 Hike #4: Petit Balcon Sud to Chalet de la Floria and Les Praz

5 Hike #5: Arve Riverbank Stroll

Other

6 Hôtel l'Aiguille du Midi

7 Refuge-Hôtel du Montenvers

8 Refuge-Plan de l'Aiguille

9 Refuge-Hôtel La Flégère

10 Micro Brasserie de Chamonix (MBC) & Paragliding Landing Field

Montenvers (overlooking the Mer de Glace glacier). You'll do lots of boulder-stepping and cross occasional streams that can dampen your shoes and make the rocks very slippery. Pay attention.

After about an hour at a steady pace, the trail splits. Follow signs up the steep trail to *Le Signal* (more scenic and easier), rather than to the left toward Montenvers (looks easier, but becomes very difficult). At this point you'll grind it out up switchbacks for about 30 minutes to the best views of the trail at Le Signal. Take time to savor the views you worked so hard to reach. Scramble about the rocks and create your own rock pile. From here it's a long, sometimes steep, but always memorable drop to Montenvers

and the Mer de Glace. As you drop, notice the dirt path the receding glacier left in its wake. In Montenvers, take the train back to Chamonix. Don't walk the rest of the trail down from Montenvers (long, steep, disappointing views).

▲▲**Hike #2: La Flégère to Planpraz (Grand Balcon Sud)**—This lovely hike undulates for two hours above Chamonix Valley, with staggering views of Mont Blanc and countless other peaks, glaciers, and wildflowers. There's just 370 feet of difference in elevation between the La Flégère and Planpraz lift stations—so this hike, though not without its ups and downs, is manageable (but still requires serious stamina and appropriate shoes). The trail is a mix of dirt paths, ankle-twisting rocky sections, and short stretches of service roads. You'll pass by winter lifts, and walk through meadows and along small sections of forest. Keep your eyes out for signs to *La Flégère* or *Planpraz,* depending on your direction; red-and-white markers also help identify the trail.

You can hike the trail in either direction, but I prefer starting at La Flégère, as Mont Blanc stays in your sights the entire walk. Ask for the round-trip rate allowed with La Flégère and Planpraz (Le Brévent) lifts, available at either lift (saves about €6). Remember that these lifts are closed from late April to mid-June and from October until ski season starts (generally in November).

To start at La Flégère, take free bus #1 or #2 (get departure times to Les Praz/La Flégère at TI; see page 884), or walk 40 minutes along the Arve River to Les Praz (see Hike #5, described later). In Les Praz, take the lift to La Flégère, and exit following signs down to *Planpraz* (you don't want *Les Praz-Chamonix*—that's straight down). Hike the rolling Grand Balcon Sud to Planpraz station, the midway stop on the Le Brévent lift line, and return to Chamonix from there.

If starting from the Le Brévent lift, take the *télécabine* up to Planpraz (automated cars leave every minute). As you ride up with your back to Mont Blanc, your destination lift station (La Flégère) is visible to the right. From the Planpraz lift station, don't take what appears to be the direct way there down the big dirt road. Instead, leave the station, walking behind it (not past La Bergerie Restaurant), then climb above, following signs to *La Flégère*. When you reach the La Flégère lift, ride it down to Les Praz (the hike down is not worth the trouble), then walk back to Chamonix following Hike #5 (described later), or take the free Chamonix bus (about 2/hour, 10-minute ride). Bus #1 stops at the shelter on the road in front of the lift station; bus #2 stops in the lift station parking lot, near the main road.

▲▲**Hike #3: La Flégère to Lac Blanc**—This is the most demanding hiking trail of those I list; it climbs steeply and steadily over a rough, boulder-strewn trail for 1.5 hours to snowy Lac Blanc (pronounced "lock blah"). Some footing is tricky, and good shoes or boots are a must. I like this trail, as it gets you away from the valley edge and opens views to peaks you don't see from other hikes. The destination is a snow-white lake framed by peaks and a nifty chalet-refuge offering good lunches (and dinners, if you stay the night). The views on the return trip are breathtaking. Check for snow conditions on the trail (often a problem until July) and go early (particularly in summer), as there is no shade and this trail is popular.

Follow the directions for Hike #2 to La Flégère station, then walk out the station's rear door past the snack stand and view area, and follow signs to *Lac Blanc*. The trail is well-signed and its surface improves as you climb. You can eliminate a good part of the uphill hiking by riding the lift from La Flégère to L'Index (about €8 one-way, €10 round-trip), but make sure the trail from L'Index is free of snow as this short-cut can be dicey, especially for kids.

▲**Hike #4: Petit Balcon Sud to Chalet de la Floria and Les Praz**—This trail runs above the valley on the Brévent side from the village of Servoz to Argentière, passing Chamonix about half-way, and is handy when snow or poor weather make other hikes problematic. No lifts are required—just firm thighs to climb up to and down from the trail. Access paths link the trail to villages below. Once you're up, the trail rises and falls with some steep segments and uneven footing, but is generally easy to walk. The highlight of the trail is **Chalet de la Floria,** with food and views (allow 1 hour each way from Chamonix).

Reach the trail from Chamonix by starting at the Le Brévent lift station (find signs to *Le Petit Balcon Sud*). Begin by walking along an asphalt road to the left of the lift leading uphill (on Chemin de la Pierre à Ruskin), which turns into a dirt road

Winter Sports in Chamonix

Chamonix offers some of the best expert-level skiing in the world, a huge choice of terrain at reasonable prices (cheaper than Switzerland), access to lots of high-elevation runs (which means good snow and views), and great nightlife. Ski here for jaw-dropping views and a good balance between true mountaineer culture and touristy glitz.

The slopes are strung out along the valley for about 10 miles, so you must drive or catch the often-crowded shuttle buses to ski more than one area. There's also limitless *off-piste* (un-groomed) skiing, but first you'll need an experienced guide to help you avoid hidden crevasses, deadly patches of ice, and avalanche danger.

Non-skiers won't be bored. The lifts described in this chapter lead to top-notch views. Swimming, saunas, tennis, skating, and climbing are available at Chamonix's Centre Sportif. You can also relax in a spa, go bowling or dog-sledding, and hike along groomed winter footpaths.

When to Go

High season is usually from December to mid-May. Chamonix is packed from Christmas through New Year's Day and busy in February and March (during European winter and spring breaks). It's quieter in early December, in January after New Year's, the second half of March, and in April (but Easter can be busy). Thanks to easy access to high-elevation runs, you'll usually find good powder in April and May, when it's less crowded. Chamonix is one of the great resorts for spring skiing, and you can usually find special spring package deals. Whenever you go, get an early start to avoid the late-morning (après-ski-party-recovery) crowds.

Tickets

Adult lift tickets covering Chamonix's three main areas, including the lower-elevation beginner areas, are €42/1 day, €80/2 days, €120/3 days, €153/4 days, €190/5 days (about 15 percent less for skiers older than 64 or younger than 16). Or consider the Mont Blanc Unlimited pass—covering all the areas in the Chamonix Valley (details on the websites listed on the next page, under "Information").

Ski Rentals

Prices don't vary much, so go with something convenient to where you're staying and ask your hotel for deals with nearby shops. You'll pay about €12-20/day for skis and about €6-12/day for boots. **Technique Extrême** has the best deals on rentals and gear (tel. 04 50 53 38 25, 200 Avenue de l'Aiguille du Midi, www.technique-extreme.com). **Snell Sports** is a respected shop that's been around for many years (tel. 04 50 53 02 17, 104 Rue du Docteur Paccard, www.cham3s.com). **Sports Alpins** provides great service (tel. 04 50 53 13 60, 7 Place Edmond Désailloud, Chamonix Sud, www.cham3s.com).

Information

For general information about Chamonix and lift rates, check www.chamonix.com, www.leshouches.com, and www.compagniedumontblanc.fr, or contact the Chamonix TI. To hire a guide, see www.chamonix-guides.com (info@chamonix-guides.com).

Where to Go

It's tough to find one area in Chamonix that offers a perfect mix of terrain for every level of skier, but here's a rundown of Chamonix's key ski areas:

Le Brévent/La Flégère—A 10-minute walk from Chamonix's center, this area has one of the valley's better mixes of terrain. If you're staying in Chamonix and have just a day, ski Le Brévent/La Flégère. Runs are good for intermediates, with some expert options, but not great for beginners. You'll enjoy fantastic views of Mont Blanc.

Les Grands Montets—Above the village of Argentière (about 10 minutes from Chamonix by bus), this area is internationally renowned for its expert terrain (and killer views from the observation deck). Part of Les Grands Montets lies on the Argentière glacier, and there's plenty of vertical. Hire a local guide to explore the off-piste options.

Les Houches—A five-minute bus or train ride from Chamonix, Les Houches covers a large area with a variety of runs for most skill levels (good for families), but it has fewer expert options. This area is less crowded than other Chamonix Valley areas, and the tree skiing is good.

Domaine de Balme—The area above the nearby town of Le Tour offers good options for beginners, intermediates, and those looking for mellow cruising runs.

Lower Areas Good for Beginners—Le Savoy is at the bottom of Le Brévent, near Chamonix's center, with scads of kids and a few rope-tows. Les Planards is a short walk from the town center and the largest area for kids and beginners. These areas depend on good snow conditions.

The Vallée Blanche—This unique-to-Chamonix run starts on the sky-high Aiguille du Midi lift and takes you 13 miles down a glacier past astounding views and terrain to Montenvers (easy train back to Chamonix). It requires a lift ticket and hiring a guide or joining a group tour (figure about €300 for a private tour of up to 4 people, €25/additional person, maximum 6 people).

marked as the *Petit Balcon Sud* trail. After about 20 minutes on the dirt road, you'll see a *Petit Balcon Sud* sign pointing left and up a smaller trail. Bypass this turnoff (which doubles back above Chamonix with great views) and continue along the dirt road.

After about 30 more minutes, follow *la Floria* signs on a 20-minute round-trip detour to Chalet de la Floria, which has drinks, snacks, flowers, and magnificent views (daily mid-June-early Nov). From here, trails lead back down to Chamonix or to Les Praz village. Following signs to *Les Praz* eventually lands you on the main road; turn left to explore the village and to connect with the river trail back to Chamonix (the trail is immediately to the right after the bridge), or turn right on the road to reach the bus stop back to Chamonix (it takes bus #1 about 20 minutes to reach Les Praz from the time point posted in Le Tour; bus #2 starts a minute away at the Les Praz/La Flégère lift).

Hike #5: Arve Riverbank Stroll and Paragliding Landing Field—For a level, forested-valley stroll, follow the Arve River toward Les Praz. At Chamonix's Hôtel Alpina, follow the path upstream past red-clay tennis courts and find the green arrow to *Les Praz*. Cross two bridges to the left and turn right along the rushing Arve River, and then follow Promenade des Econtres. Several trails loop through these woods; if you continue walking straight, you'll reach Les Praz—an appealing destination with a number of cafés and a pleasing village green.

If you keep right after the tennis courts (passing piles of river sediment dredged to keep the river from flooding), you'll come to a grassy landing field, signed *Parapente,* where paragliders hope to touch down. Walk to the top of the little grassy hill for fine Mont Blanc views and a great picnic spot. The recommended Micro Brasserie de Chamonix is nearby.

Other Activities

▲**Luge (Luge d'Eté)**—Here's something for thrill-seekers: Ride a chairlift up the mountain and then scream down a twisty, banked, concrete slalom course on a wheeled sled. Chamonix has two roughly parallel luge courses: While each course is just longer than a half-mile and about the same speed, one is marked for slower sledders, the other for speed demons. Young or old, hare or tortoise, any fit person can manage a luge. *Freinez* signs tell you when to brake. Don't take your hands off your stick; the course is fast and slippery. The luge courses are set in a grassy park with kids' play areas.

Cost and Hours: €5.50/one ride, €31/six rides, kids under 8 must ride with adult, entry includes all activities in Parc de Loisirs des Planards—see "Kids' Activities" page 892; July-Aug daily 10:00-19:00; May-June and Sept-Oct Sat-Sun and some Wed-

Thu 14:00-17:30; 15-minute walk from town center, over the tracks from train station and past Montenvers train station; tel. 04 50 53 08 97, www.chamonixparc.com.

▲▲▲**Paragliding (Parapente)**—When it's sunny and clear, the skies above Chamonix sparkle with colorful parachute-like sails that circle the valley like birds of prey. For about €100, you can launch yourself off a mountain in a tandem paraglider with a trained, experienced pilot and fly like a bird for about 20 minutes. Try **Summits Parapente** (smart to reserve a day ahead, open year-round, tel. 04 50 53 50 14, mobile 06 84 01 26 00, www.summits.fr).

For a sneak preview, walk to the main landing area and watch paragliders perfect their landings (see "Chamonix Area Hikes—Hike #5," earlier).

Rainy-Day Options

If the weather disagrees with your plans, stay cool and check out the following options, which are both included in one €6 ticket (€1 off with Chamonix Guest Card). Although neither offers a word of English, the exhibits are fairly straightforward.

Alpine Museum (Musée Alpin)—Situated in one of Chamonix's oldest "palaces," this place has good exhibits about Chamonix's evolution from a farming area to one focused on skiing. The museum shows off Chamonix's mountaineering, skiing, and mineralogical history (explanations in French only) and has exhibits on the first Winter Olympics, held right here.

Cost and Hours: €6, includes Espace Tairraz, daily 14:00-19:00 plus 10:00-12:00 in summer, 89 Avenue Michel Croz, tel. 04 50 53 25 93.

Espace Tairraz—This fascinating collection features crystals from the region in every color, shape, and size. My kids loved it. Pick up the basic brochure in English for some background.

Cost and Hours: €6, includes Alpine Museum, daily 14:00-19:00 plus 10:00-12:00 in summer.

Day Trips near Chamonix

A Day in French-Speaking Switzerland—Plenty of tempting alpine and cultural thrills await just an hour or two away in Switzerland. A scenic road-and-train line sneaks you from Chamonix to the Swiss town of Martigny. Whereas train travelers cross without formalities, drivers are charged a one-time fee of 40 Swiss francs (about €33) for a permit to use Swiss autobahns (valid for one calendar year).

A Little Italy—The remote Valle d'Aosta and its historic capital city of Aosta offer a serious change of culture. Though you won't be able to take the lift over the Alps into *bella Italia* (because of construction at the Helbronner station), you can take the two-hour bus from Chamonix to Aosta (about €16 one-way, €26 round-trip, reservation required in summer, 4/day July-mid-Sept, 2/day mid-Sept-June). Get schedules at Chamonix's bus station (located at train station, tel. 04 50 53 01 15, www.sat-montblanc.com—click "download timetables" on the right). For buses using the Mont Blanc tunnel, it's a two-hour trip to Aosta (otherwise it's at least three hours via Martigny). Drivers can drive straight through the Mont Blanc tunnel (one-way-€39, round-trip-€49 with return valid for 1 week, www.tunnelmb.com).

Sleeping in Chamonix

(€1 = about $1.30, country code: 33)

Reasonable hotels and dorm-like chalets abound in Chamonix, with easy parking and quick access from the train station. The TI can help you find budget accommodations anytime—either in person or by email (reservation@chamonix.com). Outside winter, mid-July to mid-August is most difficult, when some hotels have five-day minimum-stay requirements. Prices tumble off-season (outside July-Aug and Dec-Jan). Many hotels and restaurants are closed in April, June, and November, but you can still find a room and a meal. If you want a view of Mont Blanc, ask for *côté Mont Blanc* (coat-ay mohn blah). Travelers who visit June through September should contemplate a night high above in a refuge-hotel.

All hoteliers speak English. Price ranges usually reflect low-to-high season rates (low season is roughly March-June and Sept-Dec). Ask at your hotel about the free Chamonix Guest Card, which provides free use of most buses and trains during your stay (described on page 883).

Hotels in the City Center

$$$ Hôtel l'Oustalet*** is a modern chalet hotel that makes me feel like I'm in Austria. It's warmly run by two sisters (Véronique and Agnes), who understand the importance of good service. The place is family-friendly, with lots of grass, a pool, and six family suites. All rooms are sharp, with views and balconies (Sb-€85-140, standard Db-€120-140, bigger Db with terrace-€125-150, Qb family rooms-€150-210, breakfast-€14, Wi-Fi, free parking, near Aiguille du Midi lift at 330 Rue du Lyret, tel. 04 50 55 54 99, fax 04 50 55 54 98, www.hotel-oustalet.com, infos@hotel-oustalet.com).

$$$ Hôtel Hermitage***, a 10-minute walk from the town center, is a beautiful and well-run chalet with the coziest lounges in Chamonix and a lovely garden with good kids' toys (swings, slides, ping-pong). It has a fun bar and 30 immaculate, rustic-elegant rooms, all with balconies. Rooms facing Mont Blanc have incredible views (Db-€105-120, Db with king-size bed and Mont Blanc view-€120-160, Tb-€150-170, family rooms-€175-210, Internet access and Wi-Fi, near train station at 63 Chemin du Cé, tel. 04 50 53 13 87, fax 04 50 55 98 14, www.hermitage-paccard .com, info@hermitage-paccard.com).

$$$ Hôtel Gourmets et Italy* is a 40-room place with cozy public spaces, a cool riverfront terrace, balcony views from many of its appealing rooms, and a small pool (standard Db with shower-€90-110, larger Db with bath and Mont Blanc view-€100-140, extra person-€16, closed late April-early June, pay Internet access and Wi-Fi, 2 blocks from casino on Mont Blanc side of river, 96 Rue du Lyret, tel. 04 50 53 01 38, fax 04 50 53 46 74, www .hotelgourmets-chamonix.com, info@hotelgourmets-chamonix .com).

$$ Hôtel Richemond* has a retirement-home feel in its well-worn public spaces. The same family has run this grand old hotel since it was built in 1914, and I don't think the rooms have changed much since then. Hallways are broad, and rooms are Old World comfortable and relatively spacious, though bathrooms are rustic. There's also an outdoor terrace and a game room with a pool table, "flipper" (pinball), and table tennis. Helpful Evelyn runs the day reception and speaks impeccable English (Sb-€64-72, Db-€95-115, Tb-€120-144, Qb-€132-156, includes buffet breakfast, Wi-Fi, free parking, 228 Rue du Docteur Paccard, tel. 04 50 53 08 85, fax 04 50 55 91 69, www.richemond.fr, richemond@wanadoo.fr).

$$ Hôtel Faucigny* is quiet, well-run, and set back from the street, near the TI. It's a polished place with modern alpine decor. The front terrace provides a peaceful retreat with sensational views (Db-€100-110, Tb-€115, family rooms-€150, Internet access and Wi-Fi, Jacuzzi, 118 Place de l'Eglise, tel. 04 50 53 01 17, www.hotelfaucigny-chamonix.com, reservation@hotelfaucigny -chamonix.com).

$$ Hôtel de l'Arve* offers solid two-star comfort with a contemporary alpine feel in its 37 comfortable rooms, some right on the Arve River looking up at Mont Blanc. Owners Isabelle and Beatrice run a tight ship at this hotel that comes with a fireplace lounge, a pool room, a pleasant garden, a sauna, a climbing wall, and easy parking (standard Db-€68-96, larger or view Db-€78-110, big view room-€88-125, extra person-€15, great breakfast-€11, Internet access and Wi-Fi, nice restaurant, around the corner from huge Hôtel Alpina, 60 Impasse des Anémones, tel. 04 50 53 02 31, fax 04 50 53 56 92, www.hotelarve-chamonix.com, contact @hotelarve-chamonix.com).

$$ Hôtel les Crêtes Blanches* is a central and sweet little place wrapped around a peaceful courtyard (with outdoor tables)

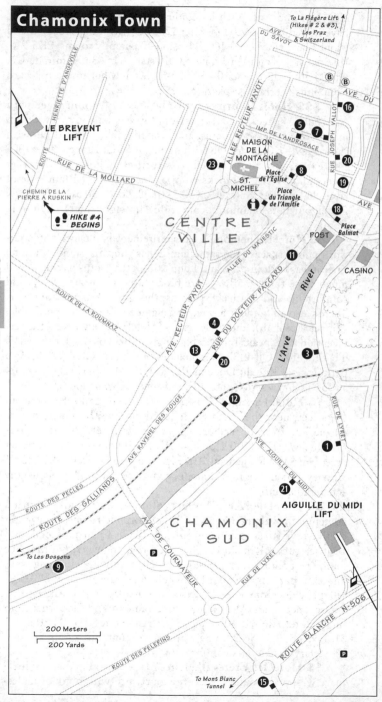

Chamonix Town

To La Flégère Lift
(Hikes # 2 & #3),
Les Praz
& Switzerland

AVE. DU SAVOY

AVE. DU

LE BREVENT LIFT

ROUTE HENRIETTE D'ANGEVILLE

RUE DE LA MOLLARD

ALLÉE RECTEUR PAYOT

IMP. DE L'ANDROSACE

RUE JOSEPH VALLOT

16

5 **7**

MAISON DE LA MONTAGNE

23

ST. MICHEL

Place de l'Eglise **8**

20

19

CHEMIN DE LA PIERRE A RUSKIN

HIKE #4 BEGINS

Place du Triangle de l'Amitié

18

AVE.

Place Balmat

CENTRE VILLE

ALLÉE DU MAJESTIC

POST

CASINO

ROUTE DE LA ROUMNAZ

AVE. RECTEUR PAYOT

RUE DU DOCTEUR PACCARD

11

L'Arve

River

4

13

20

3

12

AVE. RAVENEL DES ROUGE

RUE DE LYRET

1

AVE. AIGUILLE DU MIDI

21

ROUTE DES PECLES

ROUTE DES GALLIANDS

AVE. DE COURMAYEUR

CHAMONIX SUD

AIGUILLE DU MIDI LIFT

P

To Les Bossons & **9**

RUE DE LYRET

200 Meters

200 Yards

ROUTE DES PELERINS

ROUTE BLANCHE N-506

P

To Mont Blanc Tunnel

15

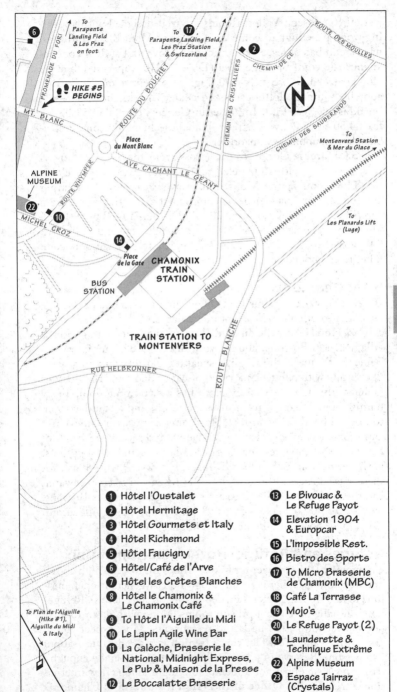

1. Hôtel l'Oustalet
2. Hôtel Hermitage
3. Hôtel Gourmets et Italy
4. Hôtel Richemond
5. Hôtel Faucigny
6. Hôtel/Café de l'Arve
7. Hôtel les Crêtes Blanches
8. Hôtel le Chamonix & Le Chamonix Café
9. To Hôtel l'Aiguille du Midi
10. Le Lapin Agile Wine Bar
11. La Calèche, Brasserie le National, Midnight Express, Le Pub & Maison de la Presse
12. Le Boccalatte Brasserie
13. Le Bivouac & Le Refuge Payot
14. Elevation 1904 & Europcar
15. L'Impossible Rest.
16. Bistro des Sports
17. To Micro Brasserie de Chamonix (MBC)
18. Café La Terrasse
19. Mojo's
20. Le Refuge Payot (2)
21. Launderette & Technique Extrême
22. Alpine Museum
23. Espace Tairraz (Crystals)

just off Rue Joseph Vallot. Rooms are well-designed with appealing wood paneling; all come with views of Mont Blanc and most have small balconies. A ceramic woodstove and stylish couches anchor the comfy lounge area (Db-€64-110, superior Db-€84-116, Tb-€94-130, Qb-€105-140, highest prices are mid-July-Aug, adorable Quint/b dollhouse-sized chalet with kitchen-€115-160, breakfast-€9, Wi-Fi, 6 Impasse du Génépy, tel. 04 50 53 05 62, fax 04 50 53 67 25, www.cretes-blanches-chamonix.com, cretes-blanches-chamonix@wanadoo.fr).

$$ Hôtel le Chamonix**, across from the TI and above a café, is simple, with 16 paneled rooms at fair rates and no elevator. The rooms facing Mont Blanc have great views, are larger and brighter, and have little balconies...but also attract noise from *le café* below, which closes at 20:00 (Db-€64-104, Tb-€90-123, Qb-€105-142, breakfast-€8, Wi-Fi, 11 Rue de l'Hôtel de Ville, tel. 04 50 53 11 07, fax 04 50 53 64 78, www.hotel-le-chamonix.com, hotel-le-chamonix@wanadoo.fr).

Near Chamonix

If Chamonix overwhelms you, spend the night in one of the valley's often-overlooked, lower-profile villages.

$$ Hôtel l'Aiguille du Midi***, a mountain retreat, lies in the village of Les Bossons, about two miles from Chamonix toward Annecy. It's run by the English-speaking Farini family in a park-like setting with point-blank views of Mont Blanc and the Bossons Glacier. This family-friendly place has a swimming pool, a clay tennis court, table tennis, a massage room, and a laundry room to boot. The alpine-comfortable rooms come with Old World bathrooms, many have decks with views, and several are good for families. The classy restaurant offers à la carte and *menu* options, with *menus* from €25 (Db-€92-145, Tb-€124, Qb-€146, ask for these special Rick Steves rates for 2013 when you reserve, elevator, Internet access and Wi-Fi, easy by train, get off at Les Bossons, tel. 04 50 53 00 65, fax 04 50 55 93 69, www.hotel-aiguilledumidi.com, info@hotel-aiguilledumidi.com).

Refuges and Refuge-Hotels near Chamonix

Chamonix has the answer for hikers who want to sleep high above, but aren't into packing it all in: refuge-hotels (generally open mid-June to mid- or late September, depending on snow levels). Refuge-hotels usually have some private rooms (along with dorm rooms), hot showers down the hall, and restaurants. Most expect you to take dinner and breakfast there (which is a good value—about €45/person). Reserve in advance (a few days is generally enough), then pack a small bag for a memorable night among new international friends. The **Office of the High Mountain** in Chamonix can explain your options (see page 892).

$ Refuge-Hôtel du Montenvers, Chamonix's oldest refuge, is a cool experience at the Montenvers train stop. It was built in 1880 as a climbing base for mountain guides before the train went there, so materials had to be gathered from nearby. The five simple wood-cozy rooms and dining room feel as though they haven't been modified since then (open July-Aug only, half-pension in a Db-€62/person, in a dorm room-€42/person, good showers down the hall, tel. 04 50 53 14 14, fax 04 50 55 38 55). For directions, see "Hike #1" on page 893.

$ Refuge-Plan de l'Aiguille is a small, easy-to-reach refuge a 15-minute walk below the Plan de l'Aiguille lift, right on the trail between the Aiguille du Midi and Montenvers-Mer de Glace. It has a cozy interior and a view café. The cook is a retired pastry chef, so the meals are good and the desserts heavenly (open May-Oct only, €19/bed, half-pension-€45/person, mobile 06 65 64 27 53).

$ Refuge-Hôtel La Flégère hangs on the edge right at the La Flégère lift station. It's simple, but ideally located for hiking to Lac Blanc or Planpraz (open mid-June-mid-Sept only, 3 private rooms with 5 beds, many dorm beds, required half-pension-€49/person, fireplace, cozy bar-café, mobile 06 03 58 28 14). For directions, see "Hike #2" on page 896.

Eating in Chamonix

You have two basic dining options in Chamonix—cozy, traditional *savoyarde* restaurants serving fondue, raclette, and the like, or big cafés in central locations serving a wide variety of dishes (including regional specialties) that allow you to watch rivers of hikers return from a full day in the mountains. Prices are roughly the same. If it's a beautiful day, take an outdoor table at a central café (see "View Cafés," later in this section); if you're dining inside, go local and consider a place in or near the town center (most are closed between lunch and dinner).

If a pre-dinner glass of wine from anywhere in the world sounds appealing, hop on into little **Le Lapin Agile** for cozy ambience and a happy-hour buffet of finger foods—free if you purchase a drink (closed Mon, a block from the train station at 11 Rue Whymper, tel. 04 50 53 33 25).

In the Town Center

La Calèche presents delectable regional dishes in a warm, hyper-decorated alpine setting (pass on the outside seating). You'll dine amid antique dolls, cuckoo clocks, copper pots, animal trophies, and more (see if you can find the luge sled from the 1924 Olympic

Games). Try the *tartiflette*—tasty scalloped potatoes with melted cheese. Don't leave without a visit to the WCs (€23 *menu*, the €29 *menu* is much better, daily, centrally located just off Place Balmat at 18 Rue du Docteur Paccard, tel. 04 50 55 94 68).

Le Boccalatte Brasserie, with a convivial atmosphere inside and out, serves a simple but good-value lunch or dinner a few blocks above the Aiguille du Midi lift. The place is family-friendly, with a playful waitstaff. Try the €19 or €29 *menus*, or choose from a large selection of local specialties, big €10 salads, good pizzas, and 20 kinds of beer. It's run by English-speaking Thierry, a friendly Alsatian (daily 12:00-22:00, 59 Avenue de l'Aiguille du Midi, tel. 04 50 53 52 14).

Le Bivouac is an unassuming but lively shoebox-sized place where you'll eat cheap and well in an informal setting. It's a youthful family affair run by son Chris, who speaks English, loves Colorado, and is monitored by gregarious owner-chef Jean-Guy (who should sing opera). The salads are good, the *plats* are tasty, and the selection is big (good kid options). Ask *le chef*'s opinion—he likes his souvlaki and *roulée savoyarde* (266 Rue du Docteur Paccard, tel. 04 50 53 34 08).

Café de l'Arve, at the recommended Hôtel de l'Arve, serves an appealing but limited selection of alpine and Italian fare at fair prices. Dine above the Arve River inside or out (€18 *plats, menus* from €25, closed Sun-Mon, tel. 04 50 53 58 57).

Brasserie le National is a fair choice for outdoor dining in the thick of the traffic-free center. The cuisine highlights local specialties, though you'll find a good selection of non-cheesy options as well (*menus* from €19, nonstop service daily 11:00-22:00, 3 Rue du Docteur Paccard, tel. 04 50 53 02 23).

Budget Meals: **Midnight Express** serves good sandwiches until late and has a few outside tables across from the recommended La Calèche restaurant. Try a *pain en rond* (round-bread rustic sandwich), served hot *(chaud)* or cold *(froid)*. **Elevation 1904** is a down-and-dirty climbers' haunt across from the train station, serving cheap and tasty sandwiches, burgers, pasta, and salads (daily until about 22:30, Wi-Fi, 263 Rue Michel Croz).

Away from the Pedestrian Center

L'Impossible, housed in a beautiful farmhouse a 10- to 20-minute walk from most recommended hotels, is *the* place to go for refined organic cuisine with an Italian bias. Even if eating organic doesn't matter to you, you'll appreciate the exquisite meals and attention to detail. Papa (who hails from Tuscany) cooks, while Mama and daughter Martha serve (€16-24 *plats*, €23-35 *menus*, daily, 5-minute walk from Aiguille du Midi lift on Route des Pélerins, tel. 04 50 53 20 36).

Après Hike: The **Bistro des Sports** is where locals hang their ice picks after a hard day in the mountains. Drinks are cheap, the crowd is loud, and the ambience works (daily until late, 176 Rue Joseph Vallot). **Le Pub** is a good spot to raise a glass with the British crowd (225 Rue du Docteur Paccard, tel. 04 50 55 92 88), and **Micro Brasserie de Chamonix (MBC),** a knockoff of microbrew pubs back home, is a cool place to hang out after a day of paragliding or rappelling. It's not central, across from the *parapente* landing strip (see "Hike #5" on page 900), but it's reasonable and lively. Come here for a homemade brew, a glass of wine, or a pub dinner, and expect crowds of twenty- and thirtysomethings (daily 16:00-1:00 in the morning, 350 Route du Bouchet, look for *MBC* sign, tel. 04 50 53 61 59).

View Cafés: Chamonix excels in outdoor café views, but here are several that I think stand above the rest. Facing the TI a block off the action-packed pedestrian core, scenic **Le Chamonix Café** sits below Chamonix's pretty little church and has terrific views of both mountain ranges (daily until 20:00, Place de l'Eglise). **Café La Terrasse** has a cool location (literally) above the rush of the Arve River and is well-positioned for Mont Blanc views (daily until late, across from the casino on Place Balmat). **Mojo's** is a relaxed place for cheap food, and lovely views of the main square and mountains (daily, 31 Place du Joseph Balmat, tel. 04 50 21 99 45).

Chamonix Connections

Bus and train service to Chamonix is surprisingly good. You'll find bus and train information desks at the train station. Some train routes pass through Switzerland to reach Chamonix (such as from Paris and Colmar) and require additional tickets if you have a France-only railpass. You can avoid passing through Switzerland if you plan ahead, but it usually takes longer, and you miss some great scenery. The **route to Colmar** (via Bern and Basel) is beautiful and costs €60 for the Swiss segment. You'll get a fun taste of Switzerland's charms and, though you'll make many changes en route, they all work like a Swiss clock.

From Chamonix by Train to: Annecy (8/day, 2.5 hours, change in St-Gervais), **Beaune** and **Dijon** (7/day, 6-7 hours, change in St-Gervais and Lyon, some require additional changes), **Nice** (4/day, 10 hours, change in St-Gervais and Lyon), **Arles** (5/day, 7-8 hours, change in St-Gervais and Lyon), **Paris'** Gare de Lyon (7/day, more in summer and winter, 5.5-7 hours, some change in Switzerland), **Colmar** (hourly, 6 hours via Switzerland with 3-4 changes), **Martigny,** Switzerland (nearly hourly, 2 hours, scenic trip), **Geneva,** Switzerland, and its airport (roughly hourly, 3.5-5 hours, two changes).

THE FRENCH ALPS

From Chamonix by Bus to: Geneva Airport, Switzerland (3/day, 2 hours), **Courmayeur,** Italy (4/day, 45 minutes), **Aosta,** Italy (4/day July-mid-Sept, 2/day mid-Sept-June, 2-3 hours). Long-distance buses depart from the train station—get information at the TI or at the bus station (tel. 04 50 53 01 15, www.sat-montblanc.com). For more on buses to Italy, see "Day Trips near Chamonix" on page 901.

Airport shuttles also provide service between Chamonix's city center and the airport in **Geneva,** Switzerland (12/day, 2 hours, from €29/person). **Chamexpress** is British-run and easy to work with (www.chamexpress.com). Also try www.chamonix-transfer .com.

BURGUNDY

Beaune • Châteauneuf-en-Auxois • Semur-en-Auxois •
Abbey of Fontenay • Flavigny-sur-Ozerain • Alise Ste-Reine
• Vézelay • Château de Guédelon • Bourges • Cluny • Taizé

The rolling hills of Burgundy gave birth to superior wine, fine cuisine, spicy mustard, and sleepy villages smothered in luscious landscapes. This deceptively peaceful region witnessed Julius Caesar's defeat of the Gauls, then saw the Abbey of Cluny rise from the ashes of the Roman Empire to vie with Rome for religious influence in the 12th century. Burgundy's last hurrah came in the 15th century, when its powerful dukes controlled an immense area stretching north to Holland.

Today, bucolic Burgundy runs from about Auxerre in the north to near Lyon in the south, and it's crisscrossed with canals and dotted with quiet farming villages. It's also the transportation funnel for eastern France and makes a convenient stopover for travelers (car or train), with easy access north to Paris or Alsace, east to the Alps, and south to Provence.

Traditions are strong. In Burgundy, both the soil and the farmers who work it are venerated. Although many of the farms you see are growing grapes, only a small part of Burgundy is actually covered by vineyards. The white cows grazing amid green meadows are Charolais, producing France's best beef (*bœuf bourguignon* and steak are good choices here).

This is a calm, cultivated, and serene region, where nature is as sophisticated as the people. If you're looking for quintessential French culture, you'll find it in Burgundy.

Planning Your Time

With limited time, stay in or near Beaune. Plan on a half-day in Beaune and a half-day for the vineyards and countryside at its doorstep. With a full day, spend the morning in Beaune and the

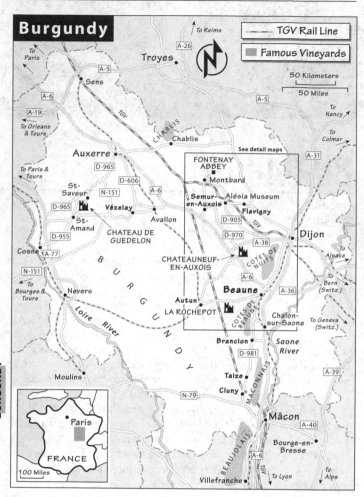

Burgundy

--- TGV Rail Line

▨ Famous Vineyards

To Reims → A-26

N

50 Kilometers
50 Miles

Troyes

A-5

To Nancy ↗

Sens

A-5

A-6
A-19

To Paris ↑
To Orleans & Tours ←

TGV

CHABLIS

Chablis

See detail maps

To Colmar ↗

A-31

Auxerre

D-965

D-606

A-6

FONTENAY ABBEY

Montbard

Alésia Museum

To Paris & Tours ←

St-Saveur

N-151

Semur-en-Auxois

Flavigny

Vézelay

Avallon

D-905

TGV

D-965

St-Amand

CHATEAU DE GUEDELON

D-970

Dijon

To Alsace →

D-955

Cosne

A-77

CHATEAUNEUF-EN-AUXOIS

A-38

COTES DE NUITS

N-151

B U R G U N D Y

Nevers

A-6

Beaune

A-36

To Bern (Switz.) →

To Bourges & Tours ←

Autun

LA ROCHEPOT

COTES DE BEAUNE

Chalon-sur-Saone

To Geneva (Switz.) →

Loire River

Brancion

Saone River

Moulins

D-981

A-39

Taize

MACONNAIS

N-79

Cluny

Mâcon

A-40

Paris

FRANCE

Bourge-en-Bresse

100 Miles

BEAUJOLAIS

A-6

TGV

Villefranche

To Lyon →

To Alps ↘

BURGUNDY

afternoon exploring the surrounding vineyards and wine villages (good by bike, car, or minibus tour). If you have a car (cheap rentals are available), or good legs and a bike, the best way to spend your afternoon is by following my scenic vineyard drive to Château de la Rochepot.

To explore off-the-beaten-path Burgundy, visit unspoiled Semur-en-Auxois or Flavigny-sur-Ozerain, the museum dedicated to the historic victory that won Gaul for Julius Caesar (in Alise Ste-Reine), and France's best-preserved medieval abbey com-

plex at Fontenay. These are all close to each other and on the way to Paris, or doable as a long day trip from Beaune. The magnificent church at Vézelay is more famous but harder to reach, and is best done as an overnight trip, or en route to Paris or the Loire Valley. If you're connecting Burgundy with the Loire, don't miss the medieval castle construction at Guédelon and the fine "High" Gothic cathedral in Bourges (either of these pairs well with Vézelay). And if you're driving between Beaune and Lyon, take the detour to adorable Brancion and once-powerful Cluny.

For up-to-date information on accommodations, restaurants, events, and shopping, see www.burgundyeye.com.

Getting Around Burgundy

Trains link Beaune with Dijon to the north and Lyon to the south; some stop in the wine villages of Meursault, Ladoix-Serrigny, and Santenay. Several buses per day cruise between vineyards north of Beaune on D-974, though precious few buses connect Beaune with villages to its south (see "Beaune Connections" on page 940). Bikes, minibus tours, and short taxi rides get non-drivers from Beaune into the countryside. Buses connect Semur-en-Auxois with the Dijon and Montbard train stations. Drivers enjoy motoring on Burgundy's lovely roads; you'll cruise along canals, past rolling hills of vineyards, and on tree-lined lanes. Drivers can navigate by the excellent (and free) map of the Côte d'Or available at all TIs.

Burgundy's Cuisine Scene

Arrive hungry. Considered by many to be France's best, Burgundian cuisine is peasant cooking elevated to an art. Entire lives are spent debating the best restaurants and bistros.

Several classic dishes were born in Burgundy: *escargots de Bourgogne* (snails served sizzling hot in garlic butter), *bœuf bourgui-*

gnon (beef simmered for hours in red wine with onions and mushrooms), coq au vin (rooster stewed in red wine), and *œufs en meurette* (poached eggs in a red wine sauce, often served on a large crouton), as well as the famous Dijon mustards. Look also for delicious *jambon persillé* (cold ham layered in a garlic-parsley gelatin), *pain d'épices* (spice bread), and *gougères* (light, puffy cheese pastries). Native cheeses are Époisses and Langres (both mushy and great) and my favorite, Montrachet (a tasty goat cheese). Crème de cassis (black currant liqueur) is another Burgundian specialty; look for it in desserts and snazzy drinks (try a *kir*).

Remember, restaurants serve only during lunch (11:30-14:00)

BURGUNDY

and dinner (19:00-21:00, later in bigger cities); some cafés serve food throughout the day.

Burgundy's Wines

Along with Bordeaux, Burgundy is why France is famous for wine. From Chablis to Beaujolais, you'll find great fruity reds, dry whites, and crisp rosés. The three key grapes are Chardonnay (dry white wines), Pinot Noir (medium-bodied red wines), and Gamay (light, fruity red wines, such as Beaujolais). Every village produces its own distinctive wine, from Chablis to Meursault to Chassagne-Montrachet. Road maps read like fine-wine lists. If the  wine village has a hyphenated name, the latter half of its name usually comes from the town's most important vineyard (such as Gevrey-Chambertin, Aloxe-Corton, and Vosne-Romanée). Look for *Dégustation Gratuite* (free tasting) signs, and prepare for serious wine-tasting—and steep prices, if you're not careful. For a more easygoing tasting experience, head for the hills: The less prestigious Hautes-Côtes (upper slopes) produce some terrific, inexpensive, and overlooked wines. The least expensive (but often worthwhile) wines are Bourgogne and Passetoutgrain (both red) and whites from the Mâcon and Chalon areas (St-Véran whites are also a good value). If you like rosé, try Marsannay, considered one of France's best. And *les famous* Pouilly-Fuissé grapes are grown near the city of Mâcon. For tips on tasting, see the sidebar on page 46.

Beaune

You'll feel comfortable right away in this prosperous, popular, and perfectly French little wine capital, where life centers on the production and consumption of the prestigious Côte d'Or wines. *Côte d'Or* means "Golden Hillside," and the slopes here are a spectacle to enjoy in late October as the leaves turn.

Medieval monks and powerful dukes of Burgundy laid the groundwork that established this town's prosperity. The monks cultivated wine and cheese, and the dukes cultivated wealth. A ring road (with a bike path) follows the foundations of the medieval walls, and parking lots just outside keep most traffic from seeping into the historic center. One of the world's most important wine auctions takes place here every year on the third weekend of November.

Orientation to Beaune

Beaune is compact (pop. 25,000), with a handful of interesting monuments and vineyards knocking at its door. Limit your Beaune ramblings to the town center, lassoed within its medieval walls and circled by a one-way ring road, and leave time to stroll into the vineyards. All roads and activities converge on the town's two squares, Place Carnot and Place de la Halle. Beaune is quiet on Sundays and Monday mornings. The city's monuments are beautifully lit at night, making Beaune ideal for a post-dinner stroll.

Tourist Information

The main TI is located across from the post office on the ring road's southeastern corner (look for *Porte Marie de Bourgogne* on the banner; daily 9:00-18:30, closed 12:00-13:00 Nov-March, tel. 03 80 26 21 30, www.beaune-tourism.com). A small TI annex (called "Point-I") is housed in the market hall, across from Hôtel Dieu. Either TI has extensive information on wine-tasting in the area, a room-finding service, a list of *chambres d'hôtes,* bus schedules, and an excellent, free road map of the region. They can also arrange a local guide (€130/2 hours, €180/4 hours). The main TI has audioguides for visiting Beaune (€5, 1.5 hours).

Ambitious sightseers may benefit by buying the **Pass Beaune,** which gets you a discount at most attractions in Beaune (including Hôtel Dieu, Wine Museum, Abbey of Fontenay, the site of the Cluny Abbey, and most major wine cellars). The catch: You have to decide what you're going to see when you buy the pass, so you're committed to visiting those attractions. Buy this pass only if your plans are set in stone (5 percent off 2 sights, 10 percent off 3 sights, 15 percent off 4 or more sights; buy at the TI).

Arrival in Beaune

By Train: To reach the city center from the train station (no baggage storage), walk straight out of the station up Avenue du 8 Septembre, cross the busy ring road, and continue up Rue du Château. Follow it as it angles left and pass the mural, veering right onto Rue des Tonneliers. A left on Rue de l'Enfant leads to Beaune's pedestrian zone and Place Carnot.

By Bus: Beaune has no bus station—only several stops along the ring road. Ask the driver for *le Centre-Ville.* The Jules Ferry (zhul fair-ee) stop is closest to the train station. (For details on bus service, see "Getting Around the Beaune Region" on page 940.)

By Car: Follow *Centre-Ville* signs to the ring road. Once on the ring road, turn right at the first signal after the modern post office (Rue d'Alsace), and park for free a block away in Place Madeleine. If the lot is full—which it often is—don't worry, as

BURGUNDY

Beaune's Best Wine and Food Stores

Beaune overflows with wine boutiques eager to convince you that their food products or wines are best. Here are a few to look for (to locate these, see the map on page 918).

The wine shop **Denis Perret** has a good selection in all price ranges and a helpful, English-speaking staff managed by friendly owner Alain. If you've tasted a wine elsewhere that you like, they can usually find a less costly bottle with similar qualities. They can chill a white for your picnic (Mon-Sat 9:00-12:00 & 14:00-19:00, Sun 9:00-12:00, 40 Place Carnot, tel. 03 80 22 35 47, www.denisperret.fr).

For an exquisite selection of fruit liqueurs (such as crème de cassis—a Burgundian treat), fruit syrups, and Burgundian brandy, find **Védrenne** at 28 Rue Carnot (closed Sun).

For food, **Alain Hess** has a beautiful display of local cheeses, mustards, and other gourmet food products (7 Place Carnot). A few doors down, welcoming **Mulot-Petitjean Pain d'Epices** shows off exquisite packages of this tasty local spice bread, also handy as gifts (1 Place Carnot).

spaces usually open up before long. You also can look for parking on surrounding streets or in other lots along the ring road. Parking inside Beaune's ring road is metered.

Helpful Hints

Market Days: Beaune hosts a smashing Saturday market and a modest Wednesday market. Both are centered on Place de la Halle and open until 12:30. The Saturday market animates much of the old town and is worth planning ahead for. For either market, watch the action from the **Baltard Café** on Place de la Halle, then do as the locals do and have lunch at an outdoor café (many good choices—see "Eating in Beaune," later, for ideas; sit down by 12:30 or forget it).

Supermarket: Supermarché Casino, with two locations in Beaune, has a great selection and a deli (Mon-Sat 8:30-20:00, closed Sun, through the arch off Place Madeleine, or in the town center on Rue Carnot).

Internet Access: Baltard Café, across from the TI annex, has pricey Internet access (€1/15 minutes for Wi-Fi or computer use, daily, 14 Place de la Halle, tel. 03 80 24 21 86). The recommended **Bistrot Bourguignon** offers Wi-Fi with wine.

Post Office: The main post office is at 7 Boulevard St Jacques. A handy PTT annex sells stamps and Colissimo boxes for international shipping (see page 1114), as well as credit for any mobile phone (Mon-Fri 10:00-12:00 & 14:00-18:00, Sat 10:00-12:00 & 14:00-17:00, closed Sun, 37 Rue Carnot).

Laundry: Beaune's two launderettes are both open daily 7:00-21:00. One is in the town center at 65 Rue Lorraine; the other is between the train station and Place Madeleine at 17-19 Rue du Faubourg St. Jean.

Bike Rental: See "Getting Around the Beaune Region—By Bike" on page 940.

Taxi: Call 06 11 83 06 10 or 06 09 35 63 12.

Car Rental: **ADA** is cheap and close to the train station (allow €50/day for a small car that includes 100 kilometers—about 60 miles, Mon-Sat 8:00-12:00 & 14:00-18:00, closed Sun, 26 Avenue 8 Septembre, tel. 03 80 22 72 90). **Avis** is at the train station (tel. 03 80 24 96 46), and **Europcar** is less centrally located (53 Route de Pommard, tel. 03 80 22 32 24).

Cooking Classes: Enthusiastic American chef **Marjorie Taylor** invites traveling foodies to her beautifully appointed, light-filled apartment to introduce them to Burgundian cuisine. She fosters a convivial environment where participants get to know each other, and she emphasizes artisanal, sustainable, locally sourced ingredients purchased directly from the producer. Marjorie's class offerings include a market-day tour of Beaune, followed by a hands-on cooking classes and a full, five-course lunch with wine (€200/person, Sat and Wed best for full market-day experience); a "dinner with the cook" class during which you're welcome to look over her shoulder as she prepares the meal (not as hands-on as the cooking class; €175/person, 10 people max); and an intensive cook's workshop for more experienced cooks (€395/person for a longer day that often includes field trips). She also conducts weekend and longer programs (mobile 06 17 36 46 60, www.thecooksatelier.com, marjorie@thecooksatelier.com).

Best Souvenir Shopping: The **Athenaeum** has a great variety of souvenirs, including wine and cooking books in English, with a good children's section upstairs...and you won't find a bookstore with a better wine bar (daily 10:00-19:00, across from Hôtel Dieu at 7 Rue de l'Hôtel Dieu). **Le Vigneron,** at 6 Rue d'Alsace, is crammed with wine-related stuff, French knives, and more.

Tours in Beaune

Tourist Train—A TGV-esque little train will show you Beaune and nearby vineyards (€7, runs April-Oct 11:00-17:00, almost hourly departures from Hôtel Dieu, no morning trips on Wed and Sat market days, 45 minutes).

Local Guides—You have several great choices. For Beaune and nearby, consider animated, athletic, and smart Canadian **Sarah**

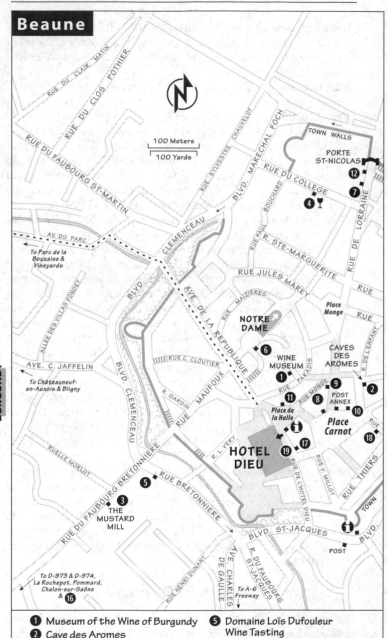

Beaune

100 Meters
100 Yards

BURGUNDY

To Parc de la Bouzaise & Vineyards

To Châteauneuf-en-Auxois & Bligny

To D-973 & D-974, La Rochepot, Pommard, Chalon-sur-Saône & 16

TOWN WALLS

PORTE ST-NICOLAS

NOTRE DAME

WINE MUSEUM

CAVES DES AROMES

POST ANNEX

Place Monge

Place de la Halle

Place Carnot

HOTEL DIEU

THE MUSTARD MILL

POST

1. Museum of the Wine of Burgundy
2. Cave des Aromes
3. The Mustard Mill
4. Patriarche Père et Fils Wine Tasting
5. Domaine Loïs Dufouleur Wine Tasting
6. Sensation Vin Wine Bar/Classes
7. Les Mille et une Vignes Wine Bar
8. Denis Perret Wine Shop
9. Védrenne Liqueurs

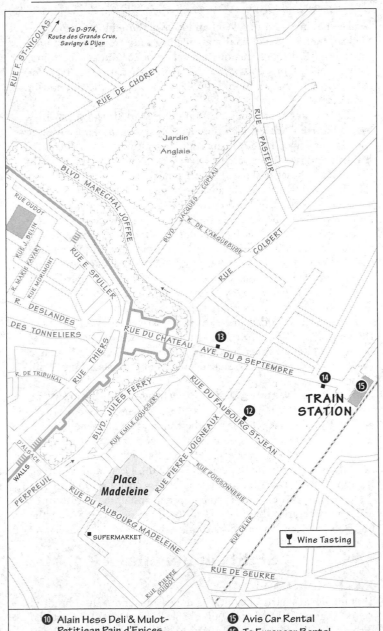

BURGUNDY

10 Alain Hess Deli & Mulot-
    Petitjean Pain d'Epices
11 Baltard Café (Internet Access)
12 Launderettes (2)
13 Bike Rental
14 ADA Car Rental
15 Avis Car Rental
16 To Europcar Rental
17 Athenaeum Bookstore
18 Le Vigneron Shop
19 Tourist Train Departures

Bird—she's married to a local and knows the region thoroughly. She can help organize your stay in Burgundy from soup to nuts (private guided tours, customized self-guided tours, wine tours, tours by bike, foot, or car for about €250/half-day, other rates for full tours on request, mobile 06 42 24 31 95, sarah@detours-in -france.com).

For tours that focus on vineyards and Burgundian history, **Colette Barbier,** a professor of gastronomy and wines at the University of Dijon, is an engaging guide who is fluent in English and passionate about her region. She knows Burgundy like a local—because she is one (her family has lived in the region for 250 years). Book well in advance, though last-minute requests sometimes work (€230/half-day, €390/day, tel. & fax 03 80 23 94 34, mobile 06 80 57 47 40, www.burgundy-guide.com, cobatour @aol.com). Her daughter **Emma,** raised in the same bottle, guides with as much passion—albeit with a more youthful perspective (mobile 06 83 43 50 78, www.burgundy-winetour.e-monsite.com).

Delightful and wine-smart **Stephanie Jones** came from her native Britain to Burgundy to learn its wines—which she has, getting her degree in oenology and working in Burgundian wine cellars for years. Today she leads informative, enjoyable tours of the vineyards while also running a B&B (price per person: €95/half-day, €180/day, 2-person minimum, tel. 03 80 61 29 61, mobile 06 10 18 04 12, www.aux-quatre-saisons.net, aux4saisons35@aol .com).

Minibus and Walking Tours of Vineyards—**Safari Wine Tours** offers two-hour van tours of the villages and vineyards around Beaune that get you into the countryside and smaller wineries (though you won't do much tasting—generally one tasting per tour). There are four itineraries (€42-52, tour #2 is best for beginners; tours depart from TI generally at 12:00, 14:30, and 17:00; tel. 03 80 24 79 12, www.burgundy-tourism-safaritours.com, or call TI to reserve). **Vinéa Tours** is more formal and upscale, with three different itineraries that last two to three hours each (€54, mobile 06 73 38 37 19, www.vineatours.com).

Sights in Beaune

▲▲▲Hôtel Dieu

This medieval charity hospital is now a museum. The Hundred Years' War and the plague (a.k.a. the Black Death) devastated Beaune, leaving three-quarters of its population destitute. Nicholas Rolin, chancellor of Burgundy (enriched, in part, by his power to collect taxes), had to do something for "his people" (or, more likely, was getting old and wanted to close out his life on a philanthropic, rather than a greedy, note). So, in 1443 Rolin paid to build this

place. It was completed in just eight years and served as a hospital until 1971, when the last patient checked out. The Hospices de Beaune began opening its doors to visitors in the 1950s, although it wasn't fully open to tourists until the early 1980s.

Cost and Hours: €7, includes audioguide, daily April-mid-Nov 9:00-18:30, mid-Nov-March 9:00-11:30 & 14:00-17:30, last entry one hour before closing; it's dead-center in Beaune, dominating Place de la Halle; tel. 03 80 24 45 00, www.hospices-de-beaune.com.

❍ **Self-Guided Tour:** While the audioguide delivers key facts and good information, this self-guided tour gives your visit more meaning. Tour the rooms, which circle the courtyard, in a clockwise direction.

Courtyard of Honor: Honor meant power, and this was all about showing off. The exterior of the hospital and the town side of the courtyard are intentionally solemn, so as not to attract pesky 15th-century brigands who would loot whatever looked most rewarding. The dazzling inner courtyard features a colorful glazed tile roof, establishing what became a style recognized in France as typically "Burgundian." The tiles, which last 300 years, are fired three times: once to harden, again to burn in the color, and finally for the glaze. They were redone in 1902. The building is lacy Flamboyant Gothic with lots of decor—and boasts more weathervanes than any other building in France.

Paupers' Ward: Enter the hospice halfway down the courtyard on the left. This grandest room of the hospital was the ward for the poorest patients. The vault, typical of big medieval rooms, was constructed like the hull of a ship. The screen separates the ward from the chapel at the front. Every three hours, the door was opened, and patients could experience Mass from their beds. Study the ceiling. Crossbeams are held by the mouths of creatively carved monsters—each mouth is stretched realistically, and each face has individual characteristics. Between the crossbars are busts of real 15th-century townsfolk—leading citizens, with animals humorously indicating their foibles (for example, a round-faced glutton next to a pig).

The carved wooden statue over the door you just entered shows a bound Christ—demonstrating graphically to patients that their Savior suffered and was able to empathize with their ordeal. Its realism shows that Gothic art had moved beyond the stiff formality of Romanesque carving. Behind the little window next to the statue, was the nuns' dorm. The sisters (who were the first nurses) would check on patients from here. Notice the scrawny candle-holder; if a patient died in the night, the candle was extinguished.

A painting halfway up on the left shows patients being treated in this room in 1949, 500 years after its founding. During epidemics, there were two to a bed. Study the glass display cases near the beds. Rolin, who believed every patient deserved dignity, provided each patient with a pewter jug, mug, bowl, and plate. But the ward didn't get heat until the 19th century (notice the heating grates on the floor), and the staff didn't get the concept of infection (and the basic practices of hand-washing and covering your mouth when coughing) until the late 19th century (thanks to Louis Pasteur). Most patients would have been better off left in a ditch outside.

Chapel: The hospice was not a place of hope. People came here to die. Care was more for the soul than the body. (Local guides are routinely instructed in writing by American tour companies not to use the word "hospice," because it turns off their clients. But this was a hospice, plain and simple, and back then, death was apparently less disturbing.) The stained glass shows Nicolas Rolin (lower left) and his wife, Guigone (lower right), dressed as a nun to show her devotion. Nicolas' feudal superior, the Duke of Burgundy, is portrayed above him. Notice the action on Golgotha. As Jesus is crucified, the souls of the two criminals crucified with him (portrayed as miniature naked humans) are being snatched up—one by an angel and the other by a red devil. At the bottom, Mary cradles the dead body of Christ. You're standing on tiles with the love symbol (or "gallant device") designed by Nicolas and Guigone to celebrate their love (as noble couples often did). The letters *N* and *G* are entwined in an oak branch, meaning that their love was strong. The word *seule* ("only one") and the lone star declare that Guigone is the only star in Nicolas' cosmos.

St. Hugue Ward: In the 17th century, this smaller ward was established for wealthy patients (who could afford better health care). They were more likely to survive, and the decor displays themes of hope, rather than resignation: The series of Baroque paintings lining the walls shows the biblical miracles that Jesus performed. As the wealthy would lie in their beds, they'd stare at the ceiling—a painting with the bottom of an angel's foot, surrounded by the sick waiting to be healed by Jesus in his scarlet robe. The syringes in the display cases with English descriptions are as delicate as caulking guns. Ouch.

St. Nicolas Room: Originally divided into smaller rooms—one used for "surgery" (a.k.a. bloodletting and amputation), the other as an extension of the kitchen that you'll see next—this room now holds a model of the steep roof support and more tools of the doctoring trade (amputation saws, pans for bloodletting, and so on). The glass panel in the floor's center shows the stream running below; the hole provided a primitive but convenient disposal system after dinner or surgery. Living downstream from the hospital was a bad idea. Notice the display case showing the *Vente aux Enchères des Hospices de Beaune*. Operation of the hospice was primarily funded through auctioning its great wines (made from land donated by grateful patients over the years). Today, the auction of Hospices de Beaune wines is an internationally followed event, and gives the first indication of prices for the previous year's wines. Proceeds from the auction still support the hospital at its current location in a Beaune suburb.

Kitchen: The kitchen display shows a 16th-century rotisserie. When fully wound, the cute robot would crank away, and the spit would spin slowly for 45 minutes. The 19th-century stove provided running hot water, which spewed from the beaks of swans. A five-minute, French-only sound-and-light show runs every 15 minutes.

Pharmacy: The nuns grew herbs out back, and strange and wondrous concoctions were stored in pottery jars. The biggest jar (by the window in the second room) was for *theriaca* ("panacea," or cure-all). The most commonly used medicine back then, it was a syrup of herbs, wine, and opium.

St. Louis Ward: A maternity ward until 1969, this room is lined with fine 16th- and 17th-century tapestries illustrating mostly Old Testament stories. Dukes traveled with tapestries to cozy up the humble places they stayed in while on the road. The 16th-century pieces have better colors but inferior perspective. (The most precious 15th-century tapestries are displayed in the next room, where everyone is enthralled by the great Van der Weyden painting.)

Roger van der Weyden's *Last Judgment:* This exquisite painting, the treasure of the Hôtel Dieu, was commissioned by Rolin in 1450 for the altar of the Paupers' Ward. He spared no cost, hiring the leading Flemish artist of his time. The entire altarpiece survives. The back side (on right wall) was sliced off so everything could be viewed at the same time. The painting is full of symbolism. Christ presides over Judgment Day. The lily is mercy, the sword is judgment, the rainbow promises salvation, and the jeweled globe at Jesus' feet symbolizes the universality of Christianity's message. As four angels blow their trumpets, St. Michael the archangel—very much in control—determines which souls are heavy with sin. Mary and the apostles pray for the souls of the dead as they emerge from their graves. But notice how both Michael and Jesus are expressionless—at this point, the cries of the damned and their loved ones are useless. In the back row are real people of the day.

The intricate detail, painted with a three-haired brush, is typical of Flemish art from this period. While Renaissance artists employed mathematical tricks of perspective, these artists captured a sense of reality by painting minute detail upon detail. (The attendant is dying to be asked to move the magnifying glass—*le loup*—into position to help you appreciate the exquisite detail in the painting.) Stare at Michael's robe and wings. Check out John's delicate feet and hands. Study the faces of the damned; you can almost hear the gnashing of teeth. The feet of the damned show the pull of a terrible force. On the far left, notice those happily entering the pearly gates. On the far right, it's the flames of hell (no, this has nothing to do with politics).

Except for Sundays and holidays, the painting was kept closed and people saw only the panels that now hang on the right wall: Nicolas and Guigone piously at the feet of St. Sebastian—invoked to fight the plague—and St. Anthony, whom patients called upon for help in combating burning skin diseases.

The unusual 15th-century tapestry *A Thousand Flowers*, hanging on the left wall, tells the medieval story of St. Eligius.

More Sights in Beaune

Collégiale Notre-Dame—Built in the 12th and 13th centuries, Beaune's cathedral was a "daughter of Cluny" (built in the style of the Cluny Abbey, described on page 975). Except for the 14th-century Gothic front porch addition, it's a good example of Cluny-style Romanesque architecture. Enter to see the 15th-century tapestries (behind the altar), a variety of stained glass, and what's left of frescoes depicting the life of Lazarus.

Cost and Hours: Free, tapestry open daily 9:30-12:30 & 14:00-17:00, until 19:00 during high season.

• *To get to the wine museum (listed next), walk 30 steps straight out of the cathedral, turn left down a cobbled alley (Rue d'Enfer, or "Hell Street," named for the fires of the Duke's kitchens once located on this street), keep left, and enter the courtyard of Hôtel des Ducs.*

Museum of the Wine of Burgundy (Musée du Vin de Bourgogne)—From this well-organized folk-wine museum, which fills the old residence of the Dukes of Burgundy, it's clear that the history and culture of Burgundy and its wine were fermented in the same bottle. Wander into the free courtyard for a look at the striking palace, antique wine presses (in the *cuverie*, or vatting shed; good English explanations), and a concrete model of Beaune's 15th-century street plan (a good chance to appreciate the town's once-impressive fortified wall). Inside the museum, you'll see a model of the region's topography, along with tools, costumes, and scenes of Burgundian wine history—but no tasting. Each room has helpful English explanations.

Cost and Hours: €5.60, ticket also includes the Musée des Beaux-Arts et Musée Marey art museum; April-Nov daily 9:30-

18:00; Dec-March Wed-Mon 9:30-17:00, closed Tue; tel. 03 80 22 08 19.

Cave des Aromes—An engaging exhibit on the sense of smell is usually set up during the summer months at Beaune's Chambre de Commerce. You'll sniff glass containers holding a great range of aromas and try to associate them with those you find in wine. It's a fun place to drop in and sniff.

Cost and Hours: Free, usually July-mid-Sept daily 10:00-12:30 & 14:00-18:00, 2 Rue Tribunal, tel. 03 80 26 35 10.

The Mustard Mill (La Moutarderie Fallot)—The last of the independent mustard mills in Burgundy opens its doors for bilingual guided tours in French and English. The tour is pricey (€10) and long, yet informative—you'll learn why Burgundy was the birthplace of mustard (it's about wine juice), and where they get their grains today (Canada). It takes over an hour to explain what could be explained in half that time—you'll see a short film, learn about the key machines used in processing mustard (with the help of audioguides), and finish with a tasting.

Cost and Hours: €10, tours daily at 10:00 and 11:30, additional tours Mon-Sat mid-June-mid-Sept at 15:30 and 17:00; must call TI to reserve or book online, as space is limited; across ring road in the appropriately yellow building at 31 Rue du Faubourg Bretonnière, tel. 03 80 22 10 02, www.fallot.com.

Walk to Parc de la Bouzaise and into the Vineyards—Stroll across the ring road, through a pleasant Impressionist-like park, and into Beaune's beautiful vineyards. This walk is ideal for picnickers, families (good play toys in park), and vine enthusiasts. Follow Avenue de la République west from the center, cross the ring road, and parallel the stream along a few grassy blocks for about five minutes, then angle right into the serene park. Pop out at the right rear (northwest) corner of the park, turn left on the small road, and enter the Côte de Beaune vineyards. Find the big poster showing how the land is sliced and diced among different plots (called *clos*, for "enclosure"). The vine-covered landscape is crisscrossed with narrow lanes and stubby stone walls (good for picnics, but no shade) and provides terrific early-morning and sunset views. Wander among the enclosures, noticing the rocky soil (wine grapes need to struggle). The highest areas of the hills far above you grow grapes that end up in wines labeled *Haute Côte de Beaune*, and are cheaper and generally less intense than those

Burgundian Wine Quality, 2002-2011

2002 Called the "vintage of the decade" by some, the reds are remarkably balanced, intense, and fruity, and can be kept a long time. The whites are excellent, with good structure, balance, and pure, clean fruit flavors.

2003 A most unusual year due to the extreme summer heat. The harvest was a month early, so the grapes were small, with thick skins, and produced only about half the usual yield. The reds are deeper in color and taste very different from usual Pinot Noirs. All wines need to be drunk sooner—the average time you can keep this year's vintage is about half the normal (10 years at most for reds; whites should be consumed right away).

2004 A lousy summer (rain, hail, and wind) but a brilliant September (three weeks of bright sunshine). The good places produced reds that are very fruity, clean, supple, and "flattering" (according to my friend). They can be drunk and appreciated early, though they will last a long time. The whites are excellent, with a precise acidity, giving them the freshness and pure fruitiness of a great vintage.

2005 The makings of a great vintage: The harvest was healthy and balanced, with great natural sugar. A local magazine called 2005 "the vintage of dreams." The reds are superb—rich, plain, concentrated, full-bodied, and intense. They will age magnificently. The whites may be a little less impressive, but they are still good.

2006 Challenged even the most experienced winemakers with capricious weather that didn't allow an idle moment in the vineyards or the cellar. The whites are of high quality with good consistency from Chablis to Mâcon. Supple and fresh, they are fruity with considerable richness. The reds are excellent across the board, with beautiful, intense color. Some are delicate and

made from the grapes in front of you. As you wander about, keep in mind that subtle differences of soil and drainage between adjacent plots of land can be enough to create very different-tasting wines—from grapes grown only feet apart. *Vive la différence.*

Wine-Tasting Around Beaune

Countless opportunities exist for you to learn the finer points of Burgundy's wines. Many shops and wineries offer free, informal, and informative tastings (with the expectation that you'll buy something)—though the limits on our ability to bring wines elegant; others are robust and full-bodied. Their aromas vary from red fruits to cherry, spices, and cocoa.

2007 A hot spring, combined with the worst Burgundian summer in 30 years, meant a light vintage for the reds—so drink them sooner rather than later. The whites are subpar as well, so you may want to skip this vintage.

2008 Another tricky year for grapes. Those who waited longest to harvest came out with the best wines, as September was a warm, dry month. The wines of Chablis are excellent, but other wines are less consistent.

2009 This was a banner year for Burgundies. The harvest provided beautiful grapes, so the expectations were sky-high after two tough years. And though the wines may not be as full-bodied as the great 2005 vintage, they are more supple and ready to drink sooner (but won't keep as long).

2010 With considerable rain in late spring, the quantity harvested was about half the usual amount—but with good concentration. Because of the low quantity, these will disappear from the shelves quickly and prices may rise. More uncertain is the quality—the harvest was quite late, so it's hard to know how well this vintage will turn out.

2011 This was yet another vintage with tricky weather—a long drought in the springtime and pouring rains in the summer meant that for the third time in less than 10 years, the harvest began in August, which doesn't allow the grapes to take advantage of September sun. So the quality of the wine will depend on the winemaker's talent. This vintage will have to be appreciated for its fruit, but will not be a wine to keep for long.

back to North America can lead to tricky dynamics, particularly at smaller places. Winemakers are busy people and, naturally, they prefer to spend their time turning folks on to their wines who can buy enough to make it worth their while—and in most cases, that's not you (as nice as you are). They hope you'll like their wines, buy several bottles or a dozen, and ask for them at your shop back home. If you're not serious about buying at least a few bottles, look for places that charge for tastings (I list several). Some shops and wineries can arrange shipping (about €15 per bottle to ship a case, though you save about 20 percent on the VAT tax when shipping—so expensive wines are worth the shipping cost). To learn more about shipping wine, **Côte d'Or Imports** works with many sellers in Burgundy and has earned a reputation for safe and reliable shipping (US tel. 971/238-1492, French tel. 03 80 61 15 15, www.cotedorpdx.com, info@cotedorpdx.com). For tips on wine-tasting, see the sidebar on page 46.

A few large cellars *(caves)* charge an entry fee, allowing you to taste a variety of wines (with less expectation that you'll buy). Most of these *caves* offer some form of introduction or self-guided tour. Don't mind the mossy ceilings. Many cellars have spent centuries growing this "angel's hair"—the result of humidity created by the evaporation of the wines stored there.

In Beaune

Here are a couple of good places to learn about Burgundy wines in Beaune.

Patriarche Père et Fils—With Burgundy's largest and most impressive wine cellar, this is the best of the major wineries to visit in the city. With a helpful videoguide, you'll tour some of their three miles of underground passages and finish in the atmospheric tasting room, where you'll try 13 Burgundian classics (3 whites and 10 reds); each bottle sits on top of its own wine barrel. The long walk back to *la sortie* helps sober you up.

Cost and Hours: €13, daily 9:30-11:30 & 14:00-17:00, 5 Rue du Collège, tel. 03 80 24 53 78, www.patriarche.com.

Sensation Vin—For a good introduction to Burgundy wines, try these short and informative wine classes. You'll gather around a small counter in the comfortable wine bar/classroom and learn while you taste. Since the young owners do not make wine, you'll get an objective education (with blind tastings) and sample from a variety of producers. Call or email ahead to arrange a class/tasting.

Cost and Hours: €22 for 1-hour class with 6 wines (3 whites, 3 reds, Sun-Fri at 10:30), €32 for 1.5-hour class with 9 wines (4 whites, 5 reds, Sun-Fri at 14:30 or 16:30)—aspirin and pillow provided, 2-person minimum, open daily, near Collégiale Notre-Dame at 1 Rue d'Enfer, tel. 03 80 22 17 57, www.sensation-vin.com, contact@sensation-vin.com.

Near Beaune

A handy way to sample village life—and prowl the vineyards—is to hop on a bike or take a taxi. These wineries are a short jaunt from Beaune (no more than a 15-minute drive). Remember that at free tastings, you're expected to buy a bottle or two, unless you're with a group tour. All of these places can ship overseas. For wine-tasting suggestions a bit farther afield, along **La Route des Grands Crus,** see page 947.

Savoring Burgundy: Wine-Tasting Tactics

If you don't want to leave Beaune: Visit the wine cellars listed under "In Beaune" on the facing page.

Visiting vineyards without wheels: Rent a bike or take a taxi to wine villages just a short drive from Beaune (see "Near Beaune," facing page), book a minibus tour or a recommended local guide (see page 917), or try Transco bus #44 for villages on La Route des Grand Crus (see page 947).

Visiting vineyards by car: Follow one of my three self-guided routes (starting on page 941). The first two routes also work well for bikes.

Villages South of Beaune

Pommard—Just five minutes from Beaune, Patrick Clémencet offers tastings in a small, traditional tasting room with minimal English. You need to know what you want to taste and have the patience to navigate the language barrier. There's a big selection of reasonably priced wines (€6-40/bottle) from most of the famous wine villages, and *bien sûr,* plenty of Pommard (generally open Mon-Sat 10:00-12:00 & 13:30-19:00, closed Sun; 1 Place de l'Europe—enter Pommard when you see Hôtel du Pont and find the winery's green sign a block down, arcing over its entry, push the *sonnez* button if no one is there; tel. 03 80 22 59 11, domaine -clemencet@orange.fr).

Puligny-Montrachet and Chassagne-Montrachet—These two villages are situated about a 15-minute drive (or 45-60 minutes by bike) south of Beaune, on the scenic route to Château de la Rochepot (see page 942).

Located on the village's central roundabout, the user-friendly **Caveau de Puligny-Montrachet** has a convivial wine-bar-like tasting room, a smart outdoor terrace, English-speaking staff, and no pressure to buy. It represents many top-quality Burgundian vintners and has a great selection from Puligny-Montrachet. Knowledgeable Julien is happy to answer your every question (about €13 for 5 wines, free if you buy 6 bottles, can ship to the US; March-Oct daily 9:30-12:00 & 14:00-19:00, sometimes open later; Nov-Feb Tue-Sat 10:00-12:00 & 15:00-18:00, closed Mon; tel. 03 80 21 96 78).

If you're looking for an upscale wine château experience, visit **Château de Chassagne-Montrachet** (look for signs in town). In this elegant mansion, an informative tour takes you through gorgeous cellars—some dating to the 11th century. You'll taste five of Michel Picard's impressive wines from throughout Burgundy (€12

BURGUNDY

includes tour, €8 without tour, allow at least an hour with tour). They also offer a well-designed wine-tasting lunch *(table dégustation)* for €45 with six wines or €55 with 12 wines...cots are provided (daily 10:00-18:00, best to call ahead, tel. 03 80 21 98 57, www .michelpicard.com).

Villages North of Beaune

Aloxe-Corton—This small village, with several good tasting opportunities, is just a 10-minute drive north of Beaune.

At the **Domaines d'Aloxe-Corton** tasting room, you can sample seven makers of the famous Aloxe-Corton wines in a comfortable and relaxed setting (no cellars to tour). Prices are affordable, and the easygoing staff speaks enough English (small fee for tasting, free if you buy 2 bottles, Thu-Mon 10:00-13:00 & 15:00-19:00, usually closed Tue-Wed, tel. 03 80 26 49 85). You'll find the *caveau* a few steps from the little square in Aloxe-Corton.

Mischief and Mayhem is a dream come true for Anglophones serious about Burgundian wine. British-born-and-raised Fiona and Michael make fine wines and sell them at fair prices (€13-60). Though eager to add their own style to their wines, they are thoroughly immersed in Burgundian culture and can help you make sense of this region's wine culture. It's a small operation, so tasting hours vary (generally late mornings and late afternoons, best to call ahead and come prepared to buy, a few blocks below the church on D-115d to Ladoix-Serrigny at 10 Impasse du Puits, tel. 03 80 26 46 15, mobile 06 30 01 23 76, www.mischiefandmayhem .com).

Domaine Comte Senard is famous for its prestigious wines and *table d'hôte,* where you get a full lunch with matching wines and thorough explanations from the wine steward as you go (Tue-Sat 12:00-14:00, €40 with 4 wines, €50 with 6 wines, €60 with 8 wines). It's a fun, convivial way to spend two hours learning about the local product—be sure to come early to make the most of the experience. It's also possible to skip lunch and just sample their wines (€10, free if you purchase wine, Tue-Sat 12:00-18:00, closed Sun-Mon, 1 Rue des Chaumes, tel. 03 80 26 41 65, www.table -comte-senard.com).

Château Corton-André offers visits to its cellars, followed by tastings in a pleasant boutique located at the far corner of the château (daily 10:00-13:00 & 14:30-18:30, Rue des Cortons, tel. 03 80 26 44 25, www.pierre-andre.com).

Savigny-lès-Beaune—About five minutes from Beaune, Savigny-lès-Beaune is home to **Henri de Villamont,** a big-time enterprise with a huge range of wines and a modern, welcoming tasting room. They grow their own grapes as well as buy grapes from other vineyards, but they make all the wines themselves. This allows them to create a great selection of wines featuring grapes from virtually all of the famous wine villages, from Pouilly-Fuissé to Chablis (Tue 14:00-18:00, Wed-Sat 10:00-12:30 & 13:30-18:00, Sun 10:00-13:00, may be open Mon mornings—call to check, Rue du Dr. Guyot, call ahead if you want to visit the cellars, tel. 03 80 21 50 59, www.hdv.fr).

Magny-les-Villers—This Hautes-Côtes village is located 15 minutes north of Beaune (beyond Aloxe-Corton). **Domaine Naudin-Ferrand** is overlooked by most, but makes terrific reds and whites at excellent prices. Its best values are wines from the Hautes-Côtes vineyards. As it's a small operation, call or email to let them know you are coming (Mon-Fri 9:00-12:00 & 13:30-17:30, Sat 10:00-18:00, closed Sun, tel. 03 80 62 91 50, www.naudin-ferrand.com, info@naudin-ferrand.com).

Sleeping in Beaune

In the Center

$$$ Hôtel le Cep**** is *the* venerable place to stay in Beaune, if you have the means. Buried in the town center, this historic building comes with fine public spaces inside and out, and 64 gorgeous wood-beamed, traditionally decorated rooms in all sizes (standard Sb-€142, Db-€175, deluxe Db-€215, suites-€255-500, continental breakfast-€20, air-con, king-size beds, Internet access and Wi-Fi, fitness center, parking-€15/day, 27 Rue Maufoux, tel. 03 80 22 35 48, www.hotel-cep-beaune.com, resa@hotel-cep-beaune.com).

   $$$ Hôtel des Remparts*** is a peaceful oasis in a manor house built around a calming courtyard. It features traditional

BURGUNDY

Sleep Code

(€1 = about $1.30, country code: 33)
S = Single, **D** = Double/Twin, **T** = Triple, **Q** = Quad, **b** = bathroom, **s** = shower only, ***** = French hotel rating system (0-5 stars). Unless otherwise noted, credit cards are accepted and English is spoken.

   To help you easily sort through these listings, I've divided the accommodations into three categories based on the price for a standard double room with bath:

   $$$ Higher Priced—Most rooms €100 or more.
   $$ Moderately Priced—Most rooms between €70-100.
   $ Lower Priced—Most rooms €70 or less.

   Prices can change without notice; verify the hotel's current rates online or by email.

Beaune Hotels & Restaurants

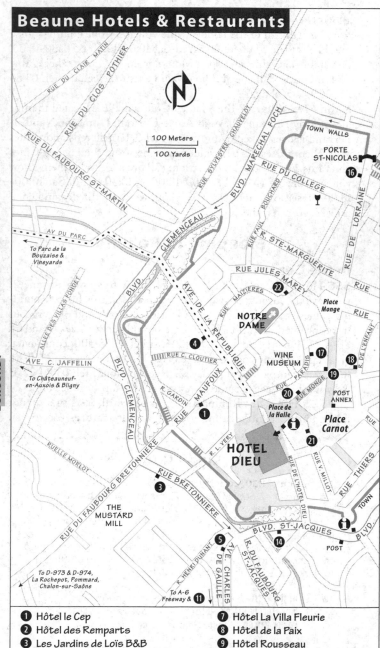

1 Hôtel le Cep	**7** Hôtel La Villa Fleurie
2 Hôtel des Remparts	**8** Hôtel de la Paix
3 Les Jardins de Loïs B&B	**9** Hôtel Rousseau
4 Hôtel Athanor	**10** To Hôtel le Home
5 Hôtel Ibis	**11** To Etap Hôtel Beaune
6 Hôtel de France & Le Tast'Vin Rest.	**12** L'Auberge Bourguignonne Rest.

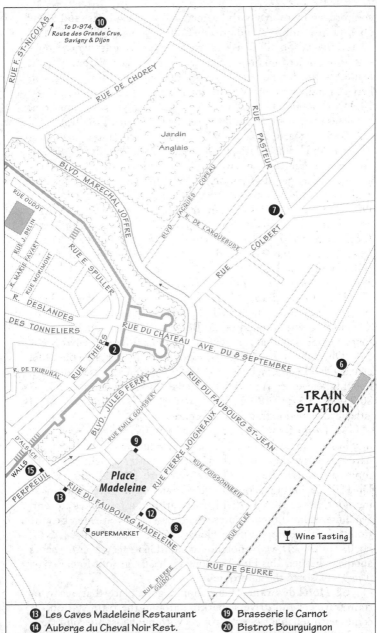

To D-974,
Route des Grands Crus,
Savigny & Dijon

RUE F. ST-NICOLAS

RUE DE CHOREY

Jardin
Anglais

RUE PASTEUR

BLVD. MARECHAL JOFFRE

RUE OUDOT

RUE J. BELIN

R. MARIE FAYART

RUE MORIMONT

RUE E. SPULLER

R. DESLANDES

DES TONNELIERS

RUE THIERS

R. DE TRIBUNAL

BLVD. JACQUES COPEAU

R. DE L'ARQUEBUSE

RUE COLBERT

RUE DU CHATEAU

AVE. DU 8 SEPTEMBRE

RUE DU FAUBOURG ST-JEAN

**TRAIN
STATION**

BLVD. JULES FERRY

RUE EMILE GOUSSERY

RUE PIERRE JOIGNEAUX

RUE FOISSONNERIE

**Place
Madeleine**

D'ALSACE

WALLS

PERPREUIL

RUE DU FAUBOURG MADELEINE

SUPERMARKET

RUE CELER

RUE DE SEURRE

RUE PIERRE GUIDOT

Y Wine Tasting

⑬ Les Caves Madeleine Restaurant
⑭ Auberge du Cheval Noir Rest.
⑮ Caveau des Arches Restaurant
⑯ La Ciboulette Restaurant
⑰ Le Petit Paradis Restaurant
⑱ Le Conty Restaurant

⑲ Brasserie le Carnot
⑳ Bistrot Bourguignon
㉑ Palais des Gourmets'
   Salon de Thé
㉒ Pickwicks Pub

comfort, many rooms with beamed ceilings, big beds, and a few good family suites (standard Db-€100-115, bigger Db-€135-155, Tb-€100-140, Qb-€160, ask for Rick Steves discount when booking, top-floor rooms have air-con, Internet access, pay Wi-Fi, laundry service, bike rental, garage-€10/day, just inside ring road between train station and main square at 48 Rue Thiers, tel. 03 80 24 94 94, fax 03 80 24 97 08, www.hotel-remparts-beaune.com, hotel.des.remparts@wanadoo.fr, run by the formal Epaillys).

$$$ **Les Jardins de Loïs****, run by welcoming winemakers Philippe and Anne-Marie, is a four-star B&B. The five big rooms all overlook gargantuan gardens lined with fruit trees, and show a no-expense-spared attention to detail and comfort. There's also a comfy lounge area and a Turkish bath (Db-€145, big Db-€170-190, Tb-€190, includes custom-order breakfasts, air-con, Wi-Fi, on the ring road a block after Hôtel de la Poste at 8 Boulevard Bretonnière, tel. 03 80 22 41 97, mobile 06 73 85 11 06, www.jardins delois.com, contact@jardinsdelois.com). Their atmospheric wine cellar, Domaine Loïs Dufouleur, also offers tastings (€8 for 4 wines, free for guests, arrange ahead).

$$$ **Hôtel Athanor*** is a good choice with a privileged location—a block from the cathedral—and offers a nice mix of modern comfort with a touch of old Beaune. The atmospheric lounge sports a pool table that's free for guests and a full-service bar (standard Db without air-con-€101, *superieure* Db with air-con-€138, deluxe Db-€164, extra bed-€20, ask for Rick Steves discount when booking, elevator, Wi-Fi, 9-11 Avenue de la République, tel. 03 80 24 09 20, fax 03 80 24 09 15, www.hotel-athanor.com, hotel .athanor@wanadoo.fr, helpful Caroline).

$$ **Hôtel Ibis**, centrally located with free and easy parking, has 73 efficient rooms. It's a good value—even better if you have kids and want a pool. The bigger and better-appointed "Club" rooms are worth the extra euros (standard Db-€90-115, "Club" Db-€90-105, extra person-€10, lower rates on website, non-smoking floor, air-con, free Wi-Fi, free parking, a few bikes to rent, 5-minute walk to town center, you'll pass it as you enter Beaune from the autoroute at 7 Rue Henri Dunant, tel. 03 80 22 75 67, fax 03 80 22 77 17, www.hotelibis.com, h1363@accor.com). There's another (cheaper) Ibis Hôtel—along with a gaggle of Motel 6-type places—closer to the autoroute.

$$ **Hôtel de France** is a simple, good place that's easy for train travelers and drivers (parking around the train station). It comes with reliable two-star rooms with big beds, air-conditioning, and fun, English-speaking owners Nicolas and Virginie (Sb-€65, Db-€72-99, Tb-€85-105, Qb-€105, Internet access and Wi-Fi, bar, good bistro, garage-€9, 35 Avenue du 8 Septembre, tel. 03 80 24 10 34, fax 03 80 24 96 78, www.hoteldefrance-beaune.com,

BURGUNDY

contact@hoteldefrance-beaune.com).

$$ Hôtel La Villa Fleurie*, an adorable 10-room refuge, is run by affable Madame Chartier on a plain street a few blocks outside the ring road (a 15-minute walk from the center). Most rooms are wood-floored, plush, and *très* traditional, and come with big bathrooms and air-conditioning; a few have some traffic noise (small Db-€72, bigger Db-€82, nifty Tb/Qb loft-€112-122, Wi-Fi, easy and free parking, cute garden, 19 Place Colbert, tel. 03 80 22 66 00, fax 03 80 22 45 46, www.lavillafleurie.fr, contact@lavilla fleurie.fr). From Beaune's ring road, turn right in front of the Bichot winery.

Place Madeleine

These hotels, on or near Place Madeleine, are a few blocks from the city center and train station, with easy parking.

$$ Hôtel de la Paix*, a few steps off Place Madeleine, is a top choice, with 24 handsome, well-appointed rooms (the suites are luxurious), several good family rooms, and elaborate public spaces. The serious owner runs a tight ship (standard Db-€85-115, bigger Db/Tb-€140-175, Qb-€140-200, air-con, Internet access and Wi-Fi, private parking-€6, 45 Rue du Faubourg Madeleine, tel. 03 80 24 78 08, fax 03 80 24 10 18, www.hotelpaix.com, contact@hotelpaix.com).

$ Hôtel Rousseau is a good-value, no-frills, frumpy manor house that turns its back on Beaune's sophistication. Cheerful, quirky, and elusive owner Madame Rousseau, her pet birds, and the quiet garden will make you smile, and the tranquility will help you sleep. The cheapest rooms are a godsend for budget travelers. The rooms with showers are like Grandma's, with enough comfort (S-€36, D-€46, D with toilet-€53, Db-€63, T with toilet-€60, Tb-€70, Q-€64, Qb-€76, showers down the hall-€3, includes breakfast, cash only, reservations preferred by email, free and easy parking, 11 Place Madeleine, tel. 03 80 22 13 59, fax 03 80 22 67 55, hotelrousseaubeaune@orange.fr). Check-ins after 19:00 and morning departures before 7:30 must be arranged in advance.

Just Outside Beaune

$$ Hôtel le Home, just off busy D-974 a half-mile north of Beaune, is a fine value, with comfy rooms in an old mansion. The rooms in the main building come in soft pastels (top-floor rooms have the most character). Rooms on the parking courtyard come with stone floors, small terraces, and bright colors, but can be dark and musty (standard Db-€77, luxury Db-€105, Tb-€98, Qb-€115, free Wi-Fi, includes parking, 138 Route de Dijon, tel. 03 80 22 16 43, fax 03 80 24 90 74, www.lehome.fr, info @lehome.fr).

BURGUNDY

$ **Etap Hôtel Beaune** is efficient, basic but clean, and a bargain just a five-minute drive from Beaune's center toward the A-6 autoroute (Db-€43, Wi-Fi, easy and free parking, 16 Rue du Moulin Noizé, tel. 03 80 24 59 00, www.etaphotel.com).

In the Wine Villages near Beaune

You'll find some exceptional hotel and *chambres d'hôte* values in wine villages a short hop from Beaune. The Côte d'Or has scads of *chambres d'hôtes;* get a list at the TI and reserve ahead in summer. Also see the suggestions along the Route des Grands Crus (page 947).

In Aloxe-Corton

$$$ **Hôtel Villa Louise***** is a romantic place burrowed in the prestigious wine hamlet of Aloxe-Corton, about 10 minutes north of Beaune. Many of its 13 *très* cozy and tastefully decorated rooms overlook the backyard vineyards, a small covered pool, and a large, grassy garden made for sipping the owner's wine (sadly, no picnics allowed). The serious owners—the Perrins—will show you their vaulted cellars (Db-€110-152—most are about €110-130, Db suite-€150-200, buffet breakfast-€15, Internet access and Wi-Fi, covered pool, sauna, near the château at 9 Rue Franche, tel. 03 80 26 46 70, fax 03 80 26 47 16, www.hotel-villa-louise.fr, hotel-villa-louise @wanadoo.fr).

In Meursault

$$$ **Hôtel les Charmes**** is a sweet two-star place with three-star prices. Although it's overpriced, I still like it here—it's got that homey Old World feel, an easygoing owner, and a nice setting: centrally located in the village of Meursault, with a veritable park in the back and a big pool. The rooms could use some updating...and some are getting it (Db-€100-120, Tb-€135, Wi-Fi, 10 Place du Murger, tel. 03 80 21 63 53, www.hotellescharmes.com, contact@hotellescharmes.com).

In Puligny-Montrachet

$$$ **Domaine des Anges** is a lovely place run by a British couple (John and Celine) who pamper their fortunate guests with the Queen's English, lovely rooms, linger-longer lounges inside and out, laundry service, fine dinners with drinks (€40, book ahead), and afternoon tea every day. It's also ideally located in the center of Puligny-Montrachet (Db-€80-145, includes a smashing breakfast, no children under 16, personalized wine tours, Place des Marronniers, tel. 03 80 21 38 28, mobile 06 23 86 63 91, www .domainedesangespuligny.com, domainedesanges@yahoo.fr).

$ **Chambres les Gagères** offers great budget accommodations: four simple but clean rooms, a common kitchen with all you need, a view terrace overlooking vineyards, and friendly Maria at the helm (Db-€55-65, 17 Rue Drouhin, tel. 03 80 21 97 46, mobile 06 15 97 64 71, maria.adao2@orange.fr).

In St-Romain

$$ La Domaine de Corgette hunkers beneath a hillside in lovely little St-Romain. Welcoming Véronique has restored an old vintner's home with style. A stay-awhile terrace, private parking, cozy common rooms, and wine-tastings are at your disposal (Db-€95-110, Tb-€130, Qb-€150, includes breakfast, cash only, 2 blocks below Hôtel les Roches—listed next, look for the *Maison d'Hôte* banner, tel. & fax 03 80 21 68 08, www.domainecorgette.com, accueil@domainecorgette.com).

$ Hôtel les Roches is an unpretentious place offering a handful of simple, clean, and perfectly sleepable rooms snuggled above a good recommended restaurant (Db-€49, bigger Db-€68, Wi-Fi, tel. 03 80 21 21 63, www.les-roches.fr, reservation@les-roches.fr).

Eating in Beaune

For a small town, Beaune offers a wide range of reasonably priced restaurants. Review my suggestions carefully before setting out, and reserve ahead to avoid frustration (especially on weekends). Many places are closed Sunday and Monday. This region offers a bounty of worthwhile upscale dining options (I've listed a few), but before you book, check their wine lists (easiest to do online)—the prices may double your total dinner cost.

At **Les Caves Madeleine,** step down into the warm little dining room that doubles as a wine shop. Choose a private table—or, better, join the communal table, where good food and wine kindle conversation, then lubricate new friendships (this is a boon for solo travelers). The owner, Monsieur Lo-Lo, speaks English and enjoys sharing his love of food and wine. Because he's also a wine merchant, he can pass his savings on to you by selling bottles at store prices plus €5 to drink them here, making top-end wines almost affordable (€14-24 *plats*, closed Thu and Sun, near Place Madeleine at 8 Rue du Faubourg Madeleine, tel. 03 80 22 93 30).

Auberge du Cheval Noir, with smart, modern decor and a location on Beaune's ring road, is normally the kind of place I avoid. But the chef's ability to cook up delicious dishes that are reasonably priced makes this a must for those who appreciate cuisine more than ambience (*menus* from €23 on weekdays, €36 on weekends, closed Tue-Wed, 17 Boulevard St-Jacques, tel. 03 80 22 07 37).

Caveau des Arches is a wise choice if you want to dine on delicious Burgundian specialties at fair prices in atmospheric stone cellars. Book ahead for this place, as it's popular with townsfolk (€24 *menu* with the classics, closed Sun-Mon, where the ring road crosses Rue d'Alsace—which leads to Place Madeleine—at 10 Boulevard Perpreuil, tel. 03 80 22 10 37).

La Ciboulette, intimate and family-run with petite Hélène as your hostess, offers good cuisine that mixes traditional Burgundian flavors with creative dishes and lovely presentation. It's worth the longer walk—and you can do your laundry next door while you dine (€20 and €32 *menus*, closed Mon-Tue; from Place Carnot, walk out Rue Carnot to 69 Rue Lorraine; tel. 03 80 24 70 72).

Le Petit Paradis does its name justice, with 10 tables crowding a sharp little room. Chef Jean-Marie's menu is inventive and ever-changing—and not traditional Burgundian (*menus* from €29, closed Sun-Mon, book ahead, just outside Museum of the Wine of Burgundy at 25 Rue de Paradis, tel. 03 80 24 91 00).

Le Tast'Vin, across from the train station at the recommended Hôtel de France, is a sharp place with a good-value €23 *menu* and fun cheeseburgers with Burgundian cheese (closed Sun-Mon, 35 Avenue du 8 Septembre, tel. 03 80 24 10 34).

Le Conty owns a privileged position at the junction of two pedestrian lanes. With its great outdoor seating, it's ideal for a big salad or good brasserie fare (€14 lunch *menus*, €24 at dinner, closed Sun-Mon, 5 Rue Ziem, tel. 03 80 22 63 94).

Brasserie le Carnot is a perennially popular café with good interior seating and better exterior tables in the thick of the pedestrian zone. It serves excellent pizza, good salads, pasta dishes, and the usual café offerings (open daily, where Rue Carnot and Rue Monge meet).

Bistrot Bourguignon is a relaxed wine bar-bistro with a lengthy wine list and 15 types of *vin* available by the glass (order by number from display behind bar). Come for a glass of wine or to enjoy a light dinner (you can get Wi-Fi with your wine). Dine at the counter, the sidewalk tables, or in the casually comfortable interior (€10 starters, €18 *plats,* €13 lunch *menu,* closed Sun-Mon, on a pedestrian-only street at 8 Rue Monge, tel. 03 80 22 23 24).

L'Auberge Bourguignonne is decidedly Burgundian, with serious service, proudly displayed awards, and a good reputation among locals. It's also open Sundays, when many other places are not. Choose from two traditional dining rooms, or eat outside on the square (*menus* from €25, some fish dishes, air-con, reservations smart, 4 Place Madeleine, tel. 03 80 22 23 53).

Palais des Gourmets' Salon de Thé provides a good-value outdoor lunch on Place Carnot, with delicious quiche, omelets, crêpes, and memorable desserts (Tue-Sun until 18:00, closed Mon, next to the Athenaeum's back-door entrance at 14 Place Carnot, tel. 03 80 22 13 39).

Before Dinner: Escape the tourists at Les Mille et une Vignes wine bar, next door to a handy launderette, which reeks with old-time ambience and local characters. Young owner Marine serves a good selection of wines by the glass at fair prices and good, split-table appetizers (Tue-Sat 11:00 until late, closed Sun-Mon, 61 Rue de Lorraine, tel. 03 80 22 03 02).

After Dinner: If you're tired of speaking French, pop into the late-night-lively **Pickwicks Pub** (Mon-Sat 17:00-5:00 in the morning, closed Sun, behind church at 2 Rue Notre-Dame).

In the Wine Villages near Beaune

In Pommard (5 minutes south of Beaune): Facing Pommard's big church, **Auprès du Clocher** has stylish, contemporary decor one floor up with windows on the village, a formal atmosphere, and a focus on *la cuisine*. Book ahead, as chef Jean-Christophe Moutet has been discovered by locals (€32, €45, and €65 *menus*; closed Tue-Wed, 1 Rue Nackenheim, tel. 03 80 22 21 79).

In Puligny-Montrachet (15 minutes south of Beaune): At **Le Montrachet,** settle in for a truly traditional Burgundian experience—a justifiable splurge if you want a refined and classy dining experience without the stuffiness, and a remarkable choice for a gourmet lunch on a lovely terrace at affordable prices (€29 lunch *menu*, €60 dinner *menu*, pricey wine list, open daily, on Puligny-Montrachet's main square at 19 Place des Marronniers, tel. 03 80 21 30 06). Come early for a glass of wine before dinner with Julien at the Caveau de Puligny-Montrachet (see page 942). **L'Estaminet de Meix,** in the heart of the village, is best for lunch or a light dinner. It serves good brasserie fare with panache, and has terrific outdoor seating and reasonable prices (€18 *menu*, closed Mon evening and all day Tue, Place des Marronniers, tel. 03 80 21 33 01).

In Pernand-Vergelesses (5 minutes north of Beaune): **La Charlemagne** is a classy place to enjoy a fusion of classic Burgundian dishes with a Japanese accent (*menus* from €35, closed Tue-Wed, 1 Route Vergelesses, tel. 03 80 21 51 45).

In Chagny (20 minutes south of Beaune): Well known as one of France's finest restaurants, **Maison Lameloise** has Michelin's top rating (three stars). The setting is elegant (as you'd expect), the service is relaxed and patient (which you might not expect), the cuisine is Burgundy's best, and the overall experience is memorable. If you're tempted to dive into the top of the top of French cuisine, book this place well ahead (*menus* from about €115, €60 main courses, very pricey wines, open daily, 36 Place d'Armes, tel. 03 85 87 65 65, www.lameloise.fr).

In Chambolle-Musigny (20 minutes north of Beaune): **Le Millésime** is a good choice (see page 949; €20 lunch *menus*,

BURGUNDY

€29-44 dinner *menus*, indoor seating only, closed Sun-Mon, 1 Rue Traversière, tel. 03 80 62 80 37).

Beaune Connections

From Beaune by Train to: Dijon (15/day, 25 minutes), **Paris'** Gare de Lyon (nearly hourly, 2.5 hours, most require reservation and easy change in Dijon; more via Dijon to Paris' Gare de Bercy, no reservation required, 3.5 hours), **Bourges** (7/day, 2.5 hours, transfer in Nevers), **Colmar** (7/day, 2.5-4 hours via TGV between Dijon and Mulhouse, reserve well ahead, changes in Dijon and Mulhouse or Belfort), **Arles** (10/day, 4.5-5 hours, 9 with transfer in Lyon and Nîmes or Avignon), **Chamonix** (7/day, 7 hours, change in Lyon and St-Gervais, some require additional changes), **Annecy** (7/day, 4-6 hours, change in Lyon), **Amboise** (2/day, 5 hours, via Dijon and Tours; plus 12/day, 6 hours, most with changes in Dijon and in Paris, arrive at Paris' Gare de Lyon, then Métro to Austerlitz or Montparnasse stations to catch the connection to Amboise).

The Beaune Region

Exploring the vineyards near Beaune, by car or by bike, is a delight.

Getting Around the Beaune Region

By Car: Driving provides the ultimate flexibility for touring the vineyards, though drivers should prepare for narrow lanes in the vineyards and make sure to sip small samples (use the handy buckets to spit back after tasting).

By Bike: If you hop on a bike in Beaune, within minutes you'll be immersed in the lush countryside and immaculate vineyards of the Côte d'Or. A sidewalk bike lane that circles Beaune's ring road—and the many quiet service roads—make this area wonderful for biking. (Beware of loose gravel on the shoulders and along the small roads.) A signed bike route runs south from Beaune all the way to Cluny, and a new route from Beaune north to Dijon may be in place by your visit.

Well-organized, English-speaking Florian and Cedric at **Bourgogne Randonnées** offer good bikes, bike racks, maps, and detailed itineraries. Ask about their favorite routes that follow only small roads and dedicated bike paths. A good one departs from Beaune's parc de la Bouzaise and connects the wine villages of Pommard, Meursault, and Volnay in a scenic, mostly level, 14-mile loop ride (can be extended to Puligny-Montrachet for a level, 22-mile loop). They can deliver your bike to your hotel anywhere in France (bikes-€5/hour, €18/day, helmets-€1, daily 9:00-12:00 &

13:30-19:00, near Beaune train station at 7 Avenue du 8 Septembre, tel. 03 80 22 06 03, fax 03 80 22 15 58, www.detours-in-france .com, info@detours-in-france.com).

By Bus: Transco bus #44 links Beaune with other wine villages to the north along the famous Route des Grands Crus, and runs to Dijon's train station (7/day). Find bus stops along Beaune's ring road. Bus service south of Beaune to villages like Meursault and Puligny-Montrachet is hopeless—take a taxi, hop a train (limited options), or rent a bike.

By Train: Hourly trains stop in the wine villages of Meursault and Santenay to the south of Beaune, and Ladoix-Serrigny to the north. Meursault's station is a 25-minute walk through vineyards to the town center.

By Minibus Tour: Try **Safari Wine Tours** or **Vinéa Tours** (see page 920).

By Taxi: Call **Gerard Rebillard** (mobile 06 11 83 06 10); for other taxis, see page 917.

Sights in the Beaune Region

In this section, you'll find three vineyard routes, all doable by car (possible by bike depending on your energy and bike-fitness),

which combine great scenery with some of my favorite wine destinations. If you only have time for one and you have a car, drive the beautiful **"Vineyard Loop South of Beaune to Château de la Rochepot"** (with off-the-beaten-path villages such as Orches, St-Romain, and St-Aubin offering ample tasting opportunities). This is a tough ride on a bike, so most bikers will prefer doing just the first section of this route (ideally to Puligny-Montrachet and back—an easy, level ride).

My **"Vineyard Loop North of Beaune to Savigny-lès-Beaune"** is good by car or bike (manageable hills and distances). I also cover the famous **"Route des Grands Crus,"** farther north of Beaune, connecting Burgundy's most prestigious wine villages (bikers should skip this one).

I try to avoid the famous wine châteaux (like some of those in Pommard and Meursault), which I find overpriced and impersonal. Although you can drop in unannounced at most wineries (*comme un cheveux sur la soupe*—"like a hair on the soup"), you'll get better service by calling ahead and letting them know you're coming. Remember that at free tastings, you're expected to buy at least a bottle or two, unless you're on a group tour.

BURGUNDY

▲▲Vineyard Loop South of Beaune to Château de la Rochepot

Take this pretty, peaceful route for the best approach to La Rochepot's romantic castle, and to glide through several of Burgundy's most reputed vineyards. Read ahead and note that if you want to see the wine-barrel-makers at work in St-Romain, you need to get there by 15:00—if that's a push, skip it or reverse this loop. Bikers can shortcut this ride by doubling back to Beaune after visiting Puligny-Montrachet (figure an hour of level riding each way)—though the bike route continues from Puligny-Montrachet on a mix of small roads and paths all the way to Cluny (eventually signed as *la Voie Verte*). The pleasant town of Santenay makes a good destination if you want to pedal a bit farther but avoid the hills to La Rochepot.

↻ Self-Guided Tour: Drivers leave Beaune's ring road, following signs for *Chalon-sur-Saône* and *Autun* (the exit after Auxerre), then follow signs to *Pommard*. Cyclists take the lovely vineyard bike path by leaving the ring road toward Auxerre and Bligny-sur-Ouche, and turning left at the signal after Lycée Viticole de Beaune—look for bike route signs.

When you come to Pommard, you'll pass many wine-tasting opportunities, including **Patrick Clémencet** (see page 929), and a cool lunch café, **Hôtel du Pont** (cheap lunch *menus* and salads, good terrace, closed Sun, tel. 03 80 22 03 41).

South of Pommard, the road gradually climbs through terrific views (bikers can take their own parallel path). From here, follow signs into *Meursault*, then follow *Toutes Directions* (and D-974) around the village, turn right on D-113b, and follow signs to *Puligny-Montrachet*.

You'll pass through low-slung vineyards south of Meursault, then enter Puligny-Montrachet. At the big roundabout with a bronze sculpture of vineyard workers, find the **Caveau de Puligny-Montrachet** and a chance to sample the world's best whites and a good selection of reds (see page 929). A block straight out the door of the *caveau* leads to the town's big square (Place des Marronniers), with **Hôtel-Restaurant Le Montrachet** and **Café de l'Estaminet de Meix** (both described on page 939).

Go back to the roundabout and follow signs *to Chassagne-Montrachet* and *St. Aubin*, leading you through more manicured vineyards. To tour **Château de Chassagne-Montrachet** (well-signed, see page 929), turn left on D-906, and you'll see it soon to the right. To continue on to Château de la Rochepot, make a hard right on D-906 to St-Aubin, where you'll follow *La Rochepot* signs onto D-33. (Bikers, this is where the going gets tough.) As you head over the hills and through the vineyards of the Hautes-Côtes (upper slopes), you'll come to a drop-dead view of the castle (stop

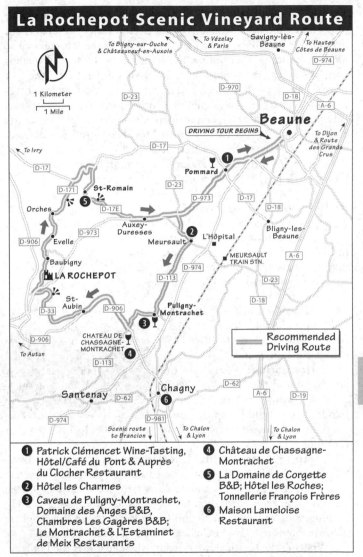

La Rochepot Scenic Vineyard Route

1 Kilometer

1 Mile

To Bligny-sur-Ouche
& Châteauneuf-en-Auxois

To Vézelay
& Paris

Savigny-lès-
Beaune

To Hautes
Côtes de Beaune

D-974

D-970

D-23

D-18

A-6

Beaune

DRIVING TOUR BEGINS

To Dijon
& Route
des Grands
Crus

To Ivry

D-17

D-17

Pommard

D-23

St-Romain

D-171

Orches

D-17E

D-973

Auxey-
Duresses

Evelle

D-906

Baubigny

LA ROCHEPOT

St-
Aubin

D-33

D-906

D-906

To Autun

CHÂTEAU DE
CHASSAGNE-
MONTRACHET

D-113

Santenay

D-62

To Chalon
& Lyon

D-974

D-981

Scenic route
to Brancion

D-973

Meursault

D-113

Puligny-
Montrachet

L'Hôpital

MEURSAULT
TRAIN STN.

Bligny-les-
Beaune

A-6

D-23

D-18

Chagny

D-62

A-6

D-19

To Chalon
& Lyon

Recommended
Driving Route

❶ Patrick Clémencet Wine-Tasting,
Hôtel/Café du Pont & Auprès
du Clocher Restaurant

❷ Hôtel les Charmes

❸ Caveau de Puligny-Montrachet,
Domaine des Anges B&B,
Chambres Les Gagères B&B;
Le Montrachet & L'Estaminet
de Meix Restaurants

❹ Château de Chassagne-
Montrachet

❺ La Domaine de Corgette
B&B; Hôtel les Roches;
Tonnellerie François Frères

❻ Maison Lameloise
Restaurant

BURGUNDY

mandatory). Turn right when you reach La Rochepot, and follow
Le Château signs to the castle (described below).

After visiting the castle, turn right out of its parking lot and
mosey through Baubigny, Evelles, and rock-solid Orches. After
Orches, climb to the top of Burgundy's world—keeping straight
on D-17, you'll pass several exceptional lookouts (the village of
St-Romain swirls below, and if it's really clear, look for Mont Blanc
on the eastern horizon).

Then drive down to St-Romain, stopping at Burgundy's most important wine-barrel-maker, **Tonnellerie François Frères.** Park in their lot just above the village and walk to the left end of the modern building, then follow the hammer noises up a few steps and take in the medieval scene. Well-stoked fires heat the oak staves to make them flexible, and sweaty workers pound iron rings around the barrels just as they've always done. No one slacks in this hardworking factory, where demand seems strong. Work starts early and ends by about 15:00 (open Mon-Fri, closed Sat-Sun, tel. 03 80 21 23 33, www.francoisfreres.com).

Next, follow signs for *Auxey-Duresses,* and then *Beaune* for a pretty finale to your journey.

▲Château de la Rochepot

This very Burgundian castle rises above the trees and its village, eight miles from Beaune. This pint-size castle—splendid both inside and out—is accessible by car, bike (hilly), or infrequent bus.

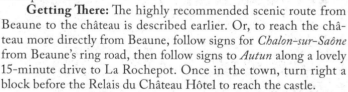

Cost and Hours: €8, open April-Sept Wed-Mon 10:00-17:30, Oct-March Wed-Mon 10:00-11:30 & 14:00-16:30, mid-Sept-Oct Wed-Mon 10:00-11:45 & 14:00-16:45, closed Tue year-round.

Information: Tour half on your own and the other half with a French guide (get the English handout; most guides speak some English and can answer questions, tel. 03 80 21 71 37, www.la rochepot.com).

Getting There: The highly recommended scenic route from Beaune to the château is described earlier. Or, to reach the château more directly from Beaune, follow signs for *Chalon-sur-Saône* from Beaune's ring road, then follow signs to *Autun* along a lovely 15-minute drive to La Rochepot. Once in the town, turn right a block before the Relais du Château Hôtel to reach the castle.

Visiting the Castle: Cross the drawbridge under the Pot family coat of arms and knock three times with the ancient knocker to enter. If no one comes, knock harder, or find a log and ram the gate.

Construction began during the end of the Middle Ages (when castles were built to defend) and was completed during the Renaissance (when castles were transformed into luxury homes). So it's neither a purely defensive structure (as in the Dordogne) nor a palace (as in the Loire)—it's a bit of both.

The furnishings are surprisingly elaborate given the military look of the exterior. I could sleep like a baby in the Captain's Room, surrounded by nine-foot-thick walls. Don't miss the 15th-century alarmed safe. Notice the colorful doorjamb. These same colors were used to paint many buildings (including castles and churches) and remind us that medieval life went beyond beige and stone. The kitchen will bowl you over; the dining room sports a 15th-century walnut high chair.

Climb the tower and see the Chinese room, sing chants in the resonant chapel, and make ripples in the 240-foot-deep well. (Can you spit a bull's-eye?) Paths outside lead you on a worthwhile walk around the castle. Don't leave without driving, walking, or pedaling up D-33 a few hundred yards toward St-Aubin (behind Hôtel Relais du Château) for a romantic view.

▲Vineyard Loop North of Beaune to Savigny-lès-Beaune

For an easy and rewarding spin (by car or ideally by bike) through waves of vineyards that smother traditional villages, follow this relatively level 10-mile loop from Beaune (with tastings, allow a half-day by bike or 1.5 hours by car). It laces together three renowned wine villages—Aloxe-Corton, Pernand-Vergelesses, and Savigny-lès-Beaune—connecting you with Burgundian nature and village wine culture. Bring water and snacks, as there is precious little available until the end of this route. Your tour concludes in Savigny-lès-Beaune, where you'll find a café-pizzeria, plenty of wine-tastings, a small grocery, and a unique château.

➋ **Self-Guided Tour:** This loop drive/pedal starts in Beaune. Drivers can also combine this loop with the Route des Grands Crus, described next.

• *From Beaune's ring road bike lane, take D-974 north toward Dijon; soon after, follow signs leading left to* Savigny-lès-Beaune. *Eventually, cross over the freeway, then veer right following signs to* Pernand-Vergelesses *on D-18 (don't turn until you see* D-18 *signs). Turn right at the first sign to* Aloxe-Corton, *and glide into the town (aim for its church spire; drivers can stop at the small parking area on Place de l'Eglise, a block above the church).*

Aloxe-Corton: This tiny town, with a world-class reputation among wine enthusiasts, is packed with top tasting opportunities (but no cafés). The easygoing **Domaines d'Aloxe-Corton,** English-owned **Mischief and Mayhem,** upscale and French **Domaine de Senard,** and traditional **Château Corton-André** all offer different kinds of tastings (see page 930).

• *Leave Aloxe and head up the hill on Rue des Chaumes toward...*

Pernand-Vergelesses: A cute little café called **La Grappe** is to the right as you enter the village (cheap food and drink, look for colorful umbrellas, closed Mon, tel. 03 80 21 59 46).

BURGUNDY

Route des Grands Crus/ Vineyard Loop Near Beaune

Vineyard Loop

1 Hôtel le Home

2 Aloxe-Corton Wine Tastings & Hotels

3 Café la Grappe

4 Domaine Naudin-Ferrand

5 Henri de Villamont Wine Tasting & R. De Famille Café-Pizzeria

Dijon

D-10

D-905

Velars-sur-Ouche

D-108

Urcy

D-35

Marsannay-la-Côte

A-311

D-122

Fixin

D-974

A-31

2 Kilometers

2 Miles

Quemigny-Poisot

Gevrey-Chambertin **10** TRAIN STN.

To Nancy & Metz and Colmar via A-36

D-31

D-122

Paris

FRANCE

100 Miles

Ternant

9 Morey-St-Denis

Broindon

Chambolle-Musigny

8

A-31

D-25

7 Vougeot

D-35

Concoeur

6 Vosne-Romanée

ROUTE DES GRANDS CRUS

DRIVING TOUR BEGINS

D-25

Nuit-St-Georges

Arcenant

D-8

D-115

D-8

TRAIN STN.

D-8

D-974

D-35

Villers-la-Faye

Echevronne

D-2

D-18

4 Magny-les-Villers

Recommended Driving Routes

Pernand-Vergelesses

3

D-974

5

Savigny-lès-Beaune

Aloxe-Corton

D-20F

A-31

To Paris

A-6

2

Ladoix-Serrigny

D-2

VINEYARD LOOP

DRIVING/BIKING TOUR BEGINS

1

Chorey

D-20

Beaune

TRAIN STN.

D-974

D-973

A-6

To La Rochepot

D-17

To Chalon & Lyon

Route des Grands Crus

6 Ferme Fruirouge

7 Château du Clos de Vougeot

8 Le Caveau des Musignys & Le Millesime Restaurant

9 Caveau des Vignerons & Le Castel des Très Girard Hôtel

10 Hôtel les Grands Crus & Chez Guy

BURGUNDY

Drivers should consider two worthwhile detours: Climbing well above the village takes you to a grand vineyard panorama. Enter Pernand-Vergelesses at the small roundabout and head up, turning right on Rue du Creux St. Germain and then continuing straight and up along Rue Copeau. Curve up past the church until you see small *Panorama* signs. Drivers can also continue north on D-18 past Pernand-Vergelesses a few minutes into the Hautes-Côtes and visit the recommended winery **Domaine Naudin-Ferrand** in Magny-les-Villers (see page 931).

• *Leaving Pernand-Vergelesses, bikers and drivers both follow the main road (D-18) back toward Beaune, and turn right into the vineyards on the first lane (about 400 yards from Pernand-Vergelesses). Keep left as it curves and rises gently to lovely views. Drop down and turn right when you come to a T, then joyride along the vine service lanes. If the spirit moves you, detour to higher ground for more views (bikers should watch for loose gravel). To reach the village of Savigny-lès-Beaune, keep going until you see a 5T sign. Turn left just before the sign, then a quick right, and right again.*

Savigny-lès-Beaune: You'll come to a three-way intersection. The left fork leads back to Beaune, the middle fork leads to *Centre-Ville,* and the road to the right leads to a good wine-tasting at **Henri de Villamont** (see page 930). Follow the middle fork to reach the town center, and find a four-towered collectors' château, **Le Château de Savigny.** This medieval castle comes with a moat, 80 fighter jets parked in the side yard, Abarth antique racing cars, fun tractor and fire-engine collections, 300 motorcycles, 2,000 airplane models, and vineyards (the owner's wine is available for tasting). The collection fills most of the interior, so don't look for the traditional château furnishings (€10, daily April-Oct 9:00-18:30, Nov-March 9:00-12:00 & 14:00-17:30, last entry 1.5 hours before closing, English handout, tel. 03 80 21 55 03, www.chateau-savigny.com). Beyond the château, you'll find the **R. De Famille** café-pizzeria facing a little square (daily, tel. 03 80 21 50 00) and a grocery shop a few blocks past the café (usually closed 12:30-15:00).

• *From Savigny-lès-Beaune, drive or pedal back into Beaune. Those with a car can continue along...*

▲Route des Grands Crus (North of Beaune)

While I prefer the areas south and west of Beaune, this route is a must for wine connoisseurs with a car, as it passes through Burgundy's most fabled vineyards. The first part, between Aloxe-Corton and Nuits St-Georges, is less interesting, as you're forced onto an unappealing highway (D-974). But from Vougeot north, the route improves—locals call this section the "Champs-Elysées of Burgundy." Between Vosne-Romanée and Gevrey-Chambertin, you'll pass 24 grand cru wineries of Côte de Nuits—Pinot Noir paradise, where 95 percent of the wines are red.

€ **Self-Guided Tour:** Begin this trip in Beaune.

• *From Beaune, take D-974 north into* **Nuits St-Georges** *and, at the north end of town, take a left at the signal onto D-25. A few minutes after leaving Nuits St-Georges, take the turnoff to* Concoeur/Corboin. *After passing fields growing red fruits* (fruits rouges), *you'll come to the hamlet of* **Concoeur** *and find the pink-signed...*

Ferme Fruirouge: This is the ultimate Back Door stop, where cassis liqueur, mustards, and jams are made with passion. Adorable owners Sylvain and Isabelle (or their equally adorable staff) will explain their time-honored process for making the famous crème de cassis, vinegars, and mustards, as well as jams made from cherries, raspberries, and black currants. You can sample everything—including their one-of-a-kind cassis-ketchup—and get free recipe cards in French (Thu-Mon 9:00-12:00 & 14:00-19:00, closed Tue-Wed, tel. 03 80 62 36 25, www.fruirouge.fr, call ahead to arrange for a good explanation of their operation).

• *Continue on same road into tiny* **Corboin**, *descend through Vosne-Romanée, and rejoin D-974 north to the next village,* **Vougeot**. *Follow signs to the famous...*

Château du Clos de Vougeot: In many ways, this is the birthplace of great Burgundian wines. In the 12th century, monks from the abbey of Cîteaux (8 miles southeast from here) created this beautiful stone structure to store equipment and make their wines. Their careful study of winemaking was the foundation for the world-famous reputation of Burgundian wines. There's little to see inside except for the fine stone construction, four ancient and massive wine presses, and the room where the Confrérie des Chevaliers Tastevin (a Burgundian brotherhood of wine-tasters) meets to celebrate their legacy—and to apply their label of quality to area wines, called *le Tastevinage*. The château has a good English handout and posted information, but no tastings (€4.20, daily April-Sept 9:00-18:30, Oct-March 9:00-11:30 & 14:00-17:30, tel. 03 80 62 86 09).

• *Follow D-122 north of Vougeot and land in the wine-soaked little village of* **Chambolle-Musigny**, *where you'll find...*

Le Caveau des Musignys: This may be the single best place to sample Burgundy's rich variety of wines. Say bonjour to baritone Paulo, who will introduce you (in fluent English) to the region's wines in his vaulted tasting room. Representing 40 producers, he has wines in all price ranges from throughout Burgundy. His whites from the Côte Challonaise are a great value, as are his mid-range reds from Chambolle-Musigny and Vosne-Romanée. If it's near summer, ask to taste his rosé from Marsannay (Wed-Sun 9:00-18:00, closed Mon-Tue, a block north of the church at 1 Rue

Traversière, tel. 03 80 62 84 01). You can eat upstairs in an elegant setting, where modern blends with tradition, at the lovely **Le Millésime** (€20 lunch *menus*, €29-44 dinner *menus,* indoor seating only, closed Sun-Mon, tel. 03 80 62 80 37).

• *The next village north is...*

Morey-St-Denis: This village houses more vineyards and another fine tasting stop at the **Caveau des Vignerons,** with reasonably priced wines from 13 small producers (each too small to have its own tasting room). Gentle Catherine works most days and speaks enough English to welcome you to this appealing and free tasting room where you can sample wines from the Côtes de Nuits (good selection of wines from Gevrey-Chambertin, though I prefer those from Morey-St-Denis; daily 9:30-19:00, next to the church, tel. 03 80 51 86 79). At the other end of the village lies an intimate, upscale hotel-restaurant, **$$$ Le Castel des Très Girard***.** Located in the heart of the Route des Grands Crus, this eight-room hotel delivers top service and classy comfort, including a pool and a restaurant that locals go out of their way for (Db-€150-190, lunch *menus* from €23, dinner *menus* from €40, poolside tables, tel. 03 80 34 33 09, fax 03 80 51 81 92, www.castel-tres-girard.com, info @castel-tres-girard.com).

• *Finally, you reach...*

Gevrey-Chambertin: For many Pinot Noir lovers, a visit to this flowery village is the pinnacle of their Burgundian pilgrimage. Gevrey-Chambertin produces nine out of the 32 grand cru wines from Burgundy. All are Pinot Noirs (no whites in sight), and all use the suffix "Chambertin" ("Gevrey" is the historic name of the village; "Chambertin" is its most important vineyard). While you drive through the countryside south of the village, look for signs identifying the famous vineyards.

You can sleep well for a steal at the **$$ Hôtel les Grands Crus***,** with traditional rooms overlooking vineyards, cozy lounges, and a nice backyard terrace (Db-€86-98, air-con, Wi-Fi, at the northwest edge of Gevrey-Chambertin on Rue de Lavaux, tel. 03 80 34 34 15, fax 03 80 51 89 07, www.hoteldesgrandscrus.com, hotel.lesgrandscrus@nerim.net). To dine well in stylish surroundings inside or out, find **Chez Guy** in the center of the village (*menus* from €27, open daily, 3 Place de la Mairie, tel. 03 80 58 51 51).

BURGUNDY

Between Beaune and Paris

North of Beaune, you'll find a handful of appealing places that string together well for a full-day excursion: towering Châteauneuf-en-Auxois, sleepy Semur-en-Auxois, remote Fontenay's abbey, pretty little Flavigny-sur-Ozerain, and Julius Caesar's victorious battlefield at Alise Ste-Reine (with its terrific new museum, MuséoParc Alésia).

As a bonus, following my self-guided driving tour of this area takes you along several stretches of the **Burgundy Canal** (Canal de Bourgogne). Like much of France, Burgundy is laced by canals dug in the early Industrial Age. Two hundred years ago, canals like these provided an affordable way to transport cargo. The Burgundy canal was among the most important of France's canals, linking Paris with the Mediterranean Sea. The canal is 145 miles long, with 209 locks, and rises over France's continental divide in Pouilly-en-Auxois, just below Châteauneuf-en-Auxois (where the canal runs underground for about two miles). Digging began on the canal in 1727 and was not completed until 1832—ironically, just in time for the invention of steam engines on rails, which would soon eliminate the need for canals.

Self-Guided Driving Tour

Back Door Burgundy

This all-day loop links Châteauneuf-en-Auxois, Alise Ste-Reine, Flavigny-sur-Ozerain, Fontenay, and Semur-en-Auxois (each of these stops is described in detail later in this chapter). The trip trades vineyards for wheat fields and pastoral landscapes. You'll drive along the Burgundy canal and visit a Cistercian abbey, two medieval villages, and the site of Gaul's last stand against the Romans. If you're heading to/from Paris, this tour works well en route or as an overnight stop; accommodations are listed. It requires a car and a good map (Michelin maps #320 or #519 work well). Stops that are bolded are described in greater detail later in this chapter.

Here's how I'd spend this day: Get out early and joyride to MuséoParc Alésia in Alise Ste-Reine (with at least a photo stop for Châteauneuf-en-Auxois), tour the museum and battle site, have lunch a few minutes away at La Grange in Flavigny, drive to Fontenay and tour the abbey, then stop in Semur-en-Auxois for a stroll on your way home (this plan also works for those continuing to Paris).

The Drive Begins: Leave Beaune following signs for *Auxerre* and *Bligny-sur-Ouche;* from Bligny-sur-Ouche, take D-33 to Pont

Back Door Burgundy Drive

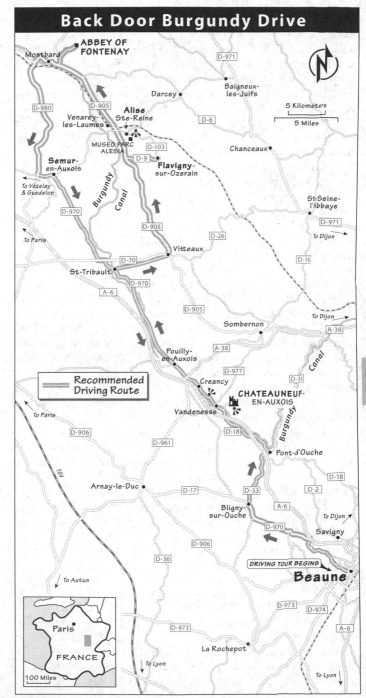

ABBEY OF FONTENAY

Montbard

D-971

D-980

D-905

Darcey

Baigneux-les-Juifs

5 Kilometers

5 Miles

Alise
Ste-Reine

Venarey-les-Laumes

D-6

MUSEO PARC ALESIA

D-103

Chanceaux

Semur-en-Auxois

D-9

Flavigny-sur-Ozerain

To Vézelay & Guedelon

Burgundy Canal

D-970

St-Seine-l'Abbaye

D-905

D-971

To Dijon

To Paris

D-26

D-16

Vitteaux

D-70

St-Tribault

D-970

A-6

D-905

Sombernon

To Dijon

A-38

Pouilly-en-Auxois

A-38

D-977

Canal

D-33

Creancy

CHATEAUNEUF-EN-AUXOIS

Recommended
Driving Route

Vandenesse

Burgundy

To Paris

D-906

D-961

D-18

Pont-d'Ouche

D-18

Arnay-le-Duc

D-17

D-33

D-2

TGV

Bligny-sur-Ouche

A-6

To Dijon

D-970

Savigny

D-906

To Autun

D-36

DRIVING TOUR BEGINS

Beaune

Paris

FRANCE

D-973

D-974

100 Miles

D-973

A-6

La Rochepot

To Lyon

To Lyon

BURGUNDY

d'Ouche (following signs to *Pont du Pany* and *Dijon*), where you'll turn left along the canal (D-18), following signs to *Château de Châteauneuf.* In five minutes, you'll see **Châteauneuf-en-Auxois'** castle looming above. Cross the canal and the freeway for great views of the hill town, even if you're not visiting it. A right on the small lane at the second farm, one kilometer after leaving D-18, leads to the best views.

After visiting Châteauneuf, return back down to the canal at Vandenesse and turn right toward Créancy (still on D-18). There's a nice picnic spot on its "port," with water views of Châteauneuf. From Créancy, drive to Pouilly-en-Auxois. The Burgundy Canal tunnels underground for several miles through Pouilly-en-Auxois, as it passes its highest point between Paris and Dijon. You'll go over it as you cross Pouilly-en-Auxois. Go through Pouilly-en-Auxois and follow signs to Vitteaux, where you'll join D-905. Go north toward **Alise Ste-Reine** and follow signs to *Alésia* and *MuséoParc.* After exploring the museum and battlefield, backtrack a short distance on D-905 and find signs to **Flavigny-sur-Ozerain** (5 minutes away on D-9).

From Flavigny-sur-Ozerain, drive back to D-905, turn right (north), and follow signs to the **Abbey of Fontenay** (you'll pass below Alise Ste-Reine again). After the abbey, continue up D-905 to Montbard, then turn onto D-980 and drive south to **Semur-en-Auxois.** From Semur-en-Auxois, take D-970 via Pouilly-en-Auxois and retrace your route past Châteauneuf-en-Auxois and Bilgny-sur-Ouche to Beaune. For a quicker option, you can dart from Semur-en-Auxois across to the A-6 autoroute and save time by taking it to Beaune (or head north to Paris).

The Museum and battlefield at Alise Ste-Reine and the Abbey of Fontenay are your primary goals; allow at least an hour to tour each. With no stops, the one-way drive from Beaune to Fontenay should take about an hour and a half. But you should be stopping—a lot.

Non-drivers can get as far as Semur-en-Auxois by bus (3/day Mon-Sat, 1/day Sun, from Montbard or Dijon—runs early morning, noon, and evening; railpass gets you a free ticket, ask TI in Semur about where to get bus ticket). There are no trains to Semur.

Châteauneuf-en-Auxois

This perfectly medieval castle used to monitor passage between Burgundy and Paris, with hawk's-eye views from its 2,000-foot setting. *Châteauneuf* means "new castle," so you'll see many in France. This one is in the Auxois area, so it's Châteauneuf-en-Auxois (not to be confused with the famous Châteauneuf-du-Pape in Provence). The living hill town hunkers in the shadow of its pit-bull château and merits exploring. Park at the lot in the very upper end of the village (where the road ends), and don't miss the **panoramic viewpoint** nearby. The military value of this site is powerfully clear from here. Find the Burgundy Canal and the three reservoirs that have maintained the canal's flow for more than 300 years. The small village below is Châteauneuf's port, Vandenesse-en-Auxois—you'll be there shortly. If not for phylloxera—the vine-loving insect that ravaged France in the early 1900s, killing all of its vineyards—you'd see more vineyards than wheat fields.

Saunter into the village, where every building feels historic and stocky farmers live side-by-side with slender artists. Walk into the courtyard, but skip the château's interior (€6, Tue-Sun 10:00-12:00 & 14:00-18:00, closed Mon, English handout). You'll get better moat views and see the more important castle entry by walking beneath the Hôstellerie du Château, and then turning right, following *Eglise* signs.

Sleeping and Eating in Châteauneuf-en-Auxois

(€1 = about $1.30, country code: 33)
$ **Hôstellerie du Château**** is a simple, cozy place for a good night's sleep in Châteauneuf. It houses an enticing budget-vacation ensemble: nine homey, inexpensive rooms with a rear garden overlooking a brooding castle that's floodlit at night (Db-€60 for tight bathrooms with showers, Db-€80 for larger rooms with tubs, Tb-€90, Wi-Fi, closed Nov-Feb, tel. 03 80 49 22 00, fax 03 80 49 21 27, www.hostellerie-de-chateauneuf.com, contact@hostellerie-de-chateauneuf.com). The restaurant offers delicious regional cuisine and four-course *menus* with a traditional cheese cart for €28 (closed Tue-Wed).

Eating: Châteauneuf has several affordable cafés and restaurants along its main drag. The **Grill du Castel,** across from the Hôstellerie du Château, offers the best value, with massive salads and good escargot and grilled meats (terrace tables in back).

Alise Ste-Reine

A united Gaul forming a single nation animated by the same spirit could defy the universe.
—Julius Caesar, *The Gallic Wars*

On these lands surrounding the small, vertical little village of Alise Ste-Reine is where historians are convinced that Julius Caesar defeated the Gallic leader Vercingétorix in 52 B.C., thus winning Gaul for the Roman Empire and forever changing France's destiny. Start below with the impressive museum and stand where Caesar did, then drive to above the village to see things from the Gauls' perspective.

Sights in Alise Ste-Reine

▲MuséoParc Alésia

This new circular museum, looking like a modern sports arena, does this important site justice with easy-to-follow exhibits and well-delivered information. The circular structure symbolizes how, more than 2,000 years ago, Caesar had the Gauls' *oppidum* (hilltop village) surrounded, allowing his forces to starve out the Gauls and win a decisive victory in spite of being vastly outnumbered (see sidebar). With  the help of a handy audioguide, touchscreens, and posted information, you'll gain a keen understanding of the events that led up to this battle, and why it happened here. You'll learn much about the two protagonists, Caesar and Vercingétorix, their armies, and their motivations, and be drawn into the conflict with a (dramatized) 18-minute film. Allow an hour for the museum's single floor of exhibits, then climb to the top floor for views from a Roman perspective. Finally, walk out back to inspect the full-scale reconstruction of a section of the Roman wall and lookouts that pinned the Gauls to that hilltop.

Cost and Hours: €9, includes essential audioguide (there's also a fun children's version), skip the €1.50 extra for the archaeological site on the hills above, daily April-Sept 9:00-18:00, until 19:00 July-Aug, Oct-Jan and March 10:00-17:00, closed Feb, tel. 03 80 96 96 23, www.alesia.com.

Nearby: After the museum, drive through the village of Alise Ste-Reine and follow the *Statue de Vercingétorix* signs leading to the park with the huge **statue** of the Gallic warrior overlooking his Waterloo (skip the archaeological site). Stand as he did—imagining yourself trapped on this hilltop—then find the orientation table under the gazebo.

BURGUNDY

The Dying Gauls

In 52 B.C., General Julius Caesar and his 60,000 soldiers surrounded Alésia (today's Alise Ste-Reine), hoping to finally end the uprising of free Gaul and establish Roman civilization in France. Holed up inside the hilltop fortress were 80,000 diehard (long-haired, tattooed) Gauls under their rebel chief, Vercingétorix (pronounced something like "verse in Genesis"). Having harassed Caesar for months with guerrilla-war attacks, they now called on their fellow Gauls to converge on Alésia to wipe out the Romans.

Rather than attack the fierce-fighting Gauls, Caesar's soldiers patiently camped at the base of the hill and began building a wall. In six weeks, they completed a 12-foot-tall, stone-and-earth wall all the way around Alésia (11 miles around—blue line on the orientation table at the hilltop site), and then a second, larger one (13 miles around—red line on the orientation table), trapping the rebel leaders with the intention of starving them out. If the Gauls tried to escape, not only would they have to breach the two walls, they'd first have to cross a steep no-man's-land dotted with a ditch, a moat, and booby traps (including sharp stakes in pits and buried iron spikes).

The starving Gauls inside Alésia sent their women and children out to beg for mercy from the Romans. The Romans (with little food themselves) refused. For days, the women and children wandered the unoccupied land, in full view of both armies, until they starved to death.

After months of siege, Vercingétorix's reinforcements finally came riding to save him. With 90,000 screaming Gallic warriors (Caesar says 250,000) converging on Alésia, and 80,000 more atop the hill, Caesar ordered his men to move between the two walls to fight a two-front battle. The Battle of Alésia raged for five days—a classic struggle between the methodical Romans and the impetuous "barbarians." When it became clear the Romans would not budge, the Gauls retreated.

Vercingétorix surrendered, and Gallic culture was finished in France. During the three-year rebellion, one in five Gauls had been killed, enslaved, or driven out. Roman rule was established for the next 500 years, strangling the Gallic/Celtic heritage. Vercingétorix spent his last years as a prisoner, paraded around as a war trophy. In 46 B.C., he was brought to Rome for Caesar's triumphal ascension to power, where he was strangled to death in a public ritual.

BURGUNDY

Flavigny-sur-Ozerain

Over the next hill from Alise Ste-Reine, little Flavigny-sur-Ozerain (flah-veen-yee sur oh-zuh-rain) had its 15 minutes of fame in 2000, when the movie *Chocolat* was filmed here. Taking its *chocolat*-covered image in stride, this unassuming and serenely situated village feels permanently stuck in the past, with one café-restaurant, one *crêperie*, a tiny grocery shop—but no counts and, alas, no Juliette Binoche.

Flavigny has been home to an abbey since 719, when the first (Benedictine) abbey of St. Pierre was built. The town thrived during the Middle Ages thanks to its proximity to Vézelay (with its relics of Mary Magdalene) and the flood of pilgrims coming through en route to Santiago de Compostela in northwest Spain. The fortifications you see hail from the 12th and 13th centuries. The little town was occupied by the Brits during the Hundred Years' War (15th century), then ever-so-gradually slid into irrelevance. By the time the French Revolution rolled around, it had no religious or defensive importance. The movie *Chocolat* put the town back on the map—at least for a while—and today, Flavigny has been reinvigorated by the return of 50 Benedictine monks at the Abbey of St. Joseph.

Getting There: The approach to Flavigny via D-9 is picture-perfect. Just south of Alise Ste-Reine, take the D-9 turnoff to Flavigny from D-905. Park at the lot just below the gate. From this lot, signs also lead to *Alise Ste-Reine*, described earlier (great views back to Flavigny after a few miles).

Tourist Information: Pick up a map at the TI (*Accueil des Visiteurs*, also called "La Maison du Notaire") and ask to see the photos of buildings used in *Chocolat* (hours vary, but generally April-Oct Tue-Sun 11:00-13:00 & 14:00-18:00, closed Mon and Nov-March, down Rue de l'Eglise in front of church, tel. 03 80 96 25 34).

Sights in Flavigny-sur-Ozerain

There's little to do here other than appreciate the setting (best from the grassy ramparts) and try the little *anis* (anise) candies.

***Chocolat* Sights**—Lovers of the movie will have to be satisfied with a few of the building facades featured in the film; there are no souvenirs or posters to be found, and nary a chocolate shop (locals, who prefer their homemade *anis* candies, weren't wowed by the movie). There are five buildings that fans should recognize. The evocative **Church of St. Genest** is the only one you can enter—stand where the preacher did and feel the heat of the congregation's angst, then find the upstairs seating (daily 10:30-12:00 &

BURGUNDY

14:00-18:30). The movie's *chocolaterie* lies across the square from the church entry, below La Grange restaurant, on Rue du Four (marked with a small sign, look for the arched window with the brown frame). The **count's home** is today's *mairie* (city hall), next to the church entry. The *coiffure* (hairdresser) is one door down from the TI—look for the white shutters. And what was the **Café de la République** is three doors up from the TI, with an austere facade and metal shutters. Johnny Depp never visited Flavigny (his loss), and there is no river here (the river scenes were filmed in the Dordogne, near Beynac).

Anis Demos and Shopping—You can buy the locally produced *anis* candies in pretty tins (they make great souvenirs). See them being made Monday through Friday mornings (9:00-11:00) in the Abbey of St. Pierre.

Ramparts—The grassy ramparts are worth a stroll for the view (behind the church, walk down Rue de la Poterne, turn right at the fork, then look for *Petite Ruelle des Remparts*). Wander out for the view and double back, or continue down to the next gate and climb back into the village from there.

Sleeping and Eating in Flavigny-sur-Ozerain

(€1 = about $1.30, country code: 33)

$ L'Ange Souriant Chambre d'Hôte is comfortable and intimate (Sb-€55, Db-€68, Tb-€86, Qb-€100, includes breakfast, a block below the TI on Rue Voltaire, tel. & fax 03 80 96 24 93, mobile 06 11 89 04 66, www.ange-souriant.fr, a.souriant@wanadoo.fr).

Eating: La Grange ("The Barn") serves dirt-cheap, farm-fresh fare, including luscious quiche, salads, *plats du jour*, fresh cheeses, pâtés, and delicious fruit pies (April-mid-Oct daily 12:30-18:00; mid-Oct-Nov & Feb-March open Sun only; closed Dec-Jan; across from church, look for brown doors and listen for lunchtime dining, tel. 03 80 35 81 78).

Le Restaurant de l'Abbaye, located just above the parking lot, is a good choice for traditional dishes, with pleasant indoor and outdoor seating and reasonable prices (€15 lunch *menu*, €28 for dinner, daily, Place des Fossés, tel. 03 80 96 27 77).

Abbey of Fontenay

The entire ensemble of buildings composing this isolated Cistercian abbey, rated ▲▲, has survived, giving visitors perhaps the best picture of medieval abbey life in France. In the Middle Ages, it was written, "To fully grasp the meaning of Fontenay and the power of its beauty, you must approach it trudging through the forest footpaths...through the brambles and bogs...in an October rain." But even if you use the parking lot, Fontenay's secluded setting—blanketed in birdsong, and with a garden lovingly used "as a stage set"—is truly magical.

Cost and Hours: €10, daily April-mid-Nov 10:00-18:00, until 19:00 July-Aug, mid-Nov-March 10:00-12:00 & 14:00-17:00, tel. 03 80 92 15 00, www.abbayedefontenay.com.

Getting There: The abbey is a 10-minute drive north of Montbard. There's no bus service—allow about €25 round-trip for a taxi from Montbard's train station (taxi mobile 06 08 26 61 55 or 06 08 99 21 13), or rent a bike at Montbard's TI and ride 45 minutes each way (Montbard TI tel. 03 80 92 53 81).

Background: This abbey—one of the oldest Cistercian abbeys in France—was founded in 1118 by St. Bernard as a back-to-basics

reaction to the excesses of Benedictine abbeys, such as Cluny. The Cistercians worked to recapture the simplicity, solitude, and poverty of the early Church. Bernard created "a horrible vast solitude" in the forest, where his monks could live like the desert fathers of the Old Testament. They chose marshland ("Cistercian" is derived from "marshy bogs") and strove to be separate from the world (which required the industrious self-sufficiency these abbeys were so adept at). The movement spread, essentially colonizing Europe religiously. In 1200, there were more than 500 such monasteries and abbeys in Europe.

Like the Cistercian movement in general, Fontenay flourished through the 13th-15th centuries. A 14th-century proverb said, "Wherever the wind blows, to Fontenay money flows." Fontenay thrived as a prosperous "mini-city" for nearly 700 years, until the French Revolution, when it became the property of the nation and was eventually sold.

Visiting the Abbey: Like visitors centuries ago, you'll enter through the abbey's **gatehouse.** The main difference: Anyone with a ticket gets in, and there's no watchdog barking angrily at you (through the small hole on the right). Pick up the English self-guided tour flier with your ticket. Your visit follows the route described here (generally clockwise). Arrows keep you on course, and signs tell you which sections of the abbey are private (as its owners still live here).

The **abbey church** is pure Romanesque and built to St. Bernard's specs: Latin cross plan, no fancy stained glass, unadorned columns, nothing to distract from prayer. The lone statue is the

13th-century *Virgin of Fontenay,* a reminder that the church was dedicated to Mary. Enjoy the ethereal light. Calm your mind and listen carefully to hear the brothers chanting.

Stairs lead from the front of the church to a vast 16th-century, oak-beamed **dormitory** where the monks slept—together, fully dressed, on thin mats. Monastic life was pretty simple: prayer, reading, work, seven services a day, one meal in the winter, two in the summer. Daily rations: a loaf of bread and a quarter-liter of wine.

Back down the stairs, enter the **cloister,** beautiful in its starkness. This was the heart of the community, where monks read, exercised, washed, did small projects—and, I imagine, gave each other those silly haircuts. The shallow alcove (next to the church door) once stored prayer books; notice the slots for shelves. Next to that, the chapter room was where the abbot led discussions and community business was discussed. The adjacent monks' hall was a general-purpose room, likely busy with monks hunched over tables copying sacred texts (a major work of abbeys). The dining hall, or refectory, also faced the cloister (closed to the public).

Across the garden stands the huge abbey **forge.** In the 13th century, the monks at Fontenay ran what many consider Europe's first metalworking plant. Iron ore was melted down in ovens with big bellows. Tools were made and sold for a profit. The hydraulic hammer, which became the basis of industrial manufacturing of iron throughout Europe, was first used here. Leaving the building, walk left around the back to see the stream, which was diverted to power the wheels that operated the forge. Water was vital to abbey life. The pond—originally practical, rather than decorative—was a fish farm (some whopper descendants still swim here). Leave through the gift shop, which was the public chapel in the days when visitors were not allowed inside the abbey grounds.

Semur-en-Auxois

This sleepy town feels real. There are 4,500 residents, few tourists, and no important sights to

digest—just a pleasing jumble of Burgundian alleys perched above the meandering Armançon River and behind the town's four massive towers, all beautifully illuminated after dark.

Locals like to believe that Hercules built Semur-en-Auxois (suh-moor-ahn-ohx-wah) on his return from Spain. But Semur's ancient origins date back to Neolithic times, long before Hercules' visit. Today the town works as a base to visit the sights described in this area, or as a handy lunch or dinner stop. Semur is also about 45 minutes from the famous church in Vézelay and two hours from Paris, making it a workable first- or last-night stop on your trip. Don't miss the smashing panorama of Semur from the viewpoint by the Citroën shop, where D-980 and D-954 intersect.

Tourist Information: The TI is across from Hôtel Côte d'Or, at Semur's medieval entry (2 Place Gaveau, tel. 03 80 97 05 96, www.tourisme-semur.fr). Pick up their city-walking brochure, information on regional sights, and bike-rental information and suggested routes (hilly terrain).

Sights in Semur-en-Auxois

Connect the following sights (and see everything of importance in Semur) with a short stroll. Begin at the TI, then stop under the Sauvigny gate.

Sauvigny and Guiller Gates—These connected gates provided safe entry to Semur in the Middle Ages. Look up at the Sauvigny gate and see the indentations for posts that held a drawbridge in place, then find a stone hinge for the original gate on the right. The Guiller gate, 100 years older, marked the town's limit in the 1300s.

• *From here, enter charming Rue Buffon, Semur's oldest commercial street. At the end of this street is the...*

Church of Notre-Dame—The town's main sight, the 13th-century church that dominates its small square, is worth a quick look. Walk counterclockwise around the ambulatory behind the altar. The first chapel on the right has unusual stained-glass windows honoring Semur's WWI soldiers. Then notice the rich colors in the next chapel. Gothic churches were usually brightly painted, not somber and gray, as you see them today. The stained-glass windows around Mary's statue date from the 13th century and are the only originals left. Before leaving the church, glance at the second-to-last chapel on your right, with a large plaque honoring American soldiers who lost their lives in World War I (Mon-Sat 9:00-12:00 & 14:00-18:30, Sun 14:00-18:30, decent English handout).

• *Leave with the church to your back and walk down the square past the half-timbered charcuterie, turn left at the bottom on Rue du Rempart, then take another left down cobbled Rue du Fourneau to the river to see...*

Semur's Towers—In the Middle Ages, 18 towers were connected by defensive ramparts to protect the center city. Caught in the crossfire between the powerful Dukes of Burgundy and the king of France, Semur's defenses were first destroyed by Louis XI in

1478, then finished off during the wars of religion in 1602.

• *For postcard-perfect views, continue your stroll for a few blocks in either direction along the Armançon River, then return back up Rue du Fourneau. Then you can head out to see a sweeping...*

▲▲**View over Semur-en-Auxois**—Drive or hike downhill from the TI along Rue du Pont Joly, cross the river, then head uphill and turn left at the top roundabout (walkers can veer left a block after the bridge for a shortcut). Across from the Citroën dealership, find the lookout with an orientation table and a memorable view of the red roofs, spires, and towers—especially striking at night. If the climb uphill feels like too much, walkers will find great views just after crossing the bridge.

Sleeping and Eating in Semur-en-Auxois

(€1 = about $1.30, country code: 33)

If Semur-en-Auxois seduces you into spending a night, try **$$ Hôtel les Cymaises****, with comfortable rooms and big beds in a manor house with a quiet courtyard (Db-€70, Tb-€80, 2-room Qb-€100, private parking, 7 Rue du Renaudot, tel. 03 80 97 21 44, fax 03 80 97 18 23, www.hotelcymaises.com, contact@hotel cymaises.com).

Eating: The various cafés along Rue du Buffon offer ambience and average quality. **L'Entract** is where everybody goes for pizza, pasta, salads, and more in a relaxed atmosphere (daily, below the church on 4 Rue Fevret, tel. 03 80 96 60 10). The historic **charcuterie** (delicatessen) across from the church can supply your picnic needs (Tue-Sat 9:00-19:30, Sun 9:00-12:00, closed Mon).

Between Burgundy and the Loire

These three sights—Vézelay and its Romanesque Basilica of Ste. Madeleine; the under-construction Château de Guédelon; and the underrated city of Bourges, with its grand "High" Gothic cathedral—make good stops for drivers connecting Burgundy and the Loire Valley. Squeezing in visits to all three in one day is tight and requires an early start (allow six hours of driving from Beaune to the Loire, plus time to stop and visit the sights). The first two also work if you're linking Burgundy and Paris (in which case, skip Bourges, which requires a long detour.)

BURGUNDY

Vézelay and the Basilica of Ste. Madeleine

For more than eight centuries, travelers have hoofed it up through this pretty little town to get to the famous hilltop church, the Basilica of Ste. Madeleine. In its 12th-century prime, Vézelay welcomed the medieval masses. Cultists of Mary Magdalene came to file past her (supposed) body. Pilgrims rendezvoused here to march to Spain to venerate St. James' (supposed) relics in Santiago de Compostela. Three Crusades were launched from this hill: the Second Crusade (1146), announced by Bernard of Clairveaux; the Third Crusade (1190), under Richard the Lionhearted and King Philippe Auguste; and the Seventh Crusade (1248), by King (and Saint) Louis IX. Today, tourists flock to Vézelay's basilica, famous for its place in history, its soul-stirring Romanesque architecture—reproduced in countless art books—and for the relics of Mary Magdalene.

Tourist Information: Vézelay's TI is at the lower end of the village (on Rue St. Etienne, which turns into Rue St. Pierre; June-Sept daily 10:00-13:00 & 14:00-18:00, until 19:00 July-Aug; Oct-May Fri-Wed 10:00-13:00 & 14:00-18:00, closed Thu, also closed Sun Nov-March; tel. 03 86 33 23 69). The TI provides Internet access.

BURGUNDY

Sights in Vézelay

▲Basilica of Ste. Madeleine

To accommodate the growing crowds of medieval pilgrims, the abbots of Vézelay enlarged their original church (1104), then rebuilt it after a disastrous 1120 fire. The building we see today—one of the largest and best-preserved Romanesque churches anywhere—was built in stages: nave (1120-1140), narthex (1132-1145), and choir (1215). The construction spanned the century-long transition from the Romanesque style (round barrel arches like the ancient Romans', thick walls, small windows) to Gothic (pointed arches, flying buttresses, high nave, lots of stained glass). Vézelay blends elements of both styles.

Cost and Hours: Free, daily 7:00-20:00; Mass Mon-Fri at 18:30, Sat at 12:30 and 18:30, Sun at 11:00; tel. 03 86 33 39 50, http://vezelay.cef.fr.

Information: Eager volunteers offer one-hour English guided tours that depart from inside the narthex in summer (donation requested, no tours 12:00-14:00). Other tours can be arranged by contacting the volunteer coordinator (tel. 03 86 33 39 50, www .basiliquedevezelay.org). Or be your own guide, either by follow-

Mary Magdalene

France has a special affection for Mary Magdalene (La Madeleine), and Vézelay is one of several churches dedicated to her—a rarity in Europe, where most churches honor Jesus' mother, the Virgin Mary.

The Bible says that Mary Magdalene, one of Jesus' followers, was exorcised of seven demons (Luke 8:2), witnessed the Crucifixion (Matthew 27:56), and was the first mortal to see the resurrected Jesus (Mark 16:9-11)—the other disciples didn't believe her.

Some theologians have fleshed out Mary's reputation by associating her with biblical passages that don't specifically name her—e.g., the sinner who washed Jesus' feet with her hair (Luke 7:36-50), the forgiven adulteress (John 8), or the woman with the alabaster jar who anointed Jesus (Matthew 26:7-13).

In medieval times, legends appeared (especially in France) that, after the Crucifixion, Mary Magdalene fled to southern France, lived in a cave, converted locals, performed miracles, and died in Provence. Renaissance artists portrayed her as a fanciful blend of Bible and legend: a red-headed, long-haired prostitute who was rescued by Jesus, symbolizing the sin of those who love too much.

In recent times, feminists have claimed Mary Magdalene was a victim of male-dominated Catholic suppression. Bible scholars cite passages in two ancient (but noncanonical) gospels that cryptically allude to Mary as Jesus' special "companion." The Da Vinci Code—a popular if unhistorical novel—seized on this, slathering it with medieval legend and asserting that Mary Magdalene was actually Jesus' wife who bore him descendants, and that her relics lie not in Vézelay but in a shopping mall in Paris.

ing my self-guided tour or buying the €6 guidebook as you enter. The view from the park behind the church is sublime.

⊘ Self-Guided Tour: The **facade**—with one tower missing its original steeple, another that's unfinished, and an inauthentic tympanum—isn't why you came. Step inside.

The **narthex,** or entrance hall, served several functions. Religiously, it was a place to cross from the profane to the sacred. Practically, it gave shelter to overflow pilgrim crowds (even overnight, if necessary) as they shuffled through one of the three doorways. And aesthetically, the dark narthex prepares the visitor for the radiant nave.

The **tympanum** (carved relief) over the central, interior doorway is one of Romanesque's signature pieces. It shows the risen Christ, ascending to heaven in an almond-shaped cloud, shooting

Holy Ghost rays at his apostles and telling them to preach the Good News to the ends of the Earth. The whole diversity of humanity (appropriate, considering Vézelay's function as a gathering place) appears beneath: hunters, fishermen, farmers, pygmies, and men with long ears, feathers, and dog heads. The signs of the zodiac arch over the scene.

Gaze through the central doorway into the **nave** at the rows and rows of arches that seem to recede into a luminous infinity—the effect is mesmerizing. The nave is long, high, and narrow (200 feet by 60 feet by 35 feet), creating a tunnel effect formed by 10 columns and arches on each side. Overhead is the church's most famous feature—barrel vaults (wide arches) built of stones alternating between creamy-white and pink-brown. The side aisles have low ceilings, whereas the nave rises up between them, lined with slender floor-to-ceiling columns that unite both stories. The interior glows with an even light from the unstained glass of the clerestory windows. The absence of distractions or bright colors makes this simple church perfect for meditation.

The capitals of the nave's **columns** are carved masterpieces by several sculptors of saints and Bible scenes. All are worth studying (the guidebook sold at the entry identifies each scene, starting in the narthex), but some you might easily recognize. On the left, look for David and Goliath (fourth column), Cain and Abel (fifth column), Moses and the Golden Calf (sixth column), Adam and Eve (ninth column), and Peter Freed from Prison (10th and final column). On the right is the well-known "Mystical Mill" (fourth column), showing Old Testament Moses and New Testament Paul working together to fill sacks with grain (and, metaphorically, the Bible with words).

The light at the end of the tunnel-like nave is the **choir** (altar area), radiating a brighter, blue-gray light. Constructed when Gothic was the rage, the choir has pointed arches and improved engineering, but the feel is monotone and sterile.

In the right transept stands a statue of the woman this church was dedicated to—not the Virgin Mary (Jesus' mother) but one of Jesus' disciples, Mary Magdalene. She cradles an alabaster jar of ointment she used (according to some Bible interpretations) to anoint Jesus.

Go down into the **crypt** for the ultimate medieval experience in one of Europe's greatest medieval churches. You're entering the foundations of the earlier ninth-century church that monks built here on the hilltop after Vikings had twice pillaged their church at the base of the hill.

File past the small container with the **relics of Mary Magdalene.** In medieval times, Vézelay claimed to possess Mary's entire body, but the relics were later damaged and scattered by anti-Catholic Huguenots (16th century) and Revolutionaries (18th century), leaving only a few pieces.

Are they really her mortal remains? We only have legends—many different versions—that first appeared in the historical record around A.D. 1000. The most popular legends say that Mary Magdalene traveled to Provence, where she died, and that her bones were brought from there by a monk to save them from Muslim pirates. In the 11th century, the abbots of Vézelay heavily marketed the notion that these were Mary's relics, and when the pope authenticated it in 1058, tourism boomed.

Vézelay prospered until the mid-13th century, when King Charles of Anjou announced that Mary's body was not in Vézelay, but had been found in another town. Vézelay's relics suddenly looked bogus, and pilgrims stopped coming. For the next five centuries, the church fell into disrepair and then was vandalized by secularists in the Revolution. The church was restored (1840-1860) by a young architect named Eugène Viollet-le-Duc, who would later revamp Notre-Dame in Paris and build the base of the Statue of Liberty.

After visiting the chapter house and cloisters (out the right transept), don't pass on the view from behind the church of the Cure River Valley.

Sleeping and Eating in Vézelay

(€1 = about $1.30, country code: 33)
You'll find pleasant cafés with reasonable food all along the street leading to the church.

$$ Hôtel de la Poste et du Lion d'Or has comfortable, country-classy rooms in Vézelay (good Db-€96, bigger Db-€108-124, extra bed-€18, Wi-Fi, easy parking, garage-€6, at the foot of the village, Place du Champ-de-Foire, tel. 03 86 33 21 23, fax 03 86 32 30 92, www.laposte-liondor.com, contact@laposte-liondor.com). Dinner in the hotel's country-elegant **restaurant**—indoors or *en plein air*—is a treat (*menus* from €25, closed Mon).

Eating: **La Dent Creuse** has the best terrace tables at the lower end of the village (left side), with salads, pizza, and more (daily until 21:30, Place du Champ-de-Foire, tel. 03 86 33 36 33).

Auberge de la Coquille is a cozy place to eat inside and out, with reasonable prices (daily until 21:30, halfway up to the church at 81 Rue St. Pierre, tel. 03 86 33 35 57).

Vézelay Connections

Vézelay is about 45 minutes northwest of **Semur-en-Auxois** (20 minutes off the autoroute to Paris). Train travelers go to **Sermizelles** (via Auxerre or Avallon, 5/day) and take the shuttle

BURGUNDY

bus (meets most trains) or taxi from there (6 miles, allow €20 one-way, taxi tel. 03 86 32 31 88 or mobile 06 85 77 89 36). Buses also run from Montbard to Avallon (with train connections to Sermizelles).

Château de Guédelon

A historian's dream (worth ▲▲, or ▲▲▲ for kids), this castle is being built by 35 enthusiasts using only the tools, techniques, and materials available in the 13th century.

Cost and Hours: €10, kids 5-17-€8.50, under 5-free, excellent English handout, picnic area and lunch café inside; castle open July-Aug daily 10:00-19:00; April-June Thu-Tue 10:00-18:00, Sun until 19:00, closed Wed; Sept Thu-Tue 10:00-17:30, Sat-Sun until 18:00, closed Wed; Oct Thu-Tue 10:00-17:30, closed Wed; closed Nov-mid-March; tel. 03 86 45 66 66, www.guedelon.fr.

Getting There: Guédelon is an hour west of Vézelay on D-955, between St-Amand-en-Puisaye and St-Saveur-en-Puisaye. It is inaccessible by public transport.

Visiting the Castle: The project is the dream of two individuals who wanted to build a medieval castle (this one is based on plans drafted in 1228). Started in 1997, it will ultimately include four towers surrounding a central courtyard with a bridge and a moat. The goal of this exciting project is to give visitors a better appreciation of medieval construction, and for the builders to learn about medieval techniques while they work. The castle won't be complete for another 11 years, so you still have time to watch the process. (It's currently about 15-50 feet tall, and the great hall is just about complete.) When the castle is done, the ambitious owners plan to build a medieval abbey.

Enter the project to the sound of chisels chipping rock and the sight of people dressed as if it were 800 years ago. A human-powered hamster wheel hoists carefully dressed stone up tower walls (the largest tower will reach six stories when completed). Carpenters whack away at massive beams, creating supports for stone arches, while weavers demonstrate how clothing was made (a sheep's pen provides the raw material). Thirteen workstations help visitors learn about castle construction, from medieval rope-making to blacksmithing. Feel free to ask the workers questions—some speak English.

Kids can't get enough of Guédelon. It's a favorite for local school field trips, so expect lots of children. And if it's been raining, be prepared for a muddy mess—you are, after all, in a construction site.

Sleeping near Guédelon: Guédelon is remote. If you need to sleep nearby, try **$$ Hôtel Les Grands Chênes,** where British Rachael and French Alain have restored a pretty manor home among trees, lakes, and waves of grass (Db-€90, Tb-€100, Qb-€115-140, Wi-Fi, on D-18 between St-Fargeau and St-Amand-en-Puisaye, tel. 03 86 74 04 05, fax 03 86 74 11 41, www.hotelles grandschenes.com, contact@hotellesgrandschenes.com).

Bourges

Nestled between rolling vineyards and thick forests in the geographical center of France, unpretentious Bourges (pronounced "boorzh") is among France's most overlooked and authentic cities. Here you'll uncover a wonderful collection of medieval houses, a Gothic cathedral to rival any you've seen, and a down-to-earth, Midwest-like friendliness. Situated three hours due south of Paris, two hours west of Beaune, and 1.5 hours east of Amboise, Bourges is a handy stopover on the drive through the French heartland between Burgundy and the Loire.

Little-known Bourges has a big story to tell those who take the time to open its pages. Its intriguing history owes much to its strategic location between two once-powerful regions, Burgundy and the Loire. It began as a Roman city of a hundred acres, became the first Christian town in Gaul, and later served as the northern boundary of the sophisticated Kingdom of Aquitaine. It hit its peak in the Middle Ages (especially 1200-1500), when its great cathedral was built. It was home to future King Charles VII (r. 1422-1461), the man who, at Joan of Arc's insistence, rallied the French and drove out the English. During that Hundred Years' War, Bourges was a provisional capital of France, which explains its impressive legacy of medieval architecture. The city is best appreciated on foot, strolling its lovely medieval lanes dotted with half-timbered buildings.

Orientation to Bourges

Tourist Information

If the cathedral had a transept, the TI would lie outside the south portal (April-Sept Mon-Sat 9:00-19:00, Sun 10:00-18:00; Oct-March daily 9:00-18:00; 21 Rue Victor Hugo, tel. 02 48 23 02 60, www.bourges-tourisme.com). Pick up one of their excellent English walking guides—wine lovers should ask for the *Route des Vignobles* map, and historians the *Route Jacques Cœur* map.

Arrival in Bourges

By Train: From the station, it's about a half-mile walk south to the cathedral, which lies at the center of town. Head straight out onto Avenue Henri Laudier, which continues as Avenue Jean Jaurès to Place Planchat. From here, turn left onto Rue du Commerce, which turns into Rue Moyenne. Continue along this street until you hit Rue Victor Hugo, where you'll find the TI, just south of the cathedral. (Efficient sightseers will want to stroll the medieval quarter en route to the cathedral: From Avenue Jean Jaurès, hang a left at Rue Cambournac—just before Place Planchat—to Place de la Barre, at the start of my "Medieval Quarter Stroll," described under "Sights in Bourges.")

By Car: On the south side of the cathedral, where Rue Victor Hugo crosses Rue Jacques Rimbault, is a big, central underground lot called Parking Mairie-Cathédrale. The stairs up to the street land you in front of the TI.

Helpful Hints

Street Markets: Bourges is known for its good morning markets (all of them shut down around 13:00). The biggest is held on Saturdays on Place de la Nation. A smaller Thursday market takes place near the cathedral on Place des Marronniers, and Place St-Bonnet has a good market on Sundays.

Internet Access: The TI has free Wi-Fi.

Sound-and-Light Show: Bourges' **Nuits Lumière** start at sundown every Thursday, Friday, and Saturday night in July and August. The town's facades, courtyards, and monuments are lit up, accompanied by medieval and Renaissance music. You don't have to understand French to enjoy it (lasts until midnight).

Music Festival: Every April, Bourges hosts **Printemps de Bourges,** a huge music festival (www.printemps-bourges .com).

Sights in Bourges

The only sights in Bourges that charge admission are the Palais Jacques Cœur and the cathedral tower/crypt (both worth paying for). The handful of municipal museums are all free.

▲▲**Cathedral of St. Etienne**—One of Europe's great Gothic churches, Bourges Cathedral is known for its simple but harmonious design, flying buttresses, stained glass, and sheer size. A Christian church has stood on this spot since the third century, including a Romanesque cathedral where Eleanor of Aquitaine received her crown in 1137. The present church was started in 1195, and largely finished just 55 years later—an astonishingly short amount of time for such a large structure. The design was inspired by Paris' Notre-Dame Cathedral, and it was built at the same time as the cathedral in Chartres. These three churches sum up the "High" Gothic style in France, and Bourges is one of the best-preserved, having been spared the ravages of the French Revolution and both world wars.

Cost and Hours: The **church interior** is free and open daily April-Sept 8:30-19:15, Oct-March 9:00-17:45, last entry 30 minutes before closing. The **tower and crypt** are covered by a €5.50 ticket (or an €11 combo-ticket with Palais Jacques Cœur) and are open Mon-Sat 9:45-11:30 & 14:00-17:30, Sun 14:00-17:30 only. Tel. 02 48 65 49 44, http://cathedrale-bourges.monuments-nationaux.fr.

❷ Self-Guided Tour: Use this commentary to get oriented, starting outside.

Exterior: The magnificent **west facade** is exceptionally wide (135 feet), dominated by five elaborately carved portals. The five doors reflect the church's unique interior—a central nave, flanked on each side by not one but two aisles. The frightening *Last Judgment* over the central doorway shows a seated Christ presiding over Judgment Day. The unfortunate condemned are on the right, while the lucky ones are saved on the left.

The church's mismatched **towers** were problematic from the start. In an age of build-'em-high-and-fast, Bourges competed with Chartres to erect the ultimate Gothic cathedral. Bourges arguably won, but at a cost. The hastily built south tower started cracking right away, and had to be shored up—hence the squat tower that sits alongside it. Since the south tower was never strong enough to house any bells, locals call it "The Deaf Tower." Meanwhile, the north tower collapsed altogether on New Year's Eve 1506 and had to be rebuilt, financed by donors who were granted an indulgence to eat butter during Lent—hence its nickname, the "Tour de Beurre."

The elegant **flying buttresses** (best seen from the garden behind the church) form two rows, supporting both the lower and upper walls. The buttresses slope upward, enfolding the church in a distinctive pyramid shape as it rises to the peaked roofline.

Interior: Step inside. The view down the **nave** is overwhelming—at 400 feet, this is the longest nave in France. It seems even longer because the church has no transepts to interrupt the tunnel effect. Notice elements of the "High" Gothic style of the 1200s: The church is tall, filled with light from many windows, and built with slender columns and thin walls (thanks to efficient flying buttresses). The church rises up like a three-tiered step-pyramid—the outermost aisles are 30 feet high, the inner aisles are 70 feet, and the central nave is a soaring 120 feet from floor to rib-arched ceiling.

BURGUNDY

The best **stained glass** (c. 1215) is at the far end of the church, in the apse. Also, the Jacques Cœur Chapel (a side chapel) has a colorful *Annunciation* in stained glass. Cœur was a traveling merchant who built a series of way-stations all over 15th-century France, and whose Bourges palace you can tour (described later).

The towering **astronomical clock** standing in the nave celebrates the most famous wedding the cathedral witnessed: that of hometown boy (and future king) Charles VII and Marie d'Anjou. The old clock, from 1424, still works.

The tower and crypt, described next, are covered by a single €5.50 ticket.

Climbing the Tower: Don't leave the cathedral without climbing the 396 steps up the north tower for terrific views.

Crypt: To see the crypt, you need to join a tour in French... but you don't have to pay attention. Once inside, find the tomb statue of Duke Jean de Berry (1340-1416), the great collector of illuminated manuscripts and patron of this church. He lies on his back atop a black marble slab, dressed in ermine. At his feet sleeps a muzzled bear, representing the duke's quiet ferocity. Nearby, the colorfully painted Holy Sepulchre statues (c. 1530) enact the story of Christ's body being prepared for burial. See how realistic the marble looks as the mourners tug the ends of Christ's shroud—remarkably supple.

Nearby: The **Archbishop's Garden** (Jardin de l'Archevêché), just behind the cathedral, has a fine classical design and point-blank views of the flying buttresses. On Sundays when the weather agrees, old-school *guinguette* balls (picture a Renoir scene) are held here. A stage and a bar are set up and locals drink and dance as if it were still the belle époque.

▲**Medieval Quarter (Vieille Ville) Stroll**—Bourges' old city is lassoed within Rues Bourbonnoux, Edouard Branly, and des Arènes. Richly decorated Renaissance mansions, many of which house small museums (none worth entering), mix it up with modest half-timbered homes and heavy cobbles. In this end of town, look for Hôtel Lallemant (home to the Musée des Arts Décoratifs), Hôtel des Echevins (Musée Estève, with contemporary paintings by Maurice Estève), and Hôtel Cujas (Musée du Berry, with Roman tombstones and the famously expressive mourner statues from the Duke of Berry's elaborate tomb).

Start your tour at **Place de la Barre,** at the far end of Rue Mirebeau (about 15 minutes' downhill walk from the cathedral toward the train station; en route, you may want to visit Palais Jaques Cœur—described next). From Place de la Barre, stroll to Rue Mirebeau's other end at Place Gordaine, then head back toward the cathedral up Rue Bourbonnoux (veer right after Rue Mirebeau). As you come upon Rue Joyeuse (on your left), notice the **Pâtisserie aux Trois Flutes.** The flutes create a column supporting the building's second floor and mark the entrance to Rue Joyeuse, the "Joyful Street" that held Bourges' red light district during the Middle Ages.

Continue up Rue Bourbonnoux to Passage Casse-Cou (look for it on the right just before the recommended Le d'Antan Sancerrois restaurant). About halfway up the stairs of the passage, turn left and walk past the ramparts, where you can spot vestiges of the Roman wall (look for the bits of red brick in the wall) before landing back near the cathedral. From there, you can walk back down Rue Moyenne (modern shopping, post office) to the Palais Jacques Cœur (one street west of Rue Moyenne—at the FNAC store, head to the left down Rue du Docteur Témoin, then take the next right down a winding alley, which lands you right in front of the palace).

▲**Palais Jacques Cœur**—Bourges matters to travelers today in large part because of Jacques Cœur (c. 1395-1456), the finance minister for Charles VII who decided to make Bourges his permanent home. Monsieur Cœur became fabulously wealthy through the spice trade, and used his wealth to bankroll Joan of Arc's call to save France from the English. He also helped establish Bourges as a capital of luxury goods and arms manufacturing, which funded construction of many of the fine mansions you see. His extravagant home is one of the most impressive examples of a Gothic civil palace, combining all the best elements of a château in an urban mansion. Though its furnishings are long gone, the stone and marble work are darned impressive. Sadly for Jacques, he didn't get to live in this glorious palace very long—shortly after moving in, he was arrested on a series of trumped-up charges (including "sorcery" and the poisoning of the king's mistress). To visit the palace, you have to join a French-only tour (pick up the English handout).

Cost and Hours: €7.50, daily 9:45-12:00 & 14:00-17:15, until 18:15 May-June, until 18:30 July-Aug, 10 bis Rue Jacques-Cœur, tel. 02 48 24 79 42, http://palais-jacques-coeur.monuments -nationaux.fr.

Sleeping in Bourges

(€1 = about $1.30, country code: 33)
Hotels and restaurants are a good value here.

$$$ Best Western Hôtel d'Angleterre Bourges*** is a fine place and as central as it gets—a stone's toss from the cathedral (standard Db-€102, bigger Db-€154, rates include buffet breakfast, air-con, Wi-Fi, 1 Place des Quatre-Piliers, tel. 02 48 24 68 51, fax 02 48 65 21 41, www.bestwestern-angleterre-bourges.com, hotel @bestwestern-angleterre-bourges.com).

BURGUNDY

$$ Hotel le Christina** is a good two-star place about 10 blocks from the cathedral (Db-€60-80, air-con, Wi-Fi, breakfast-€8.50, 5 Rue de la Halle, tel. 02 48 70 56 50, fax 02 48 70 58 13, www.le-christina.com, info@le-christina.com).

Eating in Bourges

Ground zero for dining in Bourges is **Place Gordaine,** where you'll find easygoing cafés and *bistrot*s. Consider these places as well:

Le Bourbonnoux is a top choice, with excellent *menus*, good prices, and copious servings (€13-32 *menus*, closed Sun, 44 Rue Bourbonnoux, tel. 02 48 24 14 76).

La Crêperie des Remparts offers a great range of inexpensive crêpes and salads (closed Sun-Mon, 59 Rue Bourbonnoux, tel. 02 48 24 55 44).

Au Sénat is a local favorite for good-value traditional cuisine (*menus* from €16, closed Wed-Thu, on Place Gordaine at 8 Rue de la Poissonnerie, tel. 02 48 24 02 56).

Le d'Antan Sancerrois lies in the thick of the old city, boasts a Michelin star, and is a fine place to do it up right *sans* breaking *le banque* (€54-85 *menus*, closed Sun-Mon, 50 Rue Bourbonnoux, tel. 02 48 65 96 26).

Bourges Connections

From Bourges by Train to: Paris' Gare d'Austerlitz (10/day, 2-3 hours, most with 1 change), **Amboise** (10/day, 2 hours, 1 change), **Beaune** (7/day, 2.5 hours, transfer in Nevers), **Sarlat** (7 hours, 2 changes).

Between Burgundy and Lyon

Drivers traveling south from Beaune should think about detouring into the lovely, unspoiled Mâconnais countryside. Brancion, Chapaize, Cluny, and Taizé gather a few minutes from one another, about 25 minutes west of the autoroute between Mâcon and Tournus (see map on page 912). For a lovely romp through vineyards and unspoiled villages, drive south of Beaune on D-974 to Chagny, then hook up with D-981 to Cluny (via Givry, Buxy, and Cormatin). South of Buxy, be on the lookout for a surprising château on the west side of the road in cute little Sercy. D-14 heading east to Brancion meets D-981 at Cormatin.

Brancion and Chapaize

An hour south of Beaune by car (12 miles west of Tournus on D-14) are two tiny villages, each with "daughters of Cluny"—churches that owe their existence and architectural design to the nearby and once-powerful Cluny Abbey. Between the villages you'll pass a Stonehenge-era menhir (standing stone) with a cross added on top at a later point—evidence that this was sacred ground long before Christianity (from Brancion, it's on the right just after passing the bulky Château de Nobles).

Brancion

This is a classic feudal village. Back when there were no nations in Europe, control of land was delegated from lord to vassal. The  Duke of Burgundy ruled here through his vassal, the Lord of Brancion. His vast domain—much of south Burgundy—was administered from this tiny fortified town.

Within the town's walls, the feudal lord had a castle, a church, and all the necessary administrative buildings to deliver justice, collect taxes, and so on. Strategically perched on a hill between two river valleys, he enjoyed a complete view of his domain. Brancion's population peaked centuries ago at 60. Today, it's home to only four full-time residents.

Sights in Brancion: The **castle,** part of a network of 17 castles in the region, was destroyed in 1576 by Protestant Huguenots. After the French Revolution, it was sold to be used as a quarry and spent most of the 19th century being picked apart. Though the flier gives a brief tour and the audioguide a longer one, the small castle is most enjoyable for its evocative angles and the lush views from the top of its keep (€5, audioguide-€2, daily 10:00-18:30).

Wandering from the castle to the church, you'll pass the town's lone business (l'Auberge du Vieux Brancion), a 15th-century market hall that was used by farmers from the surrounding countryside until 1900, plus a handful of other buildings from that period.

The 12th-century warm-stone **church** (with faint paintings surviving from 1330) is the town's highlight. Circumnavigate the small building—this is Romanesque at its pure, unadulterated, fortress-of-God best (thick walls, small windows, once colorfully painted interior, no-frills exterior). Notice the stone roof; inside, find the English explanations of the paintings. From its front door, enjoy a lord's view over one glorious Burgundian estate.

Sleeping and Eating in or near Brancion: You have two good choices. In the center of the village, **$ L'Auberge du Vieux Brancion** serves traditional Burgundian fare (€16 lunch *menu*, €23 dinner *menu*) and also offers a perfectly tranquil place to spend the night. Say *bonjour* to François (very simple and frumpy rooms, Ds-€38, Db-€50-58 family rooms-€55-75, tel. 03 85 51 03 83, fax 03 85 32 17 67, www.brancion.fr, no email—must call or fax to book rooms).

For a much more upscale experience, including the best Burgundian view rooms I've found, drive a mile south of the village, following the sign to **$$$ Hôtel la Montagne de Brancion*****. A vine-covered paradise awaits...for a price. Every one of the 19 sharp, deck-equipped rooms faces a territorial view over vineyards, hills, and pastures. The garden comes with swayback view chairs, and a pool lies below. The owners pride themselves on their "gourmet restaurant" and expect you to dine there (Db-€120-180, Db suite-€200-290, extra bed-€18, pricey breakfast-€18, *menus* from €48 or à la carte, tel. 03 85 51 12 40, fax 03 85 51 18 64, www.brancion.com, reservation@brancion.com).

Chapaize

This hamlet, a few miles closer to Beaune, grew up around its Benedictine monastery—only its 11th-century church survives. It's a pristine place (cars park at the edge of town), peppered with flowers and rustic decay. A ghost-town café (Le St. Martin) faces the village's classic Romanesque church—study the fine stonework by Lombard masons. (Its lean seems designed to challenge the faith of parishioners.) The WWI monument near the entry—with so many names from such a tiny hamlet—is a reminder of the 4.2 million young French men who were wounded or died in the war that *didn't* end all wars. Wander around the back for a view of the belfry, and then ponder Chapaize across the street while sipping a café au lait.

Cluny

People come from great distances to admire Cluny's great abbey that is no more. This mother of all abbeys once vied with the Vatican as the most important power center in Christendom (Cluny's abbot often served as mediator between Europe's kings and the pope). The building was destroyed during the French Revolution, and, frankly, there's not a lot to see today. Still, the abbey

History of Cluny and Its (Scant) Abbey

In 1964, St. Benedict (480-547), founder of the first monastery (in Montecassino, south of Rome) from which a great monastic movement sprang, was named the patron saint of Europe. Christians and non-Christians alike recognize the impact that monasteries had in establishing a European civilization out of the dark chaos that followed the fall of Rome.

The Abbey of Cluny was the ruling center of the first great international franchise, or chain, of monasteries in Europe. It was the heart of an upsurge in monasticism, of church reform, and an evangelical revival that spread throughout Europe—a phenomenon that historians call the Age of Faith (11th and 12th centuries). From this springboard came a vast network of abbeys, priories, and other monastic orders that kindled the establishment of modern Europe.

In 910, 12 monks founded a house of prayer at Cluny, vowing to follow the rules of St. Benedict. The cult of saints and relics was enthusiastically promoted, and the order was independent and powerful. From the start, the Abbot of Cluny answered only to the pope (not to the local bishop or secular leader). The abbots of the other Cluniac monasteries were answerable only to the Abbot of Cluny (not to their local bishop or prince). This made the Abbot of Cluny arguably the most powerful person in Europe.

The abbey's success has been attributed to a series of wise leaders, or abbots. In fact, four of the first six abbots actually became saints. They preached the principles of piety and practiced the art of shrewd fundraising. Concerning piety, the abbots got people to stop looting the monasteries. Regarding shrewd fundraising, they convinced Europe's wealthy landowners to will their estates to the monasteries in return for perpetual prayers for the benefit of their needy and frightened souls.

From all this grew the greatest monastic movement of the High Middle Ages. A huge church was built at Cluny, and by 1100 it was the headquarters of 10,000 monks who ran nearly a thousand monasteries and priories across Europe. Cluny peaked in the 12th century, then faded in influence (though monasteries continued to increase in numbers and remain a force until 1789).

makes a worthwhile visit for history buffs looking to get some idea of the scale of this vast complex. Big plans are afoot to improve the sight, making it easier for tourists to reconstruct its glory days.

The pleasant little town that grew up around the abbey maintains its street plan, with plenty of original buildings and even the same population it had in its 12th-century heyday (4,500). As you wander the town, which claims to be the finest surviving

Romanesque town in France, enjoy the architectural details on everyday buildings. Many of the town's fortified walls, gates, and towers survive.

Getting There: Drivers park at designated lots and follow *Centre-Ville* signs on foot. Bus Céphale provides a few trips to Cluny (4/day from Chalon-sur-Saône, 1.25 hours; 6/day from Mâcon, 50 minutes; toll-free tel. 08 00 07 17 10). There is no train station in Cluny.

Orientation to Cluny

Everything of interest is within a few minutes' walk of the **TI** (daily June-Sept 9:30-12:30 & 14:30-19:00, no midday closure July-Aug, until 18:00 May and Oct, until 17:00 Nov-April, 6 Rue Mercière, tel. 03 85 59 05 34).

The TI is at the base of the **"Cheese Tower,"** so named because it was used to age cheese (or perhaps for the way tourists smell after climbing to the top). The tower offers a sweeping city view (€2, same hours as TI). Facing the abbey's entrance, the TI is 100 yards to the right.

A **farmers' market** animates the old town each Saturday.

Sights in Cluny

The first two sights—the museum and the abbey—share the same ticket and schedule (€8.50, ticket covers museum and abbey entrance, both open daily May-Aug 9:30-18:00, Sept-April 9:30-12:00 & 13:30-17:00, tel. 03 85 59 15 93). Historians should invest in *The Abbey of Cluny* guidebook (€7), sold in the museum. English tours should be available on certain days July-Aug; call ahead for times.

Museum of Art and Archaeology (Musée Ochier)—The small abbey museum fills the Palace of the Abbot with bits from medieval Cluny and a terrific model of the abbey complex (visit this before you explore the ruins). I like seeing the stone carvings eye-to-eye, though the museum holds little else of interest.

Site of Cluny Abbey—Much of today's old town stands on the site of what was the largest church in Christendom. It was almost two football fields long (555 feet) and crowned with five soaring naves. The whole complex (church plus monastery) covered 25 acres. Revolutionaries destroyed it in 1790, and today the National Stud Farm and a big school obliterate much of the floor plan of the abbey. Only one tower and part of the transept still stand. The visitor's challenge: Visualize it. Get a sense of its grandeur.

The best point from which to appreciate the abbey's awesome dimensions is atop the steps across from the museum. Look out to the remaining tower (there used to be three). You're standing above the end of the nave that stretched all the way to those towers. Down the steps, a marble table shows the original floor plan (*vous êtes ici* means "you are here"). Walk past the nubs that remain of the once-massive columns.

The abbey entrance lies between the Hôtel de Bourgogne and the Brasserie du Nord. Elaborate information displays designed to introduce the abbey and put it in its historical context should be in place by your visit. You'll also see a 12-minute 3-D film, giving a virtual tour of the 1,100-year-old church that helps you grasp the tragedy of its destruction (worth the price of entry alone, English headphones). Use the English flier to tour what little of the abbey still stands. Along the way, you'll find helpful English information posted, and several backlit panels that swivel, allowing visitors to see that section of the abbey at its zenith, in three dimensions. Very cool. You'll eventually exit at the flour mill (Tour de Farine), where you can loop back along the town's pleasing main drag, Rue Mercière (cafés, shops, and the TI line this pedestrian-friendly street).

National Stud Farm (Les Haras Nationaux)—Napoleon (who needed *beaucoup de* horses for his army of 600,000) established this farm in 1806. Today, 50 thoroughbred stallions kill time in their stables. If the stalls are empty, they're out doing their current studly duty...creating strapping racehorses. The gate is next to Hôtel de Bourgogne.

Cost and Hours: €7, visits only by guided tour (some English); May-Sept daily, usually at 14:00, 15:30, and 17:00; Oct-April Wed and Sun only; call ahead for times, tel. 08 11 90 21 31, www.haras -nationaux.fr.

Sleeping in Cluny

(€1 = about $1.30, country code: 33)
If you're spending the night, bed down at the cushy, traditional **$$ Hôtel de Bourgogne***, which is built into the wall of the abbey's right transept and is as central as can be for enjoying the town (standard Db-€93-104, bigger Db-€134, parking garage-€10, Place de l'Abbaye, tel. 03 85 59 00 58, fax 03 85 59 03 73, www.hotel -cluny.com, contact@hotel-cluny.com). It also has a fine restaurant (*menus* from €26).

Taizé

To experience the latest in European monasticism, drop by the booming Christian community of Taizé (teh-zay), a few miles north of Cluny on the road to Brancion. The normal, un-cultlike ambience of this place—with thousands of mostly young, European pilgrims asking each other, "How's your soul today?"—is remarkable. Even if this sounds a little airy, you might find the 30 minutes it takes to stroll from one end of the compound to the other a worthwhile

detour. A visit to Taizé can be a thought-provoking experience, particularly after a visit to Cluny. A thousand years ago, Cluny had a similar power to draw the faithful in search of direction and meaning in life.

Getting There: Drivers follow *La Communauté* signs and park in a dirt lot. SNCF buses (free with railpass) serve Taizé from Chalon-sur-Saône to the north (4/day, 1 hour) and from Mâcon to the south (6/day, 1 hour).

Tourist Information: At the southern (Cluny) end, the Welcome Office provides an orientation and daily schedule, and makes a good first stop (pick up a copy of the bimonthly *Letter from Taizé* and the single-page information leaflet, *The Taizé Community*).

Visiting Taizé: Taizé is an ecumenical movement—prayer, silence, simplicity—welcoming Protestant as well as Catholic Christians. Though it feels Catholic, it isn't. (But, as some of the brothers are actually Catholic priests, Catholics may take the Eucharist here.) The Taizé style of worship is well-known among American Christians for its hauntingly beautiful chants—songbooks and CDs are the most popular souvenirs from here. The Exposition (next to the church) is the thriving community shop, with books, CDs, sheet music, handicrafts, and other souvenirs.

The community welcomes visitors who'd like to spend a few days getting close to God through meditation, singing, and simple living. Although designed primarily for youthful pilgrims in meditative retreat (there are about 5,000 here in a typical week), people of any age are welcome to pop in for a meal or church service. Time your visit for one of the services (Mon-Sat at 8:15, 12:20, and 20:30; Sun at 10:00 and 20:30; Catholic and Protestant communion available daily).

During services, the bells ring and worshippers file into the long, low, simple, and modern Church of Reconciliation. It's dim—

candlelit with glowing icons—as the white-robed brothers enter. The service features responsive singing of chants (from well-worn songbooks that list lyrics in 19 languages), reading of biblical passages, and silence, as worshippers on crude kneelers stare into icons. The aim: "Entering together into the mystery of God's presence." (Secondary aim: Helping Lutherans get over their fear of icons.)

Sleeping and Eating in Taizé: Those on retreat fill their days with worship services; workshops; simple, relaxed meals; and hanging out in an international festival of people searching for meaning in their lives. Visitors are welcome for free. The cost for a real stay is about €10-30 per day (based on a sliding scale; those under 18 stay for less) for monastic-style room and board. Adults (over age 30) are accommodated in a more comfortable zone, but count on simple dorms. Call or email first if you plan to stay overnight (reception open Mon-Fri 10:00-12:00 & 18:00-19:00, tel. 03 85 50 30 02). The Taizé community website explains everything—in 29 languages (www.taize.fr).

The **Oyak** (near the parking lot) is where those in a less monastic mood can get a beer or burger.

BURGUNDY

LYON

Straddling the Rhône and Saône rivers between Burgundy and Provence, Lyon has been among France's leading cities since Roman times. In spite of its workaday, business-first facade, Lyon is France's most historic and culturally important city after Paris. You'll experience two different-as-night-and-day cities: the Old World cobbled alleys, pastel Renaissance mansions, and colorful shops of Vieux Lyon; and the more staid but classy, Parisian-feeling shopping streets of the Presqu'île. Once you're settled, this big city feels small, welcoming, and surprisingly untouristy. It seems everyone's enjoying the place—and they're all French.

Planning Your Time

Just 70 minutes south of Beaune, two hours north of Avignon, and 90 minutes west of Annecy, Lyon is France's best-kept urban secret. Lyon deserves at least one night and a full day. The city makes a handy day visit for train travelers, as many trains pass through here, and both stations have baggage storage and easy connections to the city center. But those who spend the night can experience the most renowned cuisine in France at appetizing prices and enjoy one of Europe's most beautifully floodlit cities.

For a full day of sightseeing, take the funicular up to Fourvière Hill, visit the Notre-Dame Basilica, and tour the Roman Theaters and Gallo-Roman Museum. Ride the funicular back down to Vieux Lyon and have lunch, then explore the old town and its hidden passageways. Finish your day touring the Museum of Fine Arts, Resistance Center, or Lumière Museum (covering the history of early filmmaking). Most of Lyon's important sights are closed on Mondays or Tuesdays, or both. Dine well in the evening (book ahead if possible) and cap your day enjoying a stroll through the best-lit city in France.

Drivers connecting Lyon with southern destinations should consider the scenic detour via the Ardèche Gorges (described on page 746), and those connecting to Burgundy should consider taking the Beaujolais Wine Route (page 1009), then visiting Brancion and Cluny (described in the Burgundy chapter).

Lyon's Cuisine Scene

In Lyon, how well you eat determines how well you live. The best restaurants are all the buzz—a favorite conversation topic likely  to generate heated debate. Here, great chefs are more famous than professional soccer players. (Paul Bocuse is the most famous chef.) Restaurants seem to outnumber cars, and all seem busy. With an abundance of cozy, excellent restaurants in every price range, it's hard to go wrong—unless you order tripes (cow intestines, also known as *tablier de sapeur*), *foie de veau* (calf's liver), or *tête de veau* (calf's head). Beware: These questionable dishes are very common in small bistros *(bouchons)* and can be the only choices on cheaper *menus*. Look instead for these classics: St. Marcellin cheese, *salade lyonnaise* (croutons, fried bits of ham, and a poached egg on a bed of lettuce), green lentils *(lentilles)* served on a salad or with sausages, *quenelles de brochet* (fish dumplings in a creamy sauce), and *filet de sandre* (local whitefish).

Lyon Area Wines

Fruity and fresh Gamay Beaujolais grapes, which grow in vineyards just north of Lyon, produce a light, easy-to-drink red wine. Big reds made from (mostly) Syrah grapes grow to the city's south. Look for Saint-Joseph and Crozes-Hermitage wines. In the village of Condrieu, only Viognier grapes are allowed to grow; they produce a rich and perfumy white wine.

Orientation to Lyon

Despite being France's third-largest city (after Paris and Marseille), with about 1.4 million inhabitants in its metropolitan area, the traveler's Lyon (home to 485,000 people) is peaceful and manageable. Traffic noise is replaced by pedestrian friendliness in the old center—listen to how quiet this big city is. Notice the emphasis on environmentally friendly transport: Electric buses have replaced diesel buses in the historic core, and pedal taxis (called *"cyclo-politains,"* seek-loh-poh-lee-tan) are used instead of traditional taxis for short trips (about €1/ kilometer); short pedal-taxi tours are available, too. Lyon's network of more than 4,000 city-owned rental bikes was in place years

before Paris' (note that these work only with American Express or chip-and-PIN credit cards).

Lyon provides the organized traveler with a full day of activities. Sightseeing can be enjoyed on foot from any of my recom-

mended hotels, though it's smart to make use of the funiculars, trams, and Métro. Most of the town's attractions can be linked in a manageable walking-tour route. Lyon's sights are concentrated in three areas: **Fourvière Hill,** with its white Notre-Dame Basilica glimmering over the city; historic **Vieux Lyon,** which hunkers below on the bank of the Saône River; and the **Presqu'île** (home to my recommended hotels), lassoed by the Saône and Rhone rivers. Huge and curiously empty Place Bellecour, which lies in the middle of the Presqu'île, always seems to be hosting an event.

Tourist Information

The well-equipped TI is generous with helpful, free information, and can reserve a hotel for you at no charge (daily 9:00-18:00, tel. 04 72 77 69 69, www.lyon-france.com, corner of Place Bellecour, free public WCs behind the TI building). Pick up the city map (with good enlargements of central Lyon and Vieux Lyon, a handy Métro and tramway map insert, and all public parking lots; hotels have similar maps), an event schedule (ask about concerts in the Roman Theaters during Les Nuits de Fourvière—early June to early Aug—and events at the Opera House), and the *Only Lyon* booklet (with a directory of shopping and eateries, as well as articles on special aspects of the city).

Walking Tours: The TI's **audioguide** (€10/half-day) offers good, self-guided walking tours of Vieux Lyon. Live **guided walks** of Vieux Lyon are offered at 14:30 on weekends and on most days July through early September (€10, 2 hours, usually in French but in English if enough demand, depart from the TI, verify days and times with TI). Other, less-frequent English-language walks include tours of the Opera House, the La Croix-Rousse district, and the silk workshops.

Sightseeing Pass: The TI sells a good-value **Lyon City Card** for serious sightseers (€21/1 day, €31/2 consecutive days, €41/3 consecutive days, under 18 half-price). This pass includes all Lyon museums, free use of the Métro/bus system, a river cruise (April-Oct), a walking tour of Lyon with a live guide, and a 50 percent discount off the TI's audioguide. The one-day pass pays for itself if you visit the Gallo-Roman Museum and the Resistance and Deportation History Center, plus take a guided walking tour and use public transit.

Helpful Website: For useful information in English about visiting Lyon, check out http://lyon.angloinfo.com.

Arrival in Lyon

By Train: Lyon has two train stations—Part-Dieu and Lyon-Perrache. Many trains stop at both, and through-trains connect the two stations every 10 minutes. Both stations have baggage storage (daily 6:15-23:00) and are well-served by Métro, bus, airport shuttle, and taxi (figure €14 for a taxi from either station to my recommended hotels near Place Bellecour). The all-day transit ticket is a great value—buy it upon arrival at the station (described later, coin machines only), or wait to pick up a Lyon City Card—which covers transit—at the TI (for more Métro tips, see "Getting Around Lyon," later).

Arriving at Part-Dieu Station: This is where most visitors arrive. To reach the **city center,** follow *sortie Porte Rhône* signs outside the station to the Métro and a taxi stand. Buy your ticket from the machine, and take the blue Métro line B toward Stade de Gerland, transfer at Saxe-Gambetta to the Gare de Vaise route, and get off at Bellecour. At Bellecour, follow *Sortie Rue République* signs.

To get to the **airport** from Part-Dieu Station, ride the Rhône Express airport tram (described later, under "By Plane"). Exiting out the opposite (east) end of the station, follow airplane icons and *gare routière* signs to find the red tram (tickets available from machines only, bills and coins accepted, conductors can help). Also out this exit are SNCF buses to Annecy and Grenoble (but train connections are more frequent).

Arriving at Perrache Station: This station is within a 20-minute walk of Place Bellecour (follow *Place Carnot* signs out of the station, then cross Place Carnot and walk up pedestrian Rue Victor Hugo). Or take the Métro (direction: Laurent Bonnevay) two stops to Bellecour and follow *Sortie Rue République* signs.

By Car: The city center has good signage and is manageable to

---

Illuminated Lyon

The golden statue of Mary above Notre-Dame Basilica was placed atop a 16th-century chapel on December 8, 1852. Spontaneously, the entire city welcomed her with candles in their windows. Each December 8 ever since, the city glows softly with countless candles.

This tradition has spawned an actual industry. Lyon is famous as a model of state-of-the-art floodlighting, and the city hosts conventions on the topic. Each night more than 200 buildings, sites, and public spaces are gloriously flood-lit. Go for an after-dinner stroll and enjoy the view from the Bonaparte Bridge after dark. Paris calls itself the City of Light—but actually Lyon is.

---

navigate, though you'll encounter traffic on the surrounding free-ways. If autoroute A-6 is jammed (not unusual), you'll be directed to bypass freeways (such as A-46). Either way, follow *Centre-Ville* and *Presqu'île* signs, and then follow *Office de Tourisme* and *Place Bellecour* signs. Park in the lots under Place Bellecour or Place des Célestins (yellow *P* means "parking lot") or get advice from your hotel. The TI's map identifies all public parking lots. Overnight parking (generally 19:00-8:00) is only €4.50, but day rates are €2 per hour.

By Plane: Lyon's sleek little airport, Saint-Exupéry, is 15 miles from the city center, has few crowds, and is a breeze to navigate (ATMs, English information booths, tel. 08 26 80 08 26, www.lyonaeroports.com). It has connections to most major European cities, including two flights per hour to Paris' Charles de Gaulle Airport (with a TGV station). Car rental is a snap. Four **Rhône Express** trams per hour make the 30-minute trip from the airport (follow red tram car icons) to Part-Dieu Station, described earlier (€14 one-way, €24 round-trip, buy ticket from machine, bills and coins accepted). Allow €60 for a taxi if you have baggage.

Helpful Hints

Market Days: A small market stretches along the Saône River between Pont Bonaparte and Passerelle du Palais de Justice (daily until 12:30). Tuesday through Saturday, it's produce; Sunday morning, it's crafts and contemporary art on the other side of the bridge near the Court of Justice; and Monday, it's textiles. Another bustling morning produce market takes place on Boulevard de la Croix-Rousse every day except Monday until 12:30 (see page 998).

Festivals: Lyon celebrates the Virgin Mary with candlelit windows during the Festival of Lights each year on December

8-11 (www.lumieres.lyon.fr). Les Nuits de Fourvière (dance, music, and theater) takes place from early June to early August in the Roman Theaters (www.nuitsdefourviere.com).

Internet Access: Raconte Moi La Terre is a cool place to check your email (Mon-Sat 10:00-19:30, closed Sun, free Wi-Fi, air-con, drinks and snacks, 14 Rue du Plat—see map on page 1002, Métro: Bellecour, tel. 04 78 92 60 22, www.raconte moilaterre.com).

Laundry: A launderette is at 7 Rue Mercière on the Presqu'île, near the Alphonse Juin bridge (daily 6:00-21:00); another is between Place Bellecour and Perrache Station, a few steps off Rue Victor Hugo (daily 7:30-20:30, 19 Rue Sainte-Hélène). See map on page 1002 for both locations.

SNCF Train Office: The SNCF Boutique at 2 Place Bellecour is handy for train info, reservations, and tickets (Mon-Fri 9:00-18:45, Sat 10:00-18:30, closed Sun).

Chauffeur Hire: Design your own half-day or full-day tour with a car and driver (mobile 06 65 38 75 08, www.lugdunum-ips .com, contact@lugdunum-ips.com).

Riverside Bike Path: A new bike path along the mighty Rhône River is ideal for adults and children (see map on page 1002). For more information on the path and bike rentals, ask at the TI or check http://lyon.angloinfo.com.

Children's Activities: The Parc de la Tête d'Or is vast, with rental rowboats, a miniature golf course, and ponies to ride (across Rhône River from La Croix-Rousse neighborhood, Métro: Masséna, tel. 04 72 69 47 60). The riverside bike path described above makes for a good family outing.

Getting Around Lyon

Lyon has a user-friendly public transit system, with five sleek streetcar lines (tramways T1-T4 and the Rhône Express line to the airport), four underground Métro lines (A-D), an extensive bus system, and two funiculars (there are two directions heading uphill: *Fourvière* for the basilica and *Saint-Just* for the Roman Theaters). The subway is similar to Paris' Métro in many ways (e.g., routes are signed by *direction* for the last stop on the line) but is more automated (buy tickets at coin-op machines), cleaner, less crowded, and less rushed (drivers linger longer at stops). You can transfer between Métro and tramway lines with the same ticket (valid one hour), but you can't do round-trips and must revalidate your ticket whenever boarding a tram (€1.60/1 hour, €2.60/2 hours, €4.90/1 day, €14.30/10 rides, all tickets cover funicular). The one-day ticket is a great deal (even if you only use the funicular and visit one of the outlying museums—Resistance Center or Lumière Museum) and a great time-saver, as you only have to buy a ticket

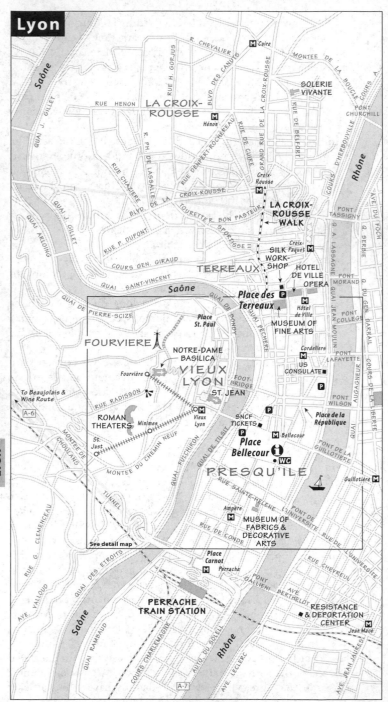

Lyon

LA CROIX-ROUSSE

R. CHEVALIER

Cuire

MONTEE DE LA BOUCLE

COURS A.

RUE H. GORJUS

BLVD DES CANUTS

SOLERIE VIVANTE

PONT CHURCHILL

Saône

QUAI J. GILLET

RUE HENON

Hénon

R. PH. DE LASSALLE

RUE CHAZIERE

RUE DEMPERT-ROCHEREAU

RUE DE CUIRE

GRAND RUE DE LA CROIX-ROUSSE

RUE DE BELFORT

Rhône

QUAI D'HERBOUVILLE

AVE. DU FOCH

QUAI J. GILLET

QUAI ARLONG

BLVD. DE LA

TOURETTE R. BON PASTEUR

Croix-Rousse

LA CROIX-ROUSSE WALK

PONT TASSIGNY

Q. A LASSAGNE

Q. SERBIE

RUE P. DUPONT

COURS GEN. GIRAUD

R. SPORSISSE

Croix-Paquet

SILK WORK-SHOP

TERREAUX

HOTEL DE VILLE OPERA

PONT MORAND

Q. DU GEN. SARRAIL

QUAI SAINT-VINCENT

Saône

QUAI DE BONDY

QUAI PECHERE

Place des Terreaux

Hôtel de Ville

QUAI JEAN MOULIN

PONT COLLEGE

QUAI DE PIERRE-SCIZE

Place St. Paul

MUSEUM OF FINE ARTS

FOURVIERE

NOTRE-DAME BASILICA

Fourvière

VIEUX LYON

FOOT-BRIDGE

St. JEAN

Cordeliers

US CONSULATE

PONT LAFAYETTE

COURS DE LA LIBERTE

To Beaujolais & Wine Route

A-6

RUE RADISSON

ROMAN THEATERS

Minimes

Vieux Lyon

QUAI FULCHIRON

QUAI DE TILSIT

SNCF TICKETS

Place Bellecour

Bellecour

Place de la République

PONT WILSON

PONT AUGAGNEUR

QUAI

St. Just

MONTEE DE CHOULANS

MONTEE DU CHEMIN NEUF

WC

PRESQU'ILE

PONT DE LA GUILLOTIERE

RUE SAINTE-HELENE

Guillotière

MONTEE DE CHOULANS

TUNNEL

Ampère

MUSEUM OF FABRICS & DECORATIVE ARTS

RUE DE L'UNIVERSITE

RUE DE L'UNIVERSITE

RUE G. CLEMENCEAU

RUE DE CONDE

See detail map

Place Carnot

Perrache

RUE CHEVREUL

AVE. VALLOUD

QUAI DES ETROITS

PERRACHE TRAIN STATION

PONT GALLIENI

AVE. BERTHELOT

RESISTANCE & DEPORTATION CENTER

Saône

QUAI RAMBAUD

COURS CHARLEMAGNE

AUTO. DU SOLEIL

Rhône

AVE. LECLERC

Jean Mace

A-7

AVE. JEAN JAURES

LYON

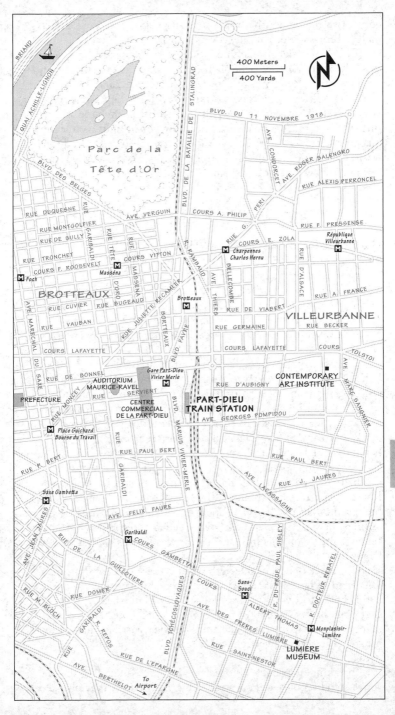

Parc de la Tête d'Or

BRIAND
QUAI ACHILLE-LIGNON
RHÔNE

BLVD. DU 11 NOVEMBRE 1918

400 Meters
400 Yards

N

BLVD DES BELGES

AVE. CONDORCET
AVE. ROGER SALENGRO
RUE ALEXIS PERRONCEL

RUE DUQUESNE
AVE. VERGUIN
COURS A. PHILIP
RUE G. PERI
RUE F. PRESSENSE

RUE MONTGOLFIER
RUE DE SULLY
RUE GARIBALDI
RUE TÊTE D'OR
RUE MASSÉNA
COURS VITTON
RUE RAMBAUD
RUE ZOLA
COURS E. ZOLA
République
Villeurbanne

RUE TRONCHET
COURS F. ROOSEVELT
Masséna
M
M Charpennes
Charles Hernu
DE BELLECOMBE

M Foch
BROTTEAUX
RUE CUVIER
RUE BUGEAUD
RUE D'OR
RUE MASSÉNA
AVE. THIERS
RUE DE VIABERT
RUE D'ALSACE
RUE A. FRANCE

Brotteaux
M

AVE. MARECHAL
RUE VAUBAN
RUE JULIETTE RECAMIER
BORTTEAUX
BLVD FAVRE
RUE GERMAINE
VILLEURBANNE
RUE BECKER

COURS LAFAYETTE
COURS LAFAYETTE
COURS
TOLSTOI

DU SAXE
RUE DE BONNEL
AUDITORIUM
MAURICE-RAVEL
Gare Part-Dieu
Vivier Merle
M
RUE D'AUBIGNY
CONTEMPORARY
ART INSTITUTE
AVE. MARC SANGNIER

PREFECTURE
RUE MONCEY
RUE SERVIENT
CENTRE
COMMERCIAL
DE LA PART-DIEU
PART-DIEU
TRAIN STATION
AVE. GEORGES POMPIDOU

M Place Guichard
Bourse du Travail
RUE GARIBALDI
RUE PAUL BERT
BLVD. MARIUS VIVIER-MERLE
RUE PAUL BERT

RUE P. BERT
RUE J. JAURES
AVE. LACASSAGNE

Saxe Gambetta
M
AVE. FELIX FAURE

AVE. JEAN JAURES
Garibaldi
M COURS GAMBETTA
R. DU PROF. PAUL SISLEY

RUE DE LA GUILLOTIERE
COURS
Sans-Souci
M
R. DOCTEUR REBATEL

RUE DOMER
AVE. DES FRERES LUMIERE
ALBERT THOMAS
M Monplaisir-
Lumière

RUE M. BLOCH
RUE GARIBALDI
R. REPOS
BLVD. TCHÉCOSLOVAQUES
RUE SAINT-NESTOR
LUMIERE
MUSEUM

AVE. BERTHELOT
RUE DE L'EPARGNE
To
Airport

LYON

once. Also remember that the Lyon City Card (described earlier, under "Tourist Information") covers transit.

To use the ticket machines, change the display language to English. Then use the black roller to *selectionner* your ticket, firmly push the top button twice to *confirmer* your request, and then insert coins (no bills, US credit cards won't work). In the Métro, insert your ticket in the turnstile, then reclaim it. If the stop has no turnstile, you must validate your ticket by punching it in a nearby machine (tramway users always validate on the trams). Study the wall maps to be sure of your direction; ask a local if you're not certain. Yellow signs lead to transfers, and green signs lead to exits *(Sortie)*.

Self-Guided Spin-Tour

Bonaparte Bridge (Pont Bonaparte)

This central bridge, just a block from Place Bellecour, is made to order for a day-or-night spin-tour.

• *Stand on the bridge and face the golden statue of the Virgin Mary marking the Notre-Dame Basilica on Fourvière Hill. (It's actually capping the smaller chapel, which predates the church by 500 years.) The basilica is named for the Roman Forum* (fourvière) *upon which it sits. Now begin to look clockwise.*

The Metallic Tower (called La Tour Métallique—not La Tour Eiffel), like the basilica, was finished just before World War I. It was originally an observation tower but today functions only as a TV tower. The husky, twin-towered church on the riverbank below (St. Jean Cathedral) marks the center of the old town. A block upstream, the Neoclassical columns are part of the Court of Justice (where Klaus Barbie, head of the local Gestapo—a.k.a. "the Butcher of Lyon"—was sentenced to life in prison). Way upstream, the hill covered with tall, pastel-colored houses is the Croix-Rousse district, former home of the city's huge silk industry. With the invention of the "Jacquard looms," which required 12-foot-tall ceilings, new factory buildings were needed and the new weaving center grew up on this hill. In 1850, it was thriving, with 30,000 looms.

The Place Bellecour side of the river is the district of Presqu'île. This strip of land is sandwiched by the Saône and Rhône rivers, and is home to Lyon's Opera House, City Hall, theater, top-end shopping, banks, and all of my recommended hotels. A morning market sets up daily under the trees (upriver, just beyond the red bridge). The simple riverfront cafés *(buvettes)* are ideal for a drink with a view (best at night).

Speaking of bridges, all of Lyon's bridges—including the one you're standing on—were destroyed by the Nazis as they checked

LYON

out in 1944. Looking downstream, you can see the stately mansions of Lyon's well-established families. Across the river, still downstream, the Neo-Gothic St. Georges Church marks the neighborhood of the first silk-weavers. The ridge behind St. Georges is dominated by a big building—once a seminary for priests, now a state high school—and leads us back to Mary.

• *Walk across the bridge and continue two blocks to find the funicular station (in the far-left corner), and ride up Fourvière Hill to the basilica (catch the train marked* Fourvière, *not* St. Just*). Sit up front and admire the funicular's funky old technology (€2.40 round-trip, Métro/tramway tickets valid). Or you can skip Fourvière Hill and go directly into the old town* **(Vieux Lyon)** *by turning right at* **St. Jean Cathedral.**

Sights in Lyon

Fourvière Hill

On Fourvière Hill, you can tour the basilica, enjoy the city view, and visit the Roman Theaters and Gallo-Roman Museum, then catch another funicular back down and explore the old town. I've listed key sights below according to this route.

▲Notre-Dame Basilica
(Basilique Notre-Dame de Fourvière)

Bam!—this ornate church fills your field of view as you exit the funicular. In about the year 1870, the bishop of Lyon vowed to

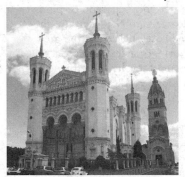

build a magnificent tribute to the Virgin Mary if the Prussians spared his city. (Similar deal-making led to the construction of the basilica of Sacré-Cœur in Paris.) Building began in 1872, and the church was ready for worship by World War I.

Cost and Hours: Free, daily 8:00-19:00; weekday Mass usually at either 7:15 or 9:30, then at 11:00 and 17:00; Sun Mass at 7:30, 9:30, 11:00, and 17:00.

Visiting the Basilica: Before entering, step back to view the fancy facade, the older chapel on the right (supporting the statue of Mary; open daily 7:00-19:00), and the top of the Eiffel-like TV tower on the left.

Climb the steps to enter. You won't find a more Mary-centered church. Everything—floor, walls, ceiling—is covered with elaborate **mosaics.** Scenes glittering on the walls tell stories of the Virgin (in Church history on the left, and in French history on the right). Amble down the center aisle at an escargot's pace and examine some of these scenes:

First scene on the left: In 431, the Council of Ephesus declared Mary to be the "Mother of God."

Across the nave, first on the right: The artist imagines Lugdunum (Lyon)—the biggest city in Roman Gaul, with 50,000 inhabitants—as the first Christian missionaries arrive. The first Christian martyrs in France (killed in A.D. 177) dance across heaven with palm branches.

Next left: In 1571, at the pivotal sea battle of Lepanto, Mary provides the necessary miracle as the outnumbered Christian forces beat the Ottomans.

Opposite (from right to left): Joan of Arc hears messages from Mary, rallies the French against the English at the Siege of Orléans in 1429 (find the Orléans coat of arms above), and is ultimately burned at the stake in Rouen at age 19 (1431).

Back across the nave on the left: In 1854, Pope Pius I proclaims the dogma of the Immaculate Conception in St. Peter's Square (establishing the belief among Catholics that Mary was born without the "Original Sin" of apple-eating Adam and Eve). To the left of the Pope, angels carry the tower of Fourvière Church; to the right is the image of the Virgin of Lourdes (who miraculously appeared in 1858).

Finally, on the right: Louis XIII offers the crown of France to the Virgin Mary. (The empty cradle hints that while he had her on the line, he asked, "Could I please have a son?" Louis XIV was born shortly thereafter.) Above marches a parade of pious French kings, from Clovis and Charlemagne to Napoleon (on the far right—with the white cross and red coat). Below are the great Marian churches of France (left to right)—Chartres, Paris' Sacré-Cœur and Notre-Dame, Reims (where most royalty was crowned), and this church. These six scenes in mosaic all lead to the altar where Mary reigns as Queen of Heaven.

Lower Church: Exit under Joan of Arc and descend to the lower church, dedicated to Mary's earthly husband, Joseph. Priorities here are painfully clear, as money ran out for Joseph's church. Today, it's used as a concert venue (notice the spongy-yellow acoustic material covering the vaulting). Return on the same stairs to the humble 16th-century chapel to the Virgin (push the door); outside, glance up to see the glorious statue of Mary that overlooks Lyon.

Nearby: Just around this chapel (past the church museum and the recommended Restaurant Panoramique) is a commanding **view** of Lyon. You can see parts of both rivers and north from the Croix-Rousse district south to the Bonaparte Bridge, with greater Lyon (pop. 1.3 million) spread out before you in the distance. The black barrel-vaulted structure to the left is the Opera House, and the rose-colored skyscraper in the distance is called, appropriately, "Le Crayon" (the pencil). On a clear afternoon you'll get a glimpse of Mont Blanc (the highest point in Europe, just left of the pencil-shaped skyscraper).

• *To get to the Roman Theaters and Gallo-Roman Museum, walk back toward the funicular station and turn left down Rue Roger Radisson. The museum hides in the concrete bunker down the steps, where Rue Roger Radisson meets Rue Cléberg. Before entering, get the best overview of the site by taking a few steps left down Rue Cléberg and finding the ramp that leads to the museum's rooftop (open the gate).*

▲▲Roman Theaters and Gallo-Roman Museum (Musée de la Civilisation Gallo-Romaine)

Founded as Lugdunum in A.D. 43, Lyon was a critical transportation hub for the administration of Roman Gaul (and much of modern-day France). The city became the central metropolis of the Three Gauls—the integrated Roman provinces of Aquitania (Aquitaine), Belgica (Belgium), and Lugdunensis (Lyon region)—and Emperors Claudius and Caracalla were both born here (for more on the Romans, see "How About Them Romans?" on page 666). This worthwhile museum—constructed in the hillside with views of the two Roman Theaters—makes clear Lyon's importance in Roman times.

Cost and Hours: Museum—€4, €6 if special exhibits, free on Thu, open Tue-Sun 10:00-18:00, closed Mon; theaters—free, daily until 19:00, 17 Rue Cléberg, tel. 04 72 38 49 30, www.musees-gallo-romains.com.

❍ Self-Guided Tour: Begin your visit in the **Gallo-Roman Museum.** The collection takes you on a chronological stroll down several floors through ancient Lyon. The displays are well organized and easy to follow, and the English explanations are excellent (signs posted in each room give a good overview of that room's exhibits).

After a brief glimpse at prehistoric objects, dive into the Gallo-Roman rooms. The artifacts you'll see were found locally. The unusual bronze chariot dates from the seventh century B.C. The model of Roman Lyon shows a city of 50,000 in its second-century A.D. glory days. (In the model, the forum stands where the basilica does today, hanging on the cliff edge.) Notice the white bits of aqueduct sections (with photos of the actual ruins nearby) and the network of gray roads leading to Lyon. The stone Roman pump behind the city model looks like an engine block (push the button on the display next to it to see how it worked).

Those curved stones you pass next were actual seats in an arena—inscribed with the names of big shots who sat there. Soon after, look for a big, black-bronze tablet placed up high. Carved

Lyon at a Glance

▲▲**Roman Theaters and Gallo-Roman Museum** Fine museum covering Roman Lyon. **Hours:** Museum—Tue-Sun 10:00-18:00, closed Mon; theaters—daily until 19:00. See page 991.

▲▲**Vieux Lyon** The city's fascinating, traffic-free historic core, with intriguing covered passageways. **Hours:** Passageways open daily 8:00-19:30. See page 994.

▲**Notre-Dame Basilica** Lyon's ornate version of Paris' Sacré-Cœur. **Hours:** Daily 8:00-19:00; weekday Mass usually at either 7:15 or 9:30, then at 11:00 and 17:00; Sun Mass at 7:30, 9:30, 11:00, and 17:00. See page 989.

▲**Museum of Fine Arts** France's second-most-important fine-arts museum (after the Louvre). **Hours:** Wed-Thu and Sat-Mon 10:00-18:00, Fri 10:30-18:00, closed Tue. See page 998.

▲**Resistance and Deportation History Center** Displays and videos telling the inspirational story of the French Resistance. **Hours:** Wed-Fri 9:00-17:30, Sat-Sun 9:30-18:00, closed Mon-Tue. See page 1000.

▲**Lumière Museum** Museum of film, dedicated to the Lumière brothers' pivotal contribution. **Hours:** Tue-Sun 10:00-18:30, closed Mon. See page 1000.

into it is the transcription of a speech given by Emperor Claudius in A.D. 48—his (longwinded) account of how he integrated the Gauls into the empire by declaring them eligible to sit in the Roman Senate (also recorded: the interjections of senators begging him to get to the point already—see the English translation on the wall).

The next section displays Roman coins, tools, and impressive models of key structures in Lyon, including the theaters you see out the window. (Find the exhibit demonstrating the mechanics of a Roman theater stage curtain, which was raised instead of lowered. Go ahead...push the button.) Lyon's wealthy merchants built large homes with interior courtyards often tiled with mosaics. One mosaic here shows a *Ben Hur*-type chariot race in a Roman circus. The museum ends with displays on Roman religious life and the onset of Christianity.

• *Exit the museum into the Roman Theaters.*

The closer **big theater** was built by Emperor Augustus and expanded by Hadrian—at its zenith, it held 10,000 spectators. Today it seats 3,000 for concerts. The **small theater,** an "odeon"

St. Jean Cathedral Gothic church with 700-year-old astronomical clock and lovely stained-glass windows. **Hours:** Mon-Fri 8:00-12:00 & 14:00-19:30, Sat-Sun 14:00-17:00. See page 994.

Gadagne Museums Two museums bringing to life Lyon's glory days and the tradition of Guignol puppets, housed in gorgeous Renaissance building. **Hours:** Wed-Sun 11:00-18:30, closed Mon-Tue. See page 996.

Atelier de la Soierie Workshop demonstrating handmade silk printing and screen painting. **Hours:** Mon-Fri 9:00-12:00 & 14:00-19:00, Sat 9:00-13:00 & 14:00-18:00, closed Sun. See page 997.

La Croix-Rousse Fun, avant-garde, historic neighborhood with great morning produce market and vertical pedestrian lanes. **Hours:** Market open Tue-Sun until 12:30; lanes always strollable. See page 998.

Museums of Fabrics and Decorative Arts Pair of museums, one tracing the development of textile weaving over 2,000 years, the other featuring 18th-century decor in a mansion. **Hours:** Tue-Sun 10:00-17:30, closed Mon, Museum of Decorative Arts closes 12:00-14:00. See page 999.

(from the Greek "ode" for song), was acoustically designed for speeches and songs. The grounds are peppered with gravestones and sarcophagi. Find a seat in the big theater and read up on Roman theaters (see page 679).

From early June through early August, the theaters host **Les Nuits de Fourvière,** an open-air festival of concerts, theater, dance, and film. Check programs at the TI and purchase tickets here at the theaters (box office at gate exit toward the Minimes funicular station, Mon-Sat 11:00-18:00, closed Sun), or online at www.nuitsdefourviere.com.

• *The ancient road between the Roman Theaters leads down and out, where you'll find the Minimes funicular station (to the right as you leave). Take the funicular to Vieux Lyon (not St. Just), where it deposits you only a few steps from St. Jean Cathedral. Take some time to explore Vieux Lyon. Or, from the Vieux Lyon funicular stop, you can take Métro*

LYON

line D directly to the Lumière Museum or (with an easy transfer) to the Resistance and Deportation History Center (both described later).

Vieux Lyon (Old Lyon)

St. Jean Cathedral—Stand back in the square for the best view of the cathedral (brilliant at night and worth returning for). This mostly Gothic cathedral took 200 years to build. It doesn't soar as high as its northern French counterparts; influenced by their Italian neighbors, churches in southern France are less vertical than those in the north. This cathedral, the seat of the "primate of the Gauls" (as Lyon's bishop is officially titled), serves what's  considered the oldest Christian city in France. Its interior sports some beautiful 13th- and 14th-century stained glass above the altar and adorning each transept (look for descriptions of the windows in English, near the altar). Under the north transept and worth a look is a medieval astronomical clock (1383); it has survived wars of all kinds, including the French Revolution. Amazingly, its 700-year-old mechanism can compute Catholic holidays (including those that change each year, such as Easter) until 2019. The 19 figures of the Annunciation do their thing four times a day (at 12:00, 14:00, 15:00, and 16:00). Find the minute hand on the right side and verify your watch.

Cost and Hours: Free, Mon-Fri 8:00-12:00 & 14:00-19:30, Sat-Sun 14:00-17:00.

Nearby: Outside (make two right turns as you leave) are the ruins of a mostly 11th-century church, destroyed during the French Revolution (the cathedral was turned into a "temple of reason"). What's left of a baptistery from an early Christian church (c. A.D. 400) is under glass.

▲▲**The Heart of Vieux Lyon**—Vieux ("Old") Lyon offers the best concentration of well-preserved Renaissance buildings in the country. The city grew rich from its trade fairs and banking, and was the capital of Europe's silk industry from the 16th to 19th centuries. The most prominent vestiges of Lyon's Golden Age are the elegant pastel buildings of the old center, which were inspired by Italy and financed by the silk industry. Rue St. Jean, leading north from the cathedral to Place du Change, is the main drag, flanked by parallel pedestrian streets and punctuated with picturesque squares (Rue de Bœuf is quieter and more appealing than busy Rue St. Jean).

• *From Rue St. Jean, take a short detour by making a left up Rue de la*

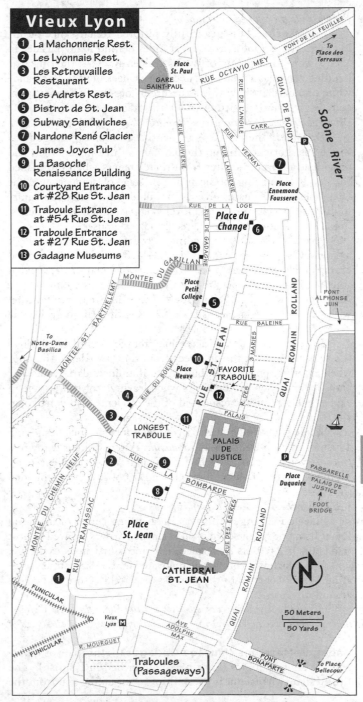

Vieux Lyon

1. La Machonnerie Rest.
2. Les Lyonnais Rest.
3. Les Retrouvailles Restaurant
4. Les Adrets Rest.
5. Bistrot de St. Jean
6. Subway Sandwiches
7. Nardone René Glacier
8. James Joyce Pub
9. La Basoche Renaissance Building
10. Courtyard Entrance at #28 Rue St. Jean
11. Traboule Entrance at #54 Rue St. Jean
12. Traboule Entrance at #27 Rue St. Jean
13. Gadagne Museums

Traboules (Passageways)

LYON

Bombarde to the colorful courtyard of...

La Basoche: This beautifully restored Renaissance building gives you a good idea of what hides behind many facades in Vieux Lyon—and a whiff of Lyon's Golden Age. (At the time, the building served as a kind of legal center.) Check out the black-and-white photos that show this structure before its 1968 renovation, and imagine most of Vieux Lyon in this state.

• *Back along Rue St. Jean, notice the heavy doors leading to Lyon's...*

Traboules: The old city's serpentine *traboules* (passageways) worked as shortcuts linking the old town's three main streets and provided important shelter from the elements when unfinished silk goods were being moved from one stage of production to the next. These hidden paths give visitors a hide-and-seek opportunity to discover pastel courtyards, lovely loggias, and delicate arches. Spiral staircases were often shared by several houses.

Several short *traboules* leading to courtyards are accessible (if a doorway is open, you can wander in—#28 Rue St. Jean is a good example). However, only a few of Vieux Lyon's many *traboules* that connect different streets are open to the public. The longest *traboule* links #54 Rue St. Jean with #27 Rue du Bœuf; my favorite, with gorgeous loggias, leads from #27 Rue St. Jean to #6 Rue de Trois Maries.

Traboules are generally accessible from 8:00 until 19:30. Press the top button next to the street-front door to release the door when entering, push the lit buttons to illuminate dark walkways, and slide the door-handle levers when leaving. You're welcome to explore—but please be respectful of the residents, and don't go up any stairs.

While you wander Vieux Lyon, look for door plaques giving a history of each building and *traboule*. After walking through a *traboule*, you'll understand why Lyon's old town was an ideal center for the Resistance fighters to slip in and out of as they confounded the Nazis.

• *At the north end of Rue St. Jean is...*

Place du Change: This was the banking center of medieval Lyon. Its money scene developed after the city was allowed to host trade fairs in 1420. Its centerpiece is France's first stock exchange, Le Loge, which was completely renovated in the 18th century (creating a stark contrast to the Renaissance architecture and colors around it).

• *With your back to the river, head to nearby Place du Petit Collège, where you can peek (for free) into the wonderfully restored courtyard of the...*

Gadagne Museums (Musées Gadagne)—This pair of museums covers two topics (both nicely described in English). The **Lyon History Museum** is overkill for most, taking you from the city's Roman period to the present day—and every era in between (the rooms devoted to its silk industry are interesting, showing looms and sample fabrics). The **Puppets of the World Museum** celebrates Guignol puppetry, the still-vibrant tradition first created in Lyon by an unemployed silk worker. Here you'll see examples of beautifully crafted Guignol puppets from around the world; the fun audioguide narrative may keep some kids engaged for a while. Don't leave the museum without enjoying *un pause* on the rooftop terrace café.

Cost and Hours: €6 for one museum, €8 for both, includes audioguide and English brochure, Wed-Sun 11:00-18:30, closed Mon-Tue, 1 Place du Petit Collège, tel. 04 78 42 03 61, www .gadagne.musees.lyon.fr.

• *From here it's a short walk across the river to Place des Terreaux and the Museum of Fine Arts (cross Pont de la Feuillée and continue straight four blocks). Ice-cream connoisseurs must stop at the recommended* **Nardone René Glacier** *before crossing the river (on river near Place du Change).*

Presqu'île

This bit of land (French for "peninsula," and liter- ally meaning "almost-an- island") between the two rivers is Lyon's shopping spine, with thriving pedes- trian streets. The neighbor- hood's northern focal point is the...

Place des Terreaux—This grand square hosts the City Hall (Hôtel de Ville), the Museum of Fine Arts, and an action-packed fountain by Frédéric-Auguste Bartholdi (the French sculptor who designed the Statue of Liberty). More importantly (for locals, at least), this square allows the last rays of sun to penetrate the café tables near City Hall. Become a member of the afternoon sun club.

The fountain features Marianne (the Lady of the Republic) riding a four-horse-powered chariot, symbolically leading Lyon's two great rivers to the sea. The square itself is usually wet, with 69 fountains spurting playfully in a vast grid (designed by Daniel Buren, who did the courtyard of the Palais Royal in Paris).

Atelier de la Soierie—This silk workshop, just off Place des Terreaux on Rue Romarin (behind Café le Moulin Joli, a Resistance hangout during World War II), welcomes the public to drop in to see silk printing and screen painting by hand. Keep in mind that this is a lost art that today has mostly been replaced by machines.

Within the shop you'll see stretched silk canvases, buckets of dye, and artists in action. Climb the staircase to visit a boutique selling handmade silk creations. Prices range from €25 to €250.

Cost and Hours: Free entry, Mon-Fri 9:00-12:00 & 14:00-19:00, Sat 9:00-13:00 & 14:00-18:00, closed Sun, tel. 04 72 07 97 83.

La Croix-Rousse—Hilly, untouristy, and SoHo-esque, this neighborhood hummed with some 30,000 silk looms in the 1800s. Today this part of town is popular with Lyon's tie-dye types, drawn here by abandoned, airy apartment spaces (built in the age of the Jacquard loom, which required exceptionally high ceilings).

The smartest way to visit is to take the Métro to the top, then follow a series of scenic slopes and stairs back down (see map on page 986). You'll pass bohemian cafés, art galleries, creative graffiti, and used-clothing shops on your way to the Presqu'île. (Or—to burn off last night's *Lyonnaise* feast—follow this suggested route in reverse.)

Begin by exiting Métro line C at the La Croix-Rousse stop. Every day except Monday, until about 12:30, a lively local produce market stretches across the square and down Boulevard de la Croix-Rousse. Start your downhill stroll from behind the Métro stop along Rue des Pierres Plantées. Pause to appreciate the views from the Jardin de la Grande Côte, and notice how the small concrete square is used as a soccer field, a tricycle track, an outdoor café, and any other purpose the neighbors can find for it. Continue down the stairs and follow the main drag, Montée de la Grande Côte. Detour a block to the right on Rue des Tables Claudiennes for a view over the Roman Amphitheater of the Three Gauls. In most other cities, a major Roman amphitheater would be big news, but in Lyon it's virtually ignored. Backpedal to the hill climb and continue your descent, working your way down to Place des Terreaux.

▲Museum of Fine Arts (Musée des Beaux-Arts)—Located in a former abbey, which was secularized by Napoleon in 1803 and made into a public museum, this fine-arts museum has an impressive collection, ranging from Egyptian antiquities to Impressionist paintings. The inner courtyard is a pleasant place to take a peaceful break from city streets.

The first floor up offers a stroll through a fine collection of ancient (especially Egyptian) art, medieval art, and Art Nouveau (furniture). The adjacent chapel is a dreamy Orsay-like display of 19th- and 20th-century statues (including work by Auguste Rodin and Bartholdi).

The second floor displays a pretty selection of paintings from the last six centuries (no famous works, but a good Impressionist collection). You'll see Renaissance and Baroque paintings by Veronese, Cranach, Rubens, and Rembrandt, and "modern" works by Monet, Matisse, and Picasso. The highlight is a series of Pre-Raphaelite-type works called *Le Poème de l'Âme* ("The Poem of the Soul"), by Louis Janmot. This cycle of 18 paintings and 16 charcoal drawings traces the story of the souls of a boy and a girl as they journey through childhood, adolescence, and into adulthood. They struggle with fears and secular temptations before gaining spiritual enlightenment on the way to heaven. The boy loses his faith and enjoys a short but delicious hedonistic fling that leads to misery in hell. But a mother's prayers intercede, and he reunites with the girl to enjoy heavenly redemption.

Cost and Hours: €7, Wed-Thu and Sat-Mon 10:00-18:00, Fri 10:30-18:00, closed Tue, pick up museum map on entering, picnic-perfect courtyard, 20 Place des Terreaux, Métro: Hôtel de Ville, tel. 04 72 10 17 40, www.mba-lyon.fr. A bar/café with calming terrace seating is on the first floor, next to the bookstore.

Museums of Fabrics and Decorative Arts (Musées des Tissus et des Arts Décoratifs)—These museums, south of Place Bellecour, fill two buildings (sharing a courtyard and connected with an interior hallway). Though packed with exquisite exhibits, the museums offer little information in English (some English information posted in the Museum of Fabrics, nothing in Museum of Decorative Arts). The Museum of Fabrics traces the development of textile weaving over the course of 2,000 years and shows off some breathtaking silk work. The Museum of Decorative Arts, billed as "an ambience museum," is a luxurious mansion decorated to the hilt with 18th-century furniture, textiles, and tapestries in a plush domestic setting.

Cost and Hours: €10, covers both museums, Tue-Sun 10:00-17:30, closed Mon, Museum of Decorative Arts closes 12:00-14:00, 34 Rue de la Charité, Métro: Bellecour, tel. 04 78 38 42 00, www.musee-des-tissus.com.

Shopping and Eating on the Presqu'île—There's more to this "almost-an-island" than the sights listed here. Join the river of shoppers on sprawling Rue de la République (north of Place Bellecour) and the teeming Rue Victor Hugo pedestrian mall (south of Place Bellecour). Peruse the *bouchons* (characteristic bistros—especially characteristic in the evening) of Rue Mercière.

Passage de l'Argue is a classy, covered shopping passage from the 1800s that predates shopping malls (78 Rue Président Edouard Herriot).

Grand Café des Négociants is ideal for an indoor break (skip the outside terrace). This *grand café*, which has been in business since 1864, feels like it hasn't changed since then, with its soft leather chairs, painted ceilings, and glass chandeliers (daily, 2 Place Francisque Régaud, near Cordeliers Métro stop, tel. 04 78 42 50 05).

Away from the Center

▲Resistance and Deportation History Center (Centre d'Histoire de la Résistance et de la Déportation)—Located near Vichy (capital of the French puppet state) and neutral Switzerland, Lyon was the center of the French Resistance from 1942 to 1945. These "underground" Resistance heroes fought the Nazis tooth and nail. Bakers hid radios inside loaves of bread to secretly contact London. Barmaids passed along tips from tipsy Nazis. Communists in black berets cut telephone lines. Farmers hid downed airmen in haystacks. Housewives spread news from the front with their gossip. Printers countered Nazi propaganda with anonymous pamphlets. Without their bravery the liberation of France would not have been possible.

This center served as a Nazi torture chamber and Gestapo headquarters under Klaus Barbie (who was finally tried and convicted in 1987 after extradition from Bolivia). More than 11,000 people were killed or deported to concentration camps during his reign.

The excellent museum, which was recently renovated, should be fully open by the time you visit (though some of the exhibits may no longer be as I describe). An audioguide, videos, reconstructed rooms, small theaters, and numerous photos with detailed English descriptions tell the inspirational story of the French Resistance. Look for portraits of witnesses who returned to the center to speak about their experiences.

Cost and Hours: €4, Wed-Fri 9:00-17:30, Sat-Sun 9:30-18:00, closed Mon-Tue, 14 Avenue Berthelot, tel. 04 78 72 23 11, www.chrd.lyon.fr.

Getting There: You have several good options: Ride the Métro line B to Jean Macé, exit toward the elevated train line, and transfer to the T2 tramway (going right) or turn right on Avenue Berthelot and walk five blocks; **walk** from Perrache Station across Pont Gallieni, then three blocks to 14 Avenue Berthelot (15 minutes); or take the T2 **tramway** from below Perrache Station to Centre Berthelot.

▲Lumière Museum (Musée Lumière)—Antoine Lumière and his two sons Louis and Auguste—the Eastman-Kodaks of France—ran a huge factory with 200 workers in the 1880s, producing four million glass photographic plates a day. Then, in 1895, they made the first *cinématographe*, or movie. In 1903 they pioneered the "autochrome" process of painting frames to make "color photos." This museum tells their story.

Cost and Hours: €6.50, essential audioguide-€3, Tue-Sun 10:00-18:30, closed Mon, tel. 04 78 78 18 95, www.institut-lumiere.org.

Getting There: Take Métro line D, enjoying your ride on

this futuristic (and driverless) train. Sit in the front and command your own underground starship. Ride the train to the Monplaisir-Lumière stop. The unsigned museum is at 25 Rue du Premier-Film, in the large mansion on the square, kitty-corner from the Métro stop.

Visiting the Museum: The museum fills Villa Lumière, the family's belle époque mansion, built in 1902. The museum does a great job of explaining the history of filmmaking, thanks to many interesting displays and the essential audioguide. After leaving this place, where the laborious yet fascinating process of creating moving images is driven home, you'll never again take the quality of today's movies for granted.

The museum's highlights are the many antique cameras and the screens playing the earliest "movies" (located on the ground floor). The first film reels held about 950 frames, which played at 19 per second, so these first movies were only 50 seconds long. About 1,500 Lumière films are catalogued between 1895 and 1907. (Notice that each movie is tagged with its "Catalog Lumière" number.) The very first movie ever made features workers piling out of the Lumière factory at the end of a work day. People attended movies at first not for the plot or the action, but rather to be mesmerized by the technology that allowed them to see moving images.

The museum's upstairs features exhibits on still photography and the Lumière living quarters (furnished c. 1900). Across the park from the mansion is a shrine of what's left of the warehouse where the first movie was actually shot. In a wonderful coincidence, *lumière* is the French word for "light."

Nightlife in Lyon

Lyon has France's second-largest cultural budget after Paris, so there are always plenty of theatrical productions and concerts to attend (in French, of course). The TI has the latest information and schedules. From mid-June through mid-September, the terrace-café at the Opera House hosts an outdoor jazz café with free concerts (usually Mon-Sat at 19:00, 20:00, and 22:00; no Sun concerts, www.opera-lyon.com).

After dinner, stroll through Lyon to savor the city's famous illuminations (see sidebar on page 984). Walk through the old town, then along the river (the view from the pedestrian bridge—*passerelle*—that leads to the Palais de la Justice is sensational), and along key streets past the main monuments of the Presqu'île.

For lively bar and people-watching scenes, prowl Rue de la Monnaie (angles off "restaurant row" Rue Mercière to the south) and the streets between Place des Terreaux and the Opera House. The **James Joyce** Irish pub, in the heart of Vieux Lyon, is

Vieux Lyon & Presqu'île

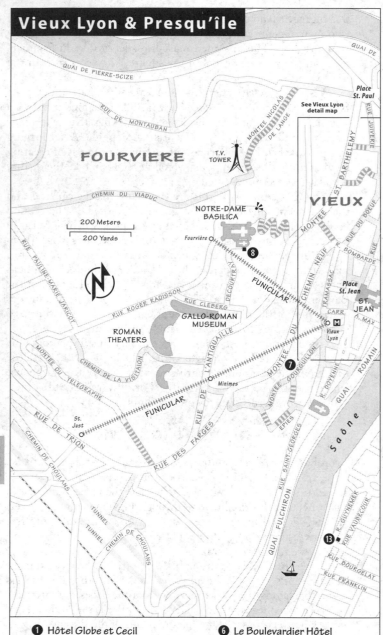

QUAI DE PIERRE-SCIZE

QUAI DE

RUE DE MONTAUBAN

Place St. Paul

See Vieux Lyon detail map

FOURVIERE

T.V. TOWER

MONTEE NICOLAS DE LANGE

ST. BARTHELEMY

RUE JUIVERIE

CHEMIN DU VIADUC

VIEUX

NOTRE-DAME BASILICA

Fourvière

FUNICULAR

MONTEE ST. BARTHELEMY

RUE DU BOEUF

R. BOMBARDE

RUE

200 Meters

200 Yards

CHEMIN NEUF

Place St. Jean

RUE PAULINE-MARIE JARICOT

RUE ROGER RADISSON

RUE CLEBERG

GALLO-ROMAN MUSEUM

MONTEE DE L'ANTIQUAILLE

ST. JEAN

TRAMASSAC

CARR.

A. MAX

RUE DOYENNE

QUAI ROMAIN

ROMAN THEATERS

CHEMIN DE LA VISITATION

M Vieux Lyon

MONTEE DU TELEGRAPHE

FUNICULAR

Minimes

RUE DE L'ANTIQUAILLE

MONTEE DU GOURGUILLON

St. Just

RUE DE TRION

RUE DES FARGES

EPIES

R. DOYENNE

Saône

CHEMIN DE CHOULANS

RUE SAINT-GEORGES

QUAI FULCHIRON

TUNNEL

TUNNEL CHEMIN DE CHOULANS

R. GUYNEMER

RUE VAUBECOUR

RUE BOURGELAT

RUE FRANKLIN

LYON

❶ Hôtel Globe et Cecil	❻ Le Boulevardier Hôtel
❷ Hôtel des Artistes	❼ Vieux Lyon Youth Hostel
❸ Hôtel des Célestins	❽ Rest. Panoramique de la Fourvière
❹ Hôtel du Théâtre	
❺ Hôtel la Residence	❾ Bistrot à Tartines

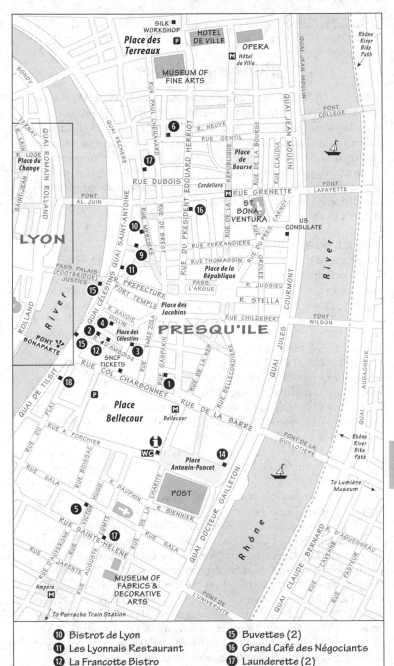

SILK WORKSHOP

Place des Terreaux

HÔTEL DE VILLE

OPERA

Hôtel de Ville

MUSEUM OF FINE ARTS

QUAI JEAN MOULIN

PONT COLLÈGE

Rhône River Bike Path

BONDY

QUAI ROMAIN ROLLAND

R. VERNAY

R. LAIN

R. LOGE

Place du Change

RUE PAUL CHENAVARD

QUAI PÊCHÈRE

R. NEUVE

RUE GENTIL

Place de Bourse

QUAI JEAN MOULIN

QUAI DE LA BOURSE

6

17

RUE DUBOIS

Cordeliers

RUE GRENETTE

ST. BONA-VENTURA

RUE DE LA CLAUDIA

RUE CLAUDIA

PONT LAFAYETTE

PONT AL. JUIN

RUE SAINT-ANTOINE

QUAI SAINT-ANTOINE

RUE DE BREST

RUE MERCIÈRE

16

RUE DE LA RÉPUBLIQUE

US CONSULATE

LYON

SAINT-JEAN

10

9

RUE FERRANDIERE

RUE DU PRÉSIDENT ÉDOUARD HERRIOT

RUE DU PRÉS CARNOT

RUE THOMASSIN

RUE GROLÉE

River

ROLLAND

River

PASS. PALAIS (FOOTBRIDGE) JUSTICE

11

R. PRÉFECTURE

PONT TEMPLE

Place de la République

PASS. L'ARGUE

R. JUSSIEU

R. STELLA

COURMONT

PONT BONAPARTE

15

R. SAVOIE

DULLIN

Place des Célestins

RUE EMILE ZOLA

RUE CHILDEBERT

PONT WILSON

QUAI CÉLESTINS

Place des Jacobins

PRESQU'ILE

2

4

R. D'AMBOISE

3

RUE DE LA REP

RUE JULES

QUAI JULES

QUAI

AUGAGNEUR

15

12

SNCF TICKETS

RUE COL. CHARBONNET

RUE GASPARIN

RUE BELLECORDIÈRE

1

18

QUAI DE TILSIT

RUE DU PLAT

P

Place Bellecour

Bellecour

RUE DE LA BARRE

PONT DE LA GUILLOTIÈRE

Rhône River Bike Path

RUE A. FORCHIER

i

WC

Place Antonin-Poncet

14

RUE BOISSAC

RUE SALA

RUE VICTOR HUGO

RUE SAINTE-HÉLÈNE

CHARITÉ

R. DAUPHIN

POST

R. BIENNIER

QUAI DOCTEUR GAILLETON

To Lumière Museum

5

17

RUE DE LA

RUE SALA

Rhône

QUAI CLAUDE BERNARD

R. D'AGUESSEAU

R. CAYENNE

R. PASTEUR

RUE D'AUVERGNE

RUE AUGUSTE COMTE

RUE D'JARENTE

MUSEUM OF FABRICS & DECORATIVE ARTS

PONT DE L'UNIVERSITÉ

Ampère

To Perrache Train Station

LYON

10 Bistrot de Lyon	**15** Buvettes (2)
11 Les Lyonnais Restaurant	**16** Grand Café des Négociants
12 La Francotte Bistro	**17** Launderette (2)
13 Chez Abel Restaurant	**18** Internet Café
14 Brasserie le Sud	

a cozy English-speaking place (daily, 68 Rue St. Jean, tel. 04 78 37 84 28).

Sleeping in Lyon

Hotels in Lyon are a steal compared with those in Paris. Weekends are generally discounted (sometimes substantially) in this city that lives off business travelers. Prices rise and rooms disappear when trade fairs are in town, so it's smart to reserve your room in advance. If you have trouble, the TI can help for free in person or by email (resa@lyon-france.com). Most of my listings are on the Presqu'île. Hotels have elevators unless otherwise noted, and air-conditioning is a godsend when it's hot (hottest June-mid-Sept). Expect to push buttons to gain access to many hotels.

On or near Place des Célestins

Book ahead to sleep in this classy yet unpretentious neighborhood (Métro: Bellecour). Just a block off the central Place Bellecour and a block to the Saône River, this area gives travelers easy access to Lyon's sights. Join shoppers perusing the upscale boutiques, or watch children playing in the small square fronting the Théâtre des Célestins. Warning: Weekend nights can be noisy if you score a room facing Place des Célestins.

$$$ Hôtel Globe et Cecil* is the most professional and elegant of my listings, with refined comfort on a refined street. Its rooms are tastefully decorated and mostly spacious (look for web deals, Sb-€148, Db-€185, includes breakfast, air-con, Wi-Fi, 21 Rue Gasparin, tel. 04 78 42 58 95, fax 04 72 41 99 06, www.globe etcecilhotel.com, accueil@globeetcecilhotel.com).

$$$ Hôtel des Artistes*, ideally located on Place des Célestins, is comfortable, professional, and a fair value (Sb-€95-135, standard Db-€128, larger Db-€155, extra bed-€10, standard rooms are comfortable but a bit tight, breakfast-€12, air-con, pay Wi-Fi, 8 Rue Gaspard-André, tel. 04 78 42 04 88, fax 04 78 42 93 76, www.artists-hotel.com, reservation@hotel-des-artistes.fr).

$$$ Hôtel des Célestins*, just off Place des Célestins, is warmly run by Cornell-grad Laurent. Its cheery rooms are filled with thoughtful touches. Streetside rooms have more light and are bigger (Sb-€70-94, Db-€94-124, bigger Db-€104-144, Tb-€120-180, beautiful suites ideal for families or those in need of room to roam-€188-228, €9 buffet breakfast served 7:00-12:00, completely non-smoking, air-con, Internet access, pay Wi-Fi, laundry service, 4 Rue des Archers, tel. 04 72 56 08 98, fax 04 72 56 08 65, www .hotelcelestins.com, info@hotelcelestins.com).

$$ Hôtel du Théâtre requires stamina to reach the lobby, which is up four flights of stairs. And it does not have air-

LYON

Sleep Code

(€1 = about $1.30, country code: 33)
S = Single, **D** = Double/Twin, **T** = Triple, **Q** = Quad, **b** = bathroom,
s = shower only, ***** = French hotel rating system (0-5 stars).
Unless otherwise noted, credit cards are accepted and English
is spoken.

To help you sort easily through these listings, I've divided
the accommodations into three categories based on the price
for a standard double room with bath:

$$$ Higher Priced—Most rooms €95 or more.
  $$ Moderately Priced—Most rooms between €65-95.
    $ Lower Priced—Most rooms €65 or less.

Prices can change without notice; verify the hotel's
current rates online or by email.

---

conditioning. But it's well-located on Place des Célestins and offers
the best deal at moderate prices that I've found. Owners Monsieur
and Madame Kuhn run a tight ship, most of the rooms and bathrooms are spacious, and the beds are firm (Db-€66-74, extra bed-
€15, Wi-Fi, enter from hotel's rear, tel. 04 78 42 33 32, fax 04 72 40
00 61, www.hotel-du-theatre.fr, contact@hotel-du-theatre.fr).

Other Places on the Presqu'île

$$ Hôtel la Residence***, south of Place Bellecour and my closest
listing to Perrache Station, feels big and institutional. The lobby is
spartan, but its 67 rooms are air-conditioned, well cared for, and a
solid value. Most are spacious and have high ceilings and bathtubs
(Sb/Db-€95, Tb-€110, Qb-€120, breakfast-€8, Internet access and
Wi-Fi, 18 Victor Hugo, tel. 04 78 42 63 28, fax 04 78 42 85 76,
www.hotel-la-residence.com, hotel-la-residence@wanadoo.fr).

$ Le Boulevardier** is a budget option located a few blocks
south of Place des Terreaux. It's particularly fun for jazz lovers, as
the 11 rooms sit above a jazz café. Don't let the dumpy facade fool
you; the well-priced rooms are surprisingly clean and sharp, and
all but two have queen-size beds (small Db-€50, bigger Db-€60
and worth the extra euros, 5 Rue de la Fromagerie, tel. 04 78 28 48
22, www.leboulevardier.fr, ccg.bernard@gmail.com).

Elsewhere in Lyon

Hostel: **$ Vieux Lyon Youth Hostel** is impressively situated a
10-minute walk above Vieux Lyon. Open 24 hours daily, it has a
lively common area with kitchen access and cheap meals (bed in
4- to 6-bed room-€23, includes sheets and breakfast, small safes

available, 45 Montée du Chemin, Métro: Hôtel de Ville, tel. 04 78 15 05 50, fax 04 78 15 05 51, www.hihostels.com, lyon@fuaj.org). Book only by email. Take the funicular to Minimes, exit the station and make a left U-turn, and follow the station wall downhill to Montée du Chemin.

Eating in Lyon

Dining is a ▲▲▲ attraction in Lyon, and it comes at a bearable price. Half the fun is joining the procession of window-shoppers mulling over where they'll *dîner ce soir*. In the evening, the city's population seems to double as locals emerge to stretch their stomachs. The tried-and-true *salade lyonnaise* (usually filling) followed by *quenelles* is one of my favorite one-two punches in France. You won't want dessert.

Lyon's characteristic *bouchons* are small bistros that evolved from the days when Mama would feed the silk workers after a long day. True *bouchons* are simple places with limited selection and seating (just like Mama's), serving only traditional fare and special 46-centiliter *pot* (pronounced "poh") wine pitchers. The lively pedestrian streets of Vieux Lyon and Rue Mercière on the Presqu'île are *bouchon* bazaars, worth strolling even if you dine elsewhere. Though food quality may be better away from these popular restaurant rows, you can't beat the atmosphere. Many of Lyon's restaurants close on Sunday and Monday and during August, except along Rue Mercière. If you plan to dine somewhere special, reserve ahead.

In or Near Vieux Lyon

Come to Vieux Lyon for an ideal blend of ambience and quality (if you choose carefully). For the epicenter of restaurant activity, go to Place Neuve St. Jean, and survey the scene and menus before sitting down. Unless otherwise noted, all of these places are located on the map on page 995.

La Machonnerie is worth booking ahead. Reputed chef Joseph Viola has created a buzz by providing wonderful cuisine at affordable prices in a classic *bouchon* setting. His are the best *quenelles* I have tasted and come with potatoes and a wonderful mac-and-cheese-like side dish that is so filling, you won't be able to eat another bite (*menus* from €27, €17 *quenelles*, indoor seating only, closed Sun-Mon, 36 Rue Tramassac, tel. 04 78 42 24 62).

Les Lyonnais is barely a block off the Rue du Bœuf action, making it a bit quieter. Its lighthearted interior has rich colors, wood tables, and a photo gallery of loyal customers. Sincere Stephane runs the place with grace (good €25 *menu* with *salade lyonnaise* and *quenelles,* fine and filling €15 salads, closed Sun, small terrace, 1 Rue Tramassac, tel. 04 78 37 64 82). A second location (described later, under "On or near Rue Mercière") faces the Saône River.

Les Retrouvailles serves tasty but less traditional Lyonnaise cuisine in a charming setting under wood-beam ceilings. Here your dining experience is carefully managed by adorable owners Pierre *(le chef)* and Odile (€23 and €29 *menus,* inside dining only, closed Sun, 38 Rue du Bœuf, tel. 04 78 42 68 84).

Les Adrets is where *bouchon* meets beer hall. This linear, heavy-beamed place, lined with velvet booths and cherry lights, is crammed with a lively crowd enjoying good-value Lyonnaise cuisine (€26-42 *menus,* indoor dining only, closed Sat-Sun and Aug, 30 Rue du Bœuf, tel. 04 78 38 24 30).

Restaurant Panoramique de la Fourvière, atop Fourvière Hill with a spectacular view overlooking Lyon, serves fine traditional cuisine in a superb setting. Choose from the modern interior or the better, leafy terrace, both with views (*menus* from €27, €14 lunch *plat du jour,* daily until 22:00, 9 Place de Fourvière, near Notre-Dame Basilica—see map on page 1002, tel. 04 78 25 21 15).

Bistrot de St. Jean is a time-warp place with an old-school owner and dirt-cheap prices. It's cheerfully located on a leafy square with fun seating inside and out (€10 *plats,* €16 three-course *menu,* closed Mon, 3 Place du Petit Collège, tel. 04 78 37 15 81).

Subway Sandwiches...*mais oui,* even gourmet diners need a slimming lunch now and then (5 Rue St. Jean, just before Place du Change).

Ice Cream: **Nardone René Glacier,** on the river near Place du Change, with pleasant outdoor seating, serves up Lyon's best ice cream (daily 10:00-24:00, 3 Place Ennemond Fousseret).

On the Presqu'île

The pedestrian Rue Mercière is the epicenter of *bouchons* on the Presqu'île. Along this street, an entertaining cancan of restaurants stretches four blocks from Place des Jacobins to Rue Grenette. Enjoy surveying the scene and choose whichever eatery appeals. All of these restaurants appear on the map on page 1002.

On or near Rue Mercière

Bistrot à Tartines is a young and fun place for nontraditional cuisine offered at unbeatable prices by a friendly staff. The interior, which feels like an antique general store, has good seating inside and out (€6 *tartines,* killer €4 desserts, daily, 2 Rue de la Monnaie,

LYON

tel. 04 78 37 70 85).

Bistrot de Lyon feels *très* touristy but still bustles with authentic Lyonnaise atmosphere and good meals. It must be famed chef-owner Jean-Paul Lacombe's least expensive establishment (€20 *quenelles*, €12 *salade lyonnaise*, limited-selection *menus* from €25, open daily, 64 Rue Mercière, tel. 04 78 38 47 47).

Les Lyonnais (recommended earlier) has a second location facing the Saône River, with a spacious terrace and stellar views up to the basilica—particularly at night (closed Sun-Mon, 1 Quai des Célestins, tel. 04 78 37 41 80).

On Place des Célestins

La Francotte is a good choice with a warm interior, a solid zinc-topped bar, and fine outdoor seating on Place des Célestins. Try the excellent fish dishes or anything served with their mouthwatering roasted garlic potatoes (*menus* from €35, closed Sun-Mon, near many recommended hotels at 8 Place des Célestins, tel. 04 78 37 38 64).

Worth a Detour

Chez Abel is the ultimate local *bouchon*, far away from restaurant rows and tourists, and catering to one kind of client only: Lyon residents. It has a warm, chalet-like interior, and servings are generous—the *quenelle de brochet* is downright massive. Consider a *plat du jour* and maybe a salad. Reserve ahead (€24 *menu*, closed Sun, about a 15-minute walk south of Place Bellecour, Métro: Ampère, a short block from Saône River, 25 Rue Guynemer, tel. 04 78 37 46 18).

Brasserie le Sud is one of four places in Lyon where you can sample legendary chef Paul Bocuse's cuisine at affordable prices. His brasseries feature international cuisine from different corners of the world (each named for the corner it represents—north, south, east, and west). Le Sud is the most accessible, with a Mediterranean feel inside and out, but less easygoing service than you'll find at my other recommended restaurants (€21-35 *menus*, reasonably priced *plats*, daily, 11 Place Antonin-Poncet, a few blocks off Place Bellecour, tel. 04 72 77 80 00).

Lyon Connections

After Paris, Lyon is France's most important rail hub. Train travelers find this gateway to the Alps, Provence, the Riviera, and Burgundy an easy stopover. Two main train stations serve Lyon: Part-Dieu and Perrache. Most trains officially depart from Part-Dieu, though many also stop at Perrache, and trains run between the stations every 10 minutes. Double-check which station your train departs from.

From Lyon by Train to: Paris (hourly, 2 hours), **Annecy** (7/day, 2 hours, most change in Aix-les-Bains, some by bus), **Chamonix** (6/day, 4 hours), **Strasbourg** (5/day, 4 hours), **Dijon** (10/day, 2 hours), **Beaune** (10/day, 1.75 hours, some change in Mâcon), **Avignon** (22/day; 12 to TGV station in 1.5 hours, 10 to main station in 2 hours), **Arles** (14/day, 2.5 hours, most change in Avignon, Marseille, or Nîmes), **Nice** (6/day, 5 hours), **Carcassonne** (6/day, 4 hours), **Venice** (3/day, 9.5-10.5 hours, 2-3 changes, night train), **Rome** (4/day, 10-12 hours, at least one change in Milan, night train), **Florence** (5/day, 8-10 hours), **Geneva** (8/day, 2 hours), **Barcelona** (2 day trains, 7 hours, change in Perpignan; 2 night trains with transfers).

Route Tips for Drivers: En route to Provence, consider a three-hour detour through the spectacular Ardèche Gorges: Exit the A-6 autoroute at Privas and follow the villages of Aubenas, Vallon Pont d'Arc (offers kayak trips), and Pont Saint-Esprit (for more on this route, see page 746). En route to Burgundy, consider a Beaujolais detour (see the next page).

Near Lyon: The Rhône Valley

The Rhône Valley is the narrow part of the hourglass that links the areas of Provence and Burgundy. The region is bordered to the west by the soft hills of the Massif Central, and with the rolling foothills of the Alps just to the east, it's the gateway to the high Alps (the region is called "Rhône-Alpes"). The mighty Rhône River rumbles through the valley from its origin in Lake Geneva to its outlet 500 miles away in the Mediterranean near Arles.

Vineyards blanket the western side of the Rhône Valley, from those of the Beaujolais just north of Lyon to the steep slopes of Tain-Hermitage below Lyon. On the eastern side of the river and closer to Avignon are the vineyards of the famous Côtes du Rhône.

The Rhône Valley has always provided the path of least resistance for access from the Mediterranean to northern Europe, and today, Roman ruins litter the valley between Lyon and Orange.

Beaujolais Wine Route

Between Cluny and Lyon, the beautiful vineyards and villages and easygoing wine-tastings of the Beaujolais region make for an appealing detour. The most scenic and interesting section lies between Mâcon and Villefranche-sur-Saône, a few minutes west of A-6 on D-306 (old N-6). The route runs from the Mâconnais wine region and the famous village of Pouilly-Fuissé south through Beaujolais' most important villages: Chiroubles, Fleurie, and Juliénas. Look for *Route de Beaujolais* signs, and expect to get lost a few times. Trains running between Lyon and Macon stop at several wine villages, including Romanèche-Thorins (described next; 6 trains/day from Lyon).

For a pricey but thorough introduction to this region's wines, visit **Le Hameau du Vin** in Romanèche-Thorins. The king of Beaujolais, Georges Dubœuf, has constructed a Disney-esque introduction to wine at his museum, which immerses you in the life of a winemaker and features impressive models, exhibits, films, and videos. You'll be escorted from the beginning of the vine to present-day winemaking, with a focus on Beaujolais wines. It also has a lovely garden with fragrant flowers, fruits, herbs, and spices that represent the rich aromas present in wine (€19, includes a small tasting and free English headphones, daily 10:00-18:00; in Romanèche-Thorins, look for signs labeled *Le Hameau du Vin* from D-306—the old N-6, then *La Gare* signs, and look for the old train-station-turned-winery; tel. 03 85 35 22 22, www.hameau duvin.com).

LYON

ALSACE

Colmar • Route du Vin • Strasbourg

The province of Alsace stands like a flower-child referee between Germany and France. Bounded by the Rhine River on the east and the Vosges Mountains on the west, this is a green region of Hansel-and-Gretel villages, ambitious vineyards, and vibrant cities. Food and wine are the primary industry, topic of conversation, and perfect excuse for countless festivals.

Alsace has changed hands between Germany and France several times because of its location, natural wealth, naked vulnerability—and the fact that Germany considered the mountains the natural border, whereas the French saw the Rhine as the dividing line.

Having been a political pawn for 1,000 years, Alsace has a hybrid culture: Natives who curse do so bilingually, and the local cuisine features sauerkraut with fine wine sauces. If you're traveling in December, come here for France's most celebrated Christmas markets and festivals—but book your hotel well in advance (and expect higher rates), as this is high season in Alsace.

Colmar is one of Europe's most enchanting cities—with a small-town warmth and world-class art. Strasbourg is a big-city version of Colmar, worth a stop for its remarkable cathedral and to feel its high-powered and trendy bustle. The small villages that dot the wine road between them are like petite Colmars, and provide a refreshing escape from the cities.

Planning Your Time

Set up for two nights in or near Colmar. Allow one day for Colmar and another for Strasbourg and the Route du Vin (Wine Road). If you have only one day, spend your morning in Colmar and your

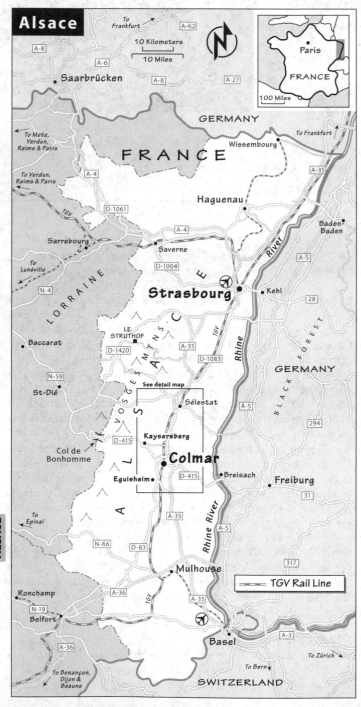

afternoon along the Route du Vin. Urban Strasbourg, with its soaring cathedral and vigorous center, is a headache for drivers but a quick 35-minute train ride from Colmar—do it by train as a day trip from Colmar.

The humbling WWI battlefields of Verdun and the bubbly vigor of Reims in northern France (both described in the next chapter) are closer to Paris than to Alsace, and follow logically only if your next destination is Paris. The high-speed TGV-Est train links Paris with Reims, Verdun, Strasbourg, Colmar, and destinations farther east, bringing the Alsace within 2.5 hours of Paris and giving train travelers easy access to Reims or Verdun en route between Paris and Alsace.

Getting Around Alsace

Frequent trains make the trip between Colmar and Strasbourg a snap (2/hour, 35 minutes). Buses and minivan excursions radiate from Colmar to villages along the Route du Vin, and you can rent bikes in Colmar and in several smaller villages if you prefer to pedal (for details on all of these options, see "Route du Vin," later).

Alsace's Cuisine Scene

Alsatian cuisine is a major tourist attraction in itself. You can't mistake the German influence: sausages, potatoes, onions, and sauerkraut. Look for *choucroute garnie* (sauerkraut and sausage—although it seems a shame to eat it in a fancy restaurant), the more traditionally Alsatian *Baeckeoffe* (see sidebar), *Rösti* (an oven-baked potato-and-cheese dish), *Spätzle* (soft egg noodles), fresh trout, and foie gras. For lighter fare, try the *poulet au Riesling,* chicken cooked ever-so-slowly in Riesling wine (*coq au Riesling* is the same dish done with rooster). At lunch, or for a lighter dinner, try a *tarte à l'oignon* (like an onion quiche, but better) or *tarte flambée* (like a thin-crust pizza with onion and bacon bits). If you're picnicking, buy some stinky Munster cheese. Dessert specialties are *tarte alsacienne* (fruit tart) and *Kuglehopf glacé* (a light cake mixed with raisins, almonds, dried fruit, and cherry liqueur).

Remember, restaurants serve only during lunch (11:30-14:00) and dinner (18:00 or 19:00-21:00, later in bigger cities), but some cafés serve food throughout the day. Many Alsatian restaurants open at 18:00, reflecting the region's Germanic heritage.

Early Crockpots

For old-school Alsatian comfort food, order the ubiquitous *Baeckeoffe,* which is still served at your table in traditional pottery. The dish gets its name from where it was cooked—in the "baker's oven." For centuries Alsatian women combined the week's leftover pork, beef, and veal with potatoes, onions, and leeks in a covered clay pot, then added white wine. Carrying the pot on their way to church on Sunday, the women would pass by the bakery and put their pot in one of the large stone ovens, still warm from baking the morning bread. During the three-hour Mass, the meat would simmer and be perfectly stewed in time for lunch. The pottery, which is still produced and sold locally, remains an integral part of every Alsatian household.

Alsatian Wines

Thanks to Alsace's Franco-Germanic culture, its wines are a kind of hybrid. The bottle shape, grapes, and much of the wine terminology are inherited from its German past, though wines made today are distinctly French in style (and generally drier than their German sisters). Alsatian wines are named for their grapes—unlike in Burgundy or Provence, where wines are commonly named after villages, or in Bordeaux, where wines are often named after châteaux. White wines rule in Alsace. You'll also come across a local version of Champagne, called Crémant d'Alsace, and several varieties of *eaux-de-vie* (strong fruit-flavored brandy). For a helpful rundown of the regional wines, see "Route du Vin Wines" (page 1039).

Colmar

Colmar is a well-pickled old place of 70,000 residents, offering a few heavyweight sights in a comfortable, midsize-town package. Historic beauty was usually a poor excuse for being spared the ravages of World War II, but it worked for Colmar. The American and British military were careful not to bomb the half-timbered old burghers' houses, characteristic red- and green-tiled roofs, and cobbled lanes of Alsace's most

ALSACE

beautiful city. The town's distinctly French shutters combined with the ye-olde German half-timbering give Colmar an intriguing ambience.

Today, Colmar is alive with colorful buildings, impressive art treasures, and German tourists. Schoolgirls park their rickety horse carriages in front of City Hall and are ready to give visitors a clip-clop tour of the old town. Antiques shops welcome browsers, and hoteliers hurry down the sleepy streets to pick up fresh croissants in time for breakfast.

Orientation to Colmar

There isn't a straight street in Colmar—count on getting lost. Thankfully, most streets are pedestrian-only, and it's a lovely town to be lost in. Navigate by the high church steeples and the helpful signs that seem to pop up whenever you need them (directing visitors to the various sights). For tourists, the town center is Place Unterlinden (a 20-minute walk from the train station), where you'll find Colmar's most important museum, the TI (close by), and a big Monoprix supermarket/department store. Every city bus starts or finishes near Place Unterlinden.

Colmar is most crowded from May through September and at its peak during its festive Christmas season (www.noel-colmar .com). Weekends are busy all year (reserve ahead). The impressive music festival fills hotels the first two weeks of July (www.festival -colmar.com), and the local wine festival rages for 10 days in early August. Open-air markets bustle next to the Dominican Church and St. Martin Cathedral on Thursdays and Saturdays.

Tourist Information

The TI is tucked behind the Monoprix store, near City Hall at 32 Cours Sainte-Anne (labeled *Mairie de Colmar*). It's well-signed from the square in front of the Unterlinden Museum. The staff is generous with printed material (April-Oct Mon-Sat 9:00-18:00, until 19:00 July-Aug, Sun 10:00-13:00; Nov-March Mon-Sat 9:00-12:00 & 14:00-18:00, Sun 10:00-13:00; tel. 03 89 20 68 92, www.ot-colmar.fr). Pick up the city map, a map of the Route du Vin (Wine Road), information on bike rental, and bus schedules (and ask where the bus stops for your trip). Get information about concerts and festivals in Colmar and in nearby villages, and ask about Colmar's Folklore Tuesdays (with folk dancing on Place de l'Ancienne Douane at 20:30 every Tue mid-May-mid-Sept, except during the July music festival). Drivers exploring the Route du Vin can buy the *Blay Foldex Alsace* map. The TI also reserves hotel rooms and has *chambres d'hôte* listings for Colmar and the region.

ALSACE

Arrival in Colmar

By Train and Bus: The old and new (TGV) parts of Colmar's train station are connected by an underground passageway. There is no baggage check.

The old train station was built during Prussian rule using the same plans as the station in Danzig (now Gdańsk, Poland). Check out the charming 1991 window that shows two local maidens about to be run over by a train and rescued by an artist. Opposite, he's shown painting their portraits.

Most buses to Route du Vin villages arrive and depart from stops to the left as you leave the old station (though stop locations tend to change regularly—ask a driver on any bus), as well as from stops closer to the city center (ask at the TI and see "Route du Vin," later).

To reach the town center, **walk** straight out past Hôtel Bristol, turn left on Avenue de la République, and keep walking (15 minutes total). For a faster trip, take **bus** #1, #3, or #4 (to the left as you leave the old station) to the Champ de Mars stop (Place Rapp) or Théâtre stop (next to the Unterlinden Museum; €1.20, pay driver, 8/hour, none on Sun, see map on page 1018). Allow €8 for a **taxi** to any hotel in central Colmar (taxi stand on the left as you leave station).

By Car: Follow signs for *Centre-Ville,* then *Place Rapp.* Parking is available at a 900-space pay-parking garage under Place Rapp, and at free lots at Place Scheurer-Kestner (across from Hôtel Primo) and off the ring road near Hôtel St. Martin (follow signs from the ring road to *Parking de la Vieille Ville*—the free parking is in the rear of the lot). Several hotels have private parking, and those that don't can advise you where to park (many get deals at pay lots for their guests—ask). When entering or leaving on the Strasbourg side of town (near the Colmar airport), look for the big Statue of Liberty replica erected on July 4, 2004, to commemorate the 100th anniversary of the death of sculptor Frédéric-Auguste Bartholdi.

Helpful Hints

Market Days: Markets take place inside the lovely market hall (*marché couvert;* Tue-Sat 8:00-18:00). The Saturday morning market on Place St. Joseph is where locals go to find fresh produce and cheese (over the train tracks, 15 minutes on foot from the center, no tourists). Textiles are on sale Thursdays on Place de la Cathédrale (all day) and Saturdays on Place des Dominicains (afternoons only). A flea market happens every Friday from June to August on Place des Dominicains.

Department/Grocery Store: The big **Monoprix,** with a super-market, is across from the Unterlinden Museum (Mon-Sat

ALSACE

8:00-20:00, closed Sun). A small Petit Casino supermarket stands across from the recommended Hôtel St. Martin (Mon-Sat 8:30-19:00, closed Sun). The **Super U** at the TGV side of the train station is open on Sunday.

Internet Access: Try **Cyber Didim,** near the Unterlinden Museum at 9 Rue du Rempart, above a kebab shop (€3/hour, no Wi-Fi; Mon-Sat 10:00-22:00, Sun 14:00-22:00, tel. 03 89 23 90 45).

Laundry: A launderette at 1 Rue Ruest is near the recommended Maison Martin Jund *chambre d'hôte* and just off the pedestrian street Rue Vauban (usually open daily 7:00-21:00). Ask your hotelier for more suggestions.

Bike Rental: There is no reliable bike rental in Colmar. It's best to drive or bus out of the city and rent a bike in Eguisheim, Kaysersberg, or Ribeauvillé (suggestions given later in this chapter). If you plan to do much biking, buy a biking map either at the TI or a *librairie* (bookstore).

Taxis: You can find one at the train station (70 yards to your left as you walk out), or call 03 89 23 10 33, mobile 06 14 47 21 80 (William), or mobile 06 72 94 65 55 (Michele). You can also ask the TI to call.

Car Rental: The least expensive is **ADA** (17 Place de Lattre de Tassigny, tel. 03 89 23 90 30, www.ada.fr). **Avis** is at the train station (tel. 03 89 23 16 89). The TI has a list of other options.

Poodle Care: To give your poodle a shampoo and a haircut (or just watch the action), drop by **Quatt Pattes** (near Hôtel Rapp at 8 Rue Berthe Molly).

Tourist Trains and Carriages: Colmar has two competing **tourist trains.** The better of the two is Le Petit Train Blanc (the white train), which departs across from the Monoprix, near the Dominican Church (€6, 45-minute tour, every 30 minutes daily 9:00-18:00, recorded commentary, hop on or off as you please, tel. 03 89 73 74 24). You can also board the train at Place des Martyrs, Place Jeanne d'Arc (beyond the cathedral), Rue Turenne in Petite Venise, and at the train station. In the summer, **horse-drawn carriages** do a similar route (€6, 30-minute tours).

Guided Tours: There are no scheduled city tours in English, but private English-speaking **guides** are available through the TI (about €120/3 hours). Several companies run good **minivan tours** of the Route du Vin (see page 1035).

Self-Guided Walk

Welcome to Colmar's Old Town

This walk—good by day, romantic by night—is a handy way to link the city's three worthwhile sights (see this chapter's Colmar

ALSACE

Colmar

1. Hôtel St. Martin
2. Hostellerie le Maréchal
3. Hôtel/Restaurant le Rapp
4. Hôtel Turenne
5. Hôtel Ibis Colmar Centre
6. Maison Martin Jund Rooms
7. Hôtel Balladins
8. Hôtel Etap
9. Grand Hôtel Bristol
10. B&B Chez Leslie
11. L'un des Sens Wine Bar
12. Sorbetière d'Isabelle & La Soï
13. Winstub de la Petite Venise
14. La Krutenau Restaurant
15. Le Comptoir de Georges Rest.
16. La Venezia Sandwiches
17. Winstub Schwendi Rest.
18. Chez Hansi Restaurant
19. La Maison Rouge Rest.
20. Le Bistrot des Copains
21. Flunch
22. Internet Café
23. Launderette
24. ADA Car Rental
25. Quatt Pattes Dog Grooming
26. Maison Pfister
27. Le Petit Train Blanc Departure Point

R. DU LOGELBACH

RUE D'ORBEY

RUE DU JURA

Best Route to Kaysersberg & Riquewihr

RUE DES POILUS

R. 5E

RUE DE PETERIMHOFF

RUE MOULINS

RUE EDOUARD RICHARD

RUE STANISLAS

RUE ROESSELMANN

R. OURDISSEURS

RUE DES 3 EPIS

RUE DES TAILLANDIERS

AVE. J. DE TASSIGNY

RUE HERTRICH

R. JACQUES PREISS

Bus #1, 3 & 4

Place Rapp

POST

Champ de

Mars

RUE DE LA REPUBLIQUE

RUE BRUAT

AVE. MARNE

AVE. DE LA REPUBLIQUE

RUE DE REIMS

RUE SCHLUMBERGER

RUE MESSIMY

RUE WILSON

RUE CAMILLE

ALSACE

To 10

TGV STN.

TRAIN STATION

To Route du Vin

Place de la Gare

To Route du Vin

To Eguisheim & D-83 to Burgundy & Alps

P

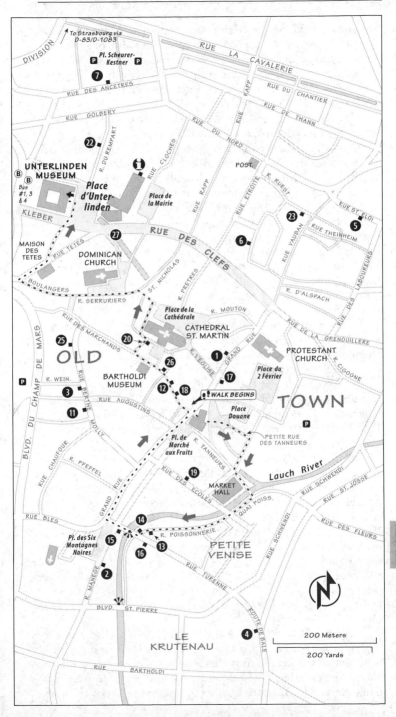

DIVISION

→ To Strasbourg via
D-83/D-1083

RUE LA CAVALERIE

Pl. Scheurer-Kestner
7

RUE DES ANCÊTRES

RUE DU CHANTIER

RUE RAPP

RUE DU NORD

RUE DE THANN

RUE GOLBERY

22

RUE DU REMPART

POST

R. RUEST

RUE CLOCHES

UNTERLINDEN
MUSEUM

Bus #1, 3 & 4

Place
d'Unterlinden

Place de
la Mairie

RUE RAPP

RUE ÉTROITE

RUE ST. ELOI

RUE VAUBAN

RUE ST. ELOI

23

RUE THEINHEIM

5

KLEBER

RUE DES CLEFS

27

6

RUE DES LABOUREURS

MAISON
DES
TÊTES

RUE TÊTES

DOMINICAN
CHURCH

R. D'ALSPACH

BOULANGERS

R. SERRURIERS

ST. NICHOLAS

R. PRÊTRES

R. MOUTON

RUE DE LA GRENOUILLÈRE

RUE DES MARCHANDS

Place de la
Cathédrale

CATHEDRAL
ST. MARTIN

25

OLD

20

R. L'ÉGLISE

GRAND RUE

PROTESTANT
CHURCH

R. CIGOGNE

BLVD. DU CHAMP DE MARS

R. WEIN.

RUE BERTHE MOLLY

BARTHOLDI
MUSEUM

26

1

Place du
2 Février

3

12 **18**

17

TOWN

11

RUE AUGUSTINS

WALK BEGINS

Place
Douane

RUE CHAUFFOUR

R. PFEFFEL

Pl. de
Marché
aux Fruits

R. TANNEURS

PETITE RUE
DES TANNEURS

RUE BLES

GRAND RUE

RUE DES ÉCOLES

19

MARKET
HALL

QUAI POISS.

Lauch River

RUE SCHWENDI

RUE ST. JOSSE

14

R. POISSONNERIE

RUE SCHWENDI

RUE DES FLEURS

Pl. des Six
Montagnes
Noires

15

16

13

PETITE
VENISE

RUE TURENNE

R. MANÈGE

2

BLVD. ST. PIERRE

LE
KRUTENAU

4

ROUTE DE BÂLE

N

200 Meters

200 Yards

RUE BARTHOLDI

ALSACE

map to help navigate). Supplement my commentary by reading the sidewalk information plaques that describe points of interest in town. Allow an hour for this walk at a peaceful pace (more if you enter sights). Colmar is wonderfully floodlit after dark. The lights can be changed to give different intensities and colors, keeping Colmar fresh and inviting.

The importance of 15th- to 17th-century Colmar is clear as you wander its pedestrian-friendly old center. It's decorated with 45 buildings classified as historic monuments. In the Middle Ages, most of Europe was fragmented into chaotic little princedoms and dukedoms. Merchant-dominated cities, natural proponents of the formation of large nation-states (a.k.a. globalization), banded together to form "trading leagues" (the World Trade Organizations of their day). The Hanseatic League was the super-league of northern Europe. Prosperous Colmar was the leading member of a smaller league of 10 Alsatian cities, called the Decapolis (founded 1354). The names of the streets you'll walk along bear witness to the merchants' historic importance to Colmar.

• *Start your tour by the Chez Hansi Restaurant, on Grand Rue, where it meets Rue des Marchands. Face the old...*

Customs House (Koïfhus): Here, delegates of the Decapolis would meet to sort out trade issues, much like the European Union does in nearby Strasbourg today. In Colmar's heyday, this was where the action was. Notice the fancy green roof tiles and the intricate railing at the base of the roof. The Dutch-looking gabled building on the left was the birthplace of Colmar's most famous son, General Jean Rapp, who distinguished himself during France's Revolutionary Wars to become one of Napoleon's most trusted generals.

Walk under the archway to Place de l'Ancienne Douane and face the Frédéric-Auguste Bartholdi statue—arm raised, à la Statue of Liberty—and do a 360-degree spin to appreciate a gaggle of gables. This was the center of business activity in Colmar, with trade routes radiating to several major European cities. All goods that entered the city were taxed here. Today, it's the festive site of outdoor cafés and, on many summer evenings, wine-tastings (open to everyone).

• *Follow the statue's left elbow and walk down Petite Rue des Tanneurs (not the larger "Rue des Tanneurs"). The half-timbered commotion of higgledy-piggledy rooftops on the downhill side of the fountain marks the...*

Tanners' Quarter: These vertical 17th- and 18th-century rooftops competed for space in the sun to dry their freshly tanned hides, while the nearby river channel flushed the waste products. Notice the openings just below the roofs where hides would be hung out to dry. This neighborhood, restored in about 1970, was a pioneer in the government-funded renovation of old quarters. Residents had to play along or move out. At the street's end, enter the small parkway, then turn back. You're looking at the city's first defensive wall. The oldest and lowest stones you see are from 1230, now built into the row of houses; later walls encircled the city farther out.

• *Walk with the old walls on your right, then take the first left along the stream.*

Old Market Hall: On your right is Colmar's historic (c. 1865) and newly renovated market hall. Here locals buy fish, produce, and other products (originally brought here by flat-bottom boat). You'll find terrific picnic fixings and produce, sandwiches and bakery items, wine tastings, and clean WCs. Several stands are run like cafés, and there's even a bar. Take a spin through the market and see what strikes your fancy (Tue-Sat 8:00-18:00, closed Sun-Mon).

• *Back on the street, cross the canal and turn right on Quai de la Poissonnerie ("Wharf of the Fish Market"), and you'll enter...*

Petite Venise: This neighborhood, a collection of Colmar's most colorful houses lining the small canal, is popular with tourists during the day. But at night it's romantic, with fewer crowds. It lies between the town's first wall (built to defend against arrows) and its later wall (built in the age of gunpowder). The river was canalized for medieval industry—to provide water for the tanners, to allow farmers to barge their goods into town, to power mills, and so on. Walk several blocks along the flower-box-lined canal to the end of Rue de la Poissonnerie. Turn right, walk to the center of the bridge, and enjoy the view. To the right  you'll see examples of the flat-bottom gondolas used to transport goods on the small river. Today, they give tourists sleepy, scenic, 30-minute canal tours (€6, departs on demand, buy tickets at the bar/restaurant La Krutenau, tel. 03 89 41 18 80).

• *Cross the bridge to find a fountain in the square to your left. Another Bartholdi work, this one was commissioned to honor a 13th-century town provost who died defending the city he loved. Take the second right on Grande Rue. Walk for several blocks to the Customs House (green-tiled roof) and land back where you started. With your back to the Customs House, look uphill along Rue des Marchands ("Merchants' Street")— one of the most scenic intersections in town. (The ruler of Malaysia was so charmed by this street that he had it re-created in Kuala Lumpur.)*

Walk up Rue des Marchands, and you'll soon come face-to-face with the...

Maison Pfister (Pfister House): This richly decorated merchant's house dates from 1537. Here the owner displayed his wealth for all to enjoy (and to envy). The external spiral-staircase turret, a fine loggia on the top floor, and the bay windows (called oriels) were pricey add-ons. The painted walls illustrate the city folks' taste for Renaissance humanism (a nice little wine shop fills the ground floor). The man carved into the side of the building next door (at #9) was a drape-maker; he's shown holding a bar, Colmar's measure of about one meter. In the Middle Ages, it was common for cities to have their own units of length; one reason merchants supported the "globalization" efforts of their time was to standardize measuring systems.

The cozy wine shop on the ground floor sells fine wines, but they are most proud of their locally made whiskey. They offer tastings, so go ahead—take a hit and see what you think.

• *Look closely at the architecture of the house next door.*

Half-Timbered Houses: The building with the guy holding the bar shows off the classic half-timbered design—the beams (upright, cross, angular supports) are grouped in what's called (and looks like) "a man." Typical houses are built with a man in the middle flanked by two "half men." Whereas houses of the rich were made of stone, anyone on a budget built half-timbered structures (though all homes here sit on a stone base to prevent them from sinking into the marshy ground). Originally, proud townsfolk would plaster over their cheap half-timbered walls to create the illusion of a stone house. Then, in the 20th century, half-timbered became charming, so they peeled away the plaster to reveal the old beams. You can identify true stone homes by their windowsills: Wooden sills mean they're half-timbered (like this one), whereas stone sills indicate the entire building is built of stone (like the Pfister House).

As you explore the town, notice how upper floors are cantilevered out. This was both a structural support trick and a tax dodge, as real-estate taxes were based on the square footage of the ground floor.

A short block along on the left is the **Bartholdi Museum** (described later, under "Sights in Colmar"), located in the home where the famous sculptor Frédéric-Auguste Bartholdi was raised. Next door (at #28) is Au Pain Dorée, with its charming Art Nouveau facade and interior. Art Nouveau was rare in Colmar. During the style's heyday in the early 20th century—which was also just after this region was taken from France by Germany—Art Nouveau was considered an anti-German statement, and therefore controversial.

• *A passage to the right leads you through the old guards' house to...*

St. Martin Cathedral: The city's golden cathedral (erected

ALSACE

in 1235), with its lone tower (two were planned) and gleaming tiles, was inspired by the Hôtel Dieu in Beaune. If you visit Strasbourg's cathedral, you'll see a very different color of stone, though both cathedrals were built with stone quarried from the nearby Vosges Mountains.

Walk left, to the front of the cathedral. Notice that the relief over the main door depicts not your typical Last Judgment scene, but the Three Kings who visited Baby Jesus. The Magi, whose remains are in the Rhine city of Köln, Germany, are popular in this region. The interior is dark, but it holds a few finely carved and beautifully painted altarpieces. The cathedral's beautiful Vosges-stone exterior radiates color in the late afternoon.

• *Walk past the cathedral, go left around Café Jupiler, and wander up the pedestrian-only Rue des Serruriers ("Locksmiths' Street") to the...*

Dominican Church: Compare St. Martin Cathedral's impressive exterior with this low-slung, sober structure that perfectly symbolizes Dominican austerity. These two very different houses of worship were built at the same time. Dominican churches were intentionally plain, symbolic of their zeal to purify their faith and compete with the growing popularity of 13th-century heretical movements, such as Catharism, which preached a simpler faith. This church is well worth entering, especially while it's playing host to *The Isenheim Altarpiece* (church and altarpiece described later, under "Sights in Colmar").

• *Continuing past the Dominican Church, Rue des Serruriers becomes Rue des Boulangers—"Bakers' Street." Turn right on Rue des Têtes (notice the beautiful swan sign over the* pharmacie *at the corner). Walk a block to the fancy old house festooned with heads (on the right) and stand in front of the Esprit boutique for the best view.*

Maison des Têtes ("House of Heads"): Colmar's other famous merchant's house, built in 1609 by a big-shot winemaker (see the grapes hanging from the wrought-iron sign and the happy man at the tip-top), is playfully decorated with 105 faces and masks. On the ground floor, the guy in the window's center has pig's feet. Look four houses to the right to see a 1947 bakery sign (above the big pretzel), which shows the *boulangerie* basics in Alsace: croissant, *kugelhopf,* and baguette. Across from the Maison des Têtes (above where you should be standing), study the early-20th-century store sign trumpeting the wonders of a butcher who once occupied these premises (with the traditional maiden chasing a goose about to be force-fed, all hung from the beak of a chicken).

ALSACE

• *Angle down Rue de l'Eau ("Water Street") for a shortcut to the TI and the Unterlinden Museum, with its namesake linden trees lining the front yard (popular locally for making the calming "Tilleul" tea).*

Sights in Colmar

▲▲▲Unterlinden Museum

Colmar's touristic claim to fame is one of my favorite museums in Europe. Its extensive yet manageable collection ranges from Roman Colmar to medieval winemaking exhibits, and from traditional wedding dresses to paintings that give vivid insight into the High Middle Ages. Make sure to allocate sufficient time for this museum, as its collection is unique and varied, and the excellent audioguide makes the curator your best friend.

Sometime in 2013, construction may force the jewel of the museum, *The Isenheim Altarpiece,* to be moved to the Dominican Church (described later). If this happens, the Unterlinden, one of the most visited museums in all of France, will be less crowded (still, it's smart to visit between 12:00 and 14:00—when most are lunching—or at the end of the day). Even without the altarpiece, this museum is worth a visit.

Cost and Hours: €8, €6 for seniors, includes entry to Dominican Church and indispensable audioguide; May-Oct daily 9:00-18:00; Nov-April Wed-Mon 9:00-12:00 & 14:00-17:00, closed Tue; 1 Rue d'Unterlinden, tel. 03 89 20 15 58, www.musee -unterlinden.com.

➋ **Self-Guided Tour:** Use this commentary to supplement the included audioguide (which doesn't start until the painting gallery in room 3 and ends before the basement rooms). Big plans are under way to expand the museum over the next two years, so be prepared for construction-related changes.

Gothic Statues (Room 1): Room 1 features 14th-century Gothic statues from nearby St. Martin Cathedral's facade and other area churches. Study the Romanesque detail of the capitals and the faces of the statues. Even though they endured the elements outdoors for more than 500 years, it's still clear that they were sculpted carefully. The reddish stone is quarried from the Vosges Mountains, giving these works their unusual coloring. Notice the faint remnants of paint still visible on some statues— then imagine all of these works brightly painted. At the far end of the room, gaze into the medieval eyes of the Byzantine-looking Magi (*un roi Mage*—the kneeling guy) and take a close look at the 15th-century stained glass; fine details are painted into the glass that no one would ever see (these windows were made 300 years after those of Paris' Sainte-Chapelle). The glass is essentially a jigsaw puzzle connected by lead. Around here, glass this old is rare—most of it was destroyed by rampaging Protestants in the Reformation wars.

Cloister: Step into the soothing cloister (the largest 13th-century cloister in Alsace) and walk right, passing the WCs in

the corner. This was a Dominican convent founded for noblewomen in 1230. It functioned until the French Revolution, when the building became a garrison. Rooms with museum exhibits branch off from here. Don't miss the wine room (next corner) with its 17th-century oak presses and finely decorated casks. Those huge presses were turned by animals. Wine revenue was used to care for Colmar's poor. The nuns owned many of the best vineyards around, and production was excellent. So was consumption. Notice (on the first cask on left) the Bacchus with the distended tummy straddling a keg. The quote from 1781 reads: "My belly's full of juice. It makes me strong. But drink too much and you lose dignity and health."

Painting Gallery (the museum audioguide begins here): To the left of the wine-press room, enter the painting gallery marked *art médiéval*. Find the spinning case of engravings by Martin Schongauer, Albrecht Dürer's master. (Schongauer also painted the *Virgin in the Rosebush,* now located at the Dominican Church.) Throughout the museum you'll see small photos of engravings illustrating how painters were influenced by other artists' engravings. Most German painters of the time were also engravers (that's how they made money—making lots of copies for sale). The following rooms are filled with paintings that are wonderfully described by the audioguide. As you enjoy the art, remember that Alsace was historically German and part of the upper Rhine River Valley. (This museum boasts France's only painting by Lucas Cranach.) Remember those Three Kings (of Bethlehem fame) from St. Martin Cathedral? They're prominently featured throughout this region, because their heads ended up as relics in Köln's cathedral (on the Rhine). You'll pass several worthwhile works by Martin Schongauer before reaching the spot where *The Isenheim Altarpiece* usually sits (if it's here now, skip ahead to read its description in the listing for the Dominican Church, next).

The Rest of the Museum: The upstairs rooms, displaying local and folk history, are worth a look. You'll see everything from iron store signs, massive church bells, and chests with intricate locking systems, to ornate armoires, medieval armor, muskets, old-time toys, and antique jewelry boxes. Back on the ground floor, near the museum's entrance, you'll find a modern-art section with a small but pleasing permanent collection, including a few works by Monet, Renoir, Picasso, Leger, de Stael, Bonnard, and a wall of Jean Dubuffet. In the basement below are impressively displayed Roman and prehistoric artifacts and temporary exhibits.

▲▲▲Dominican Church (Eglise des Dominicains)

This beautiful Gothic church is the permanent home to one medieval masterpiece (Schongauer's *Virgin in the Rosebush*), and—while the Unterlinden's renovation is under way— the temporary home of a second masterpiece (the devastatingly beautiful *Isenheim Altarpiece*, expected to be displayed here through October of 2014).

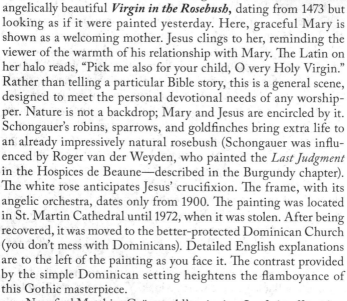

Cost and Hours: €1.50 but price may increase when *Altarpiece* arrives, included in €8 Unterlinden Museum ticket, mid-March–Dec daily 10:00-13:00 & 15:00-18:00, last entry 15 minutes before closing, closed Jan–mid-March, no photos.

❍ **Self-Guided Tour:** Start with a medieval mindblower—Martin Schongauer's angelically beautiful ***Virgin in the Rosebush,*** dating from 1473 but looking as if it were painted yesterday. Here, graceful Mary is shown as a welcoming mother. Jesus clings to her, reminding the viewer of the warmth of his relationship with Mary. The Latin on her halo reads, "Pick me also for your child, O very Holy Virgin." Rather than telling a particular Bible story, this is a general scene, designed to meet the personal devotional needs of any worshipper. Nature is not a backdrop; Mary and Jesus are encircled by it. Schongauer's robins, sparrows, and goldfinches bring extra life to an already impressively natural rosebush (Schongauer was influenced by Roger van der Weyden, who painted the *Last Judgment* in the Hospices de Beaune—described in the Burgundy chapter). The white rose anticipates Jesus' crucifixion. The frame, with its angelic orchestra, dates only from 1900. The painting was located in St. Martin Cathedral until 1972, when it was stolen. After being recovered, it was moved to the better-protected Dominican Church (you don't mess with Dominicans). Detailed English explanations are to the left of the painting as you face it. The contrast provided by the simple Dominican setting heightens the flamboyance of this Gothic masterpiece.

Now find Matthias Grünewald's gripping ***Isenheim Altarpiece*** (c. 1515)—actually a series of three paintings on hinges that pivot like shutters (study the little models on the wall, with English explanations nearby). Designed to help people in a medieval hospi-

ALSACE

tal endure horrible skin diseases (such as St. Anthony's Fire, later called rye ergotism)—long before the age of painkillers—it's one of the most powerful paintings ever produced. Germans know this painting like Americans know the *Mona Lisa*.

Stand in front of the centerpiece as if you were a medieval peasant, and let the agony and suffering of the Crucifixion drag

its fingers down your face. It's an intimate drama. The point—Jesus' suffering—is drilled home: The weight of his body bends the crossbar (unrealistically, creating to some eyes an almost crossbow effect). His elbows are pulled from their sockets by the weight of his dead body. People who are crucified die of asphyxiation, as Jesus' chest implies. His mangled feet are swollen with blood. The grief on Mary's face is agonizing. In hopes that the intended viewers (the hospital's patients) would know that Jesus understood their suffering, Jesus himself was even painted to appear as if he had a skin disease. Study the faces and the Christian symbolism. Mary is wrapped in the shroud that will cover Jesus. The sorrowful composition on the left is powerful. On the far left stands St. Sebastian (called upon by those with the plague) and on the right is St. Anthony (called upon by those with ergot poisoning from rotten rye).

Walk to the back of this panel. The Resurrection scene is unique in art history (Grünewald had no master and no students).

Jesus rockets out of the tomb as man is transformed into God. As if proclaiming once again, "I am the Light," he is radiant. His shroud is the color of light: Roy G. Biv. Around the rainbow is the "resurrection of the flesh." Jesus' perfect pink flesh would appeal to the patients who meditated on the scene. The right half of this panel depicts the Annunciation, with the normally sanguine Mary looking unsettled, as if she's been hit by some unexpected news. You wouldn't think she'd be shocked to learn of her pregnancy—she's shown reading the Bible passage that tells of this event. Find the translucent dove near Mary.

In the nativity scene on the next panel—set in the Rhineland—the much-adored Mary is tender and loving, true to the Dominican belief that she was the intercessor for all in heaven.

The three scenes of the painting changed with the church calendar. The happy ending—a psychedelic explosion of Resurrection joy—is the spiritual equivalent of jumping from the dentist's chair directly into a whirlpool tub. The scene on the left is the Concert of Angels.

Look at the last panel—zoom in on the agonizing Temptation of St. Anthony. Patients who meditated on this painting were reminded that they didn't have it so bad. They were also reminded to stay the course (religiously) and to not stray from the path of salvation. The other panel shows Anthony's visit to St. Paul the hermit. The final scene (behind you), carved in wood by Nikolaus Hagenauer, is St. Anthony on his throne.

▲Bartholdi Museum

This little museum recalls the life and work of the local boy who gained fame by sculpting America's much-loved Statue of Liberty. Frédéric-Auguste Bartholdi (1834-1904) was a dynamic painter/photographer/sculptor with a passion for the defense of liberty and freedom. Although Colmar was his home, he spent most of his career in Paris, unable to move back here without becoming a German (Prussia took control of Alsace in 1871). He devoted years of his life to realizing the vision of a statue of liberty for America that would stand in New York City's harbor. Closer to home, several Bartholdi statues grace Colmar's squares.

Cost and Hours: €5, free on July 4, open March-Dec Wed-Mon 10:00-12:00 & 14:00-18:00, closed Tue and Jan-Feb, in heart of old town at 30 Rue des Marchands, tel. 03 89 41 90 60, www.musee-bartholdi.com.

Θ **Self-Guided Tour:** Curiously, there is no English posted in this museum. The English handouts offer no help in navigating the collection, but do give worthwhile background on the Statue of Liberty and *Lion of Belfort* (the document needs an editor). The following commentary helps make sense of the three-floor museum.

On the **ground floor,** the room to the right of the ticket desk houses temporary exhibits. To the left are exhibits covering Bartholdi's works commissioned in Alsatian cities, commonly dedicated to military heroes.

Head upstairs to the **first floor,** passing a portrait of the artist at the base of the stairs. Turn left to find the tools of his trade in the glass cases. The rooms beyond re-create Bartholdi's high-society flat in Paris. The dining room is lined with portraits of his aristocratic family. In the next room hangs a beautiful portrait of the sculptor (by Jean Benner), facing his mother (on a red chair). Bartholdi was very close to his mom, writing her daily letters. Many see her features in the Statue of Liberty.

The rest of the first floor shows off Bartholdi's French work.

ALSACE

Notice how his patriotic pieces tend to have one arm raised—*Vive la France*, God bless America, *Deutschland über alles*...you can fill in the flag-waving blank.

A room dedicated to Bartholdi's most famous French work, the *Lion of Belfort*, celebrates the Alsatian town that fought so fiercely in 1871 that it was never annexed into Germany. Photos show the red sandstone lion sitting regally below the mighty Vauban fortress of Belfort—a symbol of French spirit standing strong against Germany. Small models give a sense of its gargantuan scale. (If you're linking Burgundy with Alsace by car, you'll pass the city of Belfort and see signs directing you to the *Lion*.)

Next, find Bartholdi's photo (actually a line of six photos) of New York City's harbor in 1876. The first tower of the Brooklyn Bridge is up. Bartholdi added the tiny Statue of Liberty on the far left (along with the boats). This floor ends with the thrilling statue of Gallic leader Vercingétorix victorious over a Roman soldier. In a glass case near this statue, find a lineup of French Who's Who sculpted by Bartholdi, including Claude-Joseph Rouget de Lisle (composer of *La Marseillaise*).

The **second floor** up (top floor) is dedicated to Bartholdi's American works—the paintings, photos, and statues that Bartholdi made during his many travels to the States. You'll see statues of Columbus pointing confidently, and Lafayette (who was only 19 years old when he came to America's aid) with George Washington. One room is dedicated to the evolution and completion of the dream of a Statue of Liberty. Fascinating photos show the Eiffel-designed core, the frame being covered with plaster, and then the hand-hammered copper plating, which was ultimately riveted to the frame. The statue was assembled in Paris, then un-riveted and shipped to New York, in 1886...10 years late. The big ear is half-size.

Though the statue was a gift from France, the US had to come up with the cash to build a pedestal. This was a tough sell, but Bartholdi was determined to see his statue erected. On 10 trips to the US, he worked to raise funds and lobbied for construction, bringing with him this painting and a full-size model of the torch—which the statue would ultimately hold. (Lucky for Bartholdi and his cause, his cousin was the French ambassador to the US.) Eventually, the project came together—the pedestal was built, and the Statue of Liberty has welcomed waves of immigrants into New York ever since.

Sleeping in Colmar

Hotels are busy on weekends in May, June, September, and October, and every day in July and August. But there are always rooms—somewhere. Should you have trouble finding a bed, ask

Sleep Code

(€1 = about $1.30, country code: 33)
S = Single, **D** = Double/Twin, **T** = Triple, **Q** = Quad, **b** = bathroom, **s** = shower only, * = French hotel rating system (0-5 stars). Unless otherwise noted, credit cards are accepted and English is spoken.

To help you sort easily through these listings, I've divided the accommodations into three categories based on the price for a standard double room with bath:

$$$ **Higher Priced**—Most rooms €100 or more.
 $$ **Moderately Priced**—Most rooms between €65-100.
  $ **Lower Priced**—Most rooms €55 or less.

Prices can change without notice; verify the hotel's current rates online or by email.

the TI for help, or look in a nearby village, where small hotels and bed-and-breakfasts are plentiful (see my recommendations in nearby Eguisheim, later).

In the Center

$$$ Hôtel St. Martin*,** ideally situated near the old Customs House, is a family-run place that began as a coaching inn (since 1361). Its 40 traditional yet well-equipped rooms, most with air-conditioning and big beds, are woven into its antique frame. The hotel has three sections (young, middle-aged, and elderly) joined by a peaceful courtyard. The rooms on the front are the hotel's oldest and cheapest. Twelve newer rooms are in the back, but don't have elevator access; you'll have to take the stairs. Side-wing rooms offer good comfort, character, and an elevator (Sb-€88, standard Db-€100, bigger Db-€125, still bigger Db-€165, Tb/Qb-€175, great breakfast-€12, air-con, free Internet access and Wi-Fi, free public parking nearby at Parking de la Vieille Ville, 38 Grand Rue, tel. 03 89 24 11 51, fax 03 89 23 47 78, www.hotel-saint-martin .com, colmar@hotel-saint-martin.com).

$$$ At Hostellerie le Maréchal**,** in the heart of La Petite Venise, Colmar's most famous and characteristic digs are surprisingly affordable. Though the rooms aren't big, the setting is romantic, the decor carefully selected, and the service professional (Sb-€90-100, standard Db-€105-150, Db with whirlpool tub-€180-230, suite Db-€290, breakfast-€15, garage-€15, free Wi-Fi, 4 Place des Six Montagnes Noires, tel. 03 89 41 60 32, fax 03 89 24 59 40, www.le-marechal.com, info@le-marechal.com). Their well-respected restaurant will melt a romantic's heart, and they'll heartily encourage you to dine here (€38-75 *menus,* reserve ahead).

$$$ Hôtel le Rapp*, well-located off Place Rapp and near a big park, holds a variety of rooms for many budgets, a full-service bar, a café, and a nice restaurant. The cheapest rooms are small but comfortable; the bigger rooms are tastefully designed, usually with queen-size beds. There's also a small basement pool, a sauna, and a Turkish bath. It's well-run and family-friendly (Sb-€72-85, standard Db-€98, bigger Db-€119, junior suite for 2-4 people-€156, good buffet breakfast-€12, air-con, elevator, free Internet access and Wi-Fi, 1 Rue Weinemer, tel. 03 89 41 62 10, fax 03 89 24 13 58, www.rapp-hotel.com, rapp-hotel@calixo.net).

$$ Hôtel Turenne** is a good, if less central, two-star value (a 10-minute walk from the city center, and a 15-minute walk from the train station). It sits on a busy street with easy, free parking. Rooms vary in size, and many have tight bathrooms, though all are air-conditioned and well-maintained. Rates are hard to pin down (Sb-€52-68, Db-€70-100, Tb-€78-115, family-friendly studios-€125-165, breakfast-€9, park for free on the street or book ahead to park in their lot-€7/day, elevator for most rooms, Internet access, free Wi-Fi, appealing bar and breakfast room, 10 Route de Bâle, tel. 03 89 21 58 58, fax 03 89 41 27 64, www.turenne.com, infos@turenne.com).

$$ Hôtel Ibis Colmar Centre,** on the ring road, rents pleasant rooms with small bathrooms at reasonable rates (Db-€80, bigger Db-€90, breakfast-€8, check website for deals, air-con, Internet access and Wi-Fi, 10 Rue St. Eloi, tel. 03 89 41 30 14, fax 03 89 24 51 49, www.ibishotel.com, h1377@accor.com).

$ Maison Martin Jund holds my favorite budget beds in Colmar. This ramshackle yet historic half-timbered house—the home of likeable winemakers André and Myriam—feels like a medieval tree house soaked in wine and filled with flowers. The rooms are modest but spacious and comfortable enough. Some have air-conditioning and many are equipped with kitchenettes (D-€30, Db/Tb-€45-65; big family apartments-€84-94; breakfast-€6, good organic wine for sale in their tasting room, Internet access, free Wi-Fi, 12 Rue de l'Ange, tel. 03 89 41 58 72, fax 03 89 23 15 83, www.martinjund.com, martinjund@hotmail.com). Leave your car at Place Scheurer-Kestner. Train travelers can take bus #1, #2, or #3 from the station to the Unterlinden Museum, then walk past Monoprix, and veer left on Rue des Clefs, left on Rue Etroite, and right on Rue de l'Ange. This is not a hotel, so there is no real reception—though good-natured Myriam seems to be around, somewhere, most of the time (call if you plan to arrive after 21:00).

$ Hôtel Balladins,** near the Unterlinden Museum, is a modern, efficient, clean, and cheap place to sleep. The easygoing

ALSACE

staff will hold a room for you until 18:00 if you call ahead. Rooms facing the big square *(grand place)* are far quieter (Db-€59, Tb-€69, Qb-€79, breakfast-€7.50, free Wi-Fi, free parking in big square in front, 5 Rue des Ancêtres, tel. 03 89 24 22 24, fax 03 89 24 55 96, www.balladins.com, colmar.centre@balladins.com).

$ Hôtel Etap offers tight but serviceable rooms (Db-€42-44, secure parking-€7/day or park for free on Place Scheurer-Kestner, free Wi-Fi, 10-minute walk from the city center at 15 Rue Stanislas, tel. 08 92 68 09 31, www.etaphotel.com).

Near the Train Station

$$$ Grand Hôtel Bristol*** has little personality but works if you need three-star comfort at the train station (standard Db-€118-158, big Db-€175-190, breakfast-€15, some rooms with air-con, free Wi-Fi, 7 Place de la Gare, tel. 03 89 23 59 59, fax 03 89 23 92 26, www.grand-hotel-bristol.com, reservation@grand-hotel -bristol.com).

$$ Bed-and-Breakfast Chez Leslie is run by engaging Leslie and her Franco-American family (husband Philippe and daughters Milena and Maya). Located in a neighborhood where "real people live," it's a five-minute walk from the station and a 20-minute walk from the center. The rooms are bright, big, and artfully decorated with good beds—and the garden will calm your mind (Sb-€62, Db-€81, family room-€80-110, one-night stay-€5 extra, includes breakfast, ask about apartment rental in town, 31 Rue de Mulhouse, tel. 03 89 79 98 99, mobile 06 82 58 91 98, www .chezleslie.com, info@chezleslie.com). From the train platform, exit down the stairs into the underground passageway toward Rue du Tir (away from station), walk up the stairs at the end, go left down the street, and turn right at the first corner (Rue de Soultz). Continue up to the square and turn left on Rue de Mulhouse.

Eating in Colmar

Colmar is full of good restaurants offering traditional Alsatian *menus* for €18-30, and expensive places with lighter fare. (To dine in a smaller town nearby, see "Eating in Eguisheim," later.)

Before Dinner: Slip into **L'un des Sens** wine bar for a glass of wine and an appetizer (long list of wines from many countries) and a short list of foods (meat plates, fancy foie gras, cheese plates). The colorful interior, soothing front terrace, and upbeat waitstaff make this a fun place (Tue-Fri 15:00-22:00, Sat 10:00-23:00, closed Sun-Mon, ask about blind tastings, 18 Rue Berthe Molly, tel. 03 89 24 04 37).

After Dinner: Stop by the tiny **Sorbetière d'Isabelle** for Colmar's best sorbet, and ask about her syrup toppings. Get it to go or eat there, inside or out (daily 11:00-22:00, near Maison Pfister at 13 Rue des Marchands, tel. 03 89 41 67 17). If you want lively café and bar action, find **Rue du Conseil Souverain** (just below Grand Rue and between Rue des Ecoles and Rue des Tanneurs).

In Petite Venise

For dining with a canalside view, head into Petite Venise and make your way to the photo-perfect bridge on Rue Turenne, where you'll find several picturesque places.

Winstub de la Petite Venise bucks the touristy trend in this area with caring owners Virginie and Julien and a wood-warm, collector's interior (no outside seating). The service is personal, and the menu is limited in selection—heavy on the meats—but generous in quality. Chef Julien is very proud of his *jambonneau*, though his *choucroute* is tasty, too (closed Wed, €15-23 *plats*, delicious foie gras, 4 Rue de la Poissonnerie, tel. 03 89 41 72 59).

La Krutenau's picnic tables sprawl along the canal, offering desserts and two types of *tartes flambées* (natural-€6.50, garnished-€7.50), plus cheap beer and wine. Come for a light meal with ambience (inside or out, best after dark), a dessert, or a drink on a warm evening (closed Mon, 1 Rue de la Poissonnerie, tel. 03 89 41 18 80).

Le Comptoir de Georges, Colmar's unpretentious diner (doing double-duty as a butcher shop), dishes up traditional Alsatian fare alongside French classics. The atmosphere is low-key and on the young side, with red booths, and your paper placemat doubles as the menu. The best seats are on the tiny terrace that hangs over the canal (€12-17 *plats*, big €13 salads; serves food all day—breakfast, lunch, and dinner; closed all day Sun and Mon after 13:00, 1 Place des Six Montagnes Noires, tel. 03 89 20 60 72).

La Venezia is a hole-in-the-wall across from the touristy places with a few outdoor tables, serving hot *panini* sandwiches and other budget snacks (lunch only, daily, popular with students, on Rue de Turenne).

In the Old City Center

Winstub Schwendi has fun, German pub energy inside with 10 beers on tap, animated conversation, and hustling waiters. The big terrace outside is a tad more sedate, but ideal for a warm evening. Choose from a dozen filling, robust Swiss *rösti* plates (€12) or *tartes flambées* (€9); I like the *strasbourgeoise flambée* (also good salad and main dish options, daily 12:00-22:00, slammed on weekends, facing old Customs House at 3 Grand Rue, tel. 03 89 23 66 26). If the Winstub is full, you'll find a spate of other places with good outdoor seating around Place de l'Ancienne Douane.

Chez Hansi, a half-block up from the Customs House, is where Colmarians go for a traditional meal (served by women in Alsatian dresses). This place feels real, even though it's in the thick of the touristic center. Try local specialties like *poulet au Riesling* (chicken in Riesling sauce) with *Spätzle* (soft egg noodles), or medieval "pub grub" like *choucroute garnie* (€20-40 *menus,* indoor seating only, closed Wed-Thu, 23 Rue des Marchands, tel. 03 89 41 37 84).

La Maison Rouge has a folk-museum interior and noisy sidewalk seating with good, reasonably priced, traditional Alsatian cuisine and a loyal following. You'll be greeted by the *jambon à l'os*—ham cooking on the bone (€24-40 *menus,* try the veal cordon bleu with Munster or the *tarte flambée au chèvre-basilic,* closed Sun-Mon, 9 Rue des Ecoles, tel. 03 89 23 53 22).

Hôtel-Restaurant le Rapp is a traditional place to savor a slow, elegant meal served with grace and fine Alsatian wine. If you want to order high on the menu, this is the perfect place to do it (great *Baeckeoffe* or *choucroute* for €19 that makes a whole meal, *menus* from €30, good vegetarian options, closed Thu-Fri, air-con, 1 Rue Berthe Molly, tel. 03 89 41 62 10).

La Soï ("The Sow") is a tiny, hole-in-the-wall place with an open kitchen serving meat-heavy Alsatian specialties at reasonable prices (€10-17 main dishes, closed Wed, 17 Rue des Marchands, tel. 03 89 29 63 50).

Le Bistrot des Copains is a casual, young *bistrot* with views of the cathedral, indoor and outdoor seating, and lots of traditional French—not just Alsatian—choices (€13-16 main dishes, €16-31 *menus,* daily, 18 Place de Cathédrale, tel. 03 89 29 06 44).

Flunch is family-friendly and serves cheap, cafeteria-style meals in a fast-food setting (*menus* under €10 include salad bar, main course, and drink; good kids' *menu,* open daily until 22:00, 8 Avenue de la République, tel. 03 89 23 56 56).

Colmar Connections

ALSACE

From Colmar by Train to: Strasbourg (about 2/hour, 35 minutes), **Reims** (TGV: 10/day, 3 hours, most change in Strasbourg), **Verdun** (7/day, 4-5.5 hours, 2-3 changes, many with 30-minute bus ride from Gare de Meuse), **Beaune** (7/day, 2.5-4 hours, fastest by TGV via Mulhouse, reserve well ahead, possible changes in Mulhouse or Belfort and Dijon), **Paris'** Gare de l'Est (almost hourly, 3 direct, others change in Strasbourg, 3.5 hours), **Amboise** (12/day, 5-6 hours, most with transfer in Strasbourg and Paris), **Basel,** Switzerland (hourly, 45 minutes), **Karlsruhe,** Germany (TGV: 7/day, 1.5-2.5 hours, best with change in Strasbourg; non-TGV: hourly, 2-3.5 hours, change in Strasbourg and Appenweier or Offenburg; from Karlsruhe, it's 1.5 hours to Frankfurt, 3 hours to Munich).

Route du Vin (Wine Road)

Alsace's Route du Vin is an asphalt ribbon that ties 90 miles of vineyards, villages, and feudal fortresses into an understandably popular tourist package. The gener-ally dry climate (with less rain than parts of southern France) has made for good wine and happy tourists since Roman days. Colmar and Eguisheim are well located for exploring the 30,000 acres of vineyards blanketing the hills from Marlenheim to Thann. Drivers need a detailed map of the Route du Vin, which they can pick up at any area TI.

As you tour the Route du Vin, you'll see storks' nests on church spires and city halls, thanks to a campaign to reintroduce the birds to this area. (Those nests can weigh as much as 1,000 pounds.) Look also for crucifixion monuments scattered about the vineyards—intended to prime the pump for a good harvest. Route du Vin villages are stuffed with quaint half-timbered architecture (for a refresher course, see page 1022).

Planning Your Time

If you have only a day, focus on towns within easy striking range of Colmar. World War II left many Route du Vin villages in ruins. While most have been rebuilt, they have less character than those left untouched. Villages that emerged from World War II unscathed include Eguisheim, Kaysersberg, Hunawihr, Turckheim, Ribeauvillé, and the *très* popular Riquewihr. Be careful not to overdose on all the half-timbered cuteness. Two villages meet the needs of most. For a good sampling of Route du Vin villages and countryside, start in Riquewihr (beat the crowds), then walk, ride, or drive through the vineyards to Kaysersberg. Drivers can tack on Eguisheim, or other villages and sights.

Towns are most alive during their weekly morning (until noon) farmers markets (Mon—Kaysersberg; Tue—Munster; Fri—Turckheim; Sat—Ribeauvillé and Colmar). Riquewihr and Eguisheim have no market days.

ALSACE

Getting Around the Route du Vin

By Car: A good regional map is helpful. To reach the Route du Vin north of Colmar, leave Colmar following signs to *Ingersheim* and continue to its center and join D-10 north to Sigolsheim, Bennwihr (Kaysersberg is a short detour from here), Riquewihr, Hunawihr, Ribeauvillé, and Château du Haut-Kœnigsbourg. Look for *Route du Vin* signs. For Eguisheim (south of Colmar), leave Colmar on D-83 toward Belfort.

Drivers can use some of the scenic wine service lanes known as *sentiers viticoles*—provided they drive at a snail's pace. I've recommended my favorite segments.

By Train: The only Route du Vin village accessible by train from Colmar is lovely little Turckheim (2/hour, 10 minutes). This is by far your easiest option for visiting a village outside Colmar.

By Bus: Several bus companies connect Colmar with villages along the Route du Vin (except on Sun, when there are none), but deciphering schedules and locating bus stops in Colmar is a challenge. Before setting out, be clear about bus schedules and stop locations by asking at any TI, or try these bus company websites: www.l-k.fr (French only), www.kunegel.fr/en (in English), and www.royer-voyages.fr (French only). When reading schedules, note that *année* means the bus runs all year on days listed, *vac* (for *vacances*) means it runs only during summer vacation, and *scol* (for *scolaire*) means buses run only on school days.

All buses to Route du Vin villages stop at Colmar's train station (shelters to the right as you face the station, though bus numbers may not be posted—ask any driver); some also serve the Théâtre stop in the town center (behind the Unterlinden Museum), and a few leave from Place Scheurer-Kestner, a giant parking lot two blocks north of the museum (verify stops at TI). Some towns (including Eguisheim and Kaysersberg) are served by more than one company, which can use different bus stops.

Kaysersberg has reasonable service (Kunegel bus #145 from Théâtre stop, same stop as Trace bus #25, direction: Le Bonhomme, 7/day, 25 minutes). **Riquewihr, Hunawihr,** and **Ribeauvillé** have decent service (bus #106, direction: Illhaeusern, 6/day). You can also get to Ribeauvillé on Kunegel bus #109 (direction: St-Hippolyte). Buses #106 and #109 leave from the train station or Place Scheurer-Kestner (6/day in summer, otherwise 10/day, 30-45 minutes, big midday service gaps in summer). Service to **Eguisheim** is minimal—look for bus #208 to Herrlisheim (4/day, 15 minutes, leaves from train station or Théâtre stop) or Trace bus #208 to Obermorschwihr/Herrlisheim (4/day, 30 minutes, leaves from station, Théâtre stop, same stop as Trace bus #26, or Place Scheurer-Kestner). There's also a shuttle bus to **Château du Haut-Kœnigsbourg** (explained on page 1042). Schedules may be posted

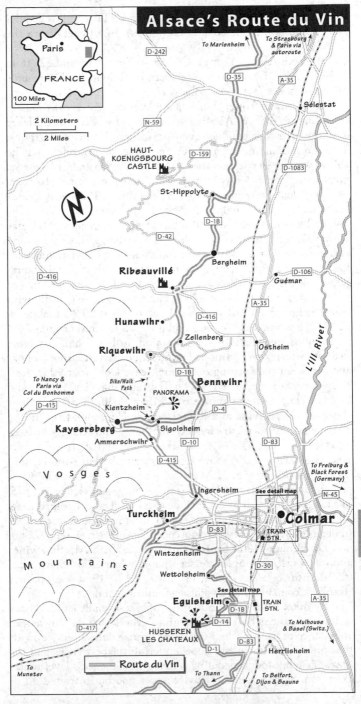

ALSACE

where buses stop—though don't count on it (TI has all schedules and can pinpoint stop locations for you). Buy tickets from the driver (€2-4 one-way).

By Taxi: Allow €12 from Colmar to Eguisheim and €25 from Colmar or Eguisheim to Kaysersberg or Riquewihr. For recommendations, see "Taxis" on page 1017.

By Minivan Tour: Jean-Claude Werner, who speaks impeccable English with an Alsatian accent, runs **Les Circuits d'Alsace** day trips in a comfortable seven-person minivan (small groups: 2-person minimum, larger groups possible, solo travelers may be able to squeeze in with another group, in English and/or Japanese, great sound system on comfy air-conditioned minibus). His tours usually include a few enjoyable, short vineyard walks. Jean-Claude's enthusiasm and personal touches add to the experience. Wine tastings and gourmet excursions can be arranged on request. Half-day tours visit three towns—generally Kaysersberg, Turckheim, and either Riquewihr or Eguisheim (€60/person). Full-day tours for €118 per person add a couple more towns and Haut-Kœnigsbourg (5 percent discount if booked 2 weeks ahead, must show current edition of this book, castle admission extra, reserve directly with Jean-Claude, pick-up at your hotel, tel. 03 89 41 90 88, mobile 06 72 37 17 11, www.alsace-travel.com, info@alsace-travel.com).

Regioscope is another good option (full- and half-day tours in 8- or 15-seat, air-conditioned minivans, departures from Colmar and Strasbourg). Morning departures leave Colmar at 9:15; afternoon departures leave at 13:45 on Tuesday, Thursday, Friday, and Sunday. Half-day trips return by 12:15 or 18:30. In the mornings they go to Ribeauvillé and Kaysersberg (€47/person); then, in the afternoons, they head to Haut-Kœnigsbourg and Riquewihr (€55, includes wine-tasting, €98 for both morning and afternoon tours). Excursions from Strasbourg depart every day but Monday and include a morning tour of Mont Sainte-Odile and Obernai (€50), and an afternoon visit of Haut-Kœnigsbourg and Riquewihr (€75; or €120 for both). All prices include entrance fees and guided tours of the castles. In December, ask about Christmas Market excursions (mobile 06 88 21 27 15, www.regioscope.com, info@regioscope.com).

Dutchman Pieter Smits is passionate about Alsatian wines and offers tasting tours to lesser-known wineries at honest rates (€59-125 for one-day tours, tel. 06 72 12 03 19, www.wijntoer -frankrijk.com, jolisoleil@wijntoer-frankrijk.com).

By Bike: With over 2,500 miles of bike-friendly lanes, Alsace is among France's best biking regions. The Route du Vin has an abundance of well-marked trails and *sentier viticole* service roads that run up and down the slopes, offering the best views and the fewest cars but tough pedaling—though more or less level routes exist, too. Start by getting advice and a good map from a TI or from where you're renting your bike.

Bikers can rent in Eguisheim, Sigolsheim (near Kaysersberg), or Ribeauvillé (I've listed rental options for each). Riding round-trip between Ribeauvillé and Kaysersberg via Hunawihr and Riquewihr along the upper *sentier viticole* yields sensational views but dang hilly terrain (you can reduce some of the climbing by following lower wine-service lanes; details provided later). The ride from Eguisheim to Turckheim is level, and makes a nice loop.

On Foot: Hikers can stroll along *sentier viticole* service roads and paths (explained above) into vineyards from each town on short loop trails (each TI has brochures), or connect the villages on longer walks. Consider taking a bus or taxi from Colmar to one village and hiking to another, then taking a bus or taxi back to Colmar (Ribeauvillé and Riquewihr, or Kaysersberg and Riquewihr make good combinations—see details later in this chapter). Hikers can also climb high to the ruined castles of the Vosges Mountains (Eguisheim and Ribeauvillé are good bases).

Route du Vin Wines

Most Route du Vin towns have wineries that give tours (some charge a fee), and scores of small producers open their courtyards with free and fun tastings (remember, it's polite to buy a bottle or two if you like the wines). The modern cooperatives at Eguisheim, Bennwihr, Hunawihr, and Ribeauvillé, created after the destruction of World War II, provide a good look at modern and efficient methods of production. Before you set off, review "French Wine-Tasting 101" (page 46).

Learn to recognize the basic grapes and wines of this region.

The simplest wines are blended from several grapes and usually called **Edelzwicker.** Despite being cheapest, these wines can be delicious and offer very good value.

Here are the key grapes to look for:

Riesling is the king of Alsatian grapes. It's more robust than Sylvaner, but drier than the German style you're probably used to. The name comes from the German word that describes its slightly smoky smell, with a note of *goût petrol* ("gasoline taste").

Sylvaner—fresh and light, fruity and cheap—is a good wine for a hot day.

Pinot Gris was called Tokay d'Alsace until recently, when the term was banned to avoid confusion with Tokaji wines in Hungary (where these grapes originated). Still, producers in Alsace call their wines Tokay Pinot Gris. These are more full-bodied, spicier, and distinctly different from other Pinot Gris wines you may have tried.

Muscat is best as a before-dinner wine. Compared with other French muscat wines, the Alsatian version is very dry, usually with a strong floral taste.

Gewürztraminer is "the lady's wine"—its bouquet is like a rosebush, its taste is fruity, and its aftertaste is spicy—as its name implies (*gewürtz* means "spice" in German). Drink this with pâtés and local cheeses.

Pinot Noir, the local red wine, is very light and fruity—if you want a red wine with body, look beyond Alsace. Pinot Noir is generally served chilled.

Crémant d'Alsace, the Alsatian sparkling wine, is very good—and much cheaper than Champagne.

You'll also see *eaux-de-vie,* powerful fruit-flavored brandies—try the *framboise* (raspberry) flavor.

In case you really get "Alsauced," the French term for headache is *mal à la tête.*

Sights Along the Route du Vin

These sights are listed from south to north, in the order you'll encounter them if you're heading north out of Colmar. The exception is the Vieil-Armand WWI Memorial, which is to the south of Colmar.

Eguisheim—This is the most appealing village of the region (described on page 1042).

Turckheim—With a charming square and a garden-filled moat, this quiet town is refreshingly untouristy, just enough off the beaten path to be overlooked. WWII buffs appreciate its **"Colmar Pocket" museum,** chronicling the American push to take Alsace from the Nazis (minimal English information but eager-to-help staff; mid-April-mid-Oct Wed-Sat 14:00-18:00, Sun 10:00-12:00 & 14:00-18:00, closed Mon-Tue except July-Sept 14:00-18:00; closed mid-Oct-mid-April, tel. 03 89 80 86 66, http://musee .turckheim-alsace.com).

Kaysersberg—This town has WWII sights, Dr. Albert Schweitzer's house, and plenty of hiking opportunities (described on page 1047).

Bennwihr—After this town was completely destroyed during World War II, the only object left standing was the statue of two girls depicting Alsace and Lorraine (outside the very modern church). The war memorials next to the statue list the names of those who died in both world wars. During World War II, 130,000 Alsatian men aged 17-37 were forced into military service under the German army (after fighting against them); most were sent to the deadly Russian front.

Riquewihr—This adorable town is the most touristed on the Route du Vin and can feel claustrophobic (described on page 1051).

Zellenberg—This place has an impressive setting and is worth a quick stop for the views from either side of its narrow perch.

Hunawihr—This bit of wine-soaked Alsatian cuteness is far less visited than its more famous neighbors, and features a 16th-century fortified church that today is shared by both Catholics and Protestants (the Catholics are buried next to the church; the Protestants are buried outside the church wall). Park at the village washbasin *(lavoir)* and follow the trail up to the church, then loop back through the village. Kids enjoy Hunawihr's small park, **Parc des Cigognes,** where they'll spot otters, over 150 storks, and more (€9, kids-€6, April-Oct daily 10:00-12:30 & 14:00-18:00, no midday closing June-Aug, until 17:00 mid-March-April and Oct-mid-Nov, closed mid-Nov-mid-March, other animals take part in the afternoon shows, tel. 03 89 73 72 62, www.cigogne-loutre.com). A nearby **butterfly exhibit** (Le Jardin des Papillons) houses thousands of the delicate insects from around the world (€7.50, kids-€5, includes audioguide, Easter-Oct daily 10:00-18:00, closed Nov-Easter, tel. 03 89 73 33 33, www.jardinsdespapillons.fr).

Ribeauvillé—This pleasant town, less visited by Americans, is well situated for hiking and biking. It's a linear place with a long pedestrian street (Grande Rue) and feels a tad less tourist-dependent than other towns. A steep but manageable trail leads from the top of the town into the Vosges Mountains, to three castle ruins, and is ideal for hikers wanting a walk in the woods to sweeping views. Follow Grand Rue uphill to the Hôtel aux Trois Châteaux and find the cobbled lane leading up from there. St. Ulrich is the most interesting of the three ruins (allow 2 hours round-trip, or 3 hours to see all three castles, or just climb 10 minutes for a view over the town—get info at TI at 1 Grand Rue, tel. 03 89 73 23 23, www.ribeauville-riquewihr.com). It's a short, sweet, and hilly bike loop from Ribeauvillé to Hunawihr and Riquewihr (can be extended to Kaysersberg if time and energy permit). You can rent a **bike** at Cycles Binder (82 Grand Rue, tel. 03 89 73 65 87) or Ribo Cycles (17 Rue de Landau, tel. 03 89 73 72 94, ribocycles@wanadoo.fr).

▲**Château du Haut-Kœnigsbourg**—This granddaddy of Alsatian castles, strategically situated on a rocky spur 2,500 feet above the flat Rhine plain, protected the passage between Alsace and Lorraine for centuries and provides remarkable insight into the 15th-century mountain fortresses of the Alsace region. The castle's pink stones were quarried from the Vosges Mountains. Rebuilt in the early 20th century, the well-furnished castle

ALSACE

highlights Germanic influence in Alsatian history with decorations that illustrate castle life from the 15th through 17th centuries. There's little English, so you'll want the informative one-hour audioguide, or better, take the English-language guided tour offered daily at 11:45.

Cost and Hours: €8, under 18 free, audioguide-€4, ticket booth open daily June-Aug 9:15-18:00, April-May and Sept 9:15-17:15, March and Oct 9:30-17:00, Nov-Feb 9:30-12:00 & 13:00-16:30, castle closes 45 minutes after ticket booth, about 15 minutes north of Ribeauvillé above St-Hippolyte, tel. 03 69 33 25 00, www.haut-koenigsbourg.fr.

Getting There: A €4 shuttle bus runs here from the Sélestat train station (10/day April 6-May 8 and June 16-Sept 16, weekends only rest of year except none Jan-mid-March, 30 minutes, timed with trains, call château for schedule or check website). Your shuttle ticket saves you €2 on the château entry fee.

Vieil-Armand WWI Memorial (Hartmannswillerkopf)—This powerful memorial evokes the slaughter of the Western Front in World War I, when Germany and France bashed heads for years in a war of attrition. It's up a windy road above Cernay (20 miles south of Colmar). From the parking lot, walk 10 minutes to the vast cemetery, and walk 30 more minutes through trenches to a hilltop with a grand Alsatian view. Here you'll find a stirring memorial statue of French soldiers storming the trenches in 1915-1916, facing near-certain death.

Eguisheim

Just a few miles south of Colmar's suburbs, this circular, flower-festooned little wine town (pop. 1,600) is overlooked by most tourists. Eguisheim ("ay-gush-I'm") is ideal for a relaxing lunch and vineyard walks, and makes a good small-town base for exploring Alsace. It's a cinch by car (easy parking) and manageable by bike (see "Getting Around the Route du Vin—By Bike," earlier), but barely accessible by bus. Consider taking the bus one way and taxi the other to Colmar or other villages (bus schedules available at TIs and posted at key stops). Eguisheim's stop is at the lower end of the village, near the post office.

Orientation to Eguisheim

The helpful **TI** has free Wi-Fi and information on accommodations, festivals, vineyard walks, and Vosges mountain hikes (Mon-Fri 9:30-12:00 & 14:00-18:00, Sat 9:30-12:00 & 13:30-17:30, closed Sun, 22 Grand Rue, tel. 03 89 23 40 33, www.ot-eguisheim.fr). They're happy to call a taxi for you (about €12 to Colmar).

Winemaker Jean-Luc Meyer has **bikes for rent** (€6/4 hours, €12/day, daily 8:30-12:00 & 13:30-19:00, 4 Rue des Trois Châteaux, tel. 03 89 24 53 66).

Public WCs are located in the lower pay parking lot, and automatic WC cabins are a few steps from the fountain on Place du Château St. Léon IX, in a courtyard off Cours Unterlinden (hidden on the right; €0.20).

Self-Guided Walk

Welcome to Eguisheim

Although Eguisheim's defensive wall is gone, the Rue des Remparts (Nord and Sud) survives, scenically circling the village. The main drag, Grand Rue, bisects the circle leading to a town square that's as darling as a Grimm fairy tale.

Start your visit at the bottom of town (near the TI) and circle the ramparts clockwise, walking up Rue du Rempart Sud. The most enchanting and higgledy-piggledy view in town is right at the start of the loop (at the tight Y in the road; go left and uphill). Rue du Rempart Sud is more picturesque than Rue du Rempart Nord, but I'd walk the entire circle. You'll see that what was once the moat is now lined with 13th- to 17th-century houses—a cancan of half-timbered charm. You're actually walking a lane between the back of fine homes (on the left) and their barns (on the right). Look for emblems of daily life, religious and magical symbols, dates on lintel stones, and so on. (The government pays 15 percent of the cost of any work locals do on their exteriors.) The loop takes a decidedly hip turn along its northern half, as you pass an art gallery, a cool coffee shop, and a trendy bar.

When you've finished the loop, walk up Grand Rue to Eguisheim's main square, **Place du Château St. Léon IX,** and lose all sense of discipline sampling the shops, cafés, and fruits of the local vine. This square, lined with fine Renaissance houses, marks the heart of the old town. The mini-castle is privately owned and closed to the public. Surviving bits of its 13th-century, eight-sided wall circle the chapel, built in Neo-Romanesque style on the site

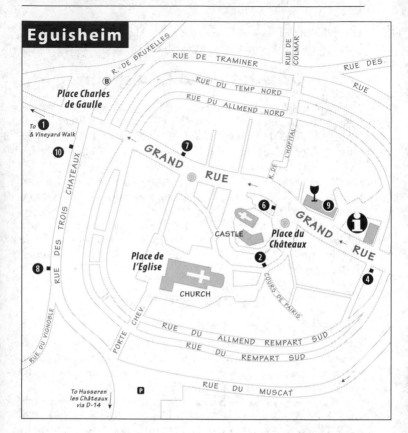

of the castle's keep in 1895. Although it is of little historic importance, it's worth a peek to see how a Romanesque chapel may have been painted (drop any coin into the €0.50 box for light). The 19th-century fountain sports a statue of St. Leo IX (1048-1054), the only Alsatian pope. Eguisheim's most famous son was a saint, to boot.

Exploring the town, you may come upon some of its 20 "tithe courtyards." Farmers who worked on land owned by the church used to come to these courtyards to pay their tithes (10 percent of their production). With so many of these courtyards, it's safe to conclude that the farming around here was excellent.

Sights in Eguisheim

Wine-Tasting—Don't leave without visiting one of Eguisheim's countless cozy wineries. The ambience and quality of wines at **Emile Beyer** is great. Enter through their Old World courtyard on Cours Unterlinden (one block from the TI) to find a welcoming counter and ample tables. Ask to visit their aromatic cellar

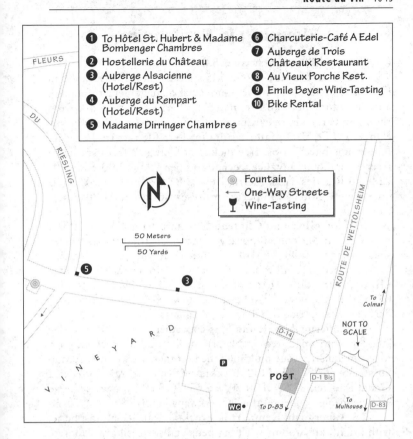

FLEURS

DU RIESLING

1 To Hôtel St. Hubert & Madame
Bombenger Chambres

2 Hostellerie du Château

3 Auberge Alsacienne
(Hotel/Rest)

4 Auberge du Rempart
(Hotel/Rest)

5 Madame Dirringer Chambres

6 Charcuterie-Café A Edel

7 Auberge de Trois
Châteaux Restaurant

8 Au Vieux Porche Rest.

9 Emile Beyer Wine-Tasting

10 Bike Rental

Fountain
One-Way Streets
Wine-Tasting

N

50 Meters
50 Yards

ROUTE DE WETTOLSHEIM

To
Colmar

VINEYARD

D-14

NOT TO
SCALE

P

POST

D-1 Bis

WC•   To D-83

To
Mulhouse   D-83

(from 1583), crammed with old wood vats. They're famous for their Rieslings, but all their wines are worth a taste ("free" tasting if you intend to buy a bottle or wines by the glass, daily in summer 10:00-19:00, shorter hours off-season, 7 Place du Château St. Léon IX, tel. 03 89 41 40 45).

Views over Eguisheim—If you have a car, follow signs up to *Husseren Les Cinq Châteaux*, then walk 20 minutes to the ruined castle towers for a good view of the Vosges Mountains above and vineyards below.

By mountain bike or on foot, find any path through the vineyards above Eguisheim for nice views (the TI has a free map). One option is to walk uphill on Grande Rue, cross the ring road leaving Eguisheim's town center, and turn left at the *Camping* arrow. Pass the campground, climb a small hill, and turn right onto the small road leading into the vineyards. From here, climb as high as you like. It's OK to walk on dirt paths between the vines. The five châteaux of Husseren float above. The TI's map shows a longer walk through the vineyards from the same starting point (signposted in English).

ALSACE

Sleeping in Eguisheim

(€1 = about $1.30, country code: 33)

$$$ Hôtel St. Hubert*** offers 15 spotless rooms with modern, German-hotelesque comfort (and strict management to match), and an indoor pool and sauna (€7). The 10-minute walk from the town center is rewarded with vineyards out your window (Db-€123, Tb-€140, family suite for four-€185, extra bed-€16, four rooms have patios, free pickup at Colmar's train station if reserved a day in advance, reception open 8:00-12:00 & 15:00-22:00, 6 Rue des Trois Pierres, tel. 03 89 41 40 50, fax 03 89 41 46 88, www.hotel-st-hubert.com, reservation@hotel-st-hubert.com).

$$ Hostellerie du Château*** is part art gallery and part hotel, providing contemporary comfort on the pleasant main square (standard Db-€75-110, Db suite with whirlpool tub-€120-135, extra bed-€20, all rooms with tubs, no air-con, Wi-Fi, garage €11/day, 2 Rue du Château St. Léon IX, tel. 03 89 23 72 00, fax 03 89 41 63 93, www.hostellerieduchateau.com, info@hostellerieduchateau.com, friendly Monsieur Wagner).

$$ Auberge Alsacienne*** is conveniently located near the bus stop, with small, reasonably priced, and traditionally designed rooms in a picturesque building. The best rooms are on the second floor (Db-€67-77, Tb-€100, breakfast-€9.50, parking-€3/day, 12 Grand Rue, tel. 03 89 41 50 20, fax 03 89 23 89 32, www.auberge-alsacienne.net, auberge-alsacienne@wanadoo.fr).

$$ Auberge du Rempart is a rockin' deal. It's atmospheric, with bright, airy rooms with big beds and surprisingly elaborate decor above a lively café/restaurant deep inside the town (standard Db-€54, grand Db-€72-95; great family suite-€120 for 4 people, €140 for 6; Wi-Fi, near TI at 3 Rue du Rempart Sud, tel. 03 89 41 16 87, fax 03 89 41 06 50, www.auberge-du-rempart.com, auberge-du-rempart@wanadoo.fr). The reception desk is in the restaurant and is usually open only during lunch and after 18:00.

Chambres d'Hôtes

Please remember to cancel if you reserve a room and can't use it.

$ Madame Dirringer rents four traditional, spotless rooms facing an atmospheric courtyard. She speaks no English, but is a creative communicator (Db-€40, good family room, breakfast-€6, cash only, 11 Rue du Riesling, tel. 03 89 41 71 87).

$ Madame Bombenger is sweet, speaks some English, and has a modern, graceful home just above Eguisheim with three rooms and nice views into the vineyards and over town (Sb-€37, Db-€46, €2 less for more than one night, includes breakfast, across from Hôtel St. Hubert at 3 Rue des Trois Pierres, tel. & fax

03 89 23 71 19, mobile 06 61 94 31 09, bombenger.marie-therese @wanadoo.fr).

Eating in Eguisheim

Charcuterie-Café A Edel, on Place du Château St. Léon IX, has killer quiche "to go" and everything you need for a fun picnic, including small tubs of chopped veggies (daily until 19:00, Mon-Fri closes 12:30-14:00 unless very busy). You can picnic by the fountain, or eat at their adjacent restaurant while listening to the trickling of the square's fountain (restaurant open Wed-Mon until 18:00, closed Tue, €9-12 *tartes flambées* and quiche, 2 Place du Château St. Léon IX, tel. 03 89 41 22 40).

Auberge de Trois Châteaux is very Alsatian, with cozy ambience and traditional cuisine (*menus* from €19 and affordable *plats du jour,* closed Tue at lunch and all day Wed, 26 Grand Rue, tel. 03 89 23 70 61).

Auberge Alsacienne offers regional cuisine in a more refined setting, and has outside seating (€16 two-course *menu,* €23-30 three-course *menu,* closed Sun evening and all day Mon, 12 Grand Rue, tel. 03 89 41 50 20).

Auberge du Rempart is best for outdoor dining in a pleasant courtyard around a big fountain. Come here for less expensive and lighter meals and, if you're in town on a summer weekend, good *tartes flambées* (€9-17 *plats,* closed Sun-Mon and sometimes Thu evenings Sept-June, 3 Rue du Rempart Sud, near TI, tel. 03 89 41 16 87).

Au Vieux Porche is a wood-beamed, white-tablecloth affair, ideal for a leisurely meal or a special occasion (*menus* from €26, closed Tue-Wed, upper end of town at 16 Rue des Trois Châteaux, tel. 03 89 24 01 90).

Kaysersberg

For much of history, Kaysersberg ("Emperor's Mountain") was of strategic importance, thanks to its location guarding the important route over the Vosges Mountains that links Colmar with the big city of Nancy. Today, philosopher-physician Albert Schweitzer's hometown offers a cute jumble of 15th-century homes under a romantically ruined castle with easy vineyard trails at its doorstep, and plenty of tourists. Reasonable bus

ALSACE

service from Colmar makes Kaysersberg a worthwhile day trip (7-10/day, 30-40 minutes).

Orientation to Kaysersberg

Tourist Information: The TI is two blocks from the town's main entry, inside the Hôtel de Ville at 39 Rue du Général de Gaulle (mid-June–mid-Sept Mon-Sat 9:00-12:30 & 14:00-18:00, Sun 10:00-12:30; mid-Sept–mid-June Mon-Sat 10:00-12:00 & 14:00-17:30, closed Sun; tel. 03 89 78 22 78, www.kaysersberg.com, WCs out the door to left under arch). The TI has free Internet access and rents iPod audioguides for touring Kaysersberg (€5, €150 deposit, allow 1-1.5 hours). Pick up the town map, the free *Sentier Viticole* bike map, bus schedules, and detailed descriptions of hiking trails between wine villages (€0.50; see "Walking/Biking Trails from Kaysersberg," later).

Getting Around: Most buses to Colmar use the Rocade Verte stop at a parking lot on the village's south side, just outside the town walls.

Services: You can rent **bikes** at the Boutique Coup de Cœur, near the 16th-century bridge (105 Rue du Général de Gaulle, tel. 03 89 78 14 28 or mobile 06 07 94 92 18) or nearby in Sigolsheim at La Pommeraie (daily 9:00-19:00, tel. 03 89 78 25 66). Find **WCs** at the top of town, across from the Schweitzer Museum.

Sights in Kaysersberg

Exploring Kaysersberg—Strolling through Kaysersberg is a treat. The town's main drag is lined with tempting bakeries and colorful shops, and cross-streets merit exploration. There's no shortage of bakeries selling tasty pretzels and *kugelhopf,* among other goodies. Here's a rundown of worthwhile places you'll pass, starting at the TI:

ALSACE

The **Caveau des Vignerons de Kaysersberg** represents 150 winemakers from around Kaysersberg, including several Grands Crus, and offers free and easy wine tastings with experts who speak "a leetl" English (Wed-Mon 10:00-12:00 & 14:00-18:00 except 10:00-19:00 in summer, closed Tue year-round, near TI at 20 Rue du Général de Gaulle, tel. 03 89 47 18 43).

Kaysersberg is known for its blown glass, and at the nice **Verrerie d'Art de Kaysersberg** you can see glassblowers at work (Tue-Sat 10:00-12:30 & 14:00-18:00, Mon

Albert Schweitzer
(1875-1965)

I don't know what your destiny will be, but one thing I do know: The only ones among you who will be really happy are those who have sought and found how to serve.

—Albert Schweitzer

Albert Schweitzer—theologian, musician, philosopher, and physician—was an unusually gifted individual who never hesitated to question accepted beliefs and practices. He is probably most famous for his work with sufferers of leprosy and tuberculosis in Africa.

Born to German parents in 1875 in Kaysersberg, he studied philosophy and theology at the University of Strasbourg, eventually becoming a pastor at his church. Not satisfied with that, Schweitzer studied music and soon gained fame as a musical scholar and organist. After trying his hand at writing with *The Quest of the Historical Jesus,* which challenged contemporary secular views of Jesus, he shifted his attention to medicine. After he married Helene Bresslau, the couple left for Africa and founded a missionary hospital in Gabon (then called Lambaréné). During World War I, Schweitzer and his wife were forced by the French to leave Africa.

After the war, Schweitzer returned to Gabon on his own, where he remained for most of the rest of his life. He received the 1952 Nobel Peace Prize for his service to humanity, particularly for founding the Albert Schweitzer Hospital in Gabon, where he died in 1965. He was 90 years old.

14:00-18:00, shop—but not workshop—also open Sun 14:00-18:00, near church at 30 Rue du Général de Gaulle, tel. 03 89 47 14 97).

The town's main sight is the medieval **St. Croix Church.** Read the pink information plaque opposite the entrance, then enter the dark interior. After your eyes adjust, study the unusual crucifix hanging high above (the church is dedicated to the Holy Cross). Next, focus on the sensational 1518 altarpiece—push the button on the right of the altar for light. The 14 brilliantly carved wood panels retrace the Passion of Christ, with Saint Christopher overseeing the event from on top (free, daily 9:00-18:00, sometimes open later and during lunch).

The courtyard at the **Musée Historique** (#66) has tables with fine ambience and reasonably priced meals. Just before the bridge, in the red house on the corner, find **Vieux Potier,** the only real potter still working in Kaysersberg—a must for pottery lovers and nostalgic types (3 Rue des Forgerons, tel. 03 89 72 87 40).

You'll eventually land on the town's beautiful **16th-century**

ALSACE

bridge. As the Nazis were preparing to evacuate, they planned to destroy the bridge. Locals reasoned with the commander, agreeing to dig an anti-tank ditch just beyond the bridge—and the symbol of the town was saved. (You can rent bikes at the Boutique Coup de Cœur, just after the bridge.)

At the top end of town, you'll come to **Dr. Albert Schweitzer's house,** a small and disappointing museum. It has two rooms of scattered photos and artifacts from his time in Africa, with some English information (€2, Easter-Oct daily 9:00-12:00 & 14:00-18:00, closed Nov-Easter, 126 Rue du Général de Gaulle). The square across the street (Place Gouraud) hosts a thriving market each Monday until noon and has public WCs.

Walking/Biking Trails from Kaysersberg—Trails start just outside the TI (get details at the TI). To find the main trail, turn left out of the TI and walk under the arch. A left on the trail leads up to the ruined **castle** (free, always open, fine views and benches, 113 steps up a dark stairway to the tower). Hikers can continue past the castle for more views and trails (TI has detailed map for €0.50, including the long route to **Riquewihr**—2.5 hours). For more great views of Kaysersberg, follow the trail described next (toward Kientzheim) for about 10 minutes.

For an easier 1.5-2-hour hike—or 40-minute bike ride—along a paved lane over vine-covered hills to Riquewihr, turn right on the main trail back down by the TI. You'll start on a bike path *(piste cyclable)* to **Kientzheim** (well-marked with bike icons). In Kientzheim, follow the *sentier viticole* route uphill along service roads past gorgeous views and vineyards to Riquewihr. If you get turned around, stop any biker or vineyard worker and ask, *"à Riquewihr?"* (ah reek-veer?)

Drivers can follow the same signs from Kientzheim to Riquewihr, but must be careful of bikers.

World War II Sights—The towns in this area with gray rather than red-tiled roofs were entirely destroyed during World War II, then rebuilt. Kientzheim has an American-made tank parked in its front yard (and a wine museum in its castle grounds). In 2004, the refreshing network of tiny streams trickling down its streets (standard before World War II) was restored. Both Sigolsheim (scene of fierce fighting—note its sterile, rebuilt Romanesque church) and Bennwihr are modern, as they were taken and lost a dozen times by the Allies and Nazis, and completely ruined.

The hill just north of Kayserberg is soaked in WWII blood and is still called "Bloody Hill," as it was nicknamed by German troops. Between its cemeteries, you'll find some of the best vines on the Route du Vin.

A **WWII Monument** stands atop Bloody Hill. The spectacular setting, best at sunset, houses a monument to the American divisions that helped liberate Alsace in World War II (find the American flag). Up the lane, a beautiful cemetery is the final resting place of 1,600 men who fought in the French army (many gravestones are Muslim, for soldiers from France's North African colonies—Morocco, Algeria, and Tunisia). From this brilliant viewpoint you can survey the entire southern section of the Route du Vin and into Germany. The castle hanging high to the north is the Château du Haut-Kœnigsbourg (described later). The road to the memorial leaves from the center of Sigolsheim (follow *Necropole* and *Cimitière* signs turning at Pierre Sparr winery, then keep straight and climb into the vineyards).

Riquewihr

This little village, wrapped in vineyards, is so picturesque today because it was so rich centuries ago. You can recognize its old wealth because it has the most stone houses of any place in Alsace. The circular village is crammed with shops, cafés, galleries, cobblestones, and flowers. Arrive early to experience an almost-peaceful Riquewihr, or sharpen your elbows if you arrive later in the day.

Orientation to Riquewihr

Buses drop you off at the lower end of the village, opposite the post office (drivers can park nearby for €2). Enter the town under the Hôtel de Ville; the main drag runs uphill from here. The **TI** is halfway up at 2 Rue de la 1ère Armée (mid-April-Sept and Dec Mon-Sat 9:30-12:00 & 14:00-18:00, Sun 10:00-13:00; Jan-mid-April and Oct-Nov Mon-Sat 10:00-12:00 & 14:00-17:00, closed Sun and every other Sat; tel. 03 89 73 23 23, www.ribeauville -riquewihr.com). A good WC is behind the TI. Quieter lanes lead off the main drag. For a taxi, call 03 89 73 73 71.

Sights in Riquewihr

Riquewihr Town—Within a few yards of the town entry, you'll see the **tourist train** (€6.50, next departure time posted, 30 minutes, recorded tour through vineyards). Next up, try the excellent, free wine-tasting at **Caves Dopff et Irion** (€7-10 bottles, just uphill from Hôtel de Ville, April-mid-Nov daily 10:00-19:00, mid-Nov-March weekends only, tel. 03 89 47 94 40). The **Musée de la Communication,** a block away (at the town's château), does a good job illustrating the evolution of man's ability to send messages, from mail delivery to mobile phones (€4.50, English brochure, April-Oct and Dec daily 10:00-17:30, closed Nov and Jan-March).

    Walking up the main street, you'll pass several **courtyard**

ALSACE

cafés with tempting tables. Two levels of nonstop holiday cheer await you at the **Käthe Wohlfahrt** shop, where Christmas comes alive even in July (daily 10:00-12:30 & 13:45-18:30, near the top of town at 1 Rue du Cerf). Just beyond, find one of the best **bell towers** in the region (Le Dolder, built in 1291). Look for the engraving of 13th-century Riquewihr by the fountain opposite the tower's entry. The steep-stepped **Dolder Museum,** inside the tower, has small rooms covering its history—but doesn't merit the climb (€3, €5 with Tour des Voleurs, July-Aug daily 14:00-18:00, Sept-Oct and mid-April-June weekends only, closed Nov-mid-April). The nearby **Tour des Voleurs** has a small museum of torture (€3, €5 with Dolder Museum, same hours).

Pass under the bell tower, take a left on Rue des Remparts, and stroll the picturesque lane. Turn right when you see steps down to the moat (and the big wine press), and double back to the top of the town along the moat. Notice how homes were built right into the defensive walls.

Scenic Walk, Ride, or Drive from Riquewihr—The *sentier viticole* lane to Kientzheim (then Kaysersberg) leads north from the TI out Rue de la 1ère Armée, climbs above Riquewihr, then drops into Kientzheim—and delivers beautiful views all the way. Leave town and follow blue signs to *Kientzheim* for a beautiful walk or ride (allow 1.5-2 hours to hike all the way to Kaysersberg). Drivers can follow the same route and get the same great views, but go slow and watch out for bikers.

Strasbourg

Strasbourg is urban Alsace at its best—it feels like a giant Colmar with rivers and streetcars. It's a progressive, livable city, with generous space devoted to pedestrians, scads of bikes, mod trams, meandering waterways, and a young, lively mix of university students, Eurocrats, and street people. This place has an Amsterdam-like feel. Situated just west of the Rhine River, Strasbourg  provides the ultimate blend of Franco-Germanic culture, architecture, and ambience. A living symbol of the hope for perpetual peace between France and Germany, Strasbourg was selected as home to the European Parliament, the European Council (sharing administrative responsibilities for the European Union with Brussels, Belgium), and the European Court of Human Rights.

ALSACE

Planning Your Time

Strasbourg makes a good day trip from Colmar. And, thanks to high-speed TGV-train service, it also makes a handy stop for train travelers en route to or from Paris (baggage storage available). None of its museums is essential (though the Alsatian Museum comes close)—you're here to see the cathedral, wander the waterways, and take a bite out of the big city. Plan on three hours to hit the highlights, starting at Strasbourg's dazzling cathedral (arrive in Strasbourg by 10:30 so you can comfortably make the noon cathedral clock performance) and ending with the district called La Petite France (ideally for lunch).

Orientation to Strasbourg

Tourist Information

Strasbourg's main TI faces the cathedral (daily 9:00-19:00, 17 Place de la Cathédrale, tel. 03 88 52 28 28, www.otstrasbourg.fr, info @otstrasbourg.fr). Another TI is in the train station's south hall (across from the station's *accueil* office, same hours, sells day passes for the tram). Buy the €1 city map, which describes a decent walking tour in English, or pay €5.50 to rent an audioguide that covers the cathedral and old city in more detail than most need (available only at the main TI, includes a cute little map of the route, allow 1.5 hours). The TI also has bike maps for the city (€1 with English explanations) and surrounding areas.

The Strasbourg Pass (€14, kids-€7), valid three days, is a good value for travelers wanting to do it all. It includes one free museum entry and half-off coupons for others, a discount on the town audioguide, a free half-day bike rental, the boat cruise, and free entry to the cathedral narthex view and the astrological clock tour.

Arrival in Strasbourg

By Train: TGV trains serve Strasbourg's gleaming train station. Baggage storage is available at platform 1 (€5.50-8, daily 6:15-21:15, allow time for its airport-type security screening). WCs are across from the stairs to platform 2, and a helpful TI is in the station's south *(sud)* hall, across from the *accueil* office. Rental bikes are available in the lower level of the glass atrium (see "Helpful Hints," later), and you'll find many budget eating options.

To **walk** to the cathedral in 15 urban minutes, go straight out of the station, cross the big square (Place de la Gare), and walk past Hôtel Vendôme and up Rue du Maire Kuss. Cross the river, and continue up serpentine, pedestrian-friendly Rue du 22 November all the way to Place Kléber. Angle a bit left into bustling Place Kléber (whose namesake graces the center of the

ALSACE

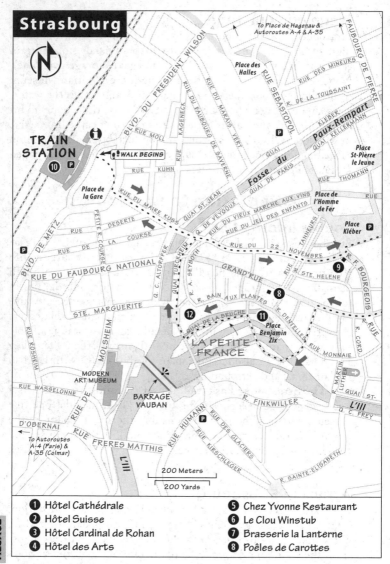

Strasbourg

N

TRAIN STATION ⑩ P

ℹ️

🚶 *WALK BEGINS*

Place de la Gare

To Place de Hagenau & Autoroutes A-4 & A-35

Place des Halles

RUE DES MINEURS

FAUBOURG DE PIERRE

RUE SEBASTOPOL

R. DE LA TOUSSAINT

BLVD. DU PRESIDENT WILSON

RUE DU FAUBOURG DE SAVERNE

RUE KAGENECK

RUE MOLL

RUE DU MARAIS VERT

RUE KUHN

Place St-Pierre le Jeune

KLÉBER

QUAI KELLERMANN

Paux-Rempart

RUE THOMANN

QUAI

Fosse du

QUAI DE PARIS

Place de l'Homme de Fer

Place Kléber P

RUE DU MAIRE KUSS

QUAI ST. JEAN

PETITE R. DESERTE

RUE DE METZ

RUE DE LA COURSE

BLVD. DE METZ

RUE DU FAUBOURG NATIONAL

PETITE R. COURSE

Q. DE VEYGOUX

RUE DU VIEUX MARCHE AUX VINS

RUE DU JEU DES ENFANTS

RUE DU 22 NOVEMBRE

TANNEURS

R. F. BOURGEOIS

⑨

Q. C. ALTORFFER

QUAI TUCKHEIM

R. A. SEYBOTH

GRAND-RUE

R. R. STE. HELENE

⑧

STE. MARGUERITE

R. BAIN AUX PLANTES

R. DENTELLES

RUE ROSHEIM

RUE DE MOLSHEIM

QUAI DE LA BRUCHE

LA PETITE FRANCE

⑫

⑪ Place Benjamin Zix

RUE MONNAIE

R. CORDI

R. MARTIN LUTHER

RUE WASSELONNE

MODERN ART MUSEUM

BARRAGE VAUBAN

R. FINKWILLER

L'ILL

QUAI ST-

Q. C. FREY

D'OBERNAI

RUE FRERES MATTHIS

RUE HUMANN

RUE DES GLACIERS

RUE KIRSCHLEGER

P

L'ILL

To Autoroutes A-4 (Paris) & A-35 (Colmar)

R. SAINTE-ELISABETH

200 Meters
200 Yards

① Hôtel Cathédrale
② Hôtel Suisse
③ Hôtel Cardinal de Rohan
④ Hôtel des Arts

⑤ Chez Yvonne Restaurant
⑥ Le Clou Winstub
⑦ Brasserie la Lanterne
⑧ Poêles de Carottes

ALSACE

square), maintaining the same direction, then turn right on the broad pedestrian street (Rue des Grandes Arcades). Turn left on Rue des Hallebardes (at *Concorde* sign on building), then follow that spire.

To get from the train station to the city center by **public transportation,** catch the caterpillar-like tram that leaves from under the station (buy €1.60 one-way ticket or €4 day pass from the station TI, or from machines on platforms—coins only, then

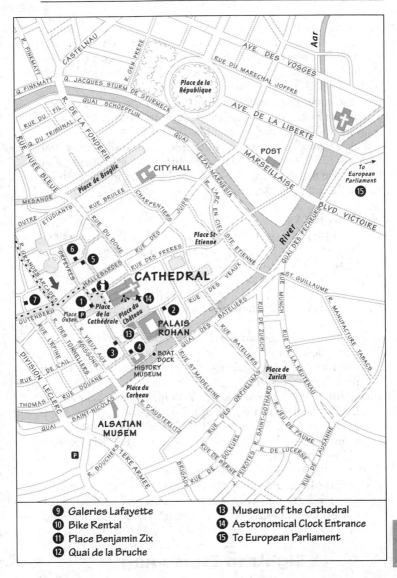

R. FINKMATT
CASTELNAU
Q. FINKMATT
Q. JACQUES STURM DE STURMECK
R. GEN FRERE
RUE DU MARECHAL JOFFRE
AVE DES VOSGES
Aar
Place de la République
QUAI SCHOEFFLIN
AVE DE LA LIBERTE
RUE DU FIL DE LA FONDERIE
RUE DU TRIBUNAL
RUE NUEE BLEUE
MESANGE
Place de Broglie
CITY HALL
POST
MARSEILLAISE
To European Parliament ⑮
OUTRE
ETUDIANTS
RUE BRULEE
RUE DU DOME
CHARPENTIERS
JUIFS
R. L'ARC EN CIEL
Place St-Etienne
BLVD VICTOIRE
River
QUAI LEZAY-MARNESIA
R. GRANDES ARCADES
ORFEVRES
⑥
⑤
HALLEBARDES
RUE DES FRERES
RUE DES
CATHEDRAL
RUE DE CIEL STE ETIENNE
QUAI DES PECHEURS
ST GUILLAUME
R. MUNCH
RUE DE ZURICH
R. MANUFACTURE TABACS
⑦
GUTENBERG
①
Place Guten.
Place de la Cathédrale
P
Place du Château
⑭
②
PALAIS ROHAN
RUE DES VEAUX
RUE DES BATELIERS
RUE DE ZURICH
RUE DE LA KRUTENAU
RUE DE L'EPINE
RUE VIEUX AUX POISSONS
⑬
⑬
④
③
RUE DES TONNELIERS
HISTORY MUSEUM
BOAT DOCK
QUAI DES BATELIERS
RUE ST MADELEINE
Place de Zurich
DIVISION LECLERC
RUE DE L'AIL
RUE DOUANE
Place du Corbeau
RUE DES ORFELINAS
THOMAS
SAINT-NICOLAS
QUAI
R. D'AUSTERLITZ
RUE SAINT-GOTHARD
R. JEU DE PAUME
ALSATIAN MUSEM
P
R. BOUCHERS 1ERE ARMEE
RUE DES
RUE DE SOLEURE
RUE DE BERNE
J. PEROLES
R. DE LUCERNE
R. DE LAUSANNE
BRIGADE

⑨ Galeries Lafayette
⑩ Bike Rental
⑪ Place Benjamin Zix
⑫ Quai de la Bruche
⑬ Museum of the Cathedral
⑭ Astronomical Clock Entrance
⑮ To European Parliament

ALSACE

validate in skinny machines). Take Tram #A (direction: Illkirch) or Tram #D (direction: Aristide Briand) three stops to Langross-Grande Rue, two blocks from the cathedral. (You can return to the station, Gare Centrale, from the same stop.)

By Car: You're better off day-tripping in by train. If you drive, you'll see signs on the autoroute for *P+R* (Parking & Relais) lots, which are located at tram stations outside the city center and make for easier driving and cheaper parking rates (€3.20/day includes round-trip tram tickets to the center; take tram in direction: Centre-Ville). To park safely in the center near the train station, follow *Gare Centrale* signs, then *Parking Aurélie* signs, then take the tram into the center (it's on Boulevard de Metz—to the right with your back to the station). To park even closer to the center (and encounter more traffic), follow *Centre-Ville/Cathédrale* signs and park at Place Gutenberg Parking (near the cathedral). Skip the train station's pricey underground lot (€3/hour).

By Plane: The user-friendly Strasbourg-Entzheim airport (tel. 03 88 64 67 67, www.strasbourg.aeroport.fr), with frequent, often inexpensive flights to Paris, is connected by train to the main rail station (€2.30, 10-minute trip).

Helpful Hints

Quiet Transportation: Beware of virtually silent trams and bicycles—look both ways before crossing streets. Bikes are allowed on pedestrian streets.

Internet Access: Several cybercafés lie on the main street into town from the station, Rue du Maire Kuss (or ask at the TI).

Car Rental: All major companies have offices at or across from the train station.

Post Office: It's at the cathedral (Mon-Fri 8:00-18:30, Sat 8:00-17:00, closed Sun).

Laundry: You'll find a handy launderette on Rue des Veaux, near my recommended hotels.

Bike Rental: You can rent bikes at **Vélhop,** one level below street level at the train station (€5/day, €150 deposit required, Mon-Fri 8:00-19:00, Sat-Sun 9:30-12:30 & 13:30-19:00; follow signs for *Parc à Vélo*, Place de la Gare; tel. 03 88 23 56 75, www .velhop.strasbourg.eu).

Taxi: Call 03 88 36 13 13 or 03 88 30 13 01.

Christmas Market: From the last Saturday of November until December 31, the city bustles and sparkles with its delightful Christkindelsmärik and all the extra visitors it draws (hotel rates climb).

ALSACE

Sights in Strasbourg

▲▲Strasbourg Cathedral (Cathédrale de Notre-Dame)

Stand in front of Hôtel de la Cathédrale and crane your neck up. If this church, with its cloud-piercing spire and pink sandstone color, wows you today, imagine its impact on medieval tourists. The delicate Gothic style of the cathedral (begun in 1176, not finished until 1429) is another Franco-German mixture that somehow survived the French Revolution, the Franco-Prussian War, World War I, and World War II.

Cost and Hours: Free, daily 7:00-11:15 & 12:45-19:00. The midday closing is for a special €2 viewing of the astronomical clock (described below).

Visiting the Cathedral: Before entering the cathedral, survey the scene. The **square** in front of the cathedral makes the ideal stage for street performers—it's like a medieval fair. This square was Roman 2,000 years ago. Then, as now, it was the center of activity.

The dark half-timbered building to your left, next to the TI, was the home of a wealthy merchant in the 16th century, and symbolizes the virtues of capitalism that Strasbourg has long revered (today it's a restaurant). Goods were sold under the ground-floor arches; owners lived above. Strasbourg made its medieval mark as a trading center, taking advantage of its position at the crossroads of Europe and its access to the important Rhine River to charge tolls for the movement of goods. Its robust economy allowed for the construction of this glorious cathedral. Strasbourg's location drew all kinds of people to the city (as it still does today), making it susceptible to new ideas. Martin Luther's theses were posted on the cathedral's main doors, and after the wars of religion, this cathedral was Protestant for more than 100 years. (Louis XIV returned it to Catholicism in 1621.) Strasbourg remains a tolerant city today.

The dark-red **stone** that differentiates this cathedral from other great Gothic churches in France is quarried from the northern part of the Vosges Mountains (compare it to the yellow stone of St. Martin's in Colmar). You'll see this stone on display in many other buildings as you tour Strasbourg.

As you enter the **cathedral,** notice the sculpture over the left portal (complacent, spear-toting Virtues getting revenge on those nasty Vices). Enter and walk down the center. English displays at a few locations give simple explanations of key aspects of the cathedral. The stained glass on the lower left windows shows various rulers of Strasbourg; the stained glass on your right depicts Bible stories. An exquisite, gold-leafed organ hangs above the second pillars. Pass the elaborately carved stone pulpit, then walk to the choir and stare at the stained-glass image of Mary; find the European Union flag at the top. Skip the short film about the cathedral that you'll see advertised in the right transept.

Inside the right transept is a high-tech, 15th-century **astronomical clock** (restored in 1883, English explanation below) that gives a ho-hum performance every 15 minutes (keep your eye on the little angel about 15 feet up, slightly left of center). The show is better on the half-hour (angel on the right) and best at 12:30 (everybody gets in the act, including a rooster and 12 apostles— for the 12 hours; this performance is viewable only with a special ticket, described next). The church is cleared out every day but Sunday between 11:15 and 12:45 for a special presentation of the clock. Visitors pay €2 to enter through the right side of the church as you face it (tickets also available from the souvenir stand inside by the clock). You'll see a 20-minute movie (with English subtitles) that explains the clock's workings, then witness the real event.

For €5 you can climb 332 steps to the **top of the narthex** for an amazing view (free first Sun of the month, access on right side of cathedral, daily April-Sept 9:00-19:15 except mid-June-Aug Fri-Sat sometimes until 21:15, Oct-March 10:00-17:15, last ascent 30 minutes before closing).

Nearby: Before leaving this area, investigate the network of small pedestrian streets that connect the cathedral with the huge Place Kléber (home to various outdoor markets, depending on the day of the week). Each street is named for the primary trade that took place there.

Museums near the Cathedral

These museums lie outside the cathedral's right transept and are interesting only for aficionados with particular interests or who have a full day in Strasbourg.

Cost and Hours: €6 for each museum, free for those under 18 and on the first Sun of the month; open Mon and Wed-Fri 12:00-18:00, Sat-Sun 10:00-18:00, closed Tue—except for Museum of the Cathedral, which is closed Mon but open Tue 12:00-18:00 (www.musees-strasbourg.org).

Palais Rohan—This stately palace houses three museums: the **Museum of Decorative Arts,** which feels like the Versailles of Strasbourg, with grand reception rooms, a king's bedroom (where Louis XV and Marie-Antoinette both slept), a big library, and rooms displaying ceramic dishes, ancient clocks, and more—borrow the English booklet; the **Museum of Fine Arts,** a small, well-displayed collection of paintings from Middle Ages to Baroque, some by artists you'll recognize; and the **Archaeological Museum,** the best of the three, with a stellar presentation of Alsatian civilization through the millennia (includes free audioguide).

Museum of the Cathedral (Musée de l'Oeuvre Notre-Dame)—This well-organized museum has plenty of artifacts from the cathedral.

Alsatian Museum—One of Strasbourg's oldest and most characteristic homes hosts this extensive, well-presented collection of Alsatian folk art. You'll see scenes from daily life, traditional home interiors (including a close-up look at half-timbered construction), lots of tools, and a good overview of the life of a winemaker. The English audioguide makes this museum a worthwhile detour (across the river and down a block to the right from the boat dock, at 23 Quai St. Nicholas—see map on page 1054, tel. 03 88 52 50 01).

Boat Ride on the Ill River

To see the cityscape from the water, take a loop cruise around Strasbourg. The glass-topped boats are air-conditioned and suf-

ficiently comfortable—both sides have fine views. You'll pass through two locks as you circle the old city clockwise. The highlight for me was cruising by the European Parliament buildings and the European Court of Human Rights.

Cost and Hours: Adults-€9.50, under 18-half-price, 70 minutes, good English commentary with live guide or audioguide; daily 2 boats/hour April-Oct 9:30-19:00, May-Sept also hourly 20:00-22:00; 2 boats/hour Dec 9:30-17:00; Nov and Jan-March boats depart only at 10:30, 13:00, 14:30, and 16:00; dock is 2 blocks outside cathedral's right transept, where Rue Rohan meets the river, tel. 03 88 84 13 13, www.batorama.fr.

▲La Petite France

The historic home to Strasbourg's tanners, millers, and fishermen, this charming area is laced with canals, crowned with magnificent half-timbered homes, carpeted with cobblestones, and filled with tourists.

From the cathedral, walk down Rue des Hallebardes to the merry-go-round, then continue straight, following Rue Gutenberg. Cross big Rue des Francs Bourgeois and keep straight (now on Grande Rue). Turn left on the third little street (Rue du Bouclier, street signs are posted behind you), and make your way to the middle of the bridge (Pont St. Martin) for a fine view. Find your way down to the river and follow the walkway over the lock deep into La Petite France. Make friends with a leafy café table on **Place Benjamin Zix,** or find the siesta-perfect parks between the canals across the bridge at Rue des Moulins. Climb the once-fortified grassy wall (Barrage Vauban) for a decent view—the glass

ALSACE

structure behind you is the splashy modern-art museum (interesting more for its architecture than its collection).

La Petite France's coziest cafés line the canal on **Quai de la Bruche** near the barrage. From here it's a 10-minute walk back to the station: With the river on your left, walk along Quai de Turckheim, cross the third bridge, and find Rue du Maire Kuss.

Sleeping in Strasbourg

(€1 = about $1.30, country code: 33)

Strasbourg is quiet in the summer (July-Aug), when 4,000 Eurocrats leave town and hotel prices fall—and slammed when the parliament is in session, throughout December (thanks to the Christmas market), and during major conferences.

$$$ Hôtel Cathédrale* ** is comfortable and contemporary, with a Jack-and-the-beanstalk spiral stairway (elevator begins one floor up) and a hopelessly confusing floor plan. This modern yet atmospheric place lets you stare at the cathedral point-blank from your room (small Db with no view-€90, medium Db with no view-€140, larger Db with view-€160-200, lower prices possible on weekends, frequent Web promotions, buffet breakfast-€13, air-con, free Wi-Fi, laundry service, free bicycles can be reserved for up to 2 hours, book ahead for one of 5 parking spaces-€18/day, 12-13 Place de la Cathédrale, tel. 03 88 22 12 12, toll-free in France 08 00 00 00 84, fax 03 88 23 28 00, www.hotel-cathedrale.fr, reserv@hotel-cathedrale.fr).

$$$ Hôtel Suisse ,** across from the cathedral's right transept and off Place du Château, is a welcoming, central, and solid two-star value (Sb-€78-106, Db-€87-115, Tb-€125, breakfast-€10, prices €10 less in Jan-Feb and July-Aug, extra person-€10, elevator, free Wi-Fi, very cozy lounge-café, 2 Place de la Râpe, tel. 03 88 35 22 11, fax 03 88 25 74 23, www.hotel-suisse.com, info@hotel-suisse.com).

$$$ Hôtel Cardinal de Rohan* ** has a classy address in the pedestrian zone just steps from the cathedral, with royal public spaces and 33 well-appointed rooms. Eight rooms are small but a good value, and four are good triples (small Db-€90, bigger Db-€170, Tb-€185, buffet breakfast-€14, air-con in most rooms, free Internet access and Wi-Fi, book ahead for one of 6 parking spaces 200 yards away-€17/day, 17 Rue du Maroquin, tel. 03 88 32 85 11, fax 03 88 75 65 37, www.hotel-rohan.com, info@hotel-rohan.com).

$$ Hôtel des Arts ,** located in the thick of things above a busy café, is a young-at-heart, simple but comfortable place with tight bathrooms. Rooms in front are fun but noisy (Sb or Db-€78, check Internet for better prices, cheap breakfast-€7, entirely non-smoking, air-con, Wi-Fi, 10 Place du Marché aux Cochons de Lait, tel. 03 88 37 98 37, fax 03 88 37 98 97, www.hotel-arts.com, info@hotel-arts.com).

Eating in Strasbourg

Atmospheric *winstubs* (wine bars) serving affordable salads and *tarte flambée* are a snap to find. If the weather is nice, head for **La Petite France** and choose ambience over cuisine—dine outside at any café/*winstub* that appeals to you. Alternatively, stock up on picnic supplies at the terrific grocery store on the main floor of the **Galeries Lafayette** department store (Mon-Sat 9:00-20:00, closed Sun, Place Kléber).

For a real meal, skip the touristy restaurants on the cathedral square and along Rue du Maroquin. Consider these nearby places instead; both are one block behind the TI (go left out of the TI, then take the first left through the passageway and keep walking): **Chez Yvonne** (marked *S'Burjerstuewel* above windows), right out of a Bruegel painting, has a tradition of good food at fair prices. Try the *coq au Riesling* or *choucroute garnie* (€16 each) or the €11.50 *salade Alsacienne* (reservations smart on weekends and holidays, dinner served from 18:00, open late daily, 10 Rue du Sanglier, tel. 03 88 32 84 15). Half a block left down Rue du Chaudron, at #3, lies the very cozy **Le Clou Winstub,** with €8-11 salads and €13-16 *plats du jour.* This place often looks closed from the outside, but don't be shy (closed Wed lunch and all day Sun, dinner served from 17:30, tel. 03 88 32 11 67).

Brasserie la Lanterne, a beloved Alsatian microbrewery, is a down-and-dirty hangout for students and hip locals. This place is famous for its home brews and cheap cuisine (€6-7 *tarte flambée*), and makes me want to plot a revolution (Mon-Sat 12:00-very late, Sun 17:00-late, near Place Kléber at 5 Rue de la Lanterne, tel. 03 88 32 10 10).

Poêles de Carottes offers vegetarians respite from porky Alsatian cuisine and has a small terrace in front (big €10-13 salads and stir-fries, closed Sun-Mon, 2 Place de Meuniers, tel. 03 88 32 33 23).

Strasbourg Connections

Strasbourg makes a good side-trip from Colmar or a stop on the way to or from Paris.

From Strasbourg by Train to: Colmar (2/hour, 35 minutes), **Reims** (TGV: 10/day, 2 hours, change at Gare Champagne-Ardennes), **Paris'** Gare de l'Est (TGV: 1-2/hour, 2.5 hours), **Lyon** (10/day, 4-5 hours), **Baden-Baden,** Germany (TGV: 2/day, 1.25

ALSACE

hours, change in Karlsruhe; non-TGV train: roughly 2/hour at rush hour but fewer midday, 70 minutes, change in Appenweier or Offenburg), **Karlsruhe,** Germany (TGV: 4/day, 40 minutes; non-TGV train: hourly, 1-1.5 hours, most with change in Appenweier or Offenburg), **Vienna,** Austria (TGV: 7/day, 9-11 hours, 2-3 changes; non-TGV train: 7/day, 9-13 hours), **Basel,** Switzerland (TGV: 4/day, 1.75 hours; non-TGV train: about 2/hour, 1-2 hours).

REIMS and VERDUN

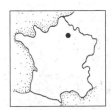

Different as night and day, bubbly Reims and brooding Verdun offer worthwhile stops between Paris and Alsace. The administrative capital of the Champagne region, bustling, modern Reims greets travelers with cellar doors wide open. It features a lively center, a historic cathedral, and, of course, Champagne tasting. Often overlooked, quiet Verdun is famous for the brutal World War I battles that surrounded the city and leveled the countryside, and offers an exceptional opportunity to learn about the Great War. High-speed TGV trains make both of these destinations easily accessible to travelers (particularly if coming from Paris).

Planning Your Time

Organized travelers in a hurry can see Reims and Verdun as they travel between Paris and the Alsace, though most will want an overnight (Reims is the better choice) to best appreciate the sights. Plan on most of a day for Reims and a half-day for Verdun. It's about 70 miles between the two towns, making a day trip from Reims to Verdun worth considering if you have a car—but it's too difficult by train. Day-tripping by train from Paris to Reims is a breeze, but day-tripping to Verdun requires careful planning.

Getting Around Reims and Verdun

Driving is a good option, even in the bigger city of Reims, and many find this a good place to pick up a rental car for a longer trip after leaving Paris (but be aware that all rental agencies are closed 12:00-14:00).

Reims offers excellent public transportation, with a tramway

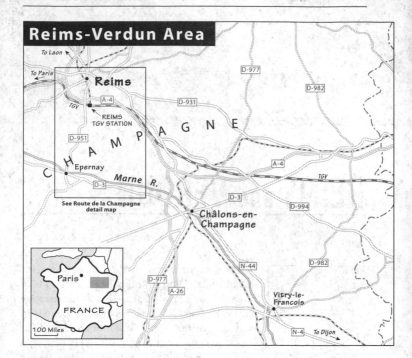

Reims-Verdun Area

To Laon

To Paris

Reims

TGV

A-4

REIMS
TGV STATION

D-977

D-982

D-931

C H A M P A G N E

D-951

A-4

TGV

Epernay

Marne R.

D-3

See Route de la Champagne
detail map

D-3

**Châlons-en-
Champagne**

D-994

Paris

FRANCE

100 Miles

D-977

A-26

N-44

D-982

**Vitry-le-
Francois**

N-4   To Dijon

and handy buses linking its major sights. In Verdun, however, public transit is nonexistent—here it's best to rent a car for the day or
take a private tour or taxi to visit the battlefields.

Frequent high-speed TGV trains link Paris and Reims in 45
minutes, and rare direct TGV trains link Paris and Verdun in 1.75
hours. Most trains between Reims and Verdun are slow, thanks to
required transfers.

Champagne's Cuisine Scene

Because traditional wines are rare here, and the Champagne drink
is not often integrated into meals, cuisine in this region suffers
from a lack of originality. Much like Paris, Champagne borrows
from other regions' recipe books. Still, be on the lookout for anything cooked in Champagne, and try the warm dandelion salad
with bacon bits *(salade de pissenlit)*. *La potée champenoise* is a blood
pudding made from rabbit. Ample rivers make for flavorful trout
(truite) dishes. *Jambon de Reims*, ham cooked in white wine or
Champagne and wrapped in a pastry shell or coated with bread-
crumbs, is popular in Reims, as is andouillette (tripe sausage).
You may also find rooster cooked in the red wine known as Bouzy
Rouge *(coq au vin de Bouzy)*. Brie cheese, made on Champagne's
border, is a good choice. Other local cheeses include Cendré de
Champagne (similar to Brie but the size of a large Camembert,

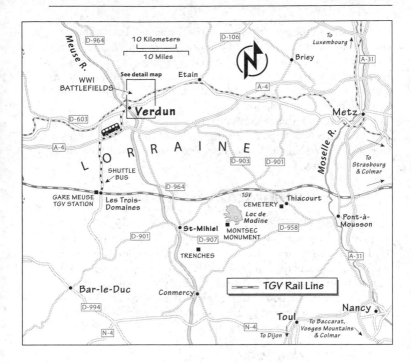

with a thin, edible ash covering), Chaource, Soumaintrain, and Langres. Fruit-flavored brandies are a common way to end an evening.

Reims

With its Roman gate, Gothic cathedral, Champagne *caves*, and vibrant pedestrian zone, Reims feels both historic and youthful. And thanks to the TGV bullet train, it's just a 45-minute ride from Paris.

Reims (pronounced "rance") has a turbulent history: This is where 26 French kings were crowned, where Champagne first bubbled, where WWI devastation met miraculous reconstruction during the Art Deco age (all but 70 buildings were damaged in 1918), and where the Germans officially surrendered in 1945, bringing World War II to a close in Europe. The town's sights give you an entertaining peek at the entire story.

Planning Your Time

You can see Reims' essential sights in an easy day, either as a day trip from Paris or as a stop en route to or from Paris. Frequent

TGV trains make the trip from Paris a breeze. Take a morning train from Paris and explore the cathedral and city center before lunch, then spend your afternoon below ground, in a cool, chalky Champagne cellar. You can be back at your Parisian hotel before dinner. Those continuing to destinations farther east find Reims a convenient place to pick up a car.

To best experience contemporary Reims, explore the busy shopping streets between the cathedral and the central train station. Rue de Vesle, Rue Condorcet, and Place Drouet d'Erlon are most interesting.

Orientation to Reims

Reims' hard-to-miss cathedral marks the city center and makes an easy orientation landmark. Many sights of interest are within a 15-minute walk from the Reims-Centre train station. Easy-to-use bus routes connect the harder-to-reach Champagne *caves* with the central train station and cathedral. The city has ambitiously renovated its downtown, converting large areas into pedestrian-friendly zones. Citizens are proud of their sleek tram system that connects Reims-Centre Station and Champagne-Ardenne TGV Station.

Tourist Information

The main TI is located outside the **cathedral**'s left (north) transept (TI open Easter-Sept Mon-Sat 9:00-19:00, Sun 10:00-18:00; Oct-Easter Mon-Sat 9:00-18:00, Sun 10:00-16:00 except March-Easter, when it's open until 18:00; public WCs across street, tel. 03 26 77 45 00, www.reims-tourisme.com). A much smaller, seasonal TI is just outside the Reims-Centre **train station** (mid-April-Dec Mon-Sat 8:30-11:00 & 12:00-18:00, Sun 12:00-17:30).

At either TI, pick up a free map of the town center and a map of the Champagne *caves*. The TI can book a visit to any *cave* that accepts visitors, and can call a taxi to get you there. Note that the most popular *caves* require advance booking (for information on reservations and specifics on reaching the *caves*, see "Champagne Tours and Sights," later). The TI also rents audioguides covering the cathedral, city center, and Art Deco architecture (single-€6, each additional set-€4, 1-2 hours each).

Arrival in Reims

By Train: From Paris' Gare de l'Est station, there are three different train routes to Reims. The fastest (and most frequent) is the direct TGV to the recently remodeled **Reims-Centre Station** (9/day, 45 minutes, no baggage check). Check the schedule before booking to avoid slower trains.

To get from the Reims-Centre station to the cathedral, it's a 15-minute walk: Follow *sortie* signs for Place de la Gare (don't use the Clairmarais exit). As you leave the station, walk toward the statue in the gardens and on toward the Grand Hôtel Continental on the pedestrianized Place Drouet d'Erlon. Turn left on Rue Condorcet, then right on Rue de Talleyrand.

To save a little time, you can jump on the tram. Find the tram stop on the square in front of the station (to the left of the statue). Take tram #A (direction: Hôpital Debré) or tram #B (direction: Gare Champagne TGV) two stops to the Opéra stop—the cathedral and TI are behind the Opéra building. For tram and bus info, see "Getting Around Reims," later.

Other TGV trains from Paris destined for Germany or Alsace stop at the **Champagne-Ardenne** TGV Station five miles away (4/day, 45 minutes). From there, you can take a local "milk-run" (TER) train to Reims-Centre Station, or ride the tram into town (tram #B, direction: Neufchâtel, walk straight out of the station and down the hill to find the stop).

There are also a few local TER trains that go from Paris through Epernay to Reims (2/day, 2 hours).

By Car: Day-trippers should follow *Centre-Ville* and *Cathédrale* signs, and park on the street approaching the cathedral (Rue Libergier) or in the well-signed Parking Cathédrale structure (€1.50/hour). If you'll be staying the night, follow *Reims-Centre* and *Gare* signs for most of my recommended hotels, and park in the Erlon parking garage.

Helpful Hints

Department Store: Monoprix, at the Espace Drouet d'Erlon shopping center, provides one-stop shopping for toiletries, cheap clothing, and groceries (Mon-Sat 9:00-20:00, closed Sun, basement level, 53 Place Drouet d'Erlon, near the recommended L'Apostrophe restaurant, follow *FNAC* signs).

Laundry: One launderette is just south of the cathedral (daily 8:00-20:00, 59 Rue Chanzy); another is a few blocks farther south (daily 7:00-21:00, 49 Rue Gambetta).

Car Rental: Avis is just outside the central train station at 20 Rue Pingat (tel. 08 20 61 17 05, use the *Clairmarais* exit from the station, turn right, and walk 200 yards). **Europcar** is at 76 Boulevard Lundy (tel. 08 25 04 52 82); **Hertz** is at 26

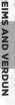

Reims

MUSEUM OF THE SURRENDER

Cemetery

RUE DES ROMAINS

R. CHAMP DE MARS

Place de la Republique ❾

PORTE DE MARS

❽

RUE DU MONT D'ARENE

RUE EDOUARD MIGNOT

REIMS-CENTRE TRAIN STATION

❿

BLVD. JOFFRE

R. DE MARS

RUE GEN. SARRAIL

RUE DU TEMPLE

❹

R. LINGUET

TOWN HALL

Place de l'Hôtel de Ville

RUE VERNOUILLET

RUE DE COURCELLAS

RUE PINGAT

P

BLVD. FOCH

T

STATUE

Square Colbert

BLVD.

RUE THIERS

RUE DE SAINT-BRICE

B

B #4

Place Drouet d'Erlon

❶

P ❶❷

❷

COURS JEAN-BAPTISTE LANGLET

Place du Forum

P

❺ Place Royale

RUE BUIRETTE

RUE J. P'ARC

RUE TALLEYRAND

RUE CHATIVESTE

CONDORCET

❻

ST. JACQUES

❸ B

❼

CATHEDRAL

BLVD. LOUIS ROEDERER

CIRQUE

BLVD. DU GENERAL LECLERC

To Paris

A-4

RUE VESLES

RUE CLOVIS

RUE LIBERGIER

❶❶ P

Place du Cardinal Luçon

RUE HINCMAR

RUE CHANZY

❶❸

la Vesle

R. PAYEN

RUE CHABAUD

RUE BRULEE

CHAUSSEE BOCQUAINE

RUE BOULARD

SYNAGOGUE

RUE CAPUCINS

RUE JARD

RUE DU

BLVD. PAUL DOUMER

Canal de l'Aisne La Marne

RUE CLOVIS

RUE R. FOLLE PEINE

RUE VENISE

RUE PASSE

RUE DEMOISELLES

STADE

Parc Léo Lagrange

STADE NAUTIQUE

CATHEDRAL EXIT

AVE. DU GENERAL DE GAULLE

RUE DE COURLANCY

AVE. PAUL MARCHANDEAU

CHAUSSEE BOCQUAINE

200 Meters

200 Yards

CHAUSSEE ST. MARTIN

A-4

BLVD. WILSON

To Verdun & Strasbourg

REIMS AND VERDUN

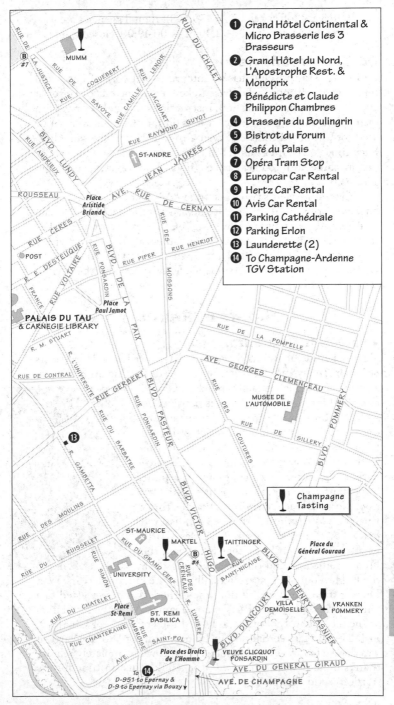

1. Grand Hôtel Continental & Micro Brasserie les 3 Brasseurs
2. Grand Hôtel du Nord, L'Apostrophe Rest. & Monoprix
3. Bénédicte et Claude Philippon Chambres
4. Brasserie du Boulingrin
5. Bistrot du Forum
6. Café du Palais
7. Opéra Tram Stop
8. Europcar Car Rental
9. Hertz Car Rental
10. Avis Car Rental
11. Parking Cathédrale
12. Parking Erlon
13. Launderette (2)
14. To Champagne-Ardenne TGV Station

REIMS AND VERDUN

Boulevard Joffre (tel. 03 26 47 98 78). Rental agencies are usually open Mon-Sat 8:00-12:00 & 14:00-19:00, closed Sun.

Getting Around Reims

By Bus or Tram: Reims has an integrated network of buses and trams (www.citura.fr). Purchase tickets from the bus driver or at any tram-stop machine (€1.60, instructions in English, pay with cash, coins only). A single ticket is valid for one hour and can be used for unlimited transfers, even a round-trip on the same line. Each time you board a bus or tram, place your ticket on the validation machine until you hear a beep (if you skip this step, you might get fined).

The tram system's two lines (tram #A—5/hour, tram #B—2-3/hour; fewer on Sun) connect Reims' two train stations—Reims-Centre and Champagne-Ardenne TGV—and serve a few key stops in town, including one near the cathedral. To get from either train station to the cathedral and town center, take a tram to the Opéra stop. The cathedral is one block away, around the back of the Opéra building.

Sights in Reims

▲▲▲Reims Cathedral

The cathedral of Reims, begun in 1211, recently celebrated its 800th birthday. It's a glorious example of Gothic architecture, and one of Europe's greatest churches. Clovis, the first king of the Franks, was baptized at a church on this site in A.D. 496, establishing France's Christian roots, which still hold firm today. Since Clovis' baptism, Reims Cathedral has served as *the* place for the coronation of 26 French kings, giving it a more important role in France's political history than Notre-Dame Cathedral in Paris—think England's Westminster Abbey. A self-assured Joan of Arc led a less-assured Charles VII to be crowned here in 1429. Thanks to Joan, the French rallied around their new king to push

the English out of France and finally end the Hundred Years' War. During the French Revolution, the cathedral was converted to a temple of reason (as was Paris' Notre-Dame). After the restoration of the monarchy, the cathedral hosted the crowning of Charles X in 1825—the last coronation in France. During World War I, it was devastated by severe bombing. Then it was completely rebuilt, thanks in large part to John D. Rockefeller...just in time for the start of World War II.

Cost and Hours: Free, daily 7:30-19:30.

> **Self-Guided Tour:** Stand on the square in front of the cathedral.

Exterior: You're admiring perhaps the best **west portal** anywhere, with more than 2,000 statues festooning its walls inside and out. (Medieval churches face east, toward the Holy Land, so you almost always enter through a church's west portal.) Like the cathedrals in Paris and in Chartres, this church is dedicated to "Our Lady" (Notre Dame). Statues depicting the crowning of the Virgin take center stage on the facade. For eight centuries Catholics have prayed to the "Mother of God," kneeling here to ask her to intervene with God on their behalf. In 1429, Joan of Arc received messages from Mary encouraging her to rally French troops against the English at the Siege of Orléans (a statue of Joan is over your left shoulder as you face the church).

Notice the **flying buttresses** soaring from the sides of the church. These massive "beams" are critical to supporting this structure. The pointed arches inside the church push the weight of the roof outward, rather than downward. The "flying" buttresses support the roof by pushing back inward, creating a delicate balance between the two forces. Gothic architects learned by trial and error—many church roofs caved in as they tested their theories and strove to build ever higher. Work on this cathedral began decades after the Notre-Dame cathedrals in Paris and Chartres, allowing architects to take advantage of what they'd learned from those magnificent earlier structures.

Contemplate the lives of the people who built this huge building, starting in 1211. Construction on a scale like this required a wholesale community effort—all hands on deck. Most townsfolk who participated donated their money or their labor knowing that neither they, nor their children, nor their children's children, would ever see it completed—such was their pride, dedication, and faith. Imagine the effort it took to raise the funds and manage the workforce. Master masons supervised, while the average Jean did much of the sweat work. Labor was something even the poorest medieval peasant could donate generously.

Interior: The weight of the roof is supported by a few towering columns that seem to sprout crisscrossing pointed arches. This technique allowed the church to grow higher, and liberated the walls to become window frames. Now, look back at the entry wall, with 120 statues filling the niches. The rose window (high above on this wall) contains the best original stained glass in the church (from 1255, removed during World War I to be spared destruction). Most of the windows are clear and newer: 18th- and 19th-century tastes called for more light, and the original, dark stained glass was replaced.

Circulate counterclockwise through the church (find help-ful information boards in English). The **south transept windows,** destroyed in World War I, were replaced in 1954 by the local Champagne makers. The windows show the connection of the Champagne industry to this town and its church with scenes por-traying the tending of vines (left), the harvest (center), and the time-honored double-fermentation process (right). Notice, around the edges, the churches representing all the grape-producing vil-lages in the area.

The apse (east end, behind the altar) holds a luminous set of **Marc Chagall stained-glass windows** from 1974. Chagall's inimitable style lends itself to stained glass, and he enjoyed opportunities to adorn great churches with his windows. The left window shows scenes from the Old Testament, and the center features the resurrection of Christ. On the right the tree of Jesse is extended to symbolically include the royalty of France—both affirm-ing the divine power of the mon-archs and stressing the responsibility to rule with wisdom and justice. For the cathedral's 800th anni-versary in 2011, six modern, abstract windows were installed on either side of the Chagall windows (they aren't working for me).

As you head for the exit, you'll find another Joan of Arc statue standing guard in her chapel.

Other Reims Sights

Palais du Tau—This former Archbishop's Palace, named after the Greek letter T *(tau)* for its shape, houses artifacts from the cathedral (with scant English information, though an audioguide is available at the TI for €6). You'll look into the weathered eyes of original statues from the cathedral's facade (taken in from the acidic open air for their own preservation). A set of precious tap-estries, telling stories from the life of Mary, are the originals that warmed the walls of the cathedral's choir in the 16th century. The coronation jewels, vestments, and other garb you see here were mostly made especially for the last French coronation (of Charles X in 1825), since the original finery had been lost a generation ear-lier in the French Revolution.

Cost and Hours: €7.50, May-Aug Tue-Sun 9:30-18:30, Sept-April Tue-Sun 9:30-12:30 & 14:00-17:30, closed Mon year-round, next to cathedral, tel. 03 26 47 81 79, www.palais-tau.monuments -nationaux.fr.

▲Museum of the Surrender (Musée de la Reddition)—
WWII buffs enjoy visiting the historic room where the Germans

signed the document of surrender of all German forces in the early morning of May 7, 1945. The news was announced the next day, turning May 8 into Victory in Europe (V-E) Day. Anyone interested in World War II will find the extensive collection of artifacts fascinating (particularly the ticker tape with the happy news, old photos, and a worthwhile 10-minute video shown on request). The room of the signing still has the maps with troop positions on the walls and the 13 chairs with name tags, each in its original spot.

Cost and Hours: €3, Wed-Mon 10:00-12:00 & 14:00-18:00, closed Tue, 12 Rue Franklin Roosevelt, tel. 03 26 47 84 19.

Getting There: It's a 15-minute walk from the central train station, or catch bus #4 in front of the station (direction: La Neuvillette Mairie), go three stops to Mignot, then continue one more block on foot.

Porte de Mars—The last vestige of Reims' ancient Roman heritage—an entry gate—is a short walk from the Reims-Centre train station. The Porte de Mars, built in the second century A.D., was one of four principal entrances into the ancient Gallo-Roman town and the only one still standing. Inspired by triumphal arches that Rome built to herald war victories, this one was constructed to celebrate the Pax Romana (a period of peace and stability—after all of Rome's foes were vanquished). Unlike most of the rest of town, the gate was undamaged in World War I, but it bears the marks of other eras, such as its integration into the medieval ramparts. Find the ruts under the arcade that guided chariots, and look for the depiction of the legend of Romulus and Remus (extremely faint on ceiling under left arch), complete with suckling she-wolf, from which Reims gets its name.

Cost and Hours: Free, always open, Place du Boulingrin.

▲Carnegie Library (Bibliothèque Carnegie)—The legacy of

the Carnegie Library network, funded generously by the 19th-century American millionaire Andrew Carnegie and his steel fortune (notice the American flag above the main entrance on the left), extends even to Reims. Built in the flurry of interwar

reconstruction, this beautiful Art Deco building still houses the city's public library. Considering that admission is free and it's just behind the cathedral, it's worth a quick look. Visitors are welcome to admire the mosaics, onyx-laden entrance hall, and Jacques Simon chandelier, but are asked not to enter the reading room (some come here to study). Peek through the reading room door to admire the stained-glass windows of this temple of thought. The gorgeous wood-paneled card-catalogue room takes older visitors back to their childhoods (notice how each card is laboriously typed), or even back to 1928, the year the library was inaugurated.

Cost and Hours: Free; Tue-Wed and Fri 10:00-13:00 & 14:00-19:00, Thu 14:00-19:00, Sat 10:00-13:00 & 14:00-18:00, closed Sun-Mon; Place Carnegie, tel. 03 26 77 81 41.

Art Deco on Place Drouet d'Erlon—Place Drouet d'Erlon is a long street-like square marking the commercial center of town. (From the central train station, it's directly across the park-like boulevards.) The square's centerpiece, a fountain with a winged figure of victory at the top, celebrates the major rivers of this district. It hasn't worked as a fountain since WWI bombings—a reminder of the devastation brought on this city. All around you'll see the stylized features—geometric reliefs, motifs in ironwork, rounded corners, and simple concrete elegance—of Art Deco. The only hints that this was once a Middle Ages town are the narrow lots that struggle to fit today's buildings. Pop into the Waida Pâtisserie (closed Mon, 3 Place Drouet d'Erlon) for a pure, typical Art Deco interior. As you stroll about, keep an eye open for "Biscuits Roses"—light, rose-colored egg-and-sugar cookies that have been made since 1756. They're the locals' favorite munchie to accompany a glass of Champagne—you're supposed to dunk them, but I like them dry (most places that sell these treats offer free samples).

▲▲Champagne Tours and Sights

Reims is the capital of the Champagne region. While the bubbly stuff's birthplace is closer to Epernay (for more on this town, see page 1083), you can tour several interesting Champagne *caves* right in Reims. All charge entry fees and most are open daily. Most have a few daily English tours, but some require a reservation. Call in advance or email from home before your trip for the schedule and to secure a spot on a tour. Martel offers the most personal and best-value tour. Pommery, Taittinger, and Mumm have the most impressive cellars. Villa Demoiselle offers a unique visit inside a mansion. Veuve Clicquot is very popular with Americans and fills up weeks in advance. Bring a sweater, even in summer, as the *caves* are cool and clammy.

Of the *caves* I list, Mumm is easiest to get to. If you don't have a car, the others involve a long **walk** (30-45 minutes) or a **bus** ride (for more, see "Getting There," under "*Caves* Southeast of the Cathedral," later). A **taxi** from either train station to the farthest Champagne *cave* will cost about €15 (many taxis wait at the station). To return, ask the staff at the *caves* to call a taxi for you (tel. 03 26 47 05 05). Warning: The meter starts running once they are called, so count on €5 extra for the return trip.

Mumm

Mumm ("moome") is one of the easiest *caves* to visit, as it's closest to the central train station (15-minute walk). Reservations are smart, especially on weekends. The basic "Cordon Rouge" visit includes a good 10-minute video, a small museum of old Champagne-making contraptions, and a tour of its industrial-size, modern-feeling chalk cellars, where 25 million bottles are stored. The video explains the place's history back to 1827 and the Champagne-making process with the enthusiasm of an advertisement ("Cordon Rouge is dedicated to the audacity and passion of exceptional men and women, with a subtle balance between freshness and intensity"). The tour ends with a glass of bubbly Cordon Rouge. You can pay more for the same tour with extra "guided" tastings.

Cost and Hours: One-hour tour with Cordon Rouge tasting-€12, Discovery tasting-€17, Grand Cru tasting-€24; daily 9:00-11:00 & 14:00-17:00, closed Sun; 34 Rue du Champ de Mars—go to the end of the courtyard and follow *Visites des Caves* signs; tel. 03 26 49 59 70, www.mumm.com, guides@mumm.com.

Getting There: To walk from the Reims-Centre train station, turn left out of the station and go four very long blocks. It's beyond Place de la République on Rue du Champ de Mars (15 minutes). Or take bus #7 from the station (direction: Béthany) to the Justice stop, turn right (south) onto Rue de la Justice, and then left onto Rue du Champ de Mars. To return to the station on bus #7 (direction: Apollinaire), catch the bus at a different Justice stop, at the junction of Rue de la Justice and Rue du Champ de Mars. If you are coming from Champagne-Ardenne TGV Station, ride the tram all the way to Reims-Centre Station, transfer to bus #7, and follow the directions above.

Caves Southeast of the Cathedral

Taittinger and Martel, offering contrasting looks at two very different *caves*, are a few blocks apart, about 30 minutes by foot from the town center. These can easily be combined in one visit. Vranken Pommery, Villa Demoiselle, and Veuve Clicquot Ponsardin are a bit farther, require reservations, and are darn pricey—but also have impressive cellars. Pommery and Villa Demoiselle have the same owners and are across the street from each other. Veuve Clicquot is a big draw for American travelers and must be booked in advance.

Getting There: From the **town center,** it's a 30-minute walk to Taittinger and Martel—take Rue de l'Université from behind the cathedral's right transept, then Rue du Barbâtre. Pommery, Villa Demoiselle, and Veuve Clicquot are about a 45-minute walk from town. To reach any of these *caves* by bus, take the small Citadine bus #1 (€1.60, 3/hour Mon-Sat, none on Sun, not to be confused with regular bus #1) from the Cathédrale stop (a block to the left behind the cathedral—see map on page 1068), and ride 10 minutes (direction: Buirette) to the St. Niçaise stop. The bus drops you close to Taittinger and Martel. It's an additional 10-minute walk to Pommery, Villa Demoiselle, and Veuve Clicquot. To return to the cathedral, catch Citadine bus #2 (around the corner on Rue du Barbâtre, bus stop Salines, direction: Hôtel de Ville), and get off at Royale.

From **Reims-Centre Station,** hop on bus #4 (6/hour Mon-Sat, 2/hour Sun, 20 minutes, direction: Hôpital Debré). Get off at the St. Timothée stop, and ask the driver to point you in the right direction. It's about a five-minute walk to Taittinger and Martel and 15 minutes to the others. To return to the station (or to reach the cathedral by getting off at the Rockefeller or Opera stops), take bus #4 from the St. Timothée stop (direction: La Neuvillette Mairie). You can get even closer to Veuve Clicquot by catching bus #6 from Reims-Centre Station to the Droits de l'Homme stop (4/hour, 20 minutes, direction: ZI Farman). To return to the station, catch bus #6 on Boulevard Dieu Lumière (opposite side of the big roundabout, bus stop Cimitière du Sud, direction: Gare Centre).

If you're coming from the **Champagne-Ardenne** TGV train station, take the tram to the Opéra stop and walk to the cathedral, then transfer to Citadine bus #1 (described earlier). Or take the tram to Reims-Centre station, then transfer to bus #4 (described earlier).

Taittinger—One of the biggest and most renowned of Reims' *caves,* Taittinger (tay-tan-zhay) runs a few morning and afternoon tours in English through their vast cellars (show up early or call for times and to reserve a spot, about 20-30 people per tour). After seeing their 10-minute promo-movie (hooray for Taittinger!), follow your guide—mine reminded me of an old-time airline hostess—for 60 chilly minutes and 80 steps down to a chalky underworld of *caves,* the deepest of which were dug by ancient Romans. You'll tour part of the three miles of *caves,* pass some of the three million bottles stored here, and learn all you need to know about the Champagne-making process from your well-informed guide. Popping corks signal when the tour's done and the tasting's begun.

Cost and Hours: €16 includes one-hour tour and tasting, tours daily mid-March–mid-Nov 9:30-13:00 & 14:00-17:30 (last tours depart at 11:50 and 16:20), closed weekends off-season, 9 Place St. Niçaise, tel. 03 26 85 84 33, www.taittinger.com, info @taittinger.com.

Martel—This offers a homey contrast to Taittinger's big-business style. It's a small operation with less extensive *caves* and is *sans* doubt the best deal in town. Call to set up a visit and expect a small group that might be yours alone. Friendly Emmanuel runs the place with a relaxed manner. Only 20 percent of their product is exported (mostly to Europe), so you won't find much of their Champagne in the US. Their visit focuses on the basics and includes an informative 10-minute film and a tour of their small cellars, which are peppered with rusted old wine-making tools. It culminates with a tasting of three different Champagnes in a casual living-room atmosphere.

Cost and Hours: €11 includes 45-minute tour and tasting, tours depart daily 10:00-13:00 & 14:00-18:00, reservations not required but smart, 17 Rue des Créneaux, tel. 03 26 82 70 67, www .champagnemartel.com, boutique@champagnemartel.com.

Vranken Pommery—This massive *domaine* is owned by Paul-François Vranken, a Belgian who now has the second-largest Champagne empire in France. While they say reservations are required, it's easy to get a same-day spot on a tour if you call early. Choose between a full tour of the chalk cellars or a shorter Cliffs Notes version. All tours finish with a tasting. The tour starts with a long, regal staircase down into the cool *caves*. Here, thousands of bottles rest in Gallo-Roman chalk quarries, each 100 feet deep, with glass skylights at ground level. These ancient "underground cathedrals" make it easier to endure the robotic tour guide and spiels lauding Pommery.

Cost and Hours: €17-21 for one-hour tour, price depends on how many tastings you take, 30-minute tour-€5 less, tour with one glass of the really good stuff-€30; daily 10:00-18:00, closes at 17:00 Nov-March; 5 Place du Général Gouraud, tel. 03 26 61 62 56, www.pommery.com, domaine@pommery.fr.

Villa Demoiselle—Across the street from Pommery, this place is also owned by Champagne mogul Vranken, but serves up a different brand. Instead of chalk *caves*, here you'll tour a beautifully restored Art Nouveau home. Built in the early 1900s, it was bought in 2002 by Vranken and has only been open to the public since 2009. Tours in English are fewer here, but all finish on the tasting room veranda.

Cost and Hours: €17-25 for one-hour tour, price depends on how many tastings you take, 30-minute tour-€5 less, call or email in advance for the schedule, 54 Boulevard Henry Vasnier, tel. 03 26

35 80 50, www.champagne-demoiselle.fr, villademoiselle@vranken pommery.fr. It's also possible to combine visits to Pommery and Villa Demoiselle (€20).

Veuve Clicquot Ponsardin—Because it's widely exported in the US, Veuve Clicquot is inundated with American travelers. Reservations are required and fill up three weeks in advance, so book early (easy via email) before you start your trip. The basic *cave* visit includes a two-flute tasting; other options add on a glass of "La Grande Dame" or pair tastings with cheese.

   Cost and Hours: €25 for 45-minute tour and tasting, €35 for one-hour tour and "La Grande Dame" Champagne, €90 for 2.5-hour tour and four tastings with cheese; mid-March-mid-Nov Tue-Sat 10:00-12:30 & 13:30-18:00, closed Sun-Mon and mid-Nov-mid-March; 1 Place des Droits de l'Homme, tel. 03 26 89 53 90, www.veuve-clicquot.com, visitscenter@veuve-clicquot.fr.

Route de la Champagne

Drivers can joyride through the pretty Montagne de Reims area just south of Reims and experience the chalky soil and rolling hills of vines that produce Champagne's prestigious wines. At the Reims TI, ask for maps of the Route de la Champagne and *The Discovery Guide* for the Marne region. Roads are clearly marked: Follow the brown *Route Touristique de la Champagne* signs. The only rail-accessible destination along this route is Epernay.

   There are thousands of small-scale producers of Champagne in these villages—unknown outside of France and producing fine-quality Champagne at less cost and without the brand names of the big houses in Reims and Epernay. Visiting these less-famous producers (known as *récoltant manipulant* because they harvest the grapes themselves and make wine only from their own grapes) requires a little more planning and perhaps the help of an hotelier or TI, but usually pays off with a more intimate, rewarding cultural experience.

   Though most village wineries require a reservation to tour their cellars, a few places are open daily for drop-in tastings. From April to October, an organization called Les Vignerons Indepéndents de Champagne (Independent Winemakers of Champagne) organizes open-house events and tastings (Sat-Sun only, usually 3-4 different wineries a day, tel. 03 26 59 55 22, www.vignerons-independants -champagne.com, contact@vignerons-independants-champagne .com). If you're doing this drive without having made reservations, do so on a weekend, when more places are open. If you plan to picnic, do your shopping in Reims: Grocery stores are scarce along this route.

   ➋ **Self-Guided Driving Tour:** For an afternoon ramble though the vineyards from Reims, try this three-hour loop drive

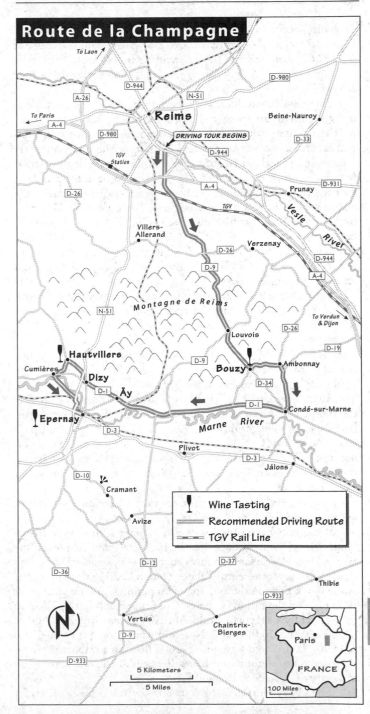

Route de la Champagne

To Laon

D-944

A-26

N-51

Reims

To Paris
A-4

D-980

D-980

Beine-Nauroy

DRIVING TOUR BEGINS

D-944

D-33

TGV
Station

A-4

D-26

TGV

Prunay

D-931

Villers-
Allerand

D-26

Verzenay

Vesle

D-944

D-9

River

A-4

N-51

Montagne de Reims

To Verdun
& Dijon

D-26

D-19

Louvois

D-9

Hautvillers

D-1

Bouzy

D-34

Ambonnay

Cumières

Dizy

Åy

Condé-sur-Marne

Epernay

D-1

D-3

Marne River

Plivot

D-3

Jálons

D-10

Cramant

Avize

Wine Tasting
Recommended Driving Route
TGV Rail Line

D-12

D-37

D-36

Thibie

D-933

N

Vertus

Chaintrix-
Bierges

Paris

D-9

D-933

FRANCE

5 Kilometers

5 Miles

100 Miles

(including stops).

• *Leave Reims on A-4 (direction: Châlons-en-Champagne), then exit south to Cormontreuil on D-9, following signs to Louvois, then to the perfectly named village of Bouzy (on D-34, 30-minute drive from Reims).*

There are 30 producers of Champagne in little **Bouzy** alone (most require reservations to visit), some of whom are also known for their Bouzy Rouge (a red wine made only from Pinot Noir grapes, and not made every year). To sample the local sauce, try **Champagne Herbert Beaufort,** a rare place that allows tastings without advance reservations (though you do need to reserve to visit the cellar). Check out the list of bottles open to taste at the bar, and admire the antique wine press. You'll probably be served by Monsieur Beaufort himself (free tastings, Mon-Fri 9:30-11:30 & 14:00-17:30, Sat 9:30-12:00 & 14:30-17:00, Sun 10:00-12:00 in summer, closed Sun Sept-Easter, first *domaine* on your left coming from Louvois at 28 Rue de Tours, tel. 03 26 57 01 34, www .champagnebeaufort.fr).

Before leaving Bouzy, find the **viewpoint** over the vineyards (follow signs uphill for *pointe de vue*; 3 minutes by car). Picnickers will find a bakery and a small grocery in Bouzy (unpredictable hours).

• *Continue toward Epernay, through Ambonnay and Condé-sur-Marne (less interesting), and along D-1 (near the Marne River), by a chalk quarry, and through the town of Aÿ.*

Aÿ (pronounced "eye") is a larger town that boasts of producing 100 percent Grand Cru Champagne from all of its vineyards. Entering the town, follow the *Route Touristique* signs and park near the Mairie (City Hall, with a small farmers market on Fri morning). While it's difficult to find winemakers with open doors, the narrow lanes are lined with half-timbered homes and make for a pleasant stroll.

• *In the next town,* **Dizy** *(which is what you get after too much Bouzy), follow signs up the hill to Hautvillers.*

If you only have time for one stop, make it this one. Hilltop **Hautvillers** ("High Village") is the most attractive hamlet in the area, with strollable lanes, houses adorned with wrought-iron shop signs, and a seventh-century abbey church housing the tombstone of the monk Dom Perignon. The main parking lot is on your right as you ascend the hill (WC here). Continuing uphill, the **TI** is on the right at the next corner (mid-April-Oct Mon-Sat 9:30-13:00 & 13:30-17.30, Sun 10:00-16.00; Nov-mid April Mon-Sat 10:00-13:00 & 14:00-17:00, closed Sun; tel. 03 26 57 06 35, www.tourisme-haut villers.com, info@tourisme-hautvillers.com). The only café is on this square (Place de la République).

The **abbey church** is to your left (better WCs here, street parking). According to the story, in about 1700, after much fiddling with double fermentation, it was here that Dom Perignon stumbled onto the bubbly treat. On that happy day, he ran through the abbey, shouting, "Brothers, come quickly...I'm drinking stars!" Find his tombstone just in front of the altar.

To taste your own stars, find **Hautvillers Champagne G. Tribaut,** with inexpensive €2 tastes (their aim is to sell their Champagne, so tastings are priced to entice you to buy). Ask about Ratafia, a local fortified wine served as an apéritif. You can linger over your *coupette* of bubbly in their garden as you survey the sea of vineyards. If you ask nicely, they'll let you picnic there—but you'll have to plan ahead, as there's only a bakery in town (daily 9:00-12:00 & 14:00-18:00; entering from Dizy, turn right at the main junction with the TI onto—what else?—Rue du Bacchus, and drive 300 yards to 88 Rue d'Eguisheim; tel. 03 26 59 40 57, www.champagne.g.tribaut.com, champagne.tribaut@wanadoo .fr). Find another beautiful picnic spot and sweeping views of the Marne River below (with tables and benches, but no WCs) by leaving on the road above the abbey church to the left (up Rue de l'Eglise, left on Avenue Chandon).

• *Exit the town downhill, toward the river, following* Cumières *signs.*

After Cumières it's less than two miles to **Epernay,** the only Champagne town accessible by train, and home to Moët et Chandon (see page 1083). True connoisseurs can continue along the *Route Touristique de Champagne* south of Epernay toward Vertus, along the Chardonnay-grape-filled **Côte des Blancs.**

Sleeping in Reims

The first two of my listings are on Place Drouet d'Erlon.

$$ Grand Hôtel Continental*** is a fine old hotel with well-priced, three-star comfort; stay-awhile public spaces; and helpful Maxeme at the desk. Rooms in the new wing are plush and modern, but smaller. Find the framed print of the original historic building before it became a hotel (standard Db-€98, "classic" Db-€129, "traditional" Db-€159-189, apartments for 3-8 available, ask about Rick Steves discount, request a nonsmoking room, aircon, elevator, laundry service, Wi-Fi, parking-€8, 5-minute walk from central train station at 93 Place Drouet d'Erlon, tel. 03 26 40 39 35, fax 03 26 47 51 12, www.grandhotelcontinental.com, reservation@grandhotelcontinental.com).

Sleep Code

(€1 = about $1.30, country code: 33)
S = Single, **D** = Double/Twin, **T** = Triple, **Q** = Quad, **b** = bathroom, **s** = shower only, ***** = French hotel rating system (0-5 stars). Unless otherwise noted, English is spoken, credit cards are accepted, and breakfast is not included.

To help you easily sort through these listings, I've divided the accommodations into two categories based on the price for a standard double room with bath:

$$ Higher Priced—Most rooms more than €100.
$ Lower Priced—Most rooms €100 or less.

Prices can change without notice; verify the hotel's current rates online or by email.

$ Grand Hôtel du Nord** has a welcoming staff and delivers clean and modern comfort at fair rates in surprisingly quiet rooms, despite being right on the square (Sb-€60-70, Db-€70-110, Tb/Qb-€110-150, free Wi-Fi, elevator, 75 Place Drouet d'Erlon, tel. 03 26 47 39 03, fax 03 26 40 92 26, www.hotel-nord-reims.com).

$ Bénédicte et Claude Philippon Chambres d'Hôte is a fine value and a lovely experience. This friendly couple offer two comfortable, homey, and centrally located rooms on Place du Chapitre (#21), 100 yards from the cathedral's north (left) transept. Look for the yellow *Chambres d'Hôte* sign (S-€50, D-€60, T-€75, €5 off for 2-night stays, cash only, includes French breakfast, shared bathroom, third floor with elevator, parking on square, tel. 03 26 91 06 22, mobile 06 77 76 20 13, claude.philippon@sfr.fr).

Eating in Reims

This is a "meaty" city: Most menus will offer *foie gras*, raw *tartares* (mostly steak but some fish too), and some dishes you may choose to avoid, such as *rognons*, *ris de veau*, *tête de veau*, *pieds de porc*, and *boudin blanc* (kidneys, sweetbreads, calf's head, pig's feet, and meat sausage, respectively). Find good people-watching opportunities—if not high cuisine—with the scads of restaurants on Place Drouet d'Erlon. All of these recommendations make good lunch or dinner options.

L'Apostrophe, an appealing place with a snazzy and cozy interior, offers a well-presented, creative cuisine that draws a loyal clientele (€14-20 *plats*, €22 and €33 *menus*, look for specials, daily, 59 Place Drouet d'Erlon, tel. 03 26 79 19 89).

Micro Brasserie les 3 Brasseurs is a rollicking, Alsatian-flavored microbrewery with copper vats and a young, inviting feel. You'll get good brasserie fare and (rare in France) more beer than wine. There's free Wi-Fi with any order—even just a drink (€9-13 salads, €10-13 *plats*, €16 *choucroute*, daily, 73 Place Drouet d'Erlon, tel. 03 26 47 86 28).

Brasserie du Boulingrin is the oldest brasserie in town, gushing with Art Deco. A Reims institution, it serves traditional French cuisine (including fresh oysters and a seafood platter) at blue-collar prices (€15-22 *plats*, €18-25 *menus*, closed Sun; 10-minute walk from the Reims-Centre train station at 48 Rue de Mars, not far from the Porte de Mars, tel. 03 26 40 96 22).

Café du Palais is appreciated by older locals who don't mind paying a premium to eat a meal or sip coffee wrapped in 1930s ambience. Reims' most venerable café-bistro stands across from the Opéra (€34 *menus*, €20-30 *plats*, daily but closed for dinner Sun-Mon, 14 Place Myron Herrick, tel. 03 26 47 52 54).

Bistrot du Forum, an informal and locally popular bistro, has small wooden tables, a cool zinc bar, and view terrace tables. They serve excellent large salads, bruschetta, and burgers, as well as traditional meat and fish dishes (€12-20); check the blackboard for their good-value daily specials. You'll also find a good selection of wines (and Champagne, *bien sûr*) by the glass (daily, 6 Place Forum, tel. 03 26 47 56 58).

For cheap picnic fixings, head to the grocery store at Monoprix (see "Helpful Hints," page 1067).

Near Reims: Epernay

Champagne purists may want to visit Epernay, about 16 miles from Reims (and also well-connected to Paris). Epernay is most famously home to Moët et Chandon, which sits along Avenue de Champagne, the Rodeo Drive of grand Champagne houses.

Arrival in Epernay: Trains run frequently between Reims-Centre Station and Epernay (10/day, 30 minutes). From the Epernay train station, walk five minutes straight up Rue Gambetta to Place de la République, and take a left to find Avenue de Champagne. Moët et Chandon (described below) is at #20, and the TI is at #7 (mid-April-mid-Oct Mon-Sat 9:30-12:30 & 13:30-19:00, Sun 11:00-16:00; mid-Oct-mid-April Mon-Sat 9:30-12:30 & 13:30-17:30, closed Sun; tel. 03 26 53 33 00, www.ot-epernay.fr).

Sights in Epernay: The granddaddy of Champagne companies, **Moët et Chandon** offers one-hour tours with three pricey tasting possibilities (€17 for single taste, €24-30 for two tastes, no reservation needed, kids under 18 can join the tour for €11—but no tasting, daily April-mid-Nov 9:30-11:30 & 14:00-16:30, closed weekends off-season, closed Jan, 20 Avenue de Champagne, tel. 03 26 51 20 20, www.moet.com, visites@moet.fr).

To sip a variety of different Champagnes from smaller producers, stop by the wine bar **C Comme Champagne** (meaning "C like Champagne"). Start with a peek in the wine cellar, then snuggle into an armchair and order by the taste, glass, or bottle. Ask about the ever-changing flight selections (daily 10:00-24:00, 8 Rue Gambetta, tel. 03 26 32 09 55).

Sleeping in Epernay: **$$ Hôtel Jean Moët***** is a stylish boutique hotel with a cozy lounge, an inviting covered terrace, and 12 pleasant rooms with all the amenities. Ask about their "green" practices (Db-€140-190, suite-€230-270, air-con, free Wi-Fi, 7 Rue Jean Moët, tel. 03 26 32 19 22, fax 03 26 32 50 84, www.hoteljeanmoet.com, contact@hoteljeanmoet.com).

Verdun

Few traces of World War I remain in Europe today, but the battlefields of Verdun provide an appropriately hard-hitting tribute to the 800,000 lives lost here in the horrific war of 1914-1918. The lunar landscape left by WWI battles is buried under thick forests and farmland. Millions of live bombs are scattered in vast cordoned-off areas—it's not unusual for French farmers or hikers to be injured by until-now-unexploded mines. Drive or ride through the eerie moguls surrounding Verdun, stopping at melted-sugar-cube forts and plaques marking spots where towns once existed. With three hours and a car, a tour, or easy taxi rides, you can see the most important sights and appreciate the horrific scale of the battles. The town of Verdun is not your destination, but rather is a starting point for your visit into the nearby battlefields. Verdun is already preparing for the 100-year anniversary (2014) of the beginning of World War I. Expect some changes at the various battlefield sites.

Orientation to Verdun

Unless you're arriving by train and have some time to spare, there's no reason to visit central Verdun's few sights. The severe Victory Monument (Monument à la Victoire), a block from the river and overlooking the pedestrian zone, has 73 steps following a watery path to a crypt storing records of the French and German soldiers who fought here. The **Citadelle Souterraine** offers a disappointing walk through the tunnels of the French Command, but it's not worth your time or money (€7; daily year-round, closed Jan).

Eating in Verdun: You'll find several inexpensive restaurants in the pedestrian zone and along the river. There's also one decent café in the battlefields, near the Ossuaire (see l'Ossuaire de Douaumont sight listing, later). If you're short on time, consider assembling a picnic from shops in Verdun or at an autoroute minimart.

Tourist Information

Verdun's two TIs are east of Verdun's city center, just across the river (cross at Pont Chausée) on Avenue du Général Mangin. The official TI is at Pavillon Japiot (March-Nov Mon-Sat 9:30-12:30 & 13:30-18:00, Sun 10:00-13:00; July-Aug open one hour later and no midday break Mon-Sat; reduced or no Sun hours in off-season; tel. 03 29 84 55 55, www.en.verdun-tourisme.com). The second TI is really a travel agency but does offer visitor information. It's farther down the road on Place de la Nation (similar hours—try here if the first TI's closed, tel. 03 29 84 14 18). The TIs have a good selection of books in English, maps of the city center with English descriptions of key monuments, and maps of the battlefields. Most important for non-drivers, the Pavillon Japiot TI is where the shuttles *(navettes)* to the battlefields depart (see next page). Either TI can arrange for private guides, but you'll need your own car and must book in advance (€150/2 hours). The pleasant park across the street provides a good picnic setting and a more cheerful break from the heavy sights.

Arrival in Verdun

By Train: Scarce TGV trains from Paris' Gare de l'Est serve the **Meuse TGV Station** (about 18 miles from Verdun); a shuttle bus connects the TGV Station with Verdun's central train station (€4, 30 minutes, leaves 5-10 minutes after train arrives, buy bus ticket with train ticket before boarding). This high-speed service puts Verdun within 1.75 hours of Paris, but with only about three direct trips a day, it's critical to confirm the schedule in advance. Less convenient trains (see "Verdun Connections" at the end of this chapter) route you through Metz or Chalôns-sur-Champagne.

Verdun's **central train station,** called Verdun SNCF, is 15 minutes by foot from the Pavillon Japiot TI. To reach the town center, walk straight out of the station (no baggage check), cross the parking lot and the roundabout, and keep straight down Avenue Garibaldi, then follow *Centre-Ville* signs on Rue St. Paul. (You'll pass a grocery store and a recommended car-rental agency soon after leaving the station.) Turn left on the first traffic-free street in the old center (Rue Chausée, good lunch options) and walk past the towers and across the river to the TI.

By Car: Drivers can bypass the town center and head straight for the battlefields. Follow signs reading *Verdun Centre-Ville,* then signs toward *Longwy,* then find signs to *Douaumont* and *Champs* *de Bataille* (battlefields) on D-112, then D-913. By following signs to *Fort de Douaumont* and *Ossuaire*, you'll pass Mémorial-Musée de Fleury, your first stop. To reach the Pavillon Japiot TI, follow signs to *Centre-Ville*, then *Office du Tourisme* (you'll pass the TI just before crossing the river).

Getting Around the Verdun Battlefields

The battlefield remains are situated on both sides of the Meuse River; the *rive droite* (right bank)—where we'll go—has more sights.

You have three choices for touring the battlefields:

By Car: Dirt-cheap car rental is available a block from the train station at **AS Location** (about €44/day with 100 km/60 miles included—easily enough to do the battlefields, Mon-Fri 8:30-12:00 & 14:00-18:00, no office hours Sat-Sun but prebooked rentals possible, 22 Rue Louis Maury, tel. 03 29 86 58 58 or mobile 06 08 91 81 71, fax 03 29 86 26 55, contact-verdun@aslocation.fr or belleville.location@orange.fr). Book ahead if possible, though they usually have cars available.

By Tour: Verdun's Pavillon Japiot **TI** offers a handy hop-on, hop-off open-roof tour bus that circulates around the key sights. Departures are on the hour from the TI and give you an hour at each monument before the next bus arrives (€10, daily Easter-Nov 11, likely departure times are 10:00, 11:00, 13:00, 14:00, and 15:00).

By Taxi: For about €35 round-trip, taxis can drop a carload at one sight and pick up at another (walk between sights). Ask to be dropped off at the Mémorial-Musée de Fleury and picked up at the Fort de Douaumont four hours later (visiting l'Ossuaire de Douaumont in between); it's about two miles from one sight to the other, so expect to walk a minimum of four miles for this plan. For less walking, ask to be dropped off at l'Ossuaire and picked up at either Fort de Douaumont or Mémorial-Musée de Fleury. Taxis normally meet trains at the station; otherwise they park at the TI (taxi mobile 06 07 02 24 16). It's easiest to arrange a taxi with the help of the TI.

Sights in Verdun

▲▲Battlefields of Verdun

Verdun's battlefields are littered with monuments and ruined forts. For most travelers, a half-day is enough, though historians could spend days here. We'll concentrate on the three most important sights: Mémorial-Musée de Fleury, l'Ossuaire de Douaumont, and Fort de Douaumont. Each offers a different perspective on the war.

Information: Sights are adequately described in English. If

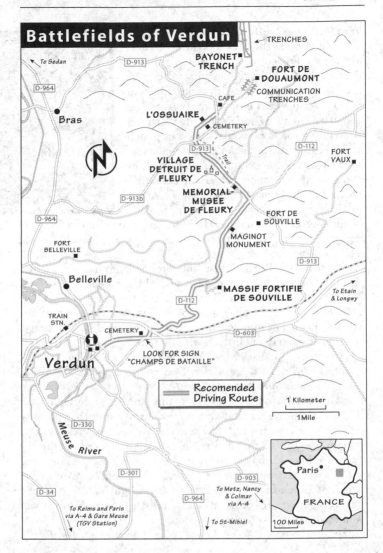

Battlefields of Verdun

TRENCHES

BAYONET TRENCH

FORT DE DOUAUMONT

To Sedan

D-913

D-964

CAFE

COMMUNICATION TRENCHES

L'OSSUAIRE

CEMETERY

Bras

D-112

FORT VAUX

D-913

Trail

VILLAGE DETRUIT DE FLEURY

MEMORIAL-MUSEE DE FLEURY

D-913b

FORT DE SOUVILLE

D-964

MAGINOT MONUMENT

FORT BELLEVILLE

D-913

Belleville

MASSIF FORTIFIE DE SOUVILLE

To Etain & Longwy

D-112

TRAIN STN.

CEMETERY

D-603

Verdun

LOOK FOR SIGN "CHAMPS DE BATAILLE"

Recomended Driving Route

1 Kilometer

1 Mile

Meuse River

D-330

D-301

Paris

D-34

D-903

FRANCE

To Reims and Paris via A-4 & Gare Meuse (TGV Station)

D-964

To Metz, Nancy & Colmar via A-4

100 Miles

To St-Mihiel

you want more, the TI and all sights sell helpful books in English describing the Battle of Verdun. The simple but adequate booklet *Verdun: Images of War* provides helpful details (in three languages) and black-and-white photos for about €5.50. More readable is *The Battle of Verdun* by Yves Buffetaut. The best is Alistair Horne's *The Price of Glory*, which sorts through the complex issues surrounding Verdun and offers perspectives from both sides of the conflict—if you can, read it ahead of your visit.

Background: After the annexation of Alsace and Lorraine following the German victory in the Franco-Prussian War in 1871,

Verdun found itself just 25 miles from the German border. This was too close for comfort for the French, who invested mightily in the fortification of Verdun, hoping to discourage German thoughts of invasion. The plan failed. World War I erupted in August 1914, and after a lengthy stalemate, the Germans elected to strike a powerful knockout punch at the heart of the French defense, to demoralize them and force a quick surrender. They chose Verdun as their target. By defeating the best of the French defenses, the Germans would cripple the French military and morale.

The French chose to fight to the bitter end. Three hundred days of nonstop trench warfare ensued. France eventually prevailed, but at a terrible cost.

Visiting the Battlefields: Soft, forested lands hide the memories of World War I's longest battles, which raged here for over 300 days in 1916. Only small monuments remind us that they ever existed. It's difficult to imagine today's lush terrain as it was just a few generations ago...a gray, treeless, crater-filled landscape, smothered in mud and littered with shattered stone.

• *Drivers (and cabbies) leave Verdun on D-603 (direction: Logwy), then take a left on D-112 (direction: Douaumont). Take the first turnoff possible (see map, previous page) into the...*

Massif Fortifié de Souville—At this parking and picnic area, find a curving trench and craters, similar to those that mark so much of the land here. A few communication trenches like this remain, though all fortified trenches were destroyed during the battles or have since been filled in. After leaving the parking area, you'll soon pass a monument to André Maginot, creator of the Maginot Line of forts erected following World War I to defend France against all future attacks from the east. Maginot was wounded during the battle of Verdun.

• *Continue following signs to* Ossuaire *and* Douaumont, *turning left on D-913.*

Mémorial-Musée de Fleury (Verdun Memorial)—This museum makes a good first visit. It's built near the site of a village (Fleury) destroyed during the fighting. The museum provides a helpful visual presentation of this war that would see the potential of mankind's destructive creativity—machine guns, flamethrowers, poisonous gas, airplanes, and observation balloons were all first used in World War I. The museum houses a manageable number of displays of weapons, uniforms (note the French colonies' contributions), models, and photos. Its centerpiece is the re-creation of a battlefield (built by veterans of the battle), and a faded-but-worthwhile 15-minute movie (request English version or read English subtitles; less important if you see the better film at l'Ossuaire de Douaumont—described below). Look for the model of the unblemished Fort de Douaumont, and remember this when you visit the fort. Basic information is posted in English.

Cost and Hours: €7, daily April-mid-Nov 9:00-18:00, mid-Nov-mid-Dec and Feb-March 9:00-12:00 & 14:00-18:00, closed mid-Dec-Jan, www.memorial-de-verdun.fr.

• *From the museum, look for signs leading to the* Village Détruit de Fleury.

Village Détruit (Destroyed Village) de Fleury—Detour in and find the church, then locate the public fountain plaque (the heart of the village) and the plaques with names of original residents and their occupations. Thirteen area villages like this one were caught in the battles and obliterated, never to be resurrected (signposted as *Villages Détruites*). Though gone, these villages have not been forgotten: Nine still have mayors and city councils.

• *Next, follow signs to the tall, missile-like building....*

L'Ossuaire de Douaumont (Douaumont Ossuary)—You'll likely see preparations in progress here for the 2014 commemoration of the beginning of World War I. All the headstones in the cemetery are being replaced, as are the grass and many plantings.

This is the tomb of 130,000 French and German soldiers whose last homes were the muddy trenches of Verdun. (Drivers can park at the rear.) The unusual artillery-shell-shaped **tower** and cross design of this building symbolizes war...and peace (imagine a sword plunged into the ground up to its hilt, and look at it again). Look through the low windows for a bony memorial to those whose political and military leaders asked them to make the "ultimate sacrifice" for their countries. The building has 22 sections with 46 granite graves, each holding remains from a different sector of the battlefield. Enter down the steps and start with the thought-provoking 20-minute **film** that remains relevant today (€5, 2/hour, ask for English headphones—you can adjust volume). The little picture boxes in the gift shop are worth a look if you don't visit the Mémorial-Musée de Fleury. Climb upstairs and experience a humbling and moving tribute to the soldiers who were convinced that this war would end all wars and that their children would grow up in a world at peace. The red lettering on the walls lists a soldier's name, rank ("Lt" is lieutenant, "Cal" is corporal, "St" is sergeant), regiment, and dates of birth and death. Skip the 204 steps up the tower.

Walk out to the **cemetery** and listen for the eerie buzz of silence and peace. Reflect on a war that ruined an entire generation, leaving half of all Frenchmen aged 15 to 30 dead or wounded. Rows of 15,000 Christian crosses and Muslim headstones (oriented toward Mecca), all with roses, decorate the cemetery. Moroccan soldiers were instrumental in France's ultimate victory at Verdun, a fact often overlooked by anti-immigration, right-wing politicians in France today.

Cost and Hours: Free entry, daily April 9:00-18:00, May-Aug 9:00-18:30, Sept 9:00-12:00 & 14:00-18:00, March and Oct-Nov 9:00-12:00 & 14:00-17:00 or 17:30, Dec and Feb 14:00-17:00, closed Jan, tel. 03 29 84 54 81.

Nearby: Looking over the cemetery from above, the road on the lower left leads 1.5 miles to Fort de Douaumont (described next). Also to the left, but behind you, a road leads to a little café, **Abri des Pelerins** (salads, omelets, €14 *menu*, March-Nov daily until 18:00, service can be slow, tel. 03 29 85 50 58). Although it's too far for walkers and there's not much to see there now, those interested can continue down the road to the **Tranchée des Baïonnettes** ("Bayonet Trench," free entry). Here, an entire company of soldiers was buried alive in their trench (the soldiers' bayonets remained aboveground for decades). The bulky concrete monument to this tragic event was donated by the US. "*Leurs frères d'Amérique*" translates as "Brothers from America."

• *Now head for...*

Fort de Douaumont—This was the most important stronghold in the network of forts built to protect Verdun after the annexation of Alsace and Lorraine to Germany in 1871. First constructed in 1882, it was built into the hillside and ultimately served as a strategic command center for both sides at various times. Soldiers were protected by a thick layer of sand (to muffle explosions) and a wall of concrete five to seven feet thick. In spite of this, German shelling in 1916 rocked the structure, leaving it useless. Inside, there's little to see except two miles of cold, damp hallways. Experiencing these corridors will add to your sympathy for the soldiers who were forced to live here like moles. Climb to the bombed-out top of the fort and check out the round, iron-gun emplacements that could rise and revolve.

Cost and Hours: €4, ask for English descriptions, daily May-Aug 10:00-18:30, April and Sept until 18:00, Oct until 17:30, Nov-Dec and Feb-March until 17:00, closed Jan.

• *Between the Ossuaire and Fort de Douaumont, on either side of the road, you'll pass what remains of the London Communication Trench. This served as a means of communication and resupply for the Fort de*

Douaumont. Notice the concrete-reinforced sides. You'll see the ruins of several abris *(shelters) on the hillside above the trench—these provided safe haven for the trench's soldiers.*

Near Verdun

St-Mihiel—If you're interested in getting a better understanding of the American role in the battles, and can afford a several-hour detour with some route-finding challenges, drive south of Verdun (other side of A-4) to the area known as the St-Mihiel salient (a salient is a territory surrounded on three sides by the enemy). Here, American and French forces joined in 1918 under the command of General John Pershing, in hopes of breaking the Germans' will by gaining the important city of Metz. The joint attack on the St-Mihiel salient caught the Germans by surprise and was initially successful, but later became bogged down by poor roads and related supply problems. The Americans didn't make it to Metz, and the Germans were able to regroup and hunker down.

Today, you can see good examples of WWI trenches (many are reconstructions) and appreciate how close the opposing trenches were. German trenches are generally still in good condition since they were built with concrete. The French ones were built mostly with dirt—they assumed the war would be short—and thus have not held up as well. Start with the trenches (maps available at Verdun's TI show their locations), then visit the cemetery.

To see the best **trenches,** take D-907 east from St-Mihiel, following signs for *Apremont le Forêt* and *Pont à Mousson,* and drive about five kilometers out of the city. You'll see signs to several trenches (first, *Bois d'Ailly/Tranchées de la Soif,* then *Tranchées des Bavarois et de Roffignac*). Both are interesting and worth a stop. The third trenches (to the right) are signed as *Bois Brûlé/ Croix des Redoutes.* Here you'll find original German trenches— still in good condition, and French trenches made from dirt. The French trenches have been rebuilt in their original locations. It's fascinating to see how close to the German trenches they were. Information panels at the trenches are in French only, but the lesson needs no explanation.

The somber **St-Mihiel American Cemetery and Memorial** at Thiaucourt has 4,153 graves (daily 9:00-17:00, WC in visitors reception on left, www.abmc.gov/cemeteries/cemeteries/sm.php). The cemetery is located about 30 kilometers (18.5 miles) east of St-Mihiel—follow signs to *Pont à Mousson.*

If you have the time, head farther south (19 km/12 miles from the cemetery) to the **Montsec Monument,** which marks the conquest of the St-Mihiel salient by the First US Army. From the monument you can appreciate views over the battlefields, and see the ruins of several forts (always open).

Skip the town of St-Mihiel, which is far away from these places of interest.

Verdun Connections

Remember, a few high-speed TGV trains serve the Verdun area from the Meuse TGV station, 30 minutes south of Verdun, whereas non-TGV trains run to Verdun's central station. For TGV connections listed below, allow an additional 30 minutes to reach Verdun's central station by shuttle bus (€4).

From Verdun by Train to: Strasbourg (9/day, 3-4 hours, most change in Metz), **Colmar** (7/day, 4-5.5 hours, 2-3 changes), **Reims** (8/day, 2-5 hours, most with change in Châlons-en-Champagne or Metz), **Paris'** Gare de l'Est (3/day direct via TGV, 1 hour; by regional train 3 hours with transfer in Châlons-en-Champagne).

FRANCE: PAST AND PRESENT

"La Marseillaise"

There's a movement in France to soften the lyrics of their national anthem. Sing it now...before it's too late.

Allons enfants de la Patrie, (Let's go, children of the motherland,)
Le jour de gloire est arrivé. (The day of glory has arrived.)
Contre nous de la tyrannie (The blood-covered flag of tyranny)
L'étendard sanglant est levé. (Is raised against us.)
L'étendard sanglant est levé. (Is raised against us.)
Entendez-vous dans les campagnes (Do you hear these ferocious soldiers)
Mugir ces féroces soldats? (Howling in the countryside?)
Qui viennent jusque dans nos bras (They're nearly in our grasp)
Egorger vos fils et vos compagnes. (To slit the throats of your sons and your women.)
Aux armes citoyens, (Grab your weapons, citizens,)
Formez vos bataillons, (Form your battalions,)
Marchons, marchons, (March on, march on,)
Qu'un sang impur (So that their impure blood)
Abreuve nos sillons. (Will fill our trenches.)

French History in an Escargot Shell

About the time of Christ, Romans "Latinized" the land of the Gauls. With the fifth-century fall of Rome, the barbarian Franks and Burgundians invaded. Today's France evolved from this unique mix of Latin and Celtic cultures.

While France wallowed with the rest of Europe in medieval darkness, it got a head start in its development as a nation-state. In 507, Clovis, the king of the Franks, established Paris as the capital

Typical Church Architecture

History comes to life when you visit a centuries-old church. Even if you wouldn't know your apse from a hole in the ground, learning a few simple terms will enrich your experience. Note that not every church has every feature, and a "cathedral" isn't a type of church architecture, but rather a designation for a church that's a governing center for a local bishop.

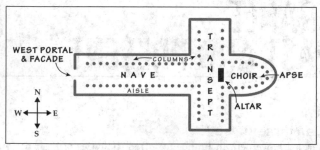

Aisles: The long, generally low-ceilinged arcades that flank the nave.

Altar: The raised area with a ceremonial table (often adorned with candles or a crucifix), where the priest prepares and serves the bread and wine for Communion.

Apse: The space beyond the altar, often bordered with small chapels.

Barrel Vault: A continuous round-arched ceiling that resembles an extended upside-down U.

Choir: A cozy area, often screened off, located within the church nave and near the high altar where services are sung in a more intimate setting.

Cloister: Covered hallways bordering a (usually square-shaped) open-air courtyard, traditionally where monks and nuns got fresh air.

Facade: The exterior surface of the church's main (west) entrance, usually highly decorated.

Groin Vault: An arched ceiling formed where two equal barrel vaults meet at right angles. Less common usage: term for a medieval jock strap.

Narthex: The area (portico or foyer) between the main entry and the nave.

Nave: The long, central section of the church (running west to east, from the entrance to the altar) where the congregation sits or stands through the service.

Transept: In a traditional cross-shaped floor plan, the transept is one of the two parts forming the "arms" of the cross. The transepts run north-south, perpendicularly crossing the east-west nave.

West Portal: The main entry to the church (on the west end, opposite the main altar).

of his Christian Merovingian dynasty. Clovis and the Franks would eventually become Louis and the French. The Frankish military leader Charles Martel stopped the spread of Islam by beating the North African Moors at the Battle of Tours (a.k.a. the Battle of Poitiers). And Charlemagne ("Charles the Great"), the most important of the "Dark Age" Frankish kings, was crowned Holy Roman Emperor by the pope in 800. Charlemagne presided over the "Carolingian Renaissance" and effectively ruled an empire that was vast for its time.

The Treaty of Verdun (843), which divided Charlemagne's empire among his grandsons, marks what could be considered the birth of Europe. For the first time, a treaty was signed in vernacular languages (French and German), rather than in Latin. This split established a Franco-Germanic divide, and heralded an age of fragmentation. While petty princes took the reigns, the Frankish king ruled only Ile de France, a small region around Paris.

Vikings, or Norsemen, settled in what became Normandy. Later, in 1066, these "Normans" invaded England. The Norman king, William the Conqueror, consolidated his English domain, accelerating the formation of modern England. But his rule also muddied the political waters between England and France, kicking off a centuries-long struggle between the two nations.

In the 12th century, Eleanor of Aquitaine (a separate country in southwest France) married Louis VII, king of France, bringing Aquitaine under French rule. They divorced, and she married Henry of Normandy (soon to be Henry II of England). This marital union gave England control of a huge swath of land from the English Channel to the Pyrenees. For 300 years, France and England would struggle over control of Aquitaine. Any enemy of the French king would find a natural ally in the English king.

In 1328, the French king Charles IV died without a son. The English king (Edward III), Charles IV's nephew, was interested in the throne, but the French resisted. This quandary pitted France, the biggest and richest country in Europe, against England, which had the biggest army. They fought from 1337 to 1453 in what was modestly called the Hundred Years' War.

Regional powers from within France actually sided with England. Burgundy took Paris, captured the royal family, and recognized the English king as heir to the French throne. England controlled France from the Loire north, and things looked bleak for the French king.

Enter Joan of Arc, a 16-year-old peasant girl driven by religious voices. France's national heroine left home to support Charles VII, the dauphin (boy prince, heir to the throne but too young to rule). Joan rallied the French, ultimately inspiring them to throw out the English. In 1430 Joan was captured by the Burgundians, who sold

Typical Castle Architecture

Castles were fortified residences for medieval nobles. Castles come in all shapes and sizes, but knowing a few general terms will help you understand them.

The Keep (or Donjon): A high, strong stone tower in the center of the castle complex that was the lord's home and refuge of last resort.

Great Hall: The largest room in the castle, serving as throne room, conference center, and dining hall.

The Yard (or Bailey or Ward): An open courtyard inside the castle walls.

Loopholes: Narrow slits in the walls (also called embrasures, arrow slits, or arrow loops) through which soldiers could shoot arrows at the enemy.

Towers: Tall structures serving as lookouts, chapels, living quarters, or the dungeon. Towers could be square or round, with either crenellated tops or conical roofs.

Turret: A small lookout tower projecting up from the top of the wall.

Moat: A ditch encircling the wall, often filled with water.

Motte-and-Bailey: A traditional form for early English castles, with a small fort on top of a hill (motte) next to an enclosed and fortified yard (bailey).

Wall Walk (or Allure): A pathway atop the wall where guards could patrol and where soldiers stood to fire at the enemy.

Parapet: Outer railing of the wall walk.

Crenellation: A gap-toothed pattern of stones atop the parapet.

Hoardings (or Gallery or Brattice): Wooden huts built onto the upper parts of the stone walls. They served as watch towers, living quarters, and fighting platforms.

her to the English, who convicted her of heresy and burned her at the stake in Rouen. But the inspiration of Joan of Arc lived on, and by 1453 English holdings on the Continent had dwindled to the port of Calais. (For more on Joan of Arc, see page 270.)

By 1500, a strong, centralized France had emerged, with borders similar to today's. Its kings (from the Renaissance François I through the Henrys and all those Louises) were model divine monarchs, setting the standards for absolute rule in Europe.

Outrage over the power plays and spending sprees of the kings—coupled with the modern thinking of the Enlightenment (whose leaders were the French *philosophes*)—led to the French Revolution (1789). In France, it was the end of the *ancien régime*, as well as its notion that some are born to rule, while others are born to be ruled.

The excesses of the Revolution in turn led to the rise of Napoleon, who ruled the French empire as a dictator. Eventually,

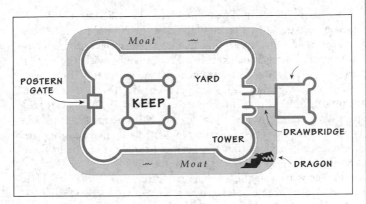

Machicolation: A stone ledge jutting out from the wall, fitted with holes in the bottom. If the enemy was scaling the walls, soldiers could drop rocks or boiling oil down through the holes and onto the enemy below.

Barbican: A fortified gatehouse, sometimes a stand-alone building located outside the main walls.

Drawbridge: A bridge that could be raised or lowered, using counterweights or a chain-and-winch.

Portcullis: A heavy iron grille that could be lowered across the entrance.

Postern Gate: A small, unfortified side or rear entrance used during peacetime. In wartime, it could become a "sally-port" used to launch surprise attacks, or as an escape route.

his excesses ushered him into a South Atlantic exile, and after another half-century of monarchy and empire, the French settled on a compromise role for their leader. The modern French "king" is ruled by a constitution. Rather than dress in leotards and powdered wigs, France's president goes to work in a suit and carries a briefcase.

The 20th century spelled the end of France's reign as a military and political superpower. Devastating wars with Germany in 1870, 1914, and 1940—and the loss of her colonial holdings—left France with not quite enough land, people, or production to be a top player on a global scale. But the 21st century may see France rise again: Paris is a cultural capital of Europe, and France—under the EU banner—is a key player in integrating Europe as a single, unified economic power. And when Europe is a superpower, Paris may yet be its capital.

France Today

Today, the main political issue in France is—like everywhere—the economy. Initially, France weathered the 2008 downturn better than the US, because it was less invested in risky home loans and the volatile stock market. But France, along with the rest of Europe, is struggling. French unemployment remains high (over 10 percent) and growth is flat-lining. Abroad, the entire eurozone is being dragged down by countries heavily in debt—Greece, Spain, Portugal, Italy, and Ireland. The challenge for French leadership is to address its economic problems while maintaining the level of social services that the French people expect from their government.

France is part of the 27-member European Union (or EU, a kind of "United States of Europe"), which has successfully dissolved borders and implemented a single currency, the euro. France's governments have been decidedly pro-EU. But many French are Euro-skeptics, afraid that EU meddling threatens their job security and social benefits.

Although France's economy may be one of the world's largest, the French remain skeptical about the virtues of capitalism and the work ethic. Business conversation is generally avoided, as it implies a fascination with money that the French find vulgar. (It's considered gauche even to ask what someone does for a living.) In France, CEOs are not glorified as celebrities—chefs are.

The French believe that the economy should support social good, not vice versa. This has produced a cradle-to-grave social security system of which the French are proud. France's poverty rate is half of that in the US, proof to the French that they are on the right track. On the other hand, if you're considering starting a business in France, think again—taxes are formidable (figure a total small-business tax rate of around 66 percent and likely to increase). France is routinely plagued with strikes, demonstrations, and slowdowns as workers try to preserve their hard-earned rights in the face of a competitive global economy.

The French political scene is complex and fascinating. France is governed by a president (currently Francois Hollande), elected by popular vote every five years. The president then selects the prime minister, who in turn chooses the cabinet ministers. Collectively, this executive branch is known as the *gouvernement*. The parliament consists of a Senate (343 seats) and the 577-seat Assemblée Nationale.

In France, compromise and coalition-building are essential to keeping power. Unlike America's two-party system, France has a half-dozen major political parties, plus more on the fringes. A simple majority is rare. Even the biggest parties rarely get more than a third of the votes. Since the parliament can force the *gouvernement* to resign at any time, it's essential that the *gouvernement* work with them.

For a snapshot of the current political landscape, look no further than the 2012 presidential elections. The various parties all chose a candidate. Incumbent president Nicolas Sarkozy headed the center-right Popular Movement Union (UMP). He defended his tough-love, carrot-and-stick approach to dealing with the sluggish economy. During his tenure, he cut taxes, reduced the size of government, limited the power of unions, cut workers' benefits, and (most controversially) raised the retirement age from 60 to 62. He also offered tax incentives to those who worked overtime, meaning above the current 35- to 39-hour workweek. Sarkozy also had to defend his flamboyant, materialist, teetotaling lifestyle (which was often criticized as un-French). His wife is Carla Bruni, a sexy Italian model-turned-singer who had previously been linked romantically with the likes of Mick Jagger and Eric Clapton (and one of your co-authors). In 2011, Bruni made her big-screen debut with a blink-and-you'll-miss-her role in the Woody Allen film, *Midnight in Paris.*

Opposing Sarkozy were a host of left-leaning candidates. Francois Hollande of the center-left Socialist Party (PS) pointed out that Sarkozy's austerity policies were not working. The more-radical Left Front Party (which includes the once-powerful Communists) proposed raising the minimum wage to $2,200 a month and establishing a "maximum wage" of $500,000, beyond which you pay 100 percent taxes. The environmental Green Party (Les Verts) promised to stimulate the economy with half a million new green jobs.

On the far-right was the National Front party (FN), led by Marine Le Pen, daughter of party founder Jean-Marie Le Pen. The FN campaigned on a "France for the French" platform, calling for expulsion of ethnic minorities, restoration of the French franc as the standard currency, secession from the EU, and broader police powers. Ms. Le Pen studiously avoided the kind of anti-Semitic, racist rants that have made her father notorious in France.

After several months and one TV debate (yes, the French election season is that short), François Hollande and the Socialists emerged victorious. And just a month after the presidential election, French voters returned to the polls to select all 577 seats of the Assemblée Nationale. Though it's almost unheard of for a single party to win an outright majority of seats, that's exactly what the Socialists did, eking out just over 50 percent. Other leftist parties also scored well, giving President Hollande a leftist mandate for change. Nevertheless, Hollande has to work closely with legislators, a strong minority of whom are from opposing parties.

Top French Notables in History

Madame and Monsieur Cro-Magnon: Prehistoric hunter-gatherers who moved to France (c. 30,000 B.C.), painted cave walls at Lascaux and Font-de-Gaume, and eventually settled down as farmers (c. 10,000 B.C.).

Vercingétorix (72 B.C.-46 B.C.): This long-haired warrior rallied the Gauls against Julius Caesar's invading Roman legions (52 B.C.). Defeated by Caesar, France fell under Roman domination, resulting in 500 years of peace and prosperity. During that time, the Romans established cities, built roads, taught in Latin, and converted people to Christianity.

Charlemagne (A.D. 742-814): For Christmas in A.D. 800, the pope gave King Charlemagne the title of Emperor, thus uniting much of Europe under the leadership of the Franks ("France"). Charlemagne stabilized France amid centuries of barbarian invasions. After his death, the empire was split, carving the outlines of modern France and Germany.

Eleanor of Aquitaine (c. 1122-1204): The beautiful, sophisticated ex-wife of the King of France married the King of England, creating an uneasy union between the two countries. During her lifetime, French culture was spread across Europe by roving troubadours, theological scholars, and skilled architects pioneering "the French style"—a.k.a. Gothic.

Joan of Arc (1412-1431): When France and England fought the Hundred Years' War to settle who would rule (1337-1453), teenager Joan of Arc—guided by voices in her head—rallied the French troops. Though Joan was captured and burned as a heretic, the French eventually drove England out of their country for good, establishing the current borders. Over the centuries, the church upgraded Joan's status from heretic to saint (canonized in 1920).

François I (1494-1547): This Renaissance king ruled a united, modern nation, making it a cultural center that hosted the Italian Leonardo da Vinci. François set the tone for future absolute monarchs, punctuating his commands with the phrase "For such is our pleasure."

Louis XIV (1638-1715): Charismatic and cunning, the "Sun King" ruled Europe's richest, most populous, most powerful nation-state. Every educated European spoke French, dressed in Louis-style leotards and powdered wigs, and built Versailles-like palaces. Though Louis ruled as an absolute monarch (distracting the nobility with courtly games), his reign also fostered the arts and philosophy, sowing the seeds of democracy and revolution.

Marie-Antoinette (1755-1793): As the wife of Louis XVI, she came to symbolize (probably unfairly) the decadence of France's ruling class. When Revolution broke out (1789), she was arrested, imprisoned, and executed—one of thousands who were guillotined on Paris' Place de la Concorde as an enemy of the people.

Napoleon Bonaparte (1769-1821): This daring young military man became a hero during the Revolution, fighting Europe's royalty. He went on to conquer much of the Continent, become leader of France, and eventually rule as a dictator with the title of emperor. In 1815, an allied Europe defeated and exiled Napoleon, reinstating the French monarchy—though future kings (including Napoleon's nephew, who ruled as Napoleon III) were subject to democratic constraints.

Claude Monet (1840-1926): Monet's Impressionist paintings captured the soft-focus beauty of the belle époque—middle-class men and women enjoying drinks in cafés, walks in gardens, and picnics along the Seine. At the turn of the 20th century, French culture reigned supreme while its economic and political clout was fading, soon to be shattered by the violence of World War I.

Charles de Gaulle (1890-1970): A career military man, de Gaulle helped France survive occupation by Nazi Germany during World War II with his rousing radio broadcasts and unbending faith in his countrymen. As president he led the country through its postwar rebuilding, divisive wars in Vietnam and Algeria (trying to preserve France's colonial empire), and turbulent student riots in the 1960s.

Contemporary French: Which recent French people will history remember? President François Mitterand (1916-1996), the driving force behind La Grande Arche and Opéra Bastille? Marcel Marceau (1923-2007), white-faced mime? Chef Paul Bocuse (b. 1926), inventor of nouvelle cuisine? Brigitte Bardot (b. 1934), film actress, crusader for animal rights, and popularizer of the bikini? Yves Saint Laurent (1936-2008), one of the world's greatest fashion designers? Jean-Marie Le Pen (b. 1928), founder of the far-right Front National party, with staunch anti-immigration policies? Bernard Kouchner (b. 1939), co-founder of Doctors without Borders and minister of foreign affairs under President Nicolas Sarkozy? Zinédine Zidane (b. 1972), France's greatest soccer player ever, whose Algerian roots helped raise the status of Arabs in France? Or Dominique Strauss-Kahn (b. 1949), disgraced International Monetary Fund chief? (I hope not.)

François Hollande is politically moderate and personally modest, even boring. Raised in a suburban Parisian middle-class home, he rose quietly through the ranks: assemblyman from a nondescript *département*, small-town mayor, secretary of the Socialist Party. He's never before held a major elected office. Though Hollande is a "Socialist" (a word that spooks Rush Limbaugh), he's in the mainstream of the European political spectrum. France's "First Lady" is Valerie Trierweiler, a well-known journalist who writes for the glossy magazine *Paris Match* (the French counterpart to *Time*). The first couple is unmarried, and Trierweiler is the first unwed first lady to occupy the Elysée Palace (French White House). *Oh-là-là*—imagine that in your country.

Hollande faces huge challenges. On the sluggish economy, he favors government stimulus rather than austerity: hiring thousands of teachers, building hundreds of thousands of homes, and taxing all income above a million euros at 75 percent. Abroad, he's working closely with Germany to shore up weaker members of the eurozone. One of his first acts in office was to return the retirement age (at least for some workers) to 60.

France must also address immigration, which is shifting the country's ethnic and cultural makeup. Ten percent of France's population is of North African descent, mainly immigrants from former colonies. The increased number of Muslims raises more questions, particularly in tight economic times. The French have (controversially) made it illegal for women to wear a full, face-covering veil *(niqāb)* in public. They continue to debate whether banning the veil enforces democracy—or squelches diversity.

Finally, Hollande must deal with high-profile members of his own turbulent party. In the run-up to the 2012 election, the front-runner was Dominique Strauss-Kahn. He was forced to drop out after being accused of sexual assault in New York City. All charges were later dropped, but the damage was done. (Strauss-Kahn has speculated he was framed by political rivals, and many in France would not find that fanciful.)

Another prominent Socialist is Ségolène Royal. She lost to Sarkozy in 2007, and lost to Hollande in the 2011 primary. As it happens, Royal and Hollande know each other well: They met in college, lived together for 30 years, and raised four children before splitting up in 2007. They never married. French politics makes strange bedfellows.

APPENDIX

Contents

Tourist Information

The website of the French national tourist office, www.franceguide
.com, is a wealth of information, with particularly good resources
for special-interest travel, and plenty of free-to-download brochures. Paris' official tourist-information website, www.parisinfo
.com, offers practical information on hotels, special events, museums, children's activities, fashion, nightlife, and more. Several private companies offer trip-planning services for a fee; try Detours in
France (tel. 03 80 22 06 03, www.detours-in-france.com) and Paris
Webservices (for Paris-specific assistance, 12 Rue de l'Exposition,
Mo: Ecole Militaire, RER: Pont de l'Alma, tel. 01 53 62 02 29,
www.pariswebservices.com, contactpws@pariswebservices.com,
helpful Gérard).

    In France, your best first stop in a new city is generally the
tourist information office—abbreviated as **TI** in this book—except

in Paris, where they aren't very necessary. In the rest of France you'll find TIs are well organized, with English-speaking staff. They're good places to get a city map and information on public transit (including bus and train schedules), walking tours, special events, and nightlife. Many TIs have information on the entire country or at least the region, so try to pick up maps for destinations you'll be visiting later in your trip. If you're arriving in town after the TI closes, call ahead or pick up a map in a neighboring town. Towns with a lot of tourism generally have English-speaking guides available for private hire (about $140 for a 2-hour guided town walk).

The French call TIs by different names. *Office de Tourisme* and *Bureau de Tourisme* are used in cities; *Syndicat d'Initiative* or *Information Touristique* are used in small towns. Also look for *Accueil* signs in airports and at popular sights. These are information booths staffed with seasonal helpers who provide tourists with limited, though generally sufficient, information. Smaller TIs often close from 12:00 to 14:00 and all day on Sundays.

While TIs are eager to book you a room, use their room-finding service only as a last resort. They are unable to give hard opinions on the relative value of one place over another. The accommodations stakes are too high to go potluck through the TI. Even if there's no "fee," you'll save yourself and your host money by going direct with the listings in this book.

Communicating

Hurdling the Language Barrier and That French Attitude

You've probably heard that the French are "mean and cold and refuse to speak English." This is an out-of-date preconception left over from the days of Charles de Gaulle. Be reasonable in your expectations: French waiters are paid to be efficient, not chatty. And postal clerks are every bit as speedy, cheery, and multilingual as ours are back home.

The biggest mistake most Americans make when traveling to France is trying to do too much with limited time. This approach is a mistake in the bustling north, and a virtual sin in the laid-back south. Hurried, impatient travelers who miss the subtle pleasures of people-watching from a sun-dappled café often misinterpret French attitudes. By slowing your pace and making an effort to understand French culture by living it, you're more likely to have a richer experience. With the five weeks of paid vacation and 35-hour workweek that many French workers consider non-negotiable rights, your hosts can't fathom why anyone would rush through their vacation.

The French take great pride in their customs, clinging to the sense of their own cultural superiority despite the fact that they're no longer a world superpower. Let's face it: It's tough to keep on smiling when you've been crushed by a Big Mac, Mickey Moused by Disney, and drowned in Starbucks coffee. Your hosts are cold only if you decide to see them that way. Polite and formal, the French respect the fine points of culture and tradition. Here, strolling down the street with a big grin on your face and saying hello to strangers is a sign of senility, not friendliness (seriously). They think that Americans, though friendly, are hesitant to pursue more serious friendships. Recognize sincerity and look for kindness. Give them the benefit of the doubt.

Communication difficulties are exaggerated. To hurdle the language barrier, start with the French survival phrases in this book (see page 1155). For a richer experience, bring a small English/French dictionary and/or a phrase book (look for mine, which contains a dictionary and menu decoder), a menu reader, and a good supply of patience. In transactions, a small notepad and pen minimize misunderstandings about prices; have vendors write the price down.

Though many French people speak English—especially those in the tourist trade, and in big cities—you'll get better treatment if you learn and use French pleasantries. If you learn only five phrases, learn and use these: *bonjour* (good day), *pardon* (pardon me), *s'il vous plaît* (please), *merci* (thank you), and *au revoir* (goodbye). The French value politeness. Begin every encounter with *"Bonjour* (or *S'il vous plaît), madame (*or *monsieur),"* and end every encounter with *"Au revoir, madame (*or *monsieur)."*

When you do make an effort to speak French, expect to be politely corrected—*c'est normal.* The French are language perfectionists—they take their language (and other languages) seriously. Often they speak more English than they let on. This isn't a tourist-baiting tactic, but timidity on their part about speaking another language less than fluently. If you want them to speak English, say, *"Bonjour, madame (*or *monsieur). Parlez-vous anglais?"* They may say *"non,"* but as you continue you'll probably find they speak more English than you speak French.

Telephones

Smart travelers use the telephone to reserve or reconfirm rooms, get tourist information, reserve restaurants, confirm tour times, or phone home. When spelling out your name on the phone, you'll find that most letters are pronounced very differently in French: *a* is pronounced "ah," *e* is pronounced "eh," and *i* is pronounced "ee." To avoid confusion, say *"a,* Anne," *"e,* euro," and *"i,* Isabelle."

This section covers dialing instructions, phone cards, and

types of phones (for more in-depth information, see www.rick steves.com/phoning).

How to Dial

Calling from the US to France, or vice versa, is simple—once you break the code. The European calling chart in this chapter will walk you through it.

Dialing Domestically Within France

France has a direct-dial 10-digit phone system (no area codes). To make domestic calls anywhere within France, just dial the number.

For example, the number of one of my recommended hotels in Nice is 04 97 03 10 70. That's the number you dial whether you're calling it from across the street or across the country.

These instructions apply to dialing from a landline (such as a pay phone or your hotel-room phone) or a French mobile phone.

If you're dialing within France using your US mobile phone, you may need to dial as if it's a domestic call, or you may need to dial as if you're calling from the US (see "Dialing Internationally," next). Try it one way, and if it doesn't work, try the other way.

Understand the various prefixes. Any number beginning with 06 or 07 is a mobile phone, and costs more to dial. France's toll-free numbers start with 0800 (like US 800 numbers, though in France you dial a 0 first rather than a 1). In France these 0800 numbers—called *numéro vert* (green number)—can be dialed free from any phone without using a phone card. But you can't call France's toll-free numbers from America, nor can you count on reaching US toll-free numbers from France.

Any 08 number that does not have a 00 directly following is a toll call, generally costing €0.10 to €0.50 per minute.

Dialing Internationally to or from France

If you want to make an international call, follow these steps:

• Dial the international access code (00 if you're calling from Europe, 011 from the US or Canada). If you're dialing from a mobile phone, you can replace the international access code with +, which works regardless of where you're calling from. (On many mobile phones, you can insert a + by pressing and holding the 0 key.)

• Dial the country code of the country you're calling (33 for France, or 1 for the US or Canada).

• Dial the local number. If you're calling France, drop the initial zero of the phone number. (The European calling chart lists specifics per country.)

Calling from the US to France: To call the Nice hotel from the US, dial 011 (the US international access code), 33 (France's country code), then 4 97 03 10 70 (the hotel's number without its initial zero).

Calling from any European country to the US: To call my office in Edmonds, Washington, from anywhere in Europe, I dial 00 (Europe's access code), 1 (the US country code), 425 (Edmonds' area code), and 771-8303.

Mobile Phones

Traveling with a mobile phone is handy and practical. Whether you're using a smartphone or a conventional cell phone, the basics for how to make calls and send texts are the same. For specifics on using your smartphone to get online, see the sidebar.

Roaming with Your Mobile Phone: Your US mobile phone works in Europe if it's GSM-enabled, tri-band or quad-band, and on a calling plan that includes international calls. Phones from AT&T and T-Mobile, which use the same GSM technology that Europe does, are more likely to work overseas than Verizon or Sprint phones (if you're not sure, ask your service provider). Most US providers will charge you $1.29-$1.99 per minute to make or receive calls while roaming internationally, and 20-50 cents to send or receive text messages. If you bother to sign up for an international calling plan with your provider, you'll save a few dimes per minute. Though pricey, roaming on your own phone is easy and can be a cost-effective way to keep in touch—especially on a short trip or if you won't be making many calls.

Buying and Using SIM Cards in Europe: You'll pay much cheaper rates if you put a European SIM card in your mobile phone; to do this, your phone must be electronically "unlocked" (ask your provider about this, buy an unlocked phone before you leave, or get one in Europe—see "Other Mobile-Phone Options," next). Then, in Europe, you can buy a fingernail-size **SIM card,** which gives you a European phone number. SIM cards are sold at mobile-phone stores, post offices, and some newsstand kiosks for $5-10, and often include at least that much prepaid domestic calling time (making the card itself virtually free). When you buy a SIM card, you may need to show ID, such as your passport.

Insert the SIM card in your phone (usually in a slot behind the battery or on the side), and it'll work like a European mobile phone. Before purchasing a SIM card, always ask about fees for domestic and international calls, roaming charges, and how to check your credit balance and buy more time. This can be tricky to accomplish if you don't speak some French, but the major mobile phone companies—SFR and Orange—usually have English-speaking staff at their stores. (Also, be aware that prompts for voice mail or topping up the card are in French.) When you're in the SIM card's

Smartphones and Data Roaming

I take my smartphone to Europe, using it to make phone calls (sparingly) and send texts, but also to check email, listen to audiotours, and browse the Internet. If you're clever, you can do all this without incurring huge data-roaming fees. Here's how.

Many smartphones, such as the iPhone, Android, and BlackBerry, work in Europe (though some older Verizon iPhones don't). For voice calls and text messaging, smartphones work like any mobile phone (as described under "Mobile Phones," previous page)—unless you're connected to free Wi-Fi, in which case you can use Skype, Google Talk, or FaceTime to call for free (or at least very cheaply; see "Calling over the Internet," opposite page).

The (potentially) *really* expensive aspect of using smartphones in Europe is not voice calls or text messages, but sky-high rates for using data: checking email, browsing the Internet, streaming videos, using certain apps, and so on. If you don't proactively adjust your settings, these charges can mount up even if you're not actually using your phone—because the phone is constantly "roaming" to update your email and such. (One tip is to switch your email settings from "push" to "fetch," so you can choose when to download your emails rather than having them automatically "pushed" over the Internet to your device.)

The best solution: Disable data roaming entirely, and use your device to access the Internet only when you find free Wi-Fi (at your hotel, for example). Then you can surf the net to your heart's content, or make free (or extremely cheap) phone calls via Skype. You can manually turn off data roaming on your phone's menu (check under the "Network" settings). For added security, you can call and ask your service provider to temporarily suspend your data account entirely for the length of your trip.

Some travelers enjoy the flexibility of getting online even when they're not on free Wi-Fi. But be careful. If you simply switch on data roaming, you'll pay exorbitant rates of about $20 per megabyte (figure around 40 cents per email downloaded, or about $3 to view a typical web page)—much more expensive than it is back home. If you know you'll be doing some data roaming, it's far more affordable to sign up for a limited international data-roaming plan through your carrier (but be very clear on your megabyte limit to avoid inflated overage charges). In general, ask your provider in advance how to avoid unwittingly roaming your way to a huge bill.

home country, domestic calls average 10 to 20 cents per minute, and incoming calls are free. Rates are higher if you're roaming in another country, and you may pay more to call a toll number than you'd pay to dial it from a fixed line.

Other Mobile-Phone Options: Many travelers like to carry two phones: both their own US mobile phone (allowing them to stay reachable on their own phone number) and a second, unlocked European phone (which lets them do all their local calling at far cheaper rates). You could either bring two phones from home, or get one in Europe. If you have an old mobile phone sitting around, ask your provider for the "unlock code" so it can be used with European SIM cards. Or buy a cheap, basic phone before you go (search your favorite online shopping site for "unlocked quad-band GSM phone"). In Europe, basic phones are sold at hole-in-the-wall vendors at many airports and train stations, and at phone desks within larger department stores. Phones that are "locked" to work with a single provider start around $40; "unlocked" phones (which work with any SIM card) start around $60. Regardless of how you get your phone, remember that you'll need a SIM card to make it work.

Car-rental companies and mobile-phone companies offer the option to rent a mobile phone with a European number. While this seems convenient, hidden fees (such as high per-minute charges or expensive shipping costs) can really add up—which usually makes it a bad value. One exception is Verizon's Global Travel Program, available only to Verizon customers.

Calling over the Internet

Some things that seem too good to be true...actually are true. If you're traveling with a laptop, tablet, or smartphone, you can make free calls over the Internet to another wireless device, anywhere in the world, for free. (Or you can pay a few cents to call from your computer to a telephone.) The major providers are Skype, Google Talk, and (on Apple devices) FaceTime (all available free for both computers and tablets/smartphones). You can get online at a Wi-Fi hotspot and use these apps to make calls without ringing up expensive roaming charges (though call quality can be spotty on slow connections). You can make Internet calls even if you're traveling without your own mobile device: Many European Internet cafés have Skype, as well as microphones and webcams, on their terminals—just log on and chat away.

Landline Telephones

As in the US, these days most French do the majority of their phoning on mobile phones. But you'll still encounter landlines in hotel rooms and at pay phones.

Hotel-Room Phones: Calling from your hotel room can be great for local calls and for international calls if you have an international phone card (described later). Otherwise, hotel-room phones can be an almost criminal rip-off for long-distance or international calls. Many hotels charge a fee for local and some-times even "toll-free" numbers—always ask for the rates before you dial. Incoming calls are free, making this a cheap way for friends and family to stay in touch (provided they have a long-distance plan with good international rates—and a list of your hotels' phone numbers).

Public Pay Phones: Coin-op phones are virtually extinct in Europe. To make calls from public phones, you'll need a prepaid phone card, described next.

Types of Telephone Cards

There are two types of phone cards: insertable (for pay phones) and international (cheap for overseas calls and usable from any type of phone). Both types of phone card work only in France. If you have a live card at the end of your trip, give it to another traveler to use—most cards expire 3-6 months after the first use.

Insertable Phone Cards: Called *télécartes* (tay-lay-kart), these cards are handy and affordable for local and domestic calls from a phone booth. (Though you can use *télécartes* to call anywhere in the world, they're a bad value for international calls.) They're sold in two denominations—*une petite* costs €7.50; *une grande* €15—at *tabacs* (tobacco shops), newsstands, post offices, and train stations. To use the card, insert it into a slot in the pay phone. Push the flag button on the phone to change the display until you see English, and follow instructions.

International Phone Cards: With a *carte international*, phone calls from France to the US can cost less than a nickel a minute. The cards can also be used to make local calls, and they work from any type of phone, including your hotel-room phone or a mobile phone with a European SIM card. To use the card, dial a toll-free access number, then enter your scratch-to-reveal PIN code.

You can buy the cards at newsstand kiosks and tobacco shops. Ask the clerk for a *"carte international pour les Etats-Unis"* (for the US; cart an-tehr-nah-see-oh-nahl poor lay-zay-tah-oo-nee). Buy a lower denomination in case the card is a dud. Some shops also sell cardless codes, printed right on the receipt.

To make a call, dial the free (usually 4-digit) access number. If the access code on the card doesn't work from your hotel-room phone, try the card's 10-digit, toll-free code that starts with 08. Either way, a voice in French (followed by English) tells you to enter your (usually 12-digit) code. Before or after entering your code, you'll probably need to press (or *touche,* pronounced toosh) the pound key (#, *dièse,* dee-ehz) or the star key (*, *étoile,* ay-twahl). At the next message, dial the number you're calling (possibly followed by pound or star key; you don't have to listen to the entire sales pitch).

Since you don't need the actual card or receipt to use the account, you can write down the access number and code and share it with friends.

US Calling Cards: These cards, such as the ones offered by AT&T, Verizon, and Sprint, are a rotten value, and are being phased out. Try any of the options outlined earlier.

Internet Access

It's useful to get online periodically as you travel—to confirm trip plans, check train or bus schedules, get weather forecasts, catch up on email, blog or post photos from your trip, or call folks back home (explained earlier, under "Calling over the Internet").

Your Mobile Device: The majority of accommodations in France offer Wi-Fi (pronounced "wee-fee" in French), as do many cafés, making it easy for you to get online with your laptop, tablet, or smartphone. Every McDonald's in France offers free Wi-Fi (handy for drivers as McD's are omnipresent on town outskirts). Access is often free, but sometimes there's a fee.

Some hotel rooms and Internet cafés have high-speed Internet jacks that you can plug into with an Ethernet cable. A cellular modem—which lets your device access the Internet over a mobile network—provides more extensive coverage, but is much more expensive than Wi-Fi.

Public Internet Terminals: Many accommodations offer a computer in the lobby with Internet access for guests. If you ask politely, smaller places may let you sit at their desk for a few minutes just to check your email. If your hotelier doesn't have access, ask to be directed to the nearest place to get online. Little hole-in-the-wall Internet-access shops, while common in the rest of Europe, are not prevalent in France. If you can't find a place to get online, look for a post office that offers Internet access *(cyberposte);* buy a chip-card (about same prices as phone cards) and you're in business.

Security: Whether you're accessing the Internet with your own device or at a public terminal, using a shared network or computer comes with the potential for increased security risks. Be careful about storing personal information online, such as passport and credit-card numbers. If you're not convinced a connection is secure, avoid accessing any sites that could be vulnerable to fraud (e.g., online banking).

European Calling Chart

Just smile and dial, using this key:
AC = Area Code, LN = Local Number.

European Country	Calling long distance within ...	Calling from the US or Canada to ...	Calling from a European country to ...
Austria	AC + LN	011 + 43 + AC (without the initial zero) + LN	00 + 43 + AC (without the initial zero) + LN
Belgium	LN	011 + 32 + LN (without initial zero)	00 + 32 + LN (without initial zero)
Bosnia-Herzegovina	AC + LN	011 + 387 + AC (without initial zero) + LN	00 + 387 + AC (without initial zero) + LN
Britain	AC + LN	011 + 44 + AC (without initial zero) + LN	00 + 44 + AC (without initial zero) + LN
Croatia	AC + LN	011 + 385 + AC (without initial zero) + LN	00 + 385 + AC (without initial zero) + LN
Czech Republic	LN	011 + 420 + LN	00 + 420 + LN
Denmark	LN	011 + 45 + LN	00 + 45 + LN
Estonia	LN	011 + 372 + LN	00 + 372 + LN
Finland	AC + LN	011 + 358 + AC (without initial zero) + LN	999 (or other 900 number) + 358 + AC (without initial zero) + LN
France	LN	011 + 33 + LN (without initial zero)	00 + 33 + LN (without initial zero)
Germany	AC + LN	011 + 49 + AC (without initial zero) + LN	00 + 49 + AC (without initial zero) + LN
Gibraltar	LN	011 + 350 + LN	00 + 350 + LN
Greece	LN	011 + 30 + LN	00 + 30 + LN
Hungary	06 + AC + LN	011 + 36 + AC + LN	00 + 36 + AC + LN
Ireland	AC + LN	011 + 353 + AC (without initial zero) + LN	00 + 353 + AC (without initial zero) + LN

APPENDIX

European Country	Calling long distance within ...	Calling from the US or Canada to ...	Calling from a European country to ...
Italy	LN	011 + 39 + LN	00 + 39 + LN
Montenegro	AC + LN	011 + 382 + AC (without initial zero) + LN	00 + 382 + AC (without initial zero) + LN
Morocco	LN	011 + 212 + LN (without initial zero)	00 + 212 + LN (without initial zero)
Netherlands	AC + LN	011 + 31 + AC (without initial zero) + LN	00 + 31 + AC (without initial zero) + LN
Norway	LN	011 + 47 + LN	00 + 47 + LN
Poland	LN	011 + 48 + LN	00 + 48 + LN
Portugal	LN	011 + 351 + LN	00 + 351 + LN
Slovakia	AC + LN	011 + 421 + AC (without initial zero) + LN	00 + 421 + AC (without initial zero) + LN
Slovenia	AC + LN	011 + 386 + AC (without initial zero) + LN	00 + 386 + AC (without initial zero) + LN
Spain	LN	011 + 34 + LN	00 + 34 + LN
Sweden	AC + LN	011 + 46 + AC (without initial zero) + LN	00 + 46 + AC (without initial zero) + LN
Switzerland	LN	011 + 41 + LN (without initial zero)	00 + 41 + LN (without initial zero)
Turkey	AC (if there's no initial zero, add one) + LN	011 + 90 + AC (without initial zero) + LN	00 + 90 + AC (without initial zero) + LN

- The instructions above apply whether you're calling a land line or mobile phone.

- The international access code (the first numbers you dial when making an international call) is 011 if you're calling from the US or Canada. It's 00 if you're calling from virtually anywhere in Europe (except Finland, where it's 999 or another 900 number, depending on the phone service you're using).

- To call the US or Canada from Europe, dial 00, then 1 (the country code for the US and Canada), then the area code and number. In short, 00 + 1 + AC + LN = Hi, Mom!

Mail

You can mail one package per day to yourself worth up to $200 duty-free from Europe to the US (mark it "personal purchases"). If you're sending a gift to someone, mark it "unsolicited gift." For details, visit www.cbp.gov and search for "Know Before You Go."

The French postal service works fine, but for quick transatlantic delivery (in either direction), consider services such as DHL (www.dhl.com). French post offices are sometimes called PTT, for "Post, Telegraph, and Telephone"—look for signs for *La Poste*. Hours vary, though most are open weekdays 8:00-19:00 and Saturday morning 8:00-12:00. Stamps and phone cards are also sold at *tabacs*. It costs about €1 to mail a postcard to the US. One convenient, if expensive, way to send packages home is to use the PTT's Colissimo International XL postage-paid mailing box (allow 6 days to reach the US). It costs €36-45 to ship boxes weighing 5-7 kilos (about 11-15 pounds).

Local and Emergency Contacts

Emergency Needs

Police: Tel. 17
Emergency Medical Assistance (called "SAMU"): Tel. 15
Ambulance in Paris: Tel. 01 45 67 50 50 (message asks for your address and name)
Collect Calls to the US: Tel. 00 00 11

Embassies and Consulates

US Consulate and Embassy in Paris: Tel. 01 43 12 22 22, (4 Avenue Gabriel, to the left as you face Hôtel Crillon, Mo: Concorde, http://france.usembassy.gov)

Canadian Consulate and Embassy in Paris: Tel. 01 44 43 29 00 (35 Avenue Montaigne, Mo: Franklin D. Roosevelt, www.amb-canada.fr). For 24/7 emergency assistance call collect to 613/996-8885 or email sos@international.gc.ca.

Australian Consulate in Paris: Tel. 01 40 59 33 00 (4 Rue Jean Rey, Mo: Bir-Hakeim, www.france.embassy.gov.au)

US Consulate in Lyon: Tel. 04 78 38 33 03 (east of the Cordeliers Métro stop at 1 Quai Jules Courmant, http://lyon.usconsulate.gov, usalyon@state.gov)

Canadian Consulate in Lyon: Tel. 04 72 77 64 07, fax 04 72 77 65 09 (21 Rue Bourgelat, www.canadainternational.gc.ca, consulat.canada-lyon@amb-canada.fr)

US Consulate in Marseille: Tel. 04 91 54 92 00, fax 04 91 55 09 47 (Place Varian Fry, http://marseille.usconsulate.gov)

US Consulate in Nice: Tel. 04 93 88 89 55, fax 04 93 87 07 38, (7 Avenue Gustave V, http://marseille.usconsulate.gov/nice.html, usca.nice@orange.fr)

Canadian Consulate in Nice: Tel. 04 93 92 93 22, fax 04 93 92 55 51 (2 Place Franklin, consulat.canada-nice@amb-canada.fr)

US Consulate in Strasbourg: Tel. 03 88 35 31 04, fax 03 88 24 06 95 (5 Avenue d'Alsace, http://strasbourg.usconsulate.gov)

US Consulate in Bordeaux: Tel. 05 56 48 63 85, fax 05 56 51 61 97 (89 Quai des Chartrons, http://bordeaux.usconsulate.gov, usa bordeaux@state.gov)

Travel Advisories

US Department of State: Tel. 888-407-4747, from outside US tel. 1-202-501-4444, www.travel.state.gov

Canadian Department of Foreign Affairs: Canadian tel. 800-267-8376, from outside Canada tel. 1-613-996-8885, www.voyage .gc.ca

US Centers for Disease Control and Prevention: Tel. 800-CDC-INFO (800-232-4636), www.cdc.gov/travel

Transportation

By Car or Public Transportation?

If you're debating between public transportation and car rental, consider these factors: Cars are best for three or more traveling together (especially families with small kids), those packing heavy, and those scouring the countryside. Trains and buses are best for solo travelers, blitz tourists, and city-to-city travelers. While a car gives you more freedom—enabling you to search for hotels more easily and carrying your bags for you—trains and buses zip you effortlessly and scenically from city to city, usually dropping you in the center, often near a TI. Cars are great in the countryside, but an expensive headache in places like Paris, Nice, and Lyon.

In cities, arriving by train in the middle of town makes hotel-hunting and sightseeing easy. But in France, many of your destinations are likely to be small, remote places far from a station, such as Honfleur, Mont St-Michel, D-Day beaches, Loire châteaux, Dordogne caves, and villages in Provence and Burgundy. In such places, taking trains and buses can require great patience, planning, and time. If you'll be relying on public transportation, focus on fewer destinations, or hire one of the excellent minivan tour guides I recommend.

I've included two sample itineraries—by car and by public transportation—to help you explore France smoothly; you'll find these in the Introduction.

Public Transportation
Trains

France's rail system (SNCF) sets the pace in Europe. Its super

France's Rail System

ENGLAND

London
Eurostar
Dover
Folkstone
Newhaven
Portsmouth

To Ireland

English   Channel

Cherbourg
Arro-manches
Le Havre
Dieppe
Le Tréport
Honfleur
Rouen

Roscoff
Brest
Morlaix
Mont St-Michel
St-Malo
Avranches
Bayeux
Caen
Lisieux
Versailles
Chartres

Quimper
Lamballe
Dinan
Pontorson
Dol

Vannes
Rennes
Le Mans
Orléans

Quiberon
Redon
TGV

Atlantic
Nantes
Angers
Saumur
Tours
Blois
Amboise

Ocean
Chinon
Langeais
Azay
Tours
St-Pierre
des Corps
TGV Stn.

Vierzon

Poitiers

F R A

La Rochelle
Oradour-sur-Glane

Saintes
Cognac
Limoges

Angoulême

Périgueux
Brive

Libourne
Bordeaux
Les Eyzies
Le Buisson
Sarlat
Soulliac

St-Emilion
Beynac

Cahors

Agen
Montauban

Biarritz
Dax
Guernica
St-Jean-de-Luz
Bayonne
Hendaye
Bilbao
Irun
PRIVATE RAIL
San Sebastián
St-Jean Pied-de-Port
Pau
Toulouse
Lourdes

Miranda de Ebro
Pamplona

Burgos
Foix
La Tour

To Madrid
SPAIN
ANDORRA
To Barcelona

Legend

- Rail
- Eurostar Rail
- TGV High Speed Rail
- Bus
- Boat
- ✈ Airports (Not All Shown)

50 Kilometers
50 Miles

APPENDIX

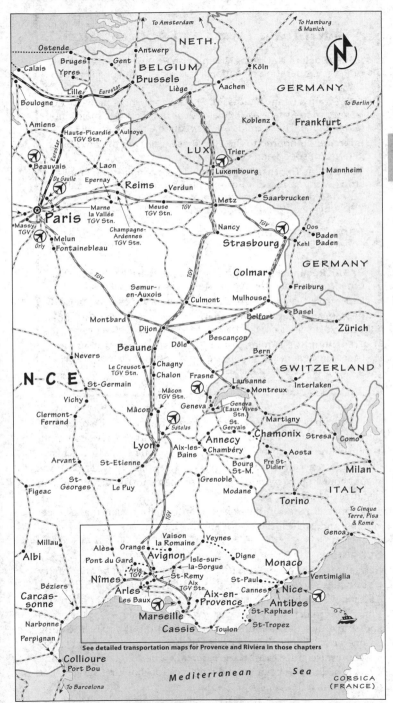

To Amsterdam

To Hamburg & Munich

Ostende

NETH.

Calais
Bruges
Ypres
Antwerp
Gent
BELGIUM
Köln
GERMANY

Boulogne
Lille
Eurostar
Brussels
Liège
Aachen

Amiens
Haute-Picardie TGV Stn.
Aulnoye
To Berlin

Beauvais
De Gaulle
Laon
Epernay
LUX
Trier
Koblenz
Frankfurt

Eurostar
Reims
Verdun
Luxembourg
Mannheim

Paris
Marne la Vallée TGV Stn.
Meuse TGV Stn.
Metz
Saarbrucken

Massy TGV
Orly
Melun
Fontainebleau
Champagne-Ardennes TGV Stn.
Nancy
TGV
Strasbourg
Oos
Baden Baden
Kehl

GERMANY

Colmar
Freiburg

TGV
Semur-en-Auxois
Culmont
Mulhouse
Basel

Montbard
Belfort
Zürich

N C E
St-Germain
Dijon
Dôle
Bescançon
Bern
SWITZERLAND

Nevers
Beaune
Le Creusot TGV Stn.
Chagny
Chalon
Frasne
Lausanne
Montreux
Interlaken

Vichy
Mâcon TGV Stn.
Geneva
Geneva (Eaux-Vives Stn.)
St. Gervais
Martigny
Chamonix
Stresa
Como

Clermont-Ferrand
Mâcon
Satolas
Annecy
Chambéry
Aosta
Milan

Arvant
Lyon
Aix-les-Bains
Bourg St-M.
Pre St-Didier
ITALY

St-Georges
St-Etienne
Grenoble
Modane
Torino

Figeac
Le Puy
To Cinque Terre, Pisa & Rome

Millau
TGV
Vaison la Romaine
Veynes
Genoa

Albi
Alès
Orange
Avignon
Digne
Monaco

Béziers
Pont du Gard
Avia. TGV
Isle-sur-la-Sorgue
St-Paul
Ventimiglia

Carcassonne
Nîmes
St-Remy
Aix TGV Stn.
Cannes
Nice

Narbonne
Arles
Les Baux
Aix-en-Provence
St-Raphael
Antibes

Perpignan
Marseille
St-Tropez

Collioure
Port Bou
Cassis
Toulon

See detailed transportation maps for Provence and Riviera in those chapters

To Barcelona

Mediterranean   Sea

CORSICA (FRANCE)

French Train Terms and Abbreviations

SNCF (Société Nationale Chemins de Fer): This is the Amtrak of France, operating all national train lines that link cities and towns.

TGV (Train à Grande Vitesse): SNCF's network of high-speed trains (twice as fast as regular trains) that connect major cities in France. These trains always require a reservation.

Intercité: Compared to the TGV, these trains are the next best in terms of speed and comfort.

TER (Trains Express Régionale): These trains serve smaller stops within a region. For example, you'll find trains called TER de Bourgogne (trains operating only in Burgundy) and TER Provence (Provence-only trains).

Paris Region Only

For more on Paris transit, see "Getting Around Paris" on page 64.

RATP (Réseau Autonome de Transport Parisienne): This organization operates subways and buses within Paris.

Le Métro: This network of subway lines serves central Paris.

RER (Réseau Express Régional): This commuter rail and subway system links central Paris with suburban destinations.

Transilien: It's similar to the RER system, but travels farther afield, serving the Ile de France region around Paris. Railpasses cover these lines.

TGV (tay zhay vay; *train à grande vitesse*) system has inspired bullet trains throughout the world. The TGV runs at 170-220 mph. Its rails are fused into one long, continuous track for a faster and smoother ride. The TGV has changed commuting patterns throughout France by putting most of the country within day-trip distance of Paris.

Any train station has schedule information, can make reservations, and can sell tickets for any destination.

Schedules

Schedules change by season, weekday, and weekend. Verify train times shown in this book—online, check www.bahn.com (Germany's all-Europe schedule site), or check locally at train stations. The French rail website (www.sncf.com) shows ticket prices and sells some tickets online (worth checking if you're traveling on one or two long-distance trains without a railpass, as advance-purchase discounts can be a great deal). The SNCF's phone line offers schedule information and a reservation-booking service, but only in French (tel. 3635).

Coping with Strikes

Going on strike *(en grève)* is a popular pastime in this rev-olution-happy country. Because bargaining between man-agement and employees is not standard procedure, workers strike to get attention. Truckers and tractors block main roads and autoroutes (they call it Opération Escargot—"Operation Snail's Pace"), baggage handlers bring airports to their knees, and museum workers make Mona Lisa off-limits to tourists. Métro and train personnel seem to strike every year—probably during your trip. What does the traveler do? You could *jeter l'éponge* (throw in the sponge) and go somewhere less strike-prone (Switzerland's nice), or learn to accept certain events as out of your control. Strikes in France generally last no lon-ger than a day or two, and if you're aware of them, you can usually plan around them. Your hotelier will know the latest (or can find out). Make a habit of asking your hotel reception-ist about strikes, or check www.americansinfrance.net (look under "Daily Life").

APPENDIX

Bigger stations have helpful information agents (wearing red or blue vests) roaming the station and at *Accueil* offices or booths. They can answer schedule questions more quickly than staff at the ticket windows. Make use of their help; don't stand in a ticket line if all you need is a train schedule.

Railpasses

Long-distance travelers can save money with a France Railpass, sold only outside Europe (through travel agents or Europe Through the Back Door). For roughly the cost of a full-fare Paris-Avignon-Paris ticket, the France Railpass offers three days of travel (within a month) anywhere in France. You can add up to six more days, each for the cost of a two-hour ride. You can save money by getting the second-class instead of the first-class version, but first class gives you more options when reserving popular TGV routes (seats are very limited for passholders, so reserving these fast trains at least several weeks in advance is recommended). The saverpass version gives two or more people traveling together a 15 percent discount.

Each day of use allows you to take as many trips as you want on one calendar day (you could go from Paris to Beaune in Burgundy, enjoy wine-tasting, then continue to Avignon, stay a few hours, and end in Nice—though I wouldn't recommend it). Buy second-class tickets in France for shorter trips, and save your valuable pass days for longer trips. Note that if you're con-necting the French Alps with Alsace, you might travel through Switzerland, a route that requires France Railpass holders to buy a

Cost of Railpasses

Prices listed are for 2012 and are subject to change. For the latest prices, details, and train schedules (and easy online ordering), see my comprehensive *Guide to Eurail Passes* at www.ricksteves.com/rail.

"Saver" prices are per person for two or more people traveling together. "Youth" means under age 26. The fare for children 4–11 is half the adult individual fare or Saver fare. Kids under age 4 travel free.

FRANCE PASS

	Adult 1st Class	Adult 2nd Class	Senior 1st Class	Youth 1st Class	Youth 2nd Class
3 days in 1 month	$299	$242	$261	$211	$178
Extra rail days (max 6)	42-47	31-39	37-40	30-32	26-29

Senior = 60 and up.

FRANCE SAVERPASS

	1st Class	2nd Class
3 days in 1 month	$255	$208
Extra rail days (max 6)	36-39	27-33

FRANCE RAIL & DRIVE PASS

Any 2 rail days and 2 car days in 1 month.

Car Category	1st Class	Extra Car Day
Economy	$270	$56
Compact	275	59
Intermediate	289	73
Full Size	302	86
Premium Automatic	310	95
Minivan	320	104

Prices are per person, two traveling together. Solo travelers pay about $100 extra. Extra rail days (3 max) cost $33 per day. To order a Rail & Drive pass, call your travel agent or Rail Europe at 800-438-7245. *This pass is not sold by Europe Through the Back Door.*

Map key:
Approximate point-to-point one-way second-class rail fares in US dollars. First class costs 50 percent more. Add up fares for your itinerary to see if a railpass will save you money.

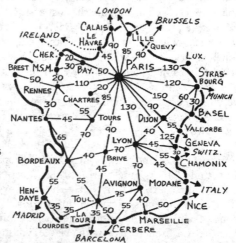

SELECTPASS

This pass covers travel in three adjacent countries. For four- and five-country options, please visit **www.ricksteves.com/rail**.

	Individual 1st Class	Saver 1st Class	Youth 2nd Class
5 days in 2 months	$447	$381	$292
6 or 7 days in 2 months	493	420	322
8 or 9 days in 2 months	583	496	380
10 or 11 days in 2 months	676	575	440

FRANCE–SWITZERLAND PASS

	Individual 1st Class	Saver 1st Class	Youth 2nd Class
4 days in 2 months	$400	$341	$282
Extra rail days (max 6)	37-57	34-51	31-35

FRANCE–ITALY PASS

	Individual 1st Class	Individual 2nd Class	Saver 1st Class	Saver 2nd Class	Youth 2nd Class
4 days in 2 months	$376	$323	$323	$275	$245
Extra rail days (max 6)	45-50	38-40	38-40	31-32	28-32

Be aware of your route. Direct Paris–Italy trains (day and overnight) and trains via Switzerland aren't covered by this pass.

FRANCE–SPAIN PASS

	Individual 1st Class	Individual 2nd Class	Saver 1st Class	Saver 2nd Class	Youth 2nd Class
4 days in 2 months	$376	$323	$323	$275	$245
Extra rail days (max 6)	45-50	38-40	38-40	31-32	28-32

If you're only dipping into a bit of Spain, you may not need the France-Spain pass. For instance, a ticket from the French border at Cerbere to Barcelona costs only $35. From the border at Hendaye to Madrid costs $75, but if you cover this ground via the fancy Paris–Madrid "Elipsos" night train, the same passholder fares ($70 and up) apply whether your pass covers one or both countries.

FRANCE–GERMANY PASS

	Individual 1st Class	Individual 2nd Class	Saver 1st Class	Saver 2nd Class	Youth 2nd Class
4 days in 2 months	$403	$364	$364	$330	$282
5 days in 2 months	446	402	402	363	312
6 days in 2 months	488	440	440	391	345
8 days in 2 months	572	517	517	449	403
10 days in 2 months	657	593	593	517	466

FRANCE–BENELUX PASS

	Individual 1st Class	Individual 2nd Class	Saver 1st Class	Saver 2nd Class	Youth 2nd Class
5 days in 2 months	$436	$376	$364	$321	$278
6 days in 2 months	478	418	402	364	309
8 days in 2 months	552	493	473	424	366
10 days in 2 months	624	563	533	481	421

APPENDIX

ticket for that segment (about €50).

For a free summary of railpass deals and the latest prices, check my Guide to Eurail Passes at www.ricksteves.com/rail. If you decide to get a railpass, this guide will help you know you're getting the right one for your trip.

Buying Tickets

While there's no deadline to buy any train ticket, the fast, reserved TGV trains get booked up. Reserve well ahead for any TGV you cannot afford to miss. Tickets go on sale 90 days in advance, and the cheapest tickets sell out early; reservations for railpass holders also go particularly fast. To buy tickets online, visit www.tgv-europe.com/en/home; for your pickup option, choose any country other than the US and outside western Europe, and you'll be able to print tickets at home or pick them up in the station (if instead you choose "France," the site will be in French, and if you choose "US," you'll be redirected to www.raileurope.com). The US company, RailEurope, delivers tickets to your home, but doesn't always have the lowest rates.

Remember that second-class tickets provide the same transportation for up to 33 percent less than first class (and many regional trains to less-trafficked places often have only second-class cars).

You can buy tickets or seat reservations on the train for a €4-10 surcharge depending on length of trip, but you must find the conductor immediately upon boarding; otherwise it's a €35 minimum charge.

Automatic Train-Ticket Machines

The ticket machines available at most stations are great time-savers for short trips when ticket window lines are long. The machines won't accept American credit cards, so you'll need euro coins instead. Some machines have English instructions, but for those that don't, here is what you are prompted to do. (The default is usually what you want; turn the dial or move the cursor to your choice, and press *"Validez"* to agree to each step.)

1. *Quelle est votre destination?* (What's your destination?)
2. *Billet Plein Tarif* (Full-fare ticket—yes for most.)
3. *1ère ou 2ème* (First or second class; normally second is fine.)
4. *Aller simple ou aller-retour?* (One-way or round-trip?)
5. *Prix en Euro* (The price should be shown if you get this far.)

Reservations

Reservations are required for any TGV train, *couchettes* (sleeping berths) on night trains, and some other trains when indicated in timetables. You can reserve any train at any station or through

---

Key Travel Phrases

Bonjour, monsieur (or **madame**), **parlez-vous anglais?**

Pron: bohn-zhoor, muhs-yur/mah-dahm, par-lay-voo ahn-glay?

Meaning: Hello, sir (or madam), do you speak English?

Je voudrais un départ pour (destination), **pour le** (date), **vers** (general time of day), **la plus direct possible.**

Pron: zhuh voo-dray uhn day-par poor (destination), poor luh (date), vehr (time), lah ploo dee-rehk poh-see-bluh.

Meaning/Example: I would like a departure for Avignon, on 23 May, about 9:00, the most direct way possible.

SNCF Boutiques (small offices in city centers).

Fast and popular TGV trains usually fill up quickly, making it a challenge to get reservations (particularly for railpass-holders, who are allocated a limited number of seats). It's wise to book well ahead for any TGV, especially on the busy Paris-Avignon-Nice line. Reservations cost €3 on top of the cost of a ticket or a France Railpass (more during busy periods, $11 if booked in the US). If you've got a multi-country railpass, they're $21. (If passholder reservations are sold out at the $11 rate, France Railpass holders can try for a seat at the "Easy Access" rate of €25.) If the TGV trains you wanted are fully booked, ask about TER trains serving the same destination, as these don't require reservations.

Reservations are generally unnecessary for non-TGV trains (verify ahead as some Intercité trains require reservations), but they are advisable during busy times (for example, Friday and Sunday afternoons, Saturday mornings, weekday rush hours, and holiday weekends; see "Holidays and Festivals" on page 1144).

International trains (such as Eurostar, Thalys, Artesia, and international TGV) have different reservation price ranges.

Validating Tickets, Reservations, and Railpasses

You are required to validate (*composter*, kohm-poh-stay) all train tickets and reservations before boarding any SNCF train. Look for a yellow machine nearby to stamp your ticket or reservation. If you have a railpass, validate it at a ticket window before the first time you use it; don't stamp it in the yellow machine.

Baggage Check

Baggage check (*consigne* or *Espaces Bagages*) is available only at the biggest train stations (about €5-11 per bag depending on size), and is noted where available in this book (depends on security concerns, so be prepared to keep your bag). For security reasons, all luggage is supposed to carry a tag with the traveler's first and last name and current address (though it's not enforced). This applies to hand luggage as well as bigger bags that are stowed. Free tags are available at train stations in France.

Other baggage-check options in cities are also listed in this book (where available). Here's a tip: Major museums and monuments usually have free baggage check for visitors. Even if the sight is not particularly interesting to you, the entry fee may be worth it if you need to stow your bags for a few hours.

Train Tips

• Arrive at the station with plenty of time before your departure to find your platform (platform numbers are posted about 15 minutes prior to departure), confirm connections, and so on.

• Small stations are minimally staffed; if there is no agent at the station, go directly to the tracks and look for the overhead sign that confirms your train stops at that track.

• Larger stations have platforms with monitors showing TGV car layouts (numbered forward or backward) so you can figure out where your *voiture* (car) will stop on the long platform and where to board it.

• Check schedules and reservation requirements in advance. Upon arrival at a station, learn your departure possibilities (don't rely exclusively on online schedules). Large stations have a separate information window or office; at small stations, the ticket office gives information.

• If you have a rail flexipass, write the date on your pass each day you travel (before or immediately after boarding your first train).

• Validate tickets and some reservations (not passes) in yellow machines before boarding. If you're traveling with a pass and have a reservation for a certain trip, you must validate the reservation.

• Reservations for all TGV trains are required and often sell out. A limited number of reservations are allocated for railpass users during peak times—reserve as far ahead as you can for Friday and Sunday afternoons and Saturday mornings.

• Before getting on a train, confirm that it's going where you think it is. For example, if you want to go to Bayeux, ask the conductor or any local passenger, *"A Bayeux?"* (ah bah-yuh; meaning, "To Bayeux?").

• Some longer trains split cars en route. Make sure your train car is continuing to your destination by asking, for example, *"Cette voiture va à Bayeux?"* (seht vwah-tewr vah ah bah-yuh; meaning, "This car goes to Bayeux?"). On my last trip, the train from

Marseille to Arles split off some cars along the way—which wasn't mentioned when I asked the conductor if this train went to Arles.

• If a non-TGV train seat is reserved, it'll likely be labeled *réservé*, with the cities to and from which it is reserved.

• If you don't understand an announcement, ask your neighbor to explain: *"Pardon madame/monsieur, qu'est-ce qui se passe?"* (kehs kee suh pahs; meaning, "Excuse me, what's going on?").

• Verify with the conductor all of the transfers you must make: *"Correspondance à?";* meaning, "Transfer to where?"

• To guard against theft, keep your bags in sight (directly overhead is ideal but not always possible—the early boarder gets the best storage space). If you must store them in the lower racks by the doors (available in most cars), pay attention at stops. Your bags are most vulnerable to theft before the train takes off and whenever it stops.

• Note your arrival time, so you'll be ready to get off.

• Use the trains' free WCs before you get off.

Buses

You can get nearly anywhere in France by rail and bus...if you're well organized, patient, and not in a hurry. Review my bus schedule information, and verify times at the local TI or bus station. Regional buses work well for many destinations not served by trains. Buses are almost always comfortable and air-conditioned.

A few bus lines are run by SNCF (France's rail system) and are included with your railpass (show railpass at station to get free bus ticket), but most bus lines are independent of the rail system and are not covered by railpasses. Bus stations *(gare routière)* are usually located next to train stations. Train stations usually have bus information where train-to-bus connections are important— and vice versa for bus companies. On Sunday, regional bus service virtually disappears.

Bus Tips

• Read the train tips described earlier, and use those that apply (check schedules in advance, arrive at the station early, confirm the destination before you board, find out if you need to transfer, etc.).

• Use TIs often to help plan your trip; they have regional bus schedules and are happy to assist you.

• Remember that service is sparse or even nonexistent on Sunday. Wednesday bus schedules often are different during the school year, because school is out this day (and regional buses generally operate school service).

• Confirm a bus stop's location before you leave (rural stops are often not signed) and be at bus stops at least five minutes early.

• On schedules *(horaires), en semaine* means Monday through

Saturday, *dimanche* is Sunday, and *jours fériés* are holidays. *Année* means the bus runs all year on the days listed, *vac* means it runs only during summer vacations, and *scol (scolaire)* means it runs only when school is on session. *Ligne* means route (or bus line) and *réseau* means network (usually all routes).

Regional Minivan Excursions

Worthwhile day tours generally are available in regions where bus and train service is sparse. For the D-Day beaches, châteaux of the Loire Valley, Dordogne Valley villages and caves, Provence's villages and vineyards, the Route du Vin (Wine Road) in Alsace, Brittany sights (including Mont St-Michel), and wine-tasting in Burgundy, I list reliable companies that provide this helpful service at fair rates for most regions in this book. Some of these minivan excursions simply offer transportation between the sights; others add a running commentary and information on regional history.

Renting a Car

If you're renting a car in France, bring your driver's license. It's recommended, but not required, that you also have an International Driving Permit (sold at your local AAA office for $15 plus the cost of two passport-type photos; see www.aaa.com); however, I've frequently rented cars in France and traveled problem-free with just my US license.

Rental companies require you to be at least 21 years old and to have held your license for one year. Drivers under the age of 25 may incur a young-driver surcharge, and some rental companies do not rent to anyone 75 and over. If you're considered too young or old, look into leasing (covered later), which has less-stringent age restrictions.

Research car rentals before you go. It's cheaper to arrange most car rentals from the US. Call several companies and look online to compare rates, or arrange a rental through your hometown travel agent.

Most of the major US rental agencies (including National, Avis, Budget, Hertz, and Thrifty) have offices throughout Europe. Also consider the two major Europe-based agencies, Europcar and Sixt. It can be cheaper to use a consolidator, such as Auto Europe (www.autoeurope.com) or Europe by Car (www.ebctravel.com), which compares rates at several companies to get you the best deal. However, my readers have reported problems with consolidators, ranging from misinformation to unexpected fees; because you're going through a middleman, it can be more challenging to resolve disputes that arise with the rental agency.

Regardless of the car-rental company you choose, always read the contract carefully. The fine print can conceal a host of common add-on charges—such as one-way drop-off fees, airport surcharges, or mandatory insurance policies—that aren't included in the "total price," but can be tacked on when you pick up your car. You may need to query rental agents pointedly to find out your actual cost.

For the best rental deal, rent by the week with unlimited mileage. To save money on fuel, ask for a diesel car. I normally rent the smallest, least-expensive model with a stick shift (cheaper than an automatic). An automatic transmission adds about 50 percent to the car-rental cost over a manual transmission. Almost all rentals are manual by default, so if you need an automatic, you must request one in advance; be aware that these cars are usually larger models. Roads and parking spaces are narrow in France, so you'll do yourself a favor by renting the smallest car that meets your needs.

For a three-week rental, allow roughly $1,000 per person (based on two people sharing a car), including insurance, tolls, gas, and parking. For trips of this length, look into leasing; you'll save money on insurance and taxes.

You can sometimes get a GPS unit with your rental car or leased vehicle for an additional fee (around $15/day; be sure it's set to English and has all the maps you need before you drive off). Or, if you have a portable GPS device at home, consider taking it with you to Europe (buy and upload European maps before your trip). GPS apps are also available for smartphones, but downloading maps on one of these apps in Europe could lead to an exorbitant data-roaming bill (for more details, see the sidebar on page 1108).

Big companies have offices in most cities; ask whether they can pick you up at your hotel. Small local rental companies can be cheaper but aren't as flexible. Compare pick-up costs (downtown can be less expensive than the airport) and explore drop-off options. When selecting a location, don't trust the agency's description of "downtown" or "city center." In some cases, a "downtown" branch can be on the outskirts of the city—a long, costly taxi ride from the center. Before choosing, plug the addresses into a mapping website. You may find that the "train station" location is handier. Returning a car at a big-city train station or downtown agency can be tricky; get precise details on the car drop-off location and hours, and allow ample time to find it. Note that rental offices often close between 12:00 and 14:00 and from midday Saturday until Monday morning.

If you want a car for only a day or two (e.g., for the D-Day beaches or Loire châteaux), you'll likely find it cheaper to rent it in France at a local agency—most US-arranged rentals make financial sense only for three days or more. You can rent a car on the spot just about anywhere in France. In many cases, this is a worthwhile splurge. All you need is your American driver's license and a major credit card (figure €65-80/day, including 100 kilometers, or 60 miles, per day).

When you pick up the rental car, check it thoroughly and make sure any damage is noted on your rental agreement. Find out how your car's lights, turn signals, wipers, and fuel cap function, and know what kind of fuel the car takes. When you return the car, make sure the agent verifies its condition with you.

A **rail-and-drive pass** allows you to mix car and train travel economically (sold only outside Europe, from your travel agent). Generally big-city connections are best done by train, and rural regions are best done by car. With a rail-and-drive pass, you can take advantage of the speed and comfort of the TGV trains for longer trips, and rent a car for as little as one day at a time for day trips that can't be done without one (such as the Loire, the Dordogne, and Provence).

The basic France Rail-and-Drive Pass comes with two days of car rental and two days of rail in one month. You can pick up a car in one city and drop it off in another. Be aware that cars are not always available on short notice: You have to reserve each car at least three days ahead, and vouchers are not honored for same-day, walk-in car rentals.

Car Insurance Options

When you rent a car, you are liable for a very high deductible, sometimes equal to the entire value of the car. Limit your financial risk by choosing one of these three options: Buy Collision Damage Waiver (CDW) coverage from the car-rental company, get coverage through your credit card (free, if your card automatically includes zero-deductible coverage), or buy coverage through Travel Guard.

CDW includes a very high deductible (typically $1,000-1,500). Though each rental company has its own variation, the basic CDW costs $15-35 a day (figure roughly 30 percent extra) and reduces your liability, but does not eliminate it. When you pick up the car, you'll be offered the chance to "buy down" the deductible to zero (for an additional $10-30/day; this is sometimes called "super CDW").

If you opt for **credit-card coverage,** there's a catch: You'll technically have to decline all coverage offered by the car-rental company, which means they can place a hold on your card (which can be up to the full value of the car). In case of damage, it can be time-consuming to resolve the charges with your credit-card company. Before you decide on this option, quiz your credit-card company about how it works.

Finally, you can buy collision insurance from **Travel Guard**

($9/day plus a one-time $3 service fee covers you for up to $35,000, $250 deductible, tel. 800-826-4919, www.travelguard.com). It's valid everywhere in Europe except the Republic of Ireland, and some Italian car-rental companies refuse to honor it. Note that various states differ on which products and policies are available to their residents.

For more on car-rental insurance, see www.ricksteves.com /cdw.

Leasing

For trips of three weeks or more, consider leasing (which automatically includes zero-deductible collision and theft insurance). By technically buying and then selling back the car, you save lots of money on tax and insurance. Leasing provides you a brand-new car with unlimited mileage and a 24-hour emergency assistance program. You can lease for as little as 21 days to as long as six months. Car leases must be arranged from the US.

Anyone age 18 or over with a driver's license is eligible. You can pick up or return cars in major cities outside of France, but you'll have to pay an additional fee.

Four reliable companies offer 21-day lease packages:
• Auto France (Peugeot cars only, US tel. 800-572-9655, fax 201/393-7801, www.autofrance.net)
• Europe by Car (Peugeot, Citroën, and Renault cars, US tel. 800-223-1516, www.ebctravel.com)
• Idea Merge (Volkswagen, Citroen, Renault and Peugeot, US tel. 888-297-0001, www.ideamerge.com)
• Kemwel (Peugeot cars only, US tel. 877-820-0668, www .kemwel.com).

RV and Campervan Rental

Even given the extra fuel costs, renting your own rolling hotel can be a great way to save money, especially if you're mainly sticking to rural areas. Keep in mind that RVs in France are much smaller than those you see at home. Companies to consider:
• **Van It** (mobile 06 70 43 11 86 www.van-it.com)
• **Idea Merge** (see listing under "Leasing," above)
• **Origin** (current-model Volkswagen vans fully equipped for 2-3 people, rates less than RVs, mobile 06 80 01 72 77, www.origin -campervans.com).

Driving

It's a pleasure to explore France by car, but you need to know the risks and rules.

Theft: Theft is a big problem, particularly in southern France. Thieves easily recognize rental cars and assume they are filled with a tourist's gear. Try to make your car look locally owned by hiding the "tourist-owned" rental-company decals and putting a French newspaper in your back window. Be sure all of your valuables are out of sight and locked in the trunk—or, even better, with you or in your room. And don't assume that just because you're parked on a main street that you'll be fine. Thieves work fast.

Road Rules: Seat belts are mandatory for all, and children under age 10 must be in the back seat. In city and town centers,

traffic merging from the right (even from tiny side streets) normally has the right-of-way *(priorité à droite)*. So even when you're driving on a major road, pay attention to cars merging from the right. In contrast, cars entering the many suburban roundabouts must yield *(cédez le passage)*. U-turns are illegal throughout France, and you cannot turn right on red lights.

Be aware of typical European road rules; for example, many countries require headlights to be turned on at all times (in France, they must be used in any case of poor visibility). It's generally illegal to drive while using your mobile phone without a hands-free headset. Ask your car-rental company about these rules, or check the US State Department website (www.travel.state.gov, click on "International Travel," then specify your country of choice and click "Traffic Safety and Road Conditions").

Speed Limits: Because speed limits are by road type, they typically aren't posted, so it's best to memorize them:
- Two-lane D and N routes outside cities and towns: 90 km/ hour
- When driving on a two-lane road through a village: 50 km/ hour (unless posted at 30 km/hour)
- Divided highways outside cities and towns: 110 km/hour
- Autoroutes: 130 km/hour
  If it's raining, subtract 10 km/hour on D and N routes and 20

APPENDIX

How to Navigate a Roundabout

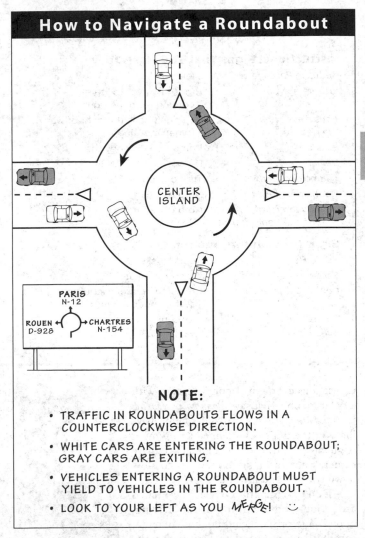

NOTE:

- TRAFFIC IN ROUNDABOUTS FLOWS IN A COUNTERCLOCKWISE DIRECTION.

- WHITE CARS ARE ENTERING THE ROUNDABOUT; GRAY CARS ARE EXITING.

- VEHICLES ENTERING A ROUNDABOUT MUST YIELD TO VEHICLES IN THE ROUNDABOUT.

- LOOK TO YOUR LEFT AS YOU MERGE! ☺

km/hour on divided highways and autoroutes. Speed-limit signs are a red circle around a number; when you see that same number again in gray with a broken line diagonally across it, this means that limit no longer applies. Speed limits drop to 30-50 km/hour in villages (always posted) and must be respected.

Road speeds are monitored regularly with camera boxes (a mere two kilometers over the limit gets a pricey ticket). The good news is that drivers are warned a few hundred yards before the camera with signs showing the proper speed, so you have no

APPENDIX

Road Signs and Driving Tips

Instructional Signs That You Must Obey

Cédez le Passage	Yield
Priorité à Droite	Right-of-way is for cars coming from the right
Vous n'avez pas la priorité	You don't have the right of way (when merging)
Rappel	Remember to obey the sign
Déviation	Detour
Allumez vos feux	Turn on your lights
Doublage Interdit	No passing
Parking Interdit/ Stationnement Interdit	No parking

Signs for Your Information

Route Barrée	Road blocked
Sortie des Camions	Work truck exit
Centre Commercial	Grouping of large, suburban stores (not city center)
Centre-Ville	City center
Feux	Traffic signal

excuse for blowing it. Look for a sign with a radar graphic that says *Pour votre sécurité, contrôles automatiques.* Anyone caught driving over the limit will be fined a minimum of about $180, though the French use these cameras not to make money but to slow down traffic—and it works.

Don't Drink and Drive: The French are serious about curbing drunk driving. Soon all motorists, including those in rental cars, will be required to have a breath-testing instrument on hand so that the drivers themselves can tell if they're over

the legal alcohol limit—which is lower in France than in the US (drinker beware). If drivers are pulled over by any reason and don't have the kit in their car, they'll be fined (driver beware). When you pick up your rental car, ask if it has a kit (if it doesn't, ask where you can get one, which should cost only around €3).

Fuel: Gas *(essence)* is expensive—about $8 per gallon. Diesel *(gazole)* is less—about $7 per gallon—and diesel cars get better mileage, so try to rent a diesel to save money. Be sure you know

Horadateur	Remote parking meter, usually at the end of the block
Parc de Stationnement	Parking lot
Rue Piétonne	Pedestrian-only street
Sauf Riverains	Local access only
Toutes Directions	All directions (passing through a city)
Autres Directions	Other directions (passing through a city)

Signs Unique to Autoroutes

Aire	Rest stop with WCs, telephones, and sometimes gas stations
Bouchon	Traffic jam ahead
Fluide	No slowing ahead (fluid conditions)
Péage	Toll
Télépéage	Toll booths—automatic toll payment only
Par temps de Pluie	When raining (modifies speed limit signs)

what type of fuel your car takes before you fill up. Gas is most expensive on autoroutes and cheapest at big supermarkets (closed at night and on Sun). Many gas stations close on Sunday. Your US credit and debit cards won't work at self-serve pumps; instead you can pay cash or find gas stations with attendants, or consider getting a card that works with the chip-and-PIN system (see page 18). To avoid unhappy surprises, fill your tank before it's very low.

Tolls: Four hours on the autoroute costs about €25 in tolls (American credit cards not accepted, but cash is—it's best to have smaller bills ready). Tolls are pricey, but the alternative to these super "feeways" usually means being marooned in countryside traffic—especially near the Riviera. Autoroutes save enough time, gas, and nausea to justify the splurge. Mix high-speed "autorouting" with scenic country-road rambling (be careful of sluggish tractors on country roads). You'll usually take a ticket when entering an autoroute and pay when you leave. At pay points, avoid the Télepéage tollbooths and those with a credit-card icon. Look instead for green arrows above the tollbooth, which indicate they accept cash. Many exits are entirely automated, with machines taking all euro bill denominations. Shorter autoroute sections have periodic tollbooths, where you can pay by dropping coins into a

Driving in France

ENGLAND

To London

Dover

Calais

BELGIUM

English Channel

Lille

LUX.

GERMANY

Arromanches (D-Day Beaches)

20m .5h

Honfleur

45m .75h

55m 1h

Bayeux

Reims

Verdun

90m·1.5h

75m·1.25h

150m·2.75h

80m·1.5h

Mont St-Michel

80m .5h

Caen

Rouen

Paris

305m·4.5h

Strasbourg

80m·1.5h

Dinan

195m·3h

Chartres

55m·1h

285m·5.5h

50m 1h

Colmar

40m .75h

225m·4.5h

Amboise

140m·2.25h

155m·2.5h

Semur-en-Auxois

50m .75h

165m·2.5h

50m·1.25h

Chinon

85m·1.5h

270m·5.5h

250m·4h

Beaune

135m·3h

F R A N C E

145m·1.5h

SWITZ.

m = miles
h = hours

Atlantic Ocean

Oradour-sur-Glane

95m·1.5h

55m·1h

360m·5.25h

220m·4.5h

200m·2.5h

Lyon

85m·1.5h

Annecy

Chamonix

St. Emilion

80m·2h

260m·5h

235m·5h

ITALY

Sarlat

30m·1.25h

Rocamadour

140m·2h

Monaco

St. Jean-de-Luz

155m·2.5h

125m·2.5h

Albi

25m .5h

Avignon

10m .5h

20m .5h

210m·4.75h

70m 1.75h

Arles

160m·2.5h

Nice

San Sebastián

250m·3.5h

Carcassonne

95m·1.5h

150m·2.25h

165m·2.5h

80m 1.25h

Cassis

105m·1.5h

Antibes

10m .5h

SPAIN

ANDORRA

Collioure

Mediterranean Sea

Note: Your times may vary based on traffic, constuction and road conditions.

basket (change given, but keep a good supply of coins handy to avoid waiting for an attendant). Autoroute gas stations usually come with well-stocked mini-marts, clean restrooms, sandwiches, maps, local products, and cheap vending-machine coffee (€1.30—I dig the *cappuccino sucré*). Many have small cafés or more elaborate cafeterias with reasonable prices.

Highways: Roads are classified into departmental (D), national (N), and autoroutes (A). D routes (usually yellow lines on maps) are often slower but the most scenic. N routes and important D routes (red lines) are the fastest after autoroutes (orange lines on maps). Green road signs are for national routes; blue are for autoroutes. Note that some key roads in France are undergoing letter designation and number changes (mostly N roads converting to D roads). If you are using an older map, the actual route name may differ from what's on your map. Navigate by destination rather than road name...or buy a new map. There are plenty of good facilities, gas stations (most closed Sun), and rest stops along most French roads.

Parking: Finding a parking place can be a headache in larger cities. Ask your hotelier for ideas, and pay to park at well-patrolled lots (blue *P* signs direct you to parking lots in French cities). Parking structures usually require that you take a ticket with you and pay at a machine (called a *caisse*) on your way back to the car. US credit cards probably won't work in these automated machines but euro coins (and sometimes bills) will. Overnight parking in lots (usually 19:00-8:00) is generally reasonable, except in Paris and Nice. Curbside metered parking also works (usually free 12:00-14:00 & 19:00-9:00, and all day and night in Aug). Look for a small machine selling time (called *horadateur,* usually one per block), plug in a few coins (€1.50 buys about an hour, varies by city), push the button, get a receipt showing the amount of time you have, and display it inside your windshield. For cheap overnight parking until the next afternoon, buy three hours worth of time after 19:00. This gets you until noon the next day, after which two more hours are usually free (12:00-14:00), so you're good until 14:00.

Driving Tips

• Be ready for many roundabouts—navigating them is an art. The key is to know your direction and be ready for your turnoff. If you miss it, take another lap (or two).

• When navigating into cities, approach intersections cautiously, stow the map, and follow the signs to *Centre-Ville* (city center). From there, head to the TI *(Office de Tourisme)* or your hotel.

• When leaving or just passing through cities, follow the signs for *Toutes Directions* or *Autres Directions* (meaning "anywhere else") until you see a sign for your specific destination.

• Driving on any roads but autoroutes will take longer than you anticipated, so allow yourself plenty of time for slower traffic (tractors, trucks, traffic, and hard-to-decipher signs all deserve blame). First-timers should estimate how long they think a drive will take...then double it. I pretend that kilometers are miles (for distances) and base my time estimates accordingly.

• While locals are eating lunch (12:00-14:00), many sights (and gas stations) are closed, so you can make great time driving—but keep it slow when passing through villages.

• Be very careful when driving on smaller roads—many are narrow, flanked by little ditches that lure inattentive drivers. I've met several readers who "ditched" their cars (which were later successfully pulled out by local farmers).

• On autoroutes, keep to the right lanes to let fast drivers by, and be careful when merging into a left lane, as cars can be coming at very high speeds. Cars and trucks keep their left blinker on while in a passing lane, indicating that they plan to get back over to the right.

• Motorcycles will scream between cars in traffic. Be ready—they expect you to make space so that they can pass.

• Fuel is tricky to find in rural areas on Sunday, so fill up on Saturday. Autoroute filling stations are always open and always staffed.

• Keep a stash of coins in your ashtray for parking and small autoroute tolls.

Biking

You'll find areas in France where public transportation is limited and bicycle touring might be a good idea. For many, biking is a romantic notion whose novelty wears off after the first hill or headwind—realistically evaluate your physical condition and be clear on the limitations bikes present. Start with an easy pedal to a nearby village or through the vineyards, then decide how ambitious you feel. Most find that two hours on a narrow, hard seat is enough. I've listed bike-rental shops where appropriate and suggested a few of my favorite rides. TIs always have addresses for bike-rental places. For a good touring bike, figure about €12 for a half-day and €18 for a full day. You'll pay more for better equipment; generally the best is available through bike shops, not at train stations or other outlets. French cyclists often do not wear helmets, though most rental outfits have them (for a small fee). Some shops even rent electric bikes.

Cheap Flights

Though trains are still the best way to connect most cities in France, a flight can save both time and money on international journeys. When comparing your options, factor in the time it takes to get to the airport and how early you'll need to arrive to check in.

The best comparison search engine for both international and intra-European flights is www.kayak.com. For inexpensive flights within Europe, try www.skyscanner.com or www.hipmunk.com.

Well-known cheapo airlines include easyJet (www.easyjet .com) and Ryanair (www.ryanair.com). Also check Air France for specials. If you're not sure who flies to your destination, check its airport's website for a list of carriers.

Be aware of the potential drawbacks of flying on the cheap: nonrefundable and nonchangeable tickets, minimal or nonexistent customer service, treks to airports far outside town, and stingy baggage allowances with steep overage fees. If you're traveling with lots of luggage, a cheap flight can quickly become a bad deal. To avoid unpleasant surprises, read the small print before you book.

Useful Phone Numbers and Websites
Airports
Paris: Charles de Gaulle and Orly—Tel. 3950 from French landlines (€0.34/minute); from the US dial 011 33 1 70 36 39 50; www.adp.fr

Beauvais (serves budget airlines such as Ryanair, Wizz Air, and Blue Air): Tel. 08 92 68 20 66, www.aeroportbeauvais.com

Lyon: Saint-Exupéry Airport—tel. 08 26 80 08 26 (€0.15/minute), www.lyon.aeroport.fr

Marseille: Aéroport Marseille-Provence—tel. 04 42 14 14 14, www.marseille.aeroport.fr

Nice: Aéroport de Nice—tel. 08 20 42 33 33 (€0.12/minute), www.nice.aeroport.fr

Airlines
The following airlines may also have alternate numbers to call from the US or other European countries.

Aer Lingus: Tel. 08 21 23 02 67 (answered Mon-Fri 9:00-17:00)

Air Canada: Tel. 08 25 88 08 81 (daily 7:30-15:00)

Air France: Tel. 3654 (daily 6:30-22:00)

Alitalia: Tel. 08 92 65 56 55 (Mon-Fri 8:00-20:00, Sat-Sun 9:00-19:00)

American Airlines: Tel. 08 26 46 09 50 (Mon-Fri 8:00-20:00, Sat-Sun 9:30-18:00)

Austrian Airlines: Tel. 08 20 81 68 16 (daily 8:00-20:00)

British Airways: Tel. 08 25 82 54 00 (Mon-Fri 9:00-18:00, Sat 9:00-14:00)

Delta: Tel. 08 92 70 26 09

Easy Jet: Tel. 08 20 42 03 15 (Mon-Fri 8:00-20:00, Sat-Sun 9:00-17:00)

Iberia: Tel. 08 25 80 09 65 (24/7)

Icelandair: Tel. 01 44 51 60 51

KLM: Tel. 08 92 70 26 08

Lufthansa: Tel. 08 92 23 16 90 (24/7)

Royal Air Maroc: Tel. 08 20 82 18 21

SAS: Tel. 08 25 32 53 35 (Mon-Fri 9:00-17:00)

Swiss International: Tel. 08 92 23 25 01

United: Tel. 08 10 72 72 72 (Mon-Fri 8:00-20:00, Sat-Sun 9:30-18:00)

US Airways: Tel. 08 10 63 22 22

APPENDIX

Resources

Resources from Rick Steves

Rick Steves' France 2013 is one of many books in my series on European travel, which includes country guidebooks, city

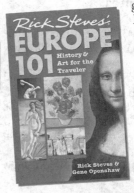

guidebooks (Paris, Rome, Florence, London, etc.), Snapshot guides (excerpted chapters from my country guides), Pocket Guides (full-color little books on big cities, including Paris), and my budget-travel skills handbook, *Rick Steves' Europe Through the Back Door.* Most of my titles are available as ebooks. My phrase books—for French, Italian, German, Spanish, and Portuguese—are practical and budget-oriented. My other books include *Europe 101* (a crash course on art and history), *Mediterranean Cruise Ports* (how to make the most of your time in port), and *Travel as a Political Act* (a travelogue sprinkled with tips for bringing home a global perspective). A more complete list of my titles appears near the end of this book.

Video: My public television series, *Rick Steves' Europe,* covers European destinations in 100 shows, with nine episodes on France. To watch episodes online, visit www.hulu.com; for scripts and local airtimes, see www.ricksteves.com/tv.

Audio: My weekly public radio show, *Travel with Rick Steves,* features interviews with travel experts from around the world. I've also produced free, self-guided audio tours of the top sights and neighborhoods in Paris. All of this audio content is available for free at Rick Steves Audio Europe, an extensive online library organized by destination. Choose whatever interests you, and download it for free via the Rick Steves Audio Europe smartphone app, www.ricksteves.com/audioeurope, iTunes, or Google Play.

Maps

The black-and-white maps in this book are concise and simple, designed to help you locate recommended places and get to local TIs, where you can pick up more in-depth maps of cities and regions (usually free). Better maps are sold at newsstands and bookstores. Before you buy a map, look at it to be sure it has the level of detail you want.

Michelin maps are available throughout France at bookstores,

Begin Your Trip at www.ricksteves.com

APPENDIX

At ricksteves.com, you'll discover a wealth of free information on European destinations, including fresh monthly news and helpful tips from thousands of fellow travelers. You'll find my latest guidebook updates (www.ricksteves.com/update), a monthly travel e-newsletter (easy and free to sign up), my personal travel blog, and my free Rick Steves Audio Europe smartphone app (if you don't have a smartphone, you can access the same content via podcasts). You can even follow me on Facebook and Twitter.

Our **online Travel Store** offers travel bags and accessories that I've designed specifically to help you travel smarter and lighter. These include my popular carry-on bags (roll-aboard and backpack versions), money belts, totes, toiletries kits, adapters, other accessories, and a wide selection of guidebooks, planning maps, and DVDs.

Choosing the right **railpass** for your trip—amid hundreds of options—can drive you nutty. We'll help you choose the best pass for your needs and ship it to you for free.

Want to travel with greater efficiency and less stress? We organize **tours** with more than three dozen itineraries and more than 500 departures reaching the best destinations in this book...and beyond. Our France tours include an 11-day Paris and the Heart of France tour (focusing on the best of the north), a seven-day French Riviera tour, a 13-day Loire to the South of France tour, a 14-day Wine Regions of Eastern France tour, and an in-depth seven-day Paris city tour. You'll enjoy great guides, a fun bunch of travel partners (with small groups of generally around 24-28), and plenty of room to spread out in a big, comfy bus. You'll find European adventures to fit every vacation length. For all the details, and to get our Tour Catalog and a free Rick Steves Tour Experience DVD (filmed on location during an actual tour), visit www.ricksteves.com or call us at 425/608-4217.

newsstands, and gas stations (about €5 each, cheaper than in the US). The Michelin #721 France map (1:1,000,000 scale) covers this book's destinations with reasonable detail. Drivers should consider the soft-cover Michelin France atlas (the entire country at 1:200,000, well-organized in a €16 book with an index and maps of major cities). Spend a few minutes learning the Michelin key to get the most sightseeing value out of these maps.

Train travelers do fine with a simple rail map (such as the one that comes with a railpass) and city maps from the TI offices.

Other Guidebooks

If you're like most travelers, this book is all you need. But if you're heading beyond my recommended destinations, $40 for extra maps and books can be money well spent. If you'll be concentrating on specific regions in France, consider *Rick Steves' Provence & the French Riviera* or *Rick Steves' Paris*.

The following books are worthwhile, though most are not updated annually; check the publication date before you buy.

I like Cadogan guides for their well-presented background information and coverage of cultural issues. Their recommendations suit upscale travelers, though updates are infrequent, so hotel and restaurant information is often dated. Lonely Planet's *France* is well-researched, with good maps and hotel recommendations for low- to moderate-budget travelers. But because it tries to cover every city in France, you'll likely find too little information on the most important places and too much information on the minor places you don't care about. The highly opinionated *Let's Go: France* is ideal for students and vagabonds traveling by train and staying in hostels. The popular, skinny, green Michelin guides are dry but informative, especially for drivers. They're known for their city and sightseeing maps, and for their succinct, helpful information on all major sights. English editions, covering most of the regions you'll want to visit, are sold in France for about €14 (or $20 in the US).

Recommended Books and Movies

To learn more about France past and present, check out a few of these books or films.

Nonfiction

For a good introduction to the French culture and people, *Culture Shock: France* (Sally Adamson Taylor), *French or Foe* (Polly Platt), and/or *Sixty Million Frenchmen Can't Be Wrong* (Jean-Benoit Nadeau and Julie Barlow). The latter is a must-read for anyone serious about understanding French culture, contemporary politics, and what makes the French tick.

The Rules of *Boules*

Throughout France you'll see people playing *boules* (also known as *pétanque*). Each player starts with three iron balls, with the object of getting them close to the target, a small wooden ball called a *cochonnet* (piglet). The first player tosses the *cochonnet* about 30 feet, then throws the first of his iron balls near the target. The next player takes a turn. As soon as a player's ball is closest, it's the other guy's turn. Once all balls have been thrown, the score is tallied—the player with the closest ball gets one point for each ball closer to the target than his opponent's. The loser gets zero. Games are generally to 15 points.

A regulation *boules* field is 10 feet by 43 feet, but the game is played everywhere—just scratch a throwing circle in the sand, toss the *cochonnet,* and you're off. Strategists can try to knock the opponent's balls out of position, knock the *cochonnet* itself out of position, or guard their best ball with the other two.

For a readable history of the country, try *The Course of French History* (Pierre Goubert). *Portraits of France* (Robert Daley) is an interesting travelogue that roams from Paris to the Pyrenees. A mix of writers explore French culture in *Travelers Tales: France* (edited by James O'Reilly, Larry Habegger, and Sean O'Reilly).

La Seduction: How the French Play the Game of Life (Elaine Sciolino) gives travelers a fun, insightful, and tantalizing peek into how seduction has been used in all aspects of French life—from small villages to the halls of national government.

Many great memoirs take place in Paris. Consider reading Ernest Hemingway's *A Moveable Feast*, Art Buchwald's *I'll Always Have Paris*, and/or *Paris to the Moon* by New Yorker writer Adam Gopnik, who takes his young son for a carousel ride in Luxembourg Garden.

If you'll be visiting Provence, pick up Peter Mayle's memoirs, *A Year in Provence* and *Toujours Provence*. Ina Caro's *The Road from the Past* is filled with enjoyable essays on her travels through France, with an accent on history. *The Da Vinci Code* fans will enjoy reading the book that inspired that book—*Holy Blood, Holy Grail* (Michael Baigent, Richard Leigh, and Henry Lincoln)—which takes place mostly in southern France. *Labyrinth* (Kate Mosse) is an intriguing tale, much of which takes place in medieval southern France during the Cathar crusade.

War buffs may want to read these classics before visiting the D-Day Beaches: *The Longest Day* (Cornelius Ryan) and *Wine*

APPENDIX

Cooking Classes and Tours

Food plays a major role in many books about France, known worldwide for its outstanding cuisine. If you'd rather knead than read, consider taking a class:

L'Atelier des Chefs is a network of cooking schools located in many cities throughout France, with top classes at good rates (half-hour-€15, 1 hour-€36, 2 hours-€72, www.atelierdeschefs.fr).

Both **Le Cordon Bleu** (tel. 01 53 68 22 50, www.lcbparis.com) and **Ritz Escoffier Ecole de Gastronomie** (tel. 01 43 16 30 50, www.ritzparis.com) have pricey demonstration courses in Paris. For a more relaxed (and cheaper) Parisian experience, try **La Cuisine Paris** (great variety of classes in English, reasonable prices, and a beautiful space in central Paris; 2-hour classes-€65-90, 4-hour class with market tour-€150, 89 Boulevard St. Michel, tel. 01 40 51 78 18, www.lacuisineparis.com) or **Cook'n with Class** (convivial cooking and wine-and-cheese classes with a maximum of six students, tasting courses offered as well; located north of Montmartre at 21 Rue Custine, mobile 06 31 73 62 77, www.cooknwithclass.com).

Acclaimed chef and author **Susan Herrmann Loomis** offers cooking courses in Paris or at her home in Normandy. Through **Edible Paris,** friendly Canadian Rosa Jackson puts together personalized "foodie" itineraries and pre-set three-hour "food guru" tours of Paris and Nice (www.edible-paris.com and www.petitsfarcis.com).

Marjorie Taylor, who lives in Beaune, gives an introduction to Burgundian cuisine in her lovely apartment (see listing on page 917). In Provence, **Barbara Schuerenberg's** reasonably priced cooking classes are held at her home in Vaison la Romaine (see listing on page 743).

& War: The French, the Nazis, and the Battle for France's Greatest Treasure (Donald and Petie Kladstrup). *Is Paris Burning?*, set in the last days of the Nazi occupation, tells the story of the French resistance and how a German general disobeyed Hitler's order to destroy Paris (Larry Collins and Dominique Lapierre).

If you'll be enjoying an extended stay in France, consider *Living Abroad in France* (Terry Link) or *Almost French* (Sarah Turnbull), a funny take on living as a Parisian native. Many appreciate the *Marling Menu-Master for France* (William E. Marling) but the most complete (and priciest) menu reader around is *A to Z of French Food, a French to English Dictionary of Culinary Terms* (G. de Temmerman). Travelers seeking green and vegetarian options in France could consider *Traveling Naturally in France* (Dorian Yates).

Fiction

"It was the best of times, it was the worst of times," begins Charles Dickens' gripping tale of the French Revolution, *A Tale of Two Cities*. In *Les Misérables* (Victor Hugo), a Frenchman tries to escape his criminal past, fleeing from a determined police captain and becoming wrapped up in the Revolutionary battles between the rich and the starving. Another recommended book set during this time is *City of Darkness, City of Light*, by Marge Piercy.

Ernest Hemingway was a fan of Georges Simenon, a Belgian who wrote mysteries based in Paris, including *The Hotel Majestic*. Other mysteries using Paris as the backdrop are *Murder in Montparnasse* (Howard Engel), *Murder in the Marais* (Cara Black), and *Sandman* (J. Robert Janes).

A Very Long Engagement (Sebastien Japrisot) is a love story set during the bleak years when World War I raged. Using a similar timeframe, *Birdsong* (Sebastian Faulks) follows a 20-year-old Englishman into France, and into the romance that follows.

Chocolat (Joanne Harris)—a book and a 2000 movie with Johnny Depp and Juliette Binoche—charms readers with its story of magic and romance.

Suite Française (Irène Némirovsky) plunges readers into the chaos of the evacuation of Paris during World War II, as well as daily life in a small rural town during the ensuing German occupation. The author, a Russian Jew living in France, wrote her account within weeks of the actual events, and died at Auschwitz in 1942.

Films

In *The Grand Illusion* (1937, directed by Jean Renoir), WWI prisoners of war hatch an escape plan. Considered a masterpiece of French film, the movie was later banned by the Nazis for its antifascism message.

Stanley Kubrick's *Paths of Glory* (1957) is a WWI story about the futility and irony of war. François Truffaut, a filmmaker of the French New Wave school, shows the Parisian streets in *Jules and Jim* (1962). Wander the streets of Paris with a small boy as he chases *The Red Balloon* (1956).

Jean de Florette (1986), a marvelous tale of greed and intolerance, follows a hunchback as he fights for the property he inherited. Its sequel, *Manon of the Spring* (1986), continues with his daughter's story. *Blue/White/Red* (1990s) is a stylish trilogy of films by Krzystof Kieslowski, based on France's national motto—"Liberty, Equality, and Fraternity."

Cyrano de Bergerac (1990) is about a homely, romantic poet who woos his love with the help of another, better-looking man. Fans of crime films—and Robert De Niro—will like *Ronin* (1998), with multiple scenes shot in France. *Saving Private Ryan* (1998) is Steven

Spielberg's intense and brilliant story of the D-Day landings.

The Gleaners & I (2000), a quiet, meditative film by Agnès Varda, follows a few working-class men and women as they gather sustenance from what's been thrown away. In *Amélie* (2001), a charming young waitress in Paris searches for love. If you'll be heading to Versailles, consider seeing *Marie Antoinette* (2006), which stars Kirsten Dunst as the infamous French queen (with a California accent). *La Vie en Rose* (2007) covers the glamorous and turbulent life of the fabled singer Edith Piaf (many scenes shot in Paris). Woody Allen's *Midnight in Paris* (2011) is a sharp comedy that shifts between today's Paris and the 1920s mecca of Picasso, Hemingway, and Fitzgerald.

Holidays and Festivals

This list includes selected festivals in major cities, plus national holidays observed throughout France. Many sights and banks close down on national holidays—keep this in mind when planning your itinerary.

Before planning a trip around a festival, verify its dates by checking with the festival's website or France's national tourism website (www.franceguide.com); www.whatsonwhen.com also lists many festival dates.

Hotels get booked up on Easter weekend, Labor Day, Ascension Day, Pentecost, Bastille Day, and the winter holidays.

For sports events, see www.sportsevents365.com for schedules and ticket information.

Here is a sampling of events and holidays in 2013:

Jan 1	New Year's Day
Jan 6	Epiphany
Feb-March	Carnival (Mardi Gras) parades and fireworks, Nice (www.nicecarnaval.com)
March	Grenoble Jazz Festival, near Lyon (www.jazzgrenoble.com)
March 31	Easter Sunday
April 1	Easter Monday
May-Mid-Oct	Festival of Gardens, Chaumont-sur-Loire (www.domaine-chaumont.fr)
May	Versailles Festival (arts), Versailles; Festival Jeanne d'Arc (pageants), Rouen
May 1	Labor Day
May 8	VE (Victory in Europe) Day
May 9	Ascension
May 15-26	Cannes Film Festival, Cannes (www.festival-cannes.fr)

APPENDIX

2013

APPENDIX

JANUARY
S	M	T	W	T	F	S
		1	2	3	4	5
6	7	8	9	10	11	12
13	14	15	16	17	18	19
20	21	22	23	24	25	26
27	28	29	30	31		

FEBRUARY
S	M	T	W	T	F	S
					1	2
3	4	5	6	7	8	9
10	11	12	13	14	15	16
17	18	19	20	21	22	23
24	25	26	27	28		

MARCH
S	M	T	W	T	F	S
					1	2
3	4	5	6	7	8	9
10	11	12	13	14	15	16
17	18	19	20	21	22	23
24/31	25	26	27	28	29	30

APRIL
S	M	T	W	T	F	S
	1	2	3	4	5	6
7	8	9	10	11	12	13
14	15	16	17	18	19	20
21	22	23	24	25	26	27
28	29	30				

MAY
S	M	T	W	T	F	S
			1	2	3	4
5	6	7	8	9	10	11
12	13	14	15	16	17	18
19	20	21	22	23	24	25
26	27	28	29	30	31	

JUNE
S	M	T	W	T	F	S
						1
2	3	4	5	6	7	8
9	10	11	12	13	14	15
16	17	18	19	20	21	22
23/30	24	25	26	27	28	29

JULY
S	M	T	W	T	F	S
	1	2	3	4	5	6
7	8	9	10	11	12	13
14	15	16	17	18	19	20
21	22	23	24	25	26	27
28	29	30	31			

AUGUST
S	M	T	W	T	F	S
				1	2	3
4	5	6	7	8	9	10
11	12	13	14	15	16	17
18	19	20	21	22	23	24
25	26	27	28	29	30	31

SEPTEMBER
S	M	T	W	T	F	S
1	2	3	4	5	6	7
8	9	10	11	12	13	14
15	16	17	18	19	20	21
22	23	24	25	26	27	28
29	30					

OCTOBER
S	M	T	W	T	F	S
		1	2	3	4	5
6	7	8	9	10	11	12
13	14	15	16	17	18	19
20	21	22	23	24	25	26
27	28	29	30	31		

NOVEMBER
S	M	T	W	T	F	S
					1	2
3	4	5	6	7	8	9
10	11	12	13	14	15	16
17	18	19	20	21	22	23
24	25	26	27	28	29	30

DECEMBER
S	M	T	W	T	F	S
1	2	3	4	5	6	7
8	9	10	11	12	13	14
15	16	17	18	19	20	21
22	23	24	25	26	27	28
29	30	31				

May 19	Pentecost
May 20	Pentecost Monday
May 23-26	Monaco Grand Prix, auto race, Monaco (www.yourmonaco.com/grand_prix)
June	Marais Festival (arts), Paris
June 6	69th Anniversary of the D-Day Landing, Normandy
Mid-June	Le Mans Auto Race, Le Mans—near Loire Valley (www.lemans.org)
June 21	Fête de la Musique, concerts and dancing in the streets throughout France
July	Nice Jazz Festival (www.nicejazz festival.fr); Avignon Festival, theater, dance, music (www.festival-avignon .com); Beaune International Music Festival; Chorégies d'Orange, Orange (performed in Roman theater,

	www.choregies.asso.fr); "Jazz à Juan" International Jazz Festival, Antibes/ Juan-les-Pins (www.jazzajuan.com); Jousting matches and medieval festivities, Carcassonne; Nights of Fourvière, Lyon (theater and music in a Roman theater, www.nuitsde fourviere.org); Colmar International Music Festival (www.festival-colmar .com); International Music and Opera Festival, Aix-en-Provence (www .festival-aix.com)
July	Tour de France, national bicycle race culminating on the Champs-Elysées in Paris (www.letour.fr)
July 14	Bastille Day (fireworks, dancing, and revelry all over France)
July-Aug	International Fireworks Festival, Cannes (www.festival-pyrotechnique -cannes.com)
Aug 15	Assumption of Mary
Late Aug-Sept	Jazz at La Villette Festival, Paris (www.villette.com)
Sept	Fall Arts Festival (Fête d'Automne), Paris; Wine harvest festivals in many towns
Early-Mid-Oct	Grape Harvest Festival in Montmartre, Paris (www.fetedesvendangesde montmartre.com)
Nov 1	All Saints' Day
Early Nov	Dijon International and Gastronomic Fair, Dijon, Burgundy
Nov 11	Armistice Day
Late Nov	Wine Auction and Festival (Les Trois Glorieuses), Beaune
Late Nov-Dec 24	Christmas Markets, Strasbourg and Colmar
Dec 8-11	Festival of Lights (celebration of Virgin Mary, candlelit windows), Lyon (www.fetedeslumieres.lyon.fr)
Dec 25	Christmas Day
Dec 31	New Year's Eve

Conversions and Climate

Numbers and Stumblers

- Europeans write a few of their numbers differently than we do: 1 = *1*, 4 = *4*, 7 = *7*.
- In Europe, dates appear as day/month/year, so Christmas is 25/12/13.
- Commas are decimal points and decimals commas. A dollar and a half is 1,50, one thousand is 1.000, and there are 5.280 feet in a mile.
- When pointing, use your whole hand, palm down.
- When counting with fingers, start with your thumb. If you hold up your first finger to request one item, you'll probably get two.
- What Americans call the second floor of a building is the first floor in Europe.
- On escalators and moving sidewalks, Europeans keep the left "lane" open for passing. Keep to the right.

Metric Conversions (approximate)

A kilogram is 2.2 pounds, and 1 liter is about a quart, or almost four to a gallon. A kilometer is six-tenths of a mile. I figure kilometers to miles by cutting them in half and adding back 10 percent of the original (120 km: 60 + 12 = 72 miles, 300 km: 150 + 30 = 180 miles).

1 foot = 0.3 meter	1 square yard = 0.8 square meter
1 yard = 0.9 meter	1 square mile = 2.6 square kilometers
1 mile = 1.6 kilometers	1 ounce = 28 grams
1 centimeter = 0.4 inch	1 quart = 0.95 liter
1 meter = 39.4 inches	1 kilogram = 2.2 pounds
1 kilometer = 0.62 mile	32°F = 0°C

Clothing Sizes

When shopping for clothing, use these US-to-European comparisons as general guidelines (but note that no conversion is perfect).

- Women's dresses and blouses: Add 30
  (US women's size 10 = European size 40)
- Men's suits and jackets: Add 10
  (US size 40 regular = European size 50)
- Men's shirts: Multiply by 2 and add about 8
  (US men's size 15 collar = European size 38)
- Women's shoes: Add about 31
  (US size 8 = European size 38-39)
- Men's shoes: Add 32-34
  (US size 9 = European size 43; US size 11 = European size 45)

France's Climate

First line, average daily high; second line, average daily low; third line, average days without rain. For more-detailed weather statistics for destinations in this book (as well as the rest of the world), check www.worldclimate.com.

	J	F	M	A	M	J	J	A	S	O	N	D
Paris												
	43°	45°	54°	60°	68°	73°	76°	75°	70°	60°	50°	44°
	34°	34°	39°	43°	49°	55°	58°	58°	53°	46°	40°	36°
	14	14	19	17	19	18	19	18	17	18	15	15
Nice												
	50°	53°	59°	64°	71°	79°	84°	83°	77°	68°	58°	52°
	35°	36°	41°	46°	52°	58°	63°	63°	58°	51°	43°	37°
	23	22	24	23	23	26	29	26	24	23	21	21

Temperature Conversion: Fahrenheit and Celsius

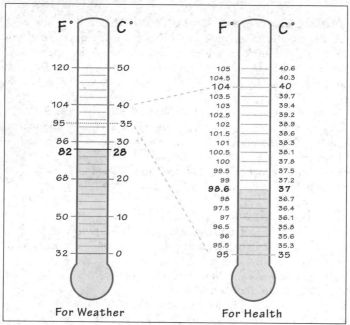

For Weather   For Health

Europe takes its temperature using the Celsius scale, whereas we opt for Fahrenheit. For a rough conversion from Celsius to Fahrenheit, double the number and add 30. For weather, remember that 28°C is 82°F—perfect. For health, 37°C is just right.

Packing Checklist

Whether you're traveling for five days or five weeks, here's what you'll need to bring. Pack light to enjoy the sweet freedom of true mobility. Happy travels!

❑ 5 shirts: long- and short-sleeve
❑ 1 sweater or lightweight fleece
❑ 2 pairs pants
❑ 1 pair shorts
❑ 1 swimsuit
❑ 5 pairs underwear and socks
❑ 1 pair shoes
❑ 1 rainproof jacket with hood
❑ Tie or scarf
❑ Money belt
❑ Money—your mix of:
  ❑ Debit card (for ATM withdrawals)
  ❑ Credit card
  ❑ Hard cash (in easy-to-exchange $20 bills)
❑ Documents plus photo-copies:
  ❑ Passport
  ❑ Printout of airline eticket
  ❑ Driver's license
  ❑ Student ID and hostel card
  ❑ Railpass/car rental voucher
  ❑ Insurance details
❑ Daypack
❑ Electronics—your choice of:
  ❑ Camera (and related gear)
  ❑ Computer/mobile devices (phone, MP3 player, ereader, etc.)
  ❑ Chargers for each of the above
  ❑ Plug adapter
❑ Empty water bottle

❑ Wristwatch and alarm clock
❑ Earplugs
❑ Toiletries kit
  ❑ Toiletries
  ❑ Medicines and vitamins
  ❑ First-aid kit
  ❑ Glasses/contacts/sunglasses (with prescriptions)
❑ Sealable plastic baggies
❑ Laundry soap
❑ Clothesline
❑ Small towel
❑ Sewing kit
❑ Travel information (guide-books and maps)
❑ Address list (for sending postcards)
❑ Postcards and photos from home
❑ Notepad and pen
❑ Journal

If you plan to carry on your luggage, note that all liquids must be in 3.4-ounce or smaller containers and fit within a single quart-size sealable baggie. For details, see www.tsa.gov/travelers.

Hotel Reservation

To: _____ _____
              hotel   *email or fax*

From:_____ _____
              name   *email or fax*

Today's date: _____ /_____ /_____
                      day   *month*   *year*

Dear Hotel _____ ,
Please make this reservation for me:

Name: _____

Total # of people: _____ # of rooms: _____ # of nights: _____

Arriving: _____ /_____ /_____   My time of arrival (24-hr clock): _____
                day *month* *year*   (I will telephone if I will be late)

Departing: ____ /____ /____
                 day *month* *year*

Room(s): Single____   Double ____   Twin ____   Triple ____   Quad____

With: Toilet ____   Shower ____   Bath ____   Sink only ____

Special needs: View____   Quiet____   Cheapest ____   Ground Floor____

Please email or fax confirmation of my reservation, along with the type of room reserved and the price. Please also inform me of your cancellation policy. After I hear from you, I will quickly send my credit-card information as a deposit to hold the room. Thank you.

_____
Name

_____
Address

_____
City   *State*   *Zip Code*   *Country*

Before hoteliers can make your reservation, they want to know the information listed above. You can use this form as the basis for your email, or you can photocopy this page, fill in the information, and send it as a fax (also available online at www.ricksteves.com/reservation).

Pronunciation Guide for Place Names

When using the phonetics: Try to nasalize the n sound (let the sound come through your nose). Note that the "ahn" combination uses the "ah" sound in "father," but the "an" combination uses the "a" sound in "sack." Pronounce the "ī" as the long "i" in "light." If your best attempt at pronunciation meets with a puzzled look, just point to the place name on the list.

In Paris

Arc de Triomphe ark duh tree-ohnf
arrondissement ah-rohn-dees-mohn
Bateaux-Mouches bah-toh moosh
Bon Marché bohn mar-shay
Carnavalet kar-nah-vah-lay
Champ de Mars shahn duh mar
Champs-Elysées shahn-zay-lee-zay
Conciergerie kon-see-ehr-zhuh-ree
Ecole Militaire eh-kohl mee-lee-tehr
Egouts ay-goo
Fauchon foh-shohn
Galeries Lafayette gah-luh-ree lah-fay-yet
gare gar
Gare d'Austerlitz gar doh-stehr-leets
Gare de l'Est gar duh less
Gare de Lyon gar duh lee-ohn
Gare du Nord gar dew nor
Gare St. Lazare gar san lah-zar
Garnier gar-nee-ay
Grand Palais grahn pah-lay
Grande Arche de la Défense grahnd arsh duh lah day-fahns
Ile de la Cité eel duh lah see-tay
Ile St. Louis eel san loo-ee
Jacquemart-André zhahk-mar-ahn-dray
Jardin des Plantes zhar-dan day plahnt
Jeu de Paume juh duh pohm
La Madeleine lah mah-duh-lehn
Le Hameau luh ah-moh
Les Halles lay ahl
Les Invalides lay-zan-vah-leed
Orangerie oh-rahn-zhuh-ree

Louvre loov-ruh
Marais mah-ray
marché aux puces mar-shay oh poos
Marmottan mar-moh-tahn
Métro may-troh
Monge mohnzh
Montmartre mohn-mart
Montparnasse mohn-par-nahs
Moulin Rouge moo-lan roozh
Musée d'Orsay mew-zay dor-say
Musée de l'Armée mew-zay duh lar-may
Notre-Dame noh-truh-dahm
Opéra Garnier oh-pay-rah gar-nee-ay
Orsay or-say
palais pah-lay
Palais de Justice pah-lay duh zhew-stees
Palais Royal pah-lay roh-yahl
Parc de la Villette park duh la vee-leht
Parc Monceau park mohn-soh
Père Lachaise pehr lah-shehz
Petit Palais puh-tee pah-lay
Pigalle pee-gahl
Place Dauphine plahs doh-feen
Place de la Bastille plahs duh lah bah-steel
Place de la Concorde plahs duh lah kohn-kord
Place de la République plahs duh lah ray-poo-bleek
Place des Vosges plahs day vohzh
Place du Tertre plahs dew tehr-truh
Place St. André-des-Arts plahs san tahn-dray day-zart
Place Vendôme plahs vahn-dohm
Pompidou pohn-pee-doo

APPENDIX

pont poh<u>n</u>
Pont Alexandre III poh<u>n</u> ah-leks-ah<u>n</u>-druh twah
Pont Neuf poh<u>n</u> nuhf
Promenade Plantée proh-meh<u>n</u>-ahd plah<u>n</u>-tay
quai kay
Rive Droite reeve dwaht
Rive Gauche reeve gohsh
Rodin roh-da<u>n</u>
rue rew
Rue Cler rew klehr
Rue Daguerre rew dah-gehr
Rue de Rivoli rew duh ree-voh-lee
Rue des Rosiers rew day roz-ee-ay
Rue Montorgueil rew moh<u>n</u>-tor-goy
Rue Mouffetard rew moof-tar
Sacré-Cœur sah-kray-koor
Sainte-Chapelle sa<u>n</u>t-shah-pehl
Seine sehn
Sèvres-Babylone seh-vruh-bah-bee-lohn
Sorbonne sor-buhn
St. Germain-des-Prés sa<u>n</u> zhehr-ma<u>n</u>-day-pray
St. Julien-le-Pauvre sa<u>n</u> zhew-lee-eh<u>n</u>-luh-poh-vruh
St. Séverin sah<u>n</u> say-vuh-ra<u>n</u>
St. Sulpice sah<u>n</u> sool-pees
Tour Eiffel toor ee-fehl
Trianon tree-ah<u>n</u>-oh<u>n</u>
Trocadéro troh-kah-day-roh
Tuileries twee-lay-ree
Venus de Milo vuh-news duh mee-loh

Outside of Paris
Abri du Cap Blanc ah-bree dew cah blah<u>n</u>
Aiguille du Midi ah-gwee dew mee-dee
Aïnhoa a<u>n</u>-oh-ah
Albi ahl-bee
Alet ah-lay
Alise Ste-Reine ah-leez sa<u>n</u>t-rehn
Aloxe-Corton ah-lohx kor-toh<u>n</u>
Alsace ahl-sahs
Amboise ahm-bwahz
Annecy ah<u>n</u>-see
Antibes ah<u>n</u>-teeb

Aosta (Italy) ay-oh-stah
Apt ahp
Aquitaine ah-kee-tehn
Arles arl
Arromanches ah-roh-mah<u>n</u>sh
Autoire oh-twahr
Auvergne oh-vehrn
Avignon ah-veen-yoh<u>n</u>
Azay-le-Rideau ah-zay luh ree-doh
Balazuc bah-lah-zook
Bayeux bī-yuh
Bayonne bī-yuhn
Beaucaire boh-kehr
Beaujolais boh-zhoh-lay
Beaune bohn
Bedoin buh-dwa<u>n</u>
Bennwihr behn-veer
Beynac bay-nak
Biarritz bee-ah-reetz
Blois blah
Bonnieux bohn-yuh
Bordeaux bor-doh
Brancion brahn-see-oh<u>n</u>
Brittany bree-tah-nee
Bruniquel brew-nee-kehl
Caen kah<u>n</u>
Cahors kah-or
Cajarc kah-zhark
Calais kah-lay
Camargue kah-marg
Cambord kah<u>n</u>-bor
Cancale kah<u>n</u>-kahl
Carcassonne kar-kah-suhn
Carennac kah-rehn-ahk
Carsac kar-sahk
Castelnaud kah-stehl-noh
Castelnau-de-Montmiral kah-stehl-noh-duh-moh<u>n</u>-mee-rahl
Caussade koh-sahd
Cavaillon kah-vī-oh<u>n</u>
Cénac say-nahk
Céret say-ray
Chambord shah<u>n</u>-bor
Chamonix shah-moh-nee
Champagne shah<u>n</u>-pahn-yuh
Chapaize shah-pehz
Chartres shart
Château de Chatonnière shah-toh duh shah-tuhn-yehr
Château de Rivau shah-toh duh ree-voh
Château du Haut-Kœnigsbourg shah-toh dew oh-koh-neegs-boorg

Châteauneuf-du-Pape shah-toh-nuhf-dew-pahp
Châteauneuf-en-Auxois shah-toh-nuhf-ehn-ohx-wah
Chaumont-sur-Loire shoh-mohn-sewr-lwahr
Chenonceau shuh-nohn-soh
Chenonceaux shuh-nohn-soh
Cherbourg shehr-boor
Cheverny shuh-vehr-nee
Chinon shee-nohn
Cluny klew-nee
Colleville kohl-veel
Collioure kohl-yoor
Collonges-la-Rouge koh-lohnzh-lah-roozh
Colmar kohl-mar
Cordes-sur-Ciel kord-sewr-see-yehl
Côte d'Azur koht dah-zewr
Cougnac koon-yahk
Courseulles-sur-Mer koor-suhl-sewr-mehr
Coustellet koo-stuh-lay
Digne deen-yuh
Dijon dee-zhohn
Dinan dee-nahn
Dinard dee-nar
Domme dohm
Dordogne dor-dohn-yuh
Eguisheim eh-geh-shīm
Entrevaux ahn-truh-voh
Epernay ay-pehr-nay
Espelette eh-speh-leht
Eze-Bord-de-Mer ehz-bor-duh-mehr
Eze-le-Village ehz-luh-vee-lahzh
Faucon foh-kohn
Flavigny-sur-Ozerain flah-veen-yee-sewr-oh-zuh-ran
Font-de-Gaume fohn-duh-gohm
Fontenay fohn-tuh-nay
Fontevraud fohn-tuh-vroh
Fontvieille fohn-vee-yeh-ee
Fougères foo-zher
Fougères-sur-Bièvre foo-zher-sewr-bee-ehv
Gaillac gī-yahk
Gigondas zhee-gohn-dahs
Giverny zhee-vehr-nee
Gordes gord
Gorges de l'Ardèche gorzh duh lar-dehsh

Grenoble gruh-noh-bluh
Grouin groo-an
Guédelon gway-duh-lohn
Hautes Corbières oht kor-bee-yehr
Hendaye ehn-dī
Honfleur ohn-flur
Huisnes-sur-Mer ween-sewr-mehr
Hunawihr uhn-ah-veer
Ile Besnard eel bay-nar
Isle-sur-la-Sorgue eel-sewr-lah-sorg
Juan-les-Pins zhwan-lay-pan
Kaysersberg kī-zehrs-behrg
Kientzheim keentz-īm
La Charente lah shah-rahnt
La Rhune lah rewn
La Rochepot lah rohsh-poh
La Roque St-Christophe lah rohk san-kree-stohf
La Roque-Gageac lah rohk-gah-zhahk
La Trophée des Alpes lah troh-fay dayz ahlp
La Turbie lah tewr-bee
Lacoste lah-kohst
Langeais lahn-zhay
Languedoc long-dohk
Lascaux lah-skoh
Lastours lahs-toor
Le Bugue luh bewg
Le Crestet luh kruh-stay
Le Havre luh hah-vruh
Le Ruquet luh rew-kay
Lémeré lay-muh-ray
Les Baux lay boh
Les Eyzies-de-Tayac lay zay-zee-duh-tī-yahk
Les Praz lay prah
Les Vosges lay vohzh
Limoges lee-mohzh
Loches lohsh
Loire lwahr
Longues-sur-Mer long-sewr-mehr
Loubressac loo-bruh-sahk
Lourmarin loo-mah-ran
Luberon lew-beh-rohn
Lyon lee-ohn
Malaucène mah-loh-sehn
Marne-la-Vallée-Chessy marn-lah-vah-lay-shuh-see
Marseille mar-say
Martel mar-tehl

Mausanne moh-sahn
Ménerbes may-nehrb
Millau mee-yoh
Minerve mee-nerv
Mirabel mee-rah-behl
Modreuc mohd-rewk
Mont Blanc moh<u>n</u> blah<u>n</u>
Mont St-Michel moh<u>n</u> sa<u>n</u>-mee-shehl
Mont Ventoux moh<u>n</u> vehn-too
Montenvers moh<u>n</u>-tuh-vehr
Montfort moh<u>n</u>-for
Montignac moh<u>n</u>-teen-yahk
Mortemart mort-mar
Munster mewn-stehr
Nantes nah<u>n</u>t
Nice nees
Normandy nor-mah<u>n</u>-dee
Nyons nee-yoh<u>ns</u>
Oradour-sur-Glane oh-rah-door-sewr-glahn
Orange oh-rahnzh
Padirac pah-dee-rahk
Paris pah-ree
Pech Merle pehsh mehrl
Peyrepertuse pay-ruh-per-tewz
Pointe du Hoc pwa<u>n</u>t dew ohk
Pont du Gard poh<u>n</u> dew gahr
Pontorson poh<u>n</u>-tor-sohn
Provence proh-vah<u>ns</u>
Puycelci pew-suhl-cee
Puyméras pwee-may-rahs
Queribus kehr-ee-bews
Reims ra<u>ns</u> (rhymes with France)
Remoulins ruh-moo-la<u>n</u>
Rennes rehn
Ribeauvillé ree-boh-vee-yay
Riquewihr reek-veer
Rocamadour roh-kah-mah-door
Rouen roo-ah<u>n</u>
Rouffignac roo-feen-yahk
Roussillon roo-see-yoh<u>n</u>
Route du Vin root dew va<u>n</u>
Sablet sah-blay
Sare sahr
Sarlat sar-lah
Savigny-les-Beaune sah-veen-yee-lay-bohn
Savoie sah-vwah
Séguret say-goo-ray
Semur-en-Auxois suh-moor-eh<u>n</u>-ohx-wah

Sigolsheim see-gohl-shīm
Souillac soo-ee-yahk
St-Cirq Lapopie sa<u>n</u>-seerk lah-poh-pee
St-Cyprien sa<u>n</u>-seep-ree-<u>ehn</u>
St-Emilion sa<u>n</u>-tay-meel-yoh<u>n</u>
St-Geniès sa<u>n</u>-zhuh-nyehs
St-Jean-de-Luz sa<u>n</u>-zhah<u>n</u>-duh-looz
St-Jean-Pied-de-Port sa<u>n</u>-zhah<u>n</u>-pee-yay-duh-por
St-Malo sa<u>n</u>-mah-loh
St-Marcellin-lès-Vaison sa<u>n</u>-mar-suh-la<u>n</u>-lay-vay-zoh<u>n</u>
St-Rémy sa<u>n</u>-ray-mee
St-Romain-en-Viennois sa<u>n</u>-roh-ma<u>n</u>-eh<u>n</u>-vee-eh<u>n</u>-nwah
St-Suliac sa<u>n</u>-soo-lee-ahk
St-Paul-de-Vence sa<u>n</u>-pohl-duh-vah<u>ns</u>
Ste-Mère Eglise sa<u>n</u>t-mehr ay-gleez
Stes-Maries-de-la-Mer sa<u>n</u>t-mah-ree-duh-lah-mehr
Strasbourg strahs-boorg
Suzette soo-zeht
Taizé teh-zay
Tarascon tah-rah-skoh<u>n</u>
Tours toor
Turckheim tewrk-hīm
Ussé oo-say
Uzès oo-zehs
Vacqueyras vah-kee-rahs
Vaison la Romaine vay-zoh<u>n</u> lah roh-mehn
Valançay vah-lah<u>n</u>-say
Valréas vahl-ray-ahs
Vence vah<u>ns</u>
Verdun vehr-duhn
Versailles vehr-sī
Veynes vay-nuh
Vézelay vay-zuh-lay
Vierville-sur-Mer vee-yehr-veel-sewr-mehr
Villandry vee-lahn-dry
Villefranche-de-Rouergue veel-frah<u>n</u>sh-duh-roo-ehrg
Villefranche-sur-Mer veel-frah<u>n</u>sh-sewr-mehr
Villeneuve-lès-Avignon veel-nuhv-lay-zah-veeh-yoh<u>n</u>
Vitrac vee-trahk
Vouvray voo-vray
Villedieu vee-luh-dyuh

French Survival Phrases

When using the phonetics, try to nasalize the <u>n</u> sound.

APPENDIX

Good day.	Bonjour.	boh<u>n</u>-zhoor
Mrs. / Mr.	Madame / Monsieur	mah-dahm / muhs-yur
Do you speak English?	Parlez-vous anglais?	par-lay-voo ah<u>n</u>-glay
Yes. / No.	Oui. / Non.	wee / noh<u>n</u>
I understand.	Je comprends.	zhuh koh<u>n</u>-prah<u>n</u>
I don't understand.	Je ne comprends pas.	zhuh nuh koh<u>n</u>-prah<u>n</u> pah
Please.	S'il vous plaît.	see voo play
Thank you.	Merci.	mehr-see
I'm sorry.	Désolé.	day-zoh-lay
Excuse me.	Pardon.	par-doh<u>n</u>
(No) problem.	(Pas de) problème.	(pah duh) proh-blehm
It's good.	C'est bon.	say boh<u>n</u>
Goodbye.	Au revoir.	oh vwahr
one / two	un / deux	uh<u>n</u> / duh
three / four	trois / quatre	twah / kah-truh
five / six	cinq / six	sa<u>n</u>k / sees
seven / eight	sept / huit	seht / weet
nine / ten	neuf / dix	nuhf / dees
How much is it?	Combien?	koh<u>n</u>-bee-a<u>n</u>
Write it?	Ecrivez?	ay-kree-vay
Is it free?	C'est gratuit?	say grah-twee
Included?	Inclus?	a<u>n</u>-klew
Where can I buy / find...?	Où puis-je acheter / trouver...?	oo pwee-zhuh ah-shuh-tay / troo-vay
I'd like / We'd like...	Je voudrais / Nous voudrions...	zhuh voo-dray / noo voo-dree-oh<u>n</u>
...a room.	...une chambre.	ewn shah<u>n</u>-bruh
...a ticket to ___.	...un billet pour ___.	uh<u>n</u> bee-yay poor
Is it possible?	C'est possible?	say poh-see-bluh
Where is...?	Où est...?	oo ay
...the train station	...la gare	lah gar
...the bus station	...la gare routière	lah gar root-yehr
...tourist information	...l'office du tourisme	loh-fees dew too-reez-muh
Where are the toilets?	Où sont les toilettes?	oo soh<u>n</u> lay twah-leht
men	hommes	ohm
women	dames	dahm
left / right	à gauche / à droite	ah gohsh / ah dwaht
straight	tout droit	too dwah
When does this open / close?	Ça ouvre / ferme à quelle heure?	sah oo-vruh / fehrm ah kehl ur
At what time?	À quelle heure?	ah kehl ur
Just a moment.	Un moment.	uh<u>n</u> moh-mah<u>n</u>
now / soon / later	maintenant / bientôt / plus tard	ma<u>n</u>-tuh-nah<u>n</u> / bee-a<u>n</u>-toh / plew tar
today / tomorrow	aujourd'hui / demain	oh-zhoor-dwee / duh-ma<u>n</u>

In a French-speaking Restaurant

I'd like / We'd like...	Je voudrais / Nous voudrions...	zhuh voo-dray / noo voo-dree-ohn
...to reserve...	...réserver...	ray-zehr-vay
...a table for one / two.	...une table pour un / deux.	ewn tah-bluh poor uhn / duh
Non-smoking.	Non fumeur.	nohn few-mur
Is this seat free?	C'est libre?	say lee-bruh
The menu (in English), please.	La carte (en anglais), s'il vous plaît.	lah kart (ahn ahn-glay) see voo play
service (not) included	service (non) compris	sehr-vees (nohn) kohn-pree
to go	à emporter	ah ahn-por-tay
with / without	avec / sans	ah-vehk / sahn
and / or	et / ou	ay / oo
special of the day	plat du jour	plah dew zhoor
specialty of the house	spécialité de la maison	spay-see-ah-lee-tay duh lah may-zohn
appetizers	hors-d'oeuvre	or-duh-vruh
first course (soup, salad)	entrée	ahn-tray
main course (meat, fish)	plat principal	plah pran-see-pahl
bread	pain	pan
cheese	fromage	froh-mahzh
sandwich	sandwich	sahnd-weech
soup	soupe	soop
salad	salade	sah-lahd
meat	viande	vee-ahnd
chicken	poulet	poo-lay
fish	poisson	pwah-sohn
seafood	fruits de mer	frwee duh mehr
fruit	fruit	frwee
vegetables	légumes	lay-gewm
dessert	dessert	duh-sehr
mineral water	eau minérale	oh mee-nay-rahl
tap water	l'eau du robinet	loh dew roh-bee-nay
milk	lait	lay
(orange) juice	jus (d'orange)	zhew (doh-rahnzh)
coffee	café	kah-fay
tea	thé	tay
wine	vin	van
red / white	rouge / blanc	roozh / blahn
glass / bottle	verre / bouteille	vehr / boo-teh-ee
beer	bière	bee-ehr
Cheers!	Santé!	sahn-tay
More. / Another.	Plus. / Un autre.	plew / uhn oh-truh
The same.	La même chose.	lah mehm shohz
The bill, please.	L'addition, s'il vous plaît.	lah-dee-see-ohn see voo play
tip	pourboire	poor-bwar
Delicious!	Délicieux!	day-lee-see-uh

For more user-friendly French phrases, check out *Rick Steves' French Phrase Book and Dictionary* or *Rick Steves' French, Italian & German Phrase Book*.

INDEX

INDEX

INDEX

INDEX

INDEX

INDEX

MAP INDEX

Audio Europe

Rick's Free Travel App

Get your FREE **Rick Steves Audio Europe**™ app to enjoy…

- Dozens of self-guided tours of Europe's top museums, sights and historic walks

- Hundreds of tracks filled with cultural insights and sightseeing tips from Rick's radio interviews

- All organized into handy geographic playlists

- For iPhone, iPad, iPod Touch, Android

With Rick whispering in your ear, Europe gets even better.

Find out more at ricksteves.com

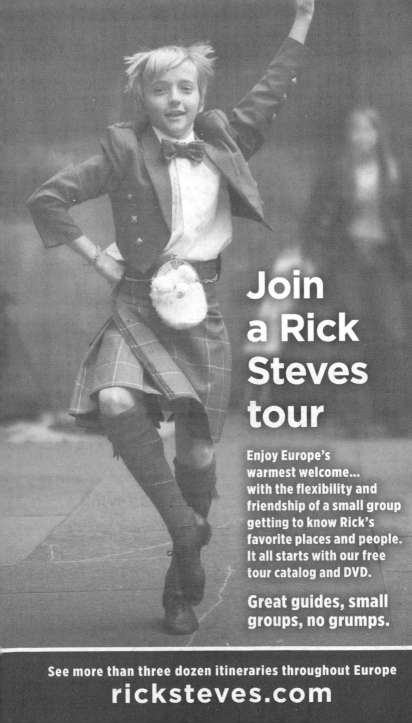

Join a Rick Steves tour

Enjoy Europe's warmest welcome... with the flexibility and friendship of a small group getting to know Rick's favorite places and people. It all starts with our free tour catalog and DVD.

Great guides, small groups, no grumps.

See more than three dozen itineraries throughout Europe

ricksteves.com

Start your trip at

Free information and great gear to

▸ Plan Your Trip

Browse thousands of articles and a wealth of money-saving tips for planning your dream trip. You'll find up-to-date information on Europe's best destinations, packing smart, getting around, finding rooms, staying healthy, avoiding scams and more.

▸ Eurail Passes

Find out, step-by-step, if a railpass makes sense for your trip—and how to avoid buying more than you need. Get free shipping on online orders

▸ Graffiti Wall & Travelers Helpline

Learn, ask, share—our online community of savvy travelers is a great resource for first-time travelers to Europe, as well as seasoned pros.

Rick Steves' Europe Through the Back Door, Inc.

ricksteves.com

turn your travel dreams into affordable reality

▶ Free Audio Tours & Travel Newsletter

Get your nose out of this guide book and focus on what you'll be seeing with Rick's free audio tours of the greatest sights in Athens, Austria, Florence, Germany, London, Paris, Rome, Turkey and Venice.

Subscribe to our free Travel News e-newsletter, and get monthly articles from Rick on what's happening in Europe.

▶ Great Gear from Rick's Travel Store

Pack light and right—on a budget—with Rick's custom-designed carry-on bags, roll-aboards, day packs, travel accessories, guidebooks, journals, maps and DVDs of his TV shows.

130 Fourth Avenue North, PO Box 2009 • Edmonds, WA 98020 USA
Phone: (425) 771-8303 • Fax: (425) 771-0833 • ricksteves.com

Rick Steves

www.ricksteves.com

EUROPE GUIDES

Best of Europe
Eastern Europe
Europe Through the Back Door
Mediterranean Cruise Ports

COUNTRY GUIDES

Croatia & Slovenia
England
France
Germany
Great Britain
Ireland
Italy
Portugal
Scandinavia
Spain
Switzerland

CITY & REGIONAL GUIDES

Amsterdam, Bruges & Brussels
Athens & the Peloponnese
Barcelona
Budapest
Florence & Tuscany
Istanbul
London
Paris
Prague & the Czech Republic
Provence & the French Riviera
Rome
Venice
Vienna, Salzburg & Tirol

SNAPSHOT GUIDES

Barcelona
Berlin
Bruges & Brussels
Copenhagen & the Best of
    Denmark
Dublin
Dubrovnik
Hill Towns of Central Italy
Italy's Cinque Terre
Krakow, Warsaw & Gdansk
Lisbon
Madrid & Toledo
Munich, Bavaria & Salzburg
Naples & the Amalfi Coast
Northern Ireland
Norway
Scotland
Sevilla, Granada & Southern Spain
Stockholm

POCKET GUIDES

Athens
London
Paris
Rome

TRAVEL CULTURE

Europe 101
European Christmas
Postcards from Europe
Travel as a Political Act

Rick Steves guidebooks are published by Avalon Travel,
a member of the Perseus Books Group.

NOW AVAILABLE:
eBOOKS, DVD & BLU-RAY

eBOOKS

Nearly all Rick Steves guides are available as eBooks. Check with your favorite bookseller.

RICK STEVES' EUROPE DVDs

10 New Shows 2011–2012
Austria & the Alps
Eastern Europe
England & Wales
European Christmas
European Travel Skills & Specials
France
Germany, BeNeLux & More
Greece & Turkey
Iran
Ireland & Scotland
Italy's Cities
Italy's Countryside
Scandinavia
Spain
Travel Extras

BLU-RAY

Celtic Charms
Eastern Europe Favorites
European Christmas
Italy Through the Back Door
Mediterranean Mosaic
Surprising Cities of Europe

PHRASE BOOKS & DICTIONARIES

French
French, Italian & German
German
Italian
Portuguese
Spanish

JOURNALS

Rick Steves' Pocket Travel Journal
Rick Steves' Travel Journal

PLANNING MAPS

Britain, Ireland & London
Europe
France & Paris
Germany, Austria & Switzerland
Ireland
Italy
Spain & Portugal

Rick Steves books and DVDs are available at bookstores and through online booksellers.

Credits

Researchers

To help update this book, Rick and Steve relied on...

Mary Bouron

Mary caught the travel bug as a child living in London, and later, as an exchange student in France. Born a Seattleite, Mary now confidently calls herself a Parisian. Deeply in love with a Frenchman, and a mother of two, she occupies her free time hunting for the city's best baguette and digging at the root causes of Franco-American cultural miscommunications.

Amy Robertson

Having studied French for many years and lived in Brittany, Amy now jumps at the chance to travel to France. For the rest of the year, Amy helps plan and manage tours in the Rick Steves tour operations department and lives near Seattle with her husband, Jeremy.

Rolinka Bloeming

While studying at the Dutch Tourism Academy, Rolinka decided to become a professional vagabond, sharing her love and enthusiasm for traveling with others. Twenty-five years later, she traded the big-city life of Paris for a new adventure: remodeling a shepherd's hut in the Languedoc countryside. Rolinka still finds time to take long walks with her dog, Risotto, and to help Rick and Steve research this guidebook.

Contributor
Gene Openshaw

Gene is the co-author of 10 Rick Steves books. For this book, he wrote material on Europe's art, history, and contemporary culture. When not traveling, Gene enjoys composing music, recovering from his 1973 trip to Europe with Rick, and living everyday life with his daughter.

Images

Location	Photographer
Title Page: Villefranche-sur-Mer	Steve Smith
Full-Page Color: Collioure	Dominic Bonuccelli
Paris: Louvre	Rick Steves
Near Paris: Versailles	Rick Steves
Normandy: Mont St-Michel	Steve Smith
Brittany: Dinan	Steve Smith
The Loire: Château d'Amboise	Steve Smith
Dordogne: Dordogne River Valley	David C. Hoerlein
Basque Country: St-Jean-de-Luz	Cameron Hewitt
Languedoc: Carcassonne	Dominic Bonuccelli
Provence: Pont du Gard Aqueduct	Rick Steves
The French Riviera: Cannes	Steve Smith
The French Alps: Chamonix Valley	David C. Hoerlein
Burgundy: Château de la Rochepot	Steve Smith
Lyon: Saône River and Bonaparte Bridge	Steve Smith
Alsace: Kaysersberg	Steve Smith
Reims and Verdun:	
The Five Defenders of Verdun	Abe Bringolf

Acknowledgments

Thanks to Steve's wife, Karen Lewis Smith, for her assistance covering French cuisine; and to Steve's children, Travis and Maria, for help with children's activities.

Thanks to Aaron Harting for his help with the "Winter Sports in Chamonix" section. Aaron is a travel advisor and assistant video editor in our Edmonds office, assists on a multitude of tours, and has skied his way through much of the Alps.

Avalon Travel
a member of the Perseus Books Group
1700 Fourth Street
Berkeley, California 94710

Text © 2012, 2011, 2009, 2008, 2007, 2006, 2005, 2004, 2003, 2002, 2001, 2000 by Rick Steves and Steve Smith. All rights reserved. Maps © 2011, 2009, 2008 by Europe Through the Back Door. All rights reserved. Paris Métro map © 2010 by La Régie Autonome des Transports Parisiens (RATP).
Used with permission.

Printed in Canada by Friesens. First printing November 2012.

ISBN 978-1-61238-383-5
ISSN 1084-4406

For the latest on Rick's lectures, guidebooks, tours, public radio show, and public television series, contact Europe Through the Back Door, Box 2009, Edmonds, WA 98020, 425/771-8303, fax 425/771-0833, rick@ricksteves.com, www.ricksteves.com.

Europe Through the Back Door
Managing Editor: Risa Laib
Editors: Jennifer Madison Davis, Glenn Eriksen, Tom Griffin, Cameron Hewitt, Suzanne Kotz, Cathy Lu, Gretchen Strauch
Editorial Interns: Emily Dugdale, Jessica Shaw
Researchers: Mary Bouron, Amy Robertson, Rolinka Bloeming
Graphic Content Director: Laura VanDeventer
Maps & Graphics: David C. Hoerlein, Twozdai Hulse, Lauren Mills

Avalon Travel
Senior Editor and Series Manager: Madhu Prasher
Editor: Jamie Andrade
Assistant Editor: Nikki Ioakimedes
Copy Editor: Patrick Collins
Proofreader: Rebecca Freed
Indexer: Stephen Callahan
Production & Typesetting: McGuire Barber Design
Cover Design: Kimberly Glyder Design
Maps & Graphics: Kat Bennett, Mike Morgenfeld, Brice Ticen, Lohnes + Wright

Front Cover Photo: Carcassonne © Cameron Hewitt
Additional Photography: Rick Steves, Steve Smith, David C. Hoerlein, Cameron Hewitt, Dominic Bonuccelli, Laura VanDeventer, Lauren Mills, Gretchen Strauch, Rich Earl, Julie Coen, Barb Geisler, Robyn Cronin, Michaelanne Jerome, Abe Bringolf, Mary Ann Cameron, Paul Orcutt, Michael Potter, Carol Ries, Dorian Yates, Rob Unck, Wikimedia Commons, Rachel Worthman pg. 34

Although the authors and publisher have made every effort to provide accurate, up-to-date information, they accept no responsibility for loss, injury, soggy crêpes, or inconvenience sustained by any person using this book.

Want More France?
Maximize the experience with Rick Steves as your guide

Guidebooks
Provence and Paris guides make side-trips smooth and affordable

Phrase Books
Rely on Rick's French Phrase Book and Dictionary

Rick's DVDs
Preview your destinations with 8 shows on France

Free! Rick's Audio Europe™ App
Free audio tours for Paris' top sights

Small-Group Tours
Rick offers 8 great itineraries through France

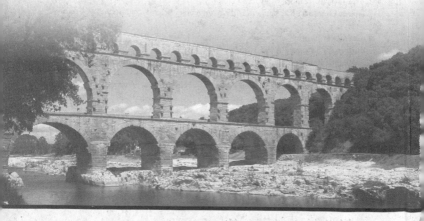

For all the details, visit ricksteves.com